159 SOVEREIGN COUNTRIES

Ranking by size	COUNTRY			POPULATION Latest Estimates	Relative to UK=1	Ranking
40	CENTRAL AFRICAN EMPIRE	622 984	2·55	2 370 000	0·04	108
41	BOTSWANA	600 372	2·46	693 000	0·01	127
42	MADAGASCAR	587 041	2·40	8 080 900	0·14	65
43	KENYA	582 646	2·38	13 847 000	0·25	46
44	FRANCE	547 026	2·24	52 944 000	0·94	15
45	THAILAND	514 000	2·10	42 960 000	0·77	18
46	SPAIN	504 782	2·07	35 971 000	0·64	21
47	CAMEROON	475 442	1·95	6 539 000	0·11	73
48	PAPUA NEW GUINEA	462 840	1·89	2 829 000	0·05	102
49	SWEDEN	449 964	1·84	8 236 000	0·15	64
50	MOROCCO	446 550	1·83	17 828 000	0·32	35
51	IRAQ	434 924	1·78	11 505 000	0·20	53
52	PARAGUAY	406 752	1·66	2 646 877	0·05	105
53	RHODESIA	390 580	1·60	6 528 000	0·12	72
54	JAPAN	372 313	1·52	112 768 000	2·01	6
55	CONGO	342 000	1·40	1 300 106	0·02	120
56	FINLAND	337 009	1·38	4 733 000	0·08	85
57	PEOPLE'S DEMOCRATIC REPUBLIC OF YEMEN	332 968	1·36	1 690 000	0·03	116
58	VIET-NAM	332 559	1·36	46 523 000	0·83	16
59	MALAYSIA	329 744	1·35	12 300 000	0·22	51
60	NORWAY	324 219	1·33	4 027 000	0·07	92
61	IVORY COAST	322 463	1·32	6 670 912	0·12	71
62	POLAND	312 677	1·28	34 552 000	0·62	23
63	ITALY	301 260	1·23	56 323 000	1·01	13
64	PHILIPPINES	300 000	1·22	43 751 000	0·78	17
65	ECUADOR	283 561	1·16	6 733 000	0·12	70
66	UPPER VOLTA	274 200	1·12	6 144 013	0·11	76
67	NEW ZEALAND	268 676	1·10	3 148 000	0·05	100
68	GABON	267 667	1·09	530 000	0·009	134
69	YUGOSLAVIA	255 804	1·04	21 672 000	0·38	32
70	GERMANY (WEST)	248 620	1·02	61 490 000	1·09	12
71	GUINEA	245 857	1·01	4 527 000	0·08	89
72	UNITED KINGDOM	244 013	1·00	55 927 600	1·00	14
73	GHANA	238 537	0·97	9 866 000	0·17	56
74	ROMANIA	237 500	0·97	21 245 000	0·38	33
75	UGANDA	236 860	0·97	11 943 000	0·21	52
76	LAOS	236 800	0·97	3 257 000	0·05	97
77	GUYANA	214 969	0·88	782 000	0·01	126
78	OMAN	212 457	0·87	600 000	0·01	130

Art Editor: David Roberts
Illustrators: Pat Gibbon, Christine Darter, Ian Cater
Map work: Alan Stone
Index: Anna Pavord

No part of this book may be reproduced or transmitted in any form or by any means, electronic,
chemical or mechanical, including photocopying, any information storage or retrieval system
without a licence or other permission in writing from the copyright owners.
Guinness is a registered trade mark of Arthur Guinness Son & Co Ltd
Made and printed in Great Britain by Redwood Burn Ltd
Trowbridge and Esher, England

THE GUINNESS BOOK OF ANSWERS

A Handbook of General Knowledge

GENERAL EDITOR
Norris McWhirter

ASSOCIATE EDITORS

John Arblaster
Dr. James Bevan
Maurice Burton D.Sc.
Clive Carpenter
Robert Dearling
Stan Greenberg

Kenneth Macksey
John Marshall
Peter Matthews
Prof. Kennedy McWhirter
John FitzMaurice Mills
Patrick Moore O.B.E.

Dr. C. T. Prime
Edward Pyatt
Alex E. Reid
Moira F. Stowe
John W. R. Taylor
Andrew Thomas

GUINNESS SUPERLATIVES LIMITED
2 CECIL COURT, LONDON ROAD, ENFIELD, MIDDLESEX

Contents

THE CALENDAR

Days of the week

ENGLISH	LATIN	SAXON
Sunday	Dies Solis	Sun's Day
Monday	Dies Lunae	Moon's Day
Tuesday	Dies Martis	Tiu's Day
Wednesday	Dies Mercurii	Woden's Day
Thursday	Dies Jovis	Thor's Day
Friday	Dies Veneris	Frigg's Day
Saturday	Dies Saturni	Saternes' Day

Tiu was the Anglo-Saxon counterpart of the Nordic Tyr, son of Odin, God of War, who came closest to Mars (Greek, Ares) son of the Roman God of War Jupiter (Greek, Zeus). Woden was the Anglo-Saxon counterpart of Odin, Nordic dispenser of victory, who came closest to Mercury (Greek, Hermes), the Roman messenger of victory. Thor was the Nordic God of Thunder, eldest son of Odin and nearest to the Roman Jupiter (Greek, Zeus), who was armed with thunder and lightning. Frigg (or Freyja), wife of Odin, was the Nordic Goddess of Love, and equivalent to Venus (Greek, Aphrodite), Goddess of Love in Roman mythology. Thus four of the middle days of the week are named after a mythological husband and wife and their two sons.

The seasons

The four seasons in the northern hemisphere are astronomically speaking:

Spring — from the vernal equinox (about 21 Mar.) to the summer solstice (about 21 June).

Summer — from the summer solstice (about 21 June) to the autumnal equinox (about 21 Sept.).

Autumn — (or Fall in USA) from the autumnal equinox (about 21 Sept.) to the winter solstice (about 21 Dec.).

Winter — from the winter solstice (about 21 Dec.) to the vernal equinox (about 21 Mar.).

In the southern hemisphere, of course, autumn corresponds to spring, winter to summer, spring to autumn and summer to winter.

The solstices (from Latin *sol*, sun; *sitium*, standing) are the two times in the year when the sun is farthest from the equator and appears to be still. The equinoxes (from Latin *aequus*, equal; *nox*, night) are the two times in the year when day and night are of equal length when the sun crosses the equator.

Longest and shortest day

The longest day (day with the longest interval between sunrise and sunset) is the day on which the *solstice* falls and in the northern hemisphere occurs on 21 June, or increasingly rarely on 22 June. The latest sunset, however, occurs on 13 or 14 June but the sunrise is still getting earlier by sufficiently large a margin to make the duration of night shorter until Midsummer's Day. At Greenwich (South London) daylight may last up to 16 h 39 min, though the longest duration sunshine is 15 h 48 min, recorded at nearby Kew (West London) on 13 June 1887. The shortest day occurs either on 21 or 22 Dec. when daylight at Greenwich may last only 7 h 50 min. The evenings, however, begin lengthening imperceptibly

on 13 or 14 Dec. when the sunset is about 2 s later than the previous day.

Equinox March 22	*Equinox* September 22
Summer solstice June 22	*Winter solstice* December 22

Old style (Julian) and new style (Gregorian) dates

In England, until 1752, Lady Day (25 Mar.) was the legal beginning of the year and 25 Mar. is still the beginning of the ecclesiastical year. Dates from 1 Jan. to 24 Mar. in any year were written e.g. 28 Feb. 1659–60 or 16$\frac{59}{60}$ indicating the historical year of 1660 but the ecclesiastical, legal and official year of 1659.

Parliament passed in March 1751 the Calendar (New Style) Act, known as Lord Chesterfield's Act (24 Geo II, c. 23), declaring that the following First of January should be the first day of the year 1752 for all ordinary purposes. It was also enacted that Wednesday 2 Sept. 1752 should be followed by Thursday 14 Sept. Thus apparent anomalies of the kind whereby William of Orange, later King William III, left Holland on 11 Nov. 1688 (New Style (NS)) by the Gregorian Calendar and landed in England on 5 Nov. 1688 (Old Style (OS)) by the Julian Calendar were eliminated.

The Julian Calendar, introduced by Julius Caesar in 45 BC, on the advice of the Egyptian astronomer Sosigenes, was in use throughout Europe until 1582 when Pope Gregory XIII ordained that 5 Oct. should be called 15 Oct. The discrepancy occurred because of the Augustinian ruling of AD 4 that every fourth year shall be of 366 days and hence include a Leap Day.

Countries switched from the Old Style (Julian) to the New Style (Gregorian) system as follows:

1582	Italy, France, Portugal, Spain
1583	Flanders, Holland, Prussia, Switzerland, and the Roman Catholic states in Germany
1586	Poland
1587	Hungary
1600	Scotland (except St Kilda)
1700	Denmark and the Protestant states in Germany
1700–40	Sweden (by gradual process)
1752	England and Wales, Ireland and the Colonies, including North America
1872	Japan (12-day lag)
1912	China (13-day lag)
1915	Bulgaria (13-day lag)
1917	Turkey and the USSR (13-day lag)
1919	Romania and Yugoslavia (13-day lag)
1923	Greece (13-day lag)

Leap year

Leap years occur in every year the number of which is divisible by four, e.g. 1964, except centennial years, e.g. 1700, 1800, or 1900, which are treated as common or non-leap years *unless* the number of the *century* is divisible by four, e.g. 1600 was (NS) a leap year and 2000 will be a leap year.

The whole process is one of compensation for over-retrenchment of the discrepancy between the calendar year of 365 days and the mean solar year of 365·24219878 days. The date when it will be necessary to suppress a further leap year, sometimes assumed to be AD 4000, AD 8000, etc., is not in fact yet clearly specifiable, owing to minute variations in the earth-sun relationship.

The word 'leap' derives from the Old Norse *hlaupár*, indicating a leap in the sense of a jump. The origin probably derives from the observation that in a bissextile (i.e. leap) year any fixed day festival falls on the next weekday but one to that on which it fell in the preceding year, and not on the next weekday as happens in common years.

The term bissextile derives literally from a double (bis) day inserted after the sixth (sextile) day before the calends of March. Thus the Julian calendar compensated (albeit inaccurately) for the discrepancy between its year and the mean solar year.

Public and bank holidays

By English Common Law the days that mark the birth and death of Christ (Christmas Day and Good Friday) are public holidays.

By custom the Bank of England at the beginning of last century was closed on at least 40 saints' days and anniversaries. In 1830 such bank holidays were cut to 18 and in 1834 to only 4.

In 1871 parliament passed the Bank Holidays Act, introduced by Rt. Hon. Sir John Lubbock, MP, 4th baronet—later Lord Avebury—and this statute regulated bank holidays as follows:

England and Wales
Good Friday (by Common Law)
Easter Monday (by Statute)
May Day (from 1978)*
Spring Holiday (last Monday in May)*
Late Summer Holiday (last Monday in August)*
Christmas Day, 25 Dec. (by Common Law)
Boxing Day, 26 Dec., or St Stephen's Day, unless this falls on a Sunday, in which case 27 Dec. (by Statute)

---

* It was announced by the President of the Board of Trade in 1965 that in England and Wales the Whitsun holiday would be replaced by the fixed Spring Holiday on the last Monday in May and that the August Bank Holiday would be replaced by the Late Summer Holiday on the last Monday in August from 1967 onwards. This was adopted also in Northern Ireland. New Year's Day also became a Bank Holiday from 1976. On 31 March 1976 a May Day (1 May) Holiday was announced by the retiring Prime Minister, effective from Monday 1 May 1978.

Scotland
New Year's Day, 1 Jan., but if this falls on a Sunday, the next day (by Statute) and the day following (by Statute)
Good Friday (by Statute)
The first Monday in May (by Statute)
The first Monday in August (by Statute)
Christmas Day, 25 Dec. (by Statute)
In addition most Scottish cities and towns have a spring and autumn holiday fixed by local custom.

Northern Ireland
March 17, St Patrick's Day, or if this falls on a Sunday, the next day (by Statute)
Good Friday (by Statute)
Easter Monday (by Statute)
Easter Tuesday (but note banks in fact remain open on this public holiday) (by Statute)
12 July (Battle of the Boyne Day), but if this falls on a Sunday, the next day★
Christmas Day, 25 Dec. (by Statute)
Boxing Day, 26 Dec. or St Stephen's Day, unless this falls on a Sunday, in which case 27 Dec. (by Statute)

In addition to the above public and bank holidays the Sovereign has power under Section 4 of the 1871 Act to proclaim a public holiday in any district, borough, town city, county or throughout the whole country. Such occasions were on her Coronation Day in 1953 and her Jubilee Day in 1977. If a Bank holiday is inexpedient it may be replaced by another date by Proclamation.

Easter Day
Easter, the Sunday on which the resurrection of Christ is celebrated in the Christian world is, unlike Christmas which is fixed, a 'moveable feast'.
The celebration of Easter is believed to have begun in about AD 68. The English word Easter probably derives from *Eostre*, a Saxon goddess whose festival was celebrated about the time of the vernal equinox.

Easter Days and Leap Years 1978–2000
(Years in bold type are leap years)

1978	26 Mar.	1990	15 Apr.
1979	15 Apr.	1991	31 Mar.
1980	6 Apr.	**1992**	19 Apr.
1981	19 Apr.	1993	11 Apr.
1982	11 Apr.	1994	3 Apr.
1983	3 Apr.	1995	16 Apr.
1984	22 Apr.	**1996**	7 Apr.
1985	7 Apr.	1997	30 Mar.
1986	30 Mar.	1998	12 Apr.
1987	19 Apr.	1999	4 Apr.
1988	3 Apr.	**2000**	23 Apr.
1989	26 Mar.		

The date of Easter has been a matter of constant dispute between the eastern and western Christian churches. Almost the entire calendar of the Christian religion revolves around the date upon which, in any given year, Easter falls. The repercussions extend in Christian countries into civil life because, for example, in England the date of the statutory Whitsun bank holiday of course depends on the date of Easter.
According to English Statute Law by Act of 1751 (24 Geo. II, **c**. 23) Easter Day is the *first* Sunday after the full moon which occurs on, or next after, 21 Mar., but if this full

moon occurs on a Sunday, Easter Day is on the Sunday after. The moon, for the purposes of this Act, is not the real moon but the paschal moon which is a hypothetical moon, the full details of which can be found in the *Book of Common Prayer*. Thus Easter may fall on any one of the thirty-five days from 22 Mar. (as last in 1818) to 25 Apr. (as last in 1943) inclusive.
Variations. It is a nautical custom that the Union flag (or more practically the Ensign) is flown upside down this is an improvised distress signal.
The House of Commons agreed in June 1928, by passing the Easter Act, to redefine Easter as 'the first Sunday after the second Saturday in Apr.'. The date would thus have fallen only between 9 Apr. and 15 Apr. inclusive (i.e. either the second or third Sunday in April). The measure failed owing to the provision that it should require the support of the various international Christian churches, which was, despite the efforts of the League of Nations, not forthcoming.
The United Nations in 1949 considered the establishment of a perpetual world calendar, which would automatically and incidentally have fixed Easter, but the proposals were shelved indefinitely in 1956.
The Vatican Council in Rome in October 1963 approved the resolution to fix the date of Easter, subject to the agreement of other Christian churches, by 2058 votes to nine against.
The boldest scheme for calendar reform, which is winning increasing support, is that the year should be divided into four quarters of thirteen weeks, with each day of the year being assigned a fixed day of the week. By this scheme it is thought likely that Easter would always fall on Sunday, 8 Apr. For this calendar to conform with the mean solar year a 'blank day' would be required each year.

Summer Time
The device of decreeing that the legal time of day should be one hour in advance of Greenwich Mean Time during the summer months was introduced by Act of Parliament in 1916.
The practice is now governed by the Summer Time Act of 1925. The *statutory* moment for putting the clocks on one hour is at 2 a.m. (GMT) on the day after the third Saturday in April, but if that Sunday happens to be Easter Day (as in 1965, 1976, 1979, 1981, 1987, 1990 and 1992) Summer Time will start a week earlier.
Statutorily, Summer Time always ends at 2 a.m. (BST) on the day after the first Saturday in October.
BUT in practice Summer Time can be extended (at either or both ends of the period) by the Home Secretary by means of an Order in Council, and this was done in 1961, 1962 and 1963 with extensions of three weeks in each direction.
As a matter of record, it may be noted that the 1925 Act operated as prescribed until 1940. Then from 1941 to 1945 and again in 1947 there was Double Summer Time, i.e. Greenwich Mean Time plus two hours. From 1948 until 1952 and since 1961, the period of Single Summer Time was extended, while the Act operated normally in the intervening years of 1953 to 1960.

The Union flag
The Union flag, commonly called the Union Jack, is described in a proclamation of 1 Jan. 1801, by authority of the Union with Ireland Act of 1800, as:
'Azure (i.e. blue), the crosses saltire (i.e. diagonal) of St Andrew (i.e. for Scotland) and St Patrick (i.e. for Ireland) quarterly per saltire, countercharged argent (i.e. white) and gules (i.e. red); the latter fimbriated (i.e. narrowly bordered) of the second, surmounted (i.e. overlaid) by the cross of St George (i.e. for England), of the third, fimbriated as the saltire.'

Every citizen in the Commonwealth may fly the Union Jack.
In the armed forces of the United Kingdom the Union flag is the personal flag of Admirals of the Fleet and Field Marshals.
The Union flag may by custom fly from 8 a.m. to sunset on public buildings.

Variations. It is a nautical custom that the Union flag (or more practically the Ensign) is flown upside down this is an improvised distress signal.

Half Mast. The Union Jack is flown at half mast in mourning (a) for the death of the Sovereign (from announcement to funeral except from 11 a.m. to sunset on the day of the Proclamation of the successor); (b) at the funerals of Prime Ministers and ex-Prime Ministers; and (c) by specific Royal Command for the funeral of members of the Royal Family, Foreign Rulers, and on other occasions. If a day for flying flags right up coincides with a half-mast occasion the former will take precedence in case (c) except for the building in which the body may be lying.

Quarter days
(England, Northern Ireland, Wales)
25 Mar. Lady Day (The Annunication of Our Lady the Virgin Mary)
24 June Midsummer (Nativity of St John The Baptist)
29 Sept. Michaelmas (Festival of St Michael and All Angels)
25 Dec. Christmas (Festival of Christ's birth)
Half quarter days are on Candlemas (2 Feb.), 9 May, 11 Aug. and Martinmas (11 Nov.).

Scottish term days
2 Feb. Candlemas (or the Feast of the Purification of the Virgin Mary)
15 May Whit Sunday (from Old English *Hƿita Sunnandaeg* or White Sunday because of the white robes of the newly baptised)
1 Aug. Lammas (from Old English *hláf maesse*, loaf-mass, hence harvest festival)
11 Nov. Martinmas (St Martin's (4th century Bishop of Tours) Day)

The zodiac
The zodiac (from the Greek *zōdiakos kyklos*, circle of animals) is an unscientific and astrological system devised in Mesopotamia *c.* 3000 BC.
The zodiac is an imaginary belt of pictorial constellations which lie as a backdrop quite arbitrarily 8 degrees on either side of the annual path or ecliptic of the sun. It is divided into twelve sections each of 30 degrees. Each has been allocated a name from the constellation which at one time coincided with that sector. The present lack of coincidence of the zodiacal sectors with the constellations from which they are named has been caused mainly by the lack of proper allowance for leap days. The old order is nonetheless adhered to.

The traditional 'signs' are:
Aries, the Ram 21 Mar.–19 Apr.
Taurus, the Bull 20 Apr.–20 May
Gemini, the Twins 21 May–21 June
Cancer, the Crab 22 June–22 July
Leo, the Lion 23 July–22 Aug.
Virgo, the Virgin 23 Aug.–22 Sept.
Libra, the Balance 23 Sept.–23 Oct.
Scorpio, the Scorpion 24 Oct.–21 Nov.
Saggittarius, the Archer 22 Nov.–21 Dec.
Capricornus, the Goat 22 Dec.–19 Jan.
Aquarius, the Water Carrier 20 Jan.–18 Feb.
Pisces, the Fish 19 Feb.–20 Mar.

Standard time

Until the last quarter of last century the time kept was a local affair, or, in the smaller countries, based on the time kept in the capital city. But the spread of railways across the vaster countries caused great time-keeping confusion to the various railway companies and their passengers. In 1880 Greenwich Mean Time (GMT) became the legal time in the British Isles (but see note re Summer Time) and by 1883 the movement to establish international time by zones was successful.

The world, for this purpose, is divided into 24 zones, or segments, each of 15° of longitude, with twelve that, being to the east, are fast on Greenwich time, and twelve that, being to the west, are slow on Greenwich time.

Each zone is 7½° on either side of its central meridian. The International Date line—with some variations to suit obvious geographical conditions—runs down the 180° meridian.

A very few countries or divisions of countries do not adhere to the Greenwich system at all and in others no zoning system is used, i.e. the whole nation, despite spanning more than one of the 24 segments, elects to keep the same time. Yet a third group (e.g. India) uses differences of half an hour.

Europe has three zones, part keeping GMT, others mid-European time (i.e. GMT + 1) and the remainder east European time (GMT + 2).

In the United States there are four zones: Eastern, Central, Mountain and Pacific, and these are 5, 6, 7 and 8 hours respectively slow on Greenwich.

The authoritative and complete reference, where the method of time keeping in every place in the world can be found, is *The Nautical Almanac*, published annually by HMSO.

Watches at sea

A watch at sea is four hours except the period between 4 p.m. and 8 p.m., which is divided into two short watches termed the first dog watch and the second dog watch. The word dog is here a corruption of 'dodge'. The object of these is to prevent the same men always being on duty during the same hours each day.

Midnight–4 a.m.	Middle Watch
4 a.m.–8 a.m.	Morning Watch
8 a.m.–noon	Forenoon Watch
noon–4 p.m.	Afternoon Watch
4 p.m.–6 p.m.	First Dog Watch
6 p.m.–8 p.m.	Second Dog Watch
8 p.m.–Midnight	First Watch

Time is marked by bells—one stroke for each half-hour elapsed during a watch which thus ends on 8 bells or 4 bells for a dog watch. The New Year is brought in with 16 bells.

Sunrise, sunset and twilight

The *Nautical Almanac* gives the GMT of sunrise and sunset for each two degrees of latitude for every third day in the year. The sunrise is the instant when the rim of the sun appears above the horizon, and the sunset when the last segment disappears below the horizon. But because of the Earth's atmosphere, the transition from day to night and vice versa is a gradual process, the length of which varies according to the declination of the sun and the latitude of the observer. The intermediate stages are called twilight.

There are three sorts of twilight:

Civil twilight. This occurs when the centre of the sun is 6° below the horizon. Before this moment in the morning and after it in the evening ordinary outdoor activities are impossible without artificial light.

Nautical twilight. This occurs when the sun is 12° below the horizon. Before this time in the morning and after it in the evening the sea horizon is invisible.

Astronomical twilight. This is the moment when the centre of the sun is 18° below the horizon. Before this time in the morning or after it in the evening there is a complete absence of sunlight.

Lighting up time for lights on vehicles occurs *half an hour* after the moment of sunset in accordance with the provisions of Section 17 of The Road Transport Lighting Act, 1957.

Lighting up time is later in the west (e.g. at Cardiff) than the east (e.g. at London). Similarly, lighting up time in the north (e.g. at Edinburgh) is also later than in London in summer but earlier in winter.

Wedding anniversaries

The choice of object or material attached to specific anniversaries is in no sense "official". The list below is a combination of commercial and traditional usage.

First	Cotton
Second	Paper
Third	Leather
Fourth	Fruit, flowers
Fifth	Wooden
Sixth	Sugar
Seventh	Wool, copper
Eighth	Bronze, pottery
Ninth	Pottery, willow
Tenth	Tin
Eleventh	Steel
Twelfth	Silk, linen
Thirteenth	Lace
Fourteenth	Ivory
Fifteenth	Crystal
Twentieth	China
Twenty-fifth	Silver
Thirtieth	Pearl
Thirty-fifth	Coral
Fortieth	Ruby
Forty-fifth	Sapphire
Fiftieth	Golden
Fifty-fifth	Emerald
Sixtieth	Diamond
Seventieth	Platinum

DAYS OF THE YEAR: BIRTHS, DEATHS & EVENTS

Below are given dates of birth and death, where accurately known, of people generally accepted as being famous or infamous. Included are also the dates of highly memorable occasions.

JANUARY (31 days)

DERIVATION

Latin, *Januarius*, or *Ianuarius*, named after Janus, the two-faced Roman god of doorways (*ianuae*) and archways (*iani*), as presiding over the 'entrance', or beginning of the year.

Daily Universal Register became *The Times* 1788; Baron Pierre de Coubertin b. 1863

Titus Livius (Livy) d. AD 18; Publius Ovidius Naso (Ovid) d. AD 18

Marcus Tullius Cicero b. 106 BC

Augustus John b. 1878; T. S. Eliot d. 1965

Edward the Confessor d. 1066; German National Socialist Party founded 1919

Joan of Arc b. c. 1412; Louis Braille d. 1852; Jet propulsion invented 1944

Sir Thomas Lawrence d. 1830

Marco Polo d. 1324; Galileo Galilei d. 1642; Lord Baden-Powell d. 1941

Richard Nixon b. 1913

Penny Post began in Britain 1840; League of Nations founded 1920

Thomas Hardy d. 1928

Edmund Burke b. 1729

13 James Joyce d. 1941
14 Albert Schweitzer b. 1875; Charles Lutwidge Dodgson (alias Lewis Carroll) d. 1898; Casablanca Conference 1943
15 Act of Supremacy 1535; Martin Luther King b. 1929
16 Ivan the Terrible crowned 1547; Federal prohibition of alcohol introduced, USA 1920
17 Benjamin Franklin b. 1706; David Lloyd George b. 1863
18 A. A. Milne b. 1882; Scott reached South Pole 1912; Rudyard Kipling d. 1936
19 James Watt b. 1736; Edgar Allan Poe b. 1809; Paul Cézanne b. 1839
20 David Garrick d. 1779; John Ruskin d. 1900; King George V d. 1936
21 Vladimir I. Ulanyov (Lenin) d. 1924
22 Francis Bacon (Viscount St Albans) b. 1561; George (later Lord) Byron b. 1788; Queen Victoria d. 1901
23 William Pitt (the younger) d. 1806; Edouard Manet b. 1832
24 Frederick the Great b. 1712; Gold discovered in California 1848; Sir Winston Churchill d. 1965

25 Robert Burns b. 1759
26 General Charles Gordon killed 1885; Baird's first demonstration of TV, Soho, London 1926
27 Wolfgang Amadeus Mozart b. 1756; Giuseppe Verdi d. 1901
28 Charlemagne b. 814; King Henry VIII d. 1547; Sir Francis Drake d. 1596
29 Victoria Cross instituted 1856; Anton Chekhov b. 1860; W. C. Fields b. 1880
30 Charles I executed 1649; Franklin Delano Roosevelt b. 1882; Mohandas Gandhi assassinated 1948
31 Franz Schubert b. 1797; *Great Eastern* launched 1858; Anna Pavlova b. 1881

FEBRUARY (29 days)

DERIVATION

Latin, *Februarius* (*februare*, to purify), from *februa*, a festival of purification held on 15 Feb.

1 Victor Herbert b. 1859; British State Labour Exchanges opened 1910

2 Nell Gwyn b. 1650; Fritz Kreisler b. 1875; Jascha Heifetz b. 1901; German capitulation at Stalingrad 1943
3 Felix Mendelssohn-Bartholdy b. 1809; Yalta conference began 1945
4 Thomas Carlyle d. 1881; Submarine warfare by Germany 1915;
5 Sir Robert Peel b. 1788
6 Charles II d. 1685; Queen Elizabeth II succeeded to throne 1952
7 Sir Thomas More b. 1478; Charles Dickens b. 1812
8 Mary, Queen of Scots, executed 1587; Russo-Japanese War began 1904
9 Fyodor Dostoyevsky d. 1881
10 Académie Française founded 1635; Charles Lamb b. 1775
11 Thomas Alva Edison b. 1847; Vatican City independence 1929
12 Abraham Lincoln b. 1809; Charles Darwin b. 1809; Marie Lloyd b. 1870; Britain's last invasion, 1797
13 Massacre of the MacDonald clan at Glencoe 1692
14 Copernicus b. 1473; Captain James Cook killed, 1779; Malthus b. 1766
15 Galileo Galilei b. 1564
16 George Macaulay Trevelyan b. 1876
17 Molière d. 1673; Edward German b. 1862; Geronimo d. 1909
18 Martin Luther d. 1546; Michelangelo d. 1564; *Pilgrim's Progress* published 1678
19 David Garrick b. 1717
20 Percy Grainger d. 1961
21 Cardinal John Henry Newman b. 1801
22 George Washington b. 1732; Rev. Sydney Smith d. 1845; Robert (later Lord) Baden-Powell b. 1857
23 Samuel Pepys b. 1633; George Frideric Handel b. 1685; John Keats d. 1821
24 Sir Samuel Hoare b. 1880
25 Sir Christopher Wren d. 1723; Enrico Caruso b. 1873
26 Victor Hugo b. 1802
27 Henry Wadsworth Longfellow b. 1807; British Labour Party founded 1900
28 Relief of Ladysmith 1900
29 Gioacchino Antonio Rossini b. 1792

MARCH (31 days)

DERIVATION
Latin, *Martius*, the month of Mars, the Roman god of war and the protector of vegetation.

1 Frédéric Chopin b. 1810
2 John Wesley d. 1791
3 Robert Adam d. 1792; Alexander Graham Bell b. 1847; Henry Wood b. 1869
4 US Constitution in force 1789; Comintern formed 1919;
5 William (later Lord) Beveridge b. 1879; Churchill's Iron Curtain speech 1946; Iosif Stalin d. 1953
6 Michelangelo b. 1475; Elizabeth Barrett Browning b. 1806
7 Bell's telephone patented 1876
8 Hector Berlioz d. 1869
9 Amerigo Vespucci b. 1451
10 Arthur Honegger b. 1892; Jan Masaryk d. 1948
11 Sir Harold Wilson b. 1916; German troops enter Austria 1938; Sir Alexander Fleming d. 1955
12 Russian revolution, 1917; Sun Yat-sen d. 1925
13 Uranus discovered 1781
14 Albert Einstein b. 1879; Karl Marx d. 1883; First trans-Atlantic broadcast 1925
15 Julius Caesar assassinated 44 BC
16 Tiberius, Emperor of Rome, d. AD 37; Lord Beveridge d. 1963

17 Marcus Aurelius d. 180
18 Ivan the Terrible d. 1584; Walpole d. 1745
19 David Livingstone b. 1813
20 Sir Isaac Newton d. 1727; Napoleon's 'Hundred Days' began 1815
21 Johann Sebastian Bach b. 1685; Modest Mussorgsky b. 1839
22 Wolfgang von Goethe d. 1832
23 Stamp Act 1765; Alfred (later Viscount) Milner b. 1854
24 Queen Elizabeth I d. 1603; Union of English and Scottish Crowns 1603
25 Rome Treaty signed by Six 1957
26 Ludwig van Beethoven d. 1827; David Lloyd George d. 1945
27 King James I d. 1625; U.S. Navy created 1794; Arnold Bennett d. 1931
28 Britain and France entered Crimean War 1854; Spanish Civil War ended 1939
29 Sir William Walton b. 1902
30 Francisco de Goya b. 1746; Vincent van Gogh b. 1853
31 Josef Haydn b. 1732; John Constable d. 1837; Charlotte Brontë d. 1855

APRIL (30 days)

DERIVATION
Latin, *Aprilis*, from *aperire* (to open), the season when trees and flowers begin to 'open'.

1 Prince Otto von Bismarck b. 1815; Royal Air Force formed 1918
2 Charlemagne b. 742; Hans Christian Andersen b. 1805; Emile Zola d. 1840
3 Pony Express established in USA 1860; Johannes Brahms d. 1897
4 North Atlantic Treaty signed 1949
5 Joseph (later Lord) Lister b. 1827; Algernon Charles Swinburne b. 1837
6 Richard I d. 1199; US Declaration of War 1917; PAYE introduced in Britain 1944
7 Dick Turpin hanged 1739; William Wordsworth b. 1770
8 Entente Cordiale signed 1904
9 Francis Bacon (Viscount St Albans) d. 1626; US Civil War ended 1865
10 William Booth b. 1829; Algernon Charles Swinburne d. 1909
11 Sir Gerald du Maurier d. 1934
12 US Civil War began 1861; Franklin Delano Roosevelt d. 1945; Yuri Gagarin orbits earth 1961
13 John Dryden became first Poet Laureate 1668; Thomas Jefferson b. 1743
14 George Frideric Handel d. 1759; Ernest Bevin d. 1951
15 Leonardo da Vinci b. 1452; Abraham Lincoln d. 1865 (wounded by assassin); "Titanic" sank, 1912
16 Battle of Culloden 1746; Francisco de Goya d. 1828; Sir Charles Chaplin b. 1889
17 John Pierpoint Morgan b. 1837; Nikita Khrushchev b. 1894
18 San Francisco earthquake 1906; Republic of Ireland established 1949; Albert Einstein d. 1955
19 Lord Byron d. 1824; Benjamin Disraeli (Earl of Beaconsfield) d. 1881; Charles Darwin d. 1882; Pierre Curie d. 1906
20 Adolf Hitler b. 1889
21 Foundation of Rome 753 BC; Charlotte Brontë b. 1816; Mark Twain d. 1910; Queen Elizabeth II b. 1926
22 Lenin b. 1870; Kathleen Ferrier b. 1912; Yehudi Menuhin b. 1916
23 William Shakespeare d. 1616; William Wordsworth d. 1850
24 Anthony Trollope b. 1815
25 Oliver Cromwell b. 1599
26 Emma, Lady Hamilton, b. 1765
27 Gen. Ulysses S. Grant b. 1822

28 Mutiny on the *Bounty* 1789; Benito Mussolini killed 1945; Japan regained independence 1952
29 William Randolph Hearst b. 1863; Emperor Hirohito of Japan b. 1901
30 George Washington became first US President 1789; Adolf Hitler committed suicide 1945

MAY (31 days)

DERIVATION
Latin, *Maius*, either from Maia, an obscure goddess, or from *maiores* (elders), on the grounds that the month honoured old people, as June honoured the young.

1 Wellington b. 1769; Great Exhibition opened at Crystal Palace 1851; David Livingstone d. 1873
2 Leonardo da Vinci d. 1519; Catherine the Great b. 1729
3 Niccolò Machiavelli b. 1469; Festival of Britain opened 1951
4 Epsom Derby first run 1780
5 Sören Kierkegaard b. 1813; Karl Marx b. 1818; Napoleon Bonaparte d. 1821
6 Pushkin b. 1799 (N.S.); Sigmund Freud b. 1856; First 4 min. mile by Roger Bannister at Oxford 1954
7 Johannes Brahms b. 1833; Pyotr Tchaikovsky b. 1840; *Lusitania* sunk 1915
8 VE-Day 1945
9 Sir James Barrie b. 1860
10 Winston Churchill became Prime Minister 1940
11 Irving Berlin b. 1888
12 Florence Nightingale b. 1820; General Strike ended 1926
13 Sir Arthur Sullivan b. 1842
14 Home Guard formed in Britain 1940; State of Israel proclaimed 1948
15 Pierre Curie b. 1859
16 First film 'Oscars' awarded 1929
17 Edward Jenner b. 1749; Mafeking relieved 1900; Paul Dukas d. 1935
18 Walter Gropius b. 1883
19 St Dunstan d. 988; Anne Boleyn executed 1536
20 Christopher Columbus d. 1506; John Stuart Mill b. 1806
21 Alexander Pope b. 1688; Elizabeth Fry b. 1780; Lindbergh landed in Paris 1927
22 Richard Wagner b. 1813; Sir Arthur Conan Doyle b. 1859
23 Thomas Hood b. 1799; Kit Carson d. 1868; Henrik Ibsen d. 1906
24 Nicolaus Copernicus d. 1543; Queen Victoria b. 1819
25 Ralph Waldo Emerson b. 1803
26 John Churchill (later Duke of Marlborough) b. 1650; Samuel Pepys d. 1703; Al Jolson b. 1886
27 John Calvin b. 1564; Habeas Corpus Act 1679; Dunkirk evacuation began, 1940; Jawaharlal Nehru d. 1964
28 William Pitt (the younger) b. 1759
29 John F. Kennedy b. 1917; Mount Everest climbed 1953
30 Joan of Arc executed 1431; Peter Paul Rubens d. 1640; Voltaire d. 1778
31 Pepy's Diary ends 1669; Josef Haydn d. 1809; Battle of Jutland 1916

JUNE (30 days)

DERIVATION
Latin, *Junius*, either the goddess Juno, or from *iuniores* (young people), as the month dedicated to youth.

1 Brigham Young b. 1801; John Masefield b. 1878; Helen Keller d. 1968
2 Thomas Hardy b. 1840; Coronation of Queen Elizabeth II 1953

3 Sydney Smith b. 1771; Johann Strauss (the younger) d. 1899
4 Giacomo Casanova d. 1798
5 Adam Smith bapt., 1723; John Maynard Keynes b. 1883; O. Henry d. 1910; Marshall Plan 1947
6 D-Day 1944
7 Robert I ('The Bruce') d. 1329; George ('Beau') Brummell b. 1778
8 Edward, the Black Prince, d. 1376
9 Peter the Great b. 1672 (N.S.); George Stephenson b. 1781; Charles Dickens d. 1870; Cole Porter b. 1893
10 Duke of Edinburgh b. 1921; Frederick Delius d. 1934
11 Ben Jonson b. 1573; John Constable b. 1776; Richard Strauss b. 1864
12 Charles Kingsley b. 1819
13 William Butler Yeats b. 1865; Boxer Rising in China 1900;
14 Battle of Naseby 1645; G K Chesterton d. 1936; John Logie Baird d. 1946
15 Magna Carta sealed 1215; Edward, the Black Prince, b. 1330
16 Duke of Marlborough d. 1722
17 John Wesley b. 1703; Battle of Bunker Hill 1775; Igor Stravinsky b. 1882
18 USA declared war on Britain 1812; Battle of Waterloo 1815
19 Sir James Barrie d. 1937
20 Black Hole of Calcutta 1756; Jacques Offenbach b. 1819
21 Machiavelli d. 1527; Inigo Jones d. 1652; Nikolay Rimsky-Korsakov d. 1908
22 Darius Milhaud d. 1974
23 Battle of Plassey 1757; Duke of Windsor b. 1894; Sterling floated 1972
24 Battle of Bannockburn 1314; Lucrezia Borgia d. 1519; John Hampden d. 1643
25 Custer's Last Stand 1876; Earl Mountbatten b. 1900; Korean War began 1950
26 King George IV d. 1830; Corn Laws repealed 1846; UN Charter signed 1945
27 Charles Stewart Parnell b. 1846
28 Rubens b. 1577; Archduke Franz Ferdinand assassinated 1914
29 Elizabeth Barrett Browning d. 1861
30 John Gay b. 1685

JULY (31 days)

DERIVATION

Latin, *Julius*, after Gaius Julius Caesar (b. 12 July, probably in 102 BC, d. 15 March 44 BC), the Roman soldier and statesman. (Formerly known by the Romans as *Quintilis* (the fifth month.)

1 Aurore Dupin (alias George Sand) b. 1804; Louis Blériot b. 1872
2 Thomas Cranmer b. 1489; Sir Robert Peel d. 1850; Joseph Chamberlain d. 1914; Ernest Hemingway d. 1961
3 Robert Adam b. 1728
4 US Declaration of Independence approved 1776; Thomas Jefferson d. 1826
5 Cecil Rhodes b. 1853; Britain's National Health Service inaugurated 1948
6 Guy de Maupassant d. 1893
7 Gustav Mahler b. 1860; Sir Arthur Conan Doyle d. 1930
8 Percy Bysshe Shelley d. 1822; Joseph Chamberlain b. 1836; Rockefeller b. 1839
9 Edward Heath b. 1916
10 John Calvin b. 1509
11 Robert I ('The Bruce') b. 1274
12 Julius Caesar b. 100 BC; Erasmus d. 1536
13 Sidney Webb b. 1859
14 Storming of the Bastille began 1789; Gerald Ford b. 1913
15 Inigo Jones b. 1573; Rembrandt van Rijn b. 1606; Anton Chekhov d. 1904
16 Sir Joshua Reynolds b. 1723; First atomic bomb exploded 1945

17 Adam Smith d. 1790; Spanish Civil War began 1936
18 William Makepeace Thackeray b. 1811
19 Edgar Degas b. 1834
20 First Moon landing by man 1969
21 Robert Burns d. 1796
22 Battle of Salamanca 1812
23 Haile Selassie b. 1892
24 Simón Bolívar b. 1783
25 Louis Blériot flew Channel 1909
26 George Bernard Shaw b. 1856; Carl Jung b. 1875; Aldous Huxley b. 1894
27 Hilaire Belloc b. 1870; Korean Armistice signed 1953
28 Johann Sebastian Bach d. 1750
29 Spanish Armada defeated 1588; Robert Schumann d. 1856; Benito Mussolini b. 1883; Vincent van Gogh d. 1890
30 William Penn d. 1718; Henry Ford b. 1863; Prince Otto Von Bismarck d. 1898
31 St Ignatius of Loyola d. 1556

AUGUST (31 days)

DERIVATION

Latin, *Augustus*, after Augustus Caesar (born Gaius Octavius), the first Roman emperor. (Originally called *Sextilis*, the sixth month.)

1 Battle of the Nile 1798
2 William Rufus d. 1100; Thomas Gainsborough d. 1788; Enrico Caruso d. 1921
3 Rupert Brooke b. 1887; Joseph Conrad d. 1924; Colette d. 1954
4 Percy Bysshe Shelley b. 1792; Britain declared War on Germany 1914
5 Guy de Maupassant b. 1850
6 Alfred, Lord Tennyson b. 1809; Alexander Fleming b. 1881; Atomic bomb dropped on Hiroshima 1945
7 British Summer Time Act 1924
9 John Dryden b. 1631; Atomic bomb dropped on Nagasaki 1945
10 Greenwich Observatory founded 1675; Herbert Hoover b. 1874
11 Cardinal John Henry Newman d. 1890
12 Robert Southey b. 1774; George Stephenson d. 1848
13 Battle of Blenheim 1704; Florence Nightingale d. 1910
14 Bertolt Brecht d. 1956
15 Napoleon Bonaparte b. 1769; Panama Canal opened 1914; VJ-Day 1945; India and Pakistan independence 1947
16 Peterloo Massacre 1819; Cyprus became independent 1960
17 Frederick the Great d. 1786; Davy Crockett b. 1786; Mae West b. 1892
18 Lord John (later 1st Earl) Russell b. 1792; Berlin Wall completed 1961
19 James Watt d. 1819
20 William Booth d. 1912
21 Princess Margaret b. 1930
22 English Civil War began 1642; Claude Debussy b. 1862
23 Rudolph Valentino d. 1926; World Council of Churches formed 1948
24 William Wilberforce b. 1759
25 David Hume d. 1776; Michael Faraday d. 1867; Paris liberated 1944
26 Battle of Crécy 1346; Sir Robert Walpole b. 1676; Prince Albert b. 1819
27 Confucius b. 551 BC; Titian d. 1576; Krakatoa erupted 1883; Sir Donald Bradman b. 1908
28 Wolfgang von Goethe b. 1749
29 Oliver Wendell Holmes, Sr. b. 1809; Brigham Young d. 1877
30 Ernest (later Lord) Rutherford b. 1871
31 John Bunyan d. 1688; Queen Wilhelmina of the Netherlands b. 1880

SEPTEMBER (30 days)

DERIVATION

Latin, from *septem* (seven), as it was originally the seventh month.

1 Germany invaded Poland 1939
2 Great Fire of London began 1666
3 Oliver Cromwell d. 1658; Britain declared War on Germany 1939
4 Albert Schweitzer d. 1965
5 Louis XIV of France b. 1638
6 *Mayflower* sailed from Plymouth 1620;
7 Queen Elizabeth I b. 1533; London Blitz began 1940; C. B. Fry d. 1956
8 Richard Coeur de Lion b. 1157; Antonín Dvořák b. 1841; First V2 landed in England 1944; Richard Strauss d. 1949
9 William the Conqueror d. 1087; Battle of Flodden Field 1513; Tolstoy b. 1828 (N.S.)
10 Mungo Park b. 1771
11 O Henry b. 1862; Jan Smuts d. 1950
12 Herbert Henry Asquith b. 1852
13 Gen. James Wolfe d. 1759
14 Gregorian Calendar in Britain 1752; Duke of Wellington d. 1852
15 James Fenimore Cooper b. 1789; Isambard Kingdom Brunel d. 1859
16 Andrew Bonar Law b. 1858
17 US Constitution signed 1787
18 Samuel Johnson b. 1709
19 Battle of Poitiers 1356
20 Battle of Lexington 1861; Sterling off Gold Standard 1931
21 Sir Walter Scott d. 1832; H G Wells b. 1866
22 Michael Faraday b. 1791; Commercial Television began in Britain 1955
23 Augustus, Emperor of Rome, b. 63 BC; Sigmund Freud d. 1939
24 Horace Walpole b. 1717; A. P. (later Sir Alan) Herbert b. 1890
25 Samuel Butler d. 1680
26 T S Eliot b. 1888; Pope Paul VI b. 1897; Degas d. 1917; *Queen Mary* launched 1934
27 St Vincent de Paul d. 1660; Stockton-Darlington Railway opened 1825; *Queen Elizabeth* launched 1938
28 Georges Clemenceau b. 1841; Louis Pasteur d. 1895; W. H. Auden d. 1973
29 Battle of Marathon 490 BC; Robert (later Lord) Clive b. 1725; Emile Zola d. 1902
30 First BBC TV Broadcast 1929

OCTOBER (31 days)

DERIVATION

Latin, from *octo* (eight), originally the eighth month.

1 Paul Dukas b. 1865; Vladimir Horowitz b. 1904; Jimmy Carter b. 1924
2 Mohandas Gandhi b. 1869
3 St Francis of Assisi b. 1226
4 Rembrandt van Rijn d. 1669; Damon Runyon b. 1884; Sputnik I launched 1957
5 Jacques Offenbach d. 1880
6 Charles Stewart Parnell d. 1891; Alfred, Lord Tennyson d. 1892
7 Oliver Wendell Holmes, Sr. d. 1894
8 Henry Fielding d. 1754
9 Universal Postal Union founded 1874
10 Henry Cavendish b. 1731
11 Battle of Camperdown 1797
12 Elizabeth Fry d. 1845; Ralph Vaughan Williams b. 1872; Nurse Edith Cavell executed 1915
13 Sir Henry Irving d. 1905
14 Battle of Hastings 1066; William Penn b. 1644; Dwight D. Eisenhower b. 1890
15 Publius Vergilius Maro (Virgil) b. 70 BC; Friedrich Wilhelm Nietzsche b. 1844
16 Marie Antoinette executed 1793; Oscar Wilde b. 1854; Eugene O'Neill b. 1888
17 Sir Philip Sidney d. 1586; Frédéric Chopin d. 1849

18 Viscount Palmerston d. 1865; Pierre Trudeau b. 1919; Thomas Alva Edison d. 1931
19 King John d. 1216; Jonathan Swift d. 1745; Lord Rutherford d. 1937
20 Sir Christopher Wren b. 1632; Viscount Palmerston b. 1784
21 Samuel Taylor Coleridge b. 1772; Battle of Trafalgar 1805
22 Franz Liszt b. 1811; Margaret Thatcher b. 1926
23 W G Grace d. 1915; Battle of El Alamein began 1942
24 UN Organization established 1945
25 Battle of Agincourt 1415; Charge of the Light Brigade at Balaklava 1854
26 King Alfred d. 899; William Hogarth d. 1764
27 Erasmus b. 1466; Theodore Roosevelt b. 1858
28 John Locke d. 1704; Evelyn Waugh b. 1903
29 Sir Walter Ralegh executed 1618; James Boswell b. 1740; New York stock market crash 1929
30 Andrew Bonar Law d. 1923
31 Vermeer bapt. 1632; John Keats b. 1795; Chiang Kai-shek b. 1887; Augustus John d. 1961

NOVEMBER (30 days)

DERIVATION
Latin, from *novem* (nine), originally the ninth month.

1 Benvenuto Cellini b. 1500; First hydrogen bomb exploded 1952
2 Marie Antoinette b. 1755; George Bernard Shaw d. 1950
3 William Cullen Bryant b. 1794; Karl Baedeker b. 1801
4 Sheridan bapt. 1751; Felix Mendelssohn-Bartholdy d. 1847
5 Gunpowder Plot 1605
6 John Philip Sousa b. 1854; Pyotr Tchaikovsky d. 1893
7 Marja Sklodowska (later Marie Curie) b. 1867
8 John Milton d. 1674; César Franck d. 1890; Munich Putsch 1923
9 Neville Chamberlain d. 1940; General Charles de Gaulle d. 1970

10 Martin Luther b. 1483; H M Stanley met David Livingstone at Ujiji 1871
11 Fyodor Dostoyevsky b. 1821; Armistice Day 1918; Sir Edward German d. 1936
12 King Canute d. 1035; Sir John Hawkins d. 1595; Auguste Rodin b. 1840
13 Robert Louis Stevenson b. 1850
14 Nell Gwyn d. 1687; Jawaharlal Nehru b. 1889; Prince of Wales b. 1948
15 William Pitt (the Elder) b. 1708; Erwin Rommel b. 1891
16 Tiberius b. 42 BC; Suez Canal opened 1869
17 Catherine the Great d. 1796; Bernard (later Viscount) Montgomery b. 1887
18 W S (later Sir William) Gilbert b. 1836; Amelita Galli-Curci b. 1889
19 Charles I b. 1600; Franz Schubert d. 1828; Mrs Indira Gandhi b. 1917
20 Count Leo Tolstoy d. 1910; Wedding of Queen Elizabeth II 1947
21 Voltaire b. 1694
22 André Gide b. 1869; Charles de Gaulle b. 1890; John F Kennedy assassinated 1963
23 Manuel de Falla b 1876
24 John Knox d. 1572; Charles Darwin's *Origin of Species* published 1859
25 Andrew Carnegie b. 1835
26 Cowper b. 1731; John McAdam d. 1836
27 Alexander Dubček b. 1921
28 William Blake b. 1757
29 Cardinal Thomas Wolsey d. 1530; Louisa May Alcott b. 1832
30 Jonathan Swift b. 1667; Samuel Clemens (alias Mark Twain) b. 1835; Sir Winston Churchill b. 1874

DECEMBER (31 days)

DERIVATION
Latin, from *decem* (ten), originally the tenth month.

1 King Henry I d. 1135; Queen Alexandra b. 1844; Beveridge Report 1942
2 Battle of Austerlitz 1805; Maria Callas b. 1923; First nuclear chain reaction 1942
3 Samuel Crompton b. 1753; Sir Rowland Hill b. 1795; Joseph Conrad b. 1857; R L Stevenson d. 1894

4 Thomas Carlyle b. 1795; Samuel Butler b. 1835; Francisco Franco b. 1892
5 Wolfgang Amadeus Mozart d. 1791; Claude Monet d. 1926
6 Warren Hastings b. 1732
7 Mary, Queen of Scots, b. 1542; Pearl Harbor attacked 1941
8 Jean Sibelius b. 1865
9 John Milton b. 1608
10 Royal Academy founded 1768; César Franck b. 1822; Alfred Nobel d. 1896
11 Hector Berlioz b. 1803; Edward VIII abdicated 1936
12 Robert Browning d. 1889; First trans-Atlantic radio signal 1901
13 Jan Vermeer d. 1675; Dr Samuel Johnson d. 1784; Heinrich Heine b. 1797
14 George Washington d. 1799; Amundsen reached South Pole 1911
15 Sitting Bull killed 1890; Queen Salote d. 1965; Walt Disney d. 1966
16 Ludwig van Beethoven b. 1770; Boston Tea Party 1773; Jane Austen b. 1775
17 Sir Humphrey Davy b. 1778; First aeroplane flight 1903
18 Antonio Stradivari d. 1737; Slavery abolished in USA 1865
19 Carl Wilhelm von Scheele b. 1742; Joseph Mallord William Turner d. 1851
20 Sir Robert Menzies b. 1894
21 Pilgrim Fathers landed 1620; Benjamin Disraeli b. 1804; Iosif Stalin b. 1879
22 Jean Racine b. 1639; James Wolfe b. 1726; Giacomo Puccini b. 1858
23 Sir Richard Arkwright b. 1732
24 St Ignatius of Loyola b. 1491; Vasco da Gama d. 1524; Matthew Arnold b. 1822
25 Sir Isaac Newton b. 1642
26 Thomas Gray b. 1716; Mao Tse-tung b. 1893; Radium discovered 1898
27 Johannes Kepler b. 1571; Louis Pasteur b. 1822; Charles Lamb d. 1834
28 Mary II d. 1694; Woodrow Wilson b. 1856; Lord Macaulay d. 1859
29 St Thomas à Becket killed 1170; William Ewart Gladstone b. 1809; Pablo Casals b. 1876; Jameson Raid 1895
30 Rudyard Kipling b. 1865; Stephen Leacock b. 1869; Grigory Rasputin assassinated 1916 (N.S.)
31 John Wycliffe d. 1384; Charles Edward Stuart (the Young Pretender) b. 1720; Henri Matisse b. 1869 ·

THE EARTH

Mass, density and volume

The Earth has a mass estimated to be 5 882 000 000 000 000 000 000 tons *5·976 × 10²¹ tonnes* and has a density 5·517 times that of water. The volume of the Earth has been estimated at 259 875 620 000 miles³ *1 083 208 840 000 km³*.

Dimensions

Its equatorial circumference is 24 901·47 miles *40 075,03 km* with a polar or meridianal circumference of 24 859·75 miles *40 007,89 km* indicating that the Earth is not a true sphere but flattened at the poles and hence an ellipsoid. The Earth also has a slight ellipticity at the equator since its long axis (about longitude 0°) is 174 yd *159 m* greater than the short axis. Artificial satellite measurements have also revealed further departures from this biaxial ellipsoid form in minor protuberances and depressions varying between extremes of 244 ft *74 m* in the area of Papua New Guinea and a depression of 354 ft *108 m* south of Sri Lanka (formerly

Ceylon) in the Indian Ocean. The equatorial diameter of the Earth is 7 926·385 miles *12 756,280 km* and the polar diameter

7 899·809 miles *12 713,510 km*.

Land and sea surfaces

The estimated total surface area of the Earth is 196 937 600 miles² *510 066 100 km²* of which the sea or hydrosphere covers five sevenths or more accurately 71·43 per cent and the land or lithosphere two sevenths or 28·57 per cent. The mean depth of the hydrosphere is 11 660 ft *3554 m*. The total volume of the oceans is 308 400 000 miles³ or *1 285 600 000 km³*, or 0·021 per cent by weight of the whole earth, viz. 1·2 × 10¹⁸ tons.

The oceans and seas

The strictest interpretations permit only three oceans—The Pacific, Atlantic and Indian. The so-called Seven Seas would require the three undisputed oceans to be divided by the equator into North and South and the addition of the Arctic Sea. The term Antarctic Ocean is not recognised by the International Hydrographic Bureau.

OCEANS

Ocean with adjacent seas	Area in millions miles²	Area in millions km²	Percentage of world area	Greatest depth (ft)	Greatest depth (m)	Greatest depth location	Average depth (ft)	Average depth (m)
Pacific	69·3	179,4	35·25	35 760	10 900	Mariana Trench	14 054	4282
Atlantic	41·0	106,1	20·9	27 498	8381	Puerto Rico Trench	12 885	3926
Indian	28·9	74,8	14·65	26 400	8046	Diamantina Trench	13 007	3963
Total	139·67	361,7	70·92					

If the adjacent seas are detached and the Arctic Sea regarded as an ocean, the oceanic areas may be listed thus:

	Area (miles²)	Area (km²)	Percentage of sea area
Pacific	63 800 000	165 240 000	45·7
Atlantic	31 800 000	82 360 000	22·8
Indian	28 400 000	73 550 000	20·3
Arctic	5 400 000	13 980 000	3·9
Other Seas	10 270 000	26 600 000	7·3
	139 670 000	361 730 000	100·0

Ocean depths are zoned by oceanographers as bathyl (down to 6560 ft or *2000 m*); abyssal (between 6560 ft and 19 685 ft *2000 m* and *6000 m*) and hadal (below 19 685 ft *6000 m*).

SEAS

Principal seas	Area (miles²)	Area (km²)	Average depth (ft)	Average depth (m)
1. Malay Sea (inc South China Sea and Malacca Straits)	3 144 000	8 142 000	4000	1200
2. Caribbean Sea	1 063 000	2 753 000	8000	2400
3. Mediterranean Sea	966 750	2 503 000	4875	1485
4. Bering Sea	875 750	2 268 180	4700	1400
5. Gulf of Mexico	595 750	1 542 985	5000	1500
6. Sea of Okhotsk	589 800	1 527 570	2750	840
7. East China Sea	482 300	1 249 150	600	180
8. Hudson Bay	475 800	1 232 300	400	120
9. Sea of Japan	389 000	1 007 500	4500	1370
10. Andaman Sea	308 000	797 700	2850	865
11. North Sea	222 125	575 300	300	90

SEAS continued

Principal seas	Area (miles²)	Area (km²)	Average depth (ft)	Average depth (m)
12. Black Sea	178 375	461 980	3600	1100
13. Red Sea	169 000	437 700	1610	490
14. Baltic Sea	163 000	422 160	190	55
15. Persian Gulf*	92 200	238 790	80	24
16. Gulf of St Lawrence	91 800	237 760	400	120
17. Gulf of California	62 530	162 000	2660	810
18. English Channel	34 700	89 900	177	54
19. Irish Sea	34 200	88 550	197	60
20. Bass Strait	28 950	75 000	230	70

* Also referred to as the Arabian Gulf.

DEEP SEA TRENCHES

Length (miles)	Length (km)	Name	Deepest point	Depth (ft)	Depth (m)
1400	2250	Mariana Trench,* W Pacific	Challenger† Deep	35 760	10 900
1600	2575	Tonga-Kermadec Trench,‡ S Pacific	Vityaz 11 (Tonga)	35 598	10 850
1400	2250	Kuril-Kamchatka Trench,* W Pacific		34 587	10 542
825	1325	Philippine Trench, W Pacific	Galathea Deep	34 578	10 539
		Idzu-Bonin Trench (sometimes included in the Japan Trench)		32 196	9810
200+	320+	New Hebrides Trench, S Pacific	North Trench	30 080	9165
400	640	Solomon or New Britain Trench, S Pacific		29 988	9140
500	800	Puerto Rico Trench, W Atlantic	Milwaukee Deep	28 374	8648
350	560	Yap Trench,* W Pacific		27 976	8527
1000	1600	Japan Trench,* W Pacific		27 591	8412
600	965	South Sandwich Trench, S Atlantic	Meteor Deep	27 112	8263
2000	3200	Aleutian Trench, N Pacific		26 574	8100
2200	3540	Pepu-Chile (Atacama) Trench, E Pacific	Bartholomew Deep	26 454	8064
		Palau Trench (sometimes included in the Yap Trench)		26 420	8050
600	965	Romanche Trench, N-S Atlantic		25 800	7864
1400	2250	Java (Sunda) Trench, Indian Ocean	Planet Deep	25 344	7725
600	965	Cayman Trench, Caribbean		24 720	7535
650	1040	Nansei Shotó (Ryukyu) Trench, W Pacific		24 630	7505
150	240	Banda Trench, Banda Sea		24 155	7360

  * These four trenches are sometimes regarded as a single 4600 mile *7400 km* long system.
  † Subsequent visits to the Challenger Deep since 1951 have produced claims for greater depths in this same longitude and latitude. In Mar. 1959 the USSR research ship Vityaz claimed 36 198 ft *11 033 m*, using echo-sounding only.
  ‡ Kermadec Trench is sometimes considered to be a separate feature. Depth 32 974 ft *10 047 m*.

THE CONTINENTS

There is ever increasing evidence that the Earth's land surface once comprised a single primeval land mass, now called Pangaea, and that this split during the Upper Cretaceous period (65 000 000 to 100 000 000 years ago) into two super-continents, called Laurasia in the North and Gondwanaland in the South. The Earth's land surface embraces seven continents, each with their attendant islands. Europe, Africa and Asia, though politically distinct, physically form one land mass known as Afro-Eurasia. Central America is often included in North America (Canada, the USA and Greenland). Europe includes all the USSR territory west of the Ural Mountains. Oceania embraces Australasia (Australia and New Zealand) and the non-Asian Pacific Islands.

Continent	Area in miles²	Area in km²	Greatest overland distance between extremities of land masses			
			North to South (miles)	North to South (km)	East to West (miles)	East to West (km)
Asia	16 993 000	44 011 000	4000	6435	4700	7560
America	16 233 000	42 043 000				
North America	8 301 000	21 500 000	2900	4665	2900	4665
Central America	1 062 000	2 750 000	820	1320	950	1530

CONTINENTS continued

South America	*6 870 000*	*17 793 000*	4500	*7240*	3200	*5150*
Africa	11 673 000	*30 232 000*	4400	*7080*	3750	*6035*
Antarctica	*c.* 5 250 000	*c. 13 600 000*	—	—	2700*	*4340*
Europe†	4 063 000	*10 523 000*	1800	*2900*	2500	*4000*
Oceania§	3 450 000	*8 935 000*	1870‡	*3000*	2300‡	*3700*
	57 270 000					

* Greatest transit from coast to coast.
† Includes 2 151 000 miles² *5 571 000 km²* of USSR territory west of the Urals.
‡ Figures applicable only to Australian mainland (2 941 526 miles² *7 618 493 km²*).
§ Includes 159 376 miles² *412 781 km²* in West Irian (West New Guinea), politically part of Indonesia, which is largely in Asia.

WORLD'S LARGEST ISLANDS

Name	Area in miles²	Area in km²	Location
* Australia	2 941 526	*7 618 493*	—
1. Greenland	840 000	*2 175 600*	Arctic Ocean
2. New Guinea	300 000	*777 000*	W Pacific
3. Borneo	280 100	*725 545*	Indian Ocean
4. Madagascar	227 800	*590 000*	Indian Ocean
5. Baffin Island	183 810	*476 065*	Arctic Ocean
6. Sumatra	182 860	*473 600*	Indian Ocean
7. Honshū	88 031	*228 000*	NW Pacific
8. Great Britain	84 186	*218 041*	North Atlantic
9. Victoria Island	81 930	*212 197*	Arctic Ocean
10. Ellesmere Island	75 767	*196 236*	Arctic Ocean
11. Celebes (Sulawesi)	72 987	*189 035*	Indian Ocean
12. South Island, New Zealand	58 093	*150 460*	SW Pacific
13. Java	48 763	*126 295*	Indian Ocean
14. North Island, New Zealand	44 281	*114 687*	SW Pacific
15. Cuba	44 217	*114 522*	Caribbean Sea
16. Newfoundland	43 359	*112 300*	North Atlantic
17. Luzon	40 420	*104 688*	W Pacific
18. Iceland	39 768	*103 000*	North Atlantic
19. Mindanao	36 381	*94 226*	W Pacific
20. Ireland (Northern Ireland and the Republic of Ireland)	31 839	*82 460*	North Atlantic
21. Hokkaido	30 077	*77 900*	NW Pacific
22. Hispaniola (Dominican Republic and Haiti)	29 418	*76 192*	Caribbean Sea
23. Sakhalin	28 597	*74 060*	NW Pacific
24. Tasmania	26 215	*67 900*	SW Pacific
25. Sri Lanka	25 332	*65 600*	Indian Ocean

* Geographically regarded as a continental land mass, as are Antarctica, Afro-Eurasia, and America.

PENINSULAS

World's largest peninsulas

	miles²	km²
Arabia	1 250 000	*3 250 000*
Southern India	800 000	*2 072 000*
Alaska	580 000	*1 500 000*
Labrador	500 000	*1 300 000*
Scandinavia	309 000	*800 300*
Iberian Peninsula	225 500	*584 000*

DESERTS

Principal deserts of the world

Name	Approx. area in miles²	Approx. area in km²	Territories
Sahara	3 250 000	*8 400 000*	Algeria, Chad, Libya, Mali, Mauritania, Niger, Sudan, Tunisia, Egypt, Morocco. Embraces the Libyan Desert (600 000 miles² *1 560 000 km²*) and the Nubian Desert (100 000 miles² *260 000 km²*)
Australian Desert	600 000	*1 550 000*	Australia. Embraces the Great Sandy (or Warburton) (160 000 miles² *420 000 km²*), Great Victoria (125 000 miles² *325 000 km²*), Simpson (Arunta) (120 000 miles² *310 000 km²*), Gibson (85 000 miles² *220 000 km²*) and Sturt Deserts

DESERTS continued

Name	Approx. area in miles²	Approx. area in km²	Territories
Arabian Desert	500 000	1 300 000	Southern Arabia, Saudi Arabia, Yemen. Includes the Ar Rab'al Khali or Empty Quarter (250 000 miles² 64 750 km²), Syrian (125 000 miles² 323 750 km²) and An Nafud (50 000 miles² 129 500 km²) Deserts
Gobi	400 000	1 040 000	Mongolia and China (Inner Mongolia)
Kalahari Desert	200 000	520 000	Botswana
Takla Makan	125 000	320 000	Sinkiang, China
Sonoran Desert	120 000	310 000	Arizona and California, USA and Mexico
Namib Desert	120 000	310 000	in S W Africa (Namibia)
*Kara Kum	105 000	270 000	Turkmenistan, USSR
Thar Desert	100 000	260 000	North-western India and Pakistan
Somali Desert	100 000	260 000	Somalia
Atacama Desert	70 000	180 000	Northern Chile
*Kyzyl Kum	70 000	180 000	Uzbekistan-Kazakhstan, USSR
Dasht-e-Lut	20 000	52 000	Eastern Iran (sometimes called Iranian Desert)
Mojave Desert	13 500	35 000	Southern California, USA
Desierto de Sechura	10 000	26 000	North-west Peru

* Together known as the Turkestan Desert.

MOUNTAINS

Mountain	Height (ft)	Height (m)	Range	Date of First Ascent (if any)
1. Mount Everest	29 028	8848	H	29 May 1953
2. K 2 (Chogori)	28 250	8610	K	31 July 1954
3. Kangchenjunga I	28 208	8597	H	25 May 1955
4. Lhotse I	27 923	8511	H	18 May 1956
Yalung Kang	27 894	8502	H	14 May 1973
Kangchenjunga S Peak	27 848	8488	H	unclimbed
5. Makalu I	27 824	8481	H	15 May 1955
Kangchenjunga Middle Peak	27 806	8475	H	unclimbed
Lhotse Shar (Lhotse II)	27 504	8383	H	12 May 1970
6. Dhaulagiri I	26 795	8167	H	13 May 1960
7. Manaslu I (Kutang I)	26 760	8156	H	9 May 1956
8. Cho Uyo	26 750	8153	H	19 Oct. 1954
9. Nanga Parbat (Diamir)	26 660	8125	H	3 July 1953
10. Annapurna I	26 546	8091	H	3 June 1950
11. Gasherbrum I (Hidden Peak)	26 470	8068	K	5 July 1958
12. Broad Peak I	26 400	8047	K	9 June 1957
13. Gasherbrum II	26 360	8034	K	7 July 1956
Broad Peak Middle	26 300	8016	K	28 July 1975
14. Shisha Pangma (Gosainthan)	26 291	8013	H	2 May 1964
15. Gasherbrum III	26 090	7952	K	11 Aug. 1975
16. Annapurna II	26 041	7937	H	17 May 1960
17. Gasherbrum IV	26 000	7924	K	6 Aug. 1958
18. Gyachung Kang	25 990	7921	H	10 Apr. 1964
19. Kangbachen	25 925	7902	H	26 May 1974
20. Disteghil Sar I	25 868	7884	K	9 June 1960
21. Himal Chuli	25 801	7864	H	24 May 1960
22. Khinyang Chhish	25 762	7852	K	26 Aug. 1971
23. Nuptse	25 726	7841	H	16 May 1961
24. Peak 29 (Manaslu II)	25 705	7835	H	Oct. 1970
25. Masherbrum East	25 660	7871	K	6 July 1960
26. Nanda Devi	25 645	7816	H	29 Aug. 1936
27. Chomo Lönzo	25 640	7815	H	30 Oct. 1954
28. Ngojumba Ri (Cho Uyo II)	25 610	7805	H	5 May 1965
Masherbrum West	25 610	7805	K	unclimbed
29. Rakaposhi	25 550	7788	K	25 June 1958
30. Batura Muztagh I (Hunza Kunji I)	25 542	7785	K	30 June 1976
31. Zemu Peak	25 526	7780	H	Unclimbed
Gasherbrum II East	25 500	7772	K	unclimbed
32. Kanjut Sar	25 460	7760	K	19 July 1959
33. Kamet	25 447	7756	H	21 June 1931
34. Namcha Barwa	25 445	7755	H	Unclimbed
35. Dhaulagiri II	25 429	7751	H	18 May 1971
36. Saltoro Kangri I	25 400	7741	K	24 July 1962
37. Batura Muztagh II (Hunza Kunji II)	25 361	7730	K	Unclimbed
38. Gurla Mandhata	25 355	7728	H	Unclimbed
39. Ulugh Muztagh	25 340	7725	KS	Unclimbed
40. Qungur II	25 326	7719	P	Unclimbed
41. Dhaulagiri II	25 318	7715	H	23 Oct. 1973
42. Jannu	25 294	7709	H	27 Apr. 1962
43. Tirich Mir	25 282	7706	HK	21 July 1950
44. Saltoro Kangri II	25 280	7705	K	Unclimbed
45. Disteghil Sar E	25 262	7700		Unclimbed
Tirich Mir, East Peak	25 236	7691	HK	25 July 1963
46. Saser Kangri I	25 170	7672	K	Unclimbed
47. Chogolisa II	25 148	7665	K	2 Aug. 1975
48. Phola Gangchhen	25 135	7661	H	Unclimbed
49. Dhaulagiri IV	25 134	7661	H	9 May 1975
50. Shahkang Sham	25 131	7660		Unclimbed
51. Makalu II (Kangshungtse)	25 120	7656	H	22 Oct. 1954
52. Chogolisa I ('Bride Peak')	25 110	7654	K	4 Aug. 1958
53. Trivor	25 098	7650	K	17 Aug. 1960
54. Ngojumba Ri II	25 085	7646		Unclimbed
55. Khinyang Chhish S	25 000	7620		Unclimbed
56. Shispare	24 997	7619	K	21 July 1974
57. Dhaulagiri V	24 993	7618	H	1 May 1975
Broad Peak North	24 935	7600	K	unclimbed
58. Qungur I	24 918	7595	P	16 Aug. 1956
59. Peak 38 (Lhotse II)	24 898	7589	H	Unclimbed
60. Minya Konka	24 891	7587	(S)	28 Oct. 1932
61. Annapurna III	24 787	7555	H	6 May 1961
62. Khula Kangri I	24 784	7554	H	Unclimbed
63. Changtse (North Peak)	24 780	7552	H	Unclimbed
64. Huztagh Ata	24 757	7546		Unclimbed
65. Skyang Kangri	24 751	7544	K	12 Aug. 1976
66. Khula Kangri II	24 740	7541	H	Unclimbed
67. Khulu Kangri III	24 710	7532	H	Unclimbed
68. Yalung Peak	24 710	7532		Unclimbed
69. Yukshin Gardas Sar	24 705	7530		Unclimbed
70. Mamostong Kangri	24 692	7526	K	Unclimbed
71. Annapurna IV	24 688	7525	H	30 May 1955
72. Khulu Kangri IV	24 659	7516	H	Unclimbed
73. Saser Kangri II	24 649	7513	K	Unclimbed

Key to Ranges: H=Himalaya K=Karakoram KS=Kunlun Shan HK=Hindu Kush P=Pamir S=in Sikiang, China.

MOUNTAINS *continued*

South America
The mountains of the Cordillera de los Andes are headed by Aconcagua at 22 834 ft *6959 m* (first climbed on 14 Jan. 1897), which has the distinction of being the highest mountain in the world outside the great ranges of Central Asia. The following list contains the 19 Andean summit peaks in excess of 21 000 ft *6400 m* above sea-level, as given in the *American Alpine Journal*, 1963.

Name	Height (ft)	Height (m)	Country	Name	Height (ft)	Height (m)	Country
1. Cerro Aconcagua	22 834	*6960*	Argentina	12. Tupungato	21 490	*6550*	Argentina–Chile
2. Ojos del Salado	22 598	*6888*	Argentina–Chile	13. Sajama	21 427	*6531*	Bolivia
3. Nevado de Pissis	22 241	*6779*	Argentina–Chile	14. Nevado Gonzalez	21 326	*6500*	Argentina
4. Huascarán, South Peak	22 205	*6768*	Peru	15. Cerro del Nacimiento	21 302	*6493*	Argentina
5. Llullaillaco volcén	22 057	*6723*	Argentina–Chile	16. Illimani	21 260	*6480*	Bolivia
6. Mercedario	21 884	*6670*	Argentina–Chile	17. El Muerto	21 253	*6478*	Argentina–Chile
7. Huascarán N	21 834	*6655*	Peru	18. Illimani S	21 201	*6462*	Bolivia
8. Yerupaja	21 758	*6632*	Peru	19. Anto Falla	21 162	*6450*	Argentina
9. Nevados de Tres Crucés C	21 270	*6620*	Argentina–Chile	20. Ancohuma (Sorata N)	21 086	*6427*	Bolivia
10. Coropuna	21 705	*6616*	Peru	21. Nevado Bonete	21 031	*6410*	Argentina
11. Nevado Incahuasi	21 657	*6601*	Argentina–Chile	22. Cerro de Ramada	21 031	*6410*	Argentina

North America
Mt McKinley (first ascent 1913) is the only peak in excess of 20 000ft *6100 m* in the entire North American continent.

Name	Height (ft)	Height (m)	Country	Name	Height (ft)	Height (m)	Country
1. McKinley, South Peak	20 320	*6193*	Alaska	8. King Peak	17 130	*5221*	Alaska
2. Logan	19 850	*6050*	Canada	9. Iztaccihuatl	17 000	*5182*	Mexico
3. Citlaltepetl or Orizaba	18 700	*5700*	Mexico	10. Steele	16 625	*5073*	Alaska
4. St Elias	18 008	*5489*	Alaska–Canada	11. Bona	16 500	*5029*	Alaska
5. Popocatépetl	17 887	*5451*	Mexico	12. Blackburn	16 390	*4996*	Alaska
6. Foraker	17 400	*5304*	Alaska	13. Sanford	16 237	*4949*	Alaska
7. Lucania	17 150	*5227*	Alaska				

Note: Mt McKinley, North Peak, is 19 470 ft *5934 m.*

Africa
All the peaks listed in the Congo (Kinshasa) and Uganda are in the Ruwenzori group.

Name	Height (ft)	Height (m)	Location
1. Kilimanjaro (Uhuru Point,* Kibo)	19 340	*5894*	Tanganyika
Hans Meyer Peak, Mawenzi	*16 890*	5148	
2. Mount Kenya (Batian)	17 058	*5199*	Kenya
Nelion	*17 022*	5188	
Point Piggott	*16 265*	4957	
Point John	*16 020*	4882	
3. Mount Stanley (Margherita Peak)	16 763	*5109*	Congo–Uganda
Albert Peak	*16 735*	5100	Congo (Kinshasa)
Alexandra Peak	*16 726*	5098	Congo–Uganda
Elena Peak	*16 388*	4995	Uganda
Great Tooth	*16 290*	4965	Uganda
Savoia Peak	*16 269*	4958	Uganda
Philip Peak	*16 239*	4949	Uganda
Elizabeth Peak	*16 236*	4948	Uganda
Moebius	*16 134*	4917	Uganda
Unnamed peak	c. *15 500*	4725	Uganda
Unnamed peak	c. *15 100*	c. *4600*	Uganda
4. Duwoni or Mt Speke (Victorio Emanuele Peak)	16 042	*4889*	Uganda
Ensonga Peak	*15 961*	4864	Congo–Uganda
Johnston Peak	*15 906*	4848	Uganda
5. Mount Baker (Edward Peak)	15 889	*4842*	Uganda
Semper Peak	*15 843*	4828	Uganda
Wollaston Peak	*15 286*	4659	Uganda
Moore Peak	*15 269*	4653	Uganda
6. Mount Emin (Umberto Peak)	15 797	*4814*	Congo (Kinshasa)
Kraepelin Peak	*15 720*	4791	Congo (Kinshasa)
7. Mount Gessi (Iolanda Peak)	15 470	*4715*	Uganda
Bottego Peak	*15 418*	4699	Uganda
8. Mount Luigi di Savoia (Sella Peak)	15 179	*4626*	Uganda
Weismann Peak	*15 157*	4619	Uganda
9. Ras Dashan (Dejen)	15 158	*4620*	Simien Mts, Ethiopia
10. Humphreys Peak	15 021	*4578*	Uganda

* Formerly called Kaiser Wilhelm Spitze.

Europe
The Caucasus range, along the spine of which runs the traditional geographical boundary between Asia and Europe, includes the following peaks which are higher than Mont Blanc (15 771 ft *4807 m*).

Name	Height (ft)	Height (m)
1. El'brus, West Peak	18 481	*5633*
El'brus, East Peak	18 356	*5594*
2. Shkara	17 060	*5199*
3. Dych Tau	17 054	*5198*
4. Pik Shota Rustaveli	17 028	*5190*
5. Koshtantau	16 880	*5154*
6. Pik Pushkin	16 732	*5100*
7. Janga, West Peak	16 572	*5051*
Janga, East Peak	*16 529*	5038
8. Dzhangi Tau	16 565	*5049*
9. Kazbek	16 558	*5046*
10. Katuintau (Adish)	16 355	*4985*
11. Mishirgitau, West Peak	16 148	*4921*
Mishirgitau, East Peak	*16 135*	4917
12. Kunjum Mishikgi	16 011	*4880*
13. Gestola	15 940	*4858*
14. Tetnuld	15 938	*4857*

MOUNTAINS continued

Highest Alps

The highest point in Italian territory is a shoulder of the main summit of Mont Blanc (Monte Bianco) through which a 4760-m *15 616–ft* contour passes. The highest top exclusively in Italian territory is Picco Luigi Amedeo (4460 m *14 632 ft*) to the south of the main Mont Blanc peak, which is itself exclusively in French territory.

Subsidiary peaks or tops on the same massif have been omitted except in the case of Mont Blanc and Monte Rosa, where they have been indented in italic type.

	Height (m)	Height (ft)	Country	First Ascent
1. Mont Blanc	4807	*15 771*	France	1786
Monte Bianco di Courmayeur	*4748*	*15 577*	France	1877
2. Monte Rosa				
Dufourspitze	*4634·0*	*15 203*	Switzerland	1855
Nordend	*4609*	*15 121*	Swiss–Italian border	1861
Ostpitze	*4596*	*15 078*	Swiss–Italian border	1854
Zumstein Spitze	*4563*	*14 970*	Swiss–Italian border	1820
Signal Kuppe	*4556*	*14 947*	Swiss–Italian border	1842
3. Dom	4545·4	*14 911*	Switzerland	1858
4. Lyskamm (Liskamm)	4527·2	*14 853*	Swiss–Italian border	1861
5. Weisshorn	4505·5	*14 780*	Switzerland	1861
6. Taschhorn	4490·7	*14 733*	Switzerland	1862
7. Matterhorn	4475·5	*14 683*	Swiss–Italian border	1865
Le Mont Maudit (Mont Blanc)	*4465*	*14 649*	Italy–France	1878
Picco Luigi Amedeo (Mont Blanc)	*4460*	*14 632*	Italy	
8. La Dent Blanche	4356·6	*14 293*	Switzerland	1862
9. Nadelhorn	4327·0	*14 196*	Switzerland	1858
10. Le Grand Combin de Grafaneire	4314	*14 153*	Switzerland	1859
Dome du Gouter (Mont Blanc)	*4304*	*14 120*	France	
11. Lenzspitze	4294	*14 087*	Switzerland	1871
12. Finsteraarhorn	4273·8	*14 021*	Switzerland	1829*

Note: In the *Dunlop Book* (1st Edition) this list was extended to include the 24 additional Alps over (13 123 ft) *4000 m.*
* Also reported climbed in 1812 but evidence lacking.

Antarctica

Large areas of Eastern Antarctica remain unsurveyed. Immense areas of the ice cap around the Pole of Inaccessibility lie over 12 000 ft *3650 m* above sea-level rising to 14 000 ft *4265 m* in 82° 25′ S 65° 30′ E.

Name	Height (ft)	Height (m)
1. Vinson Massif	16 863	*5140*
2. Mt Tyree	16 289	*4965*
3. Mt Shinn	15 750*	*4800**
4. Mt Gardner	15 354	*4688*
5. Mt Kirkpatrick	14 860	*4529*
6. Mt Elizabeth	14 698	*4480*
7. Mt Markham	14 250	*4343*
8. Mt MacKellar	14 802	*4292*
9. Mt Kaplan	13 960	*4255*
10. Mt Sidley	13 850*	*4221**
11. Mt Ostenso	13 711	*4179*
12. Mt Minto	13 648	*4160*
13. Mt Long Gables	13 622	*4152*
14. Mt Miller	13 600	*4145*
15. Mt Falla	13 500	*4115*
16. Mt Fridtjof Nansen	13 350	*4069*
17. Mt Fisher	13 340	*4066*
18. Mt Wade	13 330	*4063*
19. Mt Lister	13 205	*4025*
20. Mt Huggins	12 870	*3923*

* Volcanic as is Erebus (see Volcanoes, below).

Oceania

Name	Height (ft)	Height (m)	Location
1. Putjak Djaja (formerly Ngga Pulu and Mt Sukarno)	*c.* 16 500	*c. 5029*	Irian Jaya (W New Guinea)
2. Idenburg Peak	15 748	*4800*	West Irian
3. *Mt Mohammed Yamin (Wilhelmina Top)	15 525	*4732*	Irian Jaya (W New Guinea)
4. *Mt Trikora (Juliana Top)	15 420	*4700*	Irian Jaya (W New Guinea)
5. Mt Wilhelm	15 400	*4694*	NE New Guinea
6. Mt Kubur	14 300	*4359*	NE New Guinea
7. Mt Herbert	14 000	*4267*	NE New Guinea
8. Mt Leonard Darwin	13 887	*4233*	West Irian
9. †Mauna Kea	13 796	*4205*	Hawaii, Hawaiian Is
10. †Mauna Loa	13 680	*4170*	Hawaii, Hawaiian Is
11. Mt Giluwe	13 660	*4164*	Papua (SE New Guinea)
12. Mt Bangeta	13 473	*4107*	NE New Guinea
13. Mt Kinabalu	13 455	*4101*	Borneo
14. Mt Victoria	13 363	*4073*	Papua (SE New Guinea)
15. *Sneeuw Gebergte Peak	13 125	*4000*	Irian Jaya (W New Guinea)
16. Mt Albert Edward	13 100	*3993*	Papua (SE New Guinea)
17. †Mokuaweoweo	13 018	*3968*	Hawaii, Hawaiian Is
18. Burgess Mt	13 000	*3962*	NE New Guinea
19. †Lua Hohonu	12 805	*3903*	Hawaii, Hawaiian Is
20. Mt Auriga	12 728	*3878*	NE New Guinea
21. Mt Sirius	12 631	*3850*	NE New Guinea

* Politically regarded as in Asian territory.
† Since 21 Aug. 1959 politically part of the USA.

VOLCANOES

Volcanoes

It is estimated that there are about 535 active volcanoes of which 80 are submarine. Vulcanologists classify volcanoes as extinct, dormant or active (which includes rumbling, steaming or erupting). Areas of volcanoes and seismic activity are well defined, notably around the shores of the N Pacific and the eastern shores of the S Pacific, down the Mid-Atlantic range, the Africa Rift Valley and across from Greece and Turkey into Central Asia, the Himalayas and Meghalaya (Assam).

Cerro Aconcagua (22 834 ft) *6960 m* the highest Andean peak is an extinct volcano, while Kilimanjaro (19 340 ft *5895 m*) in Africa and Volcán Llullaillaco in Chile (22 057 ft *6725 m*) are classified as dormant. Among the principal volcanoes active in recent times are:

VOLCANOES continued

Name	Height (ft)	Height (m)	Range or Location	Country	Date of Last Notified Eruption
Guallatiri	19 882	6060	Andes	Chile	1959
Lascar	19 652	5990	Andes	Chile	1951
Cotopaxi	19 347	5897	Andes	Ecuador	1942–Steams
Volcán Misti	19 167	5842	Andes	Peru	
Tupungatito	18 504	5640	Andes	Chile	1959
Popocatépetl	17 887	5452	Altiplano de Mexico	Mexico	1932–Steams
Sangay	17 159	5230	Andes	Ecuador	1946
Cotacachi	16 192	4935	Andes	Ecuador	1955
Puracé	15 604	4756	Andes	Colombia	1950
Klyuchevskaya sopka	15 913	4850	Sredinnyy Khrebet (Kamchatka Peninsula)	USSR	1962
Tajumulco	13 812	4210		Guatemala	Rumbles
Mauna Loa	13 680	4170	Hawaii	USA	1950
Cameroon Mt	13 350	4069	(monarch)	Cameroon	1959
Tacama	13 333	4064	Sierra Madre	Guatemala	
Fuego	12 582	3835	Sierra Madre	Guatemala	1973
Erebus	12 450	3795	Ross Is	Antarctica	Steams
Rindjani	12 224	3726	Lombok	Indonesia	1964
Pico de Tiede	12 198	3718		Teneriffe	
Tolbachik	12 080	3682		USSR	1941
Semeru	12 060	3676	Java	Indonesia	1963
Nyiragongo	11 385	3470	Virunga	Zaire (Kinshasa)	1972
Koryakskaya	11 339	3456	Kamchatka Peninsula	USSR	1957
Irasu	11 268	3432	Cordillera Central	Costa Rica	1963
Chiriqui	11 253	3430	Cadelia de Talamanca	Panama	
Slamat	11 247	3428	Java	Indonesia	1953
Mt Spurr	11 070	3374	Alaska Range	USA	1953
Mt Etna	10 705	3363	Sicily	Italy	1974

Other Notable Active Volcanoes

Name	Height (ft)	Height (m)	Range or Location	Country	Date of Last Notified Eruption
Lassen Peak	10 453	3186	Cascade Rge California	USA	1915
Tambora	9351	2850	Sumbawa	Indonesia	
The Peak	6760	2060	Tristan da Cunha	S Atlantic	1961
Mt Lamington	5535	1687		Papua New Guinea	1951
La Soufrière	4813	1467	Basselerre Island	Guadaloupe	
Mt Pelée	4800	1463		Martinique	1902
Hekla	4747	1447		Iceland	1948
Vesuvius	4198	1280	Bay of Naples	Italy	1944
Kilauea	4077	1240	Hawaii	USA	1973
Stromboli	3038	926	Island	Mediterranean	1971
Santorin	1960	584	Thera	Greece	
Surtsey	568	173	off SE Iceland	Iceland	1965
Anak Krakatau	510	155	Island	Indonesia	1960

DEPRESSIONS & GLACIERS

World's deepest depressions

	Maximum depth below sea level (ft)	(m)
Dead Sea, Jordan–Israel	1296	395
Turfan Depression, Sinkiang, China	505	153
Munkhafad el Qattâra (Qattâra Depression), Egypt	436	132
Poluostrov Mangyshlak, Kazakh SSR, USSR	433	131
Danakil Depression, Ethiopia	383	116
Death Valley, California, USA	282	86
Salton Sink, California, USA	235	71
Zapadnyy Chink Ustyurta, Kazakh SSR	230	70
Prikaspiyskaya Nizmennost', Russian SFSR and Kazakh SSR	220	67
Ozera Sarykamysh, Uzbek and Turkmen SSR	148	45
El Faiyûm, Egypt	147	44
Península Valdiés Lago Enriquillo, Dominican Republic	131	40

Note: Immense areas of West Antarctica would be below sea level if stripped of their ice sheet. The deepest estimated crypto-depression is the bed rock on the Hollick–Kenyon plateau beneath the Marie Byrd Land ice cap (84° 37′ S 110° W) at −8100 ft (2468 m). The bed of Lake Baykal (USSR) is 4872 ft (1484 m) below sea level and the bed of the Dead Sea is 2600 ft (792 m) below sea-level. The ground surface of large areas of Central Greenland under the overburden of ice up to 11 190 ft 341 m thick are depressed to 1200 ft 365 m below sea-level. The world's largest exposed depression is the Prikaspiyskaya Nizmennost' stretching the whole northern third of the Caspian Sea (which is itself 92 ft 28 m below sea level) up to 250 miles 400 km inland. The Qattara Depression extends for 340 miles 547 km and is up to 80 miles 128 km wide.

World's longest glaciers

miles	km	
c. 320	515	Lambert-Fisher Ice Passage, Antarctica (disc. 1956–7)
260	418	Novaya Zemlya, North Island, USSR (1160 miles² 3004 km²)
225	362	Arctic Institute Ice Passage, Victoria Land, E Antarctica

DEPRESSIONS AND GLACIERS *continued*

180	*289*	Nimrod–Lennox–King Ice Passage, E Antarctica
150	*241*	Denman Glacier, E Antarctica
140	*225*	Beardmore Glacier, E Antarctica (disc. 1908)
140	*225*	Recovery Glacier, W Antarctica
124	*200*	*Petermanns Gletscher, Knud Rasmussen Land, Greenland
120	*193*	Unnamed Glacier, SW Ross Ice Shelf, W Antarctica
115	*185*	Slessor Glacier, W Antarctica

* Petermanns Gletscher is the largest in the Northern Hemisphere: it extends 24.8 miles *40 km* out to sea.

Glaciated areas of the world

It is estimated that 6 050 000 miles² *15 670 000 km²* or about 10·5 per cent of the world's land surface is permanently covered with ice, thus:

	miles²	km²		miles²	km²
South Polar Regions	5 250 000	*13 597 000*	Asia	14 600	*37 800*
North Polar Regions			South America	4600	*11 900*
(inc Greenland with			Europe	4128	*10 700*
695 500)	758 500	*1 965 000*	New Zealand	380	*984*
Alaska–Canada	22 700	*58 800*	Africa	92	*238*

Notable Glaciers in other areas include:

		Length (miles)	Length (km)	Area (miles²)	Area (km²)
Iceland	Vatnajökull	88	*141*	3400	*8800*
Alaska	Malaspina Glacier	26	*41*	1480	*3830*
Alaska	Nabesna Glacier	43½	*70*	770	*1990*
Pamirs	Fedtschenko	47	*75*	520	*1346*
Karakoram	Siachen Glacier	47	*75*	444	*1150*
Norway	Jostedalsbre	62	*100*	415	*1075*
Karakoram	Hispar-Biafo Ice Passage	76	*122*	125 240	*323 620*
Himalaya	Kanchenjunga	12	*19*	177	*458*
New Zealand	Tasman Glacier	18	*29*	53	*137*
Alps	Aletschgletscher	16½	*26,5*	44	*114*

Quarayaq Glacier, Greenland, flows at a velocity of 20 to 24 m (*65 to 80 ft*) a day—this is the fastest major glacier.

CAVES

World's deepest caves

Cave	ft	m
Gouffre de la Pierre Saint Martin, Basses-Pyrénées, Spain-France	4370	*1332*
Gouffre Jean Bernard, Savoie Alps, France	4258	*1298*
Gouffre Berger, Sornin Plateau, Vercors, France	3743	*1141*
Kievskaya, U.S.S.R.	3543	*1080*
Chourun des Aguilles, Dauphine Alps, France	3214	*980*
Sumidero de Cellagua, Cantabria, Spain	3182	*970*
Gouffre André Touya, Western Pyréneés, France	3116	*950*
Grotta di Monte Cuco, Perugia, Italy	3025	*922*
Abisso Michele Gortani, Julian Alps, Italy	3018	*920*
Gouffre de Cambou de Liard, Central Pyrénées, France	2979	*908*
Réseau Félix Trombe, Eastern Pyrénées, France	2952	*900*
Platteneckeishöhle, Austria	2884	*879*
Spluga Della Preta, Dolomites, Italy	2870	*875*

Note: The most extensive cave system is the Mammoth Cave system in Kentucky, USA, discovered in 1799 and in 1972 linked with the Flint Ridge system so making a combined mapped length of 181.44 miles *292 km*. The largest known cavern is the Big Room in the Carlsbad Caverns, New Mexico, USA, which has maximum measurements of 4,720 ft *1438 m* in length, 328 ft *100 m* high and 656 ft *200 m* across.
The deepest cave in Great Britain is Ogof Ffynnon Ddu, Wales with 1,010 ft *308 m*.

MOUNTAIN RANGES

World's greatest mountain ranges
The greatest mountain system is the Himalaya-Karakoram-Hindu Kush-Pamir range with 104 peaks over 24 000 ft *7315 m*. The second greatest range is the Andes with 54 peaks over 20 000 ft *6096 m*.

Length (miles)	Length (km)	Name	Location	Culminating Peak	Height (ft)	Height (m)
4500	*7200*	Cordillera de Los Andes	W South America	Aconcagua	22 834	*6960*
3750	*6000*	Rocky Mountains	W North America	Mt Robson	12 972	*3954*
2400	*3800*	Himalaya–Karakoram–Hindu Kush	S Central Asia	Mt Everest	29 028	*8847*
2250	*3600*	Great Dividing Range	E Australia	Kosciusko	7310	*2228*
2200	*3500*	Trans-Antarctic Mts	Antarctica	Mt Kirkpatrick	14 860	*4529*
1900	*3000*	Brazilian Atlantic Coast Range	E Brazil	Pico da Bandeira	9482	*2890*
1800	*2900*	West Sumatran–Javan Range	W Sumatra and Java	Kerintji	12 484	*3805*

MOUNTAIN RANGES *continued*

(miles)	(km)	Name	Location	Highest peak	(ft)	(m)
1650*	2650	Aleutian Range	Alaska and NW Pacific	Shishaldin	9387	2861
1400	2250	Tien Shan	S Central Asia	Pik Pobeda	24 406	7439
1250	2000	Central New Guinea Range	Irian Jaya–Papua/ N Guinea	Putjak Djaja†	c. 16 500	c. 5030
1250	2000	Altai Mountains	Central Asia	Gora Belukha	14 783	4505
1250	2010	Uralskiy Khrebet	Russian SFSR	Gora Narodnaya	6214	1894
1200	1930	§ Range in Kamchatka	E Russian SFSR	Klyuchevskaya Sopka	15 584	4750
1200	1930	Atlas Mountains	NW Africa	Jebel Toubkal	13 665	4165
1000	1610	Verkhoyanskiy Khrebet	E Russian SFSR	Gora Mas Khaya	9708	2959
1000	1610	Western Ghats	W India	Anai Madi	8841	2694
950	1530	Sierra Madre Oriental	Mexico	Citlaltepec (Orizaba)	18 865	5750
950	1530	Kūhhā-ye-Zāgros	Iran	Zard Kūh	14 921	4547
950	1530	Scandinavian Range	W Norway	Galdhopiggen	8104	2470
900	1450	Ethiopian Highlands	Ethiopia	Ras Dashan	c. 15 100	c. 4600
900	1450	Sierra Madre Occidental	Mexico	Nevado de Colima	13 993	4265
850	1370	Malagasy Range	Madagascar	Maromokotro	9436	2876
800	1290	Drakensberg (edge of plateau)	SE Africa	Thabana Ntlenyana	11 425	3482
800	1290	Khrebet Cherskogo	E Russian SFSR	Gora Pobeda	10 325	3147
750	1200	Caucasus	Georgia, USSR	El'brus	18 481	5633
700	1130	Alaska Range	Alaska, USA	Mt McKinley	20 320	6193
700	1130	Assam–Burma Range	Assam–W Burma	Hkakado Razi	19 296	5881
700	1130	Cascade Range	Northwest USA–Canada	Mt Rainier	14 410	4392
700	1130	Central Borneo Range	Central Borneo	Kinabulu	13 455	4101
700	1130	Tihāmat ash Shām	SW Arabia	Jebel Hadhar	12 336	3760
700	1130	Appennini	Italy	Corno Grande	9617	2931
700	1130	Appalachians	Eastern USA	Mt Mitchell	6684	2037
650	1050	Alps	Central Europe	Mt Blanc	15 771	4807
600	965	Sierra Madre del Sur	Mexico	Teotepec	12 149	3703
600	965	Khrebet Kolymskiy (Gydan)	E Russian SFSR	—	7290	2221

* Continuous mainland length (excluding islands) 450 miles *720 km.* § Comprises the Sredinnyy and Koryaskiy Khrebets.
† Also known (before 1970) as Ngga Pulu, Mount Sukarno and Cartensz Pyramide.

RIVERS

THE WORLD'S GREATEST RIVERS

The importance of rivers still tends to be judged on their length rather than by the more significant factors—their basin areas and volume of flow. In this compilation all the world's river systems with a watercourse of a length of 1500 miles *2400 km* or more are listed with all three criteria where ascertainable.

Length (miles)	(km)	Name of Watercourse	Source	Course and Outflow	Basin Area (miles²)	(km²)	Mean Discharge Rate (ft³/s)	(m³/s)	Notes
1 4145	6670	Nile (Bahr-el-Nil)– White Nile (Bahr el Jabel)–Albert Nile– Victoria Nile– Victoria Nyanza– Kagera–Luvironza	Rwanda: Luvironza branch of the Kagera, a feeder of the Victoria Nyanza	Through Tanzania (Kagera), Uganda (Victoria Nile and Albert Nile), Sudan (White Nile), Egypt to eastern Mediterranean	1 293 000	3 350 000	110 000	3120	Navigable length to first cataract (Aswan) 960 miles *1545 km* U.A.R. Irrigation Dept. states length as 4164 miles *6700 km.* Discharge 93 200 ft³/s *2600m³/s* near Aswan. Delta is 9250 miles² *23 960 km²*
2 4007	6448	Amazon (Amazonas)	Peru: Lago Villafro, head of the Apurimac branch of the Ucayali, which joins the Marañon to form the Amazonas	Through Colombia to Equatorial Brazil (Solimões) to South Atlantic (Canal do Sul)	2 722 000	7 050 000	6 350 000	180 000	Total of 15 000 tributaries, ten over 1000 miles *1600 km* including Madeira (2100 miles *3380 km).* Navigable 2300 miles *3700 km* up stream. Delta extends 250 miles *400 km* inland
3 3710	5970	Mississippi–Missouri– Jefferson–Beaver- head–Red Rock	Beaverhead County, southern Montana, U.S.A.	Through N. Dakota, S. Dakota, Nebraska–Iowa, Missouri–Kansas, Illinois, Kentucky, Tennesee, Arkansas, Mississippi, Louisiana, South West Pass into Gulf of Mexico	1 245 000	3 224 000	650 000	18 400	Missouri is 2315 miles *3725 km* the Jefferson–Beaverhead–Red Rock is 217 miles *349 km.* Lower Mississippi is 1171 miles *1884 km.* Total Mississippi from Lake Itasca, Minn., is 2348 miles *3778 km.* Longest river in one country. Delta is 13 900 miles² *36 000 km²*
4 3442	5540	Yenisey-Algara- Selenga	Mongolia: Ideriin branch of Selenga (Selenge)	Through Buryat A.S.S.R. (Selenga feeder) into Ozero Baykal, thence *via* Angara to Yenisey confluence at Strelka to Kara Sea, northern U.S.S.R.	996 000	2 580 000	670 000	19 000	Estuary 240 miles *386 km* long. Yenisey is 2200 miles *3540 km* long and has a basin of 792 000 miles² *2 050 000 km².* The length of the Angara is 1150 miles *1850 km*
5 3436	5530	Yangtze Kiang (Ch'ang Chiang)	Western China, Kunlun ShanMts. (as Dre Che and T'ungt'ien)	Begins at T'ungt'ien, then Chinsha, through Yünnan Szechwan, Hupeh, Anhwei, to Yellow Sea	756 000	1 960 000	770 000	21 800	Flood rate (1931) of 3 000 000 ft³/s *85 000 m³/s.* Estuary 120 miles *190 km* long
6 3362	5410	Ob'-Irtysh	Mongolia: Kara (Black) Irtysh *via* northern China (Sin Kiang) feeder of Ozero Zaysan	Through Kazakhstan into Russian S.F.S.R. to Ob' confluence at Khanty Mansiysk, thence Ob' to Kara Sea, northern U.S.S.R.	1 150 000	2 978 000	550 000	15 600	Estuary (Obskaya Guba) is 450 miles *725 km* long. Ob' is 2286 miles *3679 km* long, Irtysh 1840 miles *2960 km* long
7 3000	4830	Hwang Ho (Yellow River)	China: Tsaring-nor, Tsinghai Province	Through Kansu, Inner Mongolia, Hunan, Shantung to Po Hai (Gulf of Chili), Yellow Sea, North Pacific	378 000	979 000	100 000 to 800 000	2800 to 22 650	Changed mouth by 250 miles *400 km* in 1852. Only last 25 miles *40 km* navigable. Longest river in one country in Asia.
8 2920	4700	Zaïre (Congo)	Zambia Zaïre border, as Lualaba	Through Zaïre as Lualaba along to Congo border to N.W. Angola mouth into the South Atlantic	1 314 000	3 400 000	1 450 000	41 000	Navigable for 1075 miles *1730 km* from Kisangani to Kinshasa (formerly Léopoldville). Estuary 60 miles *96 km* long

RIVERS *continued*

Length (miles) (km)	Name of Watercourse	Source	Course and Outflow	Basin Area (miles²)	(km²)	Mean Discharge Rate (ft³/s)	(m³/s)	Notes
9 2734 *4400*	Lena-Kirenga	U.S.S.R. Hinterland of west central shores of Ozero Baykal as Kirenga	Northwards through Eastern Russia to Laptu Sea, Arctic Ocean	960 000	*2 490 000*	575 000	*16 300*	Lena Delta (17 375 miles² *45 000 km²*) extends 110 miles *177 km* inland, frozen 15 Oct. to 10 July Second longest solely Russian river
10 2700 *4345*	Amur–Argun' (He lung Chiang)	Northern China in Khingan Ranges (as Argun')	North along Inner Mongolian–U.S.S.R. and Manchuria–U.S.S.R. border for 2326 miles *3743 km* to Tarter Strait, Sea of Okhotsk, North Pacific	787 000	*2 038 000*	438 000	*12 400*	Amur is 1771 miles *2850 km* long (711 600 basin and 388 000 flow). *China Handbook* claims total length to be 2903 miles *4670 km* of which only 575 miles *925 km* is exclusively in U.S.S.R. territory
11 2635 *4240*	Mackenzie-Peace	Tatlatui Lake, Skeena Mts., Rockies, British Columbia, Canada, (as River Findlay)	Flows as Findlay for 250 miles *400 km* to confluence with Peace. Thence 1050 miles *1690 km* to join Slave (258 miles *415 km*) which feeds Great Slave Lake whence flows Mackenzie (1077 miles *1733 km*) to Beaufort Sea	711 000	*1 841 000*	400 000	*11 300*	Peace 1195 miles *1923 km*
12 2600 *4180*	Mekong (Me Nam Kong)	Central Tibet (as Lants'ang), slopes of Dza-Nag-Lung-Mong, 16 700 ft *5000 m*	Flows into China, thence south to form Burma–Laotian and most of Thai-Laotian frontiers, thence through Cambodia to Vietnam into South China Sea	381 000	*987 000*	388 000	*11 000*	Max flood discharge 1 700 000 ft³/s *48 000 m³/s*
13 2600 *4180*	Niger	Guinea: Loma Mts. near Sierra Leone border	Flows through Mali, Niger and along Benin border into Nigeria and Atlantic	730 000	*1 890 000*	415 000	*11 750*	Delta extends 80 miles *128 km* inland and 130 miles *200 km* in coastal length
14 2485 *4000*	Rió de la Plata–Paraná	Brazil: as Paranáiba. Flows south to eastern Paraguay border and into eastern Argentina	Emerges into confluence with River Uruguay to form Rio de la Plata, South Atlantic	1 600 000	*4 145 000*	970 000	*27 500*	After the 75-mile- *120-km*-long Delta estuary, the river shares the 210-mile- *340 km*-long estuary of the Uruguay called Rio de la Plata (River Plate)
15 2330 *3750*	Murray-Darling	Queensland, Australia: as the Culgoa continuation of the Condamine, which is an extension of the Balonne-branch of the Darling	Balome (intermittent flow) crosses into New South Wales to join Darling, which itself joins the Murray on the New South Wales–Victoria border and flows west into Lake Alexandria, in South Australia	408 000	*1 059 000*	14 000	*400*	Darling *c.* 1700 miles *2740 km* Murray 1609 miles *2590 km* or 1160 miles *1870 km*
16 2293 *3690*	Volga	USSR	Flows south and east in a great curve and empties in a delta into the north of the Caspian Sea	525 000	*1 360 000*	287 000	*8200*	Delta exceeds 175 miles *280 km* inland and arguably 280 miles *450 km*
2100 *3380*	Madeira–Mamoré–Grande (Guapay)	Bolivia rises on the Beni near Illimani	Flows north and east into Brazil to join Amazon at the Ilha Tupinambarama	Tributary of No. 2		530 000	*15 000*	World's longest tributary, navigable for 663 miles *1070 km*
2000 *3200*	Purus (formerly Coxiuara)	Peru: as the Alto Purus	Flows north and east into Brazil to join Amazon below Beruri	Tributary of No. 2		—	—	World's second longest tributary. Navigable for 1600 miles *2575 km*. Pronounced meanders
17 2200 *3540*	Zambezi (Zambeze)	Rhodesia: north-west extremity, as Zambesi	Flows after 45 miles *72 km* across eastern Angola for 220 miles *354 km* and back into Rhodesia (as Zambesi), later forming border with eastern end of Caprivi strip of South-West Africa, thence over Victoria Falls (Mosi-Oa-Toenia) into Kariba Lake. Thereafter into Mozambique and out into southern Indian Ocean	514 000	*1 330 000*	250 000	*7 000*	Navigable 380 miles *610 km* up to Quebrabasa Rapids and thereafter in stretches totalling another 1200 miles *1930 km*
18 1979 *3185*	Yukon-Teslin	North-west British Columbia, Canada, as the Teslin	Flows north into Yukon Territory and into west Alaska, USA, and thence into Bering Sea	330,000	*855 000*	—	—	Delta 85 miles *136 km* inland, navigable (shallow draft) for 1775 miles *2855 km*
19 1945 *3130*	St Lawrence	Head of St Louis River, Minn., USA	Flows into Lake Superior, thence Lakes Huron, Erie, Ontario to Gulf of St Lawrence and North Atlantic	532 000	*1 378 000*	360 000	*10 200*	Estuary 253 miles *407 km* long or 383 miles *616 km* to Anticosti Island. Discovered 1535 by Jacques Cartier
20 1885 *3033*	Rio Grande (Rio Bravo del Norte)	South-western Colorado, USA: San Juan Mts.	Flows south through New Mexico, USA, and along Texas–Mexico border into Gulf of Mexico, Atlantic Ocean	172 000	*445 000*	3000	*85*	
21 1800 *2900*	Ganges–Brahmaputra	South-western Tibet as Matsung (Tsangpo)	Flows east 770 miles *1240 km* south, then west through Assam, north-eastern India, joins Ganges (as Jamuna) to flow into Bay of Bengal, Indian Ocean	626 000	*1 620 000*	1 360 000	*38 500*	Joint delta with Ganges extends 225 miles *360 km* across and 205 miles *330 km* inland. Area 30 800 mile² *80 000 km²* the world's largest. Navigable 800 miles *1290 km*
22 1800 *2900*	São Francisco	Brazil: Serra da Canastra	Flows north and east into South Atlantic	270 000	*700 000*	—	—	Navigable 148 miles *238 km*

RIVERS continued

Length (miles) (km)	Name of Watercourse	Source	Course and Outflow	Basin Area (miles²) (km²)	Mean Discharge Rate (ft³/s) m(³/s)	Notes
23 1790 2880	Indus	Tibet: as Sengge	Flows east through Kashmir, into Pakistan and out into northern Arabian Sea	450 000 *1 166 000*	195 000 *5 500*	Delta (area 3100 miles² *8000 km²* extends 75 miles *120 km* inland
24 1770 2850	Danube	South-western Germany: Black Forest as Breg or Brigach	Flows (as Donau) east into Austria, along Czech-Hungarian border as Dunai into Hungary (273 miles *440 km*) as Duna, to Yugoslavia as Dunav along Romania–Bulgaria border and through Romania as Dunărea to Romania–USSR border as Dunay, into the Black Sea	315 000 *815 000*	250 000 *7 000*	Delta extends 60 miles *96 km* inland, Flows in territory of 8 countries
25 1750 2810	Salween (Nu Chiang)	Tibet	Flows (as Nu) east and south into western China, into eastern Burma and along Thailand border and out into Gulf of Martaban, Andaman Sea	125 000 *325 000*	— —	
26 = 1700 2740	Tigris–Euphrates (Shatt al-Arab)	Eastern Turkey as Murat	Flows west becoming the Firat, thence into Syria as Al Furāt and south and east into Iraq joining Tigris as Shatt al Arab flowing into Persian Gulf at Iran–Iraq border	430 000 *1 115 000*	50 000 *400 low 2 700 high*	
26 = 1700 2740	Tocantins	Brazil: near Brazilia as Parans	Flows north to join Pará in the Estuary Bára de Marajó and the South Atlantic	350 000 *905 000*	360 000 *10 000*	Not properly regarded as an Amazon tributary. Estuary 275 miles *440 km* in length
26 = 1700 2740	Orinoco	South-eastern Venezuela	Flows north and west to Colombia border, thence north and east to north-eastern Venezuela and the Atlantic	400 000 *1 036 000*	— —	
29 1650 2650	Si Kiang (Hsi-Chiang)	China: in Yünnan plateau as Nanp'an	Flows east as the Hungshai and later as the Hsün to emerge as the Hsi in the South China Sea, west of Hong Kong	232 300 *602 000*	— —	Delta exceeds 90 miles *145 km* inland and includes the Pearl River or Chu
30 1616 2600	Kolyma	USSR: in Khrebet Kolymskiy	Flows north across Arctic Circle into eastern Siberian Sea	206 000 *534 000*	134 000 *3 800*	
31 1600 2575	Amu-Dar'ya (Oxus)	Wakhan, Afghanistan, on the border with Sinkiang China, as Oxus	Flows west to form Tadzhik SSR–Afghan border as Pyandzh for 680 km *420 miles* and into Turkmen SSR as Amu-Dar'ya. Flows north and west into Aral'skoye More (Aral Sea)	179 500 *465 000*	— —	
32 1600 2575	Nelson–Saskatchewan	Canada: eastern Alberta as South Saskatchewan	Flows north and east through Saskatchewan and into Manitoba through Cedar Lake into Lake Winnipeg and out through northern feeder as Nelson to Hudson Bay	414 000 *1 072 000*	80 000 *2250*	Saskatchewan is 1205 miles *1940 km* in length
33 1575 2540	Ural	USSR: South-central Urals	Flows south and west into the Caspian Sea	84 900 *220 000*	— —	
34 = 1500 2410	Japurá	South-west Colombia in Cordillera Oriental as the Caquetá	Flows east into Brazil as Japurá, thence forms a left bank tributary of the Amazon opposite Tefé	Tributary of No. 2	— —	
34 = 1500 2410	Paraguay	Brazil: in the Mato Grosso as Paraguai	Flows south to touch first Bolivian then Paraguayan border, then across Paraguay and then on to form border with Argentina. Joins the Paraná south of Humaitá	444 000 *1 150 000* Tributary of No. 14	— —	

Other Rivers of 1000 miles *1600 km* or Longer

Miles	km	Name and Location	Area of Basin (miles²)	(km²)	Miles	km	Name and Location	Area of Basin (miles²)	(km²)
1450	2335	Arkansas, USA	Tributary of No. 3		1180	1900	Indigirka-Khastakh, USSR	139 000	*360 000*
1450	2335	Colorado, USA	228 000	*590 000*	1150	1850	Sungari (or Sunghua), China	Tributary of No. 9	
1420	2285	Dnepr (Dnieper), USSR	194 200	*503 000*	1150	1850	Tigris, Turkey–Iraq	Included in No. 25	
1400	2255	Río Negro, Colombia-Brazil	Tributary of No. 2		1112	1790	Pechora, USSR	126 000	*326 000*
1360	2188	Orange (Oranje), South Africa	394 000	*1 020 000*	1018	1638	Red River, USA	Tributary of No. 3	
1343	2160	Olenek, USSR	95 000	*246 000*	1000	1600	Churchill (or Missinipi), Canada	150 000	*390 000*
1330	2140	Syr-Dar'ya, USSR	175 000	*453 000*	1000	1600	Uruguay, Brazil–Uruguay–Argentina	Included in No. 14	
1306	2100	Ohio-Allegheny, USA	Tributary of No. 3						
1250	2010	Irrawaddy, China-Burma	166 000	*430 000*	1000	1600	Pilcomayo, Bolivia–Argentina–Paraguay	Tributary of Paraguay and sub-tributary of Paraná	
1224	1969	Don, USSR	163 000	*422 000*					
1210	1950	Columbia-Snake, Canada–USA	258 000	*668 000*					

Note: Some sources state that the Amazon tributary the Juruá is over 1133 miles *1823 km* and the Lena tributary the Vitim, is 1200 miles *1931 km* long.

WATERFALLS

Worlds Greatest Waterfalls
By Height

	Name	Total Drop (ft)	(m)	River	Location
1.	Angel (highest fall—2648 ft *807 m*)	3212	*979*	Carrao, an upper tributary of the Caroni	Venezuela
2.	Tugela (5 falls) (highest fall—1350 ft *410 m*	3110	*947*	Tugela	Natal, S. Africa
3.	Utigård (highest fall—1970 ft *600 m*)	2625	*800*	Jostedal Glacier	Nesdale, Norway
4.	Mongefossen	2540	*774*	Monge	Mongebekk, Norway
5.	Yosemite	2425	*739*	Yosemite Creek, a tributary of the Merced	Yosemite Valley, Yosemite National Park, Cal., USA
	(Upper Yosemite—1430 ft *435 m*; Cascades in middle section—675 ft *205 m*; Lower Yosemite —320 ft *97 m*)				
6.	Østre Mardøla Foss (highest fall—974 ft *296 m*)	2154	*656*	Mardals	Eikisdal, W. Norway
7.	Tyssestrengane (highest fall—948 ft *289 m*)	2120	*646*	Tysso	Hardanger, Norway
8.	Kukenaom (or Cuquenán)	2000	*610*	Arabopó, upper tributary of the Caroni	Venezuela
9.	Sutherland (highest fall—815 ft *248 m*)	1904	*580*	Arthur	nr. Milford Sound, Otago, S. Island, New Zealand
10.	Kile* (or Kjellfossen) (highest fall—490 ft *149 m*)	1841	*561*	Naero fjord feeder	nr. Gudvangen, Norway
11.	Takkakaw (highest fall—1200 ft *365 m*)	1650	*502*	A tributary of the Yoho	Daly Glacier, British Columbia, Canada
12.	Ribbon	1612	*491*	Ribbon Fall Stream	3 miles west of Yosemite Falls, Yosemite National Park, Cal., USA
13.	King George VI	1600	*487*	Utshi, upper tributary of the Mazaruni	Guyana
14.	Roraima	1500	*457*	an upper tributary of the Mazaruni	Guyana
15.	Cleve-Garth	1476	*449*	—	New Zealand
16.	Kalambo	1400	*426*	S.E. feeder of Lake Tanganyika	Tanzania–Zambia
17.	Gavarnie	1384	*421*	Gave de Pau	Pyrenees Glaciers, France
18.	Glass	1325	*403*	Iguazú	Brazil
19.	Krimmler fälle (4 falls, upper fall 460 ft *140 m*)	1280	*390*	Krimml Glacier	Salzburg, Austria
20.	Lofoi	1259	*383*	—	Zaïre
21.	Silver Strand (Widow's Tears)	1170	*356*	Merced tributary	Yosemite National Park, Cal., USA

*Some authorities would regard this as no more than a 'Bridal Veil' waterfall, *i.e.*, of such low volume that the fall atomizes.

Worlds Greatest Waterfalls
By Volume of Water

Name	Maximum Height (ft)	(m)	Width (ft)	Width (m)	Mean Annual Flow (ft³/s)	(m³/s)	Location
Boyoma (formerly Stanley) (7 cataracts)	200 (total)	*60*	2 400 (7th)	*730*	c. 600 000	*17 000*	Zaïre River nr. Kisangani
Guaíra (or Salto dos Sete Quedas) ('Seven Fall's)	374	*114*	15 900	*4846*	470 000*	*13 000*	Alto Paraná, River Brazil–Paraguay
Khône	70	*21*	35 000	*10 670*	400 000 to 420 000	*11 000 to 12 000*	Mekong River, Laos
Niagara:					212 000	*6 000*	
Horseshoe (Canadian)	160	*48*	2500	*760*	(Horseshoe—94%)		Niagara River, Lake Erie to Lake Ontario
American	167	*50*	1000	*300*			Niagara River, Lake Erie to Lake Ontario
Paulo Afonso	192	*58*	—	—	100 000	*2800*	São Francisco River, Brazil
Urubu-punga	40	*12*	—	—	97 000	*2700*	Alto Paraná River, Brazil
Cataratas del Iguazú (or Iguacu)	308	*93*	c. 13 000	*c. 4000*	61 660	*1700*	Iguazú (or Iguacu) River, Brazil–Argentina
Patos–Maribondo	115	*35*			53 000	*1500*	Rio Grande, Brazil
Victoria (Mosi-oa-tunya):							
Leaping Water	355	*108*	108	*33*			Zambezi River, nr. Zambia
Main Fall	(maximum)		2694	*821*	38 430	*1100*	S. Rhodesia
Rainbow Falls			1800	*550*			
Churchill (formerly Grand)	245	*75*			30 000 to 40 000	*850 to 1100*	Churchill (formerly Hamilton) River
Kaieteur (Koituok)	741	*225*	300 to 350	*90 to 105*	23 400	*660*	Potaro River, Guyana

*The peak flow has reached, 1,750,000 ft³/s.

LAKES

	Name	Country	Area (miles²)	(km²)	Length (miles)	(km)	Maximum Depth (ft)	(m)	Average Depth (ft)	(m)	Height of Surface above Sea-level (ft)	(m)
1.	Caspian Sea	USSR and Iran	143 550	*371 800*	760	*1225*	3215	*980*	675	*205*	−92	*−28*
2.	Superior	Canada and USA	31 800	*82 350*	350	*560*	1333	*406*	485	*147*	602	*183*
3.	Victoria Nyanza	Uganda, Tanzania, and Kenya	26 828	*69 500*	225	*360*	265	*80*	130	*39*	3720	*1134*
4.	Aral'skoye More (Aral Sea)	USSR	25 300	*65 500*	280	*450*	223	*68*	52	*15,8*	174	*53*
5.	Huron	Canada and USA	23 010	*59 600*	206	*330*	750	*228*	196	*59*	579	*176*
6.	Michigan	USA	22 400	*58 000*	307	*494*	923	*281*	275	*83*	579	*176*
7.	Tanganyika	Zaïre, Tanzania, and Zambia	12 700	*32 900*	450	*725*	4708	*1435*	—	—	2534	*772*
8.	Great Bear	Canada	12 275	*31 800*	232	*373*	270	*82*	—	—	390	*118*
9.	Ozero Baykal	USSR	11 780	*30 500*	385	*620*	5315	*1620*	2300	*700*	1493	*455*
10.	Malawi (formerly Nyasa)	Tanzania, Malawi, and Mozambique	11 430	*29 600*	360	*580*	2226	*678*	895	*272*	1550	*472*
11.	Great Slave	Canada	10 980	*28 500*	298	*480*	535	*163*	—	—	512	*156*
12.	Erie	Canada and USA	9930	*25 700*	241	*387*	210	*64*	60	*18,2*	572	*174*
13.	Winnipeg	Canada	9464	*24 500*	266	*428*	120	*36*	—	—	713	*217*
14.	Ontario	Canada and USA	7520	*19 500*	193	*310*	780	*237*	260	*79*	246	*75*
15.	Ozero Ladozhskoye (Lake Ladoga)	USSR	6835	*17 700*	120	*193*	738	*225*	170	*51*	13	*3,9*
16.	Ozero Balkhash	USSR	6720	*17 400*	300	*482*	85	*26*	—	—	1112	*339*
17.	Lac Tchad (Chad)	Niger, Nigeria, Chad and Cameroon	6300*	*16 300*	130	*209*	13–24	*3,9–7,3*	5	*1,5*	787	*240*
18.	Ozero Onezhskoye (Onega)	USSR	3710	*9600*	145	*233*	361	*110*	105	*32*	108	*33*
19.	Eyre	Australia	3700†	*9580*	115	*185*	65	*19,8*	—	—	−39	*−11,8*
20.	Lago Titicaca	Peru and Bolivia	3200	*8300*	130	*209*	1000	*304*	338	*103*	12 506	*3811*
21.	Athabasca	Canada	3120	*8100*	208	*334*	407	*124*	—	—	699	*213*
22.	Saimaa complex‡	Finland	c. 3100	*c. 8030*	203	*326*	—	—	—	—	249	*75*
23.	Lago de Nicaragua	Nicaragua	3089	*8000*	100	*160*	200	*60*	—	—	110	*33*

* Highly variable area between 4250 and 8500 miles² *11 000 and 22 000 km²*
† Highly variable area between 3100 and 5800 miles² *8030 and 15 000 km²*.

‡ The Saimaa proper (The Lake of a Thousand Isles) is, excluding the islands, c. 500 miles² *1300 km²*

Lakes under 3000 miles² *7770 km²* but over 2000 miles² *5180 km²*

Area (miles²)	(km²)	Name	Country
2473	*6400*	Turkana (formerly Rudolf)	Kenya and Ethiopia
2465	*6380*	Reindeer	Canada
2355	*6100*	Issyk Kul'*	USSR
2230	*5775*	Torrens	Australia
2149	*5565*	Vänern	Sweden
2105	*5450*	Winnipegosis	Canada
2075	*5375*	Mobuto Sesa Sako (formerly Albert)	Uganda and Zaïre
2050	*5300*	Kariba (dammed)	Rhodesia and Zambia

* Has a maximum depth of 2303 feet *700 m* and an average depth of 1050 ft *320 m*. The height of the surface above sea-level is 5279 ft *1600 m*.

ASTRONOMY

A guide to the scale of the Solar System and the Universe

If the Sun were reduced to the size of a beach ball of twelve in. (*30,4 cm*) in diameter, following on the same scale the nine planets would be represented *relatively* thus:

(1) Mercury = a grain of mustard seed 50 ft *15,2 m* away
(2) Venus = a pea 78 ft *23,7 m* away
(3) Earth = a pea 106 ft *32,3 m* away
    Moon = a grain of mustard seed 3½ in *8,5 cm* out from the Earth
(4) Mars = a currant 164 ft *49,9 m* away
(5) Jupiter = an orange 560 ft *170,6 m* away
(6) Saturn = a tangerine 1024 ft *312,1 m* away
(7) Uranus = a plum 2060 ft *627,8 m* away
(8) Neptune = a plum 3230 ft *984,5 m* away
(9) Pluto = a pinhead up to a mile *1,6 km* away.

The utter remoteness of the solar system from all other heavenly bodies is stressed by the fact that, still using this same scale of a one-foot (*30,48 cm*) Sun, which for this purpose we shall place in the centre of London, the nearest stars, the triple Centauri system, would lie 5350 miles (*8609,9 km*) away, say near San Francisco with the largest member having a two-foot (*60,96 cm*) diameter. Only the next six nearest stars in our Milky Way galaxy could, even on this scale, be accommodated on the Earth's surface.

Human imagination must boggle at distances greater than these, so it is necessary to switch to a much vaster scale of measurement.

Light travels at 186,282·397 miles/sec or *299 792,458 km/s* in vacuo. Thus, in the course of a tropical year (i.e. 365·24219878 mean solar days at January 0,12 hours Ephemeris time in AD 1900) light will travel 5 878 499 814 000 miles or *9 460 528 405 000 km*. This distance has conveniently, since 1888, been called a light year.

Light will thus travel to the Earth from the following heavenly bodies in the approximate times given:

From the Moon (reflected light)	1·25 s
From the Sun (at perihelion)	8 min 10·6 s
From Pluto (variable)	about 6 hrs
From nearest star (excepting the Sun)	4·28 yrs
From Rigel	900 yrs
From most distant star in Milky Way	75,000 yrs
From nearest major extra-galactic body (Larger Magellanic cloud)	160,000 yrs
From Andromeda (limit of naked eye vision)	2,200,000 yrs
By radio telescope, galaxies may be detectable up to about	17,500,000,000 yrs

Number of stars

There are 5776 stars visible to the naked eye. It is estimated that our own galaxy, the Milky Way galaxy, contains some 100 000 million (10^{11}) stars and that there are between 100 000 and 1 000 000 million (10^{11} to 10^{12}) galaxies in the detectable universe. This would indicate a total of 10^{22} to 10^{23} stars. The Milky Way galaxy is of a lens-shaped spiral form with a diameter of some 100 000 light years. The Sun is some 32 000 light years from the centre and hence the most distant star in our own galaxy is about 75 000 light years distant.

Age of stars

Being combustible, stars have a limited life. The Sun, which is classified as a Yellow Dwarf, functions like a controlled hydrogen bomb, losing four million tons in mass each second. It has been estimated that it has less than 10 000 million years to burn. It is difficult to give anything like a precise value for the age of the universe, as we are still very uncertain as to its early history. However, the Earth is over 4500 million years old, and the universe itself has most recently (Nov. 1976) estimated to be between 17,500 and 21,300 million years old.

NOTES ON THE PLANETS

Mercury

The closest of the planets to the Sun, Mercury, is never visible with the naked eye except when close to the horizon. Surface details are hard to see from Earth, even with powerful telescopes, but in 1974 the US probe Mariner 10 disclosed that the surface features are remarkably similar to those of the Moon, with mountains, valleys and craters. Mercury is virtually devoid of atmosphere, but it does have a weak but appreciable magnetic field.

Venus

Venus, almost identical in size with the Earth, is surrounded by a cloud-laden atmosphere,

---

The brightest and nearest stars (excluding the Sun)

Magnitude—a measure of stellar brightness such that the light of a star of any magnitude bears a ratio of 2·511886 to that of the star of the next magnitude. Thus a fifth magnitude star is 2·511886 times as bright, whilst one of the first magnitude is exactly 100 (or $2·511886^5$) times as bright as a sixth magnitude star. In the case of such exceptionally bright bodies as Sirius, Venus, the Moon (magnitude −12·7) or the Sun (magnitude −26·8) the magnitude is expressed as a minus quantity. Such a value for the Sun is its 'apparent magnitude' (m_v) which is the brightness as seen from the Earth, but for comparison the intrinsic brightness needs to be known and which is defined as the 'absolute magnitude' (M_v), the magnitude that would be observed if the star was placed at a distance of ten parsecs. On this basis the magnitude of the Sun is reduced to +4·8 or a four billionfold reduction in brightness.

The absolute magnitude of a star is related to its apparent magnitude and its distance in parsecs (d) by means of the equation:

$$M_v = m_v + 5 - 5 \log_{10}(d)$$

Brightest Stars

Name	Magnitude Apparent	Magnitude Absolute	Distance Light years	Distance Parsecs
Sirius	−1·46	+1·4	8·7	2·7
Canopus*	−0·73	−4·6	200	60
Alpha Centauri*	−0·29	+4·1	4·4	1·3
Arcturus	−0·06	−0·3	36	11
Vega	+0·04	+0·5	26	8·1
Capella	+0·08	−0·5	42	13
Rigel	+0·10	−7·0	850	250
Procyon	+0·35	+2·6	11	3·5
Achernar*	+0·48	−2·5	127	39
Beta Centauri*	+0·60	−4·6	360	110
Altair	+0·77	+2·3	16	5·0
Betelgeuse	+0·85 v	−5·7 v	650	200
Aldebaran	+0·85	−0·7	65	21
Alpha Crucis	+0·90	−3·7	270	85
Spica	+0·96	−3·6	260	80
Antares	+1·08	−4·5	430	130
Pollux	+1·15	+1·0	35	11
Fomalhaut	+1·16	+1·9	23	7·0
Deneb	+1·25	−7·1	1500	500
Beta Crucis	+1·25	−5·1	530	160
Regulus	+1·35	−0·7	85	26
Adhara	+1·50	−4·4	490	150

* Not visible from British Isles
v = very variable apparent magnitude, average figure.

NOTES ON THE PLANETS *continued*

so that its actual surface is never visible telescopically. Research with unmanned probes has shown that the surface temperature exceeds 900 °F *480 °C*, that the atmospheric ground pressure is about 100 times that on Earth, and that the main atmospheric constituent is carbon dioxide; the clouds contain corrosive sulphuric acid. The pictures sent back in 1975 by two Russian probes have shown rocks strewn on the surface. Venus rotates very slowly in a retrograde direction (i.e. in a sense opposite to that of the Earth).

Mars
Mars was long thought to be the one planet in the Solar System, apart from Earth, to be capable of supporting life, but results from space-probes are not encouraging. Mariner 9 (1971–2) sent back thousands of high-quality pictures, showing that Mars is a world of mountains, valleys, craters and giant volcanoes; one volcano, Olympus Mons, is some 15 miles high *over 24 000 m* and is crowned by a caldera 40 miles *64 km* in diameter. The Martian atmosphere is made up chiefly of carbon dioxide, and is very tenuous, with a ground pressure which is everywhere below ten millibars (cf. Earth's 1013 mb). The permanent polar caps are composed of ice. The Viking missions of 1976–7 disclosed no trace of organic material on Mars. The two dwarf satellites, Phobos and Demos, were discovered by A Hall in 1877; Mariner 9 pictures show that each is an irregular, crater-pitted lump of rocky material.

Jupiter
Jupiter is the largest planet in the Solar System. The outer layers are gaseous, composed of hydrogen and hydrogen compounds; it is now thought that most of the planet is liquid, and that hydrogen predominates. The famous Great Red Spot has proved to be a kind of whirling storm, as was shown by the close-range photographs sent back by the US probes Pioneer 10 and 11. Jupiter has a strong magnetic field, and is surrounded by zones of lethal radiation.

Saturn
Saturn is basically similar to Jupiter, but is less dense and is, of course, colder. The rings which make Saturn unique are composed of pieces of material (probably ices, or at least ice-covered) moving round the planet in the manner of dwarf satellites; the ring-system is 169 000 miles *270 000 km* wide, but less than 10 miles *16 km* thick. There are four main rings, two dusky and the newly detected D Ring. The main bright rings are separated by a gap known as Cassini's Division. It has been suggested that the rings were formed by the break-up of a former satellite. Opinions differ, but at least Saturn has 10 satellites left, one of which (Titan) is 3440 miles *5530 km* in diameter, and has an appreciable atmosphere which may well contain clouds.

Uranus
Just visible to the naked eye, Uranus has the same low density as Jupiter and has a diameter nearly four times that of the Earth. Its axis is tilted at 98° compared with our 23° 45′ which means that the night and day must at some points last up to 21 years each. In 1977, indirect researches showed that there are five rings round Uranus—too faint to be detected visually from Earth.

Neptune
Neptune is rather denser and probably *slightly* larger than Uranus. It requires nearly

Nearest Stars

| Name | Distance | | Magnitude | |
	Light years	Parsecs	Apparent	Absolute
Proxima Centauri	4·28	1·31	11·0	15·4
Alpha Centauri	4·38	1·34	A 0·0 B 1·3	A 4·4 B 5·7
Barnard's Star	5·91	1·81	9·5	13·2
Wolf 359	7·60	2·33	13·5	16·7
Lalande 21185	8·13	2·49	7·5	10·5
Sirius	8·65	2·65	A −1·5 B 8·7	A 1·4 B 11·6
Luyten 726-8**	8·89	2·72	A 12·5 B 13·0	A 15·3 B 15·8
Ross 154	9·45	2·90	10·6	13·3
Ross 248	10·3	3·15	12·3	14·8
Epsilon Eridani	10·8	3·30	3·7	6·1
Luyten 789-6	10·8	3·30	12·2	14·6
Ross 128	10·8	3·32	11·1	13·5
61 Cygni	11·1	3·40	A 5·2 B 6·0	A 7·6 B 8·4
Epsilon Indi	11·2	3·44	4·7	7·0
Procyon	11·4	3·50	A 0·4 B 10·7	A 2·6 B 13·0
Sigma 2398	11·5	3·53	A 8·9 B 9·7	A 11·2 B 11·9
Groombridge 34	11·6	3·55	A 8·1 B 11·0	A 10·3 B 13·3
Lacaille 9352	11·7	3·58	7·4	9·6
Tau Ceti	11·8	3·62	3·5	5·7
Luyten's Star	12·2	3·73	9·8	12·0
Luyten 725-32	12·5	3·83	11·5	13·6
Lacaille 8760	12·5	3·85	6·7	8·8
Kapteyn's Star	12·7	3·91	8·8	10·8
Kruger 60	12·9	3·95	A 9·9 B 11·3	A 11·9 B 13·3
Ross 614	13·0	4·00	A 11·2 B 14·8	A 13·2 B 16·8

** The B star component is known as UV Ceti.

165 years to make one revolution of the Sun against the 84 years of Uranus. Its axial tilt at 28° 48′ conforms more closely to those of the Earth (23° 57′), Mars (25° 12′), and Saturn (26° 44′).

Pluto
Discovered by systematic photography in 1930. The 248-year orbit of this faint planet with only 8 per cent of the volume of the Earth is so eccentric that at perihelion it will come inside Neptune on 21 Jan. 1979.

The Sun
The Sun (for statistics see Solar System table) is a yellow dwarf star with a luminosity of 3×10^{27} candle power such that each square inch of the surface emits $1·53_, \times 10^6$ candelas. Sun spots appear to be darker because they are 2700° F (1500 °C) cooler than the surface temperature of 10 220 °F (5660 °C). These may measure up to 7×10^9 miles^2 $1·8 \times 10^{10}$ km^2 and have to be 5×10^8 miles^2 $1·3 \times 10^9$ km^2 to be visible to the (*protected*) naked eye. During 1957 a record 263 were noted. Solar prominences may flare out to some 300 000 miles *480 000 km* from the Sun's surface.

EARTH-MOON SYSTEM
Creation of the Moon
It was once believed that the Moon used to be part of the Earth, and that the original combined body broke in two as a result of tidal forces. This is not now believed to be the case. It may be that the Moon was once an independent body which was captured by the Earth; however, most authorities believe that it has always been associated with the Earth. Certainly the rocks brought back by the Apollo astronauts confirm that the age of the Moon is approximately the same as that of the Earth (about 4600 million years).

Creation of the Earth
The long-popular theory that the Earth and other planets were globules thrown out from a molten Sun has long been discarded. Spectroscopic analysis has shown that the

Sun consists of 98 per cent hydrogen and helium whereas the planets are a composite of heavy non-gaseous elements.

It is now thought that the planets including the Earth were formed by accretion from a cloud of material or 'solar nebula' which used to be associated with the Sun.

ECLIPSES
An eclipse (derived from the Greek *ekleipsis* 'failing to appear') occurs when the sight of a celestial body is either obliterated or reduced by the intervention of a second body.

There are two main varieties of eclipse.
(i) Those when the eclipsing body passes between the observer on Earth and the eclipsed body. Such eclipses are those of the Sun by the Moon; occultations of various stars by the moon; transits of Venus or Mercury across the face of the Sun; and the eclipses of binary stars.
(ii) Those when the eclipsing body passes between the Sun and the eclipsed body. These can only affect planets or satellites which are not self-luminous. Such are eclipses of the Moon (by the Earth's shadow); and the eclipses of the satellites of Jupiter.

There is nothing in all the variety of natural phenomena that is quite so impressive as a total eclipse of the Sun.

Eclipses of the Sun (by the Moon) and of the Moon (by the Earth) have caused both wonder and sometimes terror since recorded history.

The element of rarity enhances the wonder of this event, which should on average only be seen from a given city or town once in about four hundred years. More specifically, Londoners saw no such eclipse between 20 March 1140 and 3 May 1715—that is, about nineteen generations later. The next will be on 14 June 2051. The next total eclipse of the Sun visible from Great Britain will occur on 11 Aug. 1999 on the Cornish coast. Eclipses of the Sun are in fact commoner than those of the Moon but the area from which they can be seen is so much smaller that the number of possible spectators is infinitely smaller.

The places from which and the times at which solar eclipses have been seen have been worked out back as far as the year 4200 BC and can be worked out far into the future, with of course an increasing, but still slight, degree of inaccuracy, for centuries ahead. The precise date of actual historical events in the Assyrian, Chinese, Greek and Roman empires have been fixed or confirmed by eclipses. For example, the battle between the Lydians and the Medes, which is reported by Herodotus, can be fixed exactly as occurring on 28 May 585 BC, because a solar eclipse caused such awe that it stopped the fight. Modern astronomy has benefited from the study of ancient eclipses because they help to determine 'secular accelerations', that is, the progressive changes in celestial motions.

Solar Eclipses (i.e. of the Sun by the Moon)

Solar eclipses are of three sorts—Total, Partial and Annular. A *total* eclipse occurs when the Moon, which, of course, must be new, comes completely between the Sun's disc and the observer on Earth. The Moon's circular shadow—its umbra—with a maximum diameter of 170 miles, *273 km* sweeps across the face of the Earth. The maximum possible duration of totality is 7 min 58 sec.

The dramatic events at the moment of totality are: sunlight vanishes in a few seconds; sudden darkness (but *not* as intense as that during a night even under a full moon); the brightest stars become visible; the Sun's corona is seen; there is a hush from the animal and bird world; cocks have been noted to crow when the light floods back.

The moon's partial shadow—its penumbra—which forms a much larger circle of about 2000 miles *3200 km* in diameter, causes a *partial* eclipse. Partial eclipses, of course, vary in their degree of completeness. There must be a minimum of two Solar eclipses each year.

An *annular* eclipse occurs when—owing to variations in the Sun's distance—the Moon's disc comes inside the Sun. In other words, the Moon's umbra stops short of the Earth's surface and an outer rim of the Sun surrounds the Moon. The maximum possible duration of containment is 12 min 24 s.

Lunar Eclipses (i.e. of the Moon by the Earth's shadow)

Lunar eclipses are caused when the Moon—which, of course must be full—passes through the shadow of the Earth and so loses its bright direct illumination by the Sun. A lunar eclipse is *partial* until the whole Moon passes into the Earth's umbra and so becomes *total*. After the Moon leaves the umbra it passes through the Earth's penumbra, which merely dims the moonlight so little that it is scarcely visible and is not even worth recording.

Other Observable Phenomena

I. During its movement across the sky the Moon may pass in front of a star, hiding or occulting it. Immersion takes place instantaneously, because the Moon has no atmosphere around its limb—in fact this was one of the earliest direct proofs of the Moon's lack of atmosphere. The emersion of the star is equally sudden. Planets may also be occulted, though in such cases both immersion and emersion are gradual because a planet presents an appreciable disk.

II. The two planets—Mercury and Venus—which are nearer the Sun than is the Earth, occasionally can be seen (with proper protection to the eyes) to pass slowly across the face of the Sun. These so-called Transits of Mercury occur on average about 14 times every century; Transits of Venus are far rarer with the last in 1882 and the next two on 8 June 2004 and 6 June 2012.

III. Some apparently single stars have been observed to vary sharply in brightness. They have been found in fact to be twin stars, revolving around each other and so eclipsing one another. Such stars are called *eclipsing binaries*, and the best-known examples are Algol and β Lyrae.

Comets

Comets are Solar System bodies moving in orbits about the Sun. Records go back to the 7th century BC. The speeds of the estimated 2 000 000 comets vary from only 700 mph in the outer reaches to 1 250 000 mph (*1100–2 million km/h*) when near the Sun. The periods of revolution vary, according to the ellipticity of orbit, from 3·3 years (Encke's comet) to millions of years as in the case of Comet 1910a (the letter 'a' indicating that it was the first classified during that year).

Comets are tenuous to the point that 10 000 cubic miles *41 000 km³* of tail might embrace only a cubic inch of solid matter. Comets are not self luminous, hence only visible only when in the inner part of the Solar System. They consist mainly of a head of dirty ice particles and a tail which always points more or less away from the Sun. In May 1910 the Earth probably passed through the tail of the famous Halley's Comet which is next due to return in 1986.

Telescopes

The prototype of modern refracting telescopes was that made in 1608 by the Dutchman Hans Lippershey (or Lippersheim) after an accidental discovery of the magnifying power of spectacle lens when held apart. The principle of the reflecting telescope was expounded by the Scot James Gregory in 1663 and the first reflector was built with a one-inch diameter mirror by Sir Isaac Newton in 1671.

Constellations

There are 31 accepted constellations in the northern and 52 in the southern hemispheres and 5 which appear at times in both hemispheres, making 88 in all. The International Astronomical Union completed the now accepted arc codification by 1945. The rectangular constellation Orion includes 3 of the 24 brightest stars in its great quadrilateral—Rigel (bottom left, Mag. 0·1), Betelgeuse (top right, Mag. 0·85 variable) and Bellatrix (top left, Mag. 1·7).

Elements of the planetary orbits

Planet	Mean Distance From Sun miles km	Perihelion Distance miles km	Aphelion Distance miles km	Orbital Eccentricity	Orbital Inclination ° ′ ″	Sidereal Period days	Orbital Velocity Mean mph km/h	Maximum mph km/h	Minimum mph km/h
Mercury	35 983 100 *57 909 100*	28 584 000 *46 001 000*	43 382 000 *69 817 000*	0·205 630	7 00 15	87·9693	105 950 *170 500*	131 930 *212 310*	86 920 *139 890*
Venus	67 237 900 *108 208 900*	66 782 000 *107 475 000*	67 694 000 *108 943 000*	0·006 783	3 23 39	224·7008	78 340 *126 070*	78 870 *126 930*	77 810 *125 220*
Earth	92 955 800 *149 597 900*	91 402 000 *147 097 000*	94 510 000 *152 099 000*	0·016 718	————	365·2564	66 620 *107 220*	67 750 *109 030*	65 520 *105 450*
Mars	141 635 700 *227 940 500*	128 410 000 *206 656 000*	154 862 000 *249 226 000*	0·093 380	1 50 59	686·9797	53 860 *86 680*	59 270 *95 390*	49 150 *79 100*
Jupiter	483 634 000 *778 333 000*	460 280 000 *740 750 000*	506 990 000 *815 920 000*	0·048 286	1 18 16	4332·62	29 210 *47 000*	30 670 *49 360*	27 840 *44 810*
Saturn	886 683 000 *1 426 978 000*	837 000 000 *1 347 020 000*	936 370 000 *1 506 940 000*	0·056 037	2 29 21	10 759·06	21 560 *34 700*	22 820 *36 730*	20 400 *32 830*
Uranus	1 783 951 000 *2 870 991 000*	1 701 660 000 *2 738 560 000*	1 866 230 000 *3 003 400 000*	0·046 125	0 46 23	30 707·79	15 200 *24 460*	15 930 *25 630*	14 520 *23 370*
Neptune	2 794 350 000 *4 497 070 000*	2 766 270 000 *4 451 880 000*	2 822 430 000 *4 542 270 000*	0·010 050	1 46 20	60 199·63	12 150 *19 560*	12 270 *19 750*	12 030 *19 360*
Pluto	3 674 490 000 *5 913 510 000*	2 761 600 000 *4 444 400 000*	4 587 300 000 *7 382 600 000*	0·248 432	17 08 22	90 777·61	10 430 *16 790*	13 660 *21 980*	8220 *13 230*

Physical Parameters of the sun and the planets

Sun or Planet		Diameters miles	Diameters km	Equatorial Sidereal Rotation Period d h m s	Equatorial Inclination	Mass tons	Mass kg	Density g/cm³	Escape Velocity mps	Escape Velocity km/s	Surface Temperature °C	On Scale Earth = 1 Equatorial Diameter	Volume	Mass	Surface Gravity	Mean Apparent Magnitude
Sun	Equ.	864,940	1 391 980	25 09 07	7° 15'	1,958 × 10²⁷	1,989 × 10³⁰	1,409	383·73	617,55	5530	109·12	1 303 700	332 946	27·90	−26·8
Mercury		3031	4878	58 15 30 32	0°	3,250 × 10²⁰	3,302 × 10²³	5,433	2·64	4,25	−180 to +420	0·3824	0·0561	0·055 27	0·3771	−0·0
Venus		7519	12 100	*243 00	178°	4,792 × 10²¹	4,869 × 10²⁴	5,249	6·44	10,36	475	0·9486	0·8563	0·815 00	0·9038	−4·4
Earth	Equ.	7926	12 756	23 56 04·091	23° 27'	5,880 × 10²¹	5,974 × 10²⁴	5,515	6·95	11,19	−88 to +58	1·0000	1·0000	1·000 00	1·0000	—
	Polar	7900	12 714													
Mars	Equ.	4221	6793	24 37 22·655	25° 12'	6,318 × 10²⁰	6,419 × 10²³	3,934	3·12	5,03	−125 to +30	0·5325	0·1507	0·107 45	0·3795	−2·0
	Polar	4196	6753													
Jupiter	Equ.	88 780	142 880	9 50 30·003	3° 04'	1,869 × 10²⁴	1,899 × 10²⁷	1,330	37·42	60,23	−25	11·201	1318	317·89	2·644	−2·6
	Polar	82 980	133 540													
Saturn	Equ.	74 600	120 000	10 14	26° 44'	5,596 × 10²³	5,686 × 10²⁶	0,705	22·52	36,25	−110	9·407	744	95·17	1·159	+0·7
	Polar	66 400	106 900													
Uranus	Equ.	31 600	50 800	10 49 *	97° 53'	8,602 × 10²²	8,740 × 10²⁵	1,31	13·38	21,53	−160	3·98	62	14·63	0·938	+5·5
	Polar	30 700	49 400													
Neptune	Equ.	30 200	48 600	15 48	28° 48'	1,013 × 10²³	1,029 × 10²⁶	1,75	14·82	23,84	−160	3·81	54	17·22	1·200	+7·8
	Polar	29 500	47 500													
Pluto		3400	5500	6 09 17	0°	2·6 × 10²⁰	2·6 × 10²³	3,0	2·21	3,56	−220	0·43	0·08	0·05	0·235	+15·0

* Retrograde

TELESCOPES

The world's most powerful astronomical telescopes are now:

Diameter of Refractors (Lens) Inches		Completion Date
40·0	Yerkes, Williams Bay, Wisconsin, USA	1897
36·0	Lick, Mt Hamilton, Cal., USA	1888
32·7	Paris Observatory, Meudon, France	1893
32·0	Astrophysical Observatory, Potsdam, Germany	1899
30.0	Nice Observatory Nice, France	1880
30·0	Alleghany Observatory, Pittsburgh, Penn., USA	1914

Diameter of Reflectors (Mirror) Inches		
236·2	Mount Semirodriki, Caucasus, USSR	1976
200	Hale, Mt Palomar, nr Pasadena, Cal., USA	1948
158	Kitt Peak Nat. Observatory, Tucson, Arizona	1970
158	Cerro Tololo, Chile	1970
153	Siding Spring, Australia	1974
150	Mount Strumlo, Canberra, Australia	1972
120	Lick, Mt Hamilton, Cal., USA	1959
107	McDonald Observatory, Fort Davis, Texas	1968
104	Crimean Astrophysical Lab., Nauchny, USSR	1960
100	Hooker, Mt Wilson, Cal., USA	1917
98	Newton, Herstmonceux, Sussex, England	1967
88	Mauna Kea Observatory, Hawaii	1970

The Russian 6 m *236·2 in* reflector is now the largest in the world; it may well remain so, as it is quite likely that future emphasis will be upon telescopes in space. The largest telescope in Great Britain in 1977 was the 98 in *248 mm* reflector at the Royal Greenwich Observatory, Herstmonceux, known as the Isaac Newton Telescope or INT. However, plans are now being made to move this telescope to the proposed Northern Hemisphere Observatory, to be set up on the island of La Palma in the Canaries.

Radio Telescope
The world's largest dish radio telescope is the non-steerable £3¾ million ionospheric apparatus at Arecibo, Puerto Rico, completed in November 1963. It utilises a natural crater which is spanned by a dish 1000 ft *305 m* in diameter. covering an area of 18½ acres *7,28 ha*. Improvements and re-plating cost a further £4½ million in 1974.

Radio Astronomy
Radio astronomy became possible with the discovery in 1887 of radio waves by Heinrich Hertz (Germany). The earliest suggestion that extra-terrestrial radio waves might exist and be detected came from Thomas Edison (USA), who corresponded with Prof A E Kennelly on the subject on 2 Nov. 1890.

It was not until 1932 that Karl Guthe Jansky (1905–49) a US scientist of Czech descent first detected radio signals from the Sagittarius constellation at Holmdel, New Jersey. This 'cosmic static' was recorded on a 15-m wave length. The pioneer radio astronomer was Grote Reber (USA) (b. 1911), who built the world's first radio telescope, a 31 ft 5-in parabolic dish, in his backyard at Wheaton, Illinois, in 1937. His first results were published in 1940.

Dr J S Hey (GB) discovered during war-time radar jamming research that sun spots emitted radio waves; that radio echoes come from meteor trails; and that the extra-galatic nebula Cygnus A was a discrete source of immense power.

In 1947 John G Bolton in Australia found that the Crab Nebula (M.1), a supernova remnant, is a strong radio source. Since then many more discrete sources have been found; some are supernova remnants in our Galaxy, while others are external galaxies and the mysterious, very remote quasars. Young science though it may be, radio astronomy is now of fundamental importance in our studies of the universe, and it has provided information which could never have been obtained in any other way.

Some milestones in astronomy
Aristotle (*c.* 385–325 BC) advanced the first argument against the flat Earth hypothesis.
Eratosthenes of Cyrene (*c.* 276–194 BC) made the earliest estimate of the Earth's circumference: very good at 24 662 miles *39 689 km*.
Ptolemy in *c.* AD 180 established the Ptolemic System i.e. Earth was the centre of the universe
Copernicus (1473–1543) established that both the Earth and Mars orbit the Sun.
Johannes Kepler published his first two laws of planetary motion in 1609 : the third in 1619.
Galileo Galilei (1564–1642) discovered in 1609 the use of the telescope and made astronomical observations with it. He was summonsed by the Roman Church to abjure his heresy that the Earth went round the Sun.
Christiaan Huygens (1629–95) built a 210 ft *64 m* refractor. In 1665 he described Saturn's rings later observing the markings on Mars.
In 1663 James Gregory put forward the principle of the reflecting telescope and *c.* 1668 Sir Isaac Newton built the first one with a 1 in *2,5 cm* metal mirror.
In the 1670's Cassini recalculated the Sun's distance at 86 million miles *138 million km*.
In 1675 Romer measured the velocity of light. His inspired answer, ignored for more than 100 years and not believed by himself, was 186 000 miles per sec *300 000 km per sec*.
Sir Isaac Newton (1642–1727) published his *Principia* in 1687.
In 1705 Halley predicted the return of Halley's comet in 1758. This was confirmed in that year by Palitzsch.
Herschel discovered Uranus in 1781.
Giuseppe Piazzi observed the first asteroid in 1801, confirmed in 1802 and named *Ceres*.
Friedrich Bessel was one of the first to realise the vastness of our galaxy discovering the star *61 Cygni* 60 million miles distant.
The steady-state or continuous creation theory was postulated in 1948 by Professors H. Bondi and T. Gold but is now considered to be incorrect. Other theories of the universe currently under discussion are the evolutionary or "big bang" theory due originally to the Abbè Lemaitre and the oscillating theory of 1965 supported by Professor A. Sandage of the USA.

Mini-Planet
It was announced on 8 Nov. 1977 by Charles Kowal of the Hale Observatory, Pasadena, California, USA that he had detected a minute planet possibly a tenth of the size of Mercury between the orbits of Saturn and Uranus on the night of 18–19 Oct.

The 20 Largest Asteroids

Size of Asteroids Relative to the Moon
(Diameter 2160 miles 3476 km)

A

Ceres   Pallas   Hygiea

Asteroid		Diameter		Year of Discovery
		miles	km	
(1)	Ceres	593	955	1801
(2)	Pallas	347	558	1802
(4)	Vesta	313	503	1807
(10)	Hygiea	237	382	1849
(15)	Eunomia	168	270	1851
(511)	Davida	165	265	1903
(16)	Psyche	158	254	1852
(324)	Bamberga	143	230	1892
(3)	Juno	140	226	1804
(19)	Fortuna	137	221	1852
(624)	Hektor	130	210	1907
(6)	Hebe	122	197	1847
(7)	Iris	120	193	1847
(29)	Amphitrite	116	187	1854
(747)	Winchester	116	187	1913
(9)	Metis	105	169	1848
(22)	Kalliope	104	168	1852
(68)	Leto	95	153	1861
(89)	Julia	95	153	1866
(8)	Flora	93	150	1847

Meteorite Craters

The most spectacular of all dry craters is the Coon Butte or Barringer crater near Canyon Diablo, Winslow, North Arizona, USA, discovered in 1891, which is now 575 ft *175 m* deep and 4150 ft *1265 m* in diameter. The next largest craters are Wolf's Creek, Western Australia (3000 ft *914 m* diameter, 170 ft *52 m* deep) and a crater discovered in N Chile in 1965 (1476 ft *450 m* diameter, 100 ft *30 m* deep). The New Quebec (formerly Chubb) 'crater' in North Ungava, Canada, discovered in June 1943, is 1325 ft *404 m* deep and 2·2 miles *3,5 km* in diameter, but is now regarded as a water-filled vulcanoid.

Ancient and oblique meteoric scars are much less spectacular though of far greater dimensions. These phenomena are known as astroblemes (Gk *astron*, a star; *blemma*, a glance).

Name	Diameter	
	miles	km
Vredefort Ring, South Africa (meteoric origin disputed, 1963)	24·8	39,9
Nordlinger Ries, Germany	15·5	24,9
Deep Bay, Saskatchewan, Canada (discovered 1956)	8·5	13,6
Lake Bosumtibi, Ghana	6·2	9,9
Serpent Mound, Ohio, USA	3·98	6,4
Wells Creek, Tennessee, USA	2·97	4,7
Al Umchaimin, Iraq	1·98	3,1

METEORITES

Approximate tonnage

Meteorites

The term meteorite must now be confined to a fallen meteor, a meteoric mass of stone (aerolite) or nickel-iron (siderite). It is loosely and incorrectly used of a meteor or shooting star which is usually only the size of a pinhead. The existence of meteorites, owing to a religious bias, was first admitted as late as 26 Apr. 1803, after a shower of some 2500 aerolites fell around L'Aigle, near Paris, France.

The majority of meteorites inevitably fall into the sea (70·8 per cent of the Earth's surface) and are not recovered. Only eight meteorites exceeding ten tons have been located. All these are of the iron-nickel type. The largest recorded stone meteorite is the one which fell in the Kirin Province, Manchuria on 8 Mar. 1976 weighing 3894 lb *1766 kg*.

The 35 megaton explosion 40 miles *64 km* north of Vanavar, Siberia, USSR on 30 June 1908 known as the Tunguska mystery was concluded in July 1977 to have been caused by a small comet.

		Approximate tonnage
Hoba	nr Grootfontein, South West Africa	60
Tent (Abnighito)	Cape York, West Greenland	30·4
Bacuberito	Mexico	27
Mbosi	Tanganyika	26
Williamette (1902)	Oregon, USA	14
Chupaero	Chihuahua, Mexico	14
Campo de Cielo	Argentina	13
Morito	Chihuahua, Mexico	11

The largest recorded in other continents are:

Australia	Cranbourne	3·5
Asia	Sikhote-Alin, USSR	1·7
Europe	Magura, Czechoslovakia	1·5

The total number of strikes recorded since the mid-17th century is nearly 1700, including 22 in the British Isles.

The largest British Isles meteorites of the 22 recorded have been:

Country	Location	Date	Weight	
Ireland	Adare, Limerick	10 Sept. 1813	65 lb (total 106 lb)	*29,5 kg* *(total 48 kg)*
England	World Cottage, nr Scarborough, Yorks	13 Dec. 1795	56 lb	*25,4 kg*
	Barwell, Leicestershire	24 Dec. 1965	17⅞ lb (total 102 lb)	*7,8 kg* *(total 46,25 kg)*
Scotland	Strathmore, Perthshire	3 Dec. 1917	22¼ lb	*10,1 kg*
Wales	Beddgelert, Caernarvonshire	21 Sept. 1949	25½ oz	*723 g*

29

ANTHROPOLOGY

Anthropology, the study of the differences and similarities between the various races of mankind, contains two autonomous sciences: physical anthropology (the study of blood groups and genetic differences) and social anthropology or ethnology (the study of custom).

Physical Anthropology

The classification of the races or gene pools of man is complex and is vulnerable to political controversy. Many terms which have been used to describe racial groupings are hypothetical, being based either upon cultural and linguistic considerations which are not genetically linked (*e.g.* the term 'the Semitic race'), or upon physical similarities (*e.g.* the term negroid).

Formerly classifications of mankind were attempted based purely upon outward physical characteristics such as skin colour (black, brown, white, yellow); body proportions (anthropometry), the shape of the head (craniometry), hair form, teeth and eyelids. A widely adopted system was that based on hair form which recognized three main types: the straight haired, woolly haired and curly haired groups. Although this remains of value no modern description of race relies solely on hair form. External bodily differences are not ignored in the definition of races but are of less scientific importance to such simply inherited or single gene traits as can be easily and precisely quantified.

One of the major factors in modern anthropological studies is the blood group. Certain blood groups predominate in some races but are almost absent in others; *e.g.* B group is very rare in Amerinds. As well as blood groups various related factors are of racial consequence: abnormal haemoglobins and pigments and deficiencies in some types of cell are all known to be racially linked.

Many metabolic differences are now used in anthropological classification: abnormalities in the sense of taste (some races cannot taste phenylthiocarbamide), the incidence of colour blindness, differences in the secretion of amino acid and other biochemical traits have all been scientifically investigated and shown to be excellent aids in the definition of gene pools. Certain medical disorders of genetic origin are useful to the science; *e.g.* thalassemia is confined to the Mediterranean type of the Caucasoid race. The Japanese have studied earwax types and found them to be genetically significant. Thus blood and other genetic traits have taken first place over body measurements and hair types in the definition of races.

The study of genetically transmitted traits has allowed anthropologists to divide man into about ten major types—the exact number depends upon individual interpretation of the scientific evidence. These major divisions, often referred to as geographical races, account for over 99% of mankind. Each geographical race contains many local groupings which, although forming breeding units separate from others to a greater or lesser degree, are nevertheless genetically related to the whole. The remaining groups are sometimes (inaccurately) termed microraces and consist of either small local genetically distinct populations, (e.g. the Ainu of Hokkaido) or peoples whose place in the anthropological jigsaw is still the subject of much controversy (*e.g.* the Bushmen of southern Africa).

The Geographical Races

1. The ASIATIC or MONGOLOID Race

Extent: most of Asia north and east of India.
Classic appearance: 'yellow-brown' skin, straight hair, round head, high cheek bones and flat face.

A northern group includes Lapps, Yakuts and Koreans; a southern group—'Oceanic Mongoloids' or Indonesians—is very mixed with a tendency to broader heads. The central (Pareoean) type with, in general, less prominent cheek bones and broader noses, includes both Chinese and Japanese.

2. The AMERINDIAN Race

Extent: the Americas.
Classic appearance: Similar to Asiatics though the Eskimos tend to have longer skulls, broader faces and narrower noses, and the Fuegans have curly hair.

Although there are undoubted links between the Indians of the New World and the Asiatics there is sufficient genetic reason to recognize them as separate races.

3. The AFRICAN or NEGROID Race

Extent: Africa south of the Sahara.
Classic appearance: tall, woolly hair, black or dark brown skin, broad nose, thickened lips.

Many sub-groups include Nilotics and the much shorter lighter skinned Pygmies (Negrillos). It is debatable whether the Bushmen belong to this geographical race.

4. The POLYNESIAN Race

Extent: Polynesia including New Zealand.
Classic appearance: similar to 'Oceanic Mongoloids' though with longer heads and some Caucasoid traits.

The ancestral home of the Polynesians was probably South-East Asia.

5. The MELANESIAN Race

Extent: Melanesia including New Guinea.
Classic appearance: similar to Africans but some Melanesian islanders tend to be lighter skinned.

This group contains isolated pockets in Asia including Semang tribes in Sumatra and Malaysia, possibly the Andaman Island Negritos, and debatably the short Aeta of the Philippines.

6. The MICRONESIAN Race

Extent: Micronesia.
Classic appearance: slight of stature, light brown skins, curly hair.

Genetically related to 'Oceanic Mongoloids'.

7. The AUSTRALOID Race

Extent: mainland Australia.
Classic appearance: curly hair, dark brown to black skin, massive skull with protruding jaws and retreating forehead, slender limbs.

The Australian aboriginals are distantly related to the Indic race, in particular to the Veddas of Sri Lanka, but long isolation has resulted in some special features.

8. The INDIC Race

Extent: Indian sub-continent.
Classic appearance: medium height, curly hair, prominent forehead, light brown skin but considerable variation in colour.

Local races include the north Indian Caucasoid type, the south Indian 'Dravidians', Singhalese Veddans and some isolated peoples in Sumatra and Sulawesi.

9. The CAUCASOID Race

Extent: Europe, Asia west of India and north Africa. Also widely diffused to the Americas and Australasia.

Classic appearance: considerable variation in height and build, and hair colour and form although there is a tendency to curly hair; 'white' or light skin, prominent forehead.

Sub-groups include Proto-Nordics (from Turkestan), Somalis Ethiops and other Caucasoid peoples of the horn of Africa and the Red Sea, Eurafricans, Arabs (including Bedouins), the Mediterranean or Romance peoples, the Nordic peoples (of Britain, Scandinavia, the Low Countries and Germany), the Pamiri, the Eurasiatics (including the Alpine type) found from central Europe to the Himalayas, and possibly the Ainu of Hokkaido, who are often categorized as a 'microrace'.

The 25 civilisations of man

If the duration of man's evolution, now estimated at 1 750 000 years, is likened to a single year, then the earliest of all history's civilisations began after 5 p.m. on 30 Dec. Put another way, 289/290ths of man's existence has been uncivilised.

Few historians have attempted to classify the world's civilisations because of the natural tendency to specialise. An early attempt was that of the Frenchman, Count de Gobineau, in his four-volume *L'Inégalité des Races Humaines* (Paris, 1853–5). His total was ten. Since that time western archaeologists have rescued five more ancient civilisations from oblivion—the Babylonic, the Hittite, the Mayan, the Minoan, and the Sumeric. This would have brought his total to 15 compared with a more modern contention of 26.

The most authoritative classification now available is the revised twelve-volume life work of Professor Arnold Toynbee, *A Study of History*, published between 1921 and 1961. This concludes that there have been 21 civilisations of which eight still survive. Those surviving are the Arabic (Islamic), the Far Eastern (began in AD 910 and now split into two), the Orthodox Christian (now also split into two), the Hindu (begun . AD 775) the Western civilisation and the Communist civilisation. The term 'civilisation' in the context of classifications relates purely to entities with separate imperial designs rather than a differing culture or ethos.

Researches published in 1960 indicate that the Yucatec and Mayan civilisations had the same cradle. The compilation below gives details. The Eskimo, Spartan, Polynesian, and Ottoman civilisations have been listed though Toynbee excludes these from his total on the grounds that they were 'arrested civilisations'.

No.	Name	Dawn	Final Collapse	Duration in Centuries	Cradle	Dominant States	Religion and Philosophy	Derivation
1.	Egyptiac	ante 4000 BC	c. AD 280	c. 43	Lower Nile	Middle Empire c. 2065–1660 BC	Osiris-worship Philosophy of Atonism	Spontaneous
2.	Sumeric or Sumerian	ante 3500 BC	c. 1700 BC	c. 18	Euphrates-Tigris Delta	Sumer and Akkad Empire c. 2298–1905 BC	Tammuz-worship	Spontaneous
3.	Indic	ante 3000 BC	c. AD 500	35	Mohenjo-Daro, Harappa Indus and Ganges valleys	Mauryan Empire 322–185 BC Gupta Empire AD 390–475	Hinduism Jainism Hinayāna Buddhism	Possibly of Sumeric origin
4.	Minoan	ante 2000 BC	c. 1400 BC	6	Cnossus, Crete and the Cyclades	Thalassocracy of Minos c. 1750–1400 BC	?Orphism	Spontaneous
5.	Hittite	2000 BC	c. 1200 BC	8	Boghazköi, Anatolia, Turkey	—	Pantheonism	Related to Minoan
6.	Mayan[1]	post 2000 BC	AD 1550	c. 35 ?	Guatemalan forests	First Empire AD c. 300–690	Human sacrifice and human penitential self-mortification	Spontaneous[2]
7.	Sinic	c. 1600 BC[3]	AD 220	18	Yellow River Basin	Ts'in and Han Empire 221 BC–AD 172	Mahāyāna Buddhism, Taoism, Confucianism	Believed unrelated
8.	Babylonic	c. 1500 BC	538 BC	10	Lower Mesopotamia	Babylonian Empire 610–539 BC	Judaism, Zoroastrianism Astrology	Related to Sumeric
9.	Hellenic	c. 1300 BC	AD 558	18½	Greek mainland and Aegean Is	Roman Empire 31 BC–AD 378	Mithraism, Platonism Stoicism, Epicureanism Christianity	Related to Minoan
10.	Syriac	c. 1200 BC	AD 970	22	Eastern Cilicia	Achaemenian Empire c. 525–332 BC	Islam and Philosophy of Zervanism	Related to Minoan
11.	Eskimo	c. 1100 BC	c. AD 1850	c. 30	Umnak, Aleutian Islands	Thule AD c. 1150–1850	Includes Sila, sky god; Sedna, seal goddess	—
12.	Spartan	c. 900 BC	AD 396	13	Laconia	620–371 BC	—	Hellenic
13.	Polynesian	c. 500 BC	c. AD 1775	22½	Samoa and Tonga	—	Ancestor spirits Mana—supernatural power	—
14.	Andean	c. 100 BC	AD 1783	19	Chimu, N Peru and Nazca, S Peru	Inca Empire AD 1430–1533	Philosophy of Viracochaism	Spontaneous
15.	Khmer[4]	c. AD 100	AD 1432	13	Cambodian coast	Ankor Kingdom AD 802–1432	—	Possibly related to Indic and Sinic
16.	Far Eastern (main)	AD 589	Scarcely survives	14 to date	Si Ngan (Sian-fu) Wei Valley	Mongol Empire AD 1280–1351 Manchu Empire AD 1644–1912	Muhayaniah Buddhism	Related to Sinic
17.	Far Eastern (Japan and Korea)	AD 645	Survives	13 to date	Yamato, Japan via Korea	Tokugawa Shogunate AD 1600–1868	Mikado-worship; Shintoism; Buddhism and Zen Philosophy	Related to Sinic
18.	Western	c. AD 675	Flourishes	13 to date	Ireland	Habsburg Monarchy AD 1526–1918 and French (Napoleonic) Empire AD 1792–1815	Philosophy of Christianity	Related to Hellenic
19.	Orthodox Christian (main)	c. AD 680	Survives	13 to date	Anatolia, Turkey	Byzantine Empire AD 395–1453	Bedreddinism Orthodox Church, Imāmi	Related to Hellenic and Western
20.	Hindu	c. AD 810	Survives	11 to date	Kanauj, Jamna-Ganges Duab	Mughal Raj AD c. 1572–1707 British Raj 1818–1947	Hinduism, Sikhism	Related to Indic

No.	Name	Dawn	Final Collapse	Duration in Centuries	Cradle	Dominant States	Religion and Philosophy	Derivation
21.	Orthodox Christian (Russia)	c. AD 950	Scarcely survives	10 to date	Upper Dnieper Basin	Muscovite Empire AD 1478–1918	Orthodox Church Sectarianism	Related to Hellenic
22.	Arabic	c. AD 975	AD 1525	5½	Arabia, Iraq, Syria	Abbasid Caliphate of Baghdad	Islām (post AD 1516)	Related to Syriac
23.	Mexic	c. AD 1075	AD 1821	7½	Mexican Plateau	Aztec Empire AD 1375–1521	Quetzalcoatl	Related to Mayan
24.	Ottoman	c. AD 1310	AD 1919	6	Turkey	Ottoman Empire AD 1372–1919	Islām	—
25.	Iranic (now Islamic)	c. AD 1320	Survives	6½ to date	Oxus-Jaxartes Basin	—	Islām (post AD 1516)	Related to Syriac
26.	Communist	1917	Flourishes	½ to date	Leningrad	U.S.S.R. and China	Atheism; Marxist-Leninism; Maoism	—

1. Toynbee regards a Yucatec civilisation (c. AD 1075–1680) as a separate entity. Archaeological discoveries in 1960 indicate that Dzibilchaltan, on the Yucatan Peninsula, was in fact the cradle of the whole Mayan civilisation.
2. There is evidence of links with Egyptiac. The early classic period at Tikal dates from c. AD 250–550.
3. The earliest archaeologically acceptable dynasty was that of Shang, variously dated 1766–1558 BC. The historicity of the First or Hsia dynasty, allegedly founded by Yü in 2205 BC, is in decided doubt.
4. Not regarded by Toynbee as a separate civilisation but as an offshoot of the Hindu civilisation. Modern evidence shows, however, that the Khmer origins antedate those of the Hindu civilisation by 7 centuries.

MAJOR ANTHROPOLOGICAL DISCOVERIES

Year	Scientific Name	Period and Estimated Date BC	Location	Description	Anthropologist
1856[1]	Homo neanderthalensis	Late middle Palaeolithic 120 000	Neander Valley, nr Düsseldorf, Germany	skull, bones	Fuhlrott
1868[2]	Homo sapiens (Cromagnon man)	Upper Palaeolithic 35 000	Cromagnon, Les Eyzies, France	4 skeletons, 1 foetus	Lartet
1890	Pithecanthropus erectus	Upper Pleistocene 400 000	Kedung Brebus, Java	mandible, tooth	Dubois
1907	Homo heidelbergensis	Lower Palaeolithic 450 000	Mauer, nr Heidelberg, Germany	lower jaw	Schoetensack
1912[3]	Eoanthropus dawsonii	Holocene (Recent) (fraud)	Piltdown, East Sussex	composite skull	Dawson
1921	Homo rhodesiensis	Upper Gamblian c. 50 000	Broken Hill, Zambia	skull	Armstrong
1924	Australopithecus africanus	Early Pleistocene 1 000 000	Taung, Botswana	skull	Dart (Izod)
1926[4]	Proconsul nyanzae	Miocene c. 25 000 000	Koru, Kenya	fragments (non-hominoid)	Hopwood
1927	Pithecanthropus pekinensis	Lower Palaeolithic 400 000	Choukoutien, nr Peking, China	tooth	Bohlin
1929–34	Neanderthaloid man	Middle Palaeolithic or Mousterian 120 000	Mt Carmel, Israel	part 16 skeletons	Garrod
1934	Ramapithecus	Miocene c. 14 000 000	Siwalik Hills, N India	Jaws, teeth	G. E. Lewis
1935[5]	Homo sapiens fossilis	Lower Palaeolithic 250 000	Boyn Hill, Swanscombe, Kent	parts skull	Marston
1935[6]	Gigantopithecus blacki	Middle Pleistocene 450 000	from Kwangsi, China (Hong Kong druggist)	teeth only	von Koenigswald
1936	Pleisianthropus transvaalensis	Early Pleistocene 1 000 000	Sterkfontein, Transvaal	skull, part femur	Broom (Barlow)
1938	Paranthropus robustus	Early Pleistocene 700 000	Kromdraai, Transvaal	skull part, bones	Broom (Terblanche)
1947	Homo sapiens fossilis	Middle Palaeolithic or Mousterian 125 000	Fontéchevade, France	2 callottes	Martin
1949	Australopithecus prometheus	Early Pleistocene 900 000	Makapansgat, Transvaal	fragments[7]	Dart
1953	Telanthropus capensis	Early Pleistocene 800 000	Swartkrans, Transvaal	jaw, skull parts	Broom
1954	Atlanthropus	Chelleo-Acheulian 500 000	Ternifine, Algeria	parietal, 3 mandibles	Arambourg
1957	Neanderthaloid man	Upper Palaeolithic 45 000	Shanidar, Iraq	skeletons	Solecki
1959	Zinjanthropus boisei	Late Pliocene c. 1 750 000	Olduvai, Tanzania	skull	Mrs Mary Leakey
1960	Homo habilis	Late Pliocene ante supra	Olduvai, Tanzania	fragments	Louis Leakey
1961	Kenyapithecus wickeri	Mid Miocene c. 14 000 000	Fort Ternan, Kenya	palate, teeth (non-hominoid)	Leakey (Mukiri)
1963	Australopithecus robustus	Middle Pleistocene 450 000	Chenchiawo, Lantien, NW China	jaw	
1964	Sinanthropus lantianensis	Middle Pleistocene c. 500 000	Kungwangling, Lantien, Shensi, China	skull cap and female jaw in 1963	Wu Ju Kang
1969	Homo erectus	Middle Pleistocene 500 000–1 000 000	Sangiran, Java	skull	Sartono
1972	Homo ?	Plio–Pleistocene 2 000 000	East Turkana, Kenya	mandibular, cranial and limb bones	Richard Leakey
1974/5	Australopithecus or Homo	Plio–Pleistocene 3 000 000	Hadar Afar region, Ethiopia	skull parts, jaws, teeth, skeleton	Johanson and Taieb
1975	Homo erectus	Plio-Pleistocene 1 500 000	Turkana, Kenya	skull**	Richard Leakey
1976	Homo ?	Pleistocene 400 000	Halkidiki, Greece	complete skeleton	Greek Anthropological Society

[1] Female skull discovered in Gibraltar in 1848 but unrecognised till 1864.
[2] Earliest specimen found at Engis, near Liége, Belgium, in 1832 by Schmerling.
[3] Exposed by X-Ray and radio-activity tests in Nov 1953 as an elaborate fraud.
[4] Non-hominoid. Complete skull discovered 1948 by Mrs Leakey.
[5] Further part discovered 1955.
[6] Since 1957 all the evidence is that these relate to a non-hominoid giant ape.
[7] Complete skull in 1958 (Kitching).
**Of great importance because of its uncanny resemblance to Peking man which Leakey believes is more correctly datable to triple the age advanced by the Chinese.

BIOLOGY

BIOLOGICAL CLASSIFICATION

The founder of modern taxonomy is usually regarded as Carolus Linnaeus of Sweden. He drew up rules for botanists and zoologists for the assigning of names to both plants and animals. The binomial system was introduced by him in 1758 with the still standard hierarchy of class, order and genus. The full modern hierarchy for an animal can now extend to 20 strata thus:

Kingdom	*Order*
Subkingdom	Suborder
Phylum	Superfamily
Subphylum	*Family*
Superclass	Subfamily
Class	Tribe
Subclass	Genus
Infraclass	Subgenus
Cohort	*Species*
Superorder	Subspecies

KINGDOM PROCARYOTA

The organisms are characterised by an absence of distinct nuclei. Class microtatobistes comprise viruses and the rickettsias, which are intermediate between viruses and bacteria in size and biochemistry.

Order rickettsiales comprises some 60 species, four families, and were named after the virologist Howard T. Ricketts (US) (1871–1910). No general classification of the 1000 plus viruses identified has yet been adopted. Eventual classification is expected to be based on the capsid (coat protein) symmetry in divisions between DNA—(deoxyribonucleus acid) and RNA—(ribonucleus acid)—containing forms. These infectious agents measured down to a minute 1.4×10^{-5} mm in diameter.

Bacteria unicellular micro-organisms often spherical or rod-like generally range from a micron in diameter to filaments several millimetres in length. They belong to the class Schizomycetes (Greek *Schizo* = I split; Mykēs = a fungas) in some 1500 species in ten orders.

Blue-green algae (Cyano phyta; Greek *Kyana* = corn-flower hence dark blue; phyton = a plant) have no motile flagellated cells and no sexual reproduction. Some 1500 species have been identified.

KINGDOM PROTISTA

This kingdom, first suggested by Ernst Haeckel in 1866, accommodates the mostly microscopic protozoa (Greek *protos* = first; zōon = an animal) of which some 30 000 species have been described embracing flagella, (Latin *Flagellum*, diminutive of *flagrum* = a whip) ciliates (Latin *Ciliatus* = furnished with hairs) and parasitic forms.

Algae possessing the nuclear mitochondrial and chloroplast membranes are also included in this kingdom.

KINGDOM FUNGI

The fungus group of some 80 000 species because of dissimilarities to both plants and animals are now quite usually placed in a separate kingdom.

Sac fungi (Order endomycetales) comprising yeasts (division mycota); moulds, mildews; truffles (class ascomycetes) and lichen (Order Lecanorales) which have both an algal and a fungal component.

Club fungi include smuts (Order Ustilaginales) so called because of black and dusty masses of spores; rusts (Order Uredinales) parasitic on vascular plants and hence destructive to agriculture; mushrooms (Order Agaricales); puffballs (Order Lycoperdales and Order Sclerodermatales) and stinkhorns (Order Phallales).

THE PLANT KINGDOM

Division Chlorophyta (Greek, *chlōros* = grass green; *phyton* = a plant). Green algae in which the chromatophores (i.e. plastids, or protoplasmic granules in active cells) are green and with the same pigments as vascular plants, i.e. those composed of vessels, as opposed to cells, but without their conducting system. About 5500 species. The plant body never grows by means of an apical cell (i.e. the single cell which is the origin of all longitudinal growth) and the reproductive organs are always one-celled and without a sheath of vegetative cells.

Division Euglenophyta (Greek, *eu-* = true; *glēnē* = a cavity; *phyton* = a plant). Mostly naked motile (Latin, *motus* = a moving), i.e. movable, unicellular organisms, frequently found in stagnant fresh waters. Algae with grass-green chromatophores. The food reserves are either paramylum (an insoluble carbohydrate related to starch) or fats. Flagella (Latin, *flagellum* = a whip), i.e. whip-like appendages by which the plants are able to progress through the water, differ from those of other major groups in that they are inserted in a small interior chamber at the anterior end of a cell. Reproduction is by cell division but several genera are known to form thick-walled resting stages. Sexual reproduction is not definitely known for any species.

Division Charophyta (Greek, *chairō* = to rejoice)—stoneworts, growing submerged in fresh or brackish waters. The plant body is multicellular, a slender cylindrical axis bearing nodes (Latin, *nodus* = a knot), i.e. whorls of short branches ('leaves'), separated by internodes. The growth is initiated by an apical cell. The sex organs (male and female) are surrounded by envelopes of sterile cells.

Division Phaeophyta (Greek, *phaios* = brown and swarthy; *phyton* = a plant). Brown algae. About 900 species, all but 3 being strictly marine, growing along rocky ocean shores, predominantly in the algal flora of colder seas, and usually where the water is less than 50 ft deep. These are all multicellular and the primary food reserve is laminarin, a carbohydrate dissolved in the cell sap.
 Three kinds of life history are found in the Phaeophyta which have been named as under.
  Class Isogeneratae (Greek, *isos* = equal to; Latin, *generatio* = a begetting). The life history consists of the alternation of similar generations.
  Class Heterogeneratae (Greek, *heteros* = other). The life history consists of the alternation of dissimilar generations. The gametophytes (i.e. the generations bearing the sexual organs) are always irregularly branched filaments.
  Class Cyclosporeae (Greek, *kyklos* = a circle). About 350 species, mostly in oceans. In this class there is no gametophytic generation, and the spores function as gametes. The reproductive organs are borne in round cavities (conceptacles) within tips of the sporophytic plant body, and each conceptacle contains many sex organs.

Division Rhodophyta (Greek, *rhodon* = a rose (hence a red colour); *phyton* = a plant). Red algae. About 2500 species, of which about 50 are fresh-water and the rest marine, predominantly in the algal flora of tropical seas. The Rhodophytes have chromatophores in which the photosynthetic pigments are masked by a red pigment (phycoerythrin; from Greek, *erythros* = red); sometimes there is also a blue pigment (phycocyanin). The chief food reserve is an insoluble carbohydrate, floridean starch. Sexual reproduction is unique in that non-flagellate male gametes (spermatia) are passively transported to female sex organs. The plant body is usually a simple blade, a much-divided blade or more complex and differentiated into stem- and blade-like portions.

Division Chrysophyta (Greek, *chrysos* = gold; *phyton* = a plant). These have golden-brown chromatophores and a storage of reserve foods as leucosin or fats. They form a distinctive type of spore (Greek, *spora* = a seed), the endospore, i.e. a spore formed within.

Division Xanthophyta (Greek, *xanthos* = yellow) or Heterokontae (Greek, *heteros* = other; *kontos* = a pole). Yellowish-green algae, almost exclusively fresh-water. About 200 species. These have yellowish-green chromatophores and store foods as leucosin or as oils, never as starch.

Division Bacillariophyta (Latin, *bacillus* = a staff). Diatoms. Microscopic unicellular or colonial algae. Over 5500 species. These have cell-walls composed of two overlapping halves and a bilateral or radially symmetrical ornamentation of the wall.

Division Pyrrophyta (Greek, *pyrrhos* = flame coloured; *phyton* = a plant). The Pyrrophytes are the only algae with yellowish to brownish chromatophores that store reserve foods as starch or starch-like compounds. Motile cells are biflagellate, usually with the flagella unequal in length and movement.
  Class Desmophyceae (Greek, *desmos* = a bond). All rare organisms, mostly marine. These have a cell wall vertically divided into two homogeneous, i.e. uniform, halves (valves). Motile cells have two apically inserted flattened flagella that differ from each other in type of movement.
  Class Dinophyceae (Greek, *dinos* = whirling). About 950 species, almost all marine plankton. 90 per cent of the genera are unicellular and motile. The cells of most species have numerous golden-brown to chocolate-brown chromatophores, but the cells of certain species lack chromatophores. Motile cells and zoospores are encircled by a transverse groove—the girdle. The two flagella are inserted in or near the girdle; one of them encircles the girdle, the other extends vertically backward.

Division Bryophyta (Greek, *bryon* = a moss) or Atracheata (Greek, *a-* = without; Latin, *trachia* = the wind-pipe). The Bryophytes—mosses and liverworts. The sex cells (gametes) are contained in a single-layered jacket of cells, as opposed to a simple cell-wall (as in Algae).
  Class Hepaticae (from Latin, *hepaticus* = pertaining to the liver). The typical liverworts, sometimes called the hepatics. The spore case (capsule) frequently has sterile slender cells (elaters) among the spores, or in some cases no sterile tissue. The elaters, if present, are unicellular. The cells of the sporophyte have several to many small chloroplasts (i.e. green plastids). There are both leafy and thalloid forms. The leafy members of the class often resemble

mosses, but usually have two rows of leaves, or two rows of large leaves and a third row of small leaves on the side of the stem towards the substrate. The thalloid forms are flattened ribbons or rosettes without leaflike structures on the stems.

Class Anthocerotae (Greek, *anthos* = a flower; *keras* = a horn). A group of horned liverworts, often called hornworts. Similar to Hepaticae, except for the indeterminate basal growth of the needle-shaped sporophyte, so that mature spores may be falling from the top of the apically split sporophyte while new ones are being initiated at the base. The cells of the sporophyte have two large chloroplasts containing starch-producing bodies called pyrenoids. The sporophyte has a sterile central column (columella) and pores (stomata) in the epidermis (the plant-skin or covering). The members of this class usually have irregular multicellular elaters. This class is sometimes included within the Hepaticae. There are about 9000 liverworts.

Class Musci (Latin, *muscus* = moss). The true mosses. The spore case has a cylinder of sterile tissue (columella) in the centre surrounded by many minute spores and usually has a definite lid (operculum) which opens by splitting loose when the spores are ripe. Under the operculum is a single or double row (peristome) of slender, triangular teeth which ring the mouth and are hygroscopic (i.e. susceptible to extension or shrinkage on the application or removal of water or vapour) and move in response to changes in moisture. When the teeth are dry they curl back exposing the interior of the capsule; when moist, they curve inward, effectively blocking the mouth of the capsule, thus controlling to some extent the dissemination of spores. The mosses are usually classified into three orders: *Sphagnales* (usually known as bog or peat mosses), *Andreaeales* (slit mosses), and *Bryales*. There are about 14 000 mosses.

Division Tracheophyta (or Tracheata) (Latin, *trachia* = the windpipe). The Tracheophytes—plants possessing tracheae, i.e. spiral ducts or water-conducting vessels in the woody tissue of plants, formed from the coalescence of series of cells by the disappearance of the partitions between them. The vascular plants.

Sub-division Psilophyta (Greek, *psilos* = naked, smooth). Grasslike plants with a creeping stem, small, scale-like leaves and no true roots. This class contains two orders, Psilophytales (comprising only fossil types) and Psilotales, which contains the single family Psilotaceae. These plants grow epiphytically (i.e. on other plants, but not parasitically) or in soil rich in humus.

Sub-division Lycopsida (Greek, *lykos* = a wolf). Club-mosses and quillworts. These are in fact vascular plants and quite distinct from the true mosses. The leaves are relatively small and simple in form while the sporangia are seated singly, one in the axil of each leaf of the fertile region, or spreading outwards on its base.

Sub-division Sphenopsida (Greek, *sphen* = a wedge; *opsis* = appearance). Horsetails. These are Pteridophytes which have their appendages disposed in successive whorls, with long internodes between them. The class contains three orders, Hyeniales, Sphenophyllales (both extinct now) and Equisetales (from Latin, *equus* = a horse; *seta* = a bristle), which has two families—Calamitaceae (extinct) and Equisetaceae. This latter family contains a single genus, *Equisetum*, comprising the horse-tails—semi-aquatic plants varying in height from a few inches to 30 ft or more, with erect shoots arising from richly branched, subterranean stems, which are themselves rooted in the soil.

Sub-division Pteropsida (Greek, *pteris* = a fern).

Class Filicinidae (Latin, *filix* = a fern). The ferns—over 9500 living species. The most distinctive feature of this group is that on the relatively large leaves many sporangia are borne, either singly or in groups (sori). Most ferns flourish under moist conditions with a moderate temperature, and the plant varies in size from a minute herb to a tree-like body, rising to a height of 80 ft. The life cycle is split into two distinct bodily phases, or generations—the leafy spore-bearing fern plant and the prothallus, a small green scale-like body which represents the sexual generation. This class contains five orders, the Cladoxylales, Coenopteridales (both extinct), Ophioglossales (adder's tongue ferns), Marattiales (from the genus Marattia) and Filicales (the 'true' ferns).

Class Gymnospermidae (or Gymnospermae) (Greek, *gymnos* = naked; *sperma* = seed). The Gymnosperms form the first of the two groups of living seed plants. The members of this class have naked ovules, exposed to the pollen at the time of pollination, and naked seeds, and the male gametophytes always produce more sterile cells than those of the angiosperms. The female gametophyte is comparatively large and produces large eggs in cellular structures called archegonia. The gymnosperms have several embryos beginning their development, depending upon how many eggs are fertilised, but only one usually survives the intense competition to maturity. The roots are predominantly tap-roots (i.e. straight roots tapering to a point growing directly downwards from the stem). The reproductive unit is the strobilus or cone, which consists of a large axis bearing either megasporophylls (the ovule-containing organs), each subtended, in conifers, by a sterile bract (a modified leaf), or microsporophylls (the pollen-containing organs). Living gymnosperms include only woody perennial plants which are usually evergreen trees, seldom shrubs, or lianas. The gymnosperms may be divided into three groups:

Sub-class Cycadopsida. The cycads and cycad-like plants

Order Cycadofilicales (or Pteridospermales)—the so-called seed ferns (now extinct).

Order Bennettitales (or Cycadeoidales)—cycad-like plants probably of pteridospermous origin (now extinct).

Order Cycadales (Greek, *kykas*, from *kiakos*, plural of *koix* = name of a kind of palm)—the Cycads, of which there are about 100 living species, which all grow very slowly. Those of the columnar type attain their maximum height only after many centuries of growth. They have only a scanty zone of wood surrounding a very large pith and enclosed by a very large cortex (i.e. bark or rind), so the stem is relatively weak.

Order Caytoniales. A small group, probably of pteridospermous origin with the ovules borne in hollow spherical bodies (cupules) They are sometimes included with Pteridospermales.

Sub-class Coniferopsida. The conifers and related plants.

Order Cordaitales (resembling the extinct genus *Cordaites*). These were mostly trees of considerable size, resembling modern conifers.

Order Ginkgoales. This order is almost entirely extinct, being represented by only a single living species, *Ginkgo biloba* (the maidenhair tree), which is native to China. The twigs of this tree are long shoots, bearing many dwarf branches, which continue their growth on the end of long shoots of the previous year, bearing leaves that alternate in a spiral arrangement.

Order Coniferales (Latin, *conus* = a cone; *fero* = I bear). The conifers, of which there are about 550 living species, such as the pine, spruce, cedar, larch and Douglas fir. The conifers are cone-bearing trees, which are usually evergreen and have profusely branched stems, with needlelike leaves that are usually small and simple and normally persist for about three to ten years. There is a lateral growth zone or cambium which gives rise to a large amount of wood surrounded by a thin cortex and enclosing only a small amount of pith. The seed cones may be large and made up of dozens of cone scales, but in some cases the seed-bearing scales are single ovules. All conifers have pollen borne in cones which are usually quite small.

Order Taxales. The Taxads (formerly included in Coniferales)—yew trees and related plants. The members of this order are, in most respects, similar to conifers, but it has been discovered that they have never had ovulate cones, i.e. the ovules are borne terminally and singly on axes of the plant and are not aggregated into cone-like structures.

Sub-class Gnetopsida

Order Gnetales—contains about 71 species. This order contains perennial, normally dioecious (i.e. unisexual) plants with opposite simple leaves. The cones consist of an axis bearing decussate pairs (i.e. alternately at right angles) of bracts or a number of superposed whorls of bracts, each whorl connate (united) in a cup-like form. The ovulate or staminate structures (called 'flowers') are axillary to these bracts (i.e. growing in an axil), and consist of one or two pairs of free or connate scales, the perianth, enclosing either a single ovule with a long projecting micropylar tube (i.e. from an aperture in the outer coat of the ovule), or from one to six stamens.

Class Angiospermae (from Greek, *angeion* = receptacle; *sperma* = seed). The true flowering plants, of which there are more than 250 000 species. The Angiosperms have ovules enclosed within the ovary of a pistil (gynoccium) and the seeds are enclosed within the ripened ovary, which, when matured, becomes a fruit that may be single-seeded or many-seeded. The angiosperms usually have fibrous roots and soft herbaceous stem tissue. The leaves contain extensive mesophytic tissue (i.e. requiring only an average amount of moisture). The reproductive unit is the flower, which typically consists of a very short central axis bearing one or more apical megasporophylls, commonly called carpels, subtended by microsporophylls (termed stamens) and by two sets of sterile bract-like appendages collectively termed the perianth (composed of petals and sepals). In the simplest form of the flower, the ovules are borne along the inner margin of the megasporophyll—like peas in the pod. In all modern angiosperms the megasporophyll is closed and fused marginally, with the ovules in the loculus (cavity) thus formed. In this form, the carpel is termed the pistil and consists of the ovary (the ovule-containing organ) and its apical stigma (the pollen-receiving part). The microsporophylls are closed until maturity, when they open and their pollen is released. The pollen-producing part is the anther and the supporting stalk the filament. The fertilisation (which follows pollination) takes place entirely within the carpel of the flower. After the pollen grain (microgametophyte) reaches the receptive stigmatic surface of the pistil, a pollen tube is developed within, and into it moves the generative nucleus, which divides to form two male nuclei, each of which is a male gamete. Stimulated by the environment created in the stigma, the pollen tube grows through the wall of the pollen grain and into the tissue of the stigma and its style (i.e. the usually attenuated part of a pistil between the ovary and the stigma). This growth continues down the style until the tube penetrates the ovary. Growth continues and when the tube reaches the ovule it enters the micropyle (a pore at the tip of the ovule) or elsewhere through the integuments (i.e. the two outer layers of the ovule) and finally the female gametophyte (enclosed within the ovule). As pollen-tube growth progresses from stigma to female gametophyte it carries with it both male nuclei. On approach to the egg nucleus, within the female gametophyte, the two haploid male nuclei are released. One unites with the haploid egg nucleus and forms a diploid sporophyte, called the zygote, and the other unites with the polar nuclei to form a triploid endosperm nucleus. The zygote thus formed is a new generation, and becomes the embryo within the seed. The zygote (enclosed by a membrane) undergoes a series of divisions leading to wall formation (either transverse or longitudinal) separating the terminal cell from the basal cell. The terminal cell continues to divide to produce the axis or hypocotyl of the embryo, from which are later produced the cotyledons (Greek, *kotylēdōn* = cup-shaped hollow) or seed leaves (either one or two—see below under sub-classes). The basal cell divides to form a chain of cells that functions as a suspensor, and the lowest is attached to the embryo and ultimately gives rise to the root and root cap of the embryo. The endosperm nucleus, together with the embryo sac, multiplies to form the endosperm tissue of the seed. This tissue multiplies as the embryo developes, but the bulk of it is digested by the embryo. The angiosperms may be divided into two groups:

Sub-class Dicotyledonae (Greek, *di* = two). The dicotyledons—over 200 000 species. This sub-class contains angiosperms in which the embryo has two cotyledons (seed leaves). The stems produce a secondary growth by successive cylinders of xylem tissue (Greek, *xylē* = wood), the wood element which, in angiosperms, contains vessels for water conduction and wood fibres for support. The veins of the leaves are typically arranged in a network, i.e. reticulate venation. Leaves may be simple, with entire or toothed margins, or compound with leaflets arranged on either side of, or radiating from a peticole, or footstalk. The petals and sepals of the flowers number mostly four or five, or multiples of four or five, and the pollen grains are mostly tricolpate (with three furrows). This group may be sub-divided into 40 or more orders, of which the following are among the larger and more important. They are listed in the general sequence of primitive to advanced.

Order Ranales (or Magnoliales)—Buttercup, magnolia, tulip tree, marsh marigold, barberry, lotus, custard apple, nutmeg, etc.

Order Rosales—Rose, strawberry, blackberry, apple, cherry, legumes, saxifrages, witch hazel, plane tree, etc.

Order Papaverales (or Rhoeadales)—Poppy, cabbage and relatives, mignonette, bleeding heart, the mustard family (Cruciferae), etc.

Order Geraniales—geranium, flax, castor bean, the citrus group, rubber, etc.

Order Umbellales—The carrot family, English ivy, the dogwoods, etc.

Order Rubiales—Madder, honeysuckle, coffee, cinchona, teasel, etc.

Order Campanulales—The bellflowers, the aster family (Compositae), etc.

Order Caryophyllales—The pinks, pigweed, spinach, buckwheat, sea lavender, thrift, etc.

Order Ericales—Heath, rhododendron, mountain laurel, blueberry, cranberry, etc.

Order Gentianales—Gentian, buddleia, olive, privet, ash, dogbane, milkweed, etc.

Order Polemoniales—Polemonium, morning-glory, phlox, forget-me-not, potato, tobacco, petunia, etc.

Order Lamiales—The mints, salvia, verbena, teak, lantana, etc.

Order Scrophulariales—Snapdragon, mimulus, trumpet vine, gloxinia, bladderwort, acanthus, etc.

There are several families of dicotyledons which appear to have no direct relationship with any other group. These include the Salicaceae (willows and poplars), Casuarinaceae (the Australian pine, not a true pine), Fagaceae (beeches and oaks) and the Proteaceae.

Sub-class Monocotyledonae (Greek, *monos* = one). The monocotyledons—about 50 000 species. The embryo has one cotyledon. The members of this sub-class have stems without any secondary thickening; the vascular strands are scattered through the stem and no cylinders of secondary xylem tissue are produced. The leaves have entire margins, the blades generally lack a petiole, and the veins are arranged in parallel form. The flower parts are always in multiples of three, and the sepals are often petal-like. The pollen grains are always monocolpate (i.e. with one furrow). This sub-class contains 15 orders, of which the Liliales (Lily order) is considered the most primitive, and the Orchidales (Orchid order) the most advanced. This sub-class also contains palms, grasses, and bamboos.

Principal trees in Britain

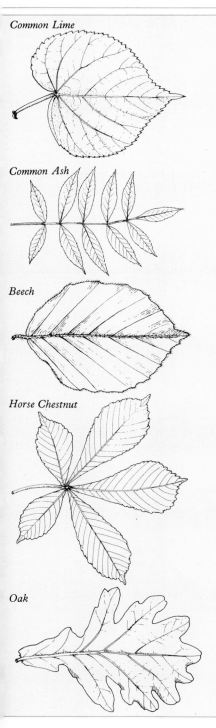

Common Lime

Common Ash

Beech

Horse Chestnut

Oak

In each case the height given is the maximum recorded living height and the girth is taken at 5 ft *1,52 m* above the ground.

1. **Grand Fir** (*Abies grandis*); height 188 ft *57,3 m* Strone, Cairndow, Strathclyde; girth 19¾ ft *6 m* at Lochanhead House, Dumfries and Galloway; intro: 1832 from W North America by David Douglas.
2. **Douglas Fir** (*Pseudotsuga menziesii*); height 181 ft *55,1 m* at Powis Castle, Powys; girth 23¼ ft *7 m* at Eggesford, Devon; intro: 1827 from W North America by David Douglas.
3. **European Silver Fir** (*Abies alba*); height *c.* 180 ft *55 m* at Kilbryde, Inverary, Strathclyde; girth 23 ft *7 m* at Ardkinglas, Strathclyde; intro: 1603 from Central Europe.
4. **Canadian** or **Sitka Spruce** (*Picea sitchensis*); height 174 ft *53 m* at Murthly, Tayside; girth 24 ft 7 in *7,5 m* at Fortescue Estates, Devon; used for aircraft and boat-oars; intro: 1831 from Canada.
5. **Wellingtonia** (*Sequoiadendron giganteum*); height 165 ft *50 m* at Endsleigh, Devon; girth 28½ ft *8,6 m* at Crichel House, Dorset; intro: 1853 from California.
= 6. **Common Lime** (*Tilia vulgaris*); height 150 ft *45,7 m* at Duncombe Park, North Yorkshire; girth 12½ ft *3,8 m* also at Duncombe Park; indigenous hybrid of *T platyphyllos* and *T cordata*.
= 6. **Black Italian Poplar** (*Populus nigra serotina*); height 150 ft *45,7 m* at Fairlawne, Kent; girth 20 ft 1 in *6,1 m* at Killagordan Farm, Truro, Cornwall; intro: 1750 from France.
8. **Common Ash** (*Fraxinus excelsior*); height 148 ft *45,1 m* at Duncombe Park, North Yorkshire; girth 19½ ft *5,9 m* at Holywell Hall, Lincolnshire; indigenous in Europe and Asia Minor.
9. **Common Larch** (*Larix decidua*); height 146 ft *44,5 m* at Hascombe, Surrey; girth 18½ ft *5,6 m* at Monzie, Perth; intro: *ante* 1629 from Central Europe.
10. **London Plane** (*Platanus acerifolia*); height 145 ft *44,2 m* at Bryanston School, Blandford, Dorset; girth 26½ ft *8,0 m* at Bishop's Palace, Ely, Cambridgeshire; intro: *ante* 1700, probably hybrid arising at Oxford Botanical Gardens.
11. **Corsican Pine** (*Pinus nigra* var. *maritima*); height 144·3 ft *44 m* at Stanage Park, Powys; girth 14¼ ft *4,4 m* at Arley Castle, Worcestershire; intro: 1759.
12. **Common** (or **Norway**) **Spruce** (*Picea excelsa* or *P abies*); height 142 ft *43,2 m* and girth 14 ft *4,2 m*, both at Inverary, Strathclyde; used as plywood and white deal; intro: *ante* 1548 from N Europe.
= 13. **Durmast Oak** (*Quercus petraea*); height 138 ft *42 m* at Whitfield, Hereford and Worcester; used for ship-building, fencing, flooring, *parquet*, panelling, furniture, charcoal; indigenous.
= 13. **Redwood** (*Sequoia sempervirens*); height 138 ft *42 m*, at an undisclosed site, North Devon, intro: 1843 from California.
15. **Beech** (*Fatus sylvatica*); height 135 ft *41 m* Whitfield House, Hereford and Worcester; girth 26 ft 1 in *7,9 m* at Eridge Park, Sussex; used for indoor furniture; indigenous in Europe.
16. **Cedar of Lebanon** (*Cedrus libani*); height 132 ft *40,2 m* at Petworth House, Sussex; girth 39¾ ft *12,1 m* at Cedar Park, Cheshunt, Hertfordshire; used for aromatic turnery; intro: *c.* 1660 from Lebanon or Syria
17. **Wych** (or **Scotch**) **Elm** (*Ulmus glabra*); height 128 ft *39 m* at Rossie Priory nr. Dundee; indigenous.
18. **Horse Chestnut** (*Aesculus hippocastanum*); height 125 ft *38,1 m* at Petworth House, West Sussex; girth 20 ft 10 in *6,3 m* in Hatfield Forest, Essex; almost valueless; intro: 1620 from Greece or Albania.
= 19. **Oak** (*Quercus robur*); height 121 ft *37 m*, Fredville, Kent; used for boat-building, flooring, *parquet*, panelling, fencing, furniture, charcoal; indigenous.
= 19. **Japanese Larch** (*Larix leptolepis*); height 121 ft *37 m* at Blair Atholl, Tayside; girth 8 ft 11 in *2,7 m* at Dunkeld House, Tayside; intro: 1861 from Japan.
21. **Scots Pine** (*Pinus sylvestris*); height 120 ft *36,6 m* in Oakley Park, Ludlow; girth 18 ft *5,4 m* in Spye Park, Wiltshire, used for yellow deal, boxes and crates; primeval British forest tree.
= 22. **Lombardy Poplar** (*Populus nigra italica*); height 118 ft *35,9 m* at Marble Hill, Twickenham; girth 14⅔ ft *4,4 m* at Upper Edgebold, Salop; intro: 1758 from Italy.
= 22. **Smooth-leaved Elm** (*Ulmus carpinifolia*); height 118 ft *35,9 m* at Kensington Gardens, London; girth 37 ft 10 in *11,5 m* at Cobham Hall, Kent; indigenous.

Elm

Sycamore

Birch

Alder

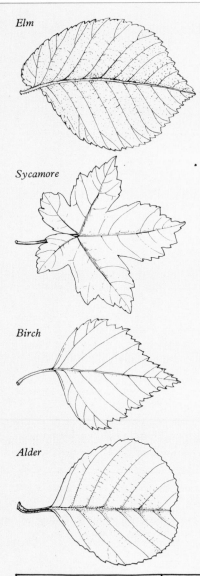

=22. **English Elm** (*Ulmus procera*); height 118 ft *35,9 m* Holkham Hall, Norfolk; girth 31 ft *9,4 m* at East Bergholt, Suffolk; used for panelling, coffins, farm buildings; indigenous.

=22. **Spanish** or **Sweet Chestnut** (*Castanea sativa*); height 118 ft *35,9 m* at Godinton Park, Kent; girth 39½ ft *12,0 m* at Canford, Dorset; used for hop poles and palings; intro: *c.* 50 BC by the Romans.

26. **Sycamore** or **Great Maple** (*Acer Pseudoplatanus*); height 112 ft *34,1 m* at Drumlarig Castle, Dumfries and Galloway, Scotland; girth 22¼ ft *6,7 m* at Birnam, Tayside; used for turnery and veneers.

27. **Hornbeam** (*Carpinus betulus*); height 98 ft *29 m* at Hutton-in-the-Forest, Cumbria; girth 17 ft 7 in *5,3 m* in Hatfield Forest, Essex; used for making piano keys; indigenous in Europe and Asia Minor.

28. **Silver** or **Common Birch** (*Betula pendula*); height 97 ft *29,5 m* at Woburn Sands, Bedfordshire; girth 11½ ft *3,5 m*; indigenous in Europe and Siberia.

=29. **Oriental Plane** (*Platanus orientalis*); height 90 ft *27,4 m* at Jesus College, Cambridge; girth 25½ ft *7,7 m* in Woodstock Park, Kent; used for lacewood furniture; intro: *c.* 1520 from SE Europe.

=29. **Monkey Puzzle** (*Araucaria araucana*); height 90 ft *27,5 m* at Bicton, Devon; girth 12 ft 1 in *3,6 m* used for decorative work; intro: 1795 from Chile.

=31. **Yew** (*Taxus baccata*); height 85 ft *25,9 m* at Midhurst, Sussex; girth 34 ft 7 in *10,5 m* at Ulcombe, Kent; used for inlay work, bows, topiary; indigenous in Europe and Central Asia.

=31. **White Willow** (*Salix alba*); height 85 ft *25,9 m* at Sandringham Park, Norfolk; girth 20 ft *6,0 m* used for osiers (cricket bats from var. *coelurea*); indigenous in Europe and N Asia.

=31. **Alder** (*Alnus glutinosa*); height 85 ft *25,9 m* at Sandling Park, Kent; used for making clogs; indigenous in Europe, Asia Minor and Africa.

=34. **Field Maple** (*Acer campestre*); height 82 ft *24,9 m* at Kinnettles, Tayside, Scotland; used for turnery small cabinet work; indigenous in Europe.

=34. **Walnut** (*Juglans regia*); height 82 ft *24,9 m* in Laverstock Park, Hampshire; girth 21½ ft *6,5 m* at Pilton Church, Northamptonshire; used for furniture, veneers, gunstocks; introduced in early times.

=34. **White Birch** (*Betula pubescens*); height *c.* 82 ft *24,9 m*; girth 10 ft *3,0 m*; indigenous.

=37. **Aspen** (*Populus tremula*); height *c.* 80 ft *24,3 m*, girth 8½ ft *2,5 m*; indigenous in Europe, N Africa and Asia Minor.

=37. **Crack Willow** (*Salix fragilis*); height 80 ft *24,3 m* at Farnham, Surrey; girth 14½ ft *4,4 m*; indigenous in Europe and N Asia.

39. **Weeping Willow** (*Salix babylonica*); height 76 ft *23,2 m*; girth 10 ft *3,0m*; at Trinity College, Cambridge, used for decorative work; intro: 1730 from China *via* Iraq.

40. **Common Holly** (*Ilex aquifolium*); height 74 ft *22,5 m* at Staverton Thicks, Surrey; girth 31¾ ft *9,6 m* at Scaftworth Hall, Doncaster; used for inlays, slide rules, pseudo ebony; indigenous in Europe, N Africa and W Asia.

41. **'Wild Service'** (*Sorbus torminalis*); height 71 ft *21,6 m* at The Grove, Penshurst, Kent; girth 9 ft *2,7 m* at Chiddingstone, Kent; used for furniture and turnery; indigenous in Europe.

=42. **Rowan** or **Mountain Ash** (*Sorbus aucuparia*); height 62 ft *18,9 m* Ramster, Chiddingfold, Surrey; girth 8 ft *2,4 m*; used for making cabinets, small turnery; indigenous in Europe and W Asia.

=42. **Whitebeam** (*Sorbus aria*); height 62 ft *18,9 m* at Tubney Wood, Berkshire; girth 7 ft *2,1 m*; used for furniture and turnery; indigenous in Europe.

44. **Juniper** (*Juniperus communis*); height 52 ft *15,8 m* at Oakley Park, Ludlow, Salop; (bush—no girth); oil of juniper is used in gin-making; indigenous in Europe.

British TREES

Average Heights

Top line, left to right:

Elm 100 ft *30 m*
Oak 75 ft *23 m*
Ash 110 ft *33 m*
Horse Chestnut 90 ft *27 m*
Silver Birch 75 ft *23 m*

Bottom line, left to right:

Alder 70 ft *21 m*
Sycamore 90 ft *27 m*
Lime 100 ft *30 m*
Beech 100 ft *30 m*

FRUIT

Common name	Scientific name	Geographical origin	Date first described or known
Apple	*Malus pumila*	Southwestern Asia	Early times; Claudius 450 BC
Apricot	*Prunus armeniaca*	Central and western China	BC (Piling and Dioscoridês)
Avocado (Pear)	*Persea americana*	Mexico and Central America	Early Spanish explorers, Clusius 1601
Banana	*Musa sapientum*	Southern Asia	Intro: Africa 1st century AD, Canary Isles 15th century
Cherry	*Prunus avium*	Europe (near Dardanelles)	Prehistoric times
Date	*Phoenix dactylifera*	unknown	Prehistoric times
Fig	*Ficus carica*	Syria westward to the Canary islands	c. 4000 BC (Egypt)
Grape	*Vitis vinifera*	around Caspian and Black Seas	c. 4000 BC
Grapefruit	*Citrus grandis*	Malay Archipelago and neighbouring islands	12th or 13th century
Lemon	*Citrus limon*	S.E. Asia	11th–13th centuries
Lime	*Citrus aurantifolia*	Northern Burma	11th–13th centuries
Mandarin (Orange)	*Citrus reticulata*	China	220 BC in China; Europe 1805
Mango	*Mangifera indica*	Southeastern Asia	c. 16th century; Cult. India 4th or 5th century BC
Olive	*Olea europaea*	Syria to Greece	Prehistoric times
Orange	*Citrus sinensis*	China	2200 BC (Europe 15th century)
Papaya	*Carica papaya*	West Indian Islands or Mexican mainland	14th–15th centuries
Peach	*Prunus persica*	China ?	300 BC (Greece)
Pear	*Pyrus communis*	Western Asia	Prehistoric times
Pineapple	*Ananas comosus*	Guadeloupe	c. 1493 (Columbus)
Plum	*Prunus domestica*	Western Asia	Possibly 100 AD
Quince	*Cydonia oblonga*	Northern Iran	BC
Rhubarb	*Rheum rhaponticum*	Eastern Mediterranean lands and Asia Minor	2700 BC (China)
Water Melon	*Citrullus laratus*	Central Africa	c. 2000 BC (Egypt)

VEGETABLES

Common name	Scientific name	Geographical origin	Date first described or known
Asparagus	*Asparagus officinalis*	Eastern Mediterranean	c. 200 BC
Beetroot	*Beta vulgaris*	Mediterranean Area	2nd century BC
Broad Bean	*Vicia faba*	—	widely cultivated in prehistoric times
Broccoli	*Brassica oleracea* (variety *Italica*)	Eastern Mediterranean	1st century AD
Brussels Sprouts	*Brassica oleracea* (variety *gemmifera*)	Northern Europe	1587 (Northern Europe)
Cabbage	*Brassica oleracea* (variety *capitata*)	Eastern Mediterranean lands and Asia Minor	c. 600 BC
Carrot	*Daucus carota*	Afghanistan	c. 500 BC
Cauliflower	*Brassica oleracea* (variety *botrytis*)	Eastern Mediterranean	6th century BC
Celery	*Apium graveolens*	Caucasus	c. 850 BC
Chive	*Allium schoenoprasum*	Eastern Mediterranean	c. 100 BC
Cucumber	*Cucumis sativus*	Northern India	2nd century BC (Egypt 1300 BC)
Endive	*Cichorium endivia*	Eastern Mediterranean lands and Asia Minor	BC
Garden Pea	*Pisum sativum*	Central Asia	3000–2000 BC
Garlic	*Allium sativum*	Middle Asia	c. 900 BC (Homer)
Gherkin (W. Indian)	*Cucumis anguria*	Northern India	2nd century BC
Globe Artichoke	*Cynara scolymus*	Western and Central Mediterranean	c. 500 BC
Kale	*Brassica oleracea* (variety *acephala*)	Eastern Mediterranean lands and Asia Minor	c. 500 BC
Leek	*Allium porrum*	Middle Asia	c. 1000 BC
Lettuce	*Lactuca sativa*	Iran	4500 BC (Egyptian tomb)
Marrow	*Cucurbita pepo*	America ?	16th–17th century (Mexican sites 7000–5500 BC)
Muskmelon	*Cucumis melo*	Africa	Roman times
Onion	*Allium cepa*	Middle Asia	c. 2400 BC 3200 BC (Egypt)
Parsnip	*Pastinaca sativa*	Caucasus	1st century BC
Pepper	*Capsicum frutescens*	Peru	Early burial sites, Peru; intro: Europe 1492
Potato	*Solanum tuberosum*	Southern Chile	c. 1530
Radish	*Raphanus sativus*	Western Asia	c. 3000 BC
Runner Bean	*Phaseolus vulgaris*	Central America	c. 1500 (known from Mexican sites 7000–5000 BC)
Soybean	*Soja max*	China	c. 2850 BC
Spinach	*Spinacia oleracea*	Iran	AD 647
Swede	*Brassica napobrassica*	Europe	1620
Sweet Corn	*Zea mays*	Andes	Cult. early times in America: intro: Europe after 1492
Tomato	*Lycopersicon esculentum*	Bolivia-Ecuador-Peru area	Europe after 1523
Turnip	*Brassica rapa*	Greece	2000 BC

THE ANIMAL KINGDOM

Animal Kingdom Metazoa (Greek, *meta* = later in time; *zōon* = an animal).
Multicellular animals composed of unlike cells that may lose their boundaries in the adult state, and with at least two cell layers. Contains 21 phyla, as listed below, with about one million described species.

Phylum Mesozoa (Greek, *mesos* = middle, the half). Minute parasitic animals, composed of a surface layer of epithelial (i.e. non-vascular) cells enclosing reproductive cells. About 50 described species, forming two orders, the *Dicyemida* (Greek, *di* = two; *kyēma* = embryo) or *Rhombozoa* (Greek, *rhombos* = turning), which are found only in the kidneys of cephalopods, and the *Orthonectida* (Greek, *orthos* = straight; *nēktos* = swimming), which infest ophiurids, polychaets, nemertines, turbellarians and possibly other groups. Members of this phylum are often considered to be degenerate members of phylum *Platyhelminthes* (see below).

Phylum Parazoa (Greek, *para* = near), **also called Porifera** (Latin, *porus* = a pore; *fero* = to bear) **or Spongiida** (Latin, *spongia* = a sponge).[1] The sponges. Porous animals whose bodies consist of a rather loose aggregation of several kinds of different cells supported by a framework of spicules or fibres which form intricate skeletal structures. There is an incomplete arrangement into tissues, so there is little co-ordination among the parts of the body. They are fixed objects often of indefinite shape, without organ systems or mouth. Reproduction may be either sexual (sponges are often bisexual) or asexual, by means of gemmules. About 4200 described species, which may be divided into two classes:
    Class Nuda (Latin, *nudus* = naked) [N.B. Class *Nuda* also occurs in phylum *Ctenophora* (see below)]. Two orders, the *Calcarea* (Latin, *calx* = lime, or chalk) or *Calcispongiae* (Latin, *calcis*, genitive of *calx*), calcareous sponges, whose skeletons have spicules made of calcite ($CaCO_3$), and the *Hexactinellida* (Greek, *hex* = six; *aktis* = a ray; Latin, *-ell*, suffix added to form diminutives), also called *Triaxonida* (Greek, *treis* = three; *axōn* = an axle) or *Hyalospongiae* (Greek, *hyaleos* = glassy, shining), the glass sponges, whose skeletons consist of siliceous spicules, i.e. made of opal ($SiO_2 nH_2O$). Includes the Venus's flower basket.
    Class Gelatinosa (Latin, *gelatina* = a gummy juice) **or Demospongiae** (Greek, *dēmos* = multitude). Two orders, the *Tetraxonida* (Greek, *tetra* = four; *axōn* = an axle), including the loggerhead sponge, and the *Keratosa* (Greek, *keratos*, genitive of *keras* = a horn) or horny sponges, including the genus *Spongia* (or *Euspongia*), the bath sponge.

Phylum Cnidaria (Greek, *knidē* = nettle) **or Coelenterata**[2] (Greek, *koilos* = hollow; *enteron* = bowel). The coelenterates, the first group of the Metazoa whose cells are completely arranged in tissues, and differentiated into nervous and muscular systems, giving efficient co-ordination of parts and powers of locomotion. The body consists of a small sac, with a single opening at one end (the blastopore). The walls of the sac contain two layers of cells (the inner known as the endoderm, the outer the ectoderm), one passing into the other at the margin of the blastopore. It thus contains only one principal internal cavity, the coelenteron, with one opening to the exterior, the mouth. Coelenterates also bear nematocysts, or stinging cells, and have two types of shape, the polyp (e.g. a sea anemone) and the medusa. Coelenterates have a tendency towards asexual reproduction, either by fission or budding. This phylum contains about 9600 described species, grouped as follows:

    Class Hydrozoa (Greek, *hydōr* = water; *zōon* = an animal) **or Hydromedusae** (Latin, *Medusa*, the Gorgon with snaky hair). Six orders, including *Siphonophora* (Greek, *siphon* = a tube; *phoros* = a bearing), which contains the genus *Physalia* (Greek, *physalis* = bubble), or Portuguese man-of-war.
    Class Scyphozoa or Scyphomedusae (Greek, *skyphos* = a cup). The jellyfish. Five orders.
    Class Anthozoa (Greek, *anthos* = a flower). Three sub-classes:
        Ceriantipatharia (Greek, *keras* = a horn; *anti-* = against; *pathos* = suffering). Two orders, including *Antipatharia* (black corals).
        Octocorallia (Latin, *octo* = eight; Greek, *korallion* = coral) or Alcyonaria. The soft corals. Three orders.
        Zoantharia (Greek, *zōon* = animal; *anthos* = flower). Five orders, including *Actiniaria* (sea anemones) and *Scleractinia* (true corals, stony corals).

Phylum Ctenophora (Greek, *ktenos*, genitive of *kteis* = comb; *phoros* = a bearing). The comb jellies. Marine animals with a body structure similar to coelenterates, i.e. a single internal cavity opening by one main aperture, the mouth, but with three layers of tissue, the ectoderm, the endoderm, producing the sex cells, and between these the jellylike mesoderm, containing

Class Anthozoa: A soft coral showing expanded Polyps

---

[1] The classification used here is by Bidder.

[2] This name is sometimes applied to a group comprising Phylum *Cnidaria* and Phylum *Ctenophora*.

cells and muscle fibres. The bilaterally symmetrical body has eight strips of modified ectoderm cells; each bearing a comb-like plate whose teeth are made up of large waving cilia (hairs). There are no nematocysts (stinging cells). This phylum contains about 80 described species, grouped as follows:

Class Tentaculata (Latin, *tentaculum* = a feeler). Four orders. Includes sea gooseberry and Venus's girdle.

Class Nuda (Latin, *nudus* = naked). A single order, *Beroida* (Greek, *Beroë* = one of the nymphs, daughter of Oceanus).

Phylum Platyhelminthes (Greek, *platys* = flat; *helminthos*, genitive of *helmins* = a worm) **or Platodaria** (Greek, *platos* = flat; Latin, *-od* = form).[1] The flatworms. Soft-bodied animals with three layers of cells and bilateral symmetry. Mostly hermaphrodites, i.e. each individual is functionally both male and female. Tissues and organs developed from three embryonic layers. Muscles render the body capable of great contraction, elongation and variability in shape. No space between digestive tube and body wall. This phylum contains about 15 000 described species, grouped as follows:

Class Turbellaria (Latin, *turbellae*, diminutive of *turba* = a disturbance). The turbellarians. Five orders.

Class Temnocephaloidea (Greek, *temnō* = to cut; *kephalē* = a head). One order, *Temnocephalidea*, also called *Dactylifera* (Greek, *daktylos* = a finger, or toe; *fero* = to bear) or *Dactyloda*.

Class Monogenea (Greek, *monas* = single; *geneos*, genitive of *genos* = a race, kind) **or Heterocotylea** (Greek, *heteros* = other, different; *kotylē* = cup-shaped). Two sub-classes:
Monopisthocotylea (Greek, *opisthen* = behind), with five orders.
Polyopisthocotylea, with four orders.

Class Cestodaria (Greek, *kestos* = a girdle). Two orders.

Class Cestoda (Greek, *kestos* = a girdle). Two sub-classes:
Didesmida (Greek, *di-* = two; *desma* = a chain, band). One order, *Pseudophyllidea* (or *Bothriocephaloidea*).
Tetradesmida (Greek, *tetra* = four). Nine orders.

Class Trematoda (Greek, *trēmatōdēs* = perforated). The flukes. Two sub-classes.
Aspidogastrea (Greek, *aspidos*, genitive of *aspis* = a shield; Greek, *gastēr* = the stomach), also called *Aspidocotylea* (Greek, *kotylē* = cup-shaped) or *Aspidobothria* (Greek, *bothrion*, diminutive of *bothros* = a hole).
Digenea (Greek, *di-* = two; *genos*, genitive of *genos* = a race, kind) or *Malacocotylea* (Greek, *malakos* = soft, gentle; *kotylē* = cup-shaped).

Phylum Nemertina, or Nemertea (Greek, *Nēmertēs* = the name of a Nereid), **also called Rhynchocoela** (Greek, *rhynchos* = a beak, snout; *koilos* = a hollow). The nemertines, or ribbon worms. These have soft, ciliated bodies without external indication of segmentation and without a distinct body cavity, the internal organs being separated by gelatinous parenchyma (soft tissue). The intestine opens at the posterior end. They have a long, muscular proboscis, used to capture food. Most species are free-living and marine, and the sexes are generally separate. This phylum contains about 550 described species, grouped as follows:

Class Anopla (Greek, *anoplos* = unarmed). The mouth posterior to the brain. Two orders. Includes the bootlace worm.

Class Enopla (Greek, *enoplos* = armed). The mouth anterior to the brain. Two orders, including *Hoplonemertina* (Greek, *hoplon* = a weapon), in which the proboscis is armed with one or more calcareous stylets.

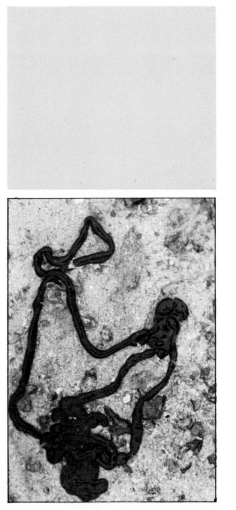

Class Anopla: Bootlace Worm

Phylum Aschelminthes (Greek, *askos* = a bag or bladder; *helminthos*, genitive of *helmins* = a worm). Small, worm-like animals with a pseudocoelom between the digestive tract and the body wall. They usually have an anus, and almost all have a mouth and digestive tract. This phylum contains about 12,000 described species, grouped as follows:

Class Rotifera (Latin, *rota* = a wheel; *fero* = to bear) **or Rotatoria**. The rotifers, or wheel animalcules. Microscopic aquatic animals. Three orders. About 1500 described species.

Class Gastrotricha (Greek, *gastros* (*gasteros*), genitive of *gastēr* = stomach; *trichos*, genitive of *thrix* = hair). Tiny aquatic animals. Two orders. About 140 described species.

Class Echinoderida (Greek, *echinōdēs* = like a hedgehog) **or Kinorhyncha** (Greek, *kineō* = to move; *rhynchos* = a beak, snout). Minute wormlike animals, living chiefly in the slime of the ocean floor. Three orders. About 100 described species.

Class Priapulida (Greek, *Priapos* = god of gardens and reproduction). Small marine worms. 5 described species.

Class Nematomorpha (Greek, *nēmatos*, genitive of *nēma* = thread; *morpha* = shape) or *Gordiacea* (Greek, *Gordios* = name of a king of Phrygia; hence the Gordian knot). The horse-hair worms. Two orders. About 250 described species.

Class Nematoda, or Nemata[1] (Greek, *nēmatos*, genitive of *nēma* = thread). The roundworms. About 10 000 described species. Two sub-classes:
Phasmidia. Nematodes with phasmids (lateral caudal pores). Eight orders.
Aphasmidia. Nematodes without phasmids. Nine orders.

Phylum Acanthocephala (Greek, *akantha* = a thorn; *kephalē* = a head). The thorny-headed worms. Parasitic animals with no specialised organs for digestion. They live in the intestines of vertebrates and absorb food through the body wall. The sexes are always separate, and males are usually smaller than females. Their length ranges from less than $\frac{1}{10}$ in to over 20 in. They have a hook-covered proboscis used as an anchor. Three orders. About 600 described species.

Phylum Entoprocta, or Endoprocta (Greek, *entos* or *endon* = within; *proktos* = the anus), **also called Clyassozoa** (Greek, *kalos* = beautiful, *yssos* = a javelin; *zōon* = an animal), **Kamptozoa** (Greek, *kamptos* = flexible, bent), **Polyzoa Endoprocta** (Greek, *poly*, singular of *polys* = much, many), **or Polyzoa Entoprocta**. These aquatic animals are similar to the *Polyzoa* (see below). In this phylum the anterior end bears the lophophore (the ridge bearing the ciliated tentacles) which is circular, and encloses both mouth and anus. Reproductive organs continuous with ducts. They have definite excretory organs. Three families. About 60 described species.

Phylum Polyzoa (Greek, *poly*, singular of *polys* = much, many; *zōon* = an animal), **also called Bryozoa** (Greek, *bryon* = a lichen), **Polyzoa Ectoprocta, or Ectoprocta** (Greek, *ektos* = outside, without; *prōktos* = the anus). In these tiny aquatic animals, the lophophore (see above) is circular or crescentic, enclosing the mouth but not the anus. Specific excretory organs are absent. Reproductive organs not continuous with ducts. They live in the compartments of tubes which they secrete, and capture their food by sweeping the water with tentacles. The individuals bud and remain attached to each other, to form colonies which are generally about an inch across and sometimes plantlike. The colonies are generally encrusting and resemble the growth of lichens. Mostly marine. About 4000 described species, grouped as follows:

  Class Phylactolaemata (Greek, *phylaktos*, genitive of *phylax* = a guard; *laimos* = the throat) **or Lophopoda** (Greek, *lophos* = the crest; *podos*, genitive of *pous* = a foot). Lophophore generally horseshoe-shaped, guarded by an epistome, a flap of tissue like a lip.
  Class Gymnolaemata (Greek, *gymnos* = naked; *laimos* = the throat) **or Stelmatopoda** (Greek, *stelma* = a crown). Lophophore circular, without epistome. Five orders, including two completely extinct.

Phylum Phoronida (Latin, *Phoronis* = surname of Io, daughter of Inachus, who was changed into a white heifer). The phoronids. Small, marine, wormlike hermaphrodite animals which live as adults in self-secreted tubes embedded in the sea bottom or attached to solid surfaces. The body is roughly elongate (from 0·3 in to 8 in) and bears at one end a crown of from 50 to over 300 tentacles, each one bearing fine hairs (cilia), and arranged in a double row around the usually crescent shaped mouth, which is covered by an episome. The digestive tract is U-shaped, and the anus is immediately outside the tentacles. The larvae are free-swimming. Only two genera and about 16 described species.

Phylum Brachiopoda (Greek, *brachiōn* = the upper part of the arm; *podos*, genitive of *pous* = a foot). The brachiopods or lamp shells. Marine animals enclosed in a bivalve shell. Inside the valves two coiled, cirrate appendages (brachia), one on each side of the mouth, serve as food-gathering organs. The sexes are usually separate. The valves are bilaterally symmetrical, and the front (ventral) valve is usually larger than the dorsal (or brachial) vavle on the back. About 260 described species, grouped as follows:

  Class Inarticulata (Latin, *in-* = not; *articulatus* = divided into joints). Two orders.
  Class Articulata (Latin, *articulatus* = divided into joints). Originally two orders (now discarded) and four sub-orders.

Phylum Mollusca (Latin, *molluscus* = soft). The molluscs. The viscera (entrails) are enclosed in a soft sheath, whose lower part is modified as a muscular organ of locomotion, the foot, while the upper part (the mantle) is extended on each side and hangs down as a free fold around the body, enclosing the mantle-cavity. The mantle usually secretes an external calcareous shell of one or more pieces. The coelom is much reduced by the extensive vascular system. Except in the *Bivalvia* (see below), the anterior tegumentary region is modified as a more or less mobile head, usually provided with sensory appendages and sense organs, and the alimentary system is characterised by a tongue (radula) beset with chitinous teeth. This phylum contains about 128 000 described species, grouped as follows:

  Class Polyplacophora[1] (Greek, *poly*, singular of *polys* = much, many; *plakos*, genitive of *plax* = tablet; *phoros* = a bearing), **or Loricata** (Latin, *loricatus* = clad in mail). Marine molluscs, including the chitons, or coat of mail shells, with eight articulated plates. From ½ in to 8 in in length. Two orders.
  Class Aplacophora[2] (Greek, *a-* = without) **or Solenogastres** (Greek, *sōlēnos*, genitive of *sōlēn* = a channel; *gastēr* = the stomach). Marine molluscs without shells and with the foot greatly reduced. Two orders.
  Class Monoplacophora (Greek, *monas* = single). Deep-sea molluscs with a single cap-shaped shell. One order. Two rare and small species.
  Class Gastropoda (Greek, *gastros* (*gasteros*), genitive of *gastēr* = the stomach; *podos*, genitive of *pous* = a foot). Land, fresh-water and marine molluscs with a flattened foot. The shell is generally a spirally coiled single structure, though may be modified, and sometimes covered by a mantle or entirely absent. From 1 mm to 2 ft in length. Three sub-classes:
    Prosobranchia (Greek, *pros* = forward, towards, in advance of; *branchia* = fins, or the gills of fishes) or *Streptoneura* (Greek, *streptos* = twisted; *neuron* = tendon). Includes the limpet, periwinkle, cowrie and whelk. Three orders.
    Opisthobranchia (Greek, *opisthen* = behind). Includes the sea-hare, sea-butterflies and sea-slugs. Eleven orders.
    Pulmonata (Latin, *pulmonatus* = having lungs). Includes the pond snail, fresh-water limpet, land snail and land slugs. Three orders.
  Class Scaphopoda (Greek, *skaphē* = a bowl; *podos*, genitive of *pous* = a foot). Marine, tubular-shelled, burrowing molluscs, commonly called tusk-shells.
  Class Bivalvia (Latin, *bi-* = two; *valva* = a leaf of a folding door), **also called Lamellibranchia** (Latin, *lamella*, diminutive of *lamina* = a thin plate; Greek, *branchia* = the gills of fishes) **or Pelecypoda** (Greek, *pelekys* = a hatchet; *podos*, genitive of *pous* = a foot). The bivalves. Aquatic headless molluscs, mostly marine, which generally live buried in sand or mud. The shell has two hinged parts, Includes the cockle, mussel, oyster, scallop, gaper and clam. Four orders.
  Class Cephalopoda (Greek, *kephalē* = a head; *podos*, genitive of *pous* = a foot) **or Siphonopoda** (Greek, *siphon* = a tube). Marine molluscs, some without shells. The head and foot are approximate, hence the mouth is situated in the middle of the foot, and the edges of the foot are drawn out into arms and tentacles, equipped with suckers. Includes the cuttlefish, squid, octopus, pearly nautilus. Three sub-classes.

Phylum Sipunculoidea (Latin, *sipunculus* = a little tube). These animals are marine worms which inhabit burrows, tubes or borrowed shells. The anus is anterior, situated on the dorsal surface near the base of the proboscis. There is apparently a total lack of segmentation. The body is divided into two regions, a trunk consisting chiefly of the elongated belly of the worm, and a retractile proboscis which bears at its anterior end the mouth, which is partly or completely surrounded by tentacles or tentacle-bearing folds. The proboscis is generally armed with chitinous spines and hooks. About 275 described species.

[1] The classification given here is by Chitwood & Chitwood (1950) and Thorne (1949).
[2] These two classes are sometimes grouped together as *Amphineura* (Greek, *amphi* = double; *neuron* = tendon).

Heather Angel

Class Gastropoda: The Common Whelk displays an erect siphon and outstretched tentacles

Heather Angel

Class Cephalopoda: The Octopus

Class Hirudinea: The Medicinal Leech

Class Insecta: The Mayflydun

Phylum Echiuroidea (Greek, *echis* = a serpent; *oura* = the tail; *-oideos* = form of). These marine worm-like animals are similar to the *Annelida* (see below), but there is an apparent lack of segmentation. The bodies are generally sac-shaped, and they inhabit U-shaped tubes on sandy-mud bottoms. Attached to the anterior end of the trunk is a preoral lobe (prostomium), about half as long as the trunk and shaped like a hemispherical fan when fully extended. It is ciliated on its ventral surface and forms a funnel around the mouth. Three orders. About 150 described species, including the spoon-worms.

Phylum Annelida or Annulata (Latin, *annela* or *annulatus* = ringed). The annelids or segmented worms. These animals are generally provided with movable bristles known as setae (or chaetae), each embedded in a setal follicle, the cell which secretes it. The body consists of an outer tube, or body wall, and an inner tube, or alimentary canal, separated by the body cavity (coelom), which is generally divided into compartments by transverse partitions, the septa. This phylum contains about 8000 described species, grouped as follows:
    Class Polychaeta (Greek, *poly*, singular or *polys* = much, many; Latin, *chaeta* = a bristle). These are primarily marine and have numerous tufts of setae, borne upon projecting lobes (parapodia) at the sides of the body. Sometimes divided into two sub-classes. *Errantia* (Latin, *errantis*, genitive of *errans* = wandering) and *Sedentaria* (Latin, *sedentarius* = sitting), which includes the lugworm.
    Class Myzostomaria (Greek, *myzō* = to suck in; *stoma* = mouth). Usually external or internal parasites.
    Class Oligochaeta (Greek, *oligos* = few; Latin, *chaeta* = a bristle). Terrestrial, limicolous or fresh-water worms, sometimes secondarily marine or parasitic. Sometimes divided into two orders. Includes the white worm and earthworms.
    Class Hirudinea (Latin, *hirudinis*, genitive of *hirudo* = a leech). The leeches. These are annelids with terminal suckers, 34 body segments or somites, no parapodia nor setae. They are hermaphrodites, and the body cavity is largely obliterated. The length is from about ¼ in to 18 in. Three orders.
    Class Archiannelida (Greek, *archi-* = first). Largely marine or brackish water inhabitants.

Phylum Arthropoda (Greek, *arthron* = a joint; *podos*, genitive of *pous* = a foot) The arthropods. Bilaterally symmetrical animals whose bodies are divided into segments, arranged in a chain along a horizontal axis, each segment typically bearing a pair of jointed appendages (legs). The skin is composed of a layer of cells (the hypodermis), a supporting internal basement membrane, and an external layer of chitinous material, which contains hardened or sclerotised areas or plates. This phylum, the largest in the animal kingdom, it grouped as follows:
    Class Onychophora (Greek, *onychos*, genitive of *onyx* = claw; *phoros* = a bearing). Tropical worm-like anthropods, apparently allied to primitive *Annelida* (see above). 100 described species.
    NB   The next four classes form the old group *Myriapoda* (Greek, *myrias* = the number 10 000, hence many; *podos*, genitive of *pous* = a foot), containing about 11 000 described species.
    Class Pauropoda (Greek, *pauros* = small; *podos*, genitive of *pous* = a foot). Minute progoneates with nine or ten pairs of legs.
    Class Diplopoda (Greek, *diploos* = double). The millipedes. Trunk composed of many double segments, each bearing two pairs of legs. Two sub-classes:
    Pselaphognatha (Greek, *psēlaphaō* = to feel about; *gnathos* = the jaw). Small, soft-bodied millipedes bearing bristles (setae) of several kinds arranged in rows and bundles (fascicles). No copulatory organs (gonopods). One order.
    Chilognatha (Greek, *cheilos* = a lip). The skin forms a hard shell bearing setae singly. Gonopods well developed. Three super-orders, containing ten orders.
    Class Chilopoda (Greek, *cheilos* = a lip; *podos*, genitive of pous = a foot). The centipedes. worm-like body divided into head and trunk. The many segments of the trunk each bear a single pair of legs. Two sub-classes:
    Epimorpha (Greek, *epi* = on, upon; *morphē* = form, shape). The young hatch with the full number of body segments and walking legs. Two orders.
    Anamorpha (Greek, *ana-* = up, throughout). The young hatch with usually 7 but sometimes 12 pairs of legs. Additional segments and legs appear later. Two orders.
    Class Symphyla (Greek, *sym-* = together; *phylē* = a tribe, race). With long antennae. Trunk with 12 or more single segments and 12 pairs of legs.
    Class Insecta (Latin, *in-* = into; *sectus* = cut, cleft) **or Hexapoda** (Greek, *hex* = six; *podos*, genitive of *pous* = a foot). The insects, Body divided into head (with mouth parts and sense organs), thorax (usually with wings and three pairs of legs) and abdomen (with the digestive, respiratory, reproductive and excretory organs). About 950 000 described species. Two sub-classes:
    Apterygota (Greek, *a-* = without; *pterygotōs* = winged) or *Ametabola* (Greek, *a-* = without; *metabola* = change). Primitive wingless insects with nine pairs of appendages on the abdomen and no true metamorphosis (i.e. change in form). Includes spring-tails and bristle-tails. Four orders.
    Pterygota (Greek, *pterygotōs* = winged) or *Metabola* (Greek, *metabola* = change). Insects which have wings, or vestiges of wings, and in which metamorphosis takes place. Two divisions:
    Palaeoptera (Greek, *palaios* = ancient; *pteron* = wing). May-flies and dragonflies. Two orders.
    Neoptera (Greek, *neos* = new, recent; *pteron* = wing). Three sections:
    Polyneoptera (Greek, *poly*, singular of *polys* = much, many). Includes cockroaches, termites, grasshoppers, crickets, locusts and earwigs. Nine orders.
    Paraneoptera (Greek, *para* = beside, near). Includes lice, thrips and bugs. Four orders.
    Oligoneoptera (Greek, *oligos* = few, small), also called *Endopterygota* (Greek, *endon* = within; *pterygotos* = winged) or *Holometabola* (Greek, *holos* = entire; *metabola* = change). Complete metamorphosis. Includes beetles, caddis flies, butterflies, moths, flies, mosquitoes, fleas, ants, wasps and bees. Ten orders.
    Class Crustacea (Latin, *crustaceus* = having a shell or rind). The crustaceans. Generally aquatic, they have two pairs of antenna-like appendages in front of the mouth. They breathe

by gills or by the general surface of the body. Head and thorax usually fused. About 25 000 described species. Seven sub-classes:

Branchiopoda (Greek, *branchion* = a fin; *podos*, genitive of *pous* = a foot). The branchiopods. Mostly in fresh water, their limbs are flattened and leaf-like. Includes the water fleas. Five orders.

Ostracoda (Greek, *ostrakōdés* = testaceous, resembling a shell). The ostracods. Minute aquatic clamlike crustaceans, whose body and limbs are completely enclosed in a hinged double shell (bivalve). Four orders.

Copepoda (Greek, *kōpē* = handle, oar; *podos*, genitive of *pous* = a foot). The copepods. Abundant microscopic aquatic crustaceans, an important source of food (as plankton) in the sea. Many are parasitic. Seven orders.

Mystacocarida (Greek, *mystakos*, genitive of *mystax* = upper lip, moustache; Latin, *caridis*, genitive of *caris* = a shrimp). One order.

Branchiura (Greek, *branchia* = the gills of fishes). Fish lice.

Cirripedia (Latin *cirrus* = a curl; *pedis*, genitive of *pes* = a foot). The cirripedes. Completely sedentary aquatic crustaceans. Many are parasitic. Includes the barnacles and acorn shells. Four orders.

Malacostraca (Greek, *malakos* = soft; *ostrakon* = a shell). Crustaceans whose bodies are composed of nineteen somites, all of which generally have appendages. The thorax has eight parts, and the abdomen six pairs of limbs. Six super-orders:

Leptostraca (Greek, *leptos* = thin, small; *ostrakon* = a shell) or *Phyllocarida* (Greek, *phyllon* = a leaf; Latin, *caridis*, genitive of *caris* = a shrimp). Marine and mud-burrowers. The abdomen has seven segments. One order.

Syncarida (Greek, *syn-* = together; Latin, *caridis*, genitive of *caris* = a shrimp). A small fresh-water group. Two orders.

Peracarida (Greek, *Pēra* = a pouch). Includes opossum-shrimps, wood-lice, the freshwater shrimp, shore hopper and whale louse. One order.

Hoplocarida (Greek, *hoplon* = a tool, weapon). The mantis shrimps. Exclusively marine, One order.

Pancarida (Greek, *pan* = all). Minute, blind, creeping crustaceans. One order.

Eucarida (Greek, *eu-* = true). The eyes are stalked, and the carapace (shell) fused dorsally with all thoracic somites. Includes krill, prawns, shrimps, crayfish, lobsters and crabs. Two orders.

Class Merostomata (Greek, *mēros* = the thigh; *stomatos*, genitive of *stoma* = mouth). The king crabs. Large marine arthropods whose bodies are composed of a cephalothorax bearing six pairs of appendages and an abdomen terminated by a long, strong spine. Respiration aquatic. One order. Four described species.

Class Arachnida (Greek, *arachnē* = a spider). Arthropods whose bodies are composed of cephalothorax, generally bearing four pairs of legs, and abdomen. There are no antennae. Respiration aerial by means of book-lungs or by tracheae. Includes scorpions, spiders, phalangids, mites and ticks. Ten orders. About 60 000 described species.

Class Pycnogonida (Greek, *pyknos* = solid, strong; *gōnia* = a joint), **or Pantopoda** (Greek, *pantos*, genitive of *pan* = all; *podos*, genitive of *pous* = a foot). Sea spiders. Marine anthropods whose bodies are composed of a five-segmented cephalothorax and a minute abdomen, with 4–9 pairs of very long legs. The genital pores are paired, on the second segment of the last two legs of the male and all legs of female. There are no respiratory or excretory organs. Four orders. About 440 described species.

Class Pentastomida (Greek, *penta-* = five; *stoma* = mouth) **or Linguatulida** (Latin, *linguatus* = with a tongue). The pentastomes. Unsegmented but superficially annulated, worm-like, bloodsucking arthropods which live as internal parasites of vertebrates. Two orders. About 60 described species.

Class Tardigrada (Latin, *tardus* = slow; *gradior* = to walk). The tardigrades, or waterbears (bear animalcules). Minute free-living arthropods whose bodies are divided into a well-developed head region and a trunk of four fused segments, each bearing a pair of short unjointed legs. generally with several claws. Found among aquatic vegetation and other damp places. Two orders. About 280 described species.

Phylum Chaetognatha (Latin, *chaeta* = a bristle; Greek, *gnathos* = the jaw). The arrow worms. Transparent, mostly pelagic, worm-like animals. The body is usually between 0·4 in and 1·2 in, divided into head, trunk and tail, separated from each other by two transverse septa. The head is covered by a retractable hood, and bears upon its side a number of sickle-shaped, chitinous hooks and rows of low spines. They are hermaphrodite and have no gill-slits. About 50 described species.

Phylum Pogonophora (Greek, *pōgōnos*, genitive of *pōgōn* = beard; *phoros* = a bearing) **or Brachiata** (Latin, *brachiatus* = having arms). The beard worms. Worm-like animals which live on the sea-floor. Enclosed in a chitinous tube and may be up to 12 in long. A 'beard' of tentacles at the front end. No mouth or anus. Separate sexes. Two orders. 100 known species.

Phylum Echinodermata (Greek, *echinos* = a hedgehog; *dermatos*, genitive of *derma* = skin). The echinoderms, Marine headless animals in which most of the body structures are divided into five sectors, often giving a radial appearance. The skin contains minute spicules of calcite, which usually grow together into plates, small bones or prickles. There is no definite excretory system. The mouth is originally in a median position but moves to the left as the animal develops. The blood system consists of a number of spaces, and there is no heart or regular circulation. About 5700 described species, grouped as follows:

Sub-phylum Pelmatozoa (Greek, *pelmatos*, genitive of *pelma* = a stalk; *zōon* = an animal). Mostly deep-water echinoderms. The body is normally borne on a stem, with five arms (brachia) containing the organs and systems. One class:

Class Crinoidea (Latin, *crinis* = hair; *oideus* = form of). Includes feather stars and sea lilies. One order.

Sub-phylum Eleutherozoa (Greek, *eleutheros* = free; *zōon* = an animal). Free-moving echinoderms not borne on a stem. Four classes:

Class Holothuroidea (Greek, *holos* = whole; *thura (thyra)* = a door). The holothurians, or sea cucumbers. The surface turned to the sea-floor is always the same. They normally move only in the direction of the mouth. Five orders.

Class Echinoidea (Greek, *echinos* = a hedgehog). The echinoids. The prickles (radioles)

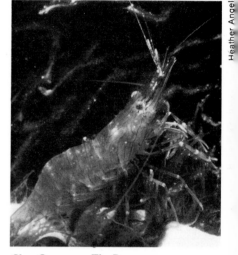

Heather Angel

Class Crustacea: The Prawn

Class Echinoidea: The Sea urchin, displaying its numerous suckered feet

Class Asteroidea: The Sunstar

Class Selachii: The Thornback Ray

are highly developed, moveable and sometimes poisonous. They live with the mouth downwards and can move sideways in any direction. Two sub-classes:

Perischoechinoidea (Greek, *peri* = near; *schoinos* = a reed). One order of sea urchins.

Euechinoidea (Greek, *eu-* = true). Four super-orders:

Diadematacea (Greek, *dia* = through; *dema* = a bundle). Two orders of sea urchins.

Echinacea (Greek, *echinos* = a hedgehog). Five orders of sea urchins.

Gnathostomata (Greek, *gnathos* = the jaw; *stoma* = mouth). Includes sand-dollars and cake urchins. Two orders.

Atelostomata (Greek, *ateles* = imperfect). Includes heart urchins. Four orders.

Class Asteroidea (Greek, *asteroeides* = like a star). The starfishes. Generally live with the mouth downwards. From it radiate five ciliated grooves. They move by crawling. Three orders.

Class Ophiuroidea (Greek, *ophis* = a snake; *oura* = the tail; *ōideos* = form of). The brittle stars. Similar to *Asteroidea*, but they move by wriggling. Most have no more than five arms. Includes the serpent stars. Two orders.

Phylum Chordata (Latin, *chordata* = having a notochord). The chordates. Sometime during their life these have an elongated skeletal rod, or notochord (Greek, 'Back-string') which stiffens the body, with a single, hollow nerve located on the dorsal side. They possess a pharynx, an enlarged chamber whose sides are perforated by gill-slits, just behind the mouth. The blood is contained within vessels and propelled by a heart located on the ventral side, and they generally have a tail extending beyond the anus. About 45 000 described species, grouped as follows:

Sub-phylum Hemichordata (Greek, *hēmi-* = half), **also called Stomochordata** (Greek, *stoma* = mouth) **or Branchiotremata** (Greek, *branchion* = a fin; *trématos*, genitive of *trēma* = a hole). the hemichordates. Soft-bodied marine worm-like chordates whose notochord is only a tiny tubular rod in the head region, 91 described species, comprising three classes:

Class Enteropneusta (Greek, *enteron* = bowel, intestine; *pneustikos* = for breathing). The acorn worms. Burrowing hemichordates whose bodies are composed of a proboscis, a mouth, a ringlike collar and a very long trunk with a terminal anus. The nerve cord is partly tubular and there are numerous gill-slits.

Class Pterobranchia (Greek, *pteron* = fin; *branchia* = the gills of fishes). The pterobranchs. Small (0·04 in to 0·3 in) hemichordates which form colonies of tubes in which they breed by budding as well as by sexual reproduction. The nerve cord is solid and there are few or no gill-slits. They have a pair tentaculated arms. Two orders.

Class Planctosphaeroidea (Greek, *plankton* = wandering; *sphaira* = a ball, sphere; *ōideos* = form of). A few larvae of unknown parentage.

Sub-phylum Urochordata (Greek, *oura* = the tail) **or Tunicata** (Latin, *tunicatus* = clothed with a tunic). The urochordates or tunicates. Exclusively marine chordates, which are mostly fixed growing organisms, roughly resembling a potato, and without a capacity for locomotion. They produce a free-swimming larva with chordate features, but these, except for the gills, are usually lost in the adult state. A rigid tunic is secreted by the skin and helps to anchor them to some solid structure. About 1600 described species, grouped as follows:

Class Ascidiacea (Greek, *askidion*, diminutive of *askos* = a bag or bladder). The ascidians, or sea squirts. Attached urochordates with a dorsal exhalant siphon. The pharynx had transverse rows of ciliated gill-slits. Two orders.

Class Thaliacea (Greek, *Thalia* = a muse, patroness of comedy). Pelagic urochordates with inhalant and exhalant siphons at opposite ends of the body. They have long, simple gill-slits. Three orders.

Class Larvacea (Latin, *larva* = the immature form of a changing animal). Small oceanic urochordates which never bud and have a permanent tail. One order, *Copelata* (Greek, *kōpēlatēs* = a rower).

Sub-phylum Cephalochordata (Greek, *kephalē* = a head), **also called Acrania** (Latin, *a-* = without; *cranium* = the skull) **or Leptocardii** (Greek, *leptos* = thin, small; *kardia* = heart). The cephalochordates. Small marine fish-like chordates that burrow in sand. Similar to *Urochordata* (see above), but they retain the notochord and powers of locomotion throughout life. 13 described species, including the lancelet.

Sub-phylum Vertebrata (Latin, *vertebratus* = joined) **or Craniata** (Latin, *cranium* = the skull). The vertebrates. Chordates with an internal skeleton, comprising a skull, a vertebral column, or backbone, usually two pairs of limb elements and a central nervous system partly enclosed within the backbone. The muscular system consists primarily of bilaterally paired masses. About 43 000 described species, grouped as follows:

The fishes, 23 000 described species of cold-blooded aquatic vertebrates which swim by fins and breathe by gills, comprising four classes:

Class Marsipobranchii (Greek, **marsypos (marsipos)** = a bag; *branchion* = a fin) **or Agnatha** (Greek, *a-* = without; *gnathos* = the jaw). The marsipobranchs. Mostly marine, eel-like fishes without jaws or paired fins. One existing sub-class:

Cyclostomata (Greek, *kyklos* = a circle; *stomatos*, genitive of *stoma* = mouth). The cyclostomes, Blood-sucking fishes, comprising lampreys, hagfishes and slime eels. Two orders.

Class Selachii (Greek, *selachos* = shark), **also called Chondropterygii** (Greek, *chondros* = a grain; *pterygos*, genitive of *pteryx* = the fin), **Chondrichthyes** (Greek, *ichthys* = a fish) **or Elasmobranchii** (Greek, *elasmos* = a thin plate; *branchion* = a fin). The selachians. Fishes with jaws, and branchial arches supporting the gills. They have median and paired fins with horny rays, and the skeleton is a series of cartilaginous rods. The mouth is on the underside of the body. There is no air bladder. Four sub-classes, three of them Palaeozoic, one existing:

Euselachii (Greek, *eu-* = true). Includes sharks, dogfishes, angel-fishes and rays. Two orders.

Class Bradyodonti (Greek, *bradys* = slow; *odontos*, genitive of *odous* = tooth). Fishes with long tapering tails and large paddle-like pectoral fins. One existing sub-class:

Holocephali (Greek, *holos* = whole, entire; *kephalē* = a head). The rabbit-fishes.

Class Pisces (Latin, *piscis* = a fish) **or Osteichthyes** (Greek, *osteon* = bone; *ichthys* = a fish). The bony fishes. The skeleton is bony, and the slimy skin is covered with scales, or bony plates. The mouth is at the front end. Three sub-classes:

Palaeopterygii (Greek, *palaios* = ancient; *pterygos*, genitive of *pteryx* = the fin). Includes the sturgeon, paddle-fish, bichir and reed-fish. Two orders.

Neopterygii (Greek, *neos* = new, recent). The ray-finned fishes. Includes the bow-fins, gar-pikes and all the typical present-day fish, such as the herring, sardine, pilchard, salmon, trout, roach, minnow, carp, cod, whiting, hake, sea-horse, perch, bass, mackerel, tunny, barracuda and eels. 34 orders.

Crossopterygii (Greek, *krossoi* = a fringe, tassels). Includes the coelacanth and lung-fishes. Two orders.

Class Amphibia (Greek, *amphibios* = leading a double life). The amphibians, Cold-blooded vertebrates who breathe air largely through their moist skin. They are mostly four-limbed, live on land, and lay their eggs in water. The larvae pass through a fish-like aquatic phase (e.g. tadpoles) before metamorphosis. About 3000 described species, grouped as follows:

Order Caudata (Latin, *caudatus* = having a tail) **or Urodela** (Greek, *oura* = the tail). Amphibians with four legs, a long body and a tail. Some live permanently in water, breathing with gills. Includes the salamanders, axolotl, newts and siren. Five sub-orders.

Order Salientia (Latin, *salientis*, genitive of *saliens*, present participle of *salio* = to jump) **or Anura** (Greek, *an-* = without; *oura* = the tail). Frogs and toads. Tail-less amphibians with long hind legs adapted for jumping. Five sub-orders.

Order Gymnophiona (Greek, *gymnos* = naked; *ophioneos* = like a serpent) **or Apoda** (Greek, *a-* = without; *podos*, genitive of *pous* = a foot). The caecilians. Small, primitive, limbless, worm-like, burrowing amphibians with a very short tail. Some have scales. Found in tropical climates.

Class Reptilia (Latin, *reptilis* = creeping). The reptiles. Dry-skinned vertebrates whose body temperature is variable, and who breathe air by lungs. The skin is usually covered with horny scales formed by the epidermis. There is a well-developed tongue. Fertilisation is internal. The typical reptile has four five-toed limbs. About 6000 described species, grouped as follows:

Order Rhynchocephalia (Greek, *rhynchos* = a beak, snout; *kephalē* = a head). Primitive lizard-like reptiles with beaked upper jaws. The only living species is the tuatara of New Zealand.

Order Testudines (Latin, *testudinis*, genitive of *testudo* = a tortoise) **or Chelonia** (Greek, *chelōnē* = a tortoise) Tortoises and turtles. Aquatic and land-dwelling reptiles whose trunk is enclosed in a hard shell built up from a series of dermal bones. They all lay their eggs on land. Two sub-orders.

Order Crocodilia (Latin, *crocodilus* = a crocodile) **or Loricata** (Latin, *loricatus* = clad in mail). Crocodiles and aligators. Reptiles with short limbs, adapted to aquatic life. They have elongated, heavily-jawed heads and long, flattened tails.

Order Squamata (Latin, *squamatus* = scaly). Horny-scaled reptiles. Two sub-orders:

Sauria (Greek, **sauros** = lizard) or *Lacertilia* (Latin, *lacerta* = a lizard). The lizards.

Serpentes (Latin, *serpentis*, genitive of *serpens* = a serpent) or *Ophidia* (Greek, *ophidion*, diminutive of *ophis* = a snake). The snakes. The jaws are joined by an elastic ligament, and there is no trace of any limbs, except in boas and pythons.

Class Aves (Latin, *aves*, plural of *avis* = a bird). The birds. Warm-blooded, egg-laying feathered vertebrates whose front limbs are modified into wings. Most are thus able to fly. About 8590 described species, grouped as follows:

Order Struthioniformes (Latin, *struthionis*, genitive of *struthio* = an ostrich; *forma* = shape, nature). The ostriches. One family.

Order Rheiformes (Greek, *Rhea* = mother of Zeus). The rheas. One family.

Order Casuariiformes (Malay, *kasuari* = the cassowary). The emu and casso-wary. Two existing families.

Order Apterygiformes (Greek, *apterygos* = without wings). The kiwis. One family.

Order Tinamiformes (from *tinamou*, the native name) **or Crypturi** (Greek, *kryptos* = hidden; oura = the tail). The tinamous. One family

Order Gaviiformes[1] (Latin, *gavia*, the name possibly of the sea-mew). The divers. One family.

Order Podicipediformes[1] (Latin, *podicis*, genitive of *podex* = the rump; *pedis*, genitive of *pes* = a foot). The grebes. One family.

Order Sphenisciformes (Greek, *sphēniskos* = a small wedge). The penguins. One existing family.

Order Procellariiformes (Latin, *procella* = a tempest) **or Turbinares** (Latin, *turbinis*, genitive of *turbo* = something which spins). Includes the petrels, shear-water, fulmar and albatross. Four families.

Order Pelecaniformes (Greek, *pelekan* = a pelican) **or Steganopodes** (Greek, *steganos* = covered; *podos* = genitive of *pous* = a foot). Includes the tropic bird, pelican, cormorant, gannet and frigate bird. Six existing families.

Order Ciconiiformes (Latin, *ciconia* = a stork) **also called Ardeiformes** (Latin, *ardea* = a heron) **or Gressores** (Latin, *gressor* = a walker). Includes the herons, bitterns, storks, ibis and spoonbill. Six families.

Order Phoenicopteriformes (Greek, *phoinikos*, genitive of *phoinix* = crimson; *pteron* = wing). The flamingos. One existing family.

Order Anseriformes (Latin, *anser* = a goose). The screamers, ducks, geese and swans. Two existing families.

Order Falconiformes (Latin, *falco* = a falcon) **or Accipitres** (Latin, *accipiter* = a bird of prey). Includes the vultures, eagles, secretary bird, hawks, kestrel, falcon and osprey. Six existing families.

Order Galliformes (Latin, *gallus* (fem. *gallina*) = a fowl). Includes the megapode, curassow, grouse, pheasant, quail, peafowl, turkeys, hoatzin and fowl. Seven existing families.

Order Gruiformes (Latin, *gruis*, genitive of *grus* = the crane). Includes the crane, rail, coot and bustard. Twelve existing families.

Order Charadriiformes (Greek, *charadrios* = a cleft-dwelling bird) **or Laro-**

Class Amphibia: Common Frog

Class Reptilia: Nile Crocodile

Class Aves: Jackass Penguin

---

[1] These two orders are also called *Pygopodes* (Greek, *pygē* = the rump; *podos*, genitive of *pous* = a foot) or *Colymbi-formes* (Greek, *kolymbos* = a diving bird).

Class Aves: Eagle Owl

Class Mammalia: Echidna

Class Mammalia: False vampire bat

limicolae (Greek, *laros* = a ravenous sea-bird (Latin *larus* = a gull); Latin, *limus* = mud; *colo* = to inhabit). Includes the plover, gulls, snipe, skua, tern, razorbill, sandpiper, oyster-catcher, puffin, woodcock and avocet. 16 existing families.

Order Columbiformes (Latin, *columba* = a dove, pigeon). Includes the sand grouse, pigeon and dove. Three families.

Order Psittaciformes (Greek, *psittakē* (*psittakos*) = a parrot). The lories, cockatoos, parrots and macaws. One family.

Order Cuculiformes (Latin, *cuculus* = the cuckoo). Includes the plantain-eater and cuckoo. Two families.

Order Strigiformes (Greek, *strigos*, genitive of *strix* = an owl). The owls. Two existing families.

Order Caprimulgiformes (Latin, *caper* (fem. *capra*) = a goat; *mulgeo* = to milk, to suck). Includes the oil bird, frogmouth and goatsucker (i.e. the nightjar). Five families.

Order Apodiformes (Greek, *a-* = without; *podos*, genitive of *pous* = a foot), **also called Micropodiformes** (Greek, *mikros* = small) **or Macrochires** (Greek, *makros* = long, large; *cheir* = head). The swifts and humming-birds. Three existing families.

Order Coliiformes (Greek, *kolios* = a king of woodpecker). The colies, or mouse birds. One family.

Order Trogoniformes (Greek, *trōgōn* = gnawing). The trogons, including the quetzal. One family.

Order Coraciiformes (Greek, *korakiao* = a kind of raven). Includes the kingfisher, tody, motmot, bee-eater, roller, hoopoe and hornbill. Nine families.

Order Piciformes (Latin, *picus* = a woodpecker). Includes the jacamar, puff-bird, toucan and woodpecker, Six families.

Order Passeriformes (Latin, *passer* = a sparrow). The perching birds. Four sub-orders:

Eurylaimi (Greek, *eurys* = wide, broad; *laimos* = the throat). The broadbills. One family.

Tyranni (Latin, *tyrannus* = a tyrant). Includes the ovenbird and cotinga. 13 families.

Menurae (Greek, *mēnē* = moon; *oura* = the tail). Includes the lyre-bird. Two families.

Passeres (Latin, *passer* = a sparrow) or *Oscines* (Latin, *oscines*, plural of *oscen* = a singing bird). The songbirds. Includes the larks, swallow, martins, crows, rook, jackdaw, magpie, jay, bird of paradise, tits, nuthatch, dippers, wren, thrush, blackbird, chats, nightingale, robin, warblers, shrikes, starling, finches and sparrow. 57 existing families.

Class Mammalia (Latin, *mammalis*, possessive of *mamma* = breast). The mammals. Warm-blooded, hairy vertebrates whose young are typically born alive and suckled, i.e. nourished with milk from the mother's breasts. About 4500 described species, grouped as follows:

Sub-class Prototheria (Greek, *prōtos* = first; *thērion* = a wild animal). The most primitive mammals. One order:

Order Monotremata (Greek, *monas* = single; *trematos*, genitive of *trema* = a hole). The monotremes. Egg-laying mammals, with a single cloaca, a common outlet for the genital, urinary and digestive organs. They have a beak instead of teeth, no external ears, and milk glands without nipples. Comprises the echidnas, or spiny ant-eaters, and the duck-billed platypus.

Sub-class Theria (Greek, *thērion* = a wild animal). Mammals with teeth, external ears, separate orifices for the intestine, bladder and reproductive organs and mammary glands with nipples.

Infra-class Metatheria (Greek, *meta* = next to). One order:

Order Marsupialia (Latin, *marsupium*, from Greek, *marsypion*, diminutive of *marsypos* = a bag). The marsupials. Mammals in which the female has a pouch on the under side, with the nipples of the mammary glands inside the pouch. The young are born in an immature state and finish their development inside the mother's pouch. Includes the opossums, kangaroo, wallaby, wombats, phalanger, bandicoot and koala.

Infra-class Eutheria (Greek, *eu-* = true). The eutherians, or placental mammals. The developing embryo is fed by the mother's blood indirectly through an organ known as the placenta. 16 orders:

Order Insectivora (Latin, *insecta* = insects; *voro* = to devour). The insectivores. Placental mammals with a dentition adapted to an insect diet. The feet generally have five toes, each with a claw. Mostly nocturnal and terrestrial. Includes the tenrec, hedgehog, shrew, mole and desman.

Order Tupaioidea (*Toepai*, native name). The tree shrews.

Order Dermoptera (Greek, *derma* = skin, leather; *pteron* = wing); Herbivorous, climbing mammals with claws and a gliding membrane. Two species of the colugo, or cobego, commonly called flying lemurs.

Order Chiroptera (Greek, *cheir* = hand; *pteron* = wing). The bats. The fore-limbs are modified to form wings, and these are the only truly flying mammals. Two sub-orders:

Megachiroptera (Greek, *megas* = great). The fruit bats, including the flying fox.
Microchiroptera (Greek, *mikros* = small). The insectivorous bats.

Order Primates (Latin, *primus* = first). The primates. Chiefly tree-dwelling mammals with hands and feet adapted for climbing. The fingers and toes are provided with nails. Three sub-orders:

Prosimii (Greek, *pro-* = before; Latin, *simia* = ape) or *Lemuroidea* (Latin, *lemures* = shades, ghosts). The lower primates. Includes the loris, bush baby, common lemur and the tarsiers.

Anthropoidea (Greek, *anthrōpos* = a man). The brain is highly developed. Includes the marmoset, monkey, baboon, chimpanzee, gorilla and man.

Order Edentata (Latin, *e-* (*ex-*) = out, without; *dentatus* = toothed). The edentates. The teeth are either completely absent or undifferentiated, and always absent in the front of the jaws. The edentates have long snouts and long tongues. Includes the sloth, armadillo and anteater.

Order Pholidota (Greek, *pholidōtos* = armed with scales). The pangolins, or scaly anteaters. Similar to the edentates, but the body is covered with overlapping horny scales, composed of cemented hairs.

Order Lagomorpha (Greek, *lagōs* = a hare; *morphē* = form, shape). Similar to **Rodentia** (see below), but the teeth include two pairs of upper incisors. Includes the pika, hares and rabbits.

Order Rodentia (Latin, *rodentis*, genitive of *rodens* = gnawing). The rodents. Gnawing mammals, with one pair of chisel-like incisor teeth, above and below. The feet are generally five-toed. They feed chiefly on plants. Three sub-orders:

Sciuromorpha (Greek, *skiouros* (Latin, *sciurus*) = a squirrel; *morphē* = form, shape). Includes the squirrel, gopher, beaver, marmot, wood-chuck and chipmunk.

Myomorpha (Greek, *myos*, genitive of *mys* = mouse). Includes the mouse, rat, dormouse, vole, hamster, lemming and jerboa.

Hystricomorpha (Greek, *hystrichos*, genitive of *hystrix* = a porcupine). Includes the guinea pig, capybara, chinchilla, coypu and porcupine.

Order Cetacea (Greek, *kētos* = a whale). Mammals adapted for aquatic life, mostly marine. The five-fingered skeletal forelimbs are enclosed as paddle-like flippers. The tail has flukes, and there is generally a dorsal fin. There is a short neck but no external hind limbs or ears. Hair absent except on lips. Two existing sub-orders:

Odontoceti (Greek, *odontos*, genitive of *odous* = tooth). The toothed whales. Includes the sperm whale, porpoises and dolphins.

Mysticeti (Greek, *mystis* = a mystic). The whalebone whales. Includes the rorqual and blue whale.

Order Carnivora (Latin, *carnis*, genitive of *caro* = flesh; *voro* = to devour). The carnivores. Mostly flesh-eating mammals, with the teeth adapted for tearing flesh. There are never less than four toes on each foot, each toe with a compressed claw. Carnivores with paw-like feet divided into toes. The cheek-teeth are of several kinds. Includes the dog, wolf, jackal, fox, bear, raccoon, panda, ferret, weasel, mink, ermine, polecat, stoat, marten, sable, badger, skunk, otter, mongoose, hyaena, civet, cat, lion, tiger, jaguar, panther, leopard and cheetah.

Order Pinnipedia (Latin, *pinna* = a wing). Aquatic with limbs adapted to fins. The upper limbs are short and the feet are swimming paddles. The cheek-teeth are all alike. Includes the seals, sea lion and walrus.

Order Tubulidentata (Latin, *tubulus*, diminutive of *tubus* = a tube; *dentatus* = toothed). The aardvark (Dutch, 'earth-pig'), or African antbear. A nocturnal burrowing anteater, similar to *Edentata* (see above), but with a tubular mouth and long ears.

Order Proboscidea (Latin, *proboscidis*, genitive of *proboscis*, from Greek, *proboskis* = an elephant's trunk). The elephants. Large mammals whose heads bear a proboscis (the trunk), a long flexible muscle organ with one or two finger-like processes at its tip.

Order Hyracoidea (Greek, *hyrakos*, genitive of *hyrax* = a shrew mouse). Small hoofed mammals, with squat, almost tail-less bodies. Includes the hyrax, dassie and coney (or cony).

Order Sirenia (Latin, *siren* = a Siren, a mermaid). Aquatic mammals with torpedo-shaped bodies. The body has a horizontal tail fluke and very mobile lips. Comprises the dugong and manatees.

Order Perissodactyla (Greek, *perisso* = uneven, odd; *daktylos* = a finger, toe). The perissodactyls, or odd-toed ungulates (hoofed mammals). Herbivorous mammals whose hindfeet each have one or three digits. Two sub-orders:

Hippomorpha (Greek, *hippos* = a horse; *morphē* = form, shape). Includes the horse, donkey and zebra.

Ceratomorpha (Greek, *keratos*, genitive of *keras* = a horn). Includes the tapir and rhinoceros.

Order Artiodactyla (Greek, *artios* = even-numbered; *daktylos* = a finger, toe). The artiodactyls, or even-toed ('cloven-hoofed') ungulates. The hindfeet each have two or four digits. Three sub-orders:

Suiformes (Latin, *suis*, genitive of *sus* = the pig; *forma* = appearance). Includes the pig, peccary, warthog and hippopotamus.

Tylopoda (Greek, *tylos* = a knot; *podos*, genitive of *pous* = a foot). Includes the llama, alpaca, vicuna, camel and dromedary.

Ruminantia (Latin, *ruminantis*, genitive of *ruminans* = chewing again). The ruminants, Artiodactyls who 'chew the cud'. Includes the deer, giraffe, buffalo, cattle, bison, antelope, gazelle, goat and sheep.

Class Mammalia: The Black Backed Jackal

Class Mammalia: Hippopotamus

BRITISH MAMMALS

The Mammalia are represented in the British Isles by 64 land species (94 if all the dubious sub-species of insular field mice and voles are included) and 25 marine mammals, making a total of 99 (or 129).

This total includes 5 introduced species of deer, the brown rat (1728), the grey squirrel (1889 from North America), and the coypu (1927 from Argentina) which are non-indigenous. The American mink is now becoming established.

Among British mammals which have become extinct in historic times are brown bears (A.D. c. 1075); beavers (c. 1250); wild boar (1683), and wolves (1743 in Scotland and c. 1766 in Ireland).

Order Insectivora (The Insectivores, or insect-eating mammals)
Family Erinaceidae (The Hedgehogs and Rat-shrews)
Genus *Erinaceus*
Erinaceus europaeus   Common Hedgehog

BRITISH MAMMALS continued

Family Talpidae (The Moles and Desmans)
  Genus *Talpa*
   Talpa europaea — Common Mole
Family Soricidae (The Tree Shrews)
  Genus *Sorex*
   Sorex minutus — Pygmy or Lesser Shrew
   Sorex araneus — Common Shrew
   Sorex araneus fretalis — Jersey Red-toothed Shrew
   Sorex araneus granti — Islay Shrew
  Genus *Neomys*
   Neomys fodiens — Water Shrew
  Genus *Crocidura*
   Crocidura suaveolens — Scilly Islands Shrew or Lesser White-toothed Shrew
   Crocidura russula — Guernsey White-toothed Shrew

Order Chiroptera (The Bats)
  Suborder Microchiroptera (Insectivorous Bats)
  Family Rhinolophidae (The Leaf-nosed Bats)
   Genus *Rhinolophus*
   Rhinolophus ferrum-equinum — Greater Horseshoe Bat
   Rhinolophus hipposideros — Lesser Horseshoe Bat
  Family Vespertilionidae (The Typical Bats)
   Genus *Myotis*
   Myotis mystacinus — Whiskered Bat
   Myotis nattereri — Natterer's Bat
   Myotis bechsteini — Bechstein's Bat
   Myotis daubentoni — Daubenton's or Water Bat
   Myotis brandti — Brandt's Bat
   Myotis myotis — Mouse-eared Bat
   Genus *Eptesicus*
   Eptesicus serotinus — Serotine
   Genus *Nyctalus*
   Nyctalus leisleri — Leisler's Bat
   Nyctalus noctula — Noctule Bat
   Genus *Pipistrellus*
   Pipistrellus pipistrellus — Pipistrelle
   Genus *Barbastella*
   Barbastella barbastellus — Barbastelle
   Genus *Plecotus*
   Plecotus auritus — Long-eared Bat
   Plecotus austriacus — Grey Long-eared Bat
   Genus *Vespertilio*
   Vespertilio murinus — Parti-coloured Bat

Order Lagomorpha (The Pikas, Hares and Rabbits)
  Family Leporidae (The Hares and Rabbits)
   Genus *Lepus*
   Lepus capensis — Brown Hare
   Lepus timidus hibernicus — Irish Hare
   Lepus timidus scoticus — Scottish Mountain or Blue Hare
   Genus *Oryctolagus*
   Oryctolagus cuniculus — European Rabbit

Order Rodentia (The Rodents, or gnawing mammals)
  Suborder Sciuromorpha (Squirrels, Marmots, Beavers, Gophers, etc.
  Family Sciuridae (The Typical Squirrels and marmots)
   Genus *Sciurus*
   Sciurus vulgaris leucourus — Red Squirrel
   Sciurus carolinensis[1] — Grey squirrel
  Suborder Myomorpha (Dormice, Rats, Mice, Voles)
  Family Gliridae or Muscardinidae (The Dormice)
   Genus *Glis*
   Glis glis[2] — Fat or Edible Dormouse
   Genus *Muscardinus*
   Muscardinus avellanarius — Dormouse
  Family Muridae (The Rats and Mice)
   Genus *Micromys*
   Micromys minutus — Harvest Mouse
   Genus *Apodemus*
   Apodemus sylvaticus — Field or Wood Mouse
   Apodemus flavicollis wintoni — Yellow-necked Field Mouse
   Genus *Rattus*
   Rattus rattus — Black or Ship Rat
   Rattus norvegicus — Brown Rat
   Genus *Mus*
   Mus musculus — House Mouse
  Family Cricetidae (The Voles)
   Genus *Clethrionomys*
   Clethrionomys glareolus britannicus — Bank Vole
   Clethrionomys glareolus skomerensis — Skomer Vole
   Clethrionomys glareolus alstoni — Mull Vole

[1] Introduced from North America, beginning in 1889.
[2] Introduced from continental Europe, *c.* 1910.

BIOLOGY

BRITISH MAMMALS *continued*

Clethrionomys glareolus caesarius	Jersey Vole
Clethrionomys rufocanus erica	Raasay Vole
Genus *Arvicola*	
Arvicola terrestris amphibius	Water Vole
Genus *Microtus*	
Microtus avalis sarnius	Guernsey Vole
Microtus arvalis orcadensis	Orkney Vole

Suborder Hystricomorpha (Porcupines, Guinea Pigs, Chinchillas, etc.)
  Family Capromyidae (The Tuco-tucos, Hutias, etc.)
    Genus *Myocaster*
    Myocastor coypus[1]   Nutria or Coypu Rat

Order Carnivora (The Carnivores, or flesh-eating mammals)
  Family Canidae (The Dogs, Wolves, Jackals, and Foxes)
    Genus *Vulpes*
    Vulpes vulpes   Fox
  Family Mustelidae (Martens, Weasels, Badgers, Otters, Skunks, Sables, Ferrets, Minks, Ermines, Wolverines, etc.)
    Genus *Martes*
    Martes martes   Pine Marten
    Genus *Mustela*
    Mustela erminea hibernica   Irish Stoat
    Mustela erminea stabilis   Stoat
    Mustela erminea ricinae   Islay Stoat
    Mustela nivalis   Weasel
    Mustela putorius   Polecat
    Genus *Meles*
    Meles meles   Common Badger
    Genus *Lutra*
    Lutra lutra   Common Otter
  Family Felidae (The Cats)
    Genus *Felis*
    Felis silvestris grampia   Scottish Wild Cat

Order Pinnipedia (The fin-footed Carnivores—Seals, Sea-lions and Walruses)
  Family Phocidae (The True Seals)
    Genus *Halichoerus*
    Halichoerus grypus   Grey, or Atlantic Seal
    Genus *Phoca*
    Phoca vitulina   Common seal

Order Artiodactyla (The even-toed Ungulates, or hoofed mammals)
  Suborder Ruminantia (The Ruminants—Cattle, Sheep, Goats, Antelopes, Deer, Giraffe, etc.)
    Family Cervidae (The True Deer)
      Genus *Cervus*
      Cervus elaphus   Red Deer
      Cervus nippon nippon[2]   Japanese Sika
      Genus *Dama*
      Dama dama   Fallow Deer
      Genus *Capreolus*
      Capreolus capreolus   Common Roe Deer
      Genus *Hydropotes*
      Hydropotes inermis[3]   Chinese Water Deer
      Genus *Muntiacus*
      Muntiacus reevesi[4]   Chinese Muntjac or Barking Deer

Order Cetacea (The Whales, Dolphins and Porpoises)
  Suborder Mysticeti (The Whalebone Whales)
    Family Balaenidae (The Right Whales)
      Genus *Eubalaena*
      Eubalaena glacialis   North Atlantic Right Whale
    Family Balaenopteridae (The Rorquals or Fin Whales)
      Genus *Megaptera*
      Megaptera novaeangliae   Humpback Whale
      Genus *Balaenoptera*
      Balaenoptera physalus   Common Rorqual or Fin Whale
      Balaenoptera acutorostrata   Lesser Rorqual or Pike Whale
      Balaenoptera musculus   Blue Whale
      Balaenoptera borealis   Sei Whale
  Suborder Odontoceti (The Toothed Whales)
    Family Physeteridae (The Sperm Whales)
      Genus *Physeter*
      Physeter catodon   Sperm Whale or Cachalot
    Family Ziphiidae (The Bottle-nosed or Beaked Whales)
      Genus *Hyperoodon*
      Hyperoodon ampullatus   Bottle-nosed Whale
      Genus *Ziphius*
      Ziphius cavirostris   Cuvier's Beaked Whale
      Genus *Mesoplodon*
      Mesoplodon bidens   Sowerby's Whale
      Mesoplodon mirus   True's Whale

[1] Introduced from Argentina in 1927.
[2-4] These occur in the wild state as a result of escapes from parks and zoological gardens, for which they have been imported at various times since *c.* 1860.

BRITISH MAMMALS continued
 Family Monodontidae (The Narwhals)
  Genus *Monodon*
   Monodon monoceros   Narwhal
  Genus *Delphinapterus*
   Delphinapterus leucas   White Whale or Beluga
 Family Delphinidae (The Dolphins)
  Genus *Globicephala*
   Globicephala melaena   Blackfish, Pilot Whale or Caa'ing Whale
  Genus *Grampus*
   Grampus griseus   Risso's Dolphin
  Genus *Orcinus*
   Orcinus orca   Killer Whale or Grampus
  Genus *Pseudorca*
   Pseudorca crassidens   False Killer
  Genus *Tursiops*
   Tursiops truncatus   Bottle-nosed Dolphin
  Genus *Lagenorhynchus*
   Lagenorhynchus albirostris   White-beaked Dolphin
   Lagenorhynchus acutus   White-sided Dolphin
  Genus *Delphinus*
   Delphinus delphis   Common Dolphin
  Genus *Stenella*
   Stenella styx   Euphrosyne Dolphin
 Family Phocaenidae (The Porpoises)
  Genus *Phocaena*
   Phocaena phocaena   Porpoise

ANIMAL DIMENSIONS BY SPECIES

Mollusca—128 000 species: ranging in size between the minute coin shell *Neolepton sykesi* 0.05 in *1·3 mm* long, and a giant octopus weighing 6–7 tons, which is the heaviest of all invertebrates.
Insecta—950 000 (1974) described species of a suspected total of perhaps some 3 million: ranging in size between the Battledore wing fairy fly (*Hymenoptera mymaridae*) 0·008 in *0·2 mm* long to the bulky 3½-oz *100 gram* African goliath beetle (*Goliathus goliathus*).
Crustacea—25 000 species: ranging in size from the water flea *Alonella* species at 0·01 in *0·25 mm* long to the Giant Japanese Spider crab (*Macrocheira kaempferi*) with a spread of 12 ft *3·66 m* between claws.
Amphibia—3000 species: ranging in size between minute poisonous frogs ½ in *12·5 mm* long and the 5 ft *1·5 m* long giant salamander (*Megalobatrachus davidianus*) weighing up to 88 lb.
Reptilia—6000 species: ranging in size between 1·5 in *38 mm* long geckoes and the South American snake anaconda (*Eunectes murinus*), which has been reported to attain 37½ ft *11·4 m* in length.
Aves—*c.* 8950 species: ranging in size from the 0·07-oz *2 gram* Helena's humming bird (*Mellisuga helenae*) up to the 345 lb *156·5 kg*, 9 ft *2·7 m* tall ostrich (*Struthio camelus*).
Mammalia—*c.* 4500 species: ranging in size, on land, between the 0·1-oz *2·5-gram* Etruscan shrew (*Suncus etruscus*) and the African elephant (*Loxodonta africana*) which may very rarely attain 11 tons; and, at sea, between the 90-lb *41-kg* Heaviside's dolphin (*Cephalorhynchus heavisidei*) and the 174-ton *177-tonne* Blue Whale (*Balaenoptera musculus*).

ANIMAL LONGEVITY

Data are still sparse and in many species unreliable or non-existent. Animals in captivity may not reflect the life span of those in their natural habitat.

Maximum life span (yrs) — *species*

yrs	species
152	Marion's Tortoise (*Testudo sumerii*)
116	Tortoise (*Testudo graeca*)
113	Man (*Homo sapiens*)—highest proven age
c. 100	Deep Sea Clam (*Tindaria callistiformis*)
>90	Killer Whale (*Orcinus orca*)
90	Blue Whale (*Balaenoptera musculus*)
90	Fin Whale (*Balaenoptera physalus*)
82	Sturgeon (*Acipenser transmontanus*)
80	Fresh Water Oyster (*Ostrea edulis*)
73	Cockatoo (*Cacatua galerita*)
72+	Andean Condor (*Vultur gryphus*)
72	African Grey Parrot (*Psittacus erithacus*)
c. 70	Indian Elephant (*Elephas maximus*)
70	Mute Swan (*Cygnus olor*)
69	Raven (*Corvus corax*)
62	Ostrich (*Struthio camelus*)
62	Horse (*Equus caballus*)
57	Aligator Snapping Turtle
57	Orangutan
55	Giant Salamander (*Megalobatrachus japonicus*)
54	Hippopotamus (*Hippopotamus amphibius*)
50	Chimpanzee (*Pan troglodytes*)
>50	Koi Fish
50	Lobster (*Humarus americanus*)
>50	Termites (*Isoptera*)
49½	Goose (*Anser anser*)
c. 49	Carp, mirror (*Cyprinus carpio* var.)
47	Rhinoceros, Indian (*Rhinoceros unicornis*)
47	Monkey (*Cebus capucinus*)
46	Grey Seal (*Halichoerus grypus*)
43	Ringed Seal (*Pusa hispida*)
40	Common Boa (*Boa constrictor*)
38	Common Boa (*Boa constrictor*)
35	Pigeon, domestic (*Columba livia domestica*)
34	Canary (*Severius canaria*)
34	Cat (domestic) (*Felis catus*)
33	Polar Bear (*Thalarctos maritimus*)
30	Giant Clam (*Tridacna gigas*)
29¾	Goldfish (*Carassius auratus*)
29	Dog (Labrador) (*Canis familiaris*)
28	Budgerigar (*Melopsittacus undulatus*)
28	Tarantula (*Mygalomorphae*)
27	Camel, Bactrian (*Camelas bactriarus*)
27	Pig (*Sus scofa*)
26½	Red Deer (*Cervus elphus*)
>24	Bat (*Myotis lucifugus*)
24	Pike (*Esox lucius*)
22	Porcupine (*Atherurus africanus*)
20	Sheep (*Ovis aries*)
19	Wallaroo (*Macropus rubustus*)
18	Goat (*Capra hircus*)
18	Rabbit (*Oryctolagus cuniculus*)
17	Cicada (*Magicicada septendecim*)
13⅓	Guinea Pig (*Cavia porcellus*)
10	Golden Hamster (*Mesocricetus auratus*)

ANIMAL LONGEVITY continued
- 7½ Gerbil (*Gerbillus gerbillus*)
- 6 House Mouse (*Mus musculus*)
- 4·5 Snail (both freshwater and land)
- 4·0 Rat, house (*Rattus rattus*)
- 0·5 Bedbug (*Cimex lectularius*)
- 0·2 Fly, house (*Musca domestica*)

VELOCITY OF ANIMAL MOVEMENT

The data on this topic are notoriously unreliable because of the many inherent difficulties of timing the movement of most animals—whether running, flying, or swimming—and because of the absence of any standardisation of the method of timing, of the distance over which the performance is measured, or of allowance for wind conditions.

The most that can be said is that a specimen of the species below has been timed to have attained as a maximum the speed given.

MPH
- 110·07* Racing Pigeon (*Columba palumbus*)
- 106·25 Spine-tailed swift (*Chaetura caudacuta*)
- 88 Spurwing Goose (*Plectropterus gambensis*)
- 82* Peregrine Falcon (*Falco peregrinus*)
- 80 Red-breasted merganser (*Mergus serrator*)
- 68 Sailfish (*Istiophorus platypterus*)
- 65 Mallard (*Anas platyrhyncha*)
- 61 Pronghorn Antelope (*Antilocapra americana*)

- 60–63† Cheetah (*Acinonyx jubatus*)
- 57 Quail (*Coturnix coturnix*)
- 57 Swift (*Apus apus*)
- 56 Red Grouse (*Lagopus scoticus*)
- 55 Swan (*Cygnus* sp.)
- 53 Partridge (*Perdix perdix*)
- 50 House Martin (*Delichon urbica*)
- 50 Starling (*Sturnus vulgaris*)
- 45 English Hare (*Lepus timidus*)
- 45 Red Kangaroo (*Megaleia rufa*)
- 43·4 Bluefin Tuna (*Thunnus thynnus*)
- 43·26 Race Horse (*Equus caballus*) (mounted)
- 43 Saluki (*Canis familiaris*)
- 42 Red Deer (*Cervus elephus*)
- 41·72‡ Greyhound (*Canis familiaris*)
- 40 Emu (*Dromiceus novaehollandiae*)
- 40 Jackdaw (*Corvus monedula*)
- 40 Flying Fish (*Cypselurus heterururs*) (airborne)
- 38 Swallow (*Hirundo rustica*)
- 37 Dolphin (*Delphinus* sp.)
- 36 Dragonfly (*Austrophlebia*)
- 35 Rhinoceros (*Cerathotherium simus*)
- 35 Wolf (*Canis lupus*)
- 33 Hawk Moth (*Sphingidae*)
- 32 Giraffe (*Giraffa camelopardalis*)
- 32 Guano Bat (*Tadarida mexicana*)
- 30 Blackbird (*Turdus merula*)
- 28 Fox (*Vulpes fulva*)
- 28 Grey Heron (*Ardea cinerea*)
- 27·89§ Man (*Homo sapiens*)
- 27 Cuckoo (*Cuculus canorus*)
- 25 California Sealion (*Zalophys californianus*)
- 24 African Elephant (*Loxodonta africana*)
- 24 Deer Bot-fly (*Cephenemyia pratti*)
- 23 Salmon (*Salmo salar*)
- 22·8 Blue Whale (*Sibbaldus musculus*)
- 22·3 Gentoo Penguin (*Pygosterlis papua*)

- 22 Pacific Leatherneck Turtle (*Dermochelys coriacea schlegelii*)
- 22 Wren (*Troglodytes troglodytes*)
- 20 Monarch Butterfly (*Danaus plexippus*)
- 18 Race Runner Lizard (*Cnemidophorus sexlineatus*)
- 16 Flying Frog (*Hyla venulosa*) (gravity glide)
- 15‖ Black mamba (*Dendroaspis polylepsis*)
- 13·3 Hornet (*Vespula maculata*)
- 12 Wasp (*Vespa vulgaris*)
- 11 Bee
- 8·5¶ Penguin (Adélie) (*Pygoscelis adeliae*)
- 4·5** Flea (Order *Siphonaptera*)
- 1·36 Sloth (*Bradypus tridactylus*)
- 1·2 Spider (*Tegenaria atrica*)
- 1·1 Centipede (*Scutigera coleoptera*)
- 0·17 Giant Tortoise (*Geochelone gigantea*)
- 0·03 Garden Snail (*Helix aspersa*)

* Strong following wind—60 m.p.h. in still air.
† Unable to sustain a speed of over 44 m.p.h. over 350 yards.
‡ Average over 410 yards.
§ Over 15 yards (flying start).
‖ Unable to sustain a speed of over 7 m.p.h.
¶ Under water.
** Jumping.

GEOLOGY

Rocks of the Earth's crust are grouped in three principal classes:

(1) Igneous rocks have been solidified from molten *Magma*. These are divided into extrusive rock, viz. larva and pumice, or intrusive rock, such as some granites or gabbro which is high in calcium and magnesium and low in silicon. It should be noted that extreme metamorphism can also produce granitic rocks from sediment.
(2) Sedimentary rocks are classically formed by the deposition of sediment in water, viz. conglomerates (e.g. gravel, shingle, pebbles), sandstones and shales (layered clay and claystone). Peat, lignite, bituminous coal and anthracite are the result of the deposition of organic matter. Gypsum, chalk and limestone are examples of chemical sedimentation.
(3) Metamorphic rocks were originally igneous or sedimentary but have been metamorphosed (transformed) by the agency of intense heat, pressure or the action of water. Gneiss is metamorphosed granite; marble is metamorphosed limestone; and slate is highly pressurised shale. Metamorphic rocks made cleavable by intense heat and

pressure are known generically as schist. Their foliate characteristics are shared by both gneiss and slate.

Geochemical abundances of the elements

	Lithosphere* (Parts per Mill. %)	Hydrosphere (Parts per Mill. %)
Oxygen	466·0	857
Silicon	277·2	0·003 to 0·00002
Aluminium	81·3	0·00001
Iron	50·0	0·00001
Calcium	36·3	0·40
Sodium	28·3	10·50
Potassium	25·9	0·38
Magnesium	20·9	1·35
Titanium	4·4	—
Hydrogen	1·40	103
Manganese	0·95	0·000002
Phosphorus	0·70	0·00007
Fluorine	0·65	0·0013
Sulfur	0·26	0·88
Carbon	0·25	0·028
Zirconium	0·17	—
Chlorine	0·13	19
Rubidium	0·09	0·0001
Nitrogen	0·02	0·0005
Chromium	0·01	0·00000005

*Assessment based on igneous rock.

Geo-chronology

Christian teaching as enunciated by Archbishop Ussher in the 17th century dated the creation of the Earth as occurring in the year 4004 BC. Lord Kelvin (1824–1907) calculated in 1899 that the earth was of the order of possibly some hundreds of millions of years old. In 1905 Lord Rutherford suggested radioactive decay could be used as a measurement and in 1907 Boltwood showed that a sample of pre-Cambrian rock dated from 1640 million years before the present (BP) measured by the uranium-lead method.

Modern dating methods using the duration of radioisotopic half-lives include also the contrasts obtained from thorium-lead, potassium-argon, rubidium-strontium, rhenium-osmium, helium-uranium and in the recent range of up to 40 000 years BP carbon-14. Other methods include thermoluminesence since 1968 and racemisation of amino acids since 1972 which latter is dependant upon the change from optically active to inactive forms which decline varies with the elapse of time.

The table below is based on the Fitch, Forster and Miller revised Potassium-Argon time scale published in 1974 and the Geological Society Phanerozoic Time Scale, 1964 as amended by Lambert (1971).

The geological past is divided into four principal eras. Going backwards in time these are the Cenozoic, the Mesozoic, the Palaeozoic and the Pre-Cambrian, which last stretches back to the formation of the Earth. This is now generally believed to be at least 4700 million years ago though some authorities prefer the earlier date of *c.* 6500 million years ago.

---

(1) Cenozoic Era (the present to 64 million years ago). The name is derived from the Gk. *kainos*, new or recent; *zo-os*, life, indicating that life-forms are all recent. The era is divided into the Quaternary Period (the Age of Man, and animals and plants of modern type) back to two million years (formerly only one million years) ago and the Tertiary Period from 2–64 million years ago. This was the age of mammals and the rise and development of the highest orders of plants such as orchids. The Cenozoic is subdivided thus:

Present to 50 000 BC
Holocene—Gk. *holos*, entirely; *kainos*, recent (all forms recent)

50 000 BC to *c.* 1 750 000 BC
Pleistocene—Gk. *pleisto*, very many (great majority of forms recent)

2 to *c.* 7 million years BP
Pliocene—Gk. *pleion*, more (majority of forms recent)

c. 7 to 26 million years BP
Miocene—Gk. *meios*, less (minority of forms recent)

26 to 38 million years BP
Oligocene—Gk. *oligos*, few (few forms recent)

38 to 54 million years BP
Eocene—Gk. *eos*, dawn (dawn of recent forms)

54 to 64 million years BP
Palaeocene—Gk. *palaious*, ancient (earliest recent forms)

(2) Mesozoic Era (65 to 225 million years ago). The name is derived from the Gk. *mesos*, middle; *zo-os*, life, indicating that life-forms are intermediate between the recent evolutions and the ancient forms. The era is divided into three periods thus:

64 to ?135 million years BP
Cretaceous (Latin *creta*, chalk; period of deposition and chalk formation). This was the age of reptiles and the fall of the dinosaurs (*c.* 120 million BP). First abundance of hardwood trees (*c.* 130 million BP) also the palms and seed-bearing plants.

?135 to *c.* 210 million years BP
Jurassic (after the Jura Mountains). This period saw the earliest gliders (*Archaeopteryx*, *c.* 150 million BP) and the earliest mammals (*Morganucodon*, *c.* 160 million BP).

c. 210 to 235 million years BP
Triassic (adj. of trias, the old three-fold German division). First appearance of dinosaurs (*c.* 210 million BP).

---

(3) Palaeozoic Era (*c.* 235 to <597 million years ago). The name is derived from the Gk. *palaios*, ancient; *zo-os*, life, indicating that fossilised life-forms are of ancient forms. The era is broadly divided into the Upper Palaeozoic (225–395 million BP) and the Lower Palaeozoic from 395–570 million years BP. The sub-divisions are as follows:

c. 235 to 280 million years BP
Permian (named in 1841 after the Russian province Perm). Earliest land reptiles (*Seymouria*) date from *c.* 250 million BP.

c. 280 to 360 million years BP
Carboniferous (carbon-bearing, so named in 1822). Earliest spider (*Palaeoteniza crassipes*) and earliest quadruped, the amphibian *Ichthyostega*, both date from *c.* 300 million BP. The earliest conifers, great coal forests, tree ferns and huge mosses date from *c.* 340 million BP. In North America the late Carboniferous is called the Pennsylvanian and the early carboniferous the Mississippian period.

c. 360 to *c.* 405 million years BP
Devonian (named after the English county). The earliest insects (*Collembola*) date from *c.* 360 million BP. Molluscs abundant.

c. 405 to ?435–460 million years BP
Silurian (named after the ancient British tribe, *Silures*). The earliest land plants date from the late Silurian. Reef-building corals active.

?435–460 to *c.* 510 million years BP
Ordovician (named after the Welsh border tribe, *Ordovices*). Earliest known fish (*Ostracoderms*) and molluscs (the still living *Neopilina*) both date from *c.* 500 million BP.

>510 to <597 million years BP
Cambrian (from the Latin, *Cambria* for Wales, scene of pioneer rock investigations). Marine invertebrates were abundant *c.* 550 million BP.

---

(4) Pre-Cambrian Era (earlier than 597 million years before the present). The name indicates merely all time pre (from Latin, *prae*, before) the Cambrian period (see above). This era includes such events as the earliest dated algal remains (*c.* 2100 million BP), problematica of the Oscillatorioid class (*c.* 2600 million BP) and the earliest certainly dated rock formations of 3980 ±170 million BP.

The Pre-Cambrian is divided into the Late Precambrian (<597 to 2400 million BP); the Middle Precambrian (2400–3500 million BP) and Early Precambrian (3500–*c.* 4600 million BP).

Gemstones

Gemstones are minerals possessing a rarity and usually a hardness, colour or translucency which gives them strong aesthetic appeal. Diamond, emerald, ruby and sapphire used to be classed as 'precious stones' and all others as 'semi-precious'. This distinction is no longer generally applied. The principal gemstones in order of hardness are listed below with data in the following order:— name; birthstone (if any); chemical formula; classic colour; degree of hardness on Mohs' Scale 10–1; principal localities where found and brief notes on outstanding specimens. A metric carat is $\frac{1}{5}$th of a gram. It should be noted that most gems are found in many colours and that only the classic colour is here described. In 1937 the National Association of Goldsmiths unified the various national lists of birthstones; their list, which completely agrees with the earlier US version, is followed here.

Diamond: (birthstone for April); C (pure crystalline isotope); fiery bluish-white; Mohs 10·0; S, SW and E Africa and India with alluvial deposits in Australia, Brazil, Congo, India, Indonesia, Liberia, Sierra Leone and USSR (Urals). Largest uncut: *Cullinan* 3106 carats (over 20 oz) by Capt M F Wells, Premier Mine, Pretoria, S Africa on 26 Jan. 1905. Cut by Jacob Asscher of Amsterdam 1909. Largest cut: *Cullinan I* or *Star of Africa* from the above in British Royal Sceptre at 530·2 carats. *Koh-i-nor* originally 186 now re-cut to 106 carats; also in British Crown Jewels. The largest coloured diamond is the 44·4 carat vivid blue *Hope Diamond* from Killur, Golconda, India (ante 1642) in the Smithsonian Institution, Washington DC since November 1958.

Ruby: (birthstone for July); Al_2O_3 (corundum with reddening trace of chromic oxide); dark red; 9·0; Brazil, Burma, Sri Lanka, Thailand. Largest recorded gem 1184 carat stone from Burma; broken red corundum originally of 3421 carats (not gem quality) July 1961, USA.

Sapphire: (birthstone for September); Al_2O_3 (corundum with bluish trace of iron or titanium); dark blue; 9·0; Australia, Burma, Sri Lanka, Kashmir, USA (Montana). Largest cut: *Star of India*, 563·5 carats from Sri Lanka now in American Museum of Natural History, New York City. Largest uncut: 1200 carats (white stone) from Anakie, Queensland, May 1956.

Alexandrite: $Al_2[BeO_4]$ (chrysoberyl); dull green (daylight) but blood red (artificial light); 8·5; Brazil, Moravia, USA (Connecticut), USSR (Urals).

Cat's Eye: $Al_2[BeO_4]$ (chrysoberyl, variety cymophane); yellowish to brownish-green with narrow silken ray; 8·5.

Topaz: (birthstone for November); $Al_2 SiO_4F_2$; tea coloured; 8·0; Australia, Brazil, Sri Lanka, Germany, Namibia, USSR. The largest recorded is one of 596 lb from Brazil.

Spinel: $MgAl_2O_4$ with reddening trace of Fe_2O_3; red; 8·0 mainly Sri Lanka and India.

Emerald: (birthstone for May); Al_2Be_3 Si_6O_{18} (beryl); vivid green; 7·5–8·0; Austria, Colombia, Norway, USA (N Carolina), USSR (Urals); largest recorded beryl prism (non-gem quality) 135 lb from Urals; largest gem: Devonshire stone of 1350 carats from Muso, Colombia.

Aquamarine: (birthstone for March); $Al_2Be_3Si_6O_{18}$ (beryl), pale limpid blue; 7·5–8·0; found in emerald localities and elsewhere, including Brazil; largest recorded 229 lb near Marambaia, Brazil, 1910.

Garnet: (birthstone for January); silicates of Al, Ca, Cr, Fe, Mg, Ti; purplish-red (Almandine, $Fe_3Al_2[SiO_4]_3$; 7·5–8·0; India, Ceylon, USA (Arizona); green (Demantoid, $Ca_3Fe_2[SiO_4]_3$; 6·5–7·0; USSR (Siberia and Urals); black (Malanite, $TiCa_3$) (Fe, Ti, Al)$_2[SiO_4]_3$, 6·5.

Zircon: $Zr(SiO_4)$; colourless but also blue and red-brown (hyacinth); 7·0–7·5; Australia (NSW), Burma, Sri Lanka, India, North America, Thailand, USSR (Siberia).

Tourmaline: complex boro-silicate of Al, Fe, Mg alkalis; notably deep green, bluish green, deep red; 7·0–7·25; Brazil, Sri Lanka, USSR (Siberia).

Rock Crystal: (birthstone for April, alternative to diamond); SiO_2; Colourless; 7·0; Brazil, Burma, France, Madagascar, Switzerland, USA (Arkansas). The largest recorded crystal ball is one of 106 lb from Burma now in the US National Museum, Washington DC.

Rose quartz: SiO_2; coarsely granular pale pink; 7·0; Bavaria, Brazil, Finland, Namibia, USA (Maine); USSR (Urals).

Cairngorm: (Smoky quartz); SiO_2; smoky yellow to brownish; 7·0; Brazil, Madagascar, Manchuria, Scotland (Cairngorm Mountains), Switzerland, USA (Colorado), USSR (Urals).

Amethyst: (birthstone for February); SiO_2; purple 7·0; Brazil, Sri Lanka, Germany, Madagascar, Uruguay, USSR (Urals).

Chrysoprase (Chalcedony form): (birthstone for May, alternative to emerald); SiO_2 with nickel hydroxide impurity; apple green (opaque); 6·5–7·0; Germany, USA.

Jade: $NaAlSi_2O_6$; dark to leek green; 6·5–7·0; Burma, China, Tibet (pale green and less valuable form is nephrite, Na_2Ca_4 $(Mg, Fe)_{10}[(OH)_2O_2Si_{16}O_{44}]$).

Cornelian (Chalcedony form); often (wrongly) spelt carnelian: (birthstone for July, alternative to ruby); SiO_2 with ferric oxide impurity; blood red to yellowish-brown; 6·5–7·0; widespread, including Great Britain.

Agate (Striped chalcedony); SiO_2; opaque white to pale grey, blue; 6·5–7·0; a variety is moss agate (milky white with moss-like inclusions, often green); Brazil, Germany, India, Madagascar, Scotland.

Onyx: a black and white banded agate (see Agate).

Sardonyx: (birthstone for August, alternative to Peridot); a reddish-brown and white-banded agate (see Agate).

Jasper (Chalcedony): SiO_2 with impurities; brown (manganese oxide), red (ferric oxide), yellow (hydrated ferric oxide); opaque; 6·5–7·0; Egypt, India.

Peridot (Green Olivine): (birthstone for August); $(Mg, Fe)_2[SiO_4]$ green; 6·0–7·0; Australia (Queensland); Brazil, Burma, Norway, St John's Island (Red Sea).

Bloodstone or Blood Jasper (Chalcedony): (birthstone for March, alternative to aquamarine); SiO_2; dark green with red spots (oxide of iron); 6·0–7·0.

Moonstone (Feldspar): (birthstone for June, alternative to pearl); $K[AlSi_3O_8]$; white to bluish, irridescent; 6·0–6·5; Brazil, Burma, Sri Lanka.

Opal: (birthstone for October); $SiO_2.nH_2O$: rainbow colours on white background; other varieties include fire opal, water opal, black opal; 5·0–6·5; Australia, Mexico and formerly Hungary. The largest recorded is one of 143 oz named *Olympic Australis* near Coober Pedy, S Australia in August 1956.

Turquoise: (birthstone for December); $CuAl_6[(OH)_8(PO_4)_4]5H_2O$; sky blue; 5·5–6·0; UAR (Sinai Peninsula), Iran, Turkey, USA (California, Nevada, New Mexico, Texas).

Lapis Lazuli: (birthstone for September, alternative to sapphire); $(Na, Ca)_8[(S, Cl, SO_4)_2(AlSiO_4)_6]$; deep azure blue, opaque; 5·5–5·75; Afghanistan, Chile, Tibet, USSR (Lake Baikal area).

Obsidian: (glassy lava); green or yellowish-brown; 5·0–5·5; volcanic areas.

Non-mineral gem material
Amber (organic): about $C_{40}H_{64}O_4$; honey yellow; clear; or paler yellow, cloudy; 2·0–2·5; Mainly Baltic and Sicily coasts. A variety is fly amber in which the body of an insect is encased.

Coral (polyps of *Coelenterata):* varied colourations including Blood or Red Coral; Australasia, Pacific and Indian Oceans.

Pearl: (birthstone for June); (secretions of molluscs, notably of the sea-water mussel genus *Pinctada* and the fresh-water mussel *Quadrula*); Western Pacific; largest recorded is the *Hope Pearl* weighing nearly 3 oz, circumference $4\frac{1}{2}$ in. Anacreous mass of 14 lb 2oz from a giant clam (*Tridacna gigas*) was recovered in the Philippines in 1934 and is known as the 'Pearl of Allah'.

Earthquakes
It was not until as recently as 1874 that subterranean slippage along overstressed faults became generally accepted as the cause of tectonic earthquakes. The collapse of caverns, volcanic action, and also possibly the very rare event of a major meteoric impact can also cause tremors. The study of earthquakes is called seismology.

The two great seismic systems are the Alps-Himalaya great circle and the circum-Pacific belt. The foci below the epicentres are classified as shallow (<50 km deep), intermediate (50–200 km) and deep (200–700 km).

The descriptive Mercalli Intensity Scale based on impression rather than measurement reads thus:

I	Just detectable by experienced observers when prone. Microseisms.
II	Felt by few. Delicately poised object may sway.
III	Vibration but still unrecognised by many. Feeble.
IV	Felt by many indoors but by few outdoors. Moderate.
V	Felt by almost all. Many awakened. Unstable objects moved.
VI	Felt by all. Heavy objects moved. Alarm. Strong.
VII	General alarm. Weak buildings considerably damaged. Very strong.
VIII	Damage general except in proofed buildings. Heavy objects overturned.
IX	Buildings shifted from foundations, collapse, ground cracks. Highly destructive.
X	Masonry buildings destroyed, rails bent, serious ground fissures. Devastating.
XI	Few if any structures left standing. Bridges down. Rails twisted. Catastrophic.
XII	Damage total. Vibrations distort vision. Objects thrown in air. Major catastrophe.

Instrumental measurements are made on seismographs on the Gutenberg-Richter scale. Cataclysmic earthquakes have an energy of the order of 3×10^{19} ergs.

Seismographs can denote P (primary) waves, S (secondary) waves with their reflections, and L (long) and M (maximum) waves. It was from a double P wave that A Mohorovičić (Croatia) in 1909 first deduced a discontinuity in the Earth's crustal structure.

On the comparative scale of the Mantle Wave magnitudes (defined in 1968) the most cataclysmic earthquakes since 1930 have been

Mag. 8.9	Prince William Sound, Alaska	28 Mar. 1964
Mag. 8.8	Kamchatka, USSR	4 Nov. 1952
Mag. 8.8	Concepción, Chile	22 May 1960

An interim magnitude of 8·9 was announced from Vienna for the South Java Sea 'quake of 18 Aug. 1977.

The Great Lisbon Earthquake of 1 Nov. 1755, 98 years before the invention of the seismograph killed 60 000: it would have rated a magnitude of $8\frac{3}{4}$ to 9.

Attendant phenomena include:
(i) *Tsunami* (wrongly called tidal waves) or gravity waves which radiate in long, low oscillations from submarine disturbances at speeds of 450–490 mph *725–790 km/h*. The 1883 Krakatoa *tsunami* reached a height of 135 ft *41 m* and that off Valolez, Alaska in 1964 attained a height of 220 ft *67 m*.
(ii) *Seiches* (a Swiss-French term of doubtful origin, pronounced sāsh). Seismic oscillations in landlocked water. Loch Lomond had a 2 ft *60 cm* seiche for 1 hr from the 1755 Lisbon 'quake.
(iii) *Fore and After Shocks.* These often occur before major 'quakes and may persist after these for months or years.

Historic Earthquakes
The five earthquakes in which the known loss of life has exceeded 100 000 have been:

830 000	Shensi Province, China	24 Jan. 1556
750 000	Tangshan, China	27 July 1976
300 000	Calcutta, India	11 Oct. 1737
180 000	Kansu Province, China	16 Dec. 1920
142 807	Kwanto Plain, Honshū, Japan	1 Sept. 1923

The material damage done in the Kwanto Plain, which includes Tōkyō, was estimated at £1 000 000 000.

Other notable earthquakes during this century, with loss of life in brackets, have been:

1906 San Francisco, USA (18 Apr.) (452)
1908 Messina, Italy (28 Dec.) (75 000)
1915 Avezzano, Italy (13 Jan.) (29 970)
1932 Kansu Province, China (26 Dec.) (70 000)
1935 Quetta, India (31 May) (60 000)
1939 Erzingan, Turkey (27 Dec.) (23 000)
1960 Agadir, Morocco (29 Feb.) (12 000)
1964 Anchorage, Alaska (28 Mar.) (131)
1970 Northern Peru (31 May) (66 800)
1972 Nicaragua (23 Dec.) (10 000)
1976 Guatemala (4 Feb.) (22 000)
1976 Tangshan, China (26 July) (c. 730,000)

Other major natural disasters
Landslides caused by earthquakes in the Kansu Province of China on 16 Dec. 1920 killed 200 000 people.

The Peruvian snow avalanches at Huaras (13 Dec. 1941) and from Huascarán (10 Jan. 1962) killed 5000 and 3000 people respectively. The Huascarán alluvion flood triggered by the earthquake of 31 May 1970 wiped out 25 000.

Both floods and famines have wreaked a greater toll of human life than have earthquakes. The greatest river floods on record are those of the Hwang-ho, China. From September into October in 1887 some 900 000 people were drowned. The flood of August 1931 killed some 3 700 000. A typhoon flood at Haiphong in North Vietnam (formerly Indo-China) on 8 Oct. 1881 killed an estimated 300 000 people. The cyclone of 12–13 Nov. 1970 which struck the Ganges Delta islands, Bangladesh drowned an estimated 1 000 000.

History's worst famines have occurred in Asia. In 1770 nearly one third of India's total population died with ten million dead in Bengal alone. From February 1877 to September 1878 an estimated 9 500 000 people died of famine in northern China.

British Earthquakes
The earliest British earthquake of which there is indisputable evidence was that of AD 974 felt over England. The earliest precisely recorded was that of 1 May 1048, in Worcester. British earthquakes of an intensity sufficient to have raised or moved the chair of the observer (Davison's Scale 8) have been recorded thus:

25 Apr. 1180 Nottinghamshire
15 Apr. 1185 Lincoln
1 June 1246 Canterbury, Kent
21 Dec. 1246 Wells
19 Feb. 1249 South Wales
11 Sept. 1275 Somerset
21 May 1382 Canterbury, Kent
28 Dec. 1480 Norfolk
26 Feb. 1575 York to Bristol
6 Apr. 1580* London
30 Apr. 1736 Menstrie, Clackmannan
1 May 1736 Menstrie, Clackmannan
14 Nov. 1769† Inverness
18 Nov. 1795 Derbyshire
13 Aug. 1816‡ Inverness
23 Oct. 1839 Comrie, Perth
30 July 1841 Comrie, Perth
6 Oct. 1863 Hereford
22 Apr. 1884§ Colchester
17 Dec. 1896 Hereford
18 Sept. 1901 Inverness
27 June 1906‖ Swansea
30 July 1926 Jersey
15 Aug. 1926 Hereford
7 June 1931 Dogger Bank
11 Feb. 1957 Midlands

* About 6 p.m. First recorded fatality—an apprentice killed by masonry falling from Christ Church.

† 'Several people' reported killed. Parish register indicates not more than one. Date believed to be 14th.
‡ At 10.45 p.m. Heard in Aberdeen (83 miles *133 km*), felt in Glasgow (115 miles *185 km*). Strongest ever in Scotland.
§ At 9.18 a.m. Heard in Oxford (108 miles *174 km*), felt in Exeter and Ostend, Belgium (95 miles *152 km*). One child and probably at least 3 others killed. Strongest ever in British Isles.
‖ At 9.45 a.m. Strongest in Wales. Felt over 37 800 miles² *98 000 km²*.

Petroleum
Most deposits of petroleum are found in sedimentary rocks representing deposition in shallow new seas which once supported flora and fauna. The assumption that oil is a downward migration of such organic decay is now modified by the abiogenic theory which maintains that some of the heavy hydrocarbons may have sprung, already polymerised, from deep layers of hot magma.

Exploration in the North Sea began on 26 Dec. 1964 from the drilling rig 'Mr Cap'. The first show of methane (CH_4) gas came on 20 Sept. 1965 from the drill of British Petroleum's 'Sea Gem' 42 miles east of the Humber estuary.

In 1965 the daily average production of the Middle East (7 610 000 bbl in 1964) surpassed that of the USA (7 665 000 bbl in 1964). It was estimated that at 1 Jan. 1975 the world's total proven oil reserves were 97,700,000,000 tonnes or 720,400,000,000 bbl. World consumption ran at 55,940,000 bbl per day in 1974 compared with the world's refining capacity of 68,440,000 bbl per day. By 1990 a world consumption of oil and natural gas of 100 million bbl per day is forecast.

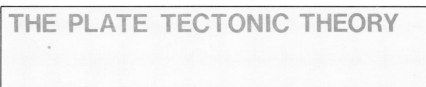

THE PLATE TECTONIC THEORY

By the end of the 19th Century the relative positions of the world's four great land masses, Afro-Eurasia, America, Antarctica and Australia were so fixed in so many minds that it was assumed that they had grown *in situ* at the original formation of the Earth's crust.

The theory of continental drift published by the German, Alfred L Wegener in 1912 was not generally accepted until 30 years after his death in 1930. The concept of large proto-continents, two in the northern hemisphere and one (possibly two) in the southern hemisphere named Gondwanaland, separated by an east-west seaway Tethys, had been published earlier by the Austrian, Eduard Suess in his *Das Antlitz der Erde* (1883–1909). Wegener held that all the continents were once part of a single land mass termed Pangaea.

One of the most striking pieces of evidence in support of the theory came with the discovery in 1968 of a fragment of the first land vertebrate (a four foot long amphibian) ever to be found in Antarctica. Fossils of this labyrinthodont from the Triassic period of 220 million years ago also occurred in the Gondwana beds of Africa, southern America and Australia.

Modern evidence is that there are at least six moving plates on the Earth's crust, of which two are oceanic and four consist of coupled continental and oceanic crust. The magnitude of motion or creep by these vast tectonic plates is estimated to range within 1 to 15 cm per annum. The driving mechanism in this highly viscous upper mantle is generally held to be thermally induced rather than tidal or gravitational.

The Earth 200 million years BC
A simplified map showing how the five continents are now thought to have fitted together to comprise Gondwanaland, a major sub-division of the super-continent Pangaea about 200 million years ago in the Triassic Period.

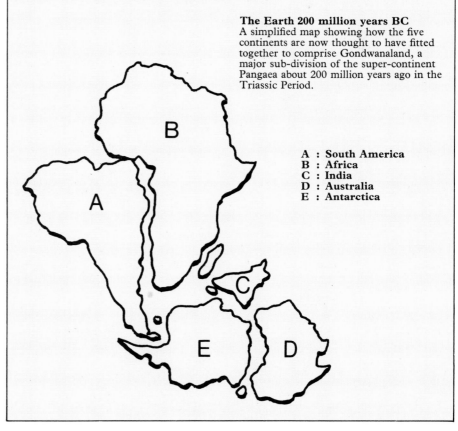

A : South America
B : Africa
C : India
D : Australia
E : Antarctica

METEOROLOGY

Beaufort Scale

A scale of numbers, designated Force 0 to Force 12, was originally devised by Commander Francis Beaufort (1774–1857) (later Rear-Admiral Sir Francis Beaufort, KCB, FRS) in 1805. Force numbers 13 to 17 were added in 1955 by the US Weather Bureau.

Force No.	Descriptive term	Wind speed mph	knots
0	Calm	0–1	0–1
1	Light air	1–3	1–3
2	Light breeze	4–7	4–6
3	Gentle breeze	8–12	7–10
4	Moderate breeze	13–18	11–16
5	Fresh breeze	19–24	17–21
6	Strong breeze	25–31	22–27
7	Moderate gale	32–38	28–33
8	Fresh gale	39–46	34–40
9	Strong gale	47–54	41–47
10	Whole gale	55–63	48–55
11	Storm	64–75	56–65
12	Hurricane	76–82	66–71
13	Hurricane	83–92	72–80
14	Hurricane	93–103	81–89
15	Hurricane	104–114	90–99
16	Hurricane	115–125	100–108
17	Hurricane	126–136	109–118

Phenomena and Terms

'Blue Moon'

The diffraction of light through very high clouds of dust or smoke, as might be caused by volcanic eruptions (notably Krakatoa, 27 Aug. 1883) or major forest fires (notably in British Columbia, 26 Sept. 1950), can change the colour of the Sun (normally white overhead and yellow or reddish at sunrise or sunset) and the Moon (normally whitish) on such rare occasions to other colours, notably green and even blue.

Ball Lightning

A very rare phenomenon. A spheroid glowing mass of energised air, usually about one ft *30 cm* in diameter. On striking an earthed object it seems to disappear, hence giving the impression that it has passed through it. Only one photograph exists of the phenomenon taken in August 1961.

Brocken Spectre

A person standing with his (or her) back to the Sun and looking down from higher ground onto a lower bank of fog or cloud, casts a shadow known by this name.

Coronae

When the Sun's or Moon's light is diffracted by water droplets in some types of cloud, a ring of light (sometimes two or more) may be seen closely and concentrically around the Sun or Moon.

Cyclone

The local name given to a tropical depression that results in a violent circular storm in the northern part of the Indian Ocean (see also Hurricane and Typhoon). The term can also be used for a low-pressure system, in contrast to the Anticyclone or high-pressure system. The cyclone of 12–13 Nov. 1970 in the Ganges Delta area, Bangladesh, resulted in about 1 000 000 deaths mainly from drowning. Cyclone Tracy which struck the Darwin area of N. Australia in 24–25 Dec. 1974 produced measured wind speeds of 134·8 mph *216,9 km/h*.

Fogbow

In rainbow conditions, when the refracting droplets of water are very small, as in fog or clouds, the colours of the rainbow may overlap and so the bow appears white. Alternative names for this phenomenon are a *Cloudbow*, or *Ulloa's Ring*.

Flachenblitz

A rare form of lightning which strikes upwards from the top of Cumulonimbus clouds and ends in clear air.

Glory

At the anti-solar point, from an observer in the situation that gives a *Brocken spectre*, a corona is seen round the head of the observer. When several people are standing side by side, each can see a *glory* round the shadow of his own head.

Haloes

When the Sun's light is refracted by ice crystals in Cirrus or Cirrostratus clouds, a bright ring of light, usually reddish on the inside and white on the outside, may be seen round the Sun with a 22° radius. Much more rarely a 46° *halo* may appear, and, very rarely indeed, haloes of other sizes with radii of 7° upwards. Halo phenomena may also be seen round the Moon.

Hurricanes

The local name given to a tropical depression that results in a violent circular storm in the southern part of the North Atlantic, notably the Caribbean Sea (see also Cyclone and Typhoon). Hurricane Betsy in 1965 caused damage estimated at more than $1000 million on which $750 million was paid out in insurance.

Iridescence (or Irisation)

When conditions giving rise to coronae illuminate clouds, the phenomena is so described.

Mirages

Mirages are caused by the refraction of light when layers of the atmosphere have sharply differing densities (due to contrasting temperature). There are two types of mirages: with the *inferior mirage*—the more common of the two—an object near the horizon appears to be refracted as in a pool of water; with the *superior mirage* the object near—or even beyond—the horizon appears to float above its true position.

Mock Suns

In halo conditions the ice crystals when orientated in a particular way can refract light so as to produce one or more *mock suns* or *parhelia* on either or both sides of the Sun and usually 22° away from it.

Nacreous Clouds and Noctilucent 'Clouds'

Nacreous, or mother-of-pearl, clouds occasionally appear after sunset over mountainous areas, at a height of from 60 000 to 80 000 ft. These are lit by sunlight from below the horizon, so may be seen hundreds of miles away, for example in Scotland over Scandinavia.

Noctilucent 'clouds' are a phenomena, possibly formed by cosmic dust, that appear bluish in colour at a very great height of 300 000 ft, say 60 miles or *100 km*. This phenomenon was reported from the Shetlands 33 times in 1967 and 15 in 1970.

Rainbows

If an observer stands with his back to the Sun and looks out on a mass of falling raindrops lit by the Sun, he will see a *rainbow*. A *primary bow* is vividly coloured with violet on the inside, followed by blue, green, yellow, orange, and red. A *secondary bow*, which, if visible, is only about a tenth of the intensity of its primary, has its colour sequence reversed. Further bows, even more feeble, can on very rare occasions be seen.

Saint Elmo's Fire (or Corposants)

A luminous electrical discharge in the atmosphere which emanates from protruding objects, such as ships' mastheads, lightning conductors and windvanes.

Sun Pillars

In halo conditions, when the ice crystals are orientated in a particular way, a *sun pillar*, which is a bright image of the Sun extending both above and below it, may appear.

Thunderbolts

These do not in fact exist, but the effect of the intense heating of a lightning strike may fuse various materials and so give the false impression that a solid object in fact hit the ground. A lightning strike may boil water almost instantaneously and so, for example, shatter damp masonry, so giving the appearance that it has been struck by a solid object.

Tornado

A *tornado* is the result of intense convection, which produces a violent whirlwind extending downwards from a storm cloud base, often reaching the ground. The width varies between about 50 m *164 ft* and 400 m *1312 ft* and it moves across country at speeds varying from 10 to 30 mph *15–50 km/h* causing great damage. The British frequency is about 12 per annum, one in 1638 causing 60 casualties at Widecombe, Devon. On 18 Mar. 1925 tornadoes in the south central states of the USA killed 689. At Wichita Falls, Texas on 2 Apr. 1958 a wind speed of 280 mph *450 km/h* was recorded.

Typhoon

The local name given to a tropical depression that results in a violent circular storm in the south-western part of the North Pacific and especially the China Sea (see also Cyclone and Hurricane). A barometer pressure as low as 877 millibars (25·90 in) was recorded

600 miles *965 km* north west of Guam in the Pacific on 24 Sept. 1958.

Waterspout
The same phenomenon as a tornado, except that it occurs over the sea, or inland water. These may reach an extreme height of 5000 feet *1524 m*.

Whiteout
When land is totally covered by snow, the intensity of the light refracted off it may be the same as that refracted off overhead cloud. This results in the obliteration of the horizon, and makes land and sky indistinguishable.

Fog
A convenient meteorological definition of fog is a 'cloud touching the ground and reducing visibility to less than one kilometre (1100 yd)'.

Fog requires the coincidence of three conditions:
(i) Minute hygroscopic particles to act as nuclei. The most usual source over land is from factory or domestic chimneys, whereas at sea salt particles serve the same purpose. Such particles exist everywhere, but where they are plentiful the fog is thickest.
(ii) Condensation of water vapour by saturation.
(iii) The temperature at or below dew point. The latter condition may arise in two ways. The air temperature may simply drop to dew point, or the dew point may rise because of increased amounts of water vapour.

Sea fog persists for up to 120 days in a year on the Grand Banks, off Newfoundland. London has twice been beset by 114 hours continuous fog recently—26 Nov. to 1 Dec. 1948 and 5–9 Dec. 1952.

Thunder and Lightning
At any given moment there are some 2200 thunderstorms on the Earth's surface which are audible at ranges of up to 18 miles *29 km*. The world's most thundery location is Bogor (formerly Buitenzorg), Java, Indonesia, which in 1916–19 averaged 322 days per year with thunder. The extreme in the United Kingdom is 38 days at Stonyhurst, Lancashire in 1912, and in Huddersfield, West Yorkshire in 1967.

Thunder arises after the separation of electrical charges in cumulonimbus (q.v.) clouds. In the bipolar thundercloud the positive charge is in the upper layer. Thunder is an audible compression wave, the source of which is the rapid heating of the air by a return lightning stroke.
Lightning: The speed of lightning varies greatly. The downward leader strokes vary between 100 and 1000 miles per second *150 to 1500 km/s*. In the case of the powerful return stroke a speed of 87 000 miles per second *140 000 km/s*, nearly half the speed of light) is attained. The length of stroke varies with cloud height and thus between 300 ft *90 m* and 4 miles *6 km* though lateral strokes as long as 20 miles *32 km* have been recorded. The central core of a lightning channel is extremely narrow—perhaps as little as a half-inch *1,27 cm*. In the case of the more 'positive giant' stroke the temperature reaches c. 30 000 °C or over five times that of the sun's surface. In Britain the frequency of strikes is only 6 per mile[2] per annum. British fatalities have averaged 11·8 per annum this century with 31 in 1914 but nil in 1937.

Constituents of Air

Gas	Formula	% By volume
Invariable component gases of dry carbon dioxide-free air		
Nitrogen	N_2	78·110
Oxygen	O_2	20·953
Argon	A	0·934
Neon	Ne	0·001818
Helium	He	0·000524
Methane	CH_4	0·0002
Krypton	Kr	0·000114
Hydrogen	H_2	0·00005
Nitrous Oxide	N_2O	0·00005
Xenon	Xe	0·0000087
		99·9997647 %
Variable components		
Water Vapour	H_2O	0 to 7·0*
Carbon dioxide	CO_2	0·01 to 0·10 average 0·034
Ozone	O_3	0 to 0·000007
Contaminants		
Sulphur dioxide	SO_2	up to 0·0001
Nitrogen dioxide	NO_2	up to 0·000002
Ammonia	NH_3	trace
Carbon monoxide	CO	trace

* This percentage can be reached at a relative humidity of 100 per cent at a shade temperature of 40 °C (104 °F).

World and UK Meteorological Absolutes and Averages
Temperature: The world's overall average annual day side temperature is 59 °F *15* °C. Highest shade (**world**): 136·4 °F *57,7 °C* Al'Aziziyah, Libya, 13 Sept. 1922. **UK**: 100·5 °F *38,0 °C* Tonbridge, Kent, 22 July 1868. The hottest place (**world**) on annual average is Dallol, Ethiopia with 94 °F *34,4 °C* (1960–66) and in **UK** Penzance, Cornwall, and Isles of Scilly, both 52·7 °F *11,5 °C*. Annual Means: England 50·3 °F *10,1 °C*; Scotland 47·6 °F *8,6 °C*. Lowest Screen (**world**): −126·9 °F *−88,3 °C* Vostock, Antarctica, 24 Aug. 1960. **UK**: −17 °F *−27,2 °C* Braemar, 11 Feb. 1895 (N.B.—Temperature of −23 °F at Blackadder, Borders, in 1879 and of −20 °F at Grantown-on-Spey, in 1955 were not standard exposures.) The coldest place (**world**) on annual average is the Pole of Cold, 150 miles *240 km* west of Vostok, Antarctica at −72 °F *−57,8 °C* and in the **UK** at Braemar, Grampian 43·7 °F *6,5 °C*.

Barometric Pressure: The world's average barometric pressure is 1013 mb. Highest (**world**): 1083·8 mb. *(32·00 in)*, Agata, Siberia, USSR, 31 Dec. 1968 and **UK**: 1054·7 mb (31·11 in) at Aberdeen, 31 Jan. 1902.
Lowest (**world**): 877 mb (25·90 in), recorded at sea 600 miles *965 km* NW of Guam, Pacific Ocean, 24 Sept. 1958 and **UK**: 925·5 mb (27·33 in), Ochtertyre, near Crieff, Tayside, 26 Jan. 1884

Wind Strength: Highest sustained surface speed (**world**) 231 mph *371 km/h*, Mt Washington (6288 ft *1916 m*), New Hampshire, USA, 24 Apr. 1934. **UK**: 144 mph *231 km/h* (125 knots). Coire Cas ski lift (3525 ft *1074 m*) Cairngorm, Highland 6 Mar. 1967. (NB—The 177·2 mph reading widely reported from Saxa Vord, Unst, Shetland Islands, on 16 Feb. 1962 was unofficially recorded with non-standard equipment.) Windiest place (**world**): Commonwealth Bay, George V coast, Antarctica, several 200 mph *320 km/h* gales each year. **UK**: Tiree, Strathclyde annual average 17·4 mph *28 km/h*.

Rainfall: Highest (**world**) **Minute**: 1·23 in *31,2 mm* Unionville, Maryland, USA, 4 July 1956; **Day**: 73·62 in *1870 mm* Cilaos, La Réunion Island, on 15–16 March 1952. S. Indian Ocean; **12 months**: 1041·78 in *26 461 mm* Cherrapunji, Assam, 1 Aug. 1860 to 31 July 1961. Highest (**UK**) **Day**: 11·00 in *279 mm* Martinstown, Dorset, 18–19 July 1955; **Year**: 257·0 in *6527 mm* Sprinkling Tarn, Cumbria, in 1954. Wettest Place (**world**) Mt Wai-'ale'ale (5148 ft *1569 m*),

Kauai I, Hawaiian Islands, annual average 451 in *11 455 mm* (1920–72). Most rainy Days in a Year (**world**) up to 350 on Mt. Wai-'ale-'ale; **British Isles**: 309 at Ballynahinch, Galway, Ireland, in 1923.

Lowest (**world**) at places in the Desierto de Atacama of Chile, including Calama, where no rain has ever been recorded in the c. 400 years to 1971. Lowest (**UK**) Year: 9·29 in *236 mm* Margate, Kent, in 1921. Longest Drought: 73 days from 4 March to 15 May 1893 at Mile End, Greater London.

Snowfall: Greatest (**world**) **Single Storm**: 175·4 in *4455 mm* Thompson Pass, Alaska, USA, 26–31 Dec. 1955; **Day**: 76 in *1870 mm* Silver Lake, Colorado, 14–15 Apr. 1921; **Year**: 1224·5 in *31 102 mm* Paradise Ranger Station, Mt Rainer, Washington, USA, in 1971–2. **UK**: Annual days of snowfall vary between extremes of 40 in the Shetland Islands and 5 in Penzance, Cornwall. The gulleys on Ben Nevis (4406 ft *1342 m*) were snowless only 7 times in the 31 years 1933–64. An accumulated level of 60 in *1524 mm* was recorded in February 1947 in both Upper Teesdale and the Clwyd Hills of North Wales.

Sunshine: Maximum (**world**): in parts of the eastern Sahara the sun shines strongly enough to cast a shadow for 4300 hours in a year or 97 per cent of possible. **UK**: The highest percentage for a month is 78·3 per cent (382 hours) at Pendennis Castle, Falmouth, Cornwall, June 1925.

Minimum (**world**): the longest periods of total darkness occur at the North Pole (over 9000 ft less altitude than South Pole) with 186 days. **UK**: the lowest monthly reading has been 6 min at Bunhill Row, London, in Dec. 1890. All 6 mins occurred on 7 December.

Ice Ages
Climatic variations occur in many time scales ranging from day to day weather changes in the shortest term and seasonal cycles up to major meteorological variations known as 'fourth order climatological changes.'

Weather is the present state of the climate in which temperature has been known to change 49 °F *27,2 °C* in 2 minutes. Second order temperature changes are those trends which now show that the mean temperature in the Northern Hemisphere which peaked in the period 1940–45 has dropped sharply by 2·7 °F *1,5 °C* to a point lower than the 1900 average when the world was emerging from the so called 'Little Ice Age' of the period 1595–1898.

Third order climatological changes are now being measured by the ratio of oxygen isotopes found in seashells. These reveal 8 Ice Ages in the last 700 000 years thus:

Ice Age	Duration BC	Nadirs BC
Last Ice Age	75 000–9000	60 000 & 18 000
Penultimate	130 000–105 000	115 000
Pre-penultimate	285 000–240 000	250 000
Fourth	355 000–325 000	330 000
Fifth	425 000–400 000	410 000
Sixth	520 000–500 000	510 000
Seventh	620 000–580 000	605 000
Eighth	685 000–645 000	670 000

Many theories have been advanced on the causes of Ice Ages which most profoundly affect human, animal and plant life. The most recent is that the Solar System which is revolving round the centre of the Milky Way at 480 000 mph *772 500 km/h* passes through dust belts which dim the Sun's heating and lighting powers.

Fourth order climatological change will be determined by the Sun's conversion from a yellow dwarf to a red giant as it burns 4 million tons of hydrogen per second. Thus in 5000 million years the oceans will boil and evaporate.

THE EARTH'S ATMOSPHERE BY LAYERS

Troposphere	—the realm of clouds, rain and snow in contact with the lithosphere (land) and hydrosphere (sea). The upper limit is 17 km *11 miles* (58 000 ft) at the equator or 6–8 km *3·7–4·9 miles* (19 700–25 000 ft) at the Poles. In middle latitudes in high pressure conditions the limits may be extended between 13 km *8 miles* to 7 km *4 miles* in low pressure conditions.
Stratosphere	—the second region of the atmosphere marked by a constant increase in temperature with altitude up to a maximum of 270°K at about 50 km *30 miles* (160 000 ft)
Mesosphere	—the third region of the atmosphere about 50 km *30 miles* (160 000 ft) marked by a rapid decrease in temperature with altitude to a minimum value even below 160 °K at about 85 km *55 miles* (290 000 ft) known as the mesopause.
Thermosphere	—the fourth region of the atmosphere above the mesosphere characterised by an unremitting rise in temperature up to a night maximum during minimum solar activity of 500 °K at about 230 km *140 miles* to above 1750 °K in a day of maximum solar activity at 500 km *310 miles* This region is sometimes termed the heterosphere because of the widely differing conditions in night and day and during solar calm and solar flare.
Exosphere	—this is the fifth and final stage at 500 km *310 miles* in which the upper atmosphere becomes space and in which temperature no longer has the customary terrestrial meaning.

CLOUD CLASSIFICATION

Genus (with abbreviation)	Ht of base (ft)	(m)	Temp at base level (°C)	Official description
Cirrus (Ci)	16 500 to 45 000	5000 to 13 700	−20 to −60	Detached clouds in the form of white delicate filaments, or white or mostly white patches or narrow bands. They have a fibrous (hair-like) appearance or a silky sheen, or both.
Cirrocumulus (Cc)	16 500 to 45 000	5000 to 13 700	−20 to −60	Thin, white patch, sheet or layer of cloud without shading, composed of very small elements in the form of grains, ripples, etc., merged or separate, and more or less regularly arranged.
Cirrostratus (Cs)	16 500 to 45 000	5000 to 13 700	−20 to −60	Transparent, whitish cloud veil of fibrous or smooth appearance, totally or partly covering the sky, and generally producing halo phenomena.
Altocumulus (Ac)	6500 to 23 000	2000 to 7000	+10 to −30	White or grey, or both white and grey, patch, sheet or layer of cloud, generally with shading, composed of laminae, rounded masses, rolls, etc. which are sometimes partly fibrous or diffuse, and which may or may not be merged.
Altostratus (As)	6500 to 23 000	2000 to 7000	+10 to −30	Greyish or bluish cloud sheet or layer of striated, fibrous or uniform appearance, totally or partly covering the sky, and having parts thin enough to reveal the sun at least vaguely.
Nimbostratus (Ns)	3000 to 10 000	900 to 3000	+10 to −15	Grey cloud layer, often dark, the appearance of which is rendered diffuse by more or less continually falling rain or snow which in most cases reaches the ground. It is thick enough throughout to blot out the sun. Low, ragged clouds frequently occur below the layer with which they may or may not merge.
Stratocumulus (Sc)	1500 to 6500	460 to 2000	+15 to −5	Grey or whitish, or both grey and whitish, patch, sheet or layer of cloud which almost always has dark parts, composed of tessellations, rounded masses, rolls, etc., which are non-fibrous (except for virga) and which may or may not be merged.
Stratus (St)	surface to 1500	surface to 460	+20 to −5	Generally grey cloud layer with a fairly uniform base, which may give drizzle, ice prisms or snow grains. When the sun is visible through the cloud its outline is clearly discernible. Stratus does not produce halo phenomena (except possibly at very low temperatures). Sometimes stratus appears in the form of ragged patches.
Cumulus (Cu)	1500 to 6500	460 to 2000	+15 to −5	Detached clouds, generally dense and with sharp outlines, developing vertically in the form of rising mounds, domes or towers, of which the bulging upper part often resembles a cauliflower. The sunlit parts of these clouds are mostly brilliant white; their bases are relatively dark and nearly horizontal.
Cumulonimbus (Cb)	1500 to 6500	460 to 2000	+15 to −5	Heavy and dense cloud, with a considerable vertical extent, in the form of a mountain or huge towers. At least part of its upper portion is usually smooth, or fibrous or striated, and nearly always flattened; this part often spreads out in the shape of an anvil or vast plume. Under the base of this cloud, which is often very dark, there are frequently low ragged clouds either merged with it or not, and precipitation, sometimes in the form of virga.

Northern and Southern Lights

Polar lights are known as Aurora Borealis in the northern hemisphere and Aurora Australis in the southern hemisphere. These luminous phenomena are caused by electrical solar discharges in the upper atmosphere between altitudes of 620 miles *1000 km* and 45 miles *72,5 km* and are usually visible only in the higher latitudes.

It is believed that in an auroral display some 100 million protons (hydrogen nuclei) strike each square centimetre of the upper atmosphere each second. Colours vary from yellow-green (attenuated oxygen), reddish (very low pressure oxygen), red below green (molecular nitrogen below ionised oxygen) or bluish (ionised nitrogen). Displays, which occur on every dark night in the year above 70° N or below 70° S (eg Northern Canada or Antarctica), vary in frequency with the 11-year sunspot cycle. Edinburgh may expect perhaps 25 displays a year against 7 in London, and Malta once a decade. The most striking recent displays over Britain occurred on 25 Jan. 1938 and 4–5 Sept. 1958. On 1 Sept. 1909, a display was reported from just above the equator at Singapore (1° 12′ N). In 1957 203 displays were recorded in the Shetland Islands (geometric Lat. 63° N).

MATHEMATICS

Mensuration

Triangle
area $= \frac{1}{2}ah$
Square
area $= a^2$
Circle
$d = 2r$
circumference $= 2\pi r$
area $= \pi r^2$
Ellipse
area $= \pi ab$
Trapezium
area $= \frac{1}{2}(m + n)h$
Cube
volume $= a^3$
surface area $= 6a^2$
Sphere
volume $= \frac{4}{3}\pi r^3$
surface area $= 4\pi r^2$
Cone
volume $= \frac{1}{3}\pi r^2 h$
surface area $= \pi r l$
Cylinder
volume $= \pi r^2 h$
curved surface area $= 2\pi r h$
total surface area $= 2\pi r h + 2\pi r^2$
$= 2\pi r(h + r)$
Pyramid
volume $= \frac{1}{3}a^2 h$
surface area $= a^2 + 2la$
Regular polygons
area $= \frac{1}{4}na^2 \cot(180/n)$
where n is the number of sides and a the
length of one side

	number of sides	area
pentagon	5	$1{\cdot}721a^2$
hexagon	6	$2{\cdot}598a^2$
heptagon	7	$3{\cdot}634a^2$
octagon	8	$4{\cdot}829a^2$

Mathematical symbols

$=$ equal to
$\neq$ not equal to
   identically equal to
$>$ greater than (or remainder)
$<$ less than
   not greater than
   not less than
$\geqslant$ equal to or greater than
$\leqslant$ equal to or less than
$\doteqdot$ approximately equal to
$+$ plus
$-$ minus
$\pm$ plus or minus
$\times$ multiplication (times)
$\div$ divided by
$()\,[]\,\{\}$ brackets, square brackets, enveloping brackets
$\parallel$ parallel
   not parallel
   numbers to follow (USA)
$\%$ per cent(um) (hundred)
$\%_0$ per mille (thousand)
$\propto$ varies with
∞ infinity
$r!$ factorial r
or $\underline{r}$
$\sqrt{}$ square root
$\sqrt[n]{}$ nth root
r^n r to the power n
$\triangle$ triangle or increment
   or $\sim$ difference
Σ summation
$\int$ integration sign
$^\circ\,'\,''$ degree, minute second $(1^\circ = 60',$
   $1' = 60'')$

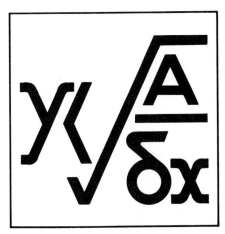

$\rightarrow$ appropriate limit of
$\therefore$ therefore
$\because$ because
$\varnothing$ diameter

Algebra

$x^m \times x^n = x^{m+n}$
$x^m \div x^n = x^{m-n}$
$(x^m)^n = x^{mn}$
$y = \log_n x$ means $x = n^y$
$\log(xy) = \log x + \log y$
$\log(x/y) = \log x - \log y$
$\log x^n = n \log x$
$\log(\sqrt[n]{x}) = \frac{1}{n} \log x$
$\log_m x = \log_n x \times \log_m n$
so that
$\log_{10} x = \log_e x \times \log_{10} e$
$= 0{\cdot}4343 \log_e x$

$x^2 - a^2 = (x + a)(x - a)$
$x^3 \pm a^3 = (x \pm a)(x^2 \mp ax + a^2)$
$(x \pm a)^2 = x^2 \pm 2ax + a^2$
$(x \pm a)^3 = x^3 \pm 3x^2 a + 3xa^2 \pm a^3$
$(x + a)^n = {}_nC_0 x^n + {}_nC_1 x^{n-1}a$
$+ {}_nC_2 x^{n-2}a^2 + \cdots$
$+ {}_nC_r x^{n-r}a^r + \cdots + {}_nC_n a^n$
where ${}_nC_r = n!/(n-r)!r!$ and
$n! = n(n-1)(n-2)\ldots 3.2.1$
Note that $0! = 1$.

The roots of the quadratic equation
$ax^2 + bx + c = 0$
are $x = \dfrac{-b \pm \sqrt{(b^2 - 4ac)}}{2a}$
If the roots are α and β then
$\alpha + \beta = -(b/a)$
and $\alpha\beta = c/a$

The sum to n terms of the arithmetic series
$a, a + d, a + 2d, \ldots$
is $S_n = \frac{1}{2}n[2a + (n-1)d]$
The sum to n terms of the geometric series
$a, ar, ar^2, \ldots$
is $S_n = \dfrac{a(1 - r^n)}{1 - r}$, where $r \neq 1$
$= na$, where $r = 1$

Trigonometry

Trigonometry (from the Greek *trigonon*, triangle; *metria*, measurement) as a science may be traced back to work attributed to Hipparchus (*fl.* 150 BC), the Greek astronomer. Further contributions were made in India, Iraq, Italy and Persia between AD 800 and 1400. The six ratios received their standard names c. 1550. The earliest com-

plete trigonometrical tables were published by Rhaeticus in 1596. The word trigonometry in English dates from 1614.

The division of the circle into 360 degrees dates from Ptolemy (AD 85–165) but at that time it was the circumference which was divided into 360 equal arcs. The sexagesimal sub-divisions of the degree are named after the latin *pars minuta prima* for the primary sub-division into 1/60th parts of a degree and *pars minuta secunda* for a second sub-division into 1/3600th parts of a degree, hence the modern terms minute ' and second ". The systematic use of decimals c. 1580 and of negative numbers c. 1610 greatly facilitated the science.

Trigonometry depends upon the fact that the corresponding sides of equiangular triangles are proportional. The three principal ratios are:
The sine (sin) of an angle
$$= \frac{\text{side opposite angle}}{\text{hypotenuse}}$$
The cosine (cos) of an angle
$$= \frac{\text{side adjacent to angle}}{\text{hypotenuse}}$$
The tangent (tan) of an angle
$$= \frac{\text{side opposite angle}}{\text{side adjacent to angle}}$$

Mnemonics
Opposite over Adjacent means Tangent (O/AMT)—Old and Ancient Motor Transport
Opposite over Hypotenuse means Sine (O/HMS)—On Her Majesty's Service
Adjacent over Hypotenuse means Cosine (A/HMC)—Algebra Helps Mental Clarity

Formulae
$\sin(A \pm B) = \sin A \cos B \pm \sin B \cos A$
$\cos(A \pm B) = \cos A \cos B \mp \sin A \sin B$
$\tan(A \pm B) = \dfrac{\tan A \pm \tan B}{1 \mp \tan A \tan B}$

$\sin A \pm \sin B$
$$= 2 \sin\left(\frac{A \pm B}{2}\right) \cos\left(\frac{A \mp B}{2}\right)$$
$\cos A + \cos B$
$$= 2 \cos\left(\frac{B - A}{2}\right) \cos\left(\frac{B + A}{2}\right)$$
$\cos A - \cos B$
$$= 2 \sin\left(\frac{B - A}{2}\right) \sin\left(\frac{B + A}{2}\right)$$

$\sin 2A = 2 \sin A \cos A$
$\cos 2A = \cos^2 A - \sin^2 A = 2\cos^2 A - 1$
$= 1 - 2\sin^2 A$

$\sin^2 A + \cos^2 A = 1$ (Pythagoras)
$\tan^2 A = \sec^2 A - 1$
$\cot^2 A = \operatorname{cosec}^2 A - 1$

Constants

$\pi = 3{\cdot}14159\ldots$ $e = 2{\cdot}71828\ldots$
$\dfrac{1}{\pi} = 0{\cdot}31831\ldots$ $\log_{10} e = 0{\cdot}43429\ldots$
$\log_{10} \pi = 0{\cdot}49715\ldots$

In the triangle ABC, sides a, b, c:
The sine rule:
$$\frac{a}{\sin A} = \frac{b}{\sin B} = \frac{c}{\sin C} = 2R$$
where R is the radius of the circumscribing circle.

$a^2 = b^2 + c^2 - 2bc \cos A$
$b^2 = c^2 + a^2 - 2ca \cos B$
$c^2 = a^2 + b^2 - 2ab \cos C$
and
$a = b \cos C + c \cos B$
$b = c \cos A + a \cos C$
$c = a \cos B + b \cos A$
If $s = \frac{1}{2}(a + b + c)$ then area of triangle
$= \sqrt{[s(s - a)(s - b)(s - c)]}$
$= \frac{1}{2}ab \sin C$

The radian

The radian is the unit of angle being the angle subtended at the centre of a circle by an arc equal in length to the radius. Thus 2π radians correspond to $360°$ and so

$$1 \text{ radian} = \frac{360}{2\pi} \text{ degrees} = 57.3°$$

Ratios greater than 90°

The sign of the three principal trigonometric ratios is shown in the accompanying diagram for the four quadrants. Those ratios which are *positive* are named in the given quadrant, the others being negative.

Calculus

y	$\dfrac{dy}{dx}$	$\displaystyle\int y\,dx$
x^n	nx^{n-1}	$\dfrac{x^{n+1}}{n+1} + C \ (n \neq -1)$
x^{-1}	$-x^{-2}$	$\log_e x + C$
e^{ax}	ae^{ax}	$\dfrac{1}{a} e^{ax} + C$
a^x	$a^x \log_e a$	$\dfrac{a^x}{\log_e a} + C$
$\log_e x$	$\dfrac{1}{x}$	$x(\log_e x - 1) + C$
$\sin ax$	$a \cos ax$	$-\dfrac{1}{a} \cos ax + C$
$\cos ax$	$-a \sin ax$	$\dfrac{1}{a} \sin ax + C$
$\tan ax$	$a \sec^2 ax$	$\dfrac{1}{a} \log_e \sec ax + C$
$\sinh ax$	$a \cosh ax$	$\dfrac{1}{a} \cosh ax + C$
$\cosh ax$	$a \sinh ax$	$\dfrac{1}{a} \sinh ax + C$
$\tanh ax$	$a \operatorname{sech}^2 ax$	$\dfrac{1}{a} \log_e (\cosh x) + C$

Where u, v are functions of x:
if $y = uv$

then $\dfrac{dy}{dx} = u\dfrac{dv}{dx} + v\dfrac{du}{dx}$;

if $y = \dfrac{u}{v}$

then $\dfrac{dy}{dx} = \dfrac{v\dfrac{du}{dx} - u\dfrac{dv}{dx}}{v^2}$

$\displaystyle\int u\dfrac{dv}{dx}\,dx = uv - \int v\dfrac{du}{dx}\,dx$

Series
Maclaurin's

$f(x) = f(0) + xf'(0) + \dfrac{x^2}{2!}f''(0)$
$$+ \dfrac{x^3}{3!}f'''(0) + \cdots$$

Taylor's

$f(x + h) = f(h) + xf'(h) + \dfrac{x^2}{2!}f''(h)$
$$+ \dfrac{x^3}{3!}f'''(h) + \cdots$$

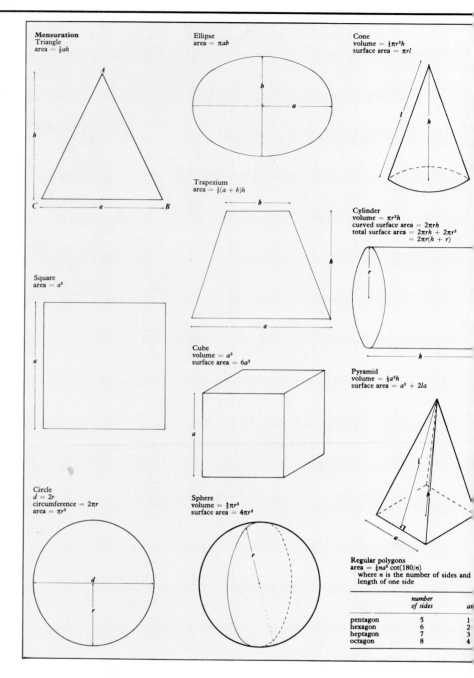

Mensuration

Triangle
area $= \frac{1}{2}ah$

Ellipse
area $= \pi ab$

Cone
volume $= \frac{1}{3}\pi r^2 h$
surface area $= \pi rl$

Trapezium
area $= \frac{1}{2}(a + b)h$

Cylinder
volume $= \pi r^2 h$
curved surface area $= 2\pi rh$
total surface area $= 2\pi rh + 2\pi r^2$
$= 2\pi r(h + r)$

Square
area $= a^2$

Cube
volume $= a^3$
surface area $= 6a^2$

Pyramid
volume $= \frac{1}{3}a^2 h$
surface area $= a^2 + 2la$

Circle
$d = 2r$
circumference $= 2\pi r$
area $= \pi r^2$

Sphere
volume $= \frac{4}{3}\pi r^3$
surface area $= 4\pi r^2$

Regular polygons
area $= \frac{1}{4}na^2 \cot(180/n)$
where n is the number of sides and length of one side

	number of sides	ar
pentagon	5	1
hexagon	6	2
heptagon	7	3
octagon	8	4

$e^x = 1 + x + \dfrac{x^2}{2!} + \dfrac{x^3}{3!} + \cdots$

$\sin x = x - \dfrac{x^3}{3!} + \dfrac{x^5}{5!} - \dfrac{x^7}{7!} + \cdots$

$\cos x = 1 - \dfrac{x^2}{2!} + \dfrac{x^4}{4!} - \dfrac{x^6}{6!} + \cdots$

$\sinh x = x + \dfrac{x^3}{3!} + \dfrac{x^5}{5!} + \dfrac{x^7}{7!} + \cdots$

$\cosh x = 1 + \dfrac{x^2}{2!} + \dfrac{x^4}{4!} + \dfrac{x^6}{6!} + \cdots$

Binary system

The numerical notation in ordinary use is the decimal or denary system with its ten symbols: 0, 1, 2, 3, 4, 5, 6, 7, 8 and 9.

The Imperial system of weights and measures utilises several other systems, viz. 3 ft to 1 yd (ternary), 12 in to 1 ft (duodenary), 20 fluid oz to 1 pint (vigesimal), etc. The most primitive notation is the unitary system of one symbol as used for instance by a cricket scorer.

Because electric switches have two essential positions, 'on' or 'off', the binary system is ideally suited to the programming of computers and is being used increasingly.

To convert the denary number, say 17, to its binary form it is necessary to divide successively through by two, recording the remainders which can only be 1 or 0 thus:

$2\ 17 = 8 > 1$ which $\div 2 = 4 > 0$ which $\div 2 = 2 > 0$ which $\div 2 = 1 > 0$, thus 17 (decimal) is 10001 binary.

This represents 1×2^4 which is 16, $0 \times 2^3, 0 \times 2^2, 0 \times 2^1$ and 1×2^0 which is 1 giving a total of 17.

To convert a binary number to its decimal or denary form, it is simplest to regard the rightermost column as the 2^0 column, thence reading to the left $2^1, 2^2, 2^3, 2^4$, etc., columns.

Thus 11101 reads $1 \times 2^4 = 16 + 1 \times 2^3 = 8 + 1 \times 2^2 = 4 + 0 \times 2^1 = 0, + 1 \times 2^0 = 1$, i.e. 29.

BINARY CONVERSION continued

A binary conversion scale thus reads:

Denary	Binary	Denary	Binary
1	1	16	10000
2	10	17	10001
3	11	18	10010
4	100	19	10011
5	101	20	10100
6	110	32	100000
7	111	64	1000000
8	1000	100	1100100
9	1001	128	10000000
10	1010	144	10010000
11	1011	150	10010110
12	1100	200	11001000
13	1101	250	11111010
14	1110	500	111110100
15	1111	1000	1111101000

Fractions are also recorded in the binary notation, thus:

Denary	Binary
·5	= ·1
·25	= ·01
·125	= ·001
·0625	= ·0001
·03125	= ·00001
·015625	= ·000001

Thus the binary fraction ·10011 is $·5 + 0 + 0 + ·0625 + 0·03125 = ·59375$.

Odds on perfect deals

The number of possible hands with four players using a full pack of 52 cards is $\dfrac{52!}{(39!)(13!)}$ or 635 013 559 600. Thus the odds against picking up a specific complete suit are 635 013 559 599 to 1 or *any* complete suit 158 753 389 899 to 1.

The number of possible deals is $\dfrac{52!}{(13!)^4 (4!)}$

or 2 235 197 406 895 366 368 301 560 000 or roughly $2·23 \times 10^{27}$. A complete suit is thus to be expected once in every 39 688 347 497 deals.

Cases throughout the world of single complete suits are in practice reported about once per year. This being so, cases of two players receiving complete suits could be expected with the present volume of card playing once every 2000 million years and this has only once been recorded. Cases of all four players picking up complete suits might be expected once in 56 000 billion years. This latter occurrence was reported in New Zealand on 8 July 1958, in Illinois, USA, on 9 Feb. 1963, again in Illinois on 30 Mar. 1963 and again 3 days later in Greybull, Wyoming. This is so unlikely, not merely to strain credulity, but to be virtually certain evidence of rigged shuffling or hoaxing.

Sets

If A is a set and x is an element of (belongs to) A then this is written:

$$x \in A$$

The symbol $\in$ is used for 'is an element of'. The negation is:

$$x \notin A$$

x is not an element of A.

Subsets

Set B is a *subset* of set A if every element of B is an element of A. This is denoted

$$B \subseteq A$$

Sometimes the symbol $\subset$ is used instead of $\subseteq$. Note that a set A is always a subset of itself:

$$A \subseteq A$$

Intersection

The *intersection* of sets A and B is denoted:

$$A \cap B$$

and is the set of all elements which belong to both A and B.

If sets A, B have no element in common they are called *disjoint* sets, in which case:

$$A \cap B = \emptyset$$

Where $\emptyset$ is the *empty set* or *null set*, i.e. the set with no elements.

Union

The union of sets A, B is denoted

$$A \cup B$$

and is the set of *all* the elements of A together with *all* the elements of B.

For all sets A, B, C:

$$A \cup B = B \cup A$$
$$A \cap B = B \cap A$$
$$A \cap (B \cup C) = (A \cap B) \cup (A \cap C)$$

Properties of number systems

If n, a, b, c are any real or complex numbers then

$a + b = b + a$
  Addition is *commutative*
$a + (b + c) = (a + b) + c$
  and *associative*
$a \times b = b \times a$
  Multiplication is *commutative*
$a \times (b \times c) = (a \times b) \times c$
  and *associative*
$n \times (a + b) = (n \times a) + (n \times b)$
  Multiplication is *distributive* over addition

METROLOGY

In essence, measurement involves *comparison*: the measurement of a physical quantity entails comparing it with an agreed and clearly defined *standard*. The result is expressed in terms of a *unit*, which is the name for a standard, preceded by a number which is the *ratio* of the measured quantity of the appropriate fixed unit.

A *system of units* is centred on a small number of *base units*. These relate to the fundamental standards of length, mass and time, together with a few others to extend the system to a wider range of physical measurements, e.g. to electrical and optical quantities. There are also two geometrical units which belong to a class known as *supplementary units*.

These few base units can be combined to form a large number of *derived units*. For example, units of area, velocity and acceleration are formed from units of length and time. Thus, very many different kinds of measurement can be made and recorded employing only about half a dozen base units.

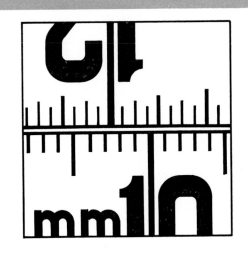

For convenience, *multiples* and *submultiples* of both base and derived units are frequently used: kilometres and millimetres.

Historically, several systems of units have evolved: in Britain, the imperial system: in the United States, the US customary units; and forms of the metric system (CGS and MKS), employed universally in science and generally in very many countries of the world.

The International System of Units (Système International d'Unités or SI) is a modern form of the metric system. It was finally agreed at the Eleventh General Conference of Weights and Measures in October 1960 and is now being adopted throughout most of the world.

The yard (yd). This is equal to 0·9144 metre exactly (Weights and Measures Act, 1963).

The pound (lb). This is equal to 0·453 592 37 kilogram exactly (Weights and Measures Act, 1963).

The gallon (gal). 'The space occupied by 10 pounds weight of distilled water of density 0·998 859 gram per millilitre weighed in air of density 0·001 217 gram per millilitre against weights of density 8·136 gram per millilitre (Weights and Measures Act, 1963). The definition of the gallon in the meaning of the 1963 Weights and Measures Act uses the 1901 definition of the litre [1 litre (1901) = 1·000 028 dm³].

Other units of length employed are:

animal stature	the hand = 4 in. *NB*—a horse of 14 hands 3 in to the withers is often written 14·3 hands.
surveying	the link = 7·92 in or a hundredth part of a chain.
approximate	the span = 9 in (from the span of the hand).
biblical	the cubit = 18 in.
approximate	the pace = 30 in (from the stride).
nautical	the cable = 120 fathoms or 240 yd.
navigation	the UK nautical mile = 6080 ft at the Equator.
navigation	the International nautical mile (adopted also by the USA on 1 July 1954) = 6076·1 ft (0·99936 of a UK nautical mile)

The use of the metric system was legalised in the United Kingdom in 1897. The Halsbury Committee recommended the introduction of decimal currency in September 1963. The intention to switch to the metric system was declared on 24 May 1965 by the President of the Board of Trade 'within ten years'. The date for the official adoption of the metric system was announced on 1 Mar. 1966 to be 'February 1971.' On Tuesday, 2 Mar. 1976, the Government decided not to proceed with the second reading of the Weights and Measures (Metrication) Act.

Base units

Quantity	Unit	Symbol	Definition
length	metre	m	the length equal to 1 650 763·73 wavelengths in vacuum of the radiation corresponding to the transition between the levels $2p_{10}$ and $5d_5$ of the krypton-86 atom.
mass	kilogram	kg	the mass of the international prototype of the kilogram, which is in the custody of the Bureau International des Poids et Mésures (BIPM) at Sevres near Paris, France.
time	second	s	the duration of 9 192 631 770 periods of the radiation corresponding to the transition between the two hyperfine levels of the ground state of the caesium-133 atom.
electric current	ampere	A	that constant current which, if maintained in two straight parallel conductors of infinite length of negligible circular cross-section, and placed 1 metre apart in vacuum, would produce between these conductors a force equal to 2×10^{-7} newton per metre of length.
thermodynamic temperature	kelvin	K	the fraction 1/273·16 of the thermodynamic temperature of the triple point of water. The triple point of water is the point where water, ice and water vapour are in equilibrium.
luminous intensity	candela	cd	the luminous intensity, in the perpendicular direction, of a surface of 1/600 000 square metre of a black body at the temperature of freezing platinum under a pressure of 101 325 newtons per square metre.
amount of substance	mole	mol	the amount of substance of a system which contains as many elementary entities as there are atoms in 0·012 kilogram of carbon-12.

Supplementary units

plane angle	radian	rad	the plane angle between two radii of a circle which cut off on the circumference an arc equal in length to the radius.
solid angle	steradian	sr	the solid angle which having its vertex in the centre of a sphere, cuts off an area of the surface of the sphere equal to that of a square having sides of length equal to the radius of the sphere.

Derived units

Quantity	Unit	Symbol	Expression in terms of other SI units
area	square metre	m^2	—
volume	cubic metre	m^3	—
velocity	metre per second	$m \cdot s^{-1}$	—
angular velocity	radian per second	$rad\ s^{-1}$	—
acceleration	metre per second squared	$m \cdot s^{-2}$	—
angular acceleration	radian per second squared	$rad\ s^{-2}$	—
frequency	hertz	Hz	s^{-1}
density	kilogram per cubic metre	$kg \cdot m^{-3}$	—
momentum	kilogram metre per second	$kg \cdot m \cdot s^{-1}$	—
angular momentum	kilogram metre squared per second	$kg \cdot m^2 \cdot s^{-1}$	—
moment of inertia	kilogram metre squared	$kg \cdot m^2$	—
force	newton	N	$kg \cdot m \cdot s^{-2}$
pressure, stress	pascal	Pa	$N \cdot m^{-2} = kg \cdot m^{-1} \cdot s^{-2}$
work, energy, quantity of heat	joule	J	$N \cdot m = kg \cdot m^2 \cdot s^{-2}$
power	watt	W	$J \cdot s^{-1} = kg \cdot m^2 \cdot s^{-3}$
surface tension	newton per metre	$N \cdot m^{-1}$	$kg \cdot s^{-2}$
dynamic viscosity	newton second per metre squared	$N \cdot s \cdot m^{-2}$	$kg \cdot m^{-1} \cdot s^{-1}$
kinematic viscosity	metre squared per second	$m^2 \cdot s^{-1}$	—
temperature	degree Celsius	°C	—
thermal coefficient of linear expansion	per degree Celsius, or per kelvin	$°C^{-1}, K^{-1}$	—
thermal conductivity	watt per metre degree C	$W \cdot m^{-1} \cdot °C^{-1}$	$kg \cdot m \cdot s^{-3} \cdot °C^{-1}$
heat capacity	joule per kelvin	$J \cdot K^{-1}$	$kg \cdot m^2 \cdot s^{-2} \cdot K^{-1}$
specific heat capacity	joule per kilogram kelvin	$J \cdot kg^{-1} \cdot K^{-1}$	$m^2 \cdot s^{-2} \cdot K^{-1}$
specific latent heat	joule per kilogram	$J\ kg^{-1}$	$m^2 \cdot s^{-2}$
electric charge	coulomb	C	$A \cdot s$
potential difference electromotive force,	volt	V	$W \cdot A^{-1} = kg \cdot m^2 \cdot s^{-3} \cdot A^{-1}$

DERIVED UNITS *continued*

electric resistance	ohm	Ω	$V \cdot A^{-1} = kg \cdot m^2 \cdot s^{-3} \cdot A^{-2}$
electric conductance	siemens	S	$A \cdot V^{-1} = kg^{-1} \cdot m^{-2} \cdot s^3 \cdot A^2$
electric capacitance	farad	F	$A \cdot s \cdot V^{-1} = kg^{-1} \cdot m^{-2} \cdot s^4 \cdot A^2$
inductance	henry	H	$V \cdot s \cdot A^{-1} = kg \cdot m^2 \cdot s^{-2} \cdot A^{-2}$
magnetic flux	weber	Wb	$V \cdot s = kg \cdot m^2 \cdot s^{-2} \cdot A^{-1}$
magnetic flux density	tesla	T	$wb \cdot m^{-2} = kg \cdot s^{-2} \cdot A^{-1}$
magnetomotive force	ampere	A	
luminous flux	lumen	lm	$cd \cdot sr$
illumination	lux	lx	$lm \cdot m^{-2} = cd \cdot sr \cdot m^{-2}$
radiation activity	becquerel	Bq	s^{-1}
radiation absorbed dose	gray	Gy	$J \cdot kg^{-1} = m^2 \cdot s^{-2}$

Multiples and Sub-Multiples
In the metric system the following decimal multiples and sub-multiples are used:

Prefix	Symbol	British Equivalent	Factor
atto- (Danish *atten* = eighteen)	a	trillionth part	$\times 10^{-18}$
femto- (Danish *femten* = fifteen)	f	thousand billionth part	$\times 10^{-15}$
pico- (L. *pico* = miniscule)	p	billionth part	$\times 10^{-12}$
nano- (L. *nanus* = dwarf)	n	thousand millionth part	$\times 10^{-9}$
micro- (Gk. *mikros* = small)	μ	millionth part	$\times 10^{-6}$
milli- (L. *mille* = thousand)	m	thousandth part	$\times 10^{-3}$
centi- (L. *centum* = hundred)	c	hundredth part	$\times 10^{-2}$
deci- (L. *decimus* = tenth)	d	tenth part	$\times 10^{-1}$
deca- (Gk. *deka* = ten)	da	tenfold	$\times 10$
hecto- (Gk. *hekaton* = hundred)	h	hundredfold	$\times 10^2$
kilo- (Gk. *chilioi* = thousand)	k	thousandfold	$\times 10^3$
mega- (Gk. *megas* = large)	M	millionfold	$\times 10^6$
giga- (Gk. *gigas* = mighty)	G	thousand millionfold	$\times 10^9$
tera- (Gk. *teras* = monster)	T	billionfold	$\times 10^{12}$
peta- (Gk. *penta* = five)	P	thousand billionfold	$\times 10^{15}$
exa- (Gk. *hexa* = six)	E	million billionfold	$\times 10^{18}$

METRIC AND IMPERIAL UNITS AND CONVERSIONS

Unit	Equivalent	To convert to:	Multiply by ($\star$ = exact)
Length			
inch (in)	—	centimetre (cm)	2·54$\star$
foot (ft)	12 ins	metre	0·3048
yard (yd)	3 ft	metre	0·9144
mile	1760 yd	kilometre (km)	1·609344
fathom	6 ft	metre	1·8288
chain	22 yd	metre	20·1168
UK nautical mile	6080 ft	kilometre	1·853184
International nautical mile	6076·1 ft	kilometre	1·852$\star$
angstrom (Å)	10^{-10} m	micron	10^{-4}
Area			
square inch	—	square centimetre	6·4516
square foot	144 sq. in.	square metre	0·092903
square yard	9 sq. ft	square metre	0·836127
acre	4840 sq. yd	hectare (ha) (10^4 m^2)	0·404686
square mile	640 acres	square kilometre	2·589988
Volume			
cubic inch	—	cubic centimetre	16·3871
cubic foot	1728 cu. in	cubic metre	0·028317
cubic yard	27 cu. ft	cubic metre	0·764555
Capacity			
litre	cubic decimetre	cubic centimetre	1000$\star$
pint	4 gills	litre or dm^3	0·568261
gallon	8 pints	litre or dm^3	4·54609
barrel (for beer)	36 gallons	hectolitre	1·63659
US gallon	0·832675 gallons	litre or dm^3	3·78541
US barrel (for petroleum)	42 US gallons	hectolitre	1·58983
fluid ounce		cubic centimetre	28·4131
Velocity			
feet per second (ft/s)	—	metres per second	0·3048
miles per hour (m.p.h.)	—	kilometres per hour	1·609344
U.K. knot	nautical mile/hour	kilometres per hour	1·853184
Acceleration			
foot per second per second (ft/s^2)	—	metres per second per second (m/s^2)	0·3048
Mass			
grain (gr)	—	gram (g)	64·7989
dram (dr)	27·3438 gr	gram	1·77185

Unit	Equivalent	To convert to:	Multiply by ($\star$ = exact)
ounce	16 drams	gram	28·3495
pound	16 ounces	kilogram	0·45359237$\star$
stone	14 pounds	kilogram	6·35029
quarter	28 pounds	kilogram	12·7006
hundredweight (cwt)	112 pounds	kilogram	50·8023
ton	2240 pounds	tonne (= 1000 kg)	1·01605
Density			
pounds per cubic inch	—	grams per cubic centimetre	27·6799
pounds per cubic foot	—	kilograms per cubic metre	16·0185
Force			
dyne (dyn)	10^{-3} Newton	—	—
poundal (pdl)	—	Newton	0·138255
pound-force (lbf)	—	Newton	4·44822
tons-force	—	kilonewton (kN)	9·9604
kilogram-force (kgf)	—	Newton	9·80665
Energy (Work, Heat)			
erg	10^{-7} Joule	—	—
horse-power (hp)	—	kilowatt (kw)	0·745700
therm	—	MJ	105·506
kilowatt hour (kwh)	—	MJ	3·6
calorie	—	Joule	4·1868$\star$
British thermal unit (Btu)	—	kilo-Joule (kJ)	1·05566
Pressure, Stress			
millibar (mbar)	100 Pa	—	—
atmosphere (atm)	—	k Pa	101·325
pounds per square inch (psi)	—	Pa	6894·76

IMPERIAL TO METRIC CONVERSIONS

A practical look at changes in measurement which affect us most frequently in daily life ..

(some of the conversions are approximations i.e. 30 m.p.h. = 48·28 k.p.h.)

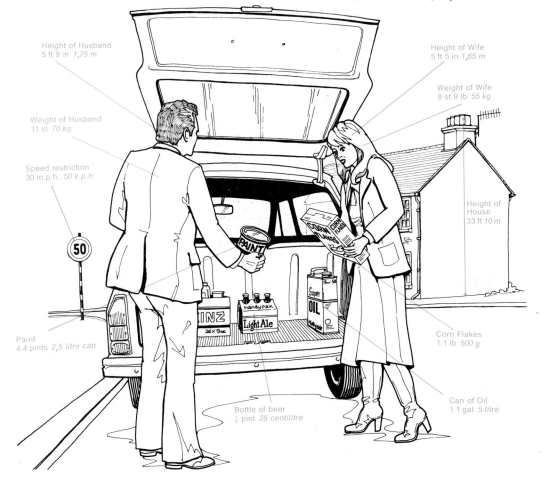

Height of Husband
5 ft 9 in *1,75 m*

Height of Wife
5 ft 5 in *1,65 m*

Weight of Wife
8 st 9 lb *55 kg*

Weight of Husband
11 st *70 kg*

Speed restriction
30 m.p.h. *50 k.p.h.*

Height of House
33 ft *10 m*

Paint
4.4 pints *2,5 litre can*

Corn Flakes
1.1 lb *500 g*

Bottle of beer
½ pint *28 centilitre*

Can of Oil
1.1 gal *5 litre*

PHYSICS

Newton's laws of motion

These three self-evident principles were discovered experimentally before Newton's time but were first formulated by him.

Law 1. The law of inertia
A particle will either remain at rest or continue to move with uniform velocity unless acted upon by a force.

Law 2
The acceleration of a particle is directly proportional to the force producing it and inversely proportional to the mass of the particle.

Law 3. The law of action and reaction
Forces, the results of interactions of two bodies, always appear in pairs. In each pair the forces are equal in magnitude and opposite in direction.

Equations of motion

Where
u is the initial velocity of a body;
v is its final velocity after time t;
s is the distance it travels in this time;
a is the uniform acceleration it undergoes.
then

$$v = u + at$$
$$s = ut + \tfrac{1}{2}at^2$$
$$v^2 = u^2 + 2as$$

Laws of Thermodynamics

Thermodynamics (Greek, *thermos*, hot; *dynamis*, power) is the quantitative treatment of the relation of heat to natural and mechanical forms of energy.

There are three Laws of Thermodynamics.

The **First Law**, derived from the principle of Conservation of Energy, may be stated 'Energy can neither be created nor destroyed, so that a given system can gain or lose energy only to the extent that it takes it from or passes it to its environment'. This is expressed as

$$E_f - E_i = \Delta$$

where E_i is the initial energy, E_f the final content of energy and Δ the change of energy. The impossibility of perpetual motion follows directly from this. The law applies only to systems of constant mass.

The **Second Law** concerns the concept of entropy (Gk. *en*, into; *tropos*, a changing) which is the relation between the temperature of and the heat content within any system. A large amount of lukewarm water may contain the same amount of heat as a little boiling water. The levelling out (equalising) of heat within a system (i.e. the pouring of a kettle of boiling water into a lukewarm bath) is said to increase the entropy of that system of two vessels. Any system, including the Universe, naturally tends to increase its entropy, i.e. to distribute its heat. If the Universe can be regarded as a closed system, it follows from the Law that it will have a finite end, i.e. when it has finally dissipated or unwound itself to the point that its entropy attains a maximal level —this is referred to as the 'Heat Death' of the Universe. From this it would also follow that the Universe must then have had a finite beginning for if it had had a creation an infinite time ago heat death would by now inevitably have set in. The second Law, published in Berlin in 1850 by Rudolf Clausius (1822–88), states 'Heat cannot of itself pass from a colder to a warmer body'. This is mathematically expressed by the inequality

$$\Delta > 0$$

i.e. the change of entropy in any heat exchanging system and its surroundings taken together is always greater than zero.

The **Third Law** is not a general law but applies only to pure crystalline solids and states that at absolute zero the entropies of such substances are zero.

Celsius and Fahrenheit Compared

The two principal temperature scales are Celsius and Fahrenheit. The former was devised in 1743 by J P Christen (1683–1755) but is referred to by its present name because of the erroneous belief that it was invented by Anders Celsius (1701–44). The latter is named after Gabriel Daniel Fahrenheit (1686–1736), a German physicist. In a meteorological context the scale is still referred to in the United Kingdom as Centigrade though the name was otherwise abandoned in 1948.

To convert C to F, multiply the C reading by 9/5 and add 32.

To convert F to C, subtract 32 from the F reading and multiply by 5/9.

Useful comparisons are:

(1)	Absolute Zero	$= -273 \cdot 15°C$	$= -459 \cdot 67°F$
(2)	Point of Equality	$= -40 \cdot 0°C$	$= -40 \cdot 0°F$
(3)	Zero Fahrenheit	$= -17 \cdot 8°C$	$= 0 \cdot 0°F$
(4)	Freezing point of Water	$= 0 \cdot 0°C$	$= 32°F$
(5)	Normal Human Blood Temperature	$= 36 \cdot 9°C$	$= 98 \cdot 4°F$
(6)	100 Degrees F	$= 37 \cdot 8°C$	$= 100°F$
(7)	Boiling Point of Water (at standard pressure)	$= 100°C$	$= 212°F$

The fundamental physical constants

The constants are called 'fundamental' since they are used universally throughout all branches of science. Because of the unprecedented amount of new experimental and theoretical work being carried out, thorough revisions are now being published about once every five years, the last being in 1973. Values are reported such that the figure in brackets following the last digit is the estimated uncertainty of that digit, i.e. the speed of light $c = 2 \cdot 997\ 924\ 58\ (1) \times 10^8$ m s^{-1} could be written $c = (2 \cdot 997\ 924\ 58 \pm 0 \cdot 000\ 000\ 01) \times 10^8$ m s^{-1}. The unit m s^{-1} represents m/s or metres per second.

	Quantity	Symbol	Value	Units
general constants	Speed of light in vacuo	c	$2 \cdot 99792458\ (1) \times 10^8$	m·s^{-1}
	elementary charge	e	$1 \cdot 6021892\ (46) \times 10^{-19}$	C
	Planck's constant	h	$6 \cdot 626176\ (36) \times 10^{-34}$	J·s
		$h = h/2\pi$	$1 \cdot 0545887\ (57) \times 10^{-34}$	J·s
	gravitational constant	G	$6 \cdot 6720\ (41) \times 10^{-11}$	m³·s^{-2}·kg^{-1}
matter in bulk	Avogadro constant	N_A	$6 \cdot 022045\ (31) \times 10^{23}$	mol^{-1}
	atomic mass unit	$u = 1/N_A$	$1 \cdot 6605655\ (86) \times 10^{-27}$	kg
			$9 \cdot 315016\ (26) \times 10^2$	Mev
	faraday	$F = N_Ae$	$9 \cdot 648456\ (27) \times 10^4$	C·mol^{-1}
	normal volume of ideal gas	V_m	$2 \cdot 241383\ (70) \times 10^{-2}$	m³·mol^{-1}
	gas constant	R	$8 \cdot 31441\ (26)$	J·mol^{-1}·K^{-1}
			$8 \cdot 20568\ (26) \times 10^{-5}$	m³·atm·mol^{-1} K^{-1}
	Boltzmann constant	$k = R/N_A$	$1 \cdot 380662\ (44) \times 10^{-23}$	J·K^{-1}
electron	electron rest mass	m_e	$9 \cdot 109534\ (47) \times 10^{-31}$	kg
			$0 \cdot 5110034\ (14)$	Mev
	electron charge to mass ratio	e/m_e	$1 \cdot 7588047\ (49) \times 10^{11}$	C·kg^{-1}
proton	proton rest mass	m_p	$1 \cdot 6726485\ (86) \times 10^{-27}$	kg
			$9 \cdot 382796\ (27) \times 10^2$	Mev
neutron	neutron rest mass	m_n	$1 \cdot 6749543\ (86) \times 10^{-27}$	kg
			$9 \cdot 395731\ (27) \times 10^2$	Mev
energy conversion	million electron volt unit	Mev	$1 \cdot 7826758\ (51) \times 10^{-30}$	kg
			$1 \cdot 6021892\ (46) \times 10^{-13}$	J

THE FORCES OF PHYSICS

	range	force-carrying particle	
gravity	very long	graviton, g	acts on all matter: weak within the atom
weak force	short, about 10^{-15} cm	W-meson	acts on all the basic particles, leptons and quarks: involved in radioactive processes.
electromagnetic force	very long	photon γ	acts on all charged particles: provides the basis to the reactions of chemistry and biology.
strong force	short, 10^{-13} cm	meson	acts on the hadrons, e.g. the proton and neutron, and is responsible for binding the nucleus together. Is involved in nuclear reactions.
colour force	short, 10^{-13} cm	gluon	acts on the quarks, allowing them freedom of movement within the hadron, e.g. proton, but holding them firmly within it.

There are considered to be four basic forces in nature which differ very considerably in strength. These are listed here in ascending order of strength, together with a fifth, the superstrong colour force, the theory of which came into being in the early part of this decade. Its existence is a matter of speculation but it is offering a satisfying explanation of phenomena at the very heart of matter.

THE PARTICLES OF PHYSICS

The Quanta

	Symbol	Anti-particle symbol	Mass MeV	Spin	Electric Charge	Strangeness	Charm
photon	γ		0	1	0	0	0
graviton	g		0	2	0	0	0

In addition to the quanta, there are thought to be only 2 families, the leptons and the quarks which are elementary.

The Leptons

	Symbol	Anti-particle symbol	Mass MeV	Spin	Electric Charge	Strangeness	Charm
electron	e^-	e^+	0·511003	$\frac{1}{2}$	—1	0	0
muon	μ^-	μ^+	105·659	$\frac{1}{2}$	—1	0	0
electron neutrino	v_e	$\bar{v}_e$	0	$\frac{1}{2}$	0	0	0
muon neutrino	v_μ	$\bar{v}_\mu$	0	$\frac{1}{2}$	0	0	0

The Quarks

	Symbol	Anti-particle symbol	Mass MeV	Spin	Electric Charge	Strangeness	Charm
up	u	$\bar{u}$	100	$\frac{1}{2}$	$+\frac{2}{3}$	0	0
down	d	$\bar{d}$	100	$\frac{1}{2}$	$-\frac{1}{3}$	0	0
strange	s	$\bar{s}$	400	$\frac{1}{2}$	$-\frac{1}{3}$	—1	0
charmed	c	$\bar{c}$	1500	$\frac{1}{2}$	$+\frac{2}{3}$	0	+1

The other particles belong to the family of hadrons, and are constructed from the quarks: the baryons from 3 quarks and the mesons from 2. The following lists a few baryons and mesons.

The Hadrons

	Symbol	Anti-particle	Composition	Mass MeV	Spin	Electric charge	Strangeness	Charm
The Baryons								
proton	p^+	p^-	uud	938·280	$\frac{1}{2}$	+1	0	0
neutron	n^0	$\bar{n}^0$	udd	939·573	$\frac{1}{2}$	0	0	0
omega minus	Ω^-	$\bar{\Omega}^+$	sss	1672·2	$\frac{3}{2}$	—1	—3	0
The Mesons								
charged pion	π^+	π^-	$u\bar{d}$	139·569	0	+1	0	0
neutral pion	π^0		$u\bar{u} + d\bar{d}$	134·965	0	0	0	0
psi	ψ		$c\bar{c}$	3098	1	0	0	0
D°	D°	$\bar{D}°$	$c\bar{u}$	1865	0	0	0	+1

MILESTONES IN MODERN PHYSICS

Introduction

Physics is very much concerned with fundamental particles – the building blocks out of which the Universe is constructed – and the forces which bind and regulate them. Many theories have been proposed from time to time to provide a better understanding of the vast number of facts and observations which have accumulated. The main development of physics is essentially a series of unifications of these theories.

1687 Sir Isaac Newton (1643–1727) produced the great unifying theory of **gravitation** which linked the falling apple with the force which keeps the stars and planets in their courses. This made available for further scientific investigation one of the basic universal forces of nature, the force of gravity. The gravitational force, F, between two bodies of masses, m_1, m_2, distance, r, apart is given by

$$F = G \frac{m_1, m_2}{r^2}$$

where G is a Universal constant

By Newton's time there existed two rival theories to explain the passage of light from source to observer. One was the **particle theory** which maintained that light consists of vast numbers of minute particles ejected by the luminous body in all directions. Newton, who made so many brilliant advances in optics, favoured this theory. It accounted in a particularly simple way for the transmission of light through the vacuum of space, for its rectilinear propagation, and for the laws of reflection. The alternative was the **wave theory,** which assumed that light was transmitted by means of a wave motion. This would imply that light would bend round corners, but when it was discovered that the wavelength of the light was very small (about 1/2000th of a millimetre), it was realised that the effect would be small as is in fact observed. Light does not cast a perfectly sharp shadow. Further phenomena were discovered which demonstrated the wave nature of light and added support to that theory, eg interference and diffraction.

1820 Hans Christian Oersted (1777–1851) of Denmark, discovered that the flow of electric current in a conductor would cause a nearby compass needle to be deflected.

1831 Michael Faraday (1791–1867) the English physicist, uncovered the principle of magnetic induction which led to the invention of the dynamo. He showed that a change in the magnetic field surrounding a conductor could cause a flow of electrical current.

1865 The unification between magnetism and electricity was brought to full flower by the Scottish physicist, James Clerk Maxwell (1831–79), in his great **electromagnetic theory**, which described every known kind of magnetic and electric behaviour. The set of equations named after him showed that electromagnetic waves travel at the velocity of light and confirmed that light is, in fact, an electromagnetic radiation. This provided further support for the wave theory of light.

1887 Heinrich Rudolph Hertz (1857–94), the German physicist, performed a classic experiment in which electromagnetic waves were produced and transmitted across the laboratory. This laid the foundation for radio transmission and provided ample vindication for Maxwell's theory.

As the 19th century drew to a close many of the problems of physics appeared to have been solved and there was a belief that, in principle, if all the observations and calculations could be made, the destiny of the universe could be revealed in full detail. However, following on Hertz's experiment, a quick succession of phenomena presented themselves which threatened to destroy the orderly structure which had been so painstakingly built up over the preceding centuries.

1895 **X-rays** were discovered by Wilhelm Konrad Röntgen (1845–1923) the German physicist. When experimenting with the passage of electrical discharges through gasses, he noticed that fluorescent material near his apparatus glowed. He won the first Nobel prize for physics in 1901 for this work.

1896 Antoine Henri Becquerel (1852–1908), the French physicist, discovered that uranium salts, even in the dark, emit a radiation similar to Röntgen's X-rays and would fog a photographic plate. This was **radioactivity.**

1898 Marie Curie (1867–1934), of Poland, working with her French husband, Pierre, (1859–1906) announced the existence of two new chemical elements which powerfully emit radiation. She named the elements radium and polonium. The active phenomenon she gave the name radioactivity. She won the Nobel prize for physics in 1903 with Becquerel and her husband, and in 1911, for chemistry on her own.

Ernest Rutherford (1871–1937), New Zealand born British physicist and Frederick Soddy (1877–1956), British chemist, formulated a theory of radioactivity which forms the basis of our present understanding of the phenomenon. Three types of radioactivity were indentified, α-rays, β-rays, and γ-rays. The γ-rays turned out to be like X-rays, more powerful than those of Röntgen. The β-rays were streams of fast moving electrons. The α-rays were found to consist of electrically charged particles being the nuclei of the element helium. The particles emitted from radioactive materials at such speed provided a means of investigating the structure of the atom itself, and enabled Rutherford to propose in 1911, a model of the atom which is the basis of our modern ideas of atomic structure.

A further important discovery which contributed to a revision of the ideas of classical physics was the **photoelectric effect.** It was observed that a polished zinc plate, when illuminated with ultra-violet light aquired a positive electric charge. In **1897** Joseph John Thomson (1856–1940), the British physicist, discovered the first of the fundamental particles, the **electron,** which is the basic unit of negative electricity, It became clear that the photoelectric effect was the result of electrons being knocked out of the metal surface by the incident light. It was further discovered that, firstly, the number of electrons emitted was greater for a greater intensity of light and, secondly, that their energy was related only to the wavelength of the light, being greater for shorter wavelengths. The first result was as expected but the second was a mystery.

Modern Physics

Modern physics could be said to have been born at the beginning of the 20th century, during the course of which a number of radical ideas were formulated and developed into theories which completely revolutionised the thinking in physics.

1900 The quantum theory was the first of these, put forward by the German physicist Max Karl Ernst Ludwig Planck (1858–1947). This arose out of yet another problem which had been insoluble up to that time. Calculations showed that the energy emitted from a hot body should be, at very short wavelengths, practically infinite: this was clearly not so. The calculations were satisfactory for radiation of longer wavelengths in that they agreed with experiment. To resolve this difficulty, Planck made the very novel suggestion that energy was radiated from the body, not in a continuous flow of waves as had been supposed up to then, but rather in distinct individual bundles. He called a bundle of energy a **quantum.** The energy of the quantum, E, is given by

$$E = \frac{hc}{\lambda}$$

where λ is the wavelength of the radiation, c is the velocity of light *in vacuo* and h is a fixed, universal constant called Planck's constant. On this theory, energy at the shorter wavelengths would require to be emitted in bigger bundles and thus there would be less of them available for emission in accordance with experimental results. Planck's constant is small and so quantum effects are also small, occurring only in the domain of atomic phenomena.

1905 Albert Einstein (1879–1955), a Bavarian Jew, published his theory of the photoelectric effect and for which he was to win the Nobel prize in 1921. Einstein followed Planck's ideas and could see that the incident light must consist of a stream of quanta, that is, bundles of light, which came to be known as **photons.** A photon striking a metal surface is absorbed by an electron in it, the electron having more energy as a result. This causes it to jump from the surface, and since photons have greater energy at shorter wavelengths, so shorter wavelength light causes the emission of higher energy electrons. And, of course, the greater the intensity of the light the more quanta will be striking the surface and so more electrons will be emitted. Thus, the idea of the quantum enabled Einstein to account for the phenomena of the photoelectric effect and this was an early triumph for the new quantum theory which was to become a ground force in the subsequent developments in physics.

1905 This year also saw the publication of Einstein's **Special (or Restricted) Theory of Relativity.** It has been said that as a child he had wondered what would happen if it were possible to travel fast enough to catch a ray of light and that this lead him some years later to formulate his celebrated theory. This theory arises from an apparent contradiction between two basic postulates:

1. The velocity of light *in vacuo* is a constant for all observers regardless of their state of motion relative to the light source.
2. The special principle of relativity which states that the laws of physics are the same for all observers in uniform motion relative to each other.

Imagine for a moment a train travelling with a uniform velocity v relative to the railway embankment, and a ray of light transmitted with velocity c along the embankment parallel, and in the direction of the train. For an observer in the train the velocity of the light should appear to be $c-v$: obviously less than c. But this violates the special principle of relativity above: the velocity of light must be the same for an observer on the embankment and an observer on the train. The reconciliation of these two apparently contradictory conclusions is the basis for the special theory and is achieved by surrendering the concepts of absolute time, absolute distance and of the absolute significance of simultaneity. From these ideas, fairly straightforward algebraic manipulation leads to equations which show that when a body is in uniform motion relative to an observer, the length of the body is diminished in the direction of travel and its mass is increased. The equations are:

$$l = l_0 \sqrt{(1 - v^2/c^2)} \text{ and } m = \frac{m_0}{\sqrt{(1 - v^2/c^2)}}$$

where l and m are the length and mass respectively of a body as seen by an observer, and moving at velocity v in the direction of its length relative to him. l_0 is the velocity of the body at rest and m_0 is its mass at rest.

Thus, if a 20m rocket came past you in space at 149 896 km per sec. (i.e. $0.5c$) it would (if you could measure it) be only about 17m long.

If two observers are moving at a constant velocity relative to each other, it appears to each that the other's clocks are slowed down and this is expressed in the equation:

$$t = t_0 \sqrt{(1 - v^2/c^2)}$$

where t is one observer's time as read by the other, and t_0 is his own time as read by himself, v being the constant relative velocity of the two observers.

From the theory it can be shown that, at rest, a body possesses energy, E given by

$$E = m c^2$$

Relativity theory confirms an important unification in physics between two of its very basic concepts: mass and energy.

1911 Ernest Rutherford proposed a model of the atom which is the basis of our ideas of atomic structure to this day. He had from the first recognised the value of the fast moving α-particles emitted naturally from radioactive materials as probes for discovering the nature of the atom. He arranged for α-particles to bombard a thin gold foil and found that while many passed straight through a few were deflected at comparatively large angles, some even 'bouncing' back towards the source. He concluded from this that the mass of the atom was concentrated at its centre in a minute nucleus consisting of positively charged particles called **protons**. Around the nucleus and at a relatively large distance from it revolved the negatively charged electrons rather like a miniature solar system. The combined negative charges of the electrons exactly balanced the total positive charge of the nucleus. This important model of the atom suffered from a number of defects. One of these was that from Maxwell's electromagnetic theory the atom should produce light of all wavelengths whereas, in fact, atoms of each element emit light consisting of a number of definite wavelengths – a spectrum – which can be measured with great accuracy. The spectrum for each element is unique.

A further major difficulty was that the electrons, moving round the nucleus, should yield up their energy in the form of radiation and so would spiral into the nucleus bringing about the collapse of the atom. In fact, nothing of the sort occurs: under normal conditions an atom is a stable structure which does not emit radiation.

1913 The difficulties of the Rutherford atom were overcome by the Danish physicist, Neils Henrik David Bohr (1885–1962) who proposed that electrons were permitted only in certain orbits but could jump from one permitted orbit to another. In so jumping the electron would gain or lose energy in the form of photons, whose wavelength followed from Planck's rule:

$$\lambda = \frac{hc}{E}$$

In this way the spectrum of light emitted, or absorbed, by an atom would relate to its individual structure. The theoretical basis to Bohr's work was confirmed by Einstein in 1917 and the Bohr theory went on successfully to explain other atomic phenomena. However, after many outstanding successes over a number of years, an increasing number of small but important discrepancies appeared with which the Bohr theory could not cope.

1919 Rutherford performed the first artificial nuclear disintegration when he bombarded nitrogen atoms with α-particles from radon-C. He demonstrated that protons were emitted as a result of the disintegration and this confirmed that the proton was, indeed, a nuclear particle.

1924 Louis-Victor de Broglie (b. 1892), French physicist, postulated that the dual wave-particle nature of light might be shown by other particles and particularly by electrons. The wavelength, λ, would be given by

$$\lambda = \frac{h}{mv}$$

where m is the mass of the particle, and v is its velocity. Electron waves were demonstrated experimentally in 1927 by C. J. Davisson (1881–1958) and L. H. Germer (b. 1896) of the USA. Subsequently, de Broglie's idea of matter waves was extended to other particles, protons, neutrons, etc. All matter has an associated wave character, but for the larger bodies of classical mecahnics, the wavelengths are too small for their effects to be detectable.

1926 Erwin Schrödinger (1887–1961), a physicist from Vienna, took up the ideas of de Broglie waves and applied them to the Bohr atom. The solutions to the resulting wave equation gave the allowed orbits or energy levels more accurately than the quantised orbits in the Bohr atom. Max Born (1882–1970), the German physicist, interpreted these solutions in terms of probability, i.e. they gave the probability of finding an electron in a given volume of space within the atom.

1927 The German physicist, Werner Karl Heisenberg (1901–76) formulated his celebrated and profound Uncertainty Principle: this states that there is a definite limit to the accuracy with which certain pairs of measurements can be made. The more accurate one quantity is known, the less accurate is our knowledge of the other. Position and momentum is an example of such a pair of measurements. The more exactly we know the position of, say, an electron, the less will we know about its momentum. This can be expressed:

$$\Delta x . \Delta p \sim h$$

where Δx represents the uncertainty in position and Δp the uncertainty in momentum. h is Planck's constant. A further important example relates to time and energy: it is not possible to know how much energy E is possessed by a particle without allowing sufficient time t for the energy to be determined.

$$\Delta E . \Delta t \sim h$$

The uncertainty principle provides the main reason why the classical mechanics of Newton do not apply to atomic and subatomic phenomena.

1928 Paul Adrien Maurice Dirac (b. 1902), the Cambridge mathematician, introduced a theory of the electron which successfully brought together the ideas of quantum mechanics thus far developed with those of relativity. As a result of this, the important concept of electron spin previously advanced by Bohr became theoretically justified.

Dirac's equations revealed a negative quantity which lead to the prediction of the existence of the antielectron, a particle identical to the electron, of the same mass but of opposite electric charge. This major idea, that there could exist **antimatter** in the universe composed of antiparticles arises from Dirac's bold prediction.

Heisenberg's uncertainty principle lead to the idea of the instantaneous creation and anihilation of short-lived 'virtual' particles in the vicinity of stable particles. The basic uncertainty in the energy of a particle enables it to acquire a loan, as it were, of energy for a short time: the length of time, in fact, being inversely related to the amount of energy lent. Provided the loan is repaid in the time available, there is no violation of the law of conservation of energy. The action of forces could now be seen in terms of these 'virtual' particles, which behave as force-carriers travelling rapidly from one particle to the other. So, it comes about that particles, not in direct contact, respond each to the presence of the other.

1932 Ernest Orlando Lawrence (1901–58), an American physicist, developed the **cyclotron.** This was one of the first machines constructed for accelerating charged particles artificially to high velocities for research. The particles, which in the first instance were protons, were caused to move with ever increasing velocity in a spiral path by the suitable application of magnetic and electric fields. Lawrence was awarded the Nobel prize in 1939 for this work.

1932 Carl David Anderson (b. 1905), an American physicist of California, announced the discovery of the antielectron predicted a few years previously by Dirac. This was the first particle of antimatter to be discovered and he named it the **positron.**

1932 James Chadwick (b. 1891), the English physicist, discovered the **neutron**, a constituent of the atomic nucleus of zero charge and only slightly heavier than the proton.

1933 Wolfgang Pauli (1900–58) of Austria postulated the existence of the **neutrino**, a neutral particle of negligible mass in order to explain the fact that in β-emission in radioactivity, there was a rather greater loss of energy than could be otherwise explained.

In 1956 Fred Reines and Clyde Cowan in Los Alamos succeeded in detecting neutrinos (electron neutrinos). In 1962 Lederman and Melvin Schwarz of Columbia University demonstrated the existence of the other neutrino, the muon neutrino.

1934 Hideki Yukawa (b. 1907), the Japanese physicist, sought to explain the forces which held the particles in the nucleus together – the **strong force** – and called the force-carrying particles in this case **mesons.** The meson predicted by Yukawa, the **pion,** was discovered by Cecil F Powell of Bristol University in 1947.

1938 **Nuclear fission** was discovered by Otto Hahn (1879–1968) and Fritz Strassman (b. 1902) by bombarding uranium with neutrons, when trying to produce transuranic elements. They succeeded in producing elements lighter than uranium from the mineral of the periodic table. The incident neutron causes the target nucleus to split into two pieces of almost equal mass. Each of the fragments consists of protons and neutrons and an enormous amount of energy is released in the process. Enrico Fermi (1901–54) suggested that the neutrons released in fission could themselves induce further fission and that it should be possible to sustain a chain reaction.

1942 The first nuclear reactor, set up by Fermi in the University of Chicago became critical.

1945 The first atomic explosion which was experimental took place in July followed by bombs dropped on Hiroshima and Nagasaki in August.

1952 The first hydrogen bomb was exploded in November. This derived its energy from the process of nuclear fusion in which two or more relatively light nuclei combined to form a heavier atomic nucleus releasing thereby a very considerable amount of energy. Considerable effort is being made to develop a fusion reactor and the main difficulty is the problem of containing the enormously high temperatures involved within the reactor for long enough to allow the reaction to proceed. In June 1954 the world's first nuclear powered generator produced electricity at Obnisk near Moscow, and in August 1956 the first large scale nuclear power generating station, Calder Hall, Northumberland, started up. It was officially opened by Her Majesty Queen Elizabeth II in October when power first flowed into the national grid.

By the 1950's a bewilderingly large number of apparently fundamental particles had been reported and their great number was becoming an embarrassment. Most particles then known fell into two classes: the **leptons** and the **hadrons** (see table page 66).

Hadrons are complex and there was evidence that they themselves possessed an internal structure. Certain of the unstable hadrons were found to take very much longer to decay than expected. These were called **strange** particles.

1953 Murray Gell-Mann (b. 1929) of the USA, introduced a concept he called **strangeness,** a quality akin in some ways to electric charge, which helped to account for the increased life-times of the strange particles. Aided by this idea, it was found that particles could be fitted into patterns according to the amount of strangeness they possessed. This lead to the prediction of the existence of a rather unusual particle and it was a great triumph for these theories when in 1964 the omega-minus particle was discovered.

1963 From considerations of these patterns, Gell-Mann was lead to the idea that the hadrons were composed of more basic particles called **quarks** (a name he borrowed from the writings of the Irish author, James Joyce). There were three kinds of quark, 'up', 'down' and 'strange' and, for each, a corresponding antiquark. These combined in only one of two ways to form either **baryons** or **mesons** as the table shows. Thus the proton can be pictured as consisting of three quarks – 2 up quarks and 1 down quark held together by force-carrying particles called **gluons.**

A free quark has not yet been detected and there is speculation that it never will. But there is experimental evidence suggesting their existence within baryons.

Current theory suggests that the gluons carry an enormously strong force called the **colour force.** This is much stronger than the strong nuclear force and permits quarks in the proton, for example, freedom of movement over a very short distance but increases with distance to hold them firmly within the proton.

1974 A particularly heavy particle, a hadron, was discovered and called the J or psi particle. Up to this time, the rules for building hadrons from quarks accounted in a complete and satisfying way for every known hadron and so it was that there appeared to be no room for the new particle. However, it could be explained by assuming it to be composed of a new quark together with its antiquark. This new, fourth quark called the charmed quark had been proposed in 1970 by Sheldon Lee Glashow (b. 1932) for other theoretical reasons. Charm, a property similar to strangeness, was first suggested in 1964 by Glashow on aesthetic grounds: there were two pairs of leptons so the up and down quark also formed a pair leaving the strange quark without a companion. Now, the charmed quark completed the team and also explained this new particle. However, the charm in this psi particle cancelled out because of the charm/anti-charm combination. The search was then for a particle exhibiting 'naked' charm, a particle containing a charmed quark in combination with an up, down or strange quark.

1976 In May the D^0 meson was discovered by Gerson Goldhaber, co-discoverer of the psi particle, and Francoise Pierre at Stanford University. The D^0 particle consisted of a charmed quark and an anti-up quark.

In August, Wonyong Lee of Columbia University announced that a charmed antiproton had been detected, consisting of three antiquarks – up, down and charmed.

New particles were thus being discovered at this time with properties predicted by the charm theory.

CHEMISTRY

INORGANIC CHEMISTRY

The nomenclature of inorganic chemistry is governed by the International Union of Pure and Applied Chemistry whose latest detailed and authoritative guidance was published in 1970 and was followed by a definite interpretation by the Association of Science Education in 1972.

Because of the difficulties in trying to produce a systematic nomenclature which will adequately cover all aspects of inorganic chemistry, trivial names have not yet been completely discarded although, for example, the use of the familiar endings 'ous' and 'ic' to denote the lower and higher valency states of metal cations is to be discouraged in favour of the Stock System in which the oxidation number of the less electronegative constituent is indicated by Roman numerals in parentheses placed immediately after the name of the atom concerned, thus $FeCl_2$ is iron (II) chloride rather than ferrous chloride and $FeCl_3$ is iron (III) chloride rather than ferric chloride. For compounds consisting of simple molecules of known composition the stoichiometry determines the name using Greek or Roman multiplying affixes (see table below), thus P_4O_{10} is tetraphosphorus decaoxide. Trivial names for acids are still in use although such alchemical leftovers as 'Aquafortis' for nitric acid, 'Oil of Vitriol' for sulfuric acid, and 'Spirit of Salt' for hydrochloric acid have long (hopefully) been discarded.

Multiplying Affixes

½	hemi	8	octa	15	pentadeca
1	mono	9	nona (Latin)	16	hexadeca
1½	sesqui		ennea (Greek)	17	heptadeca
2	di	10	deca	18	octadeca
3	tri	11	undeca (Latin)	19	nonadeca
4	tetra		henadeca (Greek)	20	eicosa
5	penta	12	dodeca	24	tetracosa
6	hexa	13	trideca	30	triaconta
7	hepta	14	tetradeca	40	tetraconta

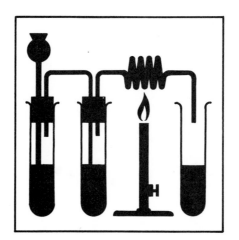

STABLE INORGANIC ACIDS OF THE NON-METALLIC ELEMENTS

Boron
boric acid (crystals) H_3BO_3

Arsenic
arsenious acid* H_3AsO_3
arsenic acid* H_3AsO_4

Bromine
hydrobromic acid (45%) HBr
hypobromous acid* HBrO
bromic acid* $HBrO_3$

Carbon
carbonic acid* H_2CO_3

Chlorine
hydrochloric acid (35%) HCl
hypochlorous acid* HClO
chlorous acid* $HClO_2$
chloric acid* $HClO_3$
perchloric acid (60%) $HClO_4$

Fluorine
hydrofluoric acid (40%) HF
fluoroboric acid (40%) HBF_4
fluorosilicic acid (40%) H_2SiF_6
fluorosulfonic acid (liquid) HSO_3F

Iodine
hydriodic acid (55%) HI
hypoiodic acid* HIO
iodic acid (crystals) HIO_3
periodic acid (crystals) HIO_4

Nitrogen
hyponitrous acid* $H_2N_2O_2$
nitrous acid* HNO_2
nitric acid (70%) HNO_3

INORGANIC ACIDS *continued*

Phosphorus
phosphinic acid (50%) H_3PO_2
(hypophosphorous acid)
phosphonic acid (crystals) H_3PO_3
(orthophosphorous acid)
diphosphonic acid (crystals) $H_4P_2O_5$
(pyrophosphorous acid)
diphosphonic acid (crystals) $H_4P_2O_6$
(hypophosphoric acid)
metaphosphoric acid (solid) $(HPO_3)_n$
orthophosphoric acid (85%) H_3PO_4
diphosphoric acid (crystals) $H_4P_2O_7$
(pyrophosphoric acid)

Selenium
selenious acid (crystals) H_2SeO_3
selenic acid (crystals) H_2SeO_4

Silicon
metasilicic acid (solid) $(H_2SiO_3)_n$
orthosilicic acid* H_4SiO_4

Sulfur
sulfurous acid* H_2SO_3
sulfuric acid (liquid) H_2SO_4
peroxomonosulfuric acid (crystals) H_2SO_5
(Caro's Acid)
dithionic acid* $H_2S_2O_6$
disulfuric acid (crystals) $H_2S_2O_7$
(pyrosulfuric acid)
peroxodisulfuric acid (crystals) $H_2S_2O_8$
(persulfuric acid)

Tellurium
tellurous acid (crystals) H_2TeO_3
orthotelluric acid (crystals) H_6TeO_6

* Stable only in aqueous solution
Values in parentheses indicate the concentration in aqueous solution of the usual commercial grades of the acid.

ORGANIC CHEMISTRY

Organic chemistry is the chemistry of hydrocarbons and their derivatives. The original division between organic chemical compounds (meaning those occurring in the Animal and Plant Kingdoms) and inorganic chemical compounds (meaning those occurring in the mineral world) was made in 1675 by Lémery. This oversimplified division was upset when in 1828 Wöhler produced urea ($NH_2.CO.NH_2$) in an attempt to produce ammonium cyanate ($NH_4.CNO$) from inorganic sources and was ended with the synthesis of acetic acid (ethanoic acid) from its elements by Kolbe in 1845, and the synthesis of methane by Berthelot in 1856. Carbon has a valency number (from the Latin *valens* = worth) of 4, i.e. a combining power expressed in terms of the number of hydrogen atoms with which the atom of carbon can combine. In addition the carbon atom has the unique property of being able to join one to another to form chains, rings, double bonds and triple bonds.

Thus there are almost limitless numbers of organic compounds and since nearly four million are known then the transition to a strict system of nomenclature from the plethora of trivial names is an essential aim of the International Union of Pure and Applied Chemistry. When all the carbon valencies are utilised in bonding with other carbon or hydrogen atoms, with all the carbon linkages as single bonds, the hydrocarbons are said to be *saturated* and may be in the form of chains or rings. When the carbon atoms are joined together by double or triple bonds then these bonds are potentially available for completion of saturation and therefore such hydrocarbons are said to be *unsaturated*. Open chain compounds are called aliphatic from the Greek *aliphos*, fat, since the first compounds in this class to be studied were the so-called fatty acids.

Saturated hydrocarbons

Straight chain hydrocarbons necessarily conform to the formula C_nH_{2n+2} and are known collectively as **alkanes** or by their trivial name paraffins (from the Latin *parvum affinis*, small affinity, which refers to their low combining power with other substances). The first four alkanes retain their semi-trivial names:

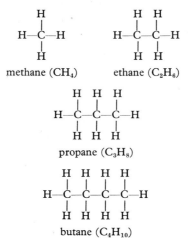

methane (CH_4)   ethane (C_2H_6)

propane (C_3H_8)

butane (C_4H_{10})

The higher alkanes are named by utilising the recommended multiplying affixes listed in the Inorganic Section to indicate the number of carbon atoms in the chain, i.e. C_5H_{12} is pentane, C_7H_{16} is heptane, and C_9H_{20} is nonane.

Ring compounds, in which the carbon atoms form a closed ring, are known as the **napthene** family and of the formula C_nH_{2n}. They take their names from the corresponding alkanes by adding the prefix *cyclo-*, e.g.

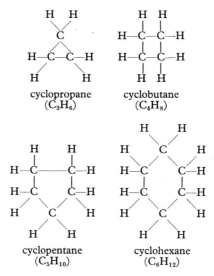

cyclopropane (C_3H_6)   cyclobutane (C_4H_8)

cyclopentane (C_5H_{10})   cyclohexane (C_6H_{12})

Unsaturated hydrocarbons

Compounds with one double bond are of the structure type $>C=C<$ and are of the formula C_nH_{2n}. They are known as **alkenes** or by the trivial name olefins (from the Latin *oleum*, oil, *faceo* = to make). They are named after their alkane equivalents by substituting the ending *-ene* to the root of the name, although the old system was to substitute the ending *-ylene*, e.g.

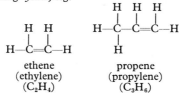

ethene (ethylene) (C_2H_4)   propene (propylene) (C_3H_6)

The higher alkenes are similarly named:
C_4H_8 butene (butylene)
C_5H_{10} pentene (pentylene)
C_6H_{12} hexene (hexylene) et seq.

where the letter ending 'a' in buta, penta, hexa, etc. is dropped for ease of pronunciation. When more than one double bond is present the endings *diene, triene* etc. are used with the positions of the double bonds being carefully noted, i.e. $CH_2=CH-CH=CH_2$ is buta-1,3-diene.

Compounds with one triple bond are called **alkynes** or by their trivial name acetylenes (from the Latin *acetum* = vinegar) and are of the general formula C_nH_{2n-2}. The same rules for nomenclature are used with the ending *-yne* being added to the root of the name of the equivalent alkane. The first member of the group is named ethyne although the more common name acetylene still has a semi-trivial standing. Typical group members include:

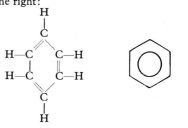

ethyne (C_2H_2)   propyne (C_3H_4)

butyne (C_4H_6)

Aromatic hydrocarbons

Substances based on the hydrocarbon benzene C_6H_6 have the family name **aromatic** (from the Greek *aroma*, fragrant smell). They are characterised by the six membered ring represented as having alternating or conjugate double bonds as shown on the left below, although because the double bonds have no fixed positions it is usual to symbolise the structure as shown on the right:

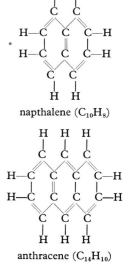

It is possible to produce multiple rings based on the benzene structure, e.g.

napthalene ($C_{10}H_8$)

anthracene ($C_{14}H_{10}$)

Organic radicals

Removal of a hydrogen atom from hydrocarbon molecules forms a radical which is named by replacing the suffix -ane by -yl, e.g.

$(CH_3)^-$ methyl; from Greek methy, wine, hyle = wood
$(C_2H_5)^-$ ethyl; from Greek aither, clean air (i.e. odourless)
$(C_3H_7)^-$ propyl; from Greek pro, before, and peon, fat, hence radical of fatty acid
$(C_4H_9)^-$ butyl; from Greek butyrum = butter (rancid smell)

Higher radicals are again based on the use of multiplying affixes, i.e. pentane becomes pentyl $(C_5H_{11})^-$ and hexane becomes hexyl $(C_6H_{13})^-$. These radicals are generically known as **alkyls** and being covalent they can be substituted for hydrogen in other molecules.

The general designation for radicals of aromatic hydrocarbons is **aryl** and the monovalent radical formed from benzene $(C_6H_5)^-$ is called phenyl and not benzyl which is reserved for the radical $(C_6H_5CH_2)^-$. The use of these radical names leads to a better description of a molecule's structure, i.e. the semi-trivial name toluene does not immediately convey an indication of molecular structure but its systematic equivalent methyl benzene indicates the replacement of one of the hydrogen atoms in the benzene ring by a methyl group.

Isomers and organic nomenclature

It is evident that except in the cases of the simplest organic molecules, it is possible to rearrange the positions of carbon atoms along the molecule skeleton (chain isomerism), or to a limited extent reposition double and triple bonds along the chain, or substitute radicals for hydrogen atoms at specific points along the chain (position isomerism).

In the case of the alkanes (paraffins) methane, ethane, and propane exist only as single molecular species, but butane exists in two—the normal straight chain (n) and a branched isomeric chain (iso), and pentane in three—normal, isomeric, and neopentane:

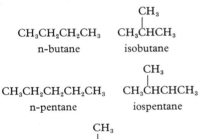

n-butane   isobutane

n-pentane   iospentane

neopentane

From then on there is a rapid increase with the alkane $C_{15}H_{32}$ exhibiting no less than 4347 possible isomeric states!

However in the IUPAC system of nomenclature the use of these prefixes becomes unnecessary since the longest possible chain is chosen as the *parent* chain and the positions of sites on the chain are indicated by numbers, the direction of numbering being so chosen as to give the lowest series of numbers for the *side* chains.

Thus isobutane becomes 2-methyl propane (since the methyl radical is attached to the second carbon atom in the chain), isopentane becomes 2-methyl butane for the same reason, and neopentane becomes 2,2-dimethyl propane (since two of the methyl radicals are regarded as forming a 'chain' with the central carbon atom and the two other methyl radicals are both attached to the 'second' carbon atom). For single bonding the treatment of more complex molecules is a simple extension of this principle with apparent side chains being regarded as belonging to the parent chain where necessary, e.g. the structure below is 3-methyl hexane and *not* 2-propyl butane:

$$CH_3CHCH_2CH_3$$
$$|$$
$$CH_2$$
$$|$$
$$CH_2$$
$$|$$
$$CH_3$$

For alkenes (olefins) and alkynes (acetylenes) the chain is always numbered from the end closest to the double or triple bond and the positions of these bonds are also specified:

$CH_3CH_2CH{=}CH_2$ $CH_3CH{=}CHCH_3$

but-1-ene   but-2-ene
α butylene)   (β butylene)

$$\begin{array}{c} CH_3 \\ {>}C{=}CH_2 \\ CH_3 \end{array}$$

2-methyl propene
(isobutylene)

$CH_3CH_2C{\equiv}CH$ $CH_3C{\equiv}CCH_3$

but-1-yne   but-2-yne

In compounds containing mixed bonds the double bond takes preference over triple bonds in numbering the chain and double and triple bonds take preference over single bonds in deciding the length of the parent chain.

When there is more than one type of radical attached to the parent chain then these are listed in strict alphabetical order without regard to the position on the chain, e.g. for the first five radicals the order will be: butyl, ethyl, methyl, pentyl, and propyl. The multiplying affixes used to indicate the total number of a particular type of radical are ignored in this sequence, e.g. ethyl still precedes dimethyl and triethyl before methyl.

For radicals the same rules apply and apart from the prefixes *normal*, *iso*, and *neo* discussed previously, the old system also includes *secondary* (*sec*) isomers (so called because two hydrogen atoms have been repositioned from the principal carbon atom and their bonds replaced by two of the carbon bonds) and *tertiary* (*tert*) isomers (so called because three hydrogen atoms have been repositioned). In the IUPAC system these prefixes are no longer required since the longest chain principal is applied and numbering specified from the carbon atom which has the free valency. In the examples of the propyl and butyl isomers listed below the names isopropyl and isobutyl are still retained on a semi-trivial basis:

Trivial Name	Structure	I.U.P.A.C. Name
n-propyl	$CH_3CH_2CH_2{-}$	propyl
iso-propyl	CH_3CHCH_3	1-methylethyl
n-butyl	$CH_3CH_2CH_2CH_2{-}$	butyl
iso-butyl	$(CH_3)_2CHCH_2{-}$	2-methylpropyl
sec-butyl	$CH_3CH_2CHCH_3$	1-methylpropyl
tert-butyl	$(CH_3)_3C{-}$	1,1-dimethylethyl

In the case of aromatic hydrocarbons, when two or more substituents are present in the benzene ring, the old nomenclature technique was to assign prefixes ortho, meta, and para to the name of the compound to indicate the differences in the positions of the radicals, i.e.

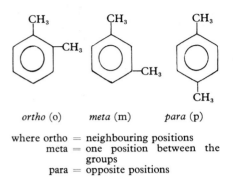

ortho (o)   *meta* (m)   *para* (p)

where ortho = neighbouring positions
meta = one position between the groups
para = opposite positions

In the IUPAC system these prefixes are again rendered unnecessary by simply numbering the benzene ring as shown below with the main functional group substituted usually assigned to position 1:

Thus a comparison of the different naming systems for the above examples clearly indicates the superiority of the IUPAC system:

Trivial Name	Semi-Trivial Name	I.U.P.A.C. Name
o-xylene	o-dimethylbenzene	1,2-dimethylbenzene
m-xylene	m-dimethylbenzene	1,3-dimethylbenzene
p-xylene	p-dimethylbenzene	1,4-dimethylbenzene

Substitution radicals

(*a*) *Alcohols*. Replacement of hydrogen atoms by hydroxyl groups (OH) leads to the **alcohols**. If the hydroxyl radical is the *principal* group (see end of this section) then the alcohol molecule is named after the hydrocarbon base with the ending -ol substituted for the ending -e, e.g. methanol (methyl alcohol) CH_3OH and ethanol (ethyl alcohol) C_2H_5OH. However, with longer chains the position of the attachment has to be specified and this is achieved by selecting the longest chain containing the hydroxyl group and assigning the lowest possible number to this side chain hydroxyl radical using the suffix -ol, e.g.

$CH_3CH_2CH_2OH$ propan-1-ol (propyl alcohol)

$$CH_3CHCH_3$$
$$|$$
$$OH$$
propan-2-ol (isopropyl alcohol)

This simplified procedure can be extended to much more complex alcohols provided that the hydroxyl radical is the principal group. To represent a number of alcohols present in a single molecule the multiplying affixes are used to obtain the endings -diol, -triol, etc.

In the case of aromatic hydrocarbons the single hydroxyl attachment is known as *phenol* whilst multi-hydroxyl groups are named on the *benzene . . . ol* system, even though the true aromatic alcohols are compounds containing the hydroxyl group in a side chain and may be regarded as aryl derivatives of the aliphatic alcohols, i.e. benzyl alcohol $C_6H_5CH_2OH$ is a true aromatic alcohol. Use of the new nomenclature gives a clearer understanding of molecular structure, e.g.

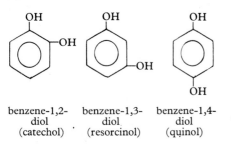

| benzene-1,2-
diol
(catechol) | benzene-1,3-
diol
(resorcinol) | benzene-1,4-
diol
(quinol) |

(b) Ethers. Derivatives of alcohols in which the hydrogen atoms in the hydroxyl groups are replaced by carbon are known as **ethers**. Thus $(C_6H_5)_2O$ is diphenyl ether and $CH_3.O.C_2H_5$ is ethylmethyl ether (using the rule that where there is no preference then the radicals are named alphabetically) but there is a tendency to treat the ether radical as a group (O.R) where 'R' is an alkyl radical part of the ether compound, so the above mixed radical compound would be methoxyethane since the group are known generically as **alkoxy** groups. Similarly $(C_2H_5)_2O$ becomes ethoxyethane rather than diethyl ether. When the two alkyl groups are the same the ether is said to be symmetrical or simple (i.e. ethoxyethane) but if the two alkyl groups are different the ether is said to be unsymmetrical or mixed (i.e. methoxyethane).

(c) Aldehydes. The substitution by the radical (CHO) leads to compounds known as the **aldehydes** although the suffix *carbaldehyde* is used if the carbon atom in the radical is not part of the base hydrocarbon, i.e. C_6H_5CHO is benzene carbaldehyde rather than its former name benzaldehyde. Where the carbon in the aldehyde is part of the original base hydrocarbon then the compound is named by substituting the ending *-al* for the hydrocarbon containing the same number of atoms in the parent group. Thus HCHO is methanal (formerly formaldehyde) and CH_3-CHO is ethanal (formerly acetaldehyde)

(d) Ketones. Ketones are based on the double bonded ($>CO$) radical. The trivial naming technique is to add the name ketone to the ends of the names of the radicals connected by the bond, i.e. $(CH_3)_2CO$ is dimethyl ketone and $CH_3.CO.C_2H_5$ is ethyl methyl ketone. However the new recommended technique is to name the molecule after the longest structural chain by adding the ending *-one*. Thus dimethyl ketone or acetone is in reality propanone. For similar reasons ethylmethyl ketone becomes butanone, etc.

(e) Acids. The functional group (COOH) is known as carboxylic acid and is used as such if the carbon atom is not part of the main base hydrocarbon, e.g.

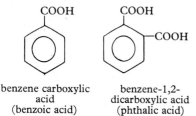

| benzene carboxylic
acid
(benzoic acid) | benzene-1,2-
dicarboxylic acid
(phthalic acid) |

However if the carbon atom is part of the base chain then the acid molecule is named by substituting the ending *-oic* to the name of the hydrocarbon containing the same number of carbon atoms, i.e.

HCOOH	methanoic acid (formic acid)
CH_3COOH	ethanoic acid (acetic acid)
CH_3CH_2COOH	propanoic acid
$CH_3CH_2CH_2COOH$	butanoic acid

(f) Amines. Amines are formed by substituting (NH_2) groups in place of hydrogen and the class name is added to the alkyl radical, i.e. CH_3NH_2 is methylamine. Further substitution can take place leading to dimethylamine $(CH_3)_2NH$ and even trimethylamine $(CH_3)_3N$. The aromatic amine $C_6H_5NH_2$ is phenylamine (aniline).

(g) Principal Groups. Since a large number of different radicals can attach to the base hydrocarbon it is important to produce an order of preference for listing these radicals. With a mixture of radicals the principal group is named as described above but the secondary groups are now named using prefixes to identify the type. Thus for hydroxy groups as secondary groups the ending *-ol* is dropped in favour of the prefix *hydroxy*. This occurs for many alcoholic compounds since this group is towards the bottom of the list. The carboxylic radical (COOH) heads the list and ethers, aldehydes, and ketones are intermediate.

Stereoisomerism

Where the carbon atoms are linked by double bonds, rotation of the kind exhibited by chain and position isomerism is not possible. In this case isomerism can occur geometrically. For example, dichloroethene which has a double bond may occur in a *cis* form (from the Latin *cis*, on the near side) which indicates that the chlorine atoms are on the same side of the molecule, and a *trans* form (from the Latin *trans*, on the far side) which indicates that the atoms are diagonally opposed across the double bond, i.e.

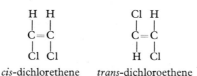

cis-dichlorethene   *trans*-dichloroethene

The third class of isomerism is optical isomerism. In this the molecule of one is in one form but the molecule of the other is laterally inverted as in a mirror image. Using the instrument known as a *polarimeter* it can be shown that one isomer has the effect of twisting the plane of light shone through it to the right while its isomer twists it to the left. These optically active forms are known as the *d*-form (*dextro* or right rotating) and the *l*-form (*laevo* or left rotating). When the isomers are mixed in equal proportions the rotating effect is cancelled out to give an optically inactive or *racemic* form (from the Latin *racemus* = a bunch of grapes, because the mother liquid of fermented grape juice exhibits this characteristic). The practical importance of this phenomenon can be

illustrated by the ability of yeast to convert *d*-grape sugar to alcohol and its powerlessness to affect the *l*-compound.

Carbohydrates

These are an important source of energy for living organisms as well as a means by which chemical energy can be stored. The name originally indicated the belief that compounds of this group could be represented as hydrates of carbon of general formula $C_x(H_2O)_y$, but it is now realised that many important carbohydrates do not have the required 2 to 1 hydrogen to oxygen ratio whilst other compounds which conform to this structure, such as methanal (formaldehyde) (CH_2O) and ethanoic acid (acetic acid) ($C_2H_4O_2$) are obviously not of this group. Further, other carbohydrates contain sulfur and nitrogen as important constituents. Carbohydrates can be defined as polyhydroxy aldehydes or ketones or as a substance which yield these compounds on hydrolysis. Glucose and fructose (both of general formula $C_6H_{12}O_6$) are typical examples, respectively of an 'aldose' and a 'ketose', e.g.

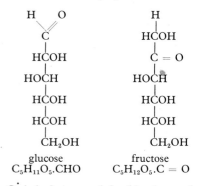

| glucose
$C_5H_{11}O_5.CHO$ | fructose
$C_5H_{12}O_5.C = O$ |

Carbohydrates are defined by the number of carbon atoms in the molecule using the usual multiplying affixes, i.e. tetrose for 4 carbon atoms, pentose for 5, hexose for 6, etc. They are divided into two main groups known as sugars and polysaccharides, where the former is subdivided into monosaccharides of general formula $C_nH_{2n}O_n$ (where $n = 2$ to 10) which cannot be hydrolysed into smaller molecules, and oligosaccharides such as disaccharides ($C_{12}H_{22}O_{11}$), trisaccharides ($C_{18}H_{32}O_{16}$), and tetrasaccharides ($C_{24}H_{42}O_{21}$) which yield two, three, and four monosaccharide molecules respectively on hydrolysis.

The polysaccharides yield a large number of monosaccharides on hydrolysis and have molecular weights ranging from thousands to several million. The most widely spread polysaccharides are of the general formula $(C_6H_{10}O_5)_n$ and include *starch*, which occurs in all green plants and is obtained from maize, wheat, barley, rice and potatoes, and from which dextrins are produced by boiling with water under pressure; *glycogen*, which is the reserve carbohydrate of animals and is often known as 'animal starch'; and *cellulose*, the main constituent of the cell walls of plants.

Of the naturally-occurring sugars (which are all optically active), the most familiar monosaccharides are the dextrorotary (D+) aldohexose *glucose* (dextrose or grape sugar) and the laevorotary (D—) ketohexose *fructose* (laevulose or fruit sugar), both of formula $C_6H_{12}O_6$.

The most important disaccharides are those of the formula $C_{12}H_{22}O_{11}$ and include *sucrose* (cane sugar or beet sugar) obtained from sugar cane or sugar beet after chemical treatment; *maltose* (malt sugar) produced by the action of malt on starch; and *lactose* (milk sugar) which occurs naturally in the milk of all animals.

TABLE OF THE 107 ELEMENTS

Atomic Number	Symbol	Name of Element	Derived From	Discoverers	Year	Atomic Weight (Note 3)	Density at 20°C (unless otherwise stated) (g/cm³) (Note 4)	Melting Point °C (Note 5)	Boiling Point °C (Note 5)	Physical Description	Valency Number	Number of Nuclides
1	H	Hydrogen	Greek, 'hydor genes' = water producer	H Cavendish (UK)	1766	1·0079	0·0867 (solid at mp); 0·00008989 (gas at 0°C)	-259·194	-252·753	Colourless gas	1	3
2	He	Helium	Greek, 'helios' = sun	J N Lockyer (UK) and P- J- C Janssen (France)	1868	4·00260	0·1908 (solid at mp); 0·0001785 (gas at 0°C)	-272·375 at 24·985 atm (Note 6)	-268·926	Colourless gas	0	6
3	Li	Lithium	Greek, 'lithos' = stone	J A Arfwedson (Sweden)	1817	6·941	0·5334	180·57	1344	Silvery-white metal	1	5
4	Be	Beryllium	Greek, 'beryllion' = beryl	N-L Vauquelin (France)	1798	9·01218	1·846	1289	2476	Grey metal	2	7
5	B	Boron	Persian, 'burah' = borax	L-J Gay Lussac and L-J Thenard (France) and H Davy (UK)	1808	10·81	2·297 (β Rhombohedral); 2·465 (α Rhombohedral)	2130	3865	Dark brown powder	3	6
6	C	Carbon	Latin, carbo = charcoal	Prehistoric	—	12·011	2·396 (β Tetragonal); 2·266 (Graphite); 3·515 (Diamond)	4550 at 103 atm	3700 sublimes	Colourless solid (diamond) or black solid (graphite)	2 or 4	9
7	N	Nitrogen	Greek, 'nitron genes' = saltpetre producer	D Rutherford (UK)	1772	14·0067	0·9426 (solid at mp); 0·001250 (gas at 0°C)	-210·004	-195·806	Colourless gas	3 or 5	7
8	O	Oxygen	Greek, oxys genes' = acid producer	C W Scheele (Sweden) and J Priestley (UK)	1771-4	15·9994	1·350 (solid at mp); 0·001429 (gas at 0°C)	-218·789	-182·962	Colourless gas	2	8
9	F	Fluorine	Latin, fluo = flow	H Moissan (France)	1886	18·99840	1·780 (solid at mp); 0·001696 (gas at 0°C)	-219·669	-188·200	Pale greenish-yellow gas	1	6
10	Ne	Neon	Greek, 'neos' = new	W Ramsay and M W Travers (UK)	1898	20·179	1·433 (solid at mp); 0·0008999 (gas at 0°C)	-248·589	-246·048	Colourless gas	0	8
11	Na	Sodium (Natrium)	English, soda	H Davy (UK)	1807	22·98977	0·9688	97·86	884	Silvery-white metal	1	7
12	Mg	Magnesium	Magnesia, a district in Thessaly	H Davy (UK)	1808	24·305	1·737	649	1097	Silvery-white metal	2	9
13	Al	Aluminium	Latin, alumen = alum	H C Oersteldt; (Denmark) F Wöhler (Germany)	1825-7	26·98154	2·699	660·46	2525	Silvery-white metal	3	7
14	Si	Silicon	Latin, silex = flint	J J Berzelius (Sweden)	1824	28·0855	2·329	1414	3225	Dark grey solid	4	8
15	P	Phosphorus	Greek, phosphoros' = light bringing	H Brand (Germany)	1669	30·97376	1·825 (white); 2·361 (violet); 2·708 (black)	44·14; 597 at 45 atm; 606 at 48 atm	277; 431 sublimes; 453 sublimes	White to yellow, violet to red, or black solid	3 or 5	7
16	S	Sulfur (Note 1)	Sanskrit, 'solvere'; Latin, sulfurum	Prehistoric		32·06	2·068 (rhombic); 2·038 (solid at mp)	115·21	444·674	Pale yellow solid	2,4, or 6	10
17	Cl	Chlorine	Greek, 'chloros' = green	C W Scheele (Sweden)	1774	35·453	0·003214 (gas at 0°C)	-100·97	-34·03	Yellow-green gas	1,3,5, or 7	9
18	Ar	Argon	Greek, 'argos' = inactive	W Ramsay and Lord Rayleigh (UK)	1894	39·948	1·622 (solid at mp); 0·001784 (gas at 0°C)	-189·352	-185·856	Colourless gas	0	12
19	K	Potassium (Kalium)	English, potash	H Davy (UK)	1807	39·0983	0·8591	63·50	760	Silvery-white metal	1	12
20	Ca	Calcium	Latin, calx = lime	H Davy (UK)	1808	40·08	1·526	840	1493	Silvery-white metal	2	15
21	Sc	Scandium	Scandinavia	L F Nilson (Sweden)	1879	44·9559	2·989	1541	2835	Metallic	3	11
22	Ti	Titanium	Latin, Titanes = sons of the earth	M H Klaproth (Germany)	1795	47·90	4·506	1670	3360	Silvery metal	3 or 4	13
23	V	Vanadium	Vanadis, a name given to Freyja, the Norse goddess of beauty and youth	N G Sefström (Sweden)	1830	50·9414	6·119	1920	3425	Silvery-grey metal	2,3,4, or 5	9
24	Cr	Chromium	Greek, 'chromos' = colour	N-L Vauquelin (France)	1798	51·996	7·193	1860	2687	Silvery metal	2,3, or 6	10
25	Mn	Manganese	Latin, magnes = magnet	J G Gahn (Sweden)	1774	54·9380	7·472	1246	2065	Reddish-white metal	2,3,4,6, or 7	10
26	Fe	Iron (Ferrum)	Anglo-Saxon, iren	Prehistoric		55·847	7·874	1535	2865	Silvery-white metal	2 or 3	11
27	Co	Cobalt	German, kobold = goblin	G Brandt (Sweden)	1737	58·9332	8·834	1495	2900	Reddish-steel metal	2 or 3	11
28	Ni	Nickel	German, abbreviation of kupfernickel (devil's copper') or niccolite	A F Cronstedt (Sweden)	1751	58·70	8·907	1455	2920	Silvery-white metal	2 or 3	12
29	Cu	Copper (Cuprum)	Cyprus	Prehistoric (earliest known use)	c. 8000 BC	63·546	8·934	1084·88	2568	Reddish-bronze metal	1 or 2	12
30	Zn	Zinc	German, zink	A S Marggraf (Germany)	1746	65·38	7·140	419·58	908	Blue-white metal	2	18
31	Ga	Gallium	Latin, Gallia = France	L de Boisbaudran (France)	1875	69·72	5·912	29·77	2209	Grey metal	2 or 3	21
32	Ge	Germanium	Latin, Germania = Germany	C A Winkler (Germany)	1886	72·59	5·327	938·3	2835	Grey-white metal	4	20
33	As	Arsenic	Latin, arsenicum	Albertus Magnus (Germany)	c. 1220	74·9216	5·781	817 at 38 atm	603 sublimes	Steel-grey solid	3 or 5	19
34	Se	Selenium	Greek, 'selene' = moon	J J Berzelius (Sweden)	1818	78·96	4·810 (trigonal); 4·398 (α monoclinic); 4·352 (β monoclinic)	221·18	685	Greyish solid	2,4, or 6	22
35	Br	Bromine	Greek 'bromos' = stench	A-J Balard (France)	1826	79·904	3·119 (liquid at 20°C)	-7·25	59·09	Red-brown liquid	1,3,5, or 7	19
36	Kr	Krypton	Greek, 'kryptos' = hidden	W Ramsay and M W Travers (UK)	1898	83·80	2·801 (solid at mp); 0·003749 (gas at 0°C)	-157·38	-153·35	Colourless gas	0	23
37	Rb	Rubidium	Latin, rubidus = red	R W Bunsen and G R Kirchhoff (Germany)	1861	85·4678	1·529	39·30	688	Silvery-white metal	1	25
38	Sr	Strontium	Strontian, a village in Strathclyde, Scotland	H Davy (UK)	1808	87·62	2·582	768	1387	Silvery-white metal	2	20
39	Y	Yttrium	Ytterby, in Sweden	J Gadolin (Finland)	1794	88·9059	4·468	1522	3300	Steel-grey metal	3	19
40	Zr	Zirconium	Persian, 'zargun' = gold coloured	M H Klaproth (Germany)	1789	91·22	6·506	1855	4340	Steel-white metal	4	22
41	Nb	Niobium	Latin, Niobe, daughter of Tantalus	C Hatchett (UK)	1801	92·9064	8·595	2477	4860	Grey metal	3 or 5	21
42	Mo	Molybdenum	Greek, 'molybdos' = lead	P J Hjelm (Sweden)	1781	95·94	10·22	2623	4650	Silvery metal	2,3,4,5, or 6	20
43	Tc	Technetium	Greek, 'technetos' = artificial	C Perrier (France) and E Segré (Italy/USA)	1937	(96·9064)	11·28	2180	4270	Silvery-grey metal	2,3,4,6, or 7	17
44	Ru	Ruthenium	Ruthenia (The Ukraine, in USSR)	K K Klaus (Estonia/USSR)	1844	101·07	12·37	2330	4160	Bluish-white metal	3,4,6, or 8	18
45	Rh	Rhodium	Greek, 'rhodon' = rose	W H Wollaston (UK)	1804	102·9055	12·42	1963	3705	Steel-blue metal	2 or 4	16
46	Pd	Palladium	The asteroid Pallas (discovered 1802)	W H Wollaston (UK)	1803	106·4	12·01	1554	2975	Silvery-white metal	2 or 4	21
47	Ag	Silver (Argentum)	Anglo-Saxon, seolfor	Prehistoric (earliest silversmithery)	c. 4000 BC	107·868	10·50	961·93	2167	Lustrous white metal	1	24
48	Cd	Cadmium	Greek, 'kadmeia' = calamine	F Stromeyer (Germany)	1817	112·41	8·648	321·108	768	Blue-white metal	2	23
49	In	Indium	Its indigo spectrum	F Reich and H T Richter (Germany)	1863	114·82	7·289	156·634	2076	Bluish-silvery metal	1 or 3	28
50	Sn	Tin (Stannum)	Anglo-Saxon, tin	Prehistoric (intentionally alloyed c. 3500 BC with Cu to make Bronze)	c. 3500 BC	118·69	7·288	231·968	2608	Silvery-white metal	2 or 4	26

51–106 continued over page

Atomic Number	Symbol	Name of Element	Derived From	Discoverers	Year	Atomic Weight (Note 3)	Density at 20°C (unless otherwise stated) (g/cm³) (Note 4)	Melting Point °C (Note 5)	Boiling Point °C (Note 5)	Physical Description	Valency Number	Number of Nuclides
51	Sb	Antimony (Stibium)	Lower Latin, antimonium	Near Historic	c. 1000 BC	121.75	6.693	630.755	1589	Silvery metal	3 or 5	26
52	Te	Tellurium	Latin, tellus = earth	F J Muller (Baron von Reichenstein) (Austria)	1783	127.60	6.237	449.87	989	Silver-grey solid	2,4, or 6	31
53	I	Iodine	Greek, 'iodes' = violet	B Courtois (France)	1811	126.9045	4.947	113.6	185.3	Grey-black solid	1,3,5, or 7	27
54	Xe	Xenon	Greek, 'xenos' = stranger	W Ramsay and M W Travers (UK)	1898	131.30	3.399 (solid at mp)	-111.76	-108.09	Colourless gas	0	30
55	Cs	Caesium	Latin, caesius = bluish-grey	R W von Bunsen and G R Kirchhoff (Germany)	1860	132.9054	1.896	28.5	671	Silvery-white metal	1	30
56	Ba	Barium	Greek, 'barys' = heavy	H Davy (UK)	1808	137.33	3.595	729	1880	Silvery-white metal	2	25
57	La	Lanthanum	Greek, 'lanthano' = conceal	C G Mosander (Sweden)	1839	138.9055	6.145	921	3435	Metallic	3	23
58	Ce	Cerium	The asteroid Ceres (discovered 1801)	J J Berzelius and W Hisinger (Sweden); M H Klaproth (Germany)	1803	140.12	6.688 (beta) 6.770 (gamma)	799	3465	Steel-grey metal	3 or 4	20
59	Pr	Praseodymium	Greek, 'prasios didymos' = green twin	C Auer von Welsbach (Austria)	1885	140.9077	6.772	934	3480	Silvery-white metal	3	17
60	Nd	Neodymium	Greek, 'neos didymos' = new twin	C Auer von Welsbach (Austria)	1885	144.24	7.006	1021	3025	Yellowish-white metal	3	18
61	Pm	Promethium	Greek demi-god 'Prometheus'—the fire stealer	J Marinsky, L E Glendenin and C D Coryell (USA)	1945	(144.9128)	7.135	1042	2430	Metallic	3	16
62	Sm	Samarium	The mineral Samarskite, named after Col M Samarski, a Russian engineer	L de Boisbaudran (France)	1879	150.4	7.519	1077	1794	Light-grey metal	2 or 3	18
63	Eu	Europium	Europe	E A Demarçay (France)	1901	151.96	5.243	822	1560	Steel-grey metal	2 or 3	20
64	Gd	Gadolinium	Johan Gadolin (1760–1852)	J-C.- G de Marignac (Switzerland)	1880	157.25	7.899	1313	3270	Silvery-white metal	3	19
65	Tb	Terbium	Ytterby, in Sweden	C G Mosander (Sweden)	1843	158.9254	8.228	1356	3230	Silvery metal	3	18
66	Dy	Dysprosium	Greek, 'dysprositos'—hard to get at	L de Boisbaudran (France)	1886	162.50	8.549	1412	2573	Metallic	3	19
67	Ho	Holmium	Holmia, a Latinised form of Stockholm	J-L Soret (France) and P T Cleve (Sweden)	1878-9	164.9304	8.794	1474	2700	Silvery metal	3	21
68	Er	Erbium	Ytterby, in Sweden	C G Mosander (Sweden)	1843	167.26	9.064	1529	2815	Greyish-silver metal	2 or 3	21
69	Tm	Thulium	Latin and Greek, 'Thule' = Northland	P T Cleve (Sweden)	1879	168.9342	9.319	1545	1950	Metallic	2 or 3	24
70	Yb	Ytterbium	Ytterby, in Sweden	J-C.- G de Marignac (Switzerland)	1878	173.04	6.967	817	1227	Silvery metal	2 or 3	21
71	Lu	Lutetium	Lutetia, Roman name for the city of Paris	G Urbain (France)	1907	174.97	9.839	1665	3400	Metallic	3	21
72	Hf	Hafnium	Hafnia, Roman name for Copenhagen	D Coster (Netherlands) and G C de Hevesy (Hungary/Sweden)	1923	178.49	13.28	2230	4630	Steel-grey metal	4	24
73	Ta	Tantalum	'Tantalus', a mythical Greek king	A G Ekeberg (Sweden)	1802	180.9479	16.67	3020	5520	Silvery metal	3 or 5	16
74	W	Tungsten (Wolfram)	Swedish, tung sten = heavy stone	J J de Elhuyar and F de Elhuyar (Spain)	1783	183.85	19.26	3422	5730	Grey metal	2,4,5, or 6	23
75	Re	Rhenium	Latin, Rhenus = the river Rhine	W Noddack, Fr I Tacke, and O. Berg, (Germany)	1925	186.207	21.01	3185	5610	Whitish-grey metal	1,4, or 7	18
76	Os	Osmium	Greek, 'osme' = odour	S Tennant (UK)	1804	190.2	22.59	3100	5020	Grey-blue metal	2,3,4,6, or 8	30
77	Ir	Iridium	Latin, iris = a rainbow	S Tennant (UK)	1804	192.22	22.56	2447	4730	Silvery-white metal	3 or 4	28
78	Pt	Platinum	Spanish, platina, small silver	A de Ulloa (Spain)	1748	195.09	21.45	1769	3835	Bluish-white metal	2 or 4	30
79	Au	Gold (Aurum)	Anglo-Saxon, gold	Prehistoric		196.9665	19.29	1064.43	2860	Lustrous yellow metal	1 or 3	30
80	Hg	Mercury (Hydrargyrum)	Assigned the alchemical sign of the Greek god Hermes (Latin Mercurius), the divine patron of the occult sciences	Near Historic	c. 1600 BC	200.59	14.17 (solid at mp) 13.55 (liquid at 20°C)	-38.836	356.66	Silvery metallic liquid	1 or 2	30
81	Tl	Thallium	Greek, 'thallos' = a budding twig	W Crookes (UK)	1861	204.37	11.87	304	1475	Blue-grey metal	1 or 3	27
82	Pb	Lead (Plumbum)	Anglo-Saxon, lead	Prehistoric		207.2	11.35	327.502	1753	Steel-blue metal	2 or 4	30
83	Bi	Bismuth	German, weissmuth = white matter	C- F Geoffroy (France)	1753	208.9804	9.807	271.442	1566	Reddish-silvery metal	3 or 5	27
84	Po	Polonium	Poland	Mme M S Curie (Poland/France)	1898	(208.9824)	9.155	254	948	Metallic	2,3, or 4	26
85	At	Astatine	Greek, 'astatos' = unstable	D R Corson (USA), K R Mackenzie (USA), and E Segrè (Italy/USA)	1940	(209.9870)	~7.0	302	377	Metallic	1,3,5, or 7	24
86	Rn	Radon	Latin, radius = ray	F E Dorn (Germany)	1900	(222.0176)	~4.7 (solid at mp) 0.01009 (gas at 0°C)	-64.9	-61.2	Colourless gas	0	27
87	Fr	Francium	France	Mlle M Perey (France)	1939	(223.0197)	~2.8	23	657	Metallic	1	26
88	Ra	Radium	Latin, radius = ray	P Curie (France), Mme M S Curie (Poland/France), and M G Bemont (France)	1898	(226.0254)	5.50	707	1530	Silvery metal	2	25
89	Ac	Actinium	Greek, 'aktinos', genitive of 'aktis' = a ray	A Debierne (France)	1899	(227.0278)	10.04	1050	3415	Metallic	3	24
90	Th	Thorium	Thor, the Norse god of thunder	J J Berzelius (Sweden)	1829	232.0381	11.72	1760	4710	Grey metal	4	23
91	Pa	Protactinium	Greek, 'protos' = first, plus actinium	O Hahn (Germany) and Fr L Meitner (Austria); F Soddy and J A Cranston (UK)	1917	(231.0359)	15.41	1570	4530	Silvery metal	4 or 5	17
92	U	Uranium	The planet Uranus (discovered 1781)	M H Klaproth (Germany)	1789	238.029	19.05	1134	4270	Bluish-white metal	3,4,5, or 6	14

Note 1: The former spelling 'sulphur' is disallowed under International Union of Pure and Applied Chemistry rules on nomenclature.
Note 2: Because the discoveries of elements 104, 105, 106 and 107 are disputed, the International Union of Pure and Applied Chemistry have not yet assigned official names to these elements.
Note 3: A value in brackets is the atomic mass of the isotope with the longest known half-life (i.e. the period taken for its radioactivity to fall to half of its original value).
Note 4: For the highly radioactive elements the density value has been calculated for the isotope with the longest known half-life.
Note 5: All temperature values have been corrected to the International Practical Temperature Scale of 1968.
Note 6: This value is the minimum pressure under which liquid helium can be solidified.

The 107 elements *continued*

THE TRANSURANIC ELEMENTS (Metallic)

Atomic Number	Symbol	Name of Element	Derived from	Year	Atomic Weight (Note 3)	Density at 20°C (g/cm³) (Note 4)	Melting Point °C (Note 5)	Boiling Point °C (Note 5)	Number of Nuclides
93	Np	Neptunium	The planet Neptune	1940	(237·0482)	20·47	637	4030	13
94	Pu	Plutonium	The planet Pluto	1940	(244·0642)	20·26	640	3360	15
95	Am	Americium	America	1944	(243·0614)	13·77	1176	2020	11
96	Cm	Curium	The Curies—Pierre (1859–1906) and Marie (1867–1934)	1944	(247·0703)	13·69	1340	3110	13
97	Bk	Berkelium	Berkeley, a town in California, USA	1949	(247·0703)	14·67	986	——	9
98	Cf	Californium	California, USA	1950	(251·0796)	15·23	900	——	15
99	Es	Einsteinium	Dr. Albert Einstein (1879–1955)	1953	(254·0880)	——	——	——	14
100	Fm	Fermium	Dr Enrico Fermi (1901–54)	1953	(257·0951)	——	——	——	17
101	Md	Mendelevium	Dmitriy I Mendeleyev (1834–1907)	1955	(528·099)	——	——	——	10
102	No	Nobelium	Alfred B Nobel (1833–96)	1958	(259·101)	——	——	——	9
103	Lr	Lawrencium	Dr Ernest O Lawrence (1901–58)	1961	(260·105)	——	——	——	8
104	Ku	Kurchatovium (Note 2) or	Dr Igor V Kurchatov (1903–60)	1964	(261·109)	——	——	——	8
105	Rf Ns	Rutherfordium (Note 2) Nielsbohrium (Note 2) or	Lord (Ernest) Rutherford (1871–1937) Prof Niels Bohr (1885–1962)	1969 1970	(262·114)	——	——	——	3
106	Ha —	Hahnium (Note 2) (Note 2)	Prof Otto Hahn (1879–1968) (Note 2)	1970 1974	(263·120)	——	——	——	2 ?
107	—	(Note 2)	(Note 2)	1976	(261·125)	——	——	——	1 ?

MEDICINE

Notes on the National Health Service (inaugurated 1 Aug. 1948); the General Medical Council and the Nursing Services were published in the *Guinness Book of Answers* **(1976 edition) on pages 33 and 34.**

Prediction of Human Stature

The table below shows the average mean percentage of mature height for both boys and girls at each age from birth to 18 years. These percentages, taken from large samples, essentially reflect the proven average expectation of ultimate height.

Age in Years	Boys	Girls
Birth	28·6%	30·9%
¼	33·9%	36·0%
½	37·7%	39·8%
¾	40·1%	42·2%
1	42·2%	44·7%
1½	45·6%	48·8%
2	49·5%	52·8%
2½	51·6%	54·8%
3	53·8%	57·0%
4	58·0%	61·8%
5	61·8%	66·2%
6	65·2%	70·3%
7	69·0%	74·0%
8	72·0%	77·5%
9	75·0%	80·7%
10	78·0%	84·4%
11	81·1%	88·4%
12	84·2%	92·9%
13	87·3%	96·5%
14	91·5%	98·3%
15	96·1%	99·1%
16	98·3%	99·6%
17	99·3%	100·0%
18	99·8%	100·0%

Thus a boy measuring 4 ft 6 in (54 in) on his ninth birthday could be expected to be

$$54 \times \frac{100}{75\cdot0} = 72 \text{ in or 6 ft 0 in as a man.}$$

In practice because of maternal factors, the prediction of adult stature becomes of value

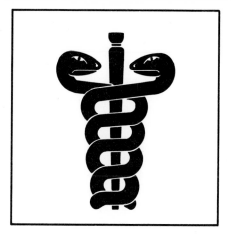

only after the age of 2 or 2½ years. After the age of 9½ prediction is more accurately based on skeletal rather than chronological age. The accuracy tends to be greater throughout for girls than for boys, who, at 14 are subject to a standard deviation of error of 4 per cent, *viz.* the 91·5 per cent figure can be 95·8 per cent for a physically advanced boy, and 87·6 per cent for a retarded one.

Human Expenditure of Energy

	Rate in calories per hour
Lying at ease	90
Sitting at ease (man)	108
Sitting and writing	114
Standing at ease	118
Driving a car	168
Washing up (woman)	198
Driving a motor cycle	204
Dressing, washing, shaving	212
Bed making (woman)	420
Walking 4 mph	492
Climbing 6 in stairs at 1½ mph	620
Tree felling	640
Bicycling at 13 mph	660
Running at 5 mph	850
Running at 7½ mph	975
Rowing at 33 strokes/min	1140
Swimming breaststroke at 56 strokes/min	1212
Nordic skiing (level loose snow) at 9·15 mph	1572

Note: Women expend less calories in performing the same activity, e.g. a man washing up would expend well over 200 cals./hour.

Sense of Smell

According to the stereochemical theory of olfaction there are for man seven primary odours each associated with a typical shape of molecule:

1. camphoraceous — spherical molecules
2. ethereal — very small or thin molecules
3. floral — kite shaped molecules
4. musky — disc shaped molecules
5. peppermint — wedged shaped molecules
6. pungent — undetermined
7. putrid — undetermined

Other smells are complexes of the above basic seven, e.g. almonds are a complex of 1, 3 and 5.

Somatotypes

One of the systems used for classifying human physique is somatotyping (from the Greek *soma*, body) first published in 1940 by Sheldon of the USA.

The three components used, some degree of which is present in everyone, are: (1) Endomorphy (a tendency to globularity): (2) Mesomorphy (a tendency to muscularity);

and (3) Ectomorphy (a tendency to linearity). The degrees of tendency range from 1 to an extreme of 7.

Billy Bunter types would be 7—1—1; Hercules would be 1—7—1, and the extreme in 'weediness' would be 1—1—7. In practice such extremes are rarely encountered. The commonest somatotypes are 3—4—4, 4—3—3, and 3—5—2. The components are oblique, not orthogonal, i.e. not independent of each other to the point where it would be impossible to have a 5—5—5 or a 7—7—1.

Research (Tanner, 1964) into a sample of Olympic athletes shows that mean Endomorphy varies between 2·0 (steeplechasers) and 3·8 (shot putters); Mesomorphy between 4·1 (high jumpers) and 6·2 (discus throwers); and Ectomorphy between 4·5 (steeplechasers) and 2·0 (shot and discus throwers). Sprinters averaged 2·5—5·5—2·9 while milers have a mean rating of 2·5—4·3—4·3.

Inflammatory conditions

The suffix -itis is the feminine form of the Greek -ites, meaning connected with. Originally, for example, carditis was termed carditis nosus, meaning the disease connected with the heart. Soon the nosus was dropped and the -itis suffix was used to indicate, more narrowly, an inflammation of a part of the body.

adenitis—lymphatic glands
angiitis—blood vessels
appendicitis—vermiform appendix
arteritis—arteries
arthritis—joints
blepharitis—eyelid
bronchiolitis—bronchioles
bronchitis—bronchial tubes
bursitis—bursa
capsulitis—joint ligaments
carditis—heart
cellulitis—subcutaneous tissues
cervicitis—neck of the uterus
cheilitis—lip
cholecystitis—gall bladder
chondritis—cartilage
colitis—colon
conjunctivitis—conjunctiva
coxitis—hip joint
cystitis—bladder
dermatitis—skin
diaphragmatitis—diaphragm
diverticulitis—diverticulae of colon
duodenitis—duodenum
encephalitis—brain
encystitis—'an encysted tumour'
endocarditis—endocardium
endometritis—uterine lining
enteritis—bowels
entero-colitis—colon and small intestine
epididymitis—epididymis
ethmoiditis—ethmoid sinuses
fibrositis—fibrous tissues
gastritis—stomach
gingivitis—gums
glossitis—tongue
gnathitis—upper jaw or cheek
hepatitis—liver
hyalitis—vitreous humour of the eye
hysteritis—uterus
ileitis—ileum
iritis—iris
keratitis—cornea
laminitis—part of a vertebra
laryngitis—larynx
mastitis—the breast
mastoiditis—mastoid process
meningitis—meninges
meningomyelitis—meninges and spinal cord
mesenteritis—mesentery
metritis—uterus
myelitis—spinal cord
myocarditis—myocardium
myositis—muscle
nephritis—kidneys
neuritis—nerves

oesophagitis—oesophagus
omphalitis—navel
oophoritis—ovary
ophthalmitis—whole eye
orchitis—testes
osteitis—bone
otitis—ear
ovaritis—ovaries
pancreatitis—pancreas
parotitis—parotid glands (e.g. mumps)
pericarditis—pericardium
periodontitis—jaw (part around the tooth)
periostitis—periosteum
peritonitis—peritoneum (or of the bowels)
pharyngitis—pharynx
phlebitis—vein
pleuritis—pleura
pneumonitis—lungs
poliomyelitis—inflammation of grey matter of spinal cord (or paralysis due to this)
proctitis—rectum
prostatitis—prostate gland
pyelitis—pelvis of the kidney
rachitis—spine
rectitis—rectum
retinitis—retina
rhinitis—nose
salpingitis—salpinx
sclerotitis—sclerotic
scrotitis—scrotum
sigmoiditis—sigmoid colon
sinusitis—sinus
sphenoiditis—air cavity in the sphenoid bone
splenitis—spleen
spondylitis—vertebrae
stomatitis—mouth
synovitis—synovial membrane
tonsillitis—tonsils
tracheitis—trachea
tympanitis—ear-drum
ulitis—gums
ureteritis—ureter
urethritis—urethra
uteritis—womb
vaginitis—vagina
vulvitis—vulva

The Hippocratic Oath

A form of the following oath, attributed to Hippocrates (*c.* 460–377 BC), the Greek physician called the 'Father of Medicine', is sworn to at some medical schools on the occasion of taking a degree.

'I swear by Apollo the healer, invoking all the gods and goddesses to be my witnesses, that I will fulfil this oath and this written covenant to the best of my ability and judgement.

'I will look upon him who shall have taught me this art even as one of my own parents. I will share my substance with him, and I will supply his necessities if he be in need. I will regard his offspring even as my own brethren, and I will teach them this art, if they would learn it, without fee or covenant. I will impart this art by precept, by lecture and by every mode of teaching, not only to my own sons but to the sons of him who has taught me, and to disciples bound by covenant and oath, according to the law of medicine.

'The regimen I adopt shall be for the benefit of the patients according to my ability and judgement, and not for their hurt or for any wrong. I will give no deadly drug to any, though it be asked of me, nor will I counsel such, and especially I will not aid a woman to procure abortion. Whatsoever house I enter, there will I go for the benefit of the sick, refraining from all wrongdoing or corruption, and especially from any act of seduction, of male or female, of bond or free. Whatsoever things I see or hear concerning the life of men, in my attendance on the sick or even apart therefrom, which ought not to be noised abroad, I will keep silence thereon, counting such things to be as sacred secrets. Pure and holy will I keep my life and my art.'

Human dentifion

Man normally has two sets of teeth during his life span. The primary (milk or deciduous) set of 20 is usually acquired between the ages of 6 and 24 months. The secondary (or permanent) dentition of 32 teeth grows in usually from about the sixth year.

The four principal types of teeth are:—

Incisors (Lat. *incidere*—to cut into) total eight. Two upper central, flanked by two upper lateral with four lower.

Canine (Lat. *canis*—a dog) total four. These are next to the lateral incisors and are thus the third teeth from the mid-line in each quadrant of the mouth. These are also referred to as *cuspids* (Lat. *cuspis*—a point).

Pre-Molars (Lat. *molare*—to grind) total eight. These are next in line back from the incisors, two in each quadrant. Because these have two cusps these are alternatively known as bi-cuspids.

Molars (see above) total twelve. These are the furthest back in the mouth—three in each quadrant. The upper molars often have four cusps and the lower five cusps for grinding. The third (hindermost) molars are known also as 'wisdom teeth' and do not usually appear until the age of 18 to 20.

Human genetics

The normal human has 46 chromosomes. The chromosome is the microscopic thread-like body within cells which carries hereditary factors or genes. These are classified as 22 pairs of non-sex chromosomes or autosomes (one of each pair derived from the father and one from the mother) and two sex chromosomes or gonosomes, making 46. In a female both gonosomes are Xs, one from the father and one from the mother. In a male they are an X from the mother and a Y from the father. The X chromosome is much larger than the Y, thus women possess four per cent more deoxyribonucleic acid than males. This may have a bearing on their greater longevity. The human sometimes exhibits 47 chromosomes.

One such instance is the XXX female in which the supernumerary is an extra X. In some cases of hermaphroditism the supernumerary is a Y.

Chimpanzees, gorillas, and orang-outangs have 48 chromosomes. It has been suggested that man's emergence from the primitive man-ape population may have occurred by a process known as 'reciprocal translocation'. This is a mechanism whereby two dissimilar chromosomes break and two of the four dissimilar parts join with the possible net loss of one chromosome. It is possible that 47 and 46 chromosome hominoids enjoyed a bipedal advantage on forest edges over brachiating apes and thus the evolution of man began from this point.

Skin

The skin is by far the largest single organ of the human body. It weighs about 16 per cent of the total body weight and in an average adult male has a surface area of 2800 in² *18000 cm²*. The three main groups into which Man is divided by the colour of his skin are *Leukoderms* (white-skinned), *Melanoderms* (black-skinned) and *Xanthoderms* (yellow-skinned). Pigment-producing cells in the basal layers of the epidermis are called melanoblasts (Greek *melas*—black *blastos*—bud).

The number (up to 4000 per sq cm) and the size do not vary significantly in white and negro skin but are more active and productive in the latter so protecting the iris and the retina against the brightness of the sun.

The human brain

It is estimated that a human brain, weighing about 3 lb *1·36 kg*, contains 10 000 000 000 nerve cells. Each of these deploys a potential 25 000 interconnections with other cells. Compared with this the most advanced computers are giant electronic morons.

Sex ratio
In the United Kingdom about 1056 boys are born to every 1000 girls.

Medical and surgical specialties
There are in medicine a great number of specialties. It is possible to have Departments of Neurology, Paediatrics and Paediatric-Neurology in the same hospital. This list provides an explanation of medical departments.
Allergy—reaction of a patient to an outside substance, e.g. pollen or Penicillin, producing symptoms which may vary between being inconvenient e.g. hay fever or rashes to fatal, e.g. asthma.
Anaesthetics—the skill of putting a patient to sleep with drugs.
Anatomy—the study of the structure of the body.
Anthropology—the study of man in his environment.
Apothecary—a pharmacist or, in its old-fashioned sense, a general practitioner was once described as an apothecary.
Audiology—the assessment of hearing.
Aurology—the study of ear disease.
Bacteriology—the study of bacterial infections. This usually includes viruses as well.
Biochemistry—the study of the variation of salts and chemicals on the body.
Bio-engineering—the study of the mechanical workings of the body, particularly with reference to artificial limbs and powered appliances which the body can use.
Biophysics—the study of electrical impulses from the body. This can be seen with assessment of muscle disease etc.
Cardiology—the study of heart disease.
Community medicine—the prevention of the spread of disease and the increase of physical and mental well being within a community.
Cryo-surgery—the use of freezing techniques in surgery.
Cytogenetics—the understanding of the particles within a cell which help to reproduce the same type of being again.
Cytology—the microscopic study of body cells.
Dentistry—the treatment and extraction of teeth.
Dermatology—the treatment of skin diseases.
Diabetics—the treatment of diabetes.
Embryology—the study of the growth of the baby from the moment of conception to about the 20th week.
Endocrinology—the study of the diseases of the glands which produce hormones.
E.N.T. *see* Otorhinolaryngology
Entomology—the study of insects, moths, with particular reference to their transmission of disease.
Epidemiology—the study of epidemics and the way that diseases travel from one person to another.
Forensic medicine—the study of injury and disease caused by criminal activity and the detection of crime by medical knowledge.
Gastro-enterology—the study of stomach and intestinal diseases.
Genetics—the study of inherited characteristics, disease and malformations.
Genito-urinary disease—the study of diseases of the sexual and urine-producing organs.
Geriatrics—the study of diseases and condition of elderly people.
Gerontology—the study of diseases of elderly people and in particular the study of the ageing process.

Gynaecology—the study of diseases of women.
Haematology—the study of blood diseases.
Histochemistry—the study of the chemical environment of the body cells.
Histology—the microscopic study of cells.
Histopathology—the microscopic study of diseased or abnormal cells.
Homeopathy—is a form of treatment by administering minute doses which in larger doses would reproduce the symptoms of the disease that is being treated. The theory is that the body is thereby stimulated into coping with the problem by itself.
Immunology—the study of the way the body reacts to outside harmful diseases and influences, e.g. the production of body proteins to overcome such diseases as diphtheria or the rejection of foreign substances like transplanted kidneys.
Laryngology—the study of throat diseases.
Metabolic disease—diseases of the interior workings of the body, e.g. disorders of calcium absorption etc., thyroid disease or adrenal gland disease.
Microbiology—the study of the workings of cells.
Nephrology—the study of kidney disease.
Neurology—the study of a wide range of diseases of the brain or nervous system.
Neurosurgery—operations on the brain or nervous system.
Nuclear medicine—treatment of diseases with radio-active substances.
Obstetrics—the care of the pregnant mother and the delivery of the child.
Oncology—study of cancer.
Ophthalmology—the study of diseases of the eye.
Optician—the measurement of disorders of the lens of the eye done by a medically unqualified but trained practitioner so that spectacles can be given to correct the disorder.
Orthodontology—a dental approach to producing teeth that are straight.
Orthopaedics—fractures and bone diseases.
Orthoptics—medically unqualified but trained practitioner treatment of squints of the eye.
Orthotist—an orthopaedic appliance technician.
Otology—the study of diseases of the ear.
Otorhinolaryngology—the study of diseases of the ear, nose and throat often referred to as E.N.T.
Paediatrics—diseases of children.
Parasitology—the study of infections of the body by worms.
Pathology—the study of dead disease by *post mortem* examination either under the microscope or the whole organ.
Pharmacology—the study of the use of drugs in relation to medicine.
Physical Medicine—the treatment of damaged parts of the body with exercises, electrical treatments etc. or the preparation of the body for surgery, e.g. breathing exercises and leg exercises.
Physiology—the study and understanding of the normal workings of the body.
Physiotherapist—a trained person who works in the physical medicine department.
Plastic surgery—the reconstruction and alteration of damaged or normal parts of the body.
Proctology—the study of diseases of the rectum or back passage.
Prosthetics—the making of artificial limbs and appliances.
Psychiatry—the study and treatment of mental disease.
Psycho-analysis—the investigation of the formation of mental illness by long-term repeated discussion.
Psychology—the study of the mind with particular reference to the measurement of intellectual activity.
Psychotherapy—treatment of mental disorder.

Radiobiology—the treatment or investigation of disease using radio-active substances.
Radiography—the taking of X-rays.
Radiology—the study of X-rays.
Radiotherapy—the treatment of disease with X-rays.
Renal diseases—the diseases of the kidney or urinary tract.
Rheumatology—the study of diseases of muscles and joints.
Rhinology—the study of diseases of the nose.
Therapeutics—curative medicine, the healing of physical and/or mental disorder.
Thoracic surgery—surgery on the chest or heart.
Toxicology—the understanding and analysis of poisons.
Urology—the study of diseases of the kidney or urinary tract.
Vascular disease—diseases of the blood vessels.
Venereology—the study of sexually transmitted disease.
Virology—the study of virus diseases.

VACCINES
Anthrax—a killed vaccine which is recommended for workers at particular risk, e.g. farmers, and butchers. Doses should be given yearly.
Bubonic Plague—killed and live vaccines can be used to limit epidemics. They give about six months' protection.
Cholera—two injections of the killed organism should be given 10 days apart and will give 3–6 months' protection. Thereafter injections should be given six-monthly. It only gives moderate protection.
Diphtheria—the killed organism is given in a course of 3 injections to infants and a booster dose at the age of 5 will give long-lasting immunity. Anti-toxin is used for those who have caught diphtheria. It gives temporary protection.
German Measles (Rubella)—a modified living vaccine is recommended to be given to all girls between the age of 11 and 13, i.e. before the onset of menstruation, and protects against infection of the foetus and thus congenital malformations.
Influenza—killed vaccines will give about 70 per cent protection for 9 months to a year in epidemics of a similar virus. They are particularly useful in those who tend to have respiratory illness, the infirm or elderly. Modified living virus vaccines are at present under assessment.
Measles—a modified living vaccine is given in the second year of life and will give prolonged protection and, in about 50 per cent, will produce a very mild feverish illness. It does not produce encephalitis.
Meningococcal meningitis—killed vaccines of both types A and C have been produced. They help in the prevention of the spread of epidemics.
Mumps—a modified living vaccine gives long-lasting protection. It is often used for adults who have not had the natural infection.
Poliomyelitis—Sabin modified living oral vaccine gives long-term protection. It is usually given in 3 doses to infants and a booster dose at the age of 5, and sometimes in the early teens. It rarely causes cases of clinical poliomyelitis. Salk vaccine is the killed virus and gives short-term protection. It is seldom used nowadays.
Rabies—14 consecutive daily injections of the killed virus are given into the stomach wall of those who may have been infected with the rabies virus. Newer vaccines are at present being evaluated.
Smallpox—a live vaccine gives protection for up to 5 years. The international regulations recognise a certificate lasting 3 years. It is no longer recommended to be used routinely in

77

MEDICINE

the United Kingdom. Outbreaks of smallpox are treated by vaccinating all those who have been in contact or close to anybody who has been in contact.

Tetanus—the killed organism is usually given in 3 injections combined with diphtheria and sometimes whooping cough. A booster dose at the age of 5 and then boosters every 5 years.

Tuberculosis—Bacille Calmette-Guerin (BCG) is a modified living organism which is given to those aged between 10 and 13 in the UK by the school health authorities. It gives lifelong immunity.

Typhoid and *Paratyphoid*—Typhoid and paratyphoid A & B (TAB) vaccine is prepared from the killed organisms. Newer vaccines contain the typhoid by itself. There is a cross-protection between typhoid and paratyphoid A & B. Two injections are given at 10 days to a month apart. These will prevent the severity of the disease but may not stop the patient catching it. Booster doses should be given yearly in areas where the infection is prevalent and every 2–3 years for those visiting these areas.

Typhus—highly effective killed vaccines will give protection for about a year.

Whooping Cough—this is usually combined with the 3 injections with diphtheria and tetanus. The present view is that it may occasionally cause damage to infants and some authorities recommend it should not be given.

Yellow Fever—a modified living vaccine will give 10 years' protection and this is recognised on an international vaccination certificate.

BONES IN THE HUMAN BODY

Skull	Number
Occipital	1
Parietal—1 pair	2
Sphenoid	1
Ethmoid	1
Inferior Nasal Conchae—1 pair	2
Frontal—1 pair, fused	1
Nasal—1 pair	2
Lacrimal—1 pair	2
Temporal—1 pair	2
Maxilla—1 pair	2
Zygomatic—1 pair	2
Vomer	1
Palatine—1 pair	2
Mandible—1 pair, fused	1
	22

The Ears	
Malleus	2
Incus	2
Stapes	2
	6

Vertebrae	
Cervical	7
Thoracic	12
Lumbar	5
Sacral—5, fused to form the Sacrum	1
Coccyx—between 3 and 5, fused	1
	26

Vertebral Ribs	
Ribs, 'true'—7 pairs	14
Ribs, 'false'—5 pairs of which 2 pairs are floating	10
	24

Sternum	
Manubrium	1
'The Body' (Sternebrae)	1
Xiphisternum	1
Hyoid	1
	4

Pectoral Girdle	
Clavicle—1 pair	2
Scapula—(including Coracoid)—1 pair	2
	4

Upper Extremity (each arm)	
Humerus	1
Radius	1
Ulna	1
Carpus:	
Scaphoid	1
Lunate	1
Triquetral	1
Pisiform	1
Trapezium	1
Trapezoid	1
Capitate	1
Hamate	1
Metacarpals	5
Phalanges:	
First Digit	2
Second Digit	3
Third Digit	3
Fourth Digit	3
Fifth Digit	3
	30

Pelvic Girdle	
Ilium, Ischium and Pubis (combined)—1 pair of hip bones, innominate	2

Lower Extremity (each leg)	
Femur	1
Tibia	1
Fibula	1
Tarsus:	
Talus	1
Calcaneus	1
Navicular	1
Cuneiform medial	1
Cuneiform, intermediate	1
Cuneiform, lateral	1
Cuboid	1
Metatarsals	5
Phalanges:	
First Digit	2
Second Digit	3
Third Digit	3
Fourth Digit	3
Fifth Digit	3
	29

Total	
Skull	22
The Ears	6
Vertebrae	26
Vertebral Ribs	24
Sternum	4
Pectoral Girdle	4
Upper Extremity (arms)—2 × 30	60
Hip Bones	2
Lower Extremity (legs)—2 × 29	58
	206

Normal pulse rates in man		Beats per minute
Embryo	5 months	156
	6 months	154
	7 months	150
	8 months	142
	9 months	145
Newborn (premature)		110–185
Newborn (full term)		135
2 years		110
4 years		105
6 years		95
8 years		90
10 years		87
15 years		83
20 years		71
21–25		74
25–30		72
30–35		70
35–40		72
40–45		72
45–50		72
50–55		72
55–60		75
60–65		73
65–70		75
70–75		75
75–80		72
>80		78
Lying down (adult)		66
Sitting (adult)		73
Standing (adult)		82
Sleeping (adult)		♂59 ♀65
Waking (adult)		♂78 ♀84

PHARMACOLOGY

Below are listed a selection of the most used and important drugs in medical practice. These are listed in order of the date of their introduction so that the weakness or strength of the pharmacological and therapeutic armoury can be seen at a glance at any point in time.

Principal drugs in order of their discovery

c. 2100 ante BC *Ethyl alcohol* or *ethanol* (C_2H_5OH). One of the earliest drugs used to stupify.

c. 1550 AD *Digitalis*, a mixture of compounds from the leaf of the Foxglove (*Digitalis purpurea* L.). Myocardial stimulant, used by herbalists since c. 1550 and introduced into scientific medicine by William Withering (GB) in 1785. Its components are still in use in treating heart failure.

1805 *Morphine*. Addictive narcotic analgesic, an alkaloid of opium which is the dried latex from the unripe capsules of the poppy (*Papaver somniferum*). First recognised by Friedrich Sertürner (Germany) in 1805 but not used in medical practice till 1821. Synthesised in 1952.

1818 *Quinine*. Obtained from Cinchona tree bark. Separated by P J Pelletier and J B Caventou (France) 1818 to 1820. Anti-malarial use.

1819 *Atropine* ($C_{17}H_{23}NO_3$). A parasympatholytic. First isolated in 1819 by Rudolph Brandes from belladonna (*Atropa belladonna*). Related motion-sickness drug is hyoscine.

78

1820 *Colchicine* ($C_{22}H_{25}NO_6$). Analgesic derived from meadow saffron (*Colchicum Autumnale*), used particularly in the treatment of gout. Isolated in 1820 by P J Pelletier and J B Caventou.

1821 *Codeine or methylmorphine.* Occurs naturally in opium and is a derivative of morphine (q.v.). Anti-tussive, weak analgesic.

1842 *Ether* (diethyl ether). General anaesthetic. First administered by Dr C W Long (1815–78) in Jefferson, Georgia, on 30 Mar. 1842 for a cystectomy.

1844 *Nitrous Oxide* (N_2O) (Dinitrogen Monoxide, or Laughing Gas). Anaesthetic in operations of short duration as prolonged inhalation can cause death. Discovered in 1776 by Joseph Priestly. First used as anaesthetic in 1844 by an American dentist, Horace Wells.

1846 *Glyceryl Trinitrate* (nitroglycerin, $C_3H_5N_3O_9$). Known mainly as an explosive. Used as a vasolidator in easing cardiac pains in angina pectoris. First prepared in 1846 by Ascanio Sobrero of Italy.

1847 *Chloroform.* Introduced as an anaesthetic by Sir James Simpson (GB).

1859 *Cocaine* (from the Peruvian coca bean (*Erythroxylon coca* and *E. truxillense*)). First separated by Niemann. Formula established by Wöhler in 1860. Local anaesthetic, which results in dependence.

1867 *Phenol* (Carbolic acid (C_6H_5OH). Earliest bactericide and disinfectant, discovered by Lister in 1867. Antiseptic and antipruritic.

1891 *Thyroid Extract.* First use as injection in treatment for Myxoedema by George Murray in 1891. The active principles are *tri-iodothyronine* and *thyroxine.*

1893 *Aspirin* (a trade name for acetylsalicylic acid) ($C_9H_8O_4$). An analgesic, and the earliest antiuretic. Introduced in 1893 by Hermann Dresser.

1893 *Paracetamol* (Acetaminophen) ($C_8H_9NO_2$). First used in medicine by Joseph von Mering in 1893, but only gained popularity as an antipyretic analgesic in 1949.

1901 *Adrenaline* (epinephrine) ($C_9H_{13}NO_3$). Hormone secreted by medulla of adrenal gland in response to stress. It mimics the effects of stimulation of the sympathetic (adrenergic) autonomic nervous system. First isolated in 1901 by J Takamine (1854–1922) and T B Aldrick and synthesised in 1904 by Friedrich Stolz (1860–1936).

1903 *Barbitone.* Early example of barbituric acid derivates (barbiturates) with hypnotic, sedative and anticonvulsant properties, e.g. phenobarbitone (long-acting), pentobarbitone (intermediate), thupentone (short-acting).

1906 *Procaine* (Novocaine). Local anaesthetic, introduced as a substitute for cocaine by Alfred Einhorn. Non-habit forming but low penetrating power.

1907 *Histamine* (β-iminoazolylethylamine). Isolated by Adolf Windus (1876–1959) and Karl Vogt (b. 1880). One of a number of substances released by body tissues as part of allergic or inflammatory responses. The earliest anti-histamine was 933 F discovered by G Ungar (France, et al. in 1937.

1912 *Acriflavine.* Introduced as an antiseptic by Paul Ehrlich.

1917 *Oxygen* (O). The most plentiful element in the Earth's crust. Essential to life as we know it. Discovered c. 1772 by the Swede, Carl Wilhelm Scheele and independently in 1774 by John Priestly. First used therapeutically by J S Haldane in 1917.

1921 *Ergotmetrine.* One of a mixture of ergot alkaloids found in rye grain infected with the fungus *Claviceps purpurea.* Used as a uterine stimulant. First isolated by K Spiro and A Stoll (Germany) in 1921. Another component *Ergotamine* is used to treat migraine.

1921 *Insulin,* the specific antidiabetic hormone from the mammalian pancreas. Isolated by Sir Frederick Banting (1891–1941) and Dr C H Best (b. 1899) at Toronto, Canada, in 1921. First synthesised in 1964.

1929 *Progesterone* ($C_{21}H_{30}O_2$). Female steroid hormone secreted by ovary following ovulation to prepare uterus for, and to maintain pregnancy. Isolated by G Corner and W Allen in 1929. Related compounds are used with oestrogen, or alone, in oral contraceptives.

1929 *Testosterone* ($C_{19}H_{28}O_2$). Androgenic (masculanising) hormone. First obtained in 1929 by C Moore, T Gallagher and F Koch. Related anabolic (muscle-building) steroids used by participants in sporting activities.

1930 *Mepacrine* (or *quinacrine* or *atebrin*). Now replaced by Chloroquine. Antimalarial.

1933 *Adrenocorticotrophic hormone* (ACTH). First isolated by J B Collip (b. 1892) et al. Active against arthritis.

1935 *Pentothal.* Intravenous anaesthetic.

1935 *Tubocurarine.* Crystalline alkaloid isolated from curare in 1935 by Harold King, used as a skeletal-muscle relaxant.

1936 *Oestradiol* ($C_{25}H_{28}O_3$). The principle oestrogenic hormone, isolated by D MacCorquodale in 1936.

1937 *Dapsone* ($C_{12}H_{12}N_2O_2S$). Bacteriostatic drug, effects in treatment of leprosy noted in 1937.

1937 *Sulphonamides.* Analogues of p-aminobenzoic acid with antibacterial activity. The most used early sulpha drug was sulphapyridine (May and Baker 693), $C_{11}H_{14}N_3O_2S$ from 1937 (Dr Arthur Ewins).

1938 *Phenytoin* ($C_{15}H_{12}N_2O_2$). Anticonvulsant introduced in 1938 by Merritt and Pulman for all types of epilepsy except absence seizures.

1939 *DDT* (Dichloro-diphenyl-trichloroethane). A powerful insecticide developed by Dr Paul Müller which has vastly lowered the malarial death rate.

1939 *Pethidine.* A narcotic analgesic particularly for childbirth. Introduced 1939 from Hoechst. Synthesised by Eisleb and Schaumann.

1940 *Penicillin.* Group of antibacterial substances (e.g. penicillin G, the benzyl derivative, $C_{16}H_{17}N_2Na$(or K)O_4S). Discovered in 1928 by Sir Alexander Fleming (1881–1955) by the chance contamination of a petri dish at St Mary's Hospital, London. First concentrated in 1940 by Sir Howard Florey (b. 1898) and E B Chain (b. 1906). Not identified as *Pencillium notatum* until 1930. Penicillin G introduced 1946. In

1961 Chain *et al.* isolate *b-aminopenicillanic Acid* which is the nucleus for many semi-synthetic derivates e.g. ampicillin.

1943 *LSD* (Lysergic acid diethylamide). A hallucinogen, discovered by Albert Hofman (Switzerland) in Apr. 1943. Now has no recognised therapeutic use.

c. 1943 *Dimercaprol* (*BAL*) (Formerly Brtish Anti-Lewisite) ($C_3H_8OS_2$). Developed during the war by L Stocken and R Thompson, to combat lethal war gas, lewisite. Later uses discovered as antidote to poisoning by arsenic, gold or mercury.

1944 *Mepyramine* (*Pyrilamine*). First acceptable antihistamine.

1944 *Amphetamine* (commercial name for the sulphate is Benzedrine). Dextroamphetamine is marketed as Dexedrine. A fatigue-inhibiting mildly addictive synthetic drug.

1944 *Streptomycin.* An antibiotic discovered by S A Waksman (Russian born, USA) in 1944. Important for its activity against tuberculosis.

c. 1944 *Paludrine* (proguanil hydrochloride). An antimalarial drug.

1947 *Chloramphenicol* ($C_{11}H_{12}Cl_2N_2O_5$). An antibiotic from *Streptomyces venezuelae* used for treatment of typhoid. First isolated by Buckholder (USA) in 1947 and first synthesised in 1949.

1948 *Chlortetracycline* (*Aureomycin*). An antibiotic first isolated in 1948 at Pearl River, NY, USA, by Dr Benjamin M Duggar.

1948 *Imipramine* ($C_{11}H_{24}N_2$). A dibenzazepine derivative, synthesised by Häfliger in 1948. An antidepressant.

1949 *Cortisone.* One of a number of steroid hormones from adrenal cortical extracts so named in 1939. First used in treatment of rheumatoid arthritis in 1949 leading to development of many anti-inflammatory steroids.

1951 *Halothane* ($C_2HBrClF_3$). General anaesthetic first synthesised in 1951 by Suckling.

1952 *Chlorpromazine* ($C_{17}H_{19}ClN_2S$). Potent synthetic tranquilliser first synthesised by Charpentier in 1952. Acts selectively upon higher centres in brain as a central nervous system depressant.

1952 *Isoniazide* (Isotonic Acid Hydrazide-INH) ($C_6H_7N_3O$). Use in the treatment of tuberculosis reported on by Edward Robitzek in 1952.

1954 *Methyldopa.* Use in treatment of hypertension. Effects first noted in 1954 by Sourkes.

1954 *Reserpine* ($C_{33}H_{40}N_2O_9$). Tranquilliser from Rauwolfia, a genus of plant in the dogbane family, used in treatment of high blood pressure and hypertension. Effects noted in modern times by Kline in 1954.

1955 *Oral Contraceptives.* The first reported field studies of a pill containing synthetic hormones that prevent ovulation were those by Pincus using Enovid in 1955, in Puerto Rico.

1955 *Metronidazole* ($C_6H_9N_3O_3$). Based on discovery of Azomycin in 1955 by Nakamura. Used in treatment of trichomoniasis, and other protozoal infections.

1956 *Amphotericin.* An antifungal antibiotic used typically. Elucidated in 1956 by Vandeputte *et al.*

1957 *Interferon.* A group of proteins produced on virus-infected cells.

They inhibit the multiplication of viruses.

c. 1960 *Tolbutamide* ($C_{12}H_{18}N_2O_3S$). Reduces blood sugar level in diabetics.

1960 *Chlordiazepoxide* (Librium). Tranquilliser for treatment of anxiety and tension states, convulsive states and neuromuscular and cardiovascular disorders. Effects first noted in 1960 by Randall *et al*. Related drug *Diazepam* (Valium) also used in anxiety states and as pre-medication for surgery.

c. 1960 *Frusemide* ($C_{12}H_{11}ClN_2O_5S$). A diuretic.

1961 *Thiabendazole* ($C_{10}H_7N_3S$). Efficacy in dealing with intestinal tract infestations noted by Brown *et al* in 1961. Used to treat various worm infections.

1962–3 *Clofibrate* ($C_{12}H_{15}ClO_3$). Lowers the fatty acid and cholestrol levels in the blood. Effects noted in 1962–3 by Thorp and Waring.

1963 *Allopurinol* ($C_5H_4N_4O$). Used in treatment of gout, it slows rate at which body forms uric acid. Reported on by Hitchings, Elion *et al* in 1963.

1963 *Cephalosporins*, antibiotics discovered in 1945 in Sardinia by Prof Brotzu. First utilised in 1963. Developed by Sir Howard (now Lord) Florey and Glaxo Laboratories.

1964 *Tolnaftate*, an anti-fungal agent announced October 1964. Highly effective against epidermiphytosis (athlete's foot).

1965 *Niridazole*. Discovered 1961 (announced December 1965) by Dr Paul Schmidt of CIBA, Basle. Treatment of debilitating liver-infestation disease Bilharzia (250 million world incidence).

1966 *Pralidoxime*. Antidote for poisoning by cholinesterase inhibitors, particularly organophosphorus compounds, which are used as insecticides and 'nerve gases'.

1966 *Trometamol* (Tromethamine). A diuretic used to treat acidosis, for example during organ transplantation.

1967 *Nitrazepam* (Trade name—Mogadon) ($C_{15}H_{11}N_3O_3$). Tranquilliser and hypnotic.

1967 *Laevo-dopa* (L-Dopa) ($C_9H_{11}NO_4$) Naturally occurring amino aci reported on by Cotzias and other in 1967. Used in treatment o Parkinson's Disease.

1968 *Propranolol* (A β-adrenergic blockin drug ($C_{16}H_{21}NO_2$). Affects rate an rhythm of the heart and may b helpful in angina pectoris.

1969 *Salbutamol*. Useful in asthma for it selective bronchodilator effect whereas earlier unselective drug were more dangerous in elevating th heart rate.

1976 *Cimetidine*. Pioneer antihistamin which prevents excessive acid secre tion in the stomach, often the caus of ulcers.

Average height and weight at birth

Nationality	Boys Length in ins	Boys Weight lb	Boys Weight oz	Girls Length in ins	Girls Weight lb	Girls Weight oz
British	20·1	7	6·4	20·0	7	4·
German	20·0	7	11·2	19·8	7	4·
Swiss	20·0	7	4·8	19·7	6	12·
USA (White)	19·9	7	12·8	19·7	7	9·
Japanese	19·7	6	11·5	19·4	6	8·
French	19·6	6	12·8	19·3	6	12·
USA (Negro)	19·5	7	1·6	19·1	6	12·
Russia	19·1	7	8	19·1	7	4·
China	18·9	6	12·8	18·9	6	9·
Africa (Pygmy)	18·0	7	14·4	18·2	8	3·

In humans the musclature normally accounts for some 40 per cent of the total bodyweight There are 639 named muscles in the human anatomy.

PHOBIAS

Acerophobia	Sourness
Acrophobia	Sharpness (pinnacles)
Agoraphobia	Open spaces
Aichurophobia	Points
Ailourophobia	Cats
Akousticophobia	Sound
Algophobia	Pain
Altophobia	Heights
Amathophobia	Dust
Ancraophobia	Wind
Androphobia	Men
Anginophobia	Narrowness
Anglophobia	England or things English
Anthropophobia	Human beings
Antlophobia	Flood
Apeirophobia	Infinity
Apiphobia	Bees
Arachnophobia	Spiders
Asthenophobia	Weakness
Astraphobia	Lightning
Atephobia	Ruin
Atelophobia	Imperfection
Aulophobia	Flute
Auroraphobia	Auroral lights
Bacilliphobia	Microbes
Barophobia	Gravity
Bathophobia	Depth
Batophobia	Walking
Batrachophobia	Reptiles
Belonephobia	Needles
Bibliophobia	Books
Blennophobia	Slime
Brontophobia	Thunder
Carcinophobia	Cancer
Cardiophobia	Heart condition
Chaetophobia	Hair
Cheimatophobia	Cold
Chionophobia	Snow
Chrometophobia	Money
Chromophobia	Colour
Chronophobia	Duration
Claustrophobia	Enclosed spaces
Clinophobia	Going to bed
Cnidophobia	Stings
Coprophobia	Faeces
Cryophobia	Ice, frost
Crystallophobia	Crystals
Cymophobia	Sea swell
Cynophobia	Dogs
Demophobia	Crowds
Demonophobia	Demons
Dendrophobia	Trees
Dermatophobia	Skin
Dikephobia	Justice
Doraphobia	Fur
Eisoptrophobia	Mirrors
Elektrophobia	Electricity
Eleutherophobia	Freedom
Enetephobia	Pins
Entomophobia	Insects
Eosophobia	Dawn
Eremitophobia	Solitude
Ergophobia	Work
Erythrophobia	Blushing
Gallophobia	France or things French
Gametophobia	Marriage
Genophobia	Sex
Germanophobia	Germany or things German
Geumatophobia	Taste
Graphophobia	Writing
Gymnophobia	Nudity
Gynophobia	Women
Haematophobia	Blood
Haptophobia	Touch
Harpaxophobia	Robbers
Hedonophobia	Pleasure
Hippophobia	Horses
Hodophobia	Travel
Homichlophobia	Fog
Hormephobia	Shock
Hydrophobia	Water (see also Rabies p. 39)
Hygrophobia	Dampness
Hypegiaphobia	Responsibility
Hypnophobia	Sleep
Hypsophobia	High place
Ideophobia	Ideas
Kakorraphiaphobia	Failure
Katagelophobia	Ridicule
Kenophobia	Void
Kinesophobia (Kinetophobia)	Motion
Kleptophobia	Stealing
Koniphobia	Dust
Kopophobia	Fatigue
Kyphophobia	Stooping
Lalophobia	Speech
Limnophobia	Lakes
Linonophobia	String
Logophobia	Words
Lyssophobia	Insanity
Maniaphobia	Insanity
Mastigophobia	Flogging
Mechanophobia	Machinery
Mettallophobia	Metals
Meteorophobia	Meteors
Monophobia	One thing
Musophobia	Mice
Musicophobia	Music
Mysophobia	Dirt
Myxophobia	Slime
Necrophobia	Corpses
Negrophobia	Negroes
Nelophobia	Glass
Neophobia	New
Nephophobia	Clouds
Nosophobia	Disease
Nyctophobia	Darkness
Ochophobia	Vehicles
Odontophobia	Teeth
Oikophobia	Home
Olfactophobia	Smell

Ommetaphobia	Eyes	Pogonophobia	Beards	Syphilophobia	Syphilis
Oneirophobia	Dreams	Poinephobia	Punishment	Tachophobia	Speed
Ophiophobia	Snakes	Polyphobia	Many things	Taphophobia	Burial alive
Ornithophobia	Birds	Potophobia	Drink	Teratophobia	Monsters
Ouranophobia	Heaven	Pteronophobia	Feathers	Terdekaphobia	Number thirteen
Panphobia		Pyrophobia	Fire	Thaasophobia	Sitting idle
(Pantophobia)	Everything	Russophobia	Russia or things	Thalassophobia	Sea
Parthenophobia	Young girls		Russian	Thanatophobia	Death
Pathophobia	Disease	Rypophobia	Soiling	Theophobia	God
Patroiophobia	Heredity	Satanophobia	Satan	Thermophobia	Heat
Peccatophobia	Sinning	Sciophobia	Shadows	Thixophobia	Touching
Pediculophobia	Lice	Selaphobia	Flashes	Tocophobia	Childbirth
Peniaphobia	Poverty	Siderophobia	Stars	Toxiphobia	Poison
Phagophobia	Swallowing	Sinophobia	China or things	Traumatophobia	Wounds, injury
Phasmophobia	Ghosts		Chinese	Tremophobia	Trembling
Pharmacophobia	Drugs	Sitophobia	Food	Trypanophobia	Inoculations,
Phobophobia	Fears	Spermophobia			injections
Phonophobia	Speaking aloud	(Spermatophobia)	Germs	Xenophobia	
Photophobia	Strong light	Stasophobia	Standing	(Zenophobia)	Foreigners
Phyllophobia	Leaves	Stygiophobia		Zelophobia	Jealousy
Pnigerophobia	Smothering	(Hadephobia)	Hell	Zoophobia	Animals

EDUCATION

The 46 United Kingdom universities
There are 46 institutions of university or degree-giving status in the UK.
The list below is given in order of seniority of date of foundation.

Name	Year of Foundation	Location	(Population Full Time as at 31 Dec. 1975)
1. The University of Oxford	1249*	Oxford OX1 2JD	11 591

Men's Colleges, Halls and Societies: University (1249), Balliol (1263), Merton (1264), Exeter (1314), Oriel (1326), Queen's (1340), New College (1379), Lincoln (1427), All Souls (1438), Magdalen (1458), Brasenose (1509), Corpus Christi (1517), Christ Church (1546), Trinity (1554), St John's (1555), Jesus (1571), Wadham (1612), Pembroke (1614), Worcester (1714), Hertford (1874), St Edmund Hall (1270), Keble (1868), St Catherine's (1962), Campion Hall (1962), St Benet's Hall (1947), St Peter's (1929), St Antony's (1950), Nuffield (1937), Linacre House (1962), Mansfield (1886), Regent's Park, Greyfriars Hall.
Women's Colleges and Hall: Lady Margaret Hall (1878), Somerville (1879), St Hugh's (1886), St Hilda's (1893), St Anne's (1952).

2. The University of Cambridge	1284*	Cambridge	10 849

Men's Colleges: Peterhouse (1284), Clare (1326), Pembroke (1347), Gonville and Caius (1348), Trinity Hall (1350), Corpus Christi (1352), King's (1441), Queen's (1448), St Catharine's (1473), Jesus (1496), Christ's (1505), St John's (1511), Magdalene (1542), Trinity (1546), Emmanuel (1584), Sidney Sussex (1596), Downing (1800), Selwyn (1882), Churchill (1960), Fitzwilliam House (1869).
Women's Colleges and Halls: Girton (1869), Newnham (1871), Hughes Hall (1885), New Hall (1954).

3. The University of St Andrews	1411	St Andrews and Dundee	3037

Colleges: United College of St Salvator and St Leonard; College of St Mary; Queen's College, Dundee.

4. The University of Glasgow	1451	Gilmorehill, Glasgow G12 8QQ	9241
5. The University of Aberdeen	1494	Aberdeen AB9 1FX	5325
6. The University of Edinburgh	1582	South Bridge Edinburgh EH8 9YL	9337
7. The University of Durham	1832	Old Shire Hall, Durham DH1 3HP	4192

Colleges: University, Hatfield, Grey, St Chad's, St John's, St Mary's, St Aidan's, Bede, St Hild's, Neville's Cross, St Cuthbert's Society, Van Mildert, Trevelyan.

8. The University of London	1836	Greater London	36 135

Schools: Bedford College, Birkbeck College, Chelsea College, Imperial College of Science and Technology, King's College, London School of Economics, Queen Elizabeth College, Queen Mary College, Royal Holloway College, Royal Veterinary College, School of Oriental and African Studies, School of Pharmacy, University College, Westfield College, Wye College.
Medical Schools: Charing Cross Hospital, Guy's Hospital, King's College Hospital, The London Hospital, The Middlesex Hospital, Royal Dental Hospital of London, Royal Free Hospital, St Bartholomew's Hospital, St George's Hospital, St Mary's Hospital, St Thomas's Hospital, University College Hospital, Westminster Hospital, British post-graduate Medical Federation, London School of Hygiene and Tropical Medicine, Royal post-graduate Medical School, and numerous post-graduate teaching hospitals; and various training colleges.
Institutes: Courtauld Institute of Art, Institute of Advanced Legal Studies, Institute of Archaeology, Institute of Classical Studies, Institute of Commonwealth Studies, Inter-collegiate Computer Science, Institute of Education, Institute of Germanic Studies, Institute of Historical Research, Institute of Latin American Studies, Institute of United States Studies, School of Slavonic and East European Studies, Warburg Institute, British Institute, Paris.

9. The University of Manchester	1851	Oxford Road, Manchester M139PL	10 867
10. The University of Newcastle upon Tyne	1852	Newcastle upon Tyne NE1 7RU	6682
11. The University of Wales	1893	see colleges	17 136

Colleges: Aberystwyth, Bangor, Cardiff, Swansea, National School of Medicine (Cardiff), Institute of Science and Technology (Cardiff), St. David's College, Lampeter

12. The University of Birmingham	1900	Edgbaston, Birmingham B15 2TT	7980
13. The University of Liverpool	1903	Brownlow Hill, Liverpool L69 3BX	7151
14. The University of Leeds	1904	Leeds LS2 9JT	9480
15. The University of Sheffield	1905	Sheffield S10 2TN	7121
16. The Queen's University of Belfast	1908	Belfast and Londonderry	5735

College: Magee University College (1865), Londonderry.

17. The University of Bristol	1909	Bristol BS8 ITH	6637
18. The University of Reading	1926	London Road, Reading RG6 2AH	5329
19. The University of Nottingham	1938	University Park, Nottingham NG7 2RD	5988

20. The University of Southampton	1952	Southampton SO9 5NH		5437
21. The University of Hull	1954	Kingston upon Hull HU6 7RX		4174
22. The University of Exeter	1955	Exeter EX4 4QJ		4076
23. The University of Leicester	1957	Leicester		3774
24. The University of Sussex	1961	Falmer, Brighton BN1 9QX		4191
25. The University of Keele	1962	Keele, Staffordshire ST5 5BG		2320
26. The University of Strathclyde†	1963	George Street, Glasgow G1 1XW		5983
27. The University of East Anglia	1963	Earlham Hall, Norwich NOR 88C		3472
28. The University of York	1963	Heslington, York YO1 5DD		2814
29. The University of Lancaster	1964	Bailrigg, Lancaster		3828
30. The University of Essex	1964	Wivenhoe Park, Colchester CO4 35Q		2294
31. The University of Warwick	1965	Coventry CV4 7AL		3944
32. The University of Kent	1965	Canterbury CT2 7N2		3008
33. Heriot-Watt University	1966	Chambers Street, Edinburgh EH1 1HX		2792
34. Loughborough University of Technology	1966	Loughborough, Leicester		3684
35. The University of Aston in Birmingham	1966	Gosta Green, Birmingham 4		4529
36. The City University	1966	St John's Street, London, EC 1V 4PB		2202
37. Brunel University	1966	Uxbridge UB8 3PH		2375
38. New University of Ulster	1965	Coleraine, Co. Londonderry		1721
39. University of Bath	1966	Claverton Down, Bath BA7 7AY		3351
40. University of Bradford	1966	Bradford BD7 1DP		4175
41. University of Surrey	1966	Guildford GU2 5XH		2770
42. University of Salford	1967	Salford M5 4WT		3968
43. University of Dundee	1967	Dundee DD1 4HN		2758
44. University of Stirling	1967	Stirling FK9 4LA		2075
45. The Open University	1969	Walton Hall, Milton Keynes MK7 6AA	(1977)‡	50 000
46. The University College at Buckingham§	1976	Buckingham MK18 1EG	(1977–78)	250

* Year of foundation of oldest constituent college
‡ Tuition mainly by correspondence

† Formerly the Royal College of Science and Technology, founded 1796
§ Independently financed from the University Grants Committee and HM Treasury

Note: The Royal College of Art (1837) Kensington Gore, London (568 post graduates) and The Cranfield Institute of Technology (1969), Cranfield, Bedford (575 post graduates, 2500 short course students) grant degrees.

PHILOSOPHY

'Philosophy' is a word derived from the Greek words meaning 'love of wisdom,' and philosophy in the Western world began with the ancient Greeks. It is used to cover a wide area: the scientific arrangement of those principles which underlie all knowledge and existence.

The sphere of philosophy can be roughly delineated by stating how it is distinct from other areas of thought. It differs from religion since its quest for the underlying causes and principles of being and thinking does not depend on dogma and faith; and from science, since it does not depend solely on fact, but leans heavily on speculation. Its inter-relation with both science and religion can be seen in the large number of philosophers who were also either theologians or scientists, and the few such as Blaise Pascal and Roger Bacon, who were all three. Philosophy developed from religion, becoming distinct when thinkers sought truth independant of theological considerations. Science in turn developed from philosophy, and eventually, all the branches of science from physics to psychology broke away—psychology being the last to do so in the 20th century.

Philosophy can be split into three particularly important categories: ethics, metaphysics and epistemology. Such a division leaves out some important areas of philosophical speculation, including logic, which is the increasingly formalised technique of exact analysis of reasoning, but it serves to introduce a few of the most important writings.

1. **Ethics** is the study of human conduct and morality. Philosophers have held many points of view about ideal human conduct but their opinions tend to resolve into an opposition between two main schools. One school, the 'Idealists,' considers that the goodness or badness of a course of action must be judged by standards dictated from the other world—from God or from some force for good—external to man. The second school, who might be grouped under the term 'Utilitarians,' feels that the effect which a course of action produces in this world makes it good or bad.

The Idealist school was represented quite early in the history of Western philosophy by the Greek philosopher Plato, who wrote in the 4th century BC. Plato, in a series of dialogues, has his ex-teacher Socrates discuss the problems of philosophy with friends and opponents.

Socrates' procedure is to draw out the wisdom from the gentleman with whom he is discussing the question. Socrates, in fact, rarely makes a statement. He prefers what advertising men call 'the soft sell.' That is to say, he asks questions which compel the others either to make the statements he wants them to make or to appear foolish.

In three of these dialogues, especially—*The Protagoras*, *The Phaedo*, and *The Gorgias*—Plato develops a system of ethics which is essentially idealistic. Socrates propounds that the good comes from the realm of 'ideas' or 'forms.' This is a sort of perfect other world which projects distorted copies of everything good down to the world we have to contend with. For Plato, individual conduct is good in so far as it is governed by the emanated spirit from above. Plato does not, of course, use the word 'heaven' for the world of ideas, but he was adapted—after being modified by Aristotle, Plotinus, and others—for Christian purposes. One of the ways in which the knowledge from the realm of the 'ideas' was communicated to mortals was by a voice or 'demon.' In the *Apology*, Socrates describes how this individual conscience has prevented him from wrongdoing.

Another important work which has to be classed with the idealists is Aristotle's *Nicomachean Ethics*. Aristotle was a pupil of Plato, and, like Plato, he thinks of the good as a divine emanation, or overflow, but his ethics have a more 'practical' bent. He equates happiness with the good and is responsible for the doctrine of the 'golden mean.' This states that every virtue is a mean, or middle-point, between two vices.

Generosity, for instance, is the mean between prodigality and stinginess.

A more cynical approach was introduced by Niccolò Machiavelli, founder of the modern science of politics. In his famous book, *The Prince*, Machiavelli drew his conclusions from the very nature of man.

The same tendency to give idealism a practical bent is found in a more modern philosopher, Immanuel Kant. His idealistic aspect may be compared with Socrates' demon.' Kant maintains that there is in each man a voice which guides him as to right or wrong.

But the part of Kant's ethics which is most famous is that connected with the phrase 'categorical imperative.' In Kant's own words: 'Act only according to a maxim by which you can at the same time will that it shall become a general law.' In other words, before acting in a certain way, the individual must ask himself: 'If everybody did the same thing what would be the moral condition of the universe? This is a practical consideration in the sense that it concerns the *result* of an action, but Kant's concern is for the morality of the universe and not its happiness or earthly welfare. Kant's principal ethical works are *The Critique of Pure Reason, The Critique of Practical Reason, The Metaphysics of Morality*, and *The Metaphysics of Ethics*.

The opposing group of 'utilitarian' ethics is concerned with the matter of earthly welfare. The earliest Western philosopher to represent this tradition is Epicurus, a Greek philosopher of the 4th century BC.

Instead of deriving ideas of right and wrong from above, as did the Socratics for example, Epicurus maintained that 'we call pleasure the beginning and end of the blessed life.' The term 'Epicurean' was used —and often still is used—to describe one who indulges in excessive pleasure, but this usage is neither accurate nor just. Epicurus did not condone excesses. On the contrary, he said that pleasure was only good when moderate or 'passive.' 'Dynamic' pleasure, which caused painful after-effects, was not good.

The utilitarian tradition has on the whole had more adherents than the idealistic tradition in modern philosophy. Jeremy Bentham, for example, writing in the 18th century, acknowledged his debt to Epicurus in his *Principles of Morals and Legislation*. Bentham agreed that pain and pleasure were the 'sovereign masters' governing man's conduct. He added to this a doctrine of *utility* which argued that 'the greatest happiness of the greatest number is the measure of right and wrong.'

John Stuart Mill, is perhaps the most famous of the Utilitarians. He extended Bentham's doctrines pointing out that there were different *qualities* of pleasure and pain, and that 'some *kinds* of pleasure are more valuable than others.' These articles were later put out in book form: *Utilitarianism*.

In the USA the Utilitarians made an impact on the Pragmatists, who held that 'the *right* is only the expendient in our way of thinking'—to quote William James, whose *Pragmatism* is the best-known book produced by this school.

2. Metaphysics.
The term 'metaphysics' originated as the title of one of Aristotle's treatises. It probably meant only that he wrote it after his *Physics*, but it was once thought to signify study beyond the realm of physics. Today it is usually employed to describe the speculation as to the ultimate nature of reality and the structure of the universe.

The sort of questions asked by metaphysicians concern the origin and condition of the universe in which man lives, and, as we might expect, they came up early in the history of philosophy. Before Aristotle had invented the term 'metaphysics'—as early as the 6th Century BC—pre-Socratic Greek philosophers were offering their solutions of the mysteries of the universe.

Much of the speculation of these pre-Socratic philosophers was centered on speculation about the four *elements* which they thought made up the universe. Empedocles, who, according to legend, threw himself into the volcano at Mt. Etna to prove his immortality—and failed—first defined earth, air, fire, and water as the four basic elements. Others attempted to make one of these the most important, or *primary*, element from which the others were derived. Thales—one of the seven wise men of Greece—thought water was on top. Heraclitus' primary element was fire. Anaximander reasoned that none of the four was primary. They must, he said, exist in perpetual balance.

3. Epistemology
is the study of the nature, grounds, and validity of man's knowing—how we come to know and how far we can rely on what we think we have discovered.

Epistemologists assert that knowledge is born in the individual and has only to be drawn forth. The other point of view is that at birth the mind is a *tabula rasa*—blank sheet—on which knowledge is imprinted.

The first school is represented classically by Plato. In the *Theaetetus* especially, he discusses various theories of knowledge and discards those built on the shifting sands of sense perception. The senses are, he feels, too fallible. True knowledge comes from those general notions which are derived from the realm of the *ideas*—which the soul possesses prior to birth.

The classic representative of the second school is John Locke—a 17th century philosopher. In his *Essay on Human Understanding*, Locke defines what is really the opposite point of view to Plato's. He is the pioneer proponent of the *tabula rasa*. Locke regards the mind at birth as comparable to an empty cabinet with two compartments. As we live, one compartment is filled with our *perceptions* and the other with our *sensations*. From these two combined we get our *idea*.

This theory tends to make knowledge a matter of experience and mental processing rather than one of religious insight. As one might expect, Locke's theories were important influences in those fields which investigate the processes of mental activity—such as psychology and education.

Schools and Theories
Since the days of the early Greeks, philosophers have been divided into different schools and have advanced opposing theories. Among the many basic outlooks and theories not already discussed but which have developed since Thales of Miletus (624–550 BC) first questioned the nature of ultimate reality, the following may be listed:

1. *Absolutism:* the theory that there is an ultimate reality in which all differences are reconciled.
2. *Agnosticism:* the position that the ultimate answer to all fundamental inquiries is that we do not know.
3. *Altruism:* the principle of living and acting in the interest of others rather than oneself.
4. *Asceticism:* the belief that withdrawal from the physical world into the inner world of the spirit is the highest good attainable.
5. *Atheism:* rejection of the concept of God as a workable hypothesis.
6. *Atomism:* the belief that the entire universe is composed of distinct and indivisible units.
7. *Conceptualism:* the doctrine that universal ideas are neither created by finite (human) minds, nor entirely apart from absolute mind (God).
8. *Critical Idealism:* the concept that man cannot determine whether there is anything beyond his own experience.
9. *Critical Realism:* the theory that reality is tri-partite, that in addition to the mental and physical aspects of reality, there is a third aspect called essences.
10. *Criticism:* the theory that the path to knowledge lies midway between dogmatism and skepticism.
11. *Determinism:* the belief that the universe follows a fixed or pre-determined pattern.
12. *Dialectical Materialism:* the theory that reality is strictly material and is based on a struggle between opposing forces, with occasional interludes of harmony.
13. *Dogmatism:* assertion of a belief without authoritative support.
14. *Dualism:* the belief that the world consists of two radically independant and absolute elements, e.g., good and evil, spirit and matter.
15. *Egoism:* in ethics the belief that the serving of one's own interests is the highest end.
16. *Empiricism:* rejection of all *a priori* knowledge in favour of experience and induction.
17. *Evolutionism:* the concept of the universe as a progression of inter-related phenomena.
18. *Existentialism:* denial of objective universal values—man must create values for himself through action; the self is the ultimate reality.
19. *Hedonism:* the doctrine that pleasure is the highest good.
20. *Humanism:* any system that regards human interests and the human mind as paramount in the universe.
21. *Idealism:* any system that regards thought or the idea as the basis either of knowledge or existence; in ethics, the search for the best or the highest.
22. *Instrumentalism:* the concept of ideas as instruments, rather than as goals of living.
23. *Intuitionism:* the doctrine that the perception of truth is by intuition, not analysis.
24. *Materialism:* the doctrine that denies the independant existence of spirit, and asserts the existence of only one substance—matter; belief that physical well-being is paramount.
25. *Meliorism:* the belief that the world is capable of improvement, and that man has the power of helping in its betterment, a position between optimism and pessimism.
26. *Monism:* belief in only one ultimate reality, whatever its nature.
27. *Mysticism:* belief that the ulitmate real lies in direct contact with the divine.
28. *Naturalism:* a position that seeks to explain all phenomena by means of strictly natural (as opposed to supernatural) categories.
29. *Neutral Monism:* theory that reality is neither physical nor spiritual, but capable of expressing itself as either.
30. *Nominalism:* the doctrine that general terms have no corresponding reality either in or out of the mind, and are, in effect, nothing more than words.
31. *Optimism:* any system that holds that the universe is the best of all possible ones, and that all will work out for the best.
32. *Pantheism:* the belief that God is identical with the universe.
33. *Personalism:* theory that ultimate reality consists of a plurality of spiritual beings or independant persons.
34. *Pessimism:* belief that the universe is the

PHILOSOPHY

worst possible and that all is doomed to evil.
35. *Phenomenalism:* theory that reality is only appearance.
36. *Pluralism:* belief that there are more than two irreducible components of reality.
37. *Positivism:* the doctrine that man can have no knowledge except of phenomena, and that the knowledge of phenomena is relative, not absolute.
38. *Pragmatism:* a method that makes practical consequences the test of truth.
39. *Rationalism:* the theory that reason alone, without the aid of experience, can arrive at the basic reality of the of the universe.
40. *Relativism:* rejection of the concept of the absolute.
41. *Skepticism:* the doctrine that no facts can be certainly known.
42. *Theism:* acceptance of the concept of God as a workable hypothesis.
43. *Transcendentalism:* belief in an ultimate reality that transcends human experience.
44. *Voluntarism:* the theory that will is the determining factor in the universe.

Philosophers Through the Ages
Pre-Socratic Greeks
Thales (624–550 BC). Regarded as the starting point of Western philosophy; the first exponent of monism.
Anaximander (611–547 BC). Continued Thales' quest for universal substance, but reasoned that that substance need not resemble known substances.
Anaximenes (588–524 BC). Regarded air as the ulitmate reality.
Pythagoras (572–497 BC). Taught a dualism of body and soul.
Parmenides (*c.* 495 BC). Formulated the basic doctrine of idealism; member of Eleatic school, so-called because based at Elea in southern Italy.
Heraclitus (533–475 BC). Opposed concept of a single ultimate reality; held that one permanent thing is change.
Zeno of Elea (490–430 BC). Argued that plurality and change are appearances, not realities.
Empedocles (*c.* 495–435 BC). Held that there were four irreducible substances (water, fire, earth and air) and two forces (love and hate).
Anaxagoras (500–428 BC). Believed in an indefinite number of basic substances.
Protagoras (481–411 BC). An early relativist and humanist; doubted human ability to attain absolute truth.

Classic Greek Philosophers
Socrates (469–399 BC). Developed Socratic method of inquiry; teacher of Plato, through whose writings his idealistic philosophy was disseminated.
Democritus (460–370 BC). Began tradition in Western thought of explaining universe in mechanistic terms.
Antisthens (*c.* 406 BC). Chief of group known as the Cynics; stressed discipline and work as the essential good.
Plato (427–347 BC). Founded the Academy at Athens; developed the idealism of his teacher Socrates; teacher of Aristotle.
Aristotle (384–322 BC). Taught that there are four factors in causation: the interrelated factors of form and matter; motive cause, which produces change; and the end, for which a process of change occurs.

Hellenistic Period
Pyrrho of Elis (*c.* 365–275 BC). Initiated the skeptic school of philosophy; believed that man could not know anything for certain.
Epicurus (341–270 BC). Taught that the test of truth is in sensation; proponent of atomism and hedonism.
Zeno of Citium (335–265 BC). Chief of

Stoics, so called because they met in the Stoa Poikile or Painted Porch at Athens; proponent of pantheism, evolutionism; taught that man's role is to accept nature and all it offers, good or bad.
Lucretius (96–55 BC). Roman disciple of Epicurus; principal teacher of atomism.
Plotinus (AD 205–270). Chief expounder of Neo-Platonism, a combining of the teachings of Plato with Oriental concepts.
Augustine (AD 354–430). Known to history as St. Augustine; expounder of optimism and absolutism; believed that God trancends human comprehension; one of greatest influences on medieval Christian thought.
Boethius (AD 480–524). A Neo-Platonist, his great work, *The Consolations of Philosophy*, served to transmit Greek philosophy to medieval Europe.

Medieval Period
Avicenna (980–1037). Arabic follower of Aristotle and Neo-Platonism; his works led to a revival of interest in Aristotle in 13th-century Europe.
Anselm (1033–1109). Italian; known to history as St. Anselm; a realist, he is famous for his examination of the proof of God's existence.
Peter Abelard (1079–1142). Leading theologian and philosopher of medieval France; his nominalism caused him to be declared a heretic by the Church.
Averroes (1126–98). Great philosopher of Mohammedan Spain, and leading comentator on Aristotle; regarded religion as allegory for the common man, philosophy as the path to truth.
Moses Maimonides (1135–1204). Leading Jewish student of Aristotle in medieval Mohammedan world; sought to combine Aristotelian teaching with that of the Bible.
Roger Bacon (1214–94). English student of Aristotle, advocated return to Hebrew and Greek versions of Scripture; an empiricist.
St. Bonaventure (1221–74). Born John of Fidanza in Italy; friend of Thomas Aquinas; student of Plato and Aristotle; a mystic and ascetic.
St. Thomas Aquinas (1225–74). Italian; leading philosopher of the Scholastics or Christian philosophers of the Middle Ages; evolved a compromise between Aristotle and Scripture, based on the belief that faith and reason are in agreement; his philosophical system is known as Thomism.

The Renaissance
John Duns Scotus (*c.* 1270–1308). Scottish; student of Augustine and Anselm; stressed will rather than reason, in opposition to Aquinas; held that faith and reason cannot be fully reconciled.
Desiderius Erasmus (1466–1536). Greatest of the humanists, he helped spread the ideas of the Renaissance in his native Holland and throughout Northern Europe.
Niccolo Machiavelli (1469–1527). Italian; a realist, he placed the state as the paramount power in human affairs.

Transition to Modern Thought
Francis Bacon (1561–1626). English; in his major work, *Novum Organum*, he sought to replace the deductive logic of Aristotle with an inductive system in interpreting nature.
Thomas Hobbes (1588–1679). English materialist who believed the natural state of man is war; outlined a theory of human government in his book *Leviathan*, whereby the state and men's subordination to it form the sole solution to human selfishness and aggressiveness.
René Descartes (1596–1650). French; dualist, rationalist, theist, Descartes and his system, Cartesianism, are at the base of all

modern knowledge. What he furnished is a theory of knowledge that underlies modern science and philosophy. 'All the sciences are conjoined with one another and interdependent.' he wrote.
Blaise Pascal (1623–62). French theist who held that sense and reason are mutually deceptive; truth lies between dogmatism and skepticism.
Benedict de Spinoza (1632–77). Dutch rationalist, parallelist, pantheist, monist absolutist, he developed ideas of Descartes while rejecting his dualism.
John Locke (1632–1704). English dualist empiricist; in his great *Essay Concerning Human Understanding* he sought to refute rationalist view that all knowledge derives from first principles.

18th Century
Gottfried Wilhelm von Leibniz (1646–1716). German idealist, absolutist, optimist (his view that this is the best of all possible worlds was ridiculed by Voltaire in *Candide*) held that reality consisted of units of force called monads.
George Berkeley (1685–1753). Irish idealist and theist who taught that material things exist only in being perceived; his system of subjective idealism is called Berkeleianism.
David Hume (1711–76). English empiricist who carried on ideas of Locke, but developed a system of skepticism (Humism) according to which human knowledge is limited to experience of ideas and sensations whose truth cannot be verified.
Jean-Jacques Rousseau (1712–78). French political philosopher whose concepts have had a profound influence on modern thought; advocated a 'return to nature' to counteract the inequality among men brought about by civilized society.
Immanuel Kant (1724–1804). German founder of critical philosophy. At first influenced by Leibniz, then by Hume, he sought to find an alternative approach to the rationalism of the former and the skepticism of the latter; in ethics, formulated the Categorical Imperative—which states that what applies to oneself must apply to everyone else unconditionally—a restatement of the Christian precept 'Do unto others as you would have them do unto you.'
Jeremy Bentham (1748–1832). Believed, like Kant, that the interests of the individual are one with those of society, but regarded fear of consequences rather than basic principle as the motivation for right action.
Johann Gottlieb Fichte (1762–1814). German; formulated a philosophy of absolute idealism based on Kant's ethical concepts.

19th Century
Georg Wilhelm Friedrich Hegel (1770–1831). German; his metaphysical system, known as Hegelianism, was rationalist and absolutist, based on the belief that thought and being are one, and nature is the manifestation of an Absolute Idea.
Arthur Schopenhauer (1788–1860). German; foremost expounder of pessimism, expressed in *The World as Will and Idea*. Rejected absolute idealism as wishful thinking, and taught that the only tenable attitude lay in utter indifference to an irrational world; an idealist who held that the highest ideal was nothingness.
Auguste Comte (1798–1857). French founder of positivism, a system which denied transcendent metaphysics and stated that the Divinity and man were one, that altruism is man's highest duty, and that scientific principles explain all phenomena.
John Stuart Mill (1806–73). English; utilitarian who differed from Bentham by

recognizing differences in quality as well as quantity in pleasure.

Søren Kierkegaard (1813–55). Danish religious existentialist, whose thought is the basis of modern (atheistic) existentialism; taught that 'existence precedes essence.' that only existence has reality, and the individual has a unique value.

Karl Marx (1818–83). German revolutionist, from whom the movement known as Marxism derives its name and many of its ideas; his works became, in the late 19th century, the basis of European socialism; published *The Communist Manifesto* with Friedrich Engels in 1848.

Herbert Spencer (1820–1903). English evolutionist whose 'synthetic philosophy' interpreted all phenomena according to the principle of evolutionary progress.

Charles S. Peirce (1839–1914). American who founded philosophical school called pragmatism; regarded logic as the basis of philosophy and taught that the test of an idea is whether it works.

William James (1842–1910). American pragmatist who held that reality is always in the making and that each man should choose the philosophy best suited to him.

Friedrich Wilhelm Nietzsche (1844–1900).

German evolutionist, egoist, who held that the 'will to power' is basic in life, that the spontaneous is to be preferred to the orderly; attacked Christianity as a system that fostered the weak, whereas the function of evolution is to evolve 'supermen.'

20th Century

Edmond Husserl (1859–1938). German who developed a system called 'phenomenology,' which asserts that realities other than mere appearance exist—called essences.

Henri Bergson (1859–1941). French evolutionist who asserted the existence of a 'vital impulse' that carries the universe forward, with no fixed beginning and no fixed end—the future is determined by the choice of alternatives made in the present.

John Dewey (1859–1952). American; basically a pragmatist, he developed a system known as instrumentalism.

Alfred North Whitehead (1861–1947). English evolutionist who held that reality must not be interpreted in atomistic terms, but in terms of events; that God is intimately present in the universe, yet distinct from it, a view called panentheism, as opposed to pantheism, which simply equates God and Nature.

George Santayana (1863–1952). An American born in Spain; a foremost critical realist who held that the ultimate substance of the world is matter in motion—and the mind itself is a product of matter in motion.

Bertrand Russell (1872–1970). English agnostic who adhered to many systems of philosophy before becoming chief expounder of scientism, the view that all knowledge is solely attainable by the scientific method.

Karl Jaspers (1883–1969). German existentialist who approached the subject from man's practical concern with his own existence.

Ludwig Wittgenstein (1889–1951). Austrian; developed the philosophy of language.

Martin Heidegger (1889–1976). German student of Husserl, he furthered development of phenomenology and greatly influenced atheistic existentialists.

Jean-Paul Sartre (b. 1905). French; developed existentialist thought of Heidegger; atheistic supporter of a subjective, irrational human existence, as opposed to an orderly overall reality.

Alfred J. Ayer (b. 1910). English; principal advocate of logical positivism, a modern extension of the thinking of Hume and Comte.

RELIGION

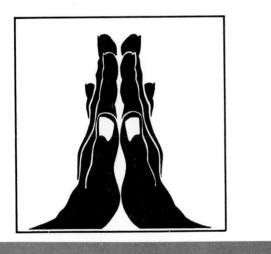

RELIGIONS OF THE WORLD (estimates in millions)

Christian	1 050	Confucian	312
Roman Catholic	630	Buddhist	160
Eastern Orthodox	160	Shintō	60
Protestant	260	Taoist	52
Moslem	600		
Hindu	437	Jewish	14·6

CHRISTIANITY

The religion Christianity takes its name from Jesus Christ*, son of the Virgin Mary, whose subsequent husband, Joseph of Nazareth, was 27 generations descended from David. His birth is now regarded as occurring at Bethlehem in the summer of 4 BC or earlier. The discrepancy is due to an error in the 6th century by Dionysius Exiguus in establishing the dating of the Christian era.

The principles of Christianity are proclaimed in the New Testament which was written in Syriac-Aramaic and of which the earliest complete surviving manuscript dates from AD c. 350.

Christ was crucified in the reign of the Roman emperor Tiberius during the procuratorship in Judaea of Pontius Pilate in AD 29 or according to the Roman Catholic chronology, 7 April, AD 30.

The primary commandment of Jesus was to believe in God, and to love Him. His second commandment (Mark xii, 31) was to 'love thy neighbour' in a way that outward performance alone did not suffice. Hate was prohibited and not only adultery but evil lust (Matt. v, 21). Unselfishness and compassion are central themes in Christianity.

Jesus appointed twelve disciples; the following are common to the lists in the books of Matthew, Mark, Luke and the Acts.

1. Peter, Saint Peter (brother of Andrew).
2. Andrew, Saint Andrew (brother of Peter).
3. James, son of Zebedee (brother of John).
4. John, Saint John (the Apostle) (brother of James).
5. Philip.
6. Bartholomew.
7. Thomas
8. Matthew, Saint Matthew.
9. James, of Alphaeus.
10. Simon the Cananaean (in Matthew and Mark) or Simon Zelotes in Luke and the Acts.)
11. Judas Iscariot (not an apostle).

Thaddaeus in the books of Matthew and Mark is the twelfth disciple, while in Luke and the Acts the twelfth is Judas of James. The former may have been a nickname or place name to distinguish Judas of James from the Iscariot. Matthias succeeded to the place of the betrayer Judas Iscariot.

*Jesus (the Saviour, from Hebrew root *yāsha'*, to save) Christ (the annointed one, from Greek, Χριω, *chrio*, to anoint).

Roman Catholicism

Roman Catholic Christianity is that practiced by those who acknowledge the supreme jurisdiction of the bishop of Rome (the Pope) and recognize him as the lawful successor of St. Peter who was appointed by Christ Himself to be head of the church. Peter visited Rome c. AD 42 and was martyred there c. AD 67. Pope Paul VI is his 261st successor.

The Roman Catholic Church claims catholicity inasmuch as she was charged (*de jure*) by Christ to 'teach all nations' and *de facto* since her

85

adherents are by far the most numerous among Christians. The Roman Catholic Church is regarded as the infallible interpreter both of the written (5 of the 12 apostles wrote) and the unwritten word of God. The organization of the Church is the Curia, the work of which is done by 11 permanent departments or congregations.

The great majority of Catholics are of the Roman rite and use the Roman liturgy. While acknowledging the hierarchical supremacy of the Holy See other Eastern Churches or Uniate Rites enjoy an autonomy. These include (1) the Byzantine or Greale rite, (2) the Armenian rite, and (3) the Coptic rite.

The doctrine of the Immaculate Conception was proclaimed on 8 Dec. 1854, and that of Papal Infallibility was adopted by the Ecumenical Council by 547 votes to 2 on 18 July 1870. The 21st Council was convened by Pope John XXIII. The election of Popes is by the College Cardinals (*see table below*).

Eastern Orthodox

The church officially described as 'The Holy Orthodox Catholic Apostolic Eastern Church' consists of those churches which accepted all the decrees of the first seven General Councils and such churches as have since sprung up in that tradition.

The origin arises from the splitting of the old Roman Empire into a Western or Latin half, centred on Rome, and an Eastern or Greek half, centred on Constantinople.

The Orthodox Church has no creed or dogma. Some features of this branch of Christianity are that bishops must be unmarried; the dogma of the immaculate conception is not admitted; icons are in the churches but the only 'graven image' is the crucifix; and fasts are frequent and rigorous.

Protestant

The term 'protestant' had never been used officially in the style of any church until the Anglican community in North America called themselves the 'Protestant Episcopal Church' during the 17th century. The name has never been officially used by the Church of England.

The origin of the term specifically derives from the formal *protestatio*, entered in 1529 by the rulers of the evangelical states of the Holy Roman Empire against the repressive Diet of Spires, which forbade further innovations. The term was not used for some years and it later became a generic term for those followers of the teaching of the Reformation against what were regarded as doctrinal and administrative abuses of Rome, and in particular the Papacy's claim of universal supremacy.

ISLAM (Mohammedanism)

Mohammedanism is a religious system founded by Mohammed (Muhammad or Mahomet) (AD *c.* 575–632) on 16 July AD 622 at Yathrib, now known as Al Madinah (Medina) in Saudi Arabia.

The religion was known by its founder as Islam (Arabic, submission) which is the term used today outside Europe. It is also known as Hanifism. Mohammed, a member of the Koreish tribe, was a caravan conductor and later became a shop-keeper in Mekkah (Mecca). There is some evidence that he was only semi-literate, at least in early manhood. He did not become a public preacher until 616. Soon after 622 [AH (anno Hegirae or the year of exile) 1] Mohammed turned the direction of his prayer southward from Jerusalem and an Israeli God to the pagan temple at Mecca and the God Allah. Mohammed soon became an administrator, general, judge and legislator in addition to being one through whom divine revelation was communicated.

Islam is based upon the word of God, the Koran (Arabic *Qur'an*, recitation) and the traditions (*hadith*) of the sayings and the life (*sunna*) of Mohammed. Other prophets are recognized including Jesus and

his gospel (*injil*) but Mohammed is the last and greatest of the prophet

Islam demands of Moslems worship five times daily, facing in the direction (*kiblah*) of Mecca, fasting in the month of Ramadan, paymer of alms (*zakat*) and the pilgrimage (*hadj*) to Mecca. Persons who hav made the pilgrimage add the word *hadj* to their names.

HINDUISM

The origin of Hinduism, or *Arya-Dharma* (Religion of the Aryans stems from the fears and ignorance which beset the early Indic civi ization. There are no beliefs common to all Hindus but caste and certai deities are widespread. Caste is of ingrained importance and withou this man has no place in society and cannot marry.

The *Veda*, or Divine Knowledge, was passed on by the Rishi inspired men, to the people in the form of hymns or *Mantras*. Brahm is the spirit which gives life to the individual, the doctrine being tha to be reunited with the spirit one should follow the path of knowledg or *jnina*.

A Hindu believes that his caste in the next life (*karma*) is determine by his actions in the present life—if he leads a good life, he will be rebor into a good caste, but if he does evil, he will become of low caste c even reincarnated as an animal. Birth in particular caste shows th relationship of one's soul with God—the perfect soul no longer has t go through the process of continual birth and death.

Hinduism is not an organized religion, in the sense that it assimilate ideas from other religions. It permits animal worship and that c numerous deities and even the animal or bird on which they ar believed to ride. Orthodox Hindus object to the killing of cattle an peacocks. There is much stress on purification rites—particularly c the occasion of inter-marriage between castes and even on touching c going close to a member of a lower caste. They strive after *dharma* (goo conduct), *kama* (satisfaction of desire), *arthra* (wealth) and *moksh* (salvation). Ceremonies for ancestors and pilgrimages to Holy Place occupy much time. The 12 yearly Kumbh-Mela at the confluence the Yamuna (Jumna), the Ganges and the invisible Sarasviti at Alla habad, Uttar Pradesh attracted 12 700 000 pilgrims in January 1977 The recent impact of Christianity has made the occidentally educate Hindus more introspective about their religion and much of the origin teaching has been modified in the last century.

CONFUCIANISM

Confucius (551–479 BC) was not the sole founder of Confucianisr but was rather a member of the founding group of *Ju* or meek one Confucius is the Latinized version of K'ung Fu-tzo or Master K'un who was a keeper of accounts from the province of Lu. He became th first teacher in Chinese history to instruct the people of all ranks i the six arts: ceremonies, music, archery, charioteering, history an numbers.

Confucius taught that the main ethic is *jen* (benevolence), and tha truth involves the knowledge of one's own faults. He believed i altruism and insisted on filial piety. He decided that people could b led by example and aimed at the rulers of his own time imitating thos in a former period of history, where he attributed the prosperity of th people to the leadership of the Emperors. Confucianism included th worship of Heaven and revered ancestors and great men, thoug Confucius himself did not advocate prayer, believing that man shoul direct his own destiny.

Confucianism can be better described as a religious philosophy c code of social behaviour, rather than a religion in the accepted sens since it has no church or clergy and is in no way an institution. For man years it had a great hold over education, its object being to emphasiz

The Popes of the 19th and 20th centuries

Elected			Died			Title	Name and Year of Birth
14	Mar.	1800	20	Aug.	1823	Pius VII	Luigi Barnabà Chiaramonti (b. 1740)
28	Sept.	1823	10	Feb.	1829	Leo XII	Annibale Sermattei della Genga (b. 1760)
31	Mar.	1829	30	Nov.	1830	Pius VIII	Francesco Savevio Castiglioni (b. 1761)
2	Feb.	1831	1	June	1846	Gregory XVI	Bartolommeo Alberto Cuppellari (b. 1765)
16	June	1846	7	Feb.	1878	Pius IX	Giovanni Marcia Matai-Ferretti (b. 1792)
20	Feb.	1878	20	July	1903	Leo XIII	Vincenzo Gioacchino Pecci (b. 1810)
4	Aug.	1903	20	Aug.	1914	Pius X*	Giuseppe Melchiorre Sarto (b. 1835)
3	Sept.	1914	22	Jan.	1922	Benedict XV	Giacomo della Chiesa (b. 1854)
6	Feb.	1922	10	Feb.	1939	Pius XI	Achille Ratti (b. 1857)
2	Mar.	1939	9	Oct.	1958	Pius XII	Eugenio Pacelli (b. 1876)
28	Oct.	1958	3	June	1963	John XXIII	Angelo Giuseppe Roncalli (b. 1881)
21	June	1963				Paul VI	Giovanni Batista Montini (b. 1897)

*Proclaimed a saint, 29 May 1954.

the development of human nature and the person. During the early 19th century attempts were made by followers to promote Confucianism to being a state religion, and though this failed, a good deal of the Confucian teachings still remain despite the onslaught of Communist ideology in the traditional area of its influence.

BUDDHISM

Buddhism is based on the teaching of the Indian prince, Siddhartha (later called Gautama) (*c*. 563–483 BC) of the Gautama clan of the Sakyas, later named Gautama Buddha (*buddha* meaning 'the enlightened one'). After seeing in *c*. 534 BC for the first time a sick man, an old man, a holy man and a dead man, he wandered fruitlessly for six years, after which he meditated for 49 days under a Bodhi tree at Gaya in Magadha. He achieved enlightenment or *nirvana* and taught salvation in Bihar, west of Bengal, until he died, aged 80. Gautama's teaching was essentially a protesting offshoot of early Hinduism. It contains four Noble Truths: (1) Man suffers from one life to the next; (2) the Origin of suffering is craving; craving for pleasure, possessions and the cessation of pain; (3) the cure for craving is non-attachment to all things including self; (4) the way to non-attachment is the Eight-fold path of right conduct, right effort, right intentions, right livelihood, right meditations, right mindfulness, right speech and right views.

Buddhism makes no provisions for God and hence has no element of divine judgement or messianic expectation. It provides an inexorable law or *dharma* of cause and effect which determines the individual's fate.

The vast body or *sangha* of monks and nuns practice celibacy, non-violence, poverty and vegetarianism. Under the *Hinayana*, or Lesser Vehicle, tradition of India only they have hope of attaining *nirvana*. Under the *Mahayana*, or Greater Vehicle, as practised in Indo-China, China and Japan, laymen as well may attain the highest ideal of *bodhisattva*, the enlightened one who liberates himself by personal sacrifice. Under Zen Buddhism enlightenment or *satori* is achieved only by prolonged meditation and mental and physical shock.

SHINTO

Shintō ('the teaching' or 'the way of the gods') came into practice during the 6th century AD to distinguish the Japanese religion from Buddhism which was reaching the islands by way of the mainland. The early forms of Shintō were a simple nature worship, and a religion for those who were not impelled by any complicated religious lore. The help of the deities was sought for the physical and spiritual needs of the people and there was great stress laid upon purification and truthfulness.

The more important national shrines were dedicated to well-known national figures, but there were also those set up for the worship of deities of mountain and forest.

During the 19th century, thirteen Sect Shintō denominations were formed and these were dependent on private support for their teaching and organization. They had very little in common and varied widely in beliefs and practices. Some adhered to the traditional Shintō deites while others did not. Of the 13 denominations *Tenrikyō* is the one with the greatest following outside Japan.

Theories of Shintō have been greatly influenced by Confucianism, Taoism and Buddhism. In 1868, however, the Department of Shintō was established and attempts were made to do away with the Shintō and Buddhist coexistence, and in 1871 Shintō was proclaimed the Japanese national religion.

TAOISM

Lao-tzu (Lao-tze or Lao-tse), the Chinese philospher and founder of Taoism, was, according to tradition, born in the sixth century BC. Lao-tzu taught that Taoism (Tao=the Ultimate and Unconditioned Being) could be attained by virtue if thrift, humility and compassion were practised.

Taoism has the following features—numerous gods (though Lao-tzu did not himself permit this); a still persisting, though now decreasing, body of superstition; and two now declining schools—the 13th-century Northern School with its emphasis on man's life, and the Southern School, probably of 10th century origin, stressing the nature of man. Various Taoist societies have been formed more recently by laymen, who though worshipping deities of many religions, promote charity and a more moral culture. The moral principles of Taoism consist of simplicity, patience, contentment and harmony. Since the decline of its espousal by the T'ang dynasty (AD 618-906), it has proved to be chiefly the religion of the semi-literate.

Philosophical Taoism or Tao-chia advocates naturalism and is thus opposed to regulations and organization of any kind. After the 4th century BC when Buddhism and Taoism began to influence each other there was a weakening of this anti-collectivist strain but the philosophy still has a strong hold over the way of life and culture in parts of China.

The religion imitates Buddhism in the matter of clergy and temple, the chief of which is the White Cloud temple in Peking, China.

JUDAISM

The word Jew is derived through the Latin *Judaeus*, from the Hebrew *Yehūdhī*, signifying a descendant of Judah, the fourth son of Jacob whose tribe, with that of his half brother Benjamin, made up the peoples of the kingdom of Judah. This kingdom was separate from the remaining tribes of Israel. The exodus of the Israelites from Egypt is believed to have occurred *c*. 1400 BC.

Judaism is monotheistic and based on the covenant that Israel is the bearer of the belief in the one and only God.

From 311 until 1790 Jews existed under severe disabilities and discrimination in most Christian and Moslem areas. Jewish emancipation began with the enfranchisement of Jews in France in Sept. 1791. This touched off anti-semitism which in return fired Zionism. The first Zionist Congress was held in Basle, Switzerland, in Aug. 1897.

The Balfour letter written on 2 Nov. 1917 by Arthur Balfour, British foreign secretary, addressed to Lord Rothschild declared 'His Majesty's Government view with favour the establishment of Palestine as a natural home for the Jewish people. . . .'

On 24 July 1922 the League of Nations approved a British mandate over Palestine. These policies led to bitter Arab resistance with revolts in 1929 and 1936–39 claiming the right of self-determination. The irreconcilable aims of Arab nationalism and Zionism led to partition with the creation of Israel (*q.v.*) on 14 May 1948 and the internationalizing of Jerusalem.

Jewish holidays including *Pesach* (Passover), celebrating the Exodus, *Shabuoth* (Pentecost), *Hashana* (New Year) and *Yom Kippur* (Day of Atonement) devoted to fasting, meditation and prayer.

Yiddish, an Eastern Vernacular form of mediaeval German, is unrelated to Semitic Hebrew.

THE CHURCH IN BRITAIN

The Church of England

The church in England renounced the supremacy of the Pope in favour of royal supremacy in 1531, but the episcopal form of church government was retained.

The Church of England is the established church with the Sovereign consecrated as its Head by his or her coronation oath. The authority of Parliament is acknowledged where secular authority is competent to exercise control.

The Church is organized into two provinces, each under an Archbishop. Canterbury has 29 dioceses, as follows:

Canterbury	Ely	Peterborough
London	Exeter	Portsmouth
Winchester	Gloucester	Rochester
Bath and Wells	Guildford	St. Albans
Birmingham	Hereford	St. Edmundsbury
Bristol	Leicester	and Ipswich
Chelmsford	Lichfield	Salisbury
Chichester	Lincoln	Southwark
Coventry	Norwich	Truro
Derby	Oxford	Worcester

York has 14 dioceses, as follows:

York	Chester	Sheffield
Durham	Liverpool	Sodor and Man
Blackburn	Manchester	Southwell
Bradford	Newcastle	Wakefield
Carlisle	Ripon	

The governing body of the Church is the National Assembly of the Church of England, usually called the Church Assembly. This has three houses: the House of Bishops, consisting of 43 diocesan bishops; the House of Clergy, comprising the Lower House of the Convocations of the Provinces of Canterbury and York (350 members): and the House of Laity, consisting of 346 elected diocesan representatives. There are 2 861 887 persons on the Electoral Roll and an estimated baptized membership of 27 484 000.

The Church in Wales

The Province of Wales consists of six dioceses under the Archbishop of Wales, who is also the Bishop of Monmouth. The other dioceses are St. Asaph, Llandaff, St. David's, Bangor, and Swansea & Brecon.

The Roman Catholic Church in Great Britain

The Roman Catholic population of Great Britain was estimated at 5 512 488 in 1977. There are six Archbishops: those of Westminster, Birmingham, Liverpool, Cardiff, St. Andrew's and Edinburgh, and Glasgow.

The Church of Scotland

The Church of Scotland is an established church, Presbyterian in constitution, presided over by a Moderator, who is chosen annually by the General Assembly, at which the Sovereign is represented by a Lord High Commissioner. The Church is divided into 16 synods and 46 presbyteries, and had a membership of 1 061 706.

ART

Painting is the visual and aesthetic expression of ideas and emotions in two dimensions, using colour, line, shapes, texture and tones.

PALAEOLITHIC ART 24 000–1000 BC

Cave painting of the Perigordian (Aurignacian period) and the later Solutrean and Magdalenian periods (18 000–11 000 BC) first discovered at Chaffaud, Vienne, France in 1834. Lascaux examples discovered 1940. Cave painting also discovered in Czechoslovakia. the Urals, USSR, India, Australia (Mootwingie dates from c. 1500 BC) and North Africa (earliest is from the Bubulus period in the Sahara post 5400 BC).

ANCIENT NEAR EAST 6000–3200 BC

Catal Hüyük, Analolin wall paintings.

EGYPTIAN ART 3100–341 BC

Covering the Protodynastic period of the 1st Dynasty (3100–2890 BC) to that of the 30th Dynasty (378–391 BC). Neither primitive nor Western.

GREEK ART 2000 BC

Minoan frescoes and Kamares painted pottery till 1700 BC. Mycenaean period ended c. 1100 BC. Black figure painting in Athens. Zenith c. 550 BC. Hellenistic period 320–150 BC.

ROMAN ART 750 BC–400 AD

Inherited Hellenistic or late Greek influence and the realistic Etruscan form. Pompeian painting c. 150 BC–70 AD.

EARLY CHRISTIAN 200 AD

Funerary fresco painting in the Roman catacombs ended with Constantine.

BYZANTINE ART

The Zenith occurred in the 9th–12th centuries.

MIGRATION PERIOD 150–1000

A general term covering the art of the Huns with strong Asian influence and the Revised post-Roman Celtic art in Ireland and Britain, the pre-Carolingian Frankish art and the art of the Vikings.

ROMANESQUE ART 1050–1200

In particular this is an architectural term and refers to that style which is based on Roman prototypes.

GOTHIC ART 1125–1450

Originally confined to a style of architecture but now applied to the contemporary decorative arts.

THE RENAISSANCE 1435–1545

Literally meaning a rebirth of forms centred in former classical styles and nurtured in Northern Italy. The High Renaissance faded with the emergence of Mannerism.

THE BAROQUE 1600–1720

The word is seemingly derived from the Portuguese word *barroco*, an irregular pearl. Noted for ceiling paintings and landscapes of illusionism with mythological figures, and extravagant decoration, which appeared not only in painting but also in architecture and sculpture.

THE ROCOCO 1735–1765

The genre of elegance yet theatricality, the use of decoration for decoration's sake.

NEO-CLASSICAL PERIOD 1750–1850

A period of great variation but conscious visual awareness of antique classical forms particularly illustrative of moral rectitude.

ROMANTIC PERIOD 1785–1835

An artist–based school of visual literacy less concerned with craftsmanship than with intellectualism. The opposite to Classicism.

REALISM 1845–1870

The period of representation of the real and existing things and persons.

PRE-RAPHAELITE 1848–1856

A brotherhood of 7 London artists formed to make a return to the pre-Raphael (hence the name) Italian forms as a protest against the frivolity of the prevailing English School of the day.

IMPRESSIONISM 1875–1886

The term was inadvertently introduced by the journalist Leroy in *Charivari* to describe the work of Monet, Sisley, Pissarro and others, taking the name from Monet's *Impression: Soleil levant*. The painters in this manner were concerned with light and its effects, and the use of 'broken' colour.

20th CENTURY FORMS

EXPRESSIONISM 1900

Romantic fantasy, which deliberately turned away from the representation of nature as the most important aspect in art; emotional ideas were expressed through distortion, exaggeration and violence in shape and colour.

CUBISM 1907

Invented by Picasso (1881–1973) and Braque (1882–1963) a style in which the subject is reduced to basic geometric solids.

ABSTRACT ART 1909

A rejection of any recognisable form of reality and a reliance on form, colour, texture and line.

CONSTRUCTIVISM 1920

A term coined in Moscow by Tatlin, after the Revolution, contending that art must be 'useful' rather than solely aesthetic. Lenin supported a 'Realism' idealising 'The Worker'.

SURREALISM 1924

Painting inspired by the exploration of the sub-conscious.

Media
TEMPERA

A loose term in painting in which the dry pigments are mixed with such substances as egg white, egg yolk, glue, gelatine or casein. True tempera is when the colours are ground with egg yolk only.

FRESCO

(Ital: *fresco*, fresh.) Developed by Minoan and other ancient civilisations. *Buon fresco* is executed with pigments ground in water or limewater on to a freshly prepared lime-plaster wall while the plaster is still damp.

OIL

Dry pigments ground in an oil; this is generally linseed, but may be poppy, walnut or other similar oils. It is a technique that gradually evolved during the latter part of the Middle Ages. The Van Eyck brothers did much to perfect the medium.

WATER COLOUR

Pigments are ground with gum arabic and thinned in use with water. The technique as used today started with Albrecht Dürer but did not achieve widespread use until the emergence of the English School of water-colourists in the first half of the 19th century. Applied with squirrel or sable brushes on white or tinted paper.

GOUACHE

A water-colour painting carried out with opaque colours as opposed to pure water colour which employs transparent colours.

ACRYLIC RESIN

A quick-drying waterproof emulsion that can be mixed with dry pigments to give paints that can be applied with heavy knife-laid impasto or diluted with water to wash-like consistency.

INKS

Liquids for drawing or painting; generally the colours are in suspension or present as a dye. Sometimes, as with Indian ink or white ink, there may be opaque pigments in suspension. Inks may be applied with different types of pen or soft hair brushes.

THE ARTISTS BY COUNTRY

Some of the world's most renowned painters with well known examples of their work

AUSTRIA
KOKOSCHKA, Oskar (b. 1886) 'View of the Thames'.

BELGIUM
BRUEGHEL, Pieter (The Elder) (*c.* 1520–69) 'The Adoration of the Kings', 'The Peasant Dance'.
GOSSAERT, Jan (*c.* 1478–1533) 'Adoration'.
JORDAENS, Jacob (1593–1678) 'The Bean King'.
MEMLINC, Hans (*c.* 1430–94) 'Mystic Marriage of St. Catherine'.
RUBENS, Peter Paul (1577–1640) 'Adoration of the Magi', 'Battle of the Amazons'.
TENIERS, David (The Younger) (1610–90) 'Peasants Playing Bowls'.
VAN DER WEYDEN, Rogier (*c.* 1400–64) 'Deposition', 'The Magdalen Reading'.
VAN DYCK, Anthony (1599–1641) 'Charles I of England'.
VAN EYCK, Hubert (*c.* 1370–*c.* 1426) Jan (*c.* 1390–1441) 'Ghent Altarpiece'.
    Jan alone 'The Arnolfini Marriage'.

FRANCE
ARP, Hans (Jean) (1887–1966) 'Berger et Nuage'.
BONNARD, Pierre (1867–1947) 'The Window'.
BOUCHER, François (1703–70) 'Diana Bathing'.
BRAQUE, Georges (1882–1963) 'Vase of Anemones'.
CÉZANNE, Paul (1839–1906) 'Mont Sainte-Victoire', 'Bathers'.
CHAGALL, Marc (b. 1887) 'I and the Village', 'Calvary'.
CHARDIN, Jean-Baptiste Siméon (1699–1779) 'The Skate', 'The Lesson'.
COROT, Jean-Baptiste Camille (1796–1875) 'Ponte de Mantes', 'Sens Cathedral'.
DAUMIER, Honoré (1808–79) 'The Third-Class Carriage'.
DAVID, Jacques Louis (1748–1825) 'The Rape of the Sabines'.
DEGAS, Hiliare-Germain-Edgar (1834–1917) 'La Danseuse au Bouquet'.
DELACROIX, Eugène (1798–1863) 'The Massacre of Chios'.
FOUQUET, Jean (*c.* 1420–*c.* 80) 'Etienne Chevalier with St. Stephen'.
FRAGONARD, Jean-Honoré (1732–1806) 'The Love Letter', 'Baigneuses'.
GAUGUIN, Paul (1848–1903) 'Ta Matete'.
INGRES, Jean-Auguste Dominique (1780–1867) 'Odalesque'.
LORRAINE, Claude (1600–82) 'Embarkation of St. Ursula'.
MANET, Edouard (1823–83) 'Déjeuner sur l'Herbe'.
MATISSE, Henri (1869–1954) 'Odalesque'.
MILLET, Jean-François (1814–75) 'Man with the Hoe', 'Angelus'.
MONET, Claude (1840–1926) 'Rouen Cathedral', 'Water-lilies'.
PISSARRO, Camille (1830–1903) 'The Harvest', 'Montfoucault'.
POUSSIN, Nicholas (1593/4–1665) 'Worship of the Golden Calf'.
RENOIR, Pierre Auguste (1841–1919) 'Luncheon of the Boating Party'.
ROUSSEAU, Henri (1844–1910) 'The Dream'.
SEURAT, Georges (1859–91) 'Sunday Afternoon on the Grande Jatte'.

FRANCE continued overleaf

FRANCE continued

SISLEY, Alfred (1839–99) 'Flood at Port Marly'.
TOULOUSE-LAUTREC, Henri de (1864–1901) 'At the Moulin Rouge'.
UTRILLO, Maurice (1883–1955) 'Port St. Martin'.
WATTEAU, Antoine (1684–1721) 'The Embarkation for Cythera'.

GERMANY
ALTDORFER, Albrecht (1480–1538) 'Battle of Arbela'.
CRANACH, Lucas (The Elder) (1472–1553) 'Venus', 'Rest on Flight into Egypt'.
DÜRER, Albrecht (1471–1528) 'The Four Apostles', 'Apocalypse'.
GRÜNEWALD, Mathias (*c.* 1460–1528) 'Isenheim Altarpiece'.
HOLBEIN, Hans (The Younger) (1497–1543) 'Henry VIII', 'The Ambassadors'.

GREAT BRITAIN
BONINGTON, Richard Parkes (1802–28) 'A Sea Piece'.
CONSTABLE, John (1776–1837) 'The Hay Wain'.
CROME, John (1768–1821) 'The Slate Quarries.
GAINSBOROUGH, Thomas (1727–88) 'Blue Boy'.
HILLIARD, Nicholas (*c.* 1547–1619) 'Elizabeth I' 'Sir Walter Raleigh'.
HOGARTH, William (1697–1764) 'Rake's Progress', 'Marriage à la Mode'.
HUNT, William Holman (1827–1910) 'The Scapegoat'.
JOHN, Augustus Edwin (1878–1961) 'The Smiling Woman'.
LANDSEER, Sir Edwin (1802–73) 'The Old Shepherd's Chief Mourner', 'Shoeing'.
MILLAIS, Sir John Everett (1829–96) 'Order of Release'.
RAEBURN, Sir Henry (1756–1823) 'Sir John Sinclair'.
REYNOLDS, Sir Joshua (1723–92) 'Mrs Siddons as the Tragic Muse', 'The Three Graces'.
ROSSETTI, Dante Gabriel (1828–82) 'Beata Beatrix'.
STUBBS, George (1724–1806) 'Horse frightened by a Lion'.
TURNER, Joseph Mallord William (1775–1851) 'The Grand Canal, Venice', 'Shipwreck'.
WILSON, Richard (1714–1782) 'Okehampton Castle'.

ITALY
BELLINI, Giovanni (*c.* 1429–1516) 'Pieta', 'Coronation of the Virgin', 'Agony in the Garden'.
BOTTICELLI, Sandro (Alessandro di Mariano Filipepi) (1445–1510) 'Birth of Venus', 'Mystic Nativity'.
CANALETTO, Giovanni Antonio Canal (1697–1768) 'Venice: A Regatta on the Grand Canal'.
CARAVAGGIO, Michelangelo Merisi (1573–1610) 'St Matthew,' 'Deposition'.
CORREGIO, Antonio Allegri (*c.* 1489–1534) 'Jupiter and Io', 'Assumption of the Virgin'.
FRANCESCA, Piero della (*c.* 1410–92) 'Nativity'.
FRA ANGELICO, Giovanni da Fiesole (1387–1455) 'Annunciation'.
FRA FILIPPO LIPPI (*c.* 1406–69) 'Tarquinia Madonna'.
GIORGIONE, Giorgio da Castelfranco (1475–1510) 'Sleeping Venus'.
GIOTTO DI BONDONE (*c.* 1267–1337) 'Life of St. Francis'.
LEONARDO DA VINCI (1452–1519) 'Mona Lisa (La Gioconda)', 'Last Supper'.
MICHELANGELO, Buonarroti (1475–1564) 'Creation of Adam'.
MODIGLIANI, Amadeo (1884–1920) 'Portrait of Madame Zborowski'.
RAPHAEL (1483–1520) 'Sistine Madonna'.
TIEPOLO, Giovanni Battista (1696–1770) 'The Finding of Moses'.
TINTORETTO, Jacopo Robusti (1518–94) 'Last Supper'. 'Il Paradiso'.
TITIAN (*c.* 1487–1576) 'The Tribute Money', 'Bacchus and Ariadne'.
VERONESE, Paolo Caliari (1528–88) 'Marriage at Cana'.

NETHERLANDS
BOSCH, Hieronymus (*c.* 1450–1516) 'Christ Crowned with Thorns', The Garden of Earthly Delights'.
HALS, Frans (*c.* 1580–1666) 'Laughing Cavalier'.
HOOCH, Pieter de (1629–83) 'An Interior'.
MONDRIAN, Piet (1872–1944) 'Composition'.
REMBRANDT, Harmensz van Rijn (1606–69) 'The Night Watch', 'The Anatomy Lesson'.
RUISDAEL, Jacob van (*c.* 1628–82) 'View of Haarlem'.
VAN GOGH, Vincent (1853–90) 'Road with Cypresses', 'Old Peasant'.
VERMEER, Jan (1632–75) 'Woman with a Water Jug'.

NORWAY
MUNCH, Edvard (1863–1944) 'Dance of Death'.

SPAIN
DALI, Salvador (b. 1904) 'Crucifixion', The Persistence of Memory'.
EL GRECO (1541–1614) 'The Burial of Count Orgaz', View of Toledo'.
GOYA, Francisco de (1746–1828) 'The Naked Maja', 'The Shootings of May 3rd'.
MURILLO, Bartolomé Esteban (1617–82) 'Virgin and Child', 'Immaculate Conception'.
PICASSO, Pablo (1881–1973) 'Guernica', 'Les Demoiselles d'Avignon'.
RIBERA, José (1591–1652) 'The Martyrdom of St. Bartholomew'.
VELAZQUEZ, Diego (1599–1660) 'Rokeby Venus', 'The Water-Carrier'.

SWITZERLAND
KLEE, Paul (1879–1940) 'Twittering Machine'.

UNITED STATES OF AMERICA
AUDUBON, John James (1785–1851) 'Birds of America'.
MOSES, Grandma (Anna Mary Robertson) (1860–1961) 'The Thanksgiving Turkey'.
POLLOCK, Jackson (1912–56) 'Autumn Rhythm'.
ROTHKO, Mark (1903–70) 'Green on Blue'.
WHISTLER, James Abbott McNeil (1834–1903) 'Arrangement in Grey and Black—The Artist's Mother.

MUSIC & THE DANCE

ORCHESTRAL INSTRUMENTS

(Woodwinds 1–10; Brass 11–14; Percussion 15–24; Strings 25–29; Keyboard 30–33)

Name (earliest concerto)	Earliest orchestral use	History
1 Piccolo or Octave Flute (Vivaldi, c. 1735)	1717 (Handel's Water Music)	Name 'piccolo' dates from 1856, but the origin goes back to prehistory via flute and sopranino recorder.
2 Recorder or Flûte-a-bec (c. 1690)	c. 1690	Earliest written mention 1388.
3 Flute—transverse or cross-blown (Vivaldi, c. 1729)	1672 (Lully)	Prehistoric (c. 18,000 BC); the modern Boehm flute dates from 1832.
4 Oboe (Marcheselli, 1708)	1657 (Lully's L'amour malade)	Originated Middle Ages in the schalmey family. The name comes from Fr. hautbois (1511) = loud wood.
5 Clarinet (Vivaldi, c. 1740?: 2 clarinets; Molter, c. 1747: 1 clarinet)	1726 (Faber: Mass)	Developed by J C Denner (1655–1707) from the recorder and schalmey families.
6 Cor anglais (J M Haydn, c. 1775?)	1760 (in Vienna)	Purcell wrote for 'tenor oboe' c. 1690: this may have originated the name English Horn. Alternatively, it may be from 'angled horn', referring to its crooked shape.
7 Bass Clarinet	1838 (Meyerbeer's Les Huguenots)	Prototype made in 1772 by Gilles Lot of Paris. Modern Boehm form from 1838.
8 Bassoon (Vivaldi, c. 1730?)	c. 1619	Introduced in Italy c. 1540 as the lowest of the double-reed group.
9 Double Bassoon	c. 1730 (Handel)	'Borrowed' from military bands for elemental effects in opera.
10 Saxophone (Debussy's Rhapsody, 1903)	1844 (Kastner's Last King of Judah)	Invented by Adolphe Sax, c. 1840.
11 Trumpet (Torelli, before 1700) (Haydn, 1796: keyed trumpet)	c. 1800 (keyed) 1835 (valved, in Halévy's La Juive)	The natural trumpet is of prehistoric origin; it formed the basis of the earliest orchestras.

Name (earliest concerto)	Earliest orchestral use	History
12 Trombone (Wagenseil, c. 1760)	c. 1600 (as part of bass-line)	From Roman *buccina* or slide-trumpet, via the mediaeval sackbut to its modern form c. 1500.
13 Horn (Bach, 1717–21, or Vivaldi) (Bach . . . Vivaldi: 2 horns; Telemann, before 1721: 1 horn)	1639 (Cavalli)	Prehistoric. The earliest music horns were the German helical horns of the mid-16th century. Rotary valve horn patented in 1832.
14 Tuba (Vaughan Williams, 1954)	1830 (Berlioz' *Symphonie Fantastique*)	Patented by W Wieprecht and Moritz, Berlin, 1835.
15 Timpani/Kettle drum (Mašek, c. 1790: 1 set; Tausch, c. 1870: 6 timpani)	1607 (Monteverdi's *Orfeo*)	Originated in the ancient Orient.
16 Bass Drum	1748 (Rameau's *Zaïs*)	As timpani.
17 Side or Snare drum	1749 (Handel's *Fireworks Music*)	Derived from the small drums of prehistory, via the Mediaeval tabor. Achieved its modern form in the 18th century.
18 Tenor Drum	1842	
19 Tambourine	1820	Dates back to the mediaeval Arabs; prototype used by Assyrians and Egyptians. Earliest use of the word 1579.
20 Cymbals	1680 (Strungk's *Esther*)	From Turkish military bands of antiquity.
21 Triangle	1774 (Glantz: Turkish Symphony)	As cymbals.
22 Xylophone	1873 (Lumbye's *Traumbilder*)	Primitive; earliest 'art' mention 1511.
23 Gong or Tam tam	1791 (Gossec's *Funeral March*)	Originating in the ancient Far East.
24 Glockenspiel	1739 (Handel's *Saul*)	Today strictly a keyboard instrument, in the 19th century the metal plates were struck by hand-held hammers. The original instrument dates from 4th century Rome.
25 Violin (Torelli, 1709)	c. 1600	Descended from the Lyre via the 6th century crwth, rebec and fiddle. Modern instrument of Lombardic origin c. 1545. The words violin and fiddle derive ultimately from Roman *vitulari*, ('to skip like a calf')
26 Viola (Giranek or Telemann, 'before 1762')	c. 1600	As violin.
27 Violoncello (Jacchini, 1701)	c. 1600	As violin.
28 Double bass (Vanhal, c. 1770)	c. 1600	Developed alongside the violin family, but is a closer relative to the bass viol or Violone.
29 Harp (Handel, 1738)	c. 1600	Possibly prehistoric: attained its modern form by 1792.
30 Vibraphone	1934	First used in dance bands in the 1920s.
31 Celesta	1880 (Widor's *Der Korrigane*)	Invented by Mustel in 1880.
32 Pianoforte (J C Bach, 1776)	1776	Descended from the dulcimer. Invented by Cristofori c. 1709. Earliest printed music: 1732. First concert use 1767 in London.
33 Organ (Handel, c. 1730)	1886 (Saint-Saëns' Symphony No. 3)	Ultimate origin lies in the antique panpipes.

MUSICAL ABBREVIATIONS

arr	arranged	ob	oboe	tpt	trumpet
clt	clarinet	orch	orchestra(l)	v d'a	viola d'amor
cor	horn	pf	pianoforte	vl	violin
fag	bassoon	pf4	piano quartet★	vla	viola
fl	flute	Rhap	Rhapsody	w	wind (woodwind and/or brass)
hps	harpsichord	Sinf Conc	Sinfonia Concertante	w5	wind quintet★
instr	instruments	str	strings		
keyb'd	keyboard	str4	string quartet★		★ and similar combinations of
misc	miscellaneous	str5	string quintet★		abbreviations.

THE HISTORY OF MUSIC

Dates (approx.)	Name of era	Musical developments	Principal composers
	Prehistoric	Improvisatory music-making. Music and magic virtually synonymous	
8th century BC to 4th century AD to 6th century AD	Primitive (Ancient Greece and Rome; Byzantium)	Improvisatory music-making in domestic surroundings. Competitive music-making in the arena.	
4th century AD	Ambrosian	The beginnings of plainsong and the establishment of order in liturgical music.	Bishop Ambrose of Milan (c. 333–97) established four scales.
6th to 10th century	Gregorian	Church music subjected to strict rules, e.g.: melodies sung only in unison.	Pope Gregory I, 'The Great' (540–604) extended the number of established scales to eight.
1100–1300	Mediaeval	Guido d'Arezzo (c. 980–1050) was called the inventor of music: his teaching methods and invention of a method of writing music transformed the art. Beginning of organised instrumental music; start of polyphony in church music.	Minstrels (10th–13th centuries). Goliards (travelling singers of Latin songs: 11th–12th centuries). Troubadours (c. 1100–1210) Trouvères (from 1100). Bernart de Ventadorn (c. 1150–95) encouraged singing in the vernacular.
1300–1600	Renaissance	The great age of polyphonic church music. Gradual emergence of instrumental music. Appearance of Madrigals, chansons, etc. The beginnings of true organisation in music and instruments.	Guillaume de Machut (c. 1300–77) John Dunstable (d. 1453) Guillaume Dufay (c. 1400–74) Johannes Ockeghem (1430–95) Josquin des Pres (1450–1521) John Taverner (c. 1495–1545) Giovanni da Palestrina (c. 1525–94) Orlando de Lasso (c. 1530–94) Thomas Morley (1557–1603) John Dowland (1563–1626) Michael Praetorius (1571–1621)
1600–1750	Baroque	Beginnings of opera and oratorio Rise of instrumental music; the first orchestras, used at first in the opera house but gradually attaining separate existence. Beginnings of sonata, concerto, suite, and symphony. The peak of polyphonic writing.	Giovanni Gabrieli (1557–1612) Claudio Monteverdi (1567–1633) Orlando Gibbons (1583–1625) Pietro Cavalli (1602–76) Jean-Baptiste Lully (1632–87) Arcangelo Corelli (1653–1713) Henry Purcell (1658–95) Alessandro Scarlatti (1660–1725) Reinhard Keiser (1674–1739) Georg Philipp Telemann (1681–1767) Jean Philippe Rameau (1683–1764) Domenico Scarlatti (1685–1757) Johann Sebastian Bach (1685–1750) George Frideric Handel (1685–1759)
1750–1800+	Classical	The age of the concert symphony and concerto. Beginning of the string quartet and sinfonia concertante. Decline of church music. Important developments in opera.	Giovanni Battista Sammartini (c. 1700–75) Christoph Willibald von Gluck (1714–87) Carl Philipp Emanuel Bach (1714–88) Franz Joseph Haydn (1732–1809) Wolfgang Amadeus Mozart (1756–91) Luigi Cherubini (1760–1842)
1800–50	Early Romantic	High maturity of the symphony and concerto, etc. in classical style. Romantic opera. The age of the piano virtuosi. Invention of the Nocturne. Beginnings of the symphonic poem. Lieder. Beginnings of nationalism.	Ludwig van Beethoven (1770–1827) Nicolo Paganini (1782–1840) Carl Maria von Weber (1786–1826) Gioacchino Rossini (1792–1868) Franz Schubert (1797–1828) Hector Berlioz (1803–69) Jakob Ludwig Felix Mendelssohn (1809–47) Frederic François Chopin (1810–49) Robert Schumann (1810–56)

HISTORY OF MUSIC continued

Dates (approx.)	Name of era	Musical developments	Principal composers
1850–1900	High Romanticism	The development of nationalism. Maturity of the symphonic and tone poems Emergence of music drama.	Mikhail Glinka (1804–57) Franz Liszt (1811–86) Richard Wagner (1813–83) Bedřich Smetana (1824–84) Johannes Brahms (1833–97) Pyotr Il'ich Tchaikovsky (1840–93) Antonín Dvořák (1841–1904) Edvard Hagerup Grieg (1843–1907)
1900–	Modern	Impressionism and post-romanticism. Gigantism. Neo-classicism and other reactionary movements. Atonalism.	Claude Debussy (1862–1918) Richard Strauss (1864–1949) Carl Nielsen (1865–1931) Jean Sibelius (1865–1957) Alexander Skryabin (1872–1915) Ralph Vaughan Williams (1872–1958) Sergei Rakhmaninoff (1873–1943) Arnold Schoenberg (1874–1951) Charles Ives (1874–1954) Béla Bartók (1881–1945) Igor Stravinsky (1882–1971) Anton Webern (1883–1945) Alban Berg (1885–1934) Samuel Barber (b. 1910) Benjamin Britten (1913–77)
Today	Avant-garde	Avant-Garde is history in the making and any list of composers would be arbitrary since one cannot tell which of the many directions taken by modern music will prove most influential. There have always been avant-garde composers, without which the art of music would never have developed: we would take many names from the above chart as good examples. Here are some names of avant-gardistes of prominence.	Luigi Dallapiccola (1904–75) John Cage (b. 1912) Iannis Xenakis (b. 1922) Luigi Nono (b. 1924) Hans Werner Henze (b. 1926) Karlheinz Stockhausen (b. 1928)

THE GREAT COMPOSERS

INTRODUCTION

A chart of the main works by history's major composers, their music listed generic columns. Lost and disputed works are ignored, as are those in sketch form, b important works which were not completed by the composer have been included (e. Schubert's Symphony No. 8, *Unfinished*) where performances are possible.

Each of the categories should be regarded as covering its respective field in a wi sense. For example, Tchaikovsky's *Manfred*, although not numbered as a symphony, included as one of his seven, and Berg's *Lyric Suite* for string quartet, even though n called a string quartet as such by the composer, is included in that column. Whe totals are unkown or obscure, only the general outline of a corpus of works has be indicated using asterisks: one for a handful of such pieces, two for a significant cont bution, and three indicating 'very many'. In some cases where the information mig be useful, these vague symbols are amplified by details in the extreme right-ha column.

In all cases the figures in the 'Concertos' columns include other major works (concer nios, rhapsodies, etc.) for the given instrument and orchestra.

Dates	Composer	symphonies	orchestral	Concertos				Chamber				Keyb'd			Vocal works				Other important works
				keyb'd	violin	other		str4	trios	vl sons	other	sonatas	solos	organ	operas	choral	lieder song, &c	other	
c. 1240–86	Hal(l)e, Adam de la French															*	**	Motets	Pastoral drama Jeu de Robin Marion.
c. 1400–53	Dunstable, John English															**			
c. 1450–1521	Des Pres, Josquin Flemish															**		Masses: ** Motets: **	
c. 1505–85	Tallis, Thomas English								**	*						** *	*		
c. 1525–94	Palestrina, Giovanni Pierluigi Italian												**			**	*	Masses: 98 Motets: 265	
1532–94	Lassus, Orlando de Flemish															** *	**	Marigals: *** Motets: ***	
1543–1623	Byrd, William English								music for viols *				** *			** *	**	Anthems ** Madrigals ** Motets: 63 Masses: 3 Canciones Sacrae and Gradualia: 170	

Dates	Composer	symphonies	orchestral	keyb'd	violin	other	str 4	trios	vl sons	other	sonatas	solos	organ	operas	choral	lieder songs, &c	other	Other important works
				Concertos			Chamber				Keyb'd			Vocal works				
c. 1548–1611	Victoria, Thomás Luis de Spanish														**	**	hymns *** Masses: 21 Motets: 46	
1557–1612	Gabrieli, Giovanni Italian									**			*		**		Madrigals ** Motets ** Vocal concerti **	
c. 1563–1626	Dowland, John English									**						**		
1567–1643	Monteverdi, Claudio Italian													19	** *	**	Madrigals etc. **	Ballets **
1571–1621	Praetorius, Michael (alias of Michael Schul(t)z(e)) German									*					*			Theoretical works
1583–1623	Gibbons, Orlando English									***		**			*	**	Psalms ** Anthems ** Madrigals **	Masks: 4
1632–87	Lully, Jean-Baptiste (b. Giovanni Battista Lulli) Italian/French		*											15	*	*		Ballets: 49
1637–1707	Buxtehude, Dietrich Danish									**			**		**	**		
1653–1713	Corelli, Arcangelo Italian					2 vl, cello: 12		48	12									
1658/9–1695	Purcell, Henry English		*					24	12	misc. *		**		6	*	** *	Anthems: 62	Incidental music: 44
c. 1660–1725	Scarlatti, Pietro Alessandro Gasparo Italian	12				str: 12 fl: 7				*		*		70	**	**	Oratorios: 24 Cantatas, Motets, etc.: c. 800 Masses: 11	
1668–1733	Couperin, François French					misc: 14		6		*		222			**	*		
1678–1741	Vivaldi, Antonio Lucio Italian	52			238	fl: 17 ob: 20 fag: 39 2 tpt: 1 2 cor: 2 cello: 27 misc str: 19 misc: 53	2	18	31	2 vl: 20 cello: 9				45	**	**	Cantatas: 36 Oratorios: 3	
1681–1767	Telemann, Georg Philipp German				20	fl: 14 ob: 10 cor: 1 tpt: 1 vla: 1 misc: 53	*	**		***		** *		40	** *		Passions: 40 Cantatas: 100	Orchestral Suites: c. 600
1683–1764	Rameau, Jean-Philippe French					*				6 tets: 6		56		20	*		Cantatas: 8	Music for ballets: 18
1685–1750	Bach, Johann Sebastian German		**	7	2	2 vl: 1 fl; vl; hps: 1 2 hps: 3 3 hps: 2 4 hps: 1 Orch: 6			7	cello: ** vl: **		** *	** *		** *	*	Magnificat: 1 Masses: 5 Cantatas: 212 Oratorios: 3 Passions: 3	Orchestral Suites: 4 Art of Fugue Musical Offering
1685–1759	Handel, George Frideric German, nat. English		**	1		ob: 3 organ: 20 2 organs: 1 conc grossi: 20 misc: *			6	**		** *		58	** *	**	Oratorios, etc: 32 Cantatas: 99	Water Music Fireworks Music
1685–1757	Scarlatti, Domenico Italian	7									555			13	*	*	Stabat Mater: 1 Oratorios: 5	
1714–88	Bach, Carl Philipp Emanuel German	18	63			2 keyb'd: 2 fl: 4 ob: 2 cello: 3 } arr		31	10	fl: 17 misc: ***	154	183	7		**	*	Passions: 2 Oratorios: 2 Magnificat: 1 Cantatas: 16	
1714–87	Gluck, Christoph Willibald von German	9						7		*				52	*	*		Pantomimes (Ballets): 4
1732–1809	Haydn, Franz Joseph Austrian	108		11	4	tpt: 1 2 lyre: 5 vl, hps: 1 cello: 2 cor: 1 sinf conc: 1	65	40 ** *	5		55	*	*	13	**	*	Oratorios: 4 Masses: 12 Te Deums: 2 Cantatas: *	Ovetures: 19 Divertimenti: c. 60 Marches: 7 Dances: *** Baryton trios: 125

Dates	Composer	symphonies	orchestral	Concertos			Chamber				Keyb'd			Vocal works				Other important works
				keyb'd	violin	other	str4	trios	vl sons	other	sonatas	solos	organ	operas	choral	lieder song, &c		
1756–91	Mozart, Wolfgang Amadeus (Johannes Chrysostomus Wolfangus Theophilus) Austrian	49	***	27	8	fl: 2 clt: 1 fag: 1 cor: 4 fl, harp: 1 2 pf: 1 3 pf: 1 Sinf conc: 2	23	**	37	str5: 6 clt5: 1 pf, w5: 1 cor5: 1 pf4: 2 fl4: 4 ob4: 1 misc: ***	18	** *	*	19	**	*	Masses: 17	Divertimenti etc. c. 40 Dances: ***
1770–1827	Beethoven, Ludwig van German	10	**	6	1	pf, vl, cello: 1	16	**	10	cello: 5 misc: **	35	**	*	1	**	80	Arias with orch: ** Masses: 2 Cantatas: 2 Oratorio: 1	Stage works: **
1786–1826	Weber, Carl Maria Friedrich Ernst von German	2		3		clt: 3 fag: 1 cello: 1			6	pf4: 1 clt4: 1 misc: *	4	**		8			Masses: 2 Cantatas: 8 Offertoria: 2	Stage works: ** Concert overture
1792–1868	Rossini, Gioacchino Italian						6			w5: 5 misc: *		*		38	*	*	Petite Messe Solonelle Stabat Mater	
1797–1828	Schubert, Franz Peter Austrian	9	**		1		15	**	4	pf5: 1 Octet: 1 str5: 1	21	** *		17	**	** *	Masses: 7 ***	Dramatic music:
1803–69	Berlioz, Louis Hector French	4	**							*				5	** *	**		
1804–57	Glinka, Mikhail Russian	1	*				2	*		str, w6: 1 vla: 1 misc: *		**		2	*	**		Prince Khomsky incidental music
1809–47	Mendelssohn-Bartholdy, Jacob Ludwig Felix German	17	**	3	2	vl, pf: 1 2pf: 1	8	2	1	str8: 1 pf4: 3 str5: 2 pf6: 1 misc: **		**	6	2	** *	** *	Elijah	Stage music: 4 Songs Without Words: 48
1810–49	Chopin, Frédéric François Polish			6					1	cello: 1 pf duets * 2pf *	3	** *				18		
1810–56	Schumann, Robert, Alexander German	5	**	2	1	cello: 1 4 cor: 1	3	3	2	pf4: 1 pf5:1	3	** *	*	1	*	** *		Manfred incidental music
1811–86	Liszt, Ferencz Hungarian	2	23	2					1	pf duets: ** 2pf: ** misc: *	1	72 +	22	1	93	** *		Symphonic poems 12
1813–1901	Verdi, Giuseppe Italian						1			*				32	**	*	Requiem Four Sacred Pieces	
1813–83	Wagner, Richard Wilhelm German	1	**				1			*	2	*		15	*	*		
1824–96	Bruckner, Anton Austrian	11	*				1			str5: 1 misc: *					**		Te Deum	Overture in G minor
1824–84	Smetana, Bedřich Bohemian	1	**				2	1				*		9	10	*		
1825–99	Strauss, Johann II Austrian		** *											16				Waltzes, Marches, Polkas, etc. ***
1833–97	Brahms, Johannes German	4	**	2	1	vl, cello: 1	3	6	3	str6: 2 str5: 2 clt5: 1 pf4: 3 cello (clt): 2	3	** *	*		**	** *	German Requiem	St Anthony Variations Overtures: 2 Serenades: 2 Hungarian Dances 21
1835–1921	Saint-Saëns, Camille French	5	**	5	4	cello: 2	4	2	2	6tet: 1 pf5: 1 pf4: 1 cello: 2 ob: 1 clt: 1 fag: 1 misc: *		**	*	13	**	**		Carnival of the Animals Incidental music
1839–81	Mussorgsky, Modest Petrovitch Russian		*									**		4	*	**		
1840–93	Tchaikovsky, Pyotr Il'ich Russian	7	**	3	1	cello: 1	3	1		str6: 1		**		11	**	** *		Ballet music: ** 1812 Overture and other concert overtures Orchestral Suites
1841–1904	Dvořák, Antonín Czech	9	**	1	1	cello: 2	14	5	2	str5: 3 pf5: 2 str6: 1 pf4: 2 pf duets: ** misc: *		**		10	**	**		Overtures: 5 Slavonic Dances 16 Slavonic Rhapsodies: 3 str Serenade: 1 w Serenade: 1 Scherzo Capricc

Dates	Composer	symphonies	orchestral	Concertos				Chamber				Keyb'd			Vocal works				Other important works
				keyb'd	violin	other	str4	trios	vl sons	other	sonatas	solos	organ	operas	choral	lieder songs, &c	other	
1843–1907	Grieg, Edvard Hagerup Norwegian	1	*	1			1		3	cello: 1 pf duets: * 2pf: *		**				*	** *		Peer Gynt incidental music Symphonic Dances: 4
1844–1908	Rimsky-Korsakov, Nikolai Russian	3	*	1		trombone: 1 ob: 1* clt: 1	3	1		str6: 1 pf, w5: 1		*		16	16	** *			Scheherazade Capriccio Espagnole Incidental music: 1
1857–1934	Elgar, Sir Edward William English	2	**		1	cello: 1 fag: 1	1		1	pf5: 1 w5: 1	1	*	*		** *	*	Dream of Gerontius	Enigma Variations incidental music: ** Pomp & Circumstance Marches: 5
1858–1924	Puccini, Giacomo Italian									*				12	*			
1860–1911	Mahler, Gustav Austrian	10												3	**	** *	Song of the Earth Lieder Eines Farenden Gesellen	
1860–1903	Wolf, Hugo Austrian						1			*		*		2	21	** *		Italian Serenade Incidental music: 2
1862–1934	Delius, Frederick English		*	1	3	vl, cello: 1	2		4	cello: 1		*		6	**	**	Mass of Life	
1864–1949	Strauss, Richard Georg German	3	**		2	horn: 2 ob: 1	1		1	w13: 2 w16: 1 pf4: 1 cello: 1		*		15	21	** *		Ballets: 2
1865–1931	Nielsen, Carl August Danish	6	**		1	fl: 1 clt: 1	4		2	w5: 1 misc: *		**	2	2	*	**		Helios Overture Little Suite for str.
1865–1957	Sibelius, Jan Julian Christian Finnish	8	** *		1		3	2	3	pf5: 1 pf4: 2 misc: *		**	*	1	** *	**		Tapiola En Saga
1872–1958	Vaughan Williams, Sir Ralph English	9	**		1	2pf: 1 tuba: 1 ob: 1	4			str5: 1		*	*	6	**	**		Ballets: 4 Incidental music: The Wasps Film music: **
1873–1943	Rakhmaninoff, Sergei Russian	3	*	5					1	cello: 1 pf duet: *	2	**		3	7	**		
1874–1951	Schoenberg, Arnold Austrian	2	*	1	1		5	1		str6: 1 misc: *		*	*	4	**	*	Gurre-Lieder	
1875–1937	Ravel, Maurice French		**	2			1	1	3	vl, cello: 1		*		2	*	**		Ballets: 4 Bolero
1881–1945	Bartók, Béla Hungarian		**	4	4	2 pf: 1 vla: 1	6	1	3	pf5: 1	2			1	*	*		Concerto for orch Ballets: 2 Suites for orch: 2 Divertimento for str
1882–1971	Stravinsky, Igor Russian, nat. French, then American	4	**	1	1	str: 1 orch: *				2 pf: 1 misc: **	2	*		4	*	*		Stage works
1883–1945	Webern, Anton Austrian	1	*			9 instr: 1	3	1		pf5: 1 pf, sax, vl, clt: 1		*			5	*		
1885–1935	Berg, Alban Austrian		*		1		2				1			2	*	*		
1890–1959	Martinů, Bohuslav Jan Czech	6	**	5	2	fl, vl: 1 cello: 2 vl; pf: 1 str4: 1 misc: **	7	2	5	str6: 1 str5: 1 w5: 1 pf4: 1 misc: ***		**		10	*	*		Ballets: 10
1891–1953	Prokofiev, Sergei Russian	7	**	5	2	cello: 1	2		2	w, str5: 1 2 vl: 1	9	**		7	10	*		Ballets: 6 Peter and the Wolf Incidental and film music **
1897–1963	Hindemith, Paul German	3	**	3	1	vla: 1 cello: 1 cor: 1 misc: *	7		7	vla: 1 v d'a: 1 cello: 1 misc: *** 2pf: *	4	*	3 +	7	*	*		Symphonic Metamorphosis on Themes of Weber Stage works: **
1906–75	Shostakovich, Dmitri Russian	15	*	2	2	cello: 2 misc: *	15	2	1	2pf: 1 cello: 2 str8: 1 pf5: 1 Vla son: 1	2	*		4	**	**		Film music: 35 Incidental music: 10 Ballets: 3
1913–77	Britten, Edward Benjamin English	3	**	2	1		2			misc: *	.	*		12	**	** *	* War Requiem	Young Person's Guide to the Orchestra Stage and film music: **

THE DANCE

MAIN TRENDS

Pre-history
Unorganised or loosely organised dances for warlike and communal purposes.

c. 50 BC
Mimes: dancing and singing spectacles (Rome).

14th Century
Danse basse: low, slow gliding steps.
Hault danse: with high fast steps.

15th Century
First true ballet, with settings by Leonardo da Vinci, danced at Tortona, 1489. Introduced at the court of Henry VIII of England as Masque.

16th Century
Ballet comique. First complete printed account (15 Oct. 1581) of a ballet to celebrate the marriage of duc de Joyeuse and Marguerite of Lorraine. It was based on the story of Circe and choreographed by Baldassarino de Belgiojoso.

17th Century
Ballet Masquerade, often with hideous and elaborate masks.

Playford's *English Dancing Master* published 1651; a collection of tunes and steps.

First waltz, developed from minuet and Landler in 1660; word 'waltz' first used in 1754 in Austria. Ballet systematique: Louis XIV established the Academie Royale de Danse 1661. 5 classic positions codified; first history of dancing published in 1682.

18th Century
Ballet steps on toe-tips (on point) (*c.* 1800).

19th Century
Square dance (*c.* 1815).

Can-can (*c.* 1835); high-kicking exhibitionist female dance popular on Parisian stages.

Age of the great waltz composers: Josef Lanner; Johann Strauss; Emil Waldteufel, etc.

20th Century
Ballet Russes established in Paris by Diaghilev, 1909.

TYPES OF DANCE POPULAR AT THE TIME
(Basic rhythmic pulse in brackets)

Pavane (4); derived from instrumental music from Padua; possibly the first stylised dance.
Galliard (3), also from Italy, where the name implies gaiety.

Court ballet: Branle (2), English clog dance with circular figures.

Allemande (2,4), ie: 'from Germany'. Courante (3), ie: 'running', from It. *corrente* (current).
Volta (3), very lively (It: *volta*: vault).

Morris dance, from Morocco.

Gigue (3,6,12), originally from English jig, the word from German *Geige*: 'fiddle'. Sarabande (3), slow and graceful, introduced to Spain *c.* 1588 from Morocco or West Indies.
Bouree (4), lively dance, starting on the upbeat.
Chaconne (3), graceful dance introduced from Peru (*guacones*, *c.* 1580) via Spain.
Gavotte (2), medium pace, from Provencale; *gavoto*: a native of the Alps.
Minuet (3), 'smale steps'; rustic minuets occur in Strasbourg in 1682, but origin in the 15th century Branle.
Passacaglia (3), as chaconne above, but in minor key.
Rigaudon; Rigadoon (2,4), lively French dance.
Landler (3), rustic dance, from *Landl*: 'small country'.
Matelot (2), Dutch sailors' clog dance.
Contredanse (2,4) from Eng.: 'country dance', but mis-translated as 'counter-dance', ie: for opposing groups, and re-introduced into England in this form.
Cotillion (6), from French word for 'petticoat', for 2 groups of 4 pairs each; developed into quadrille at the end of the 19th century.

Reel (4), stylised form of Scottish dance.

Quadrille (2,4)

Polka (2), introduced to Paris in 1843 from Bohemian courtship dance (1-2-3-hop).
Cakewalk (2), graceful walking dance of competitive type with cakes as prizes, popular in Black America in 1872; introduced into ballrooms *c.* 1900.

MAIN TRENDS cont.

TYPES OF DANCE POPULAR AT THE TIME cont.
(Basic rhythmic pulse in brackets)

New free dance forms emerging.

Samba (2), emerged from Brazil, 1885; known *c.* 1920 as Maxixe; resumed name 'samba' *c.* 1940.
Quickstep (2), invented in America 1900; reached peak of popularity in 1920's.
Tango (2), earliest contest in Nice, France, in 1907.
Barn dance (4), associated in America with festivities surrounding the completion of a new barn.
Two-step (2).
Boston (2), predecessor of the foxtrot.
Turkey Trot (2).

Ballroom dance craze, mostly couples dancing to small instrumental groups (*c.* 1920).
Growth of very energetic dancing, often to jazz or pseudo-jazz groups (from 1939).
Modern Discotheque style, ie: recorded music for dancing; originated in Parisian clubs (*c.* 1951).

Foxtrot (4), slow and quick varieties, introduced in 1912 in America, allegedly named after Harry Fox. The slow foxtrot evolved *c.* 1927 into the 'blues' dance.

Charleston (2), side kick from the knee. Named after a Mack and Johnson song about the town that saw the first ballet in America (see 1735, above).
Pasodoble (2), Spanish-style two-step.
Rumba (8 ie: 3 + 3 + 2), authentic Cuban dance.
Black Bottom (4), first mentioned in New York Times (19 Dec. 1926), a type of athletic and jerky foxtrot.
Conga (4, ie: 1-2-3-kick), single-file dance developed in 1935 from Rumba and from aboriginal African dances.
Jive (2,4) derived from Jitterbug.

Popularity of dances closely linked to the 'hit-parade' progress of popular music and the consequent invention of many new dance styles.

Mambo (8), an off-beat Rumba of Cuban origin.
Rock 'n' Roll (2), introduced in 1953 by Bill Haley and his Comets in America; heavy beat and simple melody for energetic and free dancing.
Cha cha cha (2,4) (1954), a variation of the Mambo, couples dancing with lightly linked hands.
Twist (2) (1961), body-torsion and knee-flexing lively dance, with partners rarely in contact.
Bossa nova (2), lively Latin American dance.
Go-go (2,4) (1965), repetitious dance of verve, often exhibitionist.
Reggae (4) (1969), introduced from Jamaica, strong accentuations off-beat.
Pogo (2), introduced by 'Punk Rockers' (1976). Dancers rise vertically from the floor in imitation of a pogo stick.

LANGUAGE & LITERATURE

WORLD'S PRINCIPAL LANGUAGES

The world's total of languages and dialects is now estimated to be about 5500. The most widely spoken, together with the countries in which they are used are as follows:

1. GUOYU (standardised Northern Chinese or Běifanghirà). Alphabetised into *Zhuyin Zimu* (39 letters) in 1918 and converted to the *Pinyin* Latin alphabetic system in 1958. Spoken in China (Mainland). Language family: Sino-Tibetan. 600 000 000.

2. ENGLISH. Evolved from an Anglo-Saxon, Norman-French and Latin amalgam *c.* 1350. Spoken in Australia, Bahamas, Canada, Sri Lanka (3rd), Cyprus (3rd), The Gambia, Ghana, Guyana, India (non-constitutional), Ireland, Jamaica, Kenya (official with Swahili), Malaysia, Malta (official with Maltese), New Zealand, Nigeria (official), Pakistan (now only 1 per cent), Rhodesia, Sierra Leone (official), Singapore (2nd at 24 per cent), South Africa (38 per cent of white population), Tanzania (official with swahili), Trinidad and Tobago, Uganda (official), UK, USA and also widely as the second language of educated Europeans and of citizens of the USSR. Language family: Indo-European. 375 000 000.

3. GREAT RUSSIAN. The foremost of the official languages used in the USSR

and spoken as the first language of 60 per cent of the population. Language family: Indo-European. 210 000 000.

=4. HINDUSTANI (a combination of Hindi and Urdu) foremost of the 845 languages of India of which 14 are 'constitutional'. Hindi (official) is spoken by more than 25 per cent, Urdu by nearly 4 per cent and Hindustani, as such, by 10 per cent. In Pakistan,

Hindustani is the third most prevalent language (7½ per cent). Language family: Indo-European. 200 000 000.

=4. SPANISH. Dates from the 10th century AD; spoken in Argentina, Bolivia, Canary Islands, Chile, Colombia, Costa Rica, Cuba, Dominican Republic, Guatemala, Honduras, Mexico, Nicaragua, Panama, Paraguay, Peru, Philippines, Puerto Rico, Salvador, Spain, Uruguay, Venezuela. Language family: Indo-European. 200 000 000.

6. GERMAN. Known in written form since the 8th century AD. Spoken in the Federal Republic of Germany (West) and the German Democratic Republic (East) Austria, Liechtenstein and Switzerland plus minorities in the USA, USSR, Hungary, Poland, Romania and in formerly colonised German territories in eastern and southern Africa and the Pacific. Language family: Indo-European 125 000 000.

7. BENGALI. Widely spoken in the Ganges delta area of India and Bangladesh. Language family: Indo - European. 120 000 000.

8. ARABIC. Dates from the early 6th century. Spoken in Algeria, Bahrain, Egypt, Iraq (80 per cent), Israel (16 per cent), Jordan, Kuwait, Lebanon, Libya, Maldive Is., Morocco (65 per cent), Oman, Qatar, Saudi

Arabia, Sudan (52 per cent), Syria, Tunisia, United Arab Emirates and both Yemens. Language family: Hamito - Semitic. 120 000 000.

9. PORTUGUESE. Distinct from Spanish by 14th century and, unlike it, was more influenced by French than by Arabic. Spoken in Angola, Brazil, Goa, Macao, Mozambique, Portugal, East Timor (Indonesia). Language family: Indo-European. 120 000 000.

10. JAPANESE. Earliest inscription (in Chinese characters) dates from the 5th century. Spoken in Japan, Formosa (Taiwan) Hawaii and some formerly colonised Pacific Islands. Unrelated to any other language. 110 000 000.

11. MALAY-INDONESIAN. Originated in Northern Sumatra, spoken in Indonesia (form called Bahasa is official), Malaysia, Sabah, Sarawak, Thailand (southernmost parts). Language family: Malayo-Polynesian. 95 000 000.

12. FRENCH. Developed in 9th century as a result of Frankish influence on Gaulish sub-stratum. Fixed by Academic Francaise from 17th century. Spoken in France, French Pacific Is., Belgium, Guadeloupe, Haiti, Louisiana, Luxembourg, Martinique, Monaco, Switzerland, the Italian region of Aosta, Canada, and widely in former French colonies in Africa. Language family: Indo-European. 90 000 000.

13. ITALIAN. Became very distinct from Latin by 10th century. Spoken in Eritrea, Italy, Libya, Switzerland and widely retained in USA among Italian population. Language family: Indo-European. 60 000 000.

=14. CANTONESE. A distinctive dialect of Chinese spoken in the Kwang-tung area. Language family: Sino-Tibetan. 50 000 000.

=14. TELUGU. Used in south India. Known in a written, grammatic form from the 11th century. Language family: Dravidian. 50 000 000.

=14. KOREAN. Not known to be related to any other tongue. 50 000 000.

=14. TAMIL. The second oldest written Indian language. Cave graffiti date from the 3rd century BC. Spoken in Sri Lanka, southern India, and among Tamils in Malaysia. Language family: Dravidian. 50 000 000.

=14. MARATHI. A language spoken in west and central India, including Goa and part of Hyderabad and Poona with written origins dating from about AD 500. Language family: Indo-European. 50 000 000.

=14. PUNJABI. One of the 14 constitutional languages of India spoken by the region of that name. Also spoken in parts of Pakistan. 50 000 000.

20. JAVANESE. Closely related to Malay. Serves as the language of 50 per cent of Indonesian population. Language family: Malayo-Polynesian. 45 000 000

=21. UKRAINIAN (Little Russian). Distinction from Great Russian discernible by 11th century, literary zenith late 18th and early 19th century. Banned as written language in Russia 1876–1905. Discouraged since 1931 in USSR. Spoken in Ukrainian SSR, parts of Russian SFSR and Romania. Language family: Indo - European. 40 000 000.

=21. WU. A dialect in China spoken, but not officially encouraged, in the Yang-tse delta area. Language family: Sino-Tibetan. 40 000 000.

=21. MIN (Fukien). A dialect in China which includes the now discouraged Amoy and Fuchow dialects and Hainanese. Language family: Sino-Tibetan. 40 000 000.

=21. TURKISH. Spoken in European and Asian Turkey—a member of the Oghuz division of the Turkic group of languages. 40 000 000.

25. VIETNAMESE. Used in the whole of eastern Indo-China. Classified as a Mon-Khmer by some and as a Thai language by other philologists. 35 000 000.

26. POLISH. A western Slavonic language with written records back to the 13th century, 300 years before its emergence as a modern literary language. Spoken in Poland, and western USSR and among émigré populations notably in the USA. Language family: Indo-European. 35 000 000.

ORIGINS OF THE ENGLISH LANGUAGE

The three Germanic dialects on which English is based are descended from the Indo-Germanic or Aryan family of languages, spoken since c. 3000 BC by the nomads of the Great Lowland Plain of Europe, which stretches from the Aral Sea in the Soviet Union to the Rhine in West Germany. Now only fragments of Old Lithuanian contain what is left of this ancestral tongue.

Of the three inherited Germanic dialects, the first was Jutish, brought into England in AD 449 from Jutland. This was followed 40 years later by Saxon, brought from Holstein, and Anglican, which came with the still later incursions from the area of Schleswig-Holstein.

These three dialects were superimposed on the 1000-year-old indigenous Celtic tongue, along with what Latin had survived in the towns from nearly 15 generations of Roman occupation (AD 43–410). The next major event in the history of the English language was the first of many Viking invasions, beginning in 793, from Denmark and Norway. Norse and Danish left permanent influences on the Anglo-Frisian Old English, though Norse never survived as a separate tongue in England beyond 1035, the year of the death of King Canute (Cnut), who had then reigned for 19 years over England, 16 years over Denmark and 7 years over Norway.

The Scandinavian influence now receded before Norman French, though Norse still struggled on in remote parts of Scotland until about 1630 and in the Shetland Islands until c. 1750. The Normans were, however, themselves really Vikings, who in five generations had become converts to the Latin culture and language of northern France.

For three centuries after the Norman conquest of 1066 by William I, descendant of Rollo the Viking, England lived under a trilingual system. The mother tongue of all the first 13 Kings and Queens, from William I (1066–1087) until as late as Richard II (1377–99), was Norman. English became the language of court proceedings only during the reign of Edward III, in October, 1362, and the language for teaching in the Universities of Oxford and Cambridge in c. 1380.

English did not really crystallise as an amalgam of Anglo-Saxon and Latin root forms until the 14th century, when William Langland (c. 1332–c. 1400), and Geoffrey Chaucer (?1340–1400) were the pioneers of a literary tradition, which culminated in William Shakespeare, who died in 1616, just four years before the sailing of the Mayflower.

ENGLISH LITERATURE

Nothing definite has survived of the stories or songs possessed by the ancient Britons who were invaded by Caesar on 26 Aug. 55 BC. Barely anything has survived from the 367-year-long Roman occupation until AD 410. English literature thus begins at least by being English.

The earliest known British born author was Pelagius (fl. 400–18) from whom survive some remains of theological disputations written in Rome.

The earliest English poem known to us is Widseth, about a wandering minstrel of the 6th century. In the Exeter Book 150 lines of this poem survive.

The oldest surviving record of a named English poet who composed on British soil is from the paraphrase by Bede (673–735) of a hymn attributed to Caedmon of Streaneshalch (Whitby, North Yorkshire), who was living in 670. This survives in the Cambridge manuscript of Bede (or Baeda) in a hand possibly of the 18th century.

The first great book in English prose is the Old English Chronicle supervised by King Alfred until 892. Alfred himself translated some of the writings of Baeda and of Gregory the Great's Pastoral Care into West Saxon.

The Lindisfarne Gospels, a beautiful vellum quarto Latin manuscript now in the British Museum, London, was written c. 700. In c. 950 Aldred added an interlinear gloss in Northumbrian dialect.

The leading authors of the Old English Period are:

Alfric	c. 955–c. 1020
King Alfred	849–99
Venerable Bede	c. 672–735
Caedmon	fl. 670
Cynewulf	? 9th century
Wulfstan	d. 1023

BIBLIOGRAPHY. Below are brief notes and a list of the major works of the 10 British writers who have the longest entries in the Oxford Dictionary of Quotations. They are listed in order of length of their entry.

Shakespeare, William (1564–1616)

The greatest contribution to the world's store of poetry and drama has been made by William Shakespeare (1564–1616). Born at Stratford-on-Avon, this eldest surviving child of an Alderman and trader produced in the space of the seventeen years between 1594 (Titus Andronicus) and 1611 (The Tempest) thirty-seven plays which total 814 780 words.

Shakespeare's golden outpourings of sheer genius have excited and amazed the critics of every age since. His contemporary Ben Jonson called him 'The applause! delight! the wonder of our stage!' Milton refers to him as 'Sweetest Shakespeare, Fancy's child'. To Thomas Carlyle, looking at his massive brow, he was 'The greatest of intellects'. Matthew Arnold refers to him as 'out-topping knowledge'.

Venus and Adonis	1593
The Rape of Lucrece	1594
Titus Andronicus	1594
*Henry VI Part 2	1594
*The Taming of the Shrew (see also 1623, First Folio)	1594
*Henry VI Part 3	1595
*Romeo and Juliet	1597
Richard II	1597
Richard III	1597
Henry IV Part 1	1598
Love's Labour's Lost (Revised version, original (? 1596) probably lost)	1598
Romeo and Juliet	1599
Henry IV Part 2	1600
A Midsummer Night's Dream	1600
The Merchant of Venice	1600
Much Ado About Nothing	1600
Henry V (First 'true' text published 1623 in First Folio)	1600
*Sir John Falstaff and the Merry Wives of Windsor (First 'true text published in 1623 in First Folio)	1602
*Hamlet	1603
Hamlet ('according to the true and perfect copy')	1604

King Lear 1608
Pericles, Prince of Tyre 1609
Troilus and Cressida 1609
Sonnets (1640 in 'Poems') 1609
*Bad quartos or unauthorised editions.

Posthumously Published
Othello 1622
First Folio—36 plays in all including
the first publication of *The Taming
of the Shrew* (Shakespeare's revised
version of the 1594 version) 1623

Henry VI Part 1	*Macbeth*
The Two Gentlemen	*Timon of Athens*
of Verona	*Antony and Cleopatra*
The Comedy of Errors	*Coriolanus*
King John	*Cymbeline*
As You Like It	*A Winter's Tale*
Julius Caesar	*The Tempest*
Twelfth Night	*Henry VIII*
Measure for Measure	
All's Well That Ends	
Well	

The Second Folio (1632), the Third Folio (1663 1st issue, 1664 2nd issue) and the Fourth Folio (1685) added nothing of authority to Heming and Condell's monumental First Folio.

Scientific study of Shakespeare began with Edward Capell (1713–81) and his researches published from 1768. The eminently honest and painstaking work of Alexander Dyce's edition of 1857 led to the publication in 1863–66 of what is regarded as the standard text, *The Cambridge Shakespeare*, edited by W C Clark and J Glover.

Tennyson, Alfred, First Baron (1809–92)
Poems (including *The Lotus Eaters* and
The Lady of Shallot (dated 1833) 1832
Poems (two volumes) (including
*Ulysses, Sir Galahad, Morte
d'Arthur, Locksley Hall*) 1842
In Memoriam A.H.H. (Arthur Henry
Hallam) 1850
*Ode on the Death of the Duke of
Wellington* 1852
Charge of the Light Brigade 1854
Maud and Other Poems 1859
Idylls of the King 1857–85
(completed edition 1889)
Enoch Arden (including *Old Style*) 1864
Holy Grail 1869
The Revenge: A Ballad of the Fleet 1878
Becket 1884
Locksley Hall 60 Years After 1886
Demeter and Other Poems (including
Crossing the Bar) 1889

Milton, John (1608–74)
*On the Death of Fair Infant Dying of
a Cough* 1625
L'Allegro and Il Penseroso 1632
Arcades 1633
Comus (2 Masques) 1634
Lycidas 1638
A Tractate of Education 1644
Doctrine and Discipline of Divorce 1644
Areopagitica (a Tract) 1644
Tenure of Kings and Magistrates
(a Pamphlet) 1649
Paradise Lost (written c. 1640–57) 1657
Paradise Regained (written 1665–66) 1671
Samson Agonistes 1671

Kipling, Joseph Rudyard (1865–1936)
Departmental Ditties 1886
Plain Tales from The Hills 1888
Soldiers Three 1888
Wee Willie Winkie 1888
The Light That Failed 1891
Barrack Room Ballads 1892
Many Inventions 1893

Jungle Books (Two volumes) 1894–95
The Seven Seas (including *Mandalay*) 1896
Captains Courageous 1897
Recessional 1897
Stalky & Co. 1899
Kim 1901
Just So Stories for Little Children 1902
Puck of Pook's Hill 1906
Rewards and Fairies 1910
A School History of England 1911

Wordsworth, William (1770–1850)
The Evening Walk (written 1787–92) 1793
Descriptive Sketches (written 1787–92) 1793
Guilt and Sorrow 1794
Lyrical Ballads (with Coleridge) 1798 & 1800
Prelude 1805
Poems in Two Volumes (including *Ode
to Duty* and *Ode on Intimations of
Immortality*) 1807
Excursion: a portion of the *Recluse* 1814
Poems, including the *Borderers* 1842

Shelley, Percy Bysshe (1792–1822)
Alastor 1816
Ode to The West Wind 1819
The Cenci 1819
Prometheus Unbound 1820
The Witch of Atlas 1820
To a Skylark 1820
The Cloud 1820
Epipsychidion 1821
Adonais 1821
Queen Mab 1821
Hellas 1822
Defence of Poetry (uncompleted)

Johnson, Dr Samuel (1709–84)
*A Voyage to Abyssinia by Father
Jerome Lobo* (Translation) 1735
London: a Poem, in Imitation of the
Third Satire of Juvenal (anon.) 1738
Parliamentary Reports disguised as
Debates in the Senate of Magna
Lilliputia (Senate of Lilliput)
July 1741–Mar. 1744
Life of Savage 1744
Plan of a Dictionary of the English
Language 1747
Irene (Theatrical tragedy produced
by Garrick at Drury Lane) 1748
The Vanity of Human Wishes 1749
The Rambler (essays in 208 bi-weekly
issues) Mar. 1750–Mar. 1752
A Dictionary of the English Language
(8 years' work, 1747–55) 1755
The Prince of Abyssinia, A Tale 1759
The Idler (essays in the *Universal
Chronicle* or the *Weekly Gazette*)
Apr. 1758–Apr. 1760
Rasselas 1759
Shakespeare, a new Edition 1765
A Journey to the Western Highlands 1775
The Lives of the Poets
vols. i–iv 1779, vols. v–x 1781
Dr Johnson's Diary, posthumously
published 1816

Browning, Robert (1812–89)
Paracelsus 1835
Sordello 1840
Christmas-Eve and Easter-Day 1850
Men and Women (including *One Word
More* and *Bishop Blougram's Apology*) 1855
Dramatis Personae (including *Rabi ben
Ezera* and *Caliban upon Setebos*) 1864
The Ring and The Book 1868–69
A Grammarian's Funeral
Soliloquy of the Spanish Cloister
The Pied Piper of Hamelin
Asolando posthumously 1890
New Poems (with Elizabeth Barrett
Browning) posthumously 1914

Byron, George Gordon, sixth baron (1788–1824) (adjective Byronic)
Fugitive Pieces (privately printed)
originally called *Juvenilia* 1806
Hours of Idleness (reprint of the above
with amendments) 1807
English Bards and Scotch Reviewers 1809
Childe Harold (began at Janina, 1809),
Cantos i and ii 1812
The Giaour 1813
The Corsair 1814
Lora 1814
The Siege of Corinth 1816
The Prisoner of Chillon 1816
Childe Harold (written in Switzerland),
Canto iii 1816
Childe Harold (written in Venice),
Canto iv 1817
Manfred 1817
Don Juan (first five cantos) 1818–20
Autobiography (burnt 1824)
Cain 1821
Don Juan (later cantos) 1821–22
Contribution to *The Liberal*
newspaper, 'Vision of Judgement' 1822
The Island 1823
Heaven and Earth 1824

Dickens, Charles John Huffam (1812–70) (adjective Dickensian)
*Sketches of Young Gentlemen, Sketches
of Young Couples, The Mudfog
Papers* unpublished
A Dinner at Poplar Walk (re-entitled
Mr. Minns and his Cousin) Dec. 1833
Sketches by Boz. Illustrative of Every
Day Life and Every Day People
published in *Monthly Magazine*
(1833–35) and *Evening Chronicle*
1835
*The Posthumous Papers of the
Pickwick Club* from Apr. 1836
Oliver Twist (in Bentley's *Miscellany*)
1837–39
Nicholas Nickleby (in monthly
numbers) 1838–39
Master Humphrey's Clock (*Barnaby
Rudge* and *The Old Curiosity
Shop*) 1840–41
Pic-Nic Papers (Editor) 1841
The Old Curiosity Shop (as a book) 1841
Barnaby Rudge (as a book) 1841
American Notes 1842
Martin Chuzzlewit (parts) 1843–44
A Christmas Carol 1843
The Chimes (written in Italy) 1844
The Cricket on the Hearth 1845
Pictures from Italy 1846
Daily News (later the *News
Chronicle*) Editor Jan.–Feb. 1846
The Battle of Life 1846
The Haunted Man 1847
Dombey and Son (parts) (written
in Switzerland) 1847–48
Household Word (weekly periodical)
Editor (included *Holly-Tree*) 1848–59
David Copperfield 1849–50
Bleak House (in parts) 1852–53
A Child's History of England
(in three volumes) 1852-3-4
Hard Times. For These Times
(book form) 1854
Little Dorrit 1857-8
All the Year Round (Periodical)
Editor 1859–70
Great Expectations 1860–61
The Uncommercial Traveller
(collected parts of *A Tale of
Two Cities*) 1861
Our Mutual Friend 1864–65
The Mystery of Edwin Drood
(unfinished) 1870

CLASSIC BRITISH WRITERS (14th TO 20th CENTURIES)
The writers below are listed in chronological order of year of birth, together with their best known work or works.

14th century

LANGLAND, William (c. 1332–c. 1400). *Vision of Piers Plowman.*

CHAUCER, Geoffrey (?1340–1400). *Canterbury Tales.*

15th century

MALORY, Sir Thomas (d. 1471?). *Morte D'Arthur.*

MORE, Sir Thomas (1478–1535). *Utopia.*

16th century

SPENSER, Edmund (?1552–99). *The Faerie Queene.*

LYLY, John (c. 1553–1606). *Euphues.*

SIDNEY, Sir Philip (1554–86). *The Countesse of Pembrokes Arcadia; Astrophel and Stella; The Defence of Poesie.*

BACON, Francis (Baron Verulam, Viscount St Albans) (1561–1626). *Essayes.*

MARLOWE, Christopher (1564–1593). *Tamburlaine The Great; Dr Faustus.*

DONNE, John (?1571–1631). *Poems; Songs and sonnets; Satyres; Elegies.*

JONSON, Benjamin (1572–1637). *Every Man in his humour* (produced 1598, published 1601); *Every Man out of his humour* (1600); *Volpone: or the foxe* (1607); *The Alchemist* (1610, published 1612); *Bartholomew Fayre* (1614, published 1631).

HOBBES, Thomas (1588–1679). *Leviathan.*

HERRICK, Robert (1591–1674). *Hesperides.*

17th century

BUTLER, Samuel (1612–80). *Hudibras.*

BUNYAN, John (1628–88). *The Pilgrim's Progress.*

DRYDEN, John (1631–1700). *All For Love.*

LOCKE, John (1632–1704). *Essay Concerning Human Understanding.*

PEPYS, Samuel (1633–1703). *Memoirs* (Diary).

NEWTON, Sir Isaac (1642–1727). *Philosophiae Naturalis Principia Mathematica; Opticks.*

DEFOE, Daniel (1660–1731). *The Life and Adventures of Robinson Crusoe.*

SWIFT, Jonathan (1667–1745). *Travels* (by Lemuel Gulliver).

OTWAY, Thomas (1669–85). *Venice Preserved.*

CONGREVE, William (1670–1729). *The Way of the World.*

ADDISON, Joseph (1672–1719). *The Spectator.*

POPE, Alexander (1688–1744). *An Essay on Criticism; The Rape of the Lock; The Dunciad; An Essay on Man.*

RICHARDSON, Samuel (1689–1761). *Clarissa.*

18th century

FIELDING, Henry (1707–54). *Tom Thumb; The History of Tom Jones.*

STERNE, Laurence (1713–68). *Life and Opinions of Tristram Shandy.*

GRAY, Thomas (1716–71). *An Elegy Wrote in a Country Churchyard.*

SMOLLETT, Tobias George (1721–71). *The Adventures of Peregrine Pickle.*

GOLDSMITH, Oliver (1728–74). *The Vicar of Wakefield; She Stoops to Conquer.*

BURKE, Edmund (1729–97). *Reflections on the Revolution; The Annual Register.*

COWPER, William (1731–1800). *Poems.*

GIBBON, Edward (1737–94). *A History of the Decline and Fall of the Roman Empire.*

PAINE, Thomas (1737–1809). *Rights of Man.*

BOSWELL, James (1740–95). *Life of Johnson.*

BURNEY, Frances 'Fanny' (Madame D'Arblay). (1752–1840). *Evelina.*

SHERIDAN, Richard Brinsley (1751–1816). *The Rivals; The School For Scandal.*

BLAKE, William (1757–1827). *Songs of Innocence; Songs of Experience.*

BURNS, Robert (1759–96). *Poems chiefly in the Scottish dialect* (1786); *Tam O'Shanter* (1795); *The Cotters Saturday Night* (1795); *The Jolly Beggars* (1799).

COBBETT, William (1762–1835). *Rural Rides.*

SMITH, Rev Sydney (1771–1845). *The Letters of Peter Plymley; Edinburgh Review.*

SCOTT, Sir Walter (1771–1832). *Waverley; Rob Roy; Ivanhoe; Kenilworth; Quentin Durward; Redgauntlet; Lady of the Lake.*

COLERIDGE, Samuel Taylor (1772–1834). *Lyrical Ballads (Ancient Mariner).*

SOUTHEY, Robert (1774–1843). *Quarterly Review* (contributions); *Life of Nelson.*

AUSTEN, Jane (1775–1817). *Sense and Sensibility* (1811); *Pride and Prejudice* (1813); *Mansfield Park* (1814); *Emma* (1816); *Northanger Abbey and Persuasion* (1818).

LAMB, Charles (1775–1834). *Tales from Shakespeare* [largely by his sister, Mary Lamb (1764–1847)]; *Essays of Elia.*

HAZLITT, William (1778–1830). *My First Acquaintance with Poets; Table Talk; The Plain Speaker.*

HUNT, James Henry Leigh (1784–1859). *The Story of Rimini; Autobiography.*

DE QUINCEY, Thomas (1785–1859). *Confessions of an English Opium Eater.*

PEACOCK, Thomas Love (1785–1866). *Headlong Hall; Nightmare Abbey.*

KEATS, John (1795–1821). *Endymion; Ode to a Nightingale: Ode on a Grecian Urn; Ode to Psyche; Ode to Autumn; Ode on Melancholy; La Belle Dame sans Merci; Isabella.*

CARLYLE, Thomas (1795–1881). *The French Revolution.*

HOOD, Thomas (1799–1845). *The Song of the Shirt; The Bridge of Sighs; To The Great Unknown.*

MACAULAY, Thomas Babington (Lord) (1800–59). *Lays of Ancient Rome.*

19th century

DISRAELI, Benjamin (Earl of Beaconsfield) (1804–81). *Coningsby; Sybil; Tancred.*

BROWNING, Elizabeth Barrett (1806–61). *Poems; Aurora Leigh.*

DARWIN, Charles Robert (1809–82). *On the Origin of Species; The Descent of Man.*

FITZGERALD, Edward (1809–83). *Rubáiyát of Omar Khayyám.*

GASKELL, Mrs (Elizabeth Cleghorn Stevenson) (1810–65). *Mary Barton; Cranford.*

THACKERAY, William Makepeace (1811–63). *Vanity Fair; The Newcomers.*

LEAR, Edward (1812–88). *A Book of Nonsense; Nonsense Songs.*

TROLLOPE, Anthony (1815–82). *The Five Barsetshire Novels.*

BRONTË (later Nicholls), Charlotte (1816–55). *Jane Eyre.*

BRONTË, Emily Jane (1818–48). *Wuthering Heights.*

RUSKIN, John (1819–1900). *Praeterita.*

'ELIOT, George' (Mary Ann [or Marian] Evans, later Mrs J W Cross) (1819–80). *Scenes of Clerical Life* (1858); *Adam Bede* (1859); *The Mill on the Floss* (1860); *Silas Marner* (1861); *Middlemarch* (1871–72).

KINGSLEY, Charles (1819–75). *Westward Ho!; The Water Babies.*

ARNOLD, Matthew (1822–88). *The Strayed Reveller* ('Sohrab and Rustum' and 'Scholar Gypsy').

COLLINS, William Wilkie (1824–89). *The Woman in White; Moonstone.*

MEREDITH, George (1828–1909). *Modern Love.*

ROSSETTI, Dante Gabriel (1828–82). *Poems; Ballads and Sonnets.*

'CARROLL, Lewis' (Charles Lutwidge Dodgson) (1832–98). *Alice's Adventures in Wonderland; Through The Looking Glass.*

GILBERT, Sir William Schwenck (1836–1911). *The Mikado; The Gondoliers; HMS Pinafore.*

SWINBURNE, Algernon Charles (1837–1909). *Rosamund.*

HARDY, Thomas (1840–1928). *Under The Greenwood Tree; Tess of the D'Urbervilles;*

Far From the Madding Crowd; The Return of the Native; The Mayor of Casterbridge; Jude the Obscure.

JAMES, Henry (1843–1916). *Daisy Miller* (1879); *The Portrait of a Lady* (1881); *Washington Square* (1881); *The Turn of the Screw* (1898); *The Golden Bowl* (1904).

BRIDGES, Robert Seymour (1844–1930). *The Testament of Beauty.*

HOPKINS, Gerard Manley (1844–89). *The Notebooks and Papers of Gerard Manley Hopkins.*

STEVENSON, Robert Louis (1850–94). *Travels with a Donkey in the Cévennes* (1879); *New Arabian Nights* (1882); *Treasure Island* (1883); *Strange Case of Dr Jekyll and Mr Hyde* (1886); *Kidnapped* (1886); *The Black Arrow* (1888); *The Master of Ballantrae* (1889); *Weir of Hermiston* (unfinished) (1896).

WILDE, Oscar Fingal O'Flahertie Wills (1854–1900). *The Picture of Dorion Gray* (1891); *Lady Windermere's Fan* (1893); *The Importance of Being Ernest* (1899).

SHAW, George Bernard (1856–1950) (adjective Shavian). *Plays Pleasant and Unpleasant* (1893) (including *Mrs Warren's Profession, Arms and the Man* and *Candida*); *Three Plays for Puritans* (1901) (*The Devil's Disciple, Caesar and Cleopatra* and *Captain Brassbound's Conversion*); *Man and Superman* (1903); *John Bull's Other Island* and *Major Barbara* (1907); *Androcles and the Lion, Overruled* and *Pygmalion* (1916); *Saint Joan* (1924); *Essays in Fabian Socialism* (1932).

CONRAD, Joseph (né Józef Teodor Konrad Nalecz Korzeniowski) (1857–1924). *Almayer's Folly; An Outcast of the Islands; The Nigger of the 'Narcissus'; Lord Jim; Youth; Typhoon; Nostromo; The Secret Agent.*

DOYLE, Sir Arthur Conan (1859–1930). *The White Company; The Adventures of Sherlock Holmes; The Hound of the Baskervilles.*

THOMPSON, Francis (1859–1907). *The Hound of Heaven.*

HOUSMAN, Alfred Edward (1859–1936). *A Shropshire Lad.*

GRAHAM, Kenneth (1859–1932). *Wind in the Willows.*

BARRIE, Sir James Matthew (1860–1937). *Quality Street; The Admirable Crichton; Peter Pan.*

QUILLER-COUCH, Sir Arthur ('Q') (1865–1944). *On the Art of Writing; Studies in Literature.*

YEATS, William Butler (1865–1939). *Collected Poems; The Tower; Last Poems; The Hour Glass.*

WELLS, Herbert George (1866–1946). *The Invisible Man; The History of Mr Polly; Kipps; The Shape of Things to Come.*

MURRAY, Gilbert Amié (1866–1957). *Hippolytus; The Trojan Women.*

BENNETT, Enoch Arnold (1867–1931). *Anna of the Five Towns; The Old Wives' Tale; Clayhanger; The Card; Riceyman Steps.*

GALSWORTHY, John (1867–1933). *The Forsyte Saga; Modern Comedy; The White Monkey.*

BELLOC, Joseph Hilaire Pierre (1870–1953). *The Path to Rome; The Bad Child's Book of Beasts; Hills and the Sea.*

SYNGE, John Millington (1871–1909). *The Playboy of the Western World.*

BEERBOHM, Sir Max (1872–1956). *Zuleika Dobson.*

DE LA MARE, Walter (1873–1956). *Poems; Desert Islands and Robinson Crusoe.*

CHESTERTON, Gilbert Keith (1874–1936). *The Innocence of Father Brown; The Ballad of The White Horse.*

CHURCHILL, Sir Winston Spencer (1874–1965). *Marlborough; The Second World War; A History of The English-Speaking Peoples.*

BUCHAN, John (Baron Tweedsmuir) (1875–1940). *Montrose; The Thirty-Nine Steps; Greenmantle; Prester John.*

MASEFIELD, John (1878–1967). *Barrack-Room Ballads; Ballads and Poems.*

MAUGHAM, William Somerset (1874–1965). *Of Human Bondage; The Moon and Sixpence; The Razor's Edge.*

TREVELYAN, George Macaulay (1876–1962). *History of England; English Social History.*

FORSTER, Edward Morgan (1879–1970). *Where Angels Fear to Tread; A Room with a View; Howards End; A Passage to India.*

JOYCE, James (1882–1941). *Ulysses; Finnegans Wake.*

WOOLF (*née* Stephen), Virginia (1882–1941). *The Voyage Out; Night and Day; Jacob's Room; The Years.*

KEYNES, John Maynard (Baron) (1883–1946). *The Economic Consequences of the Peace; The General Theory of Employment.*

MACKENZIE, Sir Compton (1883–1972). *Whisky Galore.*

FLECKER, James Elroy (1884–1915). *Thirty-Six Poems; Hassan.*

LAWRENCE, David Herbert (1885–1930). *Sons and Lovers; Love Poems and Others.*

SASSOON, Siegfried (1886–1967). *Memoirs of a Fox-Hunting Man.*

SITWELL, Dame Edith, DBE (1887–1964). *Collected Poems; Aspects of Modern Poetry.*

BROOKE, Rupert Chawner (1887–1915). *1914 and Other Poems; Letters from America.*

ELIOT, Thomas Stearns, OM (1888–1965). *Murder in the Cathedral; The Wasteland; Ash Wednesday; Poems.*

LAWRENCE, Thomas Edward (later Shaw) (1888–1935). *Seven Pillars of Wisdom.*

TOYNBEE, Arnold Joseph (1889–1975). *A Study of History.*

MANSFIELD, Katherine (1890–1923). *The Garden Party; Letters.*

OWEN, Wilfred (1893–1918). *Poems.*

PRIESTLY, John Boynton (b. 1894). *The Good Companions; The Linden Tree.*

HUXLEY, Aldous Leonard (1894–1963). *Brave New World; Stories, Essays and Poems.*

GRAVES, Robert Ranke (b. 1895). *Poems and Satires.*

COWARD, Sir Noel (1899–1973). *Hay Fever; Private Lives.*

20th Century

ORWELL, George (1903–50). *Animal Farm; 1984.*

WAUGH, Evelyn (1903–66). *Scoop; Vile Bodies; Brideshead Revisited; The Loved One; The Ordeal of Gilbert Pinfold.*

DAY-LEWIS, Cecil (1904–72). *Collected Poems; Overture to Death and other poems.*

GREENE, Graham (b. 1904). *Brighton Rock; Our Man in Havana; The Power and the Glory.*

BECKETT, Samuel (b. 1906). *Waiting for Godot.*

FRY, Christopher (b. 1907). *The Lady's Not for Burning.*

AUDEN, Wystan Hugh (1907–73). *Poems; Look Stranger; The Dance of Death.*

DURRELL, Lawrence (b. 1912). *The Alexandria Quartet.*

THOMAS, Dylan (1914–54). *Eighteen Poems; Twenty-Five Poems; Under Milk Wood.*

OSBORNE, John (b. 1929). *Look Back in Anger; The Entertainer; Luther.*

PINTER, Harold (b. 1930). *The Caretaker.*

WESKER, Arnold (b. 1932). *Roots; Chips with Everything.*

THE GREEK ALPHABET

The Greek alphabet consists of 24 letters—seven vowels and seventeen consonants. The seven vowels are alpha (short a), epsilon (short e), eta (long e), iota (short i), omicron (long o), upsilon (short u, usually transcribed y), and omega (short o).

Name	Capital	Lower case	English equivalent	Name	capital	Lower case	English equivalent
Alpha	*A*	*α*	a	Nu	*N*	*ν*	n
Beta	*B*	*β*	b	Xi	*Ξ*	*ξ*	x
Gamma	*Γ*	*γ*	g	Omicron	*O*	*o*	ō
Delta	*Δ*	*δ*	d	Pi	*Π*	*π*	p
Epsilon	*E*	*ε*	ĕ	Rho	*P*	*ρ*	r
Zeta	*Z*	*ζ*	z	Sigma	*Σ*	*σς*	s
Eta	*H*	*η*	ē	Tau	*T*	*τ*	t
Theta	*Θ*	*θ*	th	Upsilon	*Y*	*υ*	u or y
Iota	*I*	*ι*	i	Phi	*Φ*	*φ*	ph
Kappa	*K*	*κ*	k	Chi	*X*	*χ*	ch
Lambda	*Λ*	*λ*	l	Psi	*Ψ*	*ψ*	ps
Mu	*M*	*μ*	m	Omega	*Ω*	*ω*	o

Greek has no direct equivalent to our c, f, h, j, q, u, v, or w.

THE RUSSIAN ALPHABET

The Russian alphabet is written in Cyrillic script, so called after St Cyril, the 9th century monk who is reputed to have devised it. It contains 31 characters, including 5 hard and 5 soft vowels. Five other Cyrillic letters appear only in Bulgarian (one) and Serbian (four).

Capital	Lower case	Name	English equivalent	Capital	Lower case	Name	English equivalent
А	а	ah	ā	Т	т	teh	t
Б	б	beh	b	У	у	oo	oo
В	в	veh	v	Ф	ф	eff	f
Г	г	gheh	g	Х	х	hah	h
Д	д	deh	d	Ц	ц	tseh	ts
Е	е	yeh	ye	Ч	ч	cheh	ch
Ж	ж	zheh	j	Ш	ш	shah	sh
З	з	zeh	z	Щ	щ	shchah	shch
И	и	ee	ee	Ъ	ъ	(hard sign)	
К	к	kah	k	Ы	ы	yerih	I
Л	л	ell	l	Ь	ь	(soft sign)	—
М	м	em	m	Э	э	eh	e
Н	н	en	n	Ю	ю	you	yu
О	о	aw	aw	Я	я	ya	yā
П	п	peh	p				
Р	р	err	r	Ё	ё	yaw	yo
С	с	ess	s	Й	й	short	elided 'y'

SPORT

TABLE OF OLYMPIC MEDAL WINNERS

(SUMMER AND WINTER) BY NATIONS 1896-1976

Note: These totals include all first, second and third places, including those events no longer on the current (1980) schedule. The 1906 Games which were *officially* staged by the International Olympic Committee have also been included.

		SUMMER					WINTER					Combined
		Gold	Silver	Bronze	Total		Gold	Silver	Bronze	Total		Total
1.	USA	628	473½	410½	1512	(1)	30	38	28	96	(3)	1608
2.	USSR	260	223	209	692	(2)	51	32	35	118	(2)	810
3.	Germany[1]	135½	181	178	494½	(4)	22	19	17	58	(7)	552½
4.	Great Britain	160½	198½	168	527	(3)	5	4	10	19	(14)	546
5.	France	140	153	156	449	(5)	12	9	12	33	(=10)	482
6.	Sweden	127½	122	152	401½	(6)	25	23	26	74	(6)	475½
7.	Italy	124	115	106	345	(7)	10	7	7	24	(13)	369
8.	Finland	92	72	98	262	(9)	24	34	23	81	(4)	343
9.	Hungary	107	99	116	322	(8)	0	1	4	5	(16)	327
10.	Norway	40	30	31	101	(20)	50	52	43	145	(1)	246
11.	GDR[2]	69	57	55	181	(11)	12	10	16	38	(9)	219
=12.	Japan	73	64	63	200	(10)	1	2	1	4	(=17)	204
=12.	Switzerland	40	63	53	156	(13)	15	17	16	48	(8)	204
14.	Australia	62	51	65	178	(12)	—	—	—	—		178
15.	Netherlands	38	42	53	133	(16)	9	13	9	31	(12)	164
16.	Austria	18	27	34	79	(23)	22	31	27	80	(5)	159
=17.	Poland	38	39	74	151	(14)	1	1	2	4	(=17)	155
=17.	Canada	26	43	53	122	(19)	12	8	13	33	(=10)	155
19.	Denmark	28½	58	51	137½	(15)	—	—	—	—		137½
20.	Czechoslovakia	40	43	39½	122½	(18)	2	5	6	13	(15)	135½
21.	Belgium	35	48	43	126	(17)	1	1	2	4	(=17)	130
22.	Romania	22	31	46	99	(21)	0	0	1	1	(=21)	99
23.	Greece	22	38	35	95	(22)	—	—	—	—		95
24.	Bulgaria	19	33	22	74	(24)	—	—	—	—		74
25.	South Africa[3]	16	16	22	54	(25)	—	—	—	—		54
=26.	Yugoslavia	14	18	12	44	(=26)	—	—	—	—		44
=26.	Argentina	13	18	13	44	(=26)	—	—	—	—		44
28.	Turkey	23	12	7	42	(28)	—	—	—	—		42
29.	Cuba	15	14	10	39	(29)	—	—	—	—		39
30.	New Zealand	14	3	1	30	(30)	—	—	—	—		30
31.	Iran	4	10	15	29	(31)	—	—	—	—		29
32.	Mexico	7	8	12	27	(32)	—	—	—	—		27
33.	Estonia[4]	6	6	9	21	(33)	—	—	—	—		21
34.	Kenya	5	7	7	19	(34)	—	—	—	—		19
=35.	Brazil	3	2	13	18	(=35)	—	—	—	—		18
=35.	South Korea	1	6	11	18	(=35)	—	—	—	—		18
37.	Egypt	6	5	6	17	(37)	—	—	—	—		17
38.	Jamaica	4	7	3	14	(38)	—	—	—	—		14
=39.	India	7	3	3	13	(=39)	—	—	—	—		13
=39.	Ireland	4	3	6	13	(=39)	—	—	—	—		13

		SUMMER					WINTER				Combined
		Gold	Silver	Bronze	Total	Gold	Silver	Bronze	Total		Total
41.	Spain	1	6	3	10 (41)	1	0	0	1 (=21)		11
=42.	Uruguay	2	1	6	9 (=42)	—	—	—	—		9
=42.	Portugal	0	4	5	9 (=42)	—	—	—	—		9
44.	North Korea	2	2	3	7 (=44)	0	1	0	1 (=21)		8
=45.	Pakistan	2	3	2	7 (=44)	—	—	—	—		7
=45.	Trinidad & Tobago	1	2	4	7 (=44)	—	—	—	—		7
=45.	Chile	0	5	2	7 (=44)	—	—	—	—		7
=48.	Ethiopia	3	1	2	6 (=48)	—	—	—	—		6
=48.	Mongolia	0	3	3	6 (=48)	—	—	—	—		6
=48.	Philippines	0	1	5	6 (=48)	—	—	—	—		6
=51.	Luxembourg	3	2	0	5 (=51)	—	—	—	—		5
=51.	Tunisia	1	2	2	5 (=51)	—	—	—	—		5
=53.	Uganda	1	2	1	4 (=53)	—	—	—	—		4
=53.	Venezuela	1	1	2	4 (=53)	—	—	—	—		4
=55.	Latvia[4]	0	2	1	3 (=55)	—	—	—	—		3
=55.	Ghana	0	1	2	3 (=55)	—	—	—	—		3
=55.	Colombia	0	1	2	3 (=55)	—	—	—	—		3
=58.	Bahamas	1	0	1	2 (=58)	—	—	—	—		2
=58.	Haiti	0	1	1	2 (=58)	—	—	—	—		2
=58.	Lebanon	0	1	1	2 (=58)	—	—	—	—		2
=58.	Taiwan	0	1	1	2 (=58)	—	—	—	—		2
=58.	Panama	0	0	2	2 (=58)	—	—	—	—		2
=58.	Puerto Rico	0	0	2	2 (=58)	—	—	—	—		2
=58.	Nigeria	0	0	2	2 (=58)	—	—	—	—		2
=58.	Liechtenstein	—	—	—	—	0	0	2	2 (20)		2
=66.	Peru	1	0	0	1 (=65)	—	—	—	—		1
=66.	Ceylon (Sri Lanka)	0	1	0	1 (=65)	—	—	—	—		1
=66.	Iceland	0	1	0	1 (=65)	—	—	—	—		1
=66.	Morocco	0	1	0	1 (=65)	—	—	—	—		1
=66.	Singapore	0	1	0	1 (=65)	—	—	—	—		1
=66.	Cameroun	0	1	0	1 (=65)	—	—	—	—		1
=66.	Libya	0	1	0	1 (=65)	—	—	—	—		1
=66.	Irak	0	0	1	1 (=65)	—	—	—	—		1
=66.	Monaco	0	0	1	1 (=65)	—	—	—	—		1
=66.	Niger	0	0	1	1 (=65)	—	—	—	—		1
=66.	Bermuda	0	0	1	1 (=65)	—	—	—	—		1
=66.	Thailand	0	0	1	1 (=65)	—	—	—	—		1

[1] Germany 1896–1964; West Germany from 1968.   [2] GDR (East Germany): from 1968.   [3] South Africa: up to 1960.   [4] Estonia and Latvia: up to 1936.

Olympic sports (current schedule)

21 Summer events

1. Archery
2. Athletics (Track and Field)
3. Basketball
4. Boxing
5. Canoeing
6. Cycling
7. Equestrian Sports
8. Fencing
   Field Hockey, see Hockey (Field)
9. Football (Association)
10. Gymnastics
11. Handball
12. Hockey (Field)
13. Judo
14. Modern Pentathlon
15. Rowing
    Soccer, see Football (Association)
16. Shooting
17. Swimming, including Diving and Water Polo
    Track and Field Athletics, see Athletics
18. Volleyball
    Water Polo, see Swimming
19. Weightlifting
20. Wrestling
21. Yachting

7 Winter events

1. Nordic Skiing (including Ski-Jumping and Biathlon)
2. Alpine Skiing
3. Figure Skating
4. Speed Skating
5. Bobsleigh
6. Tobogganing (Lugeing)
7. Ice Hockey

OLYMPIC GAMES

The earliest celebration of the ancient Olympic Games of which there is a certain record is that of July 776 BC, though their origin probably dates from c. 1370 BC. A cessation in hostilities for some Games are recorded in 884 BC. The ancient Games were terminated by an order issued in Milan in AD 393 by Theodosius I, 'the Great' (c. 346–395), Emperor of Rome. At the instigation of Pierre de Fredi, Baron de Coubertin (1863–1937), the Olympic Games of the modern era were inaugurated in Athens on 6 Apr. 1896.

Celebrations have been allocated as follows:

I	Athens	6–15 Apr. 1896
II	Paris	20 May–28 Oct. 1900
III	St. Louis	1 July–23 Nov. 1904
†	Athens	22 Apr.–2 May 1906
IV	London	27 Apr.–31 Oct. 1908
V	Stockholm	5 May–22 Jul. 1912
VI	*Berlin	1916
VII	Antwerp	20 Apr.–12 Sept. 1920
VIII	Paris	4 May–27 Jul. 1924
IX	Amsterdam	17 May–12 Aug. 1928
X	Los Angeles	30 July–14 Aug. 1932
XI	Berlin	1–16 Aug. 1936
XII	*Tōkyō, then Helsinki	1940
XIII	*London	1944
XIV	London	29 July–14 Aug. 1948
XV	Helsinki	19 July–3 Aug. 1952
XVI	Melbourne	22 Nov.–8 Dec. 1956
XVII	Rome	25 Aug.–11 Sept. 1960
XVIII	Tōkyō	10–24 Oct. 1964
XIX	Mexico City	12–27 Oct. 1968
XX	Munich	26 Aug.–10 Sept. 1972
XXI	Montreal	17 July–1 Aug. 1976
XXII	Moscow	19 July–3 Aug. 1980
XXIII	Not yet allocated‡	1984

* Cancelled due to World Wars   † Intercalated Celebration not numbered but officially organised by the IOC (International Olympic Committee)
‡ Prime Candidate – Los Angeles

The Winter Olympics were inaugurated in 1924 and have been allocated as follows:

I	Chamonix, France	25 Jan.–4 Feb. 1924	VII	Cortina d'Ampezzo, Italy	26 Jan.–5 Feb. 1956
II	St Moritz, Switzerland	11–19 Feb. 1928	VIII	Squaw Valley, California	18–28 Feb. 1960
III	Lake Placid, USA	4–15 Feb. 1932	IX	Innsbruck, Austria	29 Jan.–9 Feb. 1964
IV	Garmisch-Partenkirchen, Germany	6-16 Feb. 1936	X	Grenoble, France	6–18 Feb. 1968
			XI	Sapporo, Japan	3–13 Feb. 1972
V	St Moritz, Switzerland	30 Jan.–8 Feb. 1948	XII	Innsbruck, Austria	4–15 Feb. 1976
VI	Oslo, Norway	14–25 Feb. 1952	XIII	Lake Placid, USA	14–23 Feb. 1980

ORIGINS AND ANTIQUITY OF SPORTS

Date	Sport	Location and Notes
BC		
c. 3000	Coursing	Egypt. Saluki dogs. Greyhounds used in England AD 1067. Waterloo Cup 1836.
c. 2350	Wrestling	Tomb of Ptahhotap, Egypt; ancient Olympic games c. 708 BC, Greco-Roman style, France c. AD 1860. Internationalised 1912.
c. 2050	Hockey	Beni Hasan tomb, Egypt. Lincolnshire AD 1277. Modern forms c. 1875. Some claims to be of Persian origin in 2nd millennium BC.
c. 1600	Falconry	China-Shang dynasty. Earliest manuscript evidence points to Persian origin.
c. 1520	Boxing	Thera fresco, Greece. First ring rules 1743 England. Queensberry Rules 1867.
c. 1360	Fencing	Egyptians used masks and blunted swords. Established as a sport in Germany c. AD 1450. Hand guard invented in Spain c. 1510. Foil 17th century, épée mid-19th century, and sabre in Italy, late 19th century.
c. 1300	Athletics	Ancient Olympic Games. Modern revival c. AD 1810, Sandhurst, England.
c. 800	Ice Skating	Bone skates superseded by metal blades c. AD 1600.
c. 776	Gymnastics	Ancient Olympic Games. Modern Sport developed c. AD 1780.
c. 648	Horse Racing	Thirty-third ancient Olympic Games. Roman diversion c. AD 210 Netherby, Yorkshire. Chester course 1540.
c. 600	Equestrianism	Riding of horses dates from c. 1400 BC Anatolia. Show jumping Paris AD 1886.
c. 525	Polo	As Pulu, Persia. Possibly of Tibetan origin.
c. 10	Fly Fishing	Earliest reference by the Roman Martial.
ante 1	Jiu Jitsu	Pre-Christian Chinese origin, developed as a martial art by Japan.
AD		
c. 300	Archery	Known as a neolithic skill (as opposed to a sport). Natal, South Africa ante 46 000 BC. Practised by the Genoese. Internationalised 1931.
c. 1050	Tennis (Royal)	Earliest surviving court, Paris, France, 1496. First 'world' champion c. 1740.
1278	Fox hunting	Earliest reference in England. Popularised at end 18th century. Previously deer, boar or hare hunted.
ante 1300	Bowls	On grass in Britain, descended from the Roman game of boccie.
1429	Billiards	First treatise by Marot (France) c. 1550. Rubber cushions 1835, slate beds 1836.
c. 1450	Golf	Earliest reference: parliamentary prohibition in March 1457, Scotland. Rubber core balls 1902, steel shafts 1929.
1474	Shooting	Target shooting recorded in Geneva, Switzerland.
ante 1492	Lacrosse	Originally American Indian baggataway. First non-Indian club, Montreal, 1856.
c. 1530	Football (Association)	26-a-side, Florence, Italy. Rules codified, Cambridge University, 1846. Eleven-a-side standardised 1870. Chinese ball-kicking game Tsu-chin known c. 350 BC.
c. 1550	Cricket	Earliest recorded match, Guildford, Surrey, England. Earliest depictment c. 1250. Eleven-a-side Sussex 1697. Earliest recorded women's match, Surrey, 1745.
c. 1560	Curling	Netherlands. Scotland 1716.
1600	Ice Yachting	Earliest patent in Low Countries. Sand yacht reported Belgian beach 1595.
1603	Swimming	Inter-school contests in Japan by Imperial edict. Sea-bathing at Scarborough by 1660. Earliest bath, Liverpool in 1828.
c. 1660	Ice Hockey	Netherlands. Kingston, Ontario, Canada 1855. Rules devised in Montreal 1879.
1661	Yachting	First contest Thames (1 Sept.). Earliest club in Cork, Ireland, 1720.
c. 1676	Caving	Pioneer explorer, John Beaumont, Somerset, England.
1698	Mountaineering	Rock climbing in St Kilda. First major ascent (Mont Blanc) 1786. Continuous history since only 1854.
c. 1700	Bull fighting	Francisco Romero of Ronda, Andalusia, Spain. Referred to by Romans c. 300 BC.
1716	Rowing	Earliest contest, sculling race on Thames (1 Aug.). First English regatta, 1775, Henley Regatta 1839.
1744	Baseball	Of English provenance. Cartwright Rules codified 1845.
c. 1750	Trotting	Harness racing sulky introduced 1829.
1760	Roller Skating	Developed by Joseph Merlin (Belgium). Modern type devised by J L Plimpton (USA) in 1866.
1765	Fives (Eton type)	Buttress hand-ball, Babcary, Somerset. New Courts at Eton, 1840. Rules codified 1877.
1771	Surfing	Canoe surfing first recorded by Capt. James Cook in the Hawaiian Islands. Board surfing reported by Lt. James King, 1779. Sport revived by 1900 at Waikiki, Honolulu.
1787	Beagling	Newcastle Harriers, England.
c. 1790	Shinty	Inter-village or clan game, West and Central Highlands of Scotland as gaelic lomain (driving forward). Rules suggested 1879.
1793	Lawn Tennis	Field tennis, as opposed to Court tennis, first recorded in England (29 Sept.). Leamington Club founded 1872. Patent as sphairistike by Major W C Wingfield Feb. 1874.
1798	Rackets	Earliest covered court, recorded, Exeter.
1823	Rugby	Traditional inventor Rev William Webb Ellis (c. 1807–72) at Rugby School (Nov.). Game formulated at Cambridge, 1839. The Rugby Union founded in 1871.
c. 1835	Croquet	Ireland as 'Crokey'. Country house lawn game in England, c. 1856. First rules 1857. The word dated back to 1478.
1843	Skiing (Alpine)	Tromsö, Norway. Kiandra Club, New South Wales 1855. California 1860. Alps 1883.
1845	Bowling (ten-pin)	Connecticut State, USA, to evade ban on nine-pin bowling. Kegel—a German cloister sport known since 12th century.
1847	Rodeo	Sante Fe, New Mexico, USA. Steer wrestling, 1900.
c. 1850	Fives (Rugby type)	Earliest inter-school matches c. 1872.
c. 1850	Squash rackets	Evolved at Harrow School, England. First US championship 1906.

Date	Sport	Location and Notes
1853	Gliding	Earliest flight by John Appleby, coachman to Sir George Cayley, Brompton Hall, Yorkshire. World championships 1948.
1853	Australian Rules Football	Ballarrat goldfields, Australia.
c. 1863	Badminton	Made famous at Badminton Hall, Avon, England.
1865	Canoeing	Pioneered by John Macgregor (Scotland).
1868	Cycling	First International Race 31 May, Parc de St Cloud, Paris.
1869	Water Polo	Developed in England from 'Water Soccer'. An Olympic event since 1900.
1875	Snooker	Devised by Col Sir Neville Chamberlain, Ootacamund Club, India as a variant of 'black pool'.
1876	Greyhound Racing	Railed 'hare' and windlass, Hendon, North London (Sept.). Race with mechanical hare, Emeryville, California, USA, 1919. First race in UK, Manchester 24 July 1926.
1879	Ski jumping	Huseby, near Oslo, Norway.
1882	Judo	Devised (February) by Dr Jigora Kano (Japan) from Jiu Jitsu (see above).
1884	Bobsledding	First toboggan contests, St Moritz, Switzerland. Skeleton (one-man), 1892.
1886	Equestrianism (Show Jumping)	Paris. Pignatelli's academy, Naples c. 1580.
1889	Table Tennis	Devised by James Gibb as 'Gossima' from a game known in 1881. Ping Pong Association formed in London, 1902. Sport resuscitated, 1921.
1891	Weightlifting	First international contest, Cafe Monico, London (28 Mar.).
1891	Netball	Invented in USA. Introduced to England 1895.
1891	Basketball	Invented by Dr James A Naismith. First played 20 Jan. 1892, Springfield, Mass, USA. Mayan Indian game Pok-ta-Pok dated c. 1000 BC.
1895	Motor Racing	Earliest competitive race Paris–Bordeaux, France, (11–13 June). 20 kilometre race, Longchamps, Paris, 1891.
1895	Rugby League	Professional breakaway, 1895 (29 Aug.). Team reduced from 15 to 13 in 1906, (12 June).
1895	Volleyball	Invented by William G Morgan at Holyoke, Mass, USA as Minnonette; Internationalised 1947.
1896	Marathon running	Marathon to Athens, 1896 Olympics. Standardised at 26 miles 385 yds, 42,195 km in 1924. Named after the run from the Marathon battlefield, Greece by Phidippides in 490 BC.
1897	Motorcycle Racing	Earliest race over a mile, Sheen House, Richmond, Surrey (29 Nov.).
c. 1900	Water Skiing	Aquaplaning, US Pacific coast; plank-riding behind motor boat, Scarborough, England 1914; shaped skis by Ralph Samuelson, Lake Pepin, Minnesota, USA, 1922; devised ramp jump at Miami, Florida, 1928.
1901	Small Bore Shooting	·22 calibre introduced as a Civilian Army training device.
1912	Modern Pentathlon	First formal contest, Stockholm Olympic Games.
1918	Orienteering	Invented by Major Ernst Killander, Sweden.
1922	Skiing (Slalom)	Devised by Sir Arnold Lunn, Mürren, Switzerland (21 Jan.).
1923	Speedway	West Maitland, NSW, Australia (Nov.); first World Championships Sept. 1936.
1936	Trampoline	Developed by George Nissen (US). First championships 1948. Used in show-business since 1910.
1951	Sky Diving (Parachuting)	First world championships in Yugoslavia.
1958	Hang Gliding	Modern revival by Prof. Rogallo; origins attributable to Otto Lilienthal (Germany) 1893.
1960	Aerobatics	First world championships instituted. First aerobatic manoeuvre 1913.
1966	Skate Boarding	First championship in USA; upsurge from 1975; motorized boards from 1977.

SPEED IN SPORT

mph	km/h	Record	Name	Place	Date
2193·167	3 529,56	Official air speed record (para military)	Capt Eldon Joersz & Maj George Morgan	over Beale Air Base California, USA	28 July 1976
631·367	1 016,086	Highest land speed (four wheeled rocket powered)	Gary Gabelich (US) in The Blue Flame	Bonneville Salt Flats, Utah USA	23 Oct. 1970
614	988	Parachuting free-fall in mesosphere (military research)	Capt J W Kittinger (USA)	Tularosa, New Mex, USA	16 Aug. 1960
429·311	690,909	Highest land speed (wheel driven)	Donald Campbell (GB) in Bluebird (gas turbined)	Lake Eyre, South Australia	17 Jul. 1964
418·504	673,516	Highest land speed (four wheel direct drive)	Robert Summers (USA) in Goldenrod	Bonneville Salt Flats, Utah, USA	12 Nov. 1965
328	527,8	Highest water borne speed	Donald Campbell (GB) in Bluebird K7	Coniston Water, Cumbria England	4 Jan. 1967
307·692	495,183	Highest speed motor cycle	Don Vesco (US)	Bonneville Salt Flats, Utah	28 Sept. 1975
288·3	464	Official water speed record	Ken Warby (Australia) in The Spirit of Australia	Blowering Dam, N.S.W., Australia	20 Nov. 1977
221·160	355,922	Motor racing—closed circuit	Mark Donohue Jr (US)	Talladega, Alabama, USA	9 Aug. 1975
213·70	343,92	Model aircraft (jet model)	V. Goukoune (USSR)	Klementyeva, USSR	21 Sept. 1971
202·42	325,76	Hydroplane record (propeller driven)	Larry Hill (USA)	Long Beach, California	1973
200·624	322,873	Lap record 500 miles 804 km Motor racing	Johnny Rutherford (US)	Indianapolis (USA)	13 May 1977
174	280	Pelota	Jose Areitio	Newport, RI, USA	1 June 1977
170	270	Golf ball	(Electrically timed)	USA	1960
155·627	250,457	Lap record (practice) 24 hr Endurance Motor racing	Jackie Oliver	Le Mans, France	18 Apr. 1971
140·5	226,1	Cycling, motor paced	Dr Allan V Abbott (US)	Bonneville Salt Flats, Utah	25 Aug. 1973
125·69	202,27	Water Skiing	Danny Churchill (US)	Oakland Marine Stadium, California, USA	1971
117–185	188–297	Sky-Diving—lower atmosphere	Terminal velocity (varies with attitude)		post 1950
120·849	194,489	Downhill Schuss (Alpine Skiing)	Tom Simons (USA)	Cervinia, Italy	11 July 1976
118	189	Ice hockey—puck	Bobby Hull (Canada)	Chicago, Illinois, USA	1965
108·73	175,00	Gliding (100 km triangular course)	Klaas Goudriaan (SAF) in an ASW 17	over South Africa	22 Nov. 1975
90	145	Tobogganing—Cresta Run	Poldi Berchtold (Swit.)	St Moritz, Switzerland	Jan. 1975
76·342	122,862	Cycling behind pacemaker—1 hr	Leon Vanderstuyft (Belgium)	Montlhery Motor Circuit, France	30 Sept. 1928
63·894	102,828	Downhill Alpine Skiing (Olympic course) (average)	Franz Klammer (Austria)	Innsbruck, Austria	5 Feb. 1976

continued

SPEED IN SPORT continued

mph	km/h	Record	Name	Place	Date
52·46	84,42	Speedway (4 laps of 430 yd *393 m*)	Dave Morton (GB)	Crewe, England	12 Aug. 1974
43·26	69,62	Horse racing (440 yd *402 m* in 20·8 s)	Big Racket	Mexico City, Mexico	5 Feb. 1945
42·16	67,86	Track cycling (*200 m* 219 yd) unpaced in 10·61 s	Omari Phakadze (USSR)	Mexico City, Mexico	22 Oct. 1967
41·72	67,14	Greyhound racing (410 yd *374 m* straight 26·13 s)	The Shoe (Australia)	Richmond, NSW, Australia	25 Apr. 1968
38·46	61,89	Sailing—60 ft *18,29 m* proa *Crossbow II* 33·4 kts)	T J Coleman (UK) *et al.*	Portland, Dorset, England	4 Oct. 1977
35·06	56,42	Horse racing—The Derby (1 mil 885 yd *2,41 km*)	Mahmoud	Epsom, Surrey, England	June 1936
35	56	Boxing—speed of punch	Sugar Ray Robinson (USA)	USA	Jan. 1957
30·715	49,431	Cycling—1 hr, unpaced	Eddie Merckx (Belgium)	Mexico City, Mexico	25 Oct. 1972
29·80	47,96	Steeplechasing—The Grand National (4 miles 856 yd *7,220 km*) in 9 min 1·9 s	Red Rum ridden by Brian Fletcher	Aintree, Liverpool, England	31 Mar. 1973
29·43	47,36	Ice speed skating (500 m *546 yd* in 37·00 s on 400 m *437 yd* rink)	Yevgeniy Kulikov (USSR)	Medeo, USSR	29 Mar. 1975
27·89	44,88	Sprinting (during 100 yd *91 m*)	Robert Hayes (USA)	St Louis, Missouri, USA	21 June 1963
21·49	34,58	Cycling—average maintained over 24 hr	Teuvo Louhivuori (Finland)	Tampere-Kolari, Finland	10 Sept. 1974
13·46	21,67	Rowing (2000 m *2187 yd*)	East German Eight	Montreal, Canada	16 July 1976
12·24	19,69	Marathon run (26 miles 385 yd *42,195 km*)	Derek Clayton (Australia)	Antwerp, Belgium	30 May 1969
8·84	14,24	Walking—1 hr	Bernd Kannenberg (WG)	Hamburg, W. Germany	25 May 1974
4·52	7,28	Swimming (100 m)—Long Course in 49·44 s	Jonty Skinner (SAF)	Philadelphia, USA	14 Aug. 1976
2·4	3,8	Channel swimming (effective speed)	Nasser el Sahzli (Egypt)	England to France	21 Aug. 1977
0·00084	0,00135	Tug 'o War (2 hr 41 min pull—12 ft *3,6 m*)	2nd Derbyshire Regt (UK)	Jubbulpore, India	12 Aug. 1889

WEIGHTS AND DIMENSIONS IN SPORT

Association Football	Ball circum: 27–28 in *68–71 cm* Ball wt: 14–16 oz *396–453 g* Pitch length: 100–130 yd *91–120 m* Pitch width: 50–100 yd *45–91 m*	Hockey	Ball circum: 8 $\frac{13}{16}$–9$\frac{1}{4}$ in *22,3–23,4 cm* Ball wt: 5$\frac{1}{2}$–5$\frac{3}{4}$ oz *155–163 g*	Rugby Union	Ball length: 11–11$\frac{1}{4}$ in *27,9–28,5 cm* End on diam: 28$\frac{3}{4}$–29$\frac{3}{4}$ in *73,0–75,5 cm*
Basketball	Ball circum: 29$\frac{1}{2}$–31$\frac{1}{2}$ in *74,9–80 cm*	Lawn Bowls Lawn Tennis	Ball circum: max 16$\frac{1}{2}$ in *41,9 cm* Ball diam: 2$\frac{1}{2}$–2$\frac{5}{8}$ in *6,35–6,66 cm*		Diam in width: 23–24 in *58,4–60,9 cm* Ball wt: 13$\frac{1}{2}$–15 oz *382–439 g*
Cricket	Ball circum: 8$\frac{3}{16}$–9 in *20,79–22,8 cm* Ball wt: 5$\frac{1}{2}$–5$\frac{3}{4}$ oz *155–163 g* Pitch: 22 yd *20,11 m* from stump to stump, creases 4 ft *1,21 m* apart each end.	Rugby League	Ball wt: 2–2$\frac{1}{16}$ oz *56–58 g* Court: outside dimensions 78 ft *23,77 m* long 27 ft *8,22 m* wide (singles) 36 ft *10,97 m* (doubles) Ball length: 10$\frac{3}{4}$–11$\frac{1}{2}$ in *27,3–29,2 cm* End on diam: 28$\frac{3}{4}$–29$\frac{3}{4}$ *73,0–75,5 cm*	Squash	Pitch (max): 68·58 m *75 yd* width, 91·44 m *100 yd* between goal lines. Ball diam: 1$\frac{9}{16}$–1$\frac{5}{8}$ in *3,9–4,12 cm* Ball wt: 360–380 grains *23–24 g*
Croquet Golf (UK)	Ball diam: 3$\frac{5}{8}$ in *9,2 cm* Ball min diam: 1·620 in *4,1 cm* Ball max wt: 1·62 oz *45 g* In USA min diam: 1·680 in *4,2 cm*		Diam in width: 23–24 in *58,4–60,9 cm* Ball wt: 13$\frac{1}{2}$–15$\frac{1}{2}$ oz *382–439 g* Pitch (max): 75 yd *68,58 m* wide, 110yd *100,58 m* between goal lines.	Table Tennis	Ball circum: 4$\frac{1}{2}$–4$\frac{3}{4}$ in *11,4–12,0 cm* Ball wt: 37–39 grains *2,4–2,5 g*

DEFENCE

The two great wars

History's two greatest wars have both been fought in the 20th century. World War I (1914–18) resulted in 9 700 000 fatalities including 765 399 from the United Kingdom. World War II (1939–45) resulted in 54.8 million battle and civilian deaths including 25 million in the U.S.S.R., and 6 028 000 or 22.2% of her population in Poland. The U.K. losses were 265 000.

Strategic nuclear delivery vehicles

For three decades a factor in the deterrence from world war has been the threat of nuclear attack by one or other of the major powers linked to the achievement of parity in the means of delivery. It is now possible for many nations to use tactical nuclear missiles on the battlefield by means of aircraft, rockets, artillery or from mines. For strategic delivery six major systems are available:

Inter-continental ballistic missiles with ranges in excess of 4000 miles *6400 km* ICBM

Intermediate-range ballistic missiles with ranges between 1500 and 4000 miles *2400–6400 km* IRBM

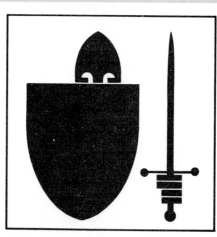

Medium-range ballistic missiles with ranges between 500 and 1500 miles *800–2400 km* MRBM

Short-range ballistic missiles with ranges less than 500 miles *800 km* SRBM

Long-range bombers with ranges over 6000 miles *9650 km*

Medium-range bombers with ranges between 3500 and 6000 miles *5600–9650 km*

Ballistic missiles can be launched from ground sites or submarines.

The warheads may be productive of explosions ranging between 25 Megaton (MT) in the largest SS 9 Scarp (USSR) ICBM, with its range of 7500 miles *12000 km* to 50 kiloton (kT) in the SRBMs. One kT is equivalent to 1000 tons of TNT and one MT to one million tons of TNT.

Naval forces

Apart from contributing to the nuclear deterrent, navies continue to pursue their time honoured role of maintaining an armed presence at sea while contributing to the protection of trade and of anti-submarine warfare.

Land and Air Forces

The many confrontations since World War II have been combined action by land and air forces with a minor naval role. The arbiters of decision since the 1930s have been close support aircraft and armoured fighting vehicles, of which the predominant weapon has been the tank.

Approximate cost of the two World Wars to the main contestants in people and money

	Mobilised (000)	Military Killed (000)	Civilians Killed (000)	Cost in $ (billion)		Mobilised (000)	Military Killed (000)	Civilians Killed (000)	Cost in $ (billion)
World War I					*World War II*				
The Central Powers					*The Axis Powers*				
Germany	11 000	1808	760	58	Germany	11 000	3250	3810	300
Austria Hungary	7800	1200	300	24	Italy	4500	330	500	50
Turkey	2850	325	2150	3·5	Japan	6095	1700	360	100
Bulgaria	1200	87	275	1					
The Allied Powers					*The Allied Powers*				
British Empire	8904	908	30	52	British Empire	8720	452	80	150
France	8410	1357	40	50	France	6000	250	360	100
Russia (USSR post-1917)	12 000	1700	2000	25·6	Poland	1000	120	5300	na
Serbia	707	45	650	2·5	USSR	12 500	7500	17 500	200
Italy	5615	650	Small	18	USA	14 900	407	Small	350
USA	4355	126	Small	33	China[1]	8000	1500	7800	na
Other Allied Powers	2200	365	—	—					
Total all countries involved	65 000	8500	6642	282	Total from above countries	72 700	15 600	35 800[2]	1600

[1] 1937–45. Figures highly speculative   [2] Does not include full total of victims of war time genocides   na—Not available

Principal wars since 1945

1945–	China and Taiwan	Nationalist Chinese (with US assistance) *versus* Communist Chinese. Intensive phase lapsed in 1949 with establishment of Communist state.
1946–75	Indo-China/Vietnam	French/South Vietnamese and then USA and South Vietnamese *versus* Communists and North Vietnamese.
1947–71	Indian sub-continent	India *versus* Pakistan, intermittently in Kashmir, plus short intensive confrontations in 1947, 1967 and 3–16 Dec. 1971.
1948–	Middle East	Israel *versus* Arab States (with interventions by Britain and France). Continuous state of war with intensive confrontations in 1948, 1956, 5–10 June 1967 (6-day war) and 6–24 Oct. 1973.
1950–1953	Korea	North Korea and China *versus* United Nations forces. 25 June 1950 invasion of South Korea. Armistice signed 27 July 1953.

Samples of defence expenditures

Due to the shifting value of currency a comparison of escalating costs cannot be fully explanatory of the rising expense of defence, but expenditure by the United Kingdom at certain crucial periods is indicative of a trend:

1901	£ 124 million	The final year of the Boer War
1917	£2436 million	The peak year of World War I
1932	£ 103 million	At a nadir during the economic depression
1940	£3220 million	The first full year of World War II
1944	£5215 million	The peak year of World War II

Since then, in the prevailing atmosphere of Cold War, and *Détente*, the following national expenditures by some major powers (quoted in $ million) have been recorded:

	USA	UK	USSR (In roubles millions)	France	Japan	West Germany
1954	42 786	4376	11 250	3346	375	1497
1964	51 213	5581	16 280	4955	781	4917
1976	113 800	10 350	70 000 (1975)	10 660	5060	12 600

Manpower as deployed by nations recently involved in major hostilities (1976)

Israel	Egypt	Syria	Vietnam (North)	India	Pakistan
158 500	342 500	225 000	615 000	1 050 000	425 000

Manpower as deployed by the world's five main nuclear powers in 1976

USA	UK	USSR	France	China
2 090 000	344 000	3 650 000	513 000	3 525 000

Weapons believed to be available (1976)

	USA	Britain	France	Germany	USSR	China
ICBM	1054	—	—	—	1527	—
IRBM	656	64	66	—	845	30
MRBM	—	—	—	—	557	50
SRBM	762	—	6	91	1300	—
Long-range bombers	387	—	—	—	135	—
Medium-range bombers	66	50	—	—	810	100

Strength of principal naval units belonging to the world's five main nuclear powers

	USA	UK	USSR	France	China
Submarines nuclear	105	8	125	—	1
Submarines non-nuclear	9	24	265	23	55
Aircraft carriers	13	1	1	2	—
Cruisers	26	10	34	2	—
Destroyers	39	3	80	20	8
Frigates/Escorts	6	61	113	28	10

Main battle tank and combat aircraft strengths of the principal NATO and Warsaw Pact powers in Europe

| | NATO | | | | | WARSAW PACT | | | |
	USA	UK	Belg.	Neths.	West Germany	USSR	Czechs	East Germany	Poland
Tanks	2500	650	325	525	2400	7900	2900	1700	3200
Aircraft	260	130	140	160	580	1300	450	400	850

Thus the Warsaw Pact has 15 700 tanks and 3000 aircraft deployed against NATO's 6755 tanks and 1320 aircraft.

Main battle tank and combat aircraft strengths of the nations recently involved in major hostilities

	Israel	Egypt	Syria	Vietnam[1]	India	Pakistan
Tanks	2700	1975	2400	900	1930	1050
Aircraft	550	450	400	200	950	220

[1] Considerably augmented by US material taken over in South Vietnam in 1975.

Ranks and the command structures of armed forces

There is a considerable similarity in the rank structure and titles of the armed services of the world, particularly, of course, with those nations using the English language. The ranks and titles used by the United Kingdom are given below.

Navy	Army	Air Force
Admiral of the Fleet	Field-Marshal (FM)	Marshal of the Royal Air Force
Admiral	General (Gen)	Air Chief Marshal
Vice Admiral (Vice-Adm)	Lieut-General (Lt-Gen)	Air Marshal
Rear-Admiral (Rear-Adm)	Major-General (Maj-Gen)	Air Vice-Marshal
Commodore (Cdre)	Brigadier (Brig)	Air Commodore (Air-Cdre)
Captain (Capt)	Colonel (Col)	Group Captain (Gp Capt)
Commander (Cdr)	Lieutenant-Colonel (Lt-Col)	Wing Commander (Wing Cdr)
Lieutenant-Commander (Lt-Cdr)	Major (Maj)	Squadron Leader (Sqn Ldr)
Lieutenant (Lt)	Captain	Flight Lieutenant (Flt Lt)
Sub-Lieutenant (Sub Lt)	Lieutenant (Lt)	Flying Officer (FO)
Acting Lieutenant	Second-Lieutenant (2-Lt)	Pilot Officer (PO)
Fleet Chief	Warrant Officer I and II	Warrant Officer
Chief Petty Officer	Staff-Sergeant	Flight-Sergeant
Petty Officer	Sergeant	Sergeant
Leading rating	Corporal	Corporal

There are many variations both in size and nomenclature of the component parts of world's fleets, armies and air fleets. Ships vary in size, air forces in components. Here, for example, because they are fairly typical, are the titles and approximate sizes of British Army units and formations, along with the ranks most likely to command them:

Title	Approx Manpower	Rank of commander
Section/tank or gun	10– 4	Corporal or Sergeant
Platoon/troop	35– 12	2nd Lieut, Lieut or Capt
Company/squadron/battery	120– 75	Major
Battalion/regiment	800– 500	Lieut-Colonel
Brigade	4000– 3000	Brigadier
Division	14 000–12 000	Major-General
Corps	Widely variable	Lieut-General
Army	Widely variable	General
Army Group	Widely variable	General or Field-Marshal

TRANSPORT

WORLD'S LARGEST SHIPS

The largest surviving liner is the *Queen Elizabeth 2* (UK) 66 852 gross tons and 963 ft *293 m* in length. The largest liner of all-time was *Queen Elizabeth* (UK) of 82 998 gross tons and 1031 ft *314 m* completed in 1940 and destroyed by fire in Hong Kong as *Seawise University* on 9 Jan. 1972. The longest liner is *France* of 66 348 gross tons and 1035 ft *315,52 m* completed in 1961 and put out of service in 1975. She was bought by Saudi Arabian interest on 24 Oct. 1977.

Shipping tonnages

There are four tonnage systems in use, viz. gross tonnage (GRT), net tonnage (NRT), deadweight tonnage (DWT) and displacement tonnage.

(1) *Gross Registered Tonnage*, used for merchantmen, is the sum in cubic ft of all the enclosed spaces divided by 100, such that 1 grt = 100 ft³ of enclosed space.

(2) *Net Registered Tonnage*, also used for merchantmen, is the gross tonnage (above) less deductions for crew spaces, engine rooms and ballast which cannot be utilised for paying passengers or cargo.

(3) *Deadweight Tonnage*, mainly used for tramp ships and oil tankers, is the number of UK long tons (of 2240 lb) of cargo, stores, bunkers and, where necessary, passengers which is required to bring down a ship from her light line to her load-water line, i.e. the carrying capacity of a ship.

(4) *Displacement Tonnage*, used for warship and US merchantmen, is the numbers of tons (each 35 ft³) of sea water displaced by a vessel charged to its load-water line, i.e. the weight of the vessel and its contents in tons.

Bulk, Ore, Bulk Oil and Ore Oil Carriers (over 250,000 tons dwt)

Name	Flag	Dwt (tons)	Length (ft)	Length (m)
Svealand	Sweden	282 450	1109	338
Docecanyon	Liberia	271 235	1113	339
Licorne Pacifique	France	271 000	1111	338
Jose Bonifacio	Brazil	270 358	1106	337
Tarfala	Sweden	265 000	1099	334
Mary R Koch	Liberia	265 000	1090	334
Torne	Sweden	265 000	1090	334
Usa Maru	Japan	264 523	1105	336
Nordic Conqueror	UK	268 728	1101	335
Lauderdale	UK	260 424	1101	335
Licorne Atlantique	France	258 268	1101	335

Oil tankers in deadweight tons over 414 000

Name	Flag	Dwt (tons)	Length (ft)	Length (m)
Bellamya	France	553 662	1359	414
Batillus	France	550 000	1312	400
Nissei Maru	Japan	484 337	1243	378
Globtik London	UK	483 939	1243	378
Globtik Tokyo	UK	483 664	1243	378
Homeric	Liberia	446 500	1241	378
Berge Empress	Norway	423 700	1252	381
Esso Deutschland	W. Germany	421 678	1240	378
Al Rekkah	Kuwait	414 366	1200	365
Berge Emperor	Norway	414 000	1285	391

MOTOR VEHICLES

Accidents

The cumulative total of fatalities since the first in the United Kingdom on 17 Aug. 1896 surpassed 250 000 in 1959 and by the end of 1975 reached about *350 000*. There are only estimated figures for Northern Ireland in the period 1923–30. The peak reached was 1941 with 9444 killed or 26 per day in Great Britain only. L plates were introduced in May 1935.

Average Mileage

The average estimated mileage for a car fell from 8900 miles in 1972 to 8500 miles in 1974. Car ownership rose in the same period from 692 per 1000 families to 730 while 4 star petrol rose from 34½p to 42p per gallon. In 1975 it rose to 72½p and in 1976 to 79p.

Traffic signals: dates of introduction

1868 Parliament Square, Westminster, London, semaphore-arms with red and green gas lamps for night use.
1925 Piccadilly Circus, London, police-operated.
1926 Wolverhampton, Staffordshire, modern type electric.
1932 First vehicle actuation sets introduced.

Petrol tax

Rate per gallon		Great Britain
30 Apr.	1909	3d
22 Sept.	1915	6d
1 Jan.	1921	repealed
25 Apr.	1928	4d
28 Apr.	1931	6d
11 Sept.	1931	8d
27 Apr.	1938	9d
19 Apr.	1950	1s 6d
4 Apr.	1951	1s 10½d
11 Mar.	1952	2s 6d
4 Dec.	1956	3s 6d
9 Apr.	1957	2s 6d
28 July	1961	2s 9d
11 Nov.	1964	3s 3d
1 Jan.	1970	4s 6d
15 Feb.	1971	22·5p
1 Apr.	1974*	27·5p
18 Nov.	1974*	35p
20 Dec.	1974*	37p

*incl. VAT

Purchase and Value Added tax on cars

		%
Oct.	1940	33⅓
June	1947	33⅓*
Apr.	1950	33⅓
Apr.	1951	66⅔
Apr.	1953	50
Oct.	1955	60
Apr.	1959	50
July	1961	55
Apr.	1962	45
Nov.	1962	25
July	1966	27½
Apr.	1973	abolished. VAT replaces
Apr.	1973	10
Apr.	1974	Nil
July	1974	8

*66⅔% if retail value exceeded £1280.

United Kingdom motor vehicles and roads

Year	No of Vehicles (Sept.)	Miles of Road (31 Mar.)	No of Yards of Road per Vehicle	Fatalities
1904	c. 18 000	—	—	—
1914	388 860	c. 176 000	796	—
1920	c. 652 000	c. 176 000	475	—
1925	1 538 235	c. 178 000	203	—
1930	2 309 515	179 286	136·7	c. 7400
1935	2 612 093	178 507	120·3	6625
1939	3 208 410	180 527	99·0	8419
1945	1 654 364	c. 183 000	194·7	5380
1950	4 511 626	197 076	77·1	5156
1955	6 567 393	201 724	54·1	5686
1960	9 610 432	207 939	38·1	7142
1961	10 148 714	208 986	36·3	7077
1962	10 763 502	209 937	34·3	6866
1963	11 729 765	212 275	31·8	7098
1964	12 671 817	213 602	29·7	8039
1965	13 263 537	214 958	28·5	8143
1970	15 322 533	222 000	25·5	7771
1974	17 626 273	221 009	22·1	7192
1975	17 870 654	220 690	21·7	6664
1976	18 218 219	221 665	21·4	6870

Notes:

Vehicles
Vehicles surpassed 1 million early in 1923.
Cars surpassed 1 million early in 1930, 5 million early in 1949.
Motor cycles (including mopeds, scooters and three-wheelers) surpassed 1 million in 1953.
Trams reached their peak in 1927 with 14 413 and sank by 1965 to 110.
Diesel vehicles surpassed 25% of all goods vehicles in 1961 (2·1% in 1935) and 35% in 1965.

Roads
The mileage includes Trunk roads, Class I, Class II and Unclassified. Statistics prior to 1925 apply to Great Britain only. The earliest dual carriageway was the Southend arterial in 1937 though parts of both the Great West Road and the Kingston by-pass were converted to separate carriageways in 1936.

Road speed limits

mph		
2	1865 Act	Town limit for steam-driven vehicles preceded by man on foot with red flag.
4	1865 Act	Country limit for steam-driven vehicles as above.
14	1897 Act	Red flag abolished. General limit.

continued

ROAD SPEED LIMITS continued

mph		
20	1903 Act	General limit under Motor Car Act. Licensing introduced on 1 Jan. 1904.
—	1930 Act	Unlimited. Motor cyclist age limit raised from 14 to 16.
30	1934 Act	Limit in built-up areas. Introduced in N Ireland on 1 Oct. 1956.
40	1957 Reg.	Experimentally introduced, confirmed 1958. N Ireland on 27 Mar. 1961.
50	1960 Reg.	Experimentally introduced on designated main roads, confirmed 1961.
70	1965 Reg.	Overall limit including motorways (experimental until September 1967).
70		Limit on motorways.
60	1974 Reg.	Limit on dual-carriageway roads.
50		Limit on hitherto decontrolled single carriageway roads.
70	1977 Reg.	Restored limit to 1965 level.

MAJOR NATIONAL RAILWAY SYSTEMS

Country	Year of first railway	Length (miles)	Length (km)	Remarks
Great Britain	1825*	11 258	18 012	*Excluding early mineral lines
Ireland (total)	1834	1360	2189	
Czechoslovakia	1839	8283	13 330	
France	1832	21 616	34 787	
Germany	1835			
Deutsche Bundesbahn		18 318	29 479	
Deutsche Reichsbahn		8938	14 384	
Hungary	1846	4728	7610	
Italy	1839	9950	16 014	
Poland	1842	14 768	23 766	
Spain	1828	8111	13 495	1,676 m gauge
Sweden	1856	7059	11 361	
Canada	1836	44 794	72 089	CPR 16 588 miles, 23 518 km CNR 23 496 miles, 37 813 km British Columbia Railway 862 miles 1387 km
USA	1830	200 916	323 344	
Mexico	1850	10 223	16 453	
Argentina	1857	24 722	39 787	All gauges
Brazil	1854	16 283	26 205	
Chile	1851	5106	8218	All gauges
USSR	1837	85 912	138 260	
China	1883	23 900	38 500	
India	1853	37 324	60 067	All gauges
Pakistan	1853	5326	8572	
Bangladesh	1853	1786	2874	1,676 m, 1,0 m gauges
Japan	1872	13 149	21 161	Standard, 1,067 m gauges
Turkey	1856	3186	5128	
Austria	1854	26 018	41 873	Including Tasmania 530 miles, 853 km
South Africa	1860	13 762	22 149	

Steam loco wheel arrangements

2–2–2   oOo

2–4–0   oOO

4–4–2 (Atlantic)   ooOOo

0–4–0   OO

0–6–0   OOO

4–6–2 (Pacific)   ooOOOo

2–8–0 (Consolidation)   oOOOO

2–10–4   oOOOOOoo

2–8–8–4   oOOOO OOOOoo

LOCOMOTIVES

Steam locomotive types are generally denoted by the system of wheel arrangements invented in 1900 by Frederic M Whyte (1865–1941), an official of the New York Central Railroad. It can easily be worked out from the examples. (*see left*) All locomotives are imagined facing to the left.

The European continental countries use an axle system, thus a 4–6–2 is a 2C1. Germany and Switzerland denote the number of driving axles as a fraction of the total number of axles: for example a 4–6–2 is a 3/6, a 2–8–0 a 4/5. By this system, however, a 3/5 could be a 4–6–0, a 2–6–2 or a 0–6–4.

In the wheel arrangements of diesel, gas-turbine and electric locomotives the number of driving axles in one frame is denoted by a letter: A = 1, B = 2, C = 3, D = 4, E = 5. Idle axles are denoted by figures, 1 and 2. Axles individually driven are denoted by a small o after the letter, e.g.: Co–Co denotes a locomotive with two 3-axle bogies with all axles individually driven. A locomotive with two 3-axle bogies of which the middle axles are not driven is A1A–A1A. Axles coupled by rods or gears are denoted by a letter only, e.g. 2–D–2 denotes a locomotive with four coupled driving axles and a 4-wheeled bogie at each end. 1C–C1 denotes a locomotive with two bogies each with three coupled axles and an idle axle, e.g. the Swiss 'Crocodiles'. Buffing or drag stresses taken through a form of articulation between the bogies are indicated by a + sign, e.g. Bo + Bo, such as the Furka-Oberalp and Brig-Visp-Zermatt locomotives in Switzerland.

WORLD'S MAJOR AIRPORTS (1976)

Name and Location	Terminal Passengers (000's)	Aircraft Movements (000's)	Date Opened to Scheduled Traffic
O'Hare, Chicago, USA	41 376	718	1 Oct. 1955
Hartsfield International, Atlanta, USA	27 299	490	3 May 1961
Los Angeles, USA	25 983	482	25 June 1961
Heathrow, London, UK	23 241	278	31 May 1946
John F Kennedy, New York, USA	21 033	305	1 July 1948
Haneda, Tokyo, Japan*	18 825	165	July 1952

* Estimated figures

AIRPORTS continued

Name and Location	Terminal Passengers (000's)	Aircraft Movements (000's)	Date Opened to Scheduled Traffic
San Francisco, USA	17 564	342	7 May 1927
La Guardia, New York, USA	14 088	313	2 Dec. 1939
Denver, USA	13 698	418	na
Miami, USA	12 884	300	1 Feb. 1959
Orly, Paris, France	10 970	89	1946
Charles de Gaulle, Paris, France	7 700	96	March 1974

MAIN COMMERCIAL AIRCRAFT IN AIRLINE SERVICE 1977

Aircraft*	Nationality	Number in Service (1 July 1977)	Wingspan	Length	Maximum cruising speed	Range	Maximum Take-off Weight	Maximum Seating Capacity
Boeing 727 (–200)	USA	1228	108 ft 0 in (32,92 m)	153 ft 2 in (46,69 m)	520 knots (964 km/h)	2500 naut miles (4635 km)	209 500 lb (95 025 kg)	189
McDonnell Douglas DC-9 (Srs 30)	USA	774	93 ft 5 in (28,47 m)	119 ft 4 in (36,37 m)	490 knots (907 km/h)	1980 naut miles (3670 km)	121 000 lb (54 885 kg)	115
Boeing 707/720 (707–320)	USA	702	145 ft 9 in (44,42 m)	152 ft 11 in (46,61 m)	525 knots (973 km/h)	6500 naut miles (12 000 km)	333 600 lb (151 315 kg)	219
Yakovlev Yak–40	USSR	630	82 ft 0 in (25,00 m)	66 ft 9 in (20,36 m)	297 knots (550 km/h)	1080 naut miles (2000 km)	35 280 lb (16 000 kg)	32
Antonov An-24/An-26 (An24V Srs II)	USSR	550	95 ft 10 in (29,20 m)	77 ft 3 in (23,53 m)	243 knots (450 km/h)	1618 naut miles (3000 km)	46 300 lb (21 000 kg)	52
McDonnell Douglas DC-8 (Srs 63)	USA	468	148 ft 5 in (45,23 m)	187 ft 5 in (57,12 m)	521 knots (965 km/h)	6686 naut miles (12 390 km)	350 000 lb (158 800 kg)	259
Boeing 737 (737–200)	USA	464	93 ft 0 in (28,35 m)	100 ft 0 in (30,48 m)	500 knots (927 km/h)	2200 naut miles (4075 km)	117 000 lb (53 070 kg)	130
Ilyushin 18	USSR	435	122 ft 8 in (37,40 m)	117 ft 9 in (35,90 m)	351 knots (650 km/h)	2805 naut miles (5200 km)	134 925 lb (61 200 kg)	110
Tupolev Tu-134	USSR	360	95 ft 2 in (29,00 m)	114 ft 8 in (34,95 m)	486 knots (898 km/h)	1888 naut miles (3500 km)	99 200 lb (45 000 kg)	72
Fokker F-27 (Mk 400)	Netherlands	354	95 ft 2 in (29,00 m)	77 ft 4 in (23,56 m)	259 knots (480 km/h)	1025 naut miles (1935 km)	45 000 lb (20 410 kg)	48
Boeing 747 (747–200)	USA	291	195 ft 8 in (59,64 m)	231 ft 4 in (70,50 m)	520 knots (965 km/h)	5625 naut miles (10 425 km)	820 000 lb (371 950 kg)	500
McDonnell Douglas DC-10 (Srs 30)	USA	234	165 ft 4½ in (50,41 m)	182 ft 1 in (55,50 m)	490 knots (908 km/h)	6250 naut miles (11 580 km)	565 000 lb (256 280 kg)	380
Tupolev Tu-154	USSR	170	123 ft 2½ in (37,55 m)	157 ft 1¾ in (47,90 m)	526 knots (975 km/h)	3723 naut miles (6900 km)	198 416 lb (90 000 kg)	167
BAC One-Eleven (Srs 500)	UK	164	93 ft 6 in (28,50 m)	107 ft 0 in (32,61 m)	470 knots (871 km/h)	1880 naut miles (3484 km)	104 500 lb (47 400 kg)	119
Lockheed L-1011 Tristar (Srs 100)	USA	138	155 ft 4 in (47,34 m)	177 ft 8½ in (54,17 m)	515 knots (954 km/h)	4820 naut miles (8932 km)	466 000 lb (211 375 kg)	400
BAC/Aérospatiale Concorde	UK/France	8	83 ft 10 in (25,56 m)	203 ft 9 in (62,10 m)	1176 knots (2179 km/h)	3550 naut miles (6580 km)	408 000 lb (185 065 kg)	128

*Note: There are many variants of the basic models of these aircraft. Versions to which data apply is indicated in parenthesis.

MAJOR WORLD AIRLINES
(1976 data)

Airline	Passenger km (000)*	Aircraft km (000)*	Passengers Carried (000)**	Aircraft Departures *	Scheduled Route Network (km)
Aeroflot, USSR†	130 000 000	na	100 000	na	805 000
United, USA	52 128 964	576 115	32 362	532 984	30 319
American, USA	40 063 700	476 639	22 963	376 390	69 911
Trans World Airlines (TWA), USA	39 413 458	449 551	16 910	303 381	320 672
Pan American, USA	32 832 753	254 795	7309	107 712	557 784
Eastern, USA	31 845 078	445 474	29 706	534 831	56 488
British Airways, UK	30 119 961	254 956	13 863	215 790	655 977
Delta, USA	29 136 679	358 896	28 409	502 817	50 558
Japan Air Lines (JAL)	19 874 336	145 721	9159	71 443	217 922
Air France	19 257 676	195 175	8598	162 553	545 498
Air Canada	18 135 796	197 533	10 623	197 123	272 992
Northwest, USA[1]	16 031 089	177 833	na	175 478	39 018
Lufthansa, Germany	15 262 295	184 171	10 418	180 429	401 530
KLM, Netherlands	11 670 540	98 559	3250	60 881	310 420
Qantas, Australia	11 619 715	65 010	1584	19 589	209 193
Braniff, USA	11 538 908	175 018	9180	198 021	48 344
Western, USA[1]	10 854 523	139 779	na	146 317	51 570
Iberia, Spain	10 606 679	126 619	10 605	162 685	313 417
Alitalia, Italy[2]	10 568 853	122 782	6135	113 733	307 211
Continental, USA[3]	9 124 564	122 441	6663	139 293	38 742
SAS, Scandinavia	8 953 319	118 713	7161	154 710	274 303
Swissair, Switzerland	8 669 045	87 050	5085	89 829	248 492
National, USA	8 588 280	102 631	5580	118 139	19 655
CP Air, Canada	7 384 960	65 892	2444	42 468	140 650
Varig, Brazil	6 116 050	92 173	3287	71 362	229 338
South African Airways	6 045 055	56 636	2937	54 487	56 044
Allegheny, USA	5 809 244	115 086	11 031	303 770	8 244

* Scheduled and non-scheduled services, including all-freight
** Scheduled services only
† data approximate
[1] 1974 data except for Scheduled Route Network which is 1976 data.
[2] 1974 data
[3] 1973 data

Milestones in civil aviation

1785 (7 Jan.)	First crossing of English Channel by balloon Jean Pierre Blanchard (FRA) and Dr John J Jeffries (USA).
1852 (24 Sept.)	First flight by navigable airship, in France
1900 (2 July)	First flight by German Zeppelin airship
1903 (17 Dec.)	First sustained flight in an aeroplane, by Wright Brothers, in United States.
1906 (12 Nov.)	First public aeroplane flight in Europe. Alberto Santos-Dumont covers a distance of 38 m near Paris, France.
1909 (25 July)	Louis Blériot (FRA) completes first aeroplane crossing of the English Channel.
1910 (27–8 Aug.)	Louis Paulhan completes first flight from London to Manchester, in 4 hr 12 min with an overnight stop.
1919 (14–15 June)	Capt John William Alcock and Lieut Arthur Whitten Brown complete first non-stop crossing of the Atlantic.
1919 (12 Nov.–10 Dec.)	Capt Ross Smith and Lieut Keith Smith complete first flight from United Kingdom (Hounslow) to Australia (Darwin).
1924 (1 Apr.)	Imperial Airways formed in Great Britain.
1928 (31 May–9 June)	First trans-Pacific flight from San Francisco to Brisbane, by Capt Charles Kingsford Smith and C T P Ulm.
1949 (21 June)	First flight of commercial jet, the De Havilland Comet (Entered service 2 May 1952).
1968 (31 Dec.)	Flight of first supersonic airliner, the Russian Tupolev TU-144.
1969 (9 Feb.)	First flight of Boeing 747, the Jumbo. (Entered service 21 Jan. 1970).
1969 (2 Mar.)	First flight of BAC/Aerospatiale Concorde. (Entered service 21 Jan. 1976).
1969 (2 Mar.)	First flight of BAC/Aerospatiale Concorde.
1976 (21 Jan.)	Concorde entered scheduled Air France and British Airways service.
1977 (26 Sept.)	Laker Airways inaugurated trans-Atlantic cheap fare Skytrain.

ENGINEERING

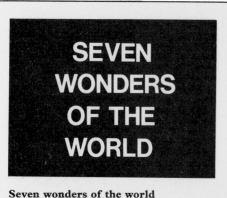

SEVEN
WONDERS
OF THE
WORLD

Seven wonders of the world

The seven Wonders of the World were first designated by Antipater of Sidon in the second century AD. They are, or were:

	Name	Location	Built (circa)	Fate
1.	Three Pyramids of Gîza (El Gîzeh)*	near El Gîzeh, Egypt	from 2580 BC	still stand
2.	Hanging Gardens of Semiramis, Babylon	Babylon, Iraq.	600 BC	no trace
3.	Statue of Zeus (Jupiter) by Phidias	Olympia, Greece	post 432 BC	destroyed by fire
4.	Temple of Artemis (Diana) of the Ephesians	Ephesus, Turkey	ante 350 BC	destroyed by Goths AD 262
5.	Tomb of King Mausolus of Caria	Halicarnassus, (now Bodrum), Turkey	post 353 BC	fragments survive
6.	Statue of Helios (Apollo) by Chares of Lindus, called the Colossus of Rhodes (117 ft 36 m tall).	Rhodes, Aegean Sea	292–280 BC	destroyed by earthquakes 224 BC
7.	Lighthouse (400 ft 122 m) on island of Pharos	off Alexandria, Egypt	200 BC	destroyed by earthquakes AD 400 and 1375

* Built by the Fourth Dynasty Pharaohs, Hwfw (Khufu or Cheops), Kha-f-Ra (Khafre or Khefren) and Menkaure (Mycerinus). The Great pyramid ('Horizon of Khufu') originally had a height of 480 ft 11 in *147 m* (now, since the loss of its topmost stone or pyramidion, reduced to 449 ft 6 in *137 m*), Khafre's pyramid was 470 ft 9 in *143 m*, and Menkaure's was 218 ft *66 m* tall.

The world's tallest inhabited buildings

Height (ft)	Height (m)	No of stories	Building	Location
1454	443	110	Sears Tower (1974)	Wacker Drive, Chicago, Illinois
1350	381	110	World Trade Centre (1973)	Barclay and Liberty Sts, New York City
1250	412	102	Empire State Building (1930)*	5th Av and 34th St, New York City
1136	346	80	Standard Oil Building (1973)	Chicago, Ilinois
1127	343	100	John Hancock Center (1968)	Chicago, Ilinois
1046	319	77	Chrysler Building (1930)	Lexington Av and 42nd St, New York City
950	290	67	60 Wall Tower	70 Pine St, New York City
935	285	72	First Canadian Place, (1977)	Toronto, Ontario
927	282	71	40 Wall Tower	New York City
914	279	59	First National City Corp (†1977)	New York City
900	274	71	Bank of Manhattan	40 Wall St, New York City
859	262	74	Water Tower Plaza (1975)	Chicago, Illinois
858	261	62	United California Bank (1974)	Los Angeles, California
853	259	48	Transamerica Pyramid	San Francisco, California
850	259	60	First National Bank of Chicago (1969)	Chicago, Illinois
850	259	70	RCA Building	Rockefeller Centre, 5th Av, New York City
841	256	64	US Steel Building (1971)	Pittsburg, Pennsylvania
813	248	60	Chase Manhattan Building	Liberty St and Nassau St, New York City
808	246	59	Pan American Building (1963)	Park Av, and 43rd St, New York City
800	243	64	MLC Office Tower (1977)	Sydney, Australia
792	241	60	Woolworth Building (1911–13)	233 Broadway, New York City
790	241	60	John Hancock Tower	Boston, Mass
787	240	28	Mikhail Lomonosov University	Moscow, USSR
784	238	57	Commerce Court	Toronto, Ontario
778	237	52	Bank of America	San Francisco, California
764	232	57	One Penn Plaza	New York City
756	230	33	Palace of Culture and Science	Warsaw, Poland
750	228	52	Prudential Tower	Boston, Mass
750	228	54	Exxon Building, 6th Av.	New York City

* The Empire State Building was completed in 1930 to a height of 1250 ft. Between 27 July 1950 and 1 May 1951 a 222 ft TV tower was added.
† Under construction

Bridges

Cantilever Bridges
The term cantilever came in only in 1883 (from *cant* and *lever*, an inclined or projecting lever). The earlier bridges of this type were termed Gerber bridges from Heinrich Gerber, engineer, of the 425 ft *129,5 m* Hassfurt am Main, Germany, bridge completed in 1867.

Length (ft)	Length (m)	Name	Completion	Location
1800	548,6	*Quebec	1917	St Lawrence, Canada
1710	521,2	*Firth of Forth	1889	Firth of Forth, Scotland
1644	501,0	Delaware River	1971	Chester, Pennsylvania, USA
1575	480,0	Greater New Orleans	1958	Algiers, Mississippi River, Louisiana, USA
1500	457,2	Howrah	1943	Calcutta, India
1400	426,7	Transbay (Oakland)	1936	San Francisco, California, USA
1250	381,0	Yokohama	1954	Yokohama, Japan
1235	376,4	Baton Rouge	1968	Mississippi River, Louisiana, USA
1212	369,4	Nyack–Tarrytown (Tappen Zee)	1955	Hudson River, NY, USA
1200	365,7	Longview	1930	Columbia River, Washington, USA
1182	360,2	Queensboro	1909	East River, NY City, USA
1164	354,7	Muscaline	1892	Mississippi River, Louisiana, USA
1160	353,5	Savanna–Sabvia	1932	Mississippi River, Illinois, USA
1100	335,2	†Carquinez Strait	1927	nr San Francisco, California, USA
1100	335,2	New Narrows	1959	Burrard Inlet, Vancouver, BC, Canada

* Rail bridge.   † New parallel bridge completed 1958.

Steel Arch Bridges
Steel was first used in bridge construction in 1828 (Danube Canal bridge, Vienna) but the first all-steel bridge was not built until the Chicago and Alton Railway Bridge over the Missouri at Glasgow, South Dakota, USA, in 1878. The longest concrete arch bridge is the Gladesville Bridge, Sydney, Australia, with a span of 1000 ft *304 m*.

Length (ft)	Length (m)	Name	Year of completion	Location
1700	518,2	New River Gorge	1977	Fayetteville, West Virginia, USA
1652	503,5	Bayonne (Kill Van Kull)	1931	Bayonne, NJ–Staten Is, NY, USA
1650	502,9	Sydney Harbour	1932	Sydney, Australia
1255	382,5	Fremont	1971	Portland, Oregon, USA
1200	365,7	Port Mann	1964	Vancouver, BC, Canada
1128	343,8	Thatcher Ferry	1962	Balboa, Panama
1100	335,2	Laviolette	1967	Trois-Rivières, Quebec, Canada
1090	332,2	Zdakov	1967	Vltava River, Czechoslovakia
1082	330,0	Runcorn–Widnes	1961	Runcorn, Cheshire–Widnes, Lancashire, England
1080	329,2	Birchenough	1935	Sabi River, Rhodesia

Suspension Bridges
The suspension principle was introduced in 1741 with a 70 ft *21 m* span iron bridge over the Tees, England. Ever since 1816 the world's largest span bridges have been of this construction except for the reign of the Forth Bridge (1889–1917) and Quebec Bridge (1917–29).

Length (ft)	Length (m)	Name	Year of completion	Location
5840	1780	*Akashi-Kaikyo	1988	Honshu–Shikoku, Japan
4626	1410	*Humber Estuary Bridge	1979	Humber, England
4260	1298	Verrazano–Narrows (6 lanes)	1964	Brooklyn–Staten Is, USA
4200	1280	Golden Gate	1937	San Francisco Bay, USA
3800	1158	Mackinac Straits	1957	Straits of Mackinac, Mich, USA
3524	1074	Atatürk Bridge	1973	Bosphorus, Istanbul, Turkey
3500	1067	George Washington (2 decks, each 7 lanes since 1962)	1931	Hudson River, NY City, USA
3323	1013	Ponte do 25 Abril (Tagus) (2 lanes and rail)	1966	Lisbon, Portugal
3300	1006	Firth of Forth Road Bridge	1964	Firth of Forth, Scotland
3240	988	Severn–Wye River (4 lanes)	1966	Severn Estuary, England
2800	853	Tacoma Narrows II	1952	Washington, USA
2336	712	Angostura	1967	Ciudad Bolívar, Venezuela
2336	712	Kanmon Straits	1973	Shimonoseki, Japan
2310	704	Transbay (2 spans)	1936	San Francisco–Oakland, Calif, USA
2300	701	Bronx–Whitestone (Belt Parkway)	1939	East River, NY City, USA
2190	668	Pierre Laporte Bridge	1970	Quebec, City, Canada
2150	655	Delaware Memorial I	1951	Wilmington, Delaware, USA
2150	655	Delaware Memorial II	1968	Wilmington, Delaware, USA
2000	610	Melville Gaspipe	1951	Atchafalaya River, Louisiana, USA
2000	610	Walt Whiteman	1957	Philadelphia, Pennsylvania, USA
1995	608	Tancarville	1959	Seine, Le Havre, France
1968	600	Lillebaelt	1970	Lillebaelt, Denmark

* Under construction.

Longest Bridging

Length (miles)	Length (km)	Name	Date Built	Location
23·87	38,422	Lake Pontchartrain Causeway II	1969	Mandeville–Jefferson, Louisiana, USA
23·83	38,352	Lake Pontchartrain Causeway I	1956	Mandeville–Jefferson, Louisiana, USA
17·65	28,400	Chesapeake Bay Bridge-Tunnel	1964	Delmarva Peninsula–Norfolk, Virginia, USA
15·0	24,5	Sunshine Skyway	1954	Lower Tampa Bay, Florida, USA
11·85*	19,070	Great Salt Lake Viaduct (Lucin cut-off)	1904	Great Salt Lake, Utah, USA
8·7	13,9	Ponte Presidente Costa e Silva	1974	Niteroi, Brazil
8·0	12,9	Chesapeake Bay I	1952	Virginia, USA
8·0	12,9	Chesapeake Bay II	1972	Virginia, USA
7·0	11,27	San Mateo–Hayward	1967	San Francisco, California, USA

Other notable bridging

Length (miles)	Length (km)	Name	Date Built	Location
4·2	6,8	Nanking	1968–9	Yangtze Kiang, China
3·77	6,06	Oeland	1972	Sweden
3·75	6,03	London Bridge–Deptford Creek (878 brick arches)	1836	London
3·5	5,63	North Beveland to Schouwen Duiveland (52 arches)	1966	Netherlands
3·12	5,02	Eastern Scheldt	1965	Netherlands
2·28*	3,67	Lower Zambezi (46 spans)	1934	Dona Ana–Vila de Sena, Mozambique
2·24*	3,60	Lake of Venice (222 arches)	1846	Mestre–Venice, Italy
2·21*	3,55	New Tay Bridge (85 spans)	1887	Wormit, Fife–Dundee, Angus, Scotland
1·99	3,20	Storstrom (3 arches, 51 piers)	1937	Sjaelland–Falster, Denmark
1·9	3,1	Upper Sone	1900	Sone River, India

* Rail viaduct.

Canals

A canal, from the Latin *canalis*—a water channel—is an artificial channel used for purposes of drainage, irrigation, water supply, navigation or a combination of these purposes.

Navigation canals were originally only for specially designed barges, but were later constructed for sea-going vessels. This important latter category consists either of improved barge canals or, since the pioneering of the Suez in 1859–69, canals specially constructed for ocean-going vessels.

The world's major deep-draught ship canals (of at least 5 m or 16·4 ft depth) in order of length

Length of Waterway (miles)	Length of Waterway (km)	Name	Year Opened	Minimum Depth (ft)	Minimum Depth (m)	No of Locks	Achievement and Notes
141	227	White Sea (Beloye More)–Baltic (formerly Stalin) Canal	1933	16·5	5,0	19	Links the Barents Sea and White Sea to the Baltic with a chain of a lake, canalised river, and 32 miles *51,5 km* of canal.
100·6	162	Suez Canal	1869	39·3	12,9	Nil	Eliminates the necessity for 'rounding the Cape'. Deepening in progress.
62·2	100	V I Lenin Volga–Don Canal	1952	—	—	13	Interconnects Black, Azov and Caspian Seas.
60·9	98	North Sea (or Kiel) Canal	1895	45	13,7	2	Shortens the North-Sea-Baltic passage; south German–Danish border. Major reconstruction 1914.
56·7	91	Houston (Texas) Canal	1940	34	10,4	Nil	Makes Houston, although 50 miles from the coast, the United States' eighth busiest port.

DEEP DRAUGHT SHIP CANALS continued

Length of Waterway (miles)	Length of Waterway (km)	Name	Year Opened	Minimum Depth (ft)	Minimum Depth (m)	No of Locks	Achievement and Notes
53	85	Alphonse XIII Canal	1926	25	7,6	13	Makes sea access to Seville safe. True canal only 4 miles 6,4 km in length.
50·71	82	Panama Canal	1914	41	12,5	6	Eliminates the necessity for 'rounding the Horn'. 49 miles 78,9 km of the length was excavated.
39·7	64	Manchester Ship Canal	1894	28	8,5	4	Makes Manchester, although 54 miles 86,9 km from the open sea, Britain's third busiest port.
28·0	45	Welland Canal	1931	29	8,8	7	Circumvents Niagara Falls and Niagara River rapids.
19·8	32	Brussels or Rupel Sea Canal	1922	21·0	6,4	4	Makes Brussels an inland port.

Notes: (1) The Volga–Baltic canal system runs 1850 miles *2300 km* from Leningrad *via* Lake Ladoga, Gor'kiy, Kuybysev and the Volga River to Astrakhan. The Grand Canal of China, completed in the 13th century over a length of 1107 miles *1780 km* from Peking to Hangchou had silted up to a maximum depth of 6 ft *1,8 m* by 1950 but is now being reconstructed.

(2) The world's longest inland navigation route is the St Lawrence Seaway of 2342 miles *3769 km* from the North Atlantic up the St Lawrence estuary and across the Great Lakes to Duluth, Minnesota, USA. It was opened on 26 Apr. 1959.

World's tallest structures

Height (ft)	Height (m)	Structure	Location
2120	646	Warszawa Radio Mast (May 1974)	Konstantynow, nr Plock, Poland
2063	629	KTHI-TV (December 1963)	Fargo, North Dakota, USA
1815	553	CN Tower, Metro Centre (April 1975)	Toronto, Canada
1762	537	Ostankino TV Tower (1967) (4 m added in 1973)	near Moscow, USSR
1749	533	WRBL-TV & WTVM (May 1962)	Columbus, Georgia, USA
1749	533	WBIR-TV (September 1963)	Knoxville, Tennessee, USA
1673	510	KFVS-TV (June 1960)	Cape Girardeau, Missouri, USA
1638	499	WPSD-TV	Paducah, Kentucky, USA
1619	493	WGAN-TV (September 1959)	Portland, Maine, USA
1610*	490	KSWS-TV (December 1956)	Roswell, New Mexico, USA
1600	487	WKY-TV	Oklahoma City, Okla, USA
1572	479	KW-TV (November 1954)	Oklahoma City, Okla, USA
1521	463	BREN Tower (unshielded atomic reactor) (April 1962)	Nevada, USA

Other tall structures

Height (ft)	Height (m)	Structure	Location
1345	410	Danish Govt Navigation Mast	Greenland
1312	399	Peking Radio Mast	Peking, China
1272†	387	Anglia TV Mast (1965–September 1967)	Belmont, Lincolnshire
1271	387	Tower Zero	North West Cape, W Australia
1253	382	Lopik Radio Mast	Netherlands
1251	381	International Nickel Co Chimney (1970)	Sudbury, Ontario, Canada
1206	368	Mitchell Power Station chimney (1969)	Cresap, West Virginia, USA
1212	369	Thule Radio Mast (1953)	Thule, Greenland
1200	366	Kennecott Copper Corp chimney (1975)	Magna, Utah, USA
1093	333	CHTV Channel II Mast	Hamilton, Ontario, Canada
1092	332	Tokyo Television Mast	Tokyo, Japan
1080	329	IBA Transmitter Tower (September 1971)	Emley Moor, West Yorkshire
1060	323	Leningrad TV Mast	Leningrad, USSR
1052	320	La Tour Eiffel (1887–9)	Paris, France

* Fell in a gale, 1960; re-erected.
† Highest structure in Great Britain.

Tallest Smokestacks and Towers in the United Kingdom

Height (ft)	Height (m)	Building	Location
850	259	Drax Power Station	Drax, Yorkshire
800	244	Grain Power Station	Isle of Grain, Kent
700	213	Pembroke Power Station	Pembroke, Pembrokeshire
669	204	Littlebrook 'D'	Dartford, Kent
650	198	Eggbrough Power Station (1 chimney)	Eggbrough, Yorkshire
650	198	Ferrybridge 'C' Power Station (2 chimneys) (1 completed, 1966)	Ferrybridge, Yorkshire
650	198	Ironbridge 'B' Power Station (1 chimney)	Ironbridge, Shropshire
650	198	Kingsnorth Power Station (1 chimney)	Kingsnorth, Kent
650	198	Fawley Power Station (1 chimney)	Fawley, Hampshire
c. 650	c. 198	West Fife Power Station (2 chimneys)	West Fife
619	188	GPO Tower (1963)	Cleveland Mews, London, W1
600	182	West Burton Power Station (2 chimneys)	West Burton, Nottinghamshire
550	167	Blyth 'B' Power Station (2 chimneys)	Blyth, Northumberland
550	167	Drakelow 'C' Power Station (2 chimneys)	Drakelow, Repton, Derbyshire
550	167	Tilbury 'B' Power Station (2 chimneys)	Tilbury, Essex

Other tall structures

Height (ft)	Height (m)	Building	Location
600	183	National Westminster Bank (1971–1977)	Old Broad Street—Bishopsgate, London
533	162	Humber Estuary Bridge Towers	
450	137	St. John's Beacon	Liverpool
404	123	Salisbury Cathedral (1334–65)	Salisbury, Wiltshire
399	121	Co-operative Insurance Society Building (1962) (tallest inhabited)	Miller Street, Manchester
387	118	Vickers Building (1959–63)	Millbank, London
385	117	Centre Point (1966)	St Giles Circus, London
370	112	Forth Rail Bridge (1882–90)	Firth of Forth, Scotland

Note: The 474 ft Townsend's stack, Port Dundas, Glasgow (1857–9) was demolished in 1928. The 455 ft Tennant's Stalk, St Rollox, Glasgow (1841–2) has also been demolished. No power stations of or below 400 ft are listed. Battersea Power Station, London, is 337 ft.

TALL STRUCTURES IN UK *continued*

Height (ft)	Height (m)	Building	Location
365	111	St Paul's Cathedral (1675–1710)	London
343	104	Shell Upstream Tower (1957–61)	South Bank, London
340	103	Victoria Tower (1840–67)	Palace of Westminster, London
328	100	Hilton Hotel (1960–63)	Park Lane, London
327	99	Portland House	Victoria, London

World's highest dams

Name	River	Country	Completion	Height (ft)	Height (m)
Nurek	Vakhsh	USSR	1979	1017	310
Grand Dixence	Dixence-Rhôde	Switzerland	1961	932	284
Ingurskaya	Inguri	USSR	Building	892	271
Vajont	Piave	Italy	1961	858	262
Mica	Columbia	Canada	Building	794	242
Sayany	Yeniseyi	USSR	Building	794	242
Chivor	Bata	Colombia	1975	778	237
Mauvoisin	Rhône	Switzerland	1957	777	237
Oroville	Feather-Sacramento	USA	1968	770	235
Chirkyi	Sulak-Caspian Sea	USSR	1975	764	233
Chicoasen	Grijalva	Mexico	1980	761	231

Longest non-vehicular tunnels

Miles	km		Location
105	168,9	Delaware Aqueduct 1937–44	New York State, USA
51·2	82,42	Orange-Fish Irrigation 1974	South Africa
44	70,8	West Delaware 1960	New York City, USA
31	50	Central Outfall 1975	Mexico City, Mexico
29·8	48	Arpa-Sevan hydro-electric u.c.	Armenia, USSR
18·8	30,3	Thames-Lea Water Supply 1960	Hampton-Walthamstow, London
18·1	29,1	Shandfaken Aqueduct 1923	Catskill, New York State
18·0	29	San Jacinto Aqueduct 1938	California, USA
17·7	28,5	Rendalen hydro-electric u.c.	Norway
17·5	28,2	Kielder Aqueduct 1980	Tyne-Tees, England
15	24,1	Lochaber-hydro-electric 1930	Ben Nevis, Scotland
13·7	22	Third Water Tunnel 1970–7	New York City, USA
13	20,9	Florence Lake Tunnel 1925	California, USA
13	20,9	Continental Divide Tunnel 1946	Colorado, USA
12	20	Ely-Ouse 1969	Cambridgeshire, England

World's longest vehicular tunnels

Miles	km		Location
33·49	53,9	Seikan (rail) 1972–82	Tsugaru Channel, Japan
17·30	27,84	Northern Line (Tube) 1939	East Finchley-Morden, London
12·31	19,82	Simplon II (rail) 1918–22	Brigue, Switzerland-Iselle, Italy
12·30	19,80	Simplon I (rail) 1898–1906	Brigue, Switzerland-Iselle, Italy
11·6	18,7	Shin-Kanmon (rail) 1975	Kanmon Strait, Japan
11·49	18,49	Great Appennine (rail) 1923–34	Vernio, Italy
10·1	16,3	St Gotthard (road) 1971–78	Goschenen-Airolo, Switzerland
10·00	16,0	Rokko (rail)	Japan
9·85	15,8	Henderson (rail) 1975	Rocky Mts, Colorado, USA
9·26	14,9	St Gotthard (rail) 1872–82	Göschenen-Airolo-Switzerland
9·03	14,5	Lötschberg (rail) 1906–13	Kandersteg-Goppenstein, Switzerland
8·61	13,85	Hokkuriku (rail) 1957–62	Tsuruga-Imajo-Japan
8·5	13,6	Mont Cenis (rail extension) (1857–81)	Modane, France-Bardonecchia, Italy
7·78	12,52	Cascade (rail) 1925–29	Berne-Senic, Washington, USA
7·27	11,69	Mont Blanc (road) 1959–65	Pèlerins, France-Entrèves, Italy

World's most massive earth and rock dams

Name	Volume (millions of cubic yards)	Volume (millions of cubic metres)
New Cornelia Tailings, Arizona (1973)	274·0	209,4
Tarbela, Indus, Pakistan (1975)	186·0	142,2
Fort Peck, Missouri, Montana, USA (1940)	125·6	96,0
Oahe, Missouri, S Dakota, USA (1963)	92·0	70,0
Mangla, Jhelum, Pakistan (1967)	85·8	65,6
Gardiner, South Saskatchewan, Canada (1968)	85.7	65,5
Afsluitdijk, Netherlands	82·9	63,3
Oroville, Feather, Calif, USA	78·0	60,0
San Luis, Calif, USA	77·6	59,3
Nurek, Vakhsh, Tadjikistan, USSR†	76·0	58,0
Garrison, Missouri, N Dakota, USA (1956)	66·5	50,8
Cochiti, USA	64·6	49,3
Tabka, Syria	60·1	45,9
Kiev, Dnieper, Ukraine, USSR (1964)	57·5	44,0
W A C Bennett (formerly Portage Mt) Peace River, BC, Canada (1968)	57·2	43,7
Aswan High Dam, (Sadd-el-Aali), Nile river, Egypt	57·2	43,7

† Under construction.

World's greatest man-made lakes
Name of Dam

Name of Dam	Capacity miles³	Capacity km³
Owen Falls, Uganda (1964)	48·5	202
Bratsk, Angara River, USSR (1964)	40·59	169,2
Aswan High Dam (Sadd-el-Aali), Nile, Egypt (1970)	39·36	164
Kariba, Rhodesia-Zambia (1959)	38·38	160
Akosombo, Volta, Ghana (1965)††	35·5	148
Daniel Johnson, Manicouagan, Quebec, Canada (1968)	34·07	142
Krasnoyarsk, Yeniseyi, USSR	17·58	73,3
WAC Bennett (Portage Mt) Peace River, BC, Canada (1967)	16·79	70
Zeya, E Siberia, USSR†	16·41	68,4
Wadi Tharthar, Tigris, Iraq (1956)	16	67
Ust-Ilim, Angara, USSR†	14·23	59,3
V I Lenin, Volga, USSR (1953)	13·68	57

    * Comprising also Jari and Soukion dams.
    † Under construction.
    †† Lake Volta, Ghana is the largest artificial lake measured by area (3275 miles² *8482 km²*).
    Note: Owen Falls Dam regulates the natural Victoria Nyanza which is the world's third largest by area.

INVENTIONS

The invention and discovery of drugs, explosives and musical instruments are treated separately (see Index)

Object	Year	Inventor	Notes
Adding Machine	1623	Wilhelm Schickard (Ger)	Earliest commercial machine invented by William Burroughs (US) in St Louis, Missouri, in 1885
Aeroplane	1903	Orville (1871–1948) and Wilbur Wright (1867–1912) (US)	Kitty Hawk, North Carolina (17 Dec.)
Airship (non-rigid)	1852	Henri Giffard (Fr) (1825–82)	Steam-powered propeller, near Paris (24 Sept.)
(rigid)	1900	Graf Ferdinand von Zeppelin (Ger) (1838–1917)	Bodensee (2 July)
Bakelite	1907	Leo H Baekeland (Belg/US) (1863–1944)	Getafe, Spain (9 Jan.) First use, electrical insulation by Loando & Co, Boonton, New Jersey
Balloon	1783	Jacques (1745–99) and Joseph Montgolfier (1740–1810) (Fr)	Tethered flight, Paris (15 Oct.) manned free flight, Paris, (21 Nov.) by François de Rozier and Marquis d'Arlandes. Father Bartolomeu de Gusmão (*né* Lourenço) (b. Brazil, 1685) demonstrated hot air balloon in Portugal on 8 Aug. 1709
Ball-Point Pen	1888	John J Loud (US)	First practical models by Lazlo and Georg Biro (Hungary) in 1938
Barbed Wire	1867	Lucien B Smith (patentee) (25 June)	Introduced to Britain in 1880 by 5th Earl Spencer in Leicestershire
Barometer	1644	Evangelista Torricelli (It) (1608–47)	Referred to in a letter of 11 June
Bicycle	1839–40	Kirkpatrick Macmillan (Scot) (1810–78)	Pedal-driven cranks. First direct drive in March 1861 by Ernest Michaux (Fr)

Object	Year	Inventor	Notes
Bicycle Tyres (pneumatic)	1888	John Boyd Dunlop (GB) (1840–1921)	Principle patented but undeveloped by Robert William Thomson (GB), 10 June 1845. First motor car pneumatic tyres adapted by André and Edouard Michelin (Fr) 1895 (see Rubber tyres)
Bifocal Lens	1780	Benjamin Franklin (1706–90) (US)	His earliest experiments began c. 1760
Bronze (copper with tin) Working	c. 2800 BC	SW Asia and Mediterranean	Copper smelting with arsenical ores was practised earlier
Bunsen Burner	1855	Robert Willhelm von Bunsen (1811–99) (Ger) at Heidelberg	Michael Faraday (1791–1867) (UK) had previously designed an adjustable burner
Burglar Alarm	1858	Edwin T Holmes (US)	Electric installed, Boston, Mass (21 Feb.)
Car (steam)	c. 1769	Nicolas Cugnot (Fr) (1725–1804)	Three-wheeled military tractor. Oldest surviving is Italian Bordino (1854) in Turin
(petrol)	1888	Karl Benz (Ger) (1844–1929)	First run Mannheim Nov. or Dec. Patented 29 Jan. 1886. First powered hand cart with internal combustion engine was by Siegfried Marcus (Austria), c. (1864)
Carburettor	1876	Gottlieb Daimler (Ger) (1834–1900)	Carburettor spray: Charles E Duryea (US) (1892)
Carpet Sweeper	1876	Melville R Bissell (US)	Grand Rapids, Mich (Patent, 19 Sept.)
Cash Register	1879	James Ritty (US) (Patent 4 Nov.)	Built in Dayton, Ohio. Taken over by National Cash Register Co 1884
Cellophane	1908	Dr Jacques Brandenberger (Switz), Zurich	Machine production not before 1911
Celluloid	1861	Alexander Parkes (GB) (1813–90)	Invented in Birmingham, Eng; developed and trade marked by J W Hyatt (US) in 1870
Cement	1824	Joseph Aspdin (GB)	Wakefield, Yorkshire (21 Oct.)
Chronometer	1735	John Harrison (GB) (1693–1776)	Received in 1772 Government's £20 000 prize on offer since 1714
Cinema	1895	Auguste Marie Louis Nicolas Lumière (1862–1954) and Louis Jean Lumière (1864–1948) (Fr)	Development pioneers were Etienne Jules Marey (Fr) (1830–1903) and Thomas A Edison (US) (1847–1931). First public showing, Blvd. des Capucines, Paris (28 Dec.)
Clock (mechanical)	725	I-Hsing and Liang Ling-Tsan (China)	Earliest escapement, 600 years before Europe
(pendulum)	1656	Christaan Huygens (Neth) (1629–95)	
Copper working	c. 4500 BC	Earliest smelting sites	Iran and Israel
Dental Plate	1817	Anthony A Plantson (US) (1774–1837)	
Dental Plate (rubber)	1855	Charles Goodyear (US) (1854–1921)	
Diesel Engine	1895	Rudolf Diesel (Ger) (1858–1913)	Lower pressure oil engine patent by Stuart Akroyd, 1890. Diesel's first commercial success, Augsberg, 1897
Disc Brake	1902	Dr F Lanchester (GB)	First used on aircraft 1953 (Dunlop Rubber Co)
Dynamo	1832	Hypolite Pixii (Fr), demonstrated, Paris 3 Sept.	Rotative dynamo, demonstrated by Joseph Saxton, Cambridge, England June 1833
Electric Blanket	1883	Exhibited Vienna, Austria Exhibition	
Electric Flat Iron	1882	H W Seeley (US)	New York City, USA (Patent 6 June)
Electric Lamp	1879	Thomas Alva Edison (US) (1847–1931)	First practical demonstration at Menlo Park, New Jersey, USA, 20 Dec.
Electric motor (DC)	1873	Zénobe Gramme (Belg) (1826–1901)	Exhibited in Vienna. Patent by Thomas Davenport (US) of Vermont, 25 Feb. 1837
Electric motor (AC)	1888	Nikola Tesla (US) (1856–1943)	
Electromagnet	1824	William Sturgeon (GB) (b. 1783)	Improved by Joseph Henry (US), 1831
Electronic Computer	1942	J G Brainerd, J P Eckert, J W Mauchly (US)	ENIAC (Electronic numerical integrator and calculator), University of Pennsylvania, Philadelphia, USA. Point-contact transistor announced by John Bardeen and Walter Brattain, July 1948. Junction transistor announced by R. L. Wallace, Morgan Sparks and Dr. William Shockley in early 1951.
Film (moving outlines)	1885	Louis le Prince	Institute for the Deaf, Washington Hts, NY, USA
(musical sound)	1923	Dr Lee de Forest (US)	New York demonstration (13 Mar.)
(talking)	1926	Warner Bros. (US)	First release *Don Juan*, Warner Theatre, New York (5 Aug.)
Fountain Pen	1884	Lewis E Waterman (US) (1837–1901)	Patented by D Hyde (US), 1830, undeveloped
Gas Lighting	1792	William Murdock (GB) (1754–1839)	Private house in Cornwall, 1792; Factory Birmingham, 1798; London Streets, 1807
Glass (stained)	c. 1080	Augsberg, Germany	Earliest English, c. 1170, York Minster
Glassware	c. 1500 BC	Egypt and Mesopotamia	Glass blowing Syria, c. 50 BC
Glider	1853	Sir George Cayley (GB) (1773–1857)	Near Brompton Hall, Yorkshire. Passenger possibly John Appleby. Emanuel Swedenborg (1688–1772) sketches dated c. 1714
Gramophone	1878	Thomas Alva Edison (US) (1847–1931)	Hand-cranked cylinder at Menlo Park, NJ. Patent, 19 Feb. First described on 30 Apr 1877 by Charles Cros (1842–88) (Fr)
Gyro-compass	1911	Elmer A Sperry (US) (1860–1930)	Tested on USS *Delaware*, (28 Aug.). Gyroscope devised 1852 by Foucault (Fr)
Helicopter	1924	Etienne Ochmichen (Fr)	First FAI world record set on 14 Apr. 1924. Earliest drawing of principal Le Mans Museum, France c. 1460. First serviceable machine by Igor Sikorsky (US), 1939
Hovercraft	1955	C S Cockerell (GB)	Patented 12 Dec. Earliest air-cushion vehicle patent was in 1877 by J I Thornycroft (1843–1928) (GB). First 'flight' Saunders Roe SR-NI at Cowes, England, 30 May 1959

Object	Year	Inventor	Notes
Iron Working (Carburized iron)	c. 1200 BC	Cyprus and Northern Israel	Introduced into Britain, c. 550 BC
Jet Engine	1937	Sir Frank Whittle (GB) (b. 1907)	First test bed run (12 Apr.). Principles announced by Merconnet (Fr) 1909 and Maxime Guillaume (Fr) 1921. First flight 27 Aug. 1939 by Heinkel He-178
Laser	1960	Dr Charles H Townes (US). First demonstration by Theodore Maiman (US)	Demonstrated at Hughes Research, Malibu, California in July. Abbreviation for Light amplification by stimulated emission of radiation
Launderette	1934	J F Cantrell (US)	Fort Worth, Texas (18 Apr.)
Lift (Mechanical)	1852	Elisha G Otis (US) (1811–61)	Earliest elevator at Yonkers, NY
Lightning Conductor	1752	Benjamin Franklin (US) (1706–90)	Philadelphia, Pennsylvania, USA in Sept.
Linoleum	1860	Frederick Walton (GB)	
Locomotive	1804	Richard Trevithick (GB) (1771–1833)	Penydarren, Wales, 9 miles 14,4 km (21 Feb.)
Loom, power	1785	Edmund Cartwright (GB) (1743–1823)	
Loudspeaker	1900	Horace Short (GB) Patentee in 1898	A compressed air Auxetophone. First used atop the Eiffel Tower, Summer 1900. Earliest open-air electric public address system used by Bell Telephone on Staten Island, NY on 30 June 1916
Machine Gun	1718	James Puckle (GB) patentee, 15 May 1718. White Cron Alley factory in use 1721	Richard Gatling (US) (1818–1903) model dates from 1861
Maps	c. 3800 BC	Sumerian (clay tablets of river Euphrates)	Earliest world map by Eratosthenes c. 220 BC. Earliest printed map printed in Bologna, Italy, 1477
Margarine	1869	Hippolyte Mège-Mouries (Fr)	Patented 15 July
Match, safety	1826	John Walker, (GB) Stockton, Teeside	
Microphone	1876	Alexander Graham Bell (1847–1922) (US)	Name coined 1878 by Prof David Hughes, who gave demonstration in London in January 1878. Compound convex-concave lens.
Microscope	1590	Zacharias Janssen (Neth)	
Motor Cycle	1885	Gottlieb Daimler of Candstatt, Germany, patent 29 Aug.	First rider Paul Daimler (10 Nov. 1885); first woman rider Mrs Edward Butler near Erith, Kent, 1888
Neon Lamp	1910	Georges Claude (Fr) (1871–1960)	First installation at Paris Motor Show (3 Dec.)
Night Club	1843	Paris, France	First was Le Bal des Anglais, Paris 5me. (Closed c. 1960)
Nylon	1937	Dr Wallace H Carothers (US) (1896–1937) at Du Pont Labs, Seaford, Delaware, USA (Patent, 16 Feb.)	First stockings made about 1937. Bristle production 24 Feb. 1938. Yarn production December 1939
Paper	AD 105	Mulberry based fibre, China	Introduced to West via Samarkand, 14th century
Parachute	1797	André-Jacques Garnerin (Fr) (1769–1823)	First descent (from 2230 ft 620 m over Paris, 22 Oct.) Earliest jump from aircraft 1 Mar. 1912 by Albert Berry (US) over St Louis, Missouri, USA
Parchment	c. 1300 BC	Egypt	Modern name from Pergamam, Asia Minor, c. 250 BC
Parking Meter	1935	Carlton C Magee (US)	Oklahoma City (16 July)
Photography (on metal)	1826	J Nicéphore Niépce (Fr) (1765–1833)	Sensitised pewter plate, 8 hr exposure at Chalon-sur-Saône, France
(on paper)	1835	W H Fox Talbot (GB) (1807–1877)	Lacock Abbey, Wiltshire (August)
(on film)	1888	John Carbutt (US)	Kodak by George Eastman (US) (1854–1932), August 1888
Porcelain	851	Earliest report from China	Reached Baghdad c. 800
Potter's Wheel	c. 6500 BC	Asia Minor	Used in Mesopotamia c. 3000 BC
Printing Press	c. 1455	Johann Gutenberg (Ger) (c. 1400–68)	Hand printing known in India in 868
Printing (rotary)	1846	Richard Hoe (US) (1812–86)	Philadelphia Public Ledger rotary printed, 1847
Propellor (ship)	1837	Francis Smith (GB) (1808–74)	
Pyramid	c. 2685 BC	Egypt	Earliest was Zoser step pyramid, Saqqara
Radar	1922	Dr Albert H Taylor and Leo C Young	Radio reflection effect first noted. First harnessed by Dr Rudolph Kühnold, Kiel, Germany 20 Mar. 1934. Word coined in 1940 by Cdr S M Tucker USN
Radio Telegraphy	1864	Dr Mahlon Loomis (US) demonstrated over 14 miles 22 km Bear's Den, Loudoun County, Virginia (October)	First advertised radio broadcast by Prof R A Fessenden (b. Canada, 1868–1932) at Brant Rock, Massachusetts on 24 Dec. 1906
Radio Telegraphy (Transatlantic)	1901	Guglielmo Marconi (It) (1874–1937)	Morse signals from Poldhu, Cornwall, to St John's, Newfoundland (12 Dec.)
Rayon	1883	Sir Joseph Swan (1828–1917) (GB)	Production at Courtauld's Ltd, Coventry, England November 1905. Name 'Rayon' adopted in 1924
Razor (electric)	1931	Col Jacob Schick (US)	First manufactured Stamford, Conn (18 Mar.)
(safety)	1895	King C Gillette (US) Patented 2 Dec. 1901	First throw-away blades. Earliest fixed safety razor by Kampfe
Record (long-playing)	1948	Dr Peter Goldmark (US)	Micro-groove developed in the CBS Research Labs and launched 21 June, so ending the 78 rpm market supremacy
Refrigerator	1850	James Harrison (GB) and Alexander Catlin Twining (US)	Simultaneous development at Rodey Point, Victoria, Australia and in Cleveland, Ohio. Earliest domestic refrigerator 1913 in Chicago, Illinois
Rubber (latex foam)	1928	Dunlop Rubber Co (GB)	Team led by E A Murphy at Fort Dunlop, Birmingham
(tyres)	1846	Thomas Hancock (GB) (1786–1865)	Introduced solid rubber tyres for vehicles (1847) (see also bicycle)
(vulcanised)	1841	Charles Goodyear (US) (1800–60)	
(waterproof)	1823	Charles Macintosh (GB) (1766–1843) Patent	First experiments in Glasgow with James Syme. G. Fox in 1821 had marketed a Gambroon clock of which no detail has survived

Object	Year	Inventor	Notes
Safety Pin	1849	William Hunt (US)	First manufactured New York City, NY (10 Apr.)
Self-Starter	1911	Charles F Kettering (US) (1876–1958)	Developed at Dayton, Ohio, sold to Cadillac
Sewing Machine	1829	Barthélemy Thimmonnier (Fr) (1793–1854)	A patent by Thomas Saint (GB) dated 17 July 1790 for an apparently undeveloped machine was found in 1874. Earliest practical domestic machine by Isaac M Singer (1811–75) of Pittstown, NY, USA, in 1851
Ship (sea-going)	c. 7250 BC	Grecian ships	Traversed from mainland to Melos
(steam)	1775	J C Périer (Fr) (1742–1818)	On the Seine, near Paris. Propulsion achieved on river Saône, France by Marquis d'Abbans, 1783
(turbine)	1894	Hon Sir Charles Parsons (GB) (1854–1931)	SS Turbinia attained 34·5 knots on first trial. Built at Heaton, County Durham.
Silk Manufacture	c. 50 BC	Reeling machines devised, China	Silk mills in Italy c. 1250, world's earliest factories
Skyscraper	1882	William Le Baron Jenny (US)	Home Insurance Co Building, Chicago, Ill, 10 storey (top 4 steel beams)
Slide Rule	1621	William Oughtred (1575–1660) (Eng)	Earliest slide between fixed stock by Robert Bissaker, 1654
Spectacles	1289	Venice, Italy (convex)	Concave lens for myopia not developed till c. 1450
Spinning Frame	1769	Sir Richard Arkwright (GB) (1732–92)	
Spinning Jenny	1764	James Hargreaves (GB) (d. 1778)	
Spinning Mule	1779	Samuel Crompton (GB) (1753–1827)	
Steam Engine	1698	Thomas Savery (GB) (c. 1650–1715)	Recorded on 25 July
Steam Engine (piston)	1712	Thomas Newcomen (GB) (1663–1729)	
Steam Engine (condenser)	1765	James Watt (Scot) (1736–1819)	
Steel Production	1855	Henry Bessemer (GB) (1813–1898)	At St Pancras, London. Cementation of wrought iron bars by charcoal contact known to Chalybes people of Asia minor c. 1400 BC
Steel (stainless)	1913	Harry Brearley (GB)	First cast at Sheffield (Eng) (20 Aug.). Krupp patent, Oct. 1912 for chromium carbon steel; failed to recognise corrosion resistance
Submarine	1776	David Bushnell (US), Saybrook, Conn	Hand propelled screw, one man crew, used off New York. A twelve man wooden and leather submersible devised by Cornelius Drebbel (Neth) demonstrated in Thames in 1624.
Tank	1914	Sir Ernest Swinton (GB) (1868–1951)	Built at Leicester, designed by William Trilton. Tested 8 Sept. 1915
Telegraph	1787	M. Lammond (Fr) demonstrated a working model, Paris	
Telegraph Code	1837	Samuel F B Morse (USA) (1791–1872)	The real credit belonged largely to his assistant Alfred Vail (US) who first transmitted at Morristown, NJ on 8 Jan. 1838
Telephone	1849	Antonio Meucci (It) in Havana, Cuba	Caveat not filed until 1871. Instrument worked imperfectly by electrical impulses
	1876	Alexander Graham Bell (US) (1847–1922) Patented 9 Mar. 1876	First exchange at Boston, Mass, 1878
Telescope	1608	Hans Lippershey (Neth)	(2 Oct.)
Television	1926	John Logie Baird (GB) (1888–1946)	First public demonstration 27 Jan., London, of moving image with gradations of light and shade at 22 Frith Street, London. First successful experiment 30 Oct. 1925. First transmission in colour on 3 July 1928 at 133 Long Acre, London
Terylene	1941	J R Whinfield (1901–1966), J T Dickson (GB) at Accrington, Lancashire	First available 1950, marketed in USA as 'Dacron'
Thermometer	1593	Galileo Galilei (It) (1564–1642)	
Transformer	1831	Michael Faraday (GB)	Built at Royal Institution, London (29 Aug.)
Transistor	1948	John Bardeen, William Shockley and Walter Brattain (US)	Researched at Bell Telephone Laboratories. First application for a patent was by Dr Julius E Lilienfeld in Canada on October 1925 (see Electronic Computer).
Typewriter	1808	Pellegrine Tarri (It)	First practical 27 character keyed machine with carbon paper built in Reggio Emilia, Italy
Washing Machine (electric)	1907	Hurley Machine Co (US)	Marketed under name of 'Thor' in Chicago, Illinois, USA
Watch	1462	Bartholomew Manfredi (It)	Earliest mention of a named watchmaker (November) but in reference to an earlier watchmaker
Water Closet	1589	Designed by Sir John Harington (GB)	Installed at Kelston, near Bath. Built by 'T C' (full name unknown)
Welder (electric)	1877	Elisha Thomson (US) (1853–1937)	
Wheel	c. 330 BC	Sumerian civilisation	Spoked as opposed to solid wheels intro. c. 1900 BC
Windmill	c. 600	Persian corn grinding	Oldest known English port mill, 1191, Bury St Edmunds
Writing	c. 3500 BC	Sumerian civilisation	Earliest evidence found in SE Iran, 1970.
X-Ray	1895	Wilhelm von Röntgen (Ger)	University of Wurzburg (8 Nov.)
Zip Fastener	1891	Whitcomb L Judson (US) Exhibited 1893 at Chicago Exposition	First practical fastener invented in USA by Gideon Sundback (Sweden) in 1913

MEDIA &
COMMUNICATIONS

The Cinema
The milestones of the cinema industry are the first public showing in the Hotel Scribe, Boulevard des Capucines, Paris, on 28 Dec. 1895; and the earliest sound on film motion picture demonstrated in New York City on 13 Mar. 1923.

The leading countries in the production of full-length films (1974 data) are:

India	435
Japan	405
Italy	237
France	234
USSR	162
USA	156

The United Kingdom produced 78 in the year ending 31 Mar. 1974.

Number of cinemas
These figures for 1974 include, where known, mobile cinemas, drive-in cinemas and those only used in certain seasons.[1]

USSR	163 400
USA	14 950
Italy	12 906
India	8946[2]

The United Kingdom had 1535[5], Canada—1434[2], Australia—976[3], New Zealand—194.

Cinema attendances
The highest attendances, by country[1] (1974 data) are:

USSR	4 566 900 000
India	2 424 000 000[2]
Italy	546 100 000
Philippines	318 000 000[4]

Comparative figures include the United Kingdom–138 500 000; Canada–89 000 000[2]; and New Zealand–13 100 000.

But some of the highest attendances per capita per annum are:
USSR 18·1, Singapore 17·8, Hong Kong 14·8, Rwanda 14·6, and Cuba 14·2. By comparison India was 4·1, the United Kingdom 2·5 and Canada 3·9[2].

[1] No data avialable for China.
[2] 1973 data.   [3] 1972 data.
[4] 1975 data.   [5] 1977 data.

Television
The estimated world total of television receivers in 1975 was 363 770 000.

Television receivers by country (1974 data):

USA	121 000 000[1]
USSR	52 500 000
Japan	25 564 000
West Germany	18 920 000
United Kingdom	18 056 058[1]
France	12 335 000
Italy	11 817 000
Brazil	8 650 000
Canada	8 232 000

Other countries include: Australia 3 013 000[2] and New Zealand, 791 000.

[1] 1977 data.   [2] 1973 data.

In the United Kingdom colour receivers constituted 55·1 per cent by March 1977.

Telephones
In 1976 there were 379 524 000 telephones in use in the world.

USA	149 011 000
Japan	45 514 000
United Kingdom	21 035 602
West Germany	19 602 606
USSR	16 949 000
Italy	14 495 677
Canada	13 142 235

Other comparative totals include: Australia—5 266 843 and New Zealand—1 570 784.

The principality of Monaco has the highest availability rate with 84 telephones per 100 inhabitants. Comparative figures include 69·4—USA, 57·15—Canada, 50·18—New Zealand, 39·01—Australia and 37·5—United Kingdom.

Radio
The first advertised broadcast was on 24 Dec. 1906 from Brant Rock, Mass., USA. The first regular broadcast entertainment in the United Kingdom started on 14 Feb. 1922.

The World total of radio sets in 1974 was 922 000 000[1]. In the United States there were 401 600 000 and in the USSR the number was 116 100 000. The next countries in order were: the United Kingdom, 42 000 000; West Germany, 20 909 000; Canada 20 252 000; and Mexico 17 514 000. By comparison New Zealand had 2 700 000.

In 1974 the United States had an ownership ratio of 1·8 sets per inhabitant; the next highest was the US Virgin Islands, 0·93, followed by Bermuda with 0·90 and Canada with 0·89.

[1] No data available for China or Japan.

United Kingdom National Press
The principal national newspapers in order of circulation are:

Name	Year Established	Circulation (Apr.–Sept. 1977)
Morning Newspapers		
Daily Mirror	1903	3 889 457
The Sun (prior to 1964 the		
Daily Herald)	1912	3 793 975
Daily Express	1900	2 310 698
Daily Mail (incorporating the News Chronicle)	1896	1 847 115
Daily Telegraph	1855	1 315 919
The Times	1785	296 809
The Guardian	1821	272 951
Financial Times	1888	175 887
Sunday Newspapers		
News of the World	1843	4 934 284[1]
Sunday Mirror	1915	3 954 642
Sunday People	1881	3 943 465
Sunday Express	1918	3 181 763
Sunday Times	1822	1 324 758
Sunday Post (Glasgow)	1914	[1] [2]
Sunday Mail (Glasgow)	1919	755 670[1]
Sunday Telegraph	1961	802 077
The Observer	1791	662 326
Evening Newspapers		
Evening News	1881	539 689[3]
Evening Standard	1827	390 676[3]
Media Journals		
Radio Times	1923	3 645 603[1]
TV Times	1955	3 489 571[1]

(*Source:* Audit Bureau of Circulations).
[1] January–June 1977.   [2] Over 1 million.
[3] Monday–Friday issues.

World Press
(Source: UNESCO Statistical Yearbook 1975—data for 1974 unless otherwise stated).

The total of daily newspapers published in the world is 8100.

Greatest Number of Daily Papers[1].

USA	1798
India	822
USSR	675
Turkey	450[2]
West Germany	320
Brazil	280[2]
Mexico	249
Japan	180
Indonesia	170
Argentina	167
Canada	121[2]
Spain	115

United Kingdom 109, Australia 58[2], New Zealand 40.

[1] No data available for China.   [2] 1973 data.

Largest total circulation of daily newspapers[1]

USSR	97 664 000
USA	62 156 000
Japan	57 820 000
United Kingdom	24 800 000
West Germany	17 872 000
France	11 458 000[2]
India	9 222 000
Poland	7 994 000
East Germany	7 753 000
Italy	6 963 000
Canada[2]	5 207 000[2]
Australia[2]	5 126 000[2]

In 1974 Sweden had the highest sale rate of 536 per 1000 inhabitants. Other comparable figures include the United Kingdom—443, Australia—386[2], New Zealand—376[3], and Canada—235[2].

[1] No data available for China.
[2] 1973 data.   [3] 1972 data.

INTERNATIONAL ORGANISATIONS

The United Nations

'A general international organisation ... for the maintenance of international peace and security' was recognised as desirable in Clause 4 of the proposals of the Four-Nation Conference of Foreign Ministers signed in Moscow on 30 Oct. 1943 by R Anthony Eden, later the Earl of Avon (1897–1977) (UK), Cordell Hull (1871–1955) (USA), Vyacheslav M Skryabin, *alias* Molotov (USSR), (b. 1893) and Ambassador Foo Ping-Sheung (China).

Ways and means were resolved at the mansion of Dumbarton Oaks, Washington, DC, USA, between 21 Aug. and 7 Oct. 1944. A final step was taken at San Francisco, California, USA between 25 Apr. and 26 June 1945 when delegates of 50 participating states signed the Charter (Poland signed on 15 Oct. 1945). This came into force on 24 Oct. 1945, when the four above-mentioned states, plus France and a majority of the other 46 states, had ratified the Charter. The first regular session was held in London on 10 Jan.–14 Feb. 1946.

Of the 159 *de facto* sovereign states of the world 146 are now in membership plus the two USSR republics of Byelorussia and the Ukraine which have separate membership.

The non-members are:
Andorra
China (Taiwan)
Korea, Republic of
Korea, Democratic People's Republic of
Liechtenstein
Monaco
Nauru
San Marino
South Africa★
Switzerland
Tonga
Vatican City (Holy See)
Western Samoa
★ Credentials rejected on 30 Sept. 1974. Suspended from General Assembly 12 Nov. 1974.

The United Nations' principal organs are:

The General Assembly consisting of all member nations, each with up to five delegates but one vote, and meeting annually in regular sessions with provision for special sessions. The Assembly has seven main committees, on which there is the right of representation by all member nations. These are (1) Political Security, (2) Economic and Financial, (3) Social, Humanitarian and Cultural, (4) Trust and Non-Self-Governing Territories, (5) Administration and Budgetary, (6) Legal, and the Special Political.

The Security Council, consisting of 15 members, each with one representative, of whom there are five permanent members (China, France, UK, USA and USSR) and ten elected members serving a two-year term. Apart from procedural questions, an affirmative majority vote of at least nine must include that of all five permanent members. It is from this stipulation that the so-called veto arises.

The Economic and Social Council, consisting of 54 members elected for three-

year terms, is responsible for carrying out the functions of the General Assembly's second and third Committees, viz. economic, social, educational, health and cultural matters. It had the following Functional Commissions in 1974: (1) Statistical (2) Population (3) Social Development (4) Narcotic Drugs (5) Human Rights (and its sub-commission on the Prevention of Discrimination and the Protection of Minorities) (6) Status of Women. The Council has also established Economic Commissions, as follows: (1) for Europe (ECE), (2) for Asia and the Far East (ESCAP), (3) for Latin America (ECLA), (4) for Africa (ECA) and (5) for Western Asia (ECWA).

The International Court of Justice, comprising 15 Judges (quorum of nine) of different nations, each serving a nine-year term and meeting at 's Gravenhage (The Hague), Netherlands. Only states may be parties in contentious cases. In the event of a party's failing to adhere to a judgment, the other party may have recourse to the Security Council. Judgements are final and without appeal but can be reopened on grounds of a new decisive factor within ten years.

The Secretariat. The principal administrative officer is the Secretary General who is appointed by the General Assembly for a five-year term. This office has been held thus:
Trygve Halvdan Lie (1896–1968) (Norway) 1 Feb. 1946–10 Nov. 1952.
Dag Hjalmar Agne Carl Hammarskjöld (1905–61) (Sweden) 10 Apr. 1953–18 Sept. 1961.
U Maung Thant 1909–1974 (Burma) (acting) 3 Nov. 1961–30 Nov. 1962, (permanent) 30 Nov. 1962–31 Dec. 1971.
Kurt Waldheim (b. 21 Dec. 1918) (Austria) 1 Jan. 1972 (in office).

Agencies in Relationship with the United Nations

There are 14 specialised agencies, which in order of absorption or creation are as follows:

ILO
International Labour Organisation (Headquarters—Geneva). Founded 11 Apr. 1919 in connection with The League of Nations.

Re-established as the senior UN specialised agency, 14 Dec. 1946. Especially concerned with social justice, hours of work, unemployment, wages, industrial sickness, and protection of foreign workers.

FAO
Food and Agriculture Organisation of the United Nations (Headquarters—Rome). Established, 16 Oct. 1945. Became UN agency, 14 Dec. 1946. Objects: to raise levels of nutrition and standards of living; to improve the production and distribution of agricultural products. FAO provides an Intelligence Service on Agriculture, Forestry and Fisheries.

UNESCO
United Nations Educational, Scientific and Cultural Organisation (Headquarters—Paris). Established, 4 Nov. 1946. Objects: to stimulate popular education and the spread of culture, and to diffuse knowledge through all means of mass communication; to further universal respect for justice, the rule of law, human rights, and fundamental freedoms. Became a UN agency, 14 Dec. 1946.

ICAO
International Civil Aviation Organisation (Headquarters—Montreal). Established, 4 Apr. 1947. Objects: to study the problems of international civil aviation; to encourage safety measures and co-ordinate facilities required for safe international flight. A UN agency from 13 May 1947.

IBRD
International Bank For Reconstruction and Development (The World Bank) (Headquarters—Washington). Established, 27 Dec. 1945. Objects: to assist in the reconstruction and development of territories of members by aiding capital investment. Became a UN agency, 15 Nov. 1947. The *International Development Association* Headquarters—Washington) is affiliated to the IBRD. Established 24 Sept. 1960. Object: Making special term loans to less developed countries. Membership limited as in IFC.

IMF
International Monetary Fund (Headquarters—Washington). Established, 27 Dec. 1945. Objects: to promote international monetary co-operation, the expansion of international trade and stability of exchange rates. A UN agency from 15 Nov. 1947.

GATT
General Agreement on Tariffs and Trade (Headquarters—Geneva). Established, 1 Jan. 1948. Objects: to reduce or stabilise customs duties and assist the trade of developing countries. A major advancement of its aims was the establishment of the European Economic Community (EEC) or Common Market by The Treaty of Rome (signed, 2 Mar. 1957).

UPU
Universal Postal Union (Headquarters—Berne, Switzerland). Established, 1 July 1875, became UN specialised agency 1 July 1948. Objects: to unite members in a single postal territory.

E.E.C. MEMBERSHIP STATISTICS

	WEST GERMANY	UK	ITALY	FRANCE	NETHERLANDS	BELGIUM	DENMARK	REPUBLIC OF IRELAND	LUXEM-BOURG
Population	61 832 000	55 962 000	55 810 000	52 786 000	13 653 000	9 801 000	5 059 000	3 127 000	358 000
Area km²	248 577	244 046	301 225	547 026	40 844	30 513	43 069	70 283	2586
Capital	Bonn	London	Rome	Paris	Amsterdam	Brussels	Copenhagen	Dublin	Luxembourg
Capital's Pop (million)	·283	7·379	2·842	2·317	·770	1·075	1·320	·567	·078
Pop Density (per km²)	249	229	185	96	334	321	117	44	138
Av Income per Head ($)	6029	3684	2759	5639	5345	5851	6245	2329	5435
Motor Vehicles (1/1/76)	19 578 252	15 639 000	15 435 963*	17 810 000	3 740 000	2 846 972	1 673 100	567 004	128 479
Telephones per 1000	302	366	246	236	344	272	428	127	397
TV and Radio per 1000	630	1006	435	566	542†	619	637	442	746
Currency	1 Deutsche Mark = 100 Pfennige	£1 = 100 New Pence	1 Lira = 100 Centesimi	1 Franc = 100 Centimes	1 Guilder or florin = 100 Cents	1 Franc = 100 Centimes	1 Krone = 100 Ore	1 Pound = 100 New Pence	1 Franc = 100 Centimes
Merchant Shipping Vessels Owned (grt)	8 517 000	33 157 422	10 136 989	10 745 999	5 679 413	1 358 425	4 478 112	210 000	—
Of Which—Oil Tankers	2 725 000	16 096 000	4 061 000	6 938 000	2 637 000	367 000	2 161 000	6000	—
Crude Steel (tonnes)	40 415 000	19 780 000	21 837 000	21 530 000	4 826 000	11 584 000	558 000	81 000	4 624 000
Housing (Dwellings Completed) (1975)	435 900	322 100	214 700	514 900	120 800	76 500‡	35 500	26 000	3000

* 1974.
† 1972.
‡ Dwellings begun.

WHO
World Health Organisation (Headquarters—Geneva). Established, 7 Apr. 1948. Objects: to promote the attainment by all peoples of the highest possible standard of health. Its services are both advisory and technical. A UN agency from 10 July 1948.

ITU
International Telecommunication Union (Headquarters—Geneva). Founded 17 May 1865; incorporated in the United Nations, 10 Jan. 1949. Objects: to seek the standardisation of procedures concerning greater efficacy of telecommunications and to allocate frequencies.

WMO
World Meteorological Organisation (Headquarters—Geneva). Established 23 Mar. 1950. Objects: to standardise meteorological observations; to secure their publication, and apply the information for the greater safety of aviation and shipping and benefit of agriculture, etc. A UN agency from 20 Dec. 1951.

IFC
International Finance Corporation (Headquarters—Washington). Established 24 July 1956. Objects: to promote the flow of private capital internationally and to stimulate the capital markets. Membership is open only to those countries that are members of the World Bank. A UN agency from 20 Feb. 1957.

IAEA
International Atomic Energy Agency (Headquarters—Vienna). Established 29 July 1957. Objects: to accelerate and enlarge the contribution of non-military atomic energy to peace, health and prosperity. A UN agency from 14 Nov. 1957.

IMCO
Inter-Governmental Maritime Consultative Organisation (Headquarters—London). Established 17 Mar. 1958. Objects: to co-ordinate safety at sea and to secure the freedom of passage. A UN agency from 13 Jan. 1959.

North Atlantic Treaty Organisation —NATO
NATO, an idea first broached by the Secretary of State for External Affairs for Canada on 28 Apr. 1948, came into existence on 4 Apr. 1949 and into force on 24 Aug. 1949 with Belgium, Canada, Denmark, France, Iceland, Italy, Luxembourg, the Netherlands, Norway, Portugal, the United Kingdom and the USA. In February 1952 Greece and Turkey were admitted and West Germany on 5 May 1955 bringing the total of countries to 15. In 1966 France withdrew from NATO's military affairs and the HQ was moved from Paris to Brussels. Greece withdrew her military forces in August 1974.

Organisation for Economic Co-operation and Development (OECD)
Founded as a European body of 30 Sept. 1961 (OEEC) the Organisation after 14 years was reconstituted to embrace other Western countries. It now comprises 24 countries: Australia, Austria, Belgium, Canada, Denmark, Finland, France, Greece, Iceland, Ireland, Italy, Japan, Luxembourg, the Netherlands, New Zealand, Norway, Portugal, Spain, Sweden, Switzerland, Turkey, United Kingdom, USA and West Germany, with Yugoslavia (special status).

Headquarters are in Paris. The aims are to achieve the highest sustainable economic growth and level of employment with a rising standard of living compatible with financial stability.

European Free Trade Association (EFTA)
With the departure of the United Kingdom and Denmark, EFTA comprised six countries viz. Austria, Iceland, Norway, Portugal, Sweden and Switzerland with Finland as an associate member. EFTA was established on 27 Mar. 1961.

The EFTA countries (except Norway) signed a free trade agreement with the EEC on 22 July 1972 and Norway did so on 14 May 1973.

South-East Asia Collective Defence Treaty (Seato)
On 8 Sept. 1954 eight countries (Australia, France, New Zealand, Pakistan, the Philippines, Thailand, United Kingdom and USA) signed a collective defence system on South-East Asia in Manila with the acronym SEATO.

Central Treaty Organisation (Cento)
The Baghdad mutual defence pact between Iraq and Turkey was signed on 24 Feb. 1955. This was joined by the United Kingdom, Pakistan and Iran within nine months and the USA joined the military committee in March 1957. In October 1958 the HQ was transferred to Ankara, Turkey with the post-revolution withdrawal of Iraq in July 1958.

Organisation of African Unity (OAU)
In Addis Ababa, Ethiopia on 25 May 1963, 30 African countries established the organisation for common defence of independence, the elimination of colonialism and co-

The Trusteeship Council administers territories under UN trusteeship. Twelve territories have been under UN trusteeship:

Original Trust Territory	Subsequent Status
Tanganyika (UK)	Independent, 9 Dec. 1961; merged with Zanzibar, 26 Apr. 1964 as Tanzania
Ruanda–Urundi (Belgium)	Two independent states, 1 July 1962
Somaliland (Italy)	Independent, 1 July 1960
Cameroons (UK)	Northern part joined Nigeria, 1 June 1961; southern part joined Cameroon, 1 Oct. 1961
Cameroons (France)	Independent republic of Cameroon, 1 Jan. 1960
Togoland (UK)	United with Gold Coast, to form Ghana, 6 Mar. 1957
Togoland (France)	Independent republic of Togo, 27 Apr. 1960
Western Samoa (NZ)	Independent, 1 Jan. 1962
Nauru (Australia, NZ and UK)	Independent 31 Jan. 1968
Papua New Guinea (Australia)	Self-Government, 1 Dec. 1973
Pacific Islands (USA) comprising the Carolines, Marshalls and Marianas (excepting Guam)	

ordination of economic policies. English and French are recognised as official languages in addition to African languages.

Europe

European Economic Community (EEC or Common Market) was established by the treaty signed in Rome (the Treaty of Rome) on 25 Mar. 1957 by Belgium, France, West Germany, Luxembourg, Italy and the Netherlands (known as The Six). Denmark, the Irish Republic and the United Kingdom became members on 1 Jan. 1973, having signed the Treaty of Accession to the Community on 22 Jan. 1972. On 25 Sept. 1972 a referendum in Norway rejected membership with a vote of 53·5% in a 77·7% poll.

The object was to weld a complete customs union between The Nine (as was forged by 1 July 1968 between The Six) by 1 July 1977. A common transport and external trade policy and co-ordination of financial, commercial, economic and social policy is a future target. Economic and monetary union was scheduled for the end of 1980 and the extension of the Common Agricultural Policy to The Nine by 1 Jan. 1978.

COUNTRIES OF THE WORLD

By the summer of 1977, there were 159 sovereign countries in the world. In this book the United Kingdom has been treated separately and in the pages which follow the salient details of both non-sovereign territories and the 158 other sovereign countries are given.

NON-SOVEREIGN COUNTRIES

The trend towards full national sovereign status has substantially reduced the total number of non-sovereign territories. With a few obvious exceptions these territories now tend to have too small a population and/or resources to sustain statehood.

The non-sovereign territories are divided below into four parts:
- (a) Territories administered by the United Kingdom.
- (b) Territories administered by Australia or New Zealand.
- (c) Territories administered by the United States of America.
- (d) Other non-sovereign territories.

TERRITORIES ADMINISTERED BY THE UNITED KINGDOM (excluding the Channel Islands and the Isle of Man)

Antigua

Location: An island about 20 miles *32 km* to the north-east of Montserrat, in the Leeward Islands, West Indies. The dependencies are Barbuda, 25 miles *40 km* north of Antigua, and Redonda, 25 miles *40 km* west-south-west of Antigua.
Area: 170½ miles² *442 km²* (Antigua 108 miles² *280 km²*, Barbuda 62 miles² *161 km²*, Redonda ½ mile² *1 km²*).
Population: 65 525 (census of 1 Apr. 1970); 70 000 (estimate for 1 July 1975).
Capital: St John's (St John City) (population 21 814 in 1970), on north-west coast.

Belize (formerly British Honduras)

Location: On the east (Caribbean) coast of the Yucatán Peninsula, Central America. Bordered on the north by Mexico, on the west and south by Guatemala.

Area: 8867 miles² *22 965 km²*, including offshore islands (212 miles² *549 km²*).
Population: 119 934 (census of 7 Apr. 1970); 140 000 (UN estimate for mid-1975).
Capital (population, 1973): Belmopan (3500)

Bermuda

Location: The Bermudas (or Somers Islands) are a group of islands in the western North Atlantic Ocean, about 570 miles *917 km* east of Cape Hatteras in North Carolina, USA.
Area: 20·59 miles² *53,3 km²*.
Population: 52 330 (census of 29 Oct. 1970); 56 000 (estimate for 1 July 1975). 20 islands are inhabited.
Capital: Hamilton (population 2060 in 1970), on Bermuda I.

British Antarctic Territory (Constituted 3 Mar. 1962)

Location: Comprises all the land south of latitude 60° south, situated between longitude 20° and 80° west. This includes the South Shetland Islands, the South Orkney Islands, Graham Land and a part of the mainland of Antarctica.
Area: The total area within the sector is about 2 200 000 miles² *5 698 000 km²* of which land (excluding ice-shelves) occupies about 150 000 miles² *388 498 km²*. The South Shetland Is. are about 130 miles² *336 km²* and the South Orkney Is 240 miles² *621 km²*.
Population: There are no permanent inhabitants. The only occupants are scientific workers, of whom UK personnel numbered 79 in the winter of 1972.
Capital: There being no settlements, the Territory is administered from Stanley, Falkland Is (*q.v.*).

British Indian Ocean Territory (Constituted 8 Nov. 1965)

Location: The territory is now confined to the Chagos Archipelago (or Oil Islands) which is 1180 miles *1899 km* northeast of (and formerly administered by) Mauritius. The islands of Aldabra, Farquhar, and Desroches (originally parts of the territory) were restored to the Seychelles when the latter became independent on 29 June 1976.
Area: about 20 miles² *52 km²*
Population: 747 (30 June 1962). The territory has a 'floating' population of contract labourers.

British Virgin Islands

Location and Composition: Comprises the eastern part of the Virgin Islands group (the western part is a US colony), and lies to the east of Puerto Rico, in the West Indies.
Area: About 59 miles² *153 km²* (Tortola 21 miles² *54 km²*, Virgin Gorda 8¼ miles² *21 km²*, Anegada 15 miles² *39 km²*, Jost van Dyke 3¼ miles² *8 km²*).
Population: 10 030 (Tortola 8666, Virgin Gorda 904, Anegada 269, Jost van Dyke 123, others 68) at census of 7 Apr. 1970; 10 500 (1975 estimate).
Capital: Road Town (population 2183 in 1970), on Tortola.

The State of Brunei

Location: On the north-west of the East Indian island of Borneo, completely surrounded on the landward side by Sarawak, a state of Malaysia.
Area: 2226 miles² *5765 km²*.
Population: 136 256 (census of 10 Aug. 1971); 162 000 (estimate for 1 July 1975). Figures exclude transients afloat.

Capital: Bandar Seri Begawan (population 36 987 in 1971).

Canton and Enderbury Islands
Location: In the north of the Phoenix Islands, in the mid-Pacific Ocean.
Area: 27 miles² *70 km²*.
Population: uninhabited.
Status and Government: A condominium, administered jointly by the UK and the USA.

Cayman Islands
Location: A group of three islands, in the Caribbean Sea, south of Cuba. The principal island, Grand Cayman, is 178 miles *286 km* west of Jamaica.
Area: approximately 100 miles² *259 km²* (Grand Cayman 76 miles² *197 km²*, Cayman Brac 14 miles² *36 km²*, Little Cayman 10 miles² *26 km²*).
Population: 10 460 (Grand Cayman 9151, Cayman Brac 1289, Little Cayman 20) at census of 7 Apr. 1970; 13 000 (1975 estimate).
Capital: George Town (population 3975 in 1970).

Dominica
Location: An island about 20 miles *32 km* north of Martinique, in the West Indies.
Area: 289·8 miles² *751 km²*.
Population: 70 302 (census of 7 Apr. 1970); mid-1975 population was 75 000 (UN estimate).
Capital: Roseau (population 10 157 in 1970).

Falkland Islands and Dependencies
Location: A group of islands in the south-western Atlantic Ocean, about 480 miles *772 km* north-east of Cape Horn, South America. The Dependencies are South Georgia, an island 800 miles *1287 km* to the east, and the South Sandwich Islands, 470 miles *756 km* south-east of South Georgia.
Area: approximately 6280 miles² *16 265 km²*, of which the Falklands are approximately 4700 miles² *12 173 km²* (East Falkland and adjacent islands 2610 miles² *6760 km²*, West Falkland, etc., 2090 miles² *5413 km²*). South Georgia is 1450 miles² *3755 km²* and the Sandwich Is 130 miles² *336 km²*.
Population: Falkland Islands 1957 (census of 3 Dec. 1972); 1905 (estimate for 31 Dec. 1975). South Georgia has a small population (499 in 1964) which is highest during the summer whaling season.
Capital: Port Stanley (population 1081 in 1972), on East Falkland.

City of Gibraltar
Location: A narrow peninsula on the south coast of Spain, commanding the north side of the Atlantic entrance to the Mediterranean Sea.
Area: 2¼ miles² *5,8 km²* (2¾ miles *4,4 km* long, greatest breadth nearly 1 mile *1,6 km*).
Population: 26 833 (census of 6 Oct. 1970); 30 000 (estimate for 1 July 1976). Figures exclude armed forces.
Chief (and only) Town: Gibraltar, at north-western corner of the Rock.

Gilbert Islands
Location: A group of 33 atolls within an area of more than 1 600 000 miles² *4 144 000 km²* in the mid-Pacific Ocean. Comprises the Gilbert Isands (16 atolls), Phoenix Islands (8), the Northern Line Islands (3: Washington Is, Fanning Is and Christmas Is), the Central and Southern Line Islands (5) and Ocean Island (Banaba), about 240 miles *386 km* south-west of Tarawa Atoll, Gilbert Islands.
Area: 253 miles² *655 km²* (Gilbert Is

114 miles² *295 km²*, Christmas Island 135 miles² *350 km²*)
Population (Census 8 Dec. 1973): 51 929 (Gilbert Is 47 714, Ocean Is 2314).
Headquarters: A residency on island of Bairiki, in the south of the Tarawa Atoll (population 17 188 in 1973), Gilbert Islands.

Hong Kong
Location: A peninsula in the central south coast of the Kwangtung province of southern China, the island of Hong Kong and some 235 other islands, the largest of which is Lantao (58 miles² *150 km²*).
Area: 404.0 miles² *1046 km²* (Hong Kong Island 29.2 miles² *76 km²* Kowloon peninsula 4.05 miles² *10 km²*, Stonecutters Island ¼ mile² *0,6 km²*, New Territories (leased) 370·5 miles² *960 km²*). Including the ocean area within administrative boundaries, the total is 1126 miles² *2916 km²*.
Population: 3 948 179 (census of 9 March 1971, excluding adjustment underenumeration, estimated at 1·05 %); 4 383 000 (estimate for 30 June 1976). Over 98% are Chinese, many being British subjects by virtue of birth in the Colony.
Languages: mainly Chinese (Cantonese); English 8·5%.
Religion: Predominantly Buddhist.
Capital City and Other Principal Towns (population at Census, 1971): Victoria (520 932), on Hong Kong Island; Kowloon; New Kowloon; North Point; Tsuen Wan; Cheung Chau (an island).
Status and Government: A Crown Colony with the Governor assisted by an Executive Council (14 in 1976) and a Legislative Council (42, including 22 elected, in 1976). There is also an urban council of 26 members (ten elected).
Recent History: British colony, 1841. New Territories leased in 1898 for 99 years. Attacked by Japan, 8 Dec. 1941. Surrendered, 25 Dec. 1941. Recaptured by UK forces, 30 Aug. 1945. UK military administration, 3 Sept. 1945 to May 1946. Formal Japanese surrender, 16 Sept. 1945. Many refugees during Chinese civil war 1948–50, and subsequently, notably on 1–25 May 1962.
Economic Situation: The principal occupations are manufacturing (notably cotton piece goods, shirts, electric products, cameras, toys and games, footwear), services and commerce. Agriculture (poultry and pigs), fishing and mining (notably iron) are carried on.
Currency: 100 cents = 1 Hong Kong dollar (U.S. $1 = H.K.$4.65 in July 1977).
Climate: The sub-tropical summer (82° F July) is hot and humid with the winter cool and dry (59° F February). The average annual rainfall is 85 in, three-quarters of which falls from June to August in the south-west monsoon season.

Montserrat
Location: An island about 35 miles *56 km* north of Basse Terre, Guadeloupe, in the Leeward Islands, West Indies.
Area: 38 miles² *98 km²*.
Population: 11 698 (census of 7 Apr. 1970); 13 291 (estimate for 31 Dec. 1975).
Capital: Plymouth (population 1267 in 1970), on south-west coast.

The Anglo-French Condominium of the New Hebrides (Nouvelles-Hébrides)
Location: In the south-western Pacific Ocean about 500 miles *804 km* west of Fiji. Includes the New Hebrides, Banks Islands and Torres Islands.
Area: Approximately 5700 miles² *14 763 km²*, of which Espiritu Santo Island (Ile Marina) is approximately 1500 miles² *3885 km²*.

Population: 77 988 (census of 28 May 1967); 97 000 (estimate for 31 Dec. 1975).
Administrative Headquarters: Port Vila (Fila) (population 3072 in 1967), on south coast of Efate (Ile Vaté).

Pitcairn Islands Group
Location: Four islands in the south Pacific Ocean, about 3000 miles *4828 km* east of New Zealand and 3500 miles *5632 km* south-west of Panama: Pitcairn, Henderson, Dulcie, Oeno.
Area: 18.5 miles² *48 km²*, including Pitcairn 1.75 miles² *4,5 km²*.
Population: Pitcairn 92 (census of Dec. 1971); 67 (1975 estimate).
Principal settlement: Adamstown.

St Christopher (St Kitts), Nevis and Anguilla
Location: In the northern part of the Leeward Islands, in the West Indies. The main island is St Christopher (or St Kitts), with Nevis 3 miles *5 km* to the south-east, Anguilla (with Scrub I and other offshore islands) 60 miles *96 km* to the north-west and Sombrero 30 miles *48 km* north of Anguilla.
Area: 138 miles² *357 km²* (St Christopher 65 miles² [*168 km²*], Nevis 36 miles² [*93 km²*], Anguilla 35 miles² [*91 km²*], Sombrero 2 miles² [*5 km²*]).
Population: 64 000 (census of 7 Apr. 1970); 66 000 (UN estimate for mid-1975).
Capital: Basse-terre (population 12 771 in 1970), on south coast of St Christopher.

St Helena and Dependencies
Location and Composition: An island in the South Atlantic Ocean, 1200 miles *1931 km* west of Africa. The dependencies are: (a) Ascension, an island 700 miles *1126 km* to the north-west; (b) the Tristan da Cunha group, comprising: Tristan da Cunha, 1320 miles *2124 km* south-west of St Helena; Inaccessible Island, 20 miles *32 km* west of Tristan; the three Nightingale Islands (Nightingale, Middle Island and Stoltenhoff Island), 20 miles *32 km* south of Tristan; Gough Island (Diego Alvarez), 220 miles *354 km* south of Tristan.
Area: 162 miles² *419 km²* (St Helena 47·3 miles² *122 km²*, Ascension 34 miles² *88 km²*, Tristan da Cunha 38 miles² *98 km²*, Gough 35 miles² *90 km²*, Inaccessible 4 miles² *10 km²*, Nightingale ¾ mile² *2 km²*).
Population: St Helena 5147 (census of 31 Oct. 1976); Ascension 1058 (estimate for 31 Dec. 1976); Tristan da Cunha 292 (1975 estimate).
Capital: Jamestown (population 1516 in 1976).
Principal Settlements: Ascension—Georgetown (or Garrison); Tristan da Cunha—Edinburgh.

St Lucia
Location: An island about 20 miles *32 km* south of Martinique in the Windward Islands, West Indies.
Area: 238 miles² *616 km²*.
Population: 100 893 (census of 7 Apr. 1970); 107 000 (estimate for 30 June 1973).
Capital: Castries (40 000).

St Vincent
Location: An island about 25 miles *40 km* south of St Lucia. The colony includes, as dependencies, the St Vincent Grenadines, (main islands Bequia, Canouan, Mustique, Mayreau and Union), the northerly part of a group between St Vincent and Grenada.
Area: 150·3 miles² *389 km²* (St Vincent 133 miles² *344 km²*, Grenadines 17 miles² *44 km²*).
Population: 87 305 (census of 7 Apr. 1970);

127

100 000 (estimate for 31 Dec. 1973).
Capital: Kingstown, population 22 000 (including suburbs) in 1973.

Solomon Islands
Location: In the south-western Pacific Ocean. Comprises the Solomon Islands group to the south of Bougainville (the islands to the north being part of Papua New Guinea) plus the Ontong Java Islands (Lord Howe Atoll), Rennell Island and the Santa Cruz Islands, about 300 miles *483 km* to the east.
Area: 10 983 miles² *28 446 km²*, of which Guadalcanal is about 2 500 miles² *6 475 km²*.
Population: 196 823 (1976 census).
Capital: Honiara (population 14 993 in 1976), on north coast of Guadalcanal.

Turks and Caicos Islands
Location: Two groups of islands at the south-eastern end of the Bahamas, 120 miles *193 km* north of Hispaniola (Haiti and Dominican Republic), in the West Indies. Turks Islands.
Area: 166 miles² *430 km²*.
Population: 5607 (census of 29 Oct. 1970, excluding foreign personnel employed on the three US bases in the islands); 6000 (estimate for 1 July 1975). There are six inhabited islands (two in the Turks Islands, four in the Caicos Islands).
Capital: Cockburn Town, on Grand Turk Island (population 2287 in 1970).

Tuvalu
Location: A group of 9 atolls, formerly called the Ellice (Lagoon) Islands, in the western Pacific Ocean, south of the Gilbert Islands (from which Tuvalu was separated on 1 Oct. 1975).
Area: 9·5 miles² *24,6 km²*.
Population: 5 887 (census of 8 Dec. 1973).
Capital: Funafuti.

TERRITORIES ADMINISTERED BY AUSTRALIA OR NEW ZEALAND

Australian Dependencies

The Australian Antarctic Territory
Location: Comprises all land south of latitude 60° S, between 45° E and 160° E, except for French territory of Terre Adélie, whose boundaries were fixed on 1 Apr. 1938 as between 136° E and 142° E.
Area: 2 333 624 miles² *6 044 058 km²* of land and 29 251 miles² *75 759 km²* of ice shelf.

Christmas Island
Location: In the Indian Ocean, 223 miles *360 km* south of Java Head.
Area: Approximately 52 miles² *135 km²*.
Population: 2691 (census of 30 June 1971); 3032 (1735 Chinese, 888 Malays, 316 Europeans, 93 others) at 30 June 1975 (estimate).
Chief settlement: Flying Fish Cove.

Territory of Cocos (Keeling) Islands
Location: In the Indian Ocean, about 1720 miles *2768 km* north-west of Perth. The territory contains 27 islands. North Keeling Island lies about 15 miles *24 km* north of the main group.
Area: Approximately 5½ miles² *14 km²*.
Population: 618 (census of 30 June 1971); 604 (Home Island 512, West Island 92) at 30 June 1975 (estimate).
Chief Settlement: Bantam Village on Home Is.

Coral Sea Islands Territory
Location: East of Queensland, between the Great Barrier Reef and 157° 10′E. longitude.
Population: 3 meteorologists.

Territories administered by the United States of America

Territory	Area (miles²)	Area (km²)	Population	Capital
North America				
Canal Zone	553	1432	44 000 (est 1/7/75)	Balboa Heights
Commonwealth of Puerto Rico	3435	8897	3 087 000 (est 30/6/75)	San Juan
Virgin Islands of the United States	133	344	92 000 (est 1/7/75)	Charlotte Amalie
Oceania				
American Samoa	76	197	29 000 (est. 30/6/75)	Pago Pago
Guam	212	549	104 000 (est. 1/7/75)	Agaña
Johnston and Sand Islands	<½	1	1007 (1/4/70)	—
Midway Islands	2	5	2220 (1/4/70)	—
Wake Island	3	8	1647 (1/4/70)	—
Trust Territory of the Pacific Islands	687*	1779*	126 000 (1/7/76)	Saipan

* Inhabited dry land only.

Other non-sovereign territories

Territory	Administering Country	Area (miles²)	Area (km²)	Population	Capital
Europe					
Faeroe Islands	Denmark	540	1399	41 000 (1/7/75)	Thorshavn
Svalbard and Jan Mayen Islands	Norway	24 101	62 422	3000 (31/12/65)*	Ny Alesund
Asia					
Macau (or Macao)	Portugal	6	16	271 000 (1/7/75)	Macau
Africa					
French Southern and Antarctic Territories	France	2918	7557	183 (1/7/75)	—
Namibia (South West Africa)†	South Africa‡	318 261	824 292	852 000 (1/7/74)	Windhoek
La Réunion	France	969	2510	481 000 (31/3/76)	Saint-Denis
North America					
Greenland	Denmark	840 000	2 175 600	50 000 (1/7/75)	Godthaab
St Pierre and Miquelon	France	93	242	500 (18/2/74)	St Pierre
Central America					
Guadeloupe and dependencies	France	687	1779	324 530 (16/10/74)	Pointe-à-Pitre
Martinique	France	425	1102	324 832 (16/10/74)	Fort-de-France
Netherlands Antilles	Netherlands	371	691	241 000 (1/7/76)	Willemstad
South America					
French Guiana	France	35 000	91 000	55 125 (16/10/74)	Cayenne
Oceania					
French Polynesia	France	c. 1500	4000	135 000 (31/12/75)	Papeete
New Caledonia and Dependencies	France	7358	19 058	135 000 (1/7/76)	Nouméa
Wallis and Futuna Islands	France	77	200	9000 (1/7/73)	Mata-Uta

* Inhabited only during winter season.
† Including data for Walvis Bay (area 434 miles² *1124 km²*, population 23 461 in 1970), an integral part of South Africa.
‡ South Africa's jurisdiction is disputed by the UN, which claims a protectorate over the territory.

Territory of Heard and McDonald Islands
Location: In the southern Indian Ocean, south-east of the Kerguelen Islands, and about 2500 miles *4023 km* south-west of Fremantle.
Area: 113 miles² *292 km²*. No permanent inhabitants.

Norfolk Island
Location: In south-west Pacific Ocean 1042 miles *1676 km* from Sydney and about 400 miles *643 km* from New Zealand. Philip Island is about 4 miles *6 km* south of Norfolk Island.
Area: 8528 acres (13·3 miles² [*34 km²*]).
Population: 1683 (census of 30 June 1971); 1870 (estimate for 30 June 1975). Figures include visitors. Philip Island and Nepean Island are uninhabited.
Seat of Government: Kingston.

New Zealand Dependencies

Cook Islands
Location: In the southern Pacific Ocean, between about 1750 miles *2816 km* and 2350 miles *3782 km* north-east of New Zealand between 8° S and 23° S, and 156° W and 167° W. Comprises 15 atolls or islands (Northern group 7, Lower group 8).
Area: 90·3 miles² *234 km²*. Main island (with area in acres) are Rarotonga (16 602), Mangaia (12 800), Atiu (6654), Mitiaro (5500), Mauke (Parry Is) (4552), Aitutaki (4461) and Penrhyn (Tongareva) (2432).
Population: 20 348 (census of 1 Dec. 1973, including 2241 in the Northern group and 18 107 (Rarotonga 11 115) in the Lower group. Estimate for 1 Dec. 1976 is 18 112.
Chief Town: Avarua, on Rarotonga Island.

Niue
Location: Niue (or Savage) Island is in the southern Pacific Ocean, 1343 miles *2161 km* north of Auckland, New Zealand, between Tonga and the Cook Islands.
Area: 64 028 acres (100·04 miles² [*259 km²*]).
Population: 4990 (census of 28 Sept. 1971); 4048 (estimate for 31 Dec. 1975).
Capital: Alofi.

Ross Dependency
Location: All the land between 160° E and 150° W longitude (moving eastward) and

south of 60° S latitude, comprising a sector of the mainland of Antarctica, including the Ross Ice Shelf, and some off-shore islands.
Area: The mainland area is estimated at 160 000 miles² *414 398 km²* and the permanent ice shelf at 130 000 miles² *336 698 km²*.
Population: No permanent inhabitants, but some bases are permanently occupied by scientific personnel.

Tokelau
Location: The Tokelau (formerly Union) Islands consist of three atolls in the central Pacific Ocean, about 300 miles *483 km* north of Western Samoa.
Area: Approximately 2500 acres (Nukunonu 1350, Fakaofo 650, Atafu 500), or about 4 miles² *10 km²*.
Population: 1599 (census of 21 Feb. 1972); 1603 (Nukunonu 374, Fakaofo 665, Atafu 564) at 30 Sept. 1975 (estimate).

SOVEREIGN COUNTRIES

AFGHANISTAN

Official name: Doulat i Jumhouri ye Afghanistan *or* De Afghānistān Jamhouriat (the Republic of Afghanistan).
Population: 17 050 000 (estimate for 1 July 1976).
Area: 250 000 miles² *647 494 km²*.
Languages: Dari Persian, Pashtu (Pakhto).
Religion: Muslim.
Capital City: Kabul, population 749 000 (including suburbs) at 1 July 1975.
Other principal towns (1975): Qandahar (Kandahar) 209 000; Herat 157 000; Kunduz 108 000; Charikar 98 000; Mazar-i-Sharif 97 000.
Highest point: Noshaq, 24 581 ft *7492 m* (first climbed 17 Aug. 1960).
Principal mountain ranges: Hindu Kush, Koh-i-Baba, Band-i-Baian, Band-i-Baba, Paropamisus, Paghman.
Principal rivers: Helmand, Bandihala-Khoulm, Kabul, Murghab, Kunduz, Hari Rud, Farah Rud, Ab-i-Panja.
Head of State: Lt-Gen Mohammad Da'ud (b. 18 July 1909), President and Prime Minister.
Climate: Wide variations between highlands and lowlands. Average annual rainfall 12 in. In Kabul July (61 °F to 92 °F) and August (59 °F to 91 °F) hottest; Jan. (18 °F to 36 °F) coldest; March rainiest (7 days). Maximum temperature up to 120 °F; minimum below −10 °F.
Labour force: 5 952 000 (1970): Agriculture, forestry and fishing 87·1% (ILO estimates).
Net domestic product: 57 205 million afghanis (at 1965 prices) in 1969: Agriculture, forestry and fishing 50·9%; Manufacturing 10·8%; Trade, restaurants and hotels 13·4%.

Exports: $124.5 million in 1972: Fruit and vegetables 35·1% (edible nuts 10·6%, raisins 12·7%); Hides, skins and furs 15·6% (fur skins 13·1%); Textile fibres 13·6%; Natural gas 13·7%.
Monetary unit: Afghani. 1 afghani = 100 puls.
Denominations:
Coins 1, 2, 5 afghani, 25, 50 puls.
Notes 10, 20, 50, 100, 500, 1000 afghani.
Exchange rate to US dollar: 45.00 (official rate, July 1977); free rate was 50.50 per US dollar in January 1977.
Political history and government: Formerly an hereditary kingdom, under British influence until 1919. Afghanistan became a limited constitutional monarchy, without political parties, on 1 Oct. 1964. A bicameral parliament was inaugurated on 16 Oct. 1965. The last king was deposed by a military *coup* on 17 July 1973, when a republic was proclaimed, the constitution abrogated and parliament dissolved. The king abdicated on 24 Aug. 1973. Government was assumed by a 13-man Central Council of the Republic, led by Lt.-Gen. Mohammad Da'ud, a former Prime Minister, who became President.
Afghanistan has 26 provinces, each administered by an appointed governor. A Grand Assembly, appointed from among notable elders by provincial governors, was convened on 30 Jan. 1977 and adopted a new constitution on 14 Feb. 1977. On the same day the Assembly elected Gen. Da'ud to continue as President for six years. He was sworn in on 15 Feb. 1977, when the Assembly was dissolved. The constitution provides for a new Grand Assembly which will include the members of a National Assembly (due to convene on 22 Nov. 1979) who are to be nominated by the only permitted political party, the National Revolutionary Party, and then elected by universal adult suffrage. Pending the formation of the National Assembly, its powers are exercised by the Government, appointed by the President.
Telephones: 23 000 (1974).
Daily newspapers: 18 (1973).
Total circulation: 90 000.
Radio: 450 000 (1970).
Length of roadways: 4164 miles *6700 km*.
Universities: 2.
Adult illiteracy: Over 90% (1963).
Expectation of life: Males 39·9 years; females 40·7 years (UN estimates for 1970/75).
Defence: Military service two years; total armed forces 100 000; defence expenditure, 1975/76: $60 million.
Cinemas: 24 (seating capacity 12 000) in 1970.

ALBANIA

Official name: Socialist People's Republic of Albania.
Population: 1 626 315 (census of 2 Oct. 1960); 2 432 000 (estimate for 31 Dec. 1975).
Area: 11 101 miles² *28 748 km²*.
Language: Albanian.
Religions: Muslim; Eastern Orthodox; Roman Catholic.
Capital city: Tiranë (Tirana), population 182 500 (estimate for 1 July 1973).
Other principal towns: Shkodër (Scutari) 59 100; Durrës (Durazzo) 57 300; Vlorë (Valona) 53 200; Korçë (Koritsa) 49 200; Elbasan 45 500; Berat 28 400; Fier 25 800.
Highest point: Mount Korabi, 9028 ft *2751 m*.

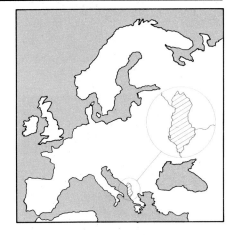

Principal mountain ranges: Albanian Alps, section of the Dinaric Alps.
Principal rivers: Semani (157 miles *253 km*), Drini (174 miles *280 km*), Vjosa (147 miles *236 km*), Mati (65 miles *105 km*). Shkumbini (91 miles *146 km*).
Head of State: Haxhi Lleshi (b. 1913), President of the Presidium of the People's Assembly.
Political leader: Enver Hoxha (b. 16 Oct. 1908), First Secretary of the Central Committee of the Albanian Party of Labour.
Head of Government: Mehmet Shehu (b. 10 Jan. 1913), Chairman of the Council of Ministers.
Climate: Mild, wet winters and dry, hot summers along coast; rainier and colder inland. Maximum temperature 45,3 °C (113·5 °F), Lezhe, 23 Aug. 1939; minimum −25,0 °C (−13·0 °F), Voskopje, 29 Jan. 1942.
Labour force: 730 762 (1960 census): 922 000 (1970): Agriculture, forestry and fishing 66·3% (ILO estimates).
Gross national product: $1450 million in 1975 (World Bank estimate).
Exports: 2 996 million old leks (299·6 million new leks) in 1964: Foodstuff 23·1%; Fuels, minerals and metals 54·2%.
Monetary unit: Lek. 1 lek = 100 qintars.
Denominations:
Coins 5, 10, 20, 50 qintars, 1 lek.
Notes 1, 3, 5, 10, 25, 50 leks.
Exchange rate to US dollar: 4·10 (July 1977).
Political history and government: Formerly part of Turkey's Ottoman Empire. On 28 Nov. 1912 a group of Albanians established a provisional government and declared the country's independence. Albania was occupied by Italy in 1914 but its independence was re-established in 1920. A republic was proclaimed on 22 Jan. 1925 and Ahmet Beg Zogu was elected President. He was proclaimed King Zog on 1 Sept. 1928 and reigned until invading Italian forces occupied Albania on 7 April 1939. Italian rule ended in 1943 but German forces then occupied Albania. After they withdrew a provisional government was established in October 1944. The Communist-led National Liberation Front, a wartime resistance group, took power on 29 Nov. 1944. The People's Republic of Albania was proclaimed on 12 Jan. 1946 and its first constitution was adopted in March 1946. A new constitution, introducing the country's present name, was adopted by the People's Assembly on 27 Dec. 1976.
The supreme organ of state power is the unicameral People's Assembly, with 264 members elected for four years by universal adult suffrage. The Assembly elects a

Presidium (13 members) to be its permanent organ. Executive and administrative authority is held by the Council of Ministers, elected by the Assembly.

Political power is held by the (Communist) Albanian Party of Labour (or Workers' Party), the only permitted political party, which dominates the Democratic Front. The Front presents a single list of approved candidates for elections to all representative bodies. The Party of Labour's highest authority is the Party Congress, convened every five years. The Congress elects a Central Committe (77 full members and 39 candidate members were elected in November 1976) to supervise Party work. To direct its policy the Committee elects a Political Bureau (Politburo), with 12 full and five candidate members.

For local government Albania is divided into 26 districts, each with a People's Council elected for three years.

Telephones: 10 150 (1963).
Daily Newspapers: 2 (1973).
Total circulation: 115 000.
Radio: 172 000 (1973).
TV: 4000 (1973).
Length of roadways: 1926 miles *3100 km.*
Length of railways: 125 miles *201 km.*
Universities: One.
Adult illiteracy: 28·5% (males 20·1%; females 36·9%) in 1955 (population aged 9 and over).
Expectation of life: Males 67·2 years; females 69·9 years (UN estimates for 1970–75).
Defence: Military service: Army two years, Air Force, Navy and special units three years; total armed forces 47 000 (22 500 conscripts); defence expenditure, 1976: $157 million.
Cinemas: 93 (seating capacity 23 700) in 1969.

ALGERIA

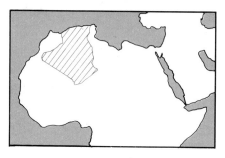

Official name: El Djemhouria El Djazaïria Demokratia Echaabia, or la République algérienne démocratique et populaire (the Democratic and Popular Republic of Algeria).
Population: 12 090 547 (census of 4 Apr. 1966); 17 304 000 (estimate for 1 July 1976).
Area: 919 595 miles² *2 381 741 km².*
Languages: Arabic 80·4%; Berber 18·7%; French 0·6% (1966).
Religion: Muslim.
Capital city: El Djazair or Alger (Algiers), population 1 839 000 (1970 est).
Other principal towns (1966): Ouahran (Oran) 328 257; Constantine 253 649; Annaba(Bône) 168 790; Sidi-Bel-Abbès 101 000; Sétif 98 000; Tlemcen 96 000; Blida 87 000.
Highest point: Mt Tahat, 9573 ft *2918 m.*
Principal mountain ranges: Atlas Saharien, Ahaggar (Hoggar), Hamada de Tinrhert.
Principal river: Chéliff (430 miles [*692 km*]).

Head of State: Col Houari Boumédienne (b. 23 Aug. 1927), President and Prime Minister.
Climate: Temperate (hot summers, fairly mild winters, adequate rainfall) along the coast, more extreme inland, hot and arid in the Sahara. In Algiers, August hottest (71 °F to 85 °F), January coldest (49 °F to 59 °F), December rainiest (12 days). Maximum temperature 53,0 °C (127·4 °F), Ouargla, 27 Aug. 1884.
Labour force: 3 254 000 (1970): Agriculture, forestry and fishing 60·7% (ILO estimates).
Gross domestic product: 20 500 million dinars in 1969: Agriculture, forestry and fishing 13%; Mining and quarrying 17%; Manufacturing 13%; Trade, restaurants and hotels 23%.
Exports: $1 796.8 million in 1973: Mineral fuels, lubricants, etc. 83·0% (crude petroleum 75·5%).
Monetary unit: Algerian dinar. 1 dinar = 100 centimes.
Denominations:
Coins 1, 2, 5, 20, 50 centimes, 1 dinar.
Notes 5, 10, 50, 100, 500 dinars.
Exchange rate to US dollar: 4·18 (July 1977).
Political history and government: A former French posession, 'attached' to metropolitan France. A nationalist revolt, led by the *Front de libération nationale* (FLN) or National Liberation Front, broke out on 1 Nov. 1954. This ended with a cease-fire and independence agreement on 18 March 1962. A provisional government was formed on 28 March 1962. Following a referendum on 1 July 1962, Algeria became independent on 3 July 1962. The provisional government transferred its functions to the Political Bureau of the FLN on 7 Aug. 1962. A National Constituent Assembly was elected, from a single list of candidates adopted by the Bureau, on 20 Sept. 1962. The Republic was proclaimed on 25 Sept. 1962 and a new government was formed with Ahmed Ben Bella as Prime Minister. The government's draft constitution, providing for a presidential régime with the FLN as sole party, was adopted by the Assembly on 28 Aug. 1963 and approved by popular referendum on 8 Sept. 1963. Ben Bella was elected President on 15 Sept. 1963 and a new National Assembly elected on 20 Sept. 1964. The President was deposed by a military *coup* on 19 June 1965, when the Assembly was dissolved and power was assumed by a Revolutionary Council, led by Col. Houari Boumédienne, Minister of Defence.

The régime's National Charter, proclaiming Algeria's adherence to socialism, was approved by referendum on 27 June 1976. A new constitution, embodying the principles of the Charter, was similarly approved on 19 Nov. 1976 and promulgated on 22 Nov. 1976. It continues the one-party system, with the FLN as sole party. Executive power is vested in the President, who is Head of State and Head of Government. He is nominated by the FLN and elected for six years by universal adult suffrage. The President appoints and presides over the Council of Ministers. Legislative power is held by the National People's Assembly, with 261 members elected by popular vote for five years (subject to dissolution by the Head of State). Boumédienne was elected President (unopposed) on 10 Dec. 1976 and members of the Assembly elected (from 783 candidates—three per constituency—nominated by the FLN) on 25 Feb. 1977.

Algeria comprises 15 departments.
Telephones: 230 000 (1974).
Daily Newspapers: 4 (1973).
Total circulation: 265 000.
Radio: 725 000 (1973).

TV: 260 000 (1973).
Length of roadways: 48 720 miles *78 408 km* (31 Dec. 1972).
Length of railways: 2531 miles *4074 km.*
Universities: 4.
Adult illiteracy: 81·2% (males 70·1%; females 92·1%) in 1966.
Expectation of life: Males 51·7 years; females 54·8 years (UN estimates for 1970–75).
Defence: Military service six months; total armed forces 69 300; defence expenditure, 1976: $312 million.
Cinemas: 440 (seating capacity 184 000) and 200 part-time (capacity 35 000) in 1970.

ANDORRA

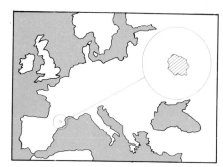

Official name: Les Valls d'Andorra (Catalán); also Los Valles de Andorra (Spanish), or Les Vallées d'Andorre (French).
Population: 29 000 (estimate for 1 July 1976).
Area: 175 miles² *453 km².*
Languages: Catalán (official), French, Spanish.
Religion: Roman Catholic.
Capital city: Andorra la Vella, population 9659.
Highest point: Pla del'Estany, 9678 ft *3011 m.*
Principal mountain range: Pyrenees.
Principal river: Valira.
Head of State: Co-Princes (the Bishop of Urgel and the President of France) each represented by a Permanent Delegate and by the Viguier Episcopal and the Viguier de France.
Head of Government: Julià Reig Ribo, First Syndic.
Climate: Mild (cool summers, cold winters) and dry. May–October are rainiest months.
Monetary unit: French and Spanish currencies (*q.v.*)
Political history and government: In 1278 Andorra was placed under the joint suzerainty of the Bishop of Urgel, in Spain, and the Comte de Foix, in France. The rights of the Comte passed to France in 1589. Andorra is an autonomous principality (*seigneurie*) in which legislative power is held by the unicameral General Council of the Valleys, with 24 members (four from each of the six parishes) elected by adult Andorran citizens for four years, half the seats being renewable every two years. Female suffrage was introduced by decree on 23 April 1970. The Council elects the First Syndic to act as chief executive for a three-year term. There are no organized political parties.
Daily Newspapers: 1.
Total circulation: 4000.
Radio: 6100 (1973).
TV: 1700 (1969).
Cinemas: 7 (seating capacity 2900) in 1969.

ANGOLA

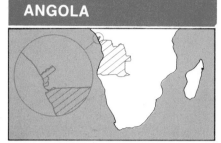

Official name: A República Popular de Angola (The People's Republic of Angola).
Population: 5 646 166 (census of 15 Dec. 1970); 6 761 000 (estimate for 31 Dec. 1975).
Area: 481 354 miles² *1 246 700 km²*.
Languages: Portuguese (official), Bantu languages.
Religions: Catholic 38%; Protestant 12%; traditional beliefs 50%.
*****Capital city:** São Paulo de Luanda, population 480 613 (1970).
*****Other principal towns (1970):** Huambo (Nova Lisboa) 61 885; Lobito 59 258; Benguela 40 996; Lubango (Sá de Bandeira) 31 674; Malange 31 559.
Highest point: Serra Môco, 8563 ft *2610 m*.
Principal mountain ranges: Rand Plateau, Benguela Plateau, Bié Plateau, Humpata Highlands, Chela mountains.
Principal rivers: Cunene (Kunene), Cuanza (Kwanza), Congo (Zaire), Cuando (Kwando), Cubango (Okavango), Zambezi, Cassai (Kasai).
Head of State: Dr (Antônio) Agostinho Neto (b. 17 Sept. 1922), President.
Prime Minister: Lopo Fortunato Ferreira do Nascimento.
Climate: Tropical, tempered locally by altitude. Two distinct seasons (wet and dry) but with little variation in temperature. Very hot and rainy in lowlands, with lower temperatures inland. Rainy season October to May; average annual rainfall 70 inches at Cabina, 11 inches at Lobito. Average annual temperature 26° C (79° F) at Santo Antônio do Zaire, 19° C (67° F) at Huambo.
Labour force: 1 421 966 (census of 30 Dec. 1960); 1 698 000 (1970): Agriculture, forestry and fishing 64·0% (ILO estimates).
Gross domestic product: $1645 million in 1970 (UN estimate).
Exports: $779.5 million in 1973: Coffee 26·9%; Other food 11·9%; Petroleum and petroleum products 31·4% (crude petroleum 30·0%); Diamonds 10·4%.
Monetary unit: Kwanza. 1 kwanza = 100 lwei.
Denominations:
    Coins 10, 20, 50 lwei, 1, 2½, 5, 10, 20 kwanza.
    Notes 20, 50, 100, 500, 1000 kwanza.
Exchange rate to US dollar: 38·48 (July 1977).
Political history and government: A former Portuguese territory, independent since 11 Nov. 1975. Before and after independence, rival nationalist groups fought for control of the country. By February 1976 the dominant group was the *Movimento Popular de Libertação de Angola* (MPLA), the Popular Movement for the Liberation of Angola, supported by troops from Cuba. Under the MPLA constitution for Angola, the supreme organ of state is the elected People's Assembly but, until Angola is completely under MPLA rule, power is held by a Revolutionary Council, led by the President. The Council comprises members of the MPLA's Political Bureau, the High Command of the armed forces and Provincial Commissars. Executive authority rests with the President, who appoints a Prime Minister and a Cabinet.

Telephones: 38 000 (1973).
Daily newspapers: 3.
Radio: 116 000 (1975).
Length of roadways: 44 939 miles *72 323 km*. (31 Dec. 1971).
Length of railways: 2200 miles *3540 km*.
Universities: 1.
Adult illiteracy: 70% plus.
Expectation of life: Males 37·0 years; females 40·1 years (UN estimates for 1970–75).
Defence: Military service voluntary; total armed forces 30 000, also 15 000 to 20 000 Cuban troops.
Cinemas: 48 (seating capacity 35 700) in 1972.

*As a result of the civil war there have been large-scale movements of population. Recent (March 1976) estimates suggest that Luanda has 800 000 inhabitants, Huambo over 100 000 and Lobito over 70 000.

ARGENTINA

Official name: La República Argentina (the Argentine Republic).
Population: 23 362 204 (census of 30 Sept. 1970); 25 719 000 (estimate for 1 July 1976).
Area: 1 072 163 miles² *2 776 889 km²*.
Language: Spanish.
Religion: Roman Catholic.
Capital city: Buenos Aires, population 2 976 000 (8 925 000, including suburbs) at 1 July 1974 (estimate).
Other principal towns (1970): Rosario 810 840; Córdoba 798 663; La Plata 506 287; Mendoza 470 896; San Miguel de Tucumán 365 757; Mar del Plata 299 700; Santa Fé 244 579; San Juan 224 000.
Highest point: Cerro Aconcagua, 22 834 ft *6960 m* (first climbed 14 Jan. 1897).
Principal mountain range: Cordillera de los Andes.
Principal rivers: Paraná (2500 miles *4023 km*), Negro, Salado.
Head of State: Lt.-Gen. Jorge Rafael Videla (b. 1925).
Climate: Sub-tropical in Chaco region (north), sunny and mild in pampas, cold and windy in southern Patagonia. In Buenos Aires, January hottest (63 °F to 85 °F), June coldest (41 °F to 57 °F), August, October and November rainiest (each 9 days). Absolute maximum temperature 48,8 °C (119·8 °F), Rivadavia, 27 Nov. 1916; absolute minimum −33,0 °C (−27·4 °F), Sarmiento.
Labour force: 9 011 450 aged 10 and over (1970 census): Agriculture, forestry and fishing 16·2%; Manufacturing 21·5%; Trade, restaurants and hotels 16·1%; Community, social and personal services 25·5%.
Gross domestic product: 1 345 000 million pesos in 1975: Agriculture, forestry and

fishing 12·2%; Manufacturing 33·3%; Trade, restaurants and hotels 10·1%.
Exports: $3 930.7 million in 1974: Meat and meat preparations 11·2%; Cereals and cereal preparations 34·8% (unmilled maize 16·8%); Other food 18·9%.
Monetary unit: Argentine peso. 1 peso = 100 centavos.
Denominations:
    Coins 1, 5, 10, 20, 50 centavos.
    1, 5, 10, 25 old pesos.
    Notes 50, 100, 500, 1000, 5000, 10 000 old pesos.
    1, 5, 10, 50, 100, 500, 1000 pesos.
Exchange rate to US dollar: 398·50 (July 1977).
Political history and government: A federal republic of 22 states and two centrally administered territories. Lt.-Gen. Juan Perón was elected President on 23 Sept. 1973 and took office on 12 Oct. 1973. Gen. Perón died on 1 July 1974 and was succeeded by his wife, the former Vice-President. She was deposed by an armed forces *coup* on 24 March 1976, when a three-man military junta took power. The bicameral Congress (a Senate and a Chamber of Deputies) and provincial legislatures were dissolved and political activities suspended. The junta's leader, Lt.-Gen. Jorge Videla, was inaugurated as President on 29 March 1976. Each province is administered by an appointed Governor.
Telephones: 2 374 000 (1974).
Daily newspapers: 179 (1973).
    Total circulation: 3 988 000 (146 dailies).
Radio: 10 000 000 (1971).
TV: 3 950 000 (1973).
Length of roadways: 193 801 miles *311 893 km* (31 Dec. 1975).
Length of railways: 24 747 miles *39 827 km*.
Universities: 37 (12 national, 2 provincial, 23 private).
Adult illiteracy: 7·4% (males 6·5%; females 8·3%) in 1970.
Expectation of life: Males 65·16 years; females 71·38 years (1970–75).
Defence: Military service: Army and Air Force one year, Navy 14 months; total armed forces 132 800; defence expenditure, 1975: $1031 million.
Cinemas: 1341 (seating capacity 776 300), 93 part-time (capacity 31 062) and 10 drive-in (capacity 3756 cars) in 1973.

AUSTRALIA

Official name: The Commonwealth of Australia.
Population: 12 755 638 (census of 30 June 1971); 13 915 500 (census of 30 June 1976, preliminary result).
Area: 2 966 150 miles² *7 682 300 km*.
Language: English.
Religions: Church of England; Roman Catholic; Methodist; Presbyterian.
Capital city: Canberra, population 214 700 at 30 June 1976.
Other principal towns (metropolitan areas, 1976): Sydney 2 935 900; Melbourne 2 603 600; Brisbane 957 700; Adelaide 900 400; Perth 805 500; Newcastle 362 980; Wollongong 211 100; Hobart 162 100; Geelong 131 600.
Highest point: Mt Kosciusko, 7316 ft *2230 m*.
Principal mountain ranges: Great Dividing Range, Macdonnell Ranges, Flinders Ranges, Australian Alps.
Principal rivers: Murray (with Darling), Flinders, Ashburton, Fitzroy.
Head of State: HM Queen Elizabeth II, represented by the Rt Hon Sir John Robert Kerr, GCMG, GCVO (b. 24 Sept. 1914), Governor General*.

Prime Minister: The Rt Hon (John) Malcolm Fraser, CH (b. 21 May 1930).
Climate: Hot and dry, with average temperatures of about 80 °F. Very low rainfall in interior. In Sydney, January and February warmest (each average 65 °F to 78 °F). July coldest (46 °F to 60 °F), each month has an average of between 11 and 14 rainy days. In Perth, average daily maximum of 63 °F (July) to 85 °F (January, February), minimum 48 °F (July, August) to 63 °F (January, February), July and August rainiest (each 19 days), January and February driest (each 3 days). In Darwin, average maximum 87 °F (July) to 94 °F (November), minimum 67 °F (July) to 78 °F (November, December), January rainiest (20 days), no rainy days in July or August. Absolute maximum temperature 127·5 °F (53,1 °C), Cloncurry, 13 Jan. 1889; absolute minimum − 8·0 °F (−22,2 °C), Charlotte Pass, 14 July 1945 and 22 Aug. 1947.
Labour force: 5 726 000 aged 15 and over (1975): Manufacturing and utilities 23·6%; Trade 19·7%; Community, social and personal services 24·5%. Figures exclude armed forces (72 000 in 1973) and unemployed (108 000 in 1973).
Gross domestic product: $A 50 699 million in 1973/74: Manufacturing and utilities 25·6% (manufacturing 22·5%); Trade 14·5%; Government services (excluding law and order) 12·5%.
Exports: US $10 787·3 million in 1974: Cereals and cereal preparations 15·9% (unmilled wheat and meslin 11·6%); Other food 17·7%; Wool 12·5%; Metalliferous ores and metal scrap 13·6%.
Monetary unit: Australian dollar ($A). 1 dollar = 100 cents.
Denominations:
  Coins 1, 2, 5, 10, 20, 50 cents.
  Notes 1, 2, 5, 10, 20, 50 dollars.
Exchange rate to US dollar: 0.890 (July 1977).
Political history and government: Britain's six Australian colonies merged to form a federation of states as the Commonwealth of Australia, a dominion under the British Crown, on 1 Jan. 1901. The Northern Territory was separated from South Australia, and the Australian Capital Territory was acquired from New South Wales, on 1 Jan. 1911. The capital was transferred from Melbourne to Canberra in May 1927. Australia became fully independent, within the Commonwealth, under the Statute of Westminster, a law promulgated in Britain on 11 Dec. 1931 and adopted by Australia on 9 Oct. 1942 (with effect from 3 Sept. 1939).
Executive power is vested in the Queen and exercised by her representative, the Governor-General, advised by the Federal Executive Council (the Cabinet), led by the Prime Minister. Legislative power is vested in the Federal Parliament. This consists of the Queen, represented by the Governor-General, an elected Senate (64 members, 10 from each State and two from each of the federal territories) and a House of Representatives (127 members, chosen in proportion to population). The Cabinet is responsible to Parliament. Australia comprises six states (each with its own Government and judicial system) and two federally-administered territories.
Telephones: 5 267 000 (30 June 1975).
Daily newspapers: 58 (1973)
  Total circulation: 5 126 000.
Radio: 2 851 230 (1974).
TV: 3 022 006 (1974).
Length of roadways: 549 501 miles 884 336 km.
Length of railways: 25 027 miles 40 277 km.
Universities: 18.
Expectation of life: Males 67·63 years;

females 74·15 years (1965–67), excluding full-blooded aborigines.
Defence: Military service voluntary; total armed forces 69 350; defence expenditure, 1976/77: US $2733 million.
Cinemas: 735 (seating capacity 478 400) and 241 drive-in (1972).

*The resignation of the Governor-General, Sir John Kerr, was announced on 14 July 1977. His successor in December is to be Sir Zelman Cowen, CMG (b. 7 Oct. 1919).

NEW SOUTH WALES

Population: 4 601 180 (1971 census); 4 914 300 (1976 census).
Area: 309 500 miles² 801 600 km².
Capital city: Sydney, population 2 935 900 at 30 June 1976.
Other principal towns (1974): Newcastle 360 090; Wollongong 208 550; Albury 31 350; Wagga Wagga 31 160; Broken Hill 28 310.
Highest point: Mt Kosciusko, 7316 ft 2230 m.
Principal mountain ranges: Great Dividing Range, Australian Alps, New England Range, Snowy Mountains, Blue Mountains, Liverpool Range.
Principal rivers: Darling, Murray.
Governor: Sir (Arthur) Roden Cutler, VC, KCMG, KCVO, CBE (b. 24 May 1916).
Premier: The Hon Neville Kenneth Wran.
Climate: Most of the state has hot summers and mild winters, with rainfall well distributed, but in the east drought and storms sometimes occur.
Telephones: 1 299 620 (1974).
Radio: 996 248 (1974).
Length of roadways: 129 745 miles 208 804 km.
Length of railways: 6061 miles 9754 km.
Universities: 6.

VICTORIA

Population: 3 502 351 (1971 census); 3 746 000 (1976 census).
Area: 87 875 miles² 227 600 km².
Capital city: Melbourne, population 2 603 600 at 30 June 1976.
Other principal towns: Geelong 131 600 (1976); Ballarat 58 620 (1971); Bendigo 45 936 (1971).
Principal mountain ranges: Australian Alps, Great Dividing Range.
Principal rivers: Murray, Yarra-Yarra.
Governor: Sir Henry Arthur Winneke, KCMG, KCVO, OBE (b. 29 Oct. 1908).
Premier: Rupert James Hamer, ED (b. 29 July 1916).
Length of roadways: 101 598 miles 163 506 km.
Length of railways: 4170 miles 6711 km.
Universities: 3.

QUEENSLAND

Population: 1 827 065 (1971 census); 2 111 700 (1976 census).
Area: 666 875 miles² 1 727 200 km².
Capital city: Brisbane, population 957 700 at 30 June 1976.
Other principal towns (1974): Townsville 79 500; Gold Coast 78 600; Toowoomba 62 250; Rockhampton 51 100; Cairns 34 350.
Highest point: Mt Bartle Frere, 5287 ft 1611 m.
Principal mountain ranges: Great Dividing Range, Selwyn, Kirby.
Principal rivers: Brisbane, Mitchell, Fitzroy, Barcoo, Flinders.
Governor: Commodore Sir James Maxwell Ramsay, CBE (b. 27 Aug. 1916).
Premier: Johannes Bjelke-Petersen (b. 13 Jan. 1911).

Radio: 429 000 (1974).
TV: 424 090 (1974).
Length of roadways: 120 076 miles 193 243 km.
Length of railways: 5797 miles 9329 km.
Universities: 3.

SOUTH AUSTRALIA

Population: 1 173 707 (1971 census); 1 261 600 (1976 census).
Area: 379 925 miles² 984 000 km².
Capital city: Adelaide, population 900 400 at 30 June 1976.
Other principal towns (1971): Whyalla 32 109; Mount Gambier 17 934; Port Pirie 15 456.
Principal mountain ranges: Middleback, Mt Lofty Range.
Principal river: Murray.
Governor: The Rev. Keith Douglas Seaman, OBE (b. 11 June 1920).
Premier: Donald Allan Dunstan (b. 21 Sept. 1926).
Climate: Mediterranean type.
Telephones: 298 300 (1974).
Radio: 339 516 (1974).
TV: 347 453 (1974).
Length of roadways: 75 517 miles 121 533 km.
Length of railways: 3756 miles 6044 km.
Universities: 2.

WESTERN AUSTRALIA

Population: 1 030 469 (1971 census); 1 169 800 (1976 census).
Area: 975 100 miles² 2 525 500 km².
Capital city: Perth, population 805 500 (including Fremantle) at 30 June 1976.
Other principal towns: Fremantle 32 100; Kalgoorlie-Boulder 20 600; Bunbury 18 550; Geraldton 15 800; Albany 12 300.
Highest point: Mt Meharry 4082 ft 1244 m.
Principal mountain ranges: Darling, Hamersley.
Principal rivers: Fitzroy, Ashburton, Fortescue, Swan, Murchison.
Governor: Air Chief Marshal Sir Wallace Hart Kyle, GCB, CBE, DSO, DFC (b. 22 Jan. 1910).
Premier: Sir Charles Walter Michael Court, OBE (b. 29 Sept. 1911).
Telephones: 304 044 (1972).
Radio: 205 230 (1972).
TV: 218 782 (1972).
Length of roadways: 58 237 miles 93 723 km.
Length of railways: 3837 miles 6175 km.
Universities: 2.

TASMANIA

Population: 390 413 (1971 census); 407 400 (1976 census).
Area: 26 175 miles² 67 800 km².
Capital city: Hobart, population 162 000 at 30 June 1976.
Other principal towns (1974): Launceston 63 210; Burnie-Somerset 20 610; Devonport 19 730.
Highest point: Cradle Mountain, 5069 ft 1545 m.
Principal mountain range: Highlands.
Principal rivers: Derwent, Gordon, Tamar
Governor: Sir Stanley Charles Burbury, KBE (b. 2 Dec. 1909).
Premier: William Arthur Neilson (b. 27 Aug. 1925).
Length of roadways: c. 12 847 miles 20 675 km.
Universities: 1

THE NORTHERN TERRITORY OF AUSTRALIA
Population: 86 390 (1971 census); 101 400 (1976 census).
Area: 519 750 miles² *1 346 200 km²*.
Administrative Headquarters: Darwin, population 41 000 (1976).
Other principal town: Alice Springs, population 11 179 (1971).
Highest point: Mount Ziel, 4955 ft *1510 m*.
Principal mountain range: MacDonnell Ranges.
Principal rivers: Victoria, Roper.
Administrator: J. A. England.
Climate: Tropical, but with considerable variations. Dry in the south, with very hot summers. On the coast the rainy season is from November to April and the dry season from May to October.
Length of roadways: 2824 miles *4545 km*.

THE AUSTRALIAN CAPITAL TERRITORY
Population: 144 063 (1971 census); 203 300 (1976 census).
Area: 925 miles² *2400 km²*.
Principal town: Canberra, population 214 700 (including Queanbeyan, NSW) at 30 June 1976.
Principal river: Murrumbidgee.
Climate: (see New South Wales).
Universities: 1.

AUSTRIA

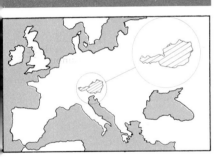

Official name: Republik Österreich (Republic of Austria).
Population: 7 456 403 (census of 12 May 1971); 7 520 000 (estimate for 1 July 1975).
Area: 32 375 miles² *83 850 km²*.
Language: German.
Religions: Roman Catholic, Protestant minority.
Capital city: Wien (Vienna), population 1 614 841 (1971).
Other principal towns (1971): Graz 248 500; Linz 202 874; Salzburg 128 845; Innsbruck 115 197; Klagenfurt 82 512.
Highest point: Grossglockner, 12 462 ft *3798 m* (first climbed in 1800).
Principal mountain range: Alps.
Principal rivers: Donau (Danube) (1770 miles *2848 km*), Inn, Mur.
Head of State: Dr Rudolf Kirchschläger (b. 20 Mar. 1915), Federal President.
Head of Government: Dr Bruno Kreisky (b. 22 Jan. 1911), Federal Chancellor.
Climate: Generally cold, dry winters and warm summers, with considerable variations due to altitude. Average annual temperature 45 °F to 48 °F. Most of rain in summer. In Vienna, July hottest (59 °F–75 °F), January coldest (26° F to 34 °F), August rainiest (10 days). Absolute maximum temperature 39,4 °C (102·9 °F), Horn, 5 July 1957; absolute minimum −36,6 °C (−33·9 °F), Zwettl, 11 Feb. 1929.
Labour force: 2 969 000 (excluding armed forces and unemployed) aged 15 and over (September 1975): Agriculture, forestry and fishing 12·6%; Mining and manufacturing 31·4% (Manufacturing 30·6%); Trade, restaurants and hotels 16·2%; Community, social and personal services 18·5%.
Gross domestic product: 533 300 million Schilling in 1973: Mining and manufacturing 35·1%; Construction 11·0%; Trade, restaurants and hotels 14·9% (trade 11·8%); Public administration and defence 11·6%.
Exports: $7 518·1 million in 1975: Iron and steel 11·8%; Machinery and transport equipment 27·4% (non-electric machinery 14·7%).
Monetary unit: Schilling. 1 Schilling = 100 Groschen.
Denominations:
Coins 1, 2, 5, 10, 50 Groschen, 1, 5, 10, 25, 50 and 100 Schilling.
Notes 20, 50, 100, 500, 1000 Schilling.
Exchange rate to US dollar: 16·15 (July 1977).
Political history and government: Formerly the centre of the Austro-Hungarian Empire. In 1918 the Empire was dissolved and Austria proper became a republic. Troops from Nazi Germany entered Austria on 11 March 1938. It was annexed on 12 March 1938 and incorporated in the German Reich. After liberation by Allied forces, a provisional government was established on 27 April 1945. Austria was divided into four occupation zones, controlled by France, the USSR, the United Kingdom and the USA. It regained independence by the Austrian State Treaty, signed on 15 May 1955 and effective from 27 July 1955. Occupation forces were withdrawn by 25 Oct. 1955.
Austria is a federal republic, divided into nine provinces. Legislative power is vested in the bicameral federal parliament, comprising the *Nationalrat* (National Council) of 183 members, directly elected by universal adult suffrage for four years (subject to dissolution), and the *Bundesrat* (Federal Council) of 58 members elected for varying terms by the provincial assemblies. The Federal President is a constitutional Head of State, elected by direct popular vote for six years. He normally acts on the advice of the Council of Ministers, led by the Federal Chancellor, which is responsible to the National Council. The President appoints the Chancellor and, on the latter's advice, other Ministers.
Telephones: 1 987 000 (1974).
Daily newspapers: 32 (1973).
Total circulation: 2 296 000.
Radio: 2 170 426 (1975).
TV: 1 910 060 (1975).
Length of roadways: 63 905 miles *102 845 km* (classified roads only, 31 Dec. 1975).
Length of railways: 3656 miles *5883 km* (state); 395 miles *636 km* (private).
Universities: 16.
Expectation of life: Males 67·4 years; females 74·7 years (1974).
Defence: Military service six months, followed by 60 days' reservist training; total armed forces 37 300 (25 000 conscripts); defence expenditure, 1976: $433 million.
Cinemas: 679 (seating capacity 228 000) and 1 drive-in (1972).

BAHAMAS

Official name: The Commonwealth of the Bahamas.
Population: 175 192 (census of 7 April 1970); 211 000 (estimate for 1 July 1976).
Area: 5 382 miles² *13 939 km²*.
Languages: English.
Religions: Anglican, Baptist, Roman Catholic, Methodist, Saints of God and Church of God.
Capital city: Nassau (on New Providence Island), population of island 101 503 (1970).
Other principal islands (1970): Grand Bahama 25 859; Andros 8845; Abaco 6501; Eleuthera 6247; Long Island 3861; Harbour Island and Spanish Wells 3221; Cat Island 2657; Inagua 1109.

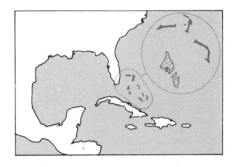

Highest point: Mount Alvernia, Cat Island.
Head of State: HM Queen Elizabeth II, represented by Sir Milo Boughton Butler, GCMG (b. 11 Aug. 1906), Governor-General.
Prime Minister: The Rt Hon Lynden Oscar Pindling (b. 22 Mar. 1930).
Climate: Equable. Winter averages of 70 °F to 75 °F (21 °C to 24 °C). Summer averages of 80 °F to 90 °F (26 °C to 32 °C). Highest recorded temperature is 94 °F and lowest 51 °F. Rainfall mainly between May and September.
Labour force: 69 791 (including unemployed) aged 14 and over (1970 census): Construction 13·6%; trade, restaurants and hotels 25·9%; community, social and personal services 27·1%.
Gross national product: US $520 million in 1975 (World Bank estimate).
Exports: US $1 443·6 million in 1974: Crude petroleum 27·3%; petroleum products 64·2% (motor spirit 11·6%; residual fuel oils 41·5%).
Monetary unit: Bahamian dollar (B$). 1 dollar = 100 cents.
Denominations:
Coins 1, 5, 10, 15, 25, 50 cents, B$ 1, 2, 5.
Notes 50 cents, B$ 1, 3, 5, 10, 20, 500, 1000.
Exchange rate to US dollar: 1.00 (July 1977).
Political history and government: A former British colony, with internal self-government from 7 Jan. 1964. Following a constitutional conference on 12–20 Dec. 1972, the Bahamas became independent, within the Commonwealth, on 10 July 1973. Executive power is vested in the Queen and exercisable by her appointed representative, the Governor-General, advised by the Cabinet. The Governor-General appoints the Prime Minister and, on the latter's advice, other members of the Cabinet. Legislative power is vested in the bicameral Parliament, comprising the Senate (16 appointed members) and the House of Assembly, with 38 members elected for five years by universal adult suffrage. The Cabinet is responsible to Parliament.
Telephones: 55 000 (1974).
Daily newspapers: 2 (1973).
Total circulation: 30 000.
Radio: 85 000 (1973).
TV: 4500 (1964).
Length of roadways: 700 miles *1126 km*.
Adult illiteracy: 10·2% (males 9·8%; females 10·5%) in 1963.
Expectation of life: Males 64·0 years; females 67·3 years (1969–71).
Cinemas: 19 and 3 drive-ins (1972).

B

BAHRAIN

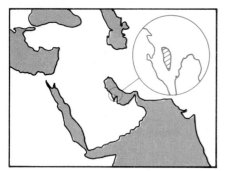

Official name: Daulat al Bahrain (State of Bahrain).

Population: 216 815 (census of 3 April 1971); 266 078 (1975 est).

Area: 240 miles² *622 km²*.

Language: Arabic.

Religions: Muslim, Christian minority.

Capital city: Manama, population 98 300 (1974).

Other principal towns: Muharraq 41 143 (1971); Rifa'a 9403 (1965); Hidd 5230 (1965).

Highest point: Jabal ad Dukhan, 440 ft *134 m.*

Head of State: H H Shaikh Isa ibn Sulman al-Khalifa, Hon KCMG (b. 3 July 1933), Amir.

Prime Minister: Shaikh Khalifa ibn Sulman al-Khalifa (b. 1935).

Climate: Very hot and humid. Average maximum 68 °F (January) to 100 °F (August), minimum 57 °F (January) to 85 °F (July, August), December and February rainiest (each two days).

Labour force: 60 301 aged 14 and over (1971 census): Manufacturing 14·1%; Construction 17·5%; Trade, restaurants and hotels 13·0%; Transport, storage and communications 13·0%; Community, social and personal services 30·9%.

Gross domestic product: $244 million in 1970.

Exports: $1 147·1 million in 1975: Petroleum products 74·1% (motor spirit 13·1%; lamp oil and white spirit 13·5%; distillate fuel oils 22·2%; residual fuel oils 23·5%).

Monetary unit: Bahrain dinar. 1 dinar = 1000 fils.

Denominations:

Coins 1, 5, 10, 25, 50, 100, 500 fils.

Notes 100 fils, ¼, ½ 1, 5, 10 dinars.

Exchange rate to US dollars: 0·396 (July 1977).

Political history and government: A shaikhdom under British protection from 1882 until full independence on 15 Aug. 1971. Now an amirate, with a Cabinet appointed by the Ruler. The National Assembly, containing Cabinet ministers and 30 elected members, was dissolved by Amiri decree on 26 Aug. 1975.

Telephones: 22 000 (1974).

Daily newspapers: 2.

Radio: 80 000 (1973).

TV: 18 000 (1973).

Adult illiteracy: 59·8% (males 50·7%; females 71·5%) in 1971.

Defence: Total armed forces 1600.

Cinemas: 10 (seating capacity 10 500) in 1973.

BANGLADESH

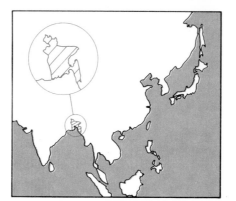

Official name: Gana Praja Tantri Bangla Desh (People's Republic of Bangladesh).

Population: 71 479 071 (census of 1 Mar. 1974, excluding underenumeration); 76 815 000 (estimate for 1 July 1975).

Area: 55 598 miles² *143 998 km².*

Language: Bengali.

Religions: Muslim with Hindu, Christian and Buddhist minorities.

Capital city: Dhaka (Dacca), population 1 679 572 (1974 census).

Other principal towns (1974): Chittagong 889 760; Khulna 437 304; Narayanganj 270 680.

Principal rivers: Ganga (Ganges), Jumna, Meghna.

Head of State: Maj.-Gen. Ziaur Rahman, President.

Climate: Tropical and monsoon. Summer temperature about 86 °F (*30 °C*); winter 68 °F (*20 °C*). Rainfall is heavy, varying from 50 in to 135 in per year in different areas, and most falling from June to September (the monsoon season).

Labour force: 23 401 000 (1970): Agriculture, forestry and fishing 85·9% (ILO estimates); 25 181 328, excluding underrenumeration (1974 census).

Gross domestic product: 102 785 million taka in 1975/76: Agriculture, forestry and fishing 56·0%; Trade, restaurants and hotels 11·7%.

Exports: 5 551·7 million taka in 1975/76: Raw jute and kenaf (mesta) 29·4%; Jute goods 50·0%.

Monetary unit: Taka. 1 taka = 100 paisa.

Denominations:

Coins 1, 2, 5, 10, 25, 50 paisa.

Notes 1, 5, 10, 100 taka.

Exchange rate to US dollar: 15.40 (July 1977).

Political history and government: Formerly the eastern wing of Pakistan, formed by the partition of British India on 15 Aug. 1947. In elections for a Pakistan National Assembly on 7 Dec. 1970 the Awami League, led by Sheikh Mujibur Rahman, won all but two seats in East Pakistan and an overall majority in the Assembly. The League advocated autonomy for East Pakistan within a loose federation but this was unacceptable to the main party in West Pakistan. When constitutional talks failed, the League declared East Pakistan's independence as Bangladesh on 26 Mar. 1971. Civil war broke out and the League was outlawed. Mujib was arrested but the League announced on 11 Apr. 1971 that he was President of Bangladesh. After Indian intervention, Pakistani forces surrendered and Bangladesh's secession became effective on 16 Dec. 1971. Mujib was released and became Prime Minister on 12 Jan. 1972. Bangladesh joined the Commonwealth or.

18 Apr. 1972. Mujib became an executive President on 25 Jan. 1975 and Bangladesh a one-party state on 25 Feb. 1975. Mujib was deposed by a *coup* and killed on 15 Aug. 1975, when martial law was imposed. After an army mutiny on 3 Nov. 1975, the new President resigned on 6 Nov. 1975, when the Chief Justice of the Supreme Court became President and Chief Martial Law Administrator. He immediately dissolved Parliament and on the next day the mutiny was crushed. His deputy, Maj.-Gen Ziaur Rahman, took over martial law powers on 29 Nov. 1976 and became President on 21 Apr. 1977. A Presidential proclamation of 22 Apr. 1977 amended the constitution to change Bangladesh from a secular to an Islamic state. A referendum on 30 May 1977 gave 99% support to President Zia.

Telephones: 48 000 (1972).

Daily newspapers: 5 (1975).

Radio: 531 000 (1969).

Length of roadways: 14 913 miles *c 24 000 km.*

Length of railways: 1776 miles *2858 km.*

Universities: 6.

Adult illiteracy: approx. 85%.

Expectation of life: Males 35·8 years; females 35·8 years (UN estimates for 1970-75).

Defence: Military service voluntary; total armed forces 63 000; defence expenditure 1975/76; $52 million.

BARBADOS

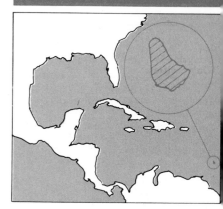

Population: 237 701 (census of 7 Apr. (1970); 247 000 (estimate for 1 July 1976).

Area: 166 miles² *430 km².*

Languages: English.

Religions: Anglican with Methodist, Roman Catholic and Moravian minorities.

Capital city: Bridgetown, population 8789 (1970); parish of Bridgetown and St Michael 96 886.

Other principal town: Speightstown.

Highest point: Mount Hillaby, 1115 ft *340 m.*

Head of State: HM Queen Elizabeth II, represented by Sir Deighton Ward, KCMG, Governor-General.

Prime Minister: The Rt Hon John Michael Geoffrey Manningham Adams (b. 24 Sept. 1931).

Climate: Pleasant, with temperatures rarely rising above 86 °F (*30 °C*) or falling below 67 °F (*18 °C*). Average annual rainfall, which varies from district to district, 50 in to 75 in (*1270 mm* to *1778 mm*). Subject to earthquakes and hurricanes.

Labour force: 91 069 (1970 census): Agriculture, forestry and fishing 17·0%; Mining and manufacturing 15·6%; (manufacturing 15·3%); Construction 13·3%; Trade, restaurants and hotels 15·1%; Services 31·9%.

Gross domestic product: B$357·0 million (at factor cost) in 1972: Agriculture, forestry and fishing 12·4%; Mining and manufacturing 12·2%; Trade 23·5%.

Exports: US$44·7 million in 1972: Sugar and honey 36·1% (raw sugar 32·0%); Petroleum products 13·4%.

Monetary unit: Barbados dollar (B$). 1 dollar = 100 cents.

Denominations:
Coins 1, 5, 10, 25 cents, B$1.
Notes B$ 1, 5, 10, 20, 100.

Exchange rate to US dollar: 2.004 (July 1977).

Political history and government: A former British colony, with internal self-government from 16 Oct. 1961. A member of the West Indies Federation from 3 Jan. 1958 to 31 May 1962. Following a constitutional conference on 20 June–4 July 1966, Barbados became independent, within the Commonwealth, on 30 Nov. 1966. Executive power is vested in the Queen and exercisable by her appointed representative, the Governor-General, advised by the Cabinet. The Governor-General appoints the Prime Minister and, on the latter's advice, other members of the Cabinet. Legislative power is vested in the bicameral Parliament, comprising the Senate (21 appointed members) and the House of Assembly, with 24 members elected by universal adult suffrage for five years (subject to dissolution) from 12 constituencies. The Cabinet, which effectively directs the government, is responsible to Parliament.

Telephones: 40 000 (1974).

Daily newspapers: One.
Total circulation: 25 642 weekdays; 35 746 Sundays.

Radio: 116 000 (1973).

TV: 42 000 (1974).

Length of roadways: 840 miles 1352 km.

Universities: 1

Expectation of life: Males 62·74 years; Females 67·43 years (1959–61).

Defence: A small volunteer force but no standing armed forces.

Cinemas: 6 (seating capacity 4700) in 1973; also two drive-ins for 395 cars.

BELGIUM

Official name: Royaume de Belgique (in French) or Koninkrijk België (in Dutch) (Kingdom of Belgium).

Population: 9 650 944 (census of 31 Dec. 1970); 9 813 000 (estimate, 31 Dec. 1975).

Area: 11 781 miles² 30 513 km².

Languages: Dutch (Flemish), French, German.

Religion: Roman Catholic.

Capital city: Bruxelles (Brussel, Brussels), population 1 050 787 (including Anderlecht,

Schaerbeek and other suburbs) at 31 Dec. 1975.

Other principal towns (1975): Antwerpen (Anvers, Antwerp) 209 200; Gent (Gand, Ghent) 142 551; Liège (Luik) 139 333; Bruges (Brugge) 119 718; Schaerbeek (Schaarbeek) 118 950 (1970); Anderlecht 103 796 (1970).

Highest point: Botrange, 2277 ft, 694 m.

Principal mountain ranges: Ardennes.

Principal rivers: Schelde, Meuse (575 miles 925 km).

Head of State: HM Baudouin Albert Charles Léopold Axel Marie Gustave, KG (b. 7 Sept. 1930), King of the Belgians. The King's name is also written Boudewijn (in Dutch) or Balduin (in German).

Prime Minister: Léo Tindemans (b. 16 Apr. 1922).

Climate: Mild and humid on coast. Hotter summers, colder winters inland. In Brussels, January coldest (31 °F to 42 °F), July hottest 54 °F to 73 °F) December rainiest (13 days). Absolute maximum temperature 40,0 °C (104 °F) on the coast, 27 June 1947; absolute minimum −29,8 °C (−21·6 °F), Vieslam, 10 Dec. 1879.

Labour force: 3 801 794 (including persons working abroad) aged 15 over (30 June 1975): Manufacturing 29·7%; Trade, restaurants and hotels 18·4%; Community, social and personal services 25·8%. Figures exclude persons on compulsory military service (32 973 in 1975) and unemployed (168 367 in 1975).

Gross domestic product: 2 081 100 million Belgian francs in 1974: Manufacturing (including garages) 32·3%; Trade 12·2%; Community, social and personal services 20·7% (government services 12·6%).

Exports: $28 760·3 million (including Luxembourg) in 1975: Chemicals 12·1%; Iron and steel 13·7%; Machinery and transport equipment 23·4% (transport equipment 10·7%).

Monetary unit: Belgian franc (frank). 1 franc = 100 centimes (centiemen).

Denominations:
Coins 25, 50 centimes, 1, 5, 10, 50, 100 francs.
Notes 20, 50, 100, 500, 1000, 5000 francs.

Exchange rate to US dollar: 35·48 (July 1977).

Political history and government: A constitutional and hereditary monarchy, comprising nine provinces. Legislative power is vested in the King and the bicameral Parliament, comprising the Senate (181 members, including 106 directly elected by universal adult suffrage, 50 elected by provincial councils and 25 co-opted by the elected members) and the Chamber of Representatives (212 members directly elected, using proportional representation). Members of both Houses serve for up to four years. Executive power, nominally vested in the King, is exercised by the Cabinet. The King appoints the Prime Minister and, on the latter's advice, other Ministers. The Cabinet is responsible to Parliament.

Telephones: 2 645 957 (1974).

Daily newspapers: 46 (1973).
Total circulation: 2 614 000.

Radio: 3 768 491 (1974).

TV: 2 464 201 (1974).

Length of roadways: 58 158 miles 93 596 km (31 Dec. 1975).

Length of railways: 2536 miles 4081 km.

Universities: 6.

Expectation of Life: Males 67·79 years; females 74·21 years (1968–72).

Defence: Military service 9 months (in Germany) or 11 months (in Belgium); total armed forces 88 300 (31 050 conscripts); defence expenditure, 1976: $1479 million.

Cinemas: 728 (seating capacity 359 000) and 39 part-time (1972).

BENIN

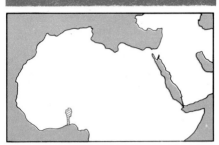

Official name: La République populaire du Bénin (the People's Republic of Benin).

Population: 3 197 000 (estimate for 1 July 1976).

Area: 43 484 miles² 112 622 km².

Languages: French (official), Fon, Adja, Bariba, Yoruba.

Religions: Animist, with Christian and Muslim minorities.

Capital city: Porto-Novo, population 104 000 (1975).

Other principal towns: Cotonou 178 000 (1975); Abomey 42 100; Ouidah 19 600; Parakou 16 300.

Highest point: 2083 ft 635 m.

Principal mountain ranges: Chaîne de l'Atakora.

Principal rivers: Ouémé, Niger (2600 miles [4184 km]) on frontier.

Head of State: Lt-Col Mathieu Kerekou (b. 2 Sept. 1933), President and Head of the Government.

Climate: Tropical (hot and humid). Average temperatures 68 °F to 93 °F. Heavy rainfall near the coast, hotter and drier inland. In Cotonou the warmest month is April (daily average high 83 °F), coldest is August (73 °F).

Labour force: 1 318 000 (1970): Agriculture, forestry and fishing 49·8% (ILO estimates); 1 445 000 (1975).

Gross domestic product: 80 800 million CFA francs in 1974/75: Agriculture, forestry and fishing 31·4%; Trade, restaurants and hotels 30·7%.

Exports: $36·5 million in 1972: Cocoa beans 19·4%; Other food 12·7%; Oil seeds, oil nuts and oil kernels 11·6%; Raw cotton 27·9%; Palm kernel oil 11·4%.

Monetary unit: Franc de la Communauté financière africaine.

Denominations:
Coins 1, 2, 5, 10, 25, 50, 100 CFA francs.
Notes 50, 100, 500, 1000, 5000 CFA francs.

Exchange rate to US dollar: 242·80 (July 1977).

Political history and government: Formerly part of French West Africa, became independent as the Republic of Dahomey on 1 Aug. 1960. Under military rule since 26 Oct. 1972. Government is controlled by a cabinet of army officers. On 1 Sept. 1973 the President announced the creation of a National Council of the Revolution (69 members, including 30 civilians), under his leadership, to develop state policy. Since 28 Nov. 1974 the Council has been directed by a 14-member National Political Bureau, also chaired by the President. The military government advocates Marxist-Leninist principles and introduced the country's present name on 1 Dec. 1975.

Telephones: 8326 (1974).

Daily newspapers: 2 (1972).
Total circulation: 2000.

Radio: 150 000 (1972).

B

TV: 100 (1972).
Length of roadways: 4310 miles *6937 km* (1973).
Length of railways: 360 miles *579 km.*
Universities: 1.
Adult illiteracy: 95·4% (males 92·3%; females 98·2%) in 1961.
Expectation of life: Males 39·4 years; females 42·6 years (UN estimates for 1970–75).
Defence: Total armed forces 1650.
Cinemas: 6 (seating capacity 9000) in 1972.

BHUTAN

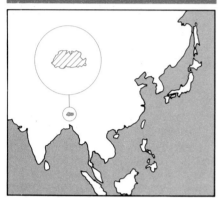

Official name: Druk-yul or, in Tibetan, Druk Gyalkhap (Realm of the Dragon). The name Bhutan is Tibetan for 'the End of the Land'.
Population: 1 034 774 (census of Nov.–Dec. 1969); 1 202 000 (UN estimate for mid-1976).
Area: 18 000 miles² *47 000 km².*
Languages: Dzongkha, Bumthangka, Sarchapkkha.
Religions: Buddhist with Hindu minority.
Capital city: Thimbu (Thimphu).
Other principal towns: Paro Dzong; Punakha; Tongsa Dzong.
Highest point: Khula Kangri 1, 24 784 ft *7554 m.*
Principal mountain range: Himalaya.
Principal rivers: Amo-Chu, Wang-chu, Ma-chu, Manas.
Head of State: Jigme Singye Wangchuk (b. 11 Nov. 1955), Druk Gyalpo ('Dragon King').
Climate: Steamy hot in lowland foothills. Cold most of the year in higher areas.
Labour force: 521 000 (1970): Agriculture, forestry and fishing 94·4% (ILO estimates).
Gross domestic products: $49 million in 1970 (UN estimate).
Exports: n.a.
Monetary unit: Ngultrum. 1 ngultrum = 100 chetrums (Indian currency is also legal tender).
Denominations:
  Coins 5, 10, 25, 50 chetrums, 1 ngultrum.
  Notes 1, 5, 10 and 100 ngultrums.
Exchange rate to US dollar: 8·8144 (July 1977).
Political history and government: A hereditary monarchy, under the Wangchuk dynasty since 1907. The Treaty of Punakha in 1910 provided that Bhutan's external relations were to be guided by British India. After the independence of India in 1947, an Indo-Bhutan Treaty of 8 Aug. 1949 transferred this protection to India.
  The King is Head of State and Head of Government but a Royal Advisory Council (nine members), established in 1965, is the principal policy-making body. Bhutan's first Cabinet was formed in May 1968. The government is assisted by the unicameral National Assembly (*Tsogdu*), established in

1953. The Assembly has 150 members, of whom 110 are indirectly elected by village headmen, 10 represent ecclesiastical bodies and 30 are appointed officials. Members of the Assembly serve a three-year term. The Royal Advisory Council and the Council of Ministers are responsible to the Assembly.
Telephones: 570 (1974).
Length of roadways: 932 miles *1500 km.*
Expectation of life: Males 42·2 years; females 45·0 years (UN estimates for 1970–75).
Defence: Army: 5000 men, Indian trained.
Cinemas: 3 (seating capacity 1500) in 1971.

BOLIVIA

Official name: La República de Bolivia.
Population: 4 687 718 (census of 29 Sept. 1976).
Area: 424 164 miles² *1 098 581 km.²*
Languages: Spanish, Amyará, Quéchua.
Religion: Roman Catholic.
Capital City: La Paz de Ayacucho, population 660 700 (estimate for 1 July 1975).
Other principal towns (1975): Cochabamba 184 340; Santa Cruz de la Sierra 149 230; Oruro 110 490; Sucre (legal capital) 106 590 (30 Sept. 1973).
Highest point: Nevado Sajama, 21 391 ft *6520 m* (first climbed in 1937).
Principal mountain ranges: Cordillera de los Andes, Cordillera Real, Cordillera Oriental, Cordillera Central.
Principal rivers: Beni, Mamoré, Pilcomayo, Paraguai (Paraguay) (1500 miles *2414 km*) on frontier.
Head of State: Gen Hugo Banzer Suárez (b. 10 May 1926), President.
Climate: Dry, with cold winds on Antiplano, hot and humid in eastern lowlands. In La Paz, average maximum 62 °F (June, July) to 67 °F (November), minimum 33 °F (July) to 43 °F (January, February), January rainiest (21 days).
Labour force: 1 586 000 (1970): Agriculture, forestry and fishing 55·5% (ILO estimates).
Gross domestic product: 37 317 million pesos in 1974: Agriculture, forestry and fishing 14·7%; Mining and quarrying 20·6%; Manufacturing 12·4%; Trade, restaurants and hotels 11·6%.
Exports: $240·4 million in 1972: Metalliferous ores and metal scrap 28·4% (non-ferrous ores and concentrates 20·7%); Mineral fuels, lubricants, etc. 17·3% (crude petroleum 13·2%); Non-ferrous metals 43·8% (tin 43·0%).
Monetary unit: Bolivian peso. 1 peso = 100 centavos.
Denominations:
  Coins 5, 10, 20, 25, 50 centavos, 1 peso.
  Notes 1, 5, 10, 20, 50, 100 pesos.
Exchange rate to US dollar: 20.00 (July 1977).
Political history and government: A republic, divided into nine departments. Under military rule since September 1969,

sometimes with the participation of political parties. An all-military Cabinet has held office since June 1974. The government has banned political activity until 1980.
Telephones: 48 950 (1973).
Daily newspapers: 17 (1973).
  Total circulation: 202 000.
Radio: 1 350 000 (1968).
TV: 11 000 (1972).
Length of roadways: 15 930 miles *25 637 km.*
Length of railways: 2190 miles *3524 km.*
Universities: 9.
Adult illiteracy: 60% (1960 estimate).
Expectation of life: Males 45·7 years; females 47·9 years (UN estimates for 1970–75).
Defence: Military service 12 months selective; total armed forces 22 000; defence expenditure, 1974: $35 million.
Cinemas: 90 with seating capacity of *c.* 42 500 (1970).

BOTSWANA

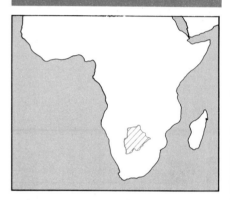

Official name: The Republic of Botswana.
Population: 608 656 (census of 31 Aug. 1971); 693 000 (estimate for 1 July 1976).
Area: 231 805 miles² *600 372 km².*
Languages: Se-Tswana, English.
Religions: Christian, ancestral beliefs.
Capital city: Gaborone, population 33 142 (1975).
Other principal towns (1975): Francistown 23 249; Selebi-Pikwe 20 572; Serowe 20 005; Kange 16 836.
Principal rivers: Chobe, Shashi.
Head of State: Sir Seretse Khama, KBE (b. 1 July 1921), President.
Climate: Sub-tropical but variable. Hot summers. In winter, warm days and cold nights in higher parts. Average annual rainfall 18 in, varying from 25 in in north, to 9 in or less in western Kalahari. Sand and dust blown by westerly wind in August.
Labour force: 299 000 (1970): Agriculture, forestry and fishing 86·6% (ILO estimates); 293 849 (excluding nomads) at 1971 census.
Gross domestic product: 152·9 million pula (provisional) in 1973/74: Agriculture, forestry and fishing 27·0%; Mining and quarrying 10·4%; Construction 12·4%; Trade, restaurants and hotels 11·5%; Services 27·3%. Revised total is 192·1 million pula.
Exports: 105·0 million pula in 1974: Meat and meat preparations 34·7%; Diamonds 30·6%; Copper and nickel ores 20·9%.
Monetary unit: Pula. 1 pula = 100 thebe.
Denominations:
  Coins 1, 5, 10, 25 and 50 thebe.
  Notes 1, 2, 5 and 10 pula.
Exchange rate to US dollar: 0·828 (July 1977).
Political history and government: Formerly the Bechuanaland Protectorate, under

British rule. In February 1965 the seat of government was moved from Mafeking, in South Africa, to Gaberones (now Gaborone). The first elections were held on 1 Mar. 1965, when internal self-government was achieved, and the first Prime Minister was appointed two days later. Bechuanaland became the independent Republic of Botswana, within the Commonwealth, on 30 Sept. 1966, when the Prime Minister became President.

Legislative power is vested in the uni-cameral National Assembly, with 38 members, including 32 directly elected by universal adult suffrage from single-member constituencies. Members of the Assembly serve for up to five years. Executive power is vested in the President, who is leader of the majority party in the Assembly. He governs with the assistance of an appointed Cabinet, responsible to the Assembly. The government is also advised by the House of Chiefs, with 15 members, including the chiefs of the eight principal tribes, four sub-chiefs and three others.

Telephones: 6699 (1974).
Daily newspapers: 2 (1971).
   Total circulation: 14 000.
Radio: 11 602 (1972).
Length of roadways (1971): 12 923 miles *20 798 km.*
Length of railways: 392 miles *630 km.*
Universities: 1.
Adult illiteracy: 67·1% (males 69·7%; females 65·0%) unable to read in 1964.
Expectation of life: Males 41·9 years; females 45·1 years (UN estimates for 1970–75).
Defence: A paramilitary police force of about 1500.
Cinemas: 11 (est seating capacity 3000) in 1971.

BRAZIL

Official name: República Federativa do Brasil (the Federative Republic of Brazil).
Population: 92 341 556 (census of 1 Sept. 1970); 109 181 000 (estimate for 1 July 1976). Figures exclude Indian jungle population (45 429 in 1950).
Area: 3 286 488 miles² *8 511 965 km².*
Language: Portuguese.
Religion: Roman Catholic.
Capital city: Brasília, population 271 570 (1970).

Other principal towns (1975): São Paulo 7 198 608; Rio de Janeiro 4 857 716; Belo Horizonte 1 557 446; Recife (Pernambuco) 1 249 821; Salvador (Bahia) 1 237 373; Fortaleza 1 109 837; Pôrto Alegre 1 043 964.
Highest point: Pico da Bandeira, 9482 ft *2890 m.*
Principal mountain ranges: Serra do Mar, Serra Geral, Serra de Mantiqueira.
Principal rivers: Amazonas (Amazon) (3910 miles *6292 km*) and tributaries, Paraná, São Francisco.
Head of State: Gen Ernesto Geisel (b. 3 Aug. 1907), President.
Climate: Hot and wet in tropical Amazon basin; sub-tropical in highlands; temperate (warm summers and mild winters) in southern uplands. In Rio de Janeiro, average maximum 75 °F (July, September) to 85 °F (February), minimum 63 °F (July) to 73 °F (January, February), December rainiest (14 days). In São Paulo maximum 71 °F (June, July) to 82 °F (February), minimum 49 °F (July) to 64 °F (February), January rainiest (19 days). Absolute maximum temperature 43·9 °C (*111·0 °F*), Ibipetuba, 16 Sept. 1927: absolute minimum −11° C (+12·2 °F), Xanxerê, 14 July 1933.
Labour force: 29 557 224 (including un-employed) aged 10 and over (1970 census): Agriculture, forestry and fishing 45·4%; Manufacturing 11·2%; Community, social and personal services 22·6%; 37 750 238 (household survey, Oct.–Dec. 1973).
Gross domestic product: 477 163 million cruzeiros in 1973: Agriculture, forestry and fishing 15·3%; Manufacturing 23·9%; Trade 17·2%; Finance, insurance and real estate 13·4%.
Exports: $8 669·5 million (excluding re-exports) in 1975: Sugar and honey 13·2% (raw sugar 11·2%); Coffee 10·8%; Other food 16·9%; Metalliferous ores and metal scrap 11·8% (iron ore and concentrates 10·6%); Machinery and transport equipment 10·3%.
Monetary unit: Cruzeiro. 1 cruzeiro = 100 centavos.
Denominations:
   Coins 1, 2, 5, 10, 20, 50 centavos, 1 cruzeiro.
   Notes 1, 5, 10, 50, 100, 500 cruzeiros.
Exchange rate of US dollar: 14.315 (July 1977).
Political history and government: Under a military-backed government since the army revolution of 31 Mar–1 Apr. 1964. New constitutions were introduced on 15 Mar. 1967 and 20 Oct. 1969. According to the 1969 constitution, Brazil is a federal republic comprising 21 States, four Territories and a Federal District (Brasília). Legislative power is exercised by the National Congress, comprising the Chamber of Deputies (364 members, elected for four years) and the Federal Senate (66 members, elected in rotation for eight years). All literate adults may vote. Executive power is exercised by the President, elected for five years by an electoral college composed of members of Congress and representatives of State legislatures. He is assisted by a Vice-President and an appointed Cabinet. The President has far-reaching powers, including authority to suspend Congress. By Presidential decrees of 14 Apr. 1977, future Presidents will hold office for six years and one-third of the Senate will be indirectly elected. Only two political parties have been legalised.
Telephones: 2 652 000 (1974).
Daily newspapers: 274 (1973).
   Total circulation: 4 058 000.
Radio: 6 250 000 (1973).
TV: 6 600 000 (1972).
Length of roadways: 868 295 miles *1 397 386 km* (31 Dec. 1975).
Length of railways: 19 381 miles *31 191 km.*

Universities: 64.
Adult illiteracy: 33·8% (males 30·6%; females 36·8%) in 1970.
Expectation of life: Males 57·61 years; females 61·10 years (1960–70).
Defence: Military service one year; total armed forces 257 200 (121 000 conscripts); defence expenditure, 1976: $1780 million.
Cinemas: 3 195 (seating capacity 1 911 200) in 1967 (35 mm films only).

BULGARIA

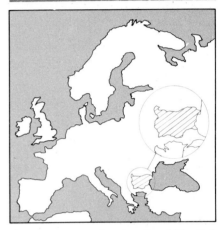

Official name: Narodna Republika Bulgaria (People's Republic of Bulgaria).
Population: 8 227 866 (census of 1 Dec. 1965); 8 721 900 (estimate for 1 July 1975).
Area: 42 823 miles² *110 912 km².*
Languages: Bulgarian 88%; Turkish and Macedonian minorities.
Religions: Eastern Orthodox with Muslim, Roman Catholic and Protestant minorities.
Capital city: Sofiya (Sofia), population 965 728 (estimate for 1 July 1975).
Other principal towns (1975): Plovdiv 300 242; Varna 231 654; Ruse (Roussé) 160 351; Burgas (Bourgas) 144 449; Stara Zagora 122 200; Pleven (Plévène) 107 567.
Highest point: Musala, 9596 ft *2925 m.*
Principal mountain ranges: Balkan Mountains.
Principal rivers: Dunav (Danube) (1770 miles *2848 km*), Iskŭr (Iskar) (229 miles *368 km*), Maritsa (326 miles *524 km*), Tundzha.
Head of State: Todor Zhivkov (b. 7 Sept. 1911), President of the State Council and First Secretary of the Central Committee of the Bulgarian Communist Party.
Head of Government: Stanko Todorov (b. 10 Dec. 1920), Chairman of the Council of Ministers.
Climate: Mild in the south, more extreme in the north. In Sofia, July (57 °F to 82 °F), August (56 °F to 82 °F), hottest, January (22 °F to 34 °F), coldest, May rainiest (11 days).
Labour force: 4 267 798 (1965 census): Agriculture and forestry 50·2%; Industry (mining, manufacturing and electricity) 30·3% (manufacturing, excluding metallurgy, 26·3%); 4 533 000 (1970): Agriculture, forestry and fishing 46·6% (ILO estimates).
Net material product: 14 289 million leva in 1975: Agriculture and forestry 22·0%; Industry 51·0%.
Exports: 3 720·8 million leva in 1974: Machinery and equipment 39·9%; Food, beverages and tobacco 24·3%.
Monetary unit: Lev. 1 lev = 100 stotinki.
Denominations:
   Coins 1, 2, 5, 10, 20, 50 stotinki, 1, 2 leva.
   Notes 1, 2, 5, 10, 20 leva.

Exchange rate to US dollar: 0.96 (July 1977).

Political history and government: Formerly part of Turkey's Ottoman Empire, becoming an autonomous principality in 1878. Bulgaria became a fully independent kingdom on 22 Sept. 1908. The government allied with Nazi Germany in the Second World War. On 9 Sept. 1944 the Fatherland, Front, a Communist-dominated coalition, seized power in a *coup*. The monarchy was abolished by a popular referendum on 8 Sept. 1946 and a republic proclaimed on 15 Sept. 1946. A constitution for a People's Republic was adopted on 4 Dec. 1947. A new constitution was promulgated, after approval by referendum, on 18 May 1971.

The supreme organ of state power is the unicameral National Assembly, with 400 members elected for five years (unopposed) by universal adult suffrage in single-member constituencies. The Assembly elects the State Council (27 members were elected on 16 June 1976) to be its permanent organ. The Council of Ministers, the highest organ of state administration, is elected by (and responsible to) the Assembly.

Political power is held by the Bulgarian Communist Party (BCP), which dominates the Fatherland Front. The Front presents an approved list of candidates for elections to all representative bodies. The BCP's highest authority is the Party Congress, convened every five years. The Congress elects a Central Committee (154 members were elected in April 1976) to supervise Party work. To direct its policy, the Committee elects a Political Bureau (Politburo), with nine full members and six candidate members in 1976.

Bulgaria comprises 27 provinces and three cities, each with a People's Council elected for 2½ years.

Telephones: 718 325 (1974).
Daily newspapers: 13 (1973).
Total circulation: 1 856 000.
Radio: 2 272 894 (1974).
TV: 1 489 640 (1975).
Length of roadways: 22 469 miles *36 161 km* (31 Dec. 1975).
Length of railways: 3830 miles *6164 km.*
Universities: 3.
Adult illiteracy: 9·8% (males 4·8%; females 14·7%) in 1965.
Expectation of life: Males 68·58 years; females 73·86 years (1969–71).
Defence: Military service: Army and Air Force two years, Navy three years; total armed forces 164 500 (100 000 conscripts); defence expenditure, 1976: $438 million.
Cinemas: 3459 (seating capacity 734 200) in 1973.

BURMA

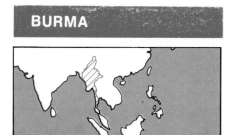

Official name: Pyidaungsu Socialist Thammada Myanma Nainggnan (The Socialist Republic of the Union of Burma).
Population: 28 885 867 (census of 31 Mar. 1973); 31 000 000 (estimate for 1 July 1976).
Area: 261 218 miles²; *676 552 km²*.
Languages: Burmese, English.
Religions: Buddhist with Muslim, Hindu and Animist minorities.

Capital city: Rangoon, population 2 056 118 (1973 census).
Other principal towns (1973): Mandalay 417 266; Moulmein 171 767; Bassein 126 152.
Highest point: Hkakado Razi, 19 296 ft *5881 m.*
Principal mountain ranges: Arakan Yoma, Pegu Yoma.
Principal rivers: Irrawaddy (including Chindwin), Salween, Sittang, Mekong (2600 miles *[4184 km]*) on frontier.
Head of State: U Ne Win (b. 24 May 1911), President.
Prime Minister: U Maung Maung Kha (b. 1919).
Climate: Hot March–April, monsoon May–October, cool November–February. In Rangoon, average maximum 85 °F (July, August) to 97 °F (April), minimum 65 °F (January) to 77 °F (May). July (26 days) and August (25 days) rainiest. Absolute maximum temperature 114 °F (*45,56 °C*), Mandalay, 29 Apr. 1906, Monywa, 15 May 1934; absolute minimum 31 °F (*−0,56 °C*), Maymyo, 29 Dec. 1913.
Labour force: 11 748 663 (1974/75): Agriculture, forestry and fishing 72·6%.
Gross domestic product: 14 852 million kyats in 1973/74: Agriculture, forestry and fishing 42·4%; Trade 26·4%.
Exports: $195·4 million (excluding re-exports) in 1974: Rice 41·9%; Other food 10·5%; Wood, lumber and cork 25·7% (sawlogs and veneer logs 16·6%).
Monetary unit: Kyat. 1 kyat = 100 pyas.
Denominations:
Coins 1, 5, 10, 25, 50 pyas, 1 kyat.
Notes 1, 5, 10, 20, 25 kyats.
Exchange rate to US dollar: 7·336 (July 1977).
Political history and government: Formerly part of British India. Burma became a separate British dependency, with limited self-government, in 1937. It was invaded and occupied by Japanese forces in February 1942 but re-occupied by British forces in May 1945. Burma became independent, outside the Commonwealth, on 4 Jan. 1948. The government was deposed by a military *coup* on 2 Mar. 1962 and Parliament was dissolved the next day. Power was assumed by a Revolutionary Council, led by Gen. Ne Win. The military régime established the Burmese Socialist Programme Party (BSPP), the only permitted party since 28 Mar. 1964.

A new one-party constitution, approved by popular referendum on 15–31 Dec. 1973, was introduced on 4 Jan. 1974, when the country's present name was adopted. Legislative power is vested in the People's Assembly, with 450 members elected for four years by universal adult suffrage. The first Assembly was elected on 27 Jan.–10 Feb. 1974 and inaugurated on 2 Mar. 1974, when the Revolutionary Council was dissolved. The Assembly elects a Council of State (29 members) to be the country's main policy-making body. The Chairman of the Council of State is President of the Republic. The Council of Ministers, elected by the Assembly, has executive responsibility. The BSPP Central Committee had 180 members (including the 15-member Central Executive Committee) in February 1977. Burma comprises seven states and seven administrative regions.

Telephones: 30 000 (1974).
Daily newspapers: 10 (1973).
Total circulation: 283 000 (9 dailies).
Radio: 627 000 (1973).
Length of roadways: c. 15 534 miles *c. 25 000 km.*
Length of railways: 1925 miles *3098 km.*
Universities: 2.
Expectation of life: Males 48·6 years; females 51·5 years (UN estimates for 1970–75).

Defence: Military service voluntary; total armed forces 169 500; defence expenditure, 1976/77: $113 million.
Cinemas: 418 (seating capacity 302 600) in 1972.

BURUNDI

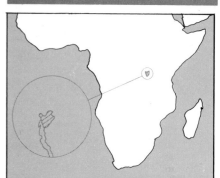

Official name: La République du Burundi or Republika y'Uburundi (the Republic of Burundi).
Population: 3 763 000 (estimate for 1 July 1975).
Area: 10 747 miles² *27 834 km²*.
Languages: French, Kirundi, Kiswahili.
Religions: Roman Catholic with Animist and Protestant minorities.
Capital city: Bujumbura (formerly Usumbura), population 78 810, including suburbs (estimate for 31 Dec. 1970).
Other principal towns: Kitega, population 5000 (1970).
Highest point: 8809 ft *2685 m.*
Principal rivers: Kagera, Ruzizi.
Head of State: Lt-Col Jean-Baptiste Bagaza (b. Aug. 1946), President.
Prime Minister: Lt-Col Edouard Nzambimana.
Climate: Hot and humid in lowlands, cool in highlands.
Labour force: 1 614 000 (1965); 1 716 000 (1970): Agriculture, forestry and fishing 87·1% (ILO estimates).
Gross domestic product: $224 million (1970 estimate).
Exports: $29·5 million (excluding re-exports) in 1974: Coffee 84·3%.
Monetary unit: Burundi franc. 1 franc = 100 centimes.
Denominations:
Coins 1, 5, 10 francs.
Notes 10, 20, 50, 100, 500, 1000, 5000 francs.
Exchange rate to US dollar: 90.00 (July 1977).
Political history and government: Formerly part of the Belgian-administered Trust Territory of Ruanda-Urundi. Burundi became independent, with the Mwami (King) as Head of State, on 1 July 1962. A one-party state since 24 Nov. 1966. The monarchy was overthrown, and a republic established, by a military *coup* on 28 Nov. 1966, when the Prime Minister, Col (later Lt-Gen) Michel Micombero, took power and became President. Another military *coup* deposed Micombero on 1 Nov. 1976.
Telephones: 4797 (1974).
Daily newspapers: 1 (1970).
Total circulation: 300.
Radio: 100 000 (1973).
Length of roadways: 1856 miles *2987 km.*
Universities: 1.
Expectation of life: Males 37·5 years; females 40·6 years (UN estimate for 1970–75).
Defence: Total forces (army and police) about 3000.
Cinemas: 4 (seating capacity 1000) in 1970.

CAMBODIA

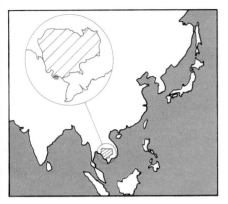

Official name: Democratic Kampuchea.
Population: 5 728 771 (census of 17 Apr. 1962); 8 349 000 (UN estimate for mid-1976).
Area: 69 898 miles², *181 035 km²*.
Languages: Khmer (official), French.
Religions: Buddhist.
Capital city: Phnom-Penh, population 393 995 (1962).
Other principal towns: Battambang, Kompong Chhnang, Kompong Cham, Kompong Som (Sihanoukville).
Highest point: Mt Ka-Kup 5722 ft *1744 m*.
Principal mountain ranges: Chaîne des Cardamomes.
Principal rivers: Mekong 2600 miles *4184 km*.
Head of State: Khieu Samphan (b. 1932), President of the State Presidium.
Prime Minister: Pol Pot.
Climate: Tropical and humid. Rainy season June–November. In Phnom-Penh, average maximum 86 °F (November, December) to 94 °F (April), minimum 70 °F (January) to 76 °F (April–October), September rainiest (19 days).
Labour force: 2 499 735 aged 10 and over (1962 census); 2 850 000 (1970): Agriculture, forestry and fishing 78·2% (ILO estimates).
Gross domestic product: 32 000 million riels in 1966 (when $1 = 35 riels); $881 million (1970 estimate).
Exports: $65·0 million in 1969: Cereals and cereal preparations 23·6% (rice 17·1%); Fruit and vegetables 11·1%; Natural rubber 40·3%.
Monetary unit: Riel. 1 riel = 100 sen.
Denominations:
   Coins 10, 20, 50 sen.
   Notes 1, 5, 10, 20, 50, 100, 500 riels.
Exchange rate to US dollar: 1675 (April 1975).
Political history and government: Formerly a monarchy and part of French Indo-China. Norodom Sihanouk became King on 26 Apr. 1941. On 6 May 1947 he promulgated a constitution providing for a bicameral Parliament, including an elected National Assembly. Cambodia became an Associate State of the French Union on 8 Nov. 1949 and fully independent on 9 Nov. 1953. Sihanouk abdicated on 2 Mar. 1955 in favour of his father, Norodom Suramarit. King Suramarit died on 3 Apr. 1960 and Parliament elected Prince Sihanouk to become Head of State (without taking the title of King) on 20 June 1960.
On 18 Mar. 1970 Prince Sihanouk was deposed by his Prime Minister, Lt-Gen (later Marshal) Lon Nol, who proclaimed the Khmer Republic on 8 Oct. 1970. Sihanouk went into exile and formed a Royal Government of National Union, supported by the pro-Communist *Khmers*

Rouges. Sihanoukists and the *Khmers Rouges* formed the National United Front of Cambodia (NUFC). Their combined forces defeated the republicans and Phnom-Penh surrendered on 17 April 1975, when the Royal Government took power. On 14 Dec. 1975 a congress of the NUFC approved a new republican constitution, promulgated on 5 Jan. 1976. Elections for a new Assembly were held on 20 Mar. 1976 and Prince Sihanouk resigned as Head of State on 4 Apr. 1976.
Legislative power is vested in the People's Representative Assembly, with 250 members elected for 5 years by universal adult suffrage. The Assembly elects a three-man State Presidium and appoints the Council of Ministers.
Telephones: 9000 (1972).
Daily newspapers: 1.
Radio: 111 000 (1974).
TV: 25 500 (1974).
Length of roadways: *c.* 6836 miles, *c. 11 000 km*.
Length of railways: 851 miles *1370 km*.
Adult illiteracy: 59·0% (males 30·1%; females 87·3%) in 1962.
Expectation of life: Males 44·0 years; females 46·9 years (UN estimates for 1970–75).
Defence: Total armed forces 80 000.
Cinemas: 52 (seating capacity 28 800) in 1967.

CAMEROON

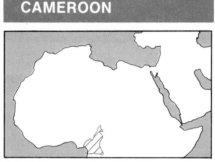

Official name: La République unie du Cameroun (the United Republic of Cameroon).
Population: 6 539 000 (estimate for 1 July 1975).
Area: 183 569 miles² *475 442 km²*.
Languages: French, English (both official).
Religions: Animist with Christian and Muslim minorities.
Capital city: Yaoundé, population 274 399 (1975).
Other principal towns (1975): Douala 485 797; Foumban 59 701; Maroua 46 077; Bafoussam 45 998; Garoua 36 661; Victoria 31 222.
Highest point: Cameroon Mt, 13 350 ft *4069 m*.
Principal mountain ranges: Massif de Ladamaoua.
Principal rivers: Sanaga, Nyong.
Head of State: Ahmadou Ahidjo (b. 24 Aug. 1924), President.
Prime Minister: Paul Biya (b. 13 Feb. 1933).
Climate: Hot and rainy on the coast; cooler and drier inland. Average temperature 80 °F. In Yaoundé average maximum 80 °F to 85 °F, minimum around 66 °F.
Labour force: 2 839 000 (1970): Agriculture, forestry and fishing 85·0% (ILO estimates); 2 985 000 Africans (1975).
Gross domestic products: 300 457 million CFA francs in 1970/71: Agriculture, forestry and fishing (excluding government) 32·3% (agriculture 28·1%); Manufacturing 11·3%; Trade, restaurants and hotels 28·4% (trade 28·1%); Community, social and personal services 11·1%.

Exports: $446·3 million in 1975: Coffee 24·2%; Cocoa 33·6% (cocoa beans 25·3%). Figures exclude trade with other members of the Customs and Economic Union of Central Africa.
Monetary unit: Franc de la Communauté financière africaine (CFA).
Denominations:
   Coins 1, 2, 5, 10, 25, 50, 100 CFA francs
   Notes 100, 500, 1000, 5000, 10 000 CFA francs.
Exchange rate to US dollar: 242.80 (July 1977).
Political history and government: The former German colony of Cameroon was divided into British and French zones, both parts becoming UN Trust Territories. The French zone became independent as the Republic of Cameroon on 1 Jan. 1960. The northern part of the British zone joined Nigeria on 1 June 1961 and the southern part became West Cameroon when it joined the former French zone (renamed East Cameroon) to form a federal republic on 1 Oct. 1961. A one-party state since 8 Sept. 1966. After approval by a referendum on 21 May 1972, the federal arrangement ended and Cameroon became a unitary state on 2 June 1972. The legislature is a unicameral National Assembly of 120 members elected for five years by universal suffrage. The President, elected by the people every five years, appoints the Prime Minister, other Ministers and a governor for each of the seven provinces.
Telephones: 21 811 (30 June 1973).
Daily newspapers: 1 (1975).
   Total circulation: 20 000.
Radio: 225 000 (1973).
Length of roadways (1972): 14 136 miles *22 750 km*.
Length of railways: 723 miles *1164 km*.
Universities: 1.
Expectation of life: Males 39·4 years; females 42·6 years (UN estimates for 1970–75).
Defence: Total armed forces 5600.
Cinemas: 41 (seating capacity 15 600) in 1972.

CANADA

Official name: The Dominion of Canada.
Population: 22 992 604 (census of 1 June 1976).
Area: 3 851 809 miles² *9 976 139 km²*.
Languages: English 60·1%; French 26·9%; German 2·6%; Italian 2·5%; Ukrainian 1·4% (1971).
Religions: Roman Catholic, United Church of Canada, Anglican.
Capital city: Ottawa, population 668 853 (metropolitan area) at 1 June 1976.
Other principal towns: Montreal 2 758 780; Toronto 2 753 112; Vancouver 1 135 774; Winnipeg 570 725; Edmonton 542 845; Quebec 534 193; Hamilton 525 222; Calgary 457 828 (metropolitan areas, 1976).
Highest point: Mt Logan, 19 850 ft *6050 m* (first climbed 23 June 1925).
Principal mountain ranges: Rocky Mts., Coast Mts, Mackenzie Mts.
Principal rivers: Mackenzie (2635 miles *4240 km*, including Peace 1195 miles *1923 km*), Yukon (1979 miles *3185 km*), St. Lawrence (1900 miles *3058 km*), Nelson (1600 miles *2575 km*, including Saskatchewan 1205 miles *1939 km*), Columbia (1150 miles *1850 km*), Churchill (1000 miles *1609 km*).
Head of State: HM Queen Elizabeth II, represented by Jules Léger (b. 4 Apr. 1913), Governor-General.
Prime Minister: The Rt Hon Pierre Elliott Trudeau (b. 18 Oct. 1919).

139

Climate: Great extremes, especially inland. Average summer temperature 65 °F, very cold winters. Light to moderate rainfall, heavy snowfalls. Below are listed a selection of towns showing the extreme monthly variations in average maximum and minimum daily temperatures and the month with the maximum number of rainy days.

Calgary: Average maximum 24 °F (January) to 76 °F (July), Average minimum 2 °F (January) to 47 °F (July). Rainiest month (rainy days) June (12).

Halifax: Average maximum 31 °F (February) to 74 °F (July, August). Average minimum 15 °F (January, February) to 56 °F (August). Rainiest month (rainy days) January (17).

Ottawa: Average maximum 21 °F (January) to 81 °F (July). Average minimum 3 °F (January, February) to 58 °F (July). Rainiest month (rainy days) December (14).

St John's: Average maximum 28 °F (February) to 69 °F (August). Average minimum 16 °F (February) to 53 °F (August). Rainiest months (rainy days) November, December (17).

Vancouver: Average maximum 41 °F (January) to 74 °F (July). Average minimum 32 °F (January) to 54 °F (July, August). Rainiest month (rainy days) December (22).

Winnipeg: Average maximum 7 °F (January) to 79 °F (July). Average minimum −13 °F (January) to 55 °F (July). Rainiest months (rainy days) January, June (12).

Yellowknife: Average maximum −10 °F (January) to 69 °F (July). Average minimum −26 °F (January) to 52 °F (July). Rainiest month (rainy days) December (13).

Absolute maximum temperature 115 °F (46,1 °C), Gleichen, Alberta, 28 July 1903; absolute minimum −81 °F (−62,8 °C), Snag, Yukon, 3 Feb. 1947.

Labour force: 9 577 000 (excluding 708 000 unemployed) in May 1976: Manufacturing 20·2%; Trade, restaurants and hotels 17·3%; Community, social and personal services 34·3%. Figures exclude Yukon Territory, the North-West Territories, armed forces and Indians living on reservations.

Gross domestic product: C$142 089 million (provisional) in 1974: Manufacturing (excluding government) 22·7%; Trade (excluding government) 12·0%; Community, social and personal services (including hotels, restaurants and business services) 23·8%. Revised total is C$145 906 million.

Exports: US$32 300·3 million in 1975: Food 11·4%; Mineral fuels, lubricants, etc. 16·5% (petroleum and petroleum products 10·4%); Machinery 10·7%; Transport equipment 19·3% (road motor vehicles and parts 17·7%).

Monetary unit: Canadian dollar (C$). One dollar = 100 cents.

Denominations:
Coins 1, 5, 10, 25, 50 cents, $1.
Notes $ 1, 2, 5, 10, 20, 50, 100, 1000.

Exchange rate to US dollar: 1.059 (July 1977).

Political history and government: The Dominion of Canada, under the British Crown, was established on 1 July 1867 by the British North America Act. It was originally a federation of four provinces (Quebec, Ontario, Nova Scotia and New Brunswick). These were later joined by Manitoba (15 July 1870), British Columbia (20 July 1871), Prince Edward Island (1 July 1873), Alberta and Saskatchewan (1 Sept. 1905). Canada acquired its Arctic islands from the United Kingdom on 1 Sept. 1880. The country achieved full independence, within the Commonwealth, by the Statute of Westminster on 11 Dec.

1931. Newfoundland, previously a separate British dependency, became the tenth province on 1 Apr. 1949.

Canada is a federal parliamentary state. Executive power is vested in the Queen and exercisable by her representative, the Governor-General, whom she appoints on the advice of the Canadian Prime Minister. The Federal Parliament comprises the Queen, a nominated Senate (104 members, appointed on a regional basis) and a House of Commons (264 members elected by universal adult suffrage). A Parliament may last no longer than 5 years. The Governor-General appoints the Prime Minister and, on the latter's recommendation, other Ministers to form the Cabinet. The Prime Minister must have majority support in Parliament, to which the Cabinet is responsible. Canada contains 10 provinces (each with a Lieutenant-Governor and a legislature from which a Premier is chosen) and two centrally-administered territories.

Telephones: 12 454 000 (1974).
Daily newspapers: 121 (1973).
Total circulation: 5 207 000.
Radio: 19 133 000 (1973).
TV: 7 705 000 (1973).
Length of roadways: 516 893 miles *831 858 km.*
Length of railways: 44 162 miles *71 071 km.*
Universities: 45 (also 22 other degree-awarding institutions).
Expectation of life: Males 69·34 years; females 76·36 years (1970–72).
Defence: Military service voluntary; total armed forces 77 900; defence expenditure, 1976/77: US$3041 million.
Cinemas: 1128 (seating capacity 651 899) in 1972; also 284 drive-ins for 117 858 cars.

ALBERTA
Population: 1 838 037 (1976 census).
Area: 255 285 miles² *661 188 km².*
Languages: English, German, Ukrainian, French.
Religions: United Church of Canada, Roman Catholic, Anglican, Lutheran.
Capital city: Edmonton, population 542 845 (metropolitan area) in 1976.
Other principal towns (1974): Calgary 433 389; Lethbridge 43 612; Red Deer 28 079; Medicine Hat 27 430; Grande Prairie 15 359.
Principal mountain range: Rocky Mountains.
Principal rivers: Peace, Athabasca.
Lieutenant-Governor: Ralph Garvin.
Premier: (Edgar) Peter Lougheed (b. 26 July 1928).
Telephones: 969 280 (1973).
Length of roadways: 86 347 miles *138 962 km.*
Length of railways: 6244 miles *10 048 km.*
Universities: 3.

BRITISH COLUMBIA
Population: 2 466 608 (1976 census).
Area: 366 255 miles² *948 600 km².*
Languages: English, German.
Religion: United Church of Canada, Anglican, Roman Catholic, Lutheran.
Capital city: Victoria, population 199 000 (1972).
Other principal towns (1971): Vancouver 1 071 081; New Westminster 42 835; Prince George 33 101; North Vancouver 31 847; Kamloops 26 168.
Principal mountain range: Rocky Mountains.
Principal rivers: Fraser, Thompson, Kootenay, Columbia.
Lieutenant-Governor: Col Walter Stewart Owen.
Premier: William R. Bennett.
Telephones: 1 160 333 (1972).

Length of roadways: 28 120 miles *45 254 km.*
Length of railways: 4826 miles *7766 km.*
Universities: 4.

MANITOBA
Population: 1 021 506 (1976 census).
Area: 251 000 miles² *652 218 km².*
Languages: English, Ukrainian, German, French.
Religions: United Church of Canada, Roman Catholic, Anglican, Lutheran.
Capital city: Winnipeg, population 570 725 (metropolitan area) in 1976.
Other principal towns: (1971) St James-Assinabora 71 800; St Boniface 46 661; St Vital 32 613; Brandon 31 150; East Kildonian 29 722.
Highest point: Duck Mountain, 2727 ft *831 m.*
Lieutenant-Governor: William John McKeag (b. 17 Mar. 1928).
Premier: Edward Richard Schreyer (b. 21 Dec. 1935).
Telephones: 433 598 (1970).
Length of roadways: 11 300 miles *18 185 km.*
Length of railways: 4900 miles *7886 km.*
Universities: 3.

NEW BRUNSWICK
Population: 677 250 (1976 census).
Area: 28 354 miles² *72 000 km².*
Languages: English, French.
Religions: Roman Catholic, Baptist, United Church of Canada, Anglican.
Capital city: Fredericton, population 42 000 (1973).
Other principal towns (1971): Saint John 106 744; Moncton 71 416; Bathurst 19 784; Edmundston 17 331; Campbellton 12 443.
Highest point: Mt Carleton, 2690 ft *820 m.*
Principal river: St John.
Lieutenant-Governor: Hédard J Robichaud (b. 2 Nov. 1911).
Premier: Richard Bennett Hatfield (b. 9 Apr. 1931).
Telephones: 260 050 (1972).
Length of roadways: 12 854 miles *20 686 km.*

NEWFOUNDLAND (Terre-Neuve)
Population: 557 725 (1976 census).
Area: 156 185 miles² *383 300 km².*
Language: English.
Religions: Roman Catholic, Anglican, United Church of Canada, Salvation Army.
Capital city: St John's, population 101 161 (1971).
Other principal towns (1971): Corner Brook 26 309; Stephenville 7770; Gander 7748; Grand Falls 7677; Windsor 6644.
Highest point: Mt Gras Morne, 2666 ft *812 m.*
Principal mountain range: Long Range Mountain.
Principal rivers: Humber, Exploits, Gander.
Lieutenant-Governor: Gordon Arnaud Winter (b. 6 Oct. 1912).
Premier: Frank Duff Moores (b. 18 Feb. 1933).
Telephones: 100 655 (1972).
Length of railways: 1085 miles *1746 km.*
Universities: 1.

NOVA SCOTIA
Population: 828 571 (1976 census).
Area: 21 425 miles² *55 000 km².*
Language: English.
Religions: Roman Catholic, United Church of Canada, Anglican, Baptist.
Capital city: Halifax, population 122 035 (1971).

Other principal towns (1971): Dartmouth 64 770; Sydney 33 230; Glace Bay 22 440; Truro 12 047; New Glasgow 10 849.
Lieutenant-Governor: Dr Clarence L Gosse.
Premier: Gerald Augustine Regan (b. 13 Feb. 1928).
Length of roadways 15 443 miles *24 853 km* (excluding cities and towns).
Length of railways: 1750 miles *2816 km.*
Universities: 6.

ONTARIO
Population: 8 264 465 (1976 census).
Area: 412 582 miles² *1 068 587 km².*
Languages: English, French, Italian, German.
Religions: Roman Catholic, United Church of Canada, Anglican, Presbyterian.
Capital city: Toronto, population 712 786 (city) in 1971; 2 753 112 (metropolitan area) in 1976.
Other principal towns (1971): Hamilton 309 173; Ottawa 302 341; London 223 222; Windsor 203 300.
Principal rivers: St Lawrence, Ottawa.
Lieutenant-Governor: Mrs Pauline M McGibbon (b. 20 Oct. 1910).
Premier: William Grenville Davis (b. 30 July 1929).
Telephones: 4 561 693 (1973).
Length of roadways: 12 990 miles *20 900 km.*
Length of railways: 10 045 miles *16 166 km*
Universities: 15.

PRINCE EDWARD ISLAND
Population: 118 229 (1976 census).
Area: 2184 miles² *5656 km².*
Languages: English, French.
Religions: Roman Catholic, United Church of Canada, Presbyterian.
Capital city: Charlottetown, population 19 133 (1971).
Other principal town: Summerside, 9439 (1971).
Lieutenant-Governor: Gordon Lockhart Bennett.
Premier: Alexander Bradshaw Campbell (b. 1 Dec. 1933).
Telephones: 42 314 (1973).
Length of roadways: 3360 miles *5406 km.*
Length of railways: 283 miles *455 km.*
Universities: 1.

QUEBEC
Population: 6 234 445 (1976 census).
Area: 594 860 miles² *1 540 668 km².*
Languages: French, English.
Religion: Roman Catholic.
Capital city: Quebec, population 187 400 (city); 499 000 (metropolitan area) in 1974.
Other principal towns (1971): Montreal 1 466 500; Laval 237 918; Sherbrooke 81 881; Verdun 76 832; Trois-Rivières 64 000; Hull 63 720.
Highest point: Mt Jacques Cartier, 4160 ft *1268 m.*
Principal mountain ranges: Notre Dame, Appalachian.
Principal river: St Lawrence.
Lieutenant-Governor: Lt-Col Hugues Lapointe (b. 3 Mar. 1911).
Premier: René Lévesque (b. 24 Aug. 1922).
Telephones: 1 500 000 (1970).
Length of roadways: 45 994 miles *74 020 km.*
Length of railways: 5360 miles *8626 km.*
Universities: 7.

SASKATCHEWAN
Population: 921 323 (1976 census).
Area: 251 700 miles² *651 903 km².*

Languages: English, German, Ukrainian.
Religions: United Church of Canada, Roman Catholic, Lutheran, Anglican.
Capital city: Regina, population 146 950 (1973).
Other principal towns (1973): Saskatoon 132 200; Moose Jaw 31 854; Prince Albert 29 150; Swift Current 15 950; Yorkton 14 500.
Highest point: 4546 ft *1385 m.*
Principal rivers: N Saskatchewan, Cree, Geokie.
Lieutenant-Governor: Dr Stephen Worobetz, MC (b. 26 Dec. 1914).
Premier: Allan Emrys Blakeney (b. 7 Sept. 1925).
Telephones: 416 163 (1973).
Length of roadways: 128 125 miles *206 197 km.*
Length of railways: 8690 miles *13 985 km*
Universities: 2.

NORTHWEST TERRITORIES
Population: 42 609 (1976 census).
Area: 1 304 903 miles² *3 379 700 km².*
Languages: Eskimo and Indian languages, English, French.
Religions: Roman Catholic, Anglican, United Church of Canada.
Capital city: Yellowknife, population 8000 (1975).
Other principal towns (1971): Inuvik 2672; Hay River 2420; Fort Smith 2372; Frobisher Bay 2014.
Principal mountain range: Mackenzie.
Principal river: Mackenzie.
Commissioner: Stuart Milton Hodgson (b. 1 Apr. 1924).

YUKON TERRITORY
Population: 21 836 (1976 census).
Area: 207 076 miles² *536 000 km².*
Languages: English, Indian languages.
Religions: Anglican, Roman Catholic, United Church of Canada.
Capital city: Whitehorse, population 12 000 (1971).
Other principal towns: Watson Lake 1115; Dawson City 500; Mayo 500.
Highest point: Mt Logan, 19 850 ft *6050 m.*
Principal mountain range: St Elias.
Principal river: Yukon.
Commissioner: James Smith.
Length of roadways: 2332 miles *3752 km.*

CAPE VERDE

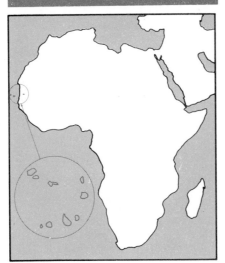

Official name: A República de Cabo Verde.

Population: 272 071 (census of 15 Dec. 1970); 303 000 (estimate for 1 July 1976).
Area: 1557 miles² *4033 km².*
Languages: Portuguese, Crioulo (a patois).
Religions: Roman Catholic 98·7% (1965).
Capital city: Praia, population 21 494 in 1970.
Other principal towns: Mindelo 29 000; São Filipe 29 500.
Highest point: 9285 ft *2829 m.*
Head of State: Aristides Maria Pereira (b. 17 Nov. 1924), President.
Prime Minister: Commandant Pedro Verona Rodrigues Pires.
Climate: Hot and semi-arid, tempered by oceanic situation. Average temperature in Praia varies from 72 °F to 80 °F Prevailing north-easterly wind. Rainfall is scarce (falling almost entirely between August and October) and drought sometimes chronic.
Labour force: 105 570 (census of 15 Dec. 1960); 63 000 (1970): Agriculture, forestry and fishing 61·9% (ILO estimates).
Gross national product: $140 million in 1974 (World Bank estimate).
Exports: $1 075 000 in 1967: Fish and fish preparations 19·3%; Fruit and vegetables 29·1% (fresh bananas and plantains 25·7%); Water and ice 10·3%; Oil seeds, oil nuts and oil kernels 10·1%.
Monetary unit: Cape Verde escudo. 1 escudo = 100 centavos.
Denominations:
Coins 5, 10, 20, 50 centavos, 1, 2½, 5, 10 escudos.
Notes 20, 50, 100, 500 escudos.
Exchange rate to US dollar: 38.48 (July 1977).
Political history and government: A former Portuguese territory, the Cape Verde Islands were part of Portuguese Guinea (now Guinea-Bissau) until 1879 and formed a separate territory from then until independence on 5 July 1975. The independence movement was dominated by the *Partido Africano da Independência da Guiné e Cabo Verde* (PAIGC), the African Party for the Independence of Guinea and Cape Verde. At independence Portugal transferred power to a PAIGC régime. Pending a constitution, the country is governed under a 'Law Establishing the Political Organization of the State'. Legislative power is vested in the National People's Assembly, with 56 members elected by universal adult suffrage on 30 June 1975. Executive power is held by the President, elected by the Assembly. He appoints and leads a Council of Minister. To provide for eventual union with Guinea-Bissau, a Council of Unity was formed on 12 Jan. 1977.
Telephones: 1482 (1971).
Radio: 31 000 (1975).
Length of roadways: 611 miles *984 km.*
Adult illiteracy: 73·2% (males 61·4%; females 82·8%) in 1960 (population aged 10 and over).
Expectation of life: Males 48·3 years; females 51·7 years (UN estimates for 1970–75).
Defence: Popular Revolutionary Armed Forces.
Cinemas: 6 (seating capacity 2800) in 1972.

CENTRAL AFRICAN REPUBLIC

Official name: L'Empire centrafricain.
Population: 2 255 536 (1968 census); 2 370 000 (estimate for 1 July 1970).
Area: 240 535 miles² *622 984 km².*
Languages: Sangho, French (official).
Religions: Protestant, Roman Catholic, Animist.

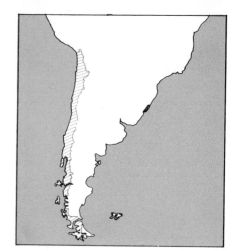

CHAD

CHILE

Capital city: Bangui, population 301 793 (1968).
Other principal towns (1964): Bouar 20 700; Bambari 19 700.
Highest point: Mt Gaou, 4659 ft *1420 m.*
Principal mountain range: Chaîne des Mongos.
Principal river: Oubangui.
Head of State: Marshal Jean-Bédel Bokassa (b. 22 Feb. 1921), Emperor.
Prime Minister: Ange Patassé (b. 25 Jan. 1937).
Climate: Tropical (hot and humid). Heavy rains June to October, especially in south-western forest areas. Average temperature 79 °F. Daily average high temperature 85 °F to 93 °F, low 66 °F to 71 °F.
Labour force: 480 000 (31 Dec. 1962); 901 000 (1970): Agriculture, forestry and fishing 91·2% (ILO estimates).
Gross domestic product: 56 983 million CFA francs in 1970: Agriculture, forestry and fishing 33·1%; Manufacturing (including diamond cutting) 14·4%; Trade, restaurants and hotels 21·3%; Government services 14·0;
Exports: $32·2 million in 1971: Coffee 23·8%; Wood, lumber and cork 10·5%; Raw cotton 23·1%; Diamonds 35·6%.
Monetary unit: Franc de la Communauté financière africaine.
Denominations:
   Coins 1, 2, 5, 10, 25, 50, 100 CFA francs.
   Notes 100, 500, 1000, 5000, 10 000 CFA francs.
Exchange rate to US dollar: 242.80 (July 1977).
Political history and government: Formerly Oubangui-Chari, part of French Equatorial Africa. Became the Central African Republic on achieving self-government, 1 Dec. 1958. Independent since 13 Aug. 1960. A one-party state since November 1962. The President was deposed on 31 Dec. 1965 by a military *coup*, led by Col (later Marshal) Jean-Bédel Bokassa. National Assembly dissolved on 1 Jan. 1966. Constitution revoked, 4 Jan. 1966. Bokassa assumed full powers and became President for life in February 1972. On 4 Dec. 1976 he proclaimed the Central African Empire, with himself as first Emperor. He rules with the assistance of an appointed Council of Ministers.
Telephones: 5000 (1973).
Daily newspapers: 1 (1972).
   Total circulation: 500.
Radio: 65 000 (1973).
Length of roadways: 13 359 miles *21 500 km* (31 Dec. 1974).
Universities: 1.
Adult illiteracy: 97·9% (males 95·6%; females 99·8%) in 1959–60 (aged 14 and over).
Expectation of life: Males 39·4 years; females 42·6 years (UN estimates for 1970–75).
Defence: Armed forces about 3000.
Cinemas: 8 (1971).

Official name: La République du Tchad.
Population: 4 116 000 (estimate for 1 July 1975).
Area: 495 750 miles² *1 284 000 km²*
Languages: French (official), Arabic, African languages.
Religions: Muslim, Animist, Christian.
Capital city: N'Djamena (formerly Fort-Lamy), population 193 000.
Other principal towns (1972): Sarh (Fort-Archambault) 43 700; Moundou 39 600; Abéché 28 100.
Highest point: Emi Koussi, 11 204 ft *3415 m.*
Principal mountain ranges: Tibesti, Ennedi.
Principal rivers: Chari, Bahr Kéita.
Head of State: Gen Félix Malloum (b. 1932), Chairman of the Supreme Military Council and President of the Council of Ministers.
Climate: Hot and dry in the Sahara desert (in the north) but milder and very wet (annual rainfall 196 in) in the south. In N'Djamena, average maximum 87 °F (August) to 107 °F (April), minimum 57 °F (December, January) to 77 °F (May), August rainiest (22 days).
Labour force: 1 357 000 (1970): Agriculture, forestry and fishing 90·2% (ILO estimates); 1 271 000 (June 1972).
Gross domestic product: 74 900 million CFA francs in 1970: Agriculture, forestry and fishing 53·7%; Trade, restaurants and hotels 17·6%; Community, social and personal services 11·9%.
Exports: $34·2 million in 1972: Meat and meat preparations 12·0%; Raw cotton 65·6%.
Monetary unit: Franc de la Communauté financière africaine.
Denominations:
   Coins 1, 2, 5, 10, 25, 50, 100 CFA francs.
   Notes 100, 500, 1000, 5000, 10 000 CFA francs.
Exchange rate to US dollar: 242.80 (July 1977).
Political history and government: Former province of French Equatorial Africa, independent since 11 Aug. 1960. Under military rule since 13 Apr. 1975. Provisional constitution announced, 16 Aug. 1975. The Supreme Military Council chooses a President who has executive and legislative powers.
Telephones: 5096 (1974).
Daily newspapers: 1.
   Total circulation: 1500.
Radio: 70 000 (1973).
Length of roadways (1971): 19 091 miles *30 725 km.*
Universities: 1.
Adult illiteracy: 94·4% (males 87·9%; females 99·4%) in 1963–4.
Expectation of life: Males 37·0 years; females 40·1 years (UN estimates for 1970–75).
Defence: Total armed forces 4700.
Cinemas: 9 (seating capacity 5900) in 1968.

Official name: La República de Chile.
Population: 8 834 820 (census of 22 Apr. 1970, excluding 8·5% underenumeration); 10 454 387 (estimate for 30 June 1976).
Area: 292 258 miles² *756 945 km².*
Language: Spanish.
Religions: Roman Catholic, Protestant minority.
Capital city: Santiago, population 3 186 000 (estimate for 30 June 1975).
Other principal towns (1975): Valparaíso 248 972; Viña del Mar 229 020; Talcahuano 183 591; Concepción 169 570; Antofagasta 149 720; Temuco 138 430.
Highest point: Ojos del Salado, 22 539 ft *6870 m* (first climbed 1937).
Principal mountain range: Cordillera de los Andes.
Principal rivers: Loa (273 miles *439 km*), Maule, Bio-Bio, Valdiva.
Head of State: Gen Augusto Pinochet Ugarte (b. 25 Nov. 1915), President.
Climate: Considerable variation north (annual rainfall 0·04 in) to south (105 in). Average temperatures 53 °F winter, 63 °F summer. In Santiago, December (51 °F to 83 °F), January (53 °F to 85 °F), and February (52 °F to 84 °F) hottest, June (37 °F to 58 °F) and July (37 °F to 59 °F) coldest and rainiest (6 days each). Absolute maximum temperature 41,6 °C (*106·9 °F*), Los Angeles, February 1944; absolute minimum −21,2 °C (*−6·16 °F*), Longuimay, July 1933.
Labour force: 2 607 360 aged 12 and over (1970 census): Agriculture, forestry and fishing 23·2%; Manufacturing 17·4%; Trade restaurants and hotels 12·7%; Community, social and personal services 28·0%.
Gross domestic product: 9 903·0 million pesos in 1974: Mining and quarrying 10·1%; Manufacturing 34·6%; Trade 23·9%.
Exports: $2 480·6 million in 1974: Metalliferous ores and metal scrap 12·1%; Non-ferrous metals 72·6% (copper 71·7%).
Monetary unit: Chilean peso. 1 peso = 100 centavos.
Denominations:
   Coins 1, 5, 10, 50 centavos, 1 peso.
   Notes 1, 5, 10, 50 pesos.
Exchange rate to US dollar: 20.87 (July 1977).
Political history and government: A republic, divided into 25 provinces. Under military control, with constitutional rule suspended, since 11 Sept. 1973. A 'state of siege' was proclaimed; the bicameral National Congress (a Senate and a Chamber of Deputies) was dissolved on 13 Sept. 1973; and the activities of political parties were

suspended on 27 Sept. 1973. Power is held by the *Junta Militar de Gobierno*, whose leader is Head of State. The junta rules through an appointed Cabinet.
Telephones: 446 000 (1974).
Daily newspapers: 128 (1972).
   Total circulation: 907 000.
Radio: 1 500 000 (1973).
TV: 525 000 (1973).
Length or roadways: 39 603 miles *63 735 km* (31 Dec. 1974).
Length of railways: 6723 miles *10 820 km.*
Universities: 8.
Adult illiteracy: 11·9% (males 11·0%; females 12·7%) in 1970.
Expectation of life: Males 60·48 years; females 66·01 years (1969–70).
Defence: Military service one year; total armed forces 79 600 (21 600 conscripts).
Cinemas: 360 (seating capacity 245 700) in 1971.

CHINA (mainland)

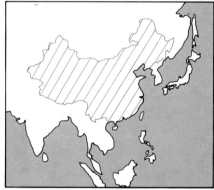

Official name: Chung-Hua Jen-Min Kung-Ho Kuo (the People's Republic of China).
Population: 582 603 417 (census of 30 June 1953), excluding Taiwan; 838 803 000 (UN estimate for mid-1975), including Taiwan (approx 16 million).
Area: 3 691 500 miles² *9 561 000 km².*
Language: Chinese (predominantly Mandarin dialect).
Religions: Confucianism, Buddhism, Taoism; Roman Catholic and Muslim minorities.
Capital city: Peking, population 7 570 000 (1970 est).
Other principal towns (1970): Shanghai 10 820 000; Tientsin 4 280 000; Shenyang 2 800 000; Wuhan 2 560 000; Kwangchow (Canton) 2 500 000; Chungking 2 400 000; Nanking 1 750 000; Harbin 1 670 000; Luta 1 650 000; Sian 1 600 000; Lanchow 1 450 000 (UN estimates except for Shanghai and Tientsin).
Highest point: Mt Everest (on Tibet-Nepal border), 29 028 ft *8848 m* (first climbed 29 May 1953).
Principal mountain ranges: Himalaya, Kunlun Shan, Tien Shan, Nan Shan, Astin Tagh.
Principal rivers: Yangtze (Ch'ang Kiang) (3436 miles *5530 km*), Huang (Yellow), Mekong.
Head of Government: Hua Kuo-feng, Premier of the State Council and Chairman of the Central Committee of the Communist Party of China.
Climate: Extreme variations. Warm, humid summers and long cold winters in north (annual average below 50 °F); sub-tropical in extreme south; monsoons in the east; arid in the north-west. In Peking, July hottest (71 °F to 89 °F) and rainiest (13 days), January coldest (15 °F to 35 °F).
Labour force: 364 612 000 (1970): Agriculture, forestry and fishing 67·8% (ILO estimates, including Taiwan).

Gross national product: $285 960 million in 1975 (World Bank estimate).
Exports: $6900 million in 1975 (unofficial estimate).
Monetary unit: Yüan. 1 yüan = 10 chiao = 100 fen.
Denominations:
   Coins 1, 2, 5 fen.
   Notes 1, 2, 5 chiao, 1, 2, 5, 10 yüan.
Exchange rate to US dollar: 1.858 (July 1977).
Political history and government: Under Communist rule since September 1949. The People's Republic was inaugurated on 1 Oct. 1949. The present constitution was adopted on 17 Jan. 1975. China is a unitary state comprising 21 provinces, 5 'autonomous' regions (including Tibet) and 3 municipalities. The Communist Party is 'the core of leadership' and the Chairman of the Party's Central Committee commands the People's Liberation Army (PLA), which includes naval and air forces. The highest organ of state power is the National People's Congress, with (in 1975) 2885 deputies indirectly elected for 5 years by provinces, regions, municipalities and the PLA. The Congress, under the leadership of the Party, elects a Standing Committee (about 140 members in 1976) to be its permanent organ. There is no Head of State but the equivalent functions are exercised by this Committee. The executive and administrative arm of government is the State Council (a Premier, Vice-Premiers and other Ministers), appointed by and accountable to the Congress.

Political power is held by the Communist Party of China (CPC). The CPC's highest authority is the Party Congress, convened normally every five years. The 11th Congress, meeting in August 1977, elected a Central Committee (201 full members) to supervise Party work. To direct its policy, the Committee elects a Political Bureau (Politburo), with 23 full members in 1977. The Politburo has a five-man Standing Committee (the Chairman and four Vice-Chairmen).
Telephones: 255 000 (1951).
Daily newspapers: n/a.
   Total circulation: 12 million (est).
Radio: *c.* 12 000 000 (1970).
TV: *c.* 500 000 (1973).
Length of roadways: *c.* 500 000 miles *c. 800 000 km.*
Length of railways: *c.* 22 000 miles *c. 36 000 km* (1965).
Universities: 24.
Adult illiteracy: 33% (1960 claim).
Expectation of life: Males 59·9 years; females 63·3 years (UN estimates for 1970–75, including Taiwan).
Defence: Military service: Army two–four years, Air Force three–five years, Navy four–six years; total regular forces 3 525 000.
Cinemas: 1386 (1958).

CHINA (Taiwan)

Official name: Chung-Hua Min-Kuo (the Republic of China).
Population: 14 678 966 (census of 16 Dec. 1970); 16 607 961 (estimate for 30 Apr. 1977).
Area: 13 892·6 miles² *35 981·8 km².*
Language: Northern Chinese (Amoy dialect).
Religions: Buddhist with Muslim and Christian minorities.
Capital city: Taipei, population 2 089 288 at 31 Dec. 1976.
Other principal towns (1976): Kaohsiung 1 019 900; Taichung 561 070; Tainan 537 217; Keelung 342 544.
Highest point: Yü Shan (Mt Morrison), 13 113 ft *3997 m.*
Principal mountain range: Chunyang Shanmo.

Principal rivers: Hsia-tan-shui Chi, Cho-shui Chi, Tan-shui Ho, Wu Chi.
Head of State: Dr Yen Chia-kan (b. 23 Oct. 1905), President.
Prime Minister: Gen Chiang Ching-kuo (b. 18 Mar. 1910).
Climate: Rainy summers and mild winters, average temperature 73 °F, average annual rainfall 101 in. In Taipei, July (76 °F to 93 °F) and August (75 °F to 91 °F) warmest, January (54 °F to 66 °F) and February (53 °F to 65 °F) coolest, April rainiest (14 days).
Labour force: 5 663 000 (exlcuding armed forces and 85 000 unemployed) in 1976: Agriculture, forestry and fishing 29·1%; Manufacturing 28·4%; Trade 13·3%.
Gross national product: NT$655 907 million in 1976: Agriculture, forestry and fishing 12·0;% Manufacturing 36·6%; Trade 10·9%.
Exports: NT$309 913 million in 1976.
Monetary unit: New Taiwan dollar (NT $). 1 dollar = 100 cents.
Denominations:
   Coins 10, 20, 50 cents, 1, 5 dollars.
   Notes 1, 5, 10, 50, 100 dollars.
Exchange rate to US dollar: 38.00 (July 1977).
Political history and government: After the Republic of China was overthrown by Communist forces on the mainland, the government withdrew to Taiwan on 8 Dec. 1949. As it claims to be the legitimate administration for all China, the régime continues to be dominated by mainlanders who came to the island in 1947–9. The first elections since the Communist victory were held in Taiwan on 23 Dec. 1972. There are five governing bodies (*yuans*). The highest legislative organ is the Legislative Yuan, comprising (in 1977) 411 life members and 52 elected for 3 years. This body submits proposals to the National Assembly (1295 life members and 53 elected for 6 years), which elects the President and Vice-President for 6 years. The Executive Yuan (Council of Ministers) is the highest administrative organ and is responsible to the Legislative Yuan.
Telephones: 986 012 (Dec. 1976).
Daily newspapers: 32 (1963).
   Total circulation: 750 000.
Radio: 1 493 057 (1976).
TV: 913 910 (1976).
Length of roadways: 10 193 miles *16 404 km.*
Length of railways: 3116 miles *5014·6 km.*
Universities: 11.
Adult illiteracy: 27·6% (males 15·2%; females 42·0%) in 1966.
Expectation of life: Males 67·92 years; females 72·82 years (1974).
Defence: Military service two years; total armed forces 470 000; defence expenditure, 1974/75: $1000 million.
Cinemas: 734 (capacity 734 000) in 1967.

COLOMBIA

Official name: La República de Colombia.
Population: 21 070 115 (census of 24 Oct. 1973).
Area: 439 737 miles² *1 138 914 km².*
Language: Spanish.

Religion: Roman Catholic.
Capital city: Santa Fe de Bogotá, population 2 855 065 (1973).
Other principal towns (1973): Medellín 1 070 924; Cali 898 253; Barranquilla 661 920; Cartagena de Indias 292 512; Bucaramanga 291 661; San José de Cúcuta 219 772; Manizales 199 904.
Highest point: Pico Cristobal Colón, 18 947 ft *5775 m* (first climbed 1939).
Principal mountain range: Cordillera de los Andes.
Principal rivers: Magdalena, Cauca, Amazonas, (Amazon, 4007 miles *6448 km*) on frontier.
Head of State: Dr Alfonso López Michelsen (b. 30 June 1913), President.
Climate: Hot and humid on the coasts and in the jungle lowlands, temperate in the Andean highlands, with rainy seasons March–May and September–November. In Bogotá, daily average low temperature 48 °F to 51 °F, high 64 °F to 68 °F, April and October rainiest (20 days).
Labour force: 5 118 475 (excluding 856 517 unemployed) aged 12 and over (1973 census): Agriculture, forestry and fishing 37·2%; Manufacturing 16·3%; Trade, restaurants and hotels 13·9%; Community, social and personal services 20·2%.
Gross domestic product: 327 786 million pesos (provisional) in 1974: Agriculture, forestry and fishing 26·6% (Agriculture 25·6%); Manufacturing 21·6%; Trade 17·4%. Revised total is 329 155 million pesos.
Exports: $1416·7 million in 1974: Coffee 44·1%; Other food 12·5%.
Monetary unit: Colombian peso. 1 peso = 100 centavos.
Denominations:
Coins 1, 5, 10, 20, 50 centavos.
Notes 1, 2, 5, 10, 20, 50, 100, 500 pesos.
Exchange rate to US dollar: 36.565 (July 1977).
Political history and government: A republic. Legislative power is vested in Congress which is composed of the Senate (112 members) and the House of Representatives (199 members). Members of both Houses are elected for 4 years. Executive power is exercised by the President (elected for 4 years by universal adult suffrage), assisted by a Cabinet. The country is divided into 22 departments, 5 intendencies and 4 commissaries.
Telephones: 1 090 000 (1974).
Daily newspapers: 52 (1973).
Total circulation: 1 299 000 (38 dailies).
Radio: 2 792 700 (1973).
TV: 1 200 000 (1972).
Length of roadways: 30 601 miles *49 248 km* (31 Dec. 1975).
Length of railways: 2128 miles *3424 km*
Universities: 38 (21 state, 17 private).
Adult illiteracy: 27·1% (males 25·2%; females 28·9%) in 1964.
Expectation of life: Males 59·2 years; females 62·7 years (UN estimates for 1970–75).
Defence: Military service two years; total armed forces 65 300; defence expenditure, 1974: $102 million.
Cinemas: 726 (seating capacity 431 400) in 1968.

THE COMOROS

Official name: Etat Comorien (Comoran State).
Population: 243 948 (census of July–Sept. 1966), including 32 494 in Mayotte prefecture; 292 000 (estimate for 1 July 1974).
Area: 838 miles² *2 171 km²* (including Mayotte, 144 miles² *374 km²*).

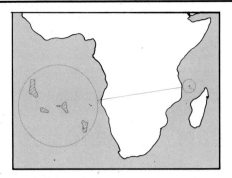

Languages: French (official), Comoran (a blend of Swahili and Arabic).
Religions: Muslim, with a Christian minority.
Capital city: Moroni, population 12 000 (estimate for 1 Jan. 1974).
Other principal towns: Dzaoudzi (on Mayotte), Mutsamudu.
Highest point: Mt Kartala, 7746 ft *2361 m.*
Head of State: Ali Soilih, President.
Prime Minister: Abdallah Mohamed.
Climate: Tropical climate with two distinct seasons. Dry between May and October, hot and humid from November to April. Most rain in January (up to 15 in). Cyclones, waterspouts and tidal waves occur in the summer. The November monsoon brings the maximum temperature of 82 °F (*28 °C*), while the minimum temperature (July) falls to 68 °F (*20 °C*).
Labour force: 106 000 (1970): Agriculture, forestry and fishing 67·0% (ILO estimates).
Gross domestic product: $28 million (1970 estimate).
Exports: 1511·2 million CFA francs in 1972: Vanilla 40·6%; Oil of ylang-ylang 33·2%; Cloves 10·9%.
Monetary unit: Franc de la Communauté financière africaine (French currency is used on Mayotte).
Denominations:
Coins 1, 2, 5, 10, 20 CFA francs.
Notes 50, 100, 500, 1000, 5000 CFA francs.
Exchange rate to US dollar: 242.80 (July 1977).
Political history and government: Formerly attached to Madagascar, the Comoro Islands became a separate French Overseas Territory in 1947. The Territory achieved internal self-government by a law of 29 Dec. 1961, with a Chamber of Deputies (in place of the Territorial Assembly) and a Government Council to control local administration. Ahmed Abdallah, President of the Council from 26 Dec. 1972, was restyled President of the Government on 15 June 1973. In a referendum on 22 Dec. 1974 the Comorans voted 95·6% in favour of independence, though on the island of Mayotte the vote was 65% against. The French Government wanted each island to ratify a new constitution separately by referendum. To avoid the expected separation of Mayotte, the Chamber of Deputies voted for immediate independence on 6 July 1975. A unilateral declaration of independence was made on the same day. On 7 July the Chamber elected Abdallah as President of the Comoros and constituted itself as the National Assembly. France kept its hold on Mayotte but the three other main islands achieved *de facto* independence. On 3 Aug. 1975 Abdallah was deposed in a *coup* by a group, led by Ali Soilih, who wished to maintain the unity of the islands. The next day a National Revolutionary Council, led by Prince Said Mohamed Jaffar, took office and abolished the National Assembly. Prince Said became President of the National Executive Council on 10 Aug. 1975. Government came under the control of a coalition of

four parties, previously in opposition, but they proved equally unsuccessful at achieving a reconciliation with Mayotte. France recognized the independence of the three islands on 31 Dec. 1975. On 2 Jan. 1976 the Executive and Revolutionary Councils elected Soilih to be President, with full executive authority, and he took office the next day. He appointed a new Council of Ministers, headed by a Prime Minister. The Revolutionary Council was replaced by a National Institutional Council to oversee the actions of the government. A National People's Council has been appointed to draw up a new constitution. A referendum on Mayotte on 8 Feb. 1976 resulted in a 99·4% vote for retaining links with France. In a second referendum, on 11 Apr. 1976, Mayotte voted against remaining a French Overseas Territory. The majority there want Mayotte to be a French Overseas Department but in December 1976 France enacted legislation to give the island a special status as a *collectivité particulière*. Meanwhile, Mayotte is governed by an appointed Prefect.
Telephones: 1378 (1975).
Radio: 36 000 (1975).
Length of roadways: 466 miles *750 km.*
Expectation of life: Males 40·9 years; females 44·1 years (UN estimates for 1970–75).
Cinemas: 2 (seating capacity 800) in 1973.

THE CONGO

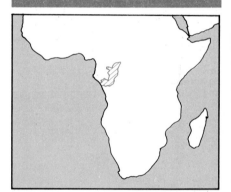

Official name: La République populaire du Congo (The People's Republic of the Congo).
Population: 1 300 106 (census of 7 Feb. 1974); 1 390 000 (estimate for 1 July 1976).
Area: 132 047 miles² *342 000 km².*
Languages: French (official), Bantu languages.
Religions: Animist, Christian minority.
Capital city: Brazzaville, population 289 700 (1974).
Other principal towns (1974): Pointe-Noire 141 700; Kayes (Jacob) 30 600; Loubomo (Dolisie) 29 600.
Highest point: 3412 ft *1040 m.*
Principal mountain range: Serro do Crystal.
Principal rivers: Congo (2718 miles *4374 km*), Oubangui.
Head of State: Col Joachim Yhombi-Opango, President of the Military Committe.
Prime Minister: Major Louis Sylvain Goma.
Climate: Tropical (hot and humid). Equatorial rains for seven to eight months per year. In Brazzaville, daily average low temperature 63 °F to 70 °F, high 82 °F to 91 °F.
Labour force: 428 000 (1970): Agriculture, forestry and fishing 41·8% (ILO estimates).
Gross domestic product: $283 million (1970 estimate).

Exports: $85·4 million in 1973: Wood, lumber and cork 29·9% (saw and veneer logs 26·6%); Petroleum and petroleum products 33·0% (crude petroleum 32·9%); Manufactured fertilizers 13·5%; Veneer sheets 15·6%.
Monetary unit: Franc de la Communauté financière africaine.
Denominations:
Coins 1, 2, 5, 10, 25, 50, 100 CFA francs.
Notes 100, 500, 1000, 5000 10 000 CFA francs.
Exchange rate to US dollar: 242.80 (July 1977).
Political history and government: Formerly, as Middle Congo, a part of French Equatorial Africa. Became independent as the Republic of the Congo on 15 Aug. 1960. A one-party state since 2 July 1964. Present name adopted on 3 Jan. 1970. A new constitution was approved by referendum on 24 June 1973, when a People's National Assembly of 115 members was elected (from a single list of candidates) to be the main legislative body. On 18 Mar. 1977 the President was assassinated and the Central Committee of the ruling party transferred its powers to an 11-member Military Committee. The new régime suspended the constitution on 5 Apr. 1977 and dissolved the National Assembly the next day. The Military Committee appoints the Council of Ministers, led by the Prime Ministers.
Telephones: 10 181 (1974).
Daily newspapers: 3 (1973).
Total circulation: 1000.
Radio: 75 000 (1973).
TV: 3800 (1973).
Length of roadways: 6835 miles *11 000 km.*
Length of railways: 494 miles *795 km.*
Universities: 1.
Adult illiteracy: 83·5% (males 76·2%; females 92·7%) in 1960–61.
Expectation of life: Males 41·9 years; females 45·1 years (UN estimates for 1970–75).
Defence: Military service voluntary; total armed forces 7000; defence expenditure, 1974: $19 million.
Cinemas: 7 (seating capacity 5100) in 1973.

COSTA RICA

Official name: República de Costa Rica (the 'rich coast').
Population: 1 871 780 (census of 14 May 1973); 2 012 000 (estimate for 1 July 1976).
Area: 19 600 miles² *50 700 km².*
Language: Spanish.
Religion: Roman Catholic.
Capital city: San José, population 218 717 (1974).
Other principal towns (1974): Alajuela 33 645; Limón 30 208; Puntarenas 26 864; Cartago 26 073; Heredia 23 133.
Highest point: Chirripó, 12 533 ft *3820 m.*
Principal mountain ranges: Cordillera del Guanacaste, Cordillera de Talamanca,
Principal river: Río Grande.
Head of State: Lic. Daniel Oduber Quirós (b. 25 Aug. 1921), President.
Climate: Hot and wet on Caribbean coast, hot but drier on Pacific coast, cooler on central plateau. In San José, May hottest (62 °F to 80 °F), December and January coolest (58 °F to 75 °F), rainy season May–November, October rainiest (25 days). Absolute maximum temperature 42 °C (*107·6 °F*), Las Cañas de Guanacaste, 26 Apr. 1952; absolute minimum −1.1 °C (*30 °F*), Cerro Buena Vista, 11 Jan. 1949.
Labour force: 585 313 (including unemployed) aged 12 and over (1973 census): Agriculture, forestry and fishing 38·4%;

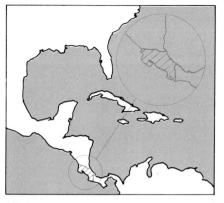

Mining and manufacturing 12·9% (manufacturing 12·6%); Trade, restaurants and hotels 12·2%; Community, social and personal services 21·5%.
Gross domestic product: 13 242 million colones (provisional) in 1974: Agriculture, forestry and fishing 18·4%; Mining and manufacturing 19·9%; Trade, restaurants and hotels 22·0%; Government services 17·1%. Revised total is 13 178 million colones.
Exports: $280·9 million in 1972: Meat and meat preparations 10·3%; Fruit and vegetables 30·4% (fresh bananas and plantains 29·7%); Coffee 27·7%.
Monetary unit: Costa Rican colón. 1 colón = 100 céntimos.
Denominations:
Coins 5, 10, 25, 50 céntimos, 1, 2, colones.
Notes 5, 10, 20, 50, 100, 500, 1000 colones.
Exchange rate to US dollar: 8.57 (July 1977).
Political history and government: A republic. Legislative power is vested in the unicameral Legislative Assembly (57 deputies elected for four years by compulsory adult suffrage). Executive power is vested in the President, similarly elected for four years. He is assisted by two Vice-Presidents and a Cabinet. There are 7 provinces, each administered by an appointed governor.
Telephones: 99 000 (1974).
Daily newspapers: 8 (1973).
Total circulation: 206 000.
Radio: 140 000 (1973).
TV: 122 000 (1973).
Length of roadways: 10 936 miles *17 600 km.*
Length of railways: 496 miles *799 km.*
Universities: 1.
Adult illiteracy: 15·6% (males 15·2%; females 16·0%) in 1963. Highest rate of literacy in Central America.
Expectation of life: Males 61·87 years; females 64·83 years (1962–64).
Defence: There have been no armed forces since 1948. Paramilitary forces number about 5000.
Cinemas: 132 with seating capacity of 90 000 (1969).

CUBA

Official name: La República de Cuba.
Population: 8 569 121 (census of 6 Sept. 1970); 9 405 000 (estimate for 31 Dec. 1975).
Area: 42 827 miles² *110 922 km².*
Languages: Spanish, English.
Religions: Roman Catholic, Protestant minority.
Capital city: San Cristóbal de la Habana (Havana), population 1 751 216 (including Marianao, Regla and other suburbs) in 1970.
Other principal towns (1970): Santiago de Cuba 277 600; Camagüey 197 720;

Holguín 131 656; Santa Clara 130 241; Guantánamo 129 005.
Highest point: Pico Turquino, 6467 ft *1971 m.*
Principal mountain range: Sierra Maestra.
Principal river: Cauto (155 miles *249 km*)
Head of State: Dr Fidel Castro Ruz (b. 13 Aug. 1927), President of the State Council and Chairman of the Council of Ministers.
Climate: Semi-tropical. Rainy season May–October. High winds, hurricanes frequent. In Havana, July and August warmest (75 °F to 89 °F), January and February coolest (65 °F to 79 °F), September and October rainiest (11 days each).
Labour force: 2 633 309 (excluding domestic servants) aged 10 and over (1970 census): Agriculture, forestry and fishing 30·4%; Mining, manufacturing, electricity and gas 20·5%; Trade, restaurants and hotels, storage and personal services 11·8%; Community and social services (including water), finance, insurance, real estate and business services 25·0%.
Gross national product: $7430 million in 1975 (World Bank estimate).
Exports: $837·9 million in 1972: Sugar and honey 73·6% (raw sugar 71·2%); Non-ferrous ores and concentrates 14·9%.
Monetary unit: Cuban peso. 1 peso = 100 centavos.
Denominations:
Coins 1, 2, 5, 20, 40 centavos.
Notes 1, 5, 10, 20, 50, 100 pesos.
Exchange rate to US dollar: 0.829 (July 1977).

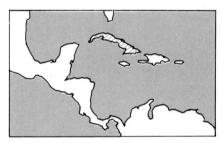

Political history and government: On 1 Jan. 1959 the dictatorship of Gen Fulgencio Batista was overthrown by revolutionary forces, led by Dr Fidel Castro. The constitution was suspended and a Fundamental Law of the Republic was instituted from 7 Feb. 1959. Executive and legislative authority was vested in the Council of Ministers, led by a Prime Minister, which appoints the Head of State. A 'Marxist-Leninist programme' was proclaimed on 2 Dec. 1961 and revolutionary groups merged into a single political movement, called the Communist Party since 2 Oct. 1965. It is the only permitted party. On 24 Nov. 1972 the government established an Executive Committee (including the President and Prime Minister) to supervise State administration. The first elections since the revolution were held for municipal offices in one province on 30 June 1974.
A new constitution, approved by referendum on 15 Feb. 1976 and in force from 24 Feb. 1976, provides for assemblies at municipal, provincial and national levels. On 10 Oct. 1976 elections were held for 169 municipal assemblies, with 'run-off' elections a week later. Members are elected by universal adult suffrage for 2½ years. On 31 Oct. 1976 the municipal assemblies elected delegates to 14 provincial assemblies. On 2 Nov. 1976 the municipal assemblies elected 481 deputies to the National Assembly of People's Power, inaugurated on 2 Dec. 1976. The National Assembly, whose members hold office for five years, is the supreme

organ of state. The Assembly elects 31 of its members to form a Council of State, its permanent organ. The Council's President is Head of State and Head of Government. Executive power is vested in the Council of Ministers, appointed by the National Assembly on the proposal of the Head of State, who presides over it.

The Communist Party of Cuba (CPC), the only permitted political party, is 'the leading force of society and the state'. The first Congress of the CPC met on 17–22 Dec. 1975 and elected a Central Committee (112 members) to supervise Party work. To direct its policy, the Committee elects a Political Bureau (Politburo), with 13 members in 1976.

Telephones: 281 000 (1973).
Daily newspapers: 14 (1973).
   Total circulation: 834 000 (10 dailies in 1972).
Radio: 2 100 000 (1976).
TV: 600 000 (1976).
Length of roadways: 8291 miles *13 343 km.*
Length of railways: 9006 miles *14 494 km.*
Universities: 4.
Adult illiteracy: 22·1% (males 24·2%; females 20·0%) in 1953.
Expectation of life: Males 68·5 years; females 71·8 years (1970).
Defence: Military service three years; total armed forces 175 000; defence expenditure, 1971: $290 million (estimate).
Cinemas: 439 (seating capacity 294 300) and one drive-in (1972).

CYPRUS

Official name: Kypriaki Dimokratia (in Greek), or Kibris Cumhuriyeti (in Turkish), meaning Republic of Cyprus.
Population: 631 778 (census of 1 Apr. 1973); 639 000 (estimate for 1 July 1974).
Area: 3572 miles² *9251 km².*
Languages: Greek 77%; Turkish 18%; English 3% (1960).
Religions: Greek Orthodox 77%; Muslim 18% (1960).
Capital city: Levkosía (Nicosía), population 117 100 (including suburbs) in 1974.
Other principal towns (1974): Lemesós (Limassol) 80 600; Famagusta 39 400; Larnaca 19 800; Paphos 9100; Kyrenia (Girne) 3900.
Highest point: Mt Olympus (Troödos), 6403 ft *1951 m.*
Principal mountain ranges: Troödos Kyrenian Mts.
Principal rivers: Seranhis, Pedieas.
Head of State: Spyros Kyprianou (b. 28 Oct. 1932), President.
Climate: Generally equable. Average rainfall is about 15 in but the summers are often rainless. The average daily high temperature in Nicosia is 97 °F (July) and the average daily low 42 °F (January).
Labour force: 258 900 (excluding armed forces and unemployed) in 1973: Agriculture, forestry and fishing 37·0%; Manufacturing

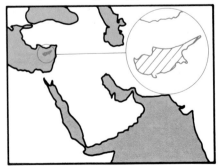

14·9%; Construction 10·8%; Commerce 12·0%; Services 18·2%.
Gross domestic product: C£355·8 million in 1973: Agriculture, forestry and fishing 13·1% (agriculture 12·7%); Manufacturing 14·0%; Trade, restaurants and hotels 19·2% (trade 15·9%); Transport, storage and communications 10·4%; Community, social and personal services 14·8%.
Exports: $146·4 million (excluding re-exports) in 1973: Fruit and vegetables 55·9% (citrus fruit 31·5%; fresh potatoes 11·6%); Alcoholic beverages 10·0%; Metalliferous ores and metal scrap 13·7% (copper ores and concentrates 12·9%).
Monetary unit: Cyprus pound. C£1 = 1000 mils.
Denominations:
   Coins 1, 3, 5, 25, 50, 100 mils.
   Notes 250, 500 mils, £1, £5.
Exchange rate to US dollar: 0.4078 (July 1977).
Political history and government: A former British dependency, independent since 16 Aug. 1960 and a member of the Commonwealth since 13 Mar. 1961. Under the 1960 constitution, Cyprus is a unitary republic with executive authority vested in the President (who must be a Greek Cypriot) and the Vice-President (who must be a Turkish Cypriot). They are elected for 5 years by universal suffrage (among the Greek and Turkish communities respectively) and jointly appoint a Council of Ministers (seven Greeks, three Turks). The national legislature is the unicameral House of Representatives, comprising 50 members (35 Greek and 15 Turkish, separately elected for 5 years). Each community was also to have a communal chamber. The President proposed amendments to the constitution on 30 Nov. 1963. These were unacceptable to the Turks, who have ceased to participate in the central government since December 1963. After the Turkish withdrawal, the all-Greek House of Representatives abolished the Greek communal chamber and the separate electoral rolls. The Turkish community continued to elect a Vice-President for Cyprus (not recognised by the Greeks) and established separate administrative, legal and judicial organs. After the temporary overthrow of President Makarios in July 1974, the armed forces of Turkey intervened and occupied northern Cyprus. On 17 Feb. 1975 the Turkish Cypriots unilaterally proclaimed this area the Turkish Federated State of Cyprus, for which a constitution was approved by referendum on 8 June 1975.
Telephones: 68 000 (1974).
Daily newspapers: 12 (1973).
   Total circulation: 92 000 (11 dailies).
Radio: 171 000 (1973).
TV: 66 000 (1973).
Length of roadways: 5899 miles *9494 km* (31 Dec. 1974).
Adult illiteracy: 24·1% (males 11·8%; females 35·6%) in 1960.
Expectation of life: Males 69·5 years; females 73·4 years (UN estimates for 1970–75).
Defence: Greek community has a National Guard; Turkish community has a Fighters' Army.
Cinemas: 150 (seating capacity 88 000) and 180 part-time (capacity 97 000) in 1972.

CZECHOSLOVAKIA

Official name: Československá Socialistická Republika (Czechoslovak Socialist Republic).
Population: 14 344 986 (census of 1 Dec.

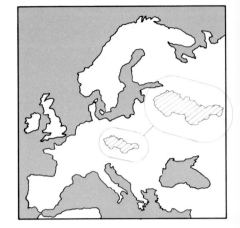

1970); 14 862 000 (estimate for 1 Jan. 1976).
Area: 49 373 miles² *127 876 km².*
Languages: Czech 64%; Slovak 30%; Hungarian 4%.
Religions: Roman Catholic 70%; Protestant 15%.
Capital city: Praha (Prague), population 1 169 567 at 1 Jan. 1976.
Other principal towns (1 Jan. 1976): Brno (Brünn) 359 540; Bratislava (Pressburg) 340 902; Ostrava (Ostrau) 300 945; Košice (Kaschau) 174 388; Plzeň (Pilsen) 156 461; Olomouc (Olmütz) 96 207; Havířov 91 653; Hradec Králóve (Königgrätz) 87 217.
Highest point: Gerlachovsky Stít, 8711 ft *2655 m.*
Principal mountain ranges: Bohemian massif, Low Tatras, High Tatras.
Principal rivers: Labe (Elbe, 525 miles *845 km*), Vltava (Moldau), Dunaj (Danube, 1770 miles *2850 km*), Morava, Váh, Nitra, Hron.
Head of State: Dr Gustáv Husák (b. 10 Jan. 1913), President; also General Secretary of the Communist Party of Czechoslovakia.
Prime Minister: Dr Lubomír Štrougal (b. 19 Oct. 1924).
Climate: Cold winters and warm, rainy summers. Average temperature 49 °F. In Prague, July warmest (58 °F to 74 °F), January coldest (25 °F to 34 °F), June and July rainiest (14 days each). Absolute maximum temperature 39,0 °C (*102·2 °F*), Hurbanovo, 5 Aug. 1905; absolute minimum −41,0 °C (*−41·8 °F*), Viglaš-Pstruša, 11 Feb. 1929.
Labour force: 7 435 000 (excluding armed forces, family workers and apprentices) aged 15 and over (1975): Agriculture, forestry and fishing 15·7%; Industry (mining, manufacturing, electricity and gas) 38·8%; Trade, restaurants and hotels 10·4%; Community, social and personal services (including water) 19·0%.
Net material product: 404 200 million korunas in 1975: Industry 65·0%; Construction 12·7%.
Exports: $7053·4 million in 1974: Iron and steel 11·7%; Machinery and transport equipment 46·3% (non-electric machinery 28·6%; transport equipment 11·4%).
Monetary unit: Koruna (Kčs) or Czechoslovak crown. 1 koruna = 100 haléřů (singular halér).
Denominations:
   Coins 1, 3, 5, 10, 20, 50 haléřů; 1, 2, 5 korunas.
   Notes 10, 20, 50, 100, 500 korunas.
Exchange rate to US dollar: 5.70 (July 1977).
Political history and government: Formerly part of Austria-Hungary, independent since 28 Oct. 1918. Under the Munich agreement, made on 29 Sept. 1938 by France, Germany, Italy and the United Kingdom,

Czechoslovakia ceded the Sudetenland to Germany and other areas to Hungary and Poland. German forces entered Czechoslovakia on 1 Oct. 1938. On 16 Mar. 1939 Germany invaded and occupied the rest of the country. At the end of the Second World War in May 1945 the pre-1938 frontiers were restored but Czechoslovakia ceded Ruthenia to the U.S.S.R. in June 1945. The Communist Party won 38% of the vote at the 1946 election and dominated the government. After Ministers of other parties resigned, Communist control became complete on 25 Feb. 1948. A People's Republic was established on 9 June 1948. A new constitution, introducing the country's present name, was proclaimed on 11 July 1960. Czechoslovakia has been a federal republic since 1 Jan. 1969.

The country comprises two nations, the Czechs and the Slovaks, each forming a republic with its own elected National Council and government. Czechoslovakia comprises 10 administrative regions and two cities.

The supreme organ of state power is the bicameral Federal Assembly, elected for 5 years by universal adult suffrage. Its permanent organ is the elected Presidium. The Assembly comprises the Chamber of the People, with 200 members (138 Czechs and 62 Slovaks), and the Chamber of Nations, with 150 members (75 from each republic). The Assembly elects the President of the Republic for a 5-year term and he appoints the Federal Government, led by the Prime Minister, to hold executive authority. Ministers are responsible to the Assembly.

Political power is held by the Communist Party of Czechoslovakia, which dominates the National Front (including four other minor parties). All candidates for representative bodies are sponsored by the Front. The Communist Party's highest authority is the Party Congress, which elects the Central Committee (121 members were elected on 16 April 1976) to supervise Party work. The Committee elects a Presidium (11 full members and two alternate members) to direct policy.

Telephones: 2 480 801 (1974).
Daily newspapers: 29.
 Total circulation: 3 987 000.
Radio: 3 916 375 (1975).
TV: 3 689 212 (1975).
Length of roadways: 90 670 miles *145 919 km.*
Length of railways: 15 032 miles *24 192 km.*
Universities: 5 (plus 4 technical universities).
Adult illiteracy: under 1%.
Expectation of life: Males 66·53 years; females 73·49 years (1973).
Defence: Military service two years; total regular forces 180 000 (110 000 conscripts); defence expenditure, 1976: $1805 million.
Cinemas: 3465 (seating capacity 985 800) in 1973.

DENMARK

Official name: Kongeriget Danmark (Kingdom of Denmark).
Population: 4 937 579 (census of 9 Nov. 1970); 5 076 000 (estimate for 1 Aug. 1976).
Area: 16 629 miles² *43 069 km².*
Language: Danish.
Religions: Evangelical Lutheran 94%, other Christian minorities.
Capital city: København (Copenhagen), population 736 951 (1 July 1974). Greater Copenhagen (including Frederiksberg and Gentofte) 1 269 938 (1 Jan. 1976).
Other principal towns (1 Jan. 1976): Århus (Aarhus) 246 355; Odense 168 206;

Ålborg (Aalborg) 154 646; Frederiksberg 95 318 (1975); Esbjerg 79 160 Randers 64 193.
Highest point: Yding Skovhøj, 568 ft *173 m.*
Principal river: Gudenå.
Head of State: HM Queen Margrethe II (b. 16 Apr. 1940).
Prime Minister: Anker Jørgensen (b. 13 July 1922).
Climate: Temperate. Mild summers (seldom above 70 °F) and cold winters (although seldom below freezing). The days are often foggy and damp. In Copenhagen, July warmest (55 °F to 72 °F), February coldest (28 °F to 36 °F), August rainiest (12 days). Absolute maximum temperature 35,8 °C (96·4 °F), Antvorskov, 13 Aug. 1911; absolute minimum −31,0 °C (−23·8 °F), Løndal, 26 Jan. 1942.
Labour force: 2 485 619 (including unemployed) aged 15 to 74 years (October 1975): Manufacturing 23·6%; Trade, restaurants and hotels 14·6%; Community, social and personal services 30·6%.
Gross domestic product: 185 289 million kroner (provisional) in 1974: Manufacturing (excluding dairies and slaughter houses) 27·1%; Trade, restaurants and hotels 13·7% (trade 12·6%); Transport, storage and communications 10·1%; Government services 19·7%. Revised total is 184 184 million kroner.

Exports: $8663·3 million in 1975: Meat and meat preparation 15·8%; Other food 16·4%; Machinery and transport equipment 29·2% (non-electric machinery 14·7%).
Monetary unit: Danish krone. 1 krone = 100 øre.
Denominations:
 Coins 5, 10, 25 øre, 1, 5 kroner.
 Notes 10, 50, 100, 500, 1000 kroner.
Exchange rate to US dollar: 5.949 (July 1977).
Political history and government: A constitutional monarchy since 1849. Under the constitutional charter (*Grundlov*) of 5 June 1953, legislative power is held jointly by the hereditary monarch (who has no personal political power) and the unicameral Parliament (*Folketing*), with 179 members (175 from metropolitan Denmark and two each from the Faeroe Islands and Greenland). Members are elected by universal adult suffrage for 4 years (subject to dissolution), using proportional representation. Executive power is exercised by the monarch through a Cabinet, led by the Prime Minister, which is responsible to Parliament. Denmark comprises 14 counties, one city and one borough.
Telephones: 2 183 847 (1975), including the Faeroes and Greenland.
Daily newspapers: 50 (1975).
 Total circulation: 1 723 000.
Radio: 1 672 000 (1975).

TV: 1 557 000 (1975).
Length of roadways: 41 096 miles *66 137 km* (31 Dec. 1975).
Length of railways: 3387 miles *5451 km.*
Universities: 5 (plus 3 technical universities).
Adult illiteracy: under 1%.
Expectation of life: Males 70·8 years; females 76·3 years (1972–73).
Defence: Military service nine months; total armed forces 34 700 (12 270 conscripts); defence expenditure, 1976/77: $844 million.
Cinemas: 356 (seating capacity 128 622) in 1973.

DJIBOUTI

Official name: La République de Djibouti.
Population: 81 200 (census of 1960–61); 106 000 (UN estimate for mid-1975). According to an unofficial estimate, the population was 220 000 in 1976.
Area: 8500 miles² *22 000 km².*
Languages: Somali, Afar, Arabic.
Religions: Muslim; Christian minority.
Capital city: Djibouti (Jibuti), population 62 000 in 1970.
Other principal towns: Tadjoura, Obock, Dikhil, Ali-Sabieh.
Head of State: Hassan Gouled Aptidon (b. 1916), President.
Prime Minister: Ahmed Dini Ahmed (b. 1932).
Climate: Very hot and dry.
Gross domestic product: $104 million (1970 estimate).
Exports: 3678 million Djibouti francs in 1974.
Monetary unit: Djibouti franc. 1 franc = 100 centimes.
Denominations:
 Coins 1, 2, 5, 10, 20, 50, 100 francs.
 Notes 50, 100, 500, 1000, 5000 francs.
Exchange rate to US dollar: 165.64 (July 1977).
Political history and government: Formerly a dependency of France. Known as French Somaliland until 5 July 1967 and from then until independence as the French Territory of the Afars and the Issas. Also in 1967 the Territorial Assembly became the Chamber of Deputies. A provisional independence agreement was signed on 8 June 1976. A popular referendum approved independence on 8 May 1977, when an enlarged Chamber of Deputies (65 members) was also elected. The Chamber elected a Prime Minister on 16 May 1977. The Territory became independent on 27 June 1977, when the Prime Minister became President and the Chamber became a Constituent Assembly. Executive power is held by the President, who is Head of State and Head of Government. The President appoints the Prime Minister and, on the latter's recommendation, other members of the Council of Ministers. The Assembly is to draw up a new constitution.
Telephones: 3000 (1974).
Radio: 10 000 (1973).
TV: 2300 (1973).
Length of roadways: 1025 miles *1650 km.*
Length of railways: 62 miles *100 km.*
Defence: At the time of independence it was agreed that 4500 French troops would remain.
Cinemas: 3 (seating capacity 4700) in 1969.

THE DOMINICAN REPUBLIC

Official name: La República Dominicana.
Population: 4 006 405 (census of 9 Jan.

D

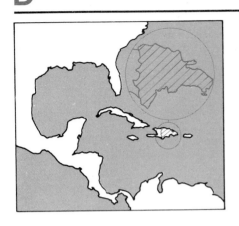

1970); 4 835 207 (estimate for 1 July 1976).
Area: 18 816 miles² *48 734 km²*.
Language: Spanish.
Religion: Roman Catholic.
Capital city: Santo Domingo de Guzmán, population 922 528 at 1 July 1975.
Other principal towns (1975): Santiago de los Caballeros 209 179; San Pedro de Macorís 61 994; San Francisco de Macorís 58 174; Barahona 51 109; La Romana 47 382.
Highest point: Pico Duarte (formerly Pico Trujillo), 10 417 ft *3175 m*.
Principal mountain range: Cordillera Central.
Principal river: Yaque del Norte.
Head of State: Dr Joaquín Balaguer (b. 1 Sept. 1907), President.
Climate: Sub-tropical. Average temperature 80 °F. The west and south-west are arid. In the path of tropical cyclones. In Santo Domingo, August is hottest (73 °F to 88 °F), January coolest (66 °F to 84 °F), June rainiest (12 days). Absolute maximum temperature 43 °C (109·4 °F), Valverde, 31 Aug. 1954; absolute minimum −3,5 °C (+25·7 °F), Valle Nuevo, 2 Mar. 1959.
Labour force: 1 241 000 (1970 census): Agriculture, forestry and fishing 56·3%; Manufacturing 10·4%; Community, social and personal services 15·8%.
Gross domestic product: 3610 million pesos in 1975: Agriculture, forestry and fishing 21·2%; Manufacturing 21·0%; Trade, restaurants and hotels 16·0%.
Exports: $636·8 million in 1974: Sugar and honey 54·8% (raw sugar 50·9%); Other food 18·7%; Metalliferous ores and metal scrap 17·4% (nickel ores and concentrates 14·6%).
Monetary unit: Dominican Republic peso. 1 peso = 100 centavos.
Denominations:
Coins 1, 5, 10, 25, 50 centavos, 1 peso.
Notes 1, 5, 10, 20, 50, 100, 500, 1000 pesos.
Exchange rate to US dollar: 1.00 (July 1977).
Political history and government: A republic comprising 26 provinces (each administered by an appointed governor) and a *Distrito Nacional* (DN) containing the capital. Legislative power is exercised by the bicameral National Congress, with a Senate of 27 members (one for each province and one for the DN) and a Chamber of Deputies (91 members). Members of both houses are elected for four years by universal adult suffrage. Executive power lies with the President, elected by direct popular vote for four years. He is assisted by a Vice-President and an appointed Cabinet containing Secretaries of State.
Telephones: 95 000 (1974).
Daily newspapers: 7 (1973).
Total circulation: 164 000 (6 dailies).
Radio: 180 000 (1973).
TV: 155 000 (1973).

Length of roadways (1971): 6504 miles *10 467 km*.
Length of railways: 1056 miles *1700 km*.
Universities: 4.
Adult illiteracy: 32·8% (males 31·2%; females 34·3%) in 1970.
Expectation of life: Males 57·15 years; females 58·59 years (1959–61).
Defence: Military service one year, selective; total armed forces 18 000; defence expenditure, 1974: $36 million.
Cinemas: 80 (seating capacity 40 700), 6 part-time (capacity 1345) and 2 drive-in (1971).

ECUADOR

Official name: La República del Ecuador ('the equator').
Population: 6 521 710 (census of 8 June 1974); 6 733 000 (estimate for 30 June 1975). Figures exclude nomadic Indian tribes.
Area: 109 484 miles² *283 561 km²*.
Language: Spanish.
Religion: Roman Catholic.
Capital city: Quito, population 557 113 (1974).
Other principal towns (1974): Guayaquil 814 064; Cuenca 104 667; Ambato 77 06?; Machala 68 379; Esmeraldas 60 132; Portoviejo 59 404; Ríobamba 58 029.
Highest point: Chimborazo, 20 561 ft *6267 m* (first climbed 1879).
Principal mountain range: Cordillera de los Andes.
Principal rivers: Napo, Pastaza, Curaray, Daule.
Head of State: Vice-Admiral Alfredo Poveda Burbano, President.
Climate: Tropical (hot and humid) in coastal lowlands. Temperate (mild days, cool nights) in highlands, average temperature 55 °F, rainy season November–May. In Quito, average maximum 70 °F (April, May) to 73 °F (August, September), minimum 44 °F(July) to 47 °F (February–May), April rainiest (22 days). Absolute maximum temperature 38 °C (100·4 °F), Babahoyo, 4 Jan. 1954; absolute minimum −3,6 °C (25·5 °F), Cotopaxi, 9 Sept. 1962.
Labour force: 1 890 431 (including unemployed) at 1974 census; Agriculture, forestry and fishing 49·8%; Manufacturing 12·4%; Trade, restaurants and hotels 10·1%; Community, social and personal services 18·0%.
Gross domestic product: 92 888 million sucres (provisional) in 1974: Agriculture, forestry and fishing 23·5% (agriculture 20·6%); Manufacturing 16·9%; Trade, restaurants and hotels 13·0% (trade 12·7%); Community, social and personal services 16·8% (public administration and defence 10·2%). Revised total is 91 500 million sucres.
Exports: $532.0 million in 1973: Fruit and vegetables 14·4% (fresh bananas and plantains 13·9%); Coffee 12·4%; Other food 13·7%; Petroleum and petroleum products 53·1% (crude petroleum 53·0%).
Monetary unit: Sucre. 1 sucre = 100 centavos.
Denominations:
Coins 5, 10, 20, 50 centavos, 1 sucre.
Notes 5, 10, 20, 50, 500, 1000 sucres.
Exchange rate to US dollar: 25.00 (July 1977).
Political history and government: A republic comprising 19 provinces (each administered by an appointed governor) and a National Territory, the Archipiélago de Colón (the Galapagos Islands). On 22 June 1970 the President dismissed the National Congress (a Senate of 54 members and a

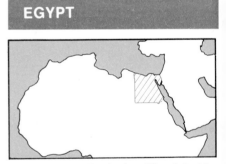

72-member Chamber of Deputies) and assumed dictatorial powers. He was deposed by the armed forces on 15 Feb. 1972 and a National Military Government was formed. All political activity was suspended on 11 July 1974. A three-man military junta took power on 11 Jan. 1976 and appointed a new Cabinet.
Telephones: 168 000 (1974).
Daily newspapers: 22 (1973).
Total circulation: 308 000.
Radio: 1 700 000 (1971).
TV: 178 000 (1972).
Length of roadways: 11 400 miles *18 345 km*.
Length of railways: 665 miles *107 km*.
Universities: 16.
Adult illiteracy: 32·7% (males 27·9%; females 36·9%) in 1962.
Expectation of life: Males 51·04 years; females 53·67 years (1961–63, excluding nomadic Indian tribes).
Defence: Military service: two years, selective; total armed forces 23 550; Defence expenditure, 1974: $52 million.
Cinemas: 113 (seating capacity 114 600) in 1972.

EGYPT

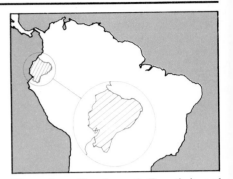

Official name: Jumhuriyat Misr al-Arabiya (Arab Republic of Egypt).
Population: 38 228 180 (census of 22–23 Nov. 1976).
Area: 386 662 miles² *1 001 449 km²*.
Language: Arabic.
Religions: Muslim 92·6% Christian 7·3% (1960).
Capital city: El Qahira (Cairo), population 5 715 000 (estimate for 1 July 1974).
Other principal towns (1974): El Iskandariyah (Alexandria) 2 259 000; El Giza 853 700; El Suwais (Suez) 368 000; Subra-El Khema 346 000; Bur Sa'id (Port Said) 342 000; El Mahalla el Kubra 287 800; Tanta 278 300; Aswan 246 000; El Mansura 232 400.
Highest point: Jebel Katherina, 8651 ft *2609 m*.
Principal mountain ranges: Sinai, Eastern Coastal Range.
Principal river: Nile 4145 miles *6671 km*.
Head of State: Col Muhammad Anwar as-Sadat (b. 25 Dec. 1918), President.
Prime Minister: Gen Mamduh Muhammad Salem (b. 1918).

Climate: Hot and dry. Over 90% is arid desert. Annual rainfall generally less than 2 in, except on Mediterranean coast (maximum of 8 in around Alexandria). Mild winters. In Cairo average maximum 65 °F (January) to 96 °F (July), minimum 47 °F (January) to 71 °F (August). In Luxor average maximum 74 °F (January) to 107 °F (July), minimum 42 °F (January) to 73 °F (July, August), rain negligible.
Labour force: 9 075 900 (excluding armed forces and unemployed) in May 1974: Agriculture, forestry and fishing 47·6%; Manufacturing 15·4%; Trade, restaurants and hotels 11·7%; Community, social and personal services 16·6%.
Gross domestic product: £E3662·8 million in 1973/74: Agriculture, forestry and fishing 32·2%; Manufacturing 18·7%; Community, social and personal services (including business services) 24·0%.
Exports: $1515·7 million in 1974: Food and live animals 15·1%; Textile fibres and waste 48·1% (raw cotton 47·0%); Textile yarn, fabrics, etc. 15·7% (cotton yarn 11·0%).
Monetary unit: Egyptian pound (£E). £E1 = 100 piastres = 1000 millièmes.
Denominations:
    Coins 1, 2, 5 millièmes, 1, 2, 5, 10 piastres.
    Notes 5, 10 piastres, ¼, ½, 1, 5, 10 pounds.
Exchange rate to US dollar: 0.391 (July 1977).
Political history and government: A former British protectorate, Egypt became independent, with the Sultan as King, on 28 Feb. 1922. Army officers staged a *coup* on 23 July 1952 and the King abdicated, in favour of his son, on 26 July 1952. Political parties were dissolved on 16 Jan. 1953. The young King was deposed, and a republic proclaimed, on 18 June 1953. Egypt merged with Syria to form the United Arab Republic on 1 Feb. 1958. Syria broke away and resumed independence on 29 Sept. 1961 but Egypt retained the union's title until the present name was adopted on 2 Sept. 1971. A new constitution, proclaiming socialist principles, was approved by referendum on 11 Sept. 1971. Legislative authority rests with the unicameral People's Assembly of 360 members (10 appointed, 12 representing occupied territories and 338 elected by universal adult suffrage for 5 years). Half the elected members must be workers or peasants. The Assembly nominates the President, who is elected by popular referendum for six years. He has executive authority and appoints one or more Vice-Presidents, a Prime Minister and a Council of Ministers to perform administrative functions. The Arab Socialist Union (ASU), created on 7 Dec. 1962, was the only recognised political organisation of the state until the formation of political parties was again legalized on 29 June 1977. The three permitted parties are based on the three 'platforms' of the ASU which presented separate candidates at the Assembly elections of 28 Oct. and 4 Nov. 1976. The country is composed of 25 governorates (5 cities, 16 provinces, 4 frontier districts).
Telephones: 503 000 (1974).
Daily newspapers: 14 (1971).
    Total circulation: 745 000.
Radio: 5 100 000 (1973).
TV: 600 000 (1973).
Length of roadways: 31 069 miles *50 000 km.*
Length of railways: 3111 miles *5006 km.*
Universities: 8.
Adult illiteracy: 73·7% (males 59·5%; females 87·6%) in 1960.
Expectation of life: Males 51·6 years; females 53·8 years (1960).
Defence: Military service: three years; total armed forces 342 500; defence expenditure 1976/77 $4859 million.
Cinemas: 151 (seating capacity 138 600) and 87 part-time (capacity 76 236) in 1970.

EL SALVADOR

Official name: La República de El Salvador ('The Saviour').
Population: 3 554 648 (census of 28 June 1971); 4 007 000 (estimate for 1 July 1975).
Area: 8124 miles² *21 041 km².*
Language: Spanish.
Religion: Roman Catholic.
Capital city: San Salvador, population 416 900 (1974 est).
Other principal towns (1971): Santa Ana 172 300; San Miguel 110 966; Zacatecoluca 57 001; Santa Tecla 55 718; Ahuachapán 53 386; Sonsonate 48 821.
Highest point: 9200 ft *2804 m.*
Principal rivers: Lempa (250 miles [*402 km*]), San Miguel.

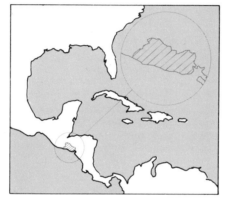

Head of State: Gen Carlos Humberto Romero, President.
Climate: Tropical (hot and humid) in coastal lowlands, temperate in uplands. In San Salvador maximum temperature is 90 °F (April and May), minimum around 60 °F (December, January, February).
Labour force: 1 314 857 (including unemployed) aged 10 and over (1971 census); Agriculture, forestry and fishing 57·7%; Manufacturing 10·1%; Community, social and personal services 16·1%.
Gross domestic product: 4565 million colones in 1975: Agriculture, forestry and fishing 24·2%; Manufacturing 17·2%; Trade, restaurants and hotels 27·0%.
Exports: $277·3 million in 1972: Coffee 38·6%; Other food 15·1%; Textile fibres and waste 14·0% (raw cotton 13·4%).
Monetary unit: Salvadorian colón. 1 colón = 100 centavos.
Denominations:
    Coins 1, 2, 3, 5, 10, 25, 50 centavos.
    Notes 1, 2, 5, 10, 25, 100 colones.
Exchange rate to US dollar: 2.50 (July 1977).
Political history and government: A republic composed of 14 departments. Legislative power is held by a single Legislative Assembly containing 52 members elected for two years by universal suffrage, using a system of proportional representation. Executive power is vested in the President, who is elected by popular vote for 5 years and may not be re-elected. The President is assisted by a Vice-President and a Council of Ministers.
Telephones: 50 000 (1974).
Daily newspapers: 13 (1973).
    Total circulation: 348 000 (10 dailies).
Radio: 350 000 (1971).
TV: 110 000 (1973).

Length of roadways: 5216 miles *8394 km.*
Length of railways: 447 miles *720 km.*
Universities: 1.
Adult illiteracy: 43·1% (1971).
Expectation of life: Males 56·56 years; females 60·42 years (1960–1).
Defence: Total armed forces 7155.
Cinemas: 57 (est seating capacity 57 000) in 1971.

EQUATORIAL GUINEA

Official name: La República de Guinea Ecuatorial.
Population: 245 989 (census of 31 Dec. 1960); 316 000 (UN estimate for mid-1976).
Area: 10 831 miles² *28 051 km².*
Languages: Spanish (official), Fang, Bubi.
Religions: Roman Catholic, Protestant minority.
Capital city: Malabo (formerly Santa Isabel), population 19 341 (1970 est).
Other principal town: Bata, population 3548.
Highest point: Pico de Moca (Moka), 9350 ft *2850 m.*
Principal rivers: Campo, Benito, Muni.
Head of State: Francisco Macías Nguema (b. 1 Jan. 1924), President.
Climate: Tropical (hot and humid), with average temperatures of over 26 °C (*80 °F*) and heavy rainfall (about 80 in per year).
Labour force: 100 000 (1970): Agriculture, forestry and fishing 80·0% (ILO estimates).
Gross domestic product: $76 million in 1970 (estimate).
Exports: 1740·9 million ekuele in 1970: Cocoa 66·2% (cocoa beans 65·3%); Coffee 24·2%.
Monetary unit: Ekuele. 1 ekuele = 100 céntimos.
Denominations:
    Coins 5, 10, 50 céntimos, 1, 2½, 5, 25, 50, 100 ekuele.
    Notes 1, 5, 25, 50, 100, 500, 1000 ekuele.
Exchange rate to US dollar: 87.80 (July 1977).
Political history and government: Formed on 20 Dec. 1963 by a merger of two Spanish territories, Rio Muni on the African mainland and the adjacent islands of Fernando Póo (now Macías Nguema Biyogo). Became an independent republic, as a federation of two provinces, on 12 Oct. 1968. All political parties were merged into one on 2 Feb. 1970. The legislature, a unicameral National Assembly of 35 members, was dissolved in 1971. Executive power lies with the President (proclaimed President for Life on 14 July 1972), assisted by a Cabinet. A revised constitution, approved by referendum on 29 July 1973 and effective from 4 Aug. 1973, gave absolute power to the President and established a unitary state, abolishing the provincial autonomy of the islands.
Telephones: 1451 (1969).
Daily newspapers: 1 (1967).
    Total circulation: 1000.

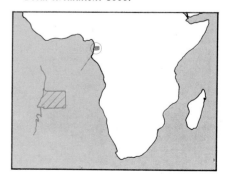

Radio: 76 000.
Length of roadways: 730 miles *1175 km.*
Expectation of life: Males 41·9 years;
females 45·1 years (UN estimates for 1970–
75).
Cinemas: 11 (seating capacity 6300) in 1967.

ETHIOPIA

Official name: Socialist Ethiopia.
Population: 28 678 000 (estimate for 1
July 1976).
Area: 471 800 miles² *1 221 900 km².*
Languages: Amharic, Galla, Somali.
Religions: Muslim 50%, Christian (mainly
Coptic).
Capital city: Addis Ababa ('New Flower'),
population 1 161 267 (1 July 1975).
Other principal towns (1974): Asmara
285 860; Dire Dawa 72 860; Dessie 54 910;
Harar 53 560; Jimma 52 420; Nazret 50 550;
Gondar 43 040.
Highest point: Ras Dashen, 15 158 ft
4620 m.
Principal mountain ranges: Eritrean
highlands, Tigre Plateau, Eastern High-
lands, Semien mountains.
Principal rivers: Abbay, Tekeze, Awash,
Omo, Sagan, Webi, Shelebe.
Head of State: Lt-Col Mengistu Haile
Mariam (b. 1937), President of the Derg
(Provisional Military Administrative Coun-
cil).
Climate: Mainly temperate and cool on the
high plateau, with average annual temperature
of 55 °F *(13 °C)*, abundant rainfall (June to
August) and low humidity. Very hot and
dry in desert lowlands and valley gorges.
In Addis Ababa, average maximum 69 °F
21 °C (July, August) to 77 °F *25 °C* (March–
May), minimum 41 °F *5 °C* (December) to
50 °F *10 °C* (April–August). Absolute maximum *47,5 °C* (117·5° F), Kelaffo, May 1959;
absolute minimum *−5,6 °C* (−22·0 °F),
Maichew, November 1956.

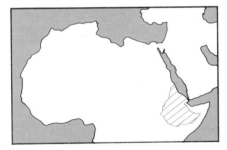

Labour force: 11 090 000 (1970): Agriculture, forestry and fishing 84·1% (ILO
estimates).
Gross domestic product: 5586 million
birr in 1973/74: Agriculture, forestry and
fishing 52·2% (agriculture 49·9%).
Exports: US$262·4 million (excluding
re-exports) in 1974: Fruit and vegetables
20·8% (dry pulses 18·7%); Coffee 27·7%;
Oil seeds, oil nuts and oil kernels 17·5%.
Monetary unit: Birr (formerly Ethiopian
dollar). 1 birr = 100 cents.
Denominations:
  Coins 1, 5, 10, 25, 50 cents.
  Notes 1, 5, 10, 20, 50, 100, 500 birr.
Exchange rate to US dollar: 2.0855 (July
1977).
Political history and government: Formerly a monarchy, ruled by an Emperor
with near-autocratic powers. Political parties
were not permitted. The former Italian
colony of Eritrea was merged with Ethiopia,
under a federal arrangement, on 15 Sept.
1952. Its federal status was ended on 14
Nov. 1962.

The last Emperor was deposed by the
armed forces on 12 Sept. 1974. The constitution and the bicameral Parliament (a
Senate and a Chamber of Deputies) were
suspended. The *coup* was engineered by the
Armed Forces Co-ordinating Committee (the
Derg). The Committee established a Provisional Military Government and on 28
Nov. 1974 created the Provisional Military
Administrative Council (PMAC) as its
executive arm. Ethiopia was declared a
socialist state on 20 Dec. 1974 and the
monarchy was abolished on 21 Mar. 1975.
Under a government re-organisation, announced on 29 Dec. 1976 and modified by
proclamation on 11 Feb. 1977, the PMAC
was renamed the Derg and was re-constituted
with three organs: a General Congress (all
members of the Derg) to determine national
policy; a Central Committee (32 members of
the Derg elected by the Congress) to supervise policy; and a Standing Committee (16
members), elected from the Central Committee by the Congress. The President of
the Derg is Head of State and Chairman of
the General Congress and the two committees. The Council of Ministers is
appointed by, and responsible to, the Derg.
Ethiopia has 14 provinces.
Telephones: 65 987 (1974).
Daily newspapers: 7 (1973).
  Total circulation: 51 000.
Radio: 200 000 (1975).
TV: 25 000 (1973).
Length of roadways: 14 292 miles
23 000 km (31 Dec. 1973).
Length of railways: 744 miles *1197 km.*
Universities: 2.
Adult illiteracy: 90% (estimate).
Expectation of life: Males 36·5 years;
females 39·6 years (UN estimates for 1970–
75).
Defence: Military service: voluntary; total
armed forces 50 800; defence expenditure,
1975: US$84 million.
Cinemas: 30 (seating capacity 26 100) in
1973.

FIJI

Population: 476 727 (census of 12 Sept.
1966); 580 000 (estimate for 1 July 1976).
Area: 7055 miles² *18 272 km².*
Languages: English, Fijian, Hindi.
Religions: Christian 50·8% (mainly Metho-
dist), Hindu 40·3%, Muslim 7·8% (1966).
Capital city: Suva, population 65 530
(1973 est).
Other principal towns: Lautoka, Vatu-
koula, Ba, Labasa, Levuka.
Highest point: Mt Victoria (Tomaniivi) on
Viti Levu, 4341 ft *1323 m.*
Principal rivers: Rewa, Sigatoka, Navua,
Nadi, Ba.
Head of State: HM Queen Elizabeth II,
represented by Ratu Sir George Kandavulevu
Cakobau, GCMG, GCVO, OBE (b. 6 Nov. 1912),
Governor-General.
Prime Minister: Ratu the Rt Hon Sir
Kamisese Kapaiwai Tuimacilau Mara, KBE
(b. 13 May 1920).
Climate: Temperate, with temperatures
rarely falling below 60 °F *(15·5 °C)* or rising
above 90 °F *(32,2 °C)*. Copious rainfall on
windward side; dry on leeward side. Rainy
season Nov.–March, driest month July.
Labour force: 120 574 (excluding 5235
unemployed) aged 15 and over (1966 census):
Agriculture, forestry and fishing 63·1%.
Gross domestic product: F$338·3 million
in 1973: Agriculture, forestry and fishing
23·4%; Manufacturing 13·1%; Trade, restaurants and hotels 19·8% (trade 16·6%).
Exports: US$79·7 million in 1974: Sugar
and honey 51·3% (raw sugar 50·2%);

Other food 10·5%; Petroleum products
10·9%.
Monetary unit: Fiji dollar ($F). 1 dollar =
100 cents.
Denominations:
  Coins 1, 2, 5, 10, 20, 50 cents.
  Notes 50 cents, 1, 2, 5, 10, 20 dollars.
Exchange rate to US dollar: 0.915 (July
1977).
Political history and government: A
former British colony, an independent
member of the Commonwealth since 10 Oct.
1970. Executive power is vested in the
Queen and exercisable by her personal
representative, the Governor-General, advised by the Prime Minister, who heads the
Cabinet. The bicameral legislature comprises
a Senate (22 members nominated for 6
years) and a House of Representatives (52
members elected for 5 years). Elections to the
House are on three rolls: Fijian (22), Indian
(22) and general (8). The Cabinet, which
effectively directs the government, is
responsible to the legislature. There are
14 provinces, each headed by a chairman.
Telephones: 26 000 (1974).
Daily newspapers: 1 (1973).
  Total circulation: 20 000.
Radio: 53 000 (1972).
Length of roadways: 1568 miles *2523 km.*
Length of railways: 400 miles *644 km.*
Universities: 1.
Expectation of life: Males 68·5 years;
females 71·7 years (UN estimates for 1970–
75).
Cinemas: 24 with seating capacity of 10 000
(1970).

FINLAND

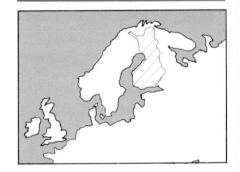

Official name: Suomen Tasavalta (Re-
public of Finland).
Population: 4 598 336 (census of 31 Dec
1970); 4 733 000 (estimate for 1 Dec. 1976).
Area: 130 120 miles² *337 009 km².*
Languages: Finnish 92·4%; Swedish 7·4%.
Religions: Lutheran 92·5%; Orthodox
1·3%.
Capital city: Helsinki (Helsingfors), popu-
lation 496 872 (31 Dec. 1975).
Other principal towns (1975): Tampere
(Tammerfors) 165 926; Turku (Åbo) 163 981;
Espoo (Esbo) 121 307; Vantaa (Vandu)
118 307; Lahti 94 818; Oulu (Uleåborg)
92 618; Pori (Björneborg) 80 242.
Highest point: Haltiatunturi, 4344 ft *1324 m*
Principal mountain ranges: Sualaselkä,
Maanselkä.
Principal rivers: Paatsjoki, Torniojoki,
Kemijoki, Kokemäenjoki.
Head of State: Dr Urho Kaleva Kekkonen,
GCB (b. 3 Sept. 1900), President.
Prime Minister: (Taisto) Kalevi Sorsa
(b. 21 Dec. 1930).
Climate: Warm summers, very cold
winters. Average annual temperature 62 °F
(17 °C). Winters are long and extreme in the
north. In Helsinki, July warmest (57 °F
14 °C to 71 °F *22 °C*), February coldest

15 °F −9 °C to 26 °F −3 °C), August and October rainiest (12 days each). Absolute maximum temperature 35,9 °C (96·6 °F), Turku, 9 July 1914; absolute minimum −48,8 °C (−55·8 °F), Sodankylä, January 868.

Labour force: 2 221 000 (excluding 30 000 persons on compulsory military service and 1 000 unemployed) aged 15 to 74 years 1975); Agriculture, forestry and fishing 4·8%; Industry (mining, quarrying, manufacturing, electricity, gas and water) 27·4%; Trade, restaurants and hotels 15·5%; Community, social and personal services 21·6%.

Gross domestic product: 82 819 million markkaa (provisional) in 1974: Agriculture, forestry and fishing 12·0%; Industry 35·8% (manufacturing 33·0%); Construction 10·0%; Trade, restaurants and hotels 11·4% (trade 10·1%). Revised total is 84 174 million markkaa.

Exports: $5489·0 million in 1975: Paper and paperboard 24·8%; Machinery and transport equipment 22·9% (transport equipment 10·6%).

Monetary unit: Markka (Finnmark). 1 markka = 100 penniä.

Denominations:
Coins 1, 5, 10, 20, 50 penniä, 1, 5 markkaa.
Notes 5, 10, 50, 100, 500 markkaa.

Exchange rate to US dollar: 4.0045 (July 1977).

Political history and government: Formerly a Grand Duchy within the Russian Empire. After the Bolshevik revolution in Russia, Finland's independence was declared on 6 Dec. 1917. A republic was established by the constitution of 17 July 1919, This combines a parliamentary system with a strong presidency. The unicameral Parliament has 200 members elected by universal adult suffrage for 4 years (subject to dissolution by the President), using proportional representation. The President, entrusted with supreme executive power, is elected for 6 years by a college of 300 electors, chosen by popular vote in the same manner as members of Parliament. Legislative power is exercised by Parliament in conjunction with the President. For general administration the President appoints a Council of State (Cabinet), headed by a Prime Minister, which is responsible to Parliament. Finland has 12 provinces, each administered by an appointed Governor.

Telephones: 1 833 993 (1975).
Daily newspapers: 61 (1973).
Radio: 2 098 938 (1975).
TV: 1 673 128 (1976).
Length of roadways: 45 701 miles 73 548 km (excluding urban streets) at 31 Dec. 1975.
Length of railways: 5487 miles 8831 km.
Universities: 8 (plus 3 technical universities).
Adult illiteracy: Under 1%.
Expectation of life: Males 66·57 years; females 74·87 years (1972).
Defence: Military service: 8 to 11 months; total armed forces 35 800 (28 000 conscripts); defence expenditure, 1976: $364 million.
Cinemas: 308 (seating capacity 94 000) in 1973.

FRANCE

Official name: La République française (the French Republic).
Population: 52 544 400 (census of 20 Feb. 1975); 52 944 000 (estimate for 1 Sept. 1976).
Area: 211 208 miles² 547 026 km².
Language: French.
Religions: Roman Catholic, Protestant, Jewish.
Capital city: Paris, population 2 290 900 (1975 census).

Other principal towns (1975): Marseille 907 900; Lyon 457 000; Toulouse 383 200; Nice 344 500; Strasbourg 257 300; Nantes 257 300; Bordeaux 221 100; Saint-Etienne 220 000; Le Havre 219 100; Rennes 195 000; Montpellier 191 100; Toulon 181 800; Reims 177 600; Lille 169 500; Brest 167 200; Grenoble 167 000; Clermont-Ferrand 157 500; Le Mans 152 200; Dijon 151 600; Limoges 147 300; Tours 140 600; Angers 137 300; Amiens 131 000; Nîmes 127 700; Caen 122 500; Besançon 120 400.
Highest point: Mont Blanc, 15 771 ft 4807 m (first climbed on 8 Aug. 1786).
Principal mountain ranges: Alps, Massif Central, Pyrenees, Jura Mts, Vosges, Cévennes.
Principal rivers: Rhône, Seine, Loire (625 miles [1006 km]), Garonne, Rhin (Rhine).
Head of State: Valéry Giscard d'Estaing (b. 2 Feb. 1926), President.
Prime Minister: Raymond Barre (b. 12 Apr. 1924).
Climate: Generally temperate, with cool summers in the west and warm summers elsewhere. Mediterranean climate (warm summers, mild winters) in the south. In Paris, average maximum 42 °F (January) to 76 °F (July), minimum 32 °F (January) to 55 °F (July, August), December rainiest (17 days). Absolute maximum temperature 44,0 °C (111·2 °F), Toulouse, 8 Aug. 1923; absolute minimum −33 °C (−27·4 °F), Langres, 9 Dec. 1879.

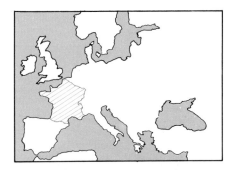

Labour force: 21 039 100 (excluding 293 800 persons on compulsory military service and 501 100 unemployed) aged 15 and over (1975): Agriculture, forestry and fishing 11·2%; Industry (mining, quarrying, manufacturing, electricity, gas and water) 29·2% (manufacturing 27·5%); Trade, restaurants and hotels 16·3%; Community, social and personal services 23·1%.
Gross domestic product: 1 279 900 million francs (provisional) in 1974: Industry (excluding wine production) and fishing 37·3%; Construction 10·0%; Trade, restaurants and hotels 17·6% (trade 14·5%); Government services 10·5%. Revised total is 1 277 600 million francs.
Exports: $51 603·9 million (including Monaco) in 1975: Food and live animals 12·6%; Machinery 21·4% (non-electric machinery 14·3%); Transport equipment 15·3% (road motor vehicles and parts 11·1%).
Monetary unit: French franc. 1 franc = 100 centimes.
Denominations:
Coins 1, 5, 10, 20, centimes, 1, 2 old francs, ½, 1, 5, 10 francs.
Notes 10, 50, 100, 500 francs.
Exchange rate to US dollar: 4.856 (July 1977).
Political history and government: A republic whose present constitution (establishing the Fifth Republic and the French Community) was approved by referendum on 28 Sept. 1958 and promulgated on 6 Oct. 1958. Legislative power is held by a bicameral parliament. The Senate has 283

members (264 for metropolitan France, 13 for the overseas departments and territories and 6 for French nationals abroad) indirectly elected for 9 years (one third renewable every three years). The National Assembly has 490 members (473 for metropolitan France and 17 for overseas departments) directly elected by universal adult suffrage (using two ballots if necessary) for 5 years, subject to dissolution. Executive power is held by the President. Since 1962 the President has been directly elected by universal adult suffrage (using two ballots if necessary) for 7 years. The President appoints a Council of Ministers, headed by the Prime Minister, which administers the country and is responsible to Parliament. Metropolitan France comprises 21 administrative regions containing 95 departments. There are also four overseas departments (French Guiana, Guadeloupe, Martinique and Réunion) which are integral parts of the French Republic. Each department is administered by an appointed Prefect.
Telephones: 12 405 054 (31 Dec. 1973).
Daily newspapers: 100 (1972).
Total circulation: 11 969 000.
Radio: 17 034 000 (1972).
TV: 13 558 551 (31 Dec. 1974).
Length of roadways: 493 797 miles 794 690 km plus 428 746 miles 690 000 km of rural roads (31 Dec. 1975).
Length of railways (1973): 21 693 miles 34 912 km (SNCF only).
Universities: 37.
Expectation of life: Males 68·6 years; females 76·4 years (1972).
Defence: Military service: 12 months; total armed forces 512 900 (279 300 conscripts); defence expenditure, 1976: $10 661 million.
Cinemas: 6126 (seating capacity 1 936 900) in 1972 (capacity refers to cinemas exhibiting 35 mm films).

GABON

Official name: La République gabonaise (The Gabonese Republic).
Population: 448 564 (census of 8 Oct. 1960 to May 1961); 530 000 (UN estimate for mid-1976).
Area: 103 347 miles² 267 667 km².
Languages: French (official), Fang, Eshira, Mbété.
Religions: Christian 60%, Animist minority.
Capital city: Libreville, population 105 080 (1970).
Other principal towns: Port-Gentil, Lambaréné.
Highest point: Mont Iboundji, 5185 ft 1580 m.
Principal river: Ogooué (Ogowe).
Head of State: Albert-Bernard Bongo (b. 30 Dec. 1935), President and Head of Government.
Prime Minister: Léon Mebiame (b. 1 Sept. 1934).

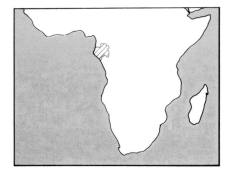

Climate: Tropical (hot and humid). Average temperature 79 °F. Heavy rainfall (annual average 98 in). In Libreville, average maximum 86 °F to 94 °F, minimum 65 °F to 71 °F.

Labour force: 220 000 (31 Dec. 1963); 264 000 (1970): Agriculture, forestry and fishing 81·8% (ILO estimates).

Gross domestic product: 108 500 million CFA francs in 1972: Agriculture, forestry and fishing 12·9%; Mining and quarrying (excluding government) 32·4%; Construction 11·3%; Trade, restaurants and hotels 15·9% (trade 14·5%).

Exports: $177·8 million in 1971: Wood, lumber and cork 23·9% (sawlogs and veneer logs 23·2%); Metalliferous ores and metal scrap 22·1% (manganese ores and concentrates 19·0%); Petroleum and petroleum products 45·2% (crude petroleum 43·8%). Figures exclude trade with other members of the Customs and Economic Union of Central Africa.

Monetary unit: Franc de la Communauté financière africaine.

Denominations:
Coins 1, 2, 5, 10, 25, 50, 100 CFA francs.
Notes 100, 500, 1000, 5000, 10 000 CFA francs.

Exchange rate to US dollar: 242.8 (July 1977).

Political history and government: Formerly part of French Equatorial Africa, independent since 17 Aug. 1960. A one-party state since March 1968. The legislature is a unicameral National Assembly of 70 members, directly elected by universal adult suffrage for 7 years. Executive power is held by the President, also directly elected for 7 years. He appoints, and presides over, a Council of Ministers, including a Prime Minister. Gabon comprises 9 regions, each administered by an appointed Prefect.

Telephones: 11 000 (1973).
Radio: 90 000 (1973).
TV: 1300 (1971).
Length of roadways: 4255 miles *6848 km* (31 Dec. 1973).
Length of railways: 231 miles *372 km.*
Universities: 1.
Expectation of life: Males 39·4 years; females 42·6 years (UN estimates for 1970–75).
Cinemas: 2 (seating capacity 1700) in 1971.

THE GAMBIA

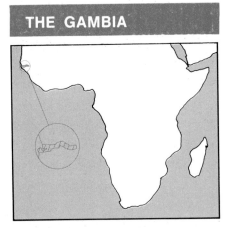

Official name: The Republic of the Gambia.
Population: 493 499 (census of 21 Apr. 1973); 538 000 (estimate for 1 July 1976, excluding seasonal farming immigrants).
Area: 4361 miles² *11 295 km²*
Languages: English (official), Mandinka, Fula, Wollof.
Religions: Muslim, Christian minority.

Capital city: Banjul (formerly Bathurst), population 42 689 (1 July 1975).
Other principal towns: Brikama; Salikeni; Bakau; Gunjur.
Principal river: Gambia.
Head of State: Sir Dawda Kairaba Jawara (b. 11 May 1924), President.
Climate: Long dry season, normally November to May, with pleasant weather on coast (best in West Africa) due to effect of the *harmattan*, a northerly wind. Hotter up-river, especially February to May. Average annual rainfall 40 in on coast, less inland. Rainy season June to October. Average annual temperature in Banjul 80 °F.
Labour force: 240 000 (1970): Agriculture, forestry and fishing 82·1% (ILO estimates).
Gross domestic product: $46 million in 1970 (estimate).
Exports: $41·1 million (excluding re-exports) in 1973: Oil-seed cake and meal 11·4%; Oil seeds, oil nuts and oil kernels 52·9% (groundnuts 52·0%); Groundnut oil 32·6%.
Monetary unit: Dalasi. 1 dalasi = 100 butut.
Denominations:
Coins 1, 5, 10, 25, 50 butut, 1 dalasi.
Notes 1, 5, 10, 25 dalasi.
Exchange rate to US dollar: 2.325 (July 1977).
Political history and government: A former British dependency, an independent member of the Commonwealth since 18 Feb. 1965. A republic since 24 April 1970. Legislative power is held by a unicameral House of Representatives containing 42 members (34 directly elected for 5 years by universal adult suffrage, 4 Chiefs' Representative Members elected by the Chiefs in Assembly, 3 non-voting nominated members and the Attorney-General). Executive power is held by the President, the leader of the majority party in the House. He appoints a Vice-President (who is leader of government business in the House) and a Cabinet from elected members of the House. The country has four political parties.
Telephones: 1942 (1973).
Radio: 60 000 (1973).
Length of roadways (1974): 1858 miles *2990 km.*
Expectation of life: Males 38·5 years; females 41·6 years (UN estimates for 1970–75).
Defence: No armed forces.
Cinemas: 8 (1971).

GERMANY (East)

Official name: Deutsche Demokratische Republik (German Democratic Republic).
Population: 17 068 318 (census of 1 Jan. 1971); 16 786 000 (estimate for 30 June 1976).
Area: 41 768 miles² *108 178 km².*
Language: German.
Religions: Protestant, Roman Catholic minority.
Capital city: (East) Berlin, population 1 094 496 (estimate for 30 June 1975).
Other principal towns (1975): Leipzig 568 877; Dresden 508 298; Karl-Marx-Stadt (Chemnitz) 304 055; Magdeburg 276 580; Halle an der Saale 239 181; Rostock 211 723; Erfurt 203 190.
Highest point: Fichtelberg (3983 ft [*1214m*])
Principal mountain ranges: Thüringer Wald, Erz Gebirge.
Principal rivers: Elbe (525 miles [*845 km*]) (with Havel and Saale), Oder (with Neisse).
Head of State: Erich Honecker (b. 25 Aug. 1912), Chairman of the Council of

State and First Secretary of the Central Committee of the Socialist Unity Party.
Head of Government: Willi Stoph (b. 9 July 1914), Chairman of the Council of Ministers.
Climate: Temperate (warm summers, cool winters), greater range inland. In Berlin, July warmest (55 °F to 74 °F), January coldest (26 °F to 35 °F), December rainiest (11 days). Absolute maximum temperature 39,3 °C (*102·7 °F*), Blankenberg, 7 July 1957; absolute minimum −33,8 °C (*−28·8 °F*), Zittau-Hirschfelde, 11 Feb. 1939.
Labour force: 8 214 251 aged 14 and over (1971 census): Agriculture, forestry and fishing 11·7%; Industry (mining, quarrying, manufacturing, electricity, gas and water) 41·2% (manufacturing 37·7%); Trade, restaurants and hotels 10·3%; Community, social and personal services (including activities not adequately defined) 21·6%.
Net material product: 141 661 million DDR Marks (at 1967 prices) in 1975: Agriculture and forestry 10·0%; Industry 62·2%; Trade, restaurants, etc. 13·3%.
Exports: $10 088 million in 1975.
Monetary unit: Mark der Deutschen Demokratischen Republik (DDR-Mark). 1 Mark = 100 Pfennige.
Denominations:
Coins 1, 5, 10, 20, 50 Pfennige, 1, 2, 5, 10, 20 M.
Notes 5, 10, 20, 50, 100 M.
Exchange rate to US dollar: 1.842 (July 1977).
Political history and government: The territory was the USSR's Zone of Occupation in Germany from May 1945. The republic, a 'people's democracy' on the Soviet pattern, was proclaimed on 7 Oct. 1949. The present constitution was promulgated on 9 Apr. 1968. The supreme organ of state power is the *Volkskammer* (People's Chamber), containing 500 members, including 434 elected for 5 years by universal adult suffrage (from a single list of candidates) and 66 representatives from East Berlin, elected by the City Assembly. The Chamber elects a 25-member *Staatsrat* (Council of State) to be its permanent organ. The executive branch of government is the *Ministerrat* (Council of Ministers), under a Chairman (Minister-President) appointed by the Chamber, which also approves his appointed Ministers. The Council's work is directed by a Presidium of 16 members. Political power is held by the (Communist) Socialist Unity Party of Germany (SED), formed in 1946 by a merger of the Communist Party and the Social Democratic Party in the Soviet Zone. The SED dominates the National Front of Democratic Germany, which also includes four minor parties and four mass organisations. The SED's highest authority is the Party Congress. The Congress elects the Central Committee to supervise Party work (on 22 May 1976 the Congress elected a Committee of 145 full members and 55 candidate members). The Central Committee elects a Political Committee (Politburo) of 19 full members and 9 candidate members to direct its policy. The country is divided into 14 districts (*Bezirke*) and the city of East Berlin.
Telephones: 2 596 200 (1975).
Daily newspapers: 40 (1973).
Total circulation: 7 527 000.
Radio: 6 166 800 (1975).
TV: 5 233 600 (1975).
Length of roadways (1974): 78 859 miles *126 911 km.*
Length of railways (1974): 8856 miles *14 252 km.*
Universities: 7.
Expectation of life: Males 68·85 years; females 74·19 years (1969–70).

Defence: Military service: 18 months; total regular forces 157 000 (92 000 conscripts); defence expenditure, 1976: $2729 million converted at $1 = 3.80 Marks).
Cinemas: 1170 (seating capacity 351 700) and 252 part-time (1973).

GERMANY (West)

Official name: Bundesrepublik Deutschland (Federal Republic of Germany).
Population: 60 650 599 (census of 27 May 1970); 61 490 000 (estimate for 30 Sept. 1976).
Area: 95 993 miles² *248 620 km²*.
Language: German.
Religions: Protestant, Roman Catholic.
Capital city: Bonn, population 283 700 (31 Dec. 1975).
Other principal towns (1974): Berlin (West) 2 002 615; Hamburg 1 751 620; München (Munich) 1 311 978; Köln (Cologne) 849 451; Essen 696 419; Frankfurt am Main 666 179; Düsseldorf 660 963; Dortmund 640 642; Stuttgart 634 202; Bremen 592 533; Hannover (Hanover) 521 003; Nürnberg (Nuremberg) 478 181; Duisberg 452 721; Wuppertal 417 694; Gelsenkirchen 347 074; Bochum 343 809; Mannheim 332 378; Kiel 271 042; Karlsruhe 259 091; Wiesbaden 250 715.
Highest point: Zugspitze, 9721 ft *2963 m* (first climbed 1820).
Principal mountain ranges: Alps, Schwarzwald (Black Forest).
Principal rivers: Rhein (Rhine) (820 miles *1320 km*), Ems, Weser, Elbe, Donau (Danube) (1770 miles [*2848 km*]).
Head of State: Walter Scheel (b. 8 July 1919), Federal President.
Head of Government: Helmut Heinrich Waldemar Schmidt (b. 23 Dec. 1918), Federal Chancellor.
Climate: Generally temperate (average annual temperature 48 °F) with considerable variations from northern coastal plain (mild) to Bavarian Alps (cool summers, cold winters). In Hamburg, July warmest (56 °F to 69 °F) January coolest (28 °F to 35 °F). January, July and December rainiest (each 12 days). Absolute maximum temperature 39,8 °C (*103·6 °F*), Amberg, 18 Aug. 1892; absolute minimum −35,4 °C (*−31·7 °F*), 12 Feb. 1929.
Labour force: 26 878 000 (including unemployed) aged 15 and over (May 1975): Manufacturing 35·5%; Trade, restaurants and hotels 14·3%; Community, social and personal services 22·3%.

Gross domestic product: 996 700 million DM (provisional) in 1974: Manufacturing (including quarrying and steel construction) 39·3%; Trade 12·1%; Government services 11·2%. Revised total is 999 700 million DM.
Exports: $90 021·4 million (excluding trade with East Germany) in 1975: Chemicals 11·6%; Machinery 31·3% (non-electric machinery 22·5%); Transport equipment 15·2% (road motor vehicles and parts 12·3%).
Monetary unit: Deutsche Mark (DM). 1 Deutsche Mark = 100 Pfennige.
Denominations:
Coins 1, 2, 5, 10, 50 Pfennige, 1, 2, 5, 10 DM.
Notes 5, 10, 20, 50, 100, 500, 1000 DM.
Exchange rate to US dollar: 2.276 (July 1977).
Political history and government: The territory was the British, French and US Zones of Occupation in Germany from May 1945. A provisional constitution, the *Grundgesetz* (Basic Law), came into force in the three Zones (excluding Saarland) on 23 May 1949 and the Federal Republic of Germany (FRG) was established on 21 Sept. 1949. Sovereignty was limited by the continuing military occupation, and subsequent defence agreements, until 5 May 1955, when the FRG became fully independent. Saarland (under French occupation) was rejoined with the FRG administratively on 1 Jan. 1957 and economically incorporated on 6 July 1959. The FRG is composed of 10 states (*Länder*)—each *Land* having its own constitution, parliament and government—plus the city of West Berlin which retains a separate status. The country has a parliamentary regime, with a bicameral legislature. The Upper House is the *Bundesrat* (Federal Council) with 45 seats, including 41 members of *Land* governments (which appoint and recall them) and 4 non-voting representatives appointed by the West Berlin Senate. The term of office varies with *Land* election dates. The Lower House, and the FRG's main legislative organ, is the *Bundestag*, with 518 deputies, including 496 elected for four years by universal adult suffrage (using a mixed system of proportional representation and direct voting) and 22 members (with limited voting rights) elected by the West Berlin House of Representatives. Executive authority rests with the *Bundesregierung* (Federal Government), led by the *Bundeskanzler* (Federal Chancellor) who is elected by an absolute majority of the *Bundestag* and appoints the other Ministers. The Head of State, who normally acts on the Chancellor's advice, is elected by a Federal Convention, consisting of the *Bundestag* and an equal number of members elected by the *Land* parliaments.
Telephones: 18 767 000 (1974).
Daily newspapers: 1211 (1973), including 807 regional editions (German language only).
Total circulation: 18 667 000.
Radio: 19 558 229 (1975).
TV: 17 796 475 (1975).
Length of roadways: 288 316 miles *464 000 km* (31 Dec. 1975).
Length of railways: 18 138 miles *29 191 km* } federal

2164 miles *3482 km* } other
Universities: 54 (incl 9 technical universities).
Expectation of life: Males 67·61 years; females 74·09 years (1971–73).
Defence: Military service: 15 months; total armed forces 495 000 (227 000 conscripts); defence expenditure, 1976: $12 605 million.
Cinemas: 3107 (seating capacity 1 229 700) in 1973; also 19 drive-ins for 1839 cars (1973).

GHANA

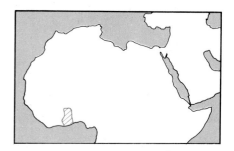

Official name: The Republic of Ghana ('land of gold').
Population: 8 559 313 (census of 1 Mar. 1970); 9 866 000 (estimate for 1 July 1975).
Area: 92 100 miles² *238 537 km²*.
Languages: English (official), Asante, Ewe, Fante.
Religions: Christian, Muslim, Animist.
Capital city: Accra, population 564 194 (1970 census).
Other principal towns (1970): Kumasi 260 286; Tamale 83 653; Tema 60 767; Takoradi 58 161; Cape Coast 51 653; Sekondi 33 713.
Highest point: Vogag (2989 ft [*911 m*]).
Principal rivers: Volta (formed by the confluence of the Black Volta and the White Volta) and its tributaries (principally the Oti), Tano, Ofin.
Head of State: Gen Ignatius Kutu Acheampong (b. 23 Sept. 1931), Chairman of the Supreme Military Council.
Climate: Tropical. In north hot and dry. Forest areas hot and humid. Eastern coastal belt warm and fairly dry. In Accra average maximum 80 °F (August) to 88 °F (February to April and December), average minimum 71 °F (August) to 76 °F (March, April), June rainiest (10 days).
Labour force: 3 331 618 aged 15 and over (1970 census); 3 352 000 (1970); Agriculture, forestry and fishing 58·4% (ILO estimates).
Gross domestic product: 2827 million new cedis in 1972: Agriculture, forestry and fishing (excluding government) 47·9%; (agriculture 43·5%); Manufacturing 10·3%; Trade, restaurants and hotels 12·1% (trade 11·6%).
Exports: $646·6 million in 1974: Cocoa 72·4% (cocoa beans 62·5%); Wood, lumber and cork 13·1%.
Monetary unit: New cedi. 1 cedi = 100 pesewas.
Denominations:
Coins ½, 1, 2½, 5, 10, 20 pesewas.
Notes 1, 2, 5, 10 cedis.
Exchange rate to US dollar: 1.15 (July 1977).
Political history and government: On 6 Mar. 1957 the British dependency of the Gold Coast merged with British Togoland to become independent, and a member of the Commonwealth, as Ghana. Became a republic on 1 July 1960. The President, Dr Kwame Nkrumah, was deposed by a military *coup* on 24 Feb. 1966. Civilian rule was restored on 30 Sept. 1969 but again overthrown by the armed forces on 13 Jan. 1972. The 1969 constitution was abolished, the National Assembly dissolved and political parties banned. Power was assumed by the National Redemption Council (NRC), comprising military commanders and Commissioners of State with ministerial responsibilities. On 14 Oct. 1975 a 7-man Supreme Military Council was established, with full legislative and administrative authority, to direct the NRC.
Telephones: 55 000 (1974).

Daily newspapers: 6 (1973).
   Total circulation: 381 000.
Radio: 775 000 (1972).
TV: 25 000 (1973).
Length of roadways: 19 236 miles *30 957 km.*
Length of railways: 593 miles *954 km.*
Universities: 3.
Expectation of life: Males 41·9 years; females 45·1 years (UN estimates for 1970–75).
Defence: Military service: voluntary; total armed forces 17 600; defence expenditure, 1974/75: $83 million.
Cinemas: 57 (seating capacity 50 400) in 1969.

GREECE

Official name: The Hellenic Republic.
Population: 8 768 640 (census of 14 Mar. 1971); 9 047 000 (estimate for 30 June 1975).
Area: 50 944 miles² *131 944 km².*
Languages: Greek.
Religions: Eastern Orthodox Church, with Roman Catholic and other minorities.
Capital city: Athínai (Athens), population 867 023 (1971 census).
Other principal towns (1971): Thessaloníki (Salonika) 345 799; Piraiévs (Piraeus) 187 362; Péristéri 118 413; Pátrai (Patras) 111 607; Iráklion (Heraklion) 78 209; Lárisa 72 760; Vólos 51 290; Kaválla 46 887.
Highest point: Óros Ólimbos (Olympus), 9550 ft *2911 m.*
Principal mountain ranges: Pindus Mountains.
Principal rivers: Aliákmon (195 miles *314 km*), Piniós, Akhelóös.
Head of State: Konstantinos Tsatsos (b. 1 July 1899), President.
Prime Minister: Konstantinos G Karamanlis (b. 23 Feb. 1907).
Climate: Mediterranean (hot, dry summers and mild, wet winters). Colder in the north and on higher ground. In Athens, July and August hottest (72 °F to 90 °F), January coolest (42 °F to 54 °F), December and January rainiest (seven days each). Absolute maximum temperature (45,7 °C *114·3 °F*), Heraklion, Crete, 16 June 1914; absolute minimum −25 °C (*−13 °F*), Kaválla, 27 Jan. 1954.
Labour force: 3 234 996 (excluding persons on compulsory military service and persons seeking work for the first time) aged 10 and over (1971 census): Agriculture, forestry and fishing 41·4%; Manufacturing 17·5%; Trade, restaurants and hotels 11·4%; Community, social and personal services 11·0%.
Gross domestic product: 575 200 million drachmae (provisional) in 1974: Agriculture, forestry and fishing 19·3%; Manufacturing 21·5%; Trade 14·2%; Community, social and personal services (including restaurants, hotels and business services) 19·1%. Revised total is 569 100 million drachmae.
Exports: $2278·3 million in 1975: Food and live animals 22·3% (fruit and vegetables 19·0%); Petroleum products 10·9%.

Monetary unit: Drachma. 1 drachma = 100 leptae.
Denominations:
   Coins 5, 10, 20, 50 leptae, 1, 2, 5, 10, 20 drachmae.
   Notes 50, 100, 500, 1000 drachmae.
Exchange rate to US dollar: 36.76 (July 1977).
Political history and government: While Greece was a monarchy a *coup* by army officers, led by Col Georgios Papadopoulos, deposed the constitutional government on 21 Apr. 1967. Parliament was suspended and political parties banned. Papadopoulos became Prime Minister on 13 Dec. 1967, a Regent was appointed and the King left the country the next day. A republic was proclaimed on 1 June 1973 and Papadopoulos became President. He was deposed by another military *coup* on 25 Nov. 1973. Civilian rule was re-established on 24 July 1974, when a Government of National Salvation took office. The ban on political parties was lifted and free elections for a Parliament were held on 17 Nov. 1974. A referendum on 8 Dec. 1974 rejected the return of the monarchy. A new republican constitution, providing for a parliamentary democracy, came into force on 11 June 1975. Executive power rests with the President, elected for 5 years by the legislature, a unicameral Parliament of 300 members directly elected by universal adult suffrage for 4 years. The President appoints a Prime Minister and, on his recommendation, the other Ministers to form a Cabinet to govern the country. The Cabinet is accountable to Parliament. The country is divided into 51 prefectures (*Nomoi*). The district of Mount Athos, with its autonomous monastic community, has a privileged status as a self-governing part of the Greek state.
Telephones: 1 972 209 (1975).
Daily newspapers: 103 (1973).
   Total circulation: 920 000.
Radio: 1 300 000 (1972).
TV: 1 140 000 (1975).
Length of roadways: 22 702 miles *36 536 km.* (31 Dec. 1974).
Length of railways: 1598 miles *2572 km.*
Universities: 6.
Adult illiteracy: 15·6% (males 6·9%; females 23·7%) in 1971.
Expectation of life: Males 67·46 years; females 70·70 years (1960–2).
Defence: Military service: 28–32 months; total armed forces 199 500 (148 000 conscripts); Defence expenditure, 1976: $1136 million.
Cinemas: 691 (seating capacity 354 600) and 932 part-time (capacity 890 584) in 1961.

GRENADA

Population: 93 858 (census of 7 Apr. 1970); 105 000 (estimate for 30 June 1975).
Area: 133 miles² *344 km².*
Language: English.
Religions: Christian.
Capital city: Saint George's, population 8644 (1971 est.)
Highest point: Mount St Catherine's, 2756 ft *840 m.*
Head of State: H.M. Queen Elizabeth II, represented by Sir Leo Victor de Gale, GCMG, CBE (b. 28 Dec. 1921), Governor-General.
Prime Minister: The Rt Hon Sir Eric Matthew Gairy (b. 18 Feb. 1922).
Climate: Tropical maritime, with equable temperature averaging 82 °F (*28 °C*) in the lowlands. Annual rainfall averages 60 in (*1524 mm*) in coastal area and 150–200 in (*3810–5080 mm*) in mountain areas. Rainy season June to December (November

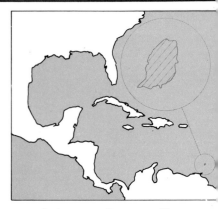

wettest), dry season January to May.
Labour force: 28 682 (1970 census).
Gross domestic product: US$ 34 million in 1970 (estimate).
Exports: EC$26·9 million in 1975.
Monetary unit: East Caribbean dollar (EC$). 1 dollar = 100 cents.
Denominations:
   Coins 1, 2, 5, 10, 25, 50 cents.
   Notes 1, 5, 20, 100 dollars.
Exchange rate to US dollar: 2.70 (July 1977).
Political history and government: A former British dependency. An Associated State, with internal self-government, from Mar. 1967 until becoming fully independent within the Commonwealth, on 7 Feb. 1974. Executive power is vested in the Queen and exercised by the Governor-General, who acts on the advice of the Cabinet, led by the Prime Minister. Legislative power is vested in the bicameral Parliament, comprising a Senate (13 members appointed by the Governor-General) and a House of Assembly (15 members elected by universal adult suffrage). The Cabinet is responsible to Parliament.
Telephones: 4700 (1974).
Daily newspapers: 2 (1971).
   Total circulation: 3000 (1 daily).
Radio: 22 000 (1975).
Length of roadways: 577 miles *928 km.*
Expectation of life: Males 60·14 years; females 65·60 years (1959–61).
Cinemas: 3 (seating capacity 2000) in 1965.

GUATEMALA

Official name: República de Guatemala.
Population: 5 160 221 (census of 26 Mar. 1973, excluding underenumeration of about 10%); 6 256 000 (estimate for 30 June 1976).
Area: 42 042 miles² *108 889 km².*
Languages: Spanish, with some twenty Indian dialects (most important is Quiché).
Religion: Mainly Roman Catholic.
Capital city: Ciudad de Guatemala (Guatemala City), population 700 504 (1973 census).
Other principal towns (1973): Quezaltenango 53 021; Escuintla 33 205; Mazatenango 23 285; Puerto Barrios 22 598; Retalhuleu 19 060; Chiquimula 16 126.
Highest point: Volcán Tajumulco, 13 845 ft *4220 m.*
Principal mountain ranges: Sierra Madre, Sierra de las Minas, Sierra de Los Cuchumatanes, Sierra de Chuacús.
Principal rivers: Motagua (249 miles *400 km*), Usumacinta (688 miles *1107 km*).
Head of State: Gen Kjell Eugenio Laugerud García (b. 24 Jan. 1930), President.
Climate: Tropical (hot and humid) on coastal lowlands, with average temperature of 83 °F. More temperate in central highlands, with average of 68 °F. Mountains cool. In Guatemala City, average maximum

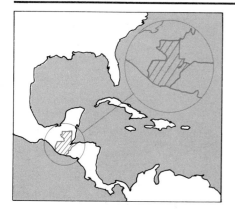

72 °F (December) to 84 °F (May), minimum 53 °F (January) to 61 °F (June), June rainiest (23 days). Absolute maximum temperature 45 °C (113 °F), Guatemala City, 17 Dec. 1957; absolute minimum −7,1 °C (19·2 °F), Quezaltenango, 15 Jan. 1956.
Labour force: 1 545 658 (excluding institutional households) at 1973 census: Agriculture, forestry and fishing 58·4%; Manufacturing 14·0%; Services 12·8%.
Gross domestic product: 2 288·4 million quetzales (at 1958 prices) in 1974: Agriculture, forestry and fishing 27·6%; Manufacturing 15·8%; Trade 28·2%.
Exports: $328·1 million in 1972: Coffee 32·7%; Other food 23·4%; Raw cotton 12·2%.
Monetary unit: Quetzal. 1 quetzal = 100 centavos.
Denominations:
Coins 1, 5, 10, 25 centavos.
Notes 50 centavos, 1, 5, 10, 20, 50, 100 quetzales.
Exchange rate to US dollar: 1.00 (July 1977).
Political history and government: A republic comprising 22 departments. Under the constitution, promulgated on 15 Sept. 1965 and effective from 1 July 1966, legislative power is vested in the unicameral National Congress, with 61 members elected for 4 years by universal adult suffrage. Executive power is held by the President, also directly elected for 4 years. He is assisted by a Vice-President and an appointed Cabinet.
Telephones: 52 905 (1973).
Daily newspapers: 11 (1973).
Total circulation: 168 000 (8 dailies).
Radio: 262 000 (1975).
TV: 110 000 (1975).
Length of roadways: 8358 miles *13 449 km.*
Length of railways: 595 miles *957 km.*
Universities: 4.
Adult illiteracy: 62·0% (males 55·7%; females 68·4%) in 1964.
Expectation of life: Males 48·29 years; females 49·74 years (1963–65).
Defence: Total armed forces 10 870.
Cinemas: 106 (seating capacity 75 200) and one drive-in for 544 cars (1972).

GUINEA

Official name: République de Guinée.
Population: 3 702 000 (estimate for 1 July 1967); 4 527 000 (UN estimate for mid-1976).
Area: 94 926 miles² *245 857 km².*
Languages: French (official), Fulani (Poular), Susu, Malinké.
Religions: Muslim, Animist minority.
Capital city: Conakry, population 525 671 (1972).
Other principal towns (1960): Kankan

29 100; Kindia 25 000; Siguiri 12 700; Labé 12 500; N'Zérékoré 8600.
Highest point: Mt Nimba, 5748 ft *1752 m.*
Principal mountain ranges: Fouta Djallon.
Principal rivers: Niger (2600 miles *4184 km*), Bafing, Konkouré, Kogon.
Head of State: Ahmed Sekou Touré (b. 9 Jan. 1922), President.
Prime Minister: Dr. Louis Lansana Beavogui (b. 1923).
Climate: Hot and moist, with heavy rainfall in coastal areas. Cooler in higher interior. In Conakry, average maximum 82 °F to 90 °F, minimum around 74 °F, annual rainfall 169 in.
Labour force: 1 870 000 (1970): Agriculture, forestry and fishing 84·7% (ILO estimates).
Gross domestic product: $320 million in 1970 (UN estimate).

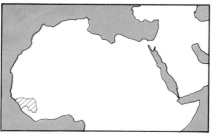

Exports: 1235 million sylis (estimate) in 1971: Pineapples 10·0%; Alumina 72·0%.
Monetary unit: Syli. 1 syli = 100 cauris (corilles).
Denominations:
Coins 50 cauris, 1, 2, 5 sylis.
Notes 10, 25, 50, 100 sylis.
Exchange rate to US dollar: 20.65 (July 1976).
Political history and government: Formerly French Guinea, part of French West Africa. Became independent, outside the French Community, on 2 Oct. 1958. A provisional constitution was adopted on 12 Nov. 1958. Legislative power is vested in the unicameral National Assembly, with 150 members elected by universal adult suffrage for 7 years. The Assembly elects a Commission to be its permanent organ. Full executive authority is vested in the President, also directly elected for 7 years. He appoints and leads a Cabinet, including a Prime Minister. Guinea has a single political party which exercises 'sovereign and exclusive control of all sections of national life'. The party's directing organ is the Central Committee, 25 members elected for 5 years at Congress.
Telephones: 10 000 (1974).
Daily newspapers: 1 (1973).
Total circulation: 5000.
Radio: 110 000 (1975).
Length of roadways: All-weather roads 2175 miles *3500 km*, dry season 4350 miles *7000 km.*
Length of railways: 510 miles *820 km.*
Adult illiteracy: 90 to 95% (estimate).
Expectation of life: Males 39·4 years; females 42·0 years (UN estimates for 1970–75).
Cinemas: 16 (1959).

GUINEA-BISSAU

Official name: A República de Guiné-Bissau.
Population: 487 448 (census of 15 Dec. 1970); 534 000 (UN estimate for mid-1976).
Area: 13 948 miles² *36 125 km².*
Languages: Portuguese (official), Creole, Balante, Fulani, Malinké.

Religions: Animist; Muslim minority.
Capital city: Bissau, population 71 169 (1970 census).
Other principal town: Bolama.
Principal rivers: Cacheu, Mansôa, Gêba, Corubel.
Head of State: Luiz de Almeida Cabral (b. 1929), President of the State Council.
Head of Government: Commdt Francisco Mendes, Chief State Commissioner.
Climate: Tropical, with an average annual temperature of 77 °F. Rainy season June to November. In dry season (December to May) the northerly *harmattan*, a dust-laden wind, blows from the Sahara.
Labour force: 157 000 (1970): Agriculture, forestry and fishing 87·3% (ILO estimates).
Gross domestic product: $127 million in 1970 (UN estimate).
Exports: 157·4 million Guinea pesos in 1975.
Monetary unit: Guinea peso. 1 peso = 100 centavos.
Denominations:
Coins 10, 20, 50 centavos, 1 2½, 5, 10, 20 pesos.
Notes 50, 100, 500 pesos.
Exchange rate to US dollar: 38.48 (July 1977).
Telephones: 2764 (1972).
Daily newspapers: 1 (1972).
Total circulation: 500.

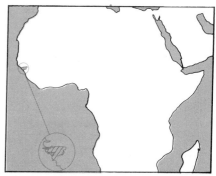

Political history and government: Formerly Portuguese Guinea. Independence declared on 24 Sept. 1973, recognized by Portugal on 10 Sept. 1974. The independence movement was dominated by the *Partido Africano da Independência da Guiné e Cabo Verde* (PAIGC), the African Party for the Independence of Guinea and Cape Verde. In 1973 the PAIGC established a National People's Assembly as the supreme organ of the state and formulated the independence constitution, which provides for the eventual union of Guinea-Bissau with Cape Verde (*qv*). In elections held between 19 Dec. 1976 and January 1977 voters chose regional councils from which a new National Assembly of 150 members was subsequently selected. The Assembly, to hold office for up to three years, was convened on 13 Mar. 1977. The Head of State is elected by the Assembly. The constitution proclaims the PAIGC, the only permitted party, to be 'the supreme expression of the sovereign will of the people'. Executive power is held by the State Council, with 15 members elected for 3 years from deputies to the Assembly. Administrative authority is exercised by the Council of State Commissioners, appointed by the Head of State.
Telephones: 3000 (1973).
Daily newspapers: 1 (1973).
Total circulation: 6000.
Radio: 10 000 (1975).
Length of roadways: 2168 miles *3489 km.*
Expectation of life: Males 37·0 years; females 40·1 years (UN estimates for 1970–75).
Cinemas: 7 (seating capacity 3000) in 1972.

GUYANA

Official name: The Co-operative Republic of Guyana.
Population: 701 885 (census of 7 Apr. 1970); 783 000 (estimate for 1 July 1976).
Area: 83 000 miles² *214 969 km²*.
Languages: English (official), Hindi, Urdu.
Religions: Christian 56·7%; Hindu 33·4%; Muslim 8·8% (1960).
Capital city: Georgetown, population 63 184 (1970 census).
Other principal cities: Linden 29 000; New Amsterdam 23 000; Mackenzie 20 000; Corriverton 17 000.
Highest point: Mt Roraima (9094 ft *2772 m*), on the Brazil-Venezuela frontier.
Principal mountain ranges: Pakaraima, Serra Acarai, Kanuku, Kamoa.
Principal rivers: Essequibo, Courantyne (on the frontier with Surinam), Mazaruni, Berbice, Demerara.
Head of State: (Raymond) Arthur Chung (b. 10 Jan. 1918), President.
Prime Minister: (Linden) Forbes Sampson Burnham (born 20 Feb. 1923).
Climate: Generally warm and pleasant. Average temperature 80 °F, with daily range of about 18 °F on coast, increasing inland. Average annual rainfall 93 in, 80 to 100 in on coast (mainly April to August and November to January), 60 in inland (May to August).
Labour force: 174 772 (including unemployed) in March 1965: Agriculture, forestry and fishing 33·5%; Manufacturing 17·1%; Commerce 13·3%; Services 19·2%; 204 000 (1970): Agriculture, forestry and fishing 27·9% (ILO estimates).
Gross domestic product: $G 643·4 million in 1973: Agriculture, forestry and fishing 18·5% (agriculture 16·3%); Mining and quarrying 14·0%; Manufacturing (excluding engineering) 10·8%; Trade 11·2%; Community, social and personal services 24·8% (public administration and defence 21·0%).
Exports: US$264·2 million (excluding re-exports) in 1974: Sugar and honey 49·5% (raw sugar 48·4%); Other food 10·2%; Bauxite and aluminium concentrates 34·1%.
Monetary unit: Guyana dollar ($G). 1 dollar = 100 cents.
Denominations:
    Coins 1, 5, 10, 25, 50 cents.
    Notes 1, 5, 10, 20 dollars.
Exchange rate to US dollar: 2.55 (July 1977).
Political history and government: Formerly the colony of British Guiana. Became independent, within the Commonwealth, on 26 May 1966, taking the name Guyana. A republic since 23 Feb. 1970. Legislative power is held by the unicameral National Assembly, with 53 members elected for 5 years by universal adult suffrage, using proportional representation. The President, a constitutional Head of State, is elected by the Assembly for 6 years. Executive power is held by the Cabinet, led by the Prime Minister, which is responsible to the Assem-

bly. Guyana comprises 6 administrative districts, each the responsibility of a Minister of State.
Telephones: 19 115 (1974).
Daily newspapers: 3 (1973).
    Total circulation: 67 000.
Radio: 280 000 (1975).
Length of roadways: 1832 miles *2948 km*.
Length of railways: 55 miles *89 km* (government owned), 50 miles *80 km* (privately owned).
Universities: 1.
Expectation of life: Males 59·03 years; females 63·01 years (1959–61), excluding Amerindians.
Defence: Total armed forces 2000.
Cinemas: 50 (seating capacity 37 500) and one drive-in for 385 cars (1974).

HAITI

Official name: République d'Haïti.
Population: 4 329 991 (census of 31 Aug. 1971); 4 668 000 (estimate for 30 Aug. 1976).
Area: 10 714 miles² *27 750 km²*.
Languages: French (official), Créole 90%.
Religions: Roman Catholic, Vodum (Voodoo).
Capital city: Port-au-Prince, population 458 675 (9 Oct. 1971).
Other principal towns: Cap Haïtien 44 000; Gonaïves 29 000; Les Cayes 23 000; Jérémie 17 000.
Highest point: Pic La Selle, 8793 ft *2680 m*.
Principal mountain range: Massif de la Hotte.
Principal river: Artibonite (147 miles *237 km*).
Head of State: Jean-Claude Duvalier (b. 3 July 1951), President.
Climate: Tropical, but cooled by sea winds. Rainy season May to September. North warmer than south. In Port-au-Prince average maximum 87 °F (December, January) to 94 °F (July), minimum 68 °F (January, February) to 74 °F (July), May rainiest (13 days).
Labour force: 2 326 201 (1971 census): Agriculture, forestry and fishing 73·8%; Trade, restaurants and hotels 10·0%.
Gross domestic product: 1 958·4 million gourdes (at 1955 prices) in 1973/74: Agriculture, forestry and fishing 43·6% (agriculture, excluding livestock, 38·6%); Manufacturing 11·0%; Trade 10·0%; Community social and personal services (including restaurants and hotels) 16·0%.
Exports: $71·3 million (excluding re-exports) in 1973/74: Coffee 33·6%; Other food 11·0%.
Monetary unit: Gourde. 1 gourde = 100 centimes.
Denominations:
    Coins 5, 10, 20, 50 centimes.
    Notes 1, 2, 5, 10, 50, 100, 250, 500 gourdes.

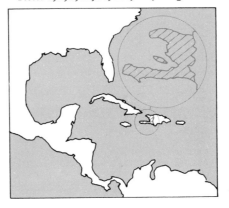

Exchange rate to US dollar: 5.00 (July 1977).
Political history and government: A republic comprising 9 departments. Dr François Duvalier was elected President on 22 Sept. 1957 and took office on 22 Oct. 1957. Under the constitution of June 1964, the unicameral Legislative Chamber has 58 members elected for 6 years by universal adult suffrage. The constitution granted absolute power to the President, who took office for life on 22 June 1964. On 14 Jan. 1971 the constitution was amended to allow the President to nominate his own successor. The President named his son, Jean-Claude, to succeed him as President for life. Dr Duvalier died on 21 Apr. 1971 and his son was sworn in on the following day. Only one political party is officially recognised.
Telephones: 8852 (1973).
Daily newspapers: 7 (1973).
    Total circulation: 82 000.
Radio: 93 000 (1975).
TV: 13 200 (1975).
Length of roadways: 1962 miles *3157 km*.
Universities: 1.
Adult illiteracy 89·5% (males 87·2%; females 91·5%) in 1950.
Expectation of life: Males 49·0 years; females 51·0 years (UN estimates for 1970–75).
Defence: Total armed forces 6550.
Cinemas: 19 and 4 drive-ins in Port-au-Prince (1974).

HONDURAS

Official name: República de Honduras ('depths').
Population: 2 656 948 (census of 6 Mar. 1974); 2 831 000 (estimate for 30 June 1976).
Area: 43 277 miles² *112 088 km²*.
Languages: Spanish, some Indian dialects.
Religion: Roman Catholic.
Capital city: Tegucigalpa, population 303 879 (1974).
Other principal towns: San Pedro Sula 102 129; La Ceiba 37 947; Puerto Cortés 27 757; Tela 12 395.
Highest point: Cerro Las Minas, 9400 ft *2865 m*.
Principal rivers: Patuca, Ulúa.

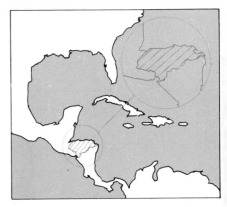

Head of State: Colonel Juan Alberto Melgar Castro (b. 1929), President.
Climate: Tropical (hot and humid) and wet on coastal plains. Rainy season, May to November. More moderate in central highlands. In Tegucigalpa, average maximum 77 °F (December, January) to 86 °F (June), September and October rainiest (each 14 days). Absolute maximum temperature 43,3 °C (*110 °F*), Nueva Octepeque, 13 March 1958; absolute minimum −0,6 °C (*31 °F*), La Esperanza, 17 Feb. 1956.
Labour force: 746 861 (1974 census):

Agriculture, forestry and fishing 60·4%; Manufacturing 11·6%; Community, social and personal services 12·5%.

Gross domestic product: 1 936·6 million lempiras in 1974: Agriculture, forestry and fishing 32·3% (agriculture 28·3%); Manufacturing 15·0%; Trade 11·9%; Community, social and personal services (including restaurants and hotels) 12·3%.

Exports: $193·1 million (excluding re-exports) in 1972: Fruit and vegetables 46·4% (fresh bananas and plantains 43·3%); Coffee 13·9%; Other food 12·1%; Wood, lumber and cork 14·0% (coniferous lumber 13·6%).

Monetary unit: Lempira. 1 lempira = 100 centavos.

Denominations:
Coins 1, 2, 5, 10, 20, 50 centavos, 1 lempira.
Notes 1, 5, 10, 20, 50, 100 lempiras.

Exchange rate to US dollar: 2.00 (July 1977).

Political history and government: A republic comprising 18 departments. The last elected President was deposed on 4 Dec. 1972 by a military *coup*, led by a former President, Brig.-Gen. Oswaldo López Arellano. The military regime suspended the legislature, a unicameral Congress of Deputies, and introduced government by decree. On 22 Apr. 1975 Gen. López was overthrown by army officers and replaced by Col. Juan Melgar Castro. The President rules with the assistance of an appointed Cabinet.

Telephones: 14 984 (1974).

Daily newspapers: 8 (1973).
Total circulation: 116 000 (6 dailies).

Radio: 160 000 (1975).

TV: 47 000 (1975).

Length of roadways: *c.* 3542 miles, *c. 5700 km.*

Length of railways: 658 miles *1059 km.*

Universities: 1.

Adult illiteracy: 55·0% (males 51·3%; females 58·5%) in 1961.

Expectation of life: Males 52·1 years; females 55·0 years (UN estimates for 1970–75).

Defence: Military service: voluntary; total armed forces 14 200.

Cinemas: About 46 with seating capacity of about 40 000 (1972).

HUNGARY

Official name: Magyar Népköztársaság (Hungarian People's Republic).

Population: 10 322 099 (census of 1 Jan. 1970); 10 560 000 (estimate for 1 July 1976).

Area: 35 920 miles², *93 032 km².*

Language: Magyar.

Religions: Roman Catholic; Protestant, Orthodox and Jewish minorities.

Capital city: Budapest, population 2 070 966 (1 Jan. 1976).

Other principal towns (1976): Miskolc 199 901; Debrecen 187 103; Szeged 170 355; Pécs 163 100; Győr 118 858; Székesfehérvár 95 683; Kecskemét 91 700; Nyírgyháza 91 362.

Highest point: Kékes 3330 ft *1015 m.*

Principal mountain ranges: Cserhát, Mátra, Bukk, Bakony.

Principal rivers: Duna (Danube) (1770 miles *2848 km*, 273 miles *439 km* in Hungary), with its tributaries (Drava, Tisza, Rába).

Head of State: Pál Losonczi (b. 18 Sept. 1919), President of the Presidential Council.

Political Leader: János Kádár (b. 22 May 1912), First Secretary of the Central Committee of the Hungarian Socialist Workers' Party.

Head of Government: György Lázár (b. 15 Sept. 1924), Chairman of the Council of Ministers.

Climate: Continental (long, dry, hot summers, cold winters). In Budapest, July warmest (61 °F to 82 °F), January coldest (26 °F to 35 °F), May and December rainiest (each nine days). Absolute maximum temperature 41,3 °C (*106·3 °F*), Pécs, 5 July 1950; absolute minimum −34,9 °C (*−30·8 °F*), Alsófügöd, 16 Feb. 1940.

Labour force: 5 085 500 (excluding persons seeking work for the first time) aged 14 and over (January 1975): Agriculture, forestry and fishing 22·7%; Industry (mining, quarrying, manufacturing, electricity, gas and water) 35·7%; Community, social and personal services (including activities not adequately defined) 16·7%.

Net material product: 369 900 million forints (in domestic prices) in 1974: Agriculture, forestry and fishing 18·6% (agriculture and fishing 17·9%); Industry 46·1%; Construction 13·5%; Trade, restaurants, etc. 15·0%.

Exports: $6093·0 million in 1975: Food and live animals 19·1%; Machinery and transport equipment 37·0% (non-electric machinery 14·9%; transport equipment 12·6%).

Monetary unit: Forint. 1 forint = 100 fillér.

Denominations:
Coins 2, 5, 10, 20, 50 fillér, 1, 2, 5, 10 forints.
Notes 10, 20, 50, 100 forints.

Exchange rate to US dollar: 20.60 (July 1977).

Political history and government: After occupation by Nazi Germany, a Hungarian provisional government signed an armistice on 20 Jan. 1945. Following elections in October 1945, a republic was proclaimed on 1 Feb. 1946. The Communist Party took power in May–June 1947. A new constitution was introduced on 18 Aug. 1949 and a People's Republic established two days later.

The highest organ of state power is the unicameral National Assembly, with 352 members elected for 5 years by universal adult suffrage (at the last election, on 15 June 1975, 318 members were elected unopposed while 34 seats were each contested by two candidates). The Assembly elects from its members a Presidential Council (21 members) to be its permanent organ and the state's executive authority, responsible to the Assembly. The Council of Ministers, the highest organ of state administration, is elected by the Assembly on the recommendation of the Presidential Council.

Political power is held by the (Communist) Hungarian Socialist Workers' Party (HSWP), the only legal party, which dominates the Patriotic People's Front. The Front presents an approved list of candidates for elections to representative bodies. The HSWP's highest authority is the Party Congress, which elects a Central Committee to supervise Party work (the 11th Congress, held on 17–22 Mar. 1975, elected a Central Committee of 125). The Central Committee elects a Political Committee (Politburo) of 15 members to direct policy.

Hungary comprises 19 counties and the capital city.

Telephones: 1 013 731 (1974).

Daily newspapers: 29 (1975).
Total circulation: 2 681 000.

Radio: 2 558 441 (1976).

TV: 2 480 000 (1976).

Length of roadways: 61 992 miles *99 767 km* (31 Dec. 1975).

Length of railways: 5227 miles *8413 km.*

Universities: 4 (also 14 specialised).

Adult illiteracy: 2·0% (males 1·6%; females 2·4%) in 1970.

Expectation of life: Males 66·87 years; females 72·59 years (1972).

Defence: Military service: 2 years; total regular forces 100 000 (60 000 conscripts); defence expenditure, 1976: $551 million (converted at $1 = 22.3 forints).

Cinemas: 3613 (seating capacity 571 300) in 1973.

ICELAND

Official name: Lýdveldid Island (Republic of Iceland).

Population: 204 930 (census of 1 Dec. 1970); 219 033 (estimate for 1 Dec. 1975).

Area: 39 769 miles² *103 000 km².*

Languages: Icelandic.

Religion: Lutheran.

Capital city Reykjavík ('Bay of Smokes'), population 84 856 (1 Dec. 1975).

Other principal towns (1975): Kópavogur 12 570; Akureyri 11 970; Hafnarfjörður 11 599; Keflavík 6179; Akranes 4629; Vestmannaeyjar 4421.

Highest point: Hvannadalshnúkur, 6952 ft *2119 m.*

Principal rivers: Thjórsá (120 miles *193 km*), Skjálfandafljót, Jökulsa á Fjöllum.

Head of State: Dr Kristján Eldjárn (b. 6 Dec. 1916), President.

Prime Minister: Geir Hallgrímsson (b. 16 Dec. 1925).

Climate: Cold. Long winters with average temperature of 34 °F. Short, cool summers with average of 50 °F. Storms are frequent. In Reykjavík, average maximum 36 °F (January) to 58 °F (July), minimum 28 °F (January, February) to 48 °F (July), December rainiest (21 days). Absolute maximum temperature 32,8 °C (*91·0 °F*), Mödrudalur, 26 July 1901; absolute minimum −44,6 °C (*−48·2 °F*), Grímsstaoir, 22 Mar. 1918.

Labour force: 95 600 (excluding unemployed) in 1974: Agriculture, forestry and fishing 18·2%; Mining and manufacturing 24·1%; Construction 11·7%; Trade, restaurants and hotels 12·0%; Community, social and personal services 21·99%.

Gross domestic product: 191 563 million krónur in 1975.

Exports: $307·5 million in 1975: Fish and fish preparations (including crustaceans and molluscs) 66·4% (fresh, chilled or frozen fish 38·0%; salted, dried or smoked fish 24·4%); Other food 10·9%; Aluminium and aluminium alloys 10·6%.

Monetary unit: Icelandic króna. 1 króna = 100 aurar.

Denominations:
Coins 1, 5, 10, 50 krónur.
Notes 100, 500, 1000, 5000 krónur.

Exchange rate to US dollar: 194.95 (July 1977).

Political history and government: Formerly ruled by Denmark. Iceland became a sovereign state, under the Danish Crown, on 1 Dec. 1918. An independent republic was declared on 17 June 1944. Legislative power is held jointly by the President (elected for 4 years by universal adult suffrage) and the Althing (Parliament), with 60 members elected by universal suffrage for 4 years (subject to dissolution by the President), using a mixed system of proportional representation. The Althing chooses 20 of its members to form the Upper House, the other 40 forming the Lower House. For some purposes the two Houses sit jointly as the United Althing. Executive power is held jointly by the President and the Cabinet he appoints. The Cabinet, led by the Prime Minister, is responsible to the Althing. Iceland has seven administrative districts.
Telephones: 87 000 (1974).
Daily newspapers: 5 (1971).
Total circulation: 96 000.
Radio: 62 785 (1976).
TV: 52 535 (1976).
Length of roadways: 7166 miles *11 533 km* (31 Dec. 1975).
Universities: 1.
Expectation of life: Males 70·7 years; females 76·3 years (1966–70).
Cinemas: 25 (seating capacity 9500) in 1970.

INDIA

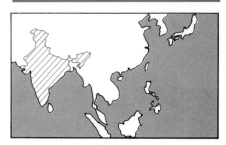

Official name: Bhartiya Ganrajya or Bharat ka Ganatantra (the Republic of India). India is called Bharat in the Hindi language.
Population: 548 159 652 (census of 1 Apr. 1971, excluding 1·67% underenumeration); 610 077 000 (estimate for 1 July 1976).
Area: 1 269 346 miles² *3 287 590 km².*
Languages: Hindi (official) 30·4%; Telugu 8·6%; Bengali 7·7%; Marathi 7·6%; Tamil 7·0%; Urdu 5·3%; Gujarati 4·6%; Kannada 4·0%; Malayalam 3·9%; Orija 3·1%; Punjabi 2·5%; Assamese 1·6% (1961).
Religions: Hindu 82·7%; Muslim 11·2%; Christian 2·6%; Sikh 1·9%; Buddhist 0·7%; Jain 0·5%; others 0·4% (1971).
Capital city: New Delhi, population 301 801 (1971 census).
Other principal towns (1971): Bombay 5 970 575; Delhi 3 287 883; Calcutta 3 148 746; Madras 2 469 449; Hyderabad 1 607 396; Ahmedabad 1 585 544; Bangalore 1 540 741; Kanpur (Cawnpore) 1 154 388; Nagpur 866 076; Pune (Poona) 856 105; Lucknow 749 239; Howrah 737 877; Jaipur 615 258; Agra 591 917; Varanasi (Banaras) 583 856; Madurai 549 114; Indore 543 381; Allahabad 490 622; Patna 473 001; Surat 471 656; Vadodara (Baroda) 466 696; Cochin 439 066; Jabalpur 426 224.
Highest point: Nanda Devi, 25 645 ft *7817 m* (first climbed 29 Aug. 1936), excluding Kashmir.
Principal mountain ranges: Himalaya, Gravalti, Sappura, Vindhya, Western Ghats, Chota Nagpur.

Principal rivers: Ganga (Ganges) (1560 miles *2510 km*) and tributaries, Brahmaputra (1800 miles *2897 km*), Sutlej, Narmeda, Tapti, Godavari, Krishna, Cauvery.
Head of State: Neelam Sanjiva Reddy (b. 19 May 1913), President.
Prime Minister: Morarji Ranchhodji Desai (b. 29 Feb. 1896).
Climate: Ranges from temperate in the north (very cold in the Himalayas) to tropical in the south. The average summer temperature in the plains is about 85 °F. The full weight of the monsoon season is felt in June and July but the rainfall figures vary widely according to locality. Average daily high temperature in Bombay 83 °F (January, February) to 91 °F (May); average daily low temperature 67 °F (January, February) 80 °F (May); rainiest month July (21 days). Average daily high temperature in Calcutta 79 °F (December) to 97 °F (April); average daily low 55 °F (December, January) to 79 °F (June, July); rainiest months July, August (each 18 days).
Labour force: 180 373 399 (excluding unemployed) at 1971 census: Agriculture, forestry and fishing 72·5%. Figures exclude Sikkim (labour force 111 607 in 1971).
Gross domestic product: 637 300 million rupees at factor cost (provisional) in 1974/75: Agriculture, forestry and fishing 49·2% (agriculture 47·2%); Manufacturing 15·0%; Trade, restaurants and hotels 11·3% (trade 10·5%). Revised total is 619 000 million rupees.
Exports: $3906·1 million in 1974: Food and live animals 27·3%; Textiles yarn, fabrics, etc. 21·1%.
Monetary unit: Indian rupee. 1 rupee = 100 paisa (singular: paise).
Denominations:
Coins 1, 2, 3, 5, 10, 20, 25, 50 paisa, 1, 10 rupees.
Notes 1, 2, 5, 10, 20, 100, 1000, 5000, 10 000 rupees.
Exchange rate to US dollar: 8.8144 (July 1977).
Political history and government: On 15 Aug. 1947 former British India was divided on broadly religious lines into two independent countries, India and Pakistan, within the Commonwealth.

India was formed as a Union of States, with a federal structure. A republican constitution was passed by the Constituent Assembly on 26 Nov. 1949 and India became a republic, under its present name, on 26 Jan. 1950. The Portuguese territories of Goa, Daman and Diu were invaded by Indian forces on 19 Dec. 1961 and incorporated in India. Sikkim, formerly an Associated State, became a State of India on 26 Apr. 1975.

Legislative power is vested in a Parliament, consisting of the President and two Houses. The Council of States (*Rajya Sabha*) has 243 members, including 231 indirectly elected by the State Assemblies for 6 years (one-third retiring every two years) and 12 nominated by the President for 6 years. The House of the People (*Lok Sabha*) has 542 members elected by universal adult suffrage for 5 years (subject to dissolution). The President is a constitutional Head of State elected for 5 years by an electoral college comprising elected members of both Houses of Parliament and the State legislatures. He exercises executive power on the advice of the Council of Ministers, which is responsible to Parliament. The President appoints the Prime Minister and, on the latter's recommendation, other Ministers.

India comprises 22 self-governing States (including the disputed territory of Jammu-Kashmir) and 9 Union Territories. Each State has a Governor (appointed by the President for 5 years), a legislature elected for 5 years and a Council of Ministers. The

Union Territories are administered by officials appointed by the President.
Telephones: 1 689 528 (1974).
Daily newspapers: 793 (1972).
Total circulation: 8 873 000
Radio: 14 908 097 (1975).
TV: 314 155 (1975).
Length of roadways: 765 716 miles *1 232 300 km* (31 Dec. 1974).
Length of railways: 37 411 miles *60 208 km.*
Universities: 92.
Adult illiteracy: 72·2% (males 58·6%; females 86·8%) in 1961.
Expectation of life: Males 50·1 years; females 48·8 years (UN estimates for 1970–75).
Defence: Military service: voluntary; total armed forces 1 055 500; defence expenditure, 1976/77: $2812 million.
Cinemas: 4787 (seating capacity 3 430 000), excluding touring cinemas (about 2500), in 1972.

INDONESIA

Official name: Republik Indonesia.
Population: 119 291 290 (census of 24 Sept. 1971; 130 597 000 (estimate for 1 July 1975).
Area: 735 272 miles² *1 904 345 km².*
Languages: Bahasa Indonesia (official), Javanese, Madurese, Sundanese.
Religions: Muslim 85%; Christian, Buddhist and Hindu minorities.
Capital city: Jakarta, population 4 915 300 (1973 est.).
Other principal towns: Surabaja 1 556 255; Bandung 1 201 730; Semarang 646 590; Medan 635 562; Palembang 582 961; Makasar 434 766; Malang 422 428; Surakarta 414 285 (1971).
Highest point: Ngga Pulu (formerly Mt Sukarno, formerly Carstensz Pyramide), 16 500 ft *5030 m* (first climbed on 13 Feb. 1962).
Principal mountain ranges: Bukit, Barisan, Pegunungan Djajawidjaja.
Principal rivers: Kapuas (715 miles *1150 km*), Digul (557 miles *896 km*), Barito (560 miles *900 km*), Mahakam, Kajan, Hari.
Head of State: Gen. Suharto (b. 8 June 1921), President and Prime Minister
Climate: Tropical (hot and rainy). Average temperature 80 °F. Mountain areas cooler. In Jakarta, average maximum 84 °F (January, February) to 88 °F (September); minimum 73 °F (July, August) to 75 °F (April, May), January rainiest (18 days).
Labour force: 40 100 070 (including unemployed) aged 10 and over (1971 census, excluding West Irian): Agriculture, forestry and fishing 65·7%; Trade, restaurants and hotels 10·9%; Community, social and personal services 10·5%.
Gross domestic product: 12 190 000 million rupiahs in 1975: Agriculture, forestry and fishing 33·2%; Mining and quarrying 20·4%.

Exports: $7426·3 million in 1974: Petroleum and petroleum products 70·2% (crude petroleum 63·0%).
Monetary unit: Rupiah. 1 rupiah = 100 sen.
Denominations:
Coins 1, 2, 5, 10, 25, 50, 100 rupiahs.
Notes 2½, 5, 10, 25, 50, 100, 500, 1000, 5000, 10 000 rupiahs.
Exchange rate to US dollar: 415.0 (July 1977).
Political history and government: Formerly the Netherlands East Indies. Occupied by Japanese forces in March 1942. On 17 Aug. 1945, three days after the Japanese surrender, a group of nationalists proclaimed the independence of the Republic of Indonesia. The Netherlands transferred sovereignty (except for West New Guinea) on 27 Dec. 1949. West New Guinea remained under Dutch control until 1 Oct. 1962, when a UN Temporary Executive Authority controlled the territory until it was transferred to Indonesia on 1 May 1963.
Military commanders, led by Gen. Suharto, assumed emergency executive powers on 11–12 Mar. 1966. The President handed all power to Suharto on 22 Feb. 1967. On 12 Mar. 1967 the People's Consultative Assembly removed the President from office and named Gen. Suharto as acting President. He became Prime Minister on 11 Oct. 1967 and, after being elected by the Assembly, was inaugurated as President on 27 Mar. 1968.
The highest authority of the state is the People's Consultative Assembly, with 920 members who serve for 5 years. The Assembly, which elects the President and Vice-President for 5 years, includes 460 members of the People's Representation Council (House of Representatives), which is the legislative organ. The Council has 100 appointed members, 351 directly elected and 9 representatives from West Irian (West New Guinea) chosen in indirect elections. The remaining 460 members of the Assembly include 207 appointed by the government, 130 elected by regional assemblies, 121 allocated to parties and groups in proportion to their elected seats in the Council and 2 allocated to minor parties. The President is assisted by an appointed Cabinet.
Indonesia comprises 27 provinces, including East (formerly Portuguese) Timor, unilaterally annexed on 17 July 1976.
Telephones: 284 831 (1974).
Daily newspapers: 154 (1973).
Total circulation: 1 110 000 (20 dailies).
Radio: 5 010 000 (1975).
TV: 300 000 (1975).
Length of roadways: 52 749 miles *84 891 km* (31 Dec. 1972).
Length of railways: 4847 miles *7801 km.*
Universities: 51 (28 state, 23 private).
Adult illiteracy: 40·4% (males 29·2%; females 51·0%) in 1971 (population aged 10 and over).
Expectation of life: Males 46·4 years; females 48·7 years (UN estimates for 1970–75).
Defence: Military service: selective; total armed forces 246 000; defence expenditure, 1975/76: $1108 million.
Cinemas: 1011 with seating capacity of 470 000 (1962).

IRAN

Official name: Keshvarē Shahanshahiyē Irān (Empire of Iran).
Population: 33 591 875 (census of November 1976).
Area: 636 296 miles² *1 648 000 km².*
Languages: Farsi (Persian), Kurdish.

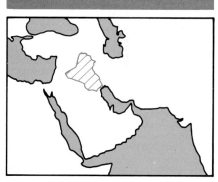

Religions: Muslim 98%; Christian, Jewish, Zoroastrian minorities.
Capital city: Tehrān (Teheran), population 4 496 159 (November 1976).
Other principal towns (1976): Eşfāhan (Isfahan) 671 825; Mashhad (Meshed) 670 180; Tabriz 598 576; Shirāz 414 408; Ahwaz 329 006; Abādān 296 081; Kermanshah 290 861.
Highest point: Qolleh-ye Damāvand (Mt Demavend), 18 386 ft *5604 m.*
Principal mountain ranges: Reshteh-ye Alborz (Elburz Mts), Kūhhā-ye Zāgros (Zagros Mts).
Principal rivers: Kārūn, Safid (Sefid Rud), Atrak, Karkheh, Zāyandeh.
Head of State: HIM Mohammad Rezā Pahlavi Aryamehr (b. 26 Oct. 1919), Shah (Emperor).
Prime Minister: Dr Jamshid Amouzegar (b. 25 June 1923).
Climate: Extremely hot on Persian Gulf, cooler and dry on central plateau, subtropical on shore of Caspian Sea. In Teheran, July hottest (77 °F to 99 °F), January coldest (27 °F to 45 °F), March rainiest (5 days). Absolute maximum temperature 52 °C (*126 °F*), Abādān, 6 July 1951.
Labour force: 6 858 396 (excluding 725 689 unemployed) aged 10 and over (settled population only, November 1966 census): Agriculture, forestry and fishing 47·1%; Manufacturing 18·8%; Services 13·8%; 7 724 000 (including unemployed) in 1972.
Gross domestic product: 2 033 200 million rials (provisional) in 1973/74: Agriculture, forestry and fishing 12·1%; Mining and manufacturing (including gas) 53·8%. Revised total is 1 860 200 million rials.
Exports: $17 792·7 million in 1974/75: Petroleum and petroleum products 96·1% (crude petroleum 88·4%).
Monetary unit: Iranian rial. 1 rial = 100 dinars.
Denominations:
Coins 1, 2, 5, 10, 20 rials.
Notes 10, 20, 50, 100, 200, 500, 1000, 5000, 10 000 rials.
Exchange rate to US dollar: 71.05 (July 1977).
Political history and government: Formerly the Empire of Persia, renamed Iran on 21 Mar. 1935. The country was an absolute monarchy until the adoption of the first constitution, approved by the Shah on 30 Dec. 1906. On 31 Oct. 1925 the National Assembly deposed the Shah and handed power to the Prime Minister, Reza Khan. He was elected Shah on 13 Dec. 1925 and took the title Reza Shah Pahlavi. During the Second World War Reza Shah favoured Nazi Germany. British and Soviet forces entered Iran on 25 Aug. 1941, forcing the Shah to abdicate in favour of his son, Mohammad Reza Pahlavi, on 16 Sept. 1941.
Iran is a limited constitutional monarchy. Executive power rests with the Shah, who appoints the Prime Minister and other Ministers. Legislative power rests with the bicameral Parliament (*Majles*), comprising a Senate of 60 members (30 appointed by the Shah and 30 elected for 4 years) and a National Consultative Assembly of 268

members elected for 4 years. Parliament must approve the Shah's nominee for Prime Minister. On 2 Mar. 1975 the Shah dissolved existing political parties and announced the formation of a single party.
Iran comprises 20 provinces, each administered by an appointed Governor-General.
Telephones: 805 560 (1974).
Daily newspapers: 39 (1972).
Total circulation: 750 000.
Radio: 7 000 000 (1972).
TV: 1 700 000 (1975).
Length of roadways: 26 994 miles *43 442 km* (31 Dec. 1972).
Length of railways: 2859 miles *4601 km.*
Universities: 8.
Adult illiteracy: 77·3% (males 67·2%; females 87·8%) in 1966.
Expectation of life: Males 50·7 years; females 51·3 years (UN estimates for 1970–75).
Defence: Military service: 2 years; total armed forces 300 000; defence expenditure, 1976/77: $9500 million.
Cinemas: 439 (seating capacity 248 000) and 45 part-time (capacity 25 000) in 1973.

IRAQ

Official name: Al Jumhuriya al 'Iraqiya (Republic of Iraq).
Population: 8 047 415 (census of 14 Oct. 1965); 11 505 000 (estimate for 14 Oct. 1976).
Area: 167 925 miles² *434 924 km².*
Languages (1965): Arabic 81·1%; Kurdish 15·5%; Turkoman 1·7%.
Religions: Muslim, Christian minority.
Capital city: Baghdād, population 2 183 760 (1970 est.)
Other principal towns (1965): Basra 310 950; Mosul 264 146; Kirkūk 175 303; Najaf 134 027.
Highest point: 12 000 ft *3658 m.*
Principal mountain ranges: Kurdistan Mts.
Principal rivers: Tigris, Euphrates (1700 miles [*2735 km*]).
Head of State: Field Marshal Ahmad Hassan al-Bakr (b. 1914), President and Prime Minister.
Climate: Extremely hot, dry summers, humid near coast. Cold damp winters with severe frosts in highlands. In Baghdad, average maximum 60 °F (January) to 110 °F (July, August), minimum 39 °F (January) to 76 °F (July, August), December rainiest (5 days). Absolute maximum temperature 52 °C (*125 °F*), Shaiba, 8 Aug. 1937; minimum −14 °C (*6 °F*), Ar Rutbah, 6 Jan. 1942.
Labour force: 2 410 000 (1970): Agriculture, forestry and fishing 46·6% (ILO estimates).
Gross domestic product: 1 483·9 million dinars (provisional) in 1971: Agriculture, forestry and fishing (excluding agricultural services, etc.) 13·5%; Mining and quarrying 37·1%. Revised total is 1465·1 million dinars.

159

Exports: $1528·7 million (excluding re-exports) in 1971: Petroleum and petroleum products 96·2% (crude and partly refined petroleum 95·8%).
Monetary unit: Iraqi dinar. 1 dinar = 5 riyals = 20 dirhams = 1000 fils.
Denominations:
Coins 1, 5, 10, 25, 50, 100, 250, 500 fils, 1, 5 dinars.
Notes ¼, ½, 1, 5, 10 dinars.
Exchange rate to US dollar: 0.296 (July 1977).
Political history and government: Formerly part of Turkey's Ottoman Empire, captured by British forces during the 1914–18 war. After the war Iraq became a Kingdom under a League of Nations mandate, administered by Britain. The mandate was ended on 3 Oct. 1932, when Iraq became independent. In an army-led revolution on 14 July 1958 the King was murdered, the bicameral parliament dissolved and a republic established. Since then Iraq has been ruled by a succession of military regimes. The present regime was established on 17 July 1968. A new constitution, proclaiming socialist principles, was introduced on 16 July 1970.

The constitution provides for the establishment of an elected National Assembly. Until the Assembly is formed the highest authority in the state is the Revolutionary Command Council (RCC), whose President is Head of State and Supreme Commander of the Armed Forces. The RCC, which has 22 members, elects the President and the Vice-President. The President appoints and leads a Council of Ministers to control administration. The only authorized political organization is the National Progressive Front, a partnership between the Arab Socialist Renaissance (Ba'ath) Party and the Iraq Communist Party.

Iraq comprises 16 provinces, each administered by an appointed Governor.
Telephones: 185 500 (1974).
Daily newspapers: 4 (1973).
Total circulation: 226 000.
Radio: 1 250 000 (1973).
TV: 520 000 (1973).
Length of roadways: 7369 miles 11 859 km (31 Dec. 1975).
Length of railways: 1571 miles 2529 km.
Universities: 5.
Adult illiteracy: 75·7% (males 64·4%; females 87·1%) in 1965.
Expectation of life: Males 51·2 years; females 54·3 years (UN estimates for 1970–75).
Defence: Military service: 2 years; total armed forces 158 000; defence expenditure, 1975/76: $1191 million.
Cinemas: 27 (seating capacity 40 500) and one part-time (capacity 400) in 1973.

IRELAND

Official name: Poblacht na h'Éireann (Republic of Ireland), abbreviated to Éire (Ireland).
Population: 2 978 248 (census of 18 Apr. 1971); 3 162 000 (estimate for 1 Apr. 1976).
Area: 27 136·3 miles² 70 282·6 km².
Languages: English, Irish Gaelic.
Religions: Roman Catholic 94·9% (1961). Church of Ireland, Presbyterian, Methodist minorities.
Capital city: Dublin (Baile Átha Cliath), population 566 034 (1971 census).
Other principal towns: Cork (Corcaigh) 128 235; Limerick (Luimneach) 57 137; Dún Laoghaire (formerly Kingstown) 52 996; Waterford (Port Láirge) 31 695; Galway (Gaillimh) 26 896.

Highest point: Carrantuohill, 3414 ft 1041 m, in Co. Kerry.
Principal mountain ranges: Macgillycuddy's Reeks, Wicklow Mts.
Principal rivers: Shannon (224 miles 360 km), Suir (85 miles 136 km), Boyne (70 miles 112 km), Barrow (119 miles 191 km), Erne (72 miles 115 km).
Head of State: Dr Patrick John Hillery (Pádraig Ó hIrighile) (b. 2 May 1923), An Uachtaran (President).
Head of Government: John Mary Lynch (Seán Ó Loinsigh) (b. 15 Aug. 1917), Taoiseach (Prime Minister).
Climate: Mild (generally between 32 °F and 70 °F). In Dublin, average maximum 47 °F (December, January, February) to 67 °F (July, August) minimum 35 °F (January, February) to 51 °F (July, August); December rainiest (14 days). Absolute maximum temperature 92 °F (33 °C), Dublin (Phoenix Park), 16 July 1876; absolute minimum −2 °F (−19 °C), Markee Castle Castle, Co. Sligo, 16 Jan. 1881.
Labour force: 1 030 000 (excluding armed forces and unemployed) aged 14 and over (April 1975): Agriculture, forestry and fishing 24·5%; Industry (mining, quarrying, manufacturing, electricity, gas and water) and construction 29·8% (manufacturing 20·4%); Trade, transport, etc. 22·6% (trade, restaurants and hotels 16·6%); Community, social and personal services 20·3%.
Gross domestic product: I£2653 million in 1973: Agriculture, forestry and fishing 19·4% (agriculture 18·8%); Industry and construction 33·0%; Trade, transport, etc. 17·3%; Government services 11·3%.
Exports: $3 178·5 million in 1975: Meat and meat preparations 16·6% (fresh, chilled or frozen meat 15·6%); Dairy products and eggs 10·6%; Other food 17·4%; Machinery and transport equipment 11·2%.
Monetary unit: Irish pound (I£). 1 pound = 100 pence.
Denominations:
Coins ½, 1, 2, 5, 10, 50 pence.
Notes 10s, 1, 5, 10, 20, 50, 100 pounds.
Exchange rate to US dollar: 0.581 (July 1977).
Political history and government: The whole of Ireland was formerly part of the United Kingdom. During an insurrection against British rule in April 1916 a republic was proclaimed but the movement was suppressed. After an armed struggle, beginning in 1919, a peace agreement was signed on 6 Dec. 1921 and became operative on 15 Jan. 1922. It provided that the six Ulster counties of Northern Ireland should remain part of the UK while the remaining 26 counties should become a dominion under the British Crown. Southern Ireland duly achieved this status as the Irish Free State on 6 Dec. 1922. A new constitution, giving full sovereignty within the Commonwealth, became effective on 29 Dec. 1937. Formal ties with the Commonwealth were ended on 18 Apr. 1949, when the 26 counties became a republic.

Legislative power is vested in the bicameral National Parliament: a Senate of 60 members (11 nominated by the Prime Minister, 49 indirectly elected for 5 years) with restricted powers; and a House of Representatives (Dáil Éireann) with 148 members elected by universal adult suffrage for 5 years (subject to dissolution), using proportional representation. The President is a constitutional Head of State elected by universal adult suffrage for 7 years. Executive power is held by the Cabinet, led by a Prime Minister, appointed by the President on the nomination of the Dáil. The President appoints other Ministers on the nomination of the Prime Minister with the previous approval

of the Dáil. The Cabinet is responsible to the Dáil.
Telephones: 404 725 (March 1975).
Daily newspapers: 7 (1973).
Total circulation: 709 000.
Radio: 865 000 (1975).
TV: 549 558 (1974).
Length of roadways: 55 306 miles 89 006 km (31 Mar. 1973).
Length of railways: 1361 miles 2190 km.
Universities: 2.
Expectation of life: Males 68·58 years; females 72·85 years (1965–67).
Defence: Military service: voluntary; total armed forces 14 000; defence budget, 1976: $134 million.
Cinemas: 183 with seating capacity of 152 000 (1961).

ISRAEL

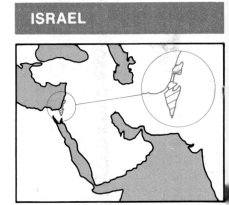

Official name: Medinat Israel (State of Israel).
Population: 3 147 683 (census of 20 May 1972, including East Jerusalem and Isreali residents in other occupied territories); 3 570 900 (estimate for 31 Dec. 1976).
Area: 8019 miles² 20 770 km².
Languages (1961): Hebrew (official) 65·9%; Arabic 15·9%; Yiddish 4·8%.
Religions (1961): Jewish 88·7%; Muslim 7·8%.
Capital city: Yerushalayim (Jerusalem), population 366 000 (January 1976), including East Jerusalem (Jordanian territory under Israeli occupation since 1967).
Other principal towns (1976): Tel Aviv-Yafo (Jaffa) 348 600; Haifa 228 000; Ramat Gan 121 800; Holon 117 600; Petah Tiqva (Petach Tikva) 109 600; Be'er Sheva (Beersheba) 98 900; Benei Beraq (Bnei Brak) 84 600.
Highest point: Mt Atzmon (Har Meron), 3963 ft 1208 m.
Lowest point: The Dead Sea, 1302 ft 397 m below sea level.
Principal mountain ranges: Mts of Judea.
Principal rivers: Jordan (200 miles 321 km), Qishon.
Head of State: Ephraim Katzir (b. 16 May 1916), President.
Prime Minister: Menachem Begin (b. 1 Aug. 1913).
Climate: Mediterranean (hot, dry, summer and mild rainy winters). More extreme in the south. Subtropical on coast. In Jerusalem average maximum 55 °F (January) to 87 °F (July, August), minimum 41 °F (January) to 64 °F (August), February rainiest (11 days). Absolute maximum temperature 54 °C (129 °F), Tirat Zevi, 22 June 1942 absolute minimum −16 °C (2 °F), Tel ha Tanim, 8 Nov. 1950.
Labour force: 1 102 500 (excluding armed forces and unemployed) aged 14 and over (1975): Mining and manufacturing 24·5% Trade, restaurants and hotels 12·4% Community, social and personal service

33·3%. Figures cover also certain occupied territories.

Gross domestic product: I£41 716 million (provisional) in 1973: Mining and manufacturing 22·7% (manufacturing 22·0%); Electricity, gas, water and construction 12·8%; Trade, restaurants and hotels 10·0%; Community, social and personal services 23·7% (government services and private non-profit institutions 20·8%). Revised total is I£38 695 million.

Exports: $1824·9 million in 1974: Fruit and vegetables 12·7%; Chemicals and petroleum products 14·5%; Diamonds (non-industrial) 35·1%.

Monetary unit: Israeli pound (I£). 1 pound = 100 agorot (singular: agora).

Denominations:
Coins 1, 5, 10, 25, 50, 100, 250 prutot, 1, 5, 10, 25 agorot.
Notes 50, 100, 250, 500 prutot, ½ 1, 5, 10, 50, 100 pounds.

Exchange rate to US dollar: 9.579 (July 1977).

Political history and government: Palestine (of which Israel forms part) was formerly part of Turkey's Ottoman Empire. During the First World War (1914–18) Palestine was occupied by British forces. After the war it was administered by Britain as part of a League of Nations mandate, established in 1922. The British Government terminated its Palestine mandate on 14 May 1948, when Jewish leaders proclaimed the State of Israel. After armed conflict with neighbouring Arab states, Israel's borders were fixed by armistice agreements in 1949. During the war of 5–10 June 1967 Israeli forces occupied parts of Egypt, Syria and Jordan, including East Jerusalem (which Israel has unilaterally incorporated into its territory).

Israel is a republic. Supreme authority rests with the unicameral Parliament (*Knesset*), with 120 members elected by universal suffrage for 4 years, using proportional representation. Parliament elects the President, a constitutional Head of State, for 5 years. Executive power rests with the Cabinet, led by the Prime Minister. The Cabinet takes office after receiving a vote of confidence in Parliament, to which it is responsible. Israel comprises 6 administrative districts.

Telephones: 869 042 (Dec. 1976).
Daily newspapers: 27 (1974).
Radio: 680 000 (1972).
TV: 385 000 (1974).
Length of roadways: 2684 miles *4320 km* (31 Dec. 1975).
Length of railways: 503 miles *809 km.*
Universities: 5 (plus 2 specialized).
Adult illiteracy: 15·8% (males 9·5%; females 22·3%) in 1961 (population aged 14 and over).
Expectation of life: Males 70·13 years; females 73·27 years (1974).
Defence: Military service: men 36 months, women 24 months (Jews and Druses only), Muslims and Christians may volunteer; annual training for reservist thereafter up to age 53/54 for men, 34 for women; total armed forces 158 500 (123 000 conscripts); defence expenditure, 1976/77: $4214 million.
Cinemas: 244 (seating capacity 165 000), 7 part-time (capacity 5000) and one drive-in for 960 cars (1972).

ITALY

Official name: Repubblica Italiana (Italian Republic), abbreviated to Italia.
Population: 53 744 737 (*de facto*, census of 24 Oct. 1971); 56 323 000 (*de jure* estimate for 31 Dec. 1976).
Area: 116 317 miles² *301 260 km².*
Language: Italian.
Religion: Roman Catholic.
Capital city: Roma (Rome), population 2 868 248 (estimate for 1 July 1975).
Other principal towns (1975): Milano (Milan) 1 731 281; Napoli (Naples) 1 223 785; Torino (Turin) 1 202 215; Genova (Genoa) 805 855; Palermo 662 567; Bologna 491 330; Firenze (Florence) 465 823; Catania 398 642; Bari 376 467; Venezia (Venice) 365 208; Verona 271 079; Trieste 270 641; Messina 261 332.
Highest point: On Monte Bianco (Mont Blanc), 15 616 ft *4759 m.*
Principal mountain range: Appennini (Appennines), Alps.
Principal rivers: Po (418 miles *672 km*), Tevere (Tiber), Arno, Volturno, Garigliano.
Head of State: Giovanni Leone (b. 3 Nov. 1908), President.
Head of Government: Giulio Andreotti (b. 14 Jan. 1919), President of the Council of Ministers (Prime Minister).
Climate: Generally Mediterranean, with warm, dry summers (average maximum 80 °F), and mild winters. Cooler and rainier in the Po Valley and the Alps. In Rome, average maximum 54 °F (January) to 88 °F (July, August), minimum 39 °F (January, February) to 64 °F (July, August), February rainiest (11 days). Absolute maximum temperature 46 °C (*114 °F*), Foggia, 6 Sept. 1946; absolute minimum −34 °C (−*29 °F*), Pian Rosa, 14 Feb. 1956.
Labour force: 19 603 000 (excluding 776 000 unemployed) in July 1976: Agriculture, forestry and fishing 15·7%; Industry (mining, quarrying, manufacturing, electricity, gas and water) 33·5% (manufacturing 31·7%); Commerce (excluding banking and insurance) 13·8%; Services (including banking and insurance) 22·2%.
Gross domestic product: 97 427 000 million lire (provisional) in 1974: Industry 33·3% (mining and manufacturing 31·5%); Trade, restaurants and hotels (including repairs) 13·8% (trade and repairs 12·1%); Government services 10·7%. Revised total is 99 239 000 million lire.
Exports: $34 825·1 million (including San Marino) in 1975: Machinery and transport equipment 35·0% (non-electric machinery 17·3%; transport equipment 10·6%).
Monetary unit: Italian lira. 1 lira = 100 centesimi.
Denominations:
Coins 1, 2, 5, 10, 20, 50, 100, 500, 1000 lire.
Notes 500, 1000, 2000, 5000, 10 000, 20 000, 50 000, 100 000 lire.
Exchange rate to US dollar: 882.4 (July 1977).
Political history and government: Formerly several independent states. The Kingdom of Italy, under the House of Savoy, was proclaimed in 1861 and the country unified in 1870. Italy was under Fascist rule from 28 Oct. 1922 to 25 July 1943. A referendum on 2 June 1946 voted to abolish the monarchy and Italy became a republic on 10 June 1946. A new constitution took effect on 1 Jan. 1948.

Legislative power is held by the bicameral Parliament, elected by universal adult suffrage for 5 years (subject to dissolution), using proportional representation. The Senate has 315 elected members (seats allocated on a regional basis) and 7 life Senators. The Chamber of Deputies has 630 members. The President of the Republic is a constitutional Head of State elected for 7 years by an electoral college comprising both Houses of Parliament and 58 regional representatives. Executive power is exercised by the Council of Ministers. The Head of State appoints the President of the Council (Prime Minister) and, on the latter's recommendation, other Ministers. The Council is responsible to Parliament.

Italy has 20 administrative regions, each with an elected legislature and a regional executive.
Telephones: 14 495 677 (1975).
Daily newspapers: 78 (1973).
Total circulation: 6 604 000.
Radio: 12 817 445 (1975).
TV: 12 102 654 (1975).
Length of roadways: 180 098 miles *289 840 km* (31 Dec. 1974).
Length of railways: 12 458 miles *20 050 km.*
Universities: 35 (28 state, 7 private).
Adult illiteracy: 9·3% (males 7·3%; females 11·2%) in 1961 (aged 14 and over).
Expectation of life: Males 68·97 years; females 74·88 years (1970–72).
Defence: Military service: Army and Air Force 12 months, Navy 18 months; total armed forces 352 000 (234 100 conscripts); defence expenditure, 1976: $3470 million.
Cinemas: 4474 plus 6302 part-time and one drive-in for 980 cars (1973).

THE IVORY COAST

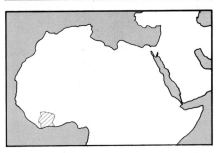

Official name: La République de la Côte d'Ivoire.
Population: 6 670 912 (census of 14 Apr. to 15 May 1975).
Area: 124 504 miles² *322 463 km².*
Languages: French (official), many African languages.
Religions: Animist, Muslim, Christian.
Capital city: Abidjan, population 650 000 (1970 est.)
Other principal towns (1969): Bouaké 100 000; Gagnoa 45 000.
Highest point: Monts de Droupole, *c.* 6900 ft *2103 m.*
Principal rivers: Bandama, Sassandra, Komoé.
Head of State: Félix Houphouët-Boigny (b. 18 Oct. 1905), President.
Climate: Generally hot, wet and humid. Temperatures from 57 °F to 103 °F. Rainy seasons May to July, October to November. In Abidjan, average maximum 82 °F to 90 °F, minimum around 74 °F.
Labour force: 2 648 360 (official estimate for 1970); 2 302 000 (1970): Agriculture, forestry and fishing 84·5% (ILO estimates).
Gross domestic product: 739 000 million CFA francs in 1974: Agriculture, forestry and fishing 27·6% (agriculture 22·9%); Manufacturing 15·4%; Trade, restaurants and hotels 22·9% (trade 22·3%); Community, social and personal services 10·2%.
Exports: $1214·3 million in 1974: Coffee 22·7%; Cocoa 25·5% (cocoa beans 21·4%); Wood, lumber and cork 21·4% (sawlogs and veneer logs 16·9%).
Monetary unit: Franc de la Communauté financière africaine.
Denominations:
Coins 1, 2, 5, 10, 25, 50, 100 CFA francs.
Notes 100, 500, 1000, 5000 CFA francs.

161

Exchange rate to US dollar: 242.8 (July 1977).

Political history and government: Formerly part of French West Africa, independent since 7 Aug. 1960. The ruling *Parti démocratique de la Côte d'Ivoire* has been the only organised political party since its establishment in 1946.

Legislative power is vested in the unicameral National Assembly, with 120 members elected for 5 years by universal adult suffrage. Executive power is held by the President, also directly elected for 5 years. He rules with the assistance of an appointed Council of Ministers, responsible to him. The country comprises 24 departments.

Telephones: 58 000 (1974).
Daily newspapers: 3 (1973).
Total circulation: 44 000.
Radio: 206 000 (1975).
TV: 100 500 (1975).
Length of roadways: 28 067 miles *45 170 km* (31 Dec. 1975).
Length of railways: 405 miles *c. 652 km.*
Universities: 1.
Adult illiteracy: 80% (est).
Expectation of life: Males 41·9 years; females 45·1 years (UN estimates for 1970–75).
Defence: Total armed forces 4100.
Cinemas: 80 (seating capacity 80 000) in 1972.

JAMAICA

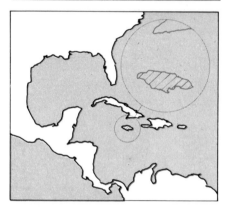

Population: 1 848 512 (census of 7 Apr. 1970); 2 060 000 (estimate for 31 Dec. 1975).
Area: 4244 miles² *10 991 km².*
Language: English.
Religions: Christian (Anglican and Baptist in majority).
Capital city: Kingston, population 169 800 (1974 est).
Other principal towns: Montego Bay 42 800; Spanish Town 41 600.
Highest point: Blue Mountain Peak (7402 ft *2256 m*).
Principal mountain range: Blue Mountains.
Head of State: H.M. Queen Elizabeth II, represented by Florizel Augustus Glasspole (b. 25 Sept. 1909), Governor-General.
Prime Minister Michael Norman Manley (b. 10 Dec. 1923).
Climate: The average rainfall is 77 in, and the rainfall is far greater in the mountains than on the coast. In Kingston, average maximum 86 °F (January to March) to 90 °F (July, August), minimum 67 °F (January, February) to 74 °F (June), wettest month is October (nine days). In the uplands the climate is pleasantly equable. Hurricanes

tend to miss the island, but there were severe storms on 20 Aug. 1944 and 17–18 Aug. 1951 (over 150 killed).
Labour force: 869 400 (including unemployed) aged 14 and over (Oct. 1975): Agriculture, forestry, fishing, mining and quarrying 31·1%; Manufacturing 11·2%; Commerce 11·8%; Services 34·6%.
Gross domestic product: J$2119·5 million (provisional) in 1974: Mining and quarrying (including petroleum refining) 15·5%; Manufacturing (excluding petroleum refining) 13·0%; Construction 10·6%; Trade, restaurants and hotels (including clubs) 16·1% (trade 14·3%); Community, social and personal services (excluding clubs) 16·8% (public administration and defence 11·6%). Revised total is J$2244·5 million.
Exports: US$718·4 million (excluding re-exports) in 1974: Sugar and honey 11·7% (raw sugar 11·4%); Bauxite and aluminium concentrates 73·7%.
Monetary unit: Jamaican dollar (J$). 1 dollar = 100 cents.
Denominations:
Coins 1, 5, 10, 20, 25, 50 cents, 1 $.
Notes 50 cents, 1, 2, 5, 10 $.
Exchange rate to US dollar: 0.9091 (July 1977).
Political history and government: A former British colony. Became independent, within the Commonwealth, on 6 Aug. 1962. Executive power is vested in the Queen and exercised by the Governor-General, who is guided by the advice of the Cabinet. Legislative power is held by the bicameral Parliament: the Senate has 21 members, appointed by the Governor-General (13 on the advice of the Prime Minister and 8 on that of the Leader of the Opposition), and the House of Representatives has 60 members elected by universal adult suffrage for 5 years (subject to dissolution). The Governor-General appoints the Prime Minister and, on the latter's recommendation, other Ministers. The Cabinet is responsible to Parliament. Jamaica has three counties.
Telephones: 96 000 (1974).
Daily newspapers: 3 (1973).
Total circulation: 180 000.
Radio: 550 000 (1975).
TV: 110 000 (1975).
Length of roadways: 2682 miles *4315 km.*
Length of railways: 205 miles *330 km.*
Universities: 1.
Adult illiteracy: 18·1% (males 21·4%; females 15·2%) in 1970.
Expectation of life: Males 62·65 years; females 66·63 years (1959–61).
Defence: Total forces about 1400.
Cinemas: 44 (seating capacity 45 000) and one part-time (capacity 725) in 1974.

JAPAN

Official name: Nippon or Nihon (Land of the Rising Sun).
Population: 111 933 818 (census of 1 Oct. 1975); 112 768 000 (estimate for 1 July 1976).
Area: 143 751 miles² *372 313 km².*
Language: Japanese.
Religions: Shintō, Buddhist.
Capital city: Tōkyō, population 8 642 800 (1 Oct. 1975).
Other principal towns (1975): Osaka 2 778 975; Yokohama 2 621 648; Nagoya 2 079 694; Kyōto 1 461 050 Kōbe 1 360 530; Sapporo 1 240 617; Kitakyushu 1 058 067; Kawasaki 1 015 022; Fukuoka (Hukuoka) 1 002 214; Hiroshima 852 607; Sakai 750 671.
Highest point: Fuji, 12 388 ft *3776 m.* First climbed before AD 806.
Principal mountain range: Hida.

Principal rivers: Tone (200 miles *321 km*) Ishikari (227 miles *365 km*), Shinano (22 miles *368 km*), Kitakami (156 miles *251 km*)
Head of State: H.I.M. Hirohito (b. 29 Apr 1901), *Nihon-koku Tennō* (Emperor o Japan).
Prime Minister: Takeo Fukuda (b. 14 Jan 1905).
Climate: Great variation, from north (warm summers with long, cold winters to south (hot, rainy summers with mile winters). In Tokyo, August warmest (72 °F to 86 °F), January coldest (20 °F to 47 °F) June and September rainiest (each 12 days). Absolute maximum temperature 41 °C (*105 °F*), Yamagata, 25 July 1933; absolut minimum −41,0 °C (−*42 °F*), Asahikawa 25 Jan. 1902.
Labour force: 51 780 000 (excluding 990 000 unemployed) aged 15 and over (1975): Agriculture, forestry and fishing 12·7%; Manufacturing 25·8%; Trade 21·6%; Community, social and personal services (including restaurants, hotels and business services) 20·2%.
Gross domestic product: 129 405 000 million yen (estimated by production method) in 1974: Manufacturing 33·0%; Trade 16·9%; Community, social and personal services (including restaurants and hotels) 17·2%.
Exports: $55 754·2 million in 1975: Iron and steel 18·2%; Non-electric machinery 12·1%; Electrical machinery, apparatus, etc. 11·0%; Transport equipment 26·1% (road motor vehicles and parts 14·6%; ships and boats 10·8%).
Monetary unit: Yen. 1 yen = 100 sen.
Denominations:
Coins 1, 5, 10, 50, 100 yen.
Notes 100, 500, 1000, 5000, 10 000 yen.
Exchange rate to US dollar: 264.0 (July 1977).
Political history and government: An hereditary monarchy, with an Emperor as Head of State. After being defeated in the Second World War, Japanese forces surrendered on 14 Aug. 1945 and the country was placed under US military occupation. A new constitution took effect from 3 May 1947 and, following the peace treaty of 8 Sept. 1951, Japan regained its sovereignty on 28 Apr. 1952. The Bonin Islands were restored on 26 June 1968 and the Ryukyu Islands (including Okinawa) on 15 May 1972.

Japan is a constitutional monarchy, with the Emperor as a symbol of the state. He has formal prerogatives but no power relating to government. Legislative power is vested in the bicameral Diet, elected by universal adult suffrage. The House of Councillors has 252 members elected for 6 years (half retiring every three years) and the House of Representatives has 511 members elected for 4 years (subject to dissolution). Executive power is vested in the Cabinet. The Prime Minister is appointed by the Emperor (on designation by the Diet) and himself appoints the other Ministers. The Cabinet is responsible to the Diet.

Japan has 47 prefectures, each administered by an elected Governor.
Telephones: 39 405 000 (31 March 1975).
Daily newspapers: 188 (1973).
Total circulation: 58 181 000.
Radio: 70 794 000 (1972).
TV: 26 692 203 (1975).
Length of roadways: 663 403 miles *1 067 643 km* (31 Mar. 1975).
Length of railways: 17 348 miles *27 919 km.*
Universities: 121 (41 national, 13 other public, 67 private) plus 21 technological universities.
Expectation of life: Males 71·16 years; females 76·31 years (Japanese nationals only, 1974).

Defence: Military service: voluntary; total armed forces 235 000; defence expenditure, 1976/77: $5058 million.
Cinemas: 2530 (seating capacity 1 138 500) in 1973.

JORDAN

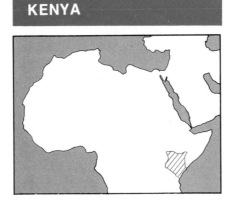

Official name: Al Mamlaka al Urduniya al Hashimiyah (The Hashemite Kingdom of Jordan).
Population: 1 706 226 (census of 18 Nov. 1961); 2 702 000 (estimate for 1 July 1975).
Area: 37 738 miles² *97 740 km²*.
Language: Arabic.
Religions: Muslim, Christian minority.
Capital city: Ammān, population 598 000 (estimate for 1 July 1974).
Other principal towns: Az Zarqa (Zarka) 226 000 (1974); Irbid 125 000 (1974); Bait Lahm (Bethlehem) 68 009 (1961); Ariha (Jericho) 66 839 (1961); Al Quds ash Sharif (Jerusalem) 60 337 (Jordanian sector, 1961).
Highest point: Jabal Ramm, 5755 ft *1754 m*.
Principal rivers: Jordan (200 miles *321 km*).
Head of State: H.M. King Husain ibn Talal, GCVO (b. 14 Nov. 1935).
Prime Minister: Mudar Badran (b. 1934).
Climate: Hot and dry, average temperature 60 °F with wide diurnal variations. Cool winters, rainy season December to March. In Ammān, August hottest (average maximum 90 °F), January coolest (average minimum 39 °F). Absolute maximum temperature 51 °C (*124 °F*), Dead Sea North, 22 June 1942; absolute minimum −7 °C (*18 °F*), Ammān, 28 Feb. 1959.
Labour force: 566 000 (1970): Agriculture, forestry and fishing 33·7% (ILO estimates).
Gross domestic product: 263·7 million dinars (provisional) in 1973: Agriculture, forestry and fishing 13·6% (agriculture 13·5%); Manufacturing 10·4%; Trade, restaurants and hotels 20·9% (trade 19·3%); Community, social and personal services 28·4%. Revised total is 268·5 million dinars.
Exports: $153·2 million in 1975: Fruit and vegetables 20·0% (citrus fruit 11·5%); Natural phosphates 40·0%; Machinery and transport equipment 14·0% (transport equipment 11·4%).
Monetary unit: Jordanian dinar. 1 dinar = 1000 fils.
Denominations:
  Coins 1, 5, 10, 20, 25, 50, 100, 250 fils.
  Notes ½, 1, 5, 10 dinars.
Exchange rate to US dollar: 0.3285 (July 1977).
Political history and government: Formerly part of Turkey's Ottoman Empire. Turkish forces were expelled in 1918. Palestine and Transjordan were administered by Britain under League of Nations mandate, established in 1922. Transjordan became an independent monarchy, under an Amir, on 22 Mar. 1946. The Amir became King, and

the country's present name was adopted, on 25 May 1946. In the Arab-Israeli war of 1948 Jordanian forces occupied part of Palestine, annexed in December 1949 and fully incorporated on 24 Apr. 1950. This territory was captured by Israel in the war of 5–10 June 1967.
Under the constitution, adopted on 7 Nov. 1951, legislative power is vested in a bi-cameral National Assembly, comprising a Chamber of Notables (30 members appointed by the King for 8 years, half retiring every 4 years) and a Chamber of Deputies with 60 members (50 Muslims and 10 Christians) elected by universal adult suffrage for 4 years (subject to dissolution). In each Chamber there is equal representation for the East Bank and the (occupied) West Bank. Executive power is vested in the King, who rules with the assistance of an appointed Council of Ministers, responsible to the Assembly. On 9 Nov. 1974 both Chambers of the Assembly approved constitutional amendments which empowered the King to dissolve the Assembly and to postpone elections for up to 12 months. The Assembly was dissolved on 22 Nov. 1974 and reconvened on 5–7 Feb. 1976, when it approved a constitutional amendment giving the King power to postpone elections indefinitely and to convene the Assembly as required.
Jordan comprises 8 administrative districts, including 3 on the West Bank (under Israeli occupation since June 1967).
Telephones: 40 511 (1974).
Daily newspapers: 4 (1973).
  Total circulation: 48 000.
Radio: 529 000 (1975).
TV: 205 000 (1975).
Length of roadways: 3711 miles *5972 km* (31 Dec. 1974).
Length of railways: 310 miles *500 km*.
Universities: 1.
Adult illiteracy: 67·6% (males 49·9%; females 84·8%) in 1961.
Expectation of life: Males 52·6 years; females 52.0 years (1959–63).
Defence: Military service: 24 months; total armed forces 67 900; defence expenditure, 1976: $155 million.
Cinemas: 39 (seating capacity 22 000) in 1974 (excluding Israeli-occupied territory).

KENYA

Official name: Djumhuri ya Kenya (Republic of Kenya).
Population: 10 942 705 (census of 24–25 Aug. 1969); 13 847 000 (estimate for 1 July 1976).
Area: 224 961 miles² *582 646 km²*.
Languages: Swahili (official), English, Kikuyu, Luo.
Religions: Christian 58% (1962).
Capital city: Nairobi, population 663 000 (1974 est).
Other principal towns: Mombasa 246 000;

Nakuru 47 800; Kisumu 30 700; Thika 18 100; Eldoret 16 900.
Highest point: Mount Kenya (17 058 ft *5199 m*).
Principal mountain range: Aberdare Mountains.
Principal rivers: Tana, Umba, Athi, Mathioya.
Head of State: Johnstone Kamau (*né* Kamau wa Ngengi), *alias* Jomo Kenyatta (b. 20 Oct. 1891), President.
Climate: Varies with altitude. Hot and humid on coast, with average temperatures of 69 °F to 90 °F, falling to 45 °F to 80 °F on land over 5000 ft. Ample rainfall in the west and on highlands, but very dry in the north. In Nairobi, average maximum 69 °F (July) to 79 °F (February), minimum 51 °F (July) to 58 °F (April), May rainiest (17 days).
Labour force: 4 570 000 (1970): Agriculture, forestry and fishing 82·1% (ILO estimates).
Gross domestic product: 19 044 million shillings (provisional) in 1974: Agriculture, forestry and fishing 30·2% (agriculture 28·6%); Manufacturing 14·2%; Government services 15·8%. Revised total is 20 452 million shillings.
Exports: $456·2 million (excluding re-exports) in 1974: Food and live animals 45·2% (coffee 23·6%; tea 11·9%); Textile fibres and waste 11·6% (sisal 10·4%); Petroleum products 19·0%. Figures exclude trade with Tanzania and Uganda in local produce and locally manufactured goods.
Monetary unit: Kenya shilling. 1 shilling = 100 cents.
Denominations:
  Coins 5, 10, 25, 50 cents, 1, 2 shillings.
  Notes 5, 10, 20, 50, 100 shillings.
Exchange rate to US dollar: 8.244 (July 1977).
Political history and government: Formerly a British colony and protectorate. Became independent, within the Commonwealth, on 12 Dec. 1963 and a republic on 12 Dec. 1964. A one-party state since 30 Oct. 1969. Legislative power is held by the unicameral National Assembly, with 171 members (158 elected by universal adult suffrage, the Attorney-General and 12 members nominated by the President) serving a term of 4 years (subject to dissolution). Executive power is held by the President, also directly elected for 4 years. He is assisted by an appointed Vice-President and Cabinet. Kenya has 7 provinces, each with an advisory Provincial Council.
Telephones: 113 688 (1974).
Daily newspapers: 3 (1973).
  Total circulation: 97 000.
Radio: 511 000 (1975).
TV: 37 500 (1975).
Length of roadways: 30 771 miles *49 521 km* (31 July 1975).
Length of railways: 1286 miles *2070 km*.
Universities: 1.
Expectation of life: Males 46·9 years; females 51·2 years (1969).
Defence: Military service: voluntary; total armed forces 7600; defence expenditure, 1976: $35 million.
Cinemas: 32 (seating capacity 18 800) and 3 drive-in for 1810 cars (1971).

KOREA (North)

Official name: Chosun Minchu-chui Inmin Konghwa-guk (Democratic People's Republic of Korea).
Population: 16 246 000 (UN estimate for mid-1976).

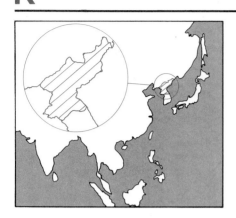

Area: 46 540 miles² *120 538 km²* (excluding demilitarised zone).
Languages: Korean.
Religions: Buddhist, Confucian, Taoist.
Capital city: Pyongyang, population 1 500 000 (1974 est).
Other principal towns (1974): Ch'ŏngjin 300 000; Kaesong 240 000; Hungnam 200 000.
Highest point: Paektu San (Pait'ou Shan), 9003 ft *2744 m* (first climbed 1886).
Principal mountain range: Nangnim Sanmaek.
Principal rivers: Imjin, Ch'ongch'ŏn, Yalu (300 miles *482 km*) on frontier.
Head of State: Marshal Kim Il Sung (*né* Kim Sung Chu, 15 Apr. 1912), President, also General Secretary of the Central Committee of the Korean Workers' Party.
Head of Government: Li Jong Ok, Premier of the Administration Council.
Climate: Continental; hot, humid, rainy summers (average temperature 77 °F) and cold, dry winters (average 21 °F).
Labour force: 5 995 000 (1970): Agriculture, forestry and fishing 54·7% (ILO estimates).
Gross national product: $6790 million in 1975 (World Bank estimate).
Monetary unit: Won. 1 won = 100 jeon.
Denominations:
Coins 1, 5, 10 jeon.
Notes 50 jeon, 1, 5, 10, 50, 100 won.
Exchange rate to US dollar: 0.979 (July 1977).
Political history and government: Korea was formerly a kingdom, for long under Chinese suzerainty. Independence was established on 17 Apr. 1895. Korea was occupied by Japanese forces in November 1905 and formally annexed by Japan on 22 Aug. 1910, when the King was deposed. After Japan's defeat in the Second World War, Korea was divided at the 38th parallel into military occupation zones, with Soviet forces in the North and US forces in the South. After the failure of negotiations in 1946 and 1947, the country remained divided. With Soviet backing, a Communist-dominated administration was established in the North. Elections were held on 25 Aug. 1948 and the Democratic People's Republic of Korea was proclaimed on 9 Sept. 1948. After the Korean War of 1950–53 a cease-fire line replaced the 38th parallel as the border between North and South.

In North Korea a new constitution was adopted on 27 Dec. 1972. The highest organ of state power is the unicameral Supreme People's Assembly, with 580 members elected (unopposed) for 4 years by universal adult suffrage. The Assembly elects for its duration the President of the Republic and, on the latter's recommendation, other members of the Central People's Committee to direct the government. The Assembly appoints the Premier and the Committee appoints other Ministers to form the Administration Council, led by the President.

Political power is held by the (Communist) Korean Workers' Party (KWP), which dominates the Democratic Front for the Reunification of the Fatherland (including two other minor parties). The Front presents an approved list of candidates for elections to representative bodies. The KWP's highest authority is the Party Congress, which elects a Central Committee to supervise Party work. The Committee elects the Politburo to direct policy.

North Korea comprises nine provinces and two cities, each with an elected People's Assembly.
Radio: 600 000 (1961).
Length of railways: 9320 miles *15 000 km*.
Universities: 1.
Adult illiteracy: 10% (est).
Expectation of life: Males 58·8 years; females 62·5 years (UN estimates for 1970–75).
Defence: Military service: Army 7 years, Navy 5 years, Air Force 3–4 years; total armed forces 495 000; defence expenditure, 1975: $878 million (converted at $1 = 2.05 won).

KOREA (South)

Official name: Daehen-Minkuk (Republic of Korea).
Population: 34 708 542 (census of 1 Oct. 1975).
Area: 38 131 miles² *98 758 km²*.
Languages: Korean.
Religions: Buddhist, Christian, Confucian, Chundo Kyo.
Capital city: Sŏul (Seoul), population 6 889 470 (1 Oct. 1975).
Other principal towns (1975): Pusan (Busan) 2 454 051; Taegu (Daegu) 1 311 078; Inchŏn (Incheon) 799 982; Kwangchu (Gwangju) 607 058; Taejŏn (Daejeon) 506 703; Masan 371 937; Chonchu (Jeonju) 311 432.
Highest point: Halla-san, 6398 ft *1950 m*.
Principal rivers: Han, Naktong (with Nam), Kum, Somjin, Yongsan.
Head of State: Gen Pak Chung Hi, *also written* Park Chung Hee (b. 14 Nov. 1917), President.
Prime Minister: Ch'oi Kyu Ha (b. 16 July 1919).
Climate: Hot, humid summers (average temperature 77 °F) and cold, dry winters (average 21 °F). In Seoul, August hottest (71 °F to 87 °F), January coldest (15 °F to 32 °F), July rainiest (16 days). Absolute maximum temperature 40 °C (*104 °F*), Taegu, 1 Aug. 1942; absolute minimum −43,6 °C (−*46·5 °F*), Chungkangjin, 12 Jan. 1933.
Labour force: 11 830 000 (excluding armed forces and 510 000 unemployed) aged 14 and over (1975); Agriculture, forestry and fishing 45·9%; Manufacturing 18·6%; Trade, restaurants and hotels 15·9%; Community, social and personal services 10·2%.
Gross domestic product: 6 844 700 million won (provisional) in 1974: Agriculture, forestry and fishing 25·6% (agriculture 21·7%); Manufacturing 28·2%; Trade, restaurants and hotels 18·9% (trade 16·8%); Community, social and personal services 10·4%. Revised total is 6 813 000 million won.
Exports: $5081·0 million in 1975: Food and live animals 11·9%; Textile yarn, fabrics etc. 12·8%; Machinery and transport equipment 13·8%; Clothing (excluding footwear) 22·6%.
Monetary unit: Won. 1 won = 100 jeon.
Denominations:
Coins 1, 5, 10, 100 won.
Notes 10, 50 jeon, 1, 5, 10, 50, 100, 500, 5000 won.
Exchange rate to US dollar: 484.0 (July 1977).
Political history and government: (For events before partition, *see* North Korea, above). After UN-supervised elections for a National Assembly on 10 May 1948, South Korea adopted a constitution and became the independent Republic of Korea on 15 Aug. 1948. North Korean forces invaded the South on 25 June 1950 and war ensued until 27 July 1953, when an armistice established a cease-fire line (roughly along the 38th parallel) between North and South. This line has become effectively an international frontier.

On 16 May 1961 South Korea's government was overthrown by a military *coup*, led by Maj-Gen Pak Chung Hi, who assumed power and dissolved the National Assembly. A new constitution was approved by referendum on 17 Dec. 1962. Gen. Pak was elected President on 15 Oct. 1963 and inaugurated on 17 Dec. 1963, when a newly-elected National Assembly was convened. Martial law was imposed on 17 Oct. 1972 and another constitution approved by referendum on 21 Nov. 1972.

Executive power is held by the President, indirectly elected for 6 years by the National Conference for Unification (NCU), which comprises 2359 delegates elected for 6 years by direct popular vote on 22 Dec. 1972. The President rules with the assistance of an appointed State Council (Cabinet), led by a Prime Minister. Legislative power is vested in the unicameral National Assembly, with 219 members (146 elected for 6 years by universal adult suffrage and 73 elected for 3 years by the NCU). An emergency decree of 13 May 1975 banned virtually all opposition activities.

South Korea comprises nine provinces and two cities.
Telephones: 1 158 000 (1974).
Daily newspapers: 33 (1972).
Total circulation: 4 400 000.
Radio: 4 115 000 (1972).
TV: 1 500 000 (1974).
Length of roadways: 27 903 miles *44 905 km* (31 Dec. 1975).
Length of railways: 3511 miles *5650 km*.
Universities: 26.
Adult illiteracy: 12·4% (males 5·6%; females 19·0%) in 1970.
Expectation of life: Males 63·00 years; females 67·00 years (1970).
Defence: Military service: Army and Marines 2½ years, Navy and Air Force 3 years; total armed forces 595 000; defence expenditure, 1976: $1500.
Cinemas: 786 (seating capacity 446 400) in 1972.

KUWAIT

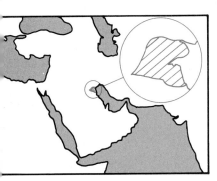

Official name: Daulat al Kuwait (State of Kuwait). Kuwait means 'little fort'.
Population: 994 837 (census of 21 Apr. 1975); 1 031 000 (estimate for 1 July 1976).
Area: 6880 miles² *17 818 km²*.
Language: Arabic.
Religions: Muslim; Christian minority.
Capital city: Kuwait City, population 93 050 (1973 est.)
Other principal towns (1970): Hawalli 106 542; Salmiya 67 346.
Highest point: 951 ft *289 m*.
Head of State: H.H. Shaikh Jabir al-Ahmad al-Jabir as-Sabah (b. 1928), Amir.
Climate: Humid, average temperature 75 °F. In Kuwait City, maximum recorded temperature 51 °C (*123·8 °F*), July 1954; minimum −2,6 °C (+*27·3 °F*), January 1964.
Labour force: 304 582 (including unemployed) aged 12 and over (1975 census): Construction 10·8%; Trade, restaurants and hotels 13·3%; Community, social and personal services 53·7%.
Gross domestic product: 2111 million dinars in 1973/74: Mining and quarrying 68·5%.
Exports: $10 954·1 million in 1974: Mineral fuels, lubricants, etc. 94·6% (crude petroleum 82·9%; petroleum products 10·1%).
Monetary unit: Kuwaiti dinar. 1 dinar = 1000 fils.
Denominations:
  Coins 1, 5, 10, 20, 50, 100 fils.
  Notes ¼, ½, 1, 5, 10 dinars.
Exchange rate to US dollar: 0.2865 (July 1977).
Political history and government: A monarchy formerly ruled by a Shaikh. Under British protection from 23 Jan. 1899 until achieving full independence, with the ruling Shaikh as Amir, on 19 June 1961. Present constitution adopted on 16 Dec. 1962. Executive power is vested in the Amir (chosen by and from members of the ruling family) and is exercised through a Council of Ministers. The Amir appoints the Prime Minister and, on the latter's recommendation, other Ministers. Legislative power is vested in the unicameral National Assembly, with 64 members, including 14 appointed and 50 elected for 4 years (subject to dissolution) by literate civilian adult male Kuwaiti citizens. On 29 Aug. 1976 the Amir dissolved the Assembly and suspended parts of the constitution, including provisions for fresh elections. Political parties are not legally permitted. Kuwait comprises three governorates.
Telephones: 108 587 (1974).
Daily newspapers: 7 (1973).
  Total circulation: 75 000.
Radio: 500 000 (1975).
TV: 180 000 (1973).
Length of roadways: 1193 miles *1920 km*.
Universities: 1.

Adult illiteracy: 45·0% (males 36·6%; females 58·1%) in 1970.
Expectation of life: Males 66·14 years; females 71·82 years (1970).
Defence: Military service: 18 months; total armed forces 9700; defence expenditure, 1975: $230 million.
Cinemas: 8 (seating capacity 11 000), one parti-time (capacity 1883) and one drive-in for 304 cars (1973).

LAOS

Official name: The Lao People's Democratic Republic.
Population: 3 257 000 (estimate for 1 July 1974).
Area: 91 400 miles² *236 800 km²*.
Languages: Lao (official), French.
Religions: Buddhist, tribal.
Capital city: Vientiane, population 176 637 (1973).
Other principal towns (1973): Savannakhet 50 690; Pakse 44 860; Luang Prabang 44 244.
Highest point: Phou Bia, 9252 ft *2820 m*.
Principal mountain range: Annamitic Range.
Principal river: Mekong (2600 miles [*4184 km*]).
Head of State: Souphanouvong (b. 1902), President.
Prime Minister: Kaysone Phomvihan (b. 1920), also General Secretary of the Lao People's Revolutionary Party.
Climate: Tropical (warm and humid). Rainy monsoon season May–October. In Vientiane average maximum 83 °F (December, January) to 93 °F (April), minimum 57 °F (January) to 75 °F (June to September), July and August rainiest (each 18 days). Maximum recorded temperature 44,8 °C (*112·6 °F*), Luang Prabang, April 1960; minimum 0,8 °C (*33·4 °F*), Luang Prabang, January 1924.
Labour force: 1 494 000 (1970): Agriculture, forestry and fishing 78·8% (ILO estimates).
Gross domestic product: $203 million in 1970 (UN estimate).
Exports: $11·3 million in 1974: Wood, lumber and cork 80·7% (non-coniferous lumber 79·8%); Metalliferous ores and metal scrap 11·9% (tin ores and concentrates 10·8%).
Monetary unit: Kip. 1 kip = 100 at.
Denominations:
  Notes 10, 20, 50, 100, 200, 500 kips.
Exchange rate to US dollar: 200.0 (July 1977).
Political history and government: Formerly the three principalities of Luang Prabang, Vientiane and Champassac. Became a French protectorate in 1893. The three principalities were merged in 1946 and an hereditary constitutional monarchy, under the Luang Prabang dynasty, was established on 11 May 1947. The Kingdom of Laos became independent, within the French Union, on 19 July 1949. Full sovereignty was recognized by France on 23 Oct. 1953. After nearly 20 years of almost continuous civil war between the Royal Government and the *Neo Lao Hak Sat* (Lao Patriotic Front or LPF), a Communist-led insurgent movement whose armed forces were known as the *Pathet Lao*, a peace agreement was signed on 21 Feb. 1973. A joint administration was established on 5 Apr. 1974 but the LPF became increasingly dominant. The National Assembly was dissolved on 13 Apr. 1975. The King abdicated on 29 Nov. 1975 and on 1 Dec. 1975 a National Congress of People's Representatives (264 delegates elected by local authorities) proclaimed the

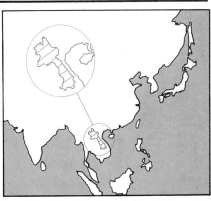

Lao People's Democratic Republic, with Prince Souphanouvong, Chairman of the LPF, as President. The Congress installed a Council of Ministers, led by a Prime Minister, and appointed a People's Supreme Council of 45 members, chaired by the President, to draft a new constitution.
Telephones: 5506 (1974).
Daily newspapers: 1 (1976).
Radio: 102 000 (1973).
Length of roadways: 4536 miles *7 300km*.
Universities: 1.
Adult illiteracy: 75% (estimate).
Expectation of life: Males 39·1 years; females 41·8 years (UN estimates for 1970–75).
Defence: Military service: conscription (term unknown); total armed forces 42 500; defence expenditure, 1974/75: $27 million.
Cinemas: 16 (seating capacity 8200) in 1969.

LEBANON

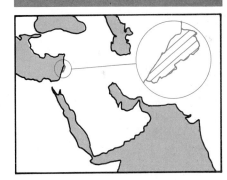

Official name Al-Jumhuriya al-Lubnaniya (the Lebanese Republic), abbreviated to al-Lubnan.
Population: 2 126 325 (survey of 15 Nov. 1970), excluding Palestinian refugees in camps (registered Palestinian refugees numbered 187 529 at 30 June 1973).
Area: 3950 miles² *10 400 km²*.
Languages: Arabic (official), French, Armenian, English.
Religions: Christian, Muslim.
Capital city: Beirut, population 474 870 (Greater Beirut 938 940) in 1970.
Other principal towns: Tripoli 175 000; Zahlé 46 800; Saida (Sidon) 24 740; Sur (Tyre) 14 000; Aley 13 800.
Highest point: Qurnat as-Sawdā, 10 131 ft *3088 m*.
Principal mountain ranges: Lebanon, Jabal ash Sharqī (Anti-Lebanon).
Principal rivers: Nahr al Litāni (Leontes).
Head of State: Elias Sarkis (b. 20 July 1924), President.
Prime Minister: Dr Selim al-Hoss (b. 1930).
Climate: Coastal lowlands are hot and humid in summer, mild (cool and damp) in winter. Mountains cool in summer, heavy

snowfall in winter. In Beirut, average maximum 62 °F (January) to 89 °F (August), minimum 51 °F (January, February) to 74 °F (August), January rainiest (15 days).
Labour force: 538 410 (excluding 33 345 unemployed) at November 1970 survey: Agriculture, forestry and fishing 19·0%; Mining, quarrying and manufacturing 17·8% (manufacturing 17·7%); Trade, restaurants and hotels 17·1%; Community, social and personal services 27·9%.
Gross domestic product: L£6365 million in 1972: Mining, quarrying and manufacturing 13·9%; Trade, restaurants and hotels 31·5%; Community, social and personal services 18·1%.
Exports: $502·5 million in 1973: Food and live animals 18·4% (fruit and vegetables 11·7%); Machinery and transport equipment 25·5% (transport equipment 11·5%).
Monetary unit: Lebanese pound (£L). 1 pound = 100 piastres.
Denominations:
Coins 1, 2, 5, 10, 25, 50 piastres.
Notes 1, 5, 10, 25, 50, 100 pounds.
Exchange rate to US dollar: 3.1205 (July 1977).
Political history and government: Formerly part of Turkey's Ottoman Empire. Turkish forces were expelled in 1918 by British and French troops, with Arab help. Administered by France under League of Nations mandate from 1 Sept. 1920. Independence declared on 26 Nov. 1941. A republic was established in 1943 and French powers transferred on 1 Jan. 1944. All foreign troops left by December 1946.

Legislative power is held by the unicameral Chamber of Deputies, with 99 members elected by universal adult suffrage for 4 years (subject to dissolution), using proportional representation. Seats are allocated on a religious basis (53 Christian, 45 Muslim). Elections to the Chamber due in April 1976 were postponed because of civil disorder. Executive power is vested in the President, elected for 6 years by the Chamber. He appoints a Prime Minister and other Ministers to form a Cabinet, responsible to the Chamber. By convention, the President is a Maronite Christian and the Prime Minister a Sunni Muslim.
Telephones: 300 000 (1971).
Daily newspapers: 32 (1973).
Total circulation: 280 000 (16 dailies).
Radio: 1 321 000 (1975).
TV: 410 000 (1975).
Length of roadways: 4598 miles *7400 km.* (31 Dec. 1971).
Length of railways: 259 miles *417 km.*
Universities: 5.
Adult illiteracy: 20% (estimate).
Expectation of life: Males 61·4 years; females 65·1 years (UN estimates for 1970–75).
Defence: Military service: 18 months, selective; total armed forces 18 250; defence expenditure, 1976: $123 million.
Cinemas: 170 (seating capacity 86 600) and 2 drive-in (1970).

LESOTHO

Official name: The Kingdom of Lesotho.
Population: 852 361 (census of 14–24 Apr. 1966); 1 039 000 (estimate for 1 July 1975). Figures exclude absentee workers (12 per cent of the total population in 1966).
Area: 11 720 miles² *30 355 km².*
Languages: Sesotho, English.
Religions: Christian 73·4% (1966).
Capital city: Maseru, population 13 312 (estimate for 31 Jan. 1972).
Highest point: Thabana Ntlenyana (Thadentsonyane), 11 425 ft *3482 m.*

Principal mountain range: Drakensberg.
Principal rivers: Orange, Caledon (on northern frontier).
Head of State: King Motlotlehi Moshoeshoe II (b. 2 May 1938).
Prime Minister: Chief (Joseph) Leabua Jonathan (b. 30 Oct. 1914).

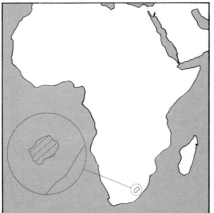

Climate: In lowlands, maximum temperature in summer 90 °F, winter minimum 20 °F. Range wider in highlands. Average annual rainfall 29 in. Rainy season October–April.
Labour force: 436 696 (excluding absentee workers) aged 15 and over (1966 census); 584 000 (1970): Agriculture, forestry and fishing 89·7% (ILO estimates).
Gross domestic product: 62·2 million rand in 1972/73: Agriculture, forestry and fishing 47·2%; Trade and catering 15·4% (trade 10·7%); Public administration and defence 10·7%.
Exports: 9·7 million rand in 1974: Live animals 15·7%; Wool 35·5%; Mohair 16·3%.
Monetary unit: South African currency (*qv*).
Political history and government: An hereditary monarchy, formerly the British colony of Basutoland. Granted internal self-government, with the Paramount Chief as King, on 30 April 1965. Became independent (under present name), within the Commonwealth, on 4 Oct. 1966. Under the constitution, legislative power was vested in a bicameral Parliament, comprising a Senate of 33 members (22 Chiefs and 11 Senators nominated by the King for 5-year terms) and a National Assembly of 60 members elected by universal adult suffrage for 5 years (subject to dissolution). Executive power is exercised by the Cabinet, led by the Prime Minister, which is responsible to Parliament. The Assembly elections of 27 Jan. 1970 were annulled three days later by the Prime Minister, who declared a state of emergency and suspended the constitution. The Cabinet assumed full power. No more elections have been held but an interim National Assembly of 93 members (the former Senate and 60 nominated members) was inaugurated on 27 Apr. 1973. Lesotho comprises 9 administrative districts, each under an appointed District Administrator.
Telephones: 3726 (1974).
Radio: 22 000 (1975).
Length of roadways: *c.* 960 miles *c. 1545 km.*
Length of railways: 1 mile *2 km.*
Universities: 1.
Adult illiteracy: 41·2% (males 55·9%; females 32·2%) in 1966 (excl. absentee workers).
Expectation of life: Males 44·4 years; females 47·6 years (UN estimates for 1970–75).
Cinemas: 2 (seating capacity 800) in 1971.

LIBERIA

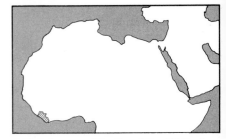

Official name: The Republic of Liberia.
Population: 1 503 368 (census of 1 Feb. 1974).
Area: 43 000 miles² *111 369 km².*
Languages: English (official), tribal languages.
Religion: Mainly Animist.
Capital city: Monrovia, population 180 000 (1974).
Other principal towns: Harbel, Buchanan, Greenville (Sinoe), Harper (Cape Palmas).
Highest point: On Mt Nimba, 4500 ft *1372 m.*
Principal mountain range: Guinea Highlands.
Principal rivers: St Paul, St John, Cess.
Head of State: William Richard Tolbert, Jr. (b. 13 May 1913), President.
Climate: Tropical (hot and humid) with temperatures from 55 °F to 120 °F. Rainy season April to October. In Monrovia, average maximum 80 °F (July, August) to 87 °F (March, April), minimum 72 °F to 74 °F all year round, June and September rainiest (each 26 days).
Labour force: 411 794 (excluding armed forces) aged 10 and over (census of 2 Apr. 1962); 607 000 (1970): Agriculture, forestry and fishing 75·6% (ILO estimates).
Gross domestic product: L$544·9 million in 1973: Agriculture, forestry and fishing 27·0% (agriculture 22·9%); Mining and quarrying 29·9%; Trade, restaurants and hotels 10·5%.
Exports: US$399·8 million in 1974: Natural rubber 16·1%; Iron ore and concentrates 65·6%.
Monetary unit: Liberian dollar. 1 dollar = 100 cents.
Denominations:
Coins 1, 2, 5, 10, 25, 50 cents, 1 Liberian dollar.
Notes 1, 5, 10, 20 US dollars (There are no Liberian banknotes).
Exchange rate to US dollar: 1.00 (July 1977).
Political history and government: Settled in 1822 by freed slaves from the USA. Became independent on 26 July 1847. The constitution was modelled on that of the USA. The bicameral legislature, elected by universal adult suffrage, comprises a Senate, with 18 members (two from each of the 9 counties) serving overlapping 6-year terms, and a House of Representatives (65 members serving 4 years). Executive power is held by the President, directly elected (with a Vice-President) for 8 years. The President rules with the assistance of an appointed Cabinet.
Telephones: 3400 (1973).
Daily newspapers: 2 (1973).
Total circulation: 7000.
Radio: 264 000 (1975).
TV: 8800 (1975).
Length of roadways: 62 298 miles *100 260 km.*
Length of railways: 291 miles *468 km.*
University: 1.
Adult illiteracy: 91·1% (males 86·1%; females 95·8%) illiterate in English in 1962.

Expectation of life: Males 45.8 years; females 44·0 years (1971).
Defence: Total armed forces 5220.
Cinemas: 26 (seating capacity 14 900) in 1971.

LIBYA

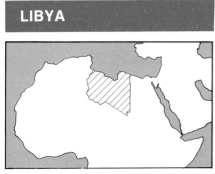

Official name: The Socialist People's Libyan Arab Jamahiriya ('state of the masses').
Population: 2 257 037 (census of 31 July 1973); 2 444 000 (estimate for 1 July 1975).
Area: 679.363 miles² *1 759 540 km².*
Language: Arabic.
Religion: Muslim.
Capital city: Tripoli, population 551 477 (1973 census).
Other principal towns: Benghazi 140 000; Misurata 103 302; Homs-Cussabat 88 695; Zawai 72 207; Gharlan 65 439; Tubruq (Tobruk) 58 869.
Highest point: Pico Bette, 7500 ft *2286 m.*
Principal mountain ranges: Jabal as Sawdā, Al Kufrah, Al Harūj al Aswad, Jabal Nafūsah, Hamada de Tinrhert.
Principal river: Wādi al Fārigh.
Head of State: Col Muammar Muhammad al-Qaddafi (b. 1938), President.
Head of Government: Abdul Ali al-Obaidi (b. 10 Oct. 1939), Chairman of the General People's Committee.
Climate: Very hot and dry, with average temperatures between 55 °F and 100 °F. Coast cooler than inland. In Tripoli, August hottest (72 °F to 86 °F), January coolest (47 °F to 61 °F). Absolute maximum temperature 57,3 °C (*135·1 °F*), Al 'Aziziyah (el Azizia), 24 Aug. 1923; absolute minimum −9 °C (*+15·8 °F*), Hon, 10 Jan. 1938.
Labour force: 387 699 (excluding aliens) aged 6 and over (census of 31 July 1964); 517 000 (1970): Agriculture, forestry and fishing 32·1% (ILO estimates).
Gross domestic product: 2193 million dinars in 1973: Mining and quarrying 50·9%; Construction 12·3%; Community, social and personal services 12·7% (public services 12·1%).
Exports: $8268·1 million in 1974: Petroleum and petroleum products 99·0% (crude petroleum 97·6%).
Monetary unit: Libyan dinar. 1 dinar = 1000 dirhams.
Denominations:
Coins 1, 5, 10, 20, 50, 100 dirhams.
Notes ¼, ½, 1, 5, 10 dinars.
Exchange rate to US dollar: 0.296 (July 1977).
Political history and government: Formerly part of Turkey's Ottoman Empire. Became an Italian colony in September 1911. Italian forces were expelled in 1942–43 and the country was under British and French administration from 1943 until becoming an independent kingdom, under the Amir of Cyrenaica, on 24 Dec. 1951. The monarchy was overthrown by an army *coup* on 1 Sept. 1969, when a Revolutionary Command Council (RCC) took power and proclaimed the Libyan Arab Republic. The bicameral Parliament was abolished and political

activity suspended. On 8 Sept. 1969 the RCC elected Col. Muammar al-Qaddafi as its Chairman. A provisional constitution, proclaimed in December 1969, vested supreme authority in the RCC, which appointed a Council of Ministers. The only legal political party is the Arab Socialist Union, established on 11 June 1971. Under a decree of 13 Nov. 1975 provision was made for the creation of a 618-member General People's Congress (GPC) comprising members of the RCC, leaders of existing 'people's congresses' and 'popular committees', and trade unions and professional organizations. The GPC held its first session on 5–18 Jan. 1976. On 2 Mar. 1977 it approved a new constitution, which adopted the country's present name. Under the constitution, the RCC and Council of Ministers were abolished and power passed to the GPC, assisted by a General Secretariat. The Head of State is the President, elected by the GPC (Col. Qaddafi became the first President). The Council of Ministers was replaced by a General People's Committee. Libya is divided into 10 governorates.
Telephones: 42 000 (1971).
Daily newspapers: 6 (1973).
Radio: 106 000 (1975).
TV: 10 000 (1975).
Length of roadways: *c.* 3232 miles *c. 5200 km.*
Length of railways: 108 miles *174 km.*
Universities: 2.
Adult illiteracy: 78·3% (males 62·5%; females 95·8%) in 1964.
Expectation of life: Males 51·4 years; females 54·5 years (UN estimates for 1970–75).
Defence: Military service: voluntary; total armed forces 29 700; defence expenditure, 1975: $203 million.

LIECHTENSTEIN

Official name: Fürstentum Liechtenstein (Principality of Liechtenstein).
Population: 21 350 (census of 1 Dec. 1970); 23 949 (estimate for 1 July 1975).
Area: 61·8 miles², *160·0 km².*
Language: German.
Religions: Roman Catholic; Protestant minority.
Capital city: Vaduz, population 4472 (1 July 1975).
Other principal towns: (1975): Schaan 4322; Balzers 3104; Triesen 2890; Eschen 2421; Mauren 2318.
Highest point: Grauspitze, 8526 ft *2599 m.*
Principal mountain range: Alps.
Principal rivers: Rhein (Rhine) (820 miles *1319 km,* 17 miles *27 km* in Liechtenstein), Samina.
Head of State: Prince Franz Josef II (b. 16 Aug. 1906).
Head of Government: Dr Walter Kieber (b. 20 Feb. 1931).
Climate: Alpine, with mild winters. Temperature extremes for Sargans, in Switzerland, a few miles from the Liechtenstein border: absolute maximum 38,0 °C

(*100·4 °F*), 29 July 1947; absolute minimum −25,6 °C (*−14·1 °F*), 12 Feb. 1929.
Labour force: 10 302 (Dec. 1974).
Exports: 522·3 million Swiss francs in 1975.
Monetary unit: Swiss currency (*qv*).
Political history and government: An hereditary principality, independent since 1866. Present constitution adopted on 5 Oct. 1921. Legislative power is exercised jointly by the Sovereign and the unicameral Diet (*Landtag*), with 15 members elected (by men only) for 4 years, using proportional representation. A 5-man Government (*Regierung*) is elected by the Diet for its duration and confirmed by the Sovereign.
Telephones: 14 745 (1974).
Daily newspapers: 1 (1972).
Total circulation: 6000.
Radio: 5462 (1975).
TV: 4696 (1975).
Length of railways: 11 miles *18 km.*
Cinemas: 3 (seating capacity 900) in 1971.

LUXEMBOURG

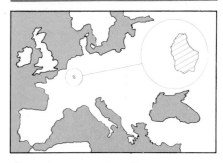

Official name: Le Grand-Duché de Luxembourg, Grousherzogdem Lezebuurg or Grossherzogtum Luxemburg (Grand Duchy of Luxembourg).
Population: 339 841 (census of 31 Dec. 1970); 358 400 (estimate for 1 July 1976).
Area: 999 miles² *2586 km².*
Languages: Letzeburgesch (Luxembourgois), French, German.
Religion: Roman Catholic.
Capital city: Luxembourg-Ville, population 78 800 (1 July 1976).
Other principal towns (1973): Esch-sur-Alzette 27 539; Differdange 17 976; Dudelange 14 625; Petange 11 903.
Highest point: Bourgplatz 1833 ft *559 m.*
Principal mountain range: Ardennes.
Principal rivers: Mosel (Moselle), Sûre (107 miles [*172 km*], 99 miles [*159 km*] in Luxembourg), Our, Alzette.
Head of State: H.R.H. Prince Jean Benoît Guillaume Marie Robert Louis Antoine Adolphe Marc d'Aviano (b. 5 Jan. 1921), Grand Duke.
Head of Government: Gaston Thorn (b. 3 Sept. 1928), President of the Government (Prime Minister).
Climate: Temperate (cool summers and mild winters). Absolute maximum temperature, 37,0 °C (*98·6 °F*), Luxembourg-Ville, 28 July 1895, and Grevenmacher, 6 July 1957; absolute minimum −24,3 °C (*−11·7 °F*), Wiltz, 5 Feb. 1917.
Labour force: 128 235 (excluding 1 020 unemployed) aged 15 and over (1970 census): Mining and manufacturing 33·9%; Trade, restaurants and hotels 18·4%; Community, social and personal services 19·4%; 150 400 (Dec. 1975).
Gross domestic product: 82 800 million Luxembourg francs (provisional) in 1974: Mining and manufacturing 44·2%; Government services 10·9%. Revised total is 85 050 million Luxembourg francs.
Exports: n.a. (included with Belgium).

Monetary unit: Luxembourg franc. 1 franc = 100 centimes.
Denominations:
 Coins 25, 50 centimes, 1, 5, 10, 100, 250 Luxembourg francs.
 Notes 10, 20, 50, 100 Luxembourg francs; 20, 50, 100, 500, 1000, 5000 Belgian francs.
Exchange rate to US dollar: 35·48 (July 1977).
Political history and government: An hereditary grand duchy, independent since 1867. Luxembourg is a constitutional monarchy. Legislative power is exercised by the unicameral Chamber of Deputies, with 59 members elected by universal adult suffrage for 5 years (subject to dissolution). Some legislative functions are also entrusted to the advisory Council of State, with 21 members appointed by the Grand Duke, but the Council can be overridden by the Chamber. Executive power is vested in the Grand Duke but is normally exercised by the Council of Ministers, led by the President of the Government. The Grand Duke appoints Ministers but they are responsible to the Chamber. Luxembourg is divided into 12 cantons.
Telephones: 141 686 (1974).
Daily newspapers: 7 (1973).
 Total circulation: 161 000 (6 dailies).
Radio: 176 000 (1972).
TV: 88 500 (1975).
Length of roadways: 2774 miles *4465 km* (31 Dec. 1975).
Length of railways: 168 miles *271 km.*
Expectation of life: Males 67·0 years; females 73·9 years (1971–73).
Defence: Military service: voluntary; total armed forces 625; defence expenditure, 1976: $20·9 million.
Cinemas: 27 (seating capacity 13 700) in 1972.

MADAGASCAR

Official name: La République démocratique de Madagascar (The Democratic Republic of Madagascar).
Population: 8 080 000 (1974 est).
Area: 226 658 miles² *587 041 km².*
Languages: Malagasy, French (both official).
Religions: Animist, Christian, Muslim.
Capital city: Antananarivo (Tananarive), population 366 530 (1972).
Other principal towns (1972): Majunga 67 458; Tamatave 59 503; Fianarantsoa 58 818; Diégo-Suarez 45 487; Tuléar 38 978; Antsirabé 33 287.
Highest point: Maromokotro, 9436 ft *2876 m.*
Principal mountain ranges: Massif du Tsaratanana, Ankaratra.
Principal rivers: Ikopa, Mania, Mangoky.
Head of State: Lt-Cdr Didier Ratsiraka (b. 4 Nov. 1936), President.
Prime Minister: Lt-Col Désiré Rakotoarijaona (b. 1934).
Climate: Hot on coast (average daily maximum 90 °F), but cooler inland. Fairly dry in south, but monsoon rains (December to April) in north. In Antananarivo, average maximum 68 °F (July) to 81 °F (November), minimum 48 °F (July, August) to 61 °F (January, February), January rainiest (21 days). Absolute maximum temperature 44,4 °C (*111·9 °F*), Behara, 20 Nov. 1940; absolute minimum −6,3 °C (*+20·7 °F*), Antsirabé, 18 June 1945.
Labour force: 3 200 000 (1 Jan. 1965); 3 620 000 (1970): Agriculture, forestry and fishing 89·4% (ILO estimates).
Gross domestic product: 268 521 million Malagasy francs in 1971: Agriculture, forestry and fishing 31·0%; Manufacturing 12·4%; Trade 15·4%; Government services 15·7%.

Exports: $244·2 million in 1974: Coffee 26·7%; Spices 16·5%; Other food 24·3%.
Monetary unit: Franc malgache (Malagasy franc). 1 franc = 100 centimes.
Denominations:
 Coins 1, 2, 5, 10, 20 francs
 Notes 50, 100, 500, 1000, 5000 francs.
Exchange rate to US dollar: 242.8 (July 1977).
Political history and government: Formerly a French colony. Became independent, as the Malagasy Republic, on 26 June 1960. Following disturbances, the President handed over full powers to the army commander on 18 May 1972, when Parliament was dissolved. A National Military Directorate was formed on 12 Feb. 1975 and suspended all political parties. On 15 June 1975 the Directorate elected Lt-Cdr Didier Ratsiraka to be Head of State, as President of the Supreme Revolutionary Council (SRC). A referendum on 21 Dec. 1975 approved a draft constitution and the appointment of Ratsiraka as Head of State for 7 years. The Democratic Republic of Madagascar was proclaimed on 30 Dec. 1975 and Ratsiraka took office as President of the Republic on 4 Jan. 1976.
 Executive power is vested in the President, who rules with the assistance of the SRC and an appointed Council of Ministers. Legislative power is vested in the National People's Assembly, with 137 members elected by universal adult suffrage for 5 years. The Assembly was first elected on 30 June 1977. The country is divided into 6 provinces.
Telephones: 30 000 (1974).
Daily newspapers: 13 (1972).
 Total circulation: 103 000.
Radio: 700 000 (1973).
TV: 7500 (1973).
Length of roadways: 16 772 miles *26 992 km* (31 Dec. 1974).
Length of railways: 549 miles *884 km.*
University: 1.
Adult illiteracy: 66·5% (males 59·2%; females 73·0%) illiterate in Malagasy in 1953 (indigenous population aged 14 and over).
Expectation of life: Males 41·9 years; females 45·1 years (UN estimates for 1970–75).
Defence: Total armed forces 4760.
Cinemas: 43 (seating capacity 15 000) in 1972.

MALAWI

Official name: The Republic of Malawi.
Population: 4 039 583 (census of 9 Aug. 1966); 5 175 000 (estimate for 1 July 1976).
Area: 45 747 miles² *118 484 km².*
Languages: English (official), Nyanja.
Religions: Mainly traditional beliefs. Christian minority.
Capital city: Lilongwe, population 19 176 (1966 census).
Other principal towns (1966): Blantyre 109 795; Zomba 19 616; Mzuzu 8490; Salima 2307.
Highest point: Mount Sapitwa 9843 ft *3000 m.*
Principal river: Shire.
Head of State: Dr. Hastings Kamuzu Banda (b. 14 May 1906), President.
Climate: In the low-lying Shire valley temperatures can rise to 115 °F in October and November, but above 3000 ft the climate is much more temperate and at the greatest heights the nights can be frosty. The dry season is May to September with the very wet season from late December to March. Rainfall in the highlands is about 50 in, and in the lowlands 35 in.
Labour force: 1 943 000 (1970); Agricul-

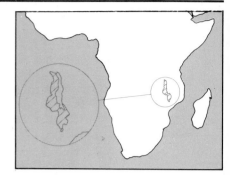

ture, forestry and fishing 89·3% (ILO estimates).
Gross domestic product: 335·9 million kwacha (provisional) in 1971: Agriculture, forestry and fishing (including all non-monetary output) 49·6%; Manufacturing 12·3%; Trade 11·9%. Revised total is 335·0 million kwacha.
Exports: $120·6 million in 1974: Tea 17·2%; Other food 18·6%; Tobacco (unmanufactured) 43·6%.
Monetary unit: Malawi kwacha. 1 kwacha = 100 tambala.
Denominations:
 Coins 1, 2, 5, 10, 20 tambala.
 Notes 50 tambala, 1, 2, 5, 10 kwacha.
Exchange rate to US dollar: 0.8973 (July 1977).
Political history and government: Formerly the British protectorate of Nyasaland. Became independent, within the Commonwealth, on 6 July 1964, taking the name Malawi. Became a republic, and a one-party state, on 6 July 1966, when Dr. Hastings Banda (Prime Minister since independence) became President. On 6 July 1971 he became President for life. Legislative power is held by the unicameral National Assembly, with 75 members (60 elected by universal adult suffrage for 5 years, subject to dissolution, and 15 nominated by the President). All members must belong to the ruling Malawi Congress Party (at the 1971 election, no voting took place as there were no opposition candidates). Executive power is vested in the President, who rules with the assistance of an appointed Cabinet. Malawi has three administrative regions, each the responsibility of a Cabinet Minister.
Telephones: 18 000 (1974).
Radio: 127 000 (1975).
Length of roadways: 6851 miles *11 025 km* (31 Dec. 1975).
Length of railways: 352 miles *566 km.*
University: 1.
Adult illiteracy: 77·9% (males 66·2%; females 87·7%) in 1966.
Expectation of life: Males 40·9 years; females 44·2 years (Africans only, 1970–72.)
Defence: Total armed forces 2300.
Cinemas: 13 (seating capacity 5000) and one drive-in for 350 cars (1972).

MALAYSIA

Official name: Persekutuan Tanah Melaysiu (Federation of Malaysia).
Population: 10 319 324 (census of 24–25 Aug. 1970, excluding persons afloat and institutional population, totalling about 94 200); 12 300 000 (estimate for 1 July 1976).
Area: 127 315 miles² *329 744 km².*
Languages: Malay (official), Chinese, Tamil, Iban, English.
Religions (1970): Muslim 50·0%; Buddhist 25·7%; Hindu; Christian.
Capital city: Kuala Lumpur, population 451 977 (1970 census).

Other principal towns (1970): George Town (Penang) 269 603; Ipoh 247 953; Johore Bahru 136 234; Klang 113 611.
Highest point: Mount Kinabalu, 13 455 ft *4101 m*, in Sabah.
Principal mountain range: Trengganu Highlands.
Principal rivers: Pahang, Kelantan.
Head of State: Tuanku Yahya Petra ibni al-Marhum Sultan Ibrahim (b. 10 Dec. 1917), Sultan of Kelantan, *Yang di-Pertuan Agong* (Supreme Head of State).
Prime Minister: Datuk Hussein bin Dato Onn (b. 12 Feb. 1922).

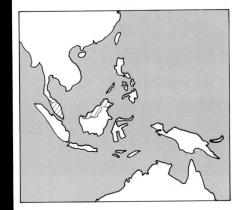

Climate: Peninsular Malaysia is hot and humid, with daytime temperatures around 85 °F *29 °C* and little variation throughout the year. The average daily range on the coast is 72 °F *22 °C* to 92 °F *33 °C*. Rainfall is regular and often heavy. Maximum record temperature 103·0 °F *39,4 °C*, Pulau Langkawi, 27 Mar. 1931; minimum 36·0 °F *2,2 °C*, Cameron Highlands, 6 Jan. 1937.
Sabah is generally fairly humid but relatively cool. In Kota Kinabalu, average temperatures are 74°F *23 °C* to 87 °F *31 °C*, average annual rainfall 104 in *264 cm*. The north-east monsoon is from mid-October to March or April, the south-west monsoon from May to August.
Sarawak is humid, with temperatures generally 72 °F *22 °C* and 88 °F *31 °C*, sometimes reaching 96 °F *36 °C*. It has heavy rainfall (annual average 120 in *305 cm* to 160 in *406 cm*), especially in the north-east monsoon season (October to March).
Labour force: 3 455 318 (including unemployed) aged 10 and over (1970 census): Agriculture, forestry and fishing 53·5%; Commerce 10·2%; Services 18·2%.
Gross domestic product: 10 936 million ringgit in 1971: Agriculture, forestry and fishing (excluding government) 28·0% (agriculture 22·4%); Manufacturing 15·8%; Trade, restaurants and hotels 12·8% (trade 11·6%); Community, social and personal services 14·8% (government services 12·4%).
Exports: US$4234·2 million in 1974: Natural rubber 28·3%; Wood, lumber and cork 15·1% (sawlogs and veneer logs 10·1%); Palm oil 10·6%; Tin metal 14·9%.
Monetary unit: Ringgit (Malaysian dollar). 1 ringgit = 100 cents (sen).
Denominations:
Coins 1, 5, 10, 20, 50 cents, 1 ringgit.
Notes 1, 5, 10, 50, 100, 1000 ringgit.
Exchange rate to US dollar: 2.479 (July 1977).
Political history and government: Peninsular (West) Malaysia comprises 11 states (nine with hereditary rulers, two with Governors) formerly under British protection. They were united as the Malayan Union on 1 Apr. 1946 and became the Federation of Malaya on 1 Feb. 1948. The Federation became independent, within the

Commonwealth, on 31 Aug. 1957. On 16 Sept. 1963 the Federation (renamed the States of Malaya) was merged with Singapore (*qv*), Sarawak (a British colony) and Sabah (formerly the colony of British North Borneo) to form the independent Federation of Malaysia, still in the Commonwealth. On 9 Aug. 1965 Singapore seceded from the Federation. On 5 Aug. 1966 the States of Malaya were renamed West Malaysia, now known as Peninsular Malaysia.
Malaysia is an elective monarchy. The nine state rulers of Peninsular Malaysia choose from their number a Supreme Head of State and a Deputy, to hold office for 5 years. Executive power is vested in the Head of State but is normally exercised on the advice of the Cabinet. Legislative power is held by the bicameral Parliament. The Senate has 58 members, including 32 appointed by the Head of State and 26 (two from each state) elected by State Legislative Assemblies. The House of Representatives has 154 members elected by universal adult suffrage for 5 years. The Head of State appoints the Prime Minister and, on the latter's recommendation, other Ministers. The Cabinet is responsible to Parliament.
Malaysia comprises 13 states and, since 1 Feb. 1974, the Federal Territory of Kuala Lumpur. Each state has a unicameral Legislative Assembly, elected by universal adult suffrage.
Telephones: 259 405 (1974).
Daily newspapers: 37 (1973).
Total circulation: 1 097 000.
Radio: 462 000 (1973).
TV: 359 000 (1973).
Length of roadways: 15 155 miles *24 389 km*.
Length of railways: 1127 miles *1814 km*.
Universities: 5.
Adult illiteracy: 42·0% (males 30·9%; females 53·2%) in 1970 (population aged 10 and over): Peninsular Malaysia 39·2%; Sabah 55·7%; Sarawak 61·7%.
Expectation of life: Males 57·5 years; females 61·3 years (UN estimates for 1970–75).
Defence: Military service: voluntary; total armed forces 62 300; defence expenditure, 1976: US$353 million.
Cinemas: 550 (seating capacity 385 000) in 1973.

MALDIVES

Official name: Divehi Jumhuriya (Republic of Maldives).
Population: 128 697 (1974 census).
Area: 115 miles² *298 km²*.
Languages: Divehi (Maldivian).
Religion: Muslim.
Capital city: Malé, population 16 246 (1974).
Head of State: Amir Ibrahim Nasir (b. 2 Sept. 1926), President.

Climate: Very warm and humid. Average temperature 27 °C (80 °F), with little daily variation. Annual rainfall from 100 inches to 150 inches.
Gross domestic product: $10 million in 1970 (estimate).
Monetary unit: Maldivian rupee. 1 rupee = 100 larees (cents).
Exchange rate to US dollar: 7.221 (July 1977).
Political history and government: Formerly an elective sultanate, called the Maldive Islands. Under British protection, with internal self-government, from December 1887 until achieving full independence, outside the Commonwealth, on 26 July 1965. Following a referendum in March 1968, the islands became a republic on 11 Nov. 1968, with Ibrahim Nasir (Prime Minister since 1954) as President. Name changed to Maldives in April 1969. Legislative power is held by the unicameral People's Council (*Majilis*), with 48 members (40 elected for 5 years by universal adult suffrage and 8 appointed by the President). Executive power is vested in the President, elected by universal adult suffrage for 5 years. He rules with the assistance of an appointed Cabinet, responsible to the *Majilis*. The country has 19 administrative districts.
Telephones: 343 (1975).
Radio: 2790 (1976).
Cinemas: 2 (seating capacity 800) in 1969.

MALI

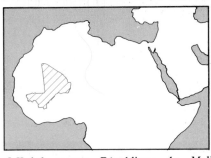

Official name: République du Mali (Republic of Mali).
Population: 6 035 272 (census of Dec. 1976).
Area: 478 767 miles² *1 240 000 km²*.
Languages: French (official language); Bambara 60%; Fulah.
Religions: Sunni Muslim 65%; traditional beliefs 30%.
Capital city: Bamako, population 310 000 (1975 est).
Other principal towns: Mopti 35 000 (1975 est); Ségou 30 000 (1975 est).
Highest point: Hombori Tondo, 3789 ft *1155 m*.
Principal mountain ranges: Mandingue Plateau, Adrar des Iforas.
Principal rivers: Sénégal, Niger, Falémé.
Head of State: Col Moussa Traoré (b. 25 Sept. 1936), President of the Military Committee for National Liberation; also President of the Government (Prime Minister).
Climate: Hot. Very dry in the north, wetter in the south (rainy season June to Oct.). Average temperatures in the south 75 °F to 90 °F, higher in the Sahara. In Bamako, average maximum 87 °F (August) to 103 °F (April), minimum 61 °F to 76 °F. In Timbuktu, average maximum 87 °F (August) to 110 °F (May), minimum 55 °F (Jan.) to 80 °F (June), July and August rainiest (each 9 days).
Labour force: 2 852 000 (1970): Agriculture, forestry and fishing 91·0% (ILO estimates).

Gross Domestic Product: 166 900 million Mali francs in 1971.

Exports: $36·7 million in 1972: Live animals 24·7% (cattle 17·7%); Other food 13·2%; Raw cotton 33·9%.

Monetary unit: Franc malien (Mali franc). 1 franc = 100 centimes.

Denominations:
Coins 5, 10, 25 francs.
Notes 50, 100, 500, 1000, 5000, 10 000 francs.

Exchange rate to US dollar: 485.60 (July 1977).

Political history and government: Formerly French Sudan, part of French West Africa. Joined Senegal to form the Federation of Mali on 4 Apr. 1959. By agreement with France, signed on 4 Apr. 1960, the Federation became independent on 20 June 1960. Senegal seceded on 20 Aug. 1960 and the remnant of the Federation was proclaimed the Republic of Mali on 22 Sept. 1960. The elected National Assembly was dissolved on 17 Jan. 1968. The government was overthrown by an army *coup* on 19 Nov. 1968, when a Military Committee for National Liberation (CMLN) was established. The constitution was abrogated and political parties banned. The CMLN rules by decree with the assistance of an appointed Council of Ministers. The President of the CMLN became also Prime Minister on 19 Sept. 1969. The CMLN published a new constitution on 26 Apr. 1974 and it was approved by referendum on 2 June 1974. This provides for a one-party state with an elected President and National Assembly, but the CMLN will remain in power for a transitional period until 1979. The formation of the ruling party was announced on 22 Sept. 1976. Mali has 19 administrative districts.

Telephones: 5062 (1969).

Daily newspapers: 3 (1968).
Total circulation: 3000.

Radio: 81 000 (1975).

Length of roadways: 9137 miles *14 704 km* (31 Dec. 1974).

Length of railways: 400 miles *645 km.*

Universities: None. There is a polytechnic.

Adult illiteracy: 97·8%.

Expectation of life: Males 36·5 years; females 39·6 years (UN estimates for 1970–75).

Defence: Total armed forces 4200.

Cinemas: 19 (seating capacity 17 100) in 1968.

MALTA

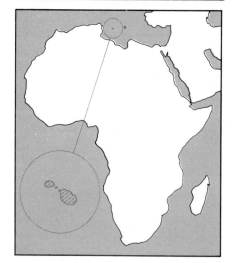

Official name: Repubblika ta Malta (Republic of Malta).

Population: 315 765 (census of 26 Nov. 1967); 327 000 (estimate for 30 Nov. 1976).

Area: 122 miles² *316 km²*, including Gozo (25·9 miles² *67 km²*) and Comino (1·07 miles² *2,77 km²*).

Languages: Maltese, English, Italian.

Religion: Mainly Roman Catholic.

Capital city: Valletta, population 14 049 at 31 Dec. 1974.

Other principal town: Sliema, population 20 120 in 1973.

Highest point: 816 ft *249 m.*

Head of State: Dr Anton Buttigieg (b. 19 Feb. 1912), President.

Prime Minister: Dominic Mintoff (b. 6 Aug. 1916).

Climate: Basically healthy without extremes. The temperature rarely drops below 40 °F, and in most years does not rise above 100 °F. The average annual rainfall in Valletta is 22·7 in. In the summer the nights are cool except when the *Sirocco* desert wind blows from the south-east.

Labour force: 106 642 (including unemployed) aged 14 and over (Nov. 1972): Manufacturing 28·8%; Commerce 12·9%; Services 38·7%.

Gross domestic product: £M131·6 million in 1974: Manufacturing 28·4%; Trade 14·9%; Government services 20·5%.

Exports: $110·5 million (excluding re-exports) in 1974: Textile yarn, fabrics, etc. 10·6%; Clothing (excluding footwear) 45·3%.

Monetary unit: Maltese pound (£M). 1 pound = 100 cents = 1000 mils.

Denominations:
Coins 2, 3, 5 mils, 1, 2, 5, 10, 50 cents.
Notes 1, 5, 10 pounds.

Exchange rate to US dollar: 0.4254 (July 1977).

Political history and government: A former British colony. Became independent, within the Commonwealth, on 21 Sept. 1964. A republic since 13 Dec. 1974, when the Governor-General became President. Legislative power is held by the unicameral House of Representatives, with 65 members elected for 5 years (subject to dissolution) by universal adult suffrage, using proportional representation. The President is a constitutional Head of State, elected for 5 years by the House, and executive power is exercised by the Cabinet. The President appoints the Prime Minister and, on the latter's recommendation, other Ministers. The Cabinet is responsible to the House.

Telephones: 48 984 (1974).

Daily newspapers: 6 (1973).

Radio: 129 000 (1973).

TV: 61 000 (1973).

Length of roadways: 774 miles *1245 km.*

Universities: 1.

Expectation of life: Males 68·10 years; females 72·02 years (1973).

Cinemas: 32 (seating capacity 25 100) and 3 part-time (capacity 1420) in 1973.

MAURITANIA

Official name: République Islamique de Mauritanie (Islamic Republic of Mauritania).

*Population: 1 318 000 (estimate for 1 July 1975).

*Area: 397 955 miles² *1 030 700 km².*

Languages: French, Arabic.

Religion: Muslim.

Capital city: Nouakchott, population 104 000 (including suburbs) at 31 Mar. 1975.

Other principal towns (1975): Nouadhibou (Port-Etienne) 23 000; Zouérate 20 800; Kaédi 20 000; Atar 19 000; Rosso 18 500.

Highest point: Kediet Ijill, 3002 ft *915 m.*

Principal river: Sénégal.

Head of State: Moktar Ould Daddah (b. 20 Dec. 1924), President.

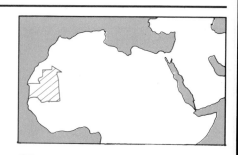

Climate: Hot and dry with breezes on coast. In Nouakchott, average maximum 83 °F to 93 °F. In interior, F'Derik has average July maximum of 109 °F.

Labour force: 363 000 (1970): Agriculture, forestry and fishing 87·3% (ILO estimates).

Gross domestic product: 13 043 million ouguiya in 1973: Agriculture, forestry and fishing (excluding government) 23·5% (agriculture 16·6%); Mining and quarrying 34·5%.

Exports: $119·2 million in 1972: Fish and fish preparations 10·0%; Metalliferous ores and metal scrap 81·3% (iron ore and concentrates 61·5%; copper ores and concentrates 19·8%).

Monetary unit: Ouguiya. 1 ouguiya = 5 khoums.

Denominations:
Coins 1 khoum, 1, 5, 10, 20 ouguiya.
Notes 100, 200, 1000 ouguiya.

Exchange rate to US dollar: 46·17 (June 1977).

Political history and government: Excluding its share of the former Spanish Sahara, Mauritania was formerly part of French West Africa and became independent on 28 Nov. 1960. The constitution was promulgated on 20 May 1961. Since 1964 the *Parti du peuple mauritanien* (PPM) has been the only legal political party. Executive power is held by the President, elected for 5 years by universal adult suffrage (the sole candidate is appointed by the PPM). The President decides and conducts the policy of the government, assisted by an appointed Council of Ministers. Legislative power is held by the unicameral National Assembly, with 70 members elected by universal adult suffrage for 5 years from a single list of PPM candidates. On 28 Feb. 1976 Spain ceded Spanish Sahara to Mauritania and Morocco, to be apportioned between them.

Telephones: 1318 (1968).

Radio: 82 000 (1975).

Length of roadways: 4290 miles *6904 km.* (31 Dec. 1972).

Length of railways: 404 miles *650 km.*

Adult illiteracy: 88·9%.

Expectation of life: Males 37·0 years; females 40·1 years (UN estimates for 1970–75).

Defence: Total armed forces 4750.

Cinemas: 10 (seating capacity 1000) in 1971.

*Figures exclude Mauritania's section of the former Spanish Sahara, partitioned between Mauritania and Morocco in April 1976.

MAURITIUS

Population: 851 335 (census of 30 June 1972); 895 000 (estimate for 30 June 1976).

Area: 789·5 miles² *2045 km².*

Languages (1962): Hindi 35·5%; Creole 31·0%; Urdu 13·2%; French 6·8%; Tamil 6·3%; Chinese 2·8%; Telegu 2·3%; Marathi 1·6%. The official language is English.

Religions (1962): Hindu 47·6%; Christian 35·4%; Muslim 15·8%.

Capital city: Port Louis, population 139 592 at 30 June 1975.

Other principal towns (1975): Beau

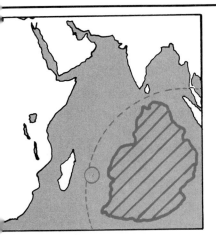

Bassin-Rose Hill 82 951; Curepipe 53 793; Quatre Bornes 52 884; Vacoas-Phoenix 49 825.
Highest point: Piton de la Rivière Noire (Black River Mountain), 2711 ft.
Head of State: H.M. Queen Elizabeth II, represented by Sir Abdul Raman Osman, CMG, CBE (b. 29 Aug. 1902), Governor-General.
Prime Minister: The Rt. Hon Sir Seewoo-sagur Ramgoolam (b. 18 Sept. 1900).
Climate: Generally humid, with south-east trade winds. Average temperatures between 19 °C (66 °F) at 2,000 ft and 23 °C (75 °F) at sea-level. At Vacoas (1394 ft) maximum 37 °C (98·6 °F), minimum 8 °C (46·4 °F). Average annual rainfall between 35 in and 200 in on highest parts. Wettest months are Jan. to Mar. Tropical cyclones between Sept. and May.
Labour force: 260 749 (including un-employed) at 1972 census (island of Mauritius only): Agriculture, forestry and fishing 33·0%; Manufacturing 13·6%; Community, social and personal services 24·7%. The island of Rodrigues had a labour force of 8206.
Gross domestic product: 3105 million rupees (provisional) in 1974: Agriculture, forestry and fishing 48·2%; Manufacturing 14·5%. Revised total is 3216 million rupees.
Exports: $137·8 million in 1973: Sugar and honey 86·6% (raw sugar 76·3%).
Monetary unit: Mauritian rupee. 1 rupee = 100 cents.
Denominations:
   Coins 1, 2, 5, 10, 25, 50 cents, 1 rupee.
   Notes 5, 10, 25, 50 rupees.
Exchange rate to US dollar: 6.582 (July 1977).
Political history and government: A former British colony. Became independent, within the Commonwealth, on 12 Mar. 1968. Executive power is held by the Queen and exercisable by the Governor-General, who is guided by the advice of the Cabinet. Legislative power is held by the unicameral Legislative Assembly, with 71 members: the Speaker, 62 members elected by univer-sal adult suffrage for 5 years and 8 'addi-tional' members (the most successful losing candidates of each community). The Gover-nor-General appoints the Prime Minister and, on the latter's recommendation, other Ministers. The Cabinet is responsible to the Assembly.
Telephones: 24 000 (1974).
Daily newspapers: 16 (1973).
   Total circulation: 100 000.
Radio: 107 000 (1972).
TV: 40 236 (1975).
Length of roadways: 1233 miles *1984 km.*
Universities: 1.
Adult illiteracy: 39·2% (males 28·5%; females 49·9%) in 1962 (population aged 13 and over).

Expectation of life: Males 58·66 years; females 61·86 years (island of Mauritius only) in 1961–63.
Cinemas: 53 (seating capacity 52 000) in 1972.

MEXICO

Official Name: Estados Unidos Mexicanos (United Mexican States).
Population: 48 225 238 (census of 28 Jan. 1970, excluding adjustment for under-enumeration); 62 329 189 (estimate for 30 June 1976).
Area: 761 605 miles² *1 972 547 km².*
Language: Spanish.
Religion: mainly Roman Catholic.
Capital city: Ciudad de México (Mexico City), population 8 628 024 at 30 June 1976.
Other principal towns (1976): Guadala-jara 1 640 902; Monterrey 1 090 226; Ciudad Juárez 544 900; Puebla de Zaragoza 498 886; Tijuana 411 643; Acapulco de Juárez 402 188; Chihuahua 365 760; Mexicali 345 493; Cuernavaca 313 029; San Luis Potosí 292 345; Veracruz Llave 277 305; Hermosillo 264 073; Culiacán Rosales 262 504; Torreón 256 955; León 252 947.
Highest point: Pico de Orizaba (Volcán Citlaltépetl), 18 865 ft *5750 m* (first climbed in 1848).
Principal mountain ranges: Sierra Madre Occidental, Sierra Madre Oriental, Sierra Madre del Sur.
Principal rivers: Rio Bravo del Norte (Rio Grande) (1885 miles [*3033 km*]), Balsas (Mexcala), Grijalva, Pánuco.
Head of State: José López Portillo y Pacheco (b. 16 June 1920), President.
Climate: Tropical (hot and wet) on coastal lowlands and in south, with average tem-perature of 64 °F. Temperate on highlands of central plateau. Arid in north and west. In Mexico City, average maximum 66 °F (December, January) to 78 °F (May), minimum 42 °F (January) to 55 °F (June), July and August rainiest (27 days each). Absolute maximum temperature 58,0 °C (*136·4 °F*), San Luis Potosí, 11 Aug. 1933; absolute minimum −28 °C (−*19·3 °F*), Balerio, 30 Jan. 1949.
Labour force: 16 597 360 aged 12 and over (June 1975): Agriculture, forestry and fishing 40·9%; Manufacturing 17·8%; Com-merce 10·0%; Services (including gas, water, sanitary services and storage) 21·9%.
Gross domestic product: 812 900 million pesos (provisional) in 1974: Manufacturing (excluding basic petroleum manufacturing) 22·7%; Trade, restaurants and hotels 32·8% (trade 30·2%); Community, social and personal services 12·0%. Revised total is 813 700 million pesos.
Exports: $2 631·5 million in 1973: Food and live animals 33·2% (fruit and vegetables 10·2%); Non-ferrous metals 10·0%; Ma-chinery and transport equipment 17·6%.
Monetary unit: Peso. 1 peso = 100 centavos.

Denominations:
   Coins 1, 5, 10, 20, 50 centavos, 1, 5, 10, 25 pesos.
   Notes 1, 5, 10, 20, 50, 100, 500, 1000, 10 000 pesos.
Exchange unit to US dollar: 22.94 (July 1977).
Political history and government: A federal republic of 31 states and a Federal District (around the capital). Present consti-tution was proclaimed on 5 Feb. 1917. Legislative power is vested in the bicameral National Congress. The Senate has 64 members—two from each state and the Federal District—elected by universal adult suffrage for 6 years. The Chamber of Depu-ties has 245 members elected by universal adult suffrage for 3 years. Executive power is held by the President, elected for 6 years by universal adult suffrage at the same time as the Senate. He appoints and leads a cabinet to assist him. Each state is admin-istered by a Governor (elected for 6 years) and an elected Chamber of Deputies.
Telephones: 2 546 186 (1974).
Daily newspapers: 227 (1973).
   Total circulation: Approx. 5 000 000.
Radio: 16 870 000 (1973).
TV: 4 339 000 (1973).
Length of roadways: 116 607 miles *187 660 km* (31 Dec. 1975).
Length of railways: 12 113 miles *19 494 km.*
Universities: 42.
Adult illiteracy: 25·8% (males 21·8%; females 29·6%) in 1970.
Expectation of life: Males 62·76 years; females 66·57 years (1975).
Defence: Military service: voluntary, with part-time conscript militia; total armed forces 89 500 regular and 250 000 part-time conscripts; defence expenditure, 1975: $586 million.
Cinemas: 1937 (seating capacity 1 552 700) and 5 drive-in for 2049 cars (1973).

MONACO

Official name: Principauté de Monaco (Principality of Monaco).
Population: 23 035 (census of 1 Mar. 1968); 25 000 (estimate for 1 July 1975).
Area: 0·73 miles² *1,89 km².*
Language: French.
Religion: Mainly Roman Catholic.
Capital city: Monaco-Ville, population 2422.
Other principal town: Monte Carlo, population 9948 (1968).
Highest point: On Chemin de Révoirés, 533 ft *162 m.*
Principal river: Vésubie.
Head of State: H.S.H. Prince Rainier III (b. 31 May 1923).

Minister of State: André Saint-Mleux.
Climate: Mediterranean, with warm summers (average July maximum 83 °F) and very mild winters (average January minimum 37 °F), 62 rainy days a year (monthly average maximum seven days in winter). Absolute maximum temperature 34 °C (*93·2 °F*), 29 June 1945 and 3 Aug. 1949; absolute minimum −2,3 °C (*27·8 °F*).
Labour force: 10 093 (excluding 232 unemployed) aged 15 and over (1968 census): Manufacturing 14·8%; Commerce 18·7%; Services 55·0%.
Exports: n.a. (included with France).
Monetary unit: French currency (*q.v.*).
Political history and government: An hereditary principality, in close association with France since 2 Feb. 1861. Monaco became a constitutional monarchy on 5 Jan. 1911. The present constitution was promulgated on 17 Dec. 1962. Legislative power is held by the unicameral National Council, with 18 members elected by universal adult suffrage for 5 years. Executive power is vested in the Sovereign and exercised by a 4-man Council of Government, headed by a Minister of State. Monaco comprises 3 *quartiers*.
Telephones: 20 612 (1974).
Radio: 7500 (1973).
TV: 16 200 (1975).
Length of railways: 1 mile *1,6 km*.
Cinemas 2 (seating capacity 1100) in 1970.

MONGOLIA

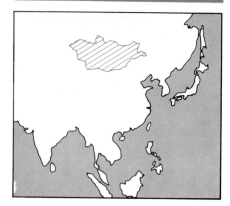

Official name: Bügd Nairamdakh Mongol Ard Uls (Mongolian People's Republic).
Population: 1 197 600 (census of 10 Jan. 1969); 1 511 900 (estimate for 1 Jan. 1977).
Area: 604 250 miles² *1 565 000 km²*.
Languages: Khalkha Mongolian.
Religion: Buddhist.
Capital city: Ulan Bator (Ulaan Baatar), population 334 400 at 1 Jan. 1976.
Other principal town: Darkhan 30 600.
Highest point: Mönh Hayrhan Uul 14 311 ft *4362 m*.
Principal mountain ranges: Altai Mts, Hangayn Nuruu.
Principal rivers: Selenge (Selenga) with Orhon, Hereleng (Kerulen).
Head of State: Marshal Yumzhagiyin Tsedenbal (b. 17 Sept. 1916), Chairman of the Presidium of the People's Great Hural and First Secretary of the Central Committee of the Mongolian People's Revolutionary Party.
Head of Government: Zhambyn Batmunkh (b. 10 Mar. 1926), Chairman of the Council of Ministers.
Climate: Dry. Summers generally mild, winters very cold. In Ulan Bator, July warmest (51 °F to 71 °F) and rainiest (10 days), January coldest (−26 °F to −2 °F).

Labour force: 488 000 (1970): Agriculture, forestry and fishing 61·9% (ILO estimates).
Gross national product: $1000 million in 1975 (World Bank estimate).
Exports: Food products 21·6%; Raw materials for food production 27·2%; Other raw materials 34·9% (1975).
Monetary unit: Tugrik. 1 tugrik = 100 möngö.
Denominations:
　Coins 1, 2, 10, 15, 20, 50 möngö, 1 tugrik.
　Notes 1, 3, 10, 25, 50, 100 tugrik.
Exchange rate to US dollar: 3.30 (May 1977).
Political history and government: Formerly a province of China. With backing from the USSR, the Mongolian People's (Communist) Party—called the Mongolian People's Revolutionary Party (MPRP) since 1924—established a Provisional People's Government on 31 Mar. 1921. After nationalist forces, with Soviet help, overthrew Chinese rule in the capital, independence was proclaimed on 11 July 1921. The USSR recognized the People's Government on 5 Nov. 1921. The Mongolian People's Republic was proclaimed on 26 Nov. 1924 but was not recognized by China. A plebiscite on 20 Oct. 1945 voted 100% for independence, recognized by China on 5 Jan. 1946. A new constitution was adopted on 6 July 1960.

The supreme organ of state power is the People's Great Hural (Assembly), with 354 members elected (unopposed) by universal adult suffrage for 4 years. The Assembly usually meets only twice a year but elects a Presidium (11 members) to be its permanent organ. The Chairman of the Presidium is Head of State. The highest executive body is the Council of Ministers, appointed by (and responsible to) the Assembly.

Political power is held by the MPRP, the only legal party. The MPRP presents a single list of approved candidates for elections to all representative bodies. The MPRP's highest authority is the Party Congress, which elects the Central Committee (91 full members and 61 candidate members were elected in June 1976) to supervise Party work. The Committee elects a Political Bureau (8 full members and 2 candidate members) to direct its policy.

For local administration, Mongolia is divided into 18 provinces and 3 municipalities.
Telephones: 33 500 (1976).
Daily newspapers: 2 (1970).
　Total circulation: 133 000.
Radio: 166 000 (1970).
TV: 33 800 (1976).
Length of roadways: *c.* 46 602 miles *c. 75 000 km*.
Length of railways: 885 miles *1425 km*.
Universities: 1.
Adult illiteracy: 4·6% (population aged 9 to 50) in 1956.
Expectation of life: Males 59·1 years; females 62·3 years (UN estimates for 1970–75).
Defence: Military service: 2 years; total armed forces 30 000; defence expenditure, 1975: $93 million (converted at $1 = 4.00 tugrik).
Cinemas: 17 fixed, 446 mobile (1970).

MOROCCO

Official name: al-Mamlaka al-Maghrebia (Kingdom of Morocco).
*Population: 15 379 259 (census of 20 July 1971); 17 828 000 (estimate for 1 July 1976).
*Area: 172 414 miles² *446 550 km²*.
Languages: Arabic, Berber.
Religions: Muslim, Christian minority.

Capital city: Rabat, population 435 510 (1971), including Salé.
Other principal cities (1971): Casablanca (Ad Dar al Baida) 1 371 330; Marrakech (Marrakesh) 330 400; Fès (Fez) 321 460; Meknès 244 520; Tanger (Tangier) 185 850; Oujda 155 800; Tétouan 137 080; Kénitra 135 960; Safi 129 100.
Highest point: Jebel Toubkal, 13 665 ft *4165 m* (first climbed in 1923).
Principal mountain ranges: Haut (Grand) Atlas, Moyen (Middle) Atlas, Anti Atlas.
Principal rivers: Oued Dra (335 miles *539 km*), Oued Oum-er-Rbia, Oued Moulouya (320 miles *515 km*), Sebou (280 miles *450 km*).
Head of State: H.M. King Hassan II (b. 9 July 1929).
Prime Minister: Dr. Ahmed Osman (b. 3 Jan. 1930).
Climate: Semi-tropical. Warm and sunny on coast, very hot inland. Rainy season November to March. Absolute maximum temperature 51,7 °C (*125·0 °F*), Agadir, 17 Aug. 1940; absolute minimum −24 °C (*−11·2 °F*), Ifrane, 11 Feb. 1935.
Labour force: 3 636 618 (excluding 343 900 unemployed) at 1971 census: Agriculture, forestry and fishing 57·1%; Manufacturing 10·6%; Community, social and personal services 14·4%. Figures for females exclude unreported family helpers in agriculture.
Gross domestic product: 26 700 million dirhams in 1974.
Exports: $1773·5 million in 1974: Food and live animals 21·3% (fruit and vegetables 15·3%); Natural phosphates 54·8%.

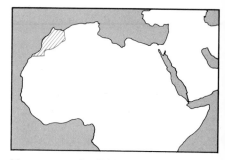

Monetary unit: Dirham. 1 dirham = 100 centimes.
Denominations:
　Coins 1, 2, 5, 10, 20, 50 centimes, 1 dirham.
　Notes 5, 10, 50, 100 dirhams.
Exchange rate to US dollar: 4.470 (July 1977).
Political history and government: An hereditary monarchy, formerly ruled by a Sultan. Most of Morocco (excluding the former Spanish Sahara) became a French protectorate on 30 Mar. 1912. A smaller part in the north became a Spanish protectorate on 27 Nov. 1912. Tangier became an international zone on 18 Dec. 1923. The French protectorate became independent on 2 Mar. 1956 and was joined by the Spanish protectorate on 7 Apr. 1956. The Tangier zone was abolished on 29 Oct. 1956. The Sultan became King on 18 Aug. 1957. The northern strip of Spanish Sahara was ceded to Morocco on 10 Apr. 1958 and the Spanish enclave of Ifni was ceded on 30 June 1969. On 28 Feb. 1976 the rest of Spanish Sahara was ceded to Morocco and Mauritania, to be apportioned between them.

A new constitution, approved by referendum on 1 Mar. 1972 and promulgated on 10 Mar. 1972, provides for a modified constitutional monarchy. Legislative power is vested in a unicameral Chamber of Representatives, with 264 members elected for 4 years (176 by direct universal adult suffrage and 88 by an electoral college). Executive

power is vested in the King, who appoints (and may dismiss) the Prime Minister and other members of the Cabinet. The King can also dissolve the Chamber.
Telephones: 189 000 (1974).
Daily newspapers: 11 (1972).
Total circulation: 234 000 (8 dailies)
Radio: 1 600 000 (1975).
TV: 459 700 (1975).
Length of roadways: 15 792 miles *25 414 km.*
Length of railways: 1091 miles *1756 km.*
Universities: 2.
Adult illiteracy: 78·6% (males 66·4%; females 90·2%) in 1971.
Expectation of life: Males 51·4 years; females 54·5 years (UN estimates for 1970–75).
Defence: Military service: 18 months; total armed forces 73 000; defence expenditure, 1976: $258 million.
Cinemas: 201 (seating capacity 147 000) in 1972.

*Figures exclude Morocco's section of the former Spanish Sahara, partitioned between Mauritania and Morocco in April 1976.

MOZAMBIQUE

Official name: A República Popular de Moçambique (The People's Republic of Mozambique).
Population: 8 233 978 (census of 15 Dec. 1970); 9 444 000 (estimate for 1 July 1976).
Area: 302 330 miles² *783 030 km²*
Languages: Portuguese (official), many African languages.
Religions: Animist; Christian and Muslim minorities.
Capital city: Maputo (formerly Lourenço Marques), population 500 000 (1974 est).
Other principal towns: Sofala (formerly Beira) 150 000 plus; Nacala, Moçambique.
Highest point: Monte Binga, 7992 ft *2436 m.*
Principal mountain range: Lebombo Range.
Principal rivers: Limpopo, Zambezi, Rovuma, Shire.
Head of State: Samora Moïsés Machel (b. Oct. 1933), President.
Climate: Varies from tropical to sub-tropical except in a few upland areas. Rainfall is irregular but the rainy season is usually from November to March, with an average temperature of 83 °F in Maputo. In the dry season, average temperatures are from 65 °F to 68 °F.
Labour force: 2 875 597 (excluding 21 689 persons on compulsory military service and 30 320 unemployed) at 1970 census: Agriculture, forestry and fishing 74·3%.
Gross domestic product: $1872 million in 1970 (UN estimate).
Exports: $175·0 million in 1972: Fruit and vegetables 27·2% (preserved and prepared fruit 17·2%); Sugar and honey 13·1%; Other food 15·5%; Textile fibres and waste 15·0% (raw cotton 13·6%).

Monetary unit: Mozambique escudo. 1 escudo = 100 centavos.
Denominations:
Coins 10, 20, 50 centavos, 1, 2½, 5, 10, 20 escudos.
Notes 50, 100, 500, 1000 escudos.
Exchange rate to US dollar: 38.48 (July 1977).
Political history and government: Formerly a Portuguese colony, independent since 25 June 1975. The independence movement was dominated by the *Frente de Libertação de Moçambique* (FRELIMO), the Mozambique Liberation Front. Before independence FRELIMO was recognized by Portugal and its leader became the first President. The independence constitution proclaims that FRELIMO is the directing power of the state and of society. Legislative power is vested in the People's Assembly, with 210 members, mainly FRELIMO officials, indirectly elected on 4 Dec. 1977. The President appoints and leads a Council of Ministers. Mozambique has 11 provinces.
Telephones: 55 708 (1974).
Daily newspapers: 5 (1973).
Total circulation: 42 000.
Radio: 200 000 (1975).
TV: 1000 (1974).
Length of roadways: 24 341 miles *39 173 km* (31 Dec. 1974).
Length of railways: 2301 miles *3703 km.*
Universities: 1
Adult illiteracy: 85–95% (est).
Expectation of life: Males 41·9 years; females 45·1 years (UN estimates for 1970–75).
Defence: National Defence Force.
Cinemas: 31 (seating capacity 20 195) in 1971.

NAURU

Official name: The Republic of Nauru.
Population: 6057 (census of 30 June 1966); 7500 (estimate for 30 June 1976).
Area: 8·2 miles² *21 km².*
Languages: English, Nauruan.
Religions: Protestant, Roman Catholic.
Highest point: 225 ft *68 m.*
Head of State: Bernard Dowiyogo (b. 14 Feb. 1946), President.
Climate: Warm and pleasant.
Labour force: 2504 aged 15 and over (1966 census).
Monetary unit: Australian currency (*qv*).
Political history and government: Annexed by Germany in December 1888. Captured by Australian forces in November 1914. Administered by Australia under League of Nations mandate (17 Dec. 1920) and later as a UN Trust Territory. Independent since 31 Jan. 1968. Nauru's first President was elected on 19 May 1968. Legislative power is held by a unicameral Parliament, with 18 members elected by universal adult suffrage for up to 3 years. Executive power is held by the President, who is elected by Parliament for its duration and rules with the assistance of an appointed Cabinet, responsible to Parliament. Nauru is a 'special member' of the Commonwealth.
Length of roadways: 12 miles *19 km.*
Length of railways: 3¼ miles *5 km.*
Radio: 3600 (1975)
Cinemas: 2 (seating capacity 800) in 1973.

NEPAL

Official name: Sri Nepāla Sarkār (Kingdom of Nepal).
Population: 11 555 983 (census of 22 June 1971); 12 904 000 (estimate for 22 June 1976).

Area: 54 362 miles² *140 797 km².*
Languages (1971): Nepali (official) 52·4%; Maithir 11·5%; Bhojpuri 7·0%; Tamang 4·8%; Tharu 4·3%; Newari 3·9%; Abadhi 2·7%; Magar 2·5%; Raikirati 2·0%.
Religions (1971): Hindu 89·4%; Buddhist 7·5%; Muslim 3·0%.
Capital city: Kathmandu, population 150 402 (1971); 353 756 (incl. suburbs).
Other principal towns (1971, including suburbs): Morang 301 557; Lalitpur 154 998; Patan 135 230; Bhaktapur 110 157.
Highest point: Mount Everest, 29 028 ft *8848 m* (on Chinese border). First climbed 29 May 1953.
Principal mountain range: Nepal Himalaya (Mahabharat Range).
Principal rivers: Karnali, Naryani, Kosi.
Head of State: H.M. King Birenda Bir Bikram Shah Dev (b. 28 Dec. 1945).
Prime Minister: Kirti Nidhi Bista (b. 27 Jan. 1927).
Climate: Varies sharply with altitude, from Arctic in Himalaya to humid subtropical in the central Vale of Kathmandu (annual average 52 °F), which is warm and sunny in summer. Rainy season June to October. In Kathmandu, average maximum 65 °F (January) to 86 °F (May), minimum 35 °F (January) to 68 °F (July, August), July (21 days) and August (20 days) rainiest. Maximum temperature recorded in Kathmandu is 99 °F (2 May 1960) and minimum is 26 °F (20 Jan. 1964).
Labour force: 4 852 524 (1971 census): Agriculture, forestry and fishing 94·4%.
Gross domestic product: 13 128 million rupees (at factor cost) in 1973/74: Agriculture, forestry and fishing 69·1%.
Exports: 1147·9 million rupees in 1975/76: Food and live animals 61·2%.
Monetary unit: Nepalese rupee. 1 rupee = 100 paisa.
Denominations:
Coins 1, 2, 5, 10, 25, 50 paisa, 1 rupee.
Notes 1, 5, 10, 100, 500, 1000 rupees.
Exchange rate to US dollar: 12.525 (July 1977).

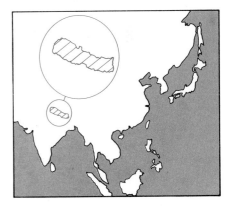

Political history and government: A hereditary kingdom. A limited constitutional monarchy was proclaimed on 18 Feb. 1951. In a royal *coup* on 15 Dec. 1960 the King dismissed the Cabinet and dissolved Parliament. A royal proclamation of 5 Jan. 1961 banned political parties. The present constitution was adopted on 16 Dec. 1962. Executive power is vested in the King but is normally exercised on the advice of an appointed Council of Ministers. Legislative power is held by the unicameral *Rashtriya Panchayat* (National Assembly) with 135 members (112 indirectly elected by zonal assemblies for staggered 4-year terms and 23 nominated by the King). All Ministers must be members of the National Assembly. Nepal comprises 14 zones, each administered by an appointed Commissioner.

Telephones: 9162 (1974).
Daily newspapers: 26 (1973).
Total circulation: c. 39 000.
Radio: 180 000 (1976).
Length of roadways: 1860 miles *c. 3000 km.*
Length of railways: 63 miles *101 km.*
Universities: 1.
Adult illiteracy: 87·5% (males 77·6%; females 97·4%) in 1971.
Expectation of life: Males 42·2 years; females 45·0 years (UN estimates for 1970–75).
Defence: Military service: voluntary; total armed forces 20 000; defence expenditure, 1973/74: $8 million.

THE NETHERLANDS (Holland)

Official name: Koninkrijk der Nederlanden (Kingdom of the Netherlands).
Population: 13 045 785 (census of 28 Feb. 1971); 13 810 000 (estimate for 1 Dec. 1976).
Area: 15 770 miles² *40 844 km².*
Language: Dutch.
Religions: Roman Catholic, Dutch Reformed Church.
Capital city: Amsterdam, population 751 156 (1976). The seat of government is 's Gravenhage (Den Haag or The Hague), population 479 369 (1976).
Other principal towns (1976): Rotterdam 614 767; Utrecht 250 887; Eindhoven 192 562; Haarlem 164 672; Groningen 163 357; Tilburg 151 513; Nijmegen 148 493; Enschede 141 597; Apeldoorn 134 055; Arnhem 126 051; Zaanstad 124 795; Breda 118 086; Maastricht 111 044; Dordrecht 101 840.
Highest point: Vaalserberg, 1053 ft *321 m.*
Principal rivers: Maas (Meuse), Waal (Rhine) (820 miles *1319 km*), IJssel.
Head of State: H.M. Queen Juliana Louise Emma Marie Wilhelmina, KG (b. 30 Apr. 1909).
Prime Minister: Andries A. M. van Agt (b. 2 Feb. 1931).
Climate: Temperate, generally between 0 °F and 70 °F. Often foggy and windy. In Amsterdam, average maximum 40 °F (January) to 69 °F (July), minimum 34 °F (January, February) to 59 °F (July, August). November, December, January rainiest (each 19 days). Absolute maximum temperature 38,6 °C (*101·5 °F*), Warnsveld, 23 Aug. 1944; absolute minimum −27,4 °C (*−17·3 °F*), Winterswijk, 27 Jan. 1942.
Labour force: 4 735 000 (excluding 55 000 unemployed) at 1971 census (sample tabulation): Manufacturing 26·2%; Construction 11·9%; Trade, restaurants and hotels 18·3%; Community, social and personal services 23·0%.
Gross domestic product: 146 730 million guilders in 1972: Manufacturing (including production of crude petroleum and natural gas) 30·0%; Trade, restaurants and hotels (excluding repairs) 12·7% (trade 11·7%); Community, social and personal services (including repairs) 23·2%.
Exports: $34 956·6 million in 1975: Food and live animals 20·1%; Petroleum and petroleum products 12·0% (petroleum products 11·8%); Chemicals 14·5%; Machinery and transport equipment 18·8%.
Monetary unit: Netherlands gulden (guilder) or florin. 1 guilder = 100 cents.
Denominations:
Coins 1, 5, 10, 25 cents, 1, 2½, 10 guilders.
Notes 1, 2½, 5, 10, 25, 100, 1000 guilders.
Exchange rate to US dollar: 2.443 (July 1977).

Political history and government: A constitutional and hereditary monarchy. Legislative power is held by the bicameral States-General. The First Chamber has 75 members indirectly elected for 6 years (half retiring every 3 years) by members of the 11 Provincial Councils. The Second Chamber has 150 members directly elected by universal suffrage for 4 years (subject to dissolution), using proportional representation. The Head of State has mainly formal prerogatives and executive power is exercised by the Council of Ministers, led by the Prime Minister, which is responsible to the States-General. Each of the 11 provinces is administered by an appointed Governor and an elected Council.

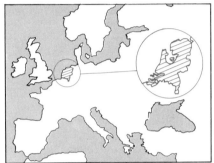

Telephones: 5 047 000 (1975).
Daily newspapers: 93 (1973).
Total circulation: 4 175 000.
Radio: 3 900 000 (1975).
TV: 3 646 000 (1975).
Length of roadways: 53 470 miles *86 052 km* (31 Dec. 1975).
Length of railways: 1760 miles *2834 km.*
Universities: 8 (plus 3 technical universities and 4 colleges of university standing).
Expectation of life: Males 71·2 years; females 77·2 years (1973).
Defence: Military service: Army 14 months, Navy and Air Force 18–21 months; total armed forces 112 200 (including 59 400 conscripts); defence expenditure, 1976: $2895 million.
Cinemas: 381 (including one drive-in) with seating capacity of 176 500 (1973).

NEW ZEALAND

Official name: Dominion of New Zealand.
Population: 3 129 383 (census of 23 Mar. 1976); 3 148 000 (estimate for 31 Dec. 1976).
Area: 103 736 miles² *268 676 km².*
Languages: English, Maori.
Religions: Church of England, Presbyterian, Roman Catholic.
Capital city: Wellington, population 141 800 (1974 est); 354 660, including suburbs, in 1975.
Other principal towns (including suburbs, 1974): Auckland 775 460; Christchurch 320 530; Hamilton 147 450; Dunedin 119 870; Napier-Hastings 105 460; Palmerston North 85 270.
Highest point: Mt Cook, 12 349 ft *3764 m.*
Principal mountain range: Southern Alps.
Principal rivers: Waikato, Clutha (210 miles [*338 km*]), Waihou, Rangitaiki, Mokau, Wanganui, Rangitikei, Manawatu.
Head of State: H.M. Queen Elizabeth II, represented by the Rt Hon Sir Keith Jacka Holyoake, GCMG, CH (b. 11 Feb. 1904), Governor-General.
Prime Minister: The Rt Hon Robert David Muldoon, CH (b. 21 Sept. 1921).
Climate: Temperate and moist. Moderate temperatures (annual average 52 °F) except

in the hotter far north. Small seasonal variations. In Wellington, January and February warmest (56 °F to 69 °F), July coolest (42 °F to 53 °F) and rainiest (18 days), February driest (nine days). In Auckland, average maximum 56 °F (July) to 73 °F (January, February), minimum 46 °F (July, August) to 60 °F (January, February), July rainiest (21 days).
Labour force: 1 206 000 (excluding 11 100 in armed forces and 4900 unemployed) aged 15 and over (April 1976): Agriculture, forestry and fishing 11·8%; Manufacturing 24·8%; Trade, restaurants and hotels 16·0%; Community, social and personal services 22·4%. Figures exclude armed forces overseas.
Gross domestic product: $NZ11 029 million in 1975/76.
Exports: US$2 437·3 million in 1974: Fresh, chilled or frozen meat 27·1% (cattle meat 10·8%; sheep and goats' meat 14·3%); Dairy products and eggs 17·2%; Wool 19·8% (greasy wool 12·1%).
Monetary unit: New Zealand dollar ($NZ). 1 dollar = 100 cents.
Denominations:
Coins 1, 2, 5, 10, 20, 25, 50 cents.
Notes 1, 2, 5, 10, 20, 100 dollars.
Exchange rate to US dollar: 1.027 (July 1977).
Political history and government: A former British colony. Became a dominion, under the British crown, on 26 Sept. 1907. Fully independent, within the Commonwealth, under the Statute of Westminster, promulgated in the United Kingdom on 11 Dec. 1931 and accepted by New Zealand on 25 Nov. 1947. Executive power is vested in the Queen and exercisable by the Governor-General, who must be guided by the advice of the Executive Council (Cabinet), led by the Prime Minister. Legislative power is held by the unicameral House of Representatives, with 87 members (including 4 Maoris) elected for 3 years by universal adult suffrage. The Governor-General appoints the Prime Minister and, on the latter's recommendation, other Ministers. The Cabinet is responsible to the House.
Telephones: 1 494 587 (1974).
Daily newspapers: 40 (1973).
Radio: 2 704 000 (1975).
TV: 815 822 (February 1977).
Length of roadways: 57 169 miles *92 005 km* (31 Mar. 1973).
Length of railways: 2912 miles *4687 km* (31 Mar. 1977).
Universities: 6.
Expectation of life: Males 68·55 years; females 74·60 years (1970–72).
Defence: Military service: voluntary, supplemented by Territorial service of 12 weeks for the Army; total armed forces 12 575; defence expenditure, 1975/76: US$243 million.
Cinemas: 238 (seating capacity 135 700) in 1973.

NICARAGUA

Official name: República de Nicaragua.
Population: 1 877 952 (census of 20 Apr. 1971); 2 233 000 (estimate for 30 June 1976).
Area: 50 193 miles² *130 000 km².*
Language: Spanish.
Religion: Roman Catholic.
Capital city: Managua, population 398 514 (1971).
Other principal towns: León 119 347; Granada 100 334; Masaya 96 830; Chinandega 95 437; Matagalpa 65 928.
Highest point: Pico Mogotón (6913 ft *2107 m*).

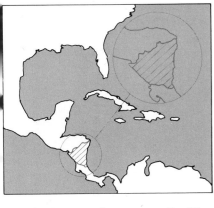

Principal mountain ranges: Cordillera Isabelia, Cordillera de Darién.

Principal rivers: Coco (Segovia) (300 miles [*482 km*]), Rio Grande, Escondido, San Juan.

Head of State: Gen Anastásio Somoza Debayle (b. 5 Dec. 1925), President.

Climate: Tropical (hot and humid) with average annual temperature of 78 °F. Rainy season May–December. Annual rainfall 100 in on east coast. In Managua, annual average over 80 °F all year round.

Labour force: 505 445 aged 10 and over (1971 census); Agriculture, forestry and fishing 47·8%; Manufacturing 12·6%; Community, social and personal services 20·1%.

Gross domestic product: 10 901 million córdobas in 1975: Agriculture, forestry and fishing 22·4%; Manufacturing 22·4%; Trade 20·9%.

Exports: $274·7 million in 1973: Meat and meat preparations 16·4% (fresh, chilled or frozen beef 16·2%); Coffee 16·3%; Other food 16·0%; Textile fibres and waste 23·5% (raw cotton 23·0%).

Monetary unit: Córdoba. 1 córdoba = 100 centavos.

Denominations:
Coins 5, 10, 25, 50 centavos, 1 córdoba.
Notes 1, 5, 10, 20, 50, 100, 500, 1000 córdobas.

Exchange rate to US dollar: 7.026 (July 1977).

Political history and government: A republic comprising 16 departments and one territory. A new constitution was approved by a Constituent Assembly on 14 Mar. 1974 and signed by the government on 3 Apr. 1974. Legislative power is vested in the bicameral National Congress, comprising a Senate of 30 members and a Chamber of Deputies (70 members), elected for 6 years by universal adult suffrage. Executive power is held by the President, also directly elected for 6 years. He appoints and leads a Council of Ministers.

Telephones: 20 447 (1974).

Daily newspapers: 6 (1973).
Total circulation: 53 000 (3 dailies).

Radio: 125 000 (1973).

TV: 70 000 (1975).

Length of roadways: 8169 miles *13 147 km.* (1971).

Length of railways: 198 miles *318 km.*

Universities: 2.

Adult illiteracy: 50·2% (males 49·9%; females 50·4%) in 1963.

Expectation of life: Males 51·2 years; females 54·6 years (UN estimates for 1970–75).

Defence: Total armed forces 7100.

Cinemas: Over 100 with seating capacity of over 60 000 (1965).

NIGER

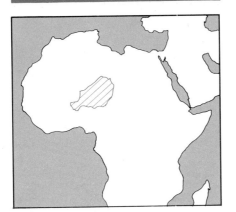

Official name: République du Niger.

Population: 4 727 000 (estimate for 1 July 1976).

Area: 489 191 miles² *1 267 000 km².*

Languages: French (official), Hausa, Tuareg, Djerma, Fulani.

Religions: Muslim 85%; Animist, Christian.

Capital city: Niamey, population 130 299 (1975 estimate).

Other principal towns (1975): Maradi 42 000; Zinder 40 000; Tahoua 30 000.

Highest point: Mont Gréboun, 6562 ft *2000 m.*

Principal mountain ranges: Aïr ou Azbine, Plateau du Djado.

Principal rivers: Niger (370 miles *595 km* in Niger), Dillia.

Head of State: Lt-Col Seyni Kountché (b. 1930), President of the Supreme Military Council.

Climate: Hot and dry. Average temperature 84 °F. In Niamey, average maximum 93 °F (January) to 108 °F (April).

Labour force: 1 313 000 (1970): Agriculture, forestry and fishing 92·8% (ILO estimates).

Gross domestic product: 97 808 million CFA francs in 1969: Agriculture, forestry and fishing 51·2%; Trade, restaurants and hotels 14·7%.

Exports: $52.6 million in 1974: Live animals 16·6% (cattle 12·4%); Metalliferous ores and metal scrap 50·1%.

Monetary unit: Franc de la Communauté financière africaine.

Denominations:
Coins 1, 2, 5, 10, 25, 50, 100 CFA francs.
Notes 100, 500, 1000, 5000 CFA francs.

Exchange rate to US dollar: 242.8 (July 1977).

Political history and government: Formerly part of French West Africa, independent since 3 Aug. 1960. Under military rule since 15 Apr. 1974, when the constitution was suspended and the National Assembly dissolved. Niger is ruled by a Supreme Military Council, composed of army officers, which has appointed a provisional government. The country has 16 administrative districts.

Telephones: 5000 (1974).

Daily newspapers: 2 (1973).
Total circulation: 2000.

Radio: 150 000 (1971).

Length of roadways: 4340 miles *6985 km* (31 Dec. 1975).

Universities: 1.

Adult illiteracy: 96% (est.).

Expectation of life: Males 37·0 years; females 40·1 years (UN estimates for 1970–75).

Defence: Total armed forces 2100.

Cinemas: 4 (seating capacity 3800) in 1970.

NIGERIA

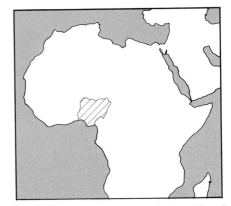

Official name: The Federal Republic of Nigeria.

Population: 64 750 000 (UN estimate for mid-1976).

Area: 356 669 miles² *923 768 km².*

Languages: English (official), Hausa, Ibo, Yoruba and other linguistic groups.

Religions: Muslim, Christian.

Capital city: Lagos, population 1 060 848 at 1 July 1975.

Other principal towns (1975): Ibadan 847 000; Ogbomosho 432 000; Kano 399 000; Oshogbo 282 000; Ilorin 282 000; Abeokuta 253 000; Port Harcourt 242 000; Zaria 224 000; Ilesha 224 000; Onitsha 220 000; Iwo 214 000; Ado-Ekiti 213 000; Kaduna 202 000; Mushin 197 000.

Highest point: Dimlang, 6700 ft *2042 m.*

Principal rivers: Niger (2600 miles [*4184 km*] in total length), Benue, Cross.

Head of State: Lt-Gen Olusegun Obasanjo (b. 5 Mar. 1937), Head of the Federal Military Government and Commander-in-Chief of the Armed Forces.

Climate: On the coast it is hot (average daily maximum temperature at Lagos 89 °F) and unpleasantly humid. In the north it is drier and semi-tropical. Annual rainfall ranges from 25 to 150 inches.

Labour force: 22 533 000 (1970): Agriculture, forestry and fishing 62·2% (ILO estimates).

Gross domestic product: 8900·5 million naira (provisional) in 1973/74: Agriculture forestry and fishing 36·9% (agriculture 30·3%); Mining and quarrying 23·5%; Trade 10·4%. Revised total is 9119·6 million naira.

Exports: $9169·7 million (excluding re-exports) in 1974: Petroleum and petroleum products 93·0% (crude and partly refined petroleum 92·8%).

Monetary unit: Naira. 1 naira = 100 kobo.

Denominations:
Coins ½, 1, 5, 10, 25 kobo.
Notes 50 kobo, 1, 5, 10 naira.

Exchange rate to US dollar: 0.651 (July 1977).

Political history and government: Formerly a British dependency. Independent, within the Commonwealth, since 1 Oct. 1960. Became a republic on 1 Oct. 1963. Under military rule since 15 Jan. 1966, when the bicameral Federal Parliament was abolished. Political parties were banned on 24 May 1966. Legislative and executive functions are vested in the Supreme Military Council (SMC), which rules by decree. The SMC's Chairman is Head of State and Government. The SMC delegates powers to the Federal Executive Council, with Commissioners in charge of government Ministries. The SMC published a draft constitution on 7 Oct.

1976. Local government councils were elected (directly in some States, indirectly in others) in Nov.–Dec. 1976. A constituent assembly of 233 members (203 selected by the local councils on 31 Aug. 1977, 22 nominated by the SMC and 8 from the constitutional drafting committee) was inaugurated on 6 Oct. 1977 to finalize the constitution in preparation for a return to civilian rule by 1 Oct. 1979. Political parties are banned until October 1978. Nigeria comprises 19 States, each administered by a Military Governor.
Telephones: 111 478 (1974).
Daily newspapers: 17 (1973).
    Total circulation: 213 000 (7 dailies).
Radio: 5 000 000 (1975).
TV: 100 000 (1975).
Length of roadways: 55 242 miles *88 904 km* (31 Dec. 1971).
Length of railways: 2178 miles *3505 km.*
Universities: 6.
Adult illiteracy: 88·5% in 1952–53 (population aged 7 and over).
Expectation of life: Males 39·4 years; females 42·6 years (UN estimates for 1970–75).
Defence: Military service: voluntary; total armed forces 230 000; defence expenditure, 1976/77: $2434 million.
Cinemas: 112 (seating capacity 56 000) in 1973.

NORWAY

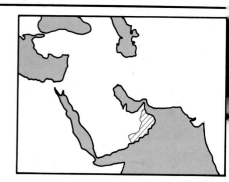

Official name: Kongeriket Norge (Kingdom of Norway).
Population: 3 874 133 (census of 1 Nov. 1970); 4 027 000 (estimate for 30 June 1976).
Area: 125 182 miles² *324 219 km².*
Languages: Norwegian; small Lappish minority.
Religion: Lutheran.
Capital city: Oslo, population 463 022 at 1 Jan. 1976.
Other principal towns (1975): Bergen 213 594; Trondheim 134 889; Stavanger 86 643; Kristiansand 59 477; Drammen 50 771.
Highest point: Galdhopiggen (8100 ft *2469 m*).
Principal mountain range: Langfjellene.
Principal rivers: Glomma (Glama) (380 miles *611 km*), Lågen (224 miles *360 km*), Tanaelv (213 miles *342 km*).
Head of State: HM King Olav V, KG, KT, GCB, GCVO (b. 2 July 1903).
Prime Minister: Odvar Nordli (b. 3 Nov. 1927).
Climate: Temperate on coast, but cooler inland. In Oslo, average maximum 30 °F (January) to 73 °F (July), minimum 20 °F (January, February) to 56 °F (July), August rainiest (11 days). Absolute maximum temperature 35,0 °C (*95·0 °F*), Oslo, 21 July 1901, and Trondheim, 22 July 1901; absolute minimum −51,4 °C (*−60·5 °F*), Karasjok, 1 Jan. 1886.
Labour force: 1 694 000 (excluding persons on compulsory military service and 40 000 unemployed) aged 16 to 74 (1975): Agriculture, forestry and fishing 10·2%; Manufac-

turing 23·9%; Trade, restaurants and hotels 15·5%; Community, social and personal services 26·5%.
Gross domestic product: 128 762 million kroner (provisional) in 1974: Manufacturing 23·5%; Trade, restaurants and hotels 14·2% (trade 12·8%); Transport, storage and communication (including oil pipelines) 15·3%; Community, social and personal services 17·9%. Revised total is 128 934 million kroner.
Exports: $7206·6 million in 1975: Mineral fuels, lubricants, etc. 13·0% (petroleum and petroleum products 12·3%); Machinery 10·6%; Transport equipment 21·9% (ships and boats 20·9%).
Monetary unit: Norwegian krone. One krone = 100 øre.
Denominations:
    Coins 1, 2, 5, 10, 25, 50 øre. 1, 5 kroner.
    Notes 5, 10, 50, 100, 500, 1000 kroner.
Exchange rate to US dollar: 5.2575 (July 1977).
Political history and government: Formerly linked with Sweden. Independence declared on 7 June 1905; union with Sweden ended on 26 Oct. 1905. Norway is a constitutional monarchy, headed by an hereditary King. Legislative power is held by the unicameral Parliament (*Storting*), with 155 members elected for 4 years by universal adult suffrage, using proportional representation. The members choose one quarter of their number to form the *Lagting* (upper house), the remainder forming the *Odelsting* (lower house). Executive power is nominally held by the King but is exercised by the Council of Ministers, led by the Prime Minister, who are appointed by the King in accordance with the will of the *Storting*, to which the Council is responsible. Norway comprises 19 counties.
Telephones: 1 406 995 (1975).
Daily newspapers: 71 (1975).
    Total circulation: 1 574 000.
Radio: 1 299 518 (1975).
TV: 1 051 125 (1975).
Length of roadways: 47 908 miles *77 101 km* (31 Dec. 1975).
Length of railways: 2635 miles *4241 km.*
Universities: 4, and 6 institutions equivalent to universities.
Expectation of life: Males 71·32 years; females 77·60 years (1972–73).
Defence: Military service: Army 12 months, Navy and Air Force 15 months; total armed forces 39 000 (including 25 000 conscripts); defence expenditure, 1976: $896 million.
Cinemas: 430 (seating capacity 138 800) in 1973.

OMAN

Official name: Sultant 'Uman (Sultanate of Oman).
Population: 600 000 (estimate for 1 July 1972).
Area: 83 000 miles² *212 457 km².*
Language: Arabic.
Religion: Muslim.
Capital city: Masqat (Muscat), population 25 000 (with port of Matrah).
Other principal towns: Matrah (14 000 in 1960); Salalah.
Highest point: Jabal ash Sham, 10 400 ft *3170 m.*
Principal mountain range: Jabal Akhdas ('Green Mountains').
Head of State: Sultan Qaboos bin Said (b. 18 Nov. 1940).
Climate: Extremely hot summers (temperatures rising to 130 °F) and mild winters. Cooler in the mountains. Average annual rainfall 3 to 6 in.

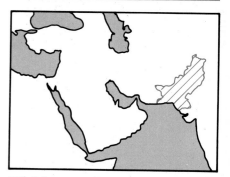

Gross domestic product: 144·5 million rials (provisional) in 1971: Agriculture, forestry and fishing 11·6%; Mining and quarrying 65·0%; Construction 14·5%. Revised total is 125·1 million rials.
Exports: $1575 million in 1976.
Monetary unit: Rial Omani. 1 rial = 1000 baiza.
Denominations:
    Coins 2, 5, 10, 25, 50, 100 baiza.
    Notes 100, 250, 500 baiza, 1, 5, 10 rials.
Exchange rate to US dollar: 0.3454 (July 1977).
Political history and government: A sultanate, formerly called Muscat and Oman, under British influence since the 19th century. Full independence was recognised by the treaty of friendship with the UK on 20 Dec. 1951. The present Sultan deposed his father on 23 July 1970 and the country adopted its present name on 9 Aug. 1970. The Sultan is an absolute ruler and legislates by decree. He is advised by an appointed Cabinet. The country has no parliament and no political parties. Oman is divided into 37 *wilayet* (governorates).
Telephones: 4 300 (1974).
Length of roadways: 3900 miles *6300 km.*
Expectation of life: Males 45·8 years; females 48·3 years (UN estimates, average for Bahrain, Oman, Qatar and the United Arab Emirates, 1970–75).
Defence: Military service: voluntary; total armed forces 14 150 (excluding expatriate personnel); defence expenditure, 1976: $768 million.

PAKISTAN

Official name: The Islamic Republic of Pakistan ('Pakistan' means 'land of the pure' in the Urdu language).
*Population: 64 979 732 (census of 16 Sept. 1972); 72 368 000 (estimate for 1 July 1976).
*Area: 310 404 miles² *803 943 km².*
Languages: Punjabi, Urdu, Sindhi, Pushtu.
Religions: Muslim 97·1%; Hindu 1·6%; Christian 1·3% (1961).
Capital city: Islamabad, population 77 318 (1972 census).
Other principal towns (1972): Karachi 3 498 634; Lahore 2 165 372; Faisalabad

(Lyallpur) 822 263; Hyderabad 628 310; Rawalpindi 615 392; Multan 542 195; Gujranwala 360 419; Peshawar 268 366.

Highest point: K2 (Mt Godwin Austen), 28 250 ft *8611 m* (first climbed 31 July 1954).

Principal mountain ranges: Hindu Kush, Pamirs, Karakoram.

Principal rivers: Indus and tributaries (Sutlej, Chenab, Ravi, Jhelum).

Head of State: Fazal Elahi Chaudhry (b. 1 Jan. 1904), President.

Head of Government: Gen Mohammad Zia ul-Haq (b. 1924), Chief Martial Law Administrator.

Climate: Dry, and generally hot, with average temperature of 80 °F except in the mountains, which have very cold winters. Temperatures range from 30 °F in winter to 120 °F in summer. In Karachi, June warmest (average 82 °F to 93 °F), January coolest (55 °F to 77 °F), rainfall negligible throughout the year. In Lahore, average maximum 69 °F (January) to 106 °F (June), minimum 40 °F (December, January) to 80 °F (July), July and August rainiest (each six days). Absolute maximum temperature 127·0 °F (*52,8 °C*), Jacobabad, 12 June 1919.

Labour force: 20 092 600 (excluding unemployed) in January 1974: Agriculture, forestry and fishing 59·2%; Manufacturing 12·9%; Trade, restaurants and hotels 10·2%.

Gross domestic product: 85 724 million rupees (provisional) in 1973/74: Agriculture, forestry and fishing 35·4% (agriculture 34·5%); Manufacturing 15·5%; Trade 15·4%; Community, social and personal services (including restaurants and hotels) 14·5%. Revised total is 85 598 million rupees.

Exports: $1118·1 million in 1974: Cereals and cereal preparations 26·4% (rice 26·1%); Textile yarn, fabrics, etc. 33·7% (textile yarn and thread 11·1%; woven cotton fabrics 11·9%).

Monetary unit: Pakistani rupee. 1 rupee = 100 paisa.

Denominations:
Coins 1, 2, 5, 10, 25, 50 paisa, 1 rupee.
Notes 1, 5, 10, 50, 100 rupees.

Exchange rate to US dollar: 9.931 (July 1977).

Political history and government: Pakistan was created as an independent dominion within the Commonwealth on 15 Aug. 1947, when former British India was partitioned. Originally in two parts, East and West Pakistan, the country became a republic on 23 Mar. 1956. Military rule was imposed on 27 Oct. 1958. Elections for a Constituent Assembly were held on 7 Dec. 1970, giving a majority to the Awami League, which sought autonomy for East Pakistan. After negotiations on a coalition government failed, East Pakistan declared independence as Bangladesh on 26 Mar. 1971. Following Indian intervention on behalf of the Bengalis, Pakistan's forces surrendered on 16 Dec. 1971, when Bangladesh's independence became a reality. Pakistan was confined to the former western wing. Military rule ended on 20 Dec. 1971. Pakistan left the Commonwealth on 30 Jan. 1972. A new constitution came into force on 14 Aug. 1973. Pakistan is a federal republic comprising four provinces (each under a Governor) plus the Federal Capital Territory and 'tribal areas' under federal administration. The bicameral Federal Legislature comprises a mainly advisory Senate (45 members, mostly elected by provincial assemblies) and a National Assembly of 216 members (200 directly elected by universal adult suffrage for 5 years plus 10 women and 6 representatives of non-Muslim minorities elected by the Assembly). The constitution provides for an increase in Senate membership to 63.

Under the constitution, the chief executive is the Prime Minister, elected by the Assembly. His advice is binding on the President, a constitutional Head of State elected at a joint sitting of the Legislature. The Prime Minister and his appointed Cabinet are answerable to the Legislature. Each province has its own elected Assembly, a Chief Minister and a Cabinet.

On 5 July 1977 the government was deposed by a military *coup*. A four-man Military Council was formed to assist the President. The national and provincial legislatures were dissolved and elections have been postponed indefinitely.

Telephones: 210 000 (1974).
Daily newspapers: 71 (1972).
Radio: 1 100 000 (1975).
TV: 415 033 (1976).
Length of roadways: 39 043 miles *62 834 km* (31 Dec. 1972).
Length of railways: 5475 miles *8811 km*.
Universities: 15.
Adult illiteracy: 81·2% (males 71·1%; females 92·6%) in 1961 (including Bangladesh).
Expectation of life: Males 49·9 years; females 49·6 years (UN estimates for 1970–75).
Defence: Military service: two years, selective; total armed forces 428 000; defence expenditure, 1976/77: $807 million.
Cinemas: 578 (seating capacity 300 000) and one drive-in for 1000 cars (1972).

* Excluding the disputed territory of Jammu and Kashmir. The Pakistan-held part has an area of 32 358 miles² *83 807 km²*.

PANAMA

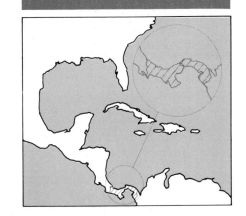

Official name: La República de Panamá.
*Population: 1 428 082 (census of 10 May 1970); 1 718 700 (estimate for 1 July 1976).
*Area: 29 209 miles² *75 650 km²*.
Language: Spanish.
Religions: Roman Catholic, Protestant minority.
Capital city: Panamá (City), population 404 190 at 1 July 1975.
Other principal town: Colón, population 63 500 (1966).
Highest point: Volcán de Chiriquí, 11 410 ft *3477 m*.
Principal mountain ranges: Serranía de Tabasará, Cordillera de San Blas.
Principal rivers: Tuira (with Chucunaque), Bayano, Santa María.
Head of State: Demetrio Basilio Lakas Bahas (b. 29 Aug. 1925), President.
Chief of Government: Brig-Gen Omar Torrijos Herrera (b. 13 Feb. 1929).
Climate: Warm, humid days with cool nights. Little seasonal temperature change. Absolute maximum temperature 98·0 °F (*36,7 °C*) at Madden Dam, Canal Zone, 13 Apr. 1920, and Panamá (City), 16 Apr.

1958; absolute minimum 59·0 °F (*15,0 °C*) at Madden Dam, Canal Zone, 4 Feb. 1924.
Labour force: 466 530 (including unemployed) aged 10 and over (1970 census): Agriculture, forestry and fishing 42·2%; Trade, restaurants and hotels 13·0%; Community, social and personal services 22·9%. Figures exclude 21 805 persons working in the Canal Zone.
Gross domestic product: 1472·5 million balboas in 1973: Agriculture, forestry and fishing 18·4%; Manufacturing 15·2%; Trade, restaurants and hotels 12·2% (trade 10·2%).
Exports: $121·1 million (excluding re-exports) in 1972: Fish and fish preparations 12·5% (crustaceans and molluscs 12·3%); Fruit and vegetables 54·2% (fresh bananas and plantains 53·5%); Other food 11·6%; Petroleum products 17·8%.
Monetary unit: Balboa. 1 balboa = 100 centésimos.
Denominations:
Coins 1, 5, 10, 25, 50 centésimos, 1 and 100 balboas.
Notes US $1 2, 5, 10, 20, 50, 100 (there are no Panamanian bank notes).
Exchange rate to US dollar: 1.00 (July 1977).
Political history and government: Formerly part of Colombia, independence declared on 3 Nov. 1903. The elected President was deposed by a *coup* on 11–12 Oct. 1968, when power was seized by the National Guard, led by Col (later Brig-Gen) Omar Torrijos Herrera. A Provisional Junta was established, the National Assembly dissolved and political activity suspended. Political parties were abolished in February 1969. On 6 Aug. 1972 elections were held for a National Assembly of Community Representatives (505 members to hold office for six years) to approve a new constitution. The Assembly elects a President and Vice-President. For a transitional period of six years from 11 Oct. 1972, full executive authority is held by Gen Torrijos as Chief of Government and Supreme Leader of the Panamanian Revolution. He rules with an appointed Cabinet Council. Panama comprises nine provinces.
Telephones: 139 241 (1975).
Daily newspapers: 9 (1973).
Total circulation: 145 000.
Radio: 265 000 (1975).
TV: 185 000 (1975).
Length of roadways: 4429 miles *7128 km* (31 Dec. 1974).
Length of railways: 447 miles *720 km*.
Universities: 2.
Adult illiteracy: 21·7% (males 21·1%; females 22·3%) in 1970.
Expectation of life: Males 64·26 years; females 67·50 years (1970, excluding tribal Indians).
Defence: National Guard of 11 000 men.
Cinemas: 45 (seating capacity 39 800), one part-time (capacity 897) and one drive-in for 330 cars (1971).

* Excluding the Canal Zone, area 553 sq miles (*1432 sq km*), population 44 198 (census of 1 April 1970).

PAPUA NEW GUINEA

Official name: The Independent State of Papua New Guinea.
Population: 2 489 935 (census of 7 July 1971); 2 829 000 (estimate for 30 June 1976).
Area: 178 704 miles² *462 840 km²*.
Languages: English (official), Pidgin, Moru.
Religion: Christian 92·8% (1966).
Capital city: Port Moresby, population 76 507 (1971).
Other principal towns (1971): Lae 34 699; Rabaul 24 778; Madang; Wewak; Goroka.

Highest point: Mt Wilhelm, 15 400 ft *4694 m*.
Principal mountain range: Bismarck Range.
Principal rivers: Fly (with Strickland), Sepik (690 miles [*1110 km*]).
Head of State: HM Queen Elizabeth II, represented by Sir Tore Lokoloko, GCMG, Governor-General.
Prime Minister: The Rt Hon Michael Thomas Somare (b. 9 Apr. 1936).
Climate: Generally hot and humid, cooler in highlands. Average annual rainfall between 40 and 250 in. In Port Moresby, average maximum temperature 82 °F (August) to 90 °F (December), minimum 73 °F (July, August) to 76 °F (November to March), rainiest month is March (9 days).
Labour force: 1 255 953 (excluding non-indigenous) at census of June–July 1966; 1 257 000 (1970): Agriculture, forestry and fishing 85·9% (ILO estimates).
Gross domestic product: 645·5 million kina in 1971/72: Agriculture, forestry and fishing 35·0%; Construction 15·1%; Community, social and personal services (including restaurants and hotels) 21·9% (public administration and defence 11·1%).
Exports: $294·2 million in 1972/73: Coffee 10·2%; Metalliferous ores and metal scrap 55·1% (non-ferrous ores and concentrates 54·9%).
Monetary unit: Kina. 1 kina = 100 toea.
Denominations:
Coins 1, 2, 5, 10, 20 toea, 1 kina.
Notes 2, 5, 10 kina.
Exchange rate to US dollar: 0.7996 (July 1977).
Political history and government: Formed by a merger of the Territory of Papua (under Australian rule from 1906) and the Trust Territory of New Guinea, administered by Australia from 1914, later under a trusteeship agreement with the United Nations. A joint administration for the two territories was established by Australia on 1 July 1949. The combined territory became independent, within the Commonwealth, on 16 Sept. 1975. Executive authority is vested in the Queen and exercisable by the Governor-General, whom she appoints on the advice of the Prime Minister, leader of the National Executive Council (the Cabinet). Legislative power is vested in the unicameral National Parliament (109 members directly elected for four years by universal adult suffrage). The Council is responsible to Parliament, where the Prime Minister, appointed by the Governor-General, must command majority support. The country comprises 19 districts.
Telephones: 16 949 (30 June 1975).
Daily newspapers: 1.
Radio: 110 000 (1975).
Length of roadways (1974): 7456 miles *12 000 km*.
Universities: 2.

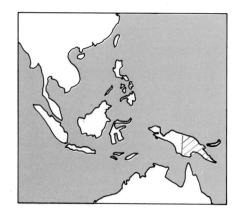

Adult illiteracy: 67·9% (males 60·7%; females 75·6%) in 1971.
Expectation of life: Males 47·7 years; females 47·6 years (UN estimates for 1970–75).
Defence: Total armed forces about 3500.
Cinemas: 28 (seating capacity 18 800) and one drive-in for 750 cars (1972).

PARAGUAY

Official name: La República del Paraguay.
Population: 2 357 955 (census of 9 July 1972); 2 646 877 (estimate for 1 July 1975).
Area: 157 048 miles² *406 752 km²*.
Languages: Spanish (official), Guaraní.
Religion: Roman Catholic.
Capital city: Asunción, population 434 922 at 1 July 1975.
Other principal towns (1962): Coronel Oviedo 44 254; Encarnación 35 186; Concepción 33 886; Mariscal Estigarribia 33 478; Luque 30 780; Villarrica 30 761.
Highest point: Cerro Tatug, 2297 ft *700 m*.
Principal mountain ranges: Cordillera Amambay, Sierra de Maracaju.
Principal rivers: Paraguay (1500 miles [*2414 km*]), Paraná (2500 miles [*4023 km*]). Pilcomayo (1000 miles [*1609 km*]).
Head of State: Gen Alfredo Stroessner (b. 3 Nov. 1912), President.
Climate: Sub-tropical and humid, average temperatures 65 °F to 85 °F. Hot December–March. Cool season May–September. Wet season March–May. In Asunción, average maximum 72 °F (June) to 95 °F (January), minimum 53 °F (June, July) to 71 °F (January, February), October, November and January rainiest (each 8 days).
Labour force: 728 320 (excluding 26 390 unemployed) aged 12 and over (1972 census, sample tabulation): Agriculture, forestry and fishing 51·8%; Manufacturing 14·8%; Community, social and personal services 17·0%.
Gross domestic product: 190 439 million guaraníes in 1975: Agriculture, forestry and fishing 36·9%; Manufacturing 15·6%; Trade and finance 22·9%.
Exports: $86·2 million in 1972: Meat and meat preparations 29·5% (fresh, chilled or frozen beef 15·6%); Other food 20·1%.
Monetary unit: Guaraní. 1 guaraní = 100 céntimos.
Denominations:
Coins (issued only for commemorative purposes).
Notes 1, 5, 10, 50, 100, 500, 1000, 5000, 10 000 guaraníes.
Exchange rate to US dollar: 126.00 (July 1977).
Political history and government: A republic comprising 16 departments. Gen. Alfredo Stroessner assumed power by a military *coup* on 5 May 1954. He was elected President on 11 July 1954 and re-elected in 1958, 1963, 1968 and 1973. A new constitution was promulgated on 25 Aug. 1967 and took effect in 1968. Legislative power is held by a bicameral National Congress, whose members serve for 5 years. The Senate has 30 members and the Chamber of Deputies

60 members. The party receiving the largest number of votes (since 1947 the National Republican Association, known as the Colorado Party) is allotted two-thirds of the seats in each chamber, the remaining seats being divided proportionately among the other contending parties. Executive power is held by the President, directly elected for 5 years at the same time as the Congress. He rules with the assistance of an appointed Council of Ministers.
Telephones: 34 531 (1974).
Daily newspapers: 11 (1973).
Total circulation: 89 000 (4 dailies).
Radio: 180 000 (1975).
TV: 54 000 (1975).
Length of roadways: 9915 miles *15 956 km* (31 Dec. 1973).
Length of railways: 309 miles *498 km*.
Universities: 2.
Adult illiteracy: 25·5% (males 19·0%; females 31·3%) in 1962.
Expectation of life: Males 60·3 years; females 63·6 years (UN estimates for 1970–75).
Defence: Military service: 18 months; total armed forces 16 600; defence expenditure, 1974: $21 million.
Cinemas: 65 in Asunción (1974).

PERU

Official name: La República del Perú.
Population: 14 121 564 (census of 4 June 1972, including adjustment for under-enumeration); 16 090 000 (estimate for 1 July 1976).
Area: 496 525 miles² *1 285 216 km²*.
Languages: Spanish, Quechua, Aymará.
Religion: Roman Catholic.
Capital city: Lima, population 2 833 609 (1972 census).
Other principal towns (1972): Arequipa 302 316; Callao 296 721; Trujillo 240 322; Chiclayo 187 809; Chimbote 159 045; Huancayo 126 754; Piura 126 010; Cuzco 121 464.
Highest point: Huascarán 22 205 ft *6768 m*.
Principal mountain ranges: Cordillera de los Andes (C. Oriental, C. Occidental, C. Blanca).
Principal rivers: Amazonas (Amazon), with Ucayali.
Head of State: Gen Francisco Morales Bermúdez (b. 4 Oct. 1921), President.

Prime Minister: Gen Guillermo Arbulú Galliani.
Climate: Varies with altitude. Daily fluctuations greater than seasonal. Rainy season October–April. Heavy rains in tropical forests. In Lima, average maximum 66 °F (August) to 83 °F (February, March), minimum 56 °F (August) to 67 °F (February), August rainiest (two days). Absolute maximum temperature 38·5 °C (*101·3 °F*), Iquitos, 19 June 1948; absolute minimum −20,2 °C (*−4·4 °F*), Imata, 1 Aug. 1947.
Labour force: 3 871 613 (including unemployed) aged 6 and over (1972 census, excluding adjustment for underenumeration): Agriculture, forestry and fishing 43·9%; Manufacturing 13·5%; Trade, restaurants and hotels 11·2%; Community, social and personal services 19·1%.
Gross domestic product: 294 700 million soles in 1972: Agriculture, forestry and fishing 16·1% (agriculture and forestry 15·0%); Manufacturing 23·1%; Trade, restaurants and hotels 16·0%; Community, social and personal services 20·9%.
Exports: $892·9 million in 1971: Meat or fish meal fodder 31·1%; Other food 13·2%; Metalliferous ores and metal scrap 18·8% (non-ferrous ores and concentrates 11·8%); Non-ferrous metals 23·0% (copper 16·6%).
Monetary unit: Sol. 1 sol = 100 centavos.
Denominations:
Coins 5, 10, 25, 50 centavos, 1, 5, 10 soles.
Notes 5, 10, 50, 100, 200, 500, 1000 soles.
Exchange rate to US dollar: 80.80 (July 1977).
Political history and government: A republic comprising 23 departments and one province. A new constitution was promulgated on 9 April 1933. The last elected President was deposed by a military *coup* on 3 Oct. 1968. The bicameral National Congress was abolished, political activity suspended and a 'revolutionary government' of military officers took power. The constitution remains only partially in force. Executive and legislative powers are exercised by the armed forces through the President, who rules by decree with the assistance of an appointed Council of Ministers. Each department is administered by an appointed prefect.
Telephones: 333 346 (1974).
Daily newspapers: 70 (1973).
Radio: 2 050 000 (1975).
TV: 500 000 (1975).
Length of roadways: 31 485 miles *50 670 km* (31 Dec. 1974).
Length of railways: 1305 miles *2100 km.*
Universities: 33.
Adult illiteracy: 38·9% (males 25·6%; females 51·6%) in 1961.
Expectation of life: Males 52·59 years; females 55·48 years (1960–5).
Defence: Military service: two years, selective; total armed forces 63 000 (including 40 000 conscripts); defence expenditure, 1975: $383 million.
Cinemas: 276 and one drive-in for 100 cars (1972); seating capacity about 243 000 (1966).

THE PHILIPPINES

Official name: República de Filipinas (in Spanish) or Repúblika ñg Pilipinas (in Tagalog).
Population: 41 831 045 (census of 1 May 1975); 43 751 000 (estimate for 1 July 1976).
Area: 115 831 miles² *300 000 km²*.
Languages (1960): Cebuano 24·1% Tagalog 21·0%; Iloco 11·7%; Panay-Hiligaynon 10·4%; Bikol 7·8%; many others.
Religions (1960): Roman Catholic 84%; Aglipayan 5%, Muslim 5%, Protestant 3%.

Capital city: Manila, population 1 479 116 at 1975 census.
Other principal towns (1975): Quezon City 956 864; Davao 484 678; Cebu 413 025; Caloocan 397 201; Zamboanga 261 978; Pasay 254 999; Iloilo 227 027; Bacolod 223 392.
Highest point: Mt Apo (on Mindanao), 9690 ft *2953 m.*
Principal mountain ranges: Cordillera Central (on Luzon), Diuata Range (on Mindanao).
Principal rivers: Cagayan (180 miles [*290 km*]), Pampanga, Abra, Agusan, Magat, Laoang, Agno.
Head of State: Ferdinand Edralin Marcos (b. 11 Sept. 1917), President and Prime Minister.
Climate: Tropical. Hot and humid, except in mountains. Heavy rainfall, frequent typhoons. In Manila, average maximum 86 °F (December, January) to 93 °F (April, May), minimum 69 °F (January, February) to 75 °F (May–August), July rainiest (24 days). Absolute maximum temperature 42,2 °C (*108·0 °F*), Tuguegarao, 29 Apr. 1912; absolute minimum 7,3 °C (*45·1 °F*), Baguio City, 1 Feb. 1930 and 11 Jan. 1932.
Labour force: 15 161 000 (including unemployed) aged 10 and over (August 1975): Agriculture, forestry and fishing 53·1%; Manufacturing 11·6%; Commerce 11·2%; Services 16·6%. Figures exclude armed forces and institutional households.
Gross domestic product: 100 123 million pesos (provisional) in 1974: Agriculture, forestry and fishing 36·4% (agriculture 28·6%); Manufacturing 24·6%. Revised total is 99 899 million pesos.
Exports: $2701·2 million in 1974: Sugar and honey 28·3% (raw sugar 27·3%); Metalliferous ores and metal scrap 16·5% (copper ores and concentrates 14·7%); Coconut (copra) oil 14·1%.
Monetary unit: Philippine peso. 1 peso = 100 centavos.
Denominations:
Coins 1, 5, 10, 25, 50 centavos, 1, 5 peso.
Notes 2, 5, 10, 20, 50, 100 pesos.
Exchange rate to US dollar: 7.3965 (July 1977).
Political history and government: Formerly a Spanish colony. After the Spanish-American War, Spain ceded the Philippines to the USA (10 Dec. 1898). A constitution, ratified by plebiscite on 14 May 1935, gave the Philippines self-government and provided for independence after 10 years. The islands were occupied by Japanese forces in 1942–45. After the restoration of US rule, the Philippines became an independent republic on 4 July 1946.
Ferdinand Marcos was elected President on 9 Nov. 1965 and inaugurated on 30 Dec. 1965. He was re-elected in 1969. Before completing his (then) maximum of two four-year terms, President Marcos proclaimed martial law, and suspended the bicameral Congress, on 23 Sept. 1972. On 2 Jan. 1973 the President ordered the formation of 'citizens' assemblies', open to all persons over 15. After discussion by these assemblies, a new constitution was ratified by the President on 17 Jan. 1973. This provides for a unicameral National Assembly and a constitutional President (both elected for 6 years), with executive power held by a Prime Minister, to be elected by the Assembly. Pending its full implementation, transitional provisions give the incumbent President the combined authority of the Presidency (under the 1935 constitution) and the Premiership under the new constitution, without any fixed term of office. The President should convene an interim National Assembly but this provision was immediately postponed (on 14 Aug. 1976 the President announced that the Assembly

would not be convened). Under martial law the definitive provisions of the constitution remain in abeyance. A referendum on 27–28 July 1973 approved the President's continuation in office beyond his elected term. Another referendum, on 27 Feb. 1975, approved the continuation of martial law, enabling the President to rule by decree. On 10 Sept. 1976 he formed the *Batasang Bayan* (Legislative Advisory Council), comprising all members of the Government, the 91 members of the executive committee of the citizens' assemblies, and others. The Council was inaugurated on 21 Sept. 1976. A referendum on 16–17 Oct. 1976 approved the further continuation of martial law and constitutional amendments, including a provision for the formation of an interim constituent assembly with 120 members (some elected and some appointed by the President). On 27 Oct. 1976 a Presidential decree amended the constitution in accordance with the referendum results. On 30 Oct. 1977 the President announced that elections for the interim assembly would be held by May 1978. The President appoints and leads a Cabinet and is Commander-in-Chief of the armed forces. The country is divided into 68 provinces.
Telephones: 489 717 (1975).
Daily newspapers: 24 (1974).
Total circulation: 1 196 239.
Radio: 1 850 000 (1975).
TV: 501 400 (1975).
Length of roadways: 57 647 miles *92 775 km* (1974).
Length of railways: 735 miles 1183 *km.*
Universities: 42.
Adult illiteracy: 16·6% (males 15·4%; females 17·8%) in 1970 (population aged 10 and over).
Expectation of life: Males 56·9 years; females 60·0 years (UN estimates for 1970–75).
Defence: Military service: selective; total armed forces 78 000; defence expenditure, 1976/77: $410 million.
Cinemas: 951 (1965).

POLAND

Official name: Polska Rzeczpospolita Ludowa (Polish People's Republic).
Population: 32 642 270 (census of 8 Dec. 1970); 34 552 000 (estimate for 1 Jan. 1977).
Area: 120 725 miles² *312 677 km²*.
Language: Polish.
Religion: Roman Catholic.
Capital city: Warszawa (Warsaw), population 1 436 100 at 31 Dec. 1975.
Other principal towns (1975): Lódź 798 300; Kraków (Cracow) 684 600; Wrocław (Breslau) 575 900; Poznań (Posen) 516 000; Gdańsk (Danzig) 421 000; Szczecin (Stettin) 369 700; Katowice 343 700; Bydgoszcz (Bromberg) 322 700; Lublin 272 000.
Highest point: Rysy, 8199 ft *2499 m.*
Principal mountain ranges: Carpathian Mountains (Tatry range), Beskids.
Principal rivers: Wisła (Vistula) with Bug, Odra (Oder).
Head of State: Dr Henryk Jabłoński (b. 27 Dec. 1909), Chairman of the Council of State.

Political Leader: Edward Gierek (b. 6 Jan. 1913), First Secretary of the Central Committee of the Polish United Workers' Party.
Head of Government: Piotr Jaroszewicz (b. 8 Oct. 1909), Chairman of the Council of Ministers.
Climate: Temperate in west, continental in east. Short, rainy summers, but occasional dry spells; cold snowy winters. In Warsaw, average maximum 30 °F (January) to 75 °F (July), minimum 21 °F (January) to 56 °F (July), June, July and August rainiest (each 11 days). Absolute maximum temperature 40,2 °C (104·4 °F), Prószków, 29 July 1921; absolute minimum −40,6 °C (−41·1 °F), Zgwiec, 10 Feb. 1929.
Labour force: 17 506 555 aged 15 and over (March 1974): Agriculture, forestry and fishing (excluding sea fishing) 34·6%; Industry (mining, quarrying, manufacturing, electricity, gas and water) and sea fishing 30·2%; Community, social and personal services (including hotels and activities not adequately described) 15·0%.
Net material product: 1 357 000 million złotys (in domestic prices) in 1975: Agriculture, forestry and fishing (excluding sea fishing) 15·1%; Industry and sea fishing 59·1%; Construction 11·2%.
Exports: 34 160·7 million złotys in 1975: Fuels and power 20·1% (hard coal 16·0%); Products of electro-engineering industries 41·4%.
Monetary unit: Złoty. 1 złoty = 100 groszy.
Denominations:
   Coins 1, 2, 5, 10, 20, 50 groszy, 1, 2, 5, 10, 50, 100 złotys.
   Notes 20, 50, 100, 500, 1000 złotys.
Exchange rate to US dollar: 3.30 (May 1977).
Political history and government: Formerly partitioned between Austria, Prussia and Russia. After the First World War an independent republic was declared on 11 Nov. 1918. Parliamentary government was overthrown in May 1926 by military leaders who ruled until 1939, when invasions by Nazi Germany (1 Sept.) and the USSR (17 Sept.) led to another partition (29 Sept.). After Germany declared war on the USSR (June 1941) its forces occupied the whole of Poland but they were driven out by Soviet forces in March 1945. With the end of the Second World War (May 1945) Poland's frontiers were redrawn. A provisional government was formed on 28 June 1945. A Communist regime took power after the elections of 19 Jan. 1947 and a People's Republic was established on 19 Feb. 1947. A new constitution was adopted on 22 July 1952.

The supreme organ of state power is the unicameral parliament (*Sejm*), with 460 members elected by universal adult suffrage for 4 years (in the elections of 21 March 1976 there were 631 candidates). The *Sejm* elects a Council of State (17 members) to be its permanent organ. The highest executive and administrative body is the Council of Ministers, appointed by (and responsible to) the *Sejm*.

Political power is held by the (Communist) Polish United Workers' Party (PUWP), which dominates the Front of National Unity (including two other smaller parties). The Front presents an approved list of candidates for elections to representative bodies. The PUWP's highest authority is the Party Congress, convened every 5 years. The Congress elects a Central Committee (140 full members and 111 candidate members were elected in December 1975) to supervise Party work. To direct its policy the Committee elects a Political Bureau (Politburo), with 15 full members (including the Committee's First Secretary) and 3 alternate members.

Poland is divided into 49 provinces (voivodships), each with a People's Council elected for 4 years.
Telephones: 2 577 600 (31 Dec. 1975).
Daily newspapers: 44 (1975).
   Total circulation: 8 429 000.
Radio: 8 127 000 (31 Dec. 1975).
TV: 6 472 000 (31 Dec. 1975).
Length of roadways: 185 058 miles *297 822 km* (excluding forest, factory and agricultural roads) at 31 Dec. 1975.
Length of railways: 16 596 miles *26 709 km* (1974).
Universities: 10.
Adult illiteracy: 2·3% (males 1·3%; females 3·1%) in 1970.
Expectation of life: Males 66·83 years; females 73·76 years (1970–2).
Defence: Military service: Army, internal security forces and Air Force 2 years, Navy and special services 3 years; total regular forces 290 000 (including 190 000 conscripts); defence expenditure, 1976: $2252 million (converted at $1 = 23·5 złotys).
Cinemas: 2336 (seating capacity 565 500) and 34 part-time (capacity 19 156) in 1973.

PORTUGAL

Official name: A República Portuguesa (The Portuguese Republic).
*Population: 8 568 703 (census of 15 Dec. 1970); 9 448 800 (estimate for 1 July 1975).
*Area: 35 553 miles² *92 082 km²*.
Language: Portuguese.
Religion: Roman Catholic.
Capital city: Lisboa (Lisbon), population 774 500 at 1 July 1974.
Other principal towns (1970): Pôrto (Oporto) 300 925; Amadora 65 870; Coímbra 55 985; Barreiro 53 690; Vila Nova de Gaia 50 805; Setúbal 49 670; Braga 48 735.
Highest point: Pico, 7713 ft *2351 m*.
Principal mountain range: The Serra da Estréla.
Principal rivers: Rio Tejo (Tagus), Douro.
Head of State: Gen António dos Santos Ramalho Eanes (b. 25 Jan. 1935), President.
Prime Minister: Dr. Mário Alberto Nobre Lopes Soares (b. 7 Dec. 1924).
Climate: Mild and temperate. Average annual temperature 61 °F, drier and hotter inland. Hot summers, rainy winters in central areas, warm and very dry in south. In Lisbon, average maximum 56 °F (January) to 80 °F (August), minimum 46 °F (January) to 64 °F (August); March, November and December rainiest (each 10 days). Absolute maximum temperature 45,8 °C (114·4 °F), Coímbra, 31 July 1944; absolute minimum −11,0 °C (12·2 °F), Penhas Douradas, 25 Jan. 1947.
Labour force: 2 997 000 (December 1975): Agriculture, forestry and fishing 28·7%; Manufacturing 24·8%; Trade, restaurants and hotels 12·4%; Community, social and personal services 16·6%. Figures exclude persons on compulsory military service (141 205 at 1970 census) and unemployed (90 805 at 1970 census).
Gross domestic product: 338 300 million escudos in 1974: Agriculture, forestry and fishing 15·6% (agriculture 12·5%); Manufacturing 35·6%; Trade, restaurants and hotels 14·1% (trade 12·2%); Community, social and personal services 11·5%.
Exports: $1939·7 million in 1975: Textile yarn, fabrics, etc. 16·1%; Machinery and transport equipment 13·2%; Clothing (excluding footwear) 11·3%.
Monetary unit: Portuguese escudo. 1 escudo = 100 centavos.

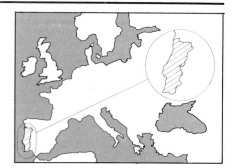

Denominations:
   Coins 10, 20, 50 centavos, 1, 2½, 5, 10, 20, 50 escudos.
   Notes 20, 50, 100, 500, 1000 escudos.
Exchange rate to US dollar: 38.48 (July 1977).
Political history and government: Formerly a kingdom. An anti-monarchist uprising deposed the King on 5 Oct. 1910, when a republic was proclaimed. The parliamentary regime was overthrown by a military *coup* on 28 May 1926. Dr. António Salazar became Prime Minister, with dictatorial powers, on 5 July 1932. A new constitution, establishing a corporate state, was adopted on 19 March 1933. Dr. Salazar retained power until illness forced his retirement on 26 Sept. 1968. His successor, Dr. Marcello Caetano, was deposed on 25 Apr. 1974 by a military *coup*, initiated by the Armed Forces Movement. Military leaders formed a Junta of National Salvation and appointed one of its members as President. He appointed a Prime Minister and, on the latter's recommendation, other Ministers to form a provisional government. The 1933 constitution was suspended and the bicameral Parliament dissolved.

On 14 Mar. 1975 the Junta was dissolved and three days later a Supreme Revolutionary Council (SRC) was established to exercise authority until a new constitution took effect. A Constitutional Assembly was elected on 25 Apr. 1975 to formulate a new constitution. After approval by the SRC, the constitution was promulgated on 2 Apr. 1976. It provides for a unicameral legislature, the Assembly of the Republic, with 262 members elected by universal adult suffrage for 4 years. Executive power is vested in the President, directly elected for 5 years. The President appoints a Prime Minister to lead a Council of Ministers, responsible to the Assembly. Portugal has 22 administrative districts.
Telephones: 1 065 974 (1975).
Daily newspapers: 29 (1973).
   Total circulation: 740 000 (est).
Radio: 1 510 703 (1975).
TV: 737 016 (June 1976).
Length of roadways: 28 699 miles *46 187 km* (31 Dec. 1974).
Length of railways: 2214 miles *3563 km*.
Universities: 11.
Adult illiteracy: 37·2% (males 30·0%; females 43·4%) in 1960.
Expectation of life: Males 65·29 years; females 72·03 years (1974).
Defence: Military service: Army 15 months; total armed forces 59 800; defence expenditure, 1976: $959 million.
Cinemas: 434 (1973).

*Metropolitan Portugal, including the Azores and Madeira Islands.

QATAR

Official name: Daulat al-Qatar (State of Qatar).
Population: 183 600 (estimate for March 1976).

Area: 4247 miles² *11 000 km²*.
Language: Arabic.
Religion: Muslim.
Capital city: Ad Dauhah (Doha), population 140 000 (1975 est).
Other principal towns: Dukhan, Umm Said.
Highest point: 240 ft *73 m*.
Head of State: Shaikh Khalifa ibn Hamad al-Thani (b. 1934), Amir and Prime Minister.
Climate: Very hot, with high humidity on the coast. Temperatures reach 120 °F in summer.

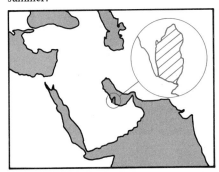

Labour force: 86 727 (March 1976).
Gross domestic product: $357 million in 1970 (UN estimate).
Exports: 8683·4 million riyals in 1976: Crude petroleum 95·5%.
Monetary unit: Qatar riyal. 1 riyal = 100 dirhams.
Denominations:
   Coins 1, 5, 10, 25, 50 dirhams.
   Notes 1, 5, 10, 100, 500 riyals.
Exchange rate to US dollar: 3.957 (May 1977).
Political history and government: Became part of Turkey's Ottoman Empire in 1872. Turkish forces evacuated Qatar at the beginning of the First World War. The UK entered into treaty relations with the ruling Shaikh on 3 Nov. 1916. A provisional constitution was adopted on 2 Apr. 1970. Qatar. remained under British protection until achieving full independence on 1 Sept. 1971. On 22 Feb. 1972 the ruler was deposed by his deputy, the Prime Minister.

Qatar is an absolute monarchy, with full powers vested in the ruler (called Amir since independence). It has no parliament or political parties. The ruler appoints and leads a Council of Ministers to exercise executive power. The Ministers are assisted by a Consultative Council with 20 nominated members.
Telephones: 18 289 (1974).
Daily newspapers: 1.
   Total circulation: 7000.
TV: 29 000 (1975).
Expectation of life: Males 45·8 years; females 48·3 years (UN estimates, average for Bahrain, Oman, Qatar and the United Arab Emirates, 1970–75).
Defence: Total armed forces 2200.
Cinemas: 8 (seating capacity 7000) in 1973.

RHODESIA

Official Name: The Republic of Rhodesia.
Population: 4 846 930 Africans (census of 21 Apr.–May 1969) and 252 414 non-Africans (census of 20 Mar. 1969); 6 220 000 Africans and 308 000 non-Africans (estimate for mid-1976).
Area: 150 804 miles². *390 580 km²*.
Languages: English (official), Sindebele, Chishona.
Religions: Tribal beliefs, Christian minority.
Capital city: Salisbury, population 568 000 at mid-1976.

Other principal towns (1976): Bulawayo 340 000; Gwelo 64 000; Umtali 61 000; Que Que 50 000; Gatooma 33 000; Wankie 28 000.
Highest point: Mount Inyangani, 8503 ft *2592 m*.
Principal mountain ranges: Enyanga, Melsetter.
Principal rivers: Zambezi and tributaries (Shangani, Umniati), Limpopo and tributaries (Umzingwani, Nuanetsi), Sabi and tributaries (Lundi, Odzi).
Head of State: John James Wrathall (b. 28 Aug. 1913), President.
Prime Minister: Ian Douglas Smith (b. 8 Apr. 1919).
Climate: Tropical, modified by altitude. Average temperature 65 °F to 75 °F. In Salisbury, average daily maximum 70 °F (June, July) to 83 °F (October), minimum 44 °F (June, July) to 60 °F (November–February), January rainiest (18 days).
Labour force: 1 859 000 (1970): Agriculture, forestry and fishing 63·9% (ILO estimates).
Gross domestic product: R$1845·5 million (provisional) in 1974: Agriculture, forestry and fishing 16·9%; Manufacturing 24·6%; Trade, restaurants and hotels 14·0% (trade 12·8%); Community, social and personal services (including business services) 16·5%. Revised total is R$1843·6 million.
Exports: R$284·9 million (excluding re-exports) in 1965: Food and live animals 10·3%; Tobacco and tobacco manufactures 34·2% (unmanufactured tobacco 33·0%).
Monetary unit: Rhodesian dollar (R$). 1 dollar = 100 cents.
Denominations:
   Coins ½ 1, 2½, 5, 10, 20, 25 cents.
   Notes 1, 2, 5, 10 dollars.
Exchange rate to US dollar: 0.617 (July 1977).
Political history and government: The British South Africa Company was granted a Royal Charter over the territory on 29 Oct. 1889. On 12 Sept. 1923 Southern Rhodesia (as it was known) was transferred from the Company to the British Empire and became a colony. It was granted full self-government (except for African interests and some other matters) on 1 Oct. 1923. The colony became part of the Federation of Rhodesia and Nyasaland (the Central African Federation), proclaimed on 1 Aug. 1953. A new constitution, which removed most of the UK's legal controls (except for foreign affairs), was promulgated on 6 Dec. 1961 and made fully operative on 1 Nov. 1962. This constitution provided for a limited African franchise and could have led to ultimate majority rule. The Federation was dissolved on 31 Dec. 1963. Ian Smith became Prime Minister on 13 Apr. 1964. Following unsuccessful negotiations with the British Government, Ian Smith made a unilateral declaration of independence (UDI) on 11 Nov. 1965. The British Government regards Rhodesia's independence as unconstitutional and having no legal validity, and no other country has formally recognized it. A new constitution was approved by referendum on 20 June 1969, adopted on 29 Nov. 1969 and took effect on 2 Mar. 1970, when a republic was proclaimed.

Legislative power is held by the bicameral Legislative Assembly. The House of Assembly has 66 members, including 50 Europeans (whites) elected by non-African voters, 8 Africans directly elected by African voters and 8 Africans elected by tribal electoral colleges. The Senate (with delaying powers only) has 23 members, including 10 Europeans elected by white members of the House, 10 Africans elected by an advisory Council of Chiefs, and 3 members (of any race) appointed by the President. Members of both

Houses serve a term of 5 years (subject to dissolution). The President is a constitutional Head of State appointed for 5 years on the nomination of the Executive Council (Cabinet). The Council, which directs the government, is led by a Prime Minister, appointed by the President. Other Ministers are appointed on the Prime Minister's recommendation.

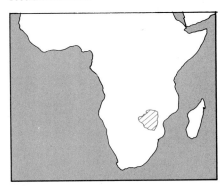

Telephones: 186 789 (30 June 1976).
Daily newspapers: 3 (1972).
   Total circulation: 84 000.
Radio: 250 000 (1975).
TV: 68 700 (1975).
Length of roadways: 49 045 miles *78 930 km*.
Length of railways: 2109 miles *3394 km*.
Universities: 1.
Adult illiteracy: 95·3% (males 94·4%; females 96·3%) in 1962 (Africans only).
Expectation of life: Males 49·8 years; females 53·3 years (UN estimates for 1970–75). Europeans: Males 66·9 years; females 74·0 years (1961–63).
Defence: Military service: 18 months (White, Asian and Coloured population); total armed forces 9200 (excluding Terriorial Army); defence expenditure, 1976/77: US $130 million.
Cinemas: 72 (seating capacity 53 900) and 5 drive-in for 2874 cars (1971).

ROMANIA

Official name: Republica Socialistă România (Socialist Republic of Romania).
Population: 19 103 163 (census of 15 Mar. 1966); 21 446 000 (estimate for 1 July 1976).
Area: 91 699 miles² *237 500 km²*.
Languages (1966): Romanian 87·8%; Hungarian 8·6%; German 2·0%.
Religions: Romanian Orthodox (85% of believers), Roman Catholic, Reformed (Calvinist).
Capital city: Bucureşti (Bucharest), population 1 565 872 at 1 July 1974.
Other principal towns (1974): Cluj 218 751; Timişoara 210 520; Iaşi 210 388; Braşov 198 753; Galaţi 197 853; Craiova 194 235; Constanţa 193 720; Ploieşti 175 527 Brăila 165 803.
Highest point: Negoiu, 8360 ft *2548 m*.
Principal mountain ranges: Carpathian Mountains, Transylvanian Alps.
Principal rivers: Dunărea (Danube) (1777 miles [*2860 km*], 668 miles [*1075 km*] in Romania), Mureş (446 miles [*718 km*]), Prut (437 miles [*703 km*]).
Head of State: Nicolae Ceauşescu (b. 26 Jan. 1918), President; also General Secretary of the Central Committee of the Romanian Communist Party.
Head of Government: Manea Mănescu (b. 9 Aug. 1916), Chairman of the Council of Ministers.

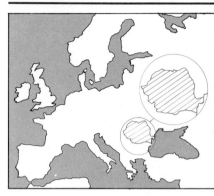

Climate: Hot and humid summers (average temperatures 70 °F); cold, windy, snowy winters (average 28 °F). Moderate rainfall. Absolute maximum temperature 44,5 °C (*112·1 °F*), Ion Sion, 10 Aug. 1951; minimum −38,5 °C (*−37·3 °F*), Bod, near Braşov, 25 Jan. 1942.
Labour force: 10 362 300 (excluding persons seeking work for the first time) aged 14 and over (1966 census): Agriculture and forestry 57·2%; Mining, quarrying, manufacturing and fishing 19·4%; 11 343 000 (1970): Agriculture, forestry and fishing 56·0% (ILO estimate).
Gross national product: $27 650 million in 1975 (World Bank estimates).
Exports: $3698·5 million in 1973: Food and live animals 16·2%; Machinery and transport equipment 24·4%.
Monetary unit: Leu (plural lei). 1 leu = 100 bani.
Denominations:
   Coins 5, 10, 15, 25 bani, 1, 3 lei.
   Notes 1, 3, 5, 10, 25, 50, 100 lei.
Exchange rate to US dollar: 4.97 (March 1977).
Political history and government: Formerly a monarchy. Under the Fascist 'Iron Guard' movement, Romania entered the Second World War as an ally of Nazi Germany. Soviet forces entered Romania in 1944. The Iron Guard regime was overthrown on 23 Aug. 1944 and a predominantly Communist government took power on 6 March 1945. The King was forced to abdicate on 30 Dec. 1947, when a People's Republic was proclaimed. A new constitution introducing the country's present name, was adopted on 21 Aug. 1965.

The supreme organ of state power is the unicameral Grand National Assembly, with 349 members elected by universal adult suffrage for 5 years (210 members were elected unopposed in 1975). The Assembly elects from its members the State Council (18 members) to be its permanent organ. The President of the Republic, elected by the Assembly for its duration, is also President of the State Council. The Council of Ministers, the highest organ of state administration, is elected by (and responsible to) the Assembly.

Political power is held by the Romanian Communist Party (RCP), the only legal party, which dominates the Front of Socialist Unity. The Front presents an approved list of candidates for elections to representative bodies. The Head of State is General Secretary of the RCP and Chairman of the Front. The RCP's highest authority is the Party Congress, convened ever 5 years. The Congress elects a Central Committee (205 full members and 156 alternate members were elected in November 1974) to supervise Party work. The Central Committee elects from its members an Executive Political Committee (23 full members and 13 alternate members) to direct policy. The Executive Committee has a five-man Permanent Bureau (including the President), which is

the Party's most powerful policy-making body.

Romania comprises 40 administrative districts, each with a People's Council elected for 5 years.
Telephones: 1 076 566 (1974).
Daily newspapers: 58 (1973).
   Total circulation: 3 736 000.
Radio: 3 111 000 (1975).
TV: 2 553 419 (1975).
Length of roadways: 48 435 miles *77 949 km* (1975).
Length of railways (1974): 6889 miles *11 086 km* plus 385 miles *619 km* (narrow-gauge).
Universities: 7.
Adult illiteracy: 11·4% (males 6·1%; females 16·3%) in 1956.
Expectation of life: Males 66·83 years; females 71·29 years (1972–74).
Defence: Military service: Army and Air Force 16 months, Navy 2 years; total armed forces 181 000 (including 100 000 conscripts); defence expenditure, 1976: $759 million (converted at $1 = 13·7 lei).
Cinemas: 6182 (1973).

RWANDA

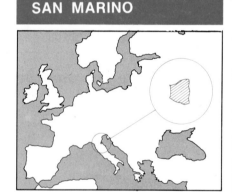

Official name: La République rwandaise (in French) *or* Republica y'u Rwanda (in Kinyarwanda).
Population: 4 289 000 (estimate for 1 July 1976).
Area: 10 169 miles² *26 338 km²*.
Languages: French, Kinyarwanda (both official), Kiswahili.
Religions: Roman Catholic, Animist, Protestant and Muslim minorities.
Capital city: Kigali, population 54 403 (including suburbs) at 31 Dec. 1970.
Other principal towns: Nyanzi, Gisenyi, Cyangugu, Sitarama.
Highest point: Mt Karisimbi, 14 787 ft *4507 m*.
Principal mountain ranges: Chaîne des Mitumba.
Principal rivers: Luvironza (headwaters of the Nile).
Head of State: Maj-Gen Juvénal Habyalimana (b. 3 Aug. 1937), President.
Climate: Tropical, tempered by altitude. Average temperature at 4800 ft *1463 m* is 73 °F. Hot and humid in lowlands, cool in highlands. Average annual rainfall 31 in. Main rainy season from February to May, dry season May to September.
Labour force: 2 065 000 (1970): Agriculture, forestry and fishing 93·3% (ILO estimates).
Gross domestic product: 28 700 million Rwanda francs in 1974.
Exports: $37·3 million in 1974: Coffee 60·2%; Metalliferous ores and metal scrap 15·6% (tin ores and concentrates 11·5%).
Monetary unit: Rwanda franc. 1 franc = 100 centimes.

Denominations:
   Coins 50 centimes, 1, 2, 5, 10 francs.
   Notes 20, 50, 100, 500, 1000 francs.
Exchange rate to US dollar: 92.84 (July 1977).
Political history and government: Formerly a monarchy, ruled by a *Mwami* (King). Part of German East Africa from 1899. Occupied in 1916 by Belgian forces from the Congo (now Zaire). From 1920 Rwanda was part of Ruanda-Urundi, administered by Belgium under League of Nations mandate and later as a UN Trust Territory. Following a referendum on 25 Sept. 1961, the monarchy was abolished and the republic proclaimed on 28 Jan. 1961 was recognised by Belgium on 2 Oct. 1961. Rwanda became independent on 1 July 1962. On 5 July 1973 the government was overthrown by a military *coup*, led by Maj.-Gen. Juvénal Habyalimana, who became President. The National Assembly was dissolved and political activity suspended. The President appoints and leads a Council of Ministers. In July 1975 a new ruling party was established.
Telephones: 2452 (1974).
Radio: 65 000 (1975).
Length of roadways: 4039 miles *6500 km* (31 Dec. 1974).
Universities: 1.
Adult illiteracy: 90% (estimate).
Expectation of life: Males 39·4 years; females 42·6 years (UN estimates for 1970–75).
Defence: Total armed forces 3750.
Cinemas: 4 (seating capacity 800) and 15 part-time (1968).

SAN MARINO

Official name: Serenissima Repubblica di San Marino (Most Serene Republic of San Marino).
Population: 19 621 (estimate for 30 June 1975).
Area: 23·4 miles² *60,5 km²*.
Language: Italian.
Religion: Roman Catholic.
Capital city: San Marino, population 4512 (1975 est).
Highest point: Mt Titano, 2424 ft *739 m*.
Head of State: There are two Captains-Regent (*Capitani reggenti*) appointed every six months.
Climate: Warm summers, average maximum 85 °F; dry, cold winters.
Exports: n.a. (included with Italy).
Monetary unit: Italian currency (*qv*).
Political history and government: Founded as a city-state in AD 301. In customs union with Italy since 1862. Legislative power is vested in the unicameral Great and General Council, with 60 members elected by universal adult suffrage for 5 years. Women have had the right to vote since 1960 but only men may stand for election. The Council elects two of its members to act jointly as Captains-Regent, with the functions of Head of State and Government, for

6 months at a time. Executive power is held by the Congress of State, with 10 members elected by the Council for the duration of its term. San Marino has a multi-party political system.
Telephones: 4 736 (1974).
Radio: 4700 (1973).
TV: 3200 (1973).
Length of roadways: 137 miles *220 km.*
Cinemas: 8 (1973).

SÃO TOMÉ AND PRÍNCIPE

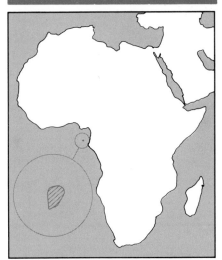

Official name: A República Democrática de São Tomé e Príncipe (The Democratic Republic of São Tomé and Príncipe).
Population: 73 811 (census of 30 Sept. 1970); 75 000 (estimate for 1 July 1972); 81 000 (UN estimate for mid-1976).
Area: 372 miles² *964 km².*
Languages: Portuguese.
Religion: Roman Catholic.
Capital city: São Tomé, population 5714 at 15 Dec. 1960.
Other principal town: Santo António.
Highest point: Pico de Tomé, 6640 ft *2024 m.*
Head of State: Dr. Manuel Pinto da Costa (b. 1910), President.
Prime Minister: Miguel Anjos da Cunha Lisboa Trovoada.
Climate: Warm and humid, with an average temperature of 80 °F.
Gross national product: $40 million in 1974 (World Bank estimate).
Exports: 322·6 million escudos in 1973: Cocoa 87·0%.
Monetary unit: Escudo. 1 escudo = 100 centavos.
Denominations:
 Coins: 10, 20, 50 centavos, 1, 2½, 5, 10, 20 escudos.
 Notes: 20, 50, 100, 500, 1000 escudos.
Exchange rate to US dollar: 38.48 (July 1977).
Political history and government: A former Portuguese territory, independent since 12 July 1975. Before independence, Portugal recognized the islands' Liberation Movement, whose leader became first President. A Constitutional Assembly, elected on 6 July 1975, is to approve a new constitution. Executive power is held by the President, who appoints and leads the Cabinet, including a Prime Minister.
Telephones: 677 (1975).
Radio: 10 000 (1975).
Length of roadways: 179 miles *288 km* (1972).
Cinemas: 1 (seating capacity 1000) in 1972.

SAUDI ARABIA

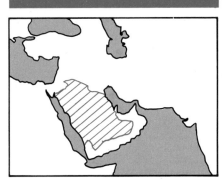

Official name: Al-Mamlaka al-'Arabiya as-Sa'udiya (Kingdom of Saudi Arabia).
Population: 7 012 642 (census of 9–14 Sept. 1974).
Area: 830 000 miles² *2 149 690 km².*
Language: Arabic.
Religion: Muslim.
Capital city: Riyadh, population 500 000 (1975 est.)
Other principal towns (1975): Jidda (Jeddah) 400 000; Mecca 250 000; Medina 100 000; Dammam 60 000; Al-Khobar 60 000.
Highest point: Jebel Razikh, 12 002 ft *3658 m.*
Principal mountain range: Tihāmatash Shām.
Principal rivers: The flows are seasonal only.
Head of State and Prime Minister: HM King Khalid ibn Abdul-Aziz (b. 1912).
Climate: Very hot and dry. Mostly desert; frequent sandstorms. Average summer temperature 100 °F to 120 °F on coast, up to 130 °F inland. High humidity. Some places have droughts for years. In Riyadh, average maximum is 107 °F June–August; January coldest (40°F to 70 °F). In Jeddah, average maximum 84 °F (January, February) to 99 °F (July, August), minimum 65 °F (February) to 80 °F (August), rainiest month is November (two days).
Labour force: 2 121 000 (1970): Agriculture, forestry and fishing 66·0% (ILO estimates).
Gross domestic product: 100 965 million riyals (provisional) in 1973/74: Mining and quarrying 79·5%. Revised total is 99 517 million riyals.
Exports: $9089·4 million in 1973: Petroleum and petroleum products 95·7% (crude petroleum 92·3%).
Monetary unit: Saudi riyal. 1 riyal = 20 qursh = 100 halalah.
Denominations:
 Coins 1, 5, 10, 25, 50 halalah, 1, 2, 4 qursh.
 Notes 1, 5, 10, 50, 100 riyals.
Exchange rate to US dollar: 3.535 (July 1977).
Political history and government: Formerly part of Turkey's Ottoman Empire. In 1913 the Sultan of Nejd overthrew Turkish rule in central Arabia. Between 1919 and 1925 he gained control of the Hijaz and was proclaimed King there on 8 Jan. 1926. On 23 Sept. 1932 the Hijaz and Nejd were combined and named Saudi Arabia. The country is an absolute monarchy, with no parliament or political parties. The King rules in accordance with the *Sharia*, the sacred law of Islam. He appoints and leads a Council of Ministers, which serves as the instrument of royal authority in both legislative and executive matters. The King is also assisted by advisory councils, nominated or approved by him.
Telephones: 84 650 (1973).

Daily newspapers: 11 (1973).
 Total circulation: 96 000.
Radio: 255 000 (1975).
TV: 124 000 (1975).
Length of roadways: 11 436 miles *18 404 km* (31 Dec. 1975).
Length of railways: 379 miles *610 km.*
Universities: 6.
Adult illiteracy: 85% (estimate).
Expectation of life: Males 44·2 years; females 46·5 years (UN estimates for 1970–75).
Defence: Military service: voluntary; total armed forces 51 500; defence expenditure, 1975/76: $6771 million.

SENEGAL

Official name: La République du Sénégal.
Population: 5 085 388 (census of 16 Apr. 1976).
Area: 75 750 miles² *196 192 km².*
Languages: French (official), Wolof, several other local dialects.
Religions: Muslim, Christian minority.
Capital city: Dakar, population 667 400 (1973 est.)
Other principal towns (1970): Kaolack 96 238; Thiès 90 456; Saint-Louis 81 204; Rufisque 48 101; Ziguinchor 45 772; Djourbel 40 230.
Highest point: Gounou Mt, 4970 ft *1515 m.*
Principal mountain ranges: Fouta Djallon.
Principal rivers: Gambia (Gambie), Casamance, Sénégal.
Head of State: Léopold-Sédar Senghor (b. 9 Oct. 1906), President.
Prime Minister: Abdou Diouf (b. 7 Sept. 1935).
Climate: Tropical. Hot, with long dry season and short, wet season. Average annual temperature about 84 °F. Heavy rainfall on coast. Average maximum 90 °F to 108 °F in interior; average minimum about 60 °F. In Dakar, on coast, average maximum 79 °F (January) to 89 °F (September, October); minimum 63 °F (February) to 76 °F (July to October); rainiest month is August (13 days).
Labour force: 1 738 000 (1970): Agriculture, forestry and fishing 79·7% (ILO estimates); 1 647 812 (official estimate for 1972–73).
Gross domestic product: 279 700 million CFA francs in 1974.
Exports: $194·7 million in 1973: Fish and fish preparations 10·8%; Oil-seed cake and meal 15·5%; Natural phosphates 11·4%; Groundnut oil 19·2%.
Monetary unit: Franc de la Communauté financière africaine.
Denominations:
 Coins 1, 2, 5, 10, 25, 50 and 100 CFA francs.
 Notes 50, 100, 500, 1000 and 5000 CFA francs.
Exchange rate to US dollar: 242·8 (July 1977).
Political history and government: Formerly part of French West Africa, Senegal

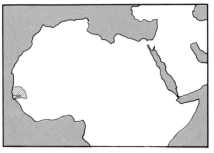

joined French Sudan (now the Republic of Mali) to form the Federation of Mali on 4 April 1959. By agreement with France, signed on 4 Apr. 1960, the Federation became independent on 20 June 1960. Senegal seceded, and became a separate independent republic, on 20 Aug. 1960. A new constitution was promulgated on 7 Mar. 1963. Senegal became a one-party state in 1966 but two legal opposition parties have since been formed (in July 1974 and February 1976). A constitutional amendment, approved by the government on 10 Mar. 1976, fixed the maximum number of permitted parties at three. Legislative power rests with the unicameral National Assembly, with 100 members elected for 5 years by universal adult suffrage (at the last election, on 28 Jan. 1973, all candidates were elected unopposed). Executive power is held by the President, also elected for 5 years at the same time as the Assembly. He appoints and leads a Cabinet, including a Prime Minister. Senegal comprises 7 regions, each with an appointed Governor and an elected local assembly.

Telephones: 36 385 (1974).
Daily newspapers: 2 (1973).
   Total circulation: 25 000 (one daily).
Radio: 287 000 (1975).
TV: 1800 (1975).
Length of roadways: 8246 miles *13 271 km* (31 Dec. 1973).
Length of roadways: 9582 miles *15 422 km* (1971).
Length of railways: 642 miles *1034 km.*
Universities: 1.
Adult illiteracy: 95% (estimate).
Expectation of life: Males 38·5 years; females 41·6 years (UN estimates for 1970–75).
Defence: Military service: two years, selective; total armed forces 5950; defence expenditure, 1976: $38 million.
Cinemas: 77 (seating capacity 33 500) in 1965.

SEYCHELLES

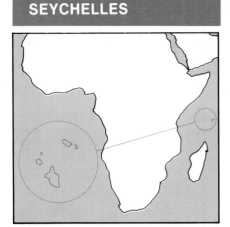

Official name: Republic of Seychelles.
Population: 53 096 (census of 5 May 1971); 59 000 (estimate for 1 July 1976).
Area: 156 miles² *404 km².*
Languages: Creole 94·4%; English 3·0%; French 1·9% (1971).
Religions: Christian (mainly Roman Catholic) 98·2% (1971).
Capital city: Port Victoria, population 13 736 (including suburbs) at 1971 census.
Other principal town: Takamaka.
Highest point: Morne Seychellois, 2992 ft *912m.*
Head of State: (France) Albert René (b. 16 Nov. 1935), President.
Climate: Warm and pleasant, with temperatures generally between 75 °F and 85 °F, cooler on high ground. Hottest during

north-west monsoon, December to May. South-east monsoon is from June to November. Average annual rainfall on Mahé between 70 in and 135 in. In Port Victoria, average annual temperature 84·5 °F, rainfall 91 in.
Labour force: 19 827 aged 15 and over (1971 census): Agriculture, forestry and fishing 29·5%; Construction 24·0%; Community, social and personal services 26·9%.
Gross national product: $30 million in 1974 (World Bank estimate).
Exports: 12·9 million rupees (excluding re-exports) in 1975: Copra 56·6%; Cinnamon bark 28·0%.
Monetary unit: Seychelles rupee. 1 rupee = 100 cents.
Denominations:
   Coins 1, 5, 25, 50 cents, 1, 5, 10 rupees.
   Notes 5, 10, 20, 50, 100 rupees.
Exchange rate to US dollar: 7.75 (July 1977).
Political history and government: Formerly a British colony, with internal self-government from 1 Oct. 1975. Following a constitutional conference on 19–22 Jan. 1976, Seychelles became an independent republic, within the Commonwealth, on 29 June 1976. At the same time three islands which formed part of the British Indian Ocean Territory (established on 8 Nov. 1965) were returned to Seychelles. The pre-independence Prime Minister became the first President, leading a Cabinet which included a Prime Minister. The President was deposed on 5 June 1977 in a *coup* by armed opponents of his rule. At the request of the *coup* leaders, the Prime Minister became President. The constitution and the elected National Assembly were dissolved. The President rules by decree with the assistance of an appointed Cabinet.
Telephones: 2857 (1974).
Daily newspapers: 2 (1973).
   Total circulation: 4000.
Radio: 16 000 (1975).
Length of roadways: 127 miles *204 km.*
Adult illiteracy: 42·2% (males 44·3%; females 40·2%) in 1971.
Expectation of life: Males 61·9 years; females 68·0 years (1970–72).
Defence: After the June 1977 *coup,* a volunteer 'people's militia' was formed.
Cinemas: 2 (seating capacity 2400) in 1972.

SIERRA LEONE

Official name: The Republic of Sierra Leone.
Population: 3 002 426 (census of 8 Dec. 1974, including 10 per cent adjustment for underenumeration); 3 111 000 (estimate for 1 July 1976).
Area: 27 699 miles² *71 740 km².*
Languages: English (official), Krio, Mende, Temne.
Religions: Animist, Muslim, Christian minorities.
Capital city: Freetown, population 214 443 at 1 July 1974.
Other principal towns: Bo 26 000; Kenema 13 000; Makeni 12 000.
Highest point: Bintimani and Kundukonko peaks, 6390 ft *1948 m.*
Principal mountain range: Loma.
Principal rivers: Siwa, Jong, Rokel.
Head of State: Dr Siaka Probyn Stevens (b. 24 Aug. 1905), President.
Prime Minister: Christian Alusine Kamara-Taylor (b. 3 June 1917).
Climate: Generally hot with two main seasons: wet (May–October) when humidity is tryingly high, and dry (November–April). The average annual rainfall at Freetown is 138 in and the average daily high temperature nearly 85 °F.

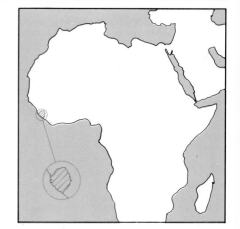

Labour force: 937 737 (excluding under-enumeration) at census of 1 Apr. 1963; 1 055 000 (1970): Agriculture, forestry and fishing 71·5% (ILO estimates).
Gross domestic product: 475·9 million leones (provisional) in 1973/74: Agriculture, forestry and fishing 30·2%; Mining and quarrying 18·4%; Trade, restaurants and hotels 15·6%; Transport, storage and communication 10·2%. Revised total is 482·6 million leones.
Exports: $141·4 million (excluding re-exports) in 1974: Metalliferous ores and metal scrap 14·3% (iron ore and concentrates 10·5%); Diamonds (non-industrial) 62·7%.
Monetary unit: Leone. 1 leone = 100 cents.
Denominations:
   Coins ½, 1, 5, 10, 20, 50 cents.
   Notes 50 cents, 1, 2, 5 leones.
Exchange rate to US dollar: 1.1624 (July 1977).
Political history of government: A former British dependency which became independent, within the Commonwealth, on 27 Apr. 1961. Following disputed elections, the army assumed power on 21 Mar. 1967. Two days later, in a counter-*coup,* another group of officers established a National Reformation Council (NRC), which suspended the constitution. The NRC was overthrown on 17–18 Apr. 1968 by junior officers who restored constitutional government and civilian rule on 26 Apr. 1968, when Dr. Siaka Stevens, appointed Prime Minister in 1967, was sworn in. A republic was established on 19 April 1971 and two days later Dr Stevens was elected President and took office. Legislative power is held by the unicameral House of Representatives, with 100 members: 85 elected by universal adult suffrage for 5 years, 12 Paramount Chiefs (one from each District) and 3 members appointed by the President. Executive power is held by the President, elected by the House for 5 years. He appoints and leads the Cabinet, including a Vice-President and a Prime Minister. The country has 4 regions, administered through the Ministry of the Interior.
Telephones: 10 331 (1974).
Daily newspapers: 5 (1970).
   Total circulation: 45 000.
Radio: 62 000 (1975).
TV: 6100 (1975).
Length of roadways: 4389 miles *7064 km* (31 Dec. 1975).
Universities: 1.
Adult illiteracy: 93·3%.
Expectation of life: Males 41·9 years; females 45·1 years (UN estimates for 1970–75).
Defence: Total armed forces 2145.
Cinemas: 10 (seating capacity 5500) in 1969.

SINGAPORE

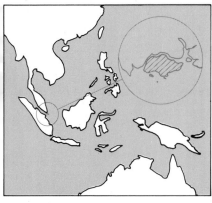

Official name: The Republic of Singapore.
Population: 2 070 507 (census of 22 June 1970); 2 278 200 (estimate for 30 June 1976).
Area: 232 miles² *602 km²*.
Languages: Malay, Mandarin Chinese, Tamil, English.
Religion: Muslim, Buddhist, Hindu.
Capital city: Singapore City, population 1 327 500 (1974).
Highest point: Bukit Timah (Hill of Tin), 581 ft *177 m*.
Principal rivers: Sungei Seletar (9 miles [*14 km*]).
Head of State: Sir Benjamin Henry Sheares, GCB (b. 12 Aug. 1907), President.
Prime Minister: Lee Kuan Yew (b. 16 Sept. 1923).
Climate: Hot and humid throughout the year, with average maximum of 86 °F to 89 °F, minimum 73 °F to 75 °F. Frequent rainfall (between 11 and 19 days each month).
Labour force: 833 525 (excluding 39 452 unemployed) aged 10 and over (June 1975): Manufacturing 26·2%; Trade, restaurants and hotels 23·0%; Community, social and personal services 24·5%.
Gross domestic product: S$12 575 million (provisional) in 1974: Manufacturing (excluding government) 23·6%; Trade, restaurants and hotels 28·6%; Transport, storage and communication 10·5%; Finance, insurance, real estate and business services (excluding government) 10·1%; Community, social and personal services 11·0%. Revised total is S$12 543 million.
Exports: US$5377·1 million in 1975: Natural rubber 10·4%; Petroleum and petroleum products 33·3% (petroleum products 32·9%); Machinery and transport equipment 22·7% (electrical machinery, apparatus, etc. 11·5%).
Monetary unit: Singapore dollar (S$). 1 dollar = 100 cents.
Denominations:
Coins 1, 5, 10, 20, 50 cents, 1 dollar.
Notes 1, 5, 10, 25, 50, 100, 500, 1000, 10 000 dollars.
Exchange rate to US dollar: 2.4635 (July 1977).
Political history and government: A former British colony, with internal self-government from 3 June 1959. Singapore became a constituent state of the independent Federation of Malaysia, within the Commonwealth, on 16 Sept. 1963 but seceded and became a separate independent country on 9 Aug. 1965. The new stated joined the Commonwealth on 16 Oct. 1965 and became a republic on 22 Dec. 1965. Legislative power rests with the unicameral Parliament, with 65 members elected by universal adult suffrage from single-member constituencies for 5 years (subject to dissolution). The President is elected by Parliament for a 4-year term as constitutional Head of State. Effective executive authority rests with the Cabinet, led by the Prime Minister, which is appointed by the President and responsible to Parliament.
Telephones: 280 280 (1974).
Daily newspapers: 10 (1976).
Total circulation: 477 018.
Radio: 369 000 (1977).
TV: 310 000 (1977).
Length of roadways: 1347 miles *2167 km* (1975).
Length of railways: 30 miles *48 km*.
Universities: 2.
Adult illiteracy: 31·1% (males 17·0%; females 45·7 %) in 1970.
Expectation of life: Males 65·1 years; females 70·0 years (1970).
Defence: Military service: 24–36 months; total armed forces 31 000; defence expenditure, 1976/77: US$340 million.
Cinemas: 75 (seating capacity 62 900) and one drive-in for 889 cars (1972).

SOMALIA

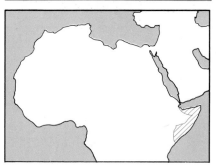

Official name: Jamhuriyadda Dimuqradiga Somaliya (Somali Democratic Republic).
Population: 2 941 000 (estimate for 1 July 1972); 3 261 000 (UN estimate for mid-1976).
Area: 246 201 miles² *637 657 km²*.
Languages: Somali, Arabic, English, Italian.
Religions: Sunni Muslim; Christian minority.
Capital city: Muqdisho (Mogadishu or Mogadiscio), population 230 000 (1972 est).
Other principal towns (1966): Hargeisa 60 000; Kisimayu 60 000; Merca 56 000; Berbera 50 000.
Highest point: Surud Ad, 7 894 ft *2406 m*.
Principal mountain range: Guban.
Principal rivers: Juba (Giuba) and Scebeli.
Head of State: Maj-Gen Muhammad Siyad Barrah (b. 1919), President and Prime Minister.
Climate: Hot and dry. Average temperature of 80 °F. Average maximum over 90 °F in interior and on Gulf of Aden. Cooler on Indian Ocean coast. Average rainfall less than 17 inches. In Mogadiscio, average maximum 83 °F (July, August), to 90 °F (April), minimum 73 °F (January, July, August), to 78 °F (April), rainiest month is July (20 days).
Labour force: 1 084 000 (1970): Agriculture, forestry and fishing 84·7% (ILO estimates).
Gross domestic product: $249 million in 1970 (UN estimate).
Exports: $43·1 million in 1972: Live animals 12·4%; Fruit and vegetables 67·7% (fresh bananas and plantains 26·2%; preserved and prepared fruit 41·4%).
Monetary unit: Somali shilling. 1 shilling = 100 centesimi.
Denominations:
Coins 1, 5, 10, 50 centesimi, 1 shilling.
Notes 5, 10, 20, 100 shillings.
Exchange rate to US dollar: 6.295 (July 1977).
Political history and government: Formed on 1 July 1960 as an independent country, called the Somali Republic, by a merger of the Trust Territory of Somaliland, under Italian protection, with British Somaliland (a protectorate until 26 June 1960). Following the assassination of the President on 15 Oct. 1969, the government was overthrown by a military *coup* on 21 Oct. 1969, when the constitution and political parties were abolished and the National Assembly dissolved. A Supreme Revolutionary Council (SRC) was established and the country's present name adopted on 22 Oct. 1969. The President of the SRC became Head of State. On 1 July 1976 the SRC was dissolved and its power transferred to the newly-formed Somali Socialist Revolutionary Party. All members of the SRC became members of the ruling party's central committee and the President is the party's secretary-general. He directs the government with the assistance of a Council of Ministers. Somalia comprises 15 regions.
Telephones: 5000 (1970).
Daily newspapers: 2 (1973).
Total circulation: 4000.
Radio: 68 000 (1975).
Length of roadways: 10 702 miles *17 223 km* (1971).
Universities: 1.
Adult illiteracy: 40% (claimed after the 1974–5 literacy campaign).
Expectation of life: Males 39·4 years; females 42·6 years (UN estimates for 1970–75).
Defence: Military service: voluntary; total armed forces 25 000; defence expenditure, 1974: $15 million.
Cinemas: 26 (seating capacity 23 000) in 1970.

SOUTH AFRICA

Official name: Republic of South Africa, or Republiek van Suid-Afrika.
Population: 21 794 328 (census of 6 May 1970); 26 129 000 (estimate for 1 July 1976).
Area: 471 445 miles² *1 221 037 km²* (excluding Walvis Bay, area 434 miles² *1124 km²*).
Languages: Afrikaans, English, Xhosa, Zulu, Sesuto, Tswana, Sepedi.
Religions: Christian; Muslim and Hindu minorities.
Capital city: Administrative: Pretoria, population 561 703 (1970).
Legislative: Cape Town (Kaapstad), 1 096 597 (1970).
Other principal towns (1970): Johannesburg 1 432 643; Durban 843 327; Port Elizabeth 468 577; Bloemfontein 180 179; Vereeniging 169 533; Pietermaritzburg 158 921; Benoni 149 563; Germiston 132 273.
Highest point: Injasuti, 11 182 ft *3408 m*.
Principal mountain range: Drakensberg.
Principal rivers: Orange (Oranje), 1300 miles *2092 km*; Limpopo; Vaal.
Head of State: Dr Nicolaas D Diederichs (b. 17 Nov. 1903), State President.

Prime Minister: Balthazar Johannes Vorster (b. 13 Dec. 1915).

Climate: Generally temperate (cool summers, mild winters). Average temperatures about 63 °F. In Cape Town, average maximum 63 °F (July) to 79 °F (February), minimum 45 °F (July) to 60 °F (January, February), rainiest month is July (10 days). In Johannesburg, average maximum 62 °F (June) to 78 °F (December, January), minimum 39 °F (June, July) to 58 °F (January, February), rainiest month is January (12 days). Absolute maximum temperature 124·8 °F (*51,56 °C*), Main, 28 Jan. 1903; absolute minimum 5·5 °F (*−14,7 °C*), Carolina, 23 July 1926.

Labour force: 7 556 930 (excluding 429 290 unemployed) at 1970 census (sample tabulation): Agriculture, forestry and fishing 29·6%; Manufacturing 13·5%; Community, social and personal services 20·8%.

Gross domestic product: 18 799 million rand (provisional) in 1973 (including South West Africa): Mining and quarrying 13·3%; Manufacturing 23·1%; Trade, restaurants and hotels 12·9%; Government services 10·0%. Revised total is 19 074 million rand.

Exports: $2605·5 million (excluding gold) in 1972: Food and live animals 28·6%; Diamonds (non-industrial) 10·4%. Figures include the trade of Botswana, Lesotho, South West Africa and Swaziland.

Monetary unit: Rand. 1 rand = 100 cents.

Denominations:
Coins ½, 1, 2, 5, 10, 20, 50 cents, 1 rand.
Notes 1, 2, 5, 10, 20 rand.

Exchange rate to US dollar: 0·87 (July 1977).

Political history and government: After the Boer War of 1899–1902 two former Boer republics, the Transvaal and the Orange Free State, became part of the British Empire. On 31 May 1910 they were merged with the British territories of Natal and Cape Colony (now Cape Province) to form the Union of South Africa, a dominion under the British crown. Under the Statute of Westminster, passed by the British Parliament in December 1931 and accepted by South Africa in June 1934, the Union was recognized as an independent country within the Commonwealth. Following a referendum among white voters on 5 Oct. 1960, South Africa became a republic, outside the Commonwealth, on 31 May 1961. Legislative power rests with the bicameral Parliament, made up exclusively of European (white) members who hold office for 5 years (subject to dissolution). The Senate has 51 members: 42 elected by electoral colleges of the four provinces and 9 nominated by the State President (two for each province and one representative of the Cape Coloured people). The House of Assembly has 165 members directly elected by Europeans only. Executive power rests with the State President, elected by a joint session of Parliament for a 7-year term as constitutional Head of State. He acts on the advice of the Executive Council (Cabinet), led by a Prime Minister, which is appointed by the President and responsible to Parliament. Each province has an Administrator appointed by the President for 5 years and a provincial council elected (by whites only) for 5 years.

South Africa has granted independence to the Transkei (26 Oct, 1976) and Bophuthatswana (6 Dec. 1977), African 'homelands' established by the government, but these acts have not received international recognition.

Telephones: 1 935 831 (1974).

Daily newspapers: 26 (including South West Africa) in 1973.
Total circulation: 1 192 000 (23 dailies).

Radio: 2 336 750 (1975).

TV: 250 000 (1976 est.).

Length of roadways: 114 973 miles *185 031 km* (31 Mar. 1975).

Length of railways: 12 373 miles *19 909 km.*

Universities: 16.

Adult illiteracy: 59·7% (males 59·3%; females 60·2%) in 1960 (Africans only).

Expectation of life:
All races: Males 47·8 years; females 50·3 years (UN estimates for 1970–75).
For non-Africans (1959–60):
Asiatic: Males 57·70 years; females 59·57 years.
Coloured: Males 49·62 years; females 54·28 years.
White: Males 64·73 years; females 71·67 years.

Defence: Military service: 12 months; total armed forces 51 500 (including 35 400 conscripts); defence expenditure, 1976/77: $1494 million.

Cinemas: 686 (seating capacity 498 000) and 120 drive-in for 6500 cars (1971).

SPAIN

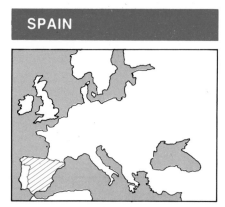

Official name: The Kingdom of Spain.

*Population: 33 956 376 (census of 31 Dec. 1970); 35 971 000 (estimate for 1 July 1976).

*Area: 194 897 miles² *504 782 km².*

Languages: Spanish (Castilian), Catalán, Basque.

Religions: Roman Catholic.

Capital city: Madrid, population 3 520 320 at 1 July 1974.

Other principal towns (1974): Barcelona 1 809 722; Valencia 713 026; Sevilla (Seville) 588 784; Zaragoza (Saragossa) 547 317; Bilbao 457 655; Málaga 402 978; Las Palmas 328 187; Valladolid 275 012; Palma de Mallorca 267 081; Córdoba 249 515.

Highest point: Mt Teide (Canary Is), 12 190 ft *3716 m.*

Principal mountain ranges: Pyrenees, Cordillera Cantábrica, Sierra Morena.

Principal rivers: Ebro (556 miles 895 *km*), Duero (Douro), Tajo (Tagus), Guadiana, Guadalquivir.

Head of State: HM King Juan Carlos (b. 5 Jan. 1938).

Head of Government: Adolfo Suárez González (b. 25 Sept. 1932), President of the Government (Prime Minister).

Climate: Cool summers and rainy winters on north coast; hot summers and cold winters in interior; hot summers and mild winters on south coast. In Madrid, average maximum 47 °F (January) to 87 °F (July), minimum 33 °F (January) to 62 °F (July, August), rainiest month is March (11 days). In Barcelona, average maximum 56 °F (January) to 82 °F (August), minimum 42 °F (January) to 69 °F (July, August), rainiest months are April, May, October (each 8 days). Absolute maximum temperature 46,2 °C (*115·2 °F*), Gualulcacin, 17 July 1943; absolute minimum −32,0 °C (*−25.6°F*), Estangento, 2 Feb. 1956.

Labour force: 13 388 000 aged 10 and over (Jan.–March 1975): Agriculture, forestry and fishing 22·3%; Manufacturing 25·2%; Trade, restaurants and hotels 16·0%; Community, social and personal services (including activities not adequately described) 18·1%.

Gross domestic product: 4 933 800 million pesetas in 1974: Manufacturing 28·2%; Trade, restaurants and hotels 15·5% (trade 11·5%).

Exports: $7675·4 million in 1975: Food and live animals 17·5% (fruit and vegetables 13·1%); Machinery and transport equipment 25·6% (transport equipment 12·5%).

Monetary unit: Spanish peseta. 1 peseta = 100 céntimos.

Denominations:
Coins 10, 50 céntimos, 1, 2½, 5, 25, 50, 100 pesetas.
Notes 100, 500, 1000 pesetas.

Exchange rate to US dollar: 87.80 (July 1977).

Political history and government: In the civil war of 1936–39 the forces of the republic (established on 14 Apr. 1931) were defeated. Gen Francisco Franco, leader of the successful insurgent forces, acted as Head of State until his death on 20 Nov. 1975. In accordance with the 1947 Law of Succession, Prince Juan Carlos de Borbón, grandson of the last reigning monarch, became King on 22 Nov. 1975. Spain is now an hereditary monarchy, with the King as Head of State. He appoints the President of the Government (Prime Minister) and, on the latter's recommendation, other members of the Council of Ministers. The government's Political Reform Bill, passed by the unicameral Legislative Assembly (*Cortes*) on 18 Nov. 1976, was approved by a popular referendum on 15 Dec. 1976. This provided for a new bicameral *Cortes*, comprising a Congress of Deputies (350 elected members) and a Senate of 248 members (207 elected, 41 nominated by the King). Elections for the new *Cortes* were held on 15 June 1977. The old *Cortes* expired on 30 June 1977; the new one was inaugurated on 13 July and formally opened on 22 July 1977. Members hold office for up to 4 years. Spain comprises 50 provinces, each with its own Assembly (*Diputación Provincial*) and an appointed Civil Governor.

Telephones: 7 836 000 (1975).

Daily newspapers: 115 (1973).
Total circulation: 3 396 000.

Radio: 8 075 000 (1975).

TV: 6 525 000 (1975).

Length of roadways: 88 598 miles *142 585 km* (31 Dec. 1974).

Length of railways: 12 016 miles *19 338 km* (1973).

Universities: 23 (plus 8 technical universities).

Adult illiteracy: 9·9% (males 5·7%; females 13·7%) in 1970.

Expectation of life: Males 69·69 years; females 74·96 years (1970, excluding Ceuta and Melilla).

Defence: Military service: 18 months; total armed forces 302 300 (including 213 400 conscripts); defence expenditure, 1975: $1766 million.

Cinemas: 5632 (seating capacity 4 380 000) in 1973 (cinemas exhibiting 35 mm films).

* Figures refer to Metropolitan Spain, including the Canary Islands and Spanish North Africa (Ceuta and Melilla).

SRI LANKA

Official name: The Republic of Sri Lanka ('Exalted Ceylon').

Population: 12 711 143 (census of 9 Oct. 1971); 13 249 000 (estimate for 1 July 1973).

Area: 25 332 miles² *65 610 km².*

Languages: Sinhala (official) 69%; Tamil 23%; English.

Religions: Buddhist 66·2%; Hindu 18·5%; Christian 8·4%; Muslim 6·8% (1963).
Capital city: Colombo, population 618 000 (1973 est.)
Other principal towns (1973): Dehiwala-Mt Lavinia 136 000; Jaffna 112 000; Kandy 93 602 (1971); Galle 72 720 (1971).
Highest point: Pidurutalagala, 8292 ft *2527 m.*
Principal rivers: Mahaweli Ganga (203 miles [*327 km*]), Kelani Ganga.
Head of State: William Gopallawa, MBE (b. 16 Sept. 1897), President.
Prime Minister: Junius Richard Jayawardene (b. 17 Sept. 1906).
Climate: Tropical, with average temperature of about 80 °F (*27 °C*). Monsoon strikes the south-west of the island. In Colombo average maximum 85 °F (June to December) to 88 °F (March, April); minimum 72 °F (December, January, February) to 78 °F (May), May and October rainiest (each 19 days).
Labour force: 3 648 875 (excluding 839 264 unemployed) at 1971 census: Agriculture, forestry and fishing 54·8%; Manufacturing 10·2%; Trade, restaurants and hotels 10·3%; Community, social and personal services 14·8%.
Gross domestic product: 21 341 million rupees (provisional) in 1974: Agriculture, forestry and fishing 39·8% (agriculture 36·1%); Manufacturing 12·4%; Trade, restaurants and hotels 16·1% (trade 14·2%); Community, social and personal services 10·6%. Revised total is 21 490 million rupees.
Exports: $519·7 million (excluding re-exports) in 1974: Tea 39·5%; Other food 12·2%; Natural rubber 21·4%.
Monetary unit: Sri Lanka rupee. 1 rupee = 100 cents.
Denominations:
    Coins 1, 2, 5, 10, 25, 50 cents, 1 rupee.
    Notes 2, 5, 10, 50, 100 rupees.
Exchange rate to US dollar: 7.221 (July 1977).
Political history and government: Ceylon (now Sri Lanka) was a British dependency until achieving independence, within the Commonwealth, on 4 Feb. 1948. The country became a republic, under the present name, on 22 May 1972, when the Governor-General became President. Legislative and executive power is vested in the unicameral National State Assembly, with 166 members elected for 6 years by universal adult suffrage. Direction of the government is vested in the Cabinet, headed by the Prime Minister, which is responsible to the Assembly. Ministers are appointed by the President, a constitutional Head of State appointed for 4 years on the nomination of the Prime Minister. The country is divided into 21 districts, each administered by an appointed government agent.

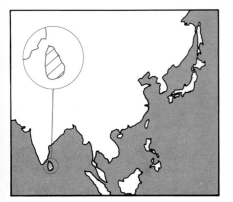

Telephones: 67 753 (1973).
Daily newspapers: 24 (1972).
    Total circulation: 536 000 (1971).
Radio: 530 000 (1975).
Length of roadways: 19 252 miles *30 983 km* (31 Dec. 1975).
Length of railways: 954 miles *1535 km.*
Universities: 1 (with six campuses).
Adult illiteracy: 24·5% (males 14·4%; females 35·9%) in 1963.
Expectation of life: Males 64·8 years; females 66·9 years (1967).
Defence: Military service: voluntary; total armed forces 13 600; defence expenditure, 1976: $19 million.
Cinemas: 303 (seating capacity 128 500) in 1971.

SUDAN

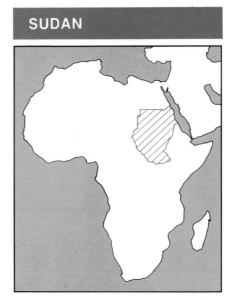

Official name: Al Jumhuriyat as-Sudan al-Dimuqratiya (The Democratic Republic of Sudan).
Population: 14 171 732 (census of 3 Apr. 1973).
Area: 967 500 miles² *2 505 813 km².*
Languages: Arabic, Nilotic, others.
Religions: Muslim (in North), Animist (in South).
Capital city: Al Khurtum (Khartoum), population 333 906 at 1973 census.
Other principal towns (1973): Omdurman 299 399; Khartoum North 150 989; Port Sudan 132 632; Wadi Medani 106 715; El Obeid 90 073.
Highest point: Mt Kinyeti, 10 456 ft *3187 m.*
Principal mountain ranges: Darfur Highlands, Nubian Mts.
Principal rivers: Nile (the Blue Nile and White Nile join at Khartoum), 4145 miles *6670 km.*
Head of State: Maj-Gen Ga'afar Muhammad an-Numairi (b. 1 Jan. 1930), President and Prime Minister.
Climate: Hot and dry in desert areas of north (average maximum up to 111 °F); rainy and humid in tropical south. Average temperature about 70 °F. In Khartoum, average maximum 90 °F (January) to 107 °F (May), minimum 59 °F (January) to 79 °F (June); rainiest month is August (6 days). Absolute maximum 49,0 °C (*120·2 °F*), Wadi Halfa, 7 and 8 June 1932, 9 and 13 June 1933, 19 June 1941; absolute minimum −0,8 °C (*30·6 °F*), Zalingei, 6 Feb. 1957.
Labour force: 4 442 921 (1973 census): Agriculture, forestry and fishing 71·5%; Community, social and personal services 11·0%.

Gross domestic product: S£1510·8 million in 1974/75: Agriculture, forestry and fishing 38·7%; Trade, restaurants and hotels 16·2%.
Exports: $429·4 million in 1975: Oil-seeds, oil nuts and oil kernels 32·7% (groundnuts 23·1%); Raw cotton 44·2%.
Monetary unit: Sudanese pound. 1 pound = 100 piastres = 1000 millièmes.
Denominations:
    Coins 1, 2, 5, 10 millièmes, 2, 5, 10 piastres.
    Notes 25, 50 piastres, 1, 5, 10 pounds.
Exchange rate to US dollar: 0.3482 (July 1977).
Political history and government: An Anglo-Egyptian condominium from 19 Jan. 1899 until becoming an independent parliamentary republic on 1 Jan. 1956. On 25 May 1969 the civilian government was overthrown by army officers, under Col. (promoted Maj-Gen) Ga'afar an-Numairi, who established a Revolutionary Command Council (RCC) and introduced the country's present name. Gen Numairi became Prime Minister on 28 Oct. 1969. On 13 Aug. 1971 the RCC promulgated a provisional constitution, proclaiming socialist principles. Gen Numairi was elected President (unopposed) in September 1971 and inaugurated for a 6-year term on 12 Oct. 1971. The RCC was dissolved and the Sudanese Socialist Union (SSU) established as the country's sole political party. A new definitive constitution was introduced on 8 May 1973. Executive power is vested in the President, nominated by the SSU, and he appoints a Council of Ministers. Legislative power is vested in the People's Assembly of 250 members (125 elected for 4 years by universal adult suffrage, 100 nominated by mass organizations and 25 appointed by the President). The Southern Region also has an elected regional assembly. Sudan comprises 15 provinces, each administered by an appointed Commissioner.
Telephones: 56 146 (1974).
Daily newspapers: 22 (1970).
    Total circulation: 127 000 (18 dailies).
Radio: 1 310 000 (1972).
TV: 100 000 (1973).
Length of roadways: *c.* 31 070 miles *c. 50 000 km.*
Length of railways: 2971 miles *4781 km.*
Universities: 2 (plus the Khartoum branch of Cairo University).
Adult illiteracy: 95·6% (males 92·6%; females 98·4%) in 1956.
Expectation of life: Males 47·3 years; females 49·9 years (UN estimates for 1970–75).
Defence: Military service: voluntary; total armed forces 52 600; defence expenditure, 1975/76: $120 million.
Cinemas: 52 (seating capacity 47 300) in 1973.

SURINAM

Official name: Republic of Surinam.
Population: 384 903 (census of 31 Dec. 1971); 405 000 (estimate for 31 Dec. 1974).
Area: 63 037 miles² *163 265 km².*
Languages: Dutch 37·1%; Hindustani 31·7%; Javanese 15·4%; Creole 13·8% (1964).
Religions: Christian 45·1%; Hindu 27·8%; Muslim 20·2% (1964).
Capital city: Paramaribo, population 151 500 (1971).
Other principal towns: Nieuw Nickerie, Nieuw Amsterdam.
Highest point: Julianatop, 4218 ft *1286 m.*
Principal mountain ranges: Wilhelmina Gebergte, Kayser Gebergte.

Principal rivers: Corantijn, Nickerie, Coppename, Saramacca, Suriname, Commewijne, Maroni (Marowijne).
Head of State: Dr Johan Henri Eliza Ferrier (b. 12 May 1910), President.
Prime Minister: Henck Alfonsius Eugene Arron (b. 24 Apr. 1936).
Climate: Sub-tropical, with fairly heavy rainfall and average temperatures of 21 °C to 30 °C (73 °F to 88 °F).
Labour force: 80 199 (excluding armed forces and Ameridians and Bush Negroes living in tribes) at census of 31 Mar. 1964; 90 000 (1970): Agriculture, forestry and fishing 22·2% (ILO estimates).
Gross domestic product: 639·8 million guilders in 1972: Mining and quarrying 33·5%; Trade, restaurants and hotels 13·9%.
Exports: $169·4 million (excluding re-exports) in 1972: Mineral slag and ash 48·4%; Bauxite and aluminium concentrates 27·1%; Aluminium metal 12·5% (bars, rods, angles, etc. 12·4%).
Monetary unit: Surinam gulden (guilder) or florin. 1 guilder = 100 cents.
Denominations:
   Coins 1, 5, 10, 25 cents, 1 guilder.
   Notes 1, 2½, 5, 10, 25, 100, 1000 guilders.
Exchange rate to US dollar: 1.785 (July 1977).
Political history and government: Formerly a Dutch possession, with full internal autonomy from 29 Dec. 1954. Surinam became an independent republic on 25 Nov. 1975. Legislative power is held by the *Staten* (Legislative Assembly) of 39 members, elected by universal adult suffrage for 4 years. The Assembly elects the President and Vice-President. Executive power is vested in the appointed Council of Ministers led by the Prime Minister, which is responsible to the Assembly. Surinam comprises 9 districts.
Telephones: 13 000 (1973).
Daily newspapers: 6 (1973).
   Total circulation: 24 000 (five dailies).
Radio: 110 000 (1975).
TV: 36 000 (1976).
Length of roadways: 2310 miles *3717 km.*
Length of railways: 54 miles *86 km.*
Universities: 1.
Adult illiteracy: 20% (estimate).
Expectation of life: Males 62·5 years; females 66·7 years (1963).
Cinemas: 31 (seating capacity 19 000) and one drive-in (1973).

SWAZILAND

Official name: The Kingdom of Swaziland.
Population: 499 046 (census of 25 Aug. 1976).
Area: 6704 miles² *17 363 km².*
Languages: English, Siswati.
Religions: Christian, Animist.
Capital city: Mbabane, population 22 262 at 1976 census.
Other principal towns Manzini 16 000; Havelock 5000; Big Bend 3500; Mhlame 2600; Pigg's Peak 2100.
Highest point: Emlembe, 6113 ft *1863 m.*
Principal mountain range: Lubombo.
Principal rivers: Usutu, Komati, Umbuluzi, Ingwavuma.
Head of State: HM King Sobhuza II, KBE (b. 22 July 1899).
Prime Minister: Col Maphevu Dlamini.
Climate: Rainy season October to March. Annual average at Mbabane, in high veld, 55 in, in low veld 25 in. Average temperatures 52 °F to 72 °F at Mbabane, 56 °F to 80 °F at Manzini, warmer on low veld.
Labour force: 131 145 aged 15 and over (census of 24 May 1966); 193 000 (1970): Agriculture, forestry and fishing 81·3% (ILO estimates).

Gross domestic product: 111·7 million emalangeni (provisional) in 1972/73: Agriculture, forestry and fishing 31·2% (agriculture 28·1%); Manufacturing 21·3%; Trade, restaurants and hotels 10·5%; Community, social and personal services 16·6%. Revised total is 112·8 million emalangeni.
Exports: 132·1 million emalangeni (excluding re-exports) in 1975: Sugar 54·2%.
*Monetary unit: Lilangeni (plural: emalangeni). 1 lilangeni = 100 cents.
Denominations:
   Coins 1, 2, 5, 10, 20, 50 cents, 1 lilangeni.
   Notes 1, 2, 5, 10 emalangeni.
Exchange rate to US dollar: 0·87 (July 1977).
Political history and government: A former British protectorate, with internal self-government from 25 Apr. 1967 and full independence, within the Commonwealth, from 6 Sept. 1968. Swaziland is a monarchy, with executive authority vested in the King. He appoints a Cabinet, led by a Prime Minister. Under the constitution, legislative power is vested in the bicameral Parliament: a House of Assembly, with 30 voting members (24 elected and 6 nominated by the King) and the Attorney-General; and a Senate of 12 members (6 appointed by the King and 6 nominated by the House). On 12 Apr. 1973, in response to a motion passed by both Houses, the King repealed the constitution, suspended political activity and assumed all legislative, executive and judicial powers. On 24 Mar. 1977 the King announced the abolition of the parliamentary system and its replacement by traditional tribal communities called *Tinkhundla*. Swaziland has 4 districts, each administered by an appointed District Commissioner.
Telephones: 6969 (1974).
Radio: 55 000 (1975).
Length of roadways: 1501 miles *2415 km.*
Length of railways: 139 miles *224 km.*
Universities: 1.
Adult illiteracy: Males 68·7%; females 72·5% (1966).
Expectation of life: Males 41·9 years; females 45·1 years (UN estimates for 1970–75).
Defence: An army of 300 men (1974).
Cinemas: 4 (seating capacity 2100) and one drive-in for 250 cars (1971).

* South African currency is also legal tender.

SWEDEN

Official name: Konungariket Sverige (Kingdom of Sweden).
Population: 8 208 544 (census of 1 Nov. 1975); 8 236 000 (estimate for 31 Dec. 1976).
Area: 173 732 miles² *449 964 km².*
Languages: Swedish; Finnish and Lapp in north.
Religion: Lutheran.
Capital city: Stockholm, population 665 202 at 31 Dec. 1975.
Other principal towns (1975): Göteborg (Gothenburg) 444 651; Malmö 243 591; Uppsala 138 116; Norrköping 119 169; Västerås 117 911; Örebro 117 837.
Highest point: Kebnekaise, 6965 ft *2123 m.*
Principal mountain ranges: Norrland Mountains, Smaland Highlands.
Principal rivers: Ume (310 miles [*499 km*]), Torne (354 miles [*569 km*]), Angerman (279 miles [*449 km*]), Klar (304 miles [*489 km*]), Dal (323 miles [*520 km*]).
Head of State: King Carl XVI Gustaf (b. 30 Apr. 1946).
Prime Minister: (Nils Olof) Thorbjörn Fälldin (b. 24 Apr. 1926).
Climate: Summers mild and warm; winters long and cold in north, more moderate in south. In Stockholm, average

maximum 31 °F (January, February) to 70 °F (July), minimum 22 °F (February) to 55 °F (July), rainiest month is August (ten days). Absolute maximum temperature 38,0 °C (*100·4 °F*), Ultana, 9 July 1933; absolute minimum, −53,3 °C (−*63·9 °F*), Laxbacken, 13 Dec. 1941.
Labour force: 4 061 900 (excluding persons on compulsory military service and persons seeking work for the first time) aged 16 to 74 years (1975): Manufacturing 28·0%; Trade, restaurants and hotels 14·4%; Community, social and personal services 30·8%.
Gross domestic product: 249 052 million kronor (provisional) in 1974: Manufacturing 32·5%; Trade, restaurants and hotels 10·0%; Community, social and personal services 22·4%. Revised total is 249 444 million kronor.
Exports: $17 434·1 million in 1975: Machinery 27·0% (non-electric machinery 17·9%); Transport equipment 16·4% (road motor vehicles and parts 10·7%).
Monetary unit: Swedish krona. 1 krona = 100 öre.
Denominations:
   Coins 5, 10, 25, 50 öre, 1, 2, 5, 10 kronor.
   Notes 5, 10, 50, 100, 1000, 10 000 kronor.
Exchange rate to US dollar: 4.346 (July 1977).
Political history and government: Sweden has been a constitutional monarchy, traditionally neutral, since the constitution of 6 June 1809. Parliamentary government was adopted in 1917 and universal adult suffrage introduced in 1921. A revised constitution was introduced on 1 Jan 1975. The King is Head of State but has very limited formal prerogatives. Legislative power is held by the Parliament (*Riksdag*), which has been unicameral since 1 Jan. 1971. It has 349 members elected by universal adult suffrage for 3 years, using proportional representation. Executive power is held by the Cabinet, led by the Prime Minister, which is responsible to the *Riksdag*. Under the 1975 constitution, the Prime Minister is nominated by the Speaker of the *Riksdag* and later confirmed in office by the whole House. After approval, the Prime Minister appoints other members of the Cabinet. Sweden is divided into 24 counties, each administered by a nominated governor.
Telephones: 5 422 795 (1975).
Daily newspapers: 114 (1970).
   Total circulation: 4 324 000.
Radio: 3 139 527 (1975).
TV: 2 909 252 (1975).
Length of roadways: 77 546 miles *124 798 km* (1 July 1975).
Length of railways: 7520 miles *12 102 km.*
Universities: 6 (plus 3 technical universities).
Expectation of life: Males 72·11 years; females 77·51 years (1970–74).
Defence: Military service: Army and Navy 7½ to 15 months; Air Force 9 to 14 months; total armed forces 65 400 (including 49 300 conscripts); defence expenditure, 1976/77: $2418 million.
Cinemas: 1329 (1974).

SWITZERLAND

Official name: Schweizerische Eidgenossenschaft (German), Confédération suisse (French), Confederazione Svizzera (Italian): The Swiss Confederation.
Population: 6 269 783 (census of 1 Dec. 1970); 6 346 000 (estimate for 1 July 1976).
Area: 15 941 miles² *41 288 km².*
Languages: German 64·9%; French 18·1%; Italian 11·9%; Spanish 2·0%; Romanche 0·8% (1970).

Religions: Roman Catholic 49·4%; Protestant 47·8% (1970).
Capital city: Bern (Berne), population 149 800 at 1 Jan. 1976.
Other principal towns (1976): Zürich 389 600; Basel (Bâle or Basle) 192 800; Genève (Genf or Geneva) 155 800; Lausanne 134 300; Winterthur 89 000; St Gallen (Saint-Gall) 77 800; Luzern (Lucerne) 65 300.
Highest point: Dufourspitze (Monte Rosa), 15 203 ft *4634 m* (first climbed 1855).
Principal mountain range: Alps.
Principal rivers: Rhein (Rhine) and Aare, Rhône, Inn, Ticino.
Head of State: Willi Ritschard (b. 28 Sept. 1918), President for 1978.
Climate: Generally temperate, with wide variations due to altitude. Cooler in north, warm on southern slopes. In Zürich, average maximum 48 °F (January) to 86 °F (July), minimum 14 °F (January) to 51 °F (July), rainiest months are June and July (each 15 days). In Geneva, January coldest (29 °F to 39 °F), July warmest (58 °F to 77 °F). Absolute maximum temperature 38,7 °C (*101·7 °F*), Basel, 29 July 1947; absolute minimum −35,8 °C (*−34·4 °F*), Jungfraujoch, 14 Feb. 1940.
Labour force: 2 990 521 (excluding 5256 unemployed) at 1970 census: Manufacturing 37·8%; Trade, restaurants and hotels 17·5%; Community, social and personal services 15·4%.
Gross domestic product: 139 800 million Swiss francs in 1975.
Exports: $12 951·8 million in 1975: Chemicals 21·4%; Machinery and transport equipment 35·6% (non-electric machinery 25·1%); Scientific instruments, watches, etc. 12·7%.
Monetary unit: Schweizer Franken (Swiss franc). 1 franc = 100 Rappen (centimes).
Denominations:
Coins 1, 2, 5, 10, 20, 50 centimes, 1, 2, 5 francs.
Notes 5, 10, 20, 50, 100, 500, 1000 francs.
Exchange rate to US dollar: 2.406 (July 1977).
Political History and government: Since 1815 Switzerland has been a neutral confederation of 19 cantons and 6 half-cantons. The present constitution, establishing a republican form of government, was adopted on 29 May 1874. The cantons hold all powers not specifically delegated to the federal authorities. Legislative power is held by the bicameral Federal Assembly: a Council of States with 44 members representing the cantons (two for each canton and one for each half-canton), elected for 3 to 4 years; and the National Council with 200 members directly elected by universal adult suffrage for 4 years, using proportional representation. The two Houses have equal rights. A referendum on 7 Feb. 1971 approved women's suffrage in federal elections. Executive power is held by the Federal Council, which has 7 members (not more than one from any canton) elected for 4 years by a joint session of the Federal Assembly. Each member of the Council has ministerial responsibility as head of a Federal Department. The Council elects one of its members to be President of the Confederation (also presiding over the Council) for one calendar year at a time. Each canton has a constitution, an elected unicameral legislature and an executive.
Telephones: 3 912 971 (1975).
Daily newspapers: 97 (1973).
Total circulation: 2 478 000.
Radio: 2 075 574 (31 Dec. 1975).
TV: 1 759 116 (31 Dec. 1975).
Length of roadways: 38 298 miles *61 635 km* (31 Dec. 1975).
Length of railways: 3084 miles *4963 km*.

Universities: 8 (plus 2 technical universities).
Expectation of life: Males 70·29 years; females 76·22 years (1968–73).
Defence: Military service: 17 weeks recruit training, followed by reservist refresher training of three weeks per year for eight years, two weeks for three years, and one week for two years; total armed forces 46 500 (including 40 000 recruits); defence expenditure, 1976: $1221 million.
Cinemas: 521 (seating capacity 193 800) in 1973.

SYRIA

Official name: Al-Jumhuriya al-Arabiya as-Suriya (The Syrian Arab Republic).
Population: 6 304 685 (census of 23 Sept. 1970); 7 596 000 (estimate for 30 June 1976).
Area: 71 498 miles² *185 180 km²*.
Languages: Arabic (official); Kurdish; Armenian; Turkish; Circassian.
Religion: Muslim.
Capital city: Dimash'q (Damascus), population 836 668 (1970).
Other principal towns (1970): Halab (Aleppo) 639 428; Homs 215 423; Hama 137 421; Latakia 125 716; Deir-ez-Zor 66 000.
Highest point: Jabal ash-Shaikh (Mt Hermon), 9232 ft *2814 m*.
Principal mountain ranges: Ansariyah range, Jabal ar Ruwā.
Principal rivers: Al Furat (Euphrates headwaters) (420 miles [*676 km*] out of 1400 miles [*2253 km*]), Asi (Orontes).
Head of State: Lt-Gen Hafiz al-Assad (b. 1928), President.
Prime Minister: Maj-Gen Abdul-Rahman Khlaifawi (b. 1927).
Climate: Variable. Hot summers, mild winters and ample rainfall on coast. Inland it is arid with hot, dry summers and cold winters. In Damascus, average maximum 53 °F (January) to 99 °F (August), minimum 36 °F (January) to 64 °F (July, August), rainiest month is January (seven days).
Labour force: 1 750 500 (excluding 88 500 unemployed) aged 10 and over (September 1975): Agriculture, forestry and fishing 51·1%; Manufacturing 11·8%; Trade, restaurants and hotels 10·6%; Community, social and personal services 13·4%.
Gross domestic product: S£20 198 million in 1975: Agriculture, forestry and fishing 17·7%; Mining and quarrying 10·0%; Manufacturing 12·2%; Trade 23·8%.
Exports: $783·7 million in 1974: Textile fibres and waste 26·9% (raw cotton 24·5%); Crude petroleum 55·2%.
Monetary unit: Syrian pound (S£). 1 pound = 100 piastres.
Denominations:
Coins 2½, 5, 10, 25, 50 piastres, 1 pound.
Notes 1, 5, 10, 25, 50, 100, 500 pounds.
Exchange rate to US dollar: 3.925 (July 1977).
Political History and government: Formerly part of Turkey's Ottoman Empire. Turkish forces were defeated in the First World War (1914–18). In 1920 Syria was occupied by French forces, in accordance with a League of Nations mandate. Nationalists proclaimed an independent republic on 16 Sept. 1941. The first elected parliament met on 17 Aug. 1943, French powers were transferred on 1 Jan. 1944 and full independence achieved on 12 Apr. 1946. Syria merged with Egypt to form the United Arab Republic, proclaimed on 1 Feb. 1958 and established on 21 Feb. 1958. Following a military *coup* in Syria on 28 Sept. 1961, the

country resumed separate independence, under its present name, on 29 Sept. 1961. Left-wing army officers overthrew the government on 8 Mar. 1963 and formed the National Council of the Revolutionary Command (NCRC), which took over all executive and legislative authority. The NCRC installed a cabinet dominated by the Arab Socialist Renaissance (Ba'ath) Party. This party has held power ever since. Lt-Gen Hafiz al-Assad became Prime Minister on 18 Nov. 1970 and assumed Presidential powers on 22 Feb. 1971. His position was approved by popular referendum on 12 Mar. 1971 and he was sworn in for a 7-year term as President on 14 Mar. 1971. Legislative power is held by the People's Council, originally comprising 173 members appointed for two years on 16 Feb. 1971 to draft a permanent constitution. The constitution, proclaiming socialist principles, was approved by referendum on 12 Mar. 1973 and adopted two days later. It declares that the Ba'ath Party is 'the leading party in the State and society'. Legislative power is held by the People's Assembly, with 195 members elected by universal adult suffrage. Political power is held by the Progressive Front of National Unity, formed on 7 Mar. 1972 by a merger of the Ba'ath Party and four others. The Head of State is leader of the Ba'ath Party and President of the Front. Syria has 13 administrative districts.
Telephones: 152 000 (1974).
Daily newspapers: 6 (1973).
Total circulation: 64 000 (5 dailies).
Radio: 1 232 500 (1 July 1976).
TV: 302 760 (1 July 1976).
Length of roadways: 10 383 miles *16 710 km*.
Length of railways: 713 miles *1148 km*.
Universities: 3.
Adult illiteracy: 60·0% (males 40·4%; females 80·0%) in 1970.
Expectation of life: Males 54·49 years; females 58·73 years (1970).
Defence: Military service: 30 months; total armed forces 227 000; defence expenditure, 1976: $1003 million.
Cinemas: 112 (seating capacity 55 000) in 1967.

TANZANIA

Official name: The United Republic of Tanzania (Jamhuri ya Muungano wa Tanzania).
Population: 12 313 469 (census of 26 Aug. 1967); 15 607 000 (estimate for 1 July 1976).
Area: 364 900 miles² *945 087 km²*.
Languages: English, Swahili.
Religions: Traditional beliefs, Christian, Muslim.
Capital city: Dar es Salaam ('haven of peace'), population 517 000 at 1 July 1975.
Other principal towns (1967): Tanga 61 058; Mwanza 34 861; Arusha 32 452; Moshi 26 853; Dodoma 23 559; Iringa 21 746.
Highest point: Mount Kilimanjaro, 19 340 ft *5894 m*.
Principal mountain range: Southern Highlands.
Principal rivers: Pangani (Ruvu), Rufiji, Rovuma.
Head of State: Dr Julius Kambarage Nyerere (b. March 1922), President.
Prime Minister: Edward Moringe Sokoine (b. 1938).
Climate: Varies with altitude. Tropical (hot and humid) on Zanzibar, and on the coast and plains. Cool and semi-temperate in the highlands. In Dar es Salaam, average maximum 83 °F to 88 °F, minimum 66 °F to 77 °F. In Zanzibar Town, average

maximum 82 °F (July) to 91 °F (February, March), minimum 72 °F (July–September) to 77 °F (March–April), average annual rainfall 62 in, April rainiest (16 days), July driest (four days).
Labour force: 5 747 096 (1967 census): Agriculture, forestry and fishing 91·6%.
Gross domestic product: 15 601 million shillings (provisional) in 1974 (Tanganyika only): Agriculture, forestry and fishing 39·6% (agriculture 36·1%); Manufacturing 10·6%; Trade, restaurants and hotels 13·2% (trade 12·5%); Community, social and personal services 11·5%. Revised total is 15 849 million shillings.
Exports: $355·2 million (excluding re-exports) in 1974: Fruit and vegetables 10·6%; Coffee 14·8%; Other food 10·7%; Textile fibres and waste 37·3% (raw cotton 18·6%; sisal 18·3%). Figures exclude trade with Kenya and Uganda in local produce and locally manufactured goods.
Monetary unit: Tanzanian shilling. 1 shilling = 100 cents.
Denominations:
Coins 5, 20, 50 cents, 1, 5 shillings.
Notes 5, 10, 20, 100 shillings.
Exchange rate to US dollar: 8.244 (July 1977).
Political history and government: Tanganyika, a former United Nations Trust Territory under British administration, became an independent member of the Commonwealth on 9 Dec. 1961 and a republic on 9 Dec. 1962. Zanzibar, a sultanate under British protection, became an independent constitutional monarchy within the Commonwealth on 10 Dec. 1963. The Sultan was overthrown by revolution on 12 Jan. 1964 and the People's Republic of Zanzibar proclaimed. The two republics merged on 26 Apr. 1964 to form the United Republic of Tanganyika and Zanzibar (renamed Tanzania on 29 Oct. 1964) and remained in the Commonwealth.

An interim constitution, declaring Tanzania a one-party state, was approved by the legislature on 5 July 1965 and received the President's assent three days later. Legislative power is held by the unicameral National Assembly, with 214 members: 96 (including four unopposed in 1975) elected from Tanganyika by universal adult suffrage for five years; 46 appointed from Zanzibar; 20 regional party secretaries; 8 nominated by the President; 9 appointed to the East African Legislative Assembly (an organ of the East African Community comprising Kenya, Tanzania and Uganda); and 35 selected by the National Assembly from other institutions. Executive power lies with the President, elected by popular vote for five years. He appoints a First Vice-President (who is Chairman of the Zanzibar Revolutionary Council), a Prime Minister and a Cabinet. Zanzibar continues to have a seperate administration for internal affairs.

At a joint conference the ruling parties of Tanganyika and Zanzibar decided on 21 Jan. 1977 to merge into a single party, *Chama Cha Mapinduzi* (the Revolutionary Party), formed on 5 Feb. 1977. The Party's leading decision-making organ is the National Executive, elected by party members.
Telephones: 58 000 (1974).
Daily newspapers: 3 (1973).
Total circulation: 41 000 (2 dailies).
Radio: 230 000 (1973).
TV: 4000 (1969).
Length of roadways: 10 403 miles *16 742 km* (1969).
Length of railways: 1591 miles *2560 km.*
Adult illiteracy: 71·9% (males 57·3%; females 85·1%) in 1967.
Universities: 1.
Expectation of life: Males 42·9 years; females 46·1 years (UN estimates, 1970–75).

Defence: Military service: voluntary; total armed forces 14 600; defence expenditure, 1975: $70 million.
Cinemas: 29 (seating capacity 13 500) in 1971.

THAILAND

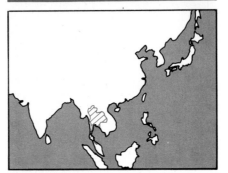

Official name: Prathet Thai (Kingdom of Thailand), also called Prades Thai or Muang-Thai (Thai means free).
Population: 35 103 000 (census of 1 Apr. 1970, including adjustment for underenumeration); 42 960 000 (estimate for 1 July 1976).
Area: 198 457 miles² *514 000 km².*
Language: Thai.
Religions: Buddhist, Muslim minority.
Capital city: Krungt'ep (Bangkok), population 1 867 297 (1970).
Other principal town (1970): Thonburi, population 627 989.
Highest point: Doi Inthanon, 8452 ft *2576 m.*
Principal rivers: Mekong (2600 miles *[4184 km]*) Chao Pyha (154 miles *[247 km]*).
Head of State: HM King Bhumibol Adulyadej (b. 5 Dec. 1927).
Prime Minister: Gen. Kriangsak Chammanand (b. 1918).
Climate: Tropical monsoon climate (humid). Three seasons–hot, rainy, and cool. Average temperature 85 °F. In Bangkok, average maximum 87 °F (November, December) to 95 °F (April), minimum 68 °F (December, January) to 77 °F (April, May), rainiest month is September (15 days). Absolute maximum 44,1 °C (*111·4 °F*), Mae Sariang, 25 Apr. 1958; absolute minimum 0,1 °C (*32·2 °F*), Loey, 13 Jan. 1955.
Labour force: 17 042 660 (excluding 73 890 unemployed) 11 and over (July–Sept. 1973): Agriculture, forestry and fishing 72·0%.
Gross domestic product: 270 017 million baht (provisional) in 1974: Agriculture, forestry and fishing 31·9% (agriculture 27·1%); Manufacturing 17·5%; Trade 20·0%; Community, social and personal services (including restaurants and hotels) 11·9%. Revised total is 268 973 million baht.
Exports: $2482·7 million in 1974: Cereals and cereal preparations 32·7% (rice 19·4%; maize 11·9%); Other food 22·3%; Natural rubber 10·0%.
Monetary unit: Baht. 1 baht = 100 satangs.
Denominations:
Coins ½, 1, 5, 10, 20, 25, 50 satangs, 1 baht.
Notes 1, 5, 10, 20, 100, 500 baht.
Exchange rate to US dollar: 20·40 (July 1977).
Political history and government: Thailand, called Siam before 1939, is a kingdom with a hereditary monarch as Head of State. The military regime established on 17 Nov. 1971 was forced to resign, following popular demonstrations, on 14 Oct. 1973. An interim government was formed and a new constitution, legalising political parties, was promulgated on 7 Oct. 1974. The constitutional government was overthrown on 6 Oct. 1976 by a military junta, the

National Administrative Reform Council (NARC), which declared martial law, annulled the 1974 constitution, dissolved the bicameral National Assembly and banned political parties. A new constitution, promulgated on 22 Oct. 1976, provided for a National Administrative Reform Assembly (340 members appointed for 4 years by the King on 20 Nov. 1976). A new Prime Minister was appointed and the NARC became the Prime Minister's Advisory Council. On 20 Oct. 1977 military leaders deposed the government, abrogated the 1976 constitution and abolished the Advisory Council. Senior military and police officers formed a 23-member Revolutionary Council. An interim constitution was promulgated on 10 Nov. 1977. The Revolutionary Council became the National Policy Council (NPC), which appoints the Prime Minister. The NPC's Chairman is to appoint a National Assembly and a committee of the Assembly is to draft a permanent constitution.
Telephones: 333 677 (1976).
Daily newspapers: 33 (1973).
Radio: 5 360 735 (1975).
TV: 761 015 (1975).
Length of roadways: 23 126 miles *37 218 km* (31 Dec. 1975).
Length of railways: 5115 miles *8233 km.*
Universities: 12.
Adult illiteracy: 21·3% (males 12·7%; females 29·5%) in 1970.
Expectation of life: Males 53·6 years; females 58·7 years (1960).
Defence: Military service: two years; total armed forces 210 000; defence expenditure, 1975/76: $542 million.
Cinemas: 900 (seating capacity 900 000) in 1972.

TOGO

Official name: La République togolaise (The Togolese Republic).
Population: 1 950 646 (census of 1 Mar.–30 Apr. 1970); 2 283 000 (estimate for 30 June 1976).
Area: 21 622 miles² *56 000 km².*
Languages: French (official), Ewe.
Religions: Animist; Christian and Muslim minorities.
Capital city: Lomé, population 229 400 (1977 est.)
Other principal towns (1977): Sokodé 33 500; Palimé 25 500; Atakpamé 21 800; Bassari 17 500; Tsévié 15 900.
Highest point: 3018 ft *919 m.*
Principal rivers: Mono, Oti.
Head of State: Major-Gen Etienne Gnassingbe Eyadéma (b. 26 Dec. 1937), President.
Climate: Equatorial (hot and humid). On coast average temperatures 76 °F to 82 °F, higher inland (average 97 °F in drier north).
Labour force: 719 308 (excluding unemployed) aged 15 and over (1970 census); 859 000 (1970): Agriculture, forestry and fishing 73·3% (ILO estimates).
Gross domestic product: 69 644 million CFA francs in 1969: Agriculture, forestry and fishing 43·0% (agriculture 38·9%); Manufacturing 11·0%; Trade, restaurants and hotels 19·0%.
Exports: $61·6 million in 1973: Coffee 13·1%; Cocoa 25·9%; Natural phosphates 45·6%.
Monetary unit: Franc de la Communauté financière africaine.
Denominations:
Coins 1, 2, 5, 10, 25, 50, 100, 500 CFA francs.
Notes 100, 500, 1000, 5000 CFA francs.
Exchange rate to US dollar: 242.8 (July 1977).
Political history and government: Formerly a United Nations Trust Territory

under French administration, an independent republic since 27 Apr. 1960. An army coup on 13 Jan. 1967 deposed the President and established military rule under Lieut-Col (later Major-Gen) Etienne Gnassingbe Eyadéma, who suspended the constitution and dissolved the National Assembly. Eyadéma proclaimed himself President on 14 Apr. 1967. Political parties were banned and the President rules by decree through an appointed Council of Ministers. On 29 Nov. 1969 the President established a single ruling party which mobilizes support for the government. Togo is divided into four regions, each administered by an appointed Inspector.

Telephones: 8000 (1974).
Daily newspapers: 3 (1973).
  Total circulation: 13 000.
Radio: 50 000 (1973).
TV: 5000 (1977).
Length of roadways: 4361 miles *7019 km.*
Length of railways: 309 miles *498 km.*
Universities: 1.
Adult illiteracy: 90–95% (estimate).
Expectation of life: Males 39·4 years; females 42·6 years (UN estimates for 1970–75).
Defence: Total armed forces 2250.
Cinemas: 2 (seating capacity 2300) in 1964.

TONGA

Official name: The Kingdom of Tonga.
Population: 90 128 (census of 1 Dec. 1976).
Area: 270 miles² *699 km².*
Languages: Tongan, English.
Religions: Christian, mainly Wesleyan.
Capital city: Nuku'alofa, population 18 396 at 1976 census.
Highest point: Kao, 3380 ft *1030 m.*
Head of State: HM King Taufa'ahau Tupou IV, GCMG, GCVO, KBE (b. 4 July 1918).
Prime Minister: HRH Prince Fatafehi Tu'ipelehake, CBE (b. 7 Jan. 1922).
Climate: Mild. Temperature from May to November rarely exceeds 84 °F in the shade, with minimum temperature of 52 °F.
Climate: Warm and pleasant. Average annual temperature is 73 °F. Hot and humid from Jan. to March (90 °F). Average annual rainfall 63 in on Tongatapu, 82 in on Vava'u.
Labour force: 18 998 (census of 30 Nov. 1966). Agriculture, forestry and fishing 74·0%; Services 18·5%.
Gross domestic product: 13·3 million pa'anga in 1970/71: Agriculture, forestry and fishing 47%.
Exports: US$6·6 million in 1974: Fruit and vegetables 24·9% (fresh fruit 12·1%; edible nuts 10·5%); Copra 69·7%.
Monetary unit: Pa'anga. 1 pa'anga = 100 seniti.
Denominations:
  Coins 1, 2, 5, 10, 20, 50 seniti; 1, 2 pa'anga.
  Notes ½, 1, 2, 5, 10 pa'anga.
Exchange rate to US dollar: 0.8052 (July 1977).
Political history and government: Tonga is a kingdom ruled by an hereditary monarchy. It was under British protection from 18 May 1900 until becoming independent, within the Commonwealth, on 4 June 1970. The King is Head of State and Head of Government. He appoints, and presides over, a Privy Council which acts as the national Cabinet. Apart from the King, the Council includes six Ministers, led by the Prime Minister (currently the King's brother), and the Governors of two island groups. The unicameral Legislative Assembly comprises 23 members: the King, the Privy Council, seven hereditary nobles elected by their peers and seven representatives elected by the

people. Elected members hold office for three years. There are no political parties.
Telephones: 1125 (1975).
Radio: 9100 (1973).
Length of roadways: 271 miles *436 km.*
Expectation of life: 55·2 years (both sexes) in 1965.
Defence: Defence budget, 1972/73: 74 100 pa'anga.
Cinemas: 5 (seating capacity 3600) in 1969.

TRINIDAD AND TOBAGO

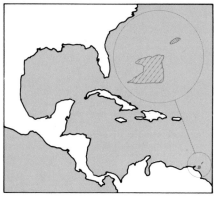

Official name: The Republic of Trinidad and Tobago.
Population: 940 719 (census of 7 Apr. 1970); 1 067 000 (estimate for 1 July 1975).
Area: 1980 miles² *5128 km².*
Languages: English (official), Hindi, French, Spanish.
Religions: Christian; Hindu, Muslim minorities.
Capital city: Port-of-Spain, population 60 450 at 1 July 1973.
Other principal towns (1973): San Fernando 36 650; Arima 12 000.
Highest point: Mount Aripo, 3085 ft *940 m.*
Principal mountain ranges: Northern and Southern, Central.
Principal rivers: Caroni, Ortoire, Oropuche.
Head of State: Ellis Emmanuel Innocent Clarke (b. 28 Dec. 1917), President.
Prime Minister: The Rt Hon Dr Eric Eustace Williams, CH (b. 25 Sept. 1911).
Climate: Tropical, with an annual average temperature of 84 °F. The dry season is January to May.
Labour force: 333 750 (excluding 60 100 unemployed) aged 15 and over (1974): Agriculture, forestry and fishing 16·4%; Mining and manufacturing 19·5%; Construction, electricity, gas, water and sanitary services 13·8%; Commerce 18·3%; Services 23·3%.
Gross domestic product: TT$4959 million (at factor cost) in 1975: Mining and quarrying (including oil refining) 39·1%; Manufacturing (excluding oil refining) 16·0%.
Exports: US$1772·7 million (excluding value of sugar preference certificates) in 1975: Crude and partly refined petroleum 37·3% (crude petroleum 32·4%); Petroleum products 49·7% (residual fuel oils 29·4%).
Monetary unit: Trinidad and Tobago dollar. 1 dollar = 100 cents.
Denominations:
  Coins 1, 5, 10, 25, 50 cents, 1 dollar.
  Notes 1, 5, 10, 20 dollars.
Exchange rate to US dollar: 2.40 (July 1977).
Political history and government: Formerly a British dependency, an independent

member of the Commonwealth since 31 Aug. 1962. Became a republic on 1 Aug. 1976. Legislative power is vested in a bicameral Parliament, comprising a Senate with 31 members, appointed for up to five years by the President (16 on the advice of the Prime Minister, 6 on the advice of the Leader of the Opposition and 9 at his own discretion), and a House of Representatives (36 members elected by universal adult suffrage for five years). The President is a constitutional Head of State elected for five years by both Houses of Parliament. He appoints the Prime Minister to form a Cabinet from members of Parliament. The Cabinet has effective control of the government and is responsible to Parliament.
Telephones: 66 385 (1975).
Daily newspapers: 2 (1974).
  Total circulation: 98 000.
Radio: 296 000 (1971).
T.V: 110 000 (1976).
Length of roadways: 2629 miles *4230 km.*
Universities: 1.
Expectation of life: Males 64·08 years; females 68·11 years (1970).
Defence: Army of about 1000.
Cinemas: 66 (seating capacity 42 700) and 5 drive-in for 1120 cars (1972).

TUNISIA

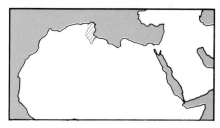

Official name: Al-Jumhuriya at-Tunisiya (The Republic of Tunisia).
Population: 5 588 209 (census of 15 May 1975); 5 737 000 (estimate for 1 July 1976).
Area: 63 170 miles² *163 610 km².*
Languages: Arabic, French.
Religions: Muslim; Jewish and Christian minorities.
Capital city: Tunis, population 550 404 (1975).
Other principal towns (1975): Sfax (Safaqis) 171 297; Djerba 70 217; Sousse 69 530; Bizerte (Bizerta) 62 856; Kairouan 54 546; Gafsa 42 225; Gabès 40 585.
Highest point: Djebel Chambi, 5066 ft *1544 m.*
Principal rivers: Medjerda (300 miles [*482 km*]).
Head of State: Habib Ben Ali Bourguiba (b. 3 Aug. 1903), President.
Prime Minister: Hedi Nouira (b. 6 Apr. 1911).
Climate: Temperate, with winter rain, on coast; hot and dry inland. In Tunis, August warmest (69 °F to 91 °F), January coolest (43 °F to 58 °F) December rainiest (14 days). Absolute maximum temperature 55,0 °C (*131·0 °F*), Kébili, 7 Dec. 1931; absolute minimum −9,0 °C (*15·8 °F*), Fort-Saint, 22 Dec. 1940.
Labour force: 1 456 000 aged 15 and over (1974): Agriculture, forestry and fishing 54·9%; Manufacturing 13·5%; Services 15·6%.
Gross domestic product: 1554·1 million dinars (provisional) in 1974: Agriculture, forestry and fishing 21·4% (agriculture and forestry 20·6%); Mining and quarrying 12·8%; Manufacturing 11·4%; Trade, restaurants and hotels 15·1% (trade 11·8%);

Public administration and defence 11·8%. Revised total is 1527·0 million dinars.

Exports: $856·2 million in 1975: Natural phosphates 13·7%; Petroleum and petroleum products 43·6% (crude and partly refined petroleum 41·8%).

Monetary unit: Tunisian dinar. 1 dinar = 1000 millimes.

Denominations:
Coins 1, 2, 5, 10, 20, 50, 100, 500 millimes.
Notes ½, 1, 5, 10 dinars.

Exchange rate to US dollar: 0.4207 (July 1977).

Political history and government: Formerly a monarchy, ruled by the Bey of Tunis. A French protectorate from 1883 until independence on 20 Mar. 1956. The campaign for independence was led by the Neo-Destour Party (founded by Habib Bourguiba), since October 1964 called the *Parti Socialiste Destourien* (PSD), the Destourian (Constitutional) Socialist Party. Elections were held on 25 Mar. 1956 for a Constitutional Assembly, which met on 8 Apr. 1956 and appointed Bourguiba as Prime Minister two days later. On 25 July 1957 the Assembly deposed the Bey, abolished the monarchy and established a republic, with Bourguiba as President. A new constitution was promulgated on 1 June 1959. Legislative power is vested in the unicameral National Assembly, first elected on 8 Nov. 1959. It has 112 members elected (unopposed in 1974) by universal adult suffrage for five years. Executive power is held by the President, elected for five years by popular vote at the same time as the Assembly (on 18 Mar. 1975 the Assembly proclaimed Bourguiba as President for life). The President, who is Head of State and Head of Government, appoints a Council of Ministers, headed by a Prime Minister, which is responsible to him. Tunisia has been a one-party state since 1963. The country is divided into 18 governorates.

Telephones: 129 000 (1975).

Daily newspapers: 4 (1974).
Total circulation: 156 000.

Radio: 277 000 (1974).

TV: 147 000 (1973).

Length of roadways: 13 241 miles *21 309 km* (31 Dec. 1974).

Length of railways: 1298 miles *2089 km* (1975).

Universities: 1.

Adult illiteracy: 76·0% (males 62·9%; females 89·4%) in 1966.

Expectation of life: Males 52·5 years; females 55·7 years (UN estimate for 1970–75).

Defence: Military service: 12 months selective; total armed forces 20 000 (including 13 000 conscripts); defence expenditure, 1976/77: $91 million.

Cinemas: 105 (seating capacity 49 800) and one part-time (capacity 300) in 1973.

TURKEY

Official name: Türkiye Cumhuriyeti (Republic of Turkey).

Population: 40 197 670 (census of 26 Oct. 1975).

Area: 301 382 miles² *780 576 km²*.

Languages: Turkish 90·2%; Kurdish 6·9%; Arabic 1·2%; Zaza 0·5% (1965).

Religion: Muslim.

Capital city: Ankara (Angora), population 1 701 004 (1975).

Other principal towns (1975): Istanbul 2 547 364; İzmir (Smyrna) 636 834; Adana 475 384; Bursa 346 103; Gaziantep 300 882; Eskişehir 259 952; Konya 246 727.

Highest point: Büyük Ağridaği (Mt Ararat), 17 011 ft *5185 m*.

Principal mountain ranges: Armenian Plateau, Toros Dağlari (Taurus Mts), Kuzey Anadolu Dağlari.

Principal rivers: Firat (Euphrates), Dicle (Tigris), Kizilirmak (Halys), Sakarya.

Head of State: Admiral Fahri S Korutürk (b. 12 Aug. 1903), President.

Prime Minister: Bülent Ecevit (b. 28 May 1925).

Climate: Hot, dry summers and cold, snowy winters in interior plateau; mild winters and warm summers on Mediterranean coast. In Ankara, average maximum 39 °F (January) to 87 °F (August), minimum 24 °F (January) to 59 °F (July, August), rainiest month is December (9 days). In Istanbul, average maximum 45 °F (January) to 81 °F (July, August), minimum 36 °F (January) to 66 °F (August), rainiest month is December (15 days). Absolute maximum temperature 46,2 °C (*115·2 °F*), Diyarbakir, 21 July 1937; absolute minimum −43,2 °C (*−45·8 °F*), Karaköse, 13 Jan. 1940.

Labour force: 15 118 887 (including unemployed) at census of 25 Oct. 1970: Agriculture, forestry and fishing 69·1%; Community, social and personal services 10·5%.

Gross domestic product: 403 500 million liras (provisional) in 1974: Agriculture, forestry and fishing 27·9% (agriculture 27·2%); Manufacturing 21·2%; Trade 13·0%. Revised total is 409 700 million liras.

Exports: $1537·8 million in 1974: Fruit and vegetables 22·1% (edible nuts 11·8%); Tobacco (unmanufactured) 13·3%; Textile fibres and waste 16·2% (raw cotton 15·3%).

Monetary unit: Turkish lira. 1 lira = 100 kurus.

Denominations:
Coins 1, 5, 10, 25, 50 kuruş, 1, 2, 5, 10 liras.
Notes 5, 10, 20, 50, 100, 500, 1000 liras.

Exchange rate to US dollar: 17·50 (July 1977).

Political history and government: Formerly a monarchy, ruled by a Sultan. Following the disintegration of the Ottoman Empire after the First World War, power passed to the Grand National Assembly which first met on 23 Apr. 1920. The Assembly approved a new constitution on 20 Jan. 1921, vesting executive and legislative authority in itself. It abolished the sultanate on 1 Nov. 1922 and declared Turkey a republic on 29 Oct. 1923. The armed forces overthrew the government on 27 May 1960, the Assembly was dissolved and political activities suspended until 12 Jan. 1961. A new constitution was approved by referendum on 9 June 1961 and took effect on 25 Oct. 1961. Legislative power is vested in the bicameral Grand National Assembly, comprising the Senate of the Republic, with 183 members (150 elected by universal suffrage for staggered six-year terms, 15 appointed by the President and 19 holding life membership in 1977), and the National Assembly (450 members elected by universal adult suffrage for four years). The Grand National Assembly elects one of its members to be President of the Republic for a seven-year term. The President appoints the Prime Minister from among members of the legislature. The Prime Minister, who must have the support of a majority in both houses, appoints a Council of Ministers to assist him in administering the government. Turkey is composed of 67 provinces.

Telephones: 1 012 000 (1975).

Daily newspapers: 450 (1973).

Radio: 4 154 000 (1975).

TV: 455 752 (1974).

Length of roadways: 116 866 miles *188 077 km* (31 Dec. 1975).

Length of railways: 6108 miles *9831 km*.

Universities: 18.

Adult illiteracy: 48·6% (males 30·9%; females 66·4%) in 1970.

Expectation of life: Males 55·2 years; females 58·7 years (UN estimates for 1970–75).

Defence: Military service: 20 months; total armed forces 480 000 (including 257 000 conscripts); defence expenditure, 1976/77 $2794 million.

Cinemas: 2424 (seating capacity 1 164 800) in 1970.

UGANDA

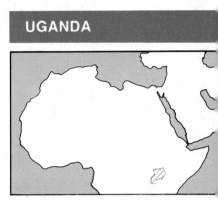

Official name: The Republic of Uganda.

Population: 9 548 847 (census of 18 Aug. 1969); 11 943 000 (estimate for 1 July 1976).

Area: 91 452 miles² *236 860 km²*.

Languages: English (official), Luganda, Ateso, Runyankore.

Religions: Christian, Muslim, traditional beliefs.

Capital city: Kampala, population 330 700 (1969).

Other principal towns (1969): Jinja/Njeru 52 509; Bugembe 46 884; Mbale 23 544; Entebbe 21 096.

Highest point: Mount Stanley, 16 763 ft *5109 m*.

Principal mountain range: Ruwenzori.

Principal rivers: Nile, Semliki.

Head of State: Field Marshal Idi Amin Dada (b. 1 Jan. 1928), President.

Climate: Tropical, with an average temperature of 71 °F. There is a seasonal variation of only 20 °F.

Labour force: 4 263 000 (1970): Agriculture, forestry and fishing 85·9% (ILO estimates).

Gross domestic product: 10 367 million shillings in 1971: Agriculture, forestry and fishing 53·6% (agriculture 49·6%); Trade, restaurants and hotels 11·6% (trade 10·7%).

Exports: $315·4 million (excluding re-exports) in 1974: Coffee 73·3%; Raw cotton 12·1%. Figures exclude trade with Kenya and Tanzania in local produce and locally manufactured goods.

Monetary unit: Uganda shilling. shilling = 100 cents.

Denominations:
Coins 5, 10, 20, 50 cents, 1, 2, 5 shillings.
Notes 10, 20, 50, 100 shillings.

Exchange rate to US dollar: 8.244 (July 1977).

Political history and government: Formerly a British dependency, an independent member of the Commonwealth since 9 Oct. 1962. Uganda became a republic, with nominal President and an executive Prime Minister, on 9 Oct. 1963. A provisional constitution, effective from 15 Apr. 1966, ended the former federal system and introduced an executive President. A unitary republic was established on 8 Sept. 1967. The president was deposed on 25 Jan. 1971 by an army *coup*, led by Major-Gen (later Field Marshal) Idi Amin Dada, who assumed full executive powers as Head of the Military Government and suspended political activity. The National Assembly was dissolved on

Feb. 1971, when Amin declared himself Head of State, took over legislative powers and suspended parts of the 1967 constitution. He was proclaimed President on 21 Feb. 1971 and rules with the assistance of an appointed Council of Ministers. On 25 June 1976 the Defence Council appointed Amin President for life. Uganda is divided into 10 provinces, each administered by a Governor.

Telephones: 58 000 (1974).
Daily newspapers: 4 (1974).
Total circulation: 58 000.
Radio: 250 000 (1973).
TV: 15 000 (1972).
Length of roadways: 14 927 miles *24 024 km.* (1974).
Length of railways: 808 miles *1301 km* (1974).
Universities: 1.
Adult illiteracy: 74·9% (males 63·2%; females 86·1%) in 1959 (African population aged 16 and over).
Expectation of life: Males 48·3 years; females 51·7 years (UN estimates for 1970–75).
Defence: Military service: voluntary; total armed forces 14 600; defence expenditure, 1975: $70 million.
Cinemas: 16 (seating capacity 8700) and 1 drive-in for 744 cars (1971).

UNION OF SOVIET SOCIALIST REPUBLICS

Official name: Soyuz Sovyetskikh Sotsialisticheskikh Respublik. (Abbreviation in Cyrillic script is CCCP).
Population: 241 720 134 (census of 15 Jan. 1970); 257 900 000 (estimate for 1 Jan. 1977).
Area: 8 649 540 miles² *22 402 200 km²*.
Languages (1970): Russian (official) 58·7%; Ukrainian 14·6%; Uzbek 3·8%; Byelorussian 3·2%; Tatar 2·4%; Kazakh 2·2%; over 50 others.
Religions: No state religion. Christian with Jewish and Muslim minorities.
Capital city: Moskva (Moscow), population 7 734 000 at 1 Jan. 1976.
Other principal towns (1976): Leningrad (St Petersburg) 4 372 000; Kiyev (Kiev) 2 013 000; Tashkent 1 643 000; Baku 1 406 000; Khar'kov 1 385 000; Gor'kiy (Nizhniy-Novgorod) 1 305 000; Novosibirsk (Novonikolayevsk) 1 286 000; Kuibyshev (Samara) 1 189 000; Minsk 1 186 000; Sverdlovsk (Yekaterinburg) 1 171 000; Tbilisi (Tiflis) 1 029 000; Odessa 1 023 000; Omsk 1 002 000.
Highest point: Pik Kommunizma, 24 589 ft *7494 m* (first climbed 3 Sept. 1933).
Principal mountain ranges: Caucasus, Urals, Pamirs, Tien Shan.
Principal rivers: 14 rivers over 1000 miles *1609 km* in length (see pages 21–3).
Head of State: Leonid Ilyich Brezhnev (b. 19 Dec. 1906), Chairman of the Presidium of the Supreme Soviet and General Secretary of the Communist Party of the Soviet Union.
Head of Government: Aleksey Nikolayevich Kosygin (b. 21 Feb. 1904), Chairman of the Council of Ministers.
Climate: Great variations. Summers generally short and hot, winters long and cold. Very hot in central Asia, extremely cold in north-east Siberia. Average maximum and minimum temperatures for selected places:
Moscow: Average maximum 21 °F (January) to 76 °F (July). Average minimum 9 °F (January) to 55 °F (July). Rainiest months July, August (each 12 days).
Archangel: Average maximum 9 °F (January) to 64 °F (July). Average minimum

0 °F (February) to 51 °F (July). Rainiest month October (12 days).
Odessa: Average maximum 28 °F (January) to 79 °F (July). Average minimum 22 °F (January) to 65 °F (July, August). Rainiest months January and June (each 7 days).
Yakutsk: Average maximum −45 °F (January) to 73 °F (July). Average minimum −53 °F (January) to 54 °F (July). Rainiest months September, October, November (each 10 days).
Absolute maximum temperature 50,0 °C (*122·0 °F*), Termez (Uzbekistan), July 1912; absolute minimum −71,1 °C (*−96·0 °F*), Oymyakon, 1964.
Labour force: 117 027 575 at 1970 census: Agriculture 26·4%; Industry (mining, manufacturing, electricity, gas and water), construction, transport and communications 45·3%; Education, cultural institutions, scientific and research institutes, public health 14·2%.
Net material product: 353 700 million roubles (provisional) in 1974: Agriculture, forestry and fishing 18·4%; Industry 52·7%; Construction 11·0%; Trade, restaurants, etc. 11·8%. Revised total is 354 000 million roubles.
Exports: $33 309·8 million in 1975: Petroleum and petroleum products 24·6% (crude petroleum 15·6%); Machinery and transport equipment 19·1%.
Monetary unit: Rubl' (ruble or rouble). 1 rouble = 100 kopeks.
Denominations:
Coins 1, 2, 3, 5, 10, 15, 20, 50 kopeks, 1 rouble.
Notes 1, 3, 5, 10, 25, 50, 100 roubles.
Exchange rate to US dollar: 0.734 (July 1977).
Political history and government: Formerly the Russian Empire, ruled by an hereditary Tsar (of the Romanov dynasty from 1613). Prompted by discontent with autocratic rule and the privations caused by the First World War, a revolution broke out on 27 Feb. (12 March New Style) 1917, causing the abdication of the last Tsar three days later and the establishment of a provisional government. During the following months Soviets (councils) were elected by some groups of industrial workers and peasants. A republic was proclaimed on 1 Sept. (14 Sept. NS) 1917. A political struggle developed between government supporters and the Bolshevik Party (called the Communist Party from 1919), which advocated the assumption of power by the Soviets. On 25 Oct. (7 Nov. NS) 1917 the Bolsheviks led an insurrection, arrested the provisional government and transferred power to the All-Russian Congress of Soviets. The Bolsheviks won only 175 out of 707 seats in the elections of 25–27 Nov. 1917 for the Constituent Assembly. The Assembly met on 18 Jan. 1918 but was forcibly dissolved by the Bolsheviks, who proclaimed a 'dictatorship of the proletariat'. On 31 Jan. 1918 Russia was proclaimed a Republic of Soviets. A constitution for the Russian Soviet Federative Socialist Republic (RSFSR) was adopted on 10 July 1918. Armed resistance to Communist rule developed into civil war (1917–22) but was eventually crushed. During the war other Soviet Republics were set up in the Ukraine, Byelorussia and Transcaucasia. These were merged with the RSFSR by a Treaty of Union, establishing the USSR, on 30 Dec. 1922. By splitting the territory of the original four, two more Republics were added in 1925 and another in 1929. A new constitution was adopted on 5 Dec. 1936, when the number of Republics was raised from seven to eleven. On 31 Mar. 1940 territory ceded to Finland became part of the newly-formed Karelo-Finnish SSR. Territory ceded by Romania on 28 June 1940 became

part of the new Moldavian SSR on 2 Aug. 1940. Lithuania, Latvia and Estonia were annexed on 3–6 Aug. 1940, raising the number of Union Republics to 16. This was reduced to the present 15 on 16 July 1956, when the Karelo-Finnish SSR was merged with the RSFSR.

A new constitution took effect on 7 Oct. 1977. According to the constitution, the Communist Party is 'the leading and guiding force of Soviet society'.

The Soviet Union is formally a federal state comprising 15 Union (constituent) Republics of equal status, voluntarily linked and having the right to secede. Some of the 15 Union Republics contain Autonomous Republics and Autonomous Regions. The RSFSR also includes 10 National Areas. The highest organ of state power is the bicameral legislature, the Supreme Soviet of the USSR, comprising the Soviet (Council) of the Union, with 767 members elected from constituencies, and the Soviet (Council) of Nationalities, with 750 members (32 from each of the 15 Union Republics; 11 from each of the 20 Autonomous Republics; five from each of the eight Autonomous Regions; one from each of the 10 National Areas). Both houses have equal rights and powers and their terms run concurrently. Members are directly elected (from a single list of candidates) for four-year terms by universal adult suffrage. At a joint session the members elect the Presidium of the Supreme Soviet (39 members) to be the legislature's permanent organ. The Supreme Soviet also appoints the Council of Ministers (called People's Commissars until 16 Mar. 1946), headed by a Chairman, to form the executive and administrative branch of government, responsible to the Supreme Soviet. Each of the 15 Union Republics has a constitution and state structure on the same pattern as the central government, with a unicameral Supreme Soviet and a Council of Ministers to deal with internal affairs.

Throughout the whole country, real power is held by the highly centralised Communist Party of the Soviet Union (CPSU), the only legal party, which has an absolute monopoly of power in all political affairs and controls government at all levels. The Party had over 16 million members in 1977. Its highest authority is, in theory, the Party Congress, which should be convened at least every five years. The Congress elects the Central Committee (287 members and 139 alternate members were chosen in 1976) which supervises Party work and directs state policy. The Committee, which meets twice a year, elects a Political Bureau (Politburo), which is the Party's most powerful policy-making body. In 1977 the Politburo had 14 members (including the General Secretary) and six candidate members. Apart from the RSFSR, each Union Republic has its own Communist Party, with a Central Committee led by a First Secretary, but they are subsidiary to, and subject to direction from, the CPSU.

Telephones: 16 949 000, excluding telephone systems of the military forces (1975).
Daily newspapers: 675 (1974).
Total circulation: 97 664 000.
Radio: 116 100 000 (1974).
TV: 55 200 000 (1975).
Length of roadways: 868 676 miles *1 398 000 km.*
Length of railways: 159 754 miles *257 100 km.*
Universities: 63 (plus 58 technical universities).
Adult illiteracy: 0·3% (males 0·2%; females 0·3%) in 1970.
Expectation of life: Males 64 years; females 74 years (1971–72).

Defence: Military service: Army and Air Force 2 years, Navy and Border Guards 2–3 years; total armed forces 3 650 000 (excluding about 750 000 uniformed civilians); defence expenditure, 1975: $124 000 million (CIA estimate).
Cinemas: 146 300 permanent; 8800 mobile (1973).

UNITED ARAB EMIRATES

Official name: Ittihād al-Imārāt al-'Arabiyah.
Population: 179 126 (census of 15 Mar.–16 Apr. 1968); 655 937 (estimate for 1975).
Area: 32 278 miles² *83 600 km²*.
Languages: Arabic.
Religions: Muslim.
Capital city: Abu Dhabi, population 150 000 (1975 est).
Other principal town (1975): Dubai 100 000.
Highest point: Western Al-Hajar, 3900 ft *1189 m*.
Principal mountain ranges: Al-Hajar.
Head of State: Shaikh Zaid ibn Sultan an-Nahayan (b. 1918), President.
Prime Minister: Shaikh Makhtum ibn Rashid al-Makhtum.
Climate: Very hot and dry, with summer temperatures of over 100 °F; cooler in the eastern mountains.
Labour force: 77 013 (1968 census).
Gross national product: $6870 million in 1975 (World Bank estimate).
Exports: 33 771 million dirhams in 1976: Crude petroleum 96·4%.
Monetary unit: UAE dirham. 1 dirham = 10 dinars = 100 fils.
Denominations:
Coins 1, 5, 10, 25, 50 fils, 1 dinar.
Notes 1, 5, 10, 50, 100, 1000 dirhams.
Exchange rate to US dollar: 3.90 (July 1977).
Political history and government: Formerly the seven shaikhdoms of Trucial Oman (the Trucial States), under British protection. An independent federation (originally of six states), under a provisional constitution, since 2 Dec. 1971. The seventh, Ras al Khaimah, joined the UAE on 11 Feb. 1972. The highest federal authority is the Supreme Council of the Union, comprising the hereditary rulers of the seven emirates (the rulers of Abu Dhabi and Dubai have the power of veto). From its seven members the Council elects a President and a Vice-President. The President appoints a Prime Minister and a Union (Federal) Council of Ministers, responsible to the Supreme Council, to hold executive authority. The legislature is the Federal National Council, a consultative assembly (comprising 40 members appointed for two years by the emirates) which considers laws proposed by the Council of Ministers. The provisional constitution, originally in force for 5 years, was extended to 1981 by a decree of 28 Nov. 1976. There are no political parties. In local affairs each ruler has absolute power over his subjects.
Telephones: 34 282 (1974).
Daily newspapers: 4.
Radio: 51 000 (1974).
TV: 16 000.
Expectation of life: Males 45·8 years; females 48·3 years (UN estimates for 1970–75, average for Bahrain, Oman, Qatar and the United Arab Emirates).
Adult illiteracy: 79·1% (males 73·0%; females 91·1%) in 1968.
Defence: Total armed forces 15 000.
Cinemas: 2 (seating capacity 1500) in 1960.

THE 50 STATES OF THE UNITED STATES OF AMERICA

Name, with date and order of (original) admission into the Union. Nicknames	Area (inc inland water). Pop. at 1970 Census (with rankings). Population density per mile² per km². State Capital. Admin. divisions	Major Cities (with population, at 1970, unless later date given)
ALABAMA (Ala.) 14 Dec. 1819 (22nd) 'Heart of Dixie' 'Cotton State' 'Yellowhammer State'	51 609 miles² *133 667 km²* (29th) 3 444 165 (21st) 66·7 *25,8* Montgomery 67 counties	Birmingham (300 910) Mobile (190 026) Huntsville (139 282) Montgomery (133 386) Tuscaloosa (65 773)
ALASKA (Aleut, 'Great Land') 3 Jan. 1959 (49th) 'The Last Frontier' 'Land of the Midnight Sun'	586 412 miles² *1 518 800 km²* (1st) 302 173 (50th) 0·5 *0,2* Juneau 19 election districts	Anchorage (48 081) Spenard (18 089) Fairbanks (14 771) Ketchikan (6994) Juneau (6050)
ARIZONA (Ariz) 14 Feb. 1912 (48th) 'Grand Canyon State' 'Apache State'	113 909 miles² *295 023 km²* (6th) 1 772 482 (33rd) 15·6 *6,0* Phoenix 14 counties	Phoenix (582 500) Tucson (262 933) Tempe (63 550) Mesa (62 853) Yuma (29 007)
ARKANSAS (Ark) 15 June 1836 (25th) 'Land of Opportunity' 'Wonder State' 'Bear State'	53 104 miles² *137 539 km²* (27th) 1 923 295 (32nd) 36·2 *14,0* Little Rock 75 counties	Little Rock (132 483) Fort Smith (65 393) North Little Rock (60 040) Pine Bluff (57 389) Hot Springs (35 631) El Dorado City (25 283)
CALIFORNIA (Cal) 9 Sept. 1850 (31st) 'Golden State'	158 693 miles² *411 013 km²* (3rd) 19 953 134 (1st) 125·7 *48,5* Sacramento 58 counties	Los Angeles City (2 809 813) San Francisco (715 674) San Diego (697 027) San Jose (445 779) Oakland (361 561) Long Beach (358 879) Sacramento (257 105) Anaheim (166 408) Fresno (165 972) Santa Ana (155 762)
Nine other towns in California have a population of over 100,000: Riverside (140,089); Torrance (134,968); Glendale (132,664); Berkeley (116,716); Huntington Beach (115,960); Pasadena (112,951); Stockton (109,963); San Bernardino (106,869); E. Los Angeles (106,033).		
COLORADO (Colo) 1 Aug. 1876 (38th) 'Centennial State'	104 247 miles² *269 998 km²* (8th) 2 207 259 (30th) 21·2 *8,2* Denver 63 counties	Denver (514 678) Colorado Springs (135 060) Pueblo (97 453) Aurora (75 974) Boulder (66 870) Fort Collins (43 337)
CONNECTICUT (Conn) 9 Jan. 1788 (5th) 'Constitution State' 'Nutmeg State'	5009 miles² *12 973 km²* (48th) 3 032 217 (24th) 605·4 *233,7* Hartford 8 counties	Hartford (158 017) Bridgeport (156 542) New Haven (137 707) Stamford (108 798) Waterbury (108 033) New Britain (83 441) Norwalk (79 113)
DELAWARE (Del) 7 Dec. 1787 (1st) 'First State' 'Diamond State'	2057 miles² *5327 km²* (49th) 548 104 (46th) 266·5 *102,9* Dover 3 counties	Wilmington (80 386) Newark (21 298) Dover (17 488) Elsmere (8415) Seaford (5537) Milford (5314)
FLORIDA (Fla) 3 Mar. 1845 (27th) 'Sunshine State' 'Peninsula State'	58 560 miles² *151 670 km²* (22nd) 6 789 443 (9th) 115·9 *44,8* Tallahassee 67 counties	Jacksonville (528 865) Miami (334 859) Tampa (277 753) St Petersburg (216 159) Fort Lauderdale (139 590) Hialeah (102 452) Orlando (99 006) Miami Beach (87 072)
GEORGIA (Ga) 2 Jan. 1788 (4th) 'Empire State of the South' 'Peach State'	58 876 miles² *152 488 km²* (21st) 4 589 575 (15th) 77·9 *30,1* Atlanta 159 counties	Atlanta (497 421) Columbus (155 028) Macon (122 423) Savannah (118 349) Albany (72 623)

UNITED STATES OF AMERICA

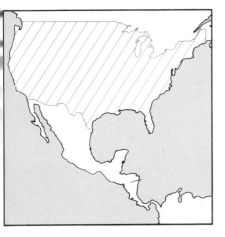

Official name: United States of America.
Population: 203 235 298 (census of 1 Apr. 1970); 216 022 000 (estimate for 1 Jan. 1977).
Area: 3 615 122 miles² *9 363 123 km²*.
Language: English.
Religions: Protestant, Roman Catholic, Jewish, Orthodox. (*see p. 198*)
Capital city: Washington, D.C., population 723 000 at 1 July 1974.
Other principal towns (1973): New York 7 646 818; Chicago 3 172 929; Los Angeles 2 746 854; Philadelphia 1 861 719; Detroit 1 386 817; Houston 1 320 018; Baltimore 877 838; Dallas 815 866; San Diego 757 148; San Antonio 756 226; Indianapolis 738 657; Milwaukee 690 685; San Francisco 687 450; Cleveland 678 615; Memphis 658 868; Phoenix 637 121; Boston 618 275.
Head of State: James Earl Carter, Jr. (b. 1 Oct. 1924), President.
Climate: Its continental dimensions ensure extreme variety, ranging in temperature between the 134 °F (56,7 °C) recorded in Death Valley, California, on 10 July 1913, and the −76 °F (−60,0 °C) at Tanana, Alaska, in January 1886. Mean annual averages range between 76·6 °F at Key West, Florida, and 10·1 °F at Barrow, Alaska. Excluding Alaska and Hawaii, rainfall averages 29 in per year and ranges between 55·6 in in Louisiana and 8·6 in in Nevada.

Climate in representative population centres are:

Anchorage, Alaska: Average daily high 65 °F July; 19 °F January. Average daily low 5 °F January; 49 °F July. Days with rain 15 in August; 4 in April.

San Francisco, Cal: Average daily high 69 °F September; 55 °F January. Average daily low 45 °F January; 55 °F September. Days with rain 11 in January–February; 0 in July–August.

Washington, DC: Average daily high 87 °F July; 42 °F January. Average daily low 27 °F January; 68 °F July. Days with rain 12 in March, May; 8 in September–October.

Honolulu, Hawaii: Average daily high 83 °F August–September; 76 °F January–February. Average daily low 67 °F February–March; 74 °F September–October. Days with rain 15 in December; 11 in February, May.

Name, with date and order of (original) admission into the Union. Nicknames	Area (inc inland water). Pop. at 1970 Census (with rankings). Population density per mile² per km². State Capital. Admin. divisions	Major Cities (with population, at 1970, unless later date given)
HAWAII 21 Aug. 1959 (50th) 'Aloha State'	6450 miles² *16 705 km²* (47th) 769 913 (40th) 119·4 *46,1* Honolulu (on Oahu) 5 counties	Honolulu (324 871) Kailua-Lanikai (33 783) Hilo (26 353) Wahiawa (17 598)
IDAHO 3 July 1890 (43rd) 'Gem State' 'Gem of the Mountains'	83 557 miles² *216 412 km²* (13th) 713 008 (42nd) 8·5 *3,3* Boise City 44 counties, plus small part of Yellowstone Park	Boise City (74 990) Pocatello (40 036) Idaho Falls (35 776) Twin Falls (21 914) Nampa (20 768) Coeur d'Alene (16 228)
ILLINOIS (Ill) 3 Dec. 1818 (21st) 'Prairie State'	56 400 miles² *146 075 km²* (24th) 11 113 976 (5th) 197·1 *76,1* Springfield 102 counties	Chicago (3 369 357) Rockford (147 370) Peoria (126 963) Springfield (91 753) Decatur (90 397) Evanston (80 113) East St Louis (69 996)
INDIANA (Ind) 11 Dec. 1816 (19th) Moosier State'	36 291 miles² *93 993 km²* (38th) 5 193 669 (11th) 143·1 *55,3* Indianapolis 92 counties	Indianapolis (746 302) Fort Wayne (178 021) Gary (175 415) Evansville (138 764) South Bend (125 580) Hammond (107 885) Terre Haute (70 335)
IOWA (Ia) 28 Dec. 1846 (29th) 'Hawkeye State'	56 290 miles² *145 790 km²* (25th) 2 825 041 (25th) 50·2 *19,4* Des Moines 99 counties	Des Moines (201 404) Cedar Rapids (110 642) Davenport (98 469) Sioux City (85 925) Waterloo (75 533) Dubuque (62 300) Council Bluffs (60 348)
KANSAS (Kan) 29 Jan. 1861 (34th) 'Sunflower State' 'Jayhawk State'	82 264 miles² *213 063 km²* (14th) 2 249 071 (28th) 27·3 *10,6* Topeka 105 counties	Wichita (276 554) Kansas City (168 213) Topeka (125 011) Lawrence (45 698) Salina (37 714) Hutchinson (36 885)
KENTUCKY (Ky) (officially the Commonwealth of Kentucky) 1 June 1792 (15th) 'Bluegrass State'	40 395 miles² *104 623 km²* (37th) 3 219 311 (23rd) 79·7 *30,8* Frankfort 120 counties	Louisville (361 706) Lexington (108 137) Covington (52 535) Owensboro (50 329) Paducah (31 627) Ashland (29 245)
LOUISIANA (La) 30 Apr. 1812 (18th) 'Pelican State' 'Creole State' 'Sugar State' 'Bayou State'	48 523 miles² *125 674 km²* (31st) 3 643 180 (20th) 75·1 *29,0* Baton Rouge 64 parishes (counties)	New Orleans (593 471) Shreveport (182 064) Baton Rouge (165 963) Lake Charles (77 998) Monroe (56 374)
MAINE (Me) 15 Mar. 1820 (23rd) 'Pine Tree State'	33 215 miles² *86 026 km²* (39th) 993 663 (38th) 30·0 *11,6* Augusta 16 counties	Portland (65 116) Lewiston (41 779) Bangor (33 168) Auburn (24 151)
MARYLAND (Md) 28 Apr. 1788 (7th) 'Old Line State' 'Free State'	10 577 miles² *27 394 km²* (42nd) 3 922 399 (18th) 370·8 *143,2* Annapolis 23 counties, plus the independent city of Baltimore	Baltimore (905 759) Dundalk (85 377) Silver Spring (77 411) Bethesda (71 621) Wheaton (66 280) Catonsville (54 812)
MASSACHUSETTS (Mass) 6 Feb. 1788 (6th) 'Bay State' 'Old Colony State'	8257 miles² *21 385 km²* (45th) 5 689 170 (10th) 689·0 *266,0* Boston 14 counties	Boston (641 071) Worcester (176 572) Springfield (163 905) New Bedford (101 777) Cambridge (100 361)

Chicago, Illinois: Average daily high 81 °F July; 32 °F January. Average daily low 18 °F January; 66 °F July. Days with rain 12 in March, May; 9 in July–October.

New York, NY: Average daily high 82 °F July; 37 °F January. Average daily low 24 °F January–February; 66 °F July–August. Days with rain 12 in January, March, July; 9 in September–November.

Miami, Florida: Average daily high 88 °F July–August; 74 °F January. Average daily low 61 °F January–February; 76 °F July–August. Days with rain 18 in September; 6 in February.

Labour force: 92 613 000 (including 7 830 000 unemployed) aged 16 and over (1975): Manufacturing 23·5%; Trade, restaurants and hotels 20·7%; Community, social and personal services 32·8%. Figures exclude armed forces (2 180 000 in 1975).
Gross domestic product: $1 297 500 million (provisional) in 1973: Manufacturing 25·1%; Trade, restaurants and hotels 17·2% (trade 16·7%); Finance, insurance, real estate and business services 10·9%; Government services 13·6%. Revised total is $1 302 000 million.
Exports: $107 651·8 million (including Puerto Rico) in 1975: Food and live animals 14·6% (cereals and cereal preparations 10·8%); Machinery and transport equipment 42·9% (non-electric machinery 19·6%; transport equipment 16·1%).
Monetary unit: US dollar ($). 1 dollar. = 100 cents.
Denominations:
 Coins 1, 5, 10, 25, 50 cents, 1 dollar.
 Notes 1, 2, 5, 10, 20, 50, 100 dollars.
Telephones: 149 012 000 (31 Dec. 1975).
Daily newspapers: 1756 (1975).
 Total circulation: 60 655 000.
Radio: 401 600 000 (1974).
TV: 121 100 000 (1974).
Length of roadways: 3 814 991 miles *6 139 633 km* (31 Dec. 1974).
Length of railways: 218 024 miles *350 875 km.*
Universities: 2606.
School leaving age: 16.
Adult illiteracy: 1·0%.
Expectation of life: Males 68·2 years; females 75·9 years (1974).
Defence: Military service voluntary; total armed forces 2 086 700; defence expenditure, 1976/77: $100 100 million.
Cinemas: 10 520 (seating capacity 10 million) and 3900 drive-in (1970).

*COUNTRIES OF THE WORLD
UNITED STATES continued*

Name, with date and order of (original) admission into the Union. Nicknames	Area (inc inland water). Pop. at 1970 Census (with rankings). Population density per mile² per km². State Capital. Admin. divisions	Major Cities (with population, at 1970, unless later date given)
MICHIGAN (Mich) 26 Jan. 1837 (26th) 'Wolverine State'	58 216 miles² *150 779 km²* (23rd) 8 875 083 (7th) 152·5 *58,9* Lansing 83 counties	Detroit (1 513 601) Grand Rapids (197 649) Flint (193 317) Lansing (131 403) Dearborn (104 199)
MINNESOTA (Minn) 11 May 1858 (32nd) 'North Star State' 'Gopher State'	84 068 miles² *217 735 km²* (12th) 3 805 069 (19th) 45·3 *17,5* St Paul 87 counties	Minneapolis (434 400) St Paul (309 714) Duluth (100 578) Bloomington (81 970) St Louis Park (48 922)
MISSISSIPPI (Miss) 10 Dec. 1817 (20th) 'Magnolia State'	47 716 miles² *123 584 km²* (32nd) 2 216 912 (29th) 46·5 *17,9* Jackson 82 counties	Jackson (153 968) Biloxi (48 486) Meridian (45 083) Greenville (39 648) Hattiesburg (38 277)
MISSOURI (Mo) 10 Aug. 1821 (24th) 'Show Me State'	69 686 miles² *180 486 km²* (19th) 4 677 399 (13th) 67·1 *25,9* Jefferson City 114 counties, plus the independent city of St Louis	St Louis (622 236) Kansas City (507 330) Springfield (120 096) Independence (111 630) St Joseph (72 691) University City (47 527)
MONTANA (Mont) 8 Nov. 1889 (41st) 'Treasure State'	147 138 miles² *381 086 km²* (4th) 694 409 (43rd) 4·7 *1,8* Helena 56 counties, plus small part of Yellowstone National Park	Billings (61 581) Great Falls (60 091) Missoula (29 497) Butte (23 368) Helena (22 730)
NEBRASKA (Nebr) 1 Mar. 1867 (37th) 'Cornhusker State' 'Beef State' 'Tree Planter's State'	77 227 miles² *200 017 km²* (15th) 1 483 791 (35th) 19·2 *7,4* Lincoln 93 counties	Omaha (346 929) Lincoln (149 518) Grand Island (31 269) Hastings (23 580) Fremont (22 962)
NEVADA (Nev) 31 Oct. 1864 (36th) 'Sagebrush State' 'Silver State' 'Battle Born State'	110 540 miles² *286 297 km²* (7th) 488 738 (47th) 4·1 *1,7* Carson City 17 counties	Las Vegas (125 787) Reno (72 863) North Las Vegas (36 216) Sparks (24 187) Henderson (16 395)
NEW HAMPSHIRE (NH) 21 June 1788 (9th) 'Granite State'	9304 miles² *24 097 km²* (44th) 737 681 (41st) 79·0 *30,6* Concord 10 counties	Manchester (87 754) Nashua (55 820) Concord (30 022) Portsmouth (25 717)
NEW JERSEY (NJ) 18 Dec. 1787 (3rd) 'Garden State'	7836 miles² *20 295 km²* (46th) 7 168 164 (8th) 914·7 *353,2* Trenton 21 counties	Newark (381 930) Jersey City (260 350) Paterson (144 824) Trenton (104 786) Camden (102 551) Elizabeth (112 654)
NEW MEXICO (NM) 6 Jan. 1912 (47th) 'Land of Enchantment' 'Sunshine State'	121 666 miles² *315 113 km²* (5th) 1 016 000 (37th) 8·4 *3,2* Santa Fe 32 counties	Albuquerque (243 751) Sante Fe (41 167) Las Cruces (37 857) Roswell (33 908) Hobbs (26 025)
NEW YORK (NY) 26 July 1788 (11th) 'Empire State'	49 576 miles² *128 401 km²* (30th) 18 190 740 (2nd) 366·9 *141,7* Albany 62 counties	New York City (7 895 563) Buffalo (462 768) Rochester (296 233) Yonkers (204 297) Syracuse (197 297) Albany (115 781) Utica (91 340) Niagara Falls (85 615)
NORTH CAROLINA (NC) 21 Nov. 1789 (12th) 'Tar Heel State' 'Old North State'	52 586 miles² *136 197 km²* (28th) 5 082 059 (12th) 96·6 *37,3* Raleigh 100 counties	Charlotte (241 178) Greensboro (144 076) Winston-Salem (133 683) Raleigh (123 793) Durham (95 438)

POPULATION

The United States of America ranks fourth in size (3 615 122 miles² *9 363 123 km²*), fourth in population (212 300 000 estimated at 1975), and first in production of all the countries in the world (40%).

The area of the 48 conterminous states comprises 3 022 260 miles² *7 827 617 km²*. The principal mountain ranges are listed on pp. 20–1. The highest point is Mount McKinley (20 320 ft [*6193 m*]) in Alaska.

There are eight US river systems involving rivers in excess of 1000 miles *1609 km* in length, of which by far the vastest is the Mississippi–Missouri.

The population is divided 88·3% white and 11·7% non-white. The population of foreign origin included at March 1972:

Jewish	6 460 000
Italian	8 764 000
German	25 543 000
British (UK)	29 548 000
Polish	5 105 000
Russian	2 188 000
Irish (Republic)	16 408 000
Spanish and Spanish origin	9 178 000
French	5 420 000

COUNTRIES OF THE WORLD
UNITED STATES continued

Name, with date and order of (original) admission into the Union. Nicknames	Area (inc inland water). Pop. at 1970 Census (with rankings). Population density per mile² per km². State Capital. Admin. divisions	Major Cities (with population, at 1970, unless later date given)
NORTH DAKOTA (ND) 2 Nov. 1889 (39th) 'Sioux State' 'Flickertail State'	70 665 miles² *183 022 km²* (17th) 617 761 (45th) 8·7 *3,4* Bismarck 53 counties	Fargo (53 365) Grand Forks (40 060) Bismarck (34 703) Minot (32 290) Jamestown (15 078)
OHIO 1 Mar. 1803 (17th) 'Buckeye State'	41 222 miles² *106 764 km²* (35th) 10 652 017 (6th) 258·4 *99,8* Columbus 88 counties	Cleveland (750 879) Columbus (540 025) Cincinnati (451 455) Toledo (383 105) Akron (275 425) Dayton (242 917) Youngstown (140 909) Canton (110 053)
OKLAHOMA (Okla) 16 Nov. 1907 (46th) 'Sooner State'	69 919 miles² *181 089 km²* (18th) 2 559 253 (27th) 36·6 *14,1* Oklahoma City 77 counties	Oklahoma City (368 377) Tulsa (330 350) Lawton (74 470) Midwest City (48 212) Enid (44 986) Muskogee (37 331)
OREGON (Ore) 14 Feb. 1859 (33rd) 'Beaver State'	96 981 miles² *251 180 km²* (10th) 2 091 385 (31st) 21·6 *8,3* Salem 36 counties	Portland (379 967) Eugene (79 028) Salem (68 480) Medford (28 454)
PENNSYLVANIA (Pa) 12 Dec. 1787 (2nd) 'Keystone State'	45 333 miles² *117 412 km²* (33rd) 11 793 909 (3rd) 260·2 *100,4* Harrisburg 67 counties	Philadelphia (1 949 996) Pittsburgh (520 117) Erie (129 231) Allentown (109 527) Scranton (103 564) Reading (87 643) Harrisburg (68 061)
RHODE ISLAND (RI) 29 May 1790 (13th) 'Little Rhody'	1214 miles² *3144 km²* (50th) 949 723 (39th) 782·3 *302,1* Providence 5 counties	Providence (179 116) Warwick (83 694) Pawtucket (76 984) Cranston (74 287) East Providence (48 207) Woonsocket (46 820) Newport (34 562)
SOUTH CAROLINA (SC) 23 May 1788 (8th) 'Palmetto State'	31 055 miles² *80 432 km²* (40th) 2 590 516 (26th) 83·4 *32,2* Columbia 46 counties	Columbia (113 542) Charleston (66 945) Greenville (61 436) Spartanburg (44 546) Anderson (27 556)
SOUTH DAKOTA (SD) 2 Nov. 1889 (40th) 'Coyote State' 'Sunshine State'	77 047 miles² *199 551 km²* (16th) 666 257 (44th) 8·6 *3,3* Pierre 67 counties (64 county governments)	Sioux Falls (72 488) Rapid City (43 836) Aberdeen (26 476) Huron (14 299) Mitchell (13 425) Watertown (13 388)
TENNESSEE (Tenn) 1 June 1796 (16th) 'Volunteer State'	42 244 miles² *109 411 km²* (34th) 3 924 164 (17th) 92·9 *35,9* Nashville 95 counties	Memphis (623 530) Nashville-Davidson (447 877) Knoxville (174 587) Chattanooga (119 923) Jackson (39 996) Johnson City (33 770)
TEXAS 29 Dec. 1845 (28th) 'Lone Star State'	267 338 miles² *692 402 km²* (2nd) 11 196 730 (4th) 41·9 *16,2* Austin 254 counties	Houston (1 232 802) Dallas (844 401) San Antonio (654 153) Fort Worth (393 476) El Paso (322 261) Austin (251 808) Corpus Christi (204 525) Lubbock (149 101) Amarillo (127 010) Beaumont (117 548) Wichita Falls (96 265) Waco (95 326) Abilene (89 653)

U

The principal religious denominations in 1972 were (in millions):

Roman Catholic	48·2
Baptist	27·3
Methodist	13·0
Lutheran	8·8
Jewish	5·6
Presbyterian	4·1
Protestant Episcopal Church	3·2
Eastern Orthodox	3·9
Mormon	2·0
United Church of Christ	1·9

The capital city is Washington, District of Columbia, with a population (estimate 1974) of 723 000. Greater Washington had a population of 1 808 423 (Census of 1960) and the metropolitan area had 3 020 000 (1973 estimate). The District of Columbia is the seat of the US Federal Government comprising 69 miles² from west central Maryland on the Potomac River opposite Virginia. The site was chosen in October 1790 by President Washington and the Capitol corner stone laid by him on 18 Sept. 1793. Washington became the capital (Philadelphia 1790–1800) on 10 June 1800. The other principal cities (with populations at 1 Apr. 1970) are listed in the separate entries for each of the 50 States.

Historical Note: Evidence from the most recent radiometric dating has backdated human habitation of North America to c. 35 000 BC. This occupation was probably achieved via the Bering Bridge (now the 55-mile-wide Bering Strait) from NE Asia.

The continent derived its name from the Italian explorer Amerigo Vespucci (1454–1512), discoverer of the NE South American coastal regions in 1498. The German cartographer Martin Waldseemüller named the New World 'Terra America' in his atlas published in St Dié, France, in April 1507.

The earliest European landing on present US territory was on 27 Mar. 1513 by the Spaniard Juan Ponce de León in Florida. The discovery of the US Pacific coast was by Juan R Cabrillo who landed from Mexico on 28 Sept. 1542, near San Diego, California. The oldest town of European origin is St Augustine, Florida, founded on 8 Sept. 1565 on the site of Seloy by Pedro Menéndez de Avilés with 1500 Spanish colonists. The British exploration of what is now US territory began with Philip Amadas and Arthur Barlowe in Virginia in 1584. Henry Hudson sailed into New York harbour in September 1609. The Plymouth Pilgrims reached Cape Cod 54 days out from Plymouth, England, in the *Mayflower* (101 passengers and 48 crew) on 9 Nov. 1620. On 6 May 1626 Peter Minuit bought Manhattan island for some trinkets valued at $39. In 1664 the area was seized by the British and granted to Charles II's brother, the Duke of York, and the city of New Amsterdam was renamed New York.

The American revolution and the War of Independence (total battle deaths 4435) occupied the years 1763–83. The incident of the Boston Tea Party occurred on 16 Dec. 1773 and the Battle of Bunker Hill on 17 June 1775. The Declaration of Independence was made on 4 July 1776. This was recognised by Britain in March 1782. General George Washington was chosen President in February 1789 and the first US Congress was called on 4 Mar. 1789.

The War of 1812 between the US and Great Britain was declared by Congress on 18 June 1812, because Britain seized US ships running her blockade of France, impressed 2800 seamen and armed Indians who raided US territory. In 1814 Maj-Gen Robert Ross burnt the Capitol and the White House in Washington. The war which

Name, with date and order of (original) admission into the Union. Nicknames	Area (inc inland water). Pop. at 1970 Census (with rankings). Population density per mile² per km². State Capital. Admin. divisions	Major Cities (with population, at 1970, unless later date given)
UTAH 4 Jan. 1896 (45th) 'Beehive State'	84 916 miles² *219 931 km²* (11th) 1 059 273 (36th) 12·5 *4,8* Salt Lake City 29 counties	Salt Lake City (75 885) Ogden (69 478) Provo (53 131) Bountiful (27 751) Orem (25 729) Logan (22 333) Kearns (17 247)
VERMONT (Vt) 4 Mar. 1791 (14th) 'Green Mountain State'	9609 miles² *24 887 km²* (43rd) 444 932 (48th) 46·3 *17,9* Montpelier 14 counties	Burlington (38 633) Rutland (19 293) Barre (10 209) Brattleboro (9055; township 12 239)
VIRGINIA (Va) (officially called the Commonwealth of Virginia) 26 June 1788 (10th) 'The Old Dominion' 'Cavalier State'	40 817 miles² *105 716 km²* (36th) 4 648 494 (14th) 113·9 *44,0* Richmond 98 counties, plus 32 independent cities	Norfolk (307 951) Richmond (249 431) Arlington County (174 284) (unincorporated) Newport News (138 177) Hampton (120 779) Portsmouth (110 963) Alexandria (110 927) Roanoke (92 115)
WASHINGTON (Wash) 11 Nov. 1889 (42nd) 'Evergreen State' 'Chinook State'	68 192 miles² *176 616 km²* (20th) 3 409 169 (22nd) 49·9 *19,3* Olympia 39 counties	Seattle (530 831) Spokane (170 516) Tacoma (154 407) Everett (53 622) Yakima (45 588) Vancouver (41 859) Bellingham (39 375) Bremerton (35 307) Walla Walla (23 619)
WEST VIRGINIA (W Va) 20 June 1863 (35th) 'Mountain State' 'Panhandle State'	24 181 miles² *62 629 km²* (41st) 1 744 237 (34th) 72·1 *27,8* Charleston 55 counties	Huntingdon (74 315) Charleston (71 505) Wheeling (48 188) Parkersburg (44 208) Weirton (27 131) Fairmont (26 093) Clarksburg (24 864)
WISCONSIN (Wisc) 29 May 1848 (30th) 'Badger State'	56 154 miles² *145 438 km²* (26th) 4 417 933 (16th) 78·7 *30,4* Madison 72 counties	Milwaukee (717 372) Madison (171 769) Racine (95 162) Green Bay (87 809) Kenosha (78 805) West Allis (71 649) Wauwatosa (58 676)
WYOMING (Wyo) 10 July 1890 (44th) 'Equality State'	97 914 miles² *253 596 km²* (9th) 332 416 (49th) 3·4 *1,3* Cheyenne 23 counties, plus most of Yellowstone National Park	Cheyenne (40 914) Casper (39 361) Laramie (23 143) Rock Springs (11 657) Sheridan (10 856) Rawlins (7855)

20th CENTURY PRESIDENTS

Name	Dates of Birth and Death	Party	Dates in Office
Theodore Roosevelt	27 Oct. 1858 to 6 Jan. 1919	Republican	1901–09
William Howard Taft	15 Sept. 1857 to 8 Mar. 1930	Republican	1909–13
Thomas Woodrow Wilson	28 Dec. 1856 to 3 Feb. 1924	Democratic	1913–21
Warren Gamaliel Harding	2 Nov. 1865 to 2 Aug. 1923	Republican	1921–23
John Calvin Coolidge	4 July 1872 to 5 Jan. 1933	Republican	1923–29
Herbert Clark Hoover	10 Aug. 1874 to 20 Oct. 1964	Republican	1929–33
Franklin Delano Roosevelt	30 Jan. 1882 to 12 Apr. 1945	Democratic	1933–45
Harry S Truman	8 May 1884 to 26 Dec. 1972	Democratic	1945–53
Dwight David Eisenhower	14 Oct. 1890 to 28 Mar. 1969	Republican	1953–61
John Fitzgerald Kennedy	29 May 1917 to 22 Nov. 1963	Democratic	1961–63
Lyndon Baines Johnson	27 Aug. 1908 to 22 Jan. 1973	Democratic	1963–69
Richard Milhous Nixon	b. 9 Jan. 1913	Republican	1969–74
Gerald Rudolph Ford	b. 14 July 1913	Republican	1974–77
James Earl Carter	b. 1 Oct. 1924	Democratic	1977–

inspired national unity cost only 2260 battle deaths. The Monroe Doctrine (the isolationism of the Americas from Europe) was declared on 2 Dec. 1823.

On 1 Nov. 1835 Texas proclaimed independence from Mexico. In the Alamo in San Antonio a US garrison was massacred (including Sen David Crockett) on 6 Mar. 1836.

The secession of States over the question of slave labour on cotton plantations began with South Carolina on 20 Dec. 1860. The Southern States of South Carolina, Georgia, Alabama, Mississippi, Louisiana and Florida formed the Confederate States of America on 8 Feb. 1861. War broke out on 12 Apr. 1861 with the bombardment of Fort Sumter in Charleston Harbor, South Carolina. The war culminated in the Battle of Gettysburg in July 1863 during which there was a total of 43 000 casualties. President A Lincoln was assassinated on 14 Apr. 1865. Slavery was abolished by the adoption of the 13th Amendment (to the Constitution) on 18 Dec. 1865.

The total fatal casualties in the Civil War were c. 547 000 of which the Union forces (North) lost 140 400 in the field and the Confederates (South) 74 500 in battle and c. 28 500 in Union prisons. The dates of the United States' entry into the World Wars of 1914–18 and 1939–45 respectively were 6 Apr. 1917 and 8 Dec. 1941.

US PRESIDENTIAL ELECTIONS

US Presidential elections occur on the first Tuesday after the first Monday of November in every fourth year—these coincide with leap years. Election is not by popular majority but by majority of votes in the Electoral College which comprises 538 Electors divided between the States on the basis of one Elector for each of the 100 Senators (upper house) and the 435 Representatives (lower house) plus, since 1964, three Electors for the District of Columbia. Thus a Presidential election victory is achieved by securing at least 270 votes. Recent results have been:

Year	Republican	Democrat	Plurality
1944	99	432	Roosevelt (D) over Dewey (R) by 333
1948	189	303	Truman (D) over Dewey (R) by 114
1952	442	89	Eisenhower (R) over Stevenson (D) by 353
1956	457	73	Eisenhower (R) over Stevenson (D) by 384
1960	219	303	Kennedy (D) over Nixon (R) by 84
1964	52	486	Johnson (D) over Goldwater (R) by 434.
1968	301	191	Nixon (R) over Humphrey (D) by 110
1972	521	17	Nixon (R) over McGovern (D) by 504
1976	241	297	Carter (D) over Ford (R) by 56

UPPER VOLTA

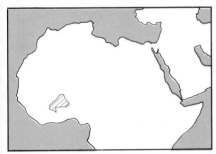

Official name: République de Haute-Volta.
Population: 6 144 013 (census of 1–7 Dec. 1975).
Area: 105 869 miles² *274 200 km².*
Languages: French (official), Mossi, other African languages.
Religions: Animist; Muslim and Christian minorities.
Capital city: Ouagadougou, population 168 607 (1975).
Other principal towns (1975): Bobo-Dioulasso 112 572; Koudougou 35 803; Ouahigouya 25 101.
Highest point: Mt Tema, 2457 ft *749 m.*
Principal rivers: Volta Noire (Black Volta), Volta Rouge (Red Volta), Volta Blanche (White Volta).
Head of State: Gen Aboubakar Sangoulé Lamizana (b. 1916), President.
Climate: Hot (average temperature 83 °F). Dry from November to March. Very dry in north and north-east. Rainy season June to October in south. In Ouagadougou average maximum temperature 87 °F (August) to 104 °F (March), minimum 60 °F to 79 °F.
Labour force: 2 999 000 (1970): Agricul-

ture, forestry and fishing 86·8% (ILO estimates); 2 856 739 (official estimate for 31 Dec. 1972).
Gross domestic product: 77 900 million CFA francs (provisional) in 1968: Agriculture, forestry and fishing 44·0%; Trade, restaurants and hotels 15·5%. Revised total is 79 000 million CFA francs.
Exports: $20·3 million in 1972: Live animals 40·8% (cattle 20·7%; sheep and goats 12·4%); Oil-seeds, oil nuts and oil kernels 16·1%; Textile fibres and waste 20·0% (raw cotton 19·9%).
Monetary unit: Franc de la Communauté financière africaine.
Denominations:
Coins 1, 2, 5, 10, 25, 50, 100 CFA francs.
Notes 50, 100, 500, 1000, 5000 CFA francs.
Exchange rate to US dollar: 242.8 (July 1977).
Political history and government: Formerly a part of French West Africa, independent since 5 Aug. 1960. Army officers, led by Lt-Col (later Gen) Sangoulé Lamizana, took power in a *coup* on 3 Jan. 1966. Col Lamizana took office as President and Prime Minister, the constitution was suspended, the National Assembly dissolved and a Supreme Council of the Armed Forces established. Political activities were suspended on 21 Sept. 1966 but the restriction was lifted in November 1969. A new constitution was approved by popular referendum on 14 June 1970 and introduced on 21 June 1970. This provided for a four-year transitional regime, under joint military and civilian control, leading to the return of civilian rule. Elections for a unicameral National Assembly of 57 members were held on 20 Dec. 1970. The leader of the majority party was appointed Prime Minister by the President, took office on 13 Feb. 1971 and formed a mixed civilian and military Council of Ministers. On 8 Feb. 1974, after a dispute

between the Premier and the Assembly, the President dismissed the former and dissolved the latter. The army again assumed power, with the constitution and political activity suspended. The Head of State also became President of the Council of Ministers on 11 Feb. 1974. Political parties were banned on 30 May 1974. The Assembly was replaced by a National Consultative Council for Renewal, formed on 2 July 1974, with 65 members nominated by the President. The country is divided into 10 departments, each under a military prefect.
Telephones: 6000 (1974).
Daily newspapers: 1 (1974).
Total circulation: 2000.
Radio: 100 000 (1973).
TV: 6000 (1971).
Length of roadways: 3262 miles *5250 km* (31 Dec. 1974).
Length of railways: 321 miles *517 km.*
Universities: 1.
Adult illiteracy: 90 to 95% (estimate).
Expectation of life: Males 36·5 years; females 39·6 years (UN estimates for 1970–75).
Defence: Total armed forces 3050.
Cinemas: 6 (seating capacity 2000) and 3 part-time (capacity 700) in 1969.

URUGUAY

Official name: La República Oriental del Uruguay (The Eastern Republic of Uruguay)
Population: 2 763 964 (census of 21 May 1975).
Area: 68 536 miles² *177 508 km².*
Language: Spanish.
Religion: Roman Catholic.
Capital city: Montevideo, population 1 229 748 (1975).
Other principal towns (1975): Salto 80 000; Paysandú 80 000; Mercedes 53 000;

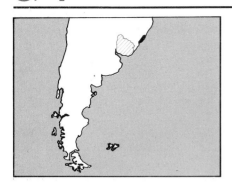

Las Piedras 42 000; Rivera 42 000; Minas 40 000; Melo 38 000.
Highest point: Cerro de las Animas, 1643 ft *500 m.*
Principal mountain ranges: Sierra de las Animas.
Principal river: Uruguay (1000 miles *[1609 km]*).
Head of State: Dr Aparicio Méndez (b. 24 Aug. 1904), President.
Climate: Temperate (average 61 °F). Warm summers and mild winters. Moderate rain. In Montevideo, average maximum 58 °F (July) to 83 °F (January), minimum 43 °F (June, July, August) to 62 °F. (January), rainiest months are August and December (each 7 days). Maximum recorded temperature 44 °C *(111·2 °F)*, Rivera, February 1953; minimum −7 °C *(19·4 °F)*, Paysandú, June 1945.
Labour force: 1 012 267 aged 10 and over (census of 16 Oct. 1963); 1 140 000 (1970): Agriculture, forestry and fishing 15·2%.
Gross domestic product: 4490·9 million new pesos (provisional) in 1974: Agriculture, forestry and fishing 16·9% (agriculture 16·8%); Manufacturing 24·2%; Trade, restaurants and hotels 17·0% (trade 14·3%); Community, social and personal services 15·6%. Revised total is 4459·7 million new pesos.
Exports: $214·1 million in 1972: Meat and meat preparations 46·1% (fresh, chilled or frozen beef 45·7%); Hides and skins 10·4%; Wool and other animal hair 25·7% (greasy wool 15·4%; wool tops 10·1%).
Monetary unit: New Uruguayan peso. 1 new peso = 100 centésimos.
Denominations:
Coins 1, 2, 5, 10 centésimos.
Notes 5, 10, 50 centésimos, 1, 5, 10 new pesos.
Exchange rate to US dollar: 4.655 (July 1977).
Political history and government: A republic comprising 19 departments. A new constitution, approved by plebiscite on 27 Nov. 1966 and taking effect on 1 Mar. 1967, provided that elections by universal adult suffrage be held every five years for a President, a Vice-President and a bicameral legislature, the General Assembly (Congress), comprising a Senate (30 elected members plus the Vice-President) and a 99-member Chamber of Representatives. Elections to both Houses were by proportional representation. Executive power is held by the President, who appoints and leads an 11-member Council of Ministers. On 27 June 1973, after agreeing to political demands by the armed forces, the President dissolved both Houses of Congress. On 19 Dec. 1973 he appointed a new legislature, a 25-member Council of State, headed by a President, to control the executive and draft plans for constitutional reform. On 12 June 1976 the President was deposed by the armed forces and replaced by the Vice-President. On 27 June 1976 the new régime established the Council of the Nation, with 46 members

(the Council of State and 21 officers of the armed forces). On 14 July 1976 the Council of the Nation elected a new President, who took office on 1 Sept. 1976.
Telephones: 247 923 (1974).
Daily newspapers: 59 (1973).
Total circulation: 960 000 (26 dailies).
Radio: 1 500 000 (1972).
TV: 351 000 (1976).
Length of roadways: 30 841 miles *49 634 km* (1973).
Length of railways: 1849 miles *2976 km.*
Universities: 2.
Adult illiteracy: 9·5% (males 9·8%; females 9·3%) in 1963.
Expectation of life: Males 65·51 years; females 71·56 years (1963–4).
Defence: Military service: voluntary; total armed forces 23 000; defence expenditure, 1973: $68 million.
Cinemas: 180 (seating capacity 124 700) in 1967 (35 mm cinemas only).

VATICAN CITY

Official name: Stato della Città del Vaticano (State of the Vatican City).
Population: 724 (estimate for 1 July 1975).
Area: 108·7 acres *44 hectares.*
Languages: Italian, Latin.
Religions: Roman Catholic.
Head of State: Pope Paul VI (b. Giovanni Battista Montini, 26 Sept. 1897).
Head of Government: Cardinal Jean Villot (b. 11 Oct. 1905), Secretary of State.
Climate: See Italy for climate of Rome.
Monetary unit: Italian currency (*q.v.*).
Political history and government: An enclave in the city of Rome, established on 11 Feb. 1929 by the Lateran Treaty with Italy. The Vatican City is under the temporal jurisdiction of the Pope, the Supreme Pontiff elected for life by the College of Cardinals (137 in 1977). He appoints a Pontifical Commission, headed by the Secretary of State, to conduct the administrative affairs of the Vatican, which serves as the international headquarters, and administrative centre, of the worldwide Roman Catholic Church.
Daily newspapers: 1.
Universities: There are 7 pontifical universities in Rome.

VENEZUELA

Official name: La República de Venezuela ('Little Venice').
Population: 10 721 522 (census of 2 Nov. 1971); 12 361 090 (estimate for 1 July 1976). Figures exclude Indian jungle population.
Area: 352 144 miles² *912 050 km².*
Languages: Spanish.
Religion: Roman Catholic.

Capital city: Santiago de León de los Caracas, population 2 105 578 (Federal District) in 1975.
Other principal towns (1971): Maracaibo 651 574; Valencia 367 171; Barquisimeto 330 815; Maracay 255 134; San Cristóbal 151 717; Ciudad Guyana 143 540.
Highest point: La Pico Columna (Pico Bolívar), 16 427 ft *5007 m.*
Principal mountain ranges: Cordillera de Mérida, Sierra de Perijá, La Gran Sabana.
Principal river: Orinoco (1700 miles *[2736 km]*).
Head of State: Carlos Andrés Pérez Rodríguez (b. 27 Oct. 1922), President.
Climate: Varies with altitude from tropical in steamy lowlands to cool in highlands. Maximum recorded temperature 38 °C *(100·4 °F)*, minimum −6 °C *(21·2 °F)*. In Caracas, average temperature 69 °F, average maximum 75 °F (January) to 81 °F (April), minimum 56 °F (January, February) to 62 °F (May, June), rainiest months are July and August (each 15 days).
Labour force: 3 416 236 (excluding 295 583 unemployed) in April 1975 (household survey): Agriculture, forestry and fishing 19·5%; Manufacturing 15·7%; Trade, restaurants and hotels 18·6%; Community, social and personal service 26·7%.
Gross domestic product: 126 699 million bolívares (provisional) in 1974: Mining and quarrying 38·3%; Manufacturing 19·3%. Revised total is 127 741 million bolívares.
Exports: $4584·3 million in 1973: Crude and partly refined petroleum 60·8% (crude petroleum 60·5%); Petroleum products 33·6% (residual fuel oils 24·4%). Figures exclude exports of iron ore ($141·6 million in 1972).
Monetary unit: Bolívar. 1 bolívar = 100 céntimos.
Denominations:
Coins 5, 12½, 25 and 50 céntimos, 1, 2, 5, 10, 20, 100 bolívares.
Notes 5, 10, 20, 50, 100, 500 bolívares.
Exchange rate to US dollar: 4.2925 (July 1977).
Political history and government: A federal republic of 20 states, two Federal Territories and a Federal District (containing the capital), each under a Governor. The last military dictatorship was overthrown by popular revolt on 21–22 Jan. 1958, after which Venezuela returned to democratic rule. A new constitution was promulgated on 23 Jan. 1961. Legislative power is held by the bicameral National Congress, comprising a Senate (49 elected members plus ex-Presidents of the Republic) and a Chamber of Deputies (203 members). Executive authority rests with the President. Senators. Deputies and the President are all elected for 5 years by universal adult suffrage. The President has wide powers and appoints a Council of Ministers to conduct the government. He may not have two consecutive terms of office.
Telephones: 554 197 (1974).

Daily newspapers: 47 (1973).
Total circulation: 963 000 (25 dailies).
Radio: 2 000 000 (1973).
TV: 995 000 (1973).
Length of roadways: 40 835 miles *65 718 km* (31 Dec. 1974).
Length of railways: 107 miles *173 km* (1975).
Universities: 11.
Adult illiteracy: 36·7% (males 32·0%; females 41·6%) in 1961.
Expectation of life: Males 62·9 years; females 66·7 years (UN estimate for 1970–75).
Defence: Military service: two years selective; total armed forces 42 000; defence expenditure, 1975: $494 million.
Cinemas: 436 and 20 drive-in for 4030 cars (1971).

VIET-NAM

Official name: Công hoa xã hôi chủ nghia Viêt Nam (Socialist Republic of Viet-Nam).
Population: 46 523 000 (estimate for 1 July 1976).
Area: 128 402 miles² *332 559 km²*.
Language: Vietnamees.
Religions: Buddhist, Taoist, Confucian, Christian.
Capital city: Hã-nôi (Hanoi), population 1 443 500 (1976).
Other principal towns (1976): Ho Chi Minh City (formerly Saigon) 3 460 500 (including Cholon); Haiphong 1 190 900; Da-Nhang (Tourane) 492 194 (1973); Nha-trang 216 227 (1973); Qui-Nhon 213 757 (1973); Hué 209 043 (1973).
Highest point: Fan si Pan, 10 308 ft *3142 m*.
Principal rivers: Mekong (2600 miles *4184 km*), Songkoi (Red River), Songbo (Black River), Ma.
Head of State: Ton Duc Thang (b. 20 Aug. 1888), President.
Political Leader: Le Duan (b. 1908), First Secretary of the Central Committee of the Communist Party of Viet-Nam.
Prime Minister: Pham Van Dong (b. 1 Mar. 1906).
Climate: Hot and wet in the north, warm and humid in the south. The rainy monsoon season is from April or May to October. In Hanoi, average maximum temperature 68 °F (January) to 92 °F (June), minimum 56 °F to 78 °F (June, July, August); rainiest month August (16 days). In Ho Chi Minh City, average maximum 87 °F (November, December) to 95 °F (April), minimum 70 °F (January) to 76 °F (April, May); rainiest month July (23 days).
Labour force: 20 344 000 (1975): Agriculture, forestry and fishing 73·6% (ILO estimates).
Gross national product: $7100 million in 1975 (World Bank estimate).
Monetary unit:
North: Dông. 1 dông = 10 hào = 100 xu.
South: New dông (Viet-Nam piastre). 1 dông = 100 xu (centimes).
Denominations:
North: *Coins* 1, 2, 5 xu.
Notes 2, 5 xu, 1, 2, 5 hào, 1, 2, 5, 10, 20 dông.
South: *Coins* 1, 2, 5 xu.
Notes 10, 20, 50 xu, 1, 2, 5, 10, 50 dông.
Exchange rates to US dollar:
North: 2.399 (July 1977).
South: 1.819 (July 1977).
Political history and government: Formerly part of French Indo-China, Viet-Nam was occupied by Japanese forces, with French co-operation, in September 1940. On 6 June 1941 nationalist and revolutionary groups, including the Communist Party of

Indo-China, formed the *Viet-Nam Doc-Lap Dong Minh Hoi* (Revolutionary League for the Independence of Viet-Nam), known as the *Viet-Minh*, to overthrow French rule. On 9 Mar. 1945 French administrative control was ended by a Japanese *coup* against their nominal allies. After Japan's surrender in August 1945, *Viet-Minh* forces entered Hanoi and formed a provisional government under Ho Chi Minh, leader of the Communist Party. On 2 Sept. 1945 the new régime proclaimed independence as the Democratic Republic of Viet-Nam (DRV), with Ho as President. On 6 Mar. 1946, after French forces re-entered Viet-Nam, an agreement between France and the DRV recognised Viet-Nam as a 'free' state within the French Union. The DRV government continued to press for complete independence but negotiations broke down and full-scale hostilities began on 19 Dec. 1946. The war continued until cease-fire agreements were made on 20–21 July 1954. These provided that DRV forces should regroup north of latitude 17° N. Thus the DRV was confined to North Viet-Nam.
On 8 Mar. 1949, during the first Indo-China war, the French government made an agreement with anti-Communist elements for the establishment of the State of Viet-Nam, under Bao Dai, Emperor of Annam. Originally within the French Union, the State made an independence agreement with France on 4 June 1954. After the cease-fire agreements of 20–21 July 1954 French forces withdrew, leaving the State's jurisdiction confined to the zone south of latitude 17° N. Complete sovereignty was transferred by France on 29 Dec. 1954. Following a referendum, Bao Dai was deposed and the Republic of Viet-Nam proclaimed on 26 Oct. 1955. In 1959 an insurgent movement, supported by North Viet-Nam, launched guerrilla warfare to overthrow the Republic. The insurgents formed the National Liberation Front (NLF) on 20 Dec. 1960. From 1961 the USA supported the Republic with troops, numbering over 500 000 by 1969. From 1964 regular forces from North Viet-Nam, numbering about 250 000 by 1975, moved south to support the NLF. On 10 June 1969 the NLF announced the formation of a Provisional Revolutionary Government (PRG) to administer 'liberated' areas. A 'peace' agreement of 27 Jan. 1973 led to the withdrawal of US forces but fighting continued until the Republic surrendered to the PRG on 30 Apr. 1975. The country was renamed the Republic of South Viet-Nam.
Following the PRG victory, it was agreed to merge North and South Viet-Nam. Elections were held on 25 Apr. 1976 for a single National Assembly (for both North and South) of 492 members. The new Assembly met on 24 June 1976 and the country was reunited as the Socialist Republic of Viet-Nam on 2 July 1976. The Assembly elected a committee of 36 to draft a new constitution.
Pending the introduction of a new constitution, the DRV constitution (adopted on 1 Jan. 1960) will remain in force. Legislative power is vested in the Assembly, a unicameral body, elected by universal adult suffrage for 4 years. The Assembly elects a Standing Committee to be its permanent organ and to supervise local government. The President and Vice-President are elected by the Assembly for 4 years. Executive authority lies with the Council of Ministers, headed by a Prime Minister, which is elected by, and responsible to, the Assembly.
Political power is held by the Communist Party of Viet-Nam, established on 20 Dec. 1976 in succession to the *Dang Lao Dong*

Viet-Nam (Viet-Nam Workers' Party), formed in 1951. The Party Congress of 14–20 Dec. 1976 elected a Central Committee (101 full members and 32 alternate members) to supervise Party work. The Central Committee elected a Political Bureau (Politburo), with 14 full and 3 alternate members, to direct its policy. The Communist Party dominates the National Fatherland Front, which also includes two minor parties and other state organizations.
Viet-Nam comprises 35 provinces and three cities.
Telephones: 47 000 (South only) in 1973.
Daily newspapers:
North: 4 (1974). *Total circulation:* 176 000
South: 28 (1973). *Total circulation:* 412 000.
Radio: 1 000 000 in the North (1974); 1 550 000 in the South (1973).
TV: 500 000 (South only) in 1973.
Length of roadways: 45 326 miles *72 945 km* (1974).
Universities: 4.
Adult illiteracy: 35·5% (population aged 12 and over) in the North (1960).
Expectation of life: Males 43·2 years; females 46·0 years (UN estimates for 1970–75).
Defence: Military service 2 years minimum; total armed forces 615 000.
Wildlife: Elephant, tiger, leopard, wild ox, wild pig, deer, monkeys, tapir, bears; wide variety of birds.
Cinemas: 41 in the North (1961); 252 (seating capacity 134 800) in the South (1971).

WESTERN SAMOA

Official name: The Independent State of Western Samoa (Samoa i Sisifo)
Population: 151 275 (census of 3 Nov. 1976).
Area: 1097 miles² *2842 km²*.
Languages: Samoan, English.
Religions: Congregational, Roman Catholic, Methodist.
Capital city: Apia, population 32 201 (1976).
Highest point: Mauga Silisli, 6094 ft *1857 m*.
Head of State: H H Malietoa Tanumafili II, CBE (b. 4 Jan. 1913).
Prime Minister: Tupuola Taisi Efi.
Climate: Warm all the year round. Rainy season November to April. In Apia, average maximum 84 °F to 86 °F, minimum 74 °F to 76 °F; rainiest month is January (22 days).
Labour force: 37 901 (including unemployed) at census of 3 Nov. 1971: Agriculture, forestry and fishing 67·3%; Community, social and personal services 15·3%.
Gross domestic product: $25 million in 1970 (estimate).
Exports: $5·6 million (excluding re-exports) in 1973: Fruit and vegetables 11·8%; Cocoa 28·1%; Oil-seeds, oil nuts and oil kernels 43·5% (copra 43·4%); Wood, lumber and cork 10·7%.
Monetary unit: Tala. 1 tala = 100 sene.
Denominations:
Coins 1, 2, 5, 10, 20, 50 sene.
Notes 1, 2, 10 tala.
Exchange rate to US dollar: 0.7794 (July 1977).
Political history and government: Formerly a United Nations Trust Territory, administered by New Zealand. Independent since 1 Jan. 1962. The position of Head of State (*O le Ao o le Malo*) was held jointly by two tribal leaders, one of whom died on 5 Apr. 1963. The other remains Head of State for life. Future Heads of State will be elected for 5 years by the Legislative Assembly. The Assembly is a unicameral body of

47 members, including 45 Samoans elected by about 11 000 *matai* (elected clan chiefs) and two members popularly elected by voters (mainly Europeans) outside the *matai* system. Members hold office for 3 years. There are no political parties. Executive power is held by the Cabinet, comprising a Prime Minister and 8 other members of the Assembly. The Prime Minister, appointed by the Head of State, must have the support of a majority in the Assembly. Western Samoa joined the Commonwealth on 28 Aug. 1970.

Telephones: 2610 (1974).
Radio: 50 000 (1972).
TV: 2800 (1973).
Length of roadways: 582 miles *936 km.*
Adult illiteracy: 2·6% (males 2·6%; females 2·5%) in 1966 (native language only).
Expectation of life: Males 60·8 years; females 65·2 years (1961–66).
Cinemas: 11 (1973).

THE YEMEN ARAB REPUBLIC

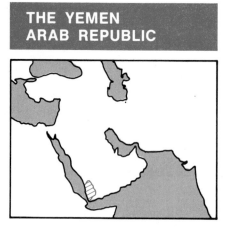

Official name: Al Jamhuriya al Arabiya al Yamaniya.
Population: 5 237 893 (census of 13 Jan. 1975).
Area: 75 290 miles² *195 000 km².*
Language: Arabic.
Religion: Muslim.
Capital city: Sana'a, population 150 000 (1974 est).
Other principal towns (1974): Hodeida 100 000; Ta'iz 100 000.
Highest point: Jebel Hadhar, 12 336 ft *3760 m.*
Principal mountain range: Yemen Highlands.
Head of State: Lt-Col Ahmad Husain al-Ghashmi, Chairman of the Military Command Council.
Prime Minister: Abdul-Aziz Abdul-Ghani (b. 4 July 1939).
Climate: Very hot (up to 130 °F) and extremely humid on semi-desert coastal strip. Cooler on highlands inland (average maximum of 71 °F in June) with heavy rainfall and winter frost. Desert in the east.
Labour force: 1 676 000 (1970): Agriculture, forestry and fishing 79·3% (ILO estimates).
Gross domestic product: 3709·7 million riyals in 1973: Agriculture, forestry and fishing 62·9%; Trade, restaurants and hotels 14·9% (trade 13·8%).
Exports: $8·0 million in 1973: Food and live animals 26·3% (coffee 16·7%); Hides and skins 15·2%; Cotton 49·4%.
Monetary unit: Yemeni riyal. 1 riyal = 100 fils.
Denominations:
  Coins 1, 5, 10, 25 and 50 fils.
  Notes 1, 5, 10, 20, 50 riyals.
Exchange rate to US dollar: 4.5625 (July 1977).

Political history and government: Formerly a monarchy, ruled by an hereditary Imam. Army officers staged a *coup* on 26–27 Sept. 1962, declared the Imam deposed and proclaimed a republic. Civil war broke out between royalist forces, supported by Saudi Arabia, and republicans, aided by Egyptian troops. The republicans gained the upper hand and Egyptian forces withdrew in 1967. A Republican Council, led by a Chairman, took power on 5 Nov. 1967 and announced a new constitution (which did not permit political parties) on 28 Dec. 1970. This provided for a unicameral legislature, the Consultative Assembly of 179 members (20 appointed by the Council and 159 elected for 4 years by general franchise on 27 Feb.–18 Mar. 1971). On 13 June 1974 power was seized by army officers who suspended the constitution, dissolved the Assembly and established a Military Command Council. On 19 June 1974 the new régime published a provisional constitution which, for a transitional period, gives full legislative and executive authority to the Command Council, whose Chairman has the powers of Head of State. The first Chairman, Lt.-Col. Ibrahim al-Hamadi, was assassinated on 11 Oct. 1977. The remaining three members of the Council continued in power. The Council appoints a Cabinet, headed by a Prime Minister, to perform administrative duties.
Telephones: 5000 (1971).
Daily newspapers: 6 (1970).
  Total circulation: 56 000.
Radio: 86 000 (1973).
Length of roadways: 1025 miles *1650 km.*
Universities: 1.
Expectation of life: Males 43·7 years; females 45·9 years (UN estimates for 1970–75).
Defence: Military service: three years; total armed forces 39 000; defence expenditure, 1975/76: $60 million.
Cinemas: 20 (1971).

THE PEOPLE'S DEMOCRATIC REPUBLIC OF YEMEN

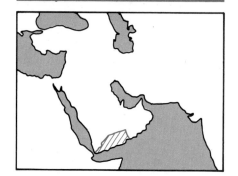

Official name: Al Jumhuria al-Yaman al-dimuqratiya ash-Sha'abiya.
Population: 1 590 275 (census of 14 May 1973); 1 749 000 (estimate for 1 July 1976).
Area: 128 560 miles² *332 968 km².*
Language: Arabic.
Religion: Muslim.
Capital city: Aden, population 264 326 (1973).
Other principal town: Al Mukalla, population 25 000.
Highest point: Qaured Audilla, 8200 ft *2499 m.*
Head of State: Salim Ali Rubayyi (b. 1934), Chairman of the Presidential Council.
Prime Minister: Ali Nasir Muhammad Hasaniya (b. 1944).

Climate: Summer extremely hot (temperatures over 130 °F) and humid. Very low rainfall (average less than 3 in per year). Winter can be very cold in high areas.
Labour force: 393 000 (1970): Agriculture, forestry and fishing 64·7% (ILO estimates); 409 742 aged 7 and over (1973 census, sample tabulation).
Gross domestic product: 59·2 million dinars in 1970: Agriculture, forestry and fishing 19·4%; Manufacturing 25·2%; Trade, restaurants and hotels 12·7%.
Exports: $143·5 million in 1969: Petroleum products 74·4% (motor spirit 13·7%; lamp oil and white spirit 17·7%; distillate fuel oils 43·0%).
Monetary unit: Yemeni dinar. 1 dinar = 1000 fils.
Denominations:
  Coins 1, 2½, 5, 25, 50 fils.
  Notes 250, 500 fils, 1, 5, 10 dinars.
Exchange rate to US dollar: 0.3454 (July 1977).
Political history and government: Formerly the British colony of Aden and the Protectorate of South Arabia. Became independent, outside the Commonwealth, on 30 Nov. 1967 as the People's Republic of Southern Yemen. Power was held by a revolutionary movement, the National Liberation Front, now the National Front (NF). The interim legislative authority was the NF's Supreme General Command. Since 22 June 1969 executive power has been held collectively by a Presidential Council (3 members in 1977), which appointed a Cabinet to administer the country. A new constitution, adopted on 30 Nov. 1970, gave the country its present name and provided for the establishment of a unicameral legislature, the Supreme People's Council (SPC). A Provisional SPC, inaugurated on 14 May 1971, has 101 members, including 86 elected by the NF's General Command and 15 elected by trade unions. It appoints members of the Presidential Council and the Cabinet. The ruling NF absorbed two smaller parties in 1975 and is now the country's only political organisation. Democratic Yemen is divided into 7 governorates.
Telephones: 9 876 (1973).
Daily newspapers: 3 (1972).
  Total circulation: 2000.
Radio: 525 000 (1973).
TV: 26 000 (1973).
Length of roadways: 1150 miles *1851 km.*
Universities: 1.
Expectation of life: Males 43·7 years; females 45·9 years (UN estimates for 1970–75).
Defence: Military service: conscription (term unknown); total armed forces 21 300; defence expenditure, 1974: $41 million.
Cinemas: 19 (seating capacity 20 000) in 1971.

YUGOSLAVIA

Official name: Socijalistička Federativna Republika Jugoslavija (Socialist Federal Republic of Yugoslavia).
Population: 20 522 972 (census of 31 Mar. 1971); 21 672 000 (estimate for 31 Dec. 1976).
Area: 98 766 miles² *255 804 km².*
Languages: Serbo-Croatian, Slovenian, Macedonian.
Religions: Eastern Orthodox, Roman Catholic, Muslim.
Capital city: Beograd (Belgrade), population 746 105 (1971).
Other principal towns (1971): Zagreb 566 224; Skoplje (Skopje) 312 980; Sarajevo 243 980; Ljubljana 173 853; Split 152 905; Novi Sad 141 375.

Highest point: Triglav, 9393 ft *2863 m.*
Principal mountain ranges: Slovene Alps, Dinaric Mts.
Principal rivers: Dunav (Danube) (1770 miles *[2848 km]*) and tributaries (Drava, Sava (584 miles *[940 km]*), Morava, Varder.
Head of State: Marshal Tito (b. Josip Broz, 25 May 1892), Federal President.
Head of Government: Veselin Djuranović (b. 1925), President of the Federal Executive Council.
Climate: Mediterranean climate on Adriatic coast (dry, warm summers; mild, rainy winters). Continental climate (cold winters) in hilly interior. In Belgrade average maximum 37 °F (January) to 85 °F. (July), minimum 27 °F (January, February) to 61 °F (July). Rainiest months are April, May, June, December (each 9 days). In Split, average maximum 57 °F (January) to 87 °F (July, August) minimum 39 °F (January, February) to 68 °F (July), rainiest month is December (11 days). Absolute maximum temperature 46,2 °C (*115·2 °F*), Monstar, 31 July 1901; absolute minimum −37,8 °C (*−36·0 °F*), Sjenica, 26 Jan. 1954.
Labour force: 8 300 648 (excluding 589 168 persons working abroad temporarily) at 1971 census: Agriculture, forestry and fishing 48·7%; Mining and manufacturing (excluding crafts) 19·3%; Services (excluding personal services), banking and social insurance 11·3%. Figures exclude unemployed dependants.
Gross material product: 407 300 million dinars in 1974: Agriculture, forestry and fishing 17·7% (agriculture 16·4%); Industry 41·7%; Construction 10·9%; Trade, restaurants, etc. 21·5%.
Exports: $3804·4 million in 1974: Chemicals 10·1%; Non-ferrous metals 11·7%; Machinery and transport equipment 23·2% (transport equipment 10·3%).
Monetary unit: Yugoslav dinar. 1 dinar = 100 para.
Denominations:
Coins 5, 10, 20, 50 para, 1, 2, 5 dinars.
Notes 5, 10, 50, 100, 500 dinars.
Exchange rate to US dollar: 18.31 (July 1977).
Political history and government: Yugoslavia was formed by a merger of Serbia, Croatia, Slovenia, Montenegro and Bosnia-Herzegovina. A pact between Serbia and other South Slavs was signed on 20 July 1917 to unite all the territories in a unitary state under the Serbian monarchy. The Kingdom of Serbs, Croats and Slovenes was proclaimed on 4 Dec. 1918. It was renamed Yugoslavia on 3 Oct. 1929. The Kingdom was invaded by German and Italian forces on 6 Apr. 1941. Resistance was divided between royalists and Partisans, led by the Communist Party under Marshal Tito. Their rivalry led to civil war, won by the Partisans, who proclaimed the Federal People's Republic of Yugoslavia, with Tito as President, on 29 Nov. 1945. A Soviet-type constitution, establishing a federation of 6 republics, was adopted on 31 Jan. 1946.

Yugoslav leaders followed independent policies and the country was expelled from the Soviet-dominated Cominform in June 1948. A new constitution, promulgated on 7 Apr. 1963, introduced the country's present name. Since 29 July 1971 national leadership has been held by a collective Presidency (led by Tito), elected by the Federal Assembly. The present constitution, which increased decentralisation, was adopted on 21 Feb. 1974. Legislative power is vested in the bicameral Federal Assembly, comprising a Federal Chamber of 220 members (30 from each of the 6 republics and 20 each from the two autonomous provinces within Serbia) and a Chamber of Republics and Provinces, with 88 members (12 from each Republican Assembly and 8 from each Provincial Assembly). Members are elected for 4 years by delegates in each Republic or Province, themselves elected by universal adult suffrage, with voters grouped according to their place of work. The collective Presidency has 9 members, the President and one each from the Republics and Provinces. The Federal Assembly elects the Federal Executive Council, led by a President, to be the administrative branch of government. The only authorised political party is the League of Communists of Yugoslavia, led by Tito, which controls political life through the Socialist Alliance of the Working People of Yugoslavia. The League's highest authority is its Congress. The 10th Congress, held on 27–30 May 1974, elected a Central Committee (165 members) to supervise the League's work. The Committee elected a Presidium of 39 members to direct its policy. The League's main policy-making body is the Presidium's Executive Bureau, with 13 members.
Telephones: 1 301 000 (1975).
Daily newspapers: 26 (1975).
Total circulation: 1 896 000.
Radio: 4 181 000 (1975).
TV: 3 076 000 (1975).
Length of roadways: 59 749 miles *96 157 km* (31 Dec. 1973).
Length of railways: 6412 miles *10 319 km.*
Universities: 15.
Adult illiteracy: 16·3% (males 7·9%; females 24·2%) in 1971.
Expectation of life: Males 65·42 years; females 70·22 years (1970–72).
Defence: Military service: Army and Air Force 15 months, Navy 18 months; total armed forces 250 000 (including 155 000 conscripts); defence expenditure, 1976: $1798 million.
Cinemas: 1344 (seating capacity 468 900) and 31 part-time (capacity 24 635) in 1973.

ZAIRE

Official name: La République du Zaïre.
Population: 25 629 000 (estimate for 1 July 1976).
Area: 905 365 miles² *2 344 885 km².*
Languages: French, Lingala, Kiswahili, Tshiluba, Kikongo.
Religions: Animist, Roman Catholic, Protestant.
Capital city: Kinshasa (formerly Léopoldville), population 2 008 352 at 1 July 1974.
Other principal towns (1974): Kananga (Luluabourg) 601 239; Lubumbashi (Elisabethville) 403 623; Mbuji-Mayi 336 654; Kisangani (Stanleyville) 310 705; Bukavu 181 774.
Highest point: Ngaliema (Mt Stanley), 16 763 ft *5109 m* (first climbed 1900).
Principal mountain ranges: Chaîne des Mitumba, Ruwenzori.
Principal rivers: Zaïre (Congo), Ubangi, Kasai.

Head of State: Lt-Gen Mobutu Sese Seko (b. 14 Oct. 1930), President.
Head of Government: Dr Mpinga Kasenda (b. 30 Aug. 1937), First State Commissioner.
Climate: Tropical. Hot and humid in Congo basin, cool in highlands. In Kinshasa (Léopoldville), March and April hottest (71 °F to 89 °F), July coolest (64 °F to 81 °F) and driest, April and November rainiest (16 days each). Absolute maximum temperature 41,0 °C (*105·8 °F*) at Yahila; absolute minimum. −1,5 °C (*29·3 °F*), Sakania, 11 Jan. 1949.
Labour force: 9 446 000 (1970): Agriculture, forestry and fishing 79·8% (ILO estimates).
Gross domestic product: 1766·5 million zaires in 1974: Agriculture, forestry and fishing 15·5%; Mining and quarrying 24·6%; Trade 14·4%; Public administration and defence 12·1%.
Exports: $1381·5 million (excluding re-exports) in 1974: Non-ferrous metals 75·2% (copper 67·0%).
Monetary unit: Zaire. 1 zaire = 10 000 sengi or 100 makuta.
Denominations:
Coins 10 sengi, 1, 5 makuta.
Notes 10, 20, 50 makuta, 1, 5, 10 zaires.
Exchange rate to US dollar: 0.8534 (July 1977).
Political history and government: Formerly the Belgian Congo, independent as the Republic of the Congo on 30 June 1960. Renamed the Democratic Republic of the Congo on 1 Aug. 1964. Power was seized on 24 Nov. 1965 by army officers, led by Lt-Gen Joseph-Désiré Mobutu (from January 1972 called Mobutu Sese Seko). The new regime, with Mobutu as President, was approved by Parliament on 28 Nov. 1965. A new constitution, approved by referendum, was adopted on 24 June 1967. The country's present name was introduced on 27 Oct. 1971. Mobutu was elected President by popular vote on 31 Oct.–1 Nov. 1970 and inaugurated for a 7-year term on 5 Dec. 1970. Under a 1974 amendment, the President's term of office is reduced to 5 years. A unicameral National Legislative Council of 244 members, led by Mobutu, was elected by acclamation for 5 years on 2 Nov. 1975. The President appoints and leads the National Executive Council, a cabinet of State Commissioners with departmental responsibilities. On 6 July 1977 the President appointed a First State Commissioner, equivalent to a Prime Minister. Since 1970 the only authorised political party has been the *Mouvement populaire de la révolution* (MPR) or People's Revolutionary Movement. The highest policy-making body is the MPR's Political Bureau. In 1977 the Bureau had 30 members, including 12 appointed by the President and 18 elected (two from each region and two from Kinshasa). The country comprises 8 regions, each headed by an

appointed Commissioner, and the city of Kinshasa, under a Governor.
Telephones: 48 000 (1975).
Daily newspapers: 13 (1973).
  Total circulation: 70 000 (4 dailies).
Radio: 100 000 (1973).
TV: 7000 (1973).
Length of roadways: 43 090 miles *69 347 km* (31 Dec. 1973).
Length of railways: 3215 miles. *5174 km.*
Universities: 1 (three campuses).
Adult illiteracy: 84·6% (males 70·8%; females 97·2%) in 1955–8.
Expectation of life: Males 41·9 years; females 45·1 years (UN estimates for 1970–75).
Defence: Military service: voluntary; total armed forces 43 400; defence expenditure, 1974: $157 million.
Cinemas: 34 (seating capacity 13 600) in 1970.

ZAMBIA

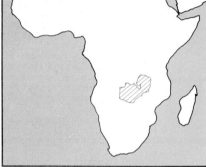

Official name: The Republic of Zambia.
Population: 4 056 995 (census of 22–30 Aug. 1969); 5 138 000 (estimate for 30 June 1976).

Area: 290 586 miles² *752 614 km².*
Languages: English (official), Nyanja, Bemba, Tonga, Lozi, Lunda, Luvale.
Religions: Roman Catholic, Protestant, Animist.
Capital city: Lusaka, population 401 000 (1974).
Other principal towns (1974): Kitwe (incl Kalulushi) 292 000; Ndola 229 000; Chingola 190 000; Mufulira 136 000; Luanshya 121 000; Kabwe (Broken Hill) 98 000; Livingstone 58 000.
Highest point: 6210 ft *1893 m.*
Principal mountain range: Muchinga Mts.
Principal rivers: Zambezi and tributaries (Kafue, Luangwa), Luapula.
Head of State: Dr Kenneth David Kaunda (b. 28 Apr. 1924), President.
Prime Minister: (Mathias) Mainza Chona (b. 1 Nov. 1930).
Climate: Hot season September–November, rainy season November–April, winter May–September. Day temperatures 80 °F to 100 °F in hot season, sharp fall at night. Average annual rainfall from 25 in in south to 50 in in north. In Lusaka, average annual minimum 64 °F, maximum 88 °F, average rainfall 33 in.
Labour force: 1 655 000 (1970): Agriculture, forestry and fishing 72·8% (ILO estimates).
Gross domestic product: 1178·2 million kwacha in 1971: Agriculture, forestry and fishing 12·9%; Mining and quarrying 25·7%; Manufacturing 12·2%; Trade, restaurants and hotels 10·8%; Community, social and personal services 12·9%.
Exports: $1136·2 million (excluding re-exports) in 1973: Non-ferrous metals 98·0% (copper 94·4%).
Monetary unit: Zambian kwacha. 1 kwacha = 100 ngwee.
Denominations:
  Coins 1, 2, 5, 10, 20 ngwee.
  Notes 50 ngwee, 1, 2, 5, 10, 20 kwacha.

Exchange rate to US dollar: 0.7867 (July 1977).
Political history and government: Formerly the British protectorate of Northern Rhodesia, an independent republic and a member of the Commonwealth since 24 Oct. 1964. A one-party state was proclaimed on 13 Dec. 1972 and inaugurated by a new constitution on 25 Aug. 1973. Legislative power is held by the unicameral National Assembly, with 135 members (10 nominated by the President and 125 elected for 5 years by universal adult suffrage, with up to three candidates per constituency). There is also an advisory House of Chiefs (27 members) to represent traditional tribal authorities. Executive power is held by the President, elected by popular vote at the same time as the Assembly. He appoints a Cabinet, led by a Prime Minister, to conduct the administration. The sole authorised party is the United National Independence Party (UNIP), led by the President. The highest policy-making body is UNIP's Central Committee (25 members), to which the Cabinet is subordinate. Zambia is divided into 9 provinces, each administered by a Cabinet Minister.
Telephones: 67 962 (1974).
Daily newspapers: 2 (1974).
  Total circulation: 105 000.
Radio: 100 000 (1973).
TV: 21 000 (1973).
Length of roadways: 21 725 miles *34 963 km* (31 Dec. 1972).
Length of railways: 1359 miles *2187 km.*
Universities: 1.
Adult illiteracy: 52·4% (males 38·5%; females 65·4%) in 1969.
Expectation of life: Males 42·9 years; females 46·1 years (UN estimates for 1970–75).
Defence: Military service: voluntary; total armed forces 7800; defence expenditure, 1974: $78 million.
Cinemas: 28 (seating capacity 13 400) and one drive-in for 300 cars (1971).

UNITED KINGDOM

PHYSICAL AND POLITICAL GEOGRAPHY

The various names used for the islands and parts of islands off the north-west coast of Europe geographically known as the British Isles are confusing. Geographical, political, legal and popular usages unfortunately differ, thus making definition necessary.

British Isles
A convenient but purely *geographical* term to describe that group of islands lying off the north-west coast of Europe, comprising principally the island of Great Britain and the

island of Ireland. There are four political units: the United Kingdom of Great Britain and Northern Ireland; the Republic of

Ireland; the Crown dependencies of the Isle of Man and, conveniently, also the Channel Islands.
Area: 121 689 miles². *Population (mid-1976 estimate):* 59 240 000.

The United Kingdom (UK) (of Great Britain and Northern Ireland)
The political style of the island of Great Britain, with its offshore islands and, since the partition of Ireland (see below), the six counties of Northern Ireland. The term United Kingdom, referring to Great Britain and (the whole island of) Ireland, first came into use officially on 1 Jan. 1801 on the Union of the two islands. With the coming into force of the Constitution of the Irish Free State as a Dominion on 6 Dec. 1922, the term 'United Kingdom of Great Britain and Ireland' had obviously become inappropriate. It was dropped by Statute from the Royal style on 13 May 1927 in favour of 'King of Great Britain, Ireland and of, etc.'. On the

same date Parliament at Westminster adopted as its style 'Parliament of the United Kingdom of Great Britain and Northern Ireland'. On 29 May 1953 by Proclamation the Royal style conformed to the Parliamentary style—Ireland having ceased to be a Dominion within the Commonwealth on 18 Apr. 1949. *Area:* 94 251 miles². *Population (mid-1976):* 55 927 600.

Great Britain (GB) is the geographical and political name of the main or principal island of the solely geographically named British Isles group. In a strict geographical sense, off-shore islands, for example the Isle of Wight, Anglesey, or Shetland, are not part of Great Britain. In the political sense Great Britain was the political name used unofficially from 24 Mar. 1603, when James VI of Scotland succeeded his third cousin twice removed upwards, Queen Elizabeth of England, so bringing about a Union of the Crowns, until on 1 May 1707 the style was formally adopted with the Union of the Parliaments of England and Scotland and was used until 1 Jan. 1801. The government of Great Britain is unitary, but in 1975 plans for separate Scottish and Welsh assemblies were first published.
Area: 88 799 miles². *Population (mid-1976):* 54 389 500.

England
Geographically the southern and greater part of the island of Great Britain. The islands off the English coast, such as the Isle of Wight and the Isles of Scilly, are administratively part of England. Politically and geographically England (historically a separate Kingdom until 1707) is that part of Great Britain governed by English law which also pertains in Wales and, since 1746, in Berwick-upon-Tweed.
The term 'England' is widely (but wrongly) used abroad to mean the United Kingdom or Great Britain.
Area: 50 366 miles². *Population (mid-1976):* 46 184 400.

Wales (The principality of) now comprises eight instead of twelve counties. The area was incorporated into England by Act of Parliament in 1536. The former county of Monmouthshire, though for all administrative intents and purposes part of Wales, only became an integral part of Wales on 1 Apr. 1974. The other boundaries between England and Wales expressly could not be altered by the ordinary processes of local government reorganisation.
Wales may not, by Statute, be represented by less than 35 MPs at Westminster.
Wales
Area: 8018 miles². *Population (mid-1976):* 2 766 800.

Scotland consists of the northern and smaller part of the island of Great Britain. The Kingdom of Scotland was united with England on 24 March 1603 when King James VI of Scotland (ascended 1567) became also King James I of England. Both countries continued, however, to have their separate Parliaments until the Union of the Parliaments at Westminster, London, on 1 May 1707. Scotland continues to have its own distinctive legal system. By Statute Scotland may not be represented by less than

BRITISH ISLES EXTREMITIES

Island of Great Britain

Great Britain, the eighth largest island in the world, has extreme (mainland) dimensions thus:

Most Northerly Point	Easter Head, Dunnet Head, Highland	Lat 58° 40′ 25″ N
Most Westerly Point	Garbhlach Mhor, Ardnamurchan, Strathclyde	Long 6° 14′ 12″ W
Most Southerly Point	Lizard Point, Cornwall	Lat 49° 57′ 33″ N
Most Easterly Point	Lowestoft Ness, Lowestoft, Suffolk	Long 1° 46′ 20″ E

Other extreme points in its 3 constituent countries are:

Most Southerly Point in Scotland	Gallie Craig, Mull of Galloway, Dumfries & Galloway	Lat 54° 38′ 27″ N
Most Easterly Point in Scotland (Mainland)	Keith Inch, Peterhead, Grampian	Long 1° 45′ 49″ W
Most Northerly Point in England	Meg's Dub, Northumberland	Lat 55° 48′ 37″ N
Most Westerly Point in England	Dr Syntax's Head, Land's End, Cornwall	Long 5° 42′ 15″ W
Most Northerly Point in Wales	Point of Air, Clwyd	Lat 53° 21′ 08″ N
Most Westerly Point in Wales	Porthtaflod, Dyfed	Long 5° 19′ 43″ W
Most Southerly Point in Wales	Rhoose Point, South Glamorgan	Lat 51° 22′ 40″ N
Most Easterly Point in Wales	Lady Park Wood, Gwent	Long 2° 38′ 49″ W

Island of Ireland (20th largest island in the world)

Most Northerly Point in Ireland	Malin Head, Donegal	Lat 55° 22′ 30″ N
Most Northerly Point in Northern Ireland	Benbane Head, Moyle, Antrim	Lat 55° 15′ 0″ N
Most Westerly Point in Ireland	Dunmore Head, Kerry	Long 10° 28′ 55″ W
Most Westerly Point in Northern Ireland	Cornaglah, Fermanagh	Long 8° 10′ 30″ W
Most Southerly Point in Ireland	Brow Head, Cork	Lat 51° 26′ 30″ N
Most Southerly Point in Northern Ireland	Cranfield Point, Newry and Mourne, Down	Lat 54° 01′ 20″ N
Most Easterly Point in Ireland (Northern)	Townhead, Ards Peninsula, Down	Long 5° 26′ 52″ W
Most Easterly Point in Republic of Ireland	Wicklow Head, Wicklow	Long 5° 59′ 40″ W

UK MOUNTAIN AND HILL RANGES

Scotland

Range	Length (miles)	Length (km)	Culminating peak	Height (ft)	Height (m)
Grampian Mountains	155	250	Ben Macdhui, Grampian	4300	1310
North West Highlands	140	225	Càrn Eige, Highland	3877	1181
*Southern Uplands (Scottish Lowlands)	125	200	Merrick Mountain, Galloway & Dumfries	2764	842
Monadh Liadth Mountains	35	55	Càrn Dearg Highland	3093	942

England

Range	Length (miles)	Length (km)	Culminating peak	Height (ft)	Height (m)
Pennines	120	195	Cross Fell, Cumbria	2930	893
North Downs	85	135	Leith Hill, Surrey	965	294
Cotswold Hills	60	95	Cleve Hill, Gloucestershire	1083	330
South Downs	55	85	Butser Hill, Hampshire	888	271
Cheviot Hills	45	70	The Cheviot, Northumberland	2676	815
Chiltern Hills	45	70	Coombe Hill, Buckinghamshire	852	259
Berkshire Downs (White Horse Hills)	35	55	Walbury Hill, Berkshire	974	296
Cumbrian Mountains	30	50	Scafell Pike, Cumbria	3210	978
Exmoor	30	50	Dunkery Beacon, Somerset	1706	519
North Yorkshire Moors (Cleveland and Hambleton Hills)	30	50	Cringle Moor, North Yorkshire	1427	434
Hampshire Downs	25	40	Pilot Hill, Hampshire	938	285
Yorkshire Wolds	22	35	Garrowby Hill, Humberside	808	246

continued over page

* Includes: Lammermuir Hills (Lammer Law, Lothian 1733 ft *528 m*); Lowther Hills (Green Lowther, Strathclyde, 2403 ft *732 m*); Pentland Hills (Scald Law, Lowthian 1898 ft *578 m*) and the Tweedsmuir Hills (Broad Law, Borders, 2754 ft *839 m*).

71 MPs at Westminster. Proposals for a separate Scottish Assembly of some 140 seats were published in 1975. On 16 May 1975 the 33 traditional counties were reduced to 9 Geographical regions and 3 island authorities.
Area: 30 415 miles². *Population (mid-1976):* 5 205 100.

Ireland

The name of the second largest island in the geographical British Isles. Henry VIII assumed the style 'King of Ireland' in 1542, although Governors of Ireland (the exact title varied) ruled on behalf of the Kings of England from 1172. The viceroyalty did not disappear until 1937. The Union of the Parliaments of Great Britain and Ireland occurred on 1 Jan. 1801.

Northern Ireland consists of six counties in the north-eastern corner of the island. County government has been replaced by 26 districts. They are all within the larger ancient province of Ulster which originally consisted of nine counties. The government's relationship to the Imperial Parliament in England was federal in nature. Certain major powers were reserved by the Imperial Parliament, the sovereignty of which was unimpaired. There is a provision in the Ireland Act of 1949 that Northern Ireland cannot cease to be part of the United Kingdom, or part of the Queen's Dominions without the express consent of her Parliament. This Parliament, known as Stormont and established in 1921, was however abolished by the Northern Ireland Constitution Act, 1973. Devolved government came into effect on 1 Jan. 1974, but the Northern Ireland Assembly was prorogued on 29 May 1974 after the Executive collapsed. Arrangements for a Constitutional Convention, under the Northern Ireland Constitution Act 1974, which came into force in July 1974, collapsed in February 1976. Northern Ireland is represented by the fixed number of twelve Members of the Imperial Parliament at Westminster.
Area: 5452 miles². *Population (mid-1976):* 1 538 100.

The Republic of Ireland

This State came into being on 15 Jan. 1922 and consists of 26 of the pre-partition total of 32 Irish counties. The original name was 'The Irish Free State' (or in Irish Gaelic 'Saorstát Eireànn') and the country had Dominion status within the British Commonwealth. A revised Constitution, which became operative on 29 Dec. 1937, abolished the former name and substituted the title 'Eire', which is the Gaelic word for 'Ireland'. On 18 Apr. 1949 the official description of the State became 'The Republic of Ireland' (Poblacht na h-Eireann), but the name of the State remains 'Ireland' in the English and 'Eire' in the Irish Gaelic language. On the same date the Republic of Ireland ceased to be a member of the British Commonwealth.
Area: 27 136 miles². *Population (mid-1976 estimate):* 3 163 000.

Isles of Scilly

Area: 4,041 acres.
Population: 2,100 (mid 1977). There are five populated islands—Bryher (pop. 80, 1964), St Agnes (pop. 65), St Martin's (pop. 125), St Mary's (pop. 1,355) and Tresco (pop. 205). There are 19 other islands and numerous rocks and islets.

The islands are administered by a Council, consisting of a Chairman, 4 aldermen and 21 councillors, which is a unique type of local government unit set up by an Order made

MOUNTAINS *continued*

Wales

Range	Length (miles)	Length (km)	Culminating peak	Height (ft)	Height (m)
Cambrian Mountains	110	175	Snowdon (Yr Wyddfa), Gwynedd	3560	1085
Berwyn Mountains	40	65	Aran Fawddwy, Gwynedd	2972	905

Northern Ireland

Range	Length (miles)	Length (km)	Culminating peak	Height (ft)	Height (m)
Sperrin Mountains	40	65	Sawel Mt, Londonderry-Tyrone	2240	682
Mountains of Mourne	30	50	Slieve Donard, County Down	2796	852
Antrim Hills	25	40	Trostan, Antrim	1817	553

Scotland's ten highest peaks

		ft	m
1.	Ben Nevis, Highland	4406	1392
2.	Ben Macdhui, Grampian	4300	1310
3.	Braeriach, Grampian-Highland border	4248	1294
	North top (Ben Macdhui)	4244	1293
4.	Cairn Toul, Grampian	4241	1292
	South Plateau (Braeriach) (also c. 4160 ft)	4149	1264
	Sgor an Lochan Uaine (Cairn Toul)	4116	1254
	Coire Sputan Dearg (Ben Macdhui)	4095	1248
5.	Cairngorm, Grampian-Highland border	4084	1244
6.	Aonach Beag,	4060	1237
	Coire an Lochain (Braeriach)	4036	1230
7.	Càrn Mor Dearg, Highland	4012	1222
8.	Aonach Mor, Highland	3999	1218
	Carn Dearg (Ben Nevis)	3990	1216
	Coire an t-Saighdeir (Cairn Toul)	3989	1215
9.	Ben Lawers, Tayside	3984	1214
	Cairn Lochan (Cairngorm)	3983	1214
10.	Beinn a' Bhùird (North Top), Grampian	3924	1196

Wales' ten highest peaks
(all in Gwynedd)

		ft	m
1.	Snowdon (Yr Wyddfa)	3560	1085
	Garnedd Ugain or Crib Y Ddisg (Yr Wyddfa)	3493	1065
2.	Carnedd Llewelyn	3484	1062
3.	Carnedd Dafydd	3426	1044
4.	Glyder Fawr	3279	999
5.	Glyder Fâch	3262	994
	Pen Yr Oleu-wen (Carnedd Dafydd)	3210	978
	Foel Grach (Carnedd Llewelyn)	3195	974
	Yr Elen (Carnedd Llewelyn)	3151	960
6.	Y Garn	3104	946
7.	Foel Fras	3091	942
8.	Elidir Fawr	3029	923
	Crib Goch (Yr Wyddfa)	3023	921
9.	Tryfan	3010	917
10.	Aran Fawddwy	2970	905

Ireland's ten highest peaks

		ft	m
1.	Carrauntual (or Carrauntoohil), Kerry	3414	1041
2.	Beenkeragh, Kerry	3314	1010
3.	Caher, Kerry	3200	975
4.	Ridge of the Reeks (*two other tops of the same height, a third* of 3141, and a *fourth* of c. 3050), Kerry	3200	c. 975
5.	Brandon, Kerry	3127	953
	Knocknapeasta (Ridge of the Reeks)	3062	933
6.	Lugnaquillia, Wicklow	3039	926
7.	Galtymore, Tipperary	3018	920
8.	Slieve Donard, County Down	*2796	852
9.	Baurtregaum, Kerry	2796	852
10.	Mullaghcleevaun, Wicklow	2788	849

* Highest peak in Northern Ireland.

England's ten highest peaks
(all in Cumbria)

		ft	m
1.	Scafell Pike	3210	978
2.	Sca Fell	3162	963
3.	Helvellyn	3118	950
	Broad Crag (Scafell Pikes)	3054	930
4.	Skiddaw	3053	930
	Lower Man (Helvellyn)	3033	922
	Ill Crags (Scafell Pikes)	c. 3025	c. 922
	Great End (Scafell Pikes)	2984	909
5.	Bow Fell	2960	902
6.	Great Gable	2949	898
7.	Cross Fell	2930	893
8.	Pillar Fell	2927	892
	Catstye Cam (Helvellyn)	2917	889
9.	Esk Pike	2903	884
	Raise (Helvellyn)	2889	880
10.	Fairfield	2863	872

under Section 292 of the Local Government Act, 1933. For some purposes the Isles are administered in company with the Cornwall County Council. The islands form part of the St Ives electoral division.

Highest peaks in the British Isles

Though the eighth largest island in the world, Great Britain does not possess any mountains of great height.

In only two Scottish regions, those of Grampian and Highland, does the terrain surpass a height of 4000 ft *1219 m*. In Great Britain there are seven mountains and five subsidiary points (tops) above 4000 ft *1219 m* all in Scotland, and a further 283 mountains and 271 tops between 3000 ft and 4000 ft *914–1219 m* of which only 21 (see below) are in England or Wales. South of the border, 3000 ft *914 m* is only surpassed in Gwynedd and Cumbria. Scotland possesses 54 mountains higher than Snowdon and 165 higher than the Scafell Pike. Ben Nevis was probably first climbed about 1720 and Ben Macdhui was thought to be Great Britain's highest mountain until as late as 1847.

See table on p. 206.
See table on p. 206.

UK WATERFALLS, LOCHS, LAKES, DEPRESSIONS AND CAVES

Waterfalls

The principal waterfalls of the British Isles are:

Height (ft)	Height (m)	Name
658	200	Eas-Coul-Aulin, Highland
370	112	Falls of Glomach, Highland
350	106	Powerscourt Falls, County Wicklow
240	73	Pistyll Rhaiadr, Clwyd
205	62	Foyers, Highland
204 (total)	62	Falls of Clyde, Strathclyde (comprises Bonnington Linn (30 ft *9 m*). Corra Linn (84 ft *25 m*), Dundaff Linn (10 ft *3 m*) and Stonebyres Linn (80 ft *24 m*) cataracts
200	60	Falls of Bruar, Tayside (upper fall)
200	60	Cauldron (or Caldron Snout), Cumbria
200	60	Grey Mare's Tail, Dumfries & Galloway

Area (miles²)	Area km²	Name and County	Max. Length (miles)	Max Length km	Max Breadth (miles)	Max Breadth km	Max Depth (ft)	Max Depth m
Northern Ireland								
147·39	381,7	Lough Neagh, Antrim, Down, Armagh, Tyrone, Londonderry	18	28	11	17	102	31
40·57	105,0	Lower Lough Erne, Fermanagh	18	28	5·5	8,8	226	68
12·25	31,7	Upper Lough Erne, Cavan	10	16	3·5	5,6	89	27
Scotland (Fresh-water (inland) lochs, in order of size of surface area)								
27·5	71,2	Loch Lomond, Strathclyde-Central	22·64	36,4	5	8	623	189
21·87	56,6	Loch Ness, Highland	22·75	36,6	2	3,2	751	228
14·95	38,7	Loch Awe, Strathclyde	25·5	41,0	2	3,2	307	93
11·0	28,4	Loch Maree, Highland	13·5	21,7	2	3,2	367	111
10·3	26,6	Loch Morar, Highland	11·5	18,5	1·5	2,4	1017	309
10·19	26,3	Loch Tay, Tayside	14·55	23,4	1·07	1,7	508	154
8·70	22,5	Loch Shin, Highland	17·25	27,7	1	1,6	162	49
7·56	19,5	Loch Shiel, Highland	17·5	28,1	0·9	1,4	420	128
7·34	19,0	Loch Rannoch, Tayside	9·75	15,6	1·1	1,7	440	134
7·18	18,5	Loch Ericht, Highland-Tayside	14·6	23,4	1·1	1,7	512	156
6·25	16,1	Loch Arkaig, Highland	12·0	19,3	0·9	1,4	359	109
5·9	15,2	Loch Lochy, Highland	9·9	15,9	1·25	2,0	531	161

England (Lake District lakes in order of size of surface area)
(all in Cumbria)

Area (miles²)	Area km²	Name	Max Length (miles)	Max Length km	Max Breadth (yd)	Max Breadth km	Max Depth (ft)	Max Depth m
5·69	14,7	Windermere	10·50	16,8	1,610	1,47	219	66
3·44	8,9	Ullswater	7·35	11,8	1,100	1,0	205	62
2·06	5,3	Bassenthwaite Water	3·83	6,1	1,300	1,18	70	21
2·06	5,3	Derwentwater	2·87	4,6	2,130	1,94	72	21
1·89	4,8	Coniston Water	5·41	8,7	870	0,79	184	56
1·12	2,9	Ennerdale Water	2·40	3,8	1,000	0,9	148	45
1·12	2,9	Wastwater	3·00	4,8	880	0,8	258	78
0·97	2,5	Crummock Water	2·50	4,0	1,000	0,9	144	43
0·54	1,3	Haweswater	2·33	3,7	600	0,54	103	31
0·36	0,9	Buttermere	1·26	2,0	670	0,61	94	28

Wales

Area (miles²)	Area km²	Name	Max Length (miles)	Max Length km	Max Breadth (miles)	Max Breadth km	Max Depth (ft)	Max Depth m
1·69	4,3	Bala Lake (Llyn Tegid)	3·8	6,1	·850	0,53	125	38
3·18	8,2	Lake Vyrnwy (dammed)	4·7	7,5	·1000	0,06	120	36

Depressions

A very small area of Great Britain is below sea-level. The largest such area is in the Fenland of East Anglia, and even here a level of 9 ft *2,7 m* below sea-level is not exceeded in the Holme Fen near Ely, Cambridgeshire. The beds of three Lake District lakes are below sea-level with the deepest being part of the bed of Windermere, Cumbria at −90 ft *−27 m*. The bed of Loch Morar, Highland, Scotland reaches 987 ft *301 m* below sea level.

Caves

Large or deep caves are few in Great Britain. Great Britain's deepest cave is Ogof Fynnon Ddu (1010 ft, *307 m*) in Powys, Wales. It is also the largest system with 23·92 miles *38,5 km* of surveyed passages. England's deepest cave is Oxlow Cavern, Giant's Hole, Derbyshire which descends 642 ft *196 m*. Scotland's largest cave is Great Smoo, Highland. Ireland's deepest is Carrowmore, County Sligo being 460 ft *140 m* deep.

UK RIVERS

Specially compiled maps issued by the Ordnance Survey in the second half of the last century are still the authority for the length of the rivers of the United Kingdom. It should, however, be noted that these measurements are strictly for the course of a river bearing the one name, thus for example where the principal head stream has a different name its additional length is ignored—unless otherwise indicated.

Length (miles)	Length km	Names	Remotest source	Mouth	Area of Basin (miles²)*	Area of Basin km²	Extreme Discharge (cusecs)†
220	355	Severn (for 158 miles)	Lake on E side of Plinlimmon, Powys	Bristol Channel	4409·7	11 421	23 100 (1937)
210	338	Thames (111 miles)—Isis (43 miles)	Trewsbury Mead	North Sea	3841·6	9950	27 900 (1894)
185	300	Trent (147)—Humber (38)	Biddulph Moor, Staffs.	North Sea (as Humber)	4029·2	10 436	5 510
161	260	Aire (78)—(Yorkshire) Ouse (45) and Humber (38)	NW of North Yorks.	North Sea (as Humber)	4388·4	11 366	4580 (Aire only)
143	230	Ouse (Great or Bedford)	nr Brackley, Northamptonshire	The Wash	3313·6	8582	11 000
135	215	Wye (or Gwy)	Plinlimmon, Powys	Into Severn 2½ miles S of Chepstow, Gwent	1615·3	4184	32 000
117	188	Tay (93·2)—Tummel	(Tay) Beinn Oss' Tayside	North Sea	1961·6	5080	49 000
100	161	Nene (formerly Nen)	nr Naseby, Northants.	The Wash	914·5	2369	13 500
98·5	158	Clyde (inc. Daer Water)	nr Earncraig Hill, extreme S Strathclyde	Atlantic Ocean (measured to Port Glasgow)	1173·8	3040	20 200
98·0	157,5	Spey	Loch Spey, Highland	North Sea	1153·5	2988	34 200
96·5	155,3	Tweed	Tweed's Well, Borders	North Sea	1992·3	5160	21 400
85·2	137,1	Dee (Aberdeenshire)	W of Cairn Toul, Grampian	North Sea	817·2	2116	40 000
85	136,7	Avon (Warwickshire or Upper)	nr Naseby, Northants.	Into Severn at Tewkesbury	(part of Severn Basin)		8560
80·5	129,5	Don (Aberdeenshire)	Carn Cuilchathaidh, Grampian	North Sea	515·7	1336	Not available
79	127	Tees	Cross Fell, Cumbria	North Sea	863·6	2237	13 600
76	122	Bann (Upper Bann—Lough Neagh—Lower Bann)	Mountains of Mourne, SW Down	Atlantic Ocean	—	—	—
73	117,5	Tyne (34)—North Tyne (39)	Cheviots between Pell Fell and Carter Fell	North Sea	1126·4	2917	42 000
70	112,5	Dee (Cheshire)	Bala Lake, Gwynedd	Irish Sea	818·1	2119	16 000

* This column gives the hydrometric area of the whole river system as per *The Surface Water Survey*.
† This column gives the highest recorded discharge in cubic feet per second (*note*: 1 cusec = 0·0283168 m³/sec 538,170 gallons per day) taken at the lowest sited gauging on the name river.

UK ISLANDS

A unique check list of more than 1000 islands of Great Britain will appear in the forthcoming *Guinness Book of British Islands*

England (12 largest)

	mile²	km²
Isle of Wight	147·09	380,99
*Sheppey	36·31	94,04
*Hayling	10·36	26,84
*Foulness	10·09	26,14
*Portsea	9·36	24,25
*Canvey	7·12	18,45
*Mersea	6·96	18,04
*Walney	5·01	12,99
*Isle of Grain	4·96	12,85
*Wallasea	4·11	10,65
St Mary's, Isles of Scilly	2·84	7,37
Thorney	1·91	4,96

*Bridged or causewayed to the mainland

Scotland (12 largest)

	mile²	km²
Lewis with Harris	844·68	2187,72
Skye	643·28	1666,08
Mainland, Shetland	373·36	967,00
Mull	347·21	899,25
Islay	246·64	614,52
Mainland, Orkney	206·99	536,10
Arran	168·08	435,32
Jura	142·99	370,35
North Uist	135·71	351,49
South Uist	128·36	332,45
Yell	82·69	214,16
Hoy, Orkney	52·84	136,85

Wales (12 largest)

	mile²	km²
*Anglesey (Ynys Mon)	275·60	713,80
Holy Is	15·22	39,44
Skomer	1·12	2,90
Ramsey	0·99	2,58
Caldey	0·84	2,79
Bardsey	0·76	1,99
Skokholm	0·41	1,06
Flat Holm	0·13	0,33
*Llanddwyn Is	0·12	0,31
Puffin Island	0·11	0,28
The Skerries	0·06	0,15
Cardigan Island	0·06	0,15

Northern Ireland's principal offshore island is Rathlin Island (5·56 mile² *14,41 km²*)

The principal Channel Isles comprise

	mile²	km²
Jersey	44·87	116,21
Guernsey	24·46	63,34
Alderney	3·07	7,94
Sark	1·99	5,15
Herm	0·50	1,29

Crown Dependency:

	mile²	km²
Isle of Man	220·72	571,66
Calf of Man	0·96	2,49

PRINCIPAL CONURBATIONS OF THE UNITED KINGDOM

Many geographers would recognize the conurbation (a term invented in 1917), a contiguous built-up area disregarding the artificial restrictions of local government boundaries, as the most significant and realistic definition of a city: such a practice is normal in Australia, Belgium, Canada, France, the Netherlands, Sweden and the United States.

Using the returns of the last census taken in the United Kingdom (25/26 Apr. 1971) it is possible to delineate 20 major conurbations (ie those with over 300 000 inhabitants): of these 8 were officially recognized by the Registrar General and in the following list they are indicated by an asterisk while the name by which they were referred to in the census is added in brackets.

1.	The LONDON conurbation (Greater London)*	7 350 000
2.	The MANCHESTER conurbation (South East Lancashire)*	2 390 000
3.	The BIRMINGHAM conurbation (West Midlands†)*	2 370 000
4.=	The GLASGOW conurbation (Clydeside)*	1 730 000
=	The LEEDS conurbation (West Yorkshire†)*	1 730 000
6.	The LIVERPOOL conurbation (Merseyside†)*	1 260 000
7.	The NEWCASTLE conurbation (Tyneside)*	800 000
8.	The SHEFFIELD conurbation	650 000
9.	The BELFAST conurbation (Belfast)*	550 000
10.	The BRISTOL conurbation	510 000
=	The NOTTINGHAM conurbation	510 000

CONURBATIONS continued

12.	The PORTSMOUTH conurbation	480 000
13.	The EDINBURGH conurbation	470 000
14.	The MIDDLESBROUGH conurbation	400 000
15.	The COVENTRY conurbation	380 000
16.	The LEICESTER conurbation	350 000
17.=	The KINGSTON UPON HULL conurbation	340 000
=	The STOKE-ON-TRENT conurbation	340 000
19.=	The BOURNEMOUTH conurbation	300 000
=	The BRIGHTON conurbation	300 000

† These do *not* cover the same areas as the present counties of these names.

THE 58 CITIES OF THE UNITED KINGDOM

The term City as used in the United Kingdom is a title of dignity applied to 58 towns of varying local Government status by virtue of their importance as either archiepiscopal or episcopal sees or former sees, or as commercial or industrial centres. The right has been acquired in the past by (1) traditional usage—for example, the Doomsday Book describes Coventry, Exeter and Norwich as *civitas*; by (2) statute; or by (3) royal prerogative, and in more recent times solely by royal charter and letters patent—the most recent examples are Lancaster (1937), Cambridge (1951) Southampton (1964), Swansea (1969), the extension of the City of Westminster to include the former Metropolitan Boroughs of Paddington and St Marylebone in 1965 and Derby (1977). ★Is styled 'Rt Hon'.

Name of City with Geographical County	First Recorded Charter	Title of Civic Head
Aberdeen, Grampian, Scotland	1179	Lord Provost
Bangor, Gwynedd, Wales	1883	Mayor
Bath, Avon	1590	Mayor
Belfast, Antrim, Northern Ireland	1613	Lord Mayor★
Birmingham, West Midlands	1838	Lord Mayor
Bradford, West Yorkshire	1847	Lord Mayor
Bristol, Avon	1188	Lord Mayor
Cambridge, Cambridgeshire	1207	Mayor
Canterbury, Kent	1448	Mayor
Cardiff, South Glamorgan, Wales	1608	Lord Mayor
Carlisle, Cumbria	1158	Mayor
Chester, Cheshire	1506	Mayor
Chichester, West Sussex	1135–54	Mayor
Coventry, West Midlands	1345	Lord Mayor
Derby, Derbyshire	1154 (present charter 1977)	Mayor
Dundee, Tayside, Scotland	c. 1179	Lord Provost
Durham, Durham	1602	Mayor
Edinburgh, Lothian, Scotland	c. 1124	Lord Provost★
Elgin, Grampian, Scotland	1234	Lord Provost
Ely, Cambridgeshire	no charter	Chairman
Exeter, Devon	1156	Mayor
Glasgow, Strathclyde, Scotland	1690	Lord Provost★
Gloucester, Gloucestershire	1483	Mayor
Hereford, Hereford and Worcester	1189	Mayor
Kingston upon Hull, Humberside	1440	Lord Mayor
Lancaster, Lancashire	1193	Mayor
Leeds, West Yorkshire	1626	Lord Mayor
Leicester, Leicestershire	1589	Lord Mayor
Lichfield, Staffordshire	1549	Mayor
Lincoln, Lincolnshire	1154	Mayor
Liverpool, Merseyside	1207	Lord Mayor
London, Greater London	1066–87	Lord Mayor★
Londonderry, Londonderry, Northern Ireland	1604	Mayor
Manchester, Greater Manchester	1838	Lord Mayor
Newcastle upon Tyne, Tyne and Wear	1157	Lord Mayor
Norwich, Norfolk	1194	Lord Mayor
Nottingham, Nottinghamshire	1155	Lord Mayor
Oxford, Oxfordshire	1154–87	Lord Mayor
Perth, Tayside, Scotland	1210	Lord Provost
Peterborough, Cambridgeshire	1874	Mayor
Plymouth, Devon	1439	Lord Mayor
Portsmouth, Hampshire	1194	Lord Mayor
Ripon, North Yorkshire	886	Mayor
Rochester, Kent	1189	Mayor
St Albans, Hertfordshire	1553	Mayor
Salford, Greater Manchester	1835	Mayor
Salisbury, Wiltshire	1227	Mayor
Sheffield, South Yorkshire	1843	Lord Mayor
Southampton, Hampshire	1447	Mayor
Stoke-on-Trent, Staffordshire	1874 (present charter 1910)	Lord Mayor
Swansea, West Glamorgan, Wales	1169 (present charter 1969)	Mayor
Truro, Cornwall	1589	Mayor
Wakefield, West Yorkshire	1848	Mayor
Wells, Somerset	1201	Mayor
Westminster, Greater London	1256 (present charter 1965)	Lord Mayor
Winchester, Hampshire	1155	Mayor
Worcester, Hereford & Worcester	1189	Mayor
York, North Yorkshire	1396	Lord Mayor★

NEW TOWNS

There are 18 New Towns ('Development Corporations') in England (15) and Scotland (3). When a New Town in England or Wales has substantially fulfilled its purpose it becomes vested in the *Commission for the New Towns*. On 1 Apr. 1962 Crawley (West Sussex) and Hemel Hempstead (Herts.) were so vested, so can be regarded as ex-New Towns.

Stevenage, Herts. (1946)
Harlow, Essex. (May 1947)
Aycliffe, Durham. (July 1947)
East Kilbride, Strathclyde. (Aug. 1947).
Peterlee, Durham. (Mar. 1948)
Welwyn Garden City, Herts. (June 1948)
Hatfield, Herts. (June 1948)
Glenrothes, Fife. (Oct. 1948)
Basildon, Essex. (Feb. 1949)
Bracknell, Berks. (Oct. 1949)
Cwmbran, Gwent. (Nov. 1949)
Corby, Northants. (1950)
Cumbernauld, Strathclyde. (1956)
Skelmersdale, Lancashire. (1962)
Livingston, Lothian. (1962)
Telford, Salop. (1963).
Runcorn, Cheshire. (1964)
Redditch, Hereford & Worcester. (1964)
Washington, Tyne & Wear. (1964)
Irvine, Strathclyde (1966)
Milton Keynes, Buckinghamshire (1967)
Newtown, Powys (1967)
Northampton, (1968)
Peterborough (1968)
Warrington, Cheshire (1968)
Central Lancashire New Town (1970)
Stonehouse, Strathclyde was scheduled in 1973 but development plans were abandoned in 1976.

POPULATIONS

Cities, towns and districts in the United Kingdom with a population of over ¼ million.

Since the recent reform of local government the definition of many towns has been difficult: a few new districts show an improved delineation of towns, but many new districts have Borough status, although the towns from which they take their nomenclature may represent but a fraction of their population. Also, some urban districts, usually with Borough status, do not bear the name of their principal town; e.g. the Borough in which West Bromich is the main town is called Sandwell.

These figures are those officially estimated by the Registrar-General for mid 1976.

1.	LONDON	Greater London	7 028 200
2.	BIRMINGHAM	West Midlands	1 058 800
3.	GLASGOW	Strathclyde	856 000
4.	LEEDS	West Yorkshire	744 500
5.	SHEFFIELD	South Yorkshire	558 000
6.	LIVERPOOL	Merseyside	539 700
7.	MANCHESTER	Greater Manchester	490 000
8.	EDINBURGH	Lothian	467 000
9.	BRADFORD	West Yorkshire	458 900
10.	BRISTOL	Avon	416 300
11.	KIRKLEES	West Yorkshire	372 500
12.	BELFAST	Belfast District, N. I.	363 000
13.	WIRRAL	Merseyside	348 200
14.	COVENTRY	West Midlands	336 800
15.	SANDWELL	West Midlands	312 900
16.	WIGAN	Greater Manchester	310 700
17.	WAKEFIELD	West Yorkshire	306 500
18.	SEFTON	Merseyside	306 000
19.	DUDLEY	West Midlands	300 200
20.	NEWCASTLE UPON TYNE	Tyne and Wear	295 800

THE CROWN DEPENDENCIES

The Isle of Man

The Isle of Man (Manx-Gaelic, *Ellan Vannin*) is a Crown dependency.

Area: 145 325 acres *58 811 ha* (227·07 miles²) (*588,1 km²*), including Calf of Man (5·4 acres *2,18 ha*) and Chicken Rock.

Population: 61 723 (census 4 April 1976).

Administrative headquarters: Douglas 20 389. The ancient capital was Castletown (2 820).

History: Continually inhabited since Mesolithic times, c. 6000 BC. By about AD 450 the island was occupied by Gaelic-speaking people. Christian missionaries came, probably from Iona, before AD 600. Invasions from Scandinavia c. 800, and Norsemen settled during the 9th century. The most notable Norse chieftain was Godred (Crovan) I, who conquered Man in 1079 and ruled until 1095. Norse kings reigned until the Treaty of Perth on 2 July 1266, when the title was sold to Alexander III of Scotland, succeeded by Margaret, the Maid of Norway. The Island was taken in 1290 by Edward I of England. Edward II lost it to Bruce, but Scotland later lost it to Edward III, who gave the kingship of the island to the 1st Earl of Salisbury. The 2nd Earl sold it to Sir William le Scrope, later executed by the order of Henry IV, who in 1406 granted the island to the Stanley family. The Stanleys (Earls of Derby after 1485) ruled as 'lords of Mann' until 1594, when Elizabeth I took over the island. James I gave it to the Earls of Salisbury in 1607, but it was returned to the Derbys in 1609. The tenth Earl died in 1736, and his daughter, the Duchess of Atholl, succeeded. The manorial rights of the Atholls were bought by Parliament in 1828. After agitation, a modified form of home rule was restored in 1866.

Administration: For administrative purposes, the island is divided into six 'sheadings'. The monarch, as lord of Man, appoints the Lieutenant Governor. The island's legislature, called the Tynwald, consists of two houses—the Legislative Council and the House of Keys. The Council president is the Lieutenant-Governor and the other members are: the Bishop of Sodor and Man, the two Deemsters (judges of the high court), the Attorney-General, two members appointed by the Lieutenant-Governor and four members appointed by the House of Keys. The 24 members of the House of Keys are made up as follows: 13 from the six sheadings, seven from Douglas, two from Ramsey, one from Castletown and one from Peel. After Bills have been passed by both houses, they are signed by the members and then sent for Royal Assent.

Highest point above sea-level: Snaefell (2034 ft *619 m*).

Leading Industries: Tourism; conferences; agriculture, chiefly oats, hay, and sheep-grazing; kippered herrings; Manx tweed; flour milling.

Places of Interest: Tynwald Hill at St Johns, where the annual reading of the laws takes place on 5 July (old midsummer day); Meayl (or Mull) circle, near Cregnish. The Laxey waterwheel (1854) of 288 ft *69 m* circumference.

The Channel Islands

The Channel Islands (French, *Îles Anglo-Normandes*) are a Crown dependency. There is a Channel Isle department in the Home Office, Whitehall, London.

Area: 48 083 acres *19 458 ha* (75·13 miles² *194,6 km²*).

Guernsey (French: *Guernesey*)—15 654 acres *6334 ha* (24·46 miles² *63,3 km²*)

Jersey—28 717 acres *11 621 ha* (44·87 miles² *116,2 km²*).

Dependencies of Guernsey:

Alderney (French: *Aurigny*) 1962 acres *794 ha* (3·07 miles² *7,9 km²*).

Sark (*Sercq*)—1274 acres *515 ha* (1·99 miles² *5,1 km²*).

(Great Sark, 1035 acres *419 ha 4,2 km²*; Little Sark 239 acres *96 ha 0,9 km²*)).

Herm—320 acres *129 ha 1,29 km²*.

Brechou (Brecqham)—74 acres *30 ha 0,3 km²*.

Jethou—44 acres *18 ha*.

Lihou (Libon)—38 acres *15 ha*.

Other islands include Ortach, Burhou, the Casquets, Les Minquiers (including Maîtresse Ile) and the Ecrehou Islands (including Marmaoutier, Blanche Ile, and Maître Ile).

Population: 126 541.

Jersey—72 532   Alderney—1785

Guernsey—51 620   Sark—604

Administrative headquarters: Jersey—St Helier, Guernsey and dependencies—St Peter Port.

History: The islands are known to have been inhabited by Acheulian man (before the last Ice Age) and by Neanderthal man. Continuously inhabited since Iberian settlers, who used flint implements, arrived in the 2nd millenium BC. The islands were later settled by the Gauls, and after them the Romans; Christian missionaries came from Cornwall and Brittany in the 6th century AD. The Vikings began raiding the islands in the 9th century. Rollo, the Viking nobleman, established the duchy of Normandy in AD 911. His son, the second duke, William I 'Longsword' annexed the Channel Islands in 933. Jethou was ceded to England in 1091. The other islands were annexed by the crown in 1106. Normandy was conquered by France, and the King (John) was declared to have forfeited all his titles to the duchy. The islanders, however, remained loyal to John. Administration has since been under the control of his successors, while maintaining a considerable degree of home rule and, until 1689, neutrality. Before the Reformation the islands formed part of the diocese of Coutances, but were later placed under the bishops of Winchester. From the 9th century everyone in the islands spoke Norman French, but English became dominant by the mid-19th century. The islands were occupied by Nazi Germany on 30 June–1 July 1940, and fortified for defence. They were relieved by British forces on 9 May 1945.

Administration: The islands are divided into two Bailiwicks, the States of Jersey and the States of Guernsey. The two Bailiwicks each have a Lieutenant-Governor and Commander-in-Chief, who is the personal representative of the Monarch and the channel of communication between HM Government and the Insular Governments. The Crown appoints Bailiffs, who are both Presidents of the Assembly of the States (the Legislature) and of the Royal Court. In Jersey the States consists of elected senators, *connétables* (constables) and deputies; in Guernsey, *conseillers* (councillors), elected by an intermediate body called the States of election, people's deputies, representatives of the *douzaines* (parish councils) and representatives of Alderney.

Highest points above sea-level:
Jersey—453 ft *138 m*
Guernsey—349 ft *106 m*
Alderney—281 ft *85,5 m*
Sark—375 ft *114 m*
Herm—235 ft *71,5 m*
Jethou—267 ft *81 m*
Lihou—68 ft *21 m*

Leading Industries: Agriculture, chiefly cattle, potatoes, tomatoes, grapes, and flowers; tourism; granite quarrying.

Places of Interest: The Museum of the Société Jersiaise; the church of St Peter Port.

THE UNITED KINGDOM COUNTIES

The United Kingdom of Great Britain and Northern Ireland's traditional 91 counties were in 1974 and 1975 reduced to 66 in Great Britain and six in Northern Ireland.

England has	46 *geographical* counties (formerly 40)
Scotland has	9 *geographical* regions and 3 island authorities(formerly 33 counties)
Wales has	8 *geographical* counties (formerly 12)
Northern Ireland has	6 *geographical* counties (divided into 26 districts)

Names of the counties: For some counties there are alternatives such as Devon and Devonshire. We however have generally only added the suffix 'shire' where there is a town of the same name as its county. This occurs in 17 cases but to these must be added four others which traditionally (but not statutorily) use 'shire': Berkshire, Cheshire, Lancashire, and Wiltshire. 'Hampshire was adopted in 1959 in favour of the County of Southampton.

Abbreviations are frequently used for counties, but we have only given the 23 that are officially listed as 'Postally acceptable' in the Post Office Guide.

County worthies by birth: The term 'worthy' is used in its sense of famous man or woman and some cases fame includes notoriety.

AVON

First recorded name and derivation: 1973. From the river of that name. (Afon is Welsh for river).
Area: 332 596 acres *134 597 ha.*
Population: 920 200
Density: 2·77 per acre *6,84 per ha*
Administrative HQ: Avon House, The Haymarket, Bristol.
Highest point above sea-level: Southern Duxbury (on southern boundary) 870 ft *265 m*

Road lengths:	miles	*km*
motorway and trunk	109	*175,4*
principal	210	*337,9*
other	2398	*3858,4*

Schools and colleges: Nursery 17; Primary 395; Secondary 64; Special 29; Colleges of further education 9; colleges of education 2; Polytechnic 1.

Places of interest: Bath (Roman remains); Bath Abbey; Clevedon Court; Bristol Cathedral; Stanton Drew (standing stones); Clifton Suspension Bridge.
County worthies by birth: John Locke (1632–1704); Thomas Chatterton (1752–70); Robert Southey (1774–1843); Samuel Plimsoll (1824–98); W G Grace (1848–1915).

BEDFORDSHIRE

First recorded use of name and derivation: 1011 (Bedanfordscir), Beda's ford, or river crossing.
Area: 305 026 acres *123 440 ha*
Population: 491 700
Density: 1·61 per acre *3,98 per ha*
Administrative HQ: County Hall, Cauldwell St, Bedford.
Highest point above sea-level: Dunstable Downs 798 ft *243 m.*

Road lengths:	miles	*km*
motorway	15·5	*24,9*
trunk	70·2	*113*
principal	132·5	*213,2*
others	1098	*1766,7*

Schools and colleges: Nursery 10; Lower/primary 233; Middle 29; Upper/secondary 31; Sixth form college 1; Special 16; Colleges of higher education 2; Colleges of further education 2; other colleges 2.
Places of interest: Woburn Abbey; Whipsnade Park (Zoo); Luton Hoo; Elstow Moot Hall; Dunstable Priory Church.
County worthies by birth: John Bunyan (1628–88); Sir Joseph Paxton (1801–65); Thomas Tompion (1638–1713).

BERKSHIRE

First recorded use of name and derivation: AD 860, wooded hill district named after Bearruc hill.
Area: 310 179 acres *125 525 ha*
Population: 659 000
Density: 2·12 per acre *5·25 per ha.*
Administrative HQ: Shire Hall, Reading.
Highest point above sea-level: Walbury Hill, 974 ft *296 m.*

Road lengths:	miles	*km*
motorway	61	*98,1*
trunk	65	*104,6*
principal	169·7	*273*
others	1540·4	*2478,5*

Schools and colleges: Nursery 19; Infant/first 76; Junior/middle 67; Primary/combined 149; Secondary 66; Special 19; Establishments of further education 10.

Places of interest: Windsor Castle (St George's Chapel; Reading Abbey (ruin); Royal Military Academy, Sandhurst; Eton College.
County worthies by birth: Edward III (1312–77); Henry VI (1421–71); Archbishop William Land (1628–88); Sir John Herschel (1792–1871).

BORDERS

First recorded use of name and derivation: 1975, from the district bordering on the boundary between England and Scotland from the Middle English word *bordure*; Term 'border' used in Act of the English Parliament, 1580.
Area: 1 154 288 acres *467 124 ha.*
Population: 99 917
Density: 0·09 per acre *0,21 per ha.*
Administrative HQ: Regional Offices, Newtown St Boswells.
Highest point above sea-level: Broad Law (Southern summit) 2754 ft *839 m.*
Districts: Berwickshire 17 728; Etterick and Lauderdale 32 498; Roxburgh 35 656; Tweeddale 14 035.

Road lengths:	miles	*km*
trunk	113	*181,8*
classified	1107	*1781,2*
unclassified	640	*1029,8*

Schools and colleges: Primary 85; Secondary 9; Special 8; Colleges of further education 3; other college 1.
Places of interest: Edin's Hall, nr. Duns; Dryburgh Abbey; Condingham Priory.
County worthies by birth: Johannes Duns Scotus (*c.* 1266–1308); James Thomson (1700–48); James Hogg (1770–1835); Mungo Park (1771–1806); Dr John Leyden (1775–1811); Sir David Brewster (1781–1868); Henry Lyte (1793–1847); Sir James Murray (1837–1915).

BUCKINGHAMSHIRE

First recorded use of name and derivation: 1016 (Buccingahamscir) the hamm (water-meadow) of Bucca's people.
Area: 464 000 acres *187 920 ha.*
Population: 512 000
Density: 1·10 per acre *2,72 per ha.*
Administrative HQ: County Hall, Aylesbury.
Highest point above sea-level: Nr. Aston Hill 857 ft *261 m.*

Road lengths:	miles	*km*
motorway	35	*56,3*
trunk	37	*59,5*
principal	247	*397,4*
others	1853	*2981,5*

Schools and colleges: Nursery 5; First 142; Middle 73; Combined 96; Secondary 50; Special 14; Colleges of further education 5; Colleges of education 2.
Places of interest: Claydon House; Cliveden; Hughenden Manor; Stowe House; Chequers; Hellfire Caves (West Wycombe).
County worthies by birth: James Brudenell, 7th Earl of Cardigan (1797–1868); Sir (George) Gilbert Scott (1811–1878); William Grenfell, Baron Desborough (1855–1945); William Malcolm, Baron Hailey (1872–1969).

CAMBRIDGESHIRE

First recorded use of name and derivation: 1010 (Grantabrycgscir), · a Norman

corruption of Grantabrice (bridge over River Granta).
Area: 842 433 acres *340 921 ha.*
Population: 563 000
Density: 0·68 per acre *1,65 per ha.*
Administrative HQ: Shire Hall, Castle Hill, Cambridge.
Highest point above sea-level: 300 yd *275 m* south of the Hall, Great Chishill. 478 ft *145 m.*

Road lengths:	miles	km
trunk	206	*331,5*
principal	216	*347,5*
classified	1072	*1724,8*
others	1214	*1953,3*

Schools and colleges: Nursery 8; Primary 291; Secondary 50; Special 14; Colleges of further education 7.
Places of interest: Burghley House; Cambridge University; The Backs, Cambridge; Ely Cathedral; Peterborough Cathedral; Sawston Hall; Peckover House.
County worthies by birth: Orlando Gibbons (1583–1625); Oliver Cromwell (1599–1658); Jeremy Taylor (1613–67); Octavia Hill (1838–1912); Lord Keynes (1883–1946).

CENTRAL SCOTLAND

First recorded use of name and derivation: self-explanatory, pertaining to the centre, the word *central*, first recorded in this sense, 1647.
Area: 622 080 acres *251 747 ha.*
Population: 270 056
Density 0·43 per acre *1,07 per ha.*
Administrative HQ: Central Region Offices, Viewforth, Stirling.
Highest point above sea-level: Ben More, 3852 ft *1174 m.*
Districts: Clackmannan 47 847; Falkirk 143 167; Stirling 79 042.

Road lengths:	miles	km
motorway	29	*46,7*
trunk	82	*131,9*
principal	196	*315,4*
classified	373	*600,2*
unclassified	416	*669,3*

Schools and colleges: Nursery 6; Primary 121; Middle 2; High 23; Special 16; Colleges of further education 2.
Places of interest: Stirling Castle; Old Stirling Bridge; Cambuskenneth Abbey; Field of Bannockburn; Loch Lomond (east side); Doune Castle.
County worthies by birth: George Buchanan (1506–1582) Marshal of the RAF Lord Tedder (1890–1967).

CHESHIRE

First recorded use of name and derivation: AD 980 (Legeceasterseir), corrupted from the camp (*castra*) of the legions (*legiones*).
Area: 573 835 acres *232 223 ha.*
Population: 916 400
Density: 1·60 per acre *3,95 per ha.*
Administrative HQ: County Hall, Chester.
Highest point above sea-level: Shining Tor 1834 ft *559 m.*

Road lengths:	miles	km
motorway	66	*106,2*
trunk	184	*296,1*
principal	363	*584,1*
classified	875	*1407,9*
unclassified	1827	*2939,6*

Schools and colleges: Nursery 8; Primary 502; Secondary 81; Special 43; Colleges of further education 8; Colleges of education 2.
Places of interest: Roman remains within walled city of Chester; Chester Cathedral; Gawsworth Hall; Jodrell Bank; Tatton Hall.
County worthies by birth: John Bradshaw (1602–59); Emma, Lady Hamilton (*c.* 1765–1815); Rev Charles Dodgson (Lewis Carroll) (1832–98).

CLEVELAND

First recorded use of name and derivation: 1110, *Clivelanda*, 'the hilly district'.
Area: 144 030 acres *582 870 ha.*
Population: 567 900.
Density: 3·94 per acre *9,74 per ha.*
Administrative HQ: Municipal Buildings, Middlesbrough.
Highest point above sea-level: Hob on the Hill 1078 ft *328 m.*

Road lengths:	miles	km
trunk	24	*39*
principal	146	*236*
others	990	*1594*

Schools and colleges: Nursery 10; Primary 279; Secondary 61; Special 20; Colleges for further education 7; colleges of education 2; Polytechnic 1.
Places of interest: Church of St Hilda (Hartlepool).
County worthies by birth: Capt James Cook (1728–79); Thomas Sheraton (1751–1806); Sir Compton Mackenzie (1823–1972).

CLWYD

First recorded use of name and derivation: 1973 from the river of that name.
Area: 599 481 acres *242 602 ha.*
Population: 376 000.
Density: 0·63 per acre *1,54 per ha.*
Administrative HQ: Shire Hall, Mold.
Highest point above sea-level: Moel Sych 2713 ft *826 m.*

Road lengths:	miles	km
trunk	119	*191,5*
principal	256	*411,9*
others	2419	*3892,2*

Schools and colleges: Nursery 1; Primary 254; Secondary 35; Special 10; Colleges of further education 5; College of education 1.
Places of interest: Denbigh Castle; Valle Crucis (Cistercian Abbey); Rhuddlan Castle (ruins); Bodrhyddan Hall; Wrexham Church; Erddig Hall; Brenig Reservoir
County worthies by birth: William Salisbury (*c.* 1520–84); Sir Hugh Myddleton (1560–1631); Judge George Jeffreys (1648–1689); Sir Henry M Stanley (1841–1904).

CORNWALL

First recorded use of name and derivation: 884 (Cornubia) and 981 (Cornwalum), possible the territory of the Welsh tribe Cornovii.
Area: 876 296 acres *354 625 ha.*
Population: 407 100.
Density: 0·46 per acre *1,15 per ha.*
Administrative HQ: County Hall, Truro.
Highest point above sea-level: Brown Willy 1375 ft *419 m.*

Road lengths:	miles	km
trunk	148	*238,1*
principal	284	*457*
classified	1892	*3044,2*
unclassified	2189	*3522,1*

Schools and colleges: Nursery 2; Primary 272; Secondary 37; Special 4; Colleges of further education 5.
Places of interest: Chun Castle (ring-fort); Chysauster (Iron Age village); Cotehele House (Tudor house); Land's End; Lanhydrock House (17th century house); Lanyon Quoit; The Lizard; Rame Head; Restormel (moated castle); St Buryan (Bronze Age stone and 15th century church); St Michael's Mount; St Neot church (stained glass); Tintagel (ruins); Kynance Cove; Truro Cathedral.
County worthies by birth: Samuel Foote (1720–77); John Opie (1761–1807); Richard Trevithick (1771–1833); Sir Humphrey Davy (1778–1829); Richard (1804–34) and John (1807–39) Lander; Sir Arthur Quiller-Couch (1863–1944); Robert Fitzsimons (1862–1917).

CUMBRIA

First recorded use of name and derivation: AD 935 Cumbra land, land of the Cumbrians from the Welsh *Cymry*.
Area: 1 701 455 acres. *688 555 ha.*
Population: 473 600.
Density: 0.28 per acre *0,69 per ha.*
Administrative HQ: The Courts, Carlisle.
Highest point above sea-level: Scafell Pike 3 210 ft *978 m.*

Road lengths:	miles	km
motorway	60	*96,5*
trunk	272	*437,6*
principal	339	*545,5*
others	3969	*6386,1*

Schools and colleges: Nursery 8; Primary 362; Secondary 62; Special 13; Colleges of further education 4; Other colleges 2; College of education 1.
Places of interest: Hadrian's Wall; Lake District; Grasmere (Wordsworth monuments—museum, cottage, grave); Levens Hall; Carlisle Cathedral.
County worthies by birth: John Dalton (1766–1844); William Wordsworth (1770–1850); John Peel (1776–1854); Sir William H Bragg (1862–1942); George Romney (1734–1802); Queen Catherine Parr (*c.* 1512–1548).

DERBYSHIRE

BENE CONSULENDO

First recorded use of name and derivation: 1049 (Deorbyscir), village with a deer park.
Area: 650 092 acres *263 083 ha.*
Population: 887 600
Density: 1·37 per acre *3,37 per ha.*
Administrative HQ: County Offices, Matlock.
Highest point above sea-level: Kinder Scout 2088 ft *636 m.*

Road lengths:	miles	km
motorway	24	*38,6*
trunk	146	*234,9*
principal	333	*535,8*

| classified | 1090 | *1753,8* |
| unclassified | 1541 | *2479,5* |

Schools and colleges: Nursery 6; Primary 488; Middle 2; Secondary 89; Special 21; Colleges of further education 8; College of education 1.

Places of interest: Peak District; Chatsworth House; Repton School; Haddon Hall; Hardwick Hall; Melbourne Hall; Dove Dale.

County worthies by birth: Samuel Richardson (1689–1761); Marquess Curzon of Kedleston (1859-·1925); James Brindley (1716–72); Thomas Cook (1808–92).

DEVON

First recorded use of name and derivation: AD 851 (Defenascir), territory of the Dumonii (An aboriginal Celtic tribal name adopted by the Saxons).
Area: 1 658 278 acres *671 082 ha.*
Population: 942 100.
Density: 0·57 per acre *1,40 per ha.*
Administrative HQ: County Hall, Exeter.
Highest point above sea-level: High Willhays 2038 ft *621 m.*

Road lengths:	miles	*km*
motorway	12	*19,3*
trunk	206	*331,5*
principal	580	*933,2*
classified	3123	*5024,9*
unclassified	4236	*6815,7*

Schools and colleges: Nursery 5; Primary 428; First schools 14; Middle 17; Secondary 83; Special 23; Establishments of further education 10; Polytechnic 1.

Places of interest: Exeter Castle (ruins); Exeter Cathedral; Devonport dockyard; Dartmoor; Buckfast Abbey; Clovelly; Powderham Castle; Dartmouth (port, castle and Royal Naval College).

County worthies by birth: St Boniface (*c.* 680–755); Sir John Hawkins (1532–95); Sir Francis Drake (*c.* 1540–96); Sir Walter Raleigh (?1552–1618); 1st Duke of Albermarle (George Monk) (1608–70); 1st Duke of Marlborough (1650–1722); Thomas Newcomen (1663–1729); Sir Joshua Reynolds (1723–92); Samuel Taylor Coleridge (1772–1834); Sir Charles Kingsley (1819–75); William Temple (1881–1944); Dame Agatha Christie (1891–1976).

DORSET

First recorded use of name and derivation: AD 940 (Dorseteschire), dwellers (*saete*) of the place of fist-play (*Dorn-gweir*).
Area: 664 116 acres *268 758 ha.*
Population: 575 800.
Density: 0·87 per acre. *2,14 per ha.*
Administrative HQ: County Hall, Dorchester.

Highest point above sea-level: Pilsdon Pen 909 ft *277 m.*

Road lengths:	miles	*km*
trunk	59	*94,9*
principal	278	*447,3*
classified	966	*1554,3*
unclassified	1977	*3181*

Schools and colleges: Primary 218; Middle 19; Secondary 50; Special 10; Colleges of further education 3; other colleges 3.

Places of interest: Corfe Castle; Sherborne Abbey; Wimborne Minster; Maiden Castle; Clouds Hill (Nat. Trust); Cerne Giant; Forde Abbey; Milton Abbey; Poole Harbour; Christchurch Priory; Compton Acres Gardens.

County worthies by birth: John, Cardinal Morton (*c.* 1420–1500); 1st Earl of Shaftesbury (1621–83); Sir James Thornhill (1676–1734); Thomas Love Peacock (1785–1866); William Barnes (1800–86); Thomas Hardy (1840–1928); Sir Frederick Treves (1853–1923).

DUMFRIES AND GALLOWAY

First recorded use of name and derivation: Dumfries *c.* 1183, Fort *Dum,* of the Welsh *prys* (copse). Galloway: *c.* 990, Gall-Gaidheal, the foreign Gael.
Area: 1 574 400 acres *637 138 ha.*
Population: 143 585
Density: 0·09 per acre *0,23 per ha.*
Administrative HQ: Regional Headquarters, Dumfries.
Highest point above sea-level: Merrick, 2770 ft *844 m.*
Districts (with population): Annadale and Eskdale 35 141; Nithsdale 56 180; Stewarty (of Kirkcudbrightshire) 22 419; Wigtown 29 845.

Road lengths:	miles	*km*
trunk	216	*347,5*
principal	309	*497,2*
classified	1121	*1803,7*
unclassified	1003	*1613,8*

Schools and colleges: Nursery 3; Primary 134; Secondary 19; Special 16; Establishments of further education 2.

Places of Interest: Stranraer Castle; Dunskey Castle; St Ninian's Cave; Glenluce Abbey; Threave Castle (ruins); Glentrool National Park; The Ruthwell Cross; Caerlaverock Castle; Drumlanrig Castle; Burn's House and Mausoleum (Dumfries).

County worthies by birth: John Dalrymple, 1st Earl of Stair (1646–95); Thomas Telford (1757–1834); Sir John Ross (1777–1856); Thomas Carlyle (1795–1881).

DURHAM

First recorded use of name and derivation: *c.* 1000 (Dunholme), the hill (old English, *dun*) crowning a holm or island.
Area: 601 939 acres *243 596 ha.*
Population: 610 400
Density: 1·01 per acre *2,51 per ha.*
Administrative HQ: County Hall, Durham.
Highest point above sea-level: Mickle Fell 2591 ft *798 m.*

Road lengths:	miles	*km*
motorway	28	*45,1*
trunk	54	*86,9*
principal	235	*378,1*
classified	726	*1168,1*
unclassified	1248	*2008*

Schools and colleges: Nursery 23; Primary 356; Secondary 65; Special 16; Colleges of further education 6; Colleges of education 2.

Places of interest: Durham Cathedral, Bowes Museum. Raby Castle.
County worthies by birth: Earl of Avon (Anthony Eden) (1897–1977); Elizabeth Barrett Browning (1806–61).

DYFED

First recorded use of name and derivation: The name of an ancient 5th century province.
Area: 1 424 668 acres *576 543 ha.*
Population: 323 100.
Density: 0·23 per acre *0,56 per ha.*
Administrative HQ: County Hall, Carmarthen.
Highest point above sea-level: Carmathen Fan Foel 2500+ ft *762+ m.*

Road lengths:	miles	*km*
trunk	237	*381,6*
principal	216	*347,8*
classified	2353	*3786,1*
unclassified	1976	*3180*

Schools and colleges: Nursery 2; Primary 339; Secondary 40; Special 6; Colleges of further education 7; other colleges 3.

Places of interest: Cardigan Castle (ruins); Aberystwyth Castle (ruins); Strata Florida Abbey; Nanteos Mansion; Kidwelly Castle; Carreg-Cennon Castle, Talley Abbey; Pendine Sands, Laugharne; St David's Cathedral and Bishop's Palace; Pentre Cfae (burial chamber), near Newport; Pembroke Castle; Carew Castle; Bishop's Palace (Lamphey) Manorbier Castle; Cilgerran Castle; Pembrokeshire Coast National Park.

County worthies by birth: Griffith Jones of Llanddowror (1684–1761); Henry VII (1457–1509); Cambrensis (Giraldus) (1146–1220); John Dyer (1700–1758); Sir Lewis Morris (1833–1907); Dafydd ap Gwilym (14th century); Sir John Rhys (1840–1915); St David (d. 601 ?); Bishop Asser (d. 909 ?); Augustus John (1878–1961); Robert Recorde (1510 ?–1558).

EAST SUSSEX

First recorded use of name and derivation: AD 722 (Suth Seaxe), the territory of the southern Saxons or suthseaxa.
Area: 443 627 acres *179 530 ha.*
Population: 655 600.
Density: 1·48 per acre. *3,65 per ha.*
Administrative HQ: County Hall, St Andrew's Lane, Lewes.
Highest point above sea-level: Ditchling Beacon 813 ft *247 m.*

Road lengths:	miles	*km*
trunk	62	*99,8*
principal	294	*473*
classified	787	*1266,3*
unclassified	1318	*2120,7*

Schools and colleges: Nursery 2; First and middle 9; Middle 21; Infants 29; Primary 119; junior 24; Secondary 45; Special 16; Colleges of further education 7; College of higher education 1; Polytechnic 1.

Places of interest: Pevensey Castle; Bodiam Castle; Brighton Pavilion; Lewes Castle; Herstmonceux (Royal Observatory).

County worthies by birth: John Fletcher (1579–1625); Aubrey Beardsley (1872–1898).

ESSEX

First recorded use of name and derivation: AD 604 (East Seaxe), territory of the eastern Saxons.
Area: 907 849 acres *367 394 ha.*
Population: 1 426 200.

Density: 1·57 per acre *3,88 per ha.*
Administrative HQ: County Hall, Chelmsford.
Highest point above sea-level: In High Wood, Langley 480 ft *146 m.*

Road lengths:

	miles	km
motorway	10	*16,1*
trunk	96	*154,5*
principal	414	*666,1*
classified	1415	*2276,7*
unclassified	2441	*3927,6*

Schools and colleges: Nursery 2; Primary 600; Secondary 115; Special 39; Colleges of further education 10; Colleges of education 2.
Places of interest: Waltham Abbey; Colchester Castle; Epping Forest (part of); Thaxted Church and Guildhall; Hadleigh Castle; Castle Hedingham Keep; St Osyth Priory.
County worthies by birth: Dick Turpin (1705–1739); Field Marshal Lord Wavell (1883–1950).

FIFE

First recorded use of name and derivation: AD *c.* 590, from Fibh (disputed), possibly one of the seven sons of Criuthne, British patriot.
Area: 322 560 acres *130 536 ha*
Population: 338 734
Density: 1·04 per acre *2,58 per ha.*
Administrative HQ: The Regional Council meets at: Fife House, North Street, Glenrothes.
Highest point above sea-level: West Lomond 1713 ft *522 m.*
Districts (with population): Dunfermline 125 027; Kirkcaldy 148 537; North East Fife 65 170.

Road lengths:

	miles	km
motorway	13	*20,9*
trunk	83	*133,5*
principal	189	*304,1*
classified	341	*548,7*
unclassified	594	*955,7*

Schools and colleges: Nursery 7; Primary 151; Secondary 22; Special 10; Establishments of further education 4.
Places of interest: St Andrew's; Dunfermline; Falkland Palace; Isle of May; Culross; Inchcolm; Dysart; East Neuk Villages; Aberdour Castle.
County worthies by birth: Sir David Lyndsay (*c.* 1486–1555); David, Cardinal Beaton (1494–1546); Charles I (1600–49); Alexander Selkirk (1676–1721); Adam Smith (1723–90); Robert (1728–92) and James (1730–94) Adams; Dr Thomas Chalmers (1780–1847); Sir David Wilkie (1785–1841); Sir Joseph Noel Paton (1821–1901); Andrew Carnegie (1835–1919).

GLOUCESTERSHIRE

First recorded use of name and derivation: AD 1016 (Gleawcestrescir), the shire around the foot (*ceaster*) at the splendid place (Old Welsh, *gloiu*).
Area: 652 229 acres *263 948 ha.*
Population: 491 500.
Density: 0·75 per acre *1,85 per ha.*
Administrative HQ: Shire Hall, Gloucester.
Highest point above sea-level: Cleeve Cloud 1083 ft *330 m.*

Road lengths:

	miles	km
motorway	32	*51,5*
trunk	157	*252,6*
principal	252	*405,5*
classified	1113	*1790,8*
unclassified	1533	*2466,6*

Schools and colleges: Nursery 1; Primary 294; Secondary 54; Special 15; Colleges of further education 5; College of education 1; other college 1.
Places of interest: Tewkesbury Abbey; Gloucester Cathedral; Roman remains at Chedworth and Cirencester; Berkeley Castle; Sudeley Castle; Forest of Dean; The Cotswolds.
County worthies by birth: Edward Jenner (1749–1823); Rev. John Keble (1792–1866); Ralph Vaughan Williams (1872–1958); Gustav Theodore Holst (1874–1934).

GRAMPIAN

First recorded use of name and derivation: 1526 possibly derived from Old Welsh crwb, a haunch or hump or more probably the Gaelic *greannich*, gloomy or rugged.
Area: 2 150 798 acres *870 398 ha.*
Population: 453 829
Density: 0·21 per acre *0,52 per ha.*
Administrative HQ: Regional Headquarters, Aberdeen.
Highest point above sea-level: Ben Macdhui, 4296 ft *1309 m.*
Districts (with population): Aberdeen (city) 209 831; Banff and Buchan 76 363; Gordon 50 976; Kincardine and Deeside 35 613; Moray 81 046.

Road lengths:

	miles	km
trunk	222	*357,2*
principal	528	*849,6*
classified	1950	*3137,6*
unclassified	1857	*2987,9*

Schools and colleges: Nursery 44; Primary 267; Secondary 41; Special 12; Colleges of further education 5.
Places of interest: Balmoral Castle (near Crathie); Kildrummy Castle (ruins); Aberdeen University; Braemar (annual Highland games); Findlater Castle; Duff House (Banff); Marden Stone; Haddo House; Leith Hall; Huntly Castle; Elgin Cathedral (ruins); Cairngorms (National Nature Reserve).
County worthies by birth: John Barbour (*c.* 1316–95); James Sharp (1618–79); Alexander Cruden (1701–1770); James Ferguson (1710–76); Sir James Clark (1788–1870); James Gordon Bennett (1795–1872); James Ramsay Macdonald (1866–1937); John Charles Walsham Reith, 1st Baron (1889–1971).

GREATER LONDON

First recorded use of name and derivation: AD 115 (*Londinium*), possibly from the Old Irish *Londo*, a wild or bold man.
Area: 390 302 acres *157 950 ha.*
Population: 7 028 200.
Density: 18·01 per acre *44,50 per ha.*
Administrative HQ: County Hall, London SE1.
Highest point above sea-level: 809 ft *246 m* 33 yd *30 m* South-east of Westerham Heights (a house) on the Kent-GLC boundary.

London Boroughs in order of population

1. Croydon	330 600	
2. Barnet	305 200	
3. Bromley	299 100	
4. Ealing	293 800	
5. Lambeth	290 300	
6. Wandsworth	284 600	
7. Enfield	260 900	
8. Brent	256 500	
9. Havering	239 200	
10. Lewisham	237 300	
11. Redbridge	231 600	
12. Hillingdon	230 800	
13. Newham	228 900	
14. Haringey	228 200	
15. Southwark	224 900	
16. Waltham Forest	223 700	
17. Westminster, City of	216 100	
18. Bexley	213 500	
19. Greenwich	207 200	
20. Harrow	200 200	
21. Hounslow	199 100	
22. Hackney	192 500	
23. Camden	185 800	
24. Islington	171 600	
25. Hammersmith	170 000	
26. Merton	169 400	
27. Richmond upon Thames	166 800	
28. Sutton	166 700	
29. Kensington and Chelsea	161 400	
30. Barking	153 800	
31. Tower Hamlets	146 100	
32. Kingston upon Thames	135 600	
33. City of London (not a London Borough)	6 800	

Road lenths:

	miles	km
trunk	163	*262,3*
metropolitan	851	*1369,1*
borough	6856	*11 031,3*

Schools and colleges: (excluding the City of London). Nursery 81; Primary *c.* 2200; Middle 17; Secondary and Sixth form Colleges *c.* 720; Special *c.* 280; Establishments of further education 61; Polytechnics 8.
Places of interest: Buckingham Palace; Houses of Parliament; St Paul's Cathedral; Tower of London; Westminster Abbey; British Museum; National Gallery; Trafalgar Square; Port of London; Hampton Court Palace; Syon House, Isleworth; Chiswick House, W.4; Osterley Park, Osterley; Harrow School; London Airport (Heathrow); Kew Gardens; Tower Bridge; Greenwich (Cutty Sark, Maritime Museum and Royal Observatory); South Kensington Museums; Westminster Cathedral; Post Office Tower.

County worthies by birth:
The following 18 Kings and Queens (see separate section for details): Mathilda, Edward I, Edward V, Henry VIII, Edward VI, Mary I, Elizabeth I, Charles II, James II, Mary II, Anne, George III, George IV, William IV, Victoria, Edward VII, George V, Elizabeth II.
The following 15 Prime Ministers (see separate section for details): Earl of Chatham, Duke of Grafton, Lord North, William Pitt, Henry Addington, Spencer Perceval, George Canning, Viscount Goderich, Viscount Melbourne, Lord John Russell, Benjamin Disraeli, Earl of Rosebery, Earl Attlee, Harold Macmillan, Lord Home of the Hirsel.

Thomas à Becket (1118–70); Geoffrey Chaucer (*c.* 1340–1400); Sir Thomas More (1478–1535); Thomas Cromwell, Earl of Essex (*c.* 1485–1540); Edmund Spenser (1552–99); Sir Francis Walsingham (*c.* 1530–1590); Francis Bacon (1561–1626); Ben Jonson (1572–1637); Inigo Jones (1573–1652); Earl of Stafford, Thomas Wentworth (1593–1641); John Hampden (*c.* 1595–1643).

Sir Thomas Browne (1605–82); John Milton (1608–74); Samuel Pepys (1633–1703); William Penn (1644–1718); Edmond Halley (1656–1742); Henry Purcell (*c.* 1658–1695); Daniel Defoe (1660–1731); Viscount Bolingbroke (1678–1751); Alexander Pope (1688–1744); Earl of Chesterfield (1694–1773).

Thomas Gray (1716–71); Horace Walpole (1717–1797); Richard Howe (1726–99); Edward Gibbon (1737–94); Charles James Fox (1749–1806); John Nash (1752–1835); Joseph Turner (1775–1851); Sir Charles Napier (1782–1853); Viscount Stratford de

Redcliffe (1786–1880); George Gordon, Lord Byron (1788–1824); Michael Faraday (1791–1867); John Keats (1795–1821); Thomas Hood (1799–1855).

John Stuart Mill (1806–73); Robert Browning (1812–89); Anthony Trollope (1815–82); George F. Watts (1817–1904); John Ruskin (1819–1900); Lord Lister (1827–1912); Dante Gabriel Rossetti (1828–82); William Morris (1834–1896); Sir William Gilbert (1836–1911); Algernon Charles Swinburne (1837–1909); Sir Arthur Sullivan (1842–1900); Lord Baden-Powell (1857–1941); Marquess of Reading (1860–1935); Gerard Manley Hopkins (1844–1889); H G Wells (1866–1946); John Galsworthy (1867–1933); Sir Max Beerbohm (1873–1956); G K Chesterton (1874–1936); Virginia Woolf (1882–1941); Sir Charles Chaplin (b. 1889); Evelyn Waugh (1903–1966).

GREATER MANCHESTER

First recorded use of name and derivation: AD 923 *Mameceaster*, first element reduced from the Old British *Mamucion* to which was added the Old English *ceaster*, a camp.
Area: 318 560 acres *128 917 ha*.
Population: 2 684 100.
Density: 8·43 per acre *20,82 per ha*.
Administrative HQ: County Hall, Piccadilly Gardens, Manchester.
Highest point above sea-level: Featherbed Moss 1774 ft *540 m*.

Road lengths:	miles	km
motorway	77	123,9
trunk	70	112,6
principal	440	708
classified	500	804,5
others	3380	5438,4

Schools and colleges: Nursery 54; Primary 1242; Middle 15; Secondary 262; Special 107; Establishments of further education 29; Polytechnic 1.
Places of interest: Foxdenton Hall; Chethams Hospital School and Library; Manchester: Cathedral, City Art Gallery; Haigh Hall; Peel Tower; Holcombe Village; Manchester Ship Canal.
County worthies by birth: Samuel Crompton (1753–1827); Sir Robert Peel (1788–1850); William Harrison Ainsworth (1805–1882); John Bright (1811–89); James Prescott Jowle (1818–89); Emmeline Pankhurst (1858–1928); 1st Earl Lloyd-George of Dwyfor (1863–1945); L. S Lowry (1887–1976); Gracie Fields (b. 1898); Sir William Walton (b. 1902).

GWENT

First recorded use of name and derivation: The name of an ancient province dating from 5th century.
Area: 339 933 acres *137 566 ha*.
Population: 439 600.
Density: 1·29 per acre *3,20 per ha*.
Administrative HQ: County Hall, Cwmbran.
Highest point above sea-level: Chwarel-y-Fan. 2228 ft *679 m*.

Road lengths:	miles	km
motorway	19	30,6
trunk	88	141,6
principal	133	214
other	560	901

Schools and colleges: Nursery 19; Primary 294; Secondary 40; Special 9; Colleges of further education 8; College of education 1.
Places of interest: Tintern Abbey; Caldicot Castle; Caerleon (Roman remains);

Chepstow Castle; Wye Valley; Raglan Castle.
County worthies by birth: Henry V (1387–1422); Bertrand Russell (1872–1970).

GWYNEDD

CADERNID · GWYNEDD

First recorded use of name and derivation: The name of an ancient province dating from the 5th century.
Area: 955 244 acres *386 574 ha*.
Population: 225 100.
Density: 0·24 per acre *0,58 per ha*.
Administrative HQ: County Offices, Caernarfon (formerly spelt Caernarvon).
Highest point above sea-level: Snowdon. 3560 ft *1085 m*.

Road lengths:	miles	km
trunk	205	329,8
principal	257	413,5
classified	1192	1917,9
unclassified	1244	2001,6

Schools and colleges: Primary 206; Secondary 24; Special 8; Establishments of further education 4.
Places of interest: Harlech Castle; Beaumaris Castle; Caernarfon Castle; Conwy (Conway) Castle; Snowdonia National Park; Bryn Celli Dhu; Portmeirion; Lloyd George Memorial and Museum, Llanystumdwy.
County worthies by birth: Edward I (1284–1327); Lewis Morris (1700–65); Goronwy Owen (1723–69); Sir Hugh Owen (1804–81); T E Lawrence (1888–1935).

HAMPSHIRE

First recorded use of name and derivation: AD 755 (Hamtunscir), the shire around Hamtun (*ham*, a meadow; *tun* a homestead).
Area: 934 474 acres *378 169 ha*.
Population: 1 456 100.
Density: 1.56 per acre *3,85 per ha*.
Administrative HQ: The Castle, Winchester.
Highest point above sea-level: Pilot Hill 937 ft *285 m*.

Road lengths:	miles	km
motorway	25	40,2
trunk	151	243
principal	474	762,7
classified	1558	2506,8
unclassified	1244	2001,6

Schools and colleges: Nursery 4; Primary 596; Secondary 125; Special 49; Colleges of further education 14; Polytechnic 1.
Places of interest: Winchester Cathedral; Beaulieu Palace House and Motor Museum; New Forest; Ocean Terminal, Southampton; Portsmouth dockyard (with HMS Victory).
County worthies by birth: Henry III (1207–72); William of Wykeham (1324–1404);

Gilbert White (1720–93); Jane Austen 1775–1817); Viscount Palmerston (1784–1865); Isambard Kingdom Brunel (1806–59); Charles Dickens (1829–1870); Sir John Everett Millais (1829–1896); Admiral Lord Jellicoe (1859–1935).

HEREFORD AND WORCESTER

First recorded use of name and derivation: AD *c.* 1038 Hereford, *herepaeth*, military road, meaning ford, a river crossing and AD 889 *Uuegorna ceastre*, the fort (Latin caester) of the Weogoran tribe, probably named from the Wyre Forest.
Area: 970 203 acres *392 628 ha*.
Population: 594 200.
Density: 0·61 per acre *1,51 per ha*.
Administrative HQ: Shire Hall, Worcester
Highest point above sea-level: In Black Mountains 2306 ft *702 m*.

Road lengths:	miles	km
motorway	60	96,5
trunk	148	238,1
principal	452	727,3
other	3415	5494,7

Schools and colleges: Nursery 1; Primary 316; Middle 37; Secondary 52; Special 16; Sixth form college 1; Colleges of further eudcation 10; Colleges of education 3.
Places of interest: Offa's Dyke; Hereford Cathedral; Worcester Cathedral; Weobley; Malvern Priory; Pershore Abbey; Dinmore Manor; Symond's Yat and Wye Valley.
County worthies by birth: Richard Hakluyt (1553–1616); Robert Devereux, Earl of Essex (1567–1601); Samuel Butler (1612–80); David Garrick (1717–79); Sir Rowland Hill (1795–1879); Sir Edward Elgar (1857–1934); A E Housman (1859–1936); Stanley Baldwin (1867–1947).

HERTFORDSHIRE

TRUST AND FEAR NOT

First recorded use of name and derivation: AD 866 (Heortfordscir), the river crossing (ford) of the stags (harts).
Area: 403 797 acres *163 411 ha*.
Population: 937 300.
Density: 2·32 per acre *5,74 per ha*.
Administrative HQ: County Hall, Hertford.
Highest point above sea-level: Hastoe 802 ft *244 m*.

Road lengths:	miles	km
motorway	35	56
trunk	106	171
principal	210	338
other	2213	3561

Schools and colleges: Nursery 17; Primary 488; Middle 11; Secondary 107; Special 35; Further education establishments 14; Polytechnic 1.
Places of interest: St Albans Cathedral, Roman remains of Verulamium (now at St Albans); Hatfield House; Knebworth House; Salisbury Hall.

County worthies by birth: Nicholas Breakspear (Pope Adrian IV) (1100–1159); Sir Henry Bessemer (1813–1898); Henry Manning (1808–1892); Queen Elizabeth, the Queen Mother (b. 1900–); Third Marquess of Salisbury (1830–1903); William Cowper (1731–1800); Cecil Rhodes (1853–1902); Sir Richard Fanshawe (1608–1666).

HIGHLAND REGION

First recorded use of name and derivation: *c.* 1425 (implied in *hielandman*) from adjective *high*, noun *land*.
Area: 6 280 320 acres *2 541 558 ha.*
Population: 186 460.
Density: 0·03 per acre *0,07 per ha.*
Administrative HQ: Regional Buildings, Glenurquhart Road, Inverness. Regional Council meets at County Buildings, Dingwall.
Highest point above sea-level: Ben Nevis 4406 ft *1342 m.*
Districts (with population): Badenoch and Strathspey 9297; Caithness 29 442; Inverness 55 045; Lochaber 19 601; Nairn 9633; Ross and Cromarty 42 031; Skye and Lochalsh 9777; Sutherland 11 634.

Road lengths:	miles	km
trunk	495	796,5
classified	2407	3872,9
other	1422	2288

Schools and colleges: Primary 210; Secondary 32; Special 7; Establishments of further education 3.
Places of interest: St Mary's Chapel (Forse Thurso); Dunbeath Castle; Site of John O'Groat's House (Pentland Firth); Girnigoe Castle; Castle of Mey; Glencoe: Callanish Stones; Reay Forest; Cape Wrath; Dunrobin Castle; Dun Dornadilla; Culloden Battlefield; Glenfinnan Monument (raising of Prince Charles Stewart's standard); Loch Ness; Eilean Donan Castle.
County worthies by birth: Hugh Mackay (1640–92); Simon Fraser, Lord Lovat (1676–1747); Duncan Forbes (1685–1746); Gen Arthur St Clair (1734–1818); Sir Alexander Mackenzie (1755–1820); Hugh Miller (1802–56); Alexander Bain (1810–77); Sir Hector MacDonald (1853–1903).

HUMBERSIDE

First recorded use of name and derivation: AD *c.* 730 *humbri*, the British river name, side.
Area: 867 784 acres *351 180 ha.*
Population: 848 600.
Density: 0·98 per acre *2,42 per ha.*
Administrative HQ: Kingston House South, Bond St, Kingston-upon-Hull.
Highest point above sea-level: Cot Nab 808 ft *246 m.*

Road lengths:	miles	km
motorway	12	19,3
trunk	94	151,2
principal	295	474,7
classified	1132	1821,4
unclassified	1879	3023,3

Schools and colleges: Nursery 9; Primary 355; Middle and secondary 142; Special 20; Colleges of further education 8; College of education 1.
Places of interest: Kingston upon Hull: Trinity House, Wilberforce House, Trinity Church, Mortimer Museum; Beverley Minster; Thornton Abbey.
County worthies by birth: Andrew Marvell (1621–78); John (1703–1791) and Charles (1707–1788) Wesley; William Wilberforce (1759–1833); Amy Johnson (1903–41); John Fisher (*c.* 1469–1535).

ISLE OF WIGHT

First recorded use of name and derivation: The Celtic name Ynys-yr-Wyth, from which the Romans derived Vectis predates the Roman conquest.
Area: 94 146 acres *38 100 ha.*
Population: 111 900.
Density: 1·18 per acre *2,92 per ha.*
Administrative HQ: County Hall, Newport
Highest point above sea-level: St Boniface Down 785 ft *239 m.*

Road lengths:	miles	km
trunk	nil	nil
principal	76	122,3
classified	156	251
unclassified	212	341,1

Schools and colleges: Primary 47; Middle 16; Secondary 5; Special 2; College of further education 1.
Places of interest: Osborne House; Carisbrooke Castle; Brading (Roman Villa); Royal Yacht Squadron at Cowes.
County worthies by birth: Sir Thomas Fleming (1544–1613); Dr Thomas James (1580–1629); Robert Hooke (1635–1703); Dr Thomas Arnold (1795–1842).

KENT

First recorded use of name and derivation: *c.* 308 BC Celtic *canto*, a rim or coastal area.
Area: 921 665 acres *372 985 ha.*
Population: 1 448 100.
Density: 1·57 per acre *3,88 per ha.*
Administrative: HQ: County Hall, Maidstone.
Highest point above sea-level: Betsom's Hill, Westerham 824 ft *251 m.*

Road lengths:	miles	km
motorway	43	69,2
trunk	141	226,9
principal	448	720,8
others	4490	7224,4

Schools and colleges: Nursery 1; Primary 617; Middle 4; Secondary 151; Special 37; Colleges of further education 11; College of education 2.
Places of interest: Canterbury Cathedral; Dover Cliffs; Pilgrim's Way; North Downs: Knole; Penshurst Place; Deal Castle; Chartwell; Rochester Castle and Cathedral; Leeds Castle.
County worthies by birth: Christopher Marlow (1564–93); Sir William Jenner (1815–98); Sir William Harvey (1578–1657); Robert Bridges (1844–1930); General James Wolfe (1727–59); William Caxton (*c.* 1422–91); Edward Richard George Heath (b. 1916); William Hazlitt (1778–1830).

LANCASHIRE

First recorded use of name and derivation: the shire around *Lancastre* AD 1087; camp, *(castrum)* on the River Lune.
Area: 753 689 acres *305 007 ha.*
Population: 1 375 500.
Density: 1·82 per acre *4,51 per ha.*
Administrative HQ: County Hall, Preston.
Highest point above sea-level: Greygarth Hill 2058 ft *627 m.*

Road lengths:	miles	km
motorway	84	135
trunk	165	265
principal	314	505
classified	1094	1761
unclassified	2732	4936

Schools and colleges: Nursery 38; Primary 698; Secondary 125; Special 48; Establishments of further education 19; Polytechnic 1.

Places of interest: Blackpool Tower; Gawthorpe Hall; Lancaster Castle; Browsholme Hall.
County worthies by birth: Sir Richard Arkwright (1732–92); James Hargreaves (?1745–78); Sir Ambrose Fleming (1849–1945).

LEICESTERSHIRE

First recorded use of name and derivation: 1087 (Laegreceastrescir) from the camp (*castra*) of the *Ligore*, dwellers on the River Legra (now the R Soar).
Area: 641 460 acres *259 590 ha.*
Population: 837 900.
Density: 1·31 per acre *3,23 per ha.*
Administrative HQ: County Hall, Glenfield, Leicester.
Highest point above sea-level: Bardon Hill 912 ft *277 m.*

Road lengths:	miles	km
motorway	42	67
trunk	129	207
principal	250	403
classified	1014	1732
unclassified	1635	2630

Schools and colleges: Nursery 1; Primary 378; Secondary 86; Sixth form colleges 4; Special 21; Colleges of further education 7; other colleges 3; Polytechnic 1.
Places of interest: Belvoir Castle; Ashby-de-la-Zouche Castle; Kirby Muxloe Castle; Stanford Hall.
County worthies by birth: Queen Jane (1537–54); George Fox (1624–91); Thomas Babbington Macauley (1800–59); George Villiers, Duke of Buckingham (1592–1628); Hugh Latimer (?*c.* 1487–1555); Titus Oates (1649–1705).

LINCOLNSHIRE

First recorded use of name and derivation: 1016 (Lincolnescire), a colony (*colonia*) by the *lindum* (a widening in the river, i.e. River Witham).
Area: 1 454 273 acres *588 524 ha.*
Population: 524 500
Density: 0·36 per acre *0,89 per ha.*
Administrative HQ: County Offices, Lincoln.
Highest point above sea-level: Normanby-le-Wold 548 ft *167 m.*

Road lenghts:	miles	km
motorway	nil	nil
trunk	209	337
principal	543	874
other	4498	7237

Schools and colleges: Nursery 6; Primary 361; Secondary 71; Special 21; Establishments of further education 9.
Places of interest: Lincoln Cathedral; Tattershall Castle; Church of St Botolph, Boston; Lincoln Castle.
County worthies by birth: Henry IV (1366–1413); John Foxe (1516–87); William Cecil, Lord Burghley (1520–1598); Sir Isaac Newton (1642-1727) Sir John Franklin (1786–1847); Alfred, Lord Tennyson (1809–92).

LOTHIAN

First recorded use of name and derivation: *c.* AD 970 from personal name, possibly a Welsh derivative of Laudinus.
Area: 433 920 acres *175 601 ha.*
Population: 755 293.
Density: 1·74 per acre *4,29 per ha.*

Administrative HQ: Regional Headquarters, George IV Bridge, Edinburgh.
Highest point above sea-level: Blackhope Scar 2137 ft *651 m.*
Length of coastline: 63 miles *101 km.*
Districts (with population): East Lothian 79 010; Edinburgh (city) 469 097; Midlothian 84 882; West Lothian 124 304.

Road lengths:	miles	km
motorway	30	*48,3*
trunk	64	*103*
principal	259	*416,7*
other	1636	*2732,3*

Schools and colleges: Nursery 36; Primary 235; Secondary 45; Special 20; Establishments of further education 6.
Places of interest: Dunbar Castle; Tantallon Castle (ruins); Muirfield Golf Centre (Gullane); Aberlady (bird sanctuary); Rosslyn chapel; Borthwick Castle; Newbattle Abbey; Dalkeith Palace; Edinburgh Castle; St Giles Cathedral; Cricktown Castle; Palace of Holyrood House; Craigmillar Castle; Linlithgow Palace; Dundas Castle; The Binns (near Queensferry); Torpichen Church; Hopetoun House; The Forth Bridges.
County worthies by birth: John Knox (*c.* 1505–72); John Napier (1550–1617); Sir Walter Scott (1771–1832); James Nasmyth (1808–90); Alexander Melville Bell (1819–1905); Sir Herbert Maxwell (1845–1937); Arthur James Balfour (1848–1930); Robert Louis Stevenson (1850–94); Alexander Graham Bell (1847–1922); Sir Arthur Conan Doyle (1859–1930); Field Marshal Douglas Haig (1861–1928); James VI of Scotland and I of England (1566–1625); Mary, Queen of Scots (1542–1587); James Boswell (1740–1795); David Hume (1711–1776); George Gordon, 4th Earl of Aberdeen (1784–1860).

MERSEYSIDE

First recorded use of name and derivation: AD 1002 *Maerse* from Old English *Maeres-ea* boundary river (between Mercia and Northumbria).
Area: 160 000 acres *64 750 ha.*
Population: 1 578 000
Density: 9·87 per acre *24,37 per ha.*
Administrative HQ: Metropolitan House, Old Hall St, Liverpool.
Highest point above sea-level: Billinge Hill 588 ft *179 m.*
Length of coastline: 56 miles *93 km.*

Road lengths:	miles	km
motorway	35	*56,6*
trunk	54	*87,2*
principal	202	*324,8*
others	2219	*3569,6*

Schools and colleges: Nursery 14; Primary 706; Combined 10; Middle 47; Secondary 172; Special 73; Colleges of further education 20; other colleges 4; Polytechnic 1.
Places of interest: Liverpool: Roman Catholic Cathedral and Anglican Cathedral, Speke Hall, Walker Art Gallery. Knowsley Safari Park; Ainsdale Nature Reserve.
County worthies by birth: George Stubbs (1724–1806); William Ewart Gladstone (1809–98); 1st Earl of Birkenhead (1872–1930); Edward Stanley, 14th Earl of Derby (1799–1869); Sir Thomas Beecham (1879–1961).

MID-GLAMORGAN

First recorded use of name and derivation: 1242 (Gwlad Morgan) the terrain of Morgan, a 10th century Welsh Prince.
Area: 251 732 acres *101 872 ha.*

Population: 540 400.
Density: 2·15 per acre *5,30 per ha.*
Administrative HQ: County Hall, Cathays Park, Cardiff, South Glamorgan (ie outside the county).
Highest point above sea-level: Near Craig-y-Llyn *c.* 1920 ft *585 m.*

Road lengths:	miles	km
motorway and trunk	54	*87*
principal	176·8	*284,5*
others	1385	*2228,4*

Schools and colleges: Nursery 21; Primary 318; Secondary 47; Special 11; Colleges of further education 6; Polytechnic 1.
Places of interest: Ewenny Priory; Caerphilly Castle.
County worthies by birth: Richard Price (1723–1791).

NORFOLK

First recorded use of name and derivation: AD 1043 (Norfolk), the territory of the *nor* (northern) *folk* (people) of East Anglia.
Area: 1 323 174 acres *535 470 ha.*
Population: 662 500.
Density: 0·50 per acre *1,24 per ha.*
Administrative HQ: County Hall, Martineau Lane, Norwich.
Highest point above sea-level: Sandy Lane, east of Sheringham 335 ft *102 m.*

Road lengths:	miles	km
trunk	132	*212,2*
principal	430	*692,2*
others	4758	*7655,4*

Schools and colleges: Nursery 4; Primary and middle 462; Secondary 70; Special 17; Colleges of further education 6.
Places of interest: The Broads; Sandringham House; Blickling Hall; Holkham Hall; Breckland; Scolt Head; Norwich Cathedral; The Castle, Norwich; Maddermarket Theatre, Norwich; Castle Acre; Grimes Graves.
County worthies by birth: Sir Edward Coke (1552–1634); 2nd Viscount Townshend (1674–1738); Sir Robert Walpole (1676–1745); Thomas Paine (1737–1809); Fanny Burney (1752–1840); 1st Viscount Nelson (1758–1805); Elizabeth Fry (1780–1845); George Borrow (1803–81); 1st Earl of Cromer (1841–1917); Edith Cavell (1865–1915); George VI (1895–1952).

NORTHAMPTONSHIRE

First recorded use of name and derivation: *c.* AD 1011 (Hamtumscir) [see Hampshire], the northern homestead.
Area: 585 009 acres *236 745 ha.*
Population: 505 900.
Density: 0·86 per acre *2,14 per ha.*
Administrative HQ: County Hall, Northampton.

Highest point above sea-level: Arbury Hill, 734 ft *223 m.*

Road lengths:	miles	km
motorway	28	*45,1*
trunk	133	*214*
principal	226	*363,6*
other	1781	*2865,6*

Schools and colleges: Nursery 9; Primary 271; Middle 20; Secondary 44; Special 34; Establishments of further education 7.
Places of interest: Earls Barton Church; Sulgrave Manor; Fotheringhay; Brixworth Church.
County worthies by birth: Richard III 1452–85); John Dryden (1631–1700); Christopher Hatton (1540–91).

NORTHUMBERLAND

First recorded use of name and derivation: AD 895 (Norohymbraland), the land to the north of the Humber.
Area: 1 243 466 acres *503 213 ha.*
Population: 287 900.
Density: 0·23 per acre *0,57 per ha.*
Administrative HQ: County Hall, Newcastle-upon-Tyne (ie outside the county) The traditional county town is Alnwick.
Highest point above sea-level: The Cheviot 2676 ft *815 m.*

Road lengths:	miles	km
trunk	134	*215,6*
principal	221	*355,6*
classified	1295	*2083,7*
unclassified	1318	*2120,7*

Schools and colleges: Primary/First 163; Middle 36; Secondary 23; Special 12; Establishments of further education 4.
Places of interest: Hadrian's Wall, Lindisfarne Priory; Alnwick Castle; Warkworth Castle; Hexham Abbey; Tynemouth Priory; Bamburgh Castle; Norham Castle; Chillingham Castle (wild cattle).
County worthies by birth: Lancelot ('Capability') Brown (1715–83); 2nd Earl Grey (1764–1845); George Stephenson (1781–1848); Grace Darling (1815–42); Robert ('Bobby') Charlton (b. 1937).

NORTH YORKSHIRE

First recorded use of name and derivation: *c.* AD 150 Ebórakon (Ptolemy); AD 1050 *Eoferwiscir*, land possessed by Eburos.
Area: 2 055 000 acres *831 630 ha.*
Population: 653 000.
Density: 0·32 per acre *0,79 per ha.*
Administrative HQ: County Hall, Northallerton.
Highest point above sea-level: Whernside 2419 ft *737 m.*

Road lengths:	miles	km
motorway	6½	*10,3*
trunk	237	*381,3*
principal	432	*695,1*
classified	2169	*3489,9*
unclassified	2953	*4751,4*

Schools and colleges: Nursery 5; Primary 442; Secondary 68; Special 17; Establishments of further education 13.
Places of interest: Richmond Castle; Scarborough Castle; City of York (the Minster and the Five Sisters Windows); Byland Abbey; Castle Howard; Rievaulx Abbey; Fountains Abbey; Bolton Priory (ruins); Ripon Cathedral; The Dales; North Yorkshire Moors; Selby Abbey.
County worthies by birth: Alcuin (735–804); Henry I (1068–1135); John Wycliffe (*c.* 1320–84); Roger Ascham (1515–1568); Guy Fawkes (1570–1606); Thomas Fairfax (1612–1671); John Flaxman (1755–1826); William Etty (1787–1849); William Stubbs

(1825–1901); Sir William Harcourt (1827–1904); Frederick, Lord Leighton (1830–78); Edith Sitwell (1887–1964); Wystan Hugh Auden (1907–73).

NOTTINGHAMSHIRE

First recorded use of name and derivation: 1016 (Snotingahamscir), the shire around the dwelling (ham) of the followers of Snot, a Norseman.
Area: 546 637 acres *221 216 ha.*
Population: 977 500.
Density: 1·79 per acre *4,42 per ha.*
Administrative HQ: County Hall, West Bridgford, Nottingham.
Highest point above sea-level: Herrod's Hill, 652 ft *198 m.*

Road lengths:	miles	km
motorway	9½	15
trunk	134	216
principal	293	472
other	2164	3482

Schools and colleges: Nursery 8; Primary 462; Secondary 104; Special 28; Further education establishments 13; Polytechnic 1.
Places of interest: Southwell Cathedral; Sherwood Forest; The Dukeries; Wollaton Hall; Newstead Abbey.
County worthies by birth: Thomas Cranmer (1489–1556); Edmund Cartwright (1743–1823); Richard Bonington (1801–28); Gen William Booth (1829–1912); Samuel Butler (1835–1902); D H Lawrence (1885–1930).

ORKNEY

First recorded use of name and derivation: *c.* 308 BC as Orkas (Pytheas) from Norse ork, a whale; old Norse-ay, island.
Area: 240 848 acres *97 468 ha.* Consists of 54 islands.
Population: 17 748
Density: 0·07 per acre *0,18 per ha.*
Administrative HQ: County Offices, Kirkwall.
Highest point above sea level: Ward Hill, Hoy 1570 ft *478 m.*

Road lengths:	miles	km
classified	325	522,9
unclassified	243	391

Schools and colleges: Primary 24; Junior secondary 5; secondary 2; Special 1; College of further education 1.
Places of interest: Noltlandcastle (ruins); the underground village of Skara Brae; the stone circle at Brogar; Old Man of Hoy; Kirkwall Cathedral; Scapa Flow.
County worthies by birth: John Rae (1813–1893); Sir Robert Strange (1721–1792)

OXFORDSHIRE

First recorded use of name and derivation: AD 1010 (Oxnfordscir), the shire around Oxford (a river ford for oxen). The town (city) was first recorded (as Osnaforda) in AD 912.
Area: 645 314 acres *261 150 ha.*

Population: 541 800.
Density: 0·84 per acre *2,07 per ha.*
Administrative HQ: County Hall, New Road, Oxford.
Highest point above sea-level: White Horse Hill, 856 ft *260 m.*

Road lengths:	miles	km
motorway	9	14,5
trunk	154	247,8
principal	237	381,3
classified	909	1462,6
unclassified	1088	1750,6

Schools and colleges: Nursery 14; First/Primary 272; Middle 15; Secondary 42; Special 12; Colleges of further education 6; Polytechnic 1.
Places of interest: Oxford University; Blenheim Palace, nr Woodstock; Rollright Stones; Broughton Castle; Radcliffe Camera; Bodleian Library, Oxford; Christ Church Cathedral, Oxford; Iffley Road running track; White Horse of Uffington.
County worthies by birth: Alfred (849–99); St Edward the Confessor (*c.* 1004–1066); Richard I (1157–99); John (1167–1216); Sir William D'Avenant (1606–68); Warren Hastings (1732–1818); Lord Randolph Churchill (1849–95); Sir Winston Churchill (1874–1965); William Morris, 1st Viscount Nuffield (1877–1963).

POWYS

First recorded use of name and derivation: The name of an ancient province probably dating from *c.* 5th century AD.
Area: 1 254 656 acres *507 742 ha.*
Population: 101 500.
Density: 0·08 per acre *0,20 per ha.*
Administrative HQ: County Hall, Llandrindod Wells.
Highest point above sea-level: Pen-y-Fan (Cadet Arthur) 2907 ft *885 m.*

Road lengths:	miles	km
trunk	268	431,2
principal	153	246,2
classified	1600	2574,4
unclassified	1490	2397,4

Schools and colleges: Nursery 3; Primary 234; Middle 2; Secondary 45; Special 10; Colleges of further education 6; College of education 1.
Places of interest: Brecon Beacons; Elan Valley Reservoirs; Brecon Cathedral; Powis Castle and gardens; Lake Vyrnwy; Montgomery Castle; Gregynog Hall.
County worthies by birth: Owain Glyndŵr (*c.* 1354–*fl* 1416); George Herbert (1593–1633); Robert Owen (1771–1858).

SALOP

First recorded use of name and derivation: AD 1094 *Salopesberia,* a Norman-French version of Scrobbesbyrig or Shrewsbury.
Area: 862 479 acres *349 033 ha.*
Population: 359 000.
Density: 0·42 per acre *1,03 per ha.*

Administrative HQ: Shire Hall, Abbey Foregate, Shrewsbury.
Highest point above sea-level: Brown Clee Hill 1790 ft *545 m.*

Road lengths:	miles	km
trunk	158	254,2
principal	254	408,7
classified	1509	2428
unclassified	1504	2419,9

Schools and colleges: Primary 136; Secondary 12; Special 4; Colleges of further education 3.
Places of interest: Offa's Dyke; Ludlow Castle; Shrewsbury Abbey and Castle; Stokesay Castle; Coalbrookdale and Ironbridge; The Wrekin; Candover Hall; Hodnet Hall.
County worthies by birth: Lord Clive of Plassey (1725–74); Charles Darwin (1809–82); Capt Matthew Webb (1848–83); Mary Webb (1881–1927).

SHETLAND

First recorded use of name and derivation: 1289, land of Hjalto (Old Norse personal name c.f. Scots, Sholto) or hilt-shaped land.
Area: 352 337 acres *142 586 ha.* Consists of 117 islands.
Population: 18 962.
Density: 0·05 per acre *0,13 per ha.*
Administrative HQ: Town Hall, Lerwick.
Highest point above sea-level: Ronas Hill, Mainland, 1475 ft *449 m.*

Road lengths:	miles	km
classified	341	548,7
unclassified	182	292,8

Schools and colleges: Primary 33; Secondary 8; College of further education 1.
Places of interest: Scalloway Castle; Jarlshof; Broch of Mousa; Broch of Clickimin; St Ninian's Isle; Lerwick Museum; Muckle Flagga lighthouse.
County worthies by birth: Arthur Anderson (1792–1868); Sir Robert Stout (1844–1930).

SOMERSET

First recorded use of name and derivation: AD 1015 *Sumaersaeton,* the land of the dwellers (Saete) dependent on Sumerton (a summer-only settlement).
Area: 854 488 acres *345 799 ha.*
Population: 404 400.
Density: 0·47 per acre *0,17 per ha.*
Administrative HQ: County Hall, Taunton
Highest point above sea-level: Dunkery Beacon 1705 ft *519 m.*

Road lengths:	miles	km
motorway	29	46,7
trunk	96	154,5
principal	355	571,2
classified	1566	2519,7
unclassified	1818	2925,2

Schools and colleges: Nursery 2; Primary 225; Middle 9; Secondary 32; Special 9; Colleges of further education 5; other colleges 7.
Places of interest: Cheddar Gorge; Wookey Hole; Wells Cathedral; Exmoor National Park; Glastonbury Abbey (ruins).
County worthies by birth: St Dunstan (*c.* 925–988); Roger Bacon (1214–94); John Pym (1584–1643); Robert Blake (1599–1657); Henry Fielding (1707–54); Sir Henry Irving (1838–1905); John Hanning Speke (1827–1864).

SOUTH GLAMORGAN

First recorded use of name and derivation: 1242 (Gwlad Morgan) the terrain of

Morgan, a 10th century Welsh Prince.
Area: 102 807 acres *41 605 ha.*
Population: 389 200.
Density: 3·79 per acre *9,35 per ha.*
Administrative HQ: County offices, Newport, Road, Cardiff.
Highest point above sea-level: Near Lisvane 866 ft *264 m.*

Road lengths:

	miles	km
motorway and trunk	22	35,4
principal	67	107,8
classified	246	395,8
unclassified	585	941,3

Schools and colleges: Nursery 12; Primary 171; Secondary 29; Special 18; Establishments of further education 4.
Places of interest: Cardiff Castle; St Fagan's Castle (Welsh Folk Museum); St Donat's Castle; Llandaff Cathedral.

SOUTH YORKSHIRE

First recorded use of name and derivation: *c.* AD 150 Ebórakon (Ptolemy). 1050 (Eoferwiscir), land possessed by Eburos.
Area: 385 610 acres *156 051 ha.*
Population: 1 318 300.
Density: 3·42 per acre *8,45 per ha.*
Administrative HQ: County Hall, Barnsley.
Highest point above sea-level: Margery Hill, 1793 ft *546 m.*

Road lengths:

	miles	km
motorway	58	94
trunk	83	134
classified	795	1279
unclassified	2040	3282

Schools and colleges: Nursery 72; Primary /Infants 556; Middle 81; Secondary 101; Special 40; Sixth form College 1; Establishments of further education 17; Polytechnic 1.
Places of interest: Sheffield: Cathedral Church of ss Peter and Paul; Cutler's Hall; Conisbrough Castle; Roche Abbey (ruins).
County worthies by birth: Thomas Osborne, Earl of Danby (1631–1712); Gordon Banks (b. 1938).

STAFFORDSHIRE

First recorded use of name and derivation: 1016 (Staeffordscir), the shire around a ford by a *staeth* or landing place.
Area: 671 184 acres *271 618 ha*
Population: 997 600.
Density: 1·49 per acre *3,67 per ha.*
Administrative HQ: County Buildings, Stafford.
Highest point above sea-level: Oliver Hill, 1684 ft *513 m.*

Road lengths:

	miles	km
motorway	51	82,1
trunk	171	275,1
principal	335	539
classified	1058	1702,3
unclassified	1978	3182,6

Schools and colleges: Nursery 26; Primary /Infants 450; Middle/Infants 46; Middle 36; Secondary 110; Sixth form college 1; Special 31; Establishments of further education 15; Polytechnic 1.
Places of interest: Lichfield Cathedral; Croxden Abbey; Cannock Chase; Alton Towers; Blithfield Hall; Tamworth Castle; Sandon Hall; Shugborough; Trentham Gardens.
County worthies by birth: Isaak Walton (1593–1683); Dr Samuel Johnson (1709–84); Josiah Wedgwood (1730–95); Admiral Earl of St Vincent (1735–1823); Arnold Bennett (1867–1931); Havergal Brian (1876–1972).

STRATHCLYDE

First recorded use of name and derivation: *c.* AD 85 Clota, the river (per Tacitus) AD 875 Straecled Wenla cyning.
Area: 3 422 520 acres *1 385 046 ha.*
Population: 2 488 643
Density: 0·73 per acre *1,81 per ha.*
Administrative HQ: Melrose House, Cadogan St, Glasgow.
Highest point above sea-level: Bidean nam Bian 3766 ft *1147 m.*
Districts (with population): Argyll and Bute 65 615; Bearsden Milngavie 38 022; Clydebank 55 902; Cumbernauld 56 268; Cumnock and Doon Valley 47 638; Cunninghame 133 296; Dumbarton 80 934; East Kilbride 83 441; Eastwood 50 598; Glasgow (city) 856 012; Hamilton 107 178; Inverclyde 104 116; Kilmarnock and Loudoun 82 520; Kyle and Carrick 112 458; Lanark 55 049; Monklands 107 561; Motherwell 161 104; Renfrew 209 476; Strathkelvin 81 455.

Road lengths:

	miles	km
motorway	47	75,6
trunk	454	730,5
other	7380	11 874,4

Schools and colleges: Nursery (no figure for nursery schools alone) nursery schools and classes 108 (of which the majority is probably classes rather than schools; Primary 945; Secondary 185; Special 115; Establishments of further education 22.
Places of interest: Fingal's Cave (in the island of Staffa); Iona: Loch Lomond; Dumbarton Rock and Castle; Newark Castle; Pollock House (Pollockshaws); Glasgow Cathedral; St Kentigern's Church (Lanark); Bothwell Castle (ruins); Culzean Castle (National Trust for Scotland); Burns' Cottage and Museum (Alloway); Inveraray Castle; Argyll National Forest Park; Brodick Castle.
County worthies by birth: Colin MacLaurin (1698–1746); James Watt (1736–1819); John Boyd Dunlop (1840–1921); James Chalmers (1841–1901); John Logie Baird (1888–1946); Robert Burns (1759–1796); Sir William Wallace (1270–1305); David Livingstone (1813–1873); Sir Alexander Fleming (1881–1955).

SUFFOLK

First recorded use of name and derivation: AD 895 (Suthfolchi), the territory of the southern folk (of East Anglia).
Area: 940 800 acres *380 729 ha.*
Population: 577 600.
Density: 0·61 per acre *1,52 per ha.*
Administrative HQ: County Hall, Ipswich (some depts. at County Hall, Bury St Edmonds).
Highest point above sea-level: Rede, 420 ft *128 m.*

Road lengths:

	miles	km
trunk	121	194,7
principal	307	494
classified	1526	2455,3
unclassified	1763	2836,7

Schools and colleges: Nursery 2; Primary 283; Middle 38; Secondary 39; Special 11; Colleges of further education 3.

Places of interest: Flatford Mill and Willy Lott's Cottage; Framlingham Castle; Kyson Hill; Saxtead Green Windmill; Gainsborough's House; Lavenham (Guild Hall, Wool Hall); Long Melford Church; Newmarket; Bury St Edmunds (Abbey ruins) and Cathedral (nave); Ickworth Mansion; The Maltings, Snape.
County worthies by birth: Sir Joseph Hooker (1817–1911); John Constable (1776–1837); Cardinal Thomas Wolsey (*c.* 1475–1530); Edward Fitzgerald (1809–83); Thomas Gainsborough (1727–88); Robert Bloomfield (1766–1823); Benjamin Britten (1913–1976).

SURREY

First recorded use of name and derivation: AD 722 (Suthrige), from the Old English, *suther-gé* or southern district.
Area: 414 922 acres *167 913 ha.*
Population: 1 002 900.
Density: 2·42 per acre *5,97 per ha.*
Administrative HQ: County Hall, Kingston upon Thames (ie outside the county) The traditional county town is Guildford.
Highest point above sea-level: Leith Hill 965 ft *294 m.*

Road lengths:

	miles	km
motorway	52	83,7
trunk	58	93,3
principal	326	524,5
classified	598	962,2
unclassified	1584	2548,7

Schools and colleges: Nursery 6; Primary 284; Middle 116; Secondary 77; Special 43; Colleges of further education 8.
Places of interest: Guildford Cathedral; Waverley Abbey; Royal Horticultural Soc Gardens, Wisley; Box Hill; Polesden Lacey; Losley House.
County worthies by birth: William of Ockham (d. 1349?); Thomas Malthus (1766–1834); Aldous Huxley (1894–1936); Sir Lawrence Olivier (b. 1907); John Evelyn (1620–1706); William Cobbett (1762–1835); Matthew Arnold (1822–1888).

TAYSIDE

First recorded use of name and derivation: *c.* AD 85 *Taus* or *Tanaus* (Tacitus).
Area: 1 894 080 acres *766 507 ha.*
Population: 402 180
Density: 0·21 per acre *0,52 per ha.*
Administrative HQ: Tayside House, Dundee.
Highest point above sea-level: Ben Lawers 3984 ft *1214 m.*
Length of coastline: 76 miles *122 km.*
Districts (with population): Angus 89 700; Dundee 194 420; Perth and Kinross 118 060.

Road lengths:

	miles	km
motorway	13	21,3
trunk	149	240,2
principal	407	654,2
classified	1055	1696,7
unclassified	1166	1876,7

Schools and colleges: Nursery 14; Primary 218; Secondary 33; Special 15; Establishments of further education 4.
Places of interest: Glamis Castle; Arbroath Abbey (ruins); Brechin Cathedral and Round Tower; Scone Palace; Bridge of Dun (near Montrose); Guthrie Castle; Blair Castle; Edzell Castle; Pitlochry Ladder and Fish Dam.
County worthies by birth: Pontius Pilate fl AD 36; Sir James Barrie (1860–1937); John Buchan 1st Baron Tweedsmuir (1875–1940); HRH The Princess Margaret, Countess of Snowdon (b. 1930).

TYNE AND WEAR

First recorded use of name and derivation: *c.* AD 150 Tina (river) (Ptolemy) and *c.* AD 720 Wirus (river) (Bede).
Population: 1 182 900.
Area: 133 390 acres *53 981 ha.*
Density: 8·86 per acre *21,91 per ha.*
Administrative HQ: Sandyford House, Newcastle-upon-Tyne.
Highest point above sea-level: Nr Chopwell 851 ft *259 m.*

Road lengths:	miles	km
motorway	5	8,1
trunk	27	43,4
classified	470	756,2
other	2122	3414,3

Schools and colleges: Nursery 29; Primary 524; Middle 21; Secondary 98; Special 40; Colleges of further education 7; Polytechnics 2.
Places of interest: Church of St Andrew Roker; Monkwearmouth (ruins); Tynemouth Castle; Washington Old Hall.
County worthies by birth: The Venerable Bede (673–735); Admiral (1st) Lord Collingwood (1750–1810); Sir Joseph Swann (1828–1914); Owen Brannigan (1908–1973).

WARWICKSHIRE

First recorded use of name and derivation: 1016 (Waerincwicsir) possibly Old English (*wering*, a weir; *wick*, cattle farm).
Area: 489 405 acres *198 055 ha.*
Population: 471 000.
Density: 0·96 per acre *2,38 per ha.*
Administrative HQ: Shire Hall, Warwick.
Highest point above sea-level: Ilmington Downs 854 ft *260 m.*

Road lengths:	miles	km
motorway	21	33,6
trunk	162	260,4
principal	187	300,7
classified	705	1134,4
unclassified	1023·6	1647,2

Schools and colleges: Nursery 9; Primary 265; Secondary 49; Special 19; Colleges of further education 4; other college 1.
Places of interest: Warwick Castle; Kenilworth Castle; Stratford-upon-Avon; (Shakespeare's birthplace); Compton Wynyates; Charlecote; Coughton Court; Ragley Hall; Arbury Hall.
County worthies by birth: William Shakespeare (1564–1616); Earl of Wilmington (1673–1743); Walter Landor (1775–1864); Richard Cosgrove (1818–99); Marion Evans (George Eliot) (1819–80); Rupert Brooke (1887–1915).

WEST GLAMORGAN

First recorded use of name and derivation: 1242 (Gwlad Morgan) the terrain of Morgan, a 10th century Welsh Prince.
Area: 201 476 acres *81 535 ha.*
Population: 371 900.
Density: 1·84 per acre *4,56 per ha.*
Administrative HQ: Guildhall, Swansea.
Highest point above sea-level: Cefnffordd 1969 ft *600 m.*

Road lengths:	miles	km
motorway	8	12,9
trunk	48	77,2
principal	110	177
classified	187	300,9
unclassified	620	997,6

Schools and colleges: Nursery 8; Primary 205; Secondary 34; Special 7; Colleges of further education 4; other college 1.
Places of interest: Neath Abbey (ruins); Penrice Castle; Gower Peninsula.
County worthies by birth: Dylan Thomas (1914–1953).

WEST MIDLANDS

First recorded use of name and derivation: 1555 mydlande, mid lands (applied to the middle counties of England).
Area: 222 250 acres *89 941 ha.*
Population: 2 743 300.
Density: 12·34 per acre *30,50 per ha.*
Administrative HQ: County Hall, Lancaster Circus, Birmingham.
Highest point above sea-level: Turner's Hill 876 ft *267 m.*

Road lengths:	miles	km
motorway	33	53,1
trunk	65	104,6
principal	330	531
other	3277	5272,7

Schools and colleges: Nursery 65; Primary 1032; Middle 32; Secondary 246; Sixth form college 1; Special 106; Colleges of further education 24; Colleges of education 7; Polytechnics 3.
Places of interest: Dudley Castle; Birmingham: Aston Hall, City Museum and Art Gallery, Museum of Science and Industry; Coventry Cathedral.
County worthies by birth: Sir Edward Burne-Jones (1833–1898); George Cadbury (1839–1922); Sir Henry Newbolt (1862–1938); Neville Chamberlain (1869–1940).

WEST SUSSEX

First recorded use of name and derivation: AD 722 (*Suth, Seaxe*), the territory of the southern Saxons or *suthseaxa*.
Area: 498 321 acres *201 664 ha.*
Population: 623 400.
Density: 1·25 per acre *3,09 per ha.*
Administrative HQ: County Hall, West St, Chichester.
Highest point above sea-level: Blackdown Hill 919 ft *280 m.*

Road lengths:	miles	km
motorway	6	9,7
trunk	63	101,4
principal	297	477,9
classified	697	1121,5
unclassified	1091	1755,4

Schools and colleges: Nursery 4; Primary 219; Middle 20; Secondary 38; Sixth form college 1; Special 13; Colleges of further education 5; other colleges 2.
Places of interest: Chichester Cathedral; Arundel Castle; Goodwood House; Petworth House; Uppark; Fishbourne Roman Palace.
County worthies by birth: John Selden (1584–1654); William Collins (1721–59); Percy Bysshe Shelley (1792–1822); Richard Cobden (1804–65).

WEST YORKSHIRE

First recorded use of name and derivation: *c.* AD 150 Ebórakon (Ptolemy), 1050 (Eoferwiscir), land possessed by Eburos.
Area: 503 863 acres *203 906 ha.*
Population: 2 072 500.
Density: 4·11 per acre *10,16 per ha.*
Administrative HQ: County Hall, Wakefield.
Highest point above sea-level: Black Hill 1908 ft *581 m.*

Road length:	miles	km
motorway	43	69,2
trunk	140	225,3
principal	454	730,5
classified	617	992,8
unclassified	2235	3596,1

Schools and colleges: Nursery 27; Primary 752; First schools 110; Middle 162; Secondary 159; Special 76; Colleges of further education 18; Colleges of education 4; Polytechnics 2.
Places of interest: Bronte Museum (Haworth); Kirkstall Abbey; Ilkley Moor; Temple Newsom House; Harewood House; Wakefield Cathedral.
County worthies by birth: Sir Martin Frobisher (*c.* 1535–94); Thomas Fairfax (1612–1671); Thomas Chippendale (1718–79); Joseph Priestley (1733–1804); Charlotte Bronte (1816–55); Anne Bronte (1820–49); Emily Bronte (18118–48); Henry Herbert, Lord Asquith (1852–1928); Frederick Delius (1862–1934); Barbara Hepworth (1903–75); John Boynton Priestley (b. 1894); Wilfred Rhodes (1877–1973); James Harold Wilson (b. 1916).

WESTERN ISLES

First recorded use of name and derivation: Possibly 14th century (during the reign of David II the style 'Lord of the Isles' appears, whereas in the Treaty of Perth, 1266, the Norse name *sudreys* is used).
Area: 716 800 acres *290 079 ha.*
Population: 29 693.
Density: 0·04 per acre *0,10 per ha.*
Administrative HQ: Council Offices, South Beach, Stornoway, Isle of Lewis.
Highest point above sea-level: Clisham, Harris 2622 ft *799 m.*
Main Islands: The largest islands in the Long Island archipelago.

	miles²	km²
Lewis with Harris	859·19	2225
North Uist	135·71	351
South Uist	128·36	332

Road lengths:	miles	km
classified	426	685,4
unclassified	270	434,4

Schools and colleges: Nursery 3; Primary 42; Secondary 15; College of further education 1.
Places of interest: Kisimul Castle (Isle of Barra); Kilpheder (south west); Callanish-stone circle and cairn (Isle of Lewis); St Kilda, Rockall.
County worthies by birth: Flora Macdonald (1722–90).

WILTSHIRE

First recorded use of name and derivation: AD 878 (Wiltunschir), the shire around *Wiltun* (tun, town) on the flooding river (Wiley).
Area: 860 099 acres *348 070 ha.*
Population: 512 800.
Density: 0·60 per acre *1,47 per ha.*
Administrative HQ: County Hall, Trowbridge.
Highest point above sea-level: Milk Hill and Tan Hill (or St Anne's Hill) 964 ft *293 m.*

Road lengths:	miles	km
motorway	33	53,1
trunk	73	116,8
principal	250	401,3
other	1389	2235,1

Schools and colleges: Primary 312; Middle 4; Secondary 49; Special 14; Establishments of further education 6.
Places of interest: Salisbury Cathedral; Longleat; Stonehenge; Avebury Stone Circle Wilton House; Stourhead; Windmill Hill.
County worthies by birth: 1st Duke of Somerset (*c.* 1500–52); Edward (Hyde) 1st Earl of Clarendon (1609–74); Sir Christopher Wren (1632–1723); Joseph Addison (1672–1719); William H F Talbot (1800–77); Sir Isaac Pitman (1813–97); Thomas Hobbes (1588–1679).

ENGLAND'S REGISES

The use of the suffix 'Regis'—meaning 'of the King'—is used in the names of 12 places in England. In most cases the term has arisen from local usage to distinguish a Royal Manor, rather than from any exercise of prerogative by the sovereign.

	Earliest Mention
Bere Regis, Dorset	1244
†Bognor Regis, West Sussex (1929)	680
Grafton Regis, Northamptonshire	1204
Houghton Regis, Bedfordshire	1353
Kingsbury Regis, Somerset	1200
Letcombe Regis, Berkshire	1136
Lyme Regis, Dorset	1285
†Lynn Regis, Norfolk (1537)	1085
Melcombe Regis, Dorset	1280
Milton Regis, Kent	
†Rowley Regis, West Midlands (1933)	1173
Wyke Regis, Dorset	998

† By royal prerogative.

NORTHERN IRELAND

Area: 3 489 150 acres (5452 miles² *14 120 km²*).
Population: 1 538 100 (mid-1976).
Density: 0.44 per acre *1,10 per ha.*
Administrative HQ: Belfast.
Districts: The province is now divided into 26 districts, whose councils have similar functions to English district councils.

District	HQ	Pop.	Area acres	Area hectares
ANTRIM	Antrim	37 600	139 001	56 253
ARDS	Newtownards	52 100	89 277	36 130
ARMAGH	Armagh	47 500	166 691	67 459
BALLYMENA	Ballymena	52 200	157 306	63 661
BALLYMONEY	Ballymoney	22 700	103 246	41 783
BANBRIDGE	Banbridge	28 800	110 029	44 528
BELFAST CITY	Belfast	368 200	28 543	11 515
CARRICKFERGUS	Carrickfergus	27 500	19 017	7696
CASTLEREAGH	in Belfast, ie out of the district	63 600	20 868	8445
COLERAINE	Coleraine	44 900	119 708	48 445
COOKSTOWN	Cookstown	27 500	150 944	61 086
CRAIGAVON	Lurgan and Portadown	71 200	95 924	38 820
DOWN	Downpatrick	48 800	159 612	64 594
DUNGANNON	Dungannon	43 000	192 731	77 997
FERMANAGH	Enniskillen	50 900	463 505	187 578
LARNE	Larne	29 000	83 982	33 987
LIMAVADY	Limavady	25 000	145 621	58 932
LISBURN	Lisburn	80 800	110 369	44 666
LONDONDERRY CITY	Londonderry	86 600	95 591	38 685
MAGHERAFELT	Magherafelt	32 200	138 902	56 213
MOYLE	Ballycastle	13 400	122 090	49 409
NEWRY AND MOURNE	Newry	75 300	224 747	90 954
NEWTOWNABBEY	Newtownabbey	71 500	34 384	13 915
NORTH DOWN	Bangor	59 600	18 174	7355
OMAGH	Omagh	41 800	277 973	112 494
STRABANE	Strabane	35 500	212 884	86 153

The six geographical counties no longer exist as administrative units. Northern Ireland is divided into nine areas: five education and library areas plus four health and social services areas (other functions such as police, planning, roads, water, housing, fire services, etc are run centrally from Stormont). The area boards are not directly elected: about a third of their members are district councillors while the rest are persons appointed by the appropriate United Kingdom minister.

Education and library areas: BELFAST AREA (HQ Belfast) Nursery 19; Primary 117; Secondary 63; Special 12; Colleges of further education 4. NORTH-EASTERN AREA (HQ Ballymena) Nursery 12; Primary 263; Intermediate 40; Grammar 18; Special 3; Colleges of further education 7; Other college 1. SOUTH-EASTERN AREA (HQ Belfast) Nursery 8; Primary 119; Secondary 22; Special 7; Colleges of further education 5. SOUTHERN AREA (HQ Armagh) Nursery 5; Primary 300; Secondary 59; Special 1; Colleges of further education 8. WESTERN AREA (HQ Omagh) Nursery 1; Primary 252; Secondary 51; Special 5; Colleges of further education 5.
Health and social security areas: BELFAST AND SOUTH-EASTERN AREA (HQ Belfast); NORTH-EASTERN AREA (HQ Ballymena); WESTERN AREA (HQ Londonderry); SOUTHERN AREA (HQ Craigavon).
Highest point above sea-level: Slieve Donard (in Newry and Mourne District) 2796 ft *852 m.*
Places of interest: Lakes of Fermanagh; Mourne Mountains; Armagh Cathedrals; Florence Court; Antrim Coast Road; Giant's Causeway; Mount Stewart; Carrickfergus Castle; Sperrin Mountains; Downpatrick Cathedral.
Worthies by birth: Lord Alexander of Tunis (1891–1969); Thomas Andrews (1813–1885); Robert Stewart, Lord Castlereagh (1769–1822); St Malachy (c. 1095–1148); John Nicholson (1822–1857); Thomas Mayne Reid (1818–1883); Sir Hans Sloane (1660–1753); Lord Kelvin (1824–1907).

The six traditional geographic counties of Northern Ireland in order of size are:

COUNTY TYRONE
First recorded use of name and derivation: From Tir Eoghan, land of Eoghan (Owen, son of Niall).
Area: 806 918 acres *326 548 ha.*
Former capital: Omagh on the river Strule.
Highest point: Sawel (in Sperrin Mts.) 2240 ft *683 m.*
Coastline length: nil.

COUNTY ANTRIM
First recorded use of name and derivation: From the 5th century monastery of Aentrebh.
Area: 718 257 acres *290 668 ha.*
Former capital: City of Belfast on the river Lagan.
Highest point: Trostan 1817 ft *544 m.*
Coastline length: 90 miles *145 km.*

COUNTY DOWN
First recorded use of name and derivation: From Dun, Irish gaelic for fort (i.e. St Patrick's fort).
Area: 609 439 acres *246 631 ha.*
Former capital: Downpatrick on the river Quoile.
Highest point: Slieve Donard 2796 ft *852 m.*
Coastline length: 125 miles *201 km.*

COUNTY LONDONDERRY
First recorded use of name and derivation: From the charter granted by James I in 1613 to the City of London (England) livery companies. 'Derry' is a corruption of the celtic *doire*, an oak grove c. AD 500.
Area: 514 376 acres *208 161 ha.*
Former capital: City of Londonderry on the river Foyle.
Highest point: Sawel 2240 ft *683 m.*
Coastline length: 18 miles *29 km.*

COUNTY FERMANAGH
First recorded use of name and derivation: From Fir Mhanach, territory of the men of Managh.
Area: 457 376 acres *185 094 ha.*
Former capital: Enniskillen.
Highest point: Caileagh 2188 ft *667 m.*
Coastline length: nil.

COUNTY ARMAGH
First recorded use of name and derivation: From Queen Macha c. 3rd century BC
Area: 312 767 acres *126 572 ha.*
Former capital: Armagh on the Blackwater tributary Callan.
Highest point: Slieve Gullion 1894 ft *577 m.*
Coastline length: 2 miles *3,2 km.*

Note: The name Ulster is sometimes (but mistakenly) used as an alternative for the Province of Northern Ireland. Ulster is in fact one of the four ancient provinces of the island of Ireland (viz Connaught (5 counties), Leinster (12 counties), Munster (6 counties) and Ulster (9 counties)) and comprised the six counties of Northern Ireland and the 3 of the 26 counties (viz Cavan, Donegal and Monaghan) in the Republic of Ireland.

BRITAIN'S PRE-HISTORY

British history starts with the earliest written references dating from *c.* 525 BC by Himilco of the Tunisian city of Carthage. Events prior to that belong to pre-history—a term invented by Daniel Wilson in 1851.

Pre-historic events are subject to continuous reassessment as new dating methods are advanced. Most notable among these has been radiocarbon dating invented by Dr Willard F Libby (US) in 1949. This is based upon the decay rate of the radioactive carbon isotope C14, whose half-life is 5730 years (formerly thought to be 5568 years). Other modern methods include dendrochronology calibration by study of tree-rings developed by Professor C W Ferguson since 1969 and thermoluminescence, pollen analysis and amino-acid testing.

BC	
—	Beestonian glaciation, possibly equivalent to the alpine Günz glaciation.
—	Cromercan interglacial.
? 350 000–250 000	Anglian glaciation possibly contemporary with the alpine Mindel glaciation with ice sheets reaching the Thames valley. Human occupation (known as pre-Hoxnian) may have occurred during a warmer interstadial phase of this glaciation, e.g. course hand-axe culture at Fordwich, Kent (published 1968) and Kents Cavern, near Torquay, Devon (reassessed 1971).
? 250 000–200 000	Hoxnian interglacial (so named after Hoxne site, Suffolk, disc. 1797). Clactonian flake assemblages followed by Acheulian hand-axe industry, which latter yielded earliest British human remains at Swanscombe, Kent found by Marston in 1935–6. Sea level 30–35 m *98–114 ft* above present datum.
200 000–125 000	Wolstonian glaciation, probably contemporary with the alpine Riss glaciation.
125 000–70 000	Ipswichian interglacial—sea level 8 m *26 ft* above present datum.
70 000–14 000	Last or Devensian glaciation, contemporary with the alpine Würm glaciation, reaching to the latitude of York. Britain probably discontinuously unpopulated but populated during the warmer Chelford interstadial of 59 000 BC and during a further interstadial of 40 000 to 36 000 BC.
26 700 ± 450	Earliest upper palaeolithic radio-carbon dating from Kent's Cavern.
18 000–14 000	Maximum extension of ice-sheets. Sea-level fall of 100–150 m *328–492 ft*.
10 500–8000	Mesolithic Creswellian period and the close of the late Upper Paleolithic era.
c. 9050	Irish Sea land-bridge breached.
8400	Start of the present Flandrian post-glacial period. Earliest (Maglemosian) to latest (Lussa, Jura) datings of Mesolithic finds. Mesolithic man may have had herds by 4300 BC.
c. 6850	The North Sea land bridge between East Yorkshire and Holland breached by rising sea-level.
c. 6450	The English Channel attained its current width under the impact of the Flandrian transgression.
6100	Earliest dated habitation in Scotland, microlithic industry at Morton in Fife.
4580	Earliest dated habitation in Ireland—neolithic site at Ballynagilly, Tyrone two centuries earlier than England's earliest neolithic sites at Broome Heath, Norfolk; Findon, West Sussex and Lambourn, Berkshire.
4210–3990	Earliest dated British farming site at Hemberg, Devon (first excavated 1934–5).
3795	Earliest dated pottery at Ballynagilly (see above).
3650–3400	Avebury Stone Circle building, Wiltshire.
2930–2560	Giant Silbury Hill round barrow, Wiltshire.
2760	Earliest Bronze Age dating with Beaker pottery from Ballynagilly, (see above) four centuries before earliest English datings at Chippenham, Cambridge and Mildenhall, Suffolk.
2285–2075	Phase I at Stonehenge (ditch construction).
1260	Earliest dated hill-fort, Ivinghoe, Buckinghamshire.
c. 750	Introduction of iron into Britain from Hallstatt by the Celts. Hill-forts proliferate.
c. 308	First circumnavigation of Great Britain by Pytheas the Greek sea-captain from Massilia (Marseille).
c. 125	Introduction of Gallo-Belgic gold coinage via Kent from the Beauvais region of France.
c. 90	Earliest British coinage—Westerham gold staters so named after the hoard find in Kent in 1927.
55 (26 Aug.)	Julius Caesar's exploratory expedition with 7th and 10th legions and 98 ships from Boulogne and Ambleteuse.
54 (18 or 21 July)	Second Julian invasion with five legions and 2000 cavalry.
AD 43	Claudian invasion and the start of the Roman Occupation.

ROMAN ERA, 55 BC-AD 410

Caesar arrived off Dover from Boulogne with 98 transports and two legions in the early hours of 26 Aug. 55 BC. He landed against beach opposition between Deal and Walmer. Repeated skirmishing prevented the reconnaisance being a success and Caesar withdrew. He returned in 54 BC (variously on 18 or 21 July) with five legions and 800 vessels, and encamped on the Kentish shore and crossed the Thames near Brentford. He was much harried by the British leader, Cassivellaunus, based on the old Belgic capital of St Albans (*Verulamium*). The occupation was not sustained.

It was nearly a century later in AD 43 when the third Roman landing was made with some 20 000 men in three waves under the command of Plautius. This invasion is referred to as the Claudian Invasion, after the Roman emperor of that time. The British leader, Cunobelinus, was aged but resistance remained bitter. Roman cruelties against the king of the Iceni tribe and his family in East Anglia fired a native 'death or liberty' revolt under his widow, Queen Bodicca (Boadicea) in AD 61. Colchester (*Camulodunum*), London (*Londinium*) and St Albans were in turn sacked. The total death roll was put at 70 000 by Tacitus. Boadicea's horde of some 80 000 was met by Suetonius' 14th and 20th Legions of 10 000 men on a battlefield perhaps near Hampstead Heath, North London. For the loss of only about 400 of the fully-armed Romans, 70 000 Britons were claimed to have been killed. Subjugation, however, was not achieved until AD 83, when Agricola, the Roman Governor, won the Battle of Mons Graupius, suggested by some to be the Pass of Killiecrankie, Tayside.

For nearly 300 years the Roman régime brought law, order, peace, food, and even unknown warmth and cleanliness for the few who aspired to villas. The legions recruited locally to maintain 40 000 troops, garrisoned at Chester, Caerleon-on-Usk, York, and Hadrian's Wall. Hadrian arrived in Britain in 122 after the annihilation of the 9th Legion by the Picts. The 74½-mile-long *120 km* wall across the Tyne–Solway isthmus was built between AD 122 and 129. The 37-mile-long *59,5 km* Forth–Clyde or Antonine Wall was built *c.* 150, but was abandoned within 40 years. Emperor Severus re-established military order in the period 208–11, but by the time of Carasius, who ruled in 287–93, raids by the Saxons (*Seax*, short, one-handed sword) from the Schleswig–Holstein area were becoming increasingly troublesome. Demands were made by the Saxons, Scots and Picts that Emperor Valentinian sent his general, Theodosius, in 367 to restore order in the Province. In 400 Theodosius in turn sent his general, Stilicho, to deliver the Province from the ever-increasing pressure of the barbarians, but by 402 he was forced to recall the Roman garrison to help resist the incursions in Northern Italy of the Visigoths under Alaric. In 405 there was mutiny in the remaining garrison in Britain, who elected Gratinius, a Briton, as rival emperor. In 410 Emperor Honorius told the Britons from Rome that they must 'defend themselves' against the Saxons, Picts, and Scots. By 449 a Jutish Kingdom had been set up in Kent by Hengist and Horsa. The 5th and 6th centuries were a period of utter confusion and misery with conflict between the English and the remaining Britons, whose last champion was reputedly King Arthur. Some time between 493 and 503 Arthur fought the Battle of Mountbadon against the cruel Saxon invaders on an uncertain site, now ascribed to Liddington Camp, Badbury, near Swindon, Wiltshire.

British rulers between the end of the Roman occupation (AD 410) and the Norman conquest (1066)
England (excluding Cumbria) did not again become a unified state before AD 954. Some earlier kings exercised direct rule over all England for intermittent periods during their reigns. Edward the Elder (899–924 or 925) son of Alfred (871–99) the most famous of the Kings of the West Saxons, had suzerainty over the whole of England though he did not directly rule the Danish kingdom of York which was not finally extinguished until 954.

The following nine kingdoms existed in England before it became a unified kingdom. All existed contemporaneously during the first half of the 7th century (*c.* AD 604 to 654) but became absorbed in each other until the Kings of Wessex established overall authority
1. Kings of Kent   *c.* 455 to 825, conquered by West Saxons.

2. Kings of the South Saxons	477–c. 786, absorbed by Wessex.
3. Kings of West Saxons	519–954, established authority over all England.
4. Kings of Bernicia	547–670, annexed by Northumbria.
5. Kings of Northumbria	c. 588–?878, reduced by the Danish Kingdom of York.
6. Kings of Mercia	c. 595–ante 883, first acknowledged over-lordship of West Saxons 829.
7. Kings of Deira	599 or 560 to 654, annexed by Bernicia.
8. Kings of the East Angles	c. 600–870, conquest by Danes.
9. Kings of the East Saxons	ante 604–825, submitted to West Saxons.
Danish Kingdom of York	875 or 876–954, expulsion by Edred, the King of West Saxons.

The West Saxon King Egbert (802–39), grandfather of King Alfred, is often quoted as the first King of All England from AD 829, but in fact he never reduced the Kingdom of Northumbria ruled by Eanred (808 or 810 to 840 or 841).

Kings of All England

Athelstan, eldest son of the eldest son of King Alfred of the West Saxons, acceded 924 or 925. The first to establish rule over all England (excluding Cumbria) in 927. d. 27 Oct. 939 aged over 40 years.

Edmund, younger half-brother of Athelstan; acceded 939 but did not regain control of all England until 944–45. Murdered, 26 May 946 by Leofa at Pucklechurch, near Bristol, Avon.

Edred, younger brother of Edmund; acceded May 946. Effectively King of All England 946–48, and from 954 to his death, on 23 Nov. 955. Also intermittently during the intervening period.

Edwy, son of Edmund, b. c. 941; acceded November 955 (crowned at Kingston, Greater London); lost control of Mercians and Northumbrians in 957. d. 1 Oct. 959 aged about 18.

Edgar, son of Edmund, b. 943; acceded October 959 as King of All England (crowned at Bath, 11 May 973). d. 8 July 975, aged c. 32.

Edward the Martyr, son of Edgar by Aethelflaed, b. c. 962; acceded 975. d. 18 Mar. 978 or 979, aged 16 or 17.

Ethelred (*Unraed*, i.e. ill-counselled), second son of Edgar by Aelfthryth, b. ?968–69; acceded 978 or 979 (crowned at Kingston, 14 Apr. 978 or 4 May 979); dispossessed by the Danish king, Swegn Forkbeard, 1013–14. d. 23 Apr. 1016, aged c. 47 or 48.

Swegn Forkbeard, King of Denmark 987–1014, acknowledged King of All England from about September 1013 to his death, 3 Feb. 1014.

Edmund Ironside, prob. 3rd son of Ethelred, b. c. 992; chosen King in London, April 1016. In summer of 1016 made agreement with Cnut whereby he retained dominion only over Wessex. d. 30 Nov. 1016.

Cnut, younger son of King Swegn Forkbeard of Denmark, b. c. 995. Secured Mercia and Danelaw, summer 1016; assumed dominion over all England December 1016; King of Denmark 1019–35; King of Norway 1028–1035; overlord of the King of the Scots and probably ruler of the Norse–Irish kingdom of Dublin. d. 12 Nov. 1035, aged c. 40 years.

Harold Harefoot, natural son of Cnut by Aelfgifu of Northampton, b. ?c. 1016–17; chosen regent for half-brother, Harthacnut, late 1035 or early 1036; sole King 1037. d. 17 Mar. 1040, aged c. 23 or 24 years.

Harthacnut, son of Cnut by Emma, widow of King Ethelred (d. 1016), b. ?c. 1018; titular King of Denmark from 1028; effectively King of England from June 1040. d. 8 June 1042, aged c. 24 years.

Edward the Confessor, senior half-brother of Harthacnut and son of King Ethelred and Emma, b. 1002–05; resided with Harthacnut from 1041, acceded 1042 crowned 3 Apr. 1043. d. 5 Jan. 1066, aged between 60 and 64. Sanctified.

Harold Godwinson, brother-in-law of Edward the Confessor and brother of his Queen Edith, son of Godwin, Earl of Wessex, b. ?c. 1020; acceded 6 Jan. 1066, d. or k. 14 Oct. 1066.

Edgar Etheling, chosen by Londoners as king after the Battle of Hastings, Oct. 1066; not apparently crowned, submitted to William I before 25 Dec. 1066; believed still living c. 1125.

Rulers in Wales (844–1289)

Province of Gwynedd (North Wales) (844–1283), last prince executed for treason by Edward I.

Province of Deheubarth (Dyfed) (South Central and South West Wales) (844–1231), last of line imprisoned in Norwich.

Province of Powys (North Central Wales) (1063–1160), split into Southern and Northern Powys. Southern Powys (1160–1277), dispossessed, Northern Powys (1160 –ante 1289), became marcher lordship.

Kings of Scotland (1005–1603)

The chronology of the early kings of Alba (north of the Clyde and the Forth) before the 10th century is highly obscure.

Malcolm II (1005–34), b. c. 954. d. 25 Nov. 1034, aged c. 80 years. Formed the Kingdom of Scotland by annexing Strathclyde, c. 1016.

Duncan I (1034–40), son of Malcolm II's daughter, Bethoc.

Macbeth (1040–57), ?son of Malcolm II's daughter, Donada. d. aged c. 52 years.

Lulach (1057–8), stepson of Macbeth and son of his wife Gruoch. d. aged c. 26.

Malcolm III (Canmore) (1058–93), son of Duncan I. d. aged c. 62.

Donald Bane (1093–94 and 1094–97), son of Duncan I, twice deposed.

Duncan II (May to October 1094), son of Malcolm III. d. aged c. 34.

Edgar (1097–1107), son of Malcolm III, half-brother of Duncan II. d. aged c. 33.

Alexander I (1107–24), son of Malcolm III, brother of Edgar. d. aged c. 47.

David I (1124–53), son of Malcolm III and brother of Edgar. d. aged c. 68.

Malcolm IV (1153–65), son of Henry, Earl of Northumberland. d. aged c. 24.

William I (*The Lion*) (1165–1214), brother of Malcolm IV. d. aged c. 72 (from 1174 to 1189 King of England acknowledged as overlord of Scotland).

Alexander II (1214–49), son of William I. d. aged 48.

Alexander III (1249–1286), son of Alexander II. d. aged 44.

Margaret (*Maid of Norway*) (1286–90), daughter of Margaret, daughter of Alexander III by King Eric II of Norway. Never visited her realm. d. aged 7.

First Interregnum 1290–92.

John (*Balliol*) (1292–96), son of Dervorguilla, a great-great-granddaughter of David I, awarded throne from 13 contestants by adjudication of Edward I who declared after four years that John would have to forfeit his throne for contumacy.

Second Interregnum 1296–1306.

Robert I (1306–29), son of Robert Bruce and grandson of a 1291 competitor. d. aged c. 55.

David II (1329–71), son of Robert I. d. aged 46.

Note: Edward Balliol, son of John, was crowned King in 1332, acknowledged Edward III of England as overlord in 1333 and surrendered all claims to Scottish crown to him in 1356.

Robert II (1371–90), founder of the Stewart dynasty, son of Walter the Steward and Marjorie Bruce. d. aged 74.

Robert III (1390–1406), legitimated natural son of Robert II. d. aged c. 69.

James I (1406–37), son of Robert III, captured by English 13 days before accession and kept prisoner in England till March 1424. d. aged 42.

James II (1437–60), son of James I. d. aged 29.

James III (1460–88), son of James II. d. aged 36.

James IV (1488–1513), son of James III and Margaret of Denmark, married Margaret Tudor. d. aged 40.

James V (1513–42), son of James IV and Margaret Tudor. d. aged 30.

Mary (*Queen of Scots*) (1542–67), daughter of James V and Mary of Lorraine, acceded aged 6 or 7 days, abdicated 24 July 1567 and was succeeded by her son (James VI) by her second husband, Henry Stuart, Lord Darnley. She was executed, 8 Feb. 1587, aged 44.

James VI (1567–1625), son of Mary and Lord Darnley (see above), succeeded to the English throne as James I on 24 Mar. 1603, so effecting a personal union of the two realms. d. aged 58.

The eleven royal houses of England since 1066

A royal dynasty normally takes its house name from the family's patronymic. It does not change by reason of a Queen Regnant's marriage—for example, Queen Victoria, a member of the House of Hanover and Brunswick, did not become a member of the House of Saxe-Coburg and Gotha (her husband's family) but her son, Edward VII, and her grandson, George V (until renamed in 1917), were members of the house of their respective fathers.

The House of Normandy (by right of conquest) (69 years)

The house name derives from the fact that William I was the 7th Duke of Normandy with the style William II. This was despite the fact that he was illegitimate because his father, Duke Robert II, had him formally instituted as his legal heir.

William I (1066–87); William II (1087–1100); Henry I (1100–35) and Matilda.

The House of Blois (19 years)

The house name derives from the fact that the father of King Stephen was Stephen (sometimes called Henry), Count of Blois.

Stephen (1135–54).

The House of Anjou (331 years)

The house name derives from the fact that the father of King Henry II was Geoffrey V, 10th Count of Anjou and Maine. This family was alternatively referred to as the Angevins, the name deriving from Angers, the town and diocese within the boundaries of Anjou.

Henry II (1154–89) and the next thirteen kings down to and including Richard III (1483–5).

Note: (1) This house, but only since the mid-15th century, and in fact less than 50 years before its male line became extinct, has been referred to as THE HOUSE OF

PLANTAGENET. This name originated from Count Geoffrey's nickname 'Plantagenet', which in turn derived, it is said, from his habit of wearing a sprig of broom (*Planta genista*) in his cap during a crusade.

(2) The House of Anjou (or Plantagenet) may be sub-divided after the deposing of Richard II in 1399 into THE HOUSE OF LANCASTER with Henry IV (1399–1413); Henry V (1413–22); Henry VI (1422–61 and 1470–1) and THE HOUSE OF YORK with Edward IV (1461–83—except 1470–1); Edward V (1483); Richard III (1483–5).

(3) The names Lancaster and York derived respectively from the titles of the 4th and 5th sons of Edward III; John of Gaunt (1340–99) was 1st Duke of Lancaster (of the second creation), and the father of Henry IV; and Edmund of Langley (1341–1402) was 1st Duke of York and a great-grandfather of Edward IV.

The House of Tudor (118 years)
This house name derives from the surname of Henry VII's father, Edmund Tudor, Earl of Richmond, and son of Sir Owen Tudor, by Catherine, widow of King Henry V.

Henry VII (1485–1509); Henry VIII (1509–47); Edward VI (1547–53); after the reign of Queen Jane, Mary I (1553–8); Elizabeth I (1558–1603).

The House of Grey (14 days)
This house name derives from the family and surname of the 3rd Marquess of Dorset, the father of Lady Guil(d)ford Dudley, who reigned as Queen Jane from 6 July, 1553 for 14 days until 19 July when the House of Tudor regained the throne.

The House of Stuart and the House of Stuart and Orange (98 years and 5 years)
This house name is derived from the family and surname of Henry Stuart, Lord Darnley and Duke of Albany, the eldest son of Matthew, 4th Earl of Lennox. Lord Darnley was the second of the three husbands and cousin of Mary Queen of Scots and the father of James VI of Scotland and I of England.

James I (1603–25); Charles I (1625–49); Charles II (*de jure* 1649 but *de facto* 1660–85); James II (1685–8).

The house name became THE HOUSE OF STUART AND ORANGE when in 1689 William III, son of William II, Prince of Orange, became the sovereign conjointly with his wife, Mary II, the 5th Stuart monarch.

The House of Stuart resumed from 1702 to 1714 during the reign of Queen Anne.

The House of Orange
William III reigned alone during his widowerhood from 1694 to 1702. William in fact possessed the sole regal power during his entire reign from 1689.

The House of Hanover and Brunswick-Lüneberg (187 years)
This house name derives from the fact that George I's father, Ernest Augustus, was the Elector of Hanover and a duke of the House of Brunswick-Lüneberg.

George I (1714–27); George II (1727–60); George III (1760–1820); George IV (1820–1830); William IV (1830–7); Queen Victoria (1837–1901).

The House of Saxe-Coburg and Gotha (16 years)
This house name derives from the princely title of Queen Victoria's husband, Prince Albert, later Prince Consort.

Edward VII (1901–10); George V (1910–1917); on 17 July 1917 King George V declared by Royal Proclamation that he had changed the name of the royal house to the House of Windsor.

The House of Windsor (59 years to date)
George V (1917–36); Edward VIII (1936); George VI (1936–52); Elizabeth II (from 1952).

In the normal course of events Prince Charles, Prince of Wales, on inheriting the throne would become the first monarch of the House of Mountbatten but by further Proclamations the Queen declared in 1952 that her children and descendants will belong to the House of Windsor, and later in 1960 that this Declaration would only affect her descendants in the male line who will bear a royal style and title. Descendants outside this class will bear the surname 'Mountbatten-Windsor'.

Titles of the Royal House
Husbands of Queens Regnant
The husband of a queen regnant derives no title from his marriage. Philip II of Spain, husband of Queen Mary I, was termed 'King Consort'. Prince George of Denmark, husband of Queen Anne, was created Duke of Cumberland. Prince Albert of Saxe-Coburg-Gotha was created 'Royal Highness' and seventeen years after his marriage 'Prince Consort'. The Duke of Edinburgh, husband of Queen Elizabeth II, is HRH and a prince of the United Kingdom of Great Britain and Northern Ireland.

Queens Consort
A queen consort ranks with and shares the king's titles. In the event of her being widowed she cannot continue to use the title 'The Queen'. She must add to it her christian name or use the style additionally, or by itself, of 'Queen Mother' (if she has children), or, as in the case of the widow of King William IV, 'Queen Dowager'.

In the event of her re-marriage, which can only be with the consent of the Sovereign, she does not forfeit her royal status. The last such example was when Queen Catherine (Parr) married, as her fourth husband, Lord Seymour of Sudeley, KG, in 1547.

The Heir to the Throne
The Heir Apparent to the throne can only be the son or grandson (as in the case of the Prince of Wales from 1751 to 1760) of the reigning Sovereign. Should the first person in the order of succession bear any relationship other than in the direct male line, they are the Heir (or Heiress) Presumptive. The last Heiress Presumptive to the Throne was HRH The Princess Elizabeth (1936–52). A female could be an Heiress Apparent if she were the only or eldest daughter of a deceased Heir Apparent who had no male issue.

The eldest surviving son of a reigning Sovereign is born The Duke of Cornwall, The Duke of Rothesay, The Earl of Carrick and The Baron Renfrew, together with the styles of Lord of the Isles, Prince and Great Steward (or Seneschel) of Scotland. The titles Prince of Wales and Earl of Chester are a matter of creation and not of birthright. The Prince of Wales is a part of the establishment of The Order of the Garter. If, however, a Prince of Wales died, as in 1751, his eldest son would automatically succeed to that title and the Earldom of Chester but not to the Dukedom of Cornwall and the other honours because they are expressly reserved for the son (and not the grandson) of a Sovereign.

Princes, Princesses and Royal Highnesses
Since 1917 the style HRH Prince or Princess has been limited to the children of the Monarch and the children of the sons of the Monarch and their wives. Grand-children of a Prince of Wales also would enjoy this style. In practice the sons of a Sovereign have a dukedom bestowed upon them after they become of age. Such 'Royal Dukedoms' only enjoy their special precedence (i.e. senior to the two Archbishops and other dukes) for the next generation. A third duke would take his seniority among the non-royal dukes according to the date of the original creation.

The title 'Princess Royal' is conferred (if vacant) for life on the eldest daughter of the Sovereign.

The order of Succession to the Crown
The order of succession is determined according to ancient Common Law rules but these may be upset by an enactment of the Crown in Parliament under powers taken in the Succession to the Crown Act of 1707, provided always (since 1931) that the parliaments of all the Members of the Commonwealth assent. At Common Law the Crown descends lineally to the legitimate issue of the sovereign, males being preferred to females, in their respective orders of age. In the event of failure of such issue (e.g. King Edward VIII in 1936) the Crown passes to the nearest collateral being an heir at law. The common law of descent of the Crown specifically departs from the normal feudal rules of land descent at two points. First, in the event of two or more sisters being next in succession the eldest alone (e.g. The Princess Elizabeth from 1936 to 1952) shall be the heiress and shall not be merely a coparcener with her sister or sisters. Secondly, male issue by a second or subsequent marriage takes precedence over half sisters (e.g. King Edward VI, son of King Henry VIII's third wife, took precedence over Queen Mary I, daughter of his first marriage, and Queen Elizabeth I, daughter of his second marriage).

Below is set out the Order of Succession to the Crown.

1. The heir apparent is HRH The Prince CHARLES Philip Arthur George, KG, KT, The Prince of Wales, The Duke of Cornwall, The Duke of Rothesay, The Earl of Carrick, and the Baron Renfrew, Lord of the Isles and Great Steward of Scotland, born 14 Nov. 1948, then follows his brother:
2. HRH The Prince ANDREW Albert Christian Edward, born 19 Feb. 1960, then his brother:
3. HRH The Prince EDWARD Antony Richard Louis, born 10 Mar. 1964, then his sister:
4. HRH The Princess ANNE Elizabeth Alice Louise, Mrs Mark Phillips, born 15 Aug. 1950, then her son:
5. PETER Mark Andrew Phillips, born 15 Nov. 1977, then his great aunt:
6. HRH The Princess MARGARET Rose, CI, GCVO, The Countess of Snowdon, born 21 Aug. 1930, then her son:
7. DAVID Albert Charles Armstrong-Jones, commonly called Viscount Linley, born 3 Nov. 1961, then his sister:
8. The Lady SARAH Frances Elizabeth Armstrong-Jones, born 1 May 1964, then her cousin, once removed:
9. HRH Prince RICHARD Alexander Walter George, Duke of Gloucester, born 26 Aug. 1944, then his son:
10. Lord ALEXANDER Patrick George Richard, Earl of Ulster, born 24 Oct. 1974, then his sister:
11. The Lady DAVINA Elizabeth Alice Benedikte Windsor, born 19 Nov. 1977, then her cousin once removed:
12. HRH Prince EDWARD George Nicholas Paul Patrick, GCVO, the (2nd) Duke of Kent, the Earl of St Andrews and the Baron Downpatrick, born 9 Oct. 1935, then his son:

13. Lord GEORGE Philip Nicholas WINDSOR, commonly called Earl of St Andrews, born 26 June 1962, then his brother:
14. Lord NICHOLAS Charles Edward Jonathan Windsor, b. 25 July 1970, then his sister:
15. The Lady HELEN Marian Lucy WINDSOR, born 28 Apr. 1964, then her uncle:
16. HRH Prince MICHAEL George Charles Franklin of Kent, born 4 July 1942, then his sister:
17. HRH Princess ALEXANDRA Helen Elizabeth Olga Christabel of Kent, GCVO, the Hon Mrs Angus J B Ogilvy, born 25 Dec. 1936, then her son:
18. JAMES Robert Bruce Ogilvy, Esq, born 29 Feb. 1964, then his sister:
19. Miss MARINA Victoria Alexandra Ogilvy, born 31 July 1966 then her second cousin, once removed upwards:
20. The Rt Hon GEORGE Henry Hubert Lascelles, the (7th) Earl of Harewood, the Viscount Lascelles, the Baron Harewood, born 7 Feb. 1923, then his son:
21. The Hon DAVID Henry George Lascelles, commonly called Viscount Lascelles, born 21 Oct. 1950, then his brother:
22. The Hon JAMES Edward Lascelles, born 5 Oct. 1953, then his daughter:
23. Sophie Lascelles, born 1 Oct. 1973, then her uncle:
24. The Hon Robert JEREMY Hugh Lascelles, born 14 Feb. 1955, then his uncle:
25. The Hon GERALD David Lascelles, born 21 Aug. 1924, then his son:
26. HENRY Ulick Lascelles, Esq, born 19 May 1953, then his third cousin once removed upwards:
27. The Most Noble JAMES George Alexander Bannerman Carnegie, the (3rd) Duke of Fife, and the Earl of Macduff, born 23 Sept. 1929, then his son:
28. DAVID Charles Carnegie, commonly called Earl of Macduff, born 3 Mar. 1961, then his sister:
29. The Lady ALEXANDRA Clare Carnegie, born 20 Jun. 1959, then her third cousin twice removed upwards:
30. HM King OLAV V of Norway (Alexander Edward Christian Frederik), KG, KT, GCB, GCVO, born 2 July 1903, then his son:
31. HRH the Crown Prince HARALD, GCVO, born 21 Feb. 1937, then his son:
32. HRH Prince HAAKON Magnus, born 20 July 1973 then his sister:
33. HRH Princess MARTHA Louise, born 22 Sept. 1971 then his aunt:
34. HH the Princess RAGNHILD Alexandra, Fru. Erling S Lorentzen, born 9 June 1930, then her son:
35. Hr HAAKON Lorentzen, born 23 Aug. 1954, then his sister:
36. Frk INGEBORG Lorentzen, born 27 Feb. 1957, then her sister:
37. Frk RAGNHILD Lorentzen, born 8 May 1968, then her aunt:
38. HH the Princess ASTRID Maud Ingeborg, Fru Johan M Ferner, born 12 Feb. 1932, then her son:
39. Hr ALEXANDER Ferner, born 15 Mar. 1965, then his brother:
40. Hr CARL-CHRISTIAN Ferner, born 22 Oct. 1972, then his sister:
41. Frk CATHRINE Ferner, born 22 July 1962, then her sister:
42. Frk BENEDIKTE Ferner, born 28 Sept. 1963, then her sister:
43. Frk ELISABETH Ferner, born 30 March 1969.

This exhausts the line of Queen Victoria's eldest son (Edward VII) and it is then necessary to move to such issue of the late Queen Marie of Rumania, CI, RRC, eldest daughter of her second son, HRH the Duke of Edinburgh, KG, KT, KP, GCB, GCSI, GCMG, GCIE, GCVO, as may not be Roman Catholics nor are, nor have been married to Roman Catholics.

Factors affecting the order
Two further factors should be borne in mind in determining the order of succession. First, no person may unilaterally renounce their right to succeed. Only an Act of Parliament can undo what another Act of Parliament (the Act of Settlement, 1701) has done. Secondly, some marriages among the descendants of George II are null and void and hence the descendants are not heirs at law, by failure to obtain the consent to marry as required by the Royal Marriage Act of 1772. In some cases this failure, prior to 1956, may have been inadvertent because it was only then confirmed by the House of Lords that every such descendant, born before 1948, is by a statute of 1705 deemed a British subject. So the escape from the requirements of the Royal Marriage Act accorded to all female descendants of George II who apparently married into *foreign* families is not so readily available as was once thought.

The Act of Settlement
On 6 Feb. 1701 the Act of Settlement came into force. It laid down that failing issue from HRH The Princess (later Queen Anne) George (of Denmark) and/or secondly from any subsequent marriage by her first cousin and brother-in-law, the widower King William III, the crown would vest in Princess Sophia, Dowager Electress of Hanover (1630–1714), the granddaughter of King James I, and the heirs of her body with the proviso that all Roman Catholics, or persons marrying Roman Catholics, were for ever to be excluded, as if they 'were naturally dead'.

The Duke of Windsor
The only subsequent change in statute law was on 11 Dec. 1936 by His Majesty's Declaration of Abdication Act, 1936, by which the late HRH The Prince Edward, MC (later HRH The Duke of Windsor), and any issue he might subsequently have had were expressly excluded from the succession.

Conditions of tenure
On succeeding to the Crown the Sovereign must (1) join in Communion with the established Church of England; (2) declare that he or she is a Protestant; (3) swear the oaths for the preservation of both the Established Church of England and the Presbyterian Church of Scotland, and (4), and most importantly, take the coronation oath, which may be said to form the basis of the contract between Sovereign and subject, last considered to have been broken, on the Royal side, by King James II in 1688.

'The King never dies'
The Sovereign can never be legally a minor, but in fact a regency is provided until he or she attains the age of 18.
There is never an interregnum on the death of a Sovereign. In pursuance of the common law maxim 'the King never dies' the new Sovereign succeeds to full prerogative rights instantly on the death of his or her predecessor.

Notes on the British peerage
There are five ranks in the British temporal peerage—in ascending order they are: 1. Barons or Baronesses; 2. Viscounts or Viscountesses; 3. Earls or Countesses; 4. Marquesses or Marchionesses (or less favoured, Marquises); 5. Dukes or Duchesses.
The British spiritual peerage is of two ranks, Archbishops (of Canterbury and of York) who rank between Royal Dukes and dukes, and twenty-four of the bishops (but always including the Bishops of London, Durham, and Winchester with the Bishop of Sodor and Man always excluded), based on their seniority, who rank between Viscounts and Barons.
A few women hold peerages in their own right and since The Peerage Act, 1963, have become peers of Parliament. The remaining category of membership of the House of Lords is life peers. These are of two sorts: (a) The Lords of Appeal in Ordinary, who are appointed by virtue of the Appellate Jurisdiction Act, 1876. Their number has been increased from the original four to six in 1913, to seven in 1929, and to nine since 1947; (b) by virtue of The Life Peerages Act, 1958, both men and women may be appointed for life membership of the House of Lords. Such creations so far have been confined to the fifth and junior temporal rank of baron or baroness.
1. Peerages of England, i.e. those created prior to the union with Scotland on 1 May 1707.
2. Peerages of Scotland, i.e. those created before the union with England.
3. Peerages of Ireland (the last creation was in 1898 and no further ones are at present likely).
4. Peerages of Great Britain, i.e. those created between the union with Scotland (1707) and the union with Ireland (2 July 1800).
5. Peerages of the United Kingdom of Great Britain and (Northern) Ireland, i.e. those created since 2 July 1800.
All holders of peerages of England, Great Britain and the United Kingdom and (only since The Peerage Act, 1963) also of Scotland, are also peers of Parliament provided they are over 21 and are not unpardoned major felons, bankrupts, lunatics or of alien nationality. Peers who are civil servants may sit but neither speak nor vote.
The single exception to the rule concerning minors is that the Duke of Cornwall (HRH The Prince of Wales) has been technically entitled to a seat from the moment of his mother's accession, when he was only three years of age.
The peers (and peeresses in their own right) of Ireland are not peers of Parliament but they are entitled to stand for election to the House of Commons for any seat in the United Kingdom. The previous system by which this category of peer could elect 28 of its number to sit in the House of Lords has now fallen into disuse because since the Partition of Ireland in 1922 there has been no machinery available to carry out that election and all the representative peers elected prior to that date have since died.
Only the holder of a substantive peerage can be described as noble. In the eyes of the law the holder of a courtesy title is a commoner. For example, the Duke of Marlborough's son is known by courtesy as Marquess of Blandford. Note the omission of the definite article 'the'. The reason is that the Duke of Marlborough is also *the* Marquess of Blandford and his secondary peerage style is merely lent to this son.

For further notes on Peerage descent, abeyance, extinction, dormancy, courtesy titles etc. see pages 107–8 in Guinness Book of Answers *1st Edition.*

KINGS & QUEENS OF ENGLAND
FROM 1066

The precise dates of all the main events in the lives of the earlier monarchs are not known, and probably now never will be. Where recognised authorities are in dispute, as quite frequently occurs in the first twenty or so reigns, we have adhered to the dates given by the Royal Historical Society's *Handbook of British Chronology* (second edition, 1961). This work includes the fruits of recent researches based on only acceptable evidence.

King or Queen Regnant, Date of Accession and Final Year of Reign; Style	Date and Place of Birth and Parentage	Marriages and No. of Children	Date, Cause and Place of Death, and Place of Burial	Notes and Succession
1. **WILLIAM I** 25 Dec. 1066–87 'The Bastard' 'The Conqueror' *Style:* 'Willielmus Rex Anglorum'	1027 or 1038 at Falaise, north France; illegitimate son of Robert I, 6th Duke of Normandy, and Arlette, dau. of Fulbert the Tanner	m. at Eu in 1050 or 1051 MATILDA (d. 1083), d. of Baldwin V, Count of Flanders. 4s 5d	d., aged 59 or 60, 9 Sept. 1087 of an abdominal injury from his saddle pommel at the Priory of St Gervais, nr. Rouen. The Abbey of St Stephen at Caen	William I succeeded by right of conquest by winning the 'Battle of Hastings,' 14 Oct. 1066, from Harold II, the nominated heir of Edward III ('The Confessor'). Succeeded as King of England by his third*, but second surviving, son, William
2. **WILLIAM II** 26 Sept. 1087–1100 'Rufus' *Style:* 'Dei Gratia Rex Anglorum'	between 1056 and 1060 in Normandy; third son of William I and Matilda	unmarried. Had illegitimate issue	d., aged between 40 and 44, 2 Aug. 1100 (according to tradition) of impalement by a stray arrow while hunting in the New Forest nr. Brockenhurst, Hants. Winchester Cathedral	Succeeded by his younger brother, Henry
3. **HENRY I** 5 Aug. 1100–35 'Beauclerc' *Style:* As No. 2 but also Duke of Normandy from 1106	in the latter half of 1068 at Selby, Yorks; fourth son of William I and Matilda	m. (1) at Westminster Abbey, 11 Nov. 1100, EADGYTH (Edith), known as MATILDA (d. 1118), d of Malcolm III, King of the Scots, and Margaret (grand-d of Edmund 'Ironside') 1s, 1d and a child who died young. m. (2) 29 Jan. 1121 ADELA (d. 1151), d of Godfrey VII, Count of Louvain. No issue	d., aged 67, 1 Dec. 1135, from a feverish illness at St Denis-le-Ferment, nr. Grisors. Reading Abbey	Succeeded by his nephew, Stephen (the third, but second surviving, son of Adela, the fifth d of William I) who usurped the throne from Henry's only surviving legitimate child and d, Matilda (1102–67)
4. **STEPHEN** 22 Dec. 1135–54 *Style:* As No. 2.	between 1096 and 1100 at Blois, France; third son of Stephen (sometimes called Henry), Count of Blois, and Adela	m. 1125, MATILDA (d. 1151), d of Eustace III, Count of Boulogne, and Mary, sister of Queen Matilda, wife of Henry I. 3s 2d	d., aged between 54 and 58, 25 Oct. 1154, from a heart attack at St Martin's Priory, Dover. Faversham Abbey	Succeeded by his first cousin once removed downwards, Henry. Between April and November 1141 he was not *de facto* King and was imprisoned in Bristol Castle
5. **MATILDA** April–Nov. 1141 'Empress Maud' *Style:* 'Imperatrix Henrici Regis filia et Anglorum domina'	Feb. 1102 in London, only legitimate d of Henry I	m. (1) 1114 HENRY V, Emperor of Germany (d 1125). No issue. m. (2) 1130 GEOFFREY V, Count of Anjou (d 1151). 3s.	d., aged 65, 10 Sept. 1167 of uncertain cause, nr. Rouen in Normandy. Fontevraud (?), France	—

King or Queen Regnant, Date of Accession and Final Year of Reign; Style	Date and Place of Birth and Parentage	Marriages and No. of Children	Date, Cause and Place of Death, and Place of Burial	Notes and Succession
6. **HENRY II** 19 Dec. 1154–1189 *Style:* 'Rex Angliae, Dux Normaniae et Aquitaniae et Comes Andigaviae'	5 Mar. 1133 at Le Mans, France; eldest son of Geoffrey V, Count of Anjou (surnamed Plantagenet), and Matilda (only d of Henry I)	m. at Bordeaux, 18 May, 1152, ELEANOR (c. 1122–1204), d of William X, Duke of Aquitaine, and divorced wife of Louis, later Louis VII, King of France, 5s 3d.	d., aged 56, 6 July 1189, of a fever at the Castle of Chinon, nr. Tours, France. Fontevraud abbey church in Anjou	Succeeded by his third and elder surviving son, Richard. On 14 June 1170, Henry II's second and eldest surviving son Henry was crowned and three years later recrowned with his wife at Winchester as King of England. Contemporaneously he was called King Henry III. He predeceased his father, 11 June 1183
7. **RICHARD I** 3 Sept. 1189–99 'Coeur de Lion' *Style:* As No. 5	8 Sept. 1157 at Oxford; third son of Henry II and Eleanor	m. at Limassol, Cyprus, 12 May 1191, BERENGARIA (d. soon after 1230), d of Sancho VI of Navarre. No issue	d., aged 41, 6 Apr. 1199, from a mortal arrow wound while besieging the Castle of Châlus in Limousin, France. Fontevraud abbey church in Anjou. Reburied Westminster Abbey	Succeeded by his younger brother, John, who usurped the throne from his nephew Arthur, the only son of Geoffrey, Duke of Brittany (1158–86); and from his niece, Eleanor (1184–1241). Arthur (b, post-humously 1187) was murdered (unmarried) 3 Apr. 1203 in his 17th year
8. **JOHN** 27 May 1199–1216 'Lackland' *Style:* 'Joannes Rex Angliae et Dominus Hiberniae' etc.	24 Dec. 1167 at Beaumont Palace, Oxford; fifth son of Henry II and Eleanor	m. (1) at Marlborough, Wilts, 29 Aug. 1189, ISABEL★ (d. 1217). No issue. m. (2) at Angoulême, 24 Aug. 1200, ISABELLA (d. 1246), d of Aimir, Count of Angoulême. 2s 3d	d., aged 48, 18–19 Oct. 1216, of dysentery at Newark Castle, Notts. Worcester Cathedral	In late 1215 the Crown was offered to Louis, son of Philip II of France but despite a visit in 1216 the claim was abandoned in Sept. 1217. Succeeded by his elder son, Henry
9. **HENRY III** 28 Oct. 1216–72 *Style:* 'Rex Angliae, Dominus Hiberniae et Dux Aquitaniea'	1 Oct. 1207 at Winchester; elder son of John and Isabella	m. at Canterbury, 20 Jan. 1236, ELEANOR (d. 1291), d of Raymond Berengar IV, Count of Provence. 2s 3d at least 4 other children who died in infancy	d., aged 65, 16 Nov. 1272, at Westminster. Westminster abbey church	The style 'Dux Normaniae' and Count of Anjou was omitted from 1259. Succeeded by Edward, his first son to survive infancy (probably his third son)
10. **EDWARD I** 20 Nov. 1272–1307 'Longshanks' *Style:* As the final style of No. 8	17/18 June 1239 at Westminster; eldest son to survive infancy (probably third son) of Henry III and Eleanor	m. (1) at the monastery of Las Huelgas, Spain, 13–31 Oct. 1254 ELEANOR (d. 1290), d of Ferdinand III, King of Castille. 4s 7d m. (2) at Canterbury, 10 Sept. 1299 MARGARET (1282–1317), d of Philip III, King of France. 2s 1d	d., aged 68, 7 July 1307, at Burgh-upon-the-Sands, nr. Carlisle. Westminster Abbey	Succeeded by the fourth, and only surviving, son of his first marriage, Edward (created Prince of Wales 7 Feb. 1301)
11. **EDWARD II** 8 July 1307 (deposed 20 Jan. 1327) 'of Caernarfon' *Style:* As the final style of No. 8	25 Apr. 1284 at Caernarfon Castle; fourth and only surviving son of Edward I and Eleanor	m. at Boulogne, c. 25 Jan. 1308, ISABELLA (1292–1358), d of Philip IV, King of France, 2s 2d	murdered, aged 43, 21 Sept. 1327 (traditionally by disembowelling with red-hot iron) at Berkeley Castle. The abbey of St Peter (now the cathedral), Gloucester	Succeeded by his elder son, Edward of Windsor. Edward II was deposed by Parliament on 20 Jan. 1327, having been imprisoned on 16 Nov. 1326
12. **EDWARD III** 25 Jan. 1327–1377 *Style:* As No. 10, until 13th year when 'Dei Gratiâ, Rex Angliae, et Franciae et Dominus Hiberniae'	13 Nov. 1312 at Windsor Castle; elder son of Edward II and Isabella	m. at York, 24 June 1328, PHILIPPA (c. 1314–69), d of William I, Count of Holland and Hainault. 7s 5d	d. peacefully, aged 64, 21 June 1377 at Sheen (now in Greater London). Westminster Abbey	Succeeded by his grandson Richard, the second and only surviving son of his eldest son Edward, the Black Prince

King or Queen Regnant, Date of Accession and Final Year of Reign; Style	Date and Place of Birth and Parentage	Marriages and No. of Children	Date, Cause and Place of Death, and Place of Burial	Notes and Succession
13. **RICHARD II** 22 June 1377–99 *Style:* As final style of No. 11	6 Jan. 1367 at Bordeaux; second, but only surviving, son of Edward, the Black Prince, and Joane, commonly called The Fair Maid of Kent (grand-d of Edward I	m. (1) at St Stephen's Chapel, Westminster, 20 Jan. 1382, ANNE of Bohemia (1366–94), d of Emperor Charles IV. No issue. m. (2) at St Nicholas' Church, Calais, probably 4 Nov. 1396, ISABELLE (1389–1409), d of Charles VI of France. No issue	d., aged 33, probably 14 Feb. 1400, a sufferer from neurasthenia at Pontefract Castle, Yorks. Westminster Abbey	He was a prisoner of Henry, Duke of Lancaster, later Henry IV, from 19 Aug. 1399 until death. He was deposed 30 Sept. 1399. Henry usurped the throne from the prior claims of the issue of his father John of Gaunt's deceased elder brother, Lionel of Antwerp
14. **HENRY IV** 30 Sept. 1399–1413 *Style:* As No. 12	probably Apr. 1366 at Bolingbroke Castle, nr. Spilsby, Lincs.; eldest son of John of Gaunt, 4th son of Edward III, and Blanche, great-great-grand-d of Henry III	m. (1) at Rochford, Essex, between July 1380 and Mar. 1381, Lady Mary de Bohun (?1368/70–94), younger d of Humphrey, Earl of Hereford. 5s 2d m. (2) at Winchester 7 Feb. 1403, JOAN (c. 1370–1437), second d of Charles II, King of Navarre. No issue	d., aged probably 46, 20 Mar. 1413, of pustulated eczema and gout in the Jerusalem Chamber, Westminster. Canterbury Cathedral	Succeeded by his second, but eldest surviving, son, Henry of Monmouth
15. **HENRY V** 21 Mar. 1413–1422 *Style:* As No. 13, until 8th year when 'Rex Angliae, Haeres, et Regens Franciae, et Dominus Hiberniae'	probably 16 Sept. 1387 at Monmouth; second and eldest surviving son of Henry IV and the Lady Mary de Bohun	m. at the church of St. John, Troyes, 2 June 1420, CATHERINE of Valois (1401–37), youngest d of Charles VI of France. 1s	d., aged probably 34, 31 Aug./Sept. 1422, of dysentery at Bois de Vincennes, France. Chapel of the Confessor, Westminster Abbey	Succeeded by his only child Henry
16. **HENRY VI** 1 Sept. 1422–1461 and 6 Oct. 1470–1471 *Style:* 'Dei Gratiâ Rex Angliae et Franciae et Dominus Hiberniae'	6 Dec. 1421 at Windsor; only son of Henry V and Catherine	m. at Tichfield Abbey, 23 Apr. 1445, MARGARET (1430–82), d of René, Duke of Anjou. 1s	murdered by stabbing, aged 49, 21 May 1471 at Tower of London. Windsor	Succeeded by the usurpation of this third cousin, Edward IV
17. **EDWARD IV** 4 Mar. 1461–1470 and 11 April 1471–1483 *Style:* As No. 15	28 Apr. 1442 at Rouen; eldest son of Richard, 3rd Duke of York ('The Protector') and the Lady Cecily Nevill	m. at Grafton, Northants, 1 May 1464, ELIZABETH (c. 1437–92), eldest d of Sir Richard Woodville 3s 7d	d., aged 40, 9 Apr. 1483, of pneumonia at Westminster. Windsor	Edward IV was a prisoner of the Earl of Warwick in Aug. and Sept. of 1469; he fled to the Netherlands 3 Oct. 1470; returned to England 14 Mar. 1471, and was restored to kingship 11 Apr. 1471. Succeeded by his eldest son, Edward
18. **EDWARD V** 9 Apr.–25 June 1483 *Style:* As No. 15	2 Nov. 1470 in the Sanctuary at Westminster; eldest son of Edward IV and Elizabeth Woodville	unmarried	d. (traditionally murdered), possibly in 1483 or in 1486, at the Tower of London. A body of the stature and dentition of a 12 year old male discovered at the Tower on 6 July 1933	Edward V was deposed 25 June 1483, when the throne was usurped by his uncle, Richard III (the only surviving brother of his father)
19. **RICHARD III** 26 June 1483–5 *Style:* As No. 15	2 Oct. 1452 at Fotheringay Castle, Northants; fourth and only surviving, son of Richard, 3rd Duke of York ('The Protector'), and the Lady Cecily Nevill	m. 12 July 1472 the Lady ANNE (1456–85), younger d of Richard Nevill, Earl of Warwick ('The King Maker') and widow of Edward, Prince of Wales, only child of Henry VI. 1s	killed aged 32, 22 Aug. 1485, at the Battle of Bosworth Field. The Abbey of the Grey Friars, Leicester	Richard III was succeeded by his third cousin once removed downwards, Henry Tudor, 2nd Earl of Richmond
20. **HENRY VII** 22 Aug. 1485–1509 *Style:* As No. 15	27 Jan. 1457 at Pembroke Castle; only child of Edmund Tudor, 1st Earl of Richmond, and Margaret Beaufort, great-great-grand-d of Edward III	m. at Westminster, 18 Jan. 1486, ELIZABETH (1466–1503) d of Edward IV. 3s and 4d, of whom 2 died in infancy	d., aged 52, 21 Apr. 1509 had rheumatoid arthritis and gout at Richmond. In his own chapel at Westminster	Succeeded by his second and only surviving son, Henry

King or Queen Regnant, Date of Accession and Final Year of Reign; Style	Date and Place of Birth and Parentage	Marriages and No. of Children	Date, Cause and Place of Death, and Place of Burial	Notes and Succession
21. **HENRY VIII** 22 Apr. 1509–47 *Style:* (from 35th year) 'Henry the eighth, by the Grace of God, King of England, France, and Ireland, Defender of the Faith and of the Church of England, and also of Ireland, on earth the Supreme Head'	28 June 1491 at Greenwich; second and only surviving son of Henry VII and Elizabeth	m. (1) secretly at the chapel of the Observant Friars, 11 June 1509, CATHERINE of Aragon (1485–1536), d of Ferdinand II, King of Spain and widow of Arthur, Prince of Wales. 2s 2d and a child who died young.	d., aged 55, 28 Jan. 1547, had chronic sinusitis and periostitis of the leg at the Palace of Westminster. Windsor	Henry was the first King to be formally styled with a post nominal number i.e. VIII. Succeeded by his only surviving son, Edward
Subsequent marriages of HENRY VIII:	m. (2) secretly 25 Jan. 1533, ANNE Marchioness of Pembroke (b. 1507, beheaded 1536), d of Sir Thomas Boleyn, the Viscount Rochford. A daughter and possibly another child	m. (3) in the Queen's Closet, York Place, London, 30 May 1536, JANE (d. 1537), eldest d of Sir John Seymour. 1s	m. (4) at Greenwich, 6 Jan. 1540, ANNE (1515–57), second d of John, Duke of Cleves. No issue. m. (5) at Oatlands, 28 July 1540, CATHERINE (beheaded 1542), d of Lord Edmund Howard. No issue	m. (6) at Hampton Court, 12 July 1543, CATHERINE (c. 1512–48), d of Sir Thomas Parr and widow of 1. Sir Edward Borough and 2. John Neville, 3rd Lord Latimer. No issue
22. **EDWARD VI** 28 Jan. 1547–53 *Style:* As No. 20	12 Oct. 1537 at Hampton Court; only surviving son of Henry VIII, by Jane Seymour	unmarried	d., aged 15, 6 July 1553, of pulmonary tuberculosis at Greenwich. Henry VII's Chapel, Westminster Abbey	Succeeded briefly by Lady Guil(d)ford Dudley (Lady Jane Grey), his first cousin once removed
23. **JANE** 6 July (proclaimed 10 July) 1553 (deposed 19 July)	Oct. 1537 at Bradgate Park, Leics.; eldest d of Henry Grey, 3rd Marquess of Dorset, and Frances (d of Mary Tudor, sister of Henry VIII)	m. at Durham House, London, 21 May 1553, Lord GUIL(D)FORD DUDLEY (beheaded 1554), 4th son of John Dudley, Duke of Northumberland. No issue	beheaded, aged 16, 12 Feb. 1554, in the Tower of London. St Peter ad Vincula, within the Tower	Succeeded by her second cousin once removed upwards, Mary
24. **MARY I** 19 July 1553–8 *Style:* As No. 20 (but supremacy title was dropped) until marriage then as footnote:	18 Feb. 1516 at Greenwich Palace; only surviving child of Henry VIII and Catherine of Aragon	m. at Winchester Cathedral, 25 July 1554, PHILIP (1527–98), King of Naples and Jerusalem, son of Emperor Charles V and widower of Maria, d of John III of Portugal. No issue	d., aged 42, 17 Nov. 1558, of endemic influenza at London. Westminster Abbey.	Philip was styled, but not crowned, king. Mary was succeeded by her half sister, Elizabeth, the only surviving child of Henry VIII
25. **ELIZABETH I** 17 Nov. 1558–1603 *Style:* 'Queen of England, France and Ireland, Defender of the Faith' etc.	7 Sept. 1533 at Greenwich; d of Henry VIII and Anne Boleyn	unmarried	d., aged 69, 24 Mar. 1603, of sepsis from tonsillar abscess at Richmond. Westminster Abbey	Succeeded by her first cousin twice removed, James
26. **JAMES I** 24 Mar. 1603–25 and VI of Scotland from 24 July 1567 *Style:* King of England, Scotland, France and Ireland, Defender of the Faith' etc.	19 June 1566 at Edinburgh Castle; only son of Henry Stuart, Lord Darnley, and Mary, Queen of Scots (d of James V of Scotland, son of Margaret Tudor, sister of Henry VIII)	m. 20 Aug. 1589 (by proxy) ANNE (1574–1619), d of Frederick II, King of Denmark and Norway. 3s 4d	d., aged 58, 27 Mar. 1625, of Bright's disease at Theobalds Park, Herts. Westminster Abbey	Succeeded by his second and only surviving son, Charles
27. **CHARLES I** 27 Mar. 1625–49 *Style:* As No. 25	19 Nov. 1600 at Dunfermline, Fife; second and only surviving son of James I and Anne	m. in Paris 1 May 1625 (by proxy) HENRIETTA MARIA (1609–69) d of Henry IV of France. 4s 5d	beheaded, aged 48, 30 Jan. 1649, in Whitehall. Windsor	The Kingship was *de facto* declared abolished 16 Mar. 1649

King or Queen Regnant, Date of Accession and Final Year of Reign; Style	Date and Place of Birth and Parentage	Marriages and No. of Children	Date, Cause and Place of Death, and Place of Burial	Notes and Succession
28. **CHARLES II** 29 May 1660 (but *de jure* 30 Jan. 1649) to 1685 *Style:* As No. 25	29 May 1630 at St James's Palace, London; eldest surviving son of Charles I and Henrietta Maria	m. at Portsmouth, 21 May 1662, CATHERINE (1638–1705), d of John, Duke of Braganza. No legitimate issue	d., aged 54, 6 Feb. 1685, of uraemia and mercurial poisoning at Whitehall. Henry VII's Chapel, Westminster Abbey	Succeeded by his younger and only surviving brother, James
29. **JAMES II** 6 Feb. 1685–8 *Style:* As No. 25	14 Oct. 1633 at St James's Palace, London; only surviving son of Charles I and Henrietta Maria	m. (1) at Worcester House, The Strand, London, 3 Sept. 1660, Anne (1637–71), eldest d of Edward Hyde. 4s 4d m. (2) at Modena (by proxy), 30 Sept. 1673, MARY D'Este (1658–1718), only d of Alfonso IV, Duke of Modena. 2s 5d	d., aged 67, 6 Sept. 1701, of a cerebral haemorrhage at St Germains, France. His remains were divided and interred at five different venues in France. All are now lost except for those at the parish church of St Germains	James II was deemed by legal fiction to have ended his reign 11 Dec. 1688 by flight. A Convention Parliament offered the Crown of England and Ireland 13 Feb. 1689 to Mary, his eldest surviving d, and her husband, his nephew, William Henry of Orange
30. **WILLIAM III** 13 Feb. 1689–1702 and	4 Nov. 1650 at The Hague; only son of William II, Prince of Orange, and Mary (Stuart), d of Charles I	T M were married at St James's Palace, London, 4 Nov. 1677. No issue	d., aged 51, 8 Mar. 1702, of pleuro-pneumonia following fracture of right collarbone, in Kensington	The widower, King William III, was succeeded by his sister-in-law, Anne, who was also his first cousin
MARY II 13 Feb. 1689–94 *Style:* 'King and Queen of England, Scotland, France and Ireland, Defenders of the Faith etc.'	30 Apr. 1662 at St James's Palace, London; elder surviving d of James II and Anne Hyde		d., aged 32, 28 Dec. 1694, of confluent haemorrhagic smallpox with pneumonia, at Kensington. T M were buried in Henry VII's Chapel, Westminster Abbey	
31. **ANNE** 8 Mar. 1702–14 *Style:* Firstly as No. 25; secondly (after Union with Scotland 6 Mar. 1707) 'Queen of Great Britain, France and Ireland, Defender of the Faith etc.'	6 Feb. 1665 at St James's Palace, London; only surviving d of James II and Anne Hyde	m. at the Chapel Royal, St James's Palace, 28 July 1683, GEORGE (1653–1708), second son of Frederick III, King of Denmark. 2s 3d from 17 confinements	d., aged 49, 1 Aug. 1714, of a cerebral haemorrhage and possibly chronic Bright's disease at Kensington. Henry VII's Chapel, Westminster Abbey	Succeeded in the terms of the Act of Settlement (which excluded all Roman Catholics and their spouses) by her second cousin, George Lewis, Elector of Hanover
32. **GEORGE I** 1 Aug. 1714–27 *Style:* 'King of Great Britain, France and Ireland, Duke of Brunswick-Lüneburg, etc., Defender of the Faith'	28 May 1660 at Osnabrück; eldest son of Ernest Augustus, Duke of Brunswick-Lüneburg and Elector of Hanover, and Princess Sophia, 5th and youngest d and 10th child of Elizabeth, Queen of Bohemia, the eldest d of James I	m. 21 Nov. 1682 (div. 1694), Sophia Dorothea (1666–1726), only d of George William, Duke of Lüneburg-Celle. 1s 1d	d., aged 67, 11 June 1727, of coronary thrombosis, at Ibbenbüren or Osnabrück. Hanover	The Kings of England were Electors of Hanover from 1714 to 1814. Succeeded by his only son, George Augustus
33. **GEORGE II** 11 June 1727–60 *Style:* As No. 31	30 Oct. 1683 at Hanover; only son of George I and Sophia Dorothea	m. 22 Aug. (O.S.), 2 Sept. (N.S.), 1705, Wilhelmina Charlotte CAROLINE (1683–1437), d of John Frederick, Margrave of Brandenburg-Auspach, 3s 5d	d. aged 76, 25 Oct. 1760, of coronary thrombosis at the Palace of Westminster. Henry VII's Chapel. Westminster Abbey	Succeeded by his elder son's eldest son, George William Frederick
34. **GEORGE III** 25 Oct. 1760–1820 *Style:* As No. 31 (until Union of Great Britain and Ireland, 1 Jan. 1801), whereafter 'By the Grace of God, of the United Kingdom of Great Britain and Ireland, King, Defender of the Faith'	24 May (O.S.) 1738 at Norfolk House, St James's Square, London; eldest son of Frederick Lewis, Prince of Wales (d. 20 Mar. 1751) and Princess Augusta of Saxe-Gotha	m. at St James's Palace, London, 8 Sept. 1761, CHARLOTTE Sophia (1744–1818), youngest d of Charles Louis Frederick, Duke of Mecklenburg-Strelitz. 9s 6d	d., aged 81 years 239 days, 29 Jan. 1820, of senility at Windsor. St George's Chapel, Windsor	His eldest son became Regent owing to his insanity 5 Feb. 1811. Hanover was made a kingdom in 1814. Succeeded by his eldest son, George Augustus Frederick

King or Queen Regnant, Date of Accession and Final Year of Reign; Style	Date and Place of Birth and Parentage	Marriages and No. of Children	Date, Cause and Place of Death, and Place of Burial	Notes and Succession
35. **GEORGE IV** 29 Jan. 1820–30 *Style:* As later style of No. 33	12 Aug. 1762 at St James's Palace, London; eldest son of George III and Charlotte	m. (2)★ at the Chapel Royal, St James's Palace, 8 Apr. 1795, CAROLINE Amelia Elizabeth (1768–1821), his first cousin, second d of Charles, Duke of Brunswick-Wolfenbüttel. 1d. ★First married Maria FitzHerbert	d., aged 67, 26 June 1830, of rupture of the stomach blood vessels; alcoholic cirrhosis; and dropsy at Windsor. St George's Chapel, Windsor	Succeeded by his eldest surviving brother, William Henry (George's only child, Princess Charlotte, having died in child-birth 6 Nov. 1817)
36. **WILLIAM IV** 26 June 1830–7 *Style:* As No. 34	21 Aug. 1765 at Buckingham Palace; third and oldest surviving son of George III and Charlotte	m. at Kew, 11 July 1818, ADELAIDE Louisa Theresa Caroline Amelia (1792–1849), eldest d of George, Duke of Saxe-Meiningen. 2d	d., aged 71, 20 June 1837, of pleuro-pneumonia and alcoholic cirrhosis at Windsor. Windsor	On William's death the crown of Hanover passed by Salic law to his brother, Ernest, Duke of Cumberland. Succeeded by his niece, Alexandrina Victoria
37. **VICTORIA** 20 June 1837–1901 *Style:* As (except for 'Queen') No. 34 until 1 May 1876, whereafter 'Empress of India' was added	24 May 1819 at Kensington Palace, London; only child of Edward, Duke of Kent and Strathearn, 4th son of George III, and Victoria, widow of Emich Charles, Prince of Leiningen and d of Francis, Duke of Saxe-Coburg-Saafeld	m. at St James's Palace, London, 10 Feb. 1840 her first cousin Francis ALBERT Augustus Charles Emmanuel (1819–61), second son of Ernest I, Duke of Saxe-Coburg-Gotha. 4s 5d	d., aged 81 years 243 days, 22 Jan. 1901 of senility at Osborne, I.o.W. Frogmore	Assumed title Empress of India 1 May 1876. Succeeded by her elder surviving son, Albert Edward
38. **EDWARD VII** 22 Jan. 1901–10 *Style:* 'By the Grace of God, of the United Kingdom of Great Britain and Ireland and of the British Dominions beyond the Seas, King, Defender of the Faith, Emperor of India'	9 Nov. 1841 at Buckingham Palace, London; elder surviving son of Victoria and Albert	m. at St George's Chapel, Windsor, 10 Mar. 1863, ALEXANDRA Caroline Maria Charlotte Louisa Julia (1844–1925), d of Christian IX of Denmark. 3s 3d	d., aged 68, 6 May, 1910, of bronchitis at Buckingham Palace. St George's Chapel, Windsor	Succeeded by his only surviving son, George Frederick Ernest Albert
39. **GEORGE V** 6 May 1910–36 *Style:* As for No. 37 until 12 May 1927, whereafter 'By the Grace of God, of Great Britain, Ireland, and of the British Dominions beyond the Seas, King, Defender of the Faith, Emperor of India'	3 June 1865 at Marlborough House, London; second and only surviving son of Edward VII and Alexandra	m. at St James's Palace, London, 6 July 1893, Victoria MARY Augusta Louise Olga Pauline Claudine Agnes (1867–1953), eldest child and only d of Francis, Duke of Teck. 5s 1d	d., aged 70, 20 Jan. 1936, of bronchitis at Sandringham House, Norfolk. St George's Chapel, Windsor	Succeeded by his eldest son, Edward Albert Christian George Andrew Patrick David
40. **EDWARD VIII** 20 Jan. 1936–11 Dec. 1936 *Style:* As for No. 38	23 June 1894 at the White Lodge, Richmond Park; eldest son of George V and Mary	m. at the Château de Candé, Monts, France, 3 June 1937, Bessie Wallis Warfield (b. 1896), previous wife of Lt. Earl Winfield Spencer, USN (div. 1927) and Ernest Simpson (div. 1936). No issue	d., aged 77, 28 May, 1972, of cancer of the throat at 4, Route du Champ, D'Entrainement, Paris XVIᵉ, France	Edward VIII abdicated for himself and his heirs and was succeeded by his eldest brother, Albert Frederick Arthur George
41. **GEORGE VI** 11 Dec. 1936–52 *Style:* As for No. 38 until the Indian title was dropped 22 June 1947	14 Dec. 1895 at York Cottage, Sandringham; second son of George V and Mary	m. at Westminster Abbey, 26 Apr. 1923, Lady ELIZABETH Angela Marguerite Bowes-Lyon (b. 1900), youngest d of 14th Earl of Strathmore and Kinghorne. 2d	d., aged 56, 6 Feb. 1952, of lung cancer at Sandringham House, Norfolk. St George's Chapel, Windsor	Succeeded by his elder d, Elizabeth Alexandra Mary

King or Queen Regnant, Date of Accession and Final Year of Reign; Style	Date and Place of Birth and Parentage	Marriages and No. of Children	Date, Cause and Place of Death, and Place of Burial	Notes and Succession
42. **ELIZABETH II** Since 6 Feb. 1952 *Style:* (from 29 May 1953) 'By the grace of God, of the United Kingdom of Great Britain and Northern Ireland and of Her other Realms and Territories, Queen, Head of the Commonwealth, Defender of the Faith'.	21 Apr. 1926 at 17 Bruton Street, London, W 1; elder d of George VI and Elizabeth	m. at Westminster Abbey, 20 Nov. 1947, her third cousin PHILIP (b. Corfu, Greece 10 June 1921), only son of Prince Andrea (Andrew) of Greece and Princess Alice (great-grand-daughter of Queen Victoria). 3s 1d	—	The Heir Apparent is Charles Philip Arthur George, Prince of Wales, b. 14 Nov. 1948

U.K. LEGISLATURE

THE COMPOSITION OF THE TWO HOUSES OF PARLIAMENT

House of Lords

Peers of the Blood Royal	4
Archbishops	2
Dukes	26
Marquesses	37
Earls	175
Countesses in their own right	6
Viscounts	116
Bishops (by seniority)	24
Barons and Scots Lords (hereditary)	462
Baronesses in their own right (hereditary)	13
Life Peers (Barons)	243
Life Peeresses (Baronesses)	38
	1146

House of Commons

The size of the House of Commons has frequently been altered:

1885 By a Representation to the People Act (RPA) membership was increased by 12 to total 670.

1918 By an RPA membership was increased by 37 to an all-time high point of 707.

1922 By two Acts of Parliament (the Partition of Ireland) membership was reduced by 92 to 615. (*Note:* Irish representation was reduced from 105 to 13 members representing Northern Ireland.)

1945 By an RPA membership was increased by 25 to 640.

1948 By an RPA membership was decreased by 15 to 625. (*Note:* This took effect in 1950 and involved the abolition of the 12 university seats and 12 double-member constituencies.)

1955 By an Order in Council under the House of Commons (Redistribution of seats) Act membership was increased by five to a total of 630.

1974 By an Order in Council membership was increased by 5 to the present total of 635.

The 21 General Elections of the Twentieth Century

1900 Lord Salisbury's Conservative Government exercised its undoubted constitutional right to cash in on the apparently victorious (Mafeking and Pretoria) outcome of the Boer War two years before its 7 years of life was expired. The Liberal opposition called these tactics immoral and dubbed the election the 'Khaki Election'. The Government were given the most triumphant encore seen since the Reform Act of 1832 with an overall majority of 134 compared with the Dissolution figure of 128. The Liberal opposition was divided into the 'pro-Boers', comprising Gladstonians with the young Lloyd George, and the followers of Asquith, Haldane and Grey, who were Empire men.

1906 By December 1905 A J Balfour, who had succeeded his uncle as Prime Minister in 1902, had his majority reduced to 68 because of losses in by-elections. Feeling out of tune with the objects of the Tariff Reform League, he resigned. The King asked Campbell-Bannerman to form a government which he did and then immediately went to the country. The result was a landslide victory for the Liberals, who won an overall majority of 84. The Conservatives lost support mainly because of alarm over Chamberlain's Tariff Reform campaign and State support for Church of England schools, which offended nonconformist opinion. Liberal policy was the trinity of Free Trade, Home Rule for Ireland, and Humanitarianism.

1910 (Jan./Feb.) Asquith took over the premiership in 1908 shortly before the death of Campbell-Bannerman. The stock of the Tories rose because of Liberal pacifism in the face of the 'German Menace' and the Government lost 10 by-elections. The Liberal hopes of securing a second term rested on their taking advantage of the Conservative peers' inevitable rejection of Lloyd George's deliberately provocative budget. The government were thus handed on a plate the priceless slogan 'Lords versus the People'. The Liberals, however, only ended up with 125 seats fewer than their 1906 highwater mark. More seriously, they were now at the mercy of the jubilant 82 Irish Nationalists and 40 Labourites.

1910 (Dec.) The Government's House of Lords policy was: (1) abolition of Lords power to veto over certified Money Bills; (2) a delaying power only of three sessions for other Bills, and (3) the life of a Parliament to be reduced from seven to five years. The ostensible reason for another General Election was that the country should vote on these policies. But the real reason was that secretly King George V, who had succeeded his father that May, had insisted on a second appeal to the nation before giving his promise to create if necessary the required number of Liberal peers to vote the Parliament Bill through. The result of the election was almost a carbon copy of that eleven months previously.

1918 The victorious wartime premier, Lloyd George, at the head of the Coalition which had superseded Asquith's Liberal administration in 1916, went to the country in December 1918. The election was called by the opposition the 'coupon election'. This was because Lloyd George (Lib.) and Bonar Law (Con.) jointly signed letters (nicknamed 'coupons') giving support to those they regarded as loyal supporters of the Coalition. The Government's election policy in terms of slogans was 'Hang the Kaiser'; make the Germans pay for the war 'until the lemon pips squeak'; and make the country 'fit for heroes to live in'. Women over 30 were first given the vote. The Coalition won a crushing victory on a very low (58·9 per cent) poll.

1922 The Coalition Government under Lloyd George progressively lost the confidence of its predominant Conservative wing. The Conservatives disliked the Liberal Prime Minister's vacillating and extravagant domestic policies, especially in regard to agriculture and what they regarded as naïve foreign policies. Left-wing opinion was displeased with the rate of social progress on the home front. Many major strikes were organised. In Oct. 1922 the Conservatives resolved to fight the next election as an independent party. Lloyd George promptly resigned. Bonar Law formed a Government and went to the country. The Conservatives, with Bonar Law's policy of 'Tranquillity', won a majority of 75 over all other parties. The Labour Party overtook the divided Liberals by nearly doubling their representation to 142 and became the official Opposition.

1923 Bonar Law, who had started his premiership a sick man, retired in May 1923, and died shortly afterwards. His successor, in preference to Lord Curzon, was Stanley Baldwin. The main domestic problem was unemployment. Baldwin took the view that protective tariffs would alleviate it: but he was bound by Bonar Law's promise not to introduce such a measure. The only way out was to appeal to the country. The election saw a tiny change from the 1922 percentages but a dramatic loss of 87 seats by the Conservatives. Baldwin, although now in a minority of 99, waited to face the new Parliament and was inevitably defeated by a Labour-Liberal alliance and then resigned in favour of Ramsay MacDonald (Labour).

1924 MacDonald found himself embarrassingly short of talented Ministers and under intense pressure and scrutiny from the National Executive of the Labour Party. His greatest success was to sort out the Franco-German squabble over war reparation payments. The Government were brought down when their often unwilling allies, the Liberals, voted with the Tories for a motion for enquiry into the circumstances under which a journalist, J R Campbell, was to have his prosecution by the Attorney General for sedition (he advocated British soldiers disobeying orders if confronted with strikers) withdrawn. The Labour Party lost 40 seats and the Conservatives, profiting from there being fewer Liberal candidates, won an overall majority of 225 seats under Baldwin.

1929 Despite Baldwin's Government's surviving overall majority of 185 seats, Labour won this election with 288 seats, but could not command an absolute majority (Conservatives 260, Liberals 59, Others 8 = 327). Over 5 million women between the ages of 21 and 30 were eligible to vote for the first time. The Conservatives had adopted the uninspiring slogan 'Safety First'. The Labour Party, with the slogan 'Socialism In Our Time', had a three-pronged policy of world peace, disarmament, and a desire to deal more energetically with unemployment. The Liberals also based their appeal on unemployment remedies. The Liberal leader, Mr Lloyd George, decided to support Labour in office.

1931 The Labour Government committed themselves to increased expenditure and the unemployment figures rose alarmingly. A crisis of loss of confidence in sterling caused a summer crisis and Ramsay MacDonald suggested to his Cabinet an economy scheme which included the reduction of unemployment insurance benefits. The National Executive of the Labour Party and the TUC characteristically flatly refused to support any such measure. On 24 Aug. the Labour Government resigned and MacDonald formed a National Government which went to the polls on 27 Oct. The extent of their victory amazed contemporary opinion as the National Government won 554 seats, including 13 by National Labour candidates, while the opposition was reduced to 52 Labour and 4 Liberal Members.

1935 Ramsay MacDonald (National Labour) resigned his premiership in June 1935 and was logically succeeded by Stanley Baldwin (Conservative), who held a snap November General Election by dissolving Parliament two days short of the fourth anniversary of the 1931 election. The main issue was simply, did the nation approve of the work of the National Government in restoring the economy after the slump and want it to continue, or did the Nation want to revert to a Labour Government? The result was a massive vote of confidence in the National (predominantly Conservative) Government

which won an overall majority of 249 seats. The Labour Party's main attack was over the 'Means Test' for unemployment assistance ('the dole'), although their own 1929 Government had accepted the principle of it, and the National Government had quickly withdrawn the new unsatisfactory regulations introduced earlier that year. Broadcasting for the first time played a significant rôle in the campaign with the public listening to a series of speeches made by the various Party Leaders every night during the first part of the election campaign.

1945 During the ten years since the previous election the country underwent the traumatic total war of 1939–45. Baldwin resigned in 1937 and was succeeded by Neville Chamberlain who resigned in 1940 at the nadir of our wartime fortunes. For the remaining five years Winston Churchill gave dynamic leadership which secured victory over Nazi Germany in May 1945. In that month the wartime Coalition broke up and was replaced by a predetermined Conservative administration. This Government, despite Churchill's premiership, was defeated by a Labour landslide. The new Government had Labour's first overall majority—146 seats.

1950 Mr Attlee's administration launched the 'Welfare State' along the lines set out by various wartime White Papers, but his nationalisation measures, especially as regards steel, met fierce resistance. A balance of payments crisis in the autumn of 1949 compelled the Government to devalue the pound against the dollar and make drastic economies. The result of the February election was a narrow Labour victory with an overall majority of only 5.

1951 After 20 months of precarious administration, during which time the Conservatives ceaselessly harried the Government ranks, especially over the nationalisation of steel, Mr Attlee resigned. The last straw was another balance of payments crisis in September following the earlier resignation of Aneurin Bevan (Minister of Labour) and Harold Wilson (Pres., Board of Trade). The nation's reply to Mr Attlee's appeal over the radio for a larger majority was to elect the Conservatives with an overall majority of 17. Winston Churchill returned as Prime Minister.

1955 In April 1955, after 4½ years of government with a small majority, Sir Winston Churchill resigned as Prime Minister in favour of Sir Anthony Eden, who seven weeks later went to the country for a vote of confidence. The Conservatives had succeeded in restoring the nation's finances, had denationalised steel and road haulage, and twice reduced the standard rate of income tax by 6d. The Government's majority rose to 58 and the five years of near deadlock in the House was broken.

1959 In Jan. 1957, following the strain of the Suez crisis, Eden resigned and Harold Macmillan became Prime Minister. The Government had been losing support, largely owing to some unpopularity over the Rent Act. The new Prime Minister, despite a number of difficulties, managed to repair Conservative fortunes. His 1959 visit to the USSR and the further reduction of income tax in April added to general contentment. The election was fought on the Conservative theme 'life is better with us' while Labour got into difficulties with Mr Gaitskell's promises of no higher taxes, yet very expensive projects. The result was that the Government again increased their overall majority to 100 seats.

1964 The Conservative Government, after 13 consecutive years of rule, went to the country in October, as required every five years by the Parliament Act of 1911. After the post-war high-water mark of 1959 (majority 100) Conservative fortunes declined owing notably to the Profumo scandal and a public wrangle over the successorship to Mr Macmillan who resigned in Oct. 1963 owing to ill health. The nation wanted a change: the Conservatives were however defeated by a rise in the Liberal vote from 5·9 per cent to 11·2 per cent rather than the Labour vote which was less than their 1959 total. Labour won by an overall majority of only 4.

1966 After 20 months in power, Mr Wilson became convinced (on the death of the Member for Falmouth in February) of the danger of continuing with his hairline majority. Labour fought the campaign on the slogan 'You Know Labour Government Works'. The Conservatives fought on a policy of entering the Common Market, reforming the 'over-mighty' Trade Unions and making the Welfare State less indiscriminate. Mr Wilson increased his overall majority from 3 to 97 and declared his intention to govern for five years to achieve 'a juster society'.

1970 Having completed four of the five years of his second term in power, Mr Wilson called the Labour Party to action in a bid for his hat-trick in May 1970. Remembered as the General Election most dominated by the pollsters, their findings consistently showed strong leads for Labour. Wages rates had risen in an unrestrained way in the five-month run-up but prices levels were also just beginning to erode the reality of these monetary gains. Within six days of polling NOP showed a massive Labour lead of 12·4 per cent. In reality, however, the voters gave the Conservatives a 3·4 per cent lead, thus an overall majority of 30 seats.

1974 (Feb.) This was the first 'crisis' election since 1931. It was called to settle 'Who governs Britain?' under the duress of the National Union of Mineworkers' coal strike against the restraints of Stage III of the Incomes Policy. The situation was exacerbated by the Arab decision the previous November to raise the price of oil fourfold. A three-day week for most industries was decreed under Emergency Powers to start on 1 Jan. A ballot inviting the miners to give the NUM authority to call a strike was announced on 4 Feb., an election was called on 7 Feb., and a strike began on 10 Feb. after 81 per cent of the miners had voted in favour of giving the NUM Executive the authority they sought. Mr Wilson spoke of conciliation in place of confrontation and the alternative possibilities under a 'Social Contract' agreed between the Labour Party and the TUC on 18 Feb. 1973. The electorate, largely due to the impact of a successful Liberal campaign, spoke equivocally, giving Labour a majority of four over the Conservatives but 10 less than the combined Conservatives and Liberals. The Liberals rejected a coalition and appealed for a government of National Unity. Two hours after Mr Heath's resignation on 4 Mar., the Queen sent for Mr Wilson for a third time.

1974 (Oct.) For the first time since 1910 there were two elections within the same year. On 11 Mar. the miners returned to full working accepting a National Coal Board offer to raise their wage bill by 29 per cent. In June and July HM Opposition, with Liberal support, defeated Mr Wilson's precarious lobby strength 29 times, notably on the Trade Union and Labour Relation Bill. An election was called by Mr Wilson on

18 Sept. The campaign was fought mainly on the issue of inflation statistics, unemployment prospects and the promise by Labour to hold an EEC ballot. Though less than 29 out of each 100 persons eligible to vote cast votes for Labour candidates, only 27 such voters supported Conservative candidates. Thus Mr Wilson won his fourth General Election, with an overall majority of three seats, but with a very secure working majority of 42 over the Conservatives, who were by far the largest party in a fragmented Opposition. Mr Wilson resigned and was replaced by Mr Callaghan, who had been elected leader of the Labour Party on 5 Apr. 1976.

THE RESULTS OF THE 21 GENERAL ELECTIONS 1900-1974

No. Election and Date	Total Seats	Result (and % share of Total Poll)			Irish Nationalists and Others	% Turn-out of Electorate
		Conservatives	Liberals	Labour		
1 1900 (28 Sept.–24 Oct.)	670	**402** (51·1)	184 (44·6)	2 (1·8)	82 (2·5)	74·6% of 6 730 935
2 1906 (12 Jan.–7 Feb.)	670	157 (43·6)	**400** (49·0)	30 (5·9)	83 (1·5)	82·6% of 7 264 608
3 1910 (14 Jan.–9 Feb.)	670	273 (46·9)	**275** (43·2)	40 (7·7)	82 (2·2)	86·6% of 7 694 741
4 1910 (2–19 Dec.)	670	272 (46·3)	272 (43·8)	42 (7·2)	84 (2·7)	81·1% of 7 709 981
5 1918 (14 Dec.)	707	**383** (38·7)	161 (25·6)	73 (23·7)	90 (12·0)	58·9% of 21 392 322
6 1922 (15 Nov.)	615	**345** (38·2)	116 (29·1)	142 (29·5)	12 (3·2)	71·3% of 21 127 663
7 1923 (6 Dec.)	615	**258** (38·1)	159 (29·6)	191 (30·5)	7 (1·8)	70·8% of 21 281 232
8 1924 (29 Oct.)	615	**419** (48·3)	40 (17·6)	151 (33·0)	5 (1·1)	76·6% of 21 731 320
9 1929 (30 May)	615	260 (38·2)	59 (23·4)	**288** (37·1)	8 (1·3)	76·1% of 28 850 870
10 1931 (27 Oct.)	615	**521** (60·5)	37 (7·0)	52 (30·6)	5 (1·7)	76·3% of 29 960 071
11 1935 (14 Nov.)	615	**432** (53·7)	20 (6·4)	154 (37·9)	9 (2·0)	71·2% of 31 379 050
12 1945 (5 July)	640	213 (39·8)	12 (9·0)	**393** (47·8)	22 (2·8)	72·7% of 33 240 391
13 1950 (23 Feb.)	625	298 (43·5)	9 (9·1)	**315** (46·4)	3 (1·3)	84·0% of 33 269 770
14 1951 (25 Oct.)	625	**321** (48·0)	6 (2·5)	295 (48·7)	3 (0·7)	82·5% of 34 465 573
15 1955 (25 May)	630	**344** (49·8)	6 (2·7)	277 (46·3)	3 (1·2)	76·7% of 34 858 263
16 1959 (8 Oct.)	630	**365** (49·4)	6 (5·9)	258 (43·8)	1 (0·9)	78·8% of 35 397 080
17 1964 (15 Oct.)	630	303 (43·4)	9 (11·1)	**317** (44·2)	1 (1·3)	77·1% of 35 894 307
18 1966 (31 Mar.)	630	253 (41·9)	12 (8·5)	**363** (47·9)	2 (1·7)	75·9% of 35 965 127
19 1970 (18 June)	630	**330** (46·4)	6 (7·5)	288 (43·0)	6 (3·1)	72·0% of 39 247 683
20 1974 (28 Feb.)	635	297 (38·2)	14 (19·3)	**301** (37·2)	23 (5·3)	78·8% of 39 752 317
21 1974 (10 Oct.)	635	277 (35·8)	13 (18·3)	**319** (39·3)	26 (6·6)	72·8% of 40 083 286

PRIME MINISTERS OF GREAT BRITAIN AND THE UNITED KINGDOM

Below is a complete compilation of the 50 Prime Ministers of Great Britain and the United Kingdom. The data run in the following order: final style as Prime Minister (with earlier or later styles); date or dates as Prime Minister with party affiliation; date and place of birth and death and place of burial; marriage or marriages with number of children; education and membership of Parliament with constituency and dates.

1. The Rt Hon, Sir Robert **WALPOLE**, KG (1726) KB (1725, resigned 1726), (PC 1714), cr. 1st Earl of Orford (of the 2nd creation) in the week of his retirement; ministry, 3 April 1721 to 8 Feb. 1742, (i) reappointed on the accession of George II on 11 June 1727, (ii) Walpole's absolute control of the Cabinet can only be said to have dated from 15 May 1730; Whig; b. 26 Aug. 1676 at Houghton, Norfolk; d. 18 Mar. 1745 at No. 5 Arlington St, Piccadilly, London; bur. Houghton, Norfolk; m. 1 (1700) Catherine Shorter (d. 1717), m. 2ndly (1738) Maria Skerrett (d. 1738); children, 1st, 3s and 2d; 2nd, 2d (born prior to the marriage); ed. Eton and King's, Camb. (scholar); MP (Whig) for Castle Rising (1701–2); King's Lynn (1702–42) (expelled from the House for a short period 1712–13).

2. The Rt Hon, the Hon Sir Spencer Compton, 1st and last Earl of **WILMINGTON**, KG (1733), KB (1725, resigned 1733), (PC 1716), cr. Baron Wilmington 1728; cr. Earl 1730; ministry, 16 Feb. 1742 to 2 July 1743; Whig; b. 1673 or 1674; d. 2 July 1743; bur. Compton Wynyates, Warwickshire; unmarried; no legitimate issue; ed. St Paul's School, London, and Trinity, Oxford; MP (originally Tory until about 1704) for Eye (1698–1710); East Grinstead (1713–15); Sussex (Whig) (1715–28); Speaker 1715–27.

3. The Rt Hon, the Hon Henry **PELHAM** (PC 1725); prior to 1706 was Henry Pelham, Esq.; ministry 27 Aug. 1743 to 6 Mar. 1754 (with an interregnum 10–12 Feb. 1746); Whig; b. c. 1695; d. 6 Mar. 1754 at Arlington St, Piccadilly, London; bur. Laughton Church, nr. Lewes, E. Sussex; m. (1726) Lady Catherine Manners; children, 2s and 6d; ed. Westminster School and Hart Hall, Oxford; MP Seaford (1717–22); Sussex (1722–54).

4. The Rt Hon Sir William Pulteney, 1st and last Earl of **BATH** (cr. 1742) PC (1716) (struck off 1731); kissed hands 10 Feb. 1746 but unable to form a ministry; Whig; b. 22 Mar. 1684 in London; d. 7 July 1764; bur. Westminster Abbey; m. Anna Maria Gumley; ed. Westminster School and Christ Church, Oxford; MP Hedon (or Heydon) 1705–34; Middlesex 1734–42.

5. His Grace the 1st Duke of **NEWCASTLE** upon Tyne and 1st Duke of Newcastle under Lyme (The Rt Hon, the Hon Sir Thomas Pelham-Holles, Bt, KG (1718). (PC 1717)); added the surname

Holles in July 1711; known as Lord Pelham of Laughton (1711–14); Earl of Claire (1714–15); cr. Duke of Newcastle upon Tyne 1715 and cr. Duke of Newcastle under Lyme 1756; ministry, (a) 16 Mar. 1754 to 26 Oct. 1756, (b) 2 July 1757 to 25 Oct. 1760, (c) 25 Oct. 1760 to 25 May 1762; Whig; b. 21 July 1693; d. 17 Nov. 1768 at Lincoln's Inn Field, London; bur. Laughton Church, nr. Lewes, E. Sussex; m. (1717) Lady Henrietta Godolphin (d. 1776); no issue; ed. Westminster School and Claire Hall, Camb.

6. His Grace the 4th Duke of **DEVONSHIRE** (Sir William Cavendish, KG (1756), (PC 1751, but struck off roll 1762)); known as Lord Cavendish of Hardwick until 1729 and Marquess of Hartington until 1755; ministry, 16 Nov. 1756 to May 1757; Whig; b. 1720; d. 2 Oct. 1764 at Spa, Belgium; bur. Derby Cathedral; m. (1748) Charlotte Elizabeth, Baroness Clifford (d. 1754); children, 3s and 1d; ed. privately; MP (Whig) for Co. Derby (1741–51). Summoned to Lords (1751) in father's Barony Cavendish of Hardwick.

7. The Rt Hon James **WALDEGRAVE**, 2nd Earl of Waldegrave (pronounced Wallgrave) from 1741, PC (1752), KG (1757); kissed hands 8 June 1757 but returned seals 12 June being unable to form Ministry; b. 14 Mar. 1715; d. 28 Apr. 1763; m. Marion Walpole (niece of No. 1); children 3d; ed. Eton; took seat in House of Lords, 1741.

8. The 3rd Earl of **BUTE** (The Rt Hon, the Hon Sir John Stuart, KG (1762), KT (1738, resigned 1762), (PC 1760)); until 1723 was The Hon John Stuart; ministry, 26 May

1762 to 8 April 1763; Tory; b. 25 May 1713 at Parliament Square, Edinburgh; d. 10 Mar. 1792 at South Audley St, Grosvenor Square, London; bur. Rothesay, Bute; m. (1736) Mary Wortley-Montagu later (1761) Baroness Mount Stuart (d. 1794); children, 4s and 4d (with other issue); ed. Eton.

9. The Rt Hon, the Hon George **GRENVILLE** (PC 1754); prior to 1749 was G. Grenville Esq.; ministry, 16 Apr. 1763 to 10 July 1765; Whig; b. 14 Oct. 1712 at ? Wotton, Bucks; d. 13 Nov. 1770 at Bolton St, Piccadilly, London; bur. Wotton, Bucks; m. (1749) Elizabeth Wyndham (d. 1769); children, 4s and 5d; ed. Eton and Christ Church, Oxford; MP for Buckingham (1741–70).

10. The Most Hon The 2nd Marquess of **ROCKINGHAM** (The Rt Hon Lord Charles Watson-Wentworth, KG (1760), (PC 1765); known as Hon Charles Watson-Wentworth until 1739; Viscount Higham (1739–46); Earl of Malton (1746–50); succeeded to Marquessate 14 Dec. 1750; ministry, (a) 13 July 1765 to July 1766, (b) 27 March 1782 to his death on 1 July 1782; Whig; b. 13 May 1730; d. 1 July 1782; bur. York Minster; m. (1752) Mary Bright (her father was formerly called Liddell) (d. 1804); no issue; ed. Westminster School (and possibly St John's Camb.). Took his seat in House of Lords 21 May 1751.

11. The 1st Earl of **CHATHAM** (The Rt Hon William Pitt (PC 1746)); cr. Earl 4 Aug. 1766; ministry, 30 July 1766 to 14 Oct. 1768; Whig; his health in 1767 prevented his being PM in other than name; b. 15 Nov. 1708 at St James's, Westminster, London; d. 11 May 1788 at Hayes, Kent; bur. Westminster Abbey; m. (1754) Hon. Hester Grenville*, later (1761) cr. Baroness Chatham in her own right (d. 1803); children, 3s and 2d; ed. Eton, Trinity, Oxford (took no degree owing to gout), and Utrecht; MP (Whig) Old Sarum (1735–47); Seaford (1747–54); Aldborough (1754–6); Okehampton (1756–7) (also Buckingham (1756)), Bath (1757–66).

12. His Grace the 3rd Duke of **GRAFTON** (The Rt Hon Sir Augustus Henry FitzRoy, KG (1769), (PC 1765); prior to 1747 known as the Hon. Augustus H. FitzRoy; 1747–57 as Earl of Euston, succeeded to dukedom in 1757; ministry, 14 Oct. 1768 to 28 Jan. 1770; Whig; he was virtually PM in 1767 when Lord Chatham's ministry broke down; b. 28 Sept. 1735 at St Marylebone, London; d. 14 Mar. 1811 at Euston Hall, Suffolk; bur. Euston, Suffolk; m. 1st (1756) Hon. Anne Liddell (sep. 1765, mar. dis. by Act of Parl. 1769) (d. 1804), m. 2ndly (1769) Elizabeth Wrottesley (d. 1822); children, 1st, 2s and 1d; 2nd, 6s and 6d (possibly also another d. who died young); ed. private school at Hackney, Westminster School, and Peterhouse, Camb; MP (Whig) Bury St Edmunds (1756–7).

13. Lord **NORTH** (The Rt Hon, the Hon Sir Frederick North, KG (1772), (PC 1766); succ. (Aug. 1790) as 2nd Earl of Guildford; ministry, 28 Jan. 1770 to 20 Mar. 1782; Tory; b. 13 Apr. 1732 at Albemarle St, Piccadilly, London; d. 5 Aug. 1792 at Lower Grosvenor Street, London; bur. All Saints' Church, Wroxton, Oxfordshire; m. (1756) Anne Speke (d. 1797); children, 4s and 3d; ed. Eton, Trinity, Oxford, and Leipzig; MP (Tory) for Banbury (1754–90) (can be regarded as a Whig from 1783). Took his seat in the House of Lords 25 Nov. 1790.

* This lady had the extraordinary distinction of being the wife, the mother, the sister and the aunt of four British Prime Ministers. They were Nos. 11, 16, 9, and 18 respectively.

14. The 2nd Earl of **SHELBURNE** (Rt Hon, the Hon Sir William Petty, KG (1782) (PC 1763)); formerly, until 1751, William Fitz-Maurice; Viscount Fitz-Maurice (1753–61); succeeded to Earldom 10 May 1761; cr. The 1st Marquess of Lansdowne (6 Dec. 1784); Col. 1760; Maj. Gen. 1765; Lt. Gen. 1772, and Gen. 1783; ministry, 4 July 1782 to 24 Feb. 1783; Whig; b. 20 May 1737 at Dublin, Ireland; d. 7 May 1805 at Berkeley Square, London; bur. High Wycombe, Bucks; m. 1st (1765) Lady Sophia Carerett (d. 1771), 2ndly (1779) Lady Louisa Fitz-Patrick (d. 1789); children, 1st, 2s, 2nd, 1s and 1d; ed. local school in S. Ireland, private tutor, and Christ Church, Oxford; MP Chipping Wycombe (1760–1). Took seat in House of Lords (as Baron Wycombe) 3 Nov. 1761.

15. His Grace the 3rd Duke of **PORTLAND** (The Most Noble Sir William Henry Cavendish Bentinck, KG (1794) (PC 1765)); assumed additional name of Bentinck in 1755; assumed by Royal Licence surname of Cavendish-Bentinck in 1801; Marquess of Titchfield from birth until he succeeded to the dukedom on 1 May 1762; ministry, (a) 2 April 1783 to Dec. 1783, (b) 31 Mar. 1807 to Oct. 1809; (a) coalition and (b) Tory; b. 14th Apr. 1738; d. 30 Oct. 1809 at Bulstrode, Bucks; bur. St Marylebone, London; m. (1766) Lady Dorothy Cavendish (d. 1794); children, 4s and 1d; ed. Westminster or Eton and Christ Church, Oxford; MP (Whig) Weobley, Herefordshire (1761–2).

16. The Rt Hon, the Hon William **PITT** (PC 1782); prior Aug. 1766 was William Pitt, Esq.; ministry, (a) 19 Dec. 1783 to 14 Mar. 1801, (b) 10 May 1804 to his death on 23 Jan. 1806; Tory; b. 28 May 1759 at Hayes, nr. Bromley, Kent; d. 23 Jan. 1806 at Bowling Green House, Putney, Surrey; bur. Westminster Abbey; unmarried. ed. privately and Pembroke Hall, Cambridge, MP (Tory) Appleby.

17. The Rt Hon Henry **ADDINGTON** (PC 1789); cr. 1st Viscount Sidmouth 1805; ministry, 17 Mar. 1801 to 30 April 1804; Tory; b. 30 May 1757 at Bedford Row, London; d. 15 Feb. 1844 at White Lodge, Richmond Park, Surrey; bur. Mortlake; m. 1st (1781) Ursula Mary Hammond (d. 1811), 2ndly (1823) Hon. Mrs Marianne Townshend (née Scott) (d. 1842); children, 1st, 3s and 4d, 2nd, no issue; ed. Cheam, Winchester Col., Lincoln's Inn, and Brasenose, Oxford (Chancellor's Medal for English Essay); MP (Tory) Devizes (1783–1805). Speaker 1789–1801. As a peer he supported the Whigs in 1807 and 1812 administrations.

18. The Rt Hon the 1st Baron **GRENVILLE** of Wotton-under-Bernewood (William Wyndham Grenville (PC (I) 1782; PC 1783)); cr. Baron 25 Nov. 1790; ministry, 10 Feb. 1806 to Mar. 1807; b. (the son of No. 9) 25 Oct. 1759; d. 12 Jan. 1834 at Dropmore Lodge, Bucks; bur. Burnham, Bucks; m. (1792) Hon Anne Pitt (d. 1864 aged 91); no issue; ed. Eton, Christ Church, Oxford (Chancellor's prize for Latin Verse), and Lincoln's Inn; MP Buckingham (1782–4), Buckinghamshire (1784–90). Speaker Jan.–June 1789.

19. The Rt Hon, the Hon Spencer **PERCEVAL** (PC 1807), KC (1796); ministry, 4 Oct. 1809 to 11 May 1812; b. 1 Nov. 1762 at Audley Sq., London; murdered 11 May 1812 in lobby of the House; bur. at Charlton; m. (1790) Jane Spencer-Wilson (later Lady Carr) (d. 1844); children, 6s and 6d; ed. Harrow; Trinity, Camb., and Lincoln's Inn; MP (Tory) Northampton (1796 and 1797).

20. The Rt Hon the 2nd Earl of **LIVERPOOL** (Sir Robert Banks Jenkinson, KG (1814) (PC 1799)); from birth to 1786 R B Jenkinson, Esq.; from 1786–96 The Hon

R B Jenkinson; from 1796–1808 (when he succeeded to the earldom) Lord Hawkesbury; ministry, (a) 8 June 1812 to 29 Jan. 1820, (b) 29 Jan. 1820 to 17 Feb., 1827; Tory; b. 7 June 1770; d. 4 Dec. 1828 at Coombe Wood, near Kingston-on-Thames; bur. at Hawkesbury; m. 1st (1795) Lady Louisa Theodosia Hervey (d. 1821), 2ndly (1822) Mary Chester (d. 1846); no issue; ed. Charterhouse and Christ Church, Oxford; summoned to House of Lords in his father's barony of Hawkesbury 15 Nov. 1803 (elected MP (Tory) for Appleby (1790) but did not sit as he was under age); Rye (1796–1803).

21. The Rt Hon George **CANNING** (PC 1800); ministry, 10 Apr. 1827 to his death; Tory; b. 11 Apr. 1770 in London; d. 8 Aug. 1827 at Chiswick Villa, London; m. (1800) Joan Scott (later, 1828, cr. Viscountess) (d. 1837); children, 3s and 1d; ed. in London; Hyde Abbey (nr. Winchester); Eton; Christ Church, Oxford (Chancellor's prize, Latin Verse), and Lincoln's Inn; MP (Tory) Newton, I. o. W. (1793–6); Wendover (1796–1802); Tralee (1802–6); Newton (1806–7); Hastings (1807–12); Liverpool (1812–23); Harwich (1823–6); Newport (1826–7), and Seaford (1827).

22. The Viscount **GODERICH** (Rt Hon, the Hon Frederick John Robinson (PC 1812, PC (I) c. 1833)); cr. Earl of Ripon 1833; ministry 31 Aug. 1827 to 8 Jan. 1828; Tory; b. 1 Nov. 1782 in London; d. 28 Jan. 1859 at Putney Heath, London; bur. Nocton, Lincs; m. (1814) Lady Sarah Albinia Louisa Hobart (d. 1867); children, 2s and 1d; ed. Harrow; St John's Col., Camb., and Lincoln's Inn; MP Carlow (1806–7); Ripon (1807–27).

23. His Grace The 1st Duke of **WELLINGTON** (The Most Noble, The Hon Sir Arthur Wellesley, KG (1813), GCB (1815), GCH (1816), (PC 1807, PC (I) 1807)); known as The Hon Arthur Wesley until 1804; then as The Hon Sir Arthur Wellesley, KB, until 1809 when cr. The Viscount Wellington; cr. Earl of Wellington 1812; Marquess of Wellington Oct. 1812 and Duke May 1814. Ensign (1787); Lieut. (1787); Capt. (1791); Major (1793); Lt-Col (1793); Col (1796); Maj. Gen. (1802); Lt. Gen. (1808); Gen. (1811); Field Marshal (1813); ministry, (a) 22 Jan. 1828 to 26 June 1830, (b) 26 June 1830 to 21 Nov. 1830, (c) 17 Nov. to 9 Dec. 1834; Tory; b. 1 May 1769 at Mornington House, Upper Merrion St., Dublin; d. 14 Sept. 1852 at Walmer Castle, Kent; bur. St Paul's Cathedral; m. (1806) the Hon Catherine Sarah Dorothea Pakenham (d. 1831); children, 2s; ed. Browns Seminary, King's Rd., Chelsea, London; Eton; Brussels, and The Academy at Angiers; MP Rye (1806); St Michael (1807); Newport, Isle of Wight (1807–9). Took seat in House of Lords as Viscount, Earl, Marquess, and Duke 28 June 1814.

24. The 2nd Earl **GREY** (The Rt Hon, the Hon Sir Charles Grey, Bt (1808), KG (1831), (PC 1806)); styled Viscount Howick 1806–7 and previously The Hon Charles Grey; ministry, 22 Nov. 1830 to July 1834; Whig; b. 13 Mar. 1764 at Fallodon, Northumberland; d. 17 July 1845 and bur. at Howick House, Northumberland; m. (1794) Hon Mary Elizabeth Ponsonby (d. 1861); children, 8s and 5d; ed. at a private school in Marylebone, London; Eton; Trinity, Camb., and Middle Temple; MP (Whig) Northumberland (1786–1807); Appleby (1807); Tavistock (1807).

25. The 3rd Viscount **MELBOURNE** (The Rt Hon, The Hon Sir William Lamb, Bt (PC (UK & I) 1827)); ministry, (a) 16 July 1834 to Nov. 1834, (b) 18 April 1835 to 20 June 1837, (c) 20 June 1837 to Aug. 1841; Whig; b. (of disputed paternity) 15 March

1779 Melbourne House, Piccadilly, London; d. 24 Nov. 1848 at Brocket; bur. at Hatfield; m. (1805) Lady Caroline Ponsonby, separated 1824 (d. 1828); only 1s survived infancy; ed. Eton; Trinity, Cambridge; Glasgow University, and Lincoln's Inn; MP (Whig) Leominster (1806); Haddington Borough (1806–7); Portarlington (1807–12); Peterborough (1816–19); Herts (1819–26); Newport, Isle of Wight (1827); Bletchingley (1827–8). Took his seat in House of Lords 1 Feb. 1829.

26. The Rt Hon Sir Robert **PEEL**, Bt (PC 1812); prior to May 1830 he was Robert Peel, Esq., MP, when he succeeded as 2nd Baronet; ministry, (a) 10 Dec. 1834 to 8 Apr. 1835, (b) 30 Aug. 1841 to 29 June 1846; Conservative; b. 5 Feb. 1788 prob. at Chamber Hall, nr. Bury, Lancashire; d. 2 July 1850 after fall from horse; bur. at Drayton-Bassett; m. (1820) Julia Floyd (d. 1859); children, 5s and 2d; ed. Harrow; Christ Church, Oxford (Double First in Classics and Mathematics), and Lincoln's Inn; MP (Tory) Cashel (Tipperary) (1809–12); Chippenham (1812–17); Univ. of Oxford (1817–29); Westbury (1829–30); Tamworth (1830–50).

27. The Rt Hon Lord John **RUSSELL** (PC 1830), and after 30 July 1861 1st Earl **RUSSELL**, KG (1862), GCMG (1869); ministry, (a) 30 June 1846 to Feb. 1852, (b) 29 Oct. 1865 to June 1866; (a) Whig and (b) Liberal; b. 18 Aug. 1792 in Hertford St, Mayfair; d. 28 May 1878 at Pembroke Lodge, Richmond Park, Surrey; bur. Chenies, Bucks; m. 1st (1835) Adelaide (née Lister), Dowager Baroness Ribblesdale (d. 1838), 2ndly (1841) Lady Frances Anna Maria Elliot-Murray-Kynynmound (d. 1898); children, 1st, 2d, 2nd 3s and 3d; ed. Westminster School and Edinburgh University; MP (Whig) Tavistock (1813–17, 1818–20 & 1830–1); Hunts (1820–6); Bandon (1826–30); Devon (1831–2); S. Devon (1832–5); Stroud (1835–41); City of London (1841–61). Took seat in the House of Lords on 30 July 1861.

28. The 14th Earl of **DERBY**, Rt Hon Sir Edward Geoffry Smith-Stanley, Bt, KG (1859), GCMG (1869), PC 1830, PC (I) 1831); prior to 1834 known as the Hon E G Stanley, MP; then known as Lord Stanley MP until 1844; ministry, (a) 23 Feb. 1852 to 18 Dec. 1852, (b) 20 Feb. 1858 to 11 June 1859, (c) 28 June 1866 to 26 Feb. 1868; Tory and Conservative; b. 19 March 1799 at Knowsley, Lancs; d. 23 Oct. 1869; and bur. at Knowsley, Lancs; m. (1825) Hon Emma Caroline Wilbraham-Bootle (d. 1876); 2s, 1d; ed. Eton; Christ Church Oxford (Chancellor's prize for Latin Verse); MP (Whig) Stockbridge (1822–6); Preston (1826–30); Windsor (1831–2); North Lancs (1832–44). Summoned 1844 to House of Lords as Lord Stanley (of Bickerstaffe); succeeded to Earldom 1851; became a Tory in 1835.

29. The Rt Hon Sir George Hamilton Gordon, Bt, 4th Earl of **ABERDEEN**, KG (1855), KT (1808), (PC 1814); prior to Oct. 1791 known as the Hon G Gordon; from 1791 to Aug. 1801 known as Lord Haddo; assumed additional name of Hamilton Nov. 1818; ministry, 19 Dec. 1852 to 5 Feb. 1855; Peelite; b. 28 Jan. 1784 in Edinburgh; d. 14 Dec. 1860 at Argyll House, St James's, London; bur. at Stanmore, G. London; m. 1st (1805) Lady Catherine Elizabeth Hamilton (d. 1812), 2ndly (1815) to her sister-in-law Harriet (née Douglas), Dowager Viscountess Hamilton (d. 1833); children, 1st, 1s and 3d, 2nd 4s and 1d; ed. Harrow and St John's, Camb.; House of Lords 1814.

30. The Rt Hon Sir Henry John Temple, 3rd and last Viscount **PALMERSTON** (a non-representative peer of Ireland), KG (1856), GCB (1832), (PC 1809); known (1784–1802) as the Hon H J Temple; ministry, (a)

6 Feb. 1855 to 19 Feb. 1858, (b) 12 June 1859 to 18 Oct. 1865; Liberal; b. 20 Oct. 1784 at Broadlands, nr. Romsey, Hants (or possibly in Park St, London); d. 18 Oct. 1865 at Brocket Hall, Herts; bur. Westminster Abbey; m. (1839) Hon. Emily Mary (née Lamb), the Dowager Countess Cowper (d. 1869); no issue; ed. Harrow; Univ. of Edinburgh, and St John's Camb.; MP (Tory) Newport, Isle of Wight (1807–11); Camb. Univ. (1811–31); Bletchingley (1831–2); S. Hants. (1832–4); Tiverton (1835–65); from 1829 a Whig and latterly a liberal.

31. The Rt Hon Benjamin **DISRAELI**, 1st and last Earl of **BEACONSFIELD**, KG (1878), (PC 1852); prior to 12 Aug. 1876 Benjamin Disraeli (except that until 1838 he was known as Benjamin D'Israeli); ministry, (a) 27 Feb. 1868 to November 1868, (b) 20 Feb. 1874 to Apr. 1880; Conservative; b. 21 Dec. 1804 at either the Adelphi, Westminster, or at 22 Theobald's Rd, or St Mary Axe; d. 19 Apr. 1881 at 19 Curzon St, Mayfair, London; bur. Hughenden Manor, Bucks (monument in Westminster Abbey); m. (1839) Mrs Mary Anne Lewis (née Evans) later (1868) Viscountess (in her own right) Beaconsfield; no issue; ed. Lincoln's Inn; MP (Con.) Maidstone (1837–41); Shrewsbury (1841–7); Buckinghamshire (1847–76), when he became a peer.

32. The Rt Hon William Ewart **GLADSTONE** (PC 1841); ministry, (a) 3 Dec. 1868 to February 1874, (b) 23 April 1880 to 12 June 1885, (c) 1 Feb. 1886 to 20 July 1886, (d) 15 Aug. 1892 to 3 March 1894; Liberal; b. 29 Dec. 1809 at 62 Rodney St, Liverpool; d. 19 May 1898 (aged 88 yr 142 days) at Hawarden Castle, Clwyd; bur. Westminster Abbey; m. (1839) Catherine Glynne (d. 1900); children, 4s and 4d; ed. Seaforth Vicarage; Eton and Christ Church, Oxford (Double First in Classics and Mathematics); MP Tory, Newark (1832–45); Univ. of Oxford (1847–65) (Peelite to 1859, thereafter a Liberal); S. Lancs. (1865–8); Greenwich (1868–80); Midlothian (1880–95).

33. The Rt Hon Robert Arthur Talbot Gascoyne-Cecil, the 3rd Marquess of **SALISBURY**, KG (1878), GCVO (1902), (PC 1866); known as Lord Robert Cecil till 1865; and as Viscount Cranbourne, MP, from 1865 to 1868; ministry, (a) 23 June 1885 to 28 Jan. 1886, (b) 25 July 1886 to Aug. 1892, (c) 25 June 1895 to 22 Jan. 1901, (d) 23 Jan. 1901 to 11 July 1902; Conservative; b. 3 Feb. 1830 at Hatfield House, Herts; d. 22 Aug. 1903 at Hatfield House; bur. at Hatfield; m. (1857) Georgiana Charlotte (née Alderson), Lady of the Royal Order of Victoria and Albert and C.I. (1899) (d. 1899); Children, 4s and 3d; ed. Eton and Christ Church, Oxford (Hon. 4th Cl. Maths.); MP (Con.) for Stamford (1853–68).

34. The Rt Hon Sir Archibald Philip Primrose, Bt, 5th Earl of **ROSEBERY**, KG (1892), KT (1895), VD (PC 1881); b. the Hon A P Primrose; known as Lord Dalmeny (1851–68); Earl of Midlothian from 1911 but style not adopted by him; ministry, 5 Mar. 1894 to 21 June 1895; Liberal; b. 7 May 1847 at Charles St, Berkeley Square, London; d. 21 May 1929 at 'The Durdans', Epsom, Surrey; bur. at Dalmeny; m. (1878) Hannah de Rothschild (d. 1890); children, 2s and 2d; ed. Eton and Christ Church, Oxford.

35. The Rt Hon Arthur James **BALFOUR** (PC 1885, PC (I) 1887); KG (1922), later (1922) the 1st Earl of Balfour, OM (1916); ministry, 12 July 1902 to 4 Dec. 1905; Conservative; b. 25 July 1848 at Whittingehame, E. Lothian, Scotland; d. 19 Mar. 1930 at Fisher's Hill, Woking, Surrey; bur. at Whittingehame; unmarried; ed. Eton and Trinity, Camb.; MP (Con.) Hertford

(1874–85); E. Manchester (1885–1906); City of London (1906–22).

36. The Rt Hon Sir Henry **CAMPBELL-BANNERMAN**, GCB (1895), (PC 1884); known as Henry Campbell until 1872; ministry, 5 Dec. 1905 to 5 Apr. 1908; Liberal; b. 7 Sept. 1836 at Kelvinside House, Glasgow; d. 22 Apr. 1908 at 10 Downing Street, London; bur. Meigle, Scotland; m. (1860) Sarah Charlotte Bruce (d. 1906); no issue; ed. Glasgow High School; Glasgow Univ. (Gold Medal for Greek); Trinity, Camb. (22nd Sen. Optime in Maths Tripos; 3rd Cl. in Classical Tripos); MP (Lib.) Stirling District (1868–1908).

37. The Rt Hon Herbert Henry **ASQUITH** (PC 1892, PC (I) 1916); later (1925) 1st Earl of **OXFORD AND ASQUITH**, KG (1925); ministry, (a) 7 Apr. 1908 to 7 May 1910, (b) 8 May 1910 to 5 Dec. 1916 (coalition from 25 May 1915); Liberal; b. 12 Sept. 1852 at Morley, W. Yorks; d. 15 Feb. 1928 at 'The Wharf', Sutton Courtney, Berks; bur. Sutton Courtney Church; m. 1st (1877) Helen Kelsall Melland (d. 1891), 2ndly (1894) Emma Alice Margaret Tennant; children, 1st, 4s and 1d, 2nd 1s and 1d; ed. City of London School; Balliol, Oxford (Scholar 1st Class Lit. Hum.); MP (Lib.) East Fife (1886–1918); Paisley (1920–4).

38. The Rt Hon (David) Lloyd **GEORGE**, OM (1919), (PC 1905); later (1945) 1st Earl **LLOYD-GEORGE** of Dwyfor; ministry, 7 Dec. 1916 to 19 Oct. 1922; Coalition; b. 17 Jan. 1863 in Manchester; d. 26 Mar. 1945 at Ty Newydd, nr. Llanystumdwy; bur. on the bank of the river Dwyfor; m. 1st (1888) Margaret Owen, GBE (1920) (d. 1941), 2ndly (1943) Frances Louise Stevenson, CBE; children, 1st 2s and 2d, 2nd no issue; ed. Llanystumdwy Church School and privately; MP Caernarvon Boroughs (1890–1945) (Lib. 1890–1931 and 1935–45; Ind. Lib. 1931–5).

39. The Rt Hon (Andrew) Bonar **LAW** (PC 1911); ministry, 23 Oct. 1922 to 20 May 1923; Conservative; b. 16 Sept. 1858 at Kingston, nr. Richibucto, New Brunswick, Canada; d. 30 Oct. 1923 at 24 Onslow Grdns., London; bur. Westminster Abbey; m. (1891) Annie Pitcairn (d. 1909); children, 4s and 2d; ed. Gilbertfield School, Hamilton; Glasgow High School; MP (Con.) Blackfriars Div. of Glasgow (1900–6); Dulwich Div. of Camberwell (1906–10); MP Bootle Div. of Lancs (1911–18); Central Div. of Glasgow (1918–23).

40. The Rt Hon Stanley **BALDWIN** (PC 1920, PC (Can.) 1927); later (1937) 1st Earl Baldwin of Bewdley, KG (1937); ministry, (a) 22 May 1923 to 22 Jan. 1924 (Con.), (b) 4 Nov. 1924 to 4 June 1929 (Con.), (c) 7 June 1935 to 20 Jan. 1936 (Nat.), (d) 21 Jan. 1936 to 11 Dec. 1936 (Nat), (e) 12 Dec. 1936 to 28 May 1937 (Nat.); b. 3 Aug. 1867 at Bewdley; d. 14 Dec. 1947; bur. Worcester Cathedral; m. (1892) Lucy Ridsdale, GBE (1937) (d. 1945); children, 2s and 4d; ed. Harrow and Trinity, Camb.; MP (Con.) Bewdley Div. of Worcestershire (1908–37).

41. The Rt Hon (James) Ramsay **MACDONALD** (PC 1924, PC (Canada) 1929); ministry, (a) 22 Jan. 1924 to 4 Nov. 1924 (Labour), (b) 5 June 1929 to 7 June 1935 (Labour and from 1931 National Coalition); b. 12 Oct. 1866 at Lossiemouth, Grampian; d. 9 Nov. 1937 at sea, mid-Atlantic; bur. Spynie Churchyard, nr. Lossiemouth, Scotland; m. (1896) Margaret Ethel Gladstone (d. 1911); children, 3s and 3d; ed. Drainie Parish Board School; MP (Lab.) Leicester (1906–18); (Lab.) Aberavon (1922–9); (Lab.) Seaham Div. Co. Durham (1929–31); (Nat. Lab.) (1931–5); MP for Scottish Univs. (1936–7).

42. The Rt Hon (Arthur) Neville

CHAMBERLAIN (PC 1922); ministry, 28 May 1937 to 10 May 1940; National; b. 18 Mar. 1869 at Edgbaston, Birmingham; d. 9 Nov. 1940 at High Field Park, Hickfield, nr. Reading; ashes interred Westminster Abbey; m. (1911) Annie Vere Cole (d. 12 Feb. 1967); children, 1s and 1d; ed. Rugby School; Mason College (later Birmingham Univ.) (Metallurgy & Engineering Design); MP (Con.) Ladywood Div. of Birmingham (1918–29); Edgbaston Div. of Birmingham (1929–40).

43. The Rt Hon Sir Winston (Leonard **SPENCER-)CHURCHILL**, KG (1953) OM (1946), CH (1922), TD (PC 1907); ministry, (a) 10 May 1940 to 26 July 1945 (Coalition but from 23 May 1945 Conservative), (b) 26 Oct. 1951 to 6 Feb. 1952 (Conservative), (c) 7 Feb. 1952 to 5 Apr. 1955 (Conservative); b. 30 Nov. 1874 at Blenheim Palace, Woodstock, Oxon; d. 24 Jan. 1965 Hyde Park Gate, London; bur. Bladen, Oxfordshire; m. (1908) Clementine Ogilvy Hozier, GBE (1946 cr. 1965 (Life) Baroness Spencer-Churchill; children, 1s and 4d; ed. Harrow School and Royal Military College; MP (Con. until 1904, then Lib.) Oldham (1900–6); (Lib.) N.-W. Manchester (1906–8); (Lib.) Dundee (1908–18 and (Coalition Lib.) until 1922); Epping Div. of Essex (1924–45); Woodford Div. of Essex (1945–64).

44. The Rt Hon Clement (Richard) **ATTLEE** CH (1945), (PC 1935); created 1955 1st Earl Attlee, KG (1956), OM (1951); ministry, 26 July 1945 to 26 Oct. 1951; Labour; b. 3 Jan. 1883 at Putney, London; d. 8 Oct. 1967; m. (1922) Violet Helen Millar; children, 1s and 3d; ed. Haileybury College and Univ. College, Oxford (2nd Cl. Hons. (Mod. Hist.)); MP Limehouse Div. of Stepney (1922–50); West Walthamstow (1950–5).

45. The Rt. Hon Sir (Robert) Anthony **EDEN**, KG (1954), MC (1917), (PC 1934); cr. 1961 1st Earl of Avon; ministry, 6 Apr. 1955 to 9 Jan. 1957; Conservative; b. 12 June 1897 Windlestone, Durham; d. 14 Jan. 1977; m. 1st (1923) Beatrice Helen Beckett (m. dis. 1950) (d. 1957), 2ndly (1952) Anne Clarissa Spencer-Churchill; children, 1st, 2s 2nd, no issue; ed. Eton and Christ Church, Oxford (1st Cl. Hons (Oriental Langs)); MP Warwick and Leamington (1923–57).

46. The 'Rt Hon (Maurice) Harold **MACMILLAN** (PC 1942); ministry, 10 Jan. 1957 to 18 Oct. 1963; Conservative; b. 10 Feb. 1894, 52 Cadogan Place, London; m. (1920) Lady Dorothy Evelyn Cavendish, GBE, 1s and 3d; ed. Eton (Scholar); Balliol, Oxford ((Exhibitioner) 1st Class Hon Mods.); MP Stockton-on-Tees (1924–9 and 1931–45); Bromley (1945–64).

47. The Rt Hon Sir Alexander (Frederick) **DOUGLAS-HOME**, KT (1962) (PC 1951); known until 30 April 1918 as the Hon A F Douglas-Home; thence until 11 July 1951 as Lord Dunglass; thence until his disclaimer of 23 Oct. 1963 as the (14th) Earl of Home; ministry, 19 Oct. 1963 to 16 Oct. 1964, Conservative; b. 2 July 1903, 28 South St, London; m. (1936) Elizabeth Hester Alington; children, 1s and 3d; ed. Eton; Christ Church, Oxford; MP South Lanark (1931–45); Lanark (1950–1); Kinross and West Perthshire (1963 to date).

48. The Rt Hon Sir (James) Harold **WILSON**, KG (1976) OBE(Civ.) (1945) (PC 1947); ministry, (a) 16 Oct. 1964 to 30 Mar. 1966, (b) 31 Mar. 1966 to 17 June 1970, (c) 4 Mar. 1974 to 10 Oct. 1974, (d) 10 Oct. 1974 to 5 Apr. 1976; Labour; b. 11 Mar. 1916; m. (1940) Gladys Mary Baldwin; children, 2s; ed. Milnsbridge C.S.; Royds Hall S.; Wirral G.S.; Jesus College, Oxford (1st Cl. Philosophy, Politics and Economics); MP Ormskirk (1945–50); Huyton (1950 to date).

49. The Rt Hon Edward Richard George **HEATH**, MBE(mil.) (1946), (PC 1955); ministry, 18 June 1970 to 3 Mar. 1974; Conservative; b. 7 July 1916 at Broadstairs, Kent; unmarried; ed. Chatham House School, Ramsgate and Balliol College, Oxford; MP Bexley (1950–74); Bexley-Sidcup from 1974.

50. The Rt Hon (Leonard) James **CALLAGHAN** (PC 1964); ministry 5 Apr. 1976 to date; Labour; b. 27 Mar. 1912 at 38, Funtingdon Rd. Portsmouth, Hampshire; m. (1938) Audrey Elizabeth Moulton, children 1s and 2d; ed. Portsmouth Northern Secondary Sch.; MP South Cardiff 1945–50; South-east Cardiff 1950 to date. Other major offices: Chancellor of the Exchequer 1964–67; Home Secretary 1967–70; Foreign Secretary 1974–76. Elected leader of Labour Party over Rt Hon Michael Foot by 176–136 votes on 5 Apr. 1976.

Leader of H.M. Opposition. Rt Hon Mrs Margaret (Hilda) Thatcher *née* Roberts (PC 1970) elected leader of Conservative Party over Rt Hon William (Stephen Ian) Whitelaw CH, MC, MP by 136–79 votes on 11 Feb. 1975—Mr Heath (see 49 above) having withdrawn after losing to her on first ballot of 130–119 on 4 Feb. b. 22 Oct. 1926, Grantham, Lincolnshire; m. (1951) Denis Thatcher MBE 1s 1d (twins) ed. Kesteven & Grantham Girls' Sch.; Somerville Coll., Oxford (MA, BSc): MP Finchley 1959–74; Barnet, Finchley 1974 to date.

AUTHORISED POST NOMINAL LETTERS IN THEIR CORRECT ORDER

There are 70 Orders, Decorations, and Medals which have been bestowed by the Sovereign that carry the entitlement to a group of letters after the name. Of these, 54 are currently awardable. The order (*vide London Gazette*, supplement 27 Oct. 1964) is as follows:

1.	VC	Victoria Cross.
2.	GC	George Cross.
3.	KG	(but *not* for Ladies of the Order), Knight of the Most Noble Order of the Garter.
4.	KT	(but *not* for Ladies of the Order), Knight of the Most Ancient and Most Noble Order of the Thistle.
5.	GCB	Knight Grand Cross of the Most Honourable Order of the Bath.
6.	OM	Member of the Order of Merit.
†7.	GCSI	Knight Grand Commander of the Most Excellent Order of the Star of India.
8.	GCMG	Knight (or Dame) Grand Cross of the Most Distinguished Order of St Michael and St George.
†9.	GCIE	Knight Grand Commander of the Most Eminent Order of the Indian Empire.
†10.	CI	Lady of The Imperial Order of the Crown of India.
11.	GCVO	Knight (or Dame) Grand Cross of the Royal Victorian Order.
12.	GBE	Knight (or Dame) Grand Cross of the Most Excellent Order of the British Empire.
13.	CH	Member of the Order of Companions of Honour.
14.	KCB	(but *not* if also a GCB), Knight Commander of the Most Honourable Order of the Bath.
15.	DCB	(but *not* if also a GCB) Dame Commander of the Most Honourable Order of the Bath.
†16.	KCSI	(but *not* if also a GCSI), Knight Commander of the Most Excellent Order of the Star of India.
17.	KCMG	(but *not* if also a GCMG), Knight Commander of the Most Distinguished Order of St Michael and St George.
18.	DCMG	(but *not* if also a GCMG) Dame Commander of the Most Distinguished Order of St Michael and St George.
†19.	KCIE	(but *not* if also a GCIE), Knight Commander of the Most Eminent Order of the Indian Empire.
20.	KCVO	(but *not* if also a GCVO), Knight Commander of the Royal Victorian Order.
21.	DCVO	(but *not* if also a GCVO), Dame Commander of the Royal Victorian Order.
22.	KBE	(but *not* if also a GBE), Knight Commander of the Most Excellent Order of the British Empire.
22.	DBE	(but *not* if also a GBE), Dame Commander of the Most Excellent Order of the British Empire.
24.	CB	(but *not* if also a GCB and/or a KCB), Companion of the Most Honourable Order of the Bath.
†25.	CSI	(but *not* if also a GCSI and/or a KCSI), Companion of the Most Excellent Order of the Star of India.
26.	CMG	(but *not* if also a GCMG and/or a KCMG or DCMG), Companion of the Most Distinguished Order of St Michael and St George.
†27.	CIE	(but *not* if also a GCIE and/or a KCIE), Companion of the Most Eminent Order of the Indian Empire.
28.	CVO	(but *not* if also a GCVO and/or a KCVO or DCVO), Commander of the Royal Victorian Order.
29.	CBE	(but *not* if also a GBE and/or a KBE or DBE), Commander of the Most Excellent Order of the British Empire.
30.	DSO	Companion of the Distinguished Service Order.
31.	MVO	(if 4th Class, but *not* if also either a GCVO and/or a KCVO or a DCVO, and/or a CVO), Member of the Royal Victorian Order.
32.	OBE	(but *not* if also either a GBE and/or a KBE or DBE and/or a CBE), Officer of the Most Excellent Order of the British Empire.
33.	ISO	Companion of the Imperial Service Order.
	MVO	(if 5th Class, but *not* if also either a GCVO and/or a KCVO or a DCVO, and/or a CVO and/or a MVO (4th Class), Member of the Royal Victorian Order.

---

† This distinction is no longer awarded, but there are surviving recipients.

---

34. MBE — (but *not* if also either a GBE and/or a KBE or DBE and/or a CBE and/or an OBE), Member of the Most Excellent Order of the British Empire.

†35. IOM — (if in Military Division), Indian Order of Merit.

†36. OB — Order of Burma (when for gallantry).

37. RRC — Member of the Royal Red Cross.

38. DSC — Distinguished Service Cross.

39. MC — Military Cross.

40. DFC — Distinguished Flying Cross.

41. AFC — Air Force Cross.

42. ARRC — (but *not* if also an RRC), Associate of the Royal Red Cross.

†43. OBI — Order of British India.

— OB — Order of Burma (when for distinguished service).

44. DCM — Distinguished Conduct Medal.

45. CGM — (both the Naval and the Flying decorations), Conspicuous Gallantry Medal.

46. GM — George Medal.

†47. KPM — King's or Queen's Police Medal.

†48. KPFSM — or Police & Fire Services Medal for Gallantry.

49. QPM

50. QFSM

DCM — (if for Royal West African Frontier Force), Distinguished Conduct Medal.

DCM — (if for the King's African Rifles), Distinguished Conduct Medal.

51. IDSM — Indian Distinguished Service Medal.

†52. BGM — Burma Gallantry Medal.

53. DSM — Distinguished Service Medal.

54. MM — Military Medal.

55. DFM — Distinguished Flying Medal.

55. AFM — Air Force Medal.

57. SGM — Medal for Saving Life at Sea (Sea Gallantry Medal).

† IOM — (if in Civil Division), Indian Order of Merit.

†58. EGM — Empire Gallantry Medal (usable only in reference to pre 1940 honorary awards unexchangeable for the G.C.

59. QGM — Queen's Gallantry Medal.

60. BEM — British Empire Medal, for Gallantry, or the British Empire Medal.

61. CM — (or for French speakers M du C, Medaille du Canada), Canada Medal.

†— KPM
†— KPFSM
— QPM
— QFSM

See 47–50 above, but for distinguished or good service.

62. MSM — (but only if awarded for Naval service prior to 20 July 1928), Medal for Meritorious Service.

63. ERD — Emergency Reserve Decoration (Army) (for either the obsolescent Volunteer Officers' Decoration (1892–1908) or Volunteer Officers' Decoration (for India and the Colonies) (1894–1930)).

†65. ED — (if for the obsolescent Colonial Auxiliary Forces Officers' Decoration (1899–1930)).

66. TD — (for either the obsolescent Territorial Decoration (1908–30) or for the current Efficiency Decoration (inst. 1930) when awarded to an officer of the (*Home*) Auxiliary Military Forces).

67. ED — (if for the current Efficiency Decoration (inst. 1930) when awarded to an officer of *Commonwealth* or Colonial Auxiliary Military Forces).

68. RD — Decoration for Officers of the Royal Naval Reserve.

69. VRD — Decoration for Officers of the Royal Naval Volunteer Reserve.

70. CD — Canadian Forces Decoration.

Any of the above post nominal letters precede any others which may relate to academic honours or professional qualifications. The unique exception is that the abbreviation 'Bt.' (or less favoured 'Bart.'), indicating a Baronetcy, should be put before *all* other letters, e.g. The Rt Hon Sir John Smyth, Bt., VC, MC.

The abbreviation PC (indicating membership of the Privy Council), which used to be placed after KG, is now not to be used, except possibly with peers, because in their case the style 'Rt Hon' cannot be used to indicate membership of the Privy Council, since Barons, Viscounts and Earls already enjoy this style *ipso facto* and Marquesses and Dukes have the superior styles 'Most Hon' and 'Most Noble' respectively.

UNITED KINGDOM COINAGE

	Standard Weight in grammes	Standard Weight in oz avoirdupois	DIAMETER cms	ins
GOLD (22 carats or 91·66%) Legal tender to any amount				
£5 quintuple sovereign	39,94028	1.40869	3,601	1.418
£2 double sovereign	15,97611	0.5635	2,839	1.118
£1 sovereign	7,98805	0.2817	2,204	0.868
50p half sovereign	3,99402	0.1408	1,9304	0.760

SILVER Silver coinage is now confined to Maundy money in 4 pence, 3 pence, 2 pence and 1 penny pieces in 92·5% silver. These do not circulate.

CUPRO-NICKEL					
50p 50 pence	Legal tender to £10	13,5	0.4761	3,0	1.1811
10p 10 pence	Legal tender to £5	11,31036	0.3989	2,8500	1.122
5p 5 pence	Legal tender to £5	5,65518	0.1994	2,3595	0.9289

BRONZE (Copper 97 parts, zinc 2½ parts, tin ½ part)					
2p 2 pence	Legal tender to 20p	7,12800	0.2514	2,5910	1.0200
1p 1 penny	Legal tender to 20p	3,56400	0.1257	2,0320	0.7999
½p ½ penny	Legal tender to 20p	1,78200	0.0628	1,7145	0.6749

Modern Imperial Coinage (Post 1816)

Imperial coinage struck by or for the Royal Mint, has existed in the following denominations and dates (hyphens indicate consecutive and inclusive dates). * Pattern or proof only.

Quarter-Farthing $\frac{1}{16}$d	1839, 1851–3, 1868
Third-Farthing $\frac{1}{12}$d	1827, 1835, 1844, 1866, 1868, 1876, 1879, 1881, 1884–5, 1902, 1913
Half-Farthing $\frac{1}{8}$d	1828, 1830, 1837, 1839, 1842–4, 1847, 1851–4, 1856, 1868
Farthings $\frac{1}{4}$d	1821–3, 1825–31, 1834–60, 1860–9, 1872–1956
Old Halfpenny $\frac{1}{2}$d	1825–7, 1831, 1834, 1837–9, 1841, 1843–8, 1851–60, 1860–1960, 1902–67
Old Penny 1d	1825–7, 1831, 1834, 1837, 1839, 1841, 1943–9, 1851, 1853–60, 1860–1922, 1926–40, 1944–51, 1953–4, 1961–7
Half New Pence ½p	1971, 1973–7
Three-halfpence 1½d	1834–43, 1860, 1862
One New Penny 1p	1971, 1973–7
Three-Pence (Nickel Brass) 3d	1937–46, 1948–67
Three-Pence (Silver) 3d	1834–7, 1838–51, 1853–1922, 1925–8, 1930–44
Groat 4d	1836–49, 1851–5, 1888
Two New Pence 2p	1971, 1975–77
Sixpence 6d	1816–21, 1824–9, 1831, 1839–46, 1848–1967
One Shilling 1s	1816–21, 1823–7, 1829, 1834–46, 1848–1966
Five New Pence 5p	1968–71, 1975, 1976*, 1977
Two Shillings (Florin) 2s	1849, 1851–60, 1862–1967
Ten New Pence 10p	1968–71, 1973–7
Half Crown 2s 6d	1816–17, 1820–21, 1823–6, 1828–9, 1834–7, 1839–46, 1848–50, 1874–1967
Double Florin 4s	1887–90
Crown 5s	1818–20, 1821–2, 1831 (proof only), 1844–5, 1847, 1887–1900, 1902, 1927–37, 1951, 1953, 1960, 1965
25 New Pence 25p	1972, 1977
50 New Pence 50p	1969–70, 1973, 1976–77
Half Sovereign £½	1817–18, 1820, 1841–61, 1863–7, 1869–80, 1883–1915, 1937* (Ed. VIII), 1937*, 1953*
Sovereign £1	1838–9, 1841–66, 1868–74, 1876, 1878–80, 1884–5, 1887–96, 1898–1917, 1925, 1937* (Ed. VIII), 1937*, 1957–9, 1962–8, 1974, 1976
Two Pound Piece £2	1887, 1893, 1902, 1911, 1937* (Edward VIII), 1937*, 1953*
Five Pound Piece £5	1839*, 1887, 1893, 1902, 1911, 1937* (Edward VIII), 1937*, 1953*

Sovereigns:
Melbourne (small M, mintmark on reverse side) 1872–4, 1881–5, 1887–1931.
Sydney (small S) 1871–5, 1877–1926. Ottawa (small C) 1908–11, 1913–14, 1916–19. Perth (small P) 1893–1931. Bombay (small I) 1918. Pretoria (small SA) 1925–32.

Half-Sovereigns:

Sydney	1871–2, 1874–6, 1878–83, 1886–7, 1891–3, 1898–1903, 1906, 1908, 1910–12, 1914–16.
Melbourne	1873, 1877, 1881–2, 1884–7, 1893, 1896, 1896, 1899–1900, 1906, 1908–09, 1915.
Perth	1900, 1904, 1908–9, 1911, 1915, 1919–20.
Pretoria	1925–6.

Bank Notes

In Britain by 1677 there were as many as **44** goldsmiths operating 'running cashes' with deposit receipts which had virtually become promissory notes. The Bank of England's earliest notes in 1694 were mostly manuscript. The first notes with printed denominations were ordered on 5 June 1695 and were of £5, £10, £20, £30, £40, £50 denominations. The oldest surviving note to bearer is a watermarked specimen dated 19 Oct. 1699 for £555. Notes of fixed denomination had again been suspended until 1725.

Bank of England Fixed Denomination Notes (Dates of issue and withdrawal)

10s.	1928	1969	£50	1725	1943
£1 (first issue)	1797	1821	£50 (re-issue)	1978	Legal tender
£1 (reissue)	1928	Legal tender	£60	1745	c. 1802
£2	1797	1821	£70	1745	c. 1802
£5	1793	Legal tender	£80	1745	c. 1802
£10	1759	1943	£90	1745	c. 1802
£10 (reissue)	1964	Legal tender	£100	1725	1943
£15	1759	1822	£200	1745	1928
£20	1725	1943	£300	1745	1885
£20 (reissue)	1970	Legal tender	£400	1745	c. 1802
£25	1765	1822			
£30	1725	1852	£500	1745	1943
£40	1725	1851	£1 000	1745	1943

The Treasury issued 10s. and £1 currency notes on 6 Aug. 1914 until the issue of the Bank of England 10s. note and the reissue of the £1 on 22 Nov. 1928.

Bank of England notes bore the manuscript signatures of various cashiers of the Bank from 1694–1853, when the signatures of the cashiers were first printed. The office of Chief Cashier has been held as follows:

6 Dec. 1866–2 July 1873,	George Forbes (signature printed from 1 Nov. 1870)	(1)
3 July 1873–8 Nov. 1893,	Frank May	(2)
9 Nov. 1893–12 Jan. 1902,	Horace George Bowen	(3)
13 Jan. 1902–8 May 1918,	John Gordon Nairne	(4)
9 May 1918–8 Apr. 1925,	Ernest Musgrave Harvey	(5)
9 Apr. 1925–26 Mar. 1929,	Cyril Patrick Mahon	(6)
27 Mar. 1929–18 Apr. 1934,	Basil Gage Catterns	(7)
19 Apr. 1934–28 Feb. 1949,	Kenneth Oswald Peppiatt	(8)
1 Mar. 1949–15 Jan. 1955,	Percy Spencer Beale	(9)
16 Jan. 1955–28 Feb. 1962,	Leslie Kenneth O'Brien	(10)
1 Mar. 1962–30 June 1966,	Jasper Quintus Hollom	(11)
1 July 1966–28 Feb. 1970,	John Standish Fforde	(12)
1 Mar. 1970 to date	John Brangwgn Page	(13)

See right for signature of the Chief Cashier listed on the left

(1) [signature]
(2) [signature]
(3) [signature]
(4) [signature]
(5) [signature]
(6) [signature]
(7) [signature]
(8) [signature]
(9) [signature]
(10) [signature]
(11) [signature]
(12) [signature]
(13) [signature]

ECONOMICS

The economic power of a nation is reflected in its Gross National Product (GNP) and its National Income.

Gross National Product is derived from Gross Domestic Product at factor cost plus net property income from overseas. National Income is GNP less capital consumption.

Gross Domestic Product at factor cost can be determined in two ways, (A) by the expenditure generating it, or (B) the incomes, rent and profits which enable the expenditure. The components in any year are thus:

A	B
Consumers' expenditure	Income from employment
Public authority current spending	Income from self-employment
Gross fixed capital formation	Gross trading profits of companies
Value of work in progress	Gross profits and surpluses of public corporations
Value of physical increase in stocks	Rent *less* stock appreciation
Exports *less* imports	
Income from abroad *less* payments abroad	
Subsidies *less* taxes on expenditure	
= Gross Domestic Product	= Gross Domestic Product

Minimum lending rate

The Bank Rate was maintained at its record low level of 2 per cent for 12 years 13 days from 26 Oct. 1939 to 7 Nov. 1951, throughout World War II and the post-war period of the Cheap Money Policy under the Atlee government. The only previous occasion that such a low rate had been available was in 1852.

On 13 Oct. 1972 the Bank Rate was more descriptively named Bank of England Minimum Lending Rate when standing at 7¼ per cent. On 13 Nov. 1973 the MLR attained its then all-time peak of 13 per cent with the Arab Oil Price crisis. The devaluation crisis of October 1976 produced a new record rate of 15 per cent. By October 1977 this had subsided to 5½ per cent.

Exports

Exports from the UK (1976)	*£ Millions f.o.b.* *
Machinery non electric	5058·0
Transport equipment	3064·2
Machinery electric	2003·9
Mineral manufacturers (non-metal)	1730·7
Petroleum and petroleum products	1161·6

Exports from the UK (1976)

Exports from the UK (1976)	£ Millions f.o.b.*
Other miscellaneous articles	1069·3
Chemical elements and compounds	1045·9
Textile yarn, fabrics	934·2
Iron and Steel	824·6
Other metal manufacturers	800·3
Non-ferrous metals	722·3
Scientific, photographic and optical instruments	628·6
Plastics and resins	531·2
Beverages	524·4
Other chemicals	498·9
Medical and pharmaceutical products	452·5
Clothing	412·3
Rubber manufacturers	299·7
Dyeing, tanning and colouring materials	282·3
Paper, Paper board	278·4
Textile fibres	260·6
Essential oils, perfumes	235·9

* f.o.b., free on board

Imports

Imports into the UK (1976)	£ Millions c.i.f*
Machinery non-electric	3254·0
Transport equipment	1751·9
Non-metallic minerals	1385·5
Machinery electric	1383·0
Non-ferrous metal	1039·0
Iron and steel	965·7
Fruit and vegetables	948·4
Textile yarn	911·4
Chemical elements and compounds	875·3
Meat	838·6
Paper and paper board	827·4
Cereals	747·9
Metal ores and scrap	685·8
Clothing	683·8
Wood, lumber and cork	585·1
Scientific, photographic and optical equipment	574·7
Dairy products and eggs	504·6
Coffee, tea and cocoa	493·3
Pulp and waste paper	464·1
Plastics and resins	463·0
Textile fibres	438·3
Sugar and honey	429·6
Metal manufacturers	415·3
Wood and cork manufacturers (excluding furniture)	290·3
Beverages	251·7
Tobacco	236·9
Oil, seeds, nuts and kernels	207·1
Animal and vegetable materials	200·7
Fertilisers and minerals—(crude)	195·2
Foreign caught fish	191·0
Animal feeding stuff	172·4
Hide, skins and fur	171·6
Footwear	165·5
Crude rubber	140·3

*c.i.f., cost, insurance and freight

Average weekly household expenditure

The average household weekly income in 1976 was £82·30 of which £16·61 went in income tax and national insurance payments. The breakdown of the average expenditure was as follows:

Food	£15·37
Transport and vehicles	£8·14
Housing	£9·21
Clothing and footwear	£4·99
Durable household goods	£4·06
Fuel, light and power	£3·53
Tobacco	£2·29
Alcoholic drink	£3·11
Other Goods	£4·49
Services	£6·19
Miscellaneous	£0·32

The United Kingdom's National Debt

The National Debt is the nominal amount of outstanding debt chargeable on the Consolidated Fund of the United Kingdom Exchequer only, i.e. the debt created by the separate Northern Ireland Exchequer is excluded.

The National Debt became a permanent feature of the country's economy as early as 1692. The table below shows how the net total Debt has increased over the years (data being for 31 March of year shown):

Year	National Debt (£ million)	Year	National Debt (£ million)	Year	National Debt (£ million)
1697	14	1918	5 871·9	1954	26 538·0
1727	52	1919	7 434·9	1955	26 933·7
1756	75	1920*	7 828·8	1956	27 038·9
1763	133	1921	7 574·4	1957	27 007·5
1775	127	1923	7 742·2	1958	27 232·0
1781	187	1931	7 413·3	1959	27 376·3
1784	243	1934	7 822·3	1960	27 732·6
1793	245	1935†	6 763·9	1961	28 251·7
1802	523	1936	6 759·3	1962	28 674·4
1815	834	1937	6 764·7	1963	29 847·6
1828	800	1938	6 993·7	1964	30 226·3
1836	832	1939	7 130·8	1965	30 440·6
1840	827	1940	7 899·2	1966	31 340·2
1854	802	1941	10 366·4	1967	31 985·6
1855	789	1942	13 041·1	1968	34 193·9
1857	837	1943	15 822·6	1969	33 984·2
1860	799	1944	18 562·2	1970	33 079·4
1899	635	1945	21 365·9	1971	33 441·9
1900	628·9	1946	23 636·5	1972	35 839·9
1903	770·8	1947	25 630·6	1973	36 884·6
1909	702·7	1948	25 620·8	1974	40 124·5
1910	713·2	1949	25 167·6	1975	45 886·0
1914	649·8	1950	25 802·3	1976	56 577·0
1915	1 105·0	1951	25 921·6	1977	54 041
1916	2 133·1	1952	25 890·5		
1917	4 011·4	1953	26 051·2		

* Beginning 1920, total excludes bonds tendered for death duties and held by the National Debt Commissioner-
† Beginning 1935, total excludes external debt, then £1036·5 million, arising out of the 1914–18 war.

Sterling—US Dollar Exchange Rates

$4·50–$5·00	Post War of Independence	1776
$12·00	All-time Peak (Civil War)	1864
$4·86 21/32	Fixed parity	1880–1914
$4·76 7/16	Pegged rate World War I	Dec. 1916
$3·40	Low point after £ floated, 19 May 1919	Feb. 1920
$4·86 21/32	Britain's return to gold standard	28 Apr. 1925
$3·14½	Low point after Britain forced off Gold Standard (21 Sept. 1931 [$3·43])	Nov. 1932
$5·20	High point during floating period	Mar. 1934
$4·03	Fixed rate World War II	4 Sept. 1939
$2·80	First post-war devaluation	18 Sept. 1949
$2·40	Second post-war devaluation	20 Nov. 1967
$2·58	£ Refloated	22 June 1972
$1·99	£ broke $2 barrier	5 Mar. 1976
$1·56	£ At new all-time low	28 Oct. 1976
$1·76	Bank of England buying pounds	10 Oct. 1977
$1·99	£ nearly breaks back to $2 level	4 Jan. 1978

25 Top Nations—Exports from UK

12 months to December 1976	£ million
1. United States	2449
2. West Germany	1834
3. France	1710
4. Netherlands	1500
5. Belgium & Luxembourg	1401
6. Ireland	1247
7. Sweden	1045
8. Switzerland	1000
9. Italy	826
10. Nigeria	774
11. Australia	688
12. Denmark	655
13. South Africa	645
14. Canada	628
15. Iran	511
16. Norway	474
17. Saudi Arabia	400
18. Spain	368
19. Japan	359
20. Finland	289

25 Top Nations—Imports into UK

12 months to December 1976	£ million
1. United States	3044
2. West Germany	2757
3. Netherlands	2428
4. France	2091
5. Belgium & Luxembourg	1300
6. Sweden	1188
7. Canada	1160
8. Italy	1106
9. Iran	1049
10. Ireland	1008
11. Saudi Arabia	978
12. Switzerland	963
13. Japan	796
14. Denmark	705
15. Soviet Union	667
16. Norway	623
17. South Africa	613
18. Kuwait	587
19. Finland	562
20. Hong Kong	440

Distribution of work force of the UK as at June 1975

Professional and scientific services	3 556 000
Distributive trades	2 763 000
Transport and communication	1 518 000
Miscellaneous services	1 376 000
Construction	1 313 000
Insurance, banking, finance and business services	1 103 000
Local government services	1 005 000
Catering, hotels etc.	826 000
National government service	650 000
Agriculture, forestry and fishing	401 000
Gas, electricity and water	353 000
Mining and quarrying	352 000
Mechanical engineering	931 000
Vehicle manufacturing	760 000
Electrical engineering	753 000
Food, drink and tobacco manufacturing	721 000
Metal good manufacturing	541 000
Paper, printing and publishing	540 000
Textile manufacturing	526,000
Metal manufacturing	481 000
Chemicals and allied industries	432 000
Clothing and footwear manufacturing	400 000
Other manufacturing industries	341 000
Bricks, pottery, glass, cement etc. manufacturing	268 000
Timber, furniture etc. manufacturing	266 000
Shipbuilding and marine engineering	182 000
Instrument engineering	149 000
Leather, leather goods and fur manufacturing	43 000
Coal and petroleum products	38 000
Employers and self-employed	1 977 000
HM Forces	345 000
Wholly unemployed	543 000
Total working population	25 453 000

Standard of living—in 20.35 million households

	1976
Colour TV	55%
Refrigerator	88.1%
Washing machine	72.3%
Car	55.2%
Telephone	52.6%
Central heating	47.1%
Average disposable income after tax and NHI	£3 415

Internal purchasing power of the £

The worth of the £ at various periods compared with its worth in January 1977 may be regarded thus:

1870	£1	worth	£13·20
1886	£1	worth	£18·00
1896	£1	worth	£17·40
1909	£1	worth	£15·60
1925	£1	worth	£8·40
1931	£1	worth	£10·10
1949	£1	worth	£5·25
1957	£1	worth	£3·60
1967	£1	worth	£3·15
1970	£1	worth	£2·40
1976 (Jan.)	£1	worth	£1·20
1977 (Jan.)	£1	worth	£1

21. New Zealand	251	21. Australia	394
22. Israel	249	22. Spain	360
23. Soviet Union	240	23. India	355
24. Portugal	223	24. New Zealand	321
25. Austria	212	25. Nigeria	317

Birth and Death Rates—Rates for 1000 of population

	1871	1901	1911	1921	1931	1951	1961	1971	1976
Birth Rate	35·0	28·6	24·6	23·1	16·3	15·8	17·8	16·2	12·1
Death Rate	22·1	17·3	14·1	12·7	12·2	12·6	12·0	11·6	12·2
Rate of Natural Increase	12·9	11·3	10·5	10·4	4·1	3·2	5·8	4·6	—0·1
Illegitimacy	60	43	45	48	48	48	55	82	91

National Employment and Unemployment

	Working Population (Thousands)	Unemployment Excluding School Leavers and Students	Percentage Rate
1965	25 504	338 200	1·4%
1970	25 293	602 000	2·6%
1971	25 124	775 800	3·4%
1972	25 234	855 000	3·7%
1973	25 578	611 000	2·6%
1974	25 515	600 100	2·6%
1975	25 665	890 300	3·8%
1976	25 886	1 219 900	5·3%
1977 Mar.	26 014	1 296 800	5·5%
June		1 247 700	5·6%
Aug.		1 346 600	5·9%

Wage Rates and Earnings (Jan. 1970 = 100)

	Index	Percentage Increase on Previous Year
1965	74·1	7·1%
1970	106·7	12·1%
1971	118·7	11·3%
1972	134·1	15·8%
1973	152·6	12·7%
1974	179·6	17·7%
1975	227·6	26·7%
1976	263·3	15·7%
1977 (mid)	288·9	9·4%

Strikes

	Working Days Lost	Workers Involved
1960	3 024 000	814 000
1965	2 933 000	867 800
1970	10 980 000	1 793 000
1973	7 197 000	1 513 000
1974	14 750 000	1 622 000
1975	6 012 000	789 000
1976	3 286 000	658 000

British Isles—Progressive population

Date	Estimate	Date	Estimate
c 500 000 BC	200	1348†	4 000 000
c 250 000 BC	1000	1355	2 500 000
12 000 BC	3000	1500	<3 000 000
2000 BC	20 000	1570‡	4 160 000
600 BC	80 000	1600‡	4 811 000
100 BC	250 000	1630‡	5 600 000
AD 43	450 000	1670‡	5 773 000
350	1 250 000	1700‡	6 045 000
1086*	1 250 000	1750‡	6 517 000

* On the evidence of the Domesday Book.
† Prior to onset of the Black Death.
‡ Figures in respect of England only based on the evidence of Parish registration.

Decennial Censuses*

Date	Total		Date	Total
1801	11 944 000		1891	34 264 000
1811	13 368 000		1901	38 237 000
1821	15 472 000		1911	42 082 000
1831	17 835 000		1921	44 027 000
1841	20 183 000		1931	46 038 000
1851	22 259 000		1951	50 225 000
1861	24 525 000		1961	52 676 000
1871	27 431 000		1971	55 515 000
1881	31 015 000		1976	est 55 928 000

* These figures are in respect of the United Kingdom (i.e. the figures for the present area of the Republic of Ireland are excluded). The 1921 and 1931 figures for Northern Ireland are estimates only but were based on censuses subsequently held in 1926 and 1937 respectively.

Expectation of life
(Average expectation at birth)

	Male	Female		Male	Female
1900	46	50	1950	66	72
1910	52	55	1958	68	74
1920	56	60	1969–71	69·2	75·2
1930	59	63	1974	69·3	75·5
1938	61	66			

Income, Expenditure and Savings

	Population Mid-Year	Gross National Product GNP	Total Personal Income	Consumer Expenditure at prices current		Personal Saving	
	Thousands	£ millions	£ millions	£ millions		£ million	as % of Disposable Income
1955	51 199	£16 945	£15 622	£13 111		£543	
1960	52 508	£22 756	£21 178	£16 971		£1203	
1965	54 218	£31 588	£30 055	£22 856	Revalued at 1970 Prices	£2179	8·7%
1970	55 421	£43 809	£43 163	£31 472		£3150	9·1%
1971	55 610	£49 298	£47 785	£35 075	£32 505	£3416	8·9%
1972	55 793	£55 259	£54 124	£39 636	£34 440	£4436	10·1%
1973	55 933	£64 321	£62 720	£45 141	£36 003	£5727	11·3%
1974	55 974	£73 977	£76 913	£51 670	£35 590	£8133	13·6%
1975	55 962	£92 841	£96 342	£63 333	£35 234	£10 972	14·8%
1976	55 928	£108 853	£111 293	£73 128	£35 290	£12 090	14·2%

Public expenditure: 1970–1 to 1975–76 and Projected to 1979–80

£ million at 1975 Survey prices

	1970–1	1971–2	1972–3	1973–4	1974–5	1975–6	1976–7	1977–8	1978–9	1979–80
1. Social security	7200	7646	8078	8080	8582	9463	10 002	10 014	9964	9963
2. Education and libraries, science and arts	5073	5434	5799	6081	6104	6164	6234	6141	6024	5995
3. Defence	4531	4593	4494	4426	4331	4538	4586	4573	4541	4541
4. Health and personal social services	4235	4405	4701	4934	5056	5285	5317	5384	5465	5548
5. Housing	2827	2492	2555	3330	4429	4018	4097	4064	4014	4090
6. Nationalised industries' capital expenditure	2669	2554	2519	2281	2822	3358	3050	2647	2789	2907
7. Other environmental services	1855	1888	2014	2156	2088	2217	2045	2062	1991	1981
8. Trade, industry and employment:										
Investment grants	808	635	384	233	102	63	23	5	2	1
Other	1080	1234	1755	2538	2763	2618	2249	2085	2121	2113
9. Roads and transport	1790	1727	1848	1964	2181	2316	2193	2032	1860	1852
10. Law, order and protective services	1093	1175	1189	1260	1339	1444	1470	1462	1439	1438
11. Agriculture, fisheries and forestry	632	718	635	751	1468	1438	987	840	641	612
12. Overseas aid and other overseas services	598	646	788	825	798	734	882	953	1027	1085
13. Northern Ireland	767	802	896	1015	1200	1321	1336	1306	1263	1258
Civil Service staff costs								—50	—140	—130
14. Common services	545	582	599	606	606	713	678	697	716	739
15. Other public services	520	560	757	587	628	682	686	686	675	679
Total programmes	36 223	37 091	39 011	41 067	44 497	46 372	45 835	44 901	44 392	44 672
Debt interest	4142	4031	4048	4764	4757	5000	6200	7000	7500	7500
Contingency reserve							700	900	1200	1400
Shortfall						—200	—250	—250	—250	—250
Total	40 365	41 122	43 059	45 831	49 254	51 172	52 485	52 551	52 842	53 322

Balance of Payments

	Visible Exports	Visible Imports	Visible Balance	Invisible Balance	Current Balance (−Deficit +Surplus)
1965	4848	5071	−223	+198	−27
1970	7907	7919	−12	+747	+735
1971	8810	8526	+282	+766	+1048
1972	9449	10 151	−702	+833	+131
1973	12 115	14 449	−2234	+1582	−752
1974	16 450	21 671	−5221	+1841	−3380
1975	19 397	22 574	−3195	+1560	−1636
1976	25 294	28 886	−3592	+2169	−1423

JUDICIAL SYSTEM IN THE U.K.

The supreme judicial court for the United Kingdom is the House of Lords as an ultimate court of appeal from all courts, except the Scottish criminal courts. Leave to appeal to it is not as of right and is usually reserved for important points of law. The work is executed by the Lord High Chancellor and nine Lords of Appeal in Ordinary. Only one case in 40,000 ever reaches them.

The Supreme Court of Judicature consists of the Court of Appeal under the Master of the Rolls and 16 Lord Justices of Appeal and The High Court of Justice with (a) the Chancery Division with 11 judges (b) the Queen's Bench Division under the Lord Chief Justice of England and 41 judges (c) the Court of Appeal (Criminal Division) with all the foregoing 59 judges excepting the Chancery Division judges (d) the Family Division with a President and currently 14 male and 2 female judges.

On 1 January 1972 the Crown Court replaced Assizes and Quarter Sessions. Under the Courts Service, First tier centres deal with both civil and criminal cases and Second tier centres with only criminal cases. Both are served by High Court (see above) and Circuit Judges. Third tier centres deal with criminal cases only but are served by Circuit Judges only. There are six circuits in England and Wales viz.

Northern Circuit	(14 Judges)
North Eastern Circuit	(25 Judges)
Midland and Oxford	(28 Judges)
Wales and Chester	(14 Judges)
South Eastern Circuit	(143 Judges)
Western Circuit	(25 Judges)

There are in addition 326 Recorders.

Major urban areas have courts presided over by whole-time salaried magistrates known as Stipendaries thus

London

Bow Street (Chief Metropolitan Stipendiary and 3 Stipendiaries).
Camberwell Green (3)
Greenwich and Woolwich (2)
Highbury Corner (3)
Horseferry Road (3)
Marlborough Street (2)
Marylebone (4)
Old Street (2)
South Western (3)
Thames (2)
Tower Bridge (2)
Wells Street (4)
West London (2)

Other Stipendiaries operate in Birmingham, Kingston-upon-Hull, Leeds, Manchester, Merseyside, Merthyr Tydfil, Mid Glamorgan, Salford, South Glamorgan, South Yorkshire and Wolverhampton.

In Scotland the Court of Session (established 1532) has an Inner House of 8 Judges (in which the Lord President presides over the First Division and the Lord Justice Clerk over the Second Division) and an Outer House of 12 Judges. The country is divided into 6 Sheriffdoms, each with a Sheriff Principal, Sheriffs and Procurators Fiscal, these are Grampian, Highland and Islands; Tayside, Central and Fife; Lothian and Borders; Glasgow and Strathkelvin; North Strathclyde; and South Strathclyde and Dumfries and Galloway.

CRIMINAL STATISTICS
Offences known to the Police, England and Wales—Year 1975

OFFENCES	Number of Offences 1975
VIOLENCE AGAINST THE PERSON	
Murder / Manslaughter / Infanticide } homicide	515
Attempted murder	449
Threat or conspiracy to murder	94
Child destruction	Nil
Causing death by dangerous driving	690
Wounding or other act endangering life	4399
Endangering railway passenger	41
Endangering life at sea	Nil
Other wounding, etc.	63 520
Assault	1141
Abandoning child under two years	7
Child stealing	63
Procuring illegal abortion	14
Concealment of birth	19
SEXUAL OFFENCES:	
Homosexual offences	5306
Rape	1040
Incest	349
Abduction	88
Bigamy	155
BURGLARY:	
Burglary in a dwelling	237 353
Burglary in a building other than a dwelling	277 551

ROBBERY:	
Robbery	11 311
THEFT AND HANDLING STOLEN GOODS:	
Theft from the person of another	20 851
Theft or unauthorised taking from mail	1584
Theft from vehicle	239 432
Shoplifting	175 552
Theft or unauthorised taking of motor vehicle	264 896
Handling stolen goods	45 578
FRAUD AND FORGERY:	
Fraud and forgery	123 055
CRIMINAL DAMAGE:	
Arson	7468
Criminal damage	70 558
OTHER OFFENCES:	
Blackmail	782
High treason	Nil
Treason felony	Nil
Riot	10
Unlawful assembly	6
Other offence against the State or public order	340
Perjury	333
Criminal libel	9
NON-INDICTABLE TRAFFIC OFFENCES	
Reckless or dangerous driving	8247
Driving while unfit through drink or drugs	57 699
In charge of motor vehicle while unfit through drink or drugs	2727
Driving while disqualified	11 784
Other motoring offences	1 152 636
OTHER SELECTED NON-INDICTABLE OFFENCES	
Cruelty to animals	922
Cruelty to children	273
Night poaching	121
Day poaching	1299
Indecent exposure	2789
Drunkenness, simple	50 116
Drunkenness with aggravation	52 104
Drug offences	11 857
Offences by pawnbrokers	5
Prostitution offences	3457
Sunday trading	542
Begging	1198
Sleeping out	311

CRIMINAL STATISTICS
Crimes and Offences known to the Police, Scotland—Year 1975

CRIMES AGAINST THE PERSON
Murder	93
Attempts to murder	272
Culpable homicide	57
Assaults	4780
Cruel and unnatural treatment of children	752
Incest	104
Rape	235
Lewd and libidinous Practices	1530
Bigamy	25

CRIMES AGAINST PROPERTY WITH VIOLENCE
Housebreaking	119 728
Robbery, and Assaults with intent	4224

CRIMES AGAINST PROPERTY WITHOUT VIOLENCE
Theft	131 889
Reset (Receiving)	2848

MALICIOUS INJURIES TO PROPERTY
Fire-raising	2035

FORGERY AND CRIMES AGAINST CURRENCY
Forgery and uttering	2923
Coining and Other	31

OTHER CRIMES
High treason and treason felony	Nil
Mobbing and rioting	27
Other crimes against the State and Public order	25
Crimes against public justice (perjury, bribery, etc.)	3436
Indecent exposure	2129

OFFENCES AGAINST INTOXICATING LIQUOR LAWS
Drunk and incapable	38 632
Drunk and disorderly	404

SELECTED MISCELLANEOUS OFFENCES
Breach of the peace, etc.	92 261
Brothel keeping	18
Prostitution	603
Contempt of court	359
Cruelty to animals	371
Furious and reckless driving	3
Offences relating to motor vehicles (excluding drunk in charge)	292 786
Drunk in charge, etc.	3043
Driving, or in charge of a motor vehicle with blood-alcohol concentration above the prescribed limit	21 244
Taking motor vehicle without consent of owner	27 582

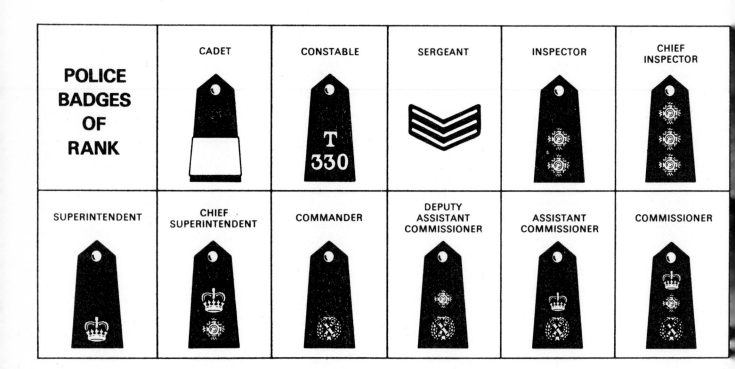

POLICE BADGES OF RANK

CADET · CONSTABLE · SERGEANT · INSPECTOR · CHIEF INSPECTOR · SUPERINTENDENT · CHIEF SUPERINTENDENT · COMMANDER · DEPUTY ASSISTANT COMMISSIONER · ASSISTANT COMMISSIONER · COMMISSIONER

Index

245

GUINNESS SUPERLATIVES
TITLES

FACTS AND FEATS SERIES

Air Facts and Feats, *2nd ed.,* John W. R. Taylor, Michael J. H. Taylor and David Mondey

Rail Facts and Feats, *2nd ed.,* John Marshall

Tank Facts and Feats, *2nd ed.,* Kenneth Macksey

Car Facts and Feats, *2nd ed.,* Anthony Harding

Yachting Facts and Feats, Peter Johnson

Plant Facts and Feats, William G. Duncalf

Animal Facts and Feats, *2nd ed.,* Gerald L. Wood

Structures – Bridges, Towers, Tunnels, Dams . . ., John H. Stephens

Business World, Henry Button and Andrew Lampert

Music Facts and Feats, Robert and Celia Dearling with Brian Rust

Art Facts and Feats, John FitzMaurice Mills

Weather Facts and Feats, Ingrid Holford

Astronomy Facts and Feats, Patrick Moore

Soccer Facts and Feats, Jack Rollin

GUIDE SERIES

Guide to Freshwater Angling, Brian Harris and Paul Boyer

Guide to Saltwater Angling, Brian Harris

Guide to Water Skiing, David Nations, Kevin Desmond

Guide to Steeplechasing, John Oaksey, Stan Mellor, Gerry Cranham

Guide to Field Sports, Wilson Stephens

Guide to Waterways of Western Europe, Hugh McKnight

Guide to Formula 1 Motor Racing, José Rosinski

Guide to Motorcycling, *2nd ed.,* Christian Lacombe

Guide to French Country Cooking, Christian Roland Délu

Guide to Bicycling, John Durry

GUINNESS SUPERLATIVES
TITLES

OTHER TITLES

Autographs, Ray Rawlins

Antique Firearms, Frederick Wilkinson

English Pottery and Porcelain, Geoffrey Wills

Kings, Rulers and Statesmen, Clive Carpenter

British Hit Singles, Jo and Tim Rice, Paul Gambaccini, Mike Read

100 Years of Wimbledon, Lance Tingay

The Guinness Book of Names, Leslie Dunkling

Battle Dress, Frederick Wilkinson

Universal Soldier, Martin Windrow and Frederick Wilkinson

History of Land Warfare, Kenneth Macksey

History of Sea Warfare, Lt.-Cmdr. Gervis Frere-Cook and
Kenneth Macksey

History of Air Warfare, David Brown, Christopher Shores and
Kenneth Macksey

The Guinness Book of Records, *24th ed.,* edited by Norris D. McWhirter

The Guinness Book of 1952, edited by Kenneth Macksey

The Guinness Book of 1953, edited by Kenneth Macksey

The Guinness Book of 1954, edited by Kenneth Macksey

Ranking by size	COUNTRY	AREA		POPULATION		
		km²	Relative to UK=1	Latest Estimates	Relative to UK=1	Ranking
79	SENEGAL	196 192	0·80	5 085 388	0·09	81
80	YEMEN ARAB REPUBLIC	195 000	0·80	5 237 893	0·09	79
81	SYRIA	185 180	0·76	7 596 000	0·13	66
82	CAMBODIA	181 035	0·74	8 349 000	0·15	63
83	URUGUAY	177 508	0·73	2 763 964	0·05	103
84	TUNISIA	163 610	0·67	5 737 000	0·10	78
85	SURINAM	163 265	0·67	405 000	0·007	136
86	BANGLADESH	143 998	0·59	76 815 000	1·37	8
87	NEPAL	140 797	0·57	12 904 000	0·23	49
88	GREECE	131 944	0·54	9 047 000	0·16	59
89	NICARAGUA	130 000	0·53	2 233 000	0·04	110
90	CZECHOSLOVAKIA	127 876	0·52	14 862 000	0·26	43
91	KOREA (NORTH)	120 538	0·49	16 256 000	0·29	40
92	MALAWI	118 484	0·48	5 175 000	0·09	80
93	BENIN	112 622	0·46	3 197 000	0·05	98
94	HONDURAS	112 088	0·45	2 653 857	0·04	106
95	LIBERIA	111 369	0·45	1 503 368	0·02	118
96	CUBA	110 922	0·45	9 405 000	0·17	58
97	BULGARIA	110 912	0·45	8 721 900	0·15	61
98	GUATEMALA	108 889	0·45	6 256 000	0·11	75
99	GERMANY (EAST)	108 178	0·44	16 786 000	0·30	38
100	ICELAND	103 000	0·42	219 033	0·004	145
101	KOREA (SOUTH)	98 758	0·40	34 708 542	0·62	22
102	JORDAN	97 740	0·40	2 702 000	0·05	104
103	HUNGARY	93 032	0·38	10 625 000	0·19	54
104	PORTUGAL	92 082	0·38	8 782 000	0·15	60
105	AUSTRIA	83 850	0·34	7 520 000	0·13	67
106	UNITED ARAB EMIRATES	83 600	0·34	655 937	0·01	128
107	PANAMA	75 650	0·31	1 718 700	0·03	115
108	SIERRA LEONE	71 740	0·29	3 111 000	0·05	101
109	IRELAND	70 282	0·29	3 162 000	0·05	99
110	SRI LANKA	65 610	0·27	13 249 000	0·23	48
111	TOGO	56 000	0·23	2 222 000	0·04	111
112	COSTA RICA	50 700	0·21	2 012 000	0·03	114
113	DOMINICAN REPUBLIC	48 734	0·19	4 835 207	0·08	84
114	BHUTAN	47 000	0·19	1 202 000	0·02	121
115	DENMARK	43 069	0·17	5 076 000	0·09	82
116	SWITZERLAND	41 293	0·17	6 333 200	0·11	74
117	NETHERLANDS	40 844	0·16	13 810 000	0·24	47
118	GUINEA-BISSAU	36 125	0·15	534 000	0·009	133